TORT LAW

Fourth Edition

A cataloguing record for this publication is available from Library and Archives Canada.

ISBN 978-0-7798-1700-9 (pbk.).—ISBN 978-0-7798-11739-9 (bound)
The paper used in this publication meets the minimum requirements of American National Standard for Information Sciences – Permanence of Paper for Printed Library Materials, ANSI Z39.48-1984.

Composition: Computer Composition of Canada Inc.

One Corporate Plaza, 2075 Kennedy Road, Toronto, Ontario M1T 3V4
Customer Service:
Toronto 1-416-609-3800
Elsewhere in Canada/U.S. 1-800-387-5164
Fax 1-416-298-5094

To
a friend and mentor
Justice Allen M. Linden

PREFACE

The last five years have seen some dramatic developments in Canadian and Commonwealth tort law. The impact on negligence law, brought about by the Supreme Court of Canada's 2001 judgments in *Cooper v. Hobart* and *Edwards v. Law Society of Upper Canada*, is now very much in evidence. Particularly in the area of public authority liability, but elsewhere as well, the refined duty of care formula has changed the way judges have approached negligence actions and has halted the expansion of negligence law. Unlike the pre-*Cooper* days, when judges spent relatively little time on the question of duty in negligence law cases, the duty issue now dominates many tort law judgments. Judges, lawyers and academics are struggling to understand the essential elements of the duty of care formula, when it is to be applied, and how these elements are to be proved. This has prompted a major re-writing of the duty of care chapter in this fourth edition. Since the existence of duty is fundamental to all negligence claims, other chapters of the book relating to such matters as the liability of public authorities, the duty to assist others, and compensation for purely economic losses, have had to be modified to reflect the new duty of care jurisprudence.

A difficult area for tort law is the issue of cause. Here again we see that a topic that seemed to attract little attention in the past, one that, on the surface at least, was easily dealt with in most tort law cases, has become somewhat of a quagmire. There have been a number of important cases, not only in Canada but also across the common law world, which have attempted to fashion new approaches to proving causation in some difficult types of cases. This jurisprudence is discussed in a significantly rewritten chapter.

Vicarious liability and the issue of non-delegable duties continued to capture the attention of the Supreme Court of Canada in the past five years. The Supreme Court's effort in *Basely v. Curry* and *Jacobi v. Griffiths*, to set the law of vicarious liability down a different path, especially in the area of sexual wrongdoing cases, has had mixed results in terms of solving these difficult cases. This has prompted the Supreme Court to go back and look at the issue of vicarious liability and non-delegable duties on a number of occasions since the writing of the last edition of this text. This jurisprudence is also discussed.

There have been many other interesting developments, albeit on a smaller, more discrete scale. Compensation for wrongful life and birth, a journalist's privilege to defame, social host liability, misfeasance in a public office, liability for nervous shock, the defence of illegality, and the business torts, among other topics, have all produced an interesting jurisprudence. Developments in all of these areas are discussed in this new edition.

As with previous editions, I have strived to describe and discuss tort law as it is reflected in the judgments of our courts, as well as elsewhere. My principal purpose is to inform and to assist law students, lawyers and judges in understanding what the important developments in this area are and how cases are being decided. Although, in this sense, this text can be seen as more 'practical' than 'theoretical' in its approach, my own ideology and views about tort law are not hidden. As I have stated in previous editions, although I am an enthusiastic supporter of tort law as the principal vehicle of our system of civil justice, there are limits to its reach and effectiveness. It is neither a no-fault compensation scheme, nor an efficient way to re-distribute accident costs or wealth. It plays a part, alongside other components of private and public law, in ordering our society. Tort law has a leading role; it is, however, not the only actor.

Interest in tort law remains strong among the judiciary, academic and legal community. New books, articles, conferences, and on-line discussion groups allow "tortaholics", to borrow a phrase from Justice Allen Linden, to indulge their passion for tort law. I have been immensely assisted in my own understanding of this area by the national and international tort law scholars, judges and practitioners who participate in the research, writing, and discussing. At my own law school, Professors Gerald Robertson, Russell Brown, Mitchell McInnes, and Erin Nelson, as well as my former colleague Justice Ellen Picard, have made significant contributions. My friend and colleague, Mr. David Cheifetz, a Toronto practitioner, whose interest and knowledge of tort law rivals that of any full-time academic, also deserves special mention for assisting me in my own understanding of some difficult tort law issues. As a result of Professor Jason Neyers' international "Obligations Discussion Group", the list of the many other scholars whose works and ideas have enriched my own understanding is too lengthy to note here, although many of these persons' works are referenced throughout this text.

One individual in particular has been instrumental in my career and my interest in tort law. That person is Allen Linden — tort scholar, author and Justice of the Federal Court of Appeal. Allen and I have been working together on a variety of projects for 30 years. I consider him a mentor and a friend. His enthusiasm for tort law is unparalleled and infectious. In recognition of his leadership and friendship, I am dedicating this fourth edition to Mr. Justice Allen M. Linden.

In preparing this book, two individuals were of enormous assistance. Kim Cordeiro, my secretarial assistant, worked tirelessly in preparing the manuscript and making sure that the publisher received it in time and in the appropriate format. It was a major task to complete and she was exceptional in seeing it through. My student research assistant was Zachary Bodmer, who not only did superb research in ferreting out interesting cases, but also in delivering them to me in a format that was easily accessible and understandable. Mr. Bodmer was a Borden, Ladner, Gervais Fellow. Due to the generosity of the law firm of Borden, Ladner, Gervais, and its commitment to legal research and education, a $10,000 fellowship was provided to Mr. Bodmer so that he could work full time during the summer months to assist in me in the research for this book. My appreciation also goes out to the University of Alberta, Faculty of Law, for its support and encouragement and to Elda Sherman and Ainsley Davison at Carswell for their assistance.

My family remains my most important partner and inspiration. Nothing would have been accomplished by me without their love and support. Thank you, Irene, Samara, Noah and Emma, and our new granddaughter Delilah. You are all very talented and exciting individuals, enriching my life enormously. I would like to particularly thank my wife, Irene, an accomplished artist, and my partner for nearly 40 years. Irene has graciously agreed to allow one of her paintings to provide the cover art for the student edition of this text.

Lewis N. Klar, Q.C.,
May 2008

TABLE OF CONTENTS

TABLE OF CASES

1

Introduction to Tort Law

1. WHAT IS A "TORT"?

In general terms, what is a "tort"? It is interesting to note that despite the fact that the law of torts has an enormous impact on people's everyday lives, very few probably have even heard of the word "tort." The word does not form part of ordinary everyday language and is rarely used outside its legal context. It derives from the Latin *tortus*, which means crooked, and the French *tort*, which means wrong. One may concede that despite its diversity, all the laws dealing with tort do in some way relate to wrongdoing, although the ambiguity of this concept turns all efforts at defining the law of torts in terms of wrongs into exercises of question-begging. This was explained by Mr. Justice La Forest in *Angus v. Hart* in the following way:

> A "tort" is a legal construct and is not to be confused with a "wrong" in the general sense. It only exists where the law says it exists, *i.e.*, where the law provides a remedy.[1]

As a starting point, however, one can do no better than to adopt the classic textbook definition:

> A tort is a civil wrong, other than a breach of contract, which the law will redress by an award of damages.[2]

More helpful perhaps to understanding "What is a tort?" is to reflect briefly on the world in which tort law operates. Interaction between individuals inevitably

---

1 (1988), 52 D.L.R. (4th) 193 at 199 (S.C.C.).

2 Linden and Feldthusen, *Canadian Tort Law*, 8th ed. (2006) at 1, citing Fleming, *The Law of Torts*, 9th ed. (1998), at 1. In *Hall v. Hebert* (1993), 15 C.C.L.T. (2d) 93 at 118 (S.C.C.), Cory J. explained the law of tort in the following terms:

> It provides a means whereby compensation, usually in the form of damages, may be paid for injuries suffered by a party as a result of the wrongful conduct of others. It may encompass damages for personal injury suffered, for example, in a motor vehicle accident or as a result of falling in dangerous premises. It can cover damages occasioned to property. It may include compensation for injury caused to the reputation of a business or a product. It may provide damages for injury to honour in cases of defamation and libel. A primary object of the law of tort is to provide compensation to persons who are injured as a result of the actions of others.

produces conflict. Expectations are disappointed, the status quo is altered to the disadvantage of one of the parties, a loss or injury is sustained. It may take the form of a personal injury, damage to proprietary interests, to one's dignity, to business interests, to the environment, to one's reputation, or one's privacy. There is a victim and an identifiable person who is responsible for the harm done. The conduct which produced the injury or loss in some cases will have been deliberate, and in others, careless, or merely accidental. Should the legal system respond? Should the victim have any entitlement to compensation, and if so, at what level? Who should provide it? Should the actor who caused the injury be accountable for it? These are the essential questions of the law of torts.

One will perceive, however, that not only is what constitutes a loss or injury a matter of debate, but as well, all losses cannot practically be, nor ought they to be, remedied. It is the law of torts that determines which losses or injuries suffered by which individuals will be remedied, how, and to what extent.

2. SOURCES OF TORT LAW

Canadian tort law is principally judge-made law, notwithstanding the growing encroachment of statutory modifications. This is significant, for those who attempt to ascribe a single ideology or function to the laws dealing with tort overlook the manner in which these laws develop. Tort laws are the product of different ideologies and philosophies residing in many judges and legislators over centuries of development. It ought not to be surprising, therefore, nor is it an indictment of tort law, that tort judgments reflect different, and often inconsistent, values and concerns. One of the strengths of tort law, as with other common law subjects, is its ability to be flexible and fluid, to represent societal concerns and values as they change. Fleming has articulated this view of tort law, noting how its emphasis has in the past shifted from a law based on causation without fault, to fault, and back to a law concerned with the efficient distribution of losses arising from the inevitable risks of an industrialized and mechanized society.[3] It is one of the theses of this book that events in the 1980s, especially with regard to the availability and affordability of liability insurance, pointed out the importance of nudging the law of torts back to a position of increased emphasis on wrongdoing as the basis for compensation. Tort law is an arbitrary, inefficient, and expensive vehicle for the distribution of accident costs for social insurance objectives. Its future strength, and even its survival, depends upon it reasserting its role as the essential element of our system for civil justice.

Canadian tort law stems from English common law, and thus its pre-Confederation history is that of English tort law as it developed from the twelfth century onwards. This is a history which has been well chronicled,[4] even though all the

---

3 Fleming, *The Law of Torts*, 9th ed. (1998), at 8ff.

4 See, among others, Wigmore, "Responsibility for Tortious Acts: Its History" (1894), 7 Harv. L. Rev. 315, 383, 441; Gregory, "Trespass to Negligence to Absolute Liability" (1951), 37 Va. L. Rev. 359; Malone, "Ruminations on the Role of Fault in the History of the Common Law of Tort" (1970), 31 La. L. Rev. 1; Fifoot, *History and Source of the Common Law*: Tort and Contract (1949); Kiralfy, *Action on the Case* (1951); Kiralfy, The English Legal System, 8th ed. (1990),

historical accounts are not in agreement. Controversy still rages today concerning the development of English tort law, particularly over the role that fault or wrongdoing, as opposed to "faultless" causation, played in decisions to find defendants liable for damages.[5] By the time tort law disputes began to be decided in the emerging nation of Canada, however, much of the previous uncertainty had been dispelled. The law of torts was a law concerned with wrongdoing, even though this notion, then as now, did not necessarily involve great moral turpitude.

Canadian tort law in the latter half of the nineteenth century had minimal importance as compared with its present status. As noted by Professor McLaren, the law of torts "was very much a 'ragbag' of disparate actions, the product of several centuries of haphazard development without much in the way of underlying theme or principle."[6] The published case reports and commentaries frequently did not regard "tort" as a subject matter in itself, but broke the subject down into smaller parts, generally relating to the most common forms of accidents.[7] Not many of the numerous editorial opinions, case commentaries, or longer articles written at this time concerned tort law subjects, although there were a few, on subjects such as "the rules relating to bicycles."[8] Not surprisingly, tort law cases dealt with the principal risk-producing activities — railway accidents,

---

at 30ff. For a good judicial account see Clyne J.'s judgment in *Walmsley v. Humenick*, [1954] 2 D.L.R. 232 (B.C. S.C.).

5 See Kretzmer, "Transformation of Tort Liability in the Nineteenth Century: The Visible Hand" (1984), 4 Oxford J. Leg. Stud. 46, for an excellent discussion. An informative review of the debate is found in Picher, "The Tortious Liability of the Insane in Canada" (1975), 13 Osgoode Hall L.J. 193. The thesis that trespass was a quasi-criminal proceeding which involved liability as a result of causation and not culpability is promoted by Prosser and Holdsworth. See also Harris, "Liability Without Fault" (1932), 6 Tul. L. Rev. 337. The theory that wrongdoing was a part of the early law of trespass *vi et armis* is expounded by Milson, *Historical Foundations of the Common Law*, 2nd ed. (1981), at 305-313. Also see, for example, Spencer, "Motor-Cars and the Rule in Rylands v. Fletcher" (1983), 42 Cambridge L.J. 65 at 65-66, where the author describes as a "misconception based on a misunderstanding of seventeenth and eighteenth-century rules of pleading" the view that trespass to the person "originally" involved strict liability.

6 McLaren, "The Convergence of Tort and Contract: A Return to More Venerable Wisdom" (1989), 68 Can. Bar Rev. 46. McLaren notes that the first significant text on the law of torts was Addison's *A Treatise on the Law of Torts*, written in 1860. John Witt, "Contingency, Immanence and Inevitability in the Law of Accidents" in *Tort Law and the Modern State* (Columbia Law School Conference, 2006) cites Francis Hilliard's *The Law of Torts or Private Wrongs* (1859) as the first English-language treatise on the law of torts. For an account of nineteenth century American tort law, see Friedman, "Civil Wrongs: Personal Injury Law in the Late 19th Century", [1987] American Bar Foundation Research Journal 351; Schwartz, "Tort Law and the Economy in Nineteenth-Century America: A Reinterpretation" (1981), 90 Yale L.J. 1717; Young, "Reconceptualizing Accountability in the Early Nineteenth Century: How the Tort of Negligence Appeared" (1989), 21 Conn. L. Rev. 197; and Schwartz, "The Character of Early American Tort Law" (1989), 36 U.C.L.A. L. Rev. 641, among others.

7 Case reports, commentaries, and notes written during this period can be found in the Canadian Law Times, published from 1881-1920, the Canada Law Journal, published between 1855 and 1922 under various names, and the Canadian Law Review, published from 1901-1907. In 1923 the Canadian Law Times and the Canada Law Times united with the Canadian Bar Review. The Digest Canadian Law Times, 1881-1899, did not include the term Tort in its Heading of Subjects. In its Notes of Cases, Tort was broken down into such titles as Bankruptcy and Insolvency, Contract, Expropriation of Land, and Negligence.

8 See, e.g., "Bicycles and the Law of the Road" (1893), 13 Canadian Law Times 261.

industrial injuries, and horse and buggy calamities. Contributory negligence and the fellow servant rule were frequently pleaded, successfully barring many plaintiffs from recovery.[9] Personal injury and property invasions formed the complaints, the law not yet being ready for losses of a more esoteric nature. Tort law was represented by numerous individual injuries in specific duty relationships, a generalized notion of duty and liability not having yet developed enabling jurists to see tort law from a larger, more global, perspective. Yet by the 1900's it was already evident that in tort law avenues to compensation could be found for many more victims, for many more injuries. Witness the following editorial written in 1900:

> It has frequently been remarked that in the development of countries certain classes of litigation from time to time prevail. In this country we have arrived at the damages-for-negligence epoch. An increasing number of these actions in proportion to other litigation are tried every year. This is not to be wondered at considering the extraordinary activity in the use of machinery, rapid production of manufactured articles, and new means of transit. In addition to actions of this nature of a legitimate character, there are, of course, many which are purely speculative; and in this connection one is compelled to recognize the fact that certain members of our profession degrade its honorable traditions by being parties to proceedings which should never have been taken, and which partake of the nature of blackmail.[10]

The debate concerning the expansion of tort law had commenced. It is a debate which still is going on.[11]

3. THE CONSTITUTIONAL CONTEXT

The law of torts relates to the protection of the individual's property and civil rights and is accordingly a matter which falls within provincial jurisdiction under s. 92(13) of the Constitution Act, 1867.[12] As pointed out above, however, the subject matter of tort law is so wide that there are substantial areas of overlap with other heads of power. One cannot restrict all questions of compensation for personal injury, property damage, and the infringement of civil rights and dignitary interests to tort law. Despite this potential for conflict, there have been surprisingly few constitutional law cases concerning the law of torts.

The most obvious clash arises between the provincial power over torts and the federal power over criminal law, found in s. 91(27) of the Constitution Act, 1867. Tort and criminal law, aside from having a common historical origin, frequently arise simultaneously out of serious human conflict. There are, of course, clear

---

9 According to Friedman, above, note 6, this evidently was also the American experience. The most frequent types of claims were against railroads and street railways. The plaintiffs had little chance of success. Not only were they barred by legal doctrines, such as contributory negligence and assumption of risk, but they also had to face the resources and power of the defendants, and a legal culture of "noncompensation." See Friedman, above, note 6, at 355.

10 Editorial (1900), 36 Can. L.J. 147.

11 See, e.g., Henderson, "Expanding the Negligence Concept: Retreat from the Rule of Law" (1976), 51 Ind. L.J. 467.

12 See the Supreme Court of Canada judgment in *C.N.R. v. Clark* (1988), 47 C.C.L.T. 1 at 15:

> Rights of action for damages for personal injury and the procedure relating thereto is a matter which, for constitutional purposes, falls within exclusive provincial legislative competence in relation to "property and civil rights" (*Constitution Act, 1867*, s. 92(13)) and "procedure in civil matters" (s. 92(14)).

differences between the two systems of justice. In most cases, tort law involves two private litigants, whereas criminal law, at least theoretically, involves the State and a private individual. The tort law process is initiated by a private person in order to recover damages as either compensation for a loss or vindication of a right which has been infringed. The criminal law process is generally initiated by the State in order to protect the interests of society by punishing offenders and deterring wrongdoing, even though there are victims involved who are increasingly demanding a larger role in the criminal justice system.[13] In view of the fact that both tort and criminal laws arise when the rights of victims have been violated, both processes involve issues of compensation, the vindication of rights, the punishment of offenders, and the deterrence of antisocial conduct. Although tort law is essentially regarded as private law, and criminal law as public, both systems, through court decisions and legislation, have public goals, such as the preservation of a peaceful and orderly society, and the respect of the rights of others. In short, tort and criminal law, in addition to a common historical origin, also express similar contemporary concerns. Several Criminal Code provisions illustrate this. The Criminal Code gives courts the power to award victims of crime restitution, or compensation, from the offender.[14] Earlier provisions have been held to be constitutionally valid, being "in pith and substance" part of the sentencing process.[15] Although orders for compensation made pursuant to these provisions could not prevent victims from exercising their civil remedies, it is probable that whatever has been recovered would be taken into account when tort damages are assessed.[16]

The federal jurisdiction over criminal law may interfere with provincial jurisdiction over tort in other ways. Section 783 of the Code permits a court to order that no civil proceedings shall be taken against certain judicial officers for exceeding their jurisdiction in certain circumstances.[17] Other provisions of the Code, while not expressly protecting individuals from civil liability, have been interpreted in such a way. These sections, found in the Code under the heading "Protection of Persons Administering and Enforcing the Law", deal with a wide range of protections for those who commit acts normally considered tortious. Section 25, for example, states that:

> Every one who is required or authorized by law to do anything in the administration or enforcement of the law . . . is, if he acts on reasonable grounds, justified in doing what he is required or authorized to do and in using as much force as is necessary for that purpose.

---

13 See, for example, Alberta's Victims of Crime Act, R.S.A. 2000, c. V-3. The legislation affords victims of crime rights to be treated with courtesy and compassion, to be kept informed and to be heard.

14 See, e.g., the Criminal Code, R.S.C. 1985, c. C-46, s. 738; 1995, c. 22, s. 6; 2000, c. 12, s. 95; 2005, c. 43, s. 7.

15 See *R. v. Zelensky*, [1978] 2 S.C.R. 940; MacPherson, "The Constitutionality of the Compensation and Restitution Provisions of the Criminal Code — The Picture After Regina v. Zelensky" (1979), 11 Ottawa L. Rev. 713.

16 The Criminal Code, R.S.C. 1985, c. C-46, s.741.2, states specifically that "a civil remedy for an act or omission is not affected by reason only that an order for restitution under section 738 or 739 has been made in respect of that act or omission."

17 See *Re Royal Can. Legion (Branch 177) and Mount Pleasant Branch 177 Savings Credit Union* (1964), 48 D.L.R. (2d) 164 (B.C. S.C.).

The Code includes many provisions which have been interpreted judicially not only as affording immunity from criminal prosecution, but immunity from civil liability as well.[18] In *Priestman v. Colangelo and Smythson*,[19] Cartwright J. expressly stated that the use of the word "justified" in these Code provisions

> means freed from civil liability as well as from criminal responsibility which might otherwise exist. The word "justified" is used in a number of sections in Part I of the *Criminal Code* in contradistinction from the phrase "protected from criminal responsibility" which is used in a number of other sections in the same Part.[20]

Can one justify this interpretation, which undoubtedly allows federal authorities to intrude significantly into areas of provincial jurisdiction? One may argue that provisions providing civil immunities to those exercising criminal enforcement functions are in pith and substance criminal law powers or necessarily incidental to criminal law powers. Or, one may argue that decisions to adopt Criminal Code defences as defences to tort actions are in essence common law decisions legitimately arrived at by courts.[21] In any event, notwithstanding its propriety, clearly this is one area where provincial power over tort law has been significantly reduced by federal legislation.[22]

In other areas as well, federal statutes have affected tort actions. Professor Hogg has pointed out several areas of overlap, including patent or copyright laws, trade mark laws, custody provisions, and company law.[23] Occasionally, federal statute law has gone too far. In *MacDonald v. Vapor Can. Ltd.*,[24] s. 7 of the Trade Marks Act,[25] which prohibited unfair trade practices, and s. 53 of the Act, which gave the court of competent jurisdiction the power to order remedies for infringements, including provisions for injunctions and damages, were struck down as being

---

18 For example, s. 25(2) relating to the execution of a process or the carrying out of a sentence; s. 25(4) relating to the right to arrest; s. 27 relating to the use of force to prevent the commission of offences; s. 30 relating to the prevention of a breach of the peace; s. 32 relating to the suppression of riots. It is important to emphasize that none of these sections speaks directly to the question of immunity from civil liability, although they have been used in this way. See, among others, *Kennedy v. Tomlinson* (1959), 20 D.L.R. (2d) 273 (Ont. C.A.); *Woodward v. Begbie* (1961), 31 D.L.R. (2d) 22 (Ont. H.C.); *Frey v. Fedoruk*, [1949] 2 W.W.R. 604, reversed [1950] S.C.R. 517; *Priestman v. Colangelo and Smythson* (1959), 19 D.L.R. (2d) 1 (S.C.C.); and *Poupart v. Lafortune* (1974), 41 D.L.R. (3d) 720 (S.C.C.).

19 *Ibid.*

20 19 D.L.R. (2d) 1 at 14. In *Green v. Lawrence*, [1998] 10 W.W.R. 427, 163 D.L.R. (4th) 115 (Man. C.A.), Huband J.A. stated that it would be too "sweeping" to suggest that s. 25 would relieve against all civil liability, including negligence.

21 Can one argue, for example, that the principle of *Geddis v. Bann Reservoir* (1878), 3 App. Cas. 430 (H.L.), is applicable here? That case established the common law principle that no action can lie for doing what the legislature has authorized if it is done without negligence, although it may cause damage to someone. As well, notwithstanding the Criminal Code provisions, these defences exist at common law as well. See *Green v. Lawrence, ibid.*, for a useful discussion.

22 Provincial laws may even incorporate federal laws so as to render the latter defences to tort claims. See, e.g., *Little v. Peers*, [1988] 3 W.W.R. 107 (B.C. C.A.).

23 See Hogg, *Constitutional Law of Canada*, 4th student ed. (2005), at Chapter 21.

24 [1977] 2 S.C.R. 134.

25 R.S.C. 1970, c. T-10 [now R.S.C. 1985, c. T-13, ss. 7, 53].

unwarranted intrusions into the area of property and civil rights.[26] In *Clark v. C.N.R.*,[27] the Supreme Court of Canada ruled that the limitation section of the federal Railway Act[28] was unconstitutional, insofar as it purported to apply to a common law action for negligence in the operation of a railway.[29]

4. TORT LAW AND THE CHARTER

A much more important constitutional issue awaits tort law in the future. To what extent will tort law be affected by the Canadian Charter of Rights and Freedoms?[30]

The case law to date clearly indicates that much of tort law will escape Charter scrutiny, at least insofar as a direct application of the Charter is concerned. As a result of *R.W.D.S.U. v. Dolphin Delivery Ltd.*,[31] common law actions in tort which are divorced from any governmental connection will not be subject to the Charter. In other words, unless a tort claim is based upon a legislative enactment,[32] or one of the litigants is a governmental official or entity, the Charter provisions will not

---

26 In *Can. v. Sask. Wheat Pool* (1983), 143 D.L.R. (3d) 9 (S.C.C.), whether the federal Parliament was constitutionally competent to provide a civil remedy to someone injured by a breach of the Canada Grain Act, S.C. 1970-71-72, c. 7, was clearly a question which Dickson J. was prepared to leave open. See 143 D.L.R. (3d) 9 at 24. See also *Ingle v. Can.*, [1984] 2 F.C. 57 at 63 (T.D.).

27 (1988), 47 C.C.L.T. 1 (S.C.C.).

28 R.S.C. 1970, c. R-2, s. 342(1) [now R.S.C. 1985, c. R-3, s. 367].

29 The issue can also arise in reverse; that is, provincial laws in the tort area can be declared inapplicable to conduct regulated by federal powers. For example, in *Shulman (Guardian ad litem of) v. McCallum*, [1991] 6 W.W.R. 470, affirmed [1993] 7 W.W.R. 567 (B.C. C.A.), it was held that the tortious liability of boat owners and operators for negligent navigation is exclusively within federal legislative jurisdiction. Thus, provisions of the Family Compensation Act, R.S.B.C. 1979, c. 120 [now R.S.B.C. 1996, c. 126], were unavailable to claimants seeking fatal accident damages. In *Bow Valley Husky (Bermuda) Ltd. v. Saint John Shipbuilding Ltd.* (1997), 153 D.L.R. (4th) 385 (S.C.C.), McLachlin J. held that the Contributory Negligence Act, R.S.N. 1990, c. C-33, did not apply to maritime tort cases.

30 Pt. 1 of the Constitution Act, 1982, being Sched. B of the Canada Act, 1982, c. 11 (U.K.). See Dale Gibson, "Tort Law and the Charter of Rights" (1986), 16 Man. L.J. 1.

31 (1986), 38 C.C.L.T. 184 (S.C.C.). Also see *Kohn v. Globerman* (1986), 36 C.C.L.T. 60, leave to appeal to S.C.C. refused 44 Man. R. (2d) 160n; *Peg-Win Real Estate Ltd. v. Winnipeg Real Estate Bd.* (1985), 19 D.L.R. (4th) 438, affirmed 27 D.L.R. (4th) 767 (Man. C.A.); *Bhindi v. B.C. Projectionists* (1985), 63 B.C.L.R. 352, affirmed 4 B.C.L.R. (2d) 145, leave to appeal to S.C.C. refused 73 N.R. 399n; *Re Blainey and Ont. Hockey Assn.* (1985), 52 O.R. (2d) 225, reversed on other grounds 26 D.L.R. (4th) 728, leave to appeal to S.C.C. refused 10 C.P.R. (3d) 450; *Cat Productions Ltd. v. Macedo*, [1985] 1 F.C. 269 (T.D.); *McKinney v. University of Guelph*, [1990] 3 S.C.R. 229; *Hill v. Church of Scientology of Toronto* (1994), 114 D.L.R. (4th) 1 (Ont. C.A.), affirmed (1995), 126 D.L.R. (4th) 129 (S.C.C.) cf. *R. v. Lerke* (1984), 41 C.R. (3d) 172, affirmed 49 C.R. (3d) 324 (Alta. C.A.). See Katherine Swinton, "Commentary", in *Canadian Charter of Rights and Freedoms* (1982), edited by Tarnopolsky and Beaudoin; McLellan and Elman, "To Whom Does the Charter Apply? Some Recent Cases on Section 32" (1986), 24 Alta. L. Rev. 361.

32 There have been numerous statutory interventions into tort law. For example, in the areas of contributory negligence, occupier's liability, the action for loss of consortium, interspousal tort immunity, guest passenger discrimination, the liability of municipalities, among others, statutes have been passed. These will all be subject to the Charter.

apply to the case.[33] This approach is less than satisfactory, and may produce anomalies. Causes of action in tort which have been modified, or supplemented, by legislative enactment, will be subject to Charter scrutiny, even if only private litigants are involved. For example, the Charter applied in the defamation case of *Coates v. The Citizen*,[34] even though the case involved private litigants, merely because relatively minor changes to the common law of defamation had been made by legislation.[35] In a subsequent defamation case, however, *Hill v. Church of Scientology of Toronto*,[36] the Charter did not apply because it was not the constitutionality of the provincial defamation legislation[37] which was being attacked, but the common law of defamation itself. Where the common law governs without statutory intervention, the Charter will apply only if a governmental connection is present.[38] It is, therefore, seemingly possible to have two "common laws" applicable in the same area, one involving private litigants, where the Charter will not apply, and one involving governmental bodies, where it would.[39] It is also possible to have valid common law rules in one province which have been declared to be contrary to the Charter, when incorporated in another province's legislation.[40]

While it is clear from *Dolphin Delivery* that the Charter will not apply to litigation between private parties if no governmental connection can be found, it

---

33 See Irvine, "Annotation" (1987), 38 C.C.L.T. 187. In *Hill v. Church of Scientology of Toronto*, above, note 31, Cory J. extensively discusses the issue of the application of the Charter to a defamation action between private persons. He notes that although the common law must be interpreted so that it is consistent with Charter "values", this is significantly different from stating that the Charter applies to the common law. For commentary, see J. Ross, "The Common Law of Defamation Fails To Enter the Age of the Charter" (1996), 35 Alta. L. Rev. 117 and D. Boivin, "Accommodating Freedom of Expression and Reputation in the Common Law of Defamation" (1997), 22 Queen's Law Journal 229. See discussion in Chapter 19. The inapplicability of the Charter to interactions between private persons or institutions, where there is no governmental connection, was confirmed by the Alberta Court of Appeal in *R. v. Dell* (2005), 256 D.L.R. (4th) 271. The issue in this case was whether the detention of the accused by an employee of a private bar leading to his ultimate arrest was subject to the Charter. The Court decided that it was not.

34 (1988), 44 C.C.L.T. 286 (N.S. T.D.).

35 Defamation Act, R.S.N.S. 1967, c. 72 [now R.S.N.S. 1989, c. 122]. This situation prevails in every common law province. See below, Chapter 19. It is important to note that in *Coates*, it was the Defamation Act itself which was subject to Charter challenge, and not the common law principles governing defamation.

36 Above, note 31.

37 The Libel and Slander Act, R.S.O. 1990, c. L.12.

38 Prior to *Dolphin Delivery*, some decisions applied the Charter in tort cases between private litigants which did not involve statutes. See, for example, *Power v. Moss* (1986), 38 C.C.L.T. 31 (Nfld. T.D.), and *Shkwarchuk v. Hansen* (1984), 30 C.C.L.T. 121 (Sask. Q.B.), where the Charter was applied to actions for loss of consortium, between private litigants, even though there was no statutory "hook." These types of decisions could not survive the *Dolphin Delivery* reasoning.

39 For an extensive discussion of the application of the Charter in a case involving a defamation action brought by a Crown Attorney, see *Hill v. Church of Scientology*, above, note 31. One of the interesting aspects of the issue was whether the fact that it is a government employee who brings the action for defamation alters the private nature of the litigation. Cory J. held that it does not. The Charter accordingly does not apply.

40 In an unpublished paper, "The Clapham Omnibus Meets the Trudeau Express", Professor Gibson discusses other possible unfortunate results of *Dolphin Delivery*.

would not be correct to assume that the common law of torts can continue to develop as if the Charter did not exist. McIntyre J. explained the Supreme Court's position in the following way:

> Where, however, private party "A" sues private party "B" relying on the common law and where no act of government is relied upon to support the action, the Charter will not apply. I should make it clear, however, that this is a distinct issue from the question whether the judiciary ought to apply and develop the principles of the common law in a manner consistent with the fundamental values enshrined in the Constitution. . . . In this sense, then, the Charter is far from irrelevant to private litigants whose disputes fall to be decided at common law.[41]

Mr. Justice Cory reaffirmed this role of the Charter in developing the common law in *Hill v. Church of Scientology*:

> . . . the common law must be interpreted in a manner which is consistent with Charter principles. This obligation is simply a manifestation of the inherent jurisdiction of the courts to modify or extend the common law in order to comply with prevailing social conditions and values.[42]

The extent to which the common law of torts will be moulded by the Charter remains to be seen.[43]

5. PURPOSES OF FAULT-BASED COMPENSATION

(a) Introduction

The diversity of the interests protected by tort law and the types of conduct sanctioned by it make it unrealistic to generalize about the purposes of tort law. Tort serves different purposes depending foremost on the area under review, the type of injury and conduct and, to a lesser extent, the philosophy and attitude of the law maker.[44]

---

41 38 C.C.L.T. 184 at 214. Another strong statement of support for using Charter values to interpret and develop the common law is found in Iacobucci J.'s judgment in *R. v. Salituro* (1990), 68 C.C.C. (3d) 289, at 304-305 (S.C.C.).

42 Above, note 31, at 126 D.L.R. (4th) 156.

43 To date, efforts to change the common law of torts to meet Charter values have been fairly unsuccessful. See, for example, *Hill v. Church of Scientology of Toronto*, above, note 31. In *Hill*, Cory J. specifically noted that Charter rights do not exist between private persons. Although Charter "values" can inform the common law, courts should be cautious in amending the common law to reflect Charter values. Accordingly, "[f]ar-reaching changes to the common law must be left to the legislature", at 126 D.L.R. (4th) 157. Change is made even more difficult by Cory J.'s assertion that the onus of proving that the common law fails to comply with Charter values and that the conflict in values favours modification of the common law rests on the person impugning the common law. On the other side of the coin, it is also interesting to note that non-tort processes which were enacted to provide alternative compensation schemes, such as Workers' Compensation, are also vulnerable to Charter attack. The Newfoundland Workers' Compensation Act, S.N. 1983, c. 48, which deprives an injured worker from pursuing an action in tort, was declared to be contrary to the Charter in *Piercey v. Gen. Bakeries Ltd.* (1986), 31 D.L.R. (4th) 373. This ruling was overturned on a subsequent reference to the Court of Appeal, 44 D.L.R. (4th) 501, whose decision was upheld by the Supreme Court of Canada at 56 D.L.R. (4th) 765. See also *Budge v. Alta. (W.C.B.)*, [1987] 6 W.W.R. 217 (Alta. Q.B.).

44 A very persuasive and exhaustive defence of the tort law system is found in a Report to the American Bar Association, *Towards a Jurisprudence of Injury: The Continuing Creation of Substantive Justice in American Tort Law*, 1984. The Report describes the pluralistic approach to tort law in the following way, at 2-10:

> The most sensible approach is to regard tort law from a pluralistic viewpoint, viewing it as

The essential characteristic of tort law's primary area of operation is that it is a fault-based system of accident compensation.[45] Even in this area, which can be defined loosely as "accident compensation law", tort laws operate differently, depending on the type of accident and injury involved.

Where injuries have been caused deliberately and with the intent to do harm,[46] tort law operates to provide justice to victims and peace and security to society. It serves to punish wrongdoers, to deter wrongdoing, to compensate victims, and to vindicate rights. Tort principles actively reflect these goals. Punitive damages may be awarded, certain defences, such as contributory negligence, may be unavailable to wrongdoers,[47] remoteness tests are broad, actual damages may not be necessary to succeed in the cause of action, and so on. The particular values and goals of tort law in the area of deliberate wrongdoing generally have been recognized and accepted, and most would agree that fault-based compensation should remain in this area.[48]

The more significant part of tort law involves injuries not deliberately caused but brought about by conduct which the law defines as having been unreasonable. This is the field covered by the action for negligence. Yet even here there are important variations. The concept of negligence itself is very wide, ranging from conduct which might be only slightly substandard to that which can be described as grossly negligent, or reckless. One must understand that all conduct can be seen as falling somewhere along a continuum, with pure accidents at one end, and deliberate misbehaviour at the other. Describing conduct as "accidental", "negligent", "reckless" or "intentional" is a matter of degree. It therefore should be evident that tort laws which sanction conduct falling at one end of the scale

---

a multifaceted response to a very varied set of problems. If one sought a natural metaphor, it might not be that of one large tree, but rather that of a densely packed forest area, where trees of different sizes and species grow together with many sorts of vegetation. This area would be seen to run into other forest areas, which might be viewed as representing statutory compensation and regulation schemes and other parts of the common law.

45 There are "strict liability" torts, which provide compensation without fault. These are, however, relatively unimportant, at least in comparison with negligence law. See below, Chapter 16. As well, tort law deals with matters other than losses caused by accidents. Tort law has a role to play in protecting reputation and privacy, in regulating business relationships, and in resolving land use conflicts. These, however, must be seen as being peripheral to its major area of operations, the compensation of those who have suffered personal injuries, property damage, or economic losses as a result of the activities of others.

46 As we will see, we must distinguish conduct which, although deliberate and legally wrongful, was not done in order to harm the claimant, from conduct which was deliberate and intended to be harmful. See below, Chapter 2.

47 As we will discuss, traditionally contributory negligence was not a defence in an intentional tort action. This position, however, may be relaxing. See discussion in Chapter 13.

48 For example, see Fleming, *The Law of Torts*, 9th ed. (1998), at 10:

> Morality will, of course, continue to dominate intentional injuries, and tort law (whatever its prospects of survival elsewhere) appears to have an assured future in this regard.

It is interesting to note, however, that the one comprehensive accident compensation scheme generally regarded as the model for all others, the New Zealand Accident Compensation Scheme, in fact did abolish the intentional torts and replace them with compulsory social insurance benefits. It was only through subsequent litigation, *Donselaar v. Donselaar*, [1982] 2 N.Z.L.R. 97 (C.A.), that the right to sue in tort for punitive damages was restored.

might have different objectives from those which deal with conduct at the other end.

As well, there are important differences among the types of activities which are dealt with by negligence law. Society's interests in regulating and compensating victims of automobile accidents, professional malpractice, defective products, or mistreatment at the hands of government and large corporations are not the same.

Having said that, however, one can generalize about the purposes of a fault-based compensation law, understanding that these purposes will vary depending upon the type of conduct and activity in question.[49]

(b) Compensation

It is trite to point out that a fault-based compensation law compensates victims only where their injuries have been caused by the fault of others. It is important to stress, though, that compensation, for its own sake, is not the purpose of tort law but rather the remedy offered by it, after liability based upon fault has been established.[50] The reasons why the law compensates victims of wrongdoing are what accurately describe the objectives of a fault-based civil justice system.[51]

Nevertheless, it is obvious that compassionate judges frequently have found it difficult to deny compensation to needy claimants and have strained tort law

---

49 Professor Weinrib makes the persuasive case for a non-instrumentalist view of tort law. According to Weinrib, tort law is a "mode of ordering whose constitutive features [a]re the causation of injury and a bipolar remedial procedure". It does not "forward independently justified goals. Rather, it gives juridical expression to the coherence of this normative unit". In simpler terms, the only purpose tort law can have is to be tort law. Professor Weinrib explains how all the elements of tort can be explained in terms of its own internal normative structure. When one, however, tries to explain tort in terms of independent, instrumentalist goals of compensation, punishment, deterrence or whatever, one discovers that tort is an inadequate, inconsistent and even incomprehensible vehicle. See Weinrib, "Understanding Tort Law" (1989), 23 Val. U.L. Rev. 485. Professor Weinrib's ideas have now been published in his book *The Idea of Private Law*, 1995. Also, see Ripstein, "Tort Law in a Liberal State" in *Tort Law and the Modern State* (Columbia University Conference, 2006). Ripstein argues that "the liberal state needs private ordering, not because of the good effects this will bring, but because it is a principal component of a system in which separate persons with separate purposes can interact on terms consistent with the freedom of all." For an argument that tort law can be explained by both deterrence and corrective justice theories that need not be in conflict, see Schwartz, "Mixed Theories of Tort Law: Affirming Both Deterrence and Corrective Justice" (1997), 75 Tex. L. Rev. 1801.

50 As stated by Joseph Little, "Up With Torts" (1987), 24 San Diego Law Rev. 861 at 862: "To perceive compensation as the prime goal of tort law is to confound consequence and purpose". A similar point is made by Leslie Bender, "Tort Law's Role as a Tool for Social Justice Struggle" (1997), 37-38 Washburn L.J. 249.

51 In his fascinating book, *Tort Law in America: An Intellectual History* (1980), G. Edward White describes the compensation function of tort actions in the following way:

> It should be recalled that tort actions, prior to 1900, had not principally been conceived as devices for compensating injured persons. Compensation had been a consequence of a successful tort action, but the primary function of tort liability had been seen as one of punishing or deterring blameworthy civil conduct. A conception of tort law as a "compensation system" is a distinctly twentieth century phenomenon, brought about by an altered view of the social consequences of injuries.

principles in order to accomplish this result.[52] This tendency has been spurred on by the presence of liability insurance, which has the effect of turning defendants into better cost absorbers than uninsured victims.[53] In other words, compensation, rather than being the result of a successful tort claim, has become, in many cases, the only reason for the tort claim's success.

This state of affairs is unsatisfactory, both for the continued viability of a civil justice system and from the social welfare perspective. Tort law's principles and their application cannot be separated from its basic rationale — it is a law dealing with the effects of wrongdoing. It is not designed to compensate needy claimants, along the lines of a social insurance or welfare program, and, in fact, its compensation role in society is a rather limited one.[54] Although one can understand the discomfort of judges forced to deny compensation to needy claimants who have not been able to establish the wrongdoing of defendants,[55] it is suggested that judges ought to resist the temptation to convert tort law into a no-fault scheme. Courts are not equipped to decide which of the disabled ought to receive priority,[56] what the levels of no-fault compensation ought to be,[57] or how it will be funded.[58]

---

52 This has been termed "intellectual dishonesty" by Mr. Justice Krever, an Ontario Court of Appeal judge, who, in a speech published in Ontario Lawyers Weekly, 21st February 1986, is reported to have stated:

> It is not satisfactory to continue to base compensation only on the necessity to find fault because there is a propensity in those cases where there will be no real compensation, unless there is fault, towards intellectual dishonesty.

53 See *Ontario Task Force on Insurance*, Vol. 1, May 1986, A Pre-Publication of the Final Report of the Ontario Task Force on Insurance to the Minister of Financial Institutions, at 92-93.

54 Numerous different studies from various jurisdictions have documented tort law's minimal compensation role, in relation to the total amount of compensation benefits paid out. See *Royal Commission on Civil Liability and Compensation for Personal Injury*, Cmnd. 7054-III, March 1978, London (Pearson Report); *Accident Compensation: A Transport Accidents Scheme for New South Wales*, N.S.W.L.R.C., May 1983; Weiler, *Protecting the Worker from Disability: Challenges for the Eighties* (1983); *Ontario Task Force on Insurance*, above (the Slater Report). The Slater Report, for example, has stated that "of the $2.5 billion that was paid out under various Ontario accident compensation schemes in 1981 to injury victims, only $250 million was paid through tort", at 91, citing a paper prepared for the Task Force by Professor P. Osborne. The situation in the United States is comparable. In Saks, "Do We Really Know Anything About the Behaviour of the Tort Litigation System — And Why Not?" (1992), 140 U. of Penn. L.R. 1147, the author points out that the tort liability system compensated only $7.7 billion of the $175.9 billion of direct personal losses due to accidental injuries. This prompted the remark that "so little compensation is achieved through the tort system that only as an act of hyperbole can it be said to be part of an injury compensation system" (at 1286).

55 Such comments of discomfort are found especially in medical litigation. See, e.g., Callaghan A.C.J.H.C.'s comments in *Koerber v. Kitchener-Waterloo Hosp.* (1987), 62 O.R. (2d) 612.

56 For example, why compensate a person who becomes disabled after an unsuccessful, but competently performed medical procedure, but not a person who becomes disabled due to an illness unconnected to medical treatment?

57 Tort claimants receive full compensation. When tort law is distorted to find liability without proof of fault, this claimant will also receive full compensation, unlike most other recipients of no-fault benefits.

58 Liability insurance funding is predicated upon the amount necessary to cover fault-based claims. If judges find liability, though there has been no fault, the basis upon which the premiums were set will be wrong.

(c) Justice

Tort law operates as an important part of Canadian society's civil *justice* system. Its theoretical underpinning — that a wrongdoer who injures another ought to be required to repair the damage and restore the victim — is clearly an integral part of our system of values. No one would suggest that the matter of wrongdoing simply ought to be ignored, although there can be legitimate debate concerning how it ought to be handled.[59]

The justice component of traditional tort law principles includes several different, but related, values. It involves the question of fairness, i.e., that it is fair that a person who causes a loss should repair it. The punishment of the wrongdoer and the consequent appeasement of the victim are bound up in it. Personal accountability and responsibility, the ability to control one's own destiny and make one's own choices, are values which are meaningful only if one assumes responsibility for one's own choices and actions. The assumption that society has become too complex and that losses result from unavoidable and inevitable risks is one that tort law rejects. It is difficult, and probably unnecessary, to empirically test for the presence or absence of these values in Canadian society.[60] It is impossible to believe that these are not values widely held in society, or to fathom what values have replaced them.[61]

The application of the principle of justice expressed in tort law doctrines varies in practice depending upon the situation. Where liability insurance proceeds are the main source of compensation for victims, as in the automobile accident field, the principle operates mainly symbolically. Although the wrongdoer is responsible for repairing the injuries caused, and is the named defendant in any subsequent litigation, it is the liability insurer who usually controls the claim and compensates the victim. Nevertheless, even in this area, there are consequences for faulty drivers. Not only are insurance premiums affected by liability claims,

---

59 For a reaffirmation of the importance of the justice component of tort law see Arthur Ripstein, "Some Recent Obituaries of Tort Law" (1998), 48 U.T.L.J. 561. Ripstein, for example, states at 565:

> A system of private ordering requires that one person not be able to displace the costs of his activities onto others. Those who take or damage the property of others in the course of pursuing their own ends need to repair what they have done. The same point applies to personal injuries: if one person carelessly injures another in the course of carrying out his purposes, it is appropriate that the injurer bear the costs of the injuries. That is why the fault system supposes that those who are wrongfully injured must be 'made whole' by their injurers, even if that means restoring a large income. Tort law thus gives expression to a familiar idea of responsibility, according to which the person who makes a mess must clean it up.

60 One study, which was done in England, was Sally Lloyd-Bostock's "Common Sense Morality and Accident Compensation", [1980] Ins. L.J. 331. The results were fairly inconclusive and can be interpreted in different ways.

61 These values seem to be universally accepted. In the Law Reform Commission of Canada's Working Paper on *Restitution and Compensation*, Working Paper 5, 1974, for example, it is argued that restitution, i.e., "making the offender pay or work to restore the damage", should be part of the criminal law process. To deny this is "a rejection of common sense." The paper submits that "if justice is to be done the violation of the individual victim's personal and property rights ought to be redressed." This is what tort law attempts to do.

but serious misconduct can result in personal liability by the insured to its insurer. As well, serious claims may exceed insurance limits and become the personal responsibility of the insured. One must also recall that liability insurance is not a factor in all tort claims. In addition, the stigmatizing effect of a finding of fault, or personal sense of blame for causing an injury, are not matters which ought to be lightly brushed aside.[62]

Looking at the principle of justice from the perspective of the victim, different considerations arise. Notwithstanding who pays for the injuries caused through the wrongdoing of a defendant, tort law allows victims to be fully compensated for their injuries. This contrasts with social insurance programs, which generally not only limit payments by considering the needs of the claimants, but have financial ceilings. This principle of full compensation raises different ideological concerns. Should all persons who suffer personal injury be entitled to the same compensation whether they have been injured by the fault of others, by the fault of no one, or by their own fault? The answer to this is clearly ideological. There is no doubt, however, that tort law clearly reflects a choice, one which distinguishes among injured parties based on the cause of their injuries.

Critics of tort law generally trivialize its role as the principal system of civil justice in our legal system by focussing on the neutralizing effect of liability insurance and emphasizing tort law's inefficiencies and large operating costs.[63] Others, however, perhaps as a result of different experiences, intuition, or even faith, sense a symbolic and important message conveyed through tort law's principles. G. Edward White has stated, for example:

> It seems to me first that there is something to be said for using tort law as a device for censure and punishment. . . . While such admonitions may not deter other potential violators, there is something to be said for a society declaring, through its legal system, that it finds certain noncriminal conduct reprehensible.[64]

---

62 This point was expressed in the following way by Southin J.A. in *Wang v. Horrod*, [1998] 9 W.W.R. 280 (B.C. C.A.), leave to appeal refused (1999), 236 N.R. 185 (note) (S.C.C.) at 297-298 [W.W.R.]. In deciding to relieve a defendant of liability for his alleged negligence in driving his bus, Southin J.A. noted that although the defendant would not undoubtedly have had to personally pay for the damages, that he was still "entitled to be absolved, not only from liability for the damages, but also, and perhaps more importantly to him, from the moral condemnation of the finding against him." As reasoned by Her Ladyship, "a decent human being is wounded in the spirit by being found to have been the cause of grave harm when he or she has done nothing untoward."

63 Some studies ignore this role completely. The Slater Report, for example, above, note 53, discusses the deterrence and compensation objectives of tort law, with no mention of values or ideology.

64 Above, note 51, at 237. Also see *The Osborne Report of Inquiry into Motor Vehicle Accident Compensation in Ontario (The Osborne Report)*, 1988, Vol. 1, at 543-44:

> Tort law's capacity for fairness and justice should not in my view be ignored. The public's sense of justice, of what is fair and reasonable, must be taken into account. . . . The concept of some individual responsibility for individual actions, at least in a humanely modified form, is central to what reasonable people regard as just.

It can be no coincidence that laws stemming from early times and in different cultures reflect similar principles of justice.[65] Efforts by some claimants in New Zealand to sue wrongdoers in tort, even for the recovery of only punitive damages which are generally very small amounts, indicate this same desire for social justice.[66]

Another aspect of tort law, not often explored, is the relationship between the values which it expresses and society's religious beliefs. H.L. Berman has expressed this concern in the following terms:

> In all cultures, including our own today, law and religion share certain elements, namely, ritual, tradition, authority, and universality. These religious elements of law are not often stressed by contemporary legal scholars. Instead, law is generally presented as a secular, rational, utilitarian system — a way of getting things done. But as soon as one goes behind the law in books to the processes by which it is made, interpreted and applied, one sees the symbols of the sanctity which infuses it.[67]

Reflecting on the "efficiency" of laws, Berman states further:

> By thinking of law solely in terms of its efficiency, we rob it of that very efficiency. By failing to give enough attention to its religious dimensions, we deprive it of its capacity to do justice and possibly even of its capacity to survive.[68]

Finally, when thinking of the justice values, the symbolism of tort laws and the principles which they espouse, one might have regard to the following statement:

> By virtue of their symbolization in judicial, legislative, and other rituals, the ideals of legal justice come into being not primarily as matters of utility but rather as matters of sanctity, not primarily as ideals, but rather as shared emotions: a common sense of rights, a common sense of duties, a demand for a fair hearing, an aversion to inconsistency, a passion for equality of treatment, an abhorrence of illegality, and a commitment to legality.[69]

(d) Deterrence

The deterrent effect of laws which impose liability on those who act carelessly is a matter of some debate. At least in theory, imposing financial sanctions on those who do not take reasonable care ought to encourage more careful behaviour. Critics of tort law, however, point to various factors which limit the deterrent function. Foremost is the existence of liability insurance, which removes the financial consequences of wrongdoing from the insured and transfers it to the

---

65 Section 206 of The Code of Hammurabi, for example, stated:

> If a man has struck another man in a dispute and wounded him, that man shall swear, "I did not strike him willingly"; and he shall pay for the doctor.

See Smith and Weisstub, *The Western Idea of Law* (1983), at 76.

66 See *Donselaar v. Donselaar*, [1982] 2 N.Z.L.R. 97 (C.A.).

67 H.L. Berman, *The Interaction of Law and Religion* (1974), at 14.

68 *Ibid.*, at 26.

69 *Ibid.*, at 33. Leslie Bender, in "Tort Law's Role as a Tool for Social Justice Struggle" (1997-1998), 37-38 Washburn L.J. 249, makes the case for tort law as an important tool of social justice. It empowers the injured by "promoting social equality and protecting human dignity."

insurer.[70] It also is suggested that in certain areas there are other more meaningful deterrent forces at work which render superfluous any deterrence from tort liability. For example, in automobile accidents, fear of personal injury, criminal sanctions, and financial penalties arguably impose sufficient deterrents on drivers.

Does tort liability deter? Some studies and authors suggest that it does,[71] others that it does not.[72] The reality probably is that the deterrent function of tort law varies depending on the activity and the actor.[73] One hardly can deny that the potential of tort liability affects behaviour while at the same time being critical of medical malpractice laws for producing "defensive medicine." Clearly, tort judgments which increase liability insurance premiums, to such an extent that insurance is no longer affordable, deter activities which terminate as a result.[74] One need not be a social scientist to suggest that ordinary people, businesses, and professionals do take into consideration the costs of liability insurance, and the potential for adverse court judgments, in conducting themselves.[75] Whether the

---

70 There are those who counter that the "dulling" effect of liability insurance on deterrence is limited. In Epstein, "A Clash Of Two Cultures: Will The Tort System Survive Automobile Insurance Reform?" (1991), 25 Val. U.L.Rev. 173, the author notes that (i) insurance may not cover the full losses caused, (ii) insurers can control risks by carefully selecting the risks which they will underwrite and by requiring that accident prevention measures be implemented, (iii) insurers will set premiums relative to the size of the risk thereby promoting safety by encouraging drivers to decrease risks, and (iv) by declining to insure at all, insurers can even prevent the activity from taking place altogether. See also, Arlen "Compensation Systems And Efficient Deterrence" (1993), 52 Maryland Rev. 1093 at 1109; and Daniel Shuman, "The Psychology of Deterrence in Tort Law" (1993), 42 Kansas Law Rev. 115.

71 See, e.g., Landes, "Insurance, Liability and Accidents: A Theoretical and Empirical Investigation of the Effect of No-Fault Accidents" (1982), 25 J.L. & Econ. 49; Grayson, "Deterrence in Automobile Liability Insurance — The Empirical Evidence" (1973), 40 Ins. Couns. J. 117; White, "The Function of Deterrence in Motor Vehicle Accident Compensation Schemes", *The Osborne Report*, Vol. 2, at 436; Arlen, "Compensation Systems And Efficient Deterrence" (1993), 52 Maryland Rev. 1053; Daniel Shuman, "The Psychology of Deterrence in Tort Law" (1993), 42 Kansas Law Rev. 115; Harry Snyder, "Serious Tort Reform Isn't: A Critique of Professor Sugarman's 'Serious Tort Law Reform'" (1987), 24 San Diego Law Rev. 893.

72 See, e.g., Sugarman, "Doing Away with Tort Law" (1985), 73 Calif. L. Rev. 558; Brown, "Deterrence in Tort and No-Fault: The New Zealand Experience" (1985), 73 Calif. L. Rev. 976; Belobaba, "Products Liability and Personal Injury Compensation in Canada: Towards Integration and Rationalization" (1983), cited in the Slater Report.

73 A study done on product liability, for example, indicated that "product liability had a notable impact on the quality of products . . .". The Study indicated that liability suits have "motivated management to positive action: for example, improving product safety, product use and warning labels, and manufacturing quality." Risk managers of 232 major American corporations were polled. See Harry Snyder, "Serious Tort Reform Isn't . . .", above, note 71, discussing Weber, *Product Liability: The Corporate Response* (1987), The Conference Board Report No. 893, at 21.

74 In some cases, tort claims and their attendant publicity reach such proportions that entire product lines are eliminated. This reportedly has happened with some reproductive devices and sports equipment. Even products such as vaccines, which may present minimal risks that are offset by great benefits, are endangered. Can one deny the deterrent effect of tort law in these cases?

75 Admittedly this is a question of degree and depends upon the actor and the activity. As Sugarman, above, note 72, points out in his criticism of the deterrent function of tort law, to be effective, deterrence depends on knowledge of the law and of the fact that proposed conduct is dangerous, on the ability to alter behaviour, on the willingness to alter behaviour, and so on.

deterrent effect of tort law is, in itself, a sufficient reason for maintaining it is a different and legitimate question.[76]

(e) Education

Activities regulated by tort law generally do not involve deliberate departures from acceptable norms and standards of behaviour but unthinking carelessness or ignorance. Automobile drivers, engineers, lawyers and doctors do not set out deliberately to injure others, but on occasion they do fail to live up to required standards or to keep themselves informed of current developments. One of tort law's purposes is to remind us of these safety requirements and, more significantly, to ensure that standards do not remain static but move ahead. Tort judgments do not only educate: in some cases they initiate change.

How important or effective is the educative effect of tort? Although this has not been the subject of systematic study,[77] tort judgments have had obvious effects on certain activities. Professionals and others who are specifically affected by tort judgments are kept abreast of important developments through university courses, seminars, conferences, newsletters, periodical literature and so on. In commenting upon the effectiveness of the civil liability system as a mechanism to ensure competence in the professions, Professor Robert Prichard, while acknowledging barriers, concluded:

> In the apparent absence of a superior alternative mechanism, civil liability, with its advantage of flexibility, dynamism, indirectness and individuality, is a relatively attractive and effective tool for achieving minimum levels of continuing competence. An enlightened policy should, in most cases, include civil liability as one element in the calculus of institutional arrangements in the search for competence.[78]

It is fairly clear that tort judgments, and the attendant publicity which they generate, inform others that certain types of activities no longer are to be considered acceptable. After the decision in *Jordan House Ltd. v. Menow*[79] was handed down, one source reported that the following occurred:

---

76 Measuring the deterrent effect of existing laws is basically a theoretical exercise. One can really only know whether a law deters by abolishing it and seeing what happens. In Lundstedt, *Superstition or Rationality in Action for Peace?*, cited by Williams, "The Aims of the Law of Tort" (1951), 4 Current Leg. Prob. 137 at 145, the author states:

> One stares one's eyes out at the *relatively rare* cases where injury has been done but forgets the infinitely greater number of cases in which injury *has not been done* owing to the fact that a social order — including, among other things criminal law and the law of torts — is operative.

Also see White's caution, above, note 71, against using "evidence" to demonstrate the deterrent effect of tort laws, in view of the fact that "experimental conditions" cannot be applied to the research.

77 There are some studies which have examined the effect of tort law judgments on specific behaviour. See, e.g., Robertson, "Informed Consent in Canada: An Empirical Study" (1984), 22 Osgoode Hall L.J. 139, which examined the effect of *Reibl v. Hughes*, [1980] 2 S.C.R. 880, on doctors.

78 Prichard, "Professional Civil Liability and Continuing Competence", in Klar (ed.), *Studies in Canadian Tort Law* (1977), Chapter 13, at 393.

79 (1973), 38 D.L.R. (3d) 105 (S.C.C.). The court held a tavern keeper liable for injuries suffered by a drunk patron on his way home.

Several reports of this case appeared in the journal of the Ontario Hotels Association which helped to finance the defendant's legal costs. A report of the decision in this case was written up in *Time* magazine and on the front page of the *Toronto Daily Star*. In the next few days, several students at the Osgoode Hall Law School did a survey of 28 tavern keepers in the Toronto area. Over 70 percent of them had read a media story about the decision. In one bar, the story from the newspaper had been clipped out and posted on the employees' notice board. When asked if they had altered their conduct as a result of this case, they denied it, insisting that they never served drunk patrons and that, if an intoxicated person would somehow make his way into their bar, they would send him home in a taxi.[80]

Law suits brought against school boards for injuries caused during physical education classes reportedly resulted in changes in the nature of these classes. Although one study has suggested that *Reibl v. Hughes* did not alter significantly the conduct of doctors in informing patients of risks of treatment,[81] clearly doctors are kept very well informed concerning their responsibilities under tort law.[82]

Tort law does more than merely reflect current standards of conduct, or educate people concerning existing norms. It is in the nature of judge-made law that standards and norms actually are advanced from time to time. For example, it is not a conclusive defence in a negligent action that the defendant was "acting like everybody else." There is in the civil justice system the power for judges and juries to respond that this is simply not good enough. The education function of tort law is not merely a passive one — it can be quite active. We not only are taught how things are done, but often we are told how things *should be done*.

(f) Ombudsman

As Linden has written, "Tort law is an ombudsman. It can be used to apply pressure upon those who wield political, economic or intellectual power."[83] With the removal of government immunities from suit and the rapid escalation of governmental tort liability,[84] the ombudsman-like function of tort law is more pronounced now than ever. Although no doubt it is true that governments and corporations often are in a much stronger economic position than those who attempt to challenge their activities in court, there have been too many successful suits to deny the importance of this ombudsman role. Tort law has been used successfully against the police, prison guards, municipal governments, provincial marketing boards, corporations and other powerful defendants.[85]

(g) Other Purposes

In addition to the above-stated functions, the important value of tort law has been expressed in other ways.

---

80 Linden and Klar, *Canadian Tort Law: Cases, Notes & Materials*, 10th ed. (1994), at 286, note 8.

81 Robertson, above, note 77.

82 Linden has written that "Each annual report of the Canadian Medical Protective Association, for example, contains a summary of some of the medical malpractice suits which go to trial each year in Canada.": Linden, *Canadian Tort Law*, 5th ed. (1993), at 13.

83 Linden, *Canadian Tort Law*, 7th ed. (2001), at 22.

84 See below, Chapter 8.

85 The "class action" undoubtedly has given claimants a powerful new weapon to be used against corporations and governments.

In its Report to the American Bar Association,[86] a Special Committee on the Tort Liability System provides an eloquent defence of American tort law. Tort law is seen as serving

> both as a grievance mechanism at a level of advanced social development and as a brake on the overt conflict that may break through the crust of civilization when injury victims have reason to believe that society is not responding to their plight.

It is seen as "an interstitial bonding agent", an "interstitial resolver of individual conflict. . . in a free, and sometimes turbulent society."[87] Tort serves "an important normative function", exerting "a subtle but pervasive influence on the views of hundreds of interest groups, and tens of millions of persons, concerning right behavior."[88] Among others, the Report identifies the following goals expressed by courts in tort law cases:

(i) reduction of the occurrence, and severity, of injury-causing events;
(ii) protecting entitlements;
(iii) responding to representations;
(iv) protecting expectations;
(v) qualitative reconciliation of individual and social interests;
(vi) providing relatively clear standards of conduct;
(viii) reconciliation through a balancing process of competing interests.

The following quote from the Report reflects the Committee's commitment to tort values:

> Tort law provides the front line principles by which American society has chosen to deal with grievances arising from allegedly wrongful injury. It is a principal barometer of the complex trade-offs that society makes among various compensation and deterrence goals, and of the resultant compromises among earnestly expounded economic principles and ethical imperatives. Undeniably tort law is sensitive to the political views of the larger society, and reflective of those views over the long term. Yet it offers the stability of a system of injury rules in which change is incremental, and within which proponents of change must engage in a sophisticated dialectical process of rationalization.[89]

6. THE FAULT/NO-FAULT DEBATE

In view of the above, it may come as somewhat of a surprise to the uninitiated to read what others have written about fault-based compensation. Professor Belobaba, for example, writes:

> If you sat down to design a system for wasting and dissipating precious medical and insurance resources, you could not do any better than what we have now.[90]

Professor Trebilcock states:

---

86 *Towards a Jurisprudence of Injury: the Continuing Creation of a System of Substantive Justice in American Tort Law*, 1984.

87 *Ibid.*, at 3-18.

88 *Ibid.*, at 3-22.

89 *Ibid.*, at 10-188.

90 Belobaba, "Products Liability and Personal Injury Compensation in Canada: Towards Integration and Rationalization" (1983), cited in the Slater Report, at 101.

> As a system of insurance or compensation, the current tort system is on most criteria, an abject failure.[91]

Professor Ison writes:

> Liability for negligence is a capricious and unsatisfactory method of compensating the victims of injury or disease . . . it is thoroughly inefficient as a method of social cost accounting, and its influence on rehabilitation is harmful in far more cases than it is beneficial. Moreover liability combines with other sources of relief not to form a comprehensive or rational system of income security or loss compensation , but a hotchpotch under which the distribution of losses and the financial destiny of the victim and his family depend on a series of chance factors interacting to produce results in each case that depend very largely on sheer luck. Finally, the cost of administering the system is so high that the burdens of liability are roughly double the benefits of compensation.[92]

Professor Sugarman writes:

> Tort law is failing — failing to promote better conduct, failing to compensate sensibly at acceptable costs, and failing to do meaningful justice to either plaintiffs or defendants.[93]

For every argument supporting the continued existence of a civil justice system in the area of accident compensation for personal injuries, there are counter-arguments denigrating the goals, costs, utility, or effectiveness of the existing system. Among the academic community generally, no-fault is favoured.[94] Among practitioners, the opposite is true. The debate is not always reasonable or objective. Lawyers who support the continuation of the existing system are accused of being motivated by self-interest and greed. Opponents of tort law, frustrated by what appears to be the slow pace of reform, steadfastly refuse to acknowledge any virtues in the existing system, but blame the lack of movement on a "conservative backlash"[95] or "right-wing governments."[96] Professor Ison concludes that tort liability does not survive due to "any virtue of the system", but due to "political power, the accidents of history, and the structure of public debate."[97]

---

91 Slater Report, *ibid.*, at 101.

92 Ison, *The Forensic Lottery* (1967), at 28-29.

93 Sugarman, "Doing Away with Tort Law" (1985), 73 Calif. L. Rev. 555 at 664.

94 Although one must note that there are several vocal supporters of tort, even among this community. See Kindregan and Swartz, "The Assault on the Captive Consumer: Emasculating the Common Law of Torts in the Name of Reform" (1987), 18 St. Mary's L.J. 673; Jerry Phillips, "In Defense Of The Tort System" (1985), 27 Arizona L. Rev. 603; Joseph Little, "Up With Torts" (1987), 24 San Diego L. Rev. 681.

95 Atiyah, "No-Fault Compensation: A Question That Will Not Go Away", [1980] Ins. L.J. 625.

96 *Ibid.*

97 Ison, "The Politics of Reform in Personal Injury Compensation" (1977), 27 U.T.L.J. 385. An interesting perspective on the politics of tort law reform is provided by Professor Sugarman in "Ideological Flip-Flop: American Liberals Are Now the Primary Supporters of Tort Law" (January 17, 2005) U.C. Berkeley Public Law Research Paper No. 92544. Sugarman's thesis is that the "conservatives" and "liberals" have switched sides in the United States with reference to their support of tort law. It is now the left that "embraces" tort law, and the right that is "pushing for 'tort reform'". Among the reasons Sugarman gives to explain this development is that the structure of tort law now is decidedly more plaintiff friendly than it traditionally has been, plaintiffs' lawyers have become a more skilful and respectable group, and victims have improved access to the system. As Sugarman notes "in the U.S. today those on the left are the ones who are the main supporters of the fault-based tort system — calling it a crucial weapon in support of progressive causes." Tort law "is depicted as *the* key barricade that prevents

The fault/no-fault debate is essentially an argument about ideology and economics. No doubt it is true that many of the criticisms of the tort liability system raised by opponents are valid. It is suggested, however, that no large legal and administrative process, be it the criminal justice system, the family law area, the taxation process, or Workers' Compensation, once put under the microscope and studied to the extent of tort law,[98] would escape demands for major reform. As well, if critics of tort law were wedded to the values and goals of the system, numerous excellent suggestions for improving the system and reducing its inefficiencies would have emerged from this very able group. No, it is not the inefficiencies of tort law, but a rejection of its ideological premises, which fuels the no-fault debate.[99]

The basic premise of no-fault is that those who have been disabled due to injury, and by extension disease, should be financially assisted, rehabilitated, and, if necessary, retrained, without regard to the cause of their disability. No-fault programs do not distinguish among victims of accidental, negligent or deliberate conduct which results in disability either in terms of eligibility or quantum of benefits. It is therefore clear that no-fault programs do not attempt to achieve, through a system of differential eligibility for compensation, those goals attempted to be achieved through tort law. If education, deterrence, and punishment are goals to be achieved, they are to be achieved outside the no-fault compensation objective. If individual responsibility and accountability between injurer and victim are values to be promoted, they must be promoted in some other way. In other words, no-fault schemes, unlike traditional tort law, keep the compensation of the "victim" separate from other objectives.

It would be nonsensical to suggest that industrialized society does not need to accomplish the objectives of accident deterrence and prevention, and repugnant to argue that we should simply ignore issues of civil justice and personal responsibility. Thus, the strategy of those seeking to eliminate and replace tort liability by no-fault programs is to convince legislators and the public that tort law does not actually achieve its objectives, or give effect to its values, rather than to denigrate the objectives, or values, themselves. As well, the costs of administering a civil justice system as compared to a no-fault program are a major part of the argument.

---

enterprises from simply rolling over consumers and workers on behalf of their owners." And what is the position from the political right? It is not to replace tort law with other mechanisms, but to downsize it; i.e., "to reduce and stabilize the exposure faced by their business and insurer allies, while remaining committed to the basic idea of private law as society's core mechanism for accident regulation and victim compensation." Thus, tort law reformers push for limits on damages, the abolition of joint and several liability, and other changes that would limit the vulnerability of tort defendants. The program of the American Tort Reform Association to fight "law suit abuse" is found on its web site at www.atra.org.

98 No self-respecting law reform commission fails to examine tort law reform at some point in time. The number of Reports and Studies, articles, conferences and seminars on tort law reform is staggering.

99 Different critics have different agenda. Governments, principally concerned about political success worry about rising insurance premiums which upset the electorate. The insurance industry worries about profits. The consumer sees the cost of insurance as being the most immediate issue. Thoughts of the intangible interests, or what seems to be the remote possibility of being seriously injured by the fault of someone else, do not have the same sense of urgency.

The *Woodhouse Report*[100] led to the implementation of what is still the most comprehensive no-fault scheme in the world. Its criticisms of the tort law system and the system's inability to achieve tort law's objectives can be summarized as follows.[101] First, it was stated that the "fault" principle is seriously flawed for the following reasons:

(a) while it focusses on the fault of defendants, it ignores the innocence of the victims and the potentially disastrous effects of their injuries;
(b) the damages awarded against defendants bear no relation to their degree of fault, but to victims' losses;
(c) the test of fault is objective and ignores the individual idiosyncrasies of defendants;
(d) liability insurance spreads the economic consequences of the defendants' fault over the whole community;
(e) the community is not concerned with fault.

Second, the litigation process was attacked. It was argued that the result of litigation was based not on the equities of the matter but on difficulties of proof, the abilities of lawyers, the reactions of juries, and mere chance. Third, the common law process was condemned as being slow and expensive. Fourth, damage assessment was characterized as speculative and opposed to the best interests of the claimant, particularly in regard to prospects for rehabilitation. The Report suggested, as well, that the objectives of tort law to deter, to punish, or its justice values were misconceived because of the externalizing effect of liability insurance. As well, the costs of the tort liability system were emphasized.[102]

Other writers have added additional objections to the continued existence of tort law. In a lengthy article written as a retort to the American Bar Association

---

100 *Royal Commission of Inquiry into Compensation for Personal Injury in New Zealand*, 1967.

101 See Klar, "New Zealand's Accident Compensation Scheme: A Tort Lawyer's Perspective" (1983), 33 U.T.L.J. 80.

102 The New Zealand no-fault system has undergone many changes since its implementation in 1974. It is now viewed as more of an insurance scheme than a system of universal compensation. The trend has been to reduce benefits and to shift the costs of accidents back onto the victims. One of its original architects, Sir Geoffrey Palmer, has written that reforms have turned the scheme into a "mean workers compensation" scheme—Palmer, "New Zealand's Accident Compensation Scheme: Some Twenty Years On" (1994), 44 U.T.L.J. 223 at 277. Another commentator has written of the 1999 reforms in the following terms: "The story of New Zealand's no-fault accident compensation scheme is one of decline: from the lofty aspiration of its creators to the 1999 reality of a lean system that has managed to regain some of the negative features of a fault-based tort system." See Colleen Flood, "New Zealand's No-Fault Accident Compensation Scheme: Paradise or Panacea" (1999/2000), 8 Health L. Rev. 3. For a good discussion of the scheme, the many changes that have been made to it over the years, and academic commentary on it, see Atkin, McLay and Hodge, *Torts in New Zealand: Cases and Materials*, 4th ed. (Auckland: Oxford University Press, 2006) at c. 3. Three points bear noting. First, it is striking how many changes have been made to the scheme over the years. The current act is the Injury Prevention, Rehabilitation, and Compensation Act 2001. Second, the editors note, at 120, that, "Parliament is aware that in removing the right to sue it has removed an important device for setting standards in the workplace, in product safety, in professions such as medicine, and in other areas." This has necessitated enacting other laws. Third, the editors note that in view of the decreasing level of compensation, lawyers on behalf of their clients are seeking ways around the Act to be able to sue. This has resulted in the same "conglomeration of different mechanisms to deal with safety and accidents" albeit with different "goal posts" that existed before accident compensation was introduced.

Committee Report,[103] Professor Sugarman outlines more of tort law's failings.[104] The deterrent function of tort law is minimized by suggesting: (a) that other forces, such as self-preservation instincts, the competitive market, personal morality and governmental regulation would deter in the absence of tort; (b) that deterrence requires knowledge of the law and the dangers of certain activities, yet such knowledge may be absent; (c) that often, even with knowledge, people cannot alter their behaviour; (d) that people may discount the threat of liability; (e) that people may prefer to run the risk; (f) that people may regard the potential penalty to be small; (g) that people may really have little to lose. Sugarman stresses the effect which liability insurance has had on the theoretical deterrent function. Sugarman also notes the failings of tort law as a system of compensation: it fails to compensate many victims; it compensates arbitrarily; it overcompensates some. The justice role is also minimized. Again, the effect of liability insurance is an important factor in Sugarman's objections to tort law's ability to achieve justice values.

Tort law's adherents counter these attacks with arguments of their own. The notions that the concept of fault is ambiguous and that the tort system is a lottery are discounted by studies which indicate that in the vast majority of instances tort cases are settled out of court, files are closed relatively quickly, and settlements are reached which significantly meet plaintiffs' realistic expectations.[105] Thus, arguments which focus on delays, difficulties of proof, lawyering skills, jury reactions, and costs — in other words, the vagaries of litigation — do not apply in the resolution of most tort disputes. The dulling effect of liability insurance on the deterrence and justice pursuits of tort law is mitigated by the realization that automobile insurance premiums are "experience-rated", there are deductibles which become the responsibility of the insured, there are monetary policy limits, all claims are not insurable, and there are uninsurable costs of claims, in terms of time required to defend, impact on reputation and goodwill, and emotional distress.[106]

Two of the most important issues in the no fault debate involve the question of values and the question of deterrence. Does wrongdoing matter? In determining the answer to this, one can draw from one's own beliefs and from the experiences of victims of wrongdoing. It is noteworthy that among the proponents for a more responsive and generous system of civil justice are victims' rights' groups. Their advocacy has been reflected, for example, in Alberta legislation that increased significantly the amount of benefits payable to the family members of those killed

103 Above, note 86.

104 Above, note 72.

105 See, for example, Danzon, "The Medical Malpractice System: Facts and Reforms", in *The Effects of Litigation On Health Care Costs* 28, 30 (Mary Ann Baily & Watkins I. Cikins, eds.) (1985), cited in Saks, "Do We Really Know Anything About the Behaviour of the Tort Litigation System — And Why Not?" (1992), 140 U. of Penn. L.R. 1147. In Bruce, "The Deterrent Effects of Automobile Insurance and Tort Law: A Survey of the Empirical Literature" (1984), 6 Law & Policy 67, at 69, the author states that an American study of 352 automobile accident insurance claims found that 90 per cent involved uncontroverted evidence of fault.

106 See Arlens, "Compensation Systems And Efficient Deterrence" (1993), 52 Maryland Rev. 1093; Shuman, "The Psychology of Deterrence In Tort Law" (1993), 42 Kansas Law Rev. 115; and Epstein, "A Class Of Two Cultures: Will The Tort System Survive Serious Automobile Insurance Reform" (1991), 25 Val. U.L.Rev. 173.

by the wrongdoing of others.[107] It is also significant to note that victims of sexual abuse have begun to see the civil justice system as a useful vehicle to remedy their wrongs.

As time passes and experience with no-fault regimes grows, new evidence emerges that wrongdoing and personal accountability remain important issues long after tort is removed. A New Zealand commentator notes, for example, that continued restrictions on the right to sue in New Zealand should not be accepted "without clear and valid reasons" and that 14 years after the implementation of no-fault in New Zealand, "individual responsibility is the catch-cry".[108] The author goes on to argue that the opportunity to bring a tort action "is a vehicle for dealing with one's own life, and "provides a public vindication of the right of individuals to expect and receive a certain standard of treatment from fellow citizens".[109]

Evidence of the deterrent effect of fault based compensation emerges from jurisdictions which have abolished tort. One author who has looked at this states that the empirical evidence demonstrates that adopting no-fault does increase expected accident costs.[110] The Quebec no-fault experience is used to highlight this conclusion. The evidence demonstrated an increase in bodily injury accidents and fatalities after the scheme's introduction.[111]

7. CONCLUSION

The lengthy arguments for and against a system of tort liability are bewildering. Proponents list all the things that the system, in their opinion, achieves; opponents are equally adamant in their denial of these benefits. What strikes one about the debate is that it is not really a debate at all, but two strongly held, but diametrically

---

107 See Fatal Accidents Amendment Act, 1994, S.A. 1994, c. 16, s. 5 [now R.S.A. 2000, c.F-8, s. 8]. The amount that can be recovered as "bereavement damages" is $75,000.

108 Catherine Yates, "Law Commission Proposals for Accident Compensation: What Place for Personal Remedies?" (1989), 19 Victoria U.L.R. 29 at 30, 38.

109 *Ibid.* There are other passages strongly supporting the value structure which underlies tort. For example, the author writes:

> In a democratic country, the determination to assert and stand by one's rights, the willingness to take control, to demand accountability, and to pursue matters that affect one personally are characteristics which need to be fostered, not frustrated. Under the ACS, a person who is injured becomes a client of the state. The person may be cushioned by the scheme, but is also muffled by it. There is no opportunity to bring attention to a state of affairs which is seen as unsatisfactory. . . . As victims are channelled into dealing with bureaucracy they are rendered impotent, are disempowered.

The author notes the value of tort to society as well as to individual victims. It "establishes the changing boundaries between acceptable and unacceptable behaviour", at 40.

110 See Arlen, "Compensation Systems And Effective Deterrence" (1993), 52 Maryland L. Rev. 1093 at 1113.

111 Marc Gaudry's study on "The Effects on Road Safety of the Compulsory Insurance, Flat Premium Rating and No-Fault Features of the 1978 Quebec Automobile Act", in the *Report Of The Inquiry Into Motor Vehicle Accident Compensation In Ontario*, 1988, is frequently cited as authority for this. The increase in bodily injury accidents was 26.3 per cent, and in fatalities 6.8 per cent, a year after the scheme. Other studies support this. See Rose Anne Devlin, "Liability Versus No-Fault Automobile Insurance Accident Regimes: An Analysis of the Experience in Quebec", in Georges Dionne, *Contributions To Insurance Economics* (1992), at 449. These are discussed by Arlens, "Compensation Systems And Efficient Deterrence", above, note 106.

opposed views, about how the legal system should deal with victims of accidents. Arguments submitted by both sides are more often than not statements of opinion, unsupported by convincing evidence. As well, there is the tendency for the two sides to simply ignore each other's statistics and arguments when they do not fit neatly into their own submissions.

When all is said and done the decision whether to retain a system of private rights of action or to abandon it comes down to a question of individual judgment. It is my judgment that to abandon the system, rather than to improve it, would be a mistake. Canadian society needs a mechanism whereby the rights of individuals are protected and advanced. We simply do not know today what protections will be required tomorrow. The private right of action is the most effective way for individuals to insist upon rights they believe they ought to have. The private action is fluid and flexible and reflects changing conceptions of what type of society Canada is. It is especially ironic, in the age of the Charter, where courts have been chosen to implement new visions of liberties, to turn away from private rights of action. Rights must be protected, not only by legislation, but by the private right of action. Law must be seen to be able to accomplish more than efficiency. Law must reflect, even if symbolically, the basic tenets of society, one of which is that persons ought to be individually responsible for the consequences of their acts. The obsession with liability insurance as an antidote to the values of tort law is unconvincing. There is a difference between receiving compensation from a wrongdoer, even if it comes from an insurer, and receiving it from a no-fault social insurance program. Liability insurance arises from a contractual arrangement between two private parties whereby for a specified premium, and on certain terms, the wrongdoer's insurer may assume financial responsibility for a judgment *obtained against the wrongdoer*. It is the wrongdoer's conduct which has given rise to the judgment, and it is the wrongdoer's responsibility to pay for it — one way or the other. Those injured by the careless or deliberate acts of others have a right to be fully restored. This is not possible in no-fault schemes which compensate everyone equally. Those injured by the fault of others ought not to be required to subsidize a no-fault social insurance scheme by accepting less than full compensation.

2

Trespass and Intentional Interferences With Persons, Property and Chattels

1. INTRODUCTION

Twentieth century tort law has been dominated by the law of negligence. Freed from the shackles of "privity of contract" by *Donoghue v. Stevenson*,[1] and operating in a society where injuries frequently are caused by carelessness and only rarely by deliberate acts of wrongdoing, negligence claims account for the vast majority of tort actions and payments for personal injury and death.[2] In view of this, tort actions for personal injuries and property damage based on causes of action other than negligence have been viewed as less important and have received little attention from academics and other observers. In many respects, however, these other tort actions, and in particular the so-called "intentional torts", personify the values and virtues of a vibrant system of civil justice.[3]

2. THE HISTORICAL CONTEXT

The tort actions dealing with direct interferences with persons, their chattels, and their land stem from the writs of trespass *vi et armis, de bonis asportatis*, and *quare clausum fregit*. Although these now commonly are referred to as the intentional torts, in Canada this reference is inaccurate. The writ of trespass was

---

1 [1932] A.C. 562 (H.L.).

2 According to the Pearson Report, above, Chapter 1, note 54, for example, 87 per cent of tort claims arose from motor vehicle and work-related accidents. Occupiers' liability claims accounted for an additional 5 per cent. Sugarman, "A Century of Change in Personal Injury Law" (2000), 88 Calif. L. Rev. 2403, citing U.S. statistics, notes that car accidents accounted for 45 per cent of accidental deaths in 1998. 1989 statistics show that the major causes of injuries were slips and falls (40 per cent), car accidents (20 per cent), products (30 per cent). Thus, it is clear that careless or accidental conduct is responsible for most injuries and deaths.

3 For an overview of this area, see Sullivan, "Trespass to the Person in Canada: A Defence of the Traditional Approach" (1987), 19 Ottawa L. Rev. 533.

developed in the thirteenth century in order to assist those who were the victims of direct and forcible interferences. There was no requirement that the interference be intended by the defendant, nor that the conduct otherwise be wrongfully motivated.[4] Fleming has suggested that direct and forcible interferences were actionable in order to preserve the peace and order in society, as this was the type of conduct ''most likely to cause breach of peace by provoking retaliation.''[5] These torts were actionable without proof of damage, consistent with the theory that the defendant's conduct was wrongful not because actual physical damage had been caused, but because the plaintiff's security, and society's tranquility, had been disrupted.

The directness requirement of these torts was rigidly adhered to. This led to the creation of a new writ, the action on the case, to provide a remedy where a consequential injury had been caused by the defendant's wrongful conduct. Case differed from trespass in certain important respects. It was not actionable without proof of damage. In addition the defendant's conduct must have been wrongful.[6] According to Fleming,

> Trespassory harm was prima facie wrongful and it was for the defendant to raise any justification or excuse . . . In contrast, the action on the case from the beginning required proof by the plaintiff of either wrongful intent or negligence on the part of the defendant.[7]

The historical differences between trespass and case have survived in Canadian tort law resulting in a somewhat confusing situation. It is necessary to distinguish between injuries which have resulted directly from the defendant's acts, as opposed to those which are indirect or consequential. As well, there are torts committed intentionally, and those committed negligently. Torts which involve direct interferences committed intentionally comprise the intentional torts of assault, battery, false imprisonment, trespass to chattels, and trespass to land. Other intentional torts, which consist of either direct or indirect injuries, are intentional infliction of mental suffering, detinue, and conversion. Complicating matters is the fact that at least certain of the direct interferences, such as assault, battery, and trespass to chattels and land may also be committed negligently, and are actionable as such. Finally, there are indirect interferences which are actionable in negligence, or case. Since there remain important practical differences between these causes of action, it is important to define their distinguishing elements.

---

4 There is, as pointed out in Chapter 1, a debate concerning the role of ''fault'' in these early tort actions. See Chapter 1, note 5.

5 Fleming, *The Law of Torts*, 9th ed. (1998), at 21.

6 See Kiralfy, *Action on the Case* (1951). According to Kiralfy there were several bases of wrongfulness — breach of a legal obligation to use care, based on custom, prescriptive duties, or statute. The origin of the action upon the case is discussed by Sharpe J.A. in *Perry, Farley & Onyschuk v. Outerbridge Management Ltd.* (2001), 54 O.R. (3d) 131 (C.A.), at para. 21 and following. The issue facing the Court of Appeal related to the limitation period for a statutory right of action for a fraudulent conveyance. The court decided that the action was not an action on the case. A similar concern faced Stinson J. in an action for deceit or fraudulent misrepresentation in *Bozzo, Re* (2005), [2005] O.J. No. 2037, 2005 CarswellOnt 1996 (S.C.J.). See below in Chapter 17.

7 Fleming, above, note 5, at 22.

3. "DIRECT" AND "INDIRECT"

The essential characteristic of those torts which stem from the writs of trespass *vi et armis, de bonis asportatis*, and *quare clausum fregit* was that they concerned injuries which resulted "directly" from the wrongdoer's act as contrasted with "indirectly" (or consequentially). The requirement of direct injury distinguished trespass from case, the latter form of action having been developed for the specific purpose of affording remedies to those who suffered consequential injuries from the wrongful conduct of others.

Although frequently ignored, there are no reasons to suggest that the directness requirement has been eliminated in the modern tort actions based on trespass. Quite to the contrary, high case authority has reaffirmed its continued importance. Lord Denning, in *Southport Corp. v. Esso Petroleum Co.*,[8] refused to consider the defendant's conduct in permitting oil to be carried onto the plaintiff's foreshore as a trespass to land, since "in order to support an action for trespass to land, the act done by the defendant must be a physical act done by him *directly* on to the plaintiff's land."[9] Lord Denning, in arriving at this conclusion, cited Viscount Simon's judgment in *Read v. J. Lyons & Co.*,[10] where Viscount Simon affirmed the same point by observing that "the circumstances in *Fletcher v. Rylands* did not constitute a case of trespass because the damage was consequential, not direct."[11]

Despite the importance of the directness requirement,[12] it is difficult to define this term, and to distinguish between injuries which are directly as opposed to indirectly produced. Judgments which have recognized the requirement invariably fail to explain it. Even scholarly literature tends to gloss over it.[13]

---

8 [1954] 2 All E.R. 561, reversed on other grounds [1955] 3 All E.R. 864 (H.L.).

9 *Ibid.*, at 570 (emphasis added).

10 [1946] 2 All E.R. 471 at 474 (H.L.).

11 See also *Fowler v. Lanning*, [1959] 1 All E.R. 290 (Q.B.), and *Cook v. Lewis*, [1951] S.C.R. 830, where, though not in issue, the directness requirement is seen as the essential characteristic of trespass actions. This point was reaffirmed by the Supreme Court of Canada in a sexual battery case, *Sansalone v. Wawanesa Mutual Insurance Co.* (2000), (sub nom. *Non-Marine Underwriters, Lloyd's of London v. Scalera*) 185 D.L.R. (4th) 1, 50 C.C.L.T. (2d) 1 (S.C.C.) at 11 [C.C.L.T.]:

> The traditional rule, as noted, is that the plaintiff in an action for trespass to the person (which includes battery) succeeds if she can prove direct interference with her person.

12 The direct/indirect dichotomy is a theme which recurs throughout tort law. In addition to distinguishing trespass from case, it is, for example, an aspect of remoteness tests in the negligence action and is a critical factor in several of the business torts.

13 The directness requirement is discussed by Trindade, "Intentional Torts: Some Thoughts on Assault and Battery" (1982), 2 Oxford J. Leg. Stud. 211 at 216, and in Trindade, Cane and Lunney, *The Law of Torts in Australia*, 4th ed. (2007), at 36-38. Trindade argues that directness is a requirement of the intentional torts and notes that this is not something sufficiently emphasized in the standard textbooks. Atrens, in "Intentional Interference with the Person", in Linden (ed.), *Studies in Canadian Tort Law* (1968), Chapter 14, acknowledges the directness requirement for torts based on trespass, but supports the American position which seemingly has abandoned it. Linden and Feldthusen, *Canadian Tort Law*, 8th ed. (2006), at 44, suggest that the directness requirement is no longer part of the battery claim, although the point is not fully discussed. Fridman, *The Law of Torts in Canada*, 2d ed. (Toronto: Carswell, 2002) at 30

An injury can be described as being directly produced by the defendant's act when it flows naturally from it, without the necessity of an intervention by another independent factor. Where, however, the defendant's act merely creates the situation of danger, and requires an additional act to produce the ultimate injury, the injury can be described as only flowing indirectly from the initial act.[14] A test of directness can be posed as follows: would the result have occurred had it not been for the intervention of another independent agency?[15]

Most cases of trespass to persons, goods or land clearly satisfy this test. Battery cases, for example, invariably involve immediate acts of violence or offensive contact created by the defendant without the involvement of other acts. There can be no question that being struck by a bullet, punched by a fist, stabbed by a knife, struck by a golf ball, a hockey puck or stick, shaken or tackled to the ground, or being operated on by a surgeon, satisfy this test of directness. It is conceded, however, that as with all situations which require the drawing of lines, cases can present themselves which are difficult to categorize.[16]

The case often mentioned to illustrate the breadth of the directness requirement is *Scott v. Shepherd.*[17] In that case the defendant threw a lighted squib into an enclosed market-house. It landed upon the stall of Y., was picked up by W. to prevent damage to Y.'s goods and thrown onto R.'s stall. R. picked it up and threw it into the market where it struck the plaintiff and exploded, blinding him in one eye. The action against the defendant was based on assault and battery. Of the four justices who decided the case, three found in favour of the plaintiff, Mr. Justice Blackstone dissenting. There was no disagreement concerning the law. Lord Chief Justice de Grey, finding in the plaintiff's favour, stated it clearly:

> For doing an unlawful act, as by laying a log in the highway whereby another is hurt, it is a nuisance, for which trespass vi et armis will not lie, but trespass upon the case; whether the injury occasioned by the act be immediate and direct or not is the criterion, and not whether the act be unlawful or not; if the injury be immediate and direct, it is trespass vi et armis, if consequential, it will be trespass on the case.[18]

---

makes it clear that directness is a requirement of trespass. Osborne, *The Law of Torts*, 3rd ed. (2007), at 239, also affirms the directness requirement.

14 Sullivan, above, note 3, at 562, defines directness as follows: "Interference is direct if it is the immediate consequence of a force set in motion by an act of the defendant."

15 In *Sansalone v. Wawanesa Mutual Insurance Co.* (2000), 50 C.C.L.T. (2d) 1 (S.C.C.) at 11, McLachlin J. defined "directness" in the following way: "Interference is direct if it is the immediate consequence of a force set in motion by an act of the defendant."

16 It is especially problematic when the victim's own involvement combines with the defendant's act to produce the result. For example, would secretly putting poison into someone's food constitute a battery? Would pulling a chair out from someone who is about to sit down be sufficiently direct? See Linden and Feldthusen, *Canadian Tort Law*, 8th ed. (2006), at 43, where these are seen as "indirect" intrusions which give rise to liability in battery. In *J. (M.I.) v. Grieve* (1996), [1996] B.C.J. No. 236, 1996 CarswellBC 260 (S.C.), the defendant secretly drugged the plaintiff by putting barbiturates into her food. The court treated this as a battery. In *Wuttunee v. Merck Frosst Canada Ltd.*, [2007] 4 W.W.R. 309 (Sask. Q.B.), the court refused to strike out a claim for battery brought against the manufacturers of an allegedly harmful drug (Vioxx) by users of that drug. While not necessarily agreeing that the defendants' actions were "sufficiently direct to constitute a battery", Klebuc C.J.S. stated that "the plaintiffs have pled sufficient facts to warrant further consideration of their claim as novel or timely expansion of the tort of battery", at para. 54.

17 (1773), 95 E.R. 1124.

18 *Ibid.*, at 1129.

There was, however, disagreement over the facts — was the injury sufficiently direct? Mr. Justice Blackstone thought not. His Lordship argued that the intervening parties:

> gave the squib two new directions, acting as free agents, not by the instigation, command, request, or as servants of the defendant, but in defence of their persons, so the injury which happened to the plaintiff was the consequence of, and not done immediately by the first act of the defendant.[19]

The other justices viewed the sequence of events as "a continuation of the first act of the defendant until the explosion;"[20] as in fact "one single act." It was "as if it had been a cracker made with gunpowder which had bounded and rebounded again and again before it had struck out the plaintiff's eye."[21] The court was concerned with leaving the plaintiff potentially without a remedy if the requirement of directness was to be applied too rigidly. Mr. Justice Nares stated that:

> the plaintiff . . . ought to receive a satisfaction . . . so we will not look with eagle's eyes to see whether the evidence applies exactly or not to the case, when we can see the plaintiff has obtained a verdict for such damages as he deserves, but we will establish such verdict if possible.[22]

As a matter of contemporary policy, there are no reasons why courts should continue to distinguish between direct and indirect injuries. Historically, the distinction served a purpose, since in the absence of a coherent theory of wrongs it did provide a basis for distinguishing between tortious and non-tortious conduct. However, in light of tort law's development and its emphasis on the nature of the defendant's conduct, rather than on the physical sequence of events which lead to the plaintiff's injury, it is anomalous to allow the directness/indirectness issue to continue to have any relevance. Conduct which results in direct injury is no more deserving of sanction or its victim more worthy of compensation than conduct which results in indirect harm.[23]

---

19 *Ibid.*, at 1128.

20 *Ibid.*, at 1129.

21 *Ibid.*

22 *Ibid.*, at 1127, quoting Lord Chief Justice Wilmot in *Slater v. Baker* (1767), 1 Wilson 359 at 362, 95 E.R. 860 at 862.

23 Trindade, Cane and Lunney, above, note 13, point out that the distinction is no longer an element in U.S. tort law. See the American Restatement (Second). As well, they note that the English Law Reform Committee on Conversion and Detinue recommended its abolition with reference to trespass to goods:

> Such distinctions as that between giving poisoned meat to a dog (trespass) and leaving poisoned meat for a dog (case) do not seem to us to have any place in a rational system of law and, in our view, if an intentional act causes injury to a chattel it ought not to matter whether the result is brought about by direct or indirect means.

See Trindade, Cane and Lunney at 38, note 62. Osborne, above, note 13, at 239 also thinks that the distinction should be jettisoned. For a contrary view, see Sullivan, above, note 3, at 562-63. Sullivan supports the continuation of the distinction for several reasons. She argues that where direct injuries are caused, the plaintiff has shown that his right to personal autonomy has been violated, and hence, the defendant *prima facie* should be required to pay, or justify his conduct. With direct interferences, the victims are more likely to be aggrieved, and it is more "just" to require compensation, or at least, justification. McLachlin J., in *Sansalone*, above, note 15, is supportive of Professor Sullivan's approach, noting that direct interferences with the plaintiff's rights have high "demoralization" costs. See Klar, "Intentional and Negligent Trespass: It is Time to Clarify the Law" (2004), 28 Advocates' Quarterly 410 at 421.

4. ACCIDENTAL, NEGLIGENT AND INTENTIONAL CONDUCT

All conduct can be seen as falling somewhere along a continuum, with accidental conduct falling at one end, and a deliberate attempt to injure falling at the other. When considering the defendant's conduct as an element of a cause of action in tort, and describing it as accidental, negligent, or intentional, one is having regard to the defendant's state of knowledge and appreciation of the *consequences* of the contemplated act, and the steps which ought to have been taken to avoid them.

Where a defendant acts and produces consequences which were either not reasonably foreseeable or not reasonably preventable, the conduct which produced the result may be seen as being accidental. Where, however, the defendant ought to have reasonably foreseen and avoided the result, the defendant's failure to have done so can be described as negligent. Finally, where a defendant acts either knowing with substantial certainty what the consequences of the act would be, or desiring them, the defendant can be said to have intended these consequences. These differences in knowledge and foreseeability of consequences, and the means which ought to have been taken to avoid them, explain the basic differences between torts of strict liability, negligence, and intention.

Direct interferences with persons, chattels and land must be committed either intentionally or negligently to be actionable in trespass. Normally, intentional trespasses are considered to be the most serious breaches, deserving the harshest of sanctions. Courts, for example, traditionally have refused to permit defendants liable for an intentional trespass to plead contributory negligence,[24] and have not limited the damages recoverable against them by the reasonable foreseeability test.[25] In most cases of intentional trespass, the wrongdoing of defendants is serious. Defendants found liable for intentional trespasses generally knew that their conduct would detrimentally affect their victims, and wanted these injuries to occur. Technically, however, the concept of "intention" in the intentional torts does not require defendants to know that their acts will result in harm to the plaintiffs. Defendants must know only that their acts will result in certain consequences. It is not necessary for defendants to realize that these intended consequences are in fact an infringement of the legal rights of others. Intention, in other

---

24 This is not a hard and fast rule, and depends upon the jurisdiction and legislation. In *Berntt v. Vancouver (City)*, [1997] 4 W.W.R. 505, 33 C.C.L.T. (2d) 1 (B.C. S.C.), reversed on other grounds and new trial ordered (1999), 46 C.C.L.T. (3d) 139, 174 D.L.R. (4th) 403 (B.C. C.A.), additional reasons at (1999), 179 D.L.R. (4th) 380, 47 C.C.L.T. (2d) 149 (B.C. C.A.), for example, contributory negligence was held to be applicable in an intentional tort case. The action was ultimately dismissed, however, based on s. 32(1) of the Criminal Code; see (2001), 209 D.L.R. (4th) 494 (B.C. S.C.). For discussion of other cases, see Chapter 13.

25 One judge, for example, stated that wrongdoers who have acted "with intent to violate the interests of others" have engaged in "such morally reprehensible conduct" so as to make them undeserving of the court's solicitude. See Borins Co. Ct. J. in *Bettel v. Yim* (1978), 20 O.R. (2d) 617 at 627, citing Atrens, "Intentional Interference with the Person", in Linden (ed.), *Studies in Canadian Tort Law* (1968). See also *Redlick v. Hallberg* (1993), 114 Sask. R. 15 (Q.B.).

words, focuses on physical consequences.[26] Mistake as to the legal or factual effect of these consequences is no defence in the intentional torts.

The clearest application of this analysis occurred in the English case, *Hollins v. Fowler*.[27] A broker was held liable in conversion — the intentional denial of the plaintiff's title to goods — by arranging for the sale of the plaintiff's goods, without his knowledge, on the mistaken belief that the goods which were being sold belonged not to the plaintiff but to another person. The broker had been led to this belief by a thief. Nevertheless, by arranging for the sale of goods the broker was knowingly transferring title to them; this transfer of title amounted to a denial of the true owner's rights to the goods, and hence was an intentional conversion.[28] Trespass to land also arises frequently as a result of an innocent act. If people enter or interfere with land on the mistaken belief that the land is their own, this nevertheless constitutes the tort of intentional trespass, should it turn out that the land belongs to another. It is relevant that the defendant, when committing the act, knew that the physical result would be the occupation of a piece of land, not that the occupation would in fact be wrongful in law.[29] Even the tort of intentional battery need not involve the intention to harm. Anyone who applies force to another person, even for the intended benefit of the other person,[30] can be liable for a battery. The same holds true for the tort of false imprisonment. The honest belief that the imprisonment of the plaintiff was justified does not negate the tort of intentional false imprisonment should the defendant's belief prove to be wrong.[31] It must be stated, however, that despite these examples of "innocent"

---

26 Quoted with approval by Iacobucci J. in *Sansalone v. Wawanesa Mutual Insurance Co.* (2000), 50 C.C.L.T. (2d) 1 (S.C.C.) at 39.

27 (1875), L.R. 7 H.L. 757.

28 There are similar Canadian cases. See *Can. Laboratory Supplies Ltd. v. Engelhard Indust. of Can. Ltd.* (1979), 97 D.L.R. (3d) 1 (S.C.C.); *Nilsson Bros. Inc. v. McNamara Estate*, [1992] 3 W.W.R. 761 (Alta. C.A.); *Portage Credit Union Ltd. v. D.E.R. Auctions Ltd.*, [1994] 4 W.W.R. 59 (Alta. C.A.); *Mutungih v. Bokun* (2006), 40 C.C.L.T. (3d) 313 (Ont.).

29 The common law's position of regarding this innocent conduct as an *intentional* wrong was articulated long ago by Oliver Wendel Holmes in his treatise on *The Common Law*, 1881 at 97-98. In Krauss, "Tort Law and Private Ordering" (1991), 35 Saint Louis University L.J. 623, at 634, note 53, the author makes the point that "if X deliberately chops down fifty trees, honestly thinking that he owns them while in reality the trees and the land belong to Y, X will be liable for the intentional tort of trespass." Holmes' book is quoted as follows:

> When a man goes upon his neighbor's land, thinking it is his own, he intends the very act or consequence complained of. He means to intermeddle with a certain thing in a certain way, and it is just that intended intermeddling for which he is sued. . . . [H]e does intend to do the damage complained of. One who diminishes the value of property by intentional damage knows it belongs to somebody. If he thinks it belongs to himself, he expects whatever harm he may do to come out of his own pocket. It would be odd if he were to get rid of the burden by discovering that it belonged to his neighbor.

30 For example, medical treatment. In *Toews (Guardian ad litem of) v. Weisner* (2001), 3 C.C.L.T. (3d) 293 (B.C. S.C.), vaccinating a student against Hepatitis B under the honest but mistaken belief that the parents had consented constituted an actionable battery.

31 See, for example, *Lebel v. Roe*, [1994] Y.J. No. 62. Hudson J. explained the point clearly:

> Conduct is intentional if a person desires to produce the consequences that follow from this act. However, conduct may also be considered to be intentional even where the defendant acts by mistake. If a defendant desires to produce a particular result which he or she

intended trespasses, most examples of intentional interferences involve not only the intention of physical results, but the knowledge that these results are legally and morally wrong.

A negligent trespass occurs when the defendant directly interferes with the plaintiff as a result of careless behaviour. For example, when a defendant unreasonably fires a gun in the plaintiff's direction and a bullet strikes the plaintiff, there has been a negligent trespass.[32] That this type of action can be maintained in Canada was affirmed in the leading case of *Cook v. Lewis*,[33] and in numerous other cases.[34] As we shall see, there are important advantages available to a plaintiff in an action for negligent trespass, which are not available in the ordinary negligence action.[35]

Accidental trespasses are not actionable. Thus, where the defendant's trespassory act was neither intended nor negligent, the plaintiff's action cannot succeed. Although this is an unlikely scenario in cases involving direct interferences with the protected interests of others, courts should allow for the defence of "innocent" contact in trespass cases.[36]

5. VOLITION AND CAPACITY

Whether dealing with torts based upon direct or indirect injuries, or intentional or negligent conduct, issues relating to the defendant's volition and capacity, and their effect on the defendant's liability, must be resolved. Not surprisingly, the issue of the effect of lack of volition, or incapacity, on liability in tort, has

---

mistakenly believes to be innocent, he or she may still be held liable for intending the consequence.

32 Although this can also be called a "negligent battery", it is apparent that battery more and more is being defined by the courts exclusively as an intentional tort. It therefore might be helpful to restrict the use of the term "battery" to intentional interferences with persons, and "negligent trespass" for negligent interferences with persons, although I personally prefer the terms intentional battery and negligent battery. See discussion on "negligent battery" below.

33 [1951] S.C.R. 830.

34 See, among others, *Teece v. Honeybourn* (1975), 54 D.L.R. (3d) 549 (B.C. S.C.) (gunshot wound); *Larin v. Goshen* (1975), 56 D.L.R. (3d) 719 (N.S. C.A.) (defendant knocking down plaintiff); *Hatton v. Webb* (1977), 81 D.L.R. (3d) 377 (Alta. Dist. Ct.) (defendant throwing wet towel at plaintiff); *Ellison v. Rogers* (1967), 67 D.L.R. (2d) 21 (Ont. H.C.) (golfing injury); *Dahlberg v. Naydiuk* (1969), 10 D.L.R. (3d) 319 (Man. C.A.) (firing gun over land). See Klar, "Intentional and Negligent Trespass: It is Time to Clarify the Law", above, note 23.

35 The plaintiff need not prove damage in order to succeed and there is a presumption of fault which the defendant must rebut. See below.

36 For example, if I am holding a gun that I accidentally discharge and the bullet hits someone, I should not be held liable for a battery. It is only where I desire to hit the person, am substantially certain that the person will be hit, or am negligent in my handling of the gun, that liability should result. *Dicta* by McLachlin J. in *Sansalone v. Wawanesa Mutual Insurance Co.* (2000), 50 C.C.L.T. (2d) 1 (S.C.C.) at 12 suggests that the mere violation of a plaintiff's right is a form of fault that is actionable. If this implies that accidental trespasses, in the sense used above, are actionable, it would represent a major departure from accepted authority. The point was not in issue in the case since the sexual contact was intended. The issue concerned the defence of consent, and not whether the sexual act itself was intentional, negligent or accidental.

stimulated legal writers.[37] The issue strikes at the heart of the debate over the purposes of fault-based compensation. The voluntariness of a defendant's act, and the capacity to understand and appreciate consequences, are essential requirements for the justice, punishment, deterrence, and education goals of tort law. Volition and capacity are not relevant if all the system seeks to do is to compensate victims. Since judicial views and preferences concerning tort law's purposes are not uniform, the treatment of volition and capacity issues is not consistent.

At a minimum, liability in tort is predicated on the requirement that the act which caused the plaintiff's injury was the defendant's act. Where, therefore, a defendant who is sued for trespass to land is able to show that he was carried upon the land by others, he will be relieved of liability because the trespass was not his act, but the act of those who carried him.[38] In other words, there was a lack of *volition.* The volition issue becomes more difficult, however, where, as happens more often, the defendant's lack of control over an act results not from external forces, but from an internal condition. The trap for the unwary here is the tendency to merge and to thereby confuse the concepts of volition and capacity.[39]

Take, for example, the case where a defendant injures another while unconscious, during a seizure, while sleepwalking, or while under the dominating influence of alcohol or drugs. In these cases, we may apply the *dicta* from *Stokes v. Carlson:*

> A contraction of muscles which is purely a reaction to some outside force, convulsive movements of an epileptic, movements of the body during sleep when will is in abeyance, and movements during periods of unconsciousness, are not "acts" of the person, and the person will not be responsible for injuries inflicted thereby, since such movements are without volition.[40]

In these cases the acts are involuntary, and the actors will not be liable in tort for the injuries which were caused due to their unconscious state.[41] One may classify

---

37 See, among others, Bohlen, "Liability in Tort of Infants and Insane Persons" (1924), 23 Mich. L. Rev. 9; Fridman, "Mental Incompetency" (1964), 80 L.Q.R. 84; Alexander and Szasz, "Mental Illness as an Excuse for Civil Wrongs" (1967-68), 43 Notre Dame Lawyer 24; Hornblower, "Insanity and the Law of Negligence" (1905), 5 Colum. L. Rev. 278; Robertson, *Mental Disability and the Law in Canada* 2nd ed. (1994), Chapter 10; Robins, "Tort Liability Of The Mentally Disabled", in Linden (ed.), *Studies in Canadian Tort Law* (1968), Chapter 4; Sharpe, "Mental State as Affecting Liability in Tort" (1975), 23 Chitty's L. J. 46; Picher, "The Tortious Liability of The Insane in Canada" (1975), 13 Osgoode Hall L.J. 191; E.J. Goldstein, "Asking the Impossible: The Negligence Liability of the Mentally Ill" (1995), 12 J. Contemp. Health L. & Pol'y 67; Harry Korrell, "The Liability of Mentally Disabled Tort Defendants" (1995), L. & Psychol. Rev. 1; and Grant Morris, "Requiring Sound Judgments of Unsound Minds: Tort Liability and Limits of Therapeutic Jurisprudence" (1994), 47 SMU L. Rev. 1837.

38 *Smith v. Stone* (1647), 82 E.R. 533.

39 Complicating the matter is the standard of care issue. There are three questions. First, was there volition? Second, did the defendant have capacity? Third, should the standard of care imposed upon the defendant take into account the defendant's reduced capacity due to mental or physical disability? This third question will be dealt with below in Chapter 9.

40 240 S.W. 2d 132 (Mo., 1951).

41 They may, nevertheless, be held liable in negligence for unreasonably allowing themselves to become incapacitated. For example, in *Dobbs v. Mayer* (1985), 32 C.C.L.T. 191 (Ont. Div. Ct.), the deceased's estate was held liable in negligence, when the deceased suffered a massive

these cases as ones where the lack of volition arose due to the defendants' "absence of consciousness or cognition."[42]

A more difficult issue arises, however, where the actor, although conscious of the act, is unable to *control* the impulse to act due to a mental illness. Is this a case of lack of volition, or lack of capacity? If it is characterized as a lack of volition, then, on the principle that a person cannot be held liable in tort for an involuntary act, there can be no judgment against the defendant. If, however, it is treated as a case of lack of capacity, the result may be different.

In *Buckley v. Smith Tpt. Ltd.*,[43] the defendant company employed a truck driver who drove through a stop sign into an intersection causing a traffic accident. The driver was labouring under the delusion that his truck was under remote control from the company's head office and that he could not control the speed or stop the vehicle. He was, however, conscious of what was occurring, unlike a sleep-walker. The manner in which the court treated this situation indicates the tendency to confuse capacity and volition in this type of case. The court spoke of the defendant's ability to understand and appreciate the duty upon him to take care and his ability to discharge that duty. The court held that if the driver was unable to either understand and appreciate the duty or unable to discharge it, there could be no liability in negligence. This language goes to the question of capacity and not volition. Yet the fact that Roach J.A. referred in his judgment to a passage from an earlier case, *Slattery v. Haley*,[44] which spoke of lunacy of such an extreme type that there was "no voluntary act at all", suggests that *Buckley* was a case concerning not capacity but volition, adopting as its test of volition the inability to control one's act even though the actor remained conscious of it.[45]

In *Roberts v. Ramsbottom*,[46] the defendant driver suffered a stroke shortly before setting out in his car. His consciousness became clouded, and as a result

---

heart attack, became unconscious, and struck the plaintiff's vehicle. The defence of "inevitable accident" failed, since the estate did not prove that the deceased had been unaware of the impending attack. See also *Telfer v. Wright* (1978), 95 D.L.R. (3d) 188 (Ont. C.A.); *Graham v. Hodgkinson* (1983), 40 D.L.R. (2d) 697 (Ont. C.A.); *Boomer v. Penn* (1966), 52 D.L.R. (2d) 673 (Ont. H.C.); *Turner's Transfer Ltd. v. Anderson* (1962), 37 D.L.R. (2d) 399 (N.S. C.A.); *Gordon v. Wallace* (1974), 42 D.L.R. (3d) 342 (Ont. H.C.); *Sheldon v. Gray* (1989), 20 M.V.R. (2d) 80 (Ont. H.C.), affirmed (1994), 8 M.V.R. (3d) 62 (Ont. C.A.); *Perry v. Banno* (1993), 80 B.C.L.R. (2d) 351 (S.C.). The defence of "inevitable accident" is discussed below, Chapter 9.

42 According to Robertson, above, note 37, this test of involuntariness traditionally has been applied by the courts in criminal law cases. A Supreme Court of Canada criminal law case involving the defence of lack of volition brought about by automatism is *R. v. Stone* (1999), 173 D.L.R. (4th) 66 (S.C.C.).

43 [1946] 4 D.L.R. 721 (Ont. C.A.).

44 [1923] 3 D.L.R. 156 (Ont. C.A.).

45 Two similar cases are *Wenden v. Trikha* (1991), 8 C.C.L.T. (2d) 138 (Q.B.), amended (1991), 118 A.R. 319 (Q.B.), additional reasons at (1992), 1 Alta. L.R. (3d) 283 (Q.B.), affirmed (1993), 14 C.C.L.T. (2d) 225 (Alta. C.A.), leave to appeal refused (1993), 17 C.C.L.T. (2d) 285 (note) (S.C.C.), and *Hutchings v. Nevin* (1992), 9 O.R. (3d) 776 (Gen. Div.). In *Fiala v. Cechmanek*, 45 C.C.L.T. (2d) 198, [1999] 9 W.W.R. 402 (Alta. Q.B.); affirmed (2001), 201 D.L.R. (4th) 680, 6 C.C.L.T. (3d) 223 (Alta. C.A.), a jogger attacked the plaintiff during an episode of severe manic behaviour. The courts approached the liability issue from the point of view of "capacity" as part of a negligence claim. See discussion, below, Chapter 9.

46 [1980] 1 All E.R. 7 (Q.B.D.).

of this impaired state he was unable to control his car and to appreciate that he was not fit to drive. He collided with the plaintiff's car. The court held that in order for lack of volition to be a defence to a civil action there must have been a complete loss of consciousness, or a total loss of control. This would amount to a lack of volition. Where, however, the defendant maintained some control, even though it was imperfect control, liability would attach.

Lack of volition is a defence to a civil action, therefore, in two situations. First, where the defendant "acted" while not conscious, and second, where the defendant, although conscious, had no control over the act, either because of external forces, such as being thrown against the plaintiff by a high wind, or because of an internal mental disease, i.e., not being able to control one's impulses.[47] Where a defendant is conscious of the act, and is able to control it, there is volition.

What is the effect of lack of capacity on civil liability? This is a more troublesome issue. As noted above, it confronts the principal dilemma of tort law — to what extent should the law focus on the compensation requirements of an innocent victim as opposed to the requirement of wrongdoing or fault on the part of the defendant?[48]

The issue has been made even more complex in light of apparently different standards of incapacity being applied depending on the cause of the incapacity and the nature of the cause of action. It has been suggested that we are less sympathetic to those who are incapable by reason of insanity, as opposed to youth, or physical disability.[49] In addition, it has been argued that the defence of incapacity gives those who have been sued for an intentional tort more protection than those who have been sued in negligence.[50]

Whatever earlier law might have been,[51] clearly there is a limited defence of lack of capacity in both the intentional and negligent torts. The civil defence, however, is not as lenient as the defence available in criminal law matters. This is explicable by the different focusses of the two legal regimes. While civil liability

---

47 In *Teece v. Honeybourn* (1974), 54 D.L.R. (3d) 549 (B.C. S.C.), the defendant police officer drew his pistol and chased the plaintiff. The defendant had his finger on the trigger of the gun. When he slipped and fell the gun discharged, and the plaintiff was shot. The court said (at 559) that "the weapon was not fired by his voluntary (intentional) act. He never intended to fire." Although the court merged the concepts of volition and intention, this was a case of lack of volition. The court did find that the defendant was negligent.

48 This will be discussed more extensively below in Chapter 9.

49 See Picher, "The Tortious Liability of the Insane in Canada" (1975), 13 Osgoode Hall L.J. 193.

50 See Robertson, above, note 37. Robertson suggests, however, that this may be illusory, since it is always open to a plaintiff to sue for negligent trespass rather than trespass and thus take advantage of the narrower defence. See, however, *A.G. Can. v. Connolly* (1989), 64 D.L.R. (4th) 84 (B.C. S.C.), where the court reached the opposite conclusion. It held that the defence of insanity is narrower in the intentional torts. Thus a person could be held liable for a battery, but due to insanity, not be accountable in negligence. The issue of capacity as it pertains to negligence law is discussed in Chapter 9, below.

51 It is not surprising that judicial attitudes towards the issue of lack of capacity change as the role of fault or wrongdoing in the law changes. A law which imposes liability as a result of causation and not culpability will not consider the defence of lack of capacity. As the law becomes more interested in morality, it will also become more interested in issues of capacity. See Picher, above, note 49, for a review of Canadian case law.

does not ignore issues of punishment and deterrence, compensation of victims is also a factor. In comparison, criminal law, focussing on punishment and deterrence, is more likely to regard issues of capacity.

Lack of capacity is a defence in intentional torts if the defendant can prove the inability by reason of mental infirmity to appreciate "the nature and quality of his acts."[52] If this cannot be shown there is no defence, even if it can be proven that the defendant was unable to appreciate that the act was wrong. In other words, to be found liable the defendant need only be able to appreciate the physical, as opposed to the moral, consequences of the act. As a practical matter, this test severely limits the scope of the incapacity defence. Once the law concedes that lack of volition, i.e., the ability to control one's act, is a defence, but that lack of appreciation of the moral quality of one's act is not, there is little room left for the defence of incapacity.[53]

The same test of incapacity operates with regard to children, in relation to the intentional torts. One of the few Canadian cases on this point is *Tillander v. Gosselin.*[54] A three-year-old defendant was sued for battery after he removed the infant plaintiff from her carriage and dragged her across the floor. The action was dismissed because the trial judge found that the child did not have the mental ability "to appreciate or know the real nature of the act he was performing."[55] A less ambiguous case is *Garratt v. Dailey.*[56] A child, slightly under the age of six, allegedly pulled a lawn chair out from under the plaintiff as she was about to sit down. The court held that as long as the defendant knew with substantial certainty his act would result in the plaintiff falling onto the ground, a battery would be made out. There was no need to prove that the defendant intended to harm the plaintiff.[57]

---

52 See *Gerigs v. Rose* (1979), 9 C.C.L.T. 222 (Ont. H.C.); *Phillips v. Soloway* (1956), 6 D.L.R. (2d) 570 (Man. Q.B.); *A.G. Can. v. Connolly* (1989), 64 D.L.R. (4th) 84 (B.C. S.C.).

53 This is perhaps why it is difficult to find cases where the defence of incapacity which did not amount to lack of volition has been held to be a successful defence.

54 [1967] 1 O.R. 203, affirmed 61 D.L.R. (2d) 192n (C.A.). It is not surprising that there are so few cases. Since parents are not vicariously liable for the torts of their children, and since children rarely have assets, law suits against them are rare. See Alexander, "Tort Liability of Children and Their Parents", in Mendes da Costa (ed.), *Studies in Canadian Family Law* (1972), Chapter 14.

55 [1967] 1 O.R. 203 at 210. The judgment unfortunately is quite obscure. The trial judge, falling into the trap noted above, confused volition and capacity. At one point he stated: "I do not believe that one can describe the act of a normal three-year-old child in doing injury to the baby plaintiff in this case as a voluntary act on his part." The trial judge also stated that the child could not formulate the genuine intention "to do harm to the child plaintiff." The intention to do harm is not, however, a necessary ingredient of the tort of battery.

56 279 P. 2d 1091 (Wash., 1955).

57 In *Olsen v. Olsen* (2006), 266 D.L.R. (4th) 209 (B.C. S.C.), the plaintiff sued his brother for sexual assaults perpetrated against him when they were young boys. The time period during which these assaults took place was in dispute. The trial judge held that whether the defendant was 12 or 16 at the time the acts occurred was irrelevant. Since the defendant "voluntarily and deliberately initiated sexual contacts" with his younger brother, "it is immaterial whether the defendant was too young to understand the nature and consequences of his actions or to know that his actions were wrong", at 218. This comment can be considered as *obiter*, since the trial judge did find that the defendant was old enough to have appreciated the nature or quality of his acts. Taken on its face, it is my view that the statement is inconsistent with Canadian law regarding the capacity required to commit an intentional tort.

6. RELATIONSHIP WITH CRIMINAL LAW

(a) Introduction

The type of conduct giving rise to actions in tort for direct and intentional interferences with persons, chattels or land may also involve a wrongdoer in a criminal prosecution. Violent acts against individuals or their property not only affect private rights but disturb the peace and order of society. Although there are marked differences between private actions in tort and criminal prosecutions, there are areas of overlap.

Tort actions are instituted by individuals to remedy wrongs committed against them. Plaintiffs generally seek damages, and occasionally injunctions, and are responsible for instituting, maintaining, and paying for the litigation. Criminal prosecutions ordinarily are brought by the Crown,[58] at the State's expense and direction, in order to punish an offender, usually by imprisonment or fine.[59] The fact, however, that both proceedings are brought against the same wrongdoer has various implications.

(b) Can Criminal Prosecutions Exclude or Suspend Civil Proceedings?

The possibility that a criminal prosecution brought against an offender can preclude the victim from bringing tort proceedings for damages has been raised in a handful of cases. The issue concerns the status and interpretation of pre-Confederation English legislation, the Offences Against The Person Act, 1828,[60] and its subsequent re-enactments. According to ss. 27 to 29 of this Act, where either a person has been charged with a "common assault or battery" and the complaint has been dismissed as evidenced by a "certificate", or where there has been a conviction with the whole amount of the fine (namely "five pounds") having been assessed against the accused, or where the accused has been imprisoned for two calendar months for nonpayment of the fine, then, "in every such Case he shall be released from all further or other Proceedings, Civil or Criminal, for the same Cause." Although it clearly would be an oddity were this legislation to have relevance today, this in fact has been considered by several courts.

In Alberta, the issue was raised in *Schultz v. Wolske*.[61] The court held that if the Act was good law in Alberta, its requirements had been met on the facts of the case before it, and that, accordingly, the plaintiff's tort action must be dismissed. Milvain J., however, accepted the plaintiff's argument that since the federal Parliament had passed its own legislation dealing with this issue,[62] it had

---

58 Private prosecutions are possible. See Law Reform Commission of Canada, *Private Prosecutions*, Working Paper 52.

59 See *Montgomery v. Black*, [1989] B.C.J. No. 1800 (B.C. S.C.), where the court, after noting the distinctions between civil and criminal proceedings, found a defendant civilly liable for assault, although the defendant was acquitted of criminal charges.

60 9 Geo. 4, c. 31.

61 (1966), 75 W.W.R. 411 (Alta. T.D.). The case concerned the Offences Against the Person Act, 1861 (24 & 25 Vict., c. 100).

62 There had been the Offences Against the Person Act, S.C. 1869, c. 20, s. 45, which was subsequently carried forward into the Criminal Code, R.S.C. 1927, c. 36, s. 734. This was repealed by S.C. 1953-54, c. 51, s. 745.

fully occupied the field, rendering the English legislation inapplicable. According to Milvain J., once ousted, the Act did not revive when the Canadian legislation which had replaced it was itself repealed. The soundness of this reasoning was of course dependent on the view that the federal legislation was constitutionally valid, which certainly is an arguable issue, in view of the provincial authority over property and civil rights.[63]

In Manitoba and British Columbia, the Imperial Act has been specifically repealed.[64]

In exceptional circumstances, civil proceedings may be suspended pending the prosecution of the criminal offence. At common law, the felonious tort rule provided that where the facts of a civil trial constituted a felony, the tort action was suspended until the plaintiff, upon whom the duty to prosecute fell, had prosecuted the defendant.[65] Since the concept of felony is no longer part of the criminal law, however, the rule has been rendered meaningless.[66] Further, s. 11 of the Criminal Code provides:

> No civil remedy for an act or omission is suspended or affected by reason that the act or omission is a criminal offence.[67]

It has been held that the purpose of this section is to abrogate the felonious tort rule.[68]

There is a discretion in civil courts to order that an action be stayed pending the determination of criminal proceedings. According to *Stickney v. Trusz*,[69] this discretion should be exercised in "extraordinary or exceptional cases." The motivation behind the order should be to ensure that the accused receives a fair trial which will not be prejudiced by the civil proceedings.[70] There is a presump-

---

63 Milvain J. referred to *Trinea v. Duleba*, [1924] 2 W.W.R. 1177 (Alta. C.A.), and *Dowsett v. Edmunds*, [1926] 3 W.W.R. 447 (Alta. C.A.), which supported the constitutional validity of the federal legislation. *Schultz v. Wolske* was followed in *Stevens v. Quinney*, [1979] 5 W.W.R. 284 (Sask. Q.B.), and *Mochoruk v. Lindquist* (1981), 12 Sask. R. 249 (Q.B.), despite earlier Saskatchewan authority to the contrary; see *Nykiforuk v. Kohut*, [1949] 1 W.W.R. 708 (Sask. Dist. Ct.).

64 See Tortfeasors and Contributory Negligence Act, R.S.M. 1987, c. T90 (also C.C.S.M., c. T90); Law and Equity Act, R.S.B.C. 1996, c. 253, s. 3.

65 See *Stickney v. Trusz* (1973), 45 D.L.R. (3d) 275 (Ont. H.C.), affirmed (1974), 46 D.L.R. (3d) 80 (Ont. Div. Ct.), which was affirmed (1974), 46 D.L.R. (3d) 80 at 82 (Ont. C.A.), where the rule is explained.

66 *Ibid.*

67 R.S.C. 1985, c. C-46.

68 Above, note 65. The felonious tort rule is briefly discussed by Morden J.A. in *Schreiber v. Canada (Attorney General)* (2001), 57 O.R. (3d) 316 (C.A.), leave to appeal refused (2002), 2002 CarswellOnt 2703, 2002 CarswellOnt 2704 (S.C.C.). Quoting from Duff J. in *M. (A.) v. P. (R.)* (1921), 62 S.C.R. 517 at 520, the rule was described in the following way:

> Where the facts constituting the foundation of a cause of action in themselves constitute a felony the right of action for tort is suspended until the plaintiff has prosecuted the defendant if the plaintiff is the person on whom the duty of prosecution falls.

69 Above, note 65.

70 See *Demeter v. Occidental Ins. Co.* (1975), 11 O.R. (2d) 369 (Master), where the plaintiff was granted the right to extend the time for delivery of his Statement of Claim, since the Senior Master felt that the additional publicity which would be generated by the civil action might prejudice him on a second trial on the criminal charge. See also *Porter v. Solloway, Mills & Co.*, [1930] 1 W.W.R. 680 (Alta. C.A.); *Czernewicz v. Winnipeg Wholesale Grocery & Con-*

tion against ordering a stay and it is accordingly up to the applicant to convince the court that there are extraordinary or exceptional circumstances that justify delaying the plaintiff's fundamental right to timely access to the court.[71]

Another matter of overlap relates to the use of criminal convictions as evidence in tort actions. The common law rule was found in the case of *Hollington v. Hewthorn & Co.*[72] This stated that evidence of conviction or acquittal of an offence based on the same acts or omissions constituting a tort was not admissible in the tort action. Similarly, a civil judgment is inadmissible to prove a fact in a criminal trial. The rule in *Hollington v. Hewthorn* has not been followed in some Canadian decisions.[73] As well, legislation has been enacted in many jurisdictions altering this rule.[74]

(c) Can Criminal Law Sanctions Affect Tort Damages?

Damages in tort are awarded to compensate an injured victim; criminal law sanctions do not seek to compensate victims but to punish wrongdoers. In the majority of instances, therefore, the fact that a wrongdoer has been punished as a result of a successful criminal prosecution does not affect the amount of damages which the victim is entitled to receive through tort. In exceptional cases, however,

---

fectionery Ltd., [1939] 2 W.W.R. 318 (Man. K.B.); *Cansulex v. Perry* (1979), 14 B.C.L.R. 105 (C.A.); *Jefferson v. Bhetcha*, [1979] 1 W.L.R. 898 (C.A.); *Jack Clark v. Clark*, [1946] 2 All E.R. 683 (C.A.); *Kozlowski v. Wkrs. Benevolent Soc.*, [1933] 3 W.W.R. 566 (Man. C.A.); *Br. Accept. Corp. v. Belzberg* (1962), 36 D.L.R. (2d) 587 (Alta. T.D.); *Saccomanno v. Swanson*, [1987] 2 W.W.R. 754 (Alta. Q.B.). See Stevenson and Coté, *Alberta Rules of Court, Annotated*, at 142-43. It has been held that the Charter of Rights and Freedoms does not affect the rule in *Stickney v. Trusz*, which remains good law. See *Seaway Trust Co. v. Kilderkin Invt. Ltd.* (1986), 29 D.L.R. (4th) 456 (Ont. H.C.); *Re Ottawa-Carleton Regional Housing Authority and Dimario* (1987), 68 O.R. (2d) 581 (Ont. Dist. Ct.).

71 See *Schreiber v. Canada (Attorney General)*, above, note 68.

72 [1943] 2 All E.R. 35 (C.A.).

73 A good discussion of this issue can be found in *Simpson v. Geswein* (1995), 25 C.C.L.T. (2d) 49 (Man. Q.B.). The court held, after reviewing the authorities, that a certificate of conviction was properly admitted in a civil case for assault and battery as evidence of the conviction and of certain facts stated therein. The court also held that the transcript of the trial judge's reasons in the criminal trial was admissible. The court upheld the decision of the Master to grant a motion for summary judgment to the plaintiff based upon the pleadings, affidavits and certificate of conviction. See also *K.(W.) v. Pornbacher* (1997), 34 C.C.L.T. (2d) 174, [1998] 3 W.W.R. 149 (B.C. S.C.), which held that a guilty plea of a sexual assault at criminal trial created a presumption of a battery in a civil case; *F. (K.) v. White* (2001), 198 D.L.R. (4th) 541 (Ont. C.A.): criminal conviction for sexual assault constitutes *prima facie* proof, subject to rebuttal. In the latter case, the court distinguished this situation (i.e., the "offensive" use of the conviction), from the situation where the convicted person is suing, for example for insurance proceeds, and the conviction is being used to deny the claim (the "defensive" use). In the latter case, courts appear to have a discretion to preclude relitigation of the criminal claim as an abuse of process. Also see *Gosse v. House* (1997), 158 Nfld. & P.E.I.R. 31 (Nfld. T.D.); and *Kuin v. 238682 Alberta Ltd.* (1997), 56 Alta. L.R. (3d) 329 (Master).

74 See, e.g., *Betterton v. Turner* (1982), 133 D.L.R. (3d) 289 (B.C. S.C.), dealing with the Evidence Act, R.S.B.C. 1979, c. 116, ss. 80, 81. See also Alberta Evidence Act, R.S.A. 2000, c. A-18, s. 26; Evidence Act, R.S.O. 1990, c. E. 23, s. 22. In *F. (K.) v. White* (2001), 198 D.L.R. (4th) 541 (Ont. C.A.), the court noted that while the legislation provides that the conviction is proof in the absence of evidence to the contrary that the crime was committed, it does not specify "the evidentiary effect of the conviction where the convicted party seeks to challenge the facts underlying the criminal offence in the subsequent civil proceedings."

punitive damages may be awarded in tort to the plaintiff in order to punish the defendant for especially outrageous conduct.[75] This has given rise to the following concern: should an award of punitive damages be disallowed in a case where the defendant already has received a criminal law punishment on the ground that this would constitute a double punishment?

There seems to be two lines of authority on this point. In *Natonson v. Lexier*, Taylor J. stated that:

> the imposition of punitive damages for the benefit of the plaintiff would be a double punishment, even if on the peculiar circumstances punitive damages ought to be awarded for the benefit of the plaintiff.[76]

In *Radovskis v. Tomn*,[77] the plaintiff was 5-and-a-half years old when she was raped by the defendant. The defendant was convicted and imprisoned. In a civil action brought against the defendant for assault and battery, Williams C.J.Q.B. followed the *Natonson* case and refused to award punitive damages.[78]

Courts have avoided this approach in some cases and recent judgments have demonstrated more flexibility. Where wrongdoers have been convicted of offences but not punished, as in the case of a conditional discharge, the rule has been held not to apply.[79] In another case, *K. (W.) v. Pornbacher*,[80] the fact that after having been found guilty in criminal proceedings for sexual assault the defendant continued to deny the allegations, requiring the plaintiff to go through a full civil trial, led to an award of punitive damages against him.[81] As well, although punitive damages might not be awarded where defendants already have been punished, it has been held that aggravated damages can be.[82]

---

75 See below.

76 [1939] 3 W.W.R. 289 at 291 (Sask. K.B.).

77 (1957), 21 W.W.R. 658 (Man Q.B.).

78 See also *Lyth v. Dagg* (1988), 46 C.C.L.T. 25 (B.C. S.C.), and *G. (E.D.) v. D. (S.)* (1993), 101 D.L.R. (4th) 101 (B.C. C.A.), other sexual assault cases where punitive damages were not awarded because the defendants had been punished criminally. In *Willington v. Marshall* (1994), 21 C.C.L.T. (2d) 198 (B.C. S.C.), the court held that it is up to the trier of fact to consider whether a criminal penalty, even one of imprisonment, should prevent an award of punitive damages from being made. In other words, whether a defendant already has been punished once and should not therefore be subject to punitive damages, is said to be a question of fact and not of law. If the trier of fact feels that the defendant has been punished, punitive damages cannot be awarded.

79 See *Loedel v. Eckert* (1977), 3 C.C.L.T. 145 (B.C. S.C.); *Kenmuir v. Huetzelmann* (1977), 3 C.C.L.T. 153 (B.C. Co. Ct.).

80 (1997), 34 C.C.L.T. (2d) 174 (B.C. S.C.).

81 The Court termed this conduct "cruel, abusive and insolent." Awarding aggravated damages might have been more appropriate in the circumstances. In *C. (S.L.) v. M. (M.J.)* (1996), 179 A.R. 200 (Q.B.), the court awarded punitive damages in a case involving serious sexual and physical assaults by a father against his children. There had been no criminal sanctions imposed, but the judge made it clear that even if there had been punitive damages would have been awarded. In *Buxbaum (Litigation Guardian of) v. Buxbaum* (1997), [1997] O.J. No 5166, 1997 CarswellOnt 4922 (C.A.), leave to appeal refused (1998), 230 N.R. 400 (note) (S.C.C.), punitive damages were awarded in favour of the plaintiff whose spouse was murdered by the defendant in his presence. The defendant was serving a life sentence for the murder.

82 See *Kirisits v. Morrell* (1965), 52 W.W.R. 123 (B.C. S.C.); *N. (J.L.) v. L. (A.M.)*, [1989] 1 W.W.R. 438 (Man. Q.B.). As discussed below, the difference between punitive and aggravated damages is a nominal one.

(d) Restitution and Compensation Under Criminal Law

The overlap between tort and criminal law becomes significant when they both attempt to accomplish the same goal — to require the offender to restore the victim's losses.[83] Although there are provisions in the Criminal Code at present which give courts the power to require an offender to make restitution to the victim, from all accounts, these are rarely used.[84] The Law Reform Commission of Canada has recommended that restitution and compensation orders be utilized more frequently, that restitution be recognized as a separate sentence, that priority be given to the victim's interests, and that such schemes should involve the co-operation of the victim and be subject to the victim's consent.[85] Despite the advantages restitution orders present to victims, it is unlikely that such a plan would have a significant impact on tort law. Tort law is rarely used against criminals at present,[86] and any increased assistance which criminal law can give to victims of crime is to be welcomed.[87]

7. ASSAULT

The tort of assault protects one's right to be free from the *threat* of imminent, physical harm. The *injuria* or legal wrong consists in the wrongdoer's act which has disturbed the victim's sense of security. The tort does not require there to have been any actual physical contact or a carrying out of the threat.[88] The tort

---

83 It is interesting to note that studies which argue for a greater use of restitution in criminal law put forward the same objective and values argued for by advocates of fault-based compensation. The Law Reform Commission of Canada's Working Paper on *Restitution and Compensation*, Working Paper 5, 1974, for example, argues that restitution should be used as a method of punishing offenders because of values of justice, the reaffirmation of society's values, deterrence, rehabilitation, recognition of the victim's psychological need that notice be taken of the wrong done, discouraging criminal activity and so on.

84 See s. 738 and following. The earlier provision, s. 653, was held to be *intra vires* in *R. v. Zelensky*, [1978] 3 W.W.R. 693 (S.C.C.). See Law Reform Commission of Canada, Working Paper, *ibid.*, at 9-10; Linden, "Restitution, Compensation for Victims of Crime and Canadian Criminal Law" (1977), 19 Can. J. Crim. & Corr. 9. The new provisions were passed in the 1988 Act to amend the Criminal Code (Victims of Crime), R.S.C. 1985, c. 23 (4th Supp.). A survey conducted by the Law Reform Commission of Canada revealed that restitution was ordered only six times out of a possible 4,294 convicted appearances, or 0.1 per cent of the time. The survey conceded that it is possible that restitution was used unofficially in more cases.

85 Law Reform Commission of Canada Report, *Dispositions and Sentences in the Criminal Process*, 1976.

86 See *The Report of the Osgoode Hall Study on Compensation for Victims of Crime* (1968).

87 There are criminal injuries' compensation schemes in every Canadian province, and the territories, which provide compensation to victims of violent crimes outside the tort law context. In Ontario, the Victims' Bill of Rights, 1995, S.O. 1995, c. 6, am. 1999, c. 6, s. 65, 2000, c. 32, 2005, c. 5, s.72, states that "a person convicted of a prescribed crime is liable in damages to every victim of the crime for emotional distress, and bodily harm resulting from distress, arising from the commission of a crime." These and other similar provisions attempt to supplement the normal tort law remedies available to crime victims. For a reference to these provisions see Rainaldi, ed., *Remedies in Tort*, Vol. 1 at 2-73 *et seq.* (Carswell).

88 See *Collins v. Wilcock*, [1984] 1 W.L.R. 1172 at 1177 (Q.B.D.), where the distinction between assault and battery is clearly drawn:

> The law draws a distinction, in terms more easily understood by philologists than by ordinary citizens, between an assault and a battery. An assault is an act which causes another person to apprehend the infliction of immediate, unlawful, force on his person; a battery is the

action indicates society's interest in ensuring that people can conduct themselves free from unwarranted intimidation or harassment.

If the number of reported cases is an adequate indicator, the tort action for assault, standing alone, rarely is instituted in Canada and other parts of the Commonwealth. In describing the elements of the cause of action, the leading texts are able to refer to few, usually very early, cases.[89] These cases have established the major features of the assault action which remain unaltered to the present day. The defendant's conduct must have caused a *reasonable* apprehension of *imminent* harm. It does not matter if the defendant did not have the actual ability to cause harm as long as a reasonable person would have felt threatened.[90] The plaintiff need not have been in fear, as long as harm was apprehended.[91] Merely because the threats of violence are conditional does not necessarily mean there is no assault. Thus, in *Mainland Sawmills Ltd. v. USW Union Local-1-3567*,[92] the fact that the threatened workers were told that they could avoid imminent harm if they obliged and did not cross the picket lines during a labour dispute did not mean that there had been no assault. The court found that they were entitled to proceed to work and were threatened with harm if they did not accede to the strikers' demands. These threats constituted an assault.

There are some aspects of the action which remain clouded. Although it seems that there is no theoretical reason why an assault cannot be committed negligently, some authors define assault as the "intentional creation" of the apprehension of harmful contact.[93] As indicated previously, Canadian tort law still recognizes the tort of negligent trespass, and there is no reason to assume that this approach is

---

actual infliction of unlawful force on another person.

This distinction is occasionally overlooked in the cases.

89 The classic cases, cited by Fleming, *The Law of Torts*, 9th ed. (1998), Linden, *Canadian Tort Law*, 7th ed. (2001), and Trindade, Cane and Lunney, *The Law of Torts in Australia*, 4th. ed. (2007), are *Stephens v. Myers* (1830), 172 E.R. 735; *Tuberville v. Savage* (1669), 86 E.R. 684; *Read v. Coker* (1853), 138 E.R. 1437; *Brady v. Schatzel*, [1911] S.R. Qd. 206.

90 Even pointing an unloaded gun amounts to assault: *Kennedy v. Hanes*, [1940] O.R. 461, affirmed [1941] S.C.R. 384.

91 A case of assault is *Peters v. Klassen*, [1993] 7 W.W.R. 465 (Man. Q.B.), reversed in part [1994] 5 W.W.R. 264 (Man. C.A.). It was alleged that the defendant swung at the plaintiff with his fist, but the plaintiff took evasive action and the punch missed its mark. This was held to be an assault. In another case, *Herbert v. Misuga* (1994), 111 D.L.R. (4th) 193 (Sask. C.A.), the defendant drove his truck towards the plaintiff cyclist intending to frighten him but not to hit him. The defendant did, however, hit the plaintiff. The court viewed the entire incident as an "assault", although clearly if there had been no contact, the issue as to whether an assault was committed would have had to been more clearly addressed. A useful discussion of "assault" from the perspective of the criminal law is found in the House of Lords' judgment in *R v. Ireland*, [1997] 4 All E.R. 225 (H.L.). The definition of assault is similar in criminal and civil law and thus the judgment is also interesting from a tort law perspective. Here the assaults emanated from repeated telephone calls, during which the caller remained silent. The Lords made it clear that even silent calls can provoke victims to fear immediate and unlawful violence.

92 [2007] B.C.S.C. No. 1433.

93 Linden and Feldthusen, *Canadian Tort Law*, 8th ed. (2006), at 46; Fleming, *The Law of Torts*, 9th ed. (1998), at 25. Not so Trindade, Cane and Lunney, *The Law of Torts in Australia*, 4th ed. (2007), at 48.

confined to battery actions.[94] As well, since the tort of assault stems from the writ of trespass *vi et armis*, the apprehension of harm must be caused by the direct act of the defendant. What this means in the context of this tort is not altogether clear. Must there be both a direct threat of direct harm or is it sufficient that the threat be direct, even though the threatened harm would not be?[95] It is argued in one text[96] that an assault is a direct threat which causes a reasonable apprehension of imminent and direct bodily contact by the defendant or someone within the defendant's control.[97] In a case dealing with "road rage", a defendant who was driving a pick-up truck chased and tailgated the plaintiffs' vehicle. The defendant then drove her truck into the rear of the plaintiffs' vehicle and forced it off the road. The court found that this conduct caused the reasonable apprehension of harm and hence constituted an assault.[98]

The fact that assault actions are rarely brought is probably the result of many factors. First, there is the question of the expense of litigation. Where the plaintiff has suffered no physical harm but merely psychological distress, it is likely that even if the assault action were maintained, the expenses of the litigation would exceed the damages awarded. In view of the fact that the assessment of punitive damages tends to be quite low, where there are no real injuries there is little point in suing. Second, it probably is felt by many that a law suit is an inappropriate way to respond to a typical assault.[99]

---

94 It is unlikely, but conceivable, that there can be a ''negligent assault.'' For example, someone rushes into what is thought to be an empty bedroom with a gun. There is someone in the room who passes out at the sight of the intruder. There may not have been the ''intention'' to create an apprehension of harm, although it might be said that the intruder was negligent.

95 This is not as unrealistic as it sounds. For example, in *Bruce v. Dyer*, [1970] 1 O.R. 482, affirming [1966] 2 O.R. 705 (C.A.), the defendant seriously injured the plaintiff in a fist fight which occurred on the highway. The defendant claimed self-defence, arguing that the plaintiff had ''assaulted'' him. One of the alleged assaults was the plaintiff's act in blocking the defendant's passage on the highway, another in preventing the defendant's car from passing the plaintiff's. If these acts caused the defendant to fear that he might be involved in a traffic collision with an oncoming vehicle, would they amount to an assault?

96 Trindade, Cane and Lunney, *The Law of Torts in Australia*, 4th ed. (2007).

97 See also Fleming, *The Law of Torts*, 8th ed. (1992), at 31 where it is pointed out that the action for assault ''remained rooted to the idea that the defendant must have committed an act in the nature of an attempted battery, and was not extended beyond threats intended to arouse apprehension of imminent physical contact.''

98 See *Herman v. Graves*, [1998] 9 W.W.R. 542 (Alta. Q.B.). The trial judge did not address the issue raised here—namely were the plaintiffs being threatened by conduct that could constitute a battery? Traditionally, car accident injury cases are pursued in negligence law, not battery. Nevertheless, threatening someone with your car merits consideration as an assault. Gesturing at someone with "the finger" is frequently used as a display of anger. Is it an assault? In *Langille v. McGrath* (2000), 233 N.B.R. (2d) 29 (Q.B.), the defendant who was being sued for defamation counter-claimed that he had been "given the finger." The trial judge, after exploring the meaning behind this gesture, determined it was not an assault. The case was appealed on the issue of the damage award for the defamation at 2001 NBCA 106 (C.A.). In *Wuttunee v. Merck Frosst Canada Ltd.*, [2007] 4 W.W.R. 309 (Sask. Q.B.) a class action was brought by the users of the drug Vioxx against the manufacturer and distributor of the drug. One of the actions claimed was "assault". The court, correctly in my view, struck out the claim. There was no threat of harmful or offensive contact in this case, even if the persons who took Vioxx were worried about the effects of Vioxx on their health.

99 Many people may not even realize that to succeed in an assault, actual physical violence is not required.

Despite the paucity of litigation, the tort of assault plays a valuable role. It is available if necessary. More significantly, it signals the common law's concern in protecting not only tangible interests, but the rights of individuals to live in peace, without fear of violence.[100]

8. BATTERY

(a) Introduction

The tort of battery protects one's right to be free from offensive physical contacts. The legal wrong consists in the act of violating an individual's bodily security. As stated in one English case:

> The fundamental principle, plain and incontestable, is that every person's body is inviolate. It has long been established that any touching of another person, however slight, may amount to a battery.[101]

The tort does not require that the contact be physically harmful to its recipient, or cause any personal injury.[102] It is the intangible right to autonomy over one's own body which is protected.

The tort of battery stems from the writ of trespass *vi et armis* and requires that the offensive contact emanate directly from the defendant's conduct. To be actionable, it must be committed either intentionally or negligently.[103] There are, therefore, two actions which must be studied separately: (a) intentional and (b) negligent battery.[104] In most instances, whether or not a battery has been committed and whether it was committed negligently or intentionally are not contentious issues. These are usually fairly straightforward matters. Legal disputes generally revolve around the applicability of one of the several defences.[105]

(b) Intentional Battery

(i) Intention

An intentional act occurs when the defendant desired the consequences or ought to have been substantially certain that they would flow from the act.[106] If

---

100 The values inherent in the intentional torts in general are discussed by J. McLaren, "The Intentional Torts To The Person Revived? Protecting Autonomy, Dignity and Emotional Welfare In A Pluralistic Society" (2002), 17 S.C.L.R. (2d) 67.

101 *Collins v. Wilcock*, [1984] 1 W.L.R. 1172 at 1177 (Q.B.D.). This was quoted with approval by McLachlin J. in *Sansalone v. Wawanesa Mutual Insurance Co.* (2000), 50 C.C.L.T. (2d) 1 (S.C.C.).

102 *Cf. Cutler v. Smith* (1977), 25 N.S.R. (2d) 5, 36 A.P.R. 5 (T.D.).

103 An accidental battery is not actionable: *Larin v. Goshen* (1974), 56 D.L.R. (3d) 719 (N.S. C.A.).

104 The tort of battery commonly is defined as the ''intentional'' infliction of unlawful force. See, for example, La Forest J. in *Norberg v. Wynrib* (1992), 12 C.C.L.T. 1 at 16 (S.C.C.): ''A battery is the intentional infliction of unlawful force on another person''. As noted above, however, Canadian tort law still recognizes a ''negligent trespass'' tort and thus a direct and offensive physical contact, i.e. a battery, can be committed either intentionally or negligently. Affirmation that Canadian tort law recognizes a negligent battery is found in numerous cases, including *Cook v. Lewis*, [1951] S.C.R. 830. See discussion of ''negligent battery'' below.

105 For a discussion of the defences, see Chapter 3.

106 The test of ''substantial certainty'', otherwise called ''constructive intention'', comes from U.S. case law and is included in Section 8A of the American Restatement (Third) of the Law

the consequences which result are tortious, even if this was not the ''intention'' of the actor, intention will have been made out. For the tort of intentional battery, the defendant must have intended an offensive, physical contact with the plaintiff.[107] The defendant need not have intended to harm or injure the plaintiff,[108] although in most battery cases there is an intention to injure.[109] Battery cases which illustrate this include incidences of stabbing,[110] shooting,[111] strangling,[112] punching[113] and fighting.[114] These were all batteries committed with the intention to cause physical harm to their victims.

(ii) Directness

To sue in battery, the physical contact must have resulted directly from the defendant's act.[115] As stated by McLachlin J., "the plaintiff in an action for trespass

---

of Torts: Liability for Physical Harm, section 1. It was used in *Herbert v. Misuga* (1991), 84 D.L.R. (4th) 645 (Sask. Q.B.), affirmed (1994), 111 D.L.R. (4th) 193 (Sask. C.A.). The defendant drove his truck towards the plaintiff intending to scare, but not to hit him. The defendant hit the plaintiff. The trial judge adopted the "substantial certainty" test, in holding that the collision was "intended". Also see Linden and Feldthusen, *Canadian Tort Law*, 8th ed. (2006), at 34; Atrens, "Intentional Interference with the Person", in Linden, ed., *Studies in Canadian Tort Law* (1977), Chapter 14, and *Bettel v. Yim* (1978), 5 C.C.L.T. 66 (Ont. Co. Ct.), where Borins Co. Ct. J. cites without disapproval the U.S. approach.

107 This raises a cloudy issue. It seems to be agreed that it is unnecessary that the defendant intended to contact the specific plaintiff, as long as physical contact with *someone* was desired or substantially certain. In other words, the identity of the victim is irrelevant, as long as it was substantially certain that there would be a victim. I know of no Canadian battery cases where this occurred. Related to this is the U.S. concept of ''transferred intent.'' Here A intends to strike B, misses, and strikes C. The doctrine of transferred intent applies and A's intent to strike B is transferred to establish that A intended to strike C. A full discussion of the doctrine, its history, its rationale, and the torts to which it applies is found in Reynolds, "Transferred Intent: Should Its "Curious Survival" Continue?" (1997), 50 Okla. L. Rev. 529. Reynolds concludes that the doctrine is unnecessary since there are other simpler ways to accomplish the same results. Reynolds also refers to early English cases, such as *James v. Campbell* (1832), 172 E.R. 1015, which applied the doctrine.

108 See *Wilson v. Pringle*, [1986] 2 All E.R. 440 at 445 (C.A.):

> It is the act and not the injury which must be intentional. An intention to injure is not essential to an action for trespass to the person.

By the word ''act'', I take it that the court meant the ''battery.''

109 Quoted with approval by Iacobucci J. in *Sansalone v. Wawanesa Mutual Insurance Co.* (2000), 50 C.C.L.T. (2d) 1 (S.C.C.) at 39.

110 *Beale v. Beale* (1982), 24 C.C.L.T. 101 (N.S. T.D.); *Long v. Gardner* (1983), 144 D.L.R. (3d) 73 (Ont. H.C.).

111 *Gerigs v. Rose* (1979), 9 C.C.L.T. 222 (Ont. H.C.); *Veinot v. Veinot* (1977), 81 D.L.R. (3d) 549 (N.S. C.A.).

112 *Rumsey v. R.*, [1984] 5 W.W.R. 585 (Fed. T.D.).

113 *Ellone v. Mesa* (1997), [1997] O.J. No. 2232, 1997 CarswellOnt 1938 (Gen. Div.); *Babiuk v. Trann* (2005), 248 D.L.R. (4th) 530 (Sask. C.A.).

114 *Holt v. Verbruggen* (1981), 20 C.C.L.T. 29 (B.C. S.C.); *Degenstein v. Riou* (1981), 129 D.L.R. (3d) 713 (Sask. Q.B.); *Rouleau v. Rex Drive-In* (1981), 16 C.C.LT. 218 (B.C. Co. Ct.); *Dolson v. Hughes* (1979), 107 D.L.R. (3d) 343 (B.C. S.C.); *Gambriell v. Caparelli* (1974), 54 D.L.R. (3d) 661 (Ont. Co. Ct.); *Shaw v. Gorter* (1977), 2 C.C.L.T. 111 (Ont. C.A.); *Kenmuir v. Huetzelmann* (1977), 3 C.C.L.T. 153 (B.C. Co. Ct.); *Loedel v. Eckert* (1977), 3 C.C.L.T. 145 (B.C. S.C.); *Bettel v. Yim* (1978), 5 C.C.L.T. 66 (Ont. Co. Ct.); *Landry v. Patterson* (1978), 7 C.C.L.T. 202 (Ont. C.A.).

115 It has been suggested that there must be an act — passive contact will not suffice. See Trindade,

to the person (which includes battery) succeeds if she can prove direct interference with her person."[116]

As indicated previously, the directness requirement poses theoretical difficulties, although in practical terms it rarely does. The test suggested: "Would the result have occurred had it not been for the intervention of another independent agency?" is adequate to deal with even the most difficult and marginal cases.[117] The direct/indirect dichotomy no longer serves any useful purpose and should be discarded. Torts should be distinguished on the basis of the interests which they protect and the conduct which they sanction, and not on the sequence of events leading up to an injury.

(iii) Offensiveness

Not all physical contacts are injurious or offensive. Some are in fact beneficial, such as the surgeon's medical intervention which saves a life or improves the patient's health. Moreover, not every contact can be avoided. The common law has had to determine which physical contacts are batteries, and which are not.

Battery requires that there be an "offensive" physical contact. As we have seen, this does not equate with harmful or injurious contact. There is no doubt that beneficial contacts, such as medical interventions, are indeed batteries, subject

---

Cane and Lunney, *The Law of Torts in Australia*, 4th ed. (2007), at 45, citing *Innes v. Wylie* (1844), 1 Car. & K. 257. See, however, *MacDonald v. Sebastian* (1987), 42 C.C.L.T. 213 (N.S. T.D.), where it was suggested that keeping silent concerning the toxicity of well water could amount to a battery. In an older case, *Parmley v. Parmley*, [1945] S.C.R. 635, a doctor and dentist were jointly responsible for a trespass because of the unauthorized extraction of the plaintiff's teeth by the dentist. The doctor's wrong consisted of failing to prevent the dentist from doing the extraction. This case can be explained, however, on the basis of joint tortfeasors. Each tortfeasor is liable for the act of the other and thus the dentist's act becomes the doctor's act.

116 Per McLachlin J. in *Sansalone v. Wawanesa Mutual Insurance Co.* (2000), 50 C.C.L.T. (2d) 1 (S.C.C.) at 11. In *E. (D.) (Guardian ad litem of) v. British Columbia* (2003), 18 C.C.L.T. (3d) 169 (B.C. S.C.), reversed (2005), 252 D.L.R. (4th) 689 (B.C. C.A.), reconsideration refused (2005), 252 D.L.R. (4th) 713 (B.C. C.A.), the directness requirement of the battery action was reaffirmed. The court held that forced sterilizations could not give rise to a battery claim against the Crown, since it was not the Crown, but an independent quasi-judicial Board and its physicians that authorized and carried out the procedures. The court applied *Sansalone* in stating that "Battery is not committed where the act of the defendant only indirectly affects the plaintiff", at 217. In *Wuttunee v. Merck Frosst Canada Ltd.*, [2007] 4 W.W.R. 309 (Sask. Q.B.), Klebuc J. allowed a battery claim to proceed based on allegations that the defendant marketed a harmful drug without disclosing its risks. Klebuc J. conceded that this would be "a novel" expansion of the tort. In my view, without a direct physical contact there cannot be a battery under current Canadian law.

117 Trindade, Cane and Lunney, *ibid.*, at 37, cite two examples from the English Criminal Injuries Compensation Board's 11th and 9th Reports which pose difficult hypotheticals. The first asks whether a defendant who intentionally presses a bell to indicate to the bus driver to start the bus, knowing that an old woman is in the process of getting off the bus, has directly injured the women when she falls at the bus's motion. In my opinion, this would not satisfy the directness test. In the second hypothetical, a person drinks a dangerous substance which secretly had been put into a drink. The directness test probably fails in this case as well, unless the victim's act can be seen as not being within his control. In *Swanson v. Mallow*, [1991] 5 W.W.R. 454 (Sask. Q.B.), affirmed [1992] 2 W.W.R. 718 (Sask. C.A.), a chemical which was sprayed into the air intake of a truck, caused the occupant of the truck to become sick. The injuries were held to be a direct consequence of the defendants' actions and hence the defendants were liable for an "assault and battery".

to the defence of consent or other protections provided by law.[118] In other words, even beneficial contacts may be offensive. What then is the definition of offensive?

The difficulty arises due to *dicta* in early cases which indicate that even trivial, almost insignificant, contact can be offensive and constitute a battery. Holt C.J.'s judgment in *Cole v. Turner* illustrates the problem:

> First, that the least touching of another in anger is a battery.
>
> Secondly, if two or more meet in a narrow passage, and without any violence or design of harm, the one touches the other gently, it will be no battery.
>
> Thirdly, if any of them use violence against the other, to force his way in a rude inordinate manner, it will be a battery; or any struggle about the passage to that degree as may do hurt, will be a battery.[119]

Not every trivial contact will constitute a battery. As stated by Fleming,[120] common day activities, such as tapping another on the shoulder to attract that person's attention,[121] or brushing someone in a narrow passage or crowd,[122] are not batteries, unless committed "in a hostile manner."

The distinction between "hostile" and "friendly" contact seems to depend upon the standard of generally acceptable conduct in society. The test is objective: what would the reasonable person consider to be acceptable? Two English cases demonstrate this proposition. In the first, *Collins v. Wilcock*,[123] the act of a police officer in taking hold of someone's arm to restrain her from walking off was deemed to constitute a battery. The test suggested by Goff L.J. was this: "whether the physical conduct so persisted in has in the circumstances gone beyond generally acceptable standards of conduct."[124] It was suggested that this is a reflection of the doctrine of implied consent:

> . . . most of the physical contacts of ordinary life are not actionable because they are impliedly consented to by all who move in society and so expose themselves to the risk of bodily contact.[125]

In the second case, *Wilson v. Pringle*,[126] a schoolboy playfully pulled the schoolbag off the plaintiff's shoulder, causing him injury. In deciding whether this was a hostile touching and consequently a battery, Croom-Johnson L.J. rejected the "implied consent" rationale and, accepting Goff L.J.'s test in *Collins v. Wilcock*, agreed that certain conduct must be judged as "acceptable in the ordinary conduct of everyday life."[127] His Lordship's test of "hostility", however, was something which could only be left "as a question of fact for the tribunal of fact."[128] In the

---

118 See Chapter 3.

119 (1705), 87 E.R. 907.

120 Fleming, *The Law of Torts*, 9th ed. (1998), at 30.

121 Citing *Wiffin v. Kincard* (1807), 127 E.R. 713; *Coward v. Baddeley* (1859), 157 E.R. 927.

122 Citing *Cole v. Turner*, above, note 119; *Campbell v. Samuels* (1980), 23 S.A.S.R. 389 (S.C.).

123 [1984] 1 W.L.R. 1172 (Q.B.).

124 *Ibid.*, at 1178. See also discussion in *F. v. West Berkshire*, [1989] 2 All E.R. 545 at 563.

125 *Ibid.*, at 1177.

126 [1986] 2 All E.R. 440 (C.A.).

127 *Ibid.*, at 447.

128 *Ibid.*, at 448. In *Newhook v. K-Mart Can. Ltd.* (1991), 116 Nfld. & P.E.I.R. 102, 363 A.P.R. 102 (Nfld. T.D.), one person grabbed another person's arm in order to stop her. The two were having an argument. The court held that although this touching was not intended to be harmful, and was not a cause for concern on the part of the person grabbed, it was technically a battery, and $100 damages were awarded.

Sansalone case, McLachlin J. adopted this definition and stated that "all contact outside the exceptional category of contact that is generally accepted or expected in the course of ordinary life, is *prima facie* offensive."[129]

The rationale of implied consent to distinguish friendly touchings from unfriendly ones is not desirable. It creates potential confusion with the general defence of consent in the intentional torts. Unlike the normal defence of consent, which must be proven by a defendant after the battery itself has been established, implied consent to everyday contact would be something which goes to the very definition of battery and would have to be refuted by the plaintiff.[130] It is also fictitious to argue that a plaintiff who demonstrated an aversion to a contact by either suing the offender, or retaliating against it, ''impliedly consented'' to the contact.[131] It is more realistic to accept the proposition that certain conduct, deemed generally acceptable by society, will not constitute a hostile act, and will not be considered to be a battery. This must be left as a question of fact to the trier of fact.

(iv) Physical Contact

The contact must be physical. It need not be person-to-person contact; the defendant can use weapons, implements, or other objects to cause the contact to occur.[132] If the contact is not physical, no battery is committed although there may be other tort actions available, such as nuisance, assault or intentional infliction of mental suffering which deal with emotional or psychological disturbances.

(v) Burden of Proof: Fault or Wrongdoing

As with all torts based on the Writs of Trespass,[133] battery must be "wrongful" in order to be actionable. In this respect, wrongfulness includes both intentional and negligent conduct; an accidental trespass is not actionable. Moreover, the

---

129 (2000), 50 C.C.L.T. (2d) 1 (S.C.C.) at 14-15. The dissenting judgment of Iacobucci J. on the question of burden of proof regarding consent to sexual touching saw consent or the absence of it as going to the issue of offensive contact. Thus, a sexual touching is only offensive or harmful if non-consensual. Under this approach, Iacobucci J. placed the burden of proving offensiveness, i.e., lack of consent, on the plaintiff.

130 As pointed out above, this is exactly what Iaccobuci J. did in *Sansalone*, which resulted in his decision to require plaintiffs, in sexual wrongdoing cases, to prove lack of consent. I would disagree with this approach.

131 What if a plaintiff clearly did not consent to the contact and made this known to the defendant? Can a person on a crowded bus loudly announce that he does not wish to be touched and that if he is he will consider it to be a hostile gesture? See *Mandel v. The Permanent* (1985), 7 O.A.C. 365 at 370 (Div. Ct.), where Henry J. stated that the defendant's act of placing his hand on the plaintiff's arm or elbow to pilot her towards the door was ''merely a polite gesture and an accepted usage in daily life in a civilized society, whether or not she was consenting to it.''

132 For example, as in *Garratt v. Dailey*, 279 P. 2d 1091 (Wash., 1955), the defendant was held liable for causing the plaintiff to fall to the ground by pulling a chair from under her. In *Sirois v. Gustafson*, [2002] S.J. No. 664, 2002 CarswellSask 722 (Sask. Q.B.), a battery occurred when the defendant struck and shattered the window of the plaintiff's car with a hammer. A piece of glass lodged in and scratched the plaintiff's eye. This was also held to constitute an assault to the persons who were in the car at the time.

133 Assault, battery, false imprisonment, trespass to goods, and trespass to land.

burden of disproving intention or negligence falls upon the defendant, once the elements of the tort have been proved by the plaintiff.[134]

Confusion does exist, however, in the cases as to what these propositions mean. Some judges and text writers refuse to acknowledge that there is such a thing as a "negligent trespass." Furthermore, what a "negligent" trespass is sometimes the subject of debate.

In the *Sansalone* case,[135] the defendant committed a sexual assault. This was clearly a battery—a physical, offensive contact to the person. It was unquestionably intentional. The defendant acted intending that physical contact with another person occur. As we shall discuss below, a negligent battery would have occurred if the defendant acted without intending to contact another person, but taking an unreasonable risk that contact could occur.[136] This, of course, did not happen in *Sansalone* and thus discussion of negligent battery in that case was moot.[137]

The defence was consent. Although McLachlin J. approved of the *dicta* from the case of *Cook v. Lewis*[138] that placed the onus of disproving "a lack of intention or negligence" upon the defendant in an action for trespass, Her Ladyship went further by using this rationale to justify imposing the burden of proving consent upon the defendant. In other words, McLachlin J. saw the issue of consent or a reasonable belief of consent as going to the issue of fault.[139]

I would not agree with this analysis. I would suggest that a person who intentionally commits a sexual act upon another person, even under the honestly held belief that the other person has consented, has committed an intentional battery. Whether the belief was reasonable or unreasonable goes to the question of consent as a defence to the battery.[140] The issue of consent goes not to the issue of whether the battery is intentional or negligent, but whether there is a defence to the intentional battery.

McLachlin J. stated that "liability in battery is based not on the defendant's fault, but on the violation of the plaintiff's right" and in this regard "the violation

---

134 *Cook v. Lewis*, [1951] S.C.R. 830, is generally cited as the leading Canadian authority although this principle has been re-iterated in a large number of Canadian cases.

135 (2000), 50 C.C.L.T. (2d) 1 (S.C.C.).

136 As Iacobucci J. illustrates in *Sansalone* this could occur where, for example, a person carelessly stretches out his arms striking someone. More examples will be given below from the case law.

137 A similar Alberta case is *S. (J.A.) v. Goss* (2002), [2002] A.J. No. 152, 2002 CarswellAlta 181 (C.A.). Both cases involved the duty of insurers to defend those who are being sued for sexual assault. Both judgments agreed that the defendant's acts were intentional and that the question of negligence did not arise on these facts.

138 [1951] S.C.R. 830.

139 This approach is illustrated in the following sentences by McLachlin J. at (2000), 50 C.C.L.T. (2d) 1 (S.C.C.) at 22:

> It is unnecessary on this appeal to comment on the relationship between battery (traditionally thought of mainly as an intentional tort) and negligence. In this case, insofar as one could speak of negligent battery, it would be to recognize the defence of reasonable belief in consent to a suit based on an intentional act.

Also referring critically to the dissenting judgment of Iacobucci J., McLachlin J. states at (2000), 50 C.C.L.T. (2d) 1 (S.C.C.) at 12 that Iacobucci J. "proposes to alter the traditional rule, at least for sexual battery, to require the plaintiff to prove fault, i.e. that the defendant either knew or ought to have known that she was not consenting."

140 And here I agree with McLachlin J. that proving consent falls to the defendant.

of another person's right can be considered a form of fault."[141] As stated above, if this *dicta* were to be interpreted as suggesting that contact that is accidental is still actionable, it would represent a major departure from precedence in the area of trespass. Liability in battery, as in all other torts of trespass is based on fault, although fault does not necessarily presume or require knowledge of the wrongfulness of one's act.[142]

(vi) Sexual Wrongdoing

Sexual contact clearly constitutes a battery, for which a defendant may be held civilly liable. Sexual contacts are direct, offensive,[143] and physical. Sexual misconduct can also constitute a breach of fiduciary duty, or a tort other than battery such as assault.[144] What is interesting to note is the growing number of tort actions based upon sexual wrongdoing that are being brought. Thus, we are seeing actions

---

141 (2000), 50 C.C.L.T. (2d) 1 (S.C.C.) at 12. McLachlin J. referred approvingly to Sullivan, "Trespass to the Person in Canada: A Defence of the Traditional Approach" (1987), 19 Ott.L.Rev. 533 with regard to this analysis.

142 What "fault" means in regard to the torts based on trespass is discussed by Sullivan, above. Sullivan argues that the wrong in a trespass is the interference with the plaintiff's "right." The absence of "fault" can be used to excuse this interference . It cannot however justify it in the sense of denying its wrongfulness. According to Sullivan, it is arguable that only proof that the interference was unavoidable by exercising the highest standard of care can excuse a trespass. This is of course much more onerous than proving only that reasonable care was taken. Sullivan concedes that modern cases tend to define even the defence of "inevitable accident" by using the language of reasonable care, and that "Canadian courts have generally assumed that negligence almost always means a failure to take care." As will be discussed below, Sullivan's view that a higher standard of reasonable care defines "fault" in torts based on trespass is not supported by recent case law. Sullivan would not agree with McLachlin J.'s view that consent is merely an excuse to a trespass, but treats it as a justification. Fridman, *The Law Of Torts*, 2d. ed., (2002) at 84-88 accepts that Canadian law recognizes that once a trespass is established, the onus of proof is upon the defendant to show lack of intent and negligence. Although Fridman states that the issue is whether the defendant behaved "in a careless manner having regard to what a reasonable man would expect to happen as a result of his actions", "negligence in this context" is not the same as in the tort of negligence. The standard is deliberate or perhaps "reckless" conduct. As I suggest in Klar, "Intentional and Negligent Trespass: It is Time to Clarify the Law" (2004), 28 Advocates' Quarterly 410, this area is ripe for judicial clarification.

143 In the sense of being not every day non-trivial contacts as defined above.

144 It has been held that sexual harassment itself is a tort—see *Lajoie v. Kelly*, [1997] 3 W.W.R. 181, 32 C.C.L.T. (2d) 115 (Man. Q.B.). In an earlier case from Alberta, *Campbell-Fowler v. Royal Trust Co.* (1993), [1994] 1 W.W.R. 193 (Alta. Master), it was decided that whether there is such a tort is an open question, and an application to strike was dismissed. Also see *Petrovics v. Canada* (1999), 209 N.B.R. (2d) 237 (Q.B.), leave to appeal refused (1999), 210 N.B.R. (2d) 109 (C.A.), *Sargeant v. Patterson Dental Canada Inc.* (January 9, 1998), Doc. 97-CU-116745, [1998] O.J. No. 82 (Div. Ct.), where motions to strike out were rejected, and *Nicholas v. Mullin* (1998), 199 N.B.R. (2d) 219 (Q.B.), where the action was struck out in deference to the human rights tribunal's jurisdiction. In *Andersen v. Ottawa (City)* (2005), 255 D.L.R. (4th) 223 (Ont. S.C.J.), an action for sexual harassment was viewed as a "workplace dispute" that fell within the exclusive jurisdiction of an arbitrator under the collective agreement. The claims relating to "sexual assault", however, were allowed to proceed as they involved a recognized tort claim. The tort of intentional infliction of emotional distress may also apply. See discussion, below.

instituted by children against their parents, relatives, or other adults,[145] by women against their dates,[146] by clients against professionals,[147] and by children against members of the clergy.[148] Claims are also being brought against employers for their vicarious liability with respect to sexual assaults committed by employees[149] and against parents or others with custodial obligations for their negligence or breach of fiduciary duties in allowing sexual assaults to be committed against those in their care.[150] The issue in most cases is not whether a battery has taken place but whether there is the defence of consent,[151] or whether the limitation period has expired.

---

145 See *B. (K.L.) v. B. (K.E.)* (1991), 7 C.C.L.T. (2d) 105 (Man. Q.B.); *Gray v. Reeves*, [1992] 3 W.W.R. 393 (B.C. S.C.); *M. (K.) v. M. (H.)* (1992), 96 D.L.R. (4th) 289 (S.C.C.); *J. (L.A.) v. J. (H.)* (1993), 102 D.L.R. (4th) 177 (Ont. Gen. Div.); *H.(S.) v. L.(R.G.)*, [1994] 2 W.W.R. 276 (B.C. S.C.); *C. (P.) v. C. (R.)* (1994), 114 D.L.R. (4th) 151 (Ont. Gen. Div.); *B. (A.) v. J. (I.)* (1991), 119 A.R. 210 (Alta. Q.B.); *B. (P.) v. B. (W.)* (1992), 11 O.R. (3d) 161 (Gen. Div.); *D. (P.A.) v. H. (A.E.)* (1998), [1999] 2 W.W.R. 139 (B.C. S.C.); *J. (A.) v. D. (W)*, [1999] 11 W.W.R. 82 (Man. Q.B.), reversed (2001), 198 D.L.R. (4th) 659 (Man. C.A.), leave to appeal refused (2001), 2001 CarswellMan 485, 2001 CarswellMan 486 (S.C.C.); *B. (T.L.) v. C. (R.E)*, [2000] 5 W.W.R. 296 (Man. Q.B.), reversed [2000] 11 W.W.R. 436 (Man. C.A.), leave to appeal refused (2001), 2001 CarswellMan 250, 2001 CarswellMan 251 (S.C.C.); and *L. (R.L.) v. L. (R.)*, [2001] 7 W.W.R. 315 (B.C. C.A), among others. In *Olsen v. Olsen* (2006), 266 D.L.R. (4th) 209 (B.C. S.C.), a brother sued his older brother for sexual assaults that occurred when the boys were young children.

146 *G. v. D.* (1993), 101 D.L.R. (4th) 101 (B.C. C.A.).

147 *H. (I.) v. Isaac*, [1994] 6 W.W.R. 381 (Man. C.A.); *Norberg v. Wynrib*, [1992] 4 W.W.R. 577 (S.C.C.); *T. (L.) v. M. (W.K.)* (1993), 110 D.L.R. (4th) 64 (N.B. Q.B.); *C. (T.) v. S. (G.D.)* (1997), [1997] O.J. No. 2389, 1997 CarswellOnt 5935 (Gen. Div.); *K. (R.) v. A. (J.)* (2001), [2001] N.B.J. No. 361, 2001 CarswellNB 353 (C.A.), leave to appeal refused (2002), 2002 CarswellNB 209, 2002 CarswellNB 210 (S.C.C.); and *C. (N.) v. Blank* (1998), [1998] O.J. No. 2544 1998 CarswellOnt 2623 (Gen. Div.).

148 *K. (W.) v. Pornbacher* (1997), 34 C.C.L.T. (2d) 174 (B.C. S.C.); *John Doe v. Bennett* (2000), 1 C.C.L.T. (3d) 261 (Nfld. T.D.), reversed (2002), 20 C.C.E.L. (3d) 24 (Nfld. C.A.). For a more exhaustive list of cases see Feldthusen, "The Civil Action For Sexual Battery: Therapeutic Jurisprudence?" (1993), 25 Ottawa L. Rev. 203. Feldthusen discusses 33 sexual battery cases litigated since 1985. See Chapter 16 for further discussion.

149 The two leading Canadian cases are *B. (P.A.). v. Curry* (1999), 46 C.C.L.T. (2d) 1, 174 D.L.R. (4th) 45 (S.C.C.) and *T. (G.)* v. *Griffiths* (1999), 46 C.C.L.T. (2d) 49, 174 D.L.R. (4th) 71 (S.C.C.). The "residential school" cases have been very significant in this category. See *B. (E.) v. Order of the Oblates of Mary* (2005), 258 D.L.R. (4th) 385 (S.C.C.) and *Blackwater v. Plint* (2005), 258 D.L.R. (4th) 275 (S.C.C.), among others. See discussion at Chapter 16.

150 See, for example, *M. (M.) v. F. (R.)*, [1999] 2 W.W.R. 446 (B.C. C.A.), additional reasons at (1998), 48 B.C.L.R. (3d) 360 (C.A.). In this case, the action against a foster mother for the sexual assaults committed against the foster child by the foster mother's son was dismissed. The issue concerned whether the defendant ought to have foreseen and prevented the abuse. In *T. (L.) v. T. (R.W.)* (1997), 36 C.C.L.T. (2d) 207 (B.C. S.C.), a Third Party claim by the sexual abuser against the victim's mother was rejected. For a discussion of the standard of care required to be observed by the parent or guardian, see Chapter 9.

151 The issue as to whether a plaintiff has the onus of proving that she did not consent or that a reasonable person would not have believed that she consented was dealt with in the *Sansalone* case. The majority of the Supreme Court of Canada per McLachlin J. held that the defendant must prove that the plaintiff had consented or that it was reasonable to believe that she had. In other words, the issue of consent went to the defences and was not seen as an element of the tort itself. Iacobucci J., writing for three of the justices, stated that in sexual battery cases, unlike in traditional battery cases, the absence of consent being an integral part of the battery

Commentators have identified the advantages and disadvantages of the civil action as a remedy for victims of sexual wrongs.[152] It is argued that the civil action presents a number of advantages to complainants which are not available through the criminal justice process. The tort action allows the plaintiff to control the proceedings and define the issues, the burden of proof is less onerous, and the claimant can receive damages, including aggravated and punitive damages.[153] More significantly, perhaps, is the ''empowering'' effect of the law suit, and its potential ''therapeutic'' value.[154]

---

itself, must be established by the plaintiff. On this point, I agree with McLachlin J. As with medical treatment, a contact will be perfectly appropriate, *if the plaintiff consented to it.* What makes it a "battery" is not that it was unconsensual contact, but that it was direct, out of the ordinary, contact. Consent will validate that contact, but only if proved as a defence by the defendant. See Chapter 3.

152 See West, ''Rape in the Criminal Law and the Victim's Tort Alternative: A Feminist Analysis'' (1992), 50 U.T. Fac. L. Rev. 96; Feldthusen, ''The Civil Action for Sexual Battery: Therapeutic Jurisprudence?'' (1993), 25 Ottawa L. Rev. 203; Des Rosiers, ''Limitation Periods and Civil Remedies for Childhood Sexual Abuse'' (1992-1993), C.F.L.Q. 43; Taylor and Singh, ''Sexual And Domestic Torts I: Types and Defences'', unpublished paper, Alberta Department of Justice; and Mosher, ''Challenging Limitation Periods: Civil Claims by Adult Survivors of Incest'' (1994), 44 U.T.L.J. 169; Feldthusen, "The Canadian Experiment with the Civil Action for Sexual Battery", in *Torts in the Nineties* (1997), and Grace and Vella, *Civil Liability for Sexual Abuse and Violence in Canada* (Markham: Butterworths, 2000). For an analysis of the English experience, see Joanne Conaghan, "Tort Litigation in the Context of Intra-familial Abuse" (1998), 61 Mod. L. Rev. 132. A study of sexual assault victims by Feldthusen, Hankivsky and Greaves, "Therapeutic Consequences of Civil Actions for Damages and Compensation Claims by Victims of Sexual Abuse" (1999), 11(1) Can. J. of Women & The Law discusses the advantages and disadvantages of the tort process and compensation schemes. Also see Barbara Micheels, "Is Justice Served? The Development Of Tort Liability Against The Passive Parent In Incest Cases" (1996-97), 41 Saint Louis U.L.J. 809, who supports the use of tort by incest victims against "passive" parents. A more cautious approach is urged by Reaume and Van Praagh, "Family Matters: Mothers As Secondary Defendants In Child Sexual Abuse Actions" (2002), 17 S.C.L.R. (2d) 179.

153 See West, above, note 152, and Feldthusen, above, note 152. Feldthusen discusses the notion that unlike the criminal law, ''the civil system is premised on the equality of the plaintiff and defendant''. Moreover, the plaintiff in the tort action controls the decision to sue, can choose the facts to be introduced, can determine the legal theory to be argued, and can discuss the consequences that the battery had on her. See Feldthusen, at 216. In terms of damages, it has been held that the cap on non-pecuniary damages imposed by the Supreme Court of Canada does not apply to victims of sexual assault: see *Y. (S.) v. C. (F.G)* (1996), 30 C.C.L.T. (2d) 82 (B.C. C.A.). In this case, a jury awarded the plaintiff $650,000 in damages, which included an award of $350,000 for non-pecuniary and aggravated damages. The Court of Appeal, while agreeing that there is no cap on non-pecuniary damages, pared down the entire award to $350,000. Also see *P. (S.) v. K. (F.)* (1996), 32 C.C.L.T. (2d) 250 (Sask. Q.B.). A contrary view was expressed in *A. (D.A.) v. B. (D.K.)* (1995), 27 C.C.L.T. (2d) 256 (Ont. Gen. Div.). The trial judge held that the cap does apply to all cases, including cases of breach of fiduciary duty and sexual assault. In *O'Neill v. MacDougall* (2006), 38 C.C.L.T. (3d) 253 (B.C. S.C.), the Court held that where the defendant had sexually assaulted many victims, awards of punitive damages to individual claimants should be moderated to reflect what the global award would be if they were all awarded that amount.

154 Feldthusen, above, note 152, discusses the issue of the therapeutic effect of the civil action. He writes that some victims have commented on the value of the litigation as part of the healing process, while others noted that they instituted action in order to see their assailant punished, in their desire for public vindication or in order to encourage others to come forward. Feldthusen's own conclusion is that the therapeutic benefits of the tort action are ''plausible'',

On the other side, tort suits are costly, time consuming, and stressful. One problem in particular has been the expiration of the limitation period for bringing action. The typical 2-year or even 4- or 6-year limitation periods have proven to be serious obstacles for adult claimants where the abuse occurred during their childhood, numerous years before they are prepared to come forward and take legal action.[155] In recent years courts and legislatures have stepped forward to alleviate this problem. In the important case of *M. (K.) v. M. (H.)*,[156] the Supreme Court of Canada established that the limitation period for a sexual battery based upon incest does not begin to run until the incest victim discovers the connection between the harm she has suffered and her childhood history. There is a presumption that this occurs when the victim undergoes therapy and through therapy becomes aware of the connection. In the specific case, the plaintiff was permitted to take action at the age of 28 for her father's sexual misconduct towards her which occurred starting when she was 8, and ending 12 years before she instituted her action.[157] In addition to this judicial approach, the legislatures of several provinces have amended their limitations legislation to incorporate the Supreme Court's approach,[158] or even to abolish any limitation period at all for actions based upon sexual misconduct.[159]

---

but yet "unproven". Mosher, above, note 152, at 183, however, is more convinced:

> For many survivors, a civil claim has a beneficial therapeutic impact. It may well represent the evolution of a process of therapy which began with the survivor blaming herself for the abuse and which, at the point of litigation, has progressed to public naming and a demand for accountability to her. There is a world of difference between the victim demanding accountability to her, and the state demanding accountability to it through its criminal law process.

155 The limitation period has been called "the most difficult legal obstacle preventing victims of childhood sexual abuse from suing their aggressor." See Des Rosiers, above, note 152, at 43. See also Mosher, above, note 152, at 181-82: "One of the most enduring legal barriers to civil claims by incest survivors is the limitation period."

156 (1992), 96 D.L.R. (4th) 289 (S.C.C.).

157 See Des Rosiers, above, note 152. This approach has been followed in a number of subsequent cases including *C. (P.) v. C. (R. J.)* (1994), 114 D.L.R. (4th) 151 (Ont. Gen. Div.); *H. (S.G.) v. Gorsline* (2001), 5 C.C.L.T. (3d) 65 (Alta. Q.B.), additional reasons at [2001] 11 W.W.R. 405 (Alta. Q.B.), affirmed (2004), 23 C.C.L.T. (3d) 65, [2005] 2 W.W.R. 716, 29 Alta. L.R. (4th) 203 (Alta. C.A.), leave to appeal refused (2005), 2005 CarswellAlta 62, 2005 CarswellAlta 63 (S.C.C.); *F. (L.) v. F. (J.R.)* (2001), [2001] O.J. No. 1720, 2001 CarswellOnt 1555 (C.A.); and *D. (S.) v. Scoles* (2001), [2001] O.J. No. 2588, 2001 CarswellOnt 2321 (S.C.J.), among others. For a discussion of the discoverability rule under the Manitoba jurisprudence see *B. (T.L.) v. C. (R.E.)*, [2000] 11 W.W.R. 436 (Man. C.A.), leave to appeal refused (2001), 2001 CarswellMan 250, 2001 CarswellMan 251 (S.C.C.). For an analysis of the test enunciated by the Supreme Court and some problems with it, see Mosher, above, note 153. There are ways of extending the limitation period, other than through this "reasonable discoverability" approach. The limitation period may be able to be extended, or even eliminated, if the cause of action is one of breach of fiduciary duty. As well, the issues of legal disability or fraudulent concealment can be argued to prevent the extinction of the cause of action. This issue tends to be complex depending as it does on the specific provincial legislation, and the cause of action that is in question.

158 For example, the Prince Edward Island amendment states that in cases involving sexual abuse, the limitation period "begins to run when the plaintiff understands the nature of the injuries and recognizes the effects of the abuse." S.P.E.I. 1992, c. 63, s. 1 (b). A similar provision is contained in the Nova Scotia amendment. See Rainaldi, ed., *Remedies in Tort* (Carswell), at

The renewed interest in the civil action for victims of egregious sexual misconduct, and the reasons why victims are seeking remedies through tort, reaffirm the importance of the principles of civil justice reflected in tort law. While one must hesitate before too quickly drawing analogies between this area of tort law and other areas, the lesson of what may be significant to victims of wrongdoing, other than purely monetary compensation, should not be lost on those contemplating tort law "reform".

(c) Negligent Battery

A negligent battery exists when the defendant causes a direct, offensive, physical contact with the plaintiff as a result of negligent conduct.[160] The defendant's negligence consists of unreasonably disregarding a foreseeable risk of contact, even though the contact was neither desired nor substantially certain to occur.[161]

Although eliminated in England,[162] there is no doubt that the tort of negligent battery still exists in Canada, and other parts of the Commonwealth.[163] Except for

2.88.2 *et seq.* for a review of the various provincial legislative provisions dealing with this issue.

159 See, for example, Saskatchewan's Limitations of Actions Act, R.S.S. 1978, c. L-15, s. 3(3.1); and the British Columbia Limitation Amendment Act, R.S.B.C. 1996, c. 266, s. 3(4).

160 As noted above, this action is a "negligent trespass". Some contemporary courts reserve the term "battery" exclusively for intentional contacts. See, for example, *Reibl v. Hughes* (1980), 14 C.C.L.T. 1 at 12 (S.C.C.), where Laskin C.J.C. states that the tort of battery "is an intentional one, consisting of an unprivileged and unconsented to invasion of one's bodily security." See also La Forest J. in *Norberg v. Wynrib* (1992), 12 C.C.L.T. (2d) 1 at 16 (S.C.C.): "A battery is the intentional infliction of unlawful force on another person", and Rosenberg J. in *Bell-Ginsburg v. Ginsburg* (1993), 17 C.C.L.T. (2d) 167 at 172 (Ont. Gen. Div.): "Battery is the intentional, unconsented touching of the person of the plaintiff by the defendant." See as well *F. (B.) v. Saskachewan Rivers School Division No. 119* (2000), 192 D.L.R. (4th) 706, [2001] 6 W.W.R. 257 (Sask. C.A.), where battery is defined exclusively as an intentional tort. In *Hurley v. Moore* (1993), 18 C.C.L.T. (2d) 78 at 85 (Nfld. C.A.), Steele J.A., while defining battery exclusively in terms of intentional conduct, also includes the following definition of battery from Halsbury's Laws of England, 4th edition, vol. 45, para. 1311: "A battery is an act of the defendant which directly and either intentionally *or negligently* causes some physical contact with the person of the plaintiff without the plaintiff's consent" (emphasis added).

161 This paragraph is quoted with approval by Iacobucci J. in *Sansalone* at (2000), 50 C.C.L.T. (2d) 1 (S.C.C.) at 48. Also see the Alberta Court of Appeal judgment in *S. (J.A.) v. Goss* (2002), [2002] A.J. No. 152, 2002 CarswellAlta 181 (C.A.). As discussed above, Professor Sullivan argues that it is arguable that fault in the torts of trespass imposes a much higher standard of care on defendants than mere reasonable care. See Sullivan, "Trespass to the Person in Canada: A Defence of the Traditional Approach" (1987), 19 Ottawa L. Rev. 533 at 553. A different view is expressed by Klar, "Intentional and Negligent Trespass: It is Time to Clarify the Law", above, note 142.

162 See *Letang v. Cooper*, [1965] 1 Q.B. 232 (C.A.); *Fowler v. Lanning*, [1959] 1 Q.B. 426; and Fleming, *The Law of Torts*, 9th ed. (1998), at 31.

163 See Trindade, Cane and Lunney, *The Law of Torts in Australia*, 4th ed. (2007), at 68 and following, and the Australian cases cited therein. The authors refer to *Leame v. Bray* (1803), 102 E.R. 724, 3 East 593 (Eng. K.B.), which is described as "one of the earliest cases of negligent trespass to the person." They refer to *Williams v. Milotin* (1957), 97 C.L.R. 465 (Aust. H.C.) as making it clear that negligent trespass and negligence are two separate torts. See, however, *Hackshaw v. Shaw* (1985), 59 A.L.J.R. 156 (Aust. H.C.), where Gibbs C.J. stated that he preferred the English view, although he found it unnecessary to decide the issue. Osborne, *The Law of Torts*, 3rd ed. (2007), at 239 also supports the view that Canadian law recognizes negligent battery.

the area of highway traffic accidents,[164] which in any event now are regulated by legislation providing favourable procedural advantages to victims hit by a vehicle,[165] plaintiffs in negligent battery cases have the same advantages as those involved in the intentional torts. Plaintiffs need prove only that the battery was committed by the defendant, who must then disprove that it was done negligently.

Cook v. Lewis[166] is the leading case establishing that a plaintiff may sue in negligent battery. The plaintiff was shot by one of two hunters. He was unable to establish by direct evidence which of the two had hit him, and attempted to reverse the burden of proof, placing it on the defendants to exculpate themselves. He was unable to do this using the tort of negligent battery because he could not establish who was responsible for the battery.[167] Nonetheless, Cartwright J. affirmed that, except for highway accidents,

> where a plaintiff is injured by force applied directly to him by the defendant his case is made by proving this fact and the onus falls upon the defendant to prove "that such trespass was utterly without his fault."[168]

This has been followed in several subsequent negligent battery cases, involving direct injuries caused, for example, by errant golf balls,[169] projectiles,[170] and bullets.[171]

Negligent conduct resulting in a direct injury is no more deserving of sanction, nor is it more difficult to prove, than negligent conduct which indirectly leads to injury. That being so, there is no justification for treating negligent battery cases differently from other negligence actions. As a practical matter, continuing to

---

164 See *Walmsley v. Humenick*, [1954] 2 D.L.R. 232 at 242 (B.C. S.C.); *Fletcher v. Rylands* (1866), L.R. 1 Ex. 265, affirmed L.R. 3 H.L. 330; *Phillips v. Britannia Hygienic Laundry Co.*, [1923] 1 K.B. 539, affirmed [1923] 2 K.B. 832 (C.A.); *Winnipeg Elec. Co. v. Geel*, [1932] 4 D.L.R. 51 (P.C.).

165 For example, s. 179 of the Highway Traffic Act, R.S.A. 2000, c. H-8, provides that where a person suffers loss or damage arising out of the operation of a motor vehicle on a highway, and where that vehicle was being operated in contravention of the Act, the onus of proof is on the owner or driver of the vehicle to show that the loss or damage did not arise by reason of the breach. Section 180 states that if a person is injured by a motor vehicle, the onus of proof that the loss or damage did not entirely or solely arise through the negligence of the owner or driver is on the owner or driver.

166 [1952] 1 D.L.R. 1 (S.C.C.).

167 The proof problem was overcome by the court's enunciation of a new rule designed to deal with this type of factual problem. See Chapter 11.

168 [1952] 1 D.LR. 1 at 15.

169 *Ellison v. Rogers* (1967), 67 D.L.R. (2d) 21 (Ont. H.C.).

170 *Goshen v. Larin* (1974), 46 D.L.R. (3d) 137 (N.S. T.D.), reversed 56 D.L.R. (3d) 719 (N.S. C.A.); *Hatton v. Webb* (1977), 81 D.L.R. (3d) 377 (Alta. Dist. Ct.).

171 *Dahlberg v. Naydiuk* (1969), 10 D.L.R. (3d) 319 (Man. C.A.). Negligent battery, as a separate cause of action, has even been argued in medical malpractice cases. If a doctor performs surgery, for which there has not been consent, a battery has been committed. If due to the doctor's negligence, surgery is performed on one part of the body, when it actually ought to have been performed on another, is this a negligent battery? This depends on why the mistake was made. If the doctor intended to perform the surgery which was performed, the battery is intentional, assuming lack of consent. The negligence in this case, refers not to the battery itself, but to the decision to perform the surgery in this way. If, however, the doctor carelessly cut in one area, when the intention was to cut in another, this battery fairly can be described as negligent. See *Gerula v. Flores* (1995), 126 D.L.R. (4th) 506 (Ont. C.A.); *Vasdani v. Sehmi*, [1993] O.J. No. 44. On the topic of "informed consent", see below, Chapter 4, 10.

treat negligent batteries independently of other negligence actions rarely has any real significance. Although it is true that a plaintiff who can pursue an action in negligent battery (i) does not have to prove damage,[172] and (2) does not have the burden of proving negligence, the burden of disproof being on the defendant, these are seldom relevant concerns. A plaintiff who has suffered no damage is unlikely to contemplate suing because of the expenses involved.[173] As well, the matter of who has the burden of proving or disproving negligence will only have importance where the trier of fact cannot come to a conclusion as to negligence after all the evidence has been heard. This has not been a factor in any of the negligent battery cases of which I am aware.[174] Canadian law ought to recognize that there are no policy reasons which justify distinguishing between negligence and negligent batteries, and discard this distinction.[175]

9. FALSE IMPRISONMENT

(a) Introduction

The tort of false imprisonment protects one's right to go where one has a lawful right to be. As with the torts of assault and battery, it stems from the writ of trespass, and accordingly, involves conduct which directly confines the victim. The legal wrong is the restriction of the plaintiff's liberty and actual damage is not necessary for a successful action. The tort usually is committed intentionally, although the possibility of a negligently committed false imprisonment remains open.

The tort is committed when a person is imprisoned without lawful justification, i.e., wrongfully. A claimant has the burden of proving the imprisonment, and having done this, the onus then lies on a defendant to prove a justification in defence.[176] Although there are some theoretical difficulties with the concept of imprisonment, litigation generally involves one of the defences to the tort, and not whether a *prima facie* case has been made out. In the contemporary context, the action most frequently arises when a person is imprisoned ostensibly according

---

172 For a contrary view see Harari, *The Place of Negligence in the Law of Torts* (1962), at 145.

173 Costs may even be awarded against the plaintiff.

174 It has been suggested that there are other functions which are met by the continued existence of the separate tort of negligent battery. See Trindade, Cane and Lunney, *The Law of Torts in Australia,* 4th ed. (2007), at 68-77. Briefly these are as follows:

(1) A duty of care must be established in an action for negligence, but not in a case of negligent trespass;

(2) There may not be legally recognized damage to support an action for negligence;

(3) There is no need for the plaintiff to prove negligence, which may have importance especially in cases where the defendant does not appear for trial.

Except for negligent false imprisonment cases, these advantages have been termed "inconsequential or illusory." See Harding and Feng, "Negligent False Imprisonment — A Problem in the Law of Trespass" (1980), 22 Malaya L. Rev. 29.

175 This would mean that all negligent acts would be treated in the same way, i.e., as an action for negligence. Tort law would distinguish between intentional conduct and negligence. See also Heffey, "Negligent Infliction of Imprisonment: Actionable 'Per Se' or 'Com Damno'?" (1983-84), 14 Mel. U. L. Rev. 53.

176 See *Dendekker v. F.W. Woolworth*, [1975] 3 W.W.R. 429 at 432 (Alta. T.D.); *Frey v. Fedoruk*, [1950] S.C.R. 517; *Little v. Peers* (1988), 47 D.L.R. (4th) 621 (B.C. C.A.).

to statutory authority, or when a person is detained on suspicion of shoplifting.[177] The action's importance resides in the fact that it is a useful remedy to challenge the numerous existing statutes which authorize the detention and confinement of individuals.[178]

Closely related to the tort of false imprisonment is that of false arrest. As has been stated: "Few values are more important to the individual in a free society such as Canada than the right not to be unlawfully arrested and detained."[179] The tort of false arrest occurs at the time a person is placed under arrest.[180] Since, however, every arrest constitutes a restraint on the subject's liberty, the tort of false arrest is subsumed in the tort of false imprisonment.[181]

---

177 This has been borne out in an empirical study. In Poirier, "Economic Analysis of False Imprisonment in Canada: A Statistical and Empirical Study" (1985), 34 U.N.B.L. J. 104, the author studied all the reported false imprisonment cases in Canada from 1950 to 1983. Of the fifty-six reported cases, 60 per cent were brought against police officers and 30 per cent against store owners.

178 For example, the Criminal Code, R.S.C. 1985, c. C-46; the Mental Health Act, R.S.A. 2000, c. M-14; the Intoxicated Persons Detention Act, R.S.N.B. 1973, c. I-14. An important decision relating to the confinement and sterilization of so-called "mentally defective persons" is *Muir v. Alberta*, 132 D.L.R. (4th) 695, [1996] 4 W.W.R. 177 (Alta. Q.B.). The plaintiff received approximately $750,000 in damages for her wrongful confinement and sterilization pursuant to Alberta's eugenics legislation. Following this judgment, the Government of Alberta settled the claims of hundreds of other persons who had been similarly treated. For a similar action, see *E. (D.) (Guardian ad litem of) v. British Columbia* (2003), 18 C.C.L.T. (3d) 169 (B.C. S.C.), reversed (2004), 28 C.C.L.T. (3d) 283 (B.C. C.A.), reconsideration refused (2005), 2005 CarswellBC 1220 (C.A.).

179 Williams J.A. in *Swansburg v. Royal Canadian Mounted Police* (1996), (*sub nom. Swansburg v. Smith*) 141 D.L.R. (4th) 94 (B.C. C.A.).

180 What constitutes an "arrest" is an interesting question frequently arising in the criminal law context. *Beckstead v. Ottawa (City)* (1997), 155 D.L.R. (4th) 382 (Ont. C.A.) held that a charge by way of summons does not constitute an arrest for the purpose of this tort.

181 In *Buck v. Canada*, [1985] F.C.J. No. 1040, Action No. T-3738-81, Muldoon J. stated that "false arrest is a kind, or mode, of false imprisonment, because the detention does not require prison walls or a dungeon so long as the plaintiff is restrained and he understands that he will not be permitted to go his way freely." It should be noted, however, that all restraints on liberty which constitute false imprisonments do not amount to arrests. See *Remedies In Tort*, Vol. 1, Rainaldi (ed.), which separates the actions of arrest and imprisonment into separate torts. One notes that the cases support the distinction between false arrest and false imprisonment, at least semantically. See, for example, *Nicely v. Waterloo Regional Police Force* (1991), 7 C.C.L.T. (2d) 61 (Ont. Div. Ct.), where the actions brought are for false arrest and false imprisonment. However, in *Newhook v. K-Mart Can. Ltd.* (1991), 116 Nfld. & P.E.I.R. 102, 363 A.P.R. 102 (Nfld. T.D.), Puddester J. noted that although separate claims for false arrest and false imprisonment were made, the counsel agreed that the false arrest claim was subsumed within the false imprisonment claim. The claims are often treated as "interchangeable". Thus, despite the theoretical difference between the act of arrest and the act of detention, it is all part of the continued process of detention. Also see *Kovacs v. Ont. Jockey Club* (1995), 126 D.L.R. (4th) 576 at 585 (Ont. Gen. Div.), where Cumming J. also notes that "in reality there would not seem to be much of a distinction between false arrest and false imprisonment." A very useful discussion of the differences between an arrest and imprisonment is found in Brooker J.'s judgment in *Chopra v. T. Eaton Co.*, [1999] 9 W.W.R. 711 (Alta. Q.B.). As Brooker J. notes an unlawful arrest always involves an imprisonment. An imprisonment does not always involve an arrest (e.g., a kidnapping). As well, an arrest can be lawful but be accompanied by an excessive use of force (a battery), or be followed by an unlawful imprisonment. In *Jensen v. Stemmer* (2007), 282 D.L.R. (4th) 340 (Man. C.A.), leave to appeal

(b) Intentional False Imprisonment

(i) Imprisonment

An imprisonment occurs when one is prevented from going where one has a lawful right to be. This does not mean, however, that a person is entitled to insist upon following an exact route. It appears from both the cases[182] and the texts[183] that a total restraint on one's liberty to go where one pleases is necessary to constitute an imprisonment. As long as a reasonable alternative route exists, the imprisonment has not been made out.[184] Nevertheless, this does not mean, and should not mean, that a person who is unreasonably prevented from proceeding along the way because of harassment or threats is without legal recourse. There very well may lie an action for assault, battery, or an action on the case, depending upon the circumstances.

An imprisonment can be brought about due to actual physical force, the threat of force, or even psychological coercion. The first two cases pose little difficulty. It is obvious that a person who is locked in a cell, physically restrained, or threatened with imminent harm should an attempt be made to leave has been imprisoned. Imprisonment by psychological coercion presents problems, however, and should be approached by courts with caution. Courts should not readily assume that individuals who have felt constrained, without there having been any actual overt acts or threats, have been imprisoned. Where someone with apparent authority to arrest or detain, such as a uniformed police officer, or even a security guard, requests that another person remain to answer questions concerning a suspicious occurrence, it is reasonable to assume that the ordinary person would

---

refused (2007), 2007 CarswellMan 379 (S.C.C.), Hamilton J.A. agreed that since the tort of false arrest is subsumed in the tort of false imprisonment, a plaintiff suing for false arrest is entitled to a jury trial pursuant to s. 64(1) of The Court of Queen's Bench Act, S.M. 1988-89, c. 4.

182 The classic case is *Bird v. Jones* (1845), 7 Q.B. 742. The plaintiff was unable to insist that he be allowed to proceed along one side of a bridge, which had been temporarily closed, when with little difficulty he could have proceeded on the other side. Coleridge J. held that there must be a total restraint on a person's ability to leave a place, and not merely a partial restraint, to constitute an imprisonment. Lord Denman C.J. dissented, holding that if a person has a right to do something, any restraint is unlawful, even if an alternative is presented to the plaintiff by the wrongdoer. See also *R. v. Macquarrie* (1875), 13 S.C.R. (N.S.W.) 264; *Burton v. Davies*, [1953] Q.S.R. 26.

183 See Fleming, *The Law of Torts*, 9th ed. (1998), at 33; Linden and Feldthusen, *Canadian Tort Law*, 8th ed. (2006), at 50; Trindade, Cane and Lunney, *The Law of Torts in Australia*, 4th ed. (2007), at 56; Fridman, *The Law of Torts in Canada*, 2nd ed. (2002), at 77; and Osborne, *The Law of Torts*, 3rd ed. (2007), at 244.

184 Thus, in *Hanson v. Wayne's Café Ltd.* (1990), 84 Sask. R. 220 (Q.B.), the fact that the plaintiff could have left the office through the back door meant that the restraint was not total and there was no false imprisonment. What about the situation of a person, who is already confined in prison, wrongfully being put in segregated or solitary confinement? Can one be imprisoned "within a prison"? In *Hill v. British Columbia* (1997), 148 D.L.R. (4th) 337, 38 C.C.L.T. (2d) 182 (B.C. C.A.), reversing (1995), 127 D.L.R. (4th) 362 (B.C. S.C.), the British Columbia Court of Appeal per Newbury J.A. held that it would constitute a false imprisonment to fail to follow regulations with respect to keeping a prisoner in segregated custody. The remedies lie not only in administrative law, but also in tort, and perhaps even with the Charter. See also *Brandon v. Canada (Correctional Service)* (1996), 131 D.L.R. (4th) 761 (Fed. T.D.), where the same conclusion is reached in so far as the tort of false imprisonment is concerned.

feel compelled to comply.[185] This should not be interpreted too generally. There are situations in which people voluntarily submit themselves to questioning and do not feel constrained.[186] Other cases have involved situations where individuals have complied with requests to remain in order to avoid embarrassing scenes.[187] In all such cases, courts must weigh competing interests. The rights of individuals to go where and when they please without harassment or obstruction must be balanced against the rights of others to make reasonable requests that the former remain to clear up suspicious circumstances. It ought not be necessary that co-operative attempts to settle disputes always be replaced by involving the police or other officials.

Although there are no Canadian cases on point, an imprisonment presumably can occur when a person makes it difficult for someone else to leave, although the victim is not personally detained. For example, taking someone's car keys away, or detaining a young child's parent, can effectively imprison the driver or child.[188]

(ii) Directness

As with the other trespasses, false imprisonment must occur directly as a result of the defendant's conduct. With the tort of false imprisonment, the directness requirement presents real difficulties.

The most important legal consequence of the directness requirement is that, unless the defendant personally has detained the plaintiff or has been responsible for the detention, the tort cannot be made out. In many instances of "official" detention, the decision to arrest and detain a suspect is not a decision which an ordinary person has the power to make, but is a decision within the discretion of officials. When will someone who has been arrested or imprisoned at the request of, or on the basis of information supplied by, a private citizen have an action against that person for false arrest or false imprisonment?

According to Canadian criminal law, private citizens have the power of arrest in certain limited cases.[189] When a private citizen, which includes a private security guard, arrests or imprisons another, the former will be *prima facie* liable for the tort of false imprisonment, subject to the applicability of the defence of legal authority.[190] Where, however, as is more common, a private citizen swears an information in front of a justice of the peace, and as a result of this information,

---

185 See, e.g., *Campbell v. S.S. Kresge Co.* (1976), 74 D.L.R. (3d) 717 (N.S. T.D.); *Lebrun v. High-Low Foods Ltd.* (1968), 69 D.L.R. (2d) 433 (B.C. S.C.); *Otto v. J. Grant Wallace Ltd.*, [1988] 2 W.W.R. 728 (Alta. Q.B.); and *Maher v. K Mart Can. Ltd.* (1991), 84 Nfld. & P.E.I.R. 271, 262 A.P.R. 271 (Nfld. T.D.).

186 See, e.g., *Cannon v. Hudson's Bay*, [1939] 4 D.L.R. 465 (B.C. S.C.).

187 See, e.g., *Conn v. David Spencer Ltd.*, [1930] 1 W.W.R. 26 (B.C. S.C.); *Chaytor v. London, New York & Paris Assn. of Fashion Ltd.* (1961), 30 D.L.R. (2d) 527 (Nfld. T.D.).

188 Trindade, Cane and Lunney, *The Law of Torts in Australia*, 4th ed. (2007), at 62, support this argument, although they could not cite any English or Australian cases.

189 The nature and history of the "citizen's arrest" is discussed in *R. v. Lerke* (1986), 67 A.R. 390, 25 D.L.R. (4th) 403 (C.A.) and more recently in *R. v. Dell* (2005), 256 D.L.R. (4th) 271 (Alta. C.A.). The issue in these, and other cases, revolves around the applicability of the Charter to citizen's arrests.

190 This will be discussed in Chapter 3.

a summons or warrant is issued for the appearance or arrest of an accused, the person who has sworn the information cannot be sued for false imprisonment should it turn out that the arrest was unjustified. The reason for this is that the arrest or imprisonment was not brought about by the direct act of the complainant but required the intervention of the judicial process.[191] Even where a police officer arrests a person, without warrant, on the information of an alleged witness or victim, it cannot be said that the arrest and imprisonment were brought about by the direct act of the complainant, since the decision to arrest was the police officer's.[192] Where, on the other hand, the informant "directs" the police to make an arrest, or otherwise utilizes the police for their own private purposes, an action may lie.[193]

This situation, while beneficial to those who provide information to the police concerning the suspicious conduct of others,[194] creates a difficulty for persons who have been arrested or imprisoned on the basis of the information. If they are innocent of the alleged charges, their civil remedies are quite limited. They do not have an action for false imprisonment against those who provided the infor-

---

191 See *Dendekker v. F.W. Woolworth*, [1975] 3 W.W.R. 429 (Alta. T.D.); *Foth v. O'Hara* (1958), 24 W.W.R. 533 (Alta. T.D.), and the several cases cited therein; *Benedetto v. Bunyan*, [1981] 5 W.W.R. 193 (Alta. Q.B.), and the cases cited therein; and *Fasken v. Time/System Inc. APS* (1986), 12 C.P.C. (2d) 1 (Ont. H.C.).

192 See, for example, *Brady v. Bank of N.S.*, [1992] O.J. No. 217; or *Webster v. Edmonton (City) Police Service* (2005), [2005] A.J. No. 225, 2005 CarswellAlta 283 (Q.B.), reversed (2007), 2007 CarswellAlta 76 (C.A.) at para. 59 [Q.B.]: "Merely making a complaint to the police does not expose a defendant to liability for false imprisonment if the police act on their own in making an arrest or detention."

193 In *Valderhaug v. Libin* (1954), 13 W.W.R. 383 (Alta. C.A.), the police arrested the plaintiff on the information of the defendant. The defendant informed the police that the plaintiff had committed a crime, writing a bad cheque, and was about to leave town. Even after the defendant became aware that this was not true, he failed to inform the police in a timely fashion. The court upheld (at 386) the plaintiff's false imprisonment action on the ground that "the arrest was the direct consequence of what he [the defendant] told them was about to happen, and without any investigation by any police officer into the facts. In so far as he had the power or influence to do so, he directed them to make the arrest." See also *Otto v. J. Grant Wallace Ltd.*, [1988] 2 W.W.R. 728 (Alta. Q.B.). The issue also arose in *Maher v. K Mart Can. Ltd.* (1991), 84 Nfld. & P.E.I.R. 271, 262 A.P.R. 271 (Nfld. T.D.). The defendant, a department store's security manager, asked the police to bring the plaintiff, who was already in police custody, into the store's security office, so that he could be given a "trespass notice". The court held that since this specific incident of giving the notice was for private purposes and outside of the police investigation, legal responsibility for it fell upon the security manager. This detention became the security manager's act, and he could be sued for false imprisonment on the basis of it. See also *Newhook v. K Mart Can. Ltd.* (1991), 116 Nfld. & P.E.I.R. 102 (Nfld. T.D.), 363 A.P.R. 102, where the court notes that the department store's false imprisonment ended when the police arrived and took over the investigation. Another approach is to find both the arresting officer and the person who directly encouraged or procured the arrest to be jointly liable for it. See *Hanisch v. Canada* (2004), 27 C.C.L.T. (3d) 1 (B.C. C.A.) and the cases cited therein. It is clear, however, that in these types of cases the defendant was actively involved in directing and encouraging the arrest. See discussion below on "joint tortfeasors".

194 It has been argued that "as a matter of public policy, the law should not discourage people from contacting the police by measuring their degree of participation too finely." See, Potts J. in *Fasken v. Time/System Int. APS* (1986), 12 C.P.C. (2d) 1 at 5, quoted by Chapnik J. in *Brady v. Bank of N.S.*, above, note 192, at 7. The argument is that people should be encouraged to contact the police rather than taking action themselves.

mation because of the absence of directness. Where they have been arrested without warrant they may have an action for false arrest and imprisonment against the police officers involved, although, as we shall see, the defences open to these officials are considerably wider than those available to ordinary persons. They may have an action for malicious prosecution, although this will normally be more difficult to establish than a simple action for false imprisonment and will require proof of damage. Is this situation satisfactory? Ought the directness requirement to be used to prevent people from suing those who effectively are responsible for their arrest? Is it realistic to suggest that the police are acting independently when they arrest a person based solely on information provided by reliable informants? These problems were recognized in *Foth v. O'Hara*,[195] where Riley J. stated:

> It seems to me that much of the confusion arises from the old forms of pleading, an action for false arrest and/or false imprisonment having been dealt with as a case of trespass whereas an action for malicious prosecution having been regarded as an action on the case. These old forms of pleadings have long since been abolished and swept away and should not now govern the judicial approach. It is common knowledge that a private person who swears to a false and unfounded charge before a magistrate does, in a very real sense, set the criminal law in motion. Neither the police nor the magistrate in such cases makes an investigation, the more so because of the great volume of work confronting them, and do not act according to their discretion, but do act on the sworn information and complaint. A private person laying such a sworn false and unfounded charge knows that as a direct result of the charge he has made, a warrant will be issued and that the accused will be arrested. Under those circumstances, the complainant then becomes, in my view, directly responsible for the arrest and imprisonment and should not in law be permitted to hide behind the magistrate's warrant.[196]

Despite these sentiments, however, it is clear that this problem still persists.[197]

(iii) Imprisonment by "Agreement"

There are numerous situations in which people enter into premises or other facilities upon the understanding that they will be required to remain for a certain period of time, or only be permitted to leave upon fulfilling a specified condition. This occurs, for example, when a person takes an airplane, train or bus, when a person drives a car into a parking lot where the fee is paid upon exiting, when the fee for riding on public transportation is determined at the end of the trip, and so on. In such circumstances, what are the rights and obligations of the parties to the agreement? Can a person be compelled to remain according to the terms of the agreement?

The classic English case of *Herd v. Weardale Steel, Coal & Coke Co.*[198] held that mine owners were entitled to refuse to allow protesting workers to avail themselves of the cage, used to take persons out of the mine, in advance of the

---

195 (1958), 24 W.W.R. 533 at 537 (Alta. T.D.).

196 *Ibid.*

197 A more hypothetical problem concerning the directness requirement involves situations where a defendant's act may cause the indirect imprisonment of the plaintiff in other ways. Where, for example, the defendant digs a pit into which the plaintiff falls, is the directness requirement met? Not only is this type of situation unlikely to occur, but even if it does, it can be argued that having caused a person's imprisonment indirectly, it is a false imprisonment to directly continue the imprisonment by failing to assist or release one's captive.

198 [1915] A.C. 67 (H.L.).

time which had been agreed upon. Applying the concept of *volenti non fit injuria*, Viscount Haldane stated that it is not a false imprisonment to "hold a man to the conditions he has accepted when he goes down into a mine. . . ."[199] The judgment followed an earlier Privy Council case, *Robinson v. Balmain New Ferry Co.*[200] In that case, the plaintiff, who was intending to take a boat, paid one penny and entered the turnstile leading to the wharf. When he discovered that the boat was not due to leave for another twenty minutes, he decided that he wished to leave the wharf. The exit provided was a second turnstile, which again required the payment of one penny. The plaintiff refused to pay the penny and was detained in the wharf area for a short period of time until he was able to escape. Was this a false imprisonment? The Privy Council judgment, per Lord Loreburn L.C., was that no false imprisonment had occurred. The court held that there had been no agreement concerning what would happen if the plaintiff wished to leave the wharf since this had not been contemplated by the parties. The defendant, accordingly, was entitled to impose a "reasonable" condition, and according to His Lordship, the payment of one penny was "a quite fair condition."

Imprisonment cannot be used to enforce a civil debt.[201] If two parties enter into a contract, and one fails to observe a contractual obligation, the proper procedure is to sue for breach of contract. This ought to be the governing principle in the imprisonment by "agreement" cases. There is, of course, an important tactical advantage to the person who refuses to abide by the contract, subject only to being sued, because of the expense and inconvenience which the other party would have to incur, to enforce a small debt by suit. Conversely, if a person is able to enforce a debt by imprisoning the alleged debtor or refusing to allow that person's car, for example, to leave an enclosed parking lot, the advantage is distinctly the creditor's. On balance, it is far preferable to require that the alleged debtor be released than to risk a breach of the peace. On the other hand, it is clear that persons who agree to *reasonable* conditions must be obliged to abide by these conditions in some circumstances.[202] The question is a matter of judgment for the court: was the detention of the plaintiff in all the circumstances of the case a reasonable one?[203] The burden of proving that the detention was justified should be a heavy one resting on the defendant.[204]

---

199 *Ibid.*, at 72 (H.L.).

200 [1910] A.C. 295.

201 See, e.g., *Bahner v. Marwest Hotel Co.* (1970), 12 D.L.R. (3d) 646 at 649 (B.C. C.A.).

202 An interesting case is *Martin v. Berends*, [1989] O.J. No. 2644 (Ont. Prov. Ct.). The defendant took an express bus which went from York University to the Wilson Avenue bus station. There are no stops. The defendant was aware of this, although he had been told by his friend that some drivers will make unauthorized stops and let passengers off. During the trip, the defendant wanted to disembark but the bus driver would not allow it. This ultimately led to an altercation between the driver and the defendant. When sued for assault, the defendant counterclaimed for false imprisonment. The court dismissed the counterclaim. Chapnik J. noted that the situation was not an emergency, and that the driver was justified in refusing to let the defendant off.

203 Trindade, Cane and Lunney, *The Law of Torts in Australia*, 4th ed. (2007), at 60, propose the following test: does the plaintiff's desire to be released from confinement sooner than that agreed to "involve the defendant in significant inconvenience, substantial expense or grave risk?"

204 In many instances, the problem is one of the creditor's own making. The creditor often can alter the system so that the risk of customers refusing to pay for a service after it has been

(iv) Knowledge of the Confinement

It is not necessary that the plaintiff be aware of the confinement at the time it occurred in order to sue for false imprisonment. In *Murray v. Min. of Defence*,[205] the English House of Lords settled a debate over this issue which had arisen in English law as a result of two earlier conflicting decisions. In *Herring v. Boyle*,[206] the Court of Exchequer held that in order to be actionable the imprisonment must have been against the plaintiff's will, and that knowledge of this confinement was necessary. In *Meering v. Grahame-White Aviation Co.*,[207] Atkin L.J. came to the opposite conclusion, stating that a person could be imprisoned without his knowledge. Lord Griffiths, in *Murray v. Min. of Defence*, agreed with Atkin L.J.'s view and stated:

> The law attaches supreme importance to the liberty of the individual and if he suffers a wrongful interference with that liberty it should remain actionable even without proof of special damage.[208]

This view is consistent with the spirit of the torts based upon trespass and should be followed in Canadian law.[209]

(c) Negligent False Imprisonment

The question as to whether a tort of negligent false imprisonment exists has been discussed in the periodical literature.[210] There is no reason to suspect that Canadian tort law, which continues to recognize that a trespass can be committed either intentionally or negligently, would treat false imprisonment any differently than assault or battery in this respect. Thus Canadian law should recognize a claim for a false imprisonment committed negligently. As with the other negligent trespasses, the tort of negligent false imprisonment would allow a person to sue without proof of damage, and with the procedural advantage of a reverse onus. Although one can conceive of some scenarios whereby a person can be imprisoned as a result of someone else's negligence,[211] there are no reported Canadian cases of negligent false imprisonment.

---

rendered is minimized. It is frequently for the convenience and profit of the creditor that the system is not so designed.

205 [1988] 2 All E.R. 521.

206 (1834), 149 E.R. 1126.

207 (1919), 122 L.T. 44 (C.A.).

208 [1988] 2 All E.R. 523 at 529.

209 As it was in *J. (M.I.) v. Grieve* (1996), [1996] B.C.J. No. 236, 1996 CarswellBC 260 (S.C.). The plaintiff was drugged without her knowledge and she passed out for the night. The fact that she was unaware of this at the time did not prevent there being a false imprisonment. In the American Restatement (Second) of Torts, consciousness of confinement or harm is made a requirement of the tort. See Prosser, "False Imprisonment — Consciousness of Confinement" (1955), 55 Colum. L. Rev. 847, regarding the position taken on this question in the first Restatement.

210 See primarily Trindade, "Some Curiosities of Negligent Trespass" (1971), 20 Int. & Comp. L.Q. 706; Harding & Feng, "Negligent False Imprisonment — A Problem in the Law of Trespass" (1980), 22 Malaya L. Rev. 29; Heffey, "Negligent Infliction of Imprisonment: Actionable 'Per Se' or 'Cum Damno'?" (1983), 14 Mel. U. L. Rev. 53; and Burnham, "Negligent False Imprisonment —Scope for Re-emergence" (1998), 61 Modern L. Rev. 573.

211 Harding and Feng, *ibid.*, recall the case of someone in Singapore being locked up overnight in a bank vault due to the actions of the bank's employees in not fully ascertaining whether everyone had left the vault. As well, in *Sayers v. Harlow Urban Dist. Council*, [1958] 1 W.L.R. 623 (C.A.), a person was locked in a lavatory cubicle because the door of the cubicle

10. MALICIOUS PROSECUTION

In exceptional circumstances, the tort of malicious prosecution can fill the void created by the directness requirement of the tort of false imprisonment.

As noted by the Supreme Court of Canada in *Nelles v. Ont.*,[212] there are four requirements for a successful malicious prosecution action:

(1) The proceedings must have been initiated by the defendant;
(2) The proceedings must have terminated in favour of the plaintiff;
(3) The plaintiff must show that the proceedings were instituted without reasonable cause;
(4) The defendant must have been actuated by malice.[213]

In view of the policy of not wishing to discourage individuals from co-operating with law enforcement agencies or utilizing judicial processes for the resolution of disputes, the malicious prosecution claim is a difficult one to establish.[214] This is especially true with regard to claims against prosecutors. As stated by Iacobucci J. and Binnie J. in the *Proulx* case, in view of the "extensive discretion and decision-making authority" given to prosecutors, "courts should be very slow indeed to second-guess a Prosecutor's judgment calls when assessing Crown liability for prosecutorial misconduct."[215]

The action is designed to remedy damage suffered by a person as a result of unjustifiably having been prosecuted. It is not intended that every unsuccessful legal action instituted against a person should result in a malicious prosecution claim merely because the defence of the action caused the person sued inconven-

---

would not open. In *W v. The Home Office, The Times,* March 14, 1997 an asylum-seeker who was subject to a long detention allegedly as a result of the carelessness of the Immigration Service sued in negligence. The action was dismissed, leading Burnham, above, note 210, to question whether there ought to be in English law a tort of negligent false imprisonment. According to the author, the decision of the English courts in *Fowler v. Lanning,* [1959] 1 Q.B. 426 (Eng. Q.B.), and *Letang v. Cooper* (1964), [1965] 1 Q.B. 232 (Eng. C.A.) not to continue to recognize negligent trespass was not only not supported by the authorities but also has created a lacuna in English law with respect to protecting the right to liberty. The author notes that these decisions "are inconsistent with the primary function of the law of trespass: the vindication of constitutional rights."

212 (1989), 60 D.L.R. (4th) 609 (S.C.C.).

213 See McIntyre J.'s judgment, *ibid.*, at 615. These elements were re-affirmed by the Supreme Court of Canada in *Proulx c. Québec (Procureur général)* (2001), 206 D.L.R. (4th) 1, 7 C.C.L.T. (3d) 157 (S.C.C.), a case emanating from Quebec.

214 See Fleming, *The Law of Torts*, 9th ed. (1998), at 673, where it is stated that "the action for malicious prosecution is held on tighter rein than any other in the law of torts." In *Gregory v. Portsmouth City Council*, [2000] 2 W.L.R. 306 (U.K. H.L.) at 311, Lord Steyn justified the narrow limits of the tort by noting that "in a democracy, which upholds the rule of law, it is a delicate matter to allow actions to be brought in respect of the regular processes of the law. Law enforcement agencies are heavily dependent on the assistance and co-operation of citizens in the enforcement of the law." A very surprising and frankly disappointing case in this regard is *Wood v. Kennedy* (1998), 165 D.L.R. (4th) 542 (Ont. Gen. Div.). A 13-year-old girl who had alleged that her uncle had repeatedly sexually assaulted her was successfully sued by her uncle for malicious prosecution. Criminal charges had been laid by the Crown against the uncle, but withdrawn on the eve of trial. The trial judge went through each allegation of sexual assault and concluded that based on the available evidence that they were unfounded. This conclusion led the trial judge to find that the elements of the malicious prosecution action had been made out. See discussion below.

215 (2001), 7 C.C.L.T. (3d) 157 (S.C.C.) at 174.

ience or expense. Thus, the action generally is brought when criminal proceedings have been instituted unjustifiably against a person, since these very proceedings may deprive the accused of liberty, threaten security and peace of mind, and damage reputation.[216] Other types of legal proceedings, such as petitioning for a person's bankruptcy, which by themselves can result in economic losses, also have been the bases for malicious prosecution actions.[217] Whether the action for

---

216 Almost all of the cases deal with criminal proceedings. See, e.g., *Carpenter v. MacDonald* (1978), 6 C.C.L.T. 159 (Ont. Dist. Ct.), affirmed (1979), 19 C.R. (3d) 400 (Ont. C.A.) — prosecution for breaking and entry and possession of stolen goods; *Whitehouse v. Reimer* (1979), 107 D.L.R. (3d) 283 (Alta. Q.B.), reversed (1981), 116 D.L.R. (3d) 594 (Alta. C.A.) — prosecution for causing a disturbance; *Curry v. Dargie* (1984), 28 C.C.L.T. 93 (N.S. C.A.) — prosecution for offence under Residential Tenancies Act, S.N.S. 1970, c. 13; *Can. v. Lukasik* (1985), 18 D.L.R. (4th) 245 (Alta. Q.B.) — prosecution for rape; *German v. Major* (1985), 34 C.C.L.T. 257 (Alta. C.A.) — prosecution for tax evasion; *Banks v. Bliefernich* (1988), 44 C.C.L.T. 144 (B.C. S.C.) — prosecution for assault and threatening death or grievous bodily harm; *Nelles v. Ont.* (1989), 60 D.L.R. (4th) 609 (S.C.C.) — prosecution for murder; *Petrovich v. Campbell*, [1992] B.C.J. No. 20, Van. Reg. No. C902219 — prosecution for criminal assault; *Forster v. MacDonald* (1993), 108 D.L.R. (4th) 690, [1994] 3 W.W.R. 364; affirmed (1995), 127 D.L.R. (4th) 184 (Alta. C.A.), additional reasons at (1995), 35 Alta. L.R. (3d) 319 (C.A.) — court martial for being absent without leave; *Wood v. Kennedy* (1998), 165 D.L.R. (4th) 542 (Ont. Gen. Div.) — prosecution for sexual assault; *Al's Steak House & Tavern Inc. v. Deloitte & Touche* (1999), 45 C.C.L.T. (2d) 98 (Ont. Gen. Div.) and *Kleysen v. Canada (Attorney General)*, [2001] 11 W.W.R. 667 (Man. Q.B.) — prosecution for tax evasion; *Klein v. Seiferling*, [1999] 10 W.W.R. 554 (Sask. Q.B.), *Proulx c. Québec (Procureur général)* (2001), 206 D.L.R. (4th) 1, 7 C.C.L.T. (3d) 157 (S.C.C.), and *Dix v. Canada (Attorney General)* (2002), [2002] A.J. No. 784, 2002 CarswellAlta 826 (Q.B.), additional reasons at (2002), [2003] 1 W.W.R. 580 (Alta. Q.B.) — prosecution for murder; *Oniel v. Metropolitan Toronto (Municipality) Police Force* (2001), 195 D.L.R. (4th) 59 (Ont. C.A.), additional reasons at (2001), 195 D.L.R. (4th) 106 (Ont. C.A.), additional reasons at (2001), 2001 CarswellOnt 1674 (C.A.), leave to appeal refused (2001), 2001 CarswellOnt 3948, 2001 CarswellOnt 3949 (S.C.C.) — prosecution for robbery; *Kvello v. Miazga*, (2007), (*sub nom. Kvello Estate v. Miazga*) 282 D.L.R. (4th) 1 (Sask. C.A.), leave to appeal allowed (2008), 2008 CarswellSask 61 (S.C.C.) — prosecution for sexual assaults. In *Gregory v. Portsmouth City Council*, above, note 214, the House of Lords confined the tort to criminal proceedings with a few limited exceptions involving abuse of legal process. This is because criminal proceedings bring into play "the coercive powers of the state."

217 See, e.g., *Flame Bar-B-Q Ltd. v. Hoar* (1979), 106 D.L.R. (3d) 438 (N.B.C.A.). See also *Stoffman v. Ont. Veterinary Assn.* (1990), 71 D.L.R. (4th) 720 (Ont. Div. Ct.), where the court refused to strike out a claim for malicious prosecution brought by the plaintiff veterinarian against the Ontario Veterinary Association. The prosecution related to disciplinary proceedings which had been brought against the plaintiff by the Association. In *Lawrie v. Law Society of Upper Can.*, [1992] O.J. No. 2440, an action for malicious prosecution was instituted against the Law Society of Upper Canada. The prosecution had been brought against the plaintiffs under the Law Society Act, R.S.O. 1980, c. 233, s. 50(1), relating to a charge of unauthorized practice. The action for malicious prosecution was struck out upon a motion for summary judgment. In the view of the court, an essential element of the action, the absence of a reasonable and probable cause for the prosecution, could not be established. Other malicious prosecution actions based on complaints to professional disciplinary bodies include *Roach v. Long* (2000), [2000] O.J. No. 3588, 2000 CarswellOnt 3441 (S.C.J.), additional reasons at (2001), 2001 CarswellOnt 57 (S.C.J.), additional reasons at (2001), 2001 CarswellOnt 4077 (S.C.J.), affirmed (2002), 2002 CarswellOnt 2032 (Div. Ct.); *Benalcazar v. Tahtadjian* (1997), [1997] O.J. No. 4498, 1997 CarswellOnt 4601 (Div. Ct.); and *Khanna v. Royal College of Dental Surgeons (Ontario)* (1999), 44 O.R. (3d) 535 (S.C.J.), additional reasons at (1999), 1999 CarswellOnt 4009 (S.C.J.), reversed (2000), 47 O.R. (3d) 95 (C.A.), leave to appeal refused (2000), 2000 CarswellOnt 3830, 2000 CarswellOnt 3831 (S.C.C.). Internal disciplinary hearings instituted by the police against the Deputy Director of police

malicious prosecution can be brought in cases of "ordinary" civil proceedings is still somewhat of an open question, although the weight of the authority seems to be against it. As noted by Fleming, extending the action to wrongful civil proceedings "has encountered anything but enthusiastic response", despite the fact that there is nothing in history nor any binding authority which confines the action to criminal proceedings.[218] Canadian cases which have examined the issue have reflected this restrictive approach.[219]

The action is brought against those responsible for initiating the proceedings. Frequently the defendants are police officers, since they are "actively instrumental in putting the law into force by advising on the swearing of the information and in instructing of the Crown Attorney."[220] Others acting in their official

---

services, which included allegations of sexual harassment, led to a successful malicious prosecution claim in *Griffin v. Summerside (City)* (2006), [2006] P.E.I.J. No. 15, 2006 CarswellPEI 13 (T.D.). In *Gregory v. Portsmouth City Council* , above, the House of Lords rejected the extension of the tort to "disciplinary proceedings of any kind." For a critique of this case see Cane, "The Scope of Malicious Prosecution" (2000), L.Q.R. 346.

218 Fleming, *The Law of Torts*, 9th ed. (1998), at 675. Professor Irvine states, however, that there is a tort of "malicious pursuit of civil proceedings", which "emerged as an offshoot of the old tort of malicious prosecution in the 19th century", to deal with the malicious institution of civil proceedings which damaged the plaintiff. Irvine concedes, however, that the requirement of legally recognized damage has "almost exclusively confined the operation of the tort to cases where the proceedings complained of would tend to involve disgrace", and gives as examples the institution of lunacy proceedings and cases involving damage to the plaintiff's financial credit. See Irvine, "The Resurrection of Tortious Abuse of Process" (1989), 47 C.C.L.T. 217 at 218. Note also that in the English Court of Appeal case of *Metall v. Donaldson*, [1989] 3 All E.R. 14 at 51, Slade L.J., after referring to several textual authorities which support the existence of such a tort, stated that "we have great doubt whether any general tort of maliciously instituting civil proceedings exists." The court was of the view that except for the malicious institution of criminal proceedings or the unjustified institution of bankruptcy or liquidation proceedings, there is no cause of action in tort in the case of "ordinary" civil actions.

219 In *Norman v. Soule* (1991), 7 C.C.L.T. (2d) 16 (B.C. S.C.) an action for malicious prosecution was brought by a plaintiff against defendants who had instituted a civil conspiracy action against him. Lander J. noted that an action for malicious prosecution arising in a civil setting is extremely rare, and suggested that the appropriate remedy was an action for abuse of process. In *Metz v. Pellegrin*, [1990] B.C.J. No. 845, Lamperson L.J.S.C. stated that "an action for malicious prosecution founded on civil proceedings would be so difficult to maintain" as to validate Fleming's view that it is practically only available for criminal prosecutions. In *Crewe v. Reichlin*, [1992] O.J. No. 659, Meehan J. stated that the action is generally reserved "for criminal prosecutions or in the alternative prosecutions wherein one's liberty or freedom can be interfered with". His Lordship noted that there must be a "moral stigma" attached to the prosecution and he refused to allow the action which related to a prosecution under a municipal by-law for an illegal fence. Mr. Justice John Sopinka in his lecture "The Tort of Malicious Prosecution: Current Scope and Future Directions", February 9, 1995, Can. Bar Assn. Ontario Continuing Legal Education Institute, questioned "whether the malicious institution of civil proceedings can ever be the subject of a civil action." Also see *AM Installations Ltd. v. Kindersley* (1985), 42 Sask. R. 79 (Q.B.).

220 See *Carpenter v. MacDonald* (1978), 6 C.C.L.T. 159 at 179 (Ont. Dist. Ct.), affirmed (1979), 19 C.R. (3d) 400 (Ont. C.A.). Other cases involving police officers as defendants are *Whitehouse v. Reimer*, above, note 216; *Banks v. Bliefernich*, above, note 216; *Klein v. Sieferling*, [1999] 10 W.W.R. 554 (Sask. Q.B.); *Reilly v. British Columbia (Attorney General)*, [2006] 12 W.W.R. 534 (S.C. [In Chambers]), reversed (2008), 2008 CarswellBC 768 (C.A.) among others. In *Hill v. Hamilton-Wentworth Regional Police Services Board* (2007), 50 C.C.L.T. (3d) 1 (S.C.C.), the plaintiff sued for both malicious prosecution and negligent police investigation. Both claims failed. The Supreme Court of Canada did affirm, however, that the

capacities can also be sued, such as a residential tenancies officer who swore an information that she had reasonable and probable grounds to believe that a statutory offence had been committed,[221] and a prosecuting counsel in a tax evasion case.[222] As a result of the Supreme Court of Canada's decision in *Nelles v. Ont.*,[223] Attorneys General now can be sued, having been deprived of an absolute immunity.[224] Prosecuting counsel can be sued "for adopting or continuing proceedings" even though not technically responsible or even involved with the initiation of these proceedings.[225] Private citizens also may be sued if they are responsible for having initiated the proceedings. In one case, a person who claimed that she had been raped by the defendant was sued successfully for malicious prosecution.[226] The proceedings must have been initiated, i.e., set in motion, by the defendant.[227] The test is whether ''the informant had done all he could do to launch criminal proceedings against the accused.''[228] In a recent case, a trial judge

---

police can be sued for their negligent investigation of a crime, which leads to the plaintiff's arrest and prosecution. See discussion below in Chapter 5.

221 See *Curry v. Dargie*, above, note 216.

222 See *German v. Major*, above, note 216. In another tax evasion case, *Kleyson v. Canada (Attorney General)*, above, note 216, the investigators and auditors of the Department of National Revenue were sued.

223 Above, note 212.

224 Although, as conceded by the court, successful claims will be very difficult to establish. The Supreme Court reaffirmed that it is only in the exceptional case that prosecutors will be found liable for malicious prosecution in *Proulx c. Québec (Procureur général)*, above. For an analysis of the *Nelles* decision and the broader issue of the liability and immunities of Crown prosecutors, see Sossin, "Crown Prosecutors and Constitutional Torts: The Promise and Politics of Charter Damages" (1993-94), 19 Queen's L.J. 372. Note that although the Crown prosecutors and Attorneys-General can be sued, the Crown itself cannot. See *Nelles v. Ontario* (1989), 60 D.L.R. (4th) 609 (S.C.C.) at 617, applied in *Walker v. Ontario* (1997), 40 C.C.L.T. (2d) 197 (Ont. Gen. Div.). Another case to the same effect is *Richardson v. Payne* (1998), 204 N.B.R. (2d) 203 (Q.B.) and *Ramsay v. Saskatchewan*, [2004] 1 W.W.R. 309 (Sask. Q.B.). In *Hawley v. Bapoo* (2000), 187 D.L.R. (4th) 533 (Ont. Div. Ct.) it was held that the Crown attorneys were immune from suit in negligence. In *Dix v. Canada (Attorney General)* (2002), [2002] A.J. No. 784, 2002 CarswellAlta 826 (Q.B.), additional reasons at (2002), [2003] 1 W.W.R. 580 (Alta. Q.B.) it was held that one cannot sue Crown attorneys, investigators, or police officers for negligence with respect to the investigation and prosecution of criminal charges. See, however, *Hill v. Hamilton-Wentworth*, above, which now recognizes the "tort of negligent police investigation".

225 See *Wilson v. Toronto Police Service* (2001), [2001] O.J. No. 2434, 2001 CarswellOnt 2226 (S.C.J.), affirmed (2002), 2002 CarswellOnt 335 (C.A.), where this point is made by Dambrot J. with reference to authorities. Also see *Ferri v. Root* (2007), 45 C.C.L.T. (3d) 159 (Ont. C.A.), leave to appeal refused (2007), 2007 CarswellOnt 5619 (S.C.C.).

226 *Can. v. Lukasik*, above, note 216. Also see *Ellacott v. Long* (1999), [1999] O.J. No. 430, 1999 CarswellOnt 1566 (Gen. Div.).

227 Even where an information subsequently was withdrawn by the complainant prior to the commencement of further legal proceedings, a malicious prosecution claim was possible. See *Casey v. Auto. Renault Can. Ltd.* (1965), 54 D.L.R. (2d) 600 (S.C.C.).

228 (1965), 54 D.L.R. (2d) 600 at 613 (S.C.C.). In *Butterfield v. Butterfield*, [1993] B.C.J. No. 2770, the action was brought by a husband against his ex-wife who had instigated a variety of criminal charges against him. In *Petrovich v. Campbell*, [1992] B.C.J. No. 20 Van. Registry No. C902219, the action was brought by a bouncer in a club against a patron who had instigated an assault charge against him. The trial judge noted that the requirement that the defendant be responsible for having initiated the prosecution would not have been met merely if the defendant had called the police and had given them a candid account of the incident. However, the defendant had been adamant in his allegations, and had not been truthful in his story to the police. He had slanted the story to ensure that charges would be laid. In *Hinde v. Skibinski*

found that a child care worker/therapist had been so involved in the investigation and prosecution of the plaintiffs, that the 'initiation of the proceedings' element was satisfied. This decision, however, was reversed by the Court of Appeal.[229] Sherstobitoff J.A. found that the trial judge erred in taking into consideration the child care worker's conduct with respect to the prosecution which came after the date that the information was sworn and filed. In addition, he found that the trial judge erred in concluding that but for the involvement of the child care worker the charges would not have been laid or prosecuted. The decision to prosecute was an independent decision by the police who had available to them all the information necessary to exercise their discretion.[230]

The proceedings must have terminated in the plaintiff's favour. It is how the proceedings ended and not why this result was reached which is critical. Thus, if the proceedings terminated in the plaintiff's favour because of a technical defect or procedural irregularity, rather than on the substantive merits, this element still

---

(1994), 21 C.C.L.T. (2d) 314 (Ont. Gen. Div.), Lederman J. allowed an action for malicious prosecution to proceed to trial based upon allegations that the defendant had participated in the decision as to the charge which should be laid against the plaintiff. In his lecture on Malicious Prosecution, above, note 219, Sopinka J. noted that the test is whether the person was ''actively instrumental in putting the law in force''. In *Wood v. Kennedy* (1998), 165 D.L.R. (4th) 542 (Ont. Gen. Div.), the information that formally launched the criminal proceedings for sexual assault was sworn by the police, and not by the 13-year-old alleged victim. She was not the one, in fact, who even went to the police. Her allegation had been made to friends who then told her teacher, who told the Vice-Principal, who told the Children's Aid Society, who went to the police. Despite this, the alleged victim was successfully sued for having initiated the proceedings. For a stricter view, see *Chopra v. T. Eaton Co.* (1999), 70 Alta. L.R. (3d) 90 (Q.B.). After an extensive review of the authorities, Brooker J. makes it clear that one must do more than merely pass on information to the police or give a "candid" account of the facts. "The defendant's role must be active and instrumental in both the actual laying of charges and the decision to law charges", at 139.

229 See *Kvello v. Miazga*, [2004] 9 W.W.R. 647 (Sask. Q.B.), reversed (2007), 49 C.C.L.T. (3d) 194 (Sask. C.A.), leave to appeal allowed (2008), 2008 CarswellSask 61 (S.C.C.). The case involved a number of bizarre sexual acts allegedly committed by several persons against children in foster care. Charges of sexual assaults were laid. After all of the charges against the plaintiffs were stayed, they brought actions for malicious prosecution, and other claims, against a number of defendants, including a child care worker/therapist. The trial judge conceded that he could not find any other case where a therapist/child care worker was sufficiently implicated in the initiation of the criminal proceedings to substantiate a malicious prosecution action. However, in light of the "very active role" of the therapist involved in this case, both in relation to the investigation of the children's allegations, and in the prosecution of the plaintiffs, the court found the therapist liable for malicious prosecution. The investigating officer and prosecutor were also found liable. The trial judgment is lengthy and deals with all elements of the tort of malicious prosecution. Although the Court of Appeal reversed the trial judge's decision that had found the therapist liable, the liability of the prosecutor was affirmed. An earlier judgment at [2004] 7 W.W.R. 547 (Sask.) dispensed with non-suit motions brought in the same action. In another recent judgment, *D.(A.A.) v. Turner*, [2005] 2 W.W.R. 466 (Man. Q.B.), an action for malicious prosecution brought against a social worker, who had informed the police of the potential sexual abuse of a teenage girl by her father was dismissed. The action was also dismissed against the police and the Attorney General based on the plaintiff's failure to establish lack of reasonable and probable grounds and malice.

230 Sherstobitoff J.A. cited *Martin v. Watson*, [1995] 3 All E.R. 559 (H.L.) as authority for this proposition.

has been satisfied.[231] Of course, it may, in this type of case, be very difficult to establish the other elements for a successful malicious prosecution claim.[232] An issue arises where a prosecution terminates in the plaintiff's favour as a result of a "plea bargain" or other type of agreement. Should a plaintiff who agrees to plead guilty to one charge if another charge is dropped be entitled to sue for malicious prosecution relating to the latter charge? It has been held that an accused person may be "estopped" from claiming that proceedings terminated in his favour in such cases.[233]

The third requirement is that the defendant did not have reasonable and probable cause to believe that the proceedings were justified.[234] This has both a subjective and objective element. The defendant must have had "an honest or actual belief in the accused's guilt, and reasonable and probable grounds upon which to base his belief."[235] "Reasonable and probable grounds", however, do not demand that the defendant believed that the accused necessarily would be found guilty, for, as

---

231 See Rainaldi, ed., *Remedies in Tort*, Vol. 1 (1987), at 15-20.1. In Sopinka J.'s lecture, above, note 219, it is stated that the following results will satisfy the requirement:

(a) an acquittal;
(b) the complainant abandons, but not due to some compromise or arrangement with the accused;
(c) the information is found to be a nullity;
(d) the Crown enters a stay of proceedings;
(e) the plaintiff is discharged at a preliminary hearing.

See *Boudreault v. Barrett* (1993), 10 Alta. L.R. (3d) 166 (Master), reversed (1995), 33 Alta. L.R. (3d) 60 (C.A.), additional reasons at (1999), 237 A.R. 399 (C.A.); *Casey v. Auto. Renault Can. Ltd.* (1965), 54 D.L.R. (2d) 600 (S.C.C.); *Romiegialli v. Marceau*, [1964] 1 O.R. 407, and *Nelles v. Ont.* (1989), 60 D.L.R. (4th) 609 (S.C.C.), as authorities for the above.

232 Such as lack of reasonable and probable grounds, or proof of malice.

233 See *Baxter v. Gordon Ironsides & Fares Co.* (1907), 13 O.L.R. 598 (C.A.), and *Banks v. Bliefernich* (1988), 44 C.C.L.T. 144 at 147 (B.C. S.C.). Sopinka J., above, note 219, agrees and adds that it would seem to follow that a discharge or conditional discharge predicated on a finding of guilt is also a bar to a malicious prosecution claim. In *Ramsay v. Saskatchewan* (2003), [2004] 1 W.W.R. 309 (Sask. Q.B.), the accused, who was charged with attempted sexual intercourse, pled guilty to indecent assault. The court dismissed his action for malicious prosecution on the ground that the criminal proceedings brought against him did not terminate in his favour. In *Ferri v. Root* (2007), 45 C.C.L.T. (3d) 159 (Ont. C.A.), the Ontario Court of Appeal refused to strike out a claim for malicious prosecution merely because the Crown and the police agreed to withdraw the charges based on an agreement or arrangement with the accused. The court held that a trial was necessary to examine the underlying reasons for the agreement. LaForme J.A. was concerned not to permit the Crown and the police to avoid a malicious prosecution action simply by requiring the accused to first enter into some sort of agreement before they will be willing to withdraw unfounded charges.

234 The question whether the existence of reasonable and probable grounds is a question for the judge to determine, or one for the jury, was carefully reviewed by Dambrot J. in *Wilson v. Toronto Police Service,* above note 225. Dambrot J. notes that in *Nelles*, Lamer J. stated that this was a matter for the judge to decide. Dambrot J. notes however that while this had been the law in Ontario, that it was changed by the Courts of Justice Act in 1984, five years prior to *Nelles*, and that the question of reasonable and probable grounds is a matter for the trier of fact to determine. This is an important point since it limits the ability of judges to strike out a claim for malicious prosecution based on the judge's finding that there were reasonable and probable grounds. Also see *Ferri v. Root*, above, note, 233.

235 See Rainaldi, ed., *Remedies in Tort*, at 15-24.1. See Lamer J. in *Nelles v. Ont.* (1989), 60 D.L.R. (4th) 609 at 639 (S.C.C.).

stated by Fleming, "a fair minded person may well feel justified in bringing a suspect to justice without, in his own mind, prejudging the issue."[236] A prosecutor need not be convinced beyond a reasonable doubt that the accused is guilty; the prosecutor however must "have sufficient evidence to believe that guilt *could* be proved beyond a reasonable doubt before reasonable and probable grounds exists, and criminal proceedings can be instituted."[237] In one case, the fact that the proceedings which were initiated required the prior approval of the Attorney General did not necessarily prove that the complainant had reasonable and probable grounds.[238] Nor does the fact that the plaintiff was committed for trial after a preliminary hearing conclusively prove that the complainant had reasonable and probable grounds.[239] As well, it has been held that the set of charges as a whole must be considered. Therefore, even if the defendant had reasonable and probable grounds to believe that some of the charges were justified, if the defen-

---

236 Fleming, *The Law of Torts*, 9th ed. (1998), at 681. See also *German v. Major* (1985), 34 C.C.L.T. 257 (Alta. C.A.). In *Lawrie v. Law Society of Upper Can.*, above, note 217, Roberts J. stated that "where there is clearly, on the objective test, reasonable and probable cause to commence the prosecution", the subjective element need not be considered. That is, the subjective element, or the state of the prosecutor's belief, need not be examined in cases where the objective test is satisfied. It is only where there are no reasonable and probable grounds that the plaintiff must meet the additional hurdle of proving an absence of subjective belief. See *Tempest v. Snowden*, [1952] All E.R. 1, where Denning L.J. argues that there may be many cases where a fair-minded prosecutor might proceed with the prosecution even though on a subjective test he has not made up his own mind as to guilt.

237 Per Iacobucci J. and Binnie J. in *Proulx* at (2001), 7 C.C.L.T. (3d) 157 (S.C.C.) at 181. In *Klein v. Seiferling*, [1999] 10 W.W.R. 554 (Sask. Q.B.), the test used was whether the ordinary prudent and cautious person would think that the accused was "probably" guilty. This was the test used in the *Dix* case as well, above note 216. In *Wilson v. Toronto Police Service* (2001), [2001] O.J. No. 2434, 2001 CarswellOnt 2226 (S.C.J.), affirmed (2002), 2002 CarswellOnt 335 (C.A.), Dambrot J. noted that in the case of Crown counsel a more appropriate test is whether they believed that "reasonable and probable cause exists for continuing a criminal proceeding", and not whether they had a personal belief in the probable guilt of the accused. In *Kvello v. Miazga*, above, note 229, at 39, Sherstobitoff J.A. affirmed the trial judge's finding that the Crown prosecutor did not have reasonable and probable grounds to prosecute since "he did not have an honest belief in the guilt of the respondents nor that he could prove each of the charges against each of them beyond a reasonable doubt." In *Ferri v. Root*, above, note 225, at 176, LaForme J.A. stated that the police "had a continuing duty to investigate and to examine the evidence, including exculpatory evidence, after the charges had been laid."

238 See *Curry v. Dargie* (1984), 28 C.C.L.T. 93 (N.S. C.A.). One of the judges conceded, however, that the Attorney General's fiat became " a formidable obstacle in the path of the appellant." (*Ibid.*, at 112.)

239 See *Temilini v. Ontario Provincial Police Commissioner* (1990), 73 O.R. (2d) 664 (Ont.C.A.), followed in *Al's Steak House & Tavern Inc. v. Deloittee & Touche* (1999), 45 C.C.L.T. (2d) 98 (Ont. Gen. Div.). In the latter case it was held that the dismissal of a motion for a non-suit is not conclusive evidence that the complainant had reasonable and probable grounds. As well in *Proulx* not only was the accused committed for trial, he was also in fact convicted by the jury. The conviction was overturned on appeal. Despite the conviction at trial, the majority judgment in the Supreme Court found that the prosecutor did not have reasonable and probable grounds. As stated in the majority's judgment, "the Prosecutor cannot bootstrap his own position on the basis of flawed court decisions that were swept away by the Court of Appeal", at (2001), 7 C.C.L.T. (3d) 157 (S.C.C.) at 181. There was a strong dissent on the point of reasonable and probable grounds by three justices in the Supreme Court.

dant did not have such a belief with respect to other charges that were brought, this ground is made out.[240]

Malice also must be established. In this respect, malice has been defined as ''some predominate wish or motive other than vindication of the law; some other motive than a desire to bring to justice a person the defendant honestly believes to be guilty.''[241] ''Malice'' and ''lack of reasonable and probable grounds'' are separate elements of the cause of action;[242] both elements must be established for a successful claim.[243] In the case of prosecutors, malice is not made out simply by showing recklessness or gross negligence, but "a wilful and intentional effort

240 See *Chopra v. T. Eaton Co.* (1999), 70 Alta. L.R. (3d) 90 (Q.B.) at 142.

241 *Carpenter v. MacDonald* (1978), 6 C.C.L.T. 159 at 180 (Ont. Dist. Ct.), affirmed (1979), 19 C.R. (3d) 400 (Ont. C.A.). Also see *Petrovich v. Campbell*, above, note 216, and *Marshall v. Greene*, [1991] O.J. No. 2106. Sopinka J., above, note 219, states that malice involves ''a deliberate improper use of the office of Attorney General or Crown Attorney''. It is not limited to spite, ill-will, or vengeance, but includes abusing the criminal justice process for ends it was not designed to serve. Sopinka J. concedes that proof of malice creates an onerous and strict burden, requiring substantial evidence. In *Griffin v. Summerside (City)*, above, note 217, the court distinguished between malice in fact and malice in law. Malice in fact requires spite or ill will against the person, or improper motives. Malice in law involves an act done without just cause or excuse, but does not necessarily require ill will. The tort of malicious prosecution involves malice in fact. The judge decided that one of the persons involved in initiating the proceedings intentionally misused his office for an improper purpose and was therefore malicious. Also see Vancise J.A.'s dissenting judgment in *Kvello v. Miazga*, above, note 229, where the difference between malice in law and malice in fact is explained.

242 A person may lack reasonable and probable grounds but may not have been malicious. Also, a person may have been malicious despite having had reasonable and probable grounds. In either case, the action for malicious prosecution would fail.

243 Note that in *Wood v. Kennedy* (1998), 165 D.L.R. (4th) 542 (Ont. Gen. Div.), the trial judge dealt with lack of reasonable and probable grounds and malice together. The trial judge held that since he found that the allegations were unfounded, the alleged victim had therefore lied, knew that she was lying, and therefore was malicious. In my opinion, this line of reasoning creates the danger that if an alleged victim goes to the police with her charges and these charges do not lead to a successful prosecution because they are not believed, the victim can successfully be sued for malicious prosecution on this basis alone. Also see *Klein v. Seiferling*, [1999] 10 W.W.R. 554 (Sask. Q.B.), where the recklessness of the police in the way they conducted their investigation and the unreasonableness of their belief in the accused's guilt established not only the lack of reasonable and probable belief element, but also the element of malice as well. In *Kvello v. Miazga*, above, note 229, the extraordinary nature of the allegations of sexual assaults, the complete failure of the defendants to perform their professional obligations as investigating officer, prosecutor, or child care worker, their "tainted tunnel vision", their aggressiveness, and a variety of other factors led the trial judge to conclude that they were malicious and had a "primary purpose other than that of carrying the law into effect." The decision as to the prosecutor was affirmed by the Court of Appeal on the basis that the prosecutor did not have an honest belief in the guilt of the accused or the credibility of the complainants. Note that these were the same factors that led to the finding that there was a lack of reasonable and probable grounds. There was a strong dissent by Vancise J.A. who stressed that the inference of malice cannot arise merely from the fact that a prosecutor lacked reasonable and probable grounds. There must be "other evidence of malice or improper purpose". In this case, Vancise J.A. held there was none and he would have dismissed the action against the prosecutor. Vancise J.A. provides a useful discussion of the history of the action, its extension to Crown prosecutors, and the reason for distinguishing between malicious prosecution actions brought against Crown prosecutors as opposed to private persons.

on the Crown's part to abuse or distort its proper role within the criminal justice system."[244]

The plaintiff must have suffered damage in order to succeed. The damage need not however be monetary, but can be to one's good name or reputation.[245] A plaintiff may recover damages for loss of freedom, damage to reputation, mental suffering, and pecuniary losses, flowing from the malicious prosecution.[246] Punitive damages also may be awarded.

11. ABUSE OF PROCESS

A related tort is that of abuse of process. This arises where a person uses the process of the court for an improper purpose and where there is a definite act or threat in furtherance of such a purpose.[247] Unlike the tort of malicious prosecu-

---

244 Per Iacobucci J. and Binnie J. in *Proulx* at (2001), 7 C.C.L.T. (3d) 157 (S.C.C.) at 183. Despite this sentiment, the majority seemed to rely predominantly on the same factors establishing the absence of reasonable and probable grounds to establish malice, with some additional considerations. This was another point of contention between the majority and minority judgments. Also see Borins J. A.'s judgment in *Oniel v. Metropolitan Toronto (Municipality) Police Force* (2001), 195 D.L.R. (4th) 59 (Ont. C.A.), additional reasons at (2001), 195 D.L.R. (4th) 106 (Ont. C.A.), additional reasons at (2001), 2001 CarswellOnt 1674 (C.A.), leave to appeal refused (2001), 2001 CarswellOnt 3948, 2001 CarswellOnt 3949 (S.C.C.), where the issue of malice is dealt with at some length. Borins J.A. defines malice as "the use of the criminal justice system for an improper purpose" but agrees that "in the appropriate case it is proper to infer malice from the absence of reasonable and probable cause to commence or to continue a prosecution". As noted in other judgments, this approach has the potential of eliminating malice as a separate element of the tort, unless the decision to prosecute without having reasonable and probable grounds is made with reckless indifference to the truth or for an improper purpose. See the discussion on this point in *Wiche v. Ontario* (2001), 9 C.C.L.T. (3d) 72 (Ont. S.C.J.), affirmed (January 27, 2003), Doc. CA C36910 (Ont. C.A.). In *Griffin v. Summerside (City)*, above, note 217, at para 51, Chevrier J. concedes that "although the final element of the tort requires the plaintiff to prove the defendants were actuated by malice, there is spillover and overlap between the reasonable and probable cause issue and the malice issue." In *Kvello v. Miazga*, above, note 229, at 221 C.C.L.T., Sherstobitoff J.A. cautioned against "permit[ting] malice to be found on the basis of lack of reasonable and probable grounds alone" as this "would, in effect, collapse the last two parts of the four part test for liability, and would allow findings of malicious prosecution where the Crown prosecutor was merely negligent or reckless."

245 See *Savile v. Roberts* (1698), 1 Ld. Raym. 374, cited by Sopinka J., above, note 219. Sopinka J. notes that with some, but not all, types of prosecutions damages can be presumed. It depends on the nature of the offence being prosecuted. Thus, as Fleming notes, damages are presumed in an accusation of a crime involving a scandalous reflection on one's name. Also see *Wiche v. Ontario* (2001), 9 C.C.L.T. (3d) 72 (Ont. S.C.J.), affirmed (January 27, 2003), Doc. CA C36910 (Ont. C.A.). See Fleming, *The Law of Torts*, 9th ed. (1998), at 686. See, however, *Teskey v. Toronto Transit Commission* (2003), [2003] O.J. No. 4546, 2003 CarswellOnt 4452 (S.C.J.), where it was held that damages are not presumed in a malicious prosecution claim.

246 Which includes legal defence fees; see *Klein v. Seiferling*, above, note 220.

247 There has been several Canadian cases dealing with this tort. See, among others, *Norman v. Soule* (1991), 7 C.C.L.T. (2d) 16 (B.C. S.C.); *C.P. Int. Freight Services Ltd. v. Starber Int. Inc.* (1992), 12 C.C.L.T. (2d) 321 (Ont. Gen. Div.), additional reasons at (July 22, 1992), Doc. 76913/910 (Ont. Gen. Div.); *Walker v. C.R.O.S.* (1993), 18 C.C.L.T. (2d) 166 (B.C. S.C.); *Teledata Communications Inc. v. Westburne Indust. Ent. Ltd.* (1990), 65 D.L.R. (4th) 636 (Ont. H.C.); *Poulos v. Matovic* (1989), 47 C.C.L.T. 207 (Ont. H.C.); *R. Cholkan & Co. v. Brinker* (1990), 1 C.C.L.T. (2d) 291 (Ont. H.C.); *Atland Containers v. Macs Corp. Ltd.* (1974), 7 O.R. (2d) 107 (H.C.); *Tsiopoulos v. Commercial Union Assur. Co.* (1986), 57 O.R. (2d) 117

tion,[248] the tort of abuse of process does not require a plaintiff to prove that the proceedings terminated favourably,[249] nor that the defendant lacked reasonable and probable grounds for initiating the prosecution.[250] The cause of action does require, however, proof of overt conduct, i.e., an act or threat, to further the improper purpose. The improper purpose must lie outside of the scope of the process which is alleged to have been abused.[251] Furthermore, it is not sufficient that the defendant used the court process for a collateral purpose, if this was not

---

(H.C.); *Pac. Aquafoods v. C.P. Koch Ltd.* (1988), 47 C.C.L.T. 214 (B.C. S.C.); and *Guilford Indust. Ltd. v. Hankinson Mgmt. Services Ltd.*, [1974] 1 W.W.R. 141 (B.C. S.C.). There have been some recent English decisions as well: *Metall v. Donaldson*, [1989] 3 All E.R. 14 (C.A.), and *Speed Seal Prod. Ltd. v. Paddington*, [1986] 1 All E.R. 91 (C.A.). In addition to these reported cases, there are literally hundreds of unreported cases where abuse of process has been raised, although successful claims are very rare. *Grainger v. Hill* (1838), 132 E.R. 769, is the case generally referred to as establishing this cause of action. A very useful discussion of this tort is provided by Irvine, ''The Resurrection of Tortious Abuse of Process'' (1989), 47 C.C.L.T. 217.

248 Fleming, *The Law of Torts*, 9th ed., (1998) at 687 distinguishes between tort actions based upon abuses of legal *procedure*, such as malicious prosecution, and the tort of abuse of process. This distinction was raised by D.S. Ferguson J. in *Brown v. Durham Regional Police Force* (1996), 134 D.L.R. (4th) 177 (Ont. Gen. Div.), additional reasons at (1996), 134 D.L.R. (4th) 177 at 221 (Ont. Gen. Div.), affirmed (1998), 167 D.L.R. (4th) 672 (Ont. C.A.), leave to appeal allowed (1999), 252 N.R. 198 (note) (S.C.C.) at 219 [134 D.L.R. (4th) 177] . Ferguson J. noted that the tort of abuse of process relates only to the commencement of civil or criminal proceedings. Other alleged improprieties relating to legal procedures abused by the parties do not fall under the abuse of process tort. See as well the judgment in *Krackovitch v. Scherer Leasing Inc.* (2001), [2001] O.J. No. 2401, 2001 CarswellOnt 2157 (S.C.J.), additional reasons at (2001), 2001 CarswellOnt 2938 (S.C.J.), where Shaugnessy J. agrees that the torts, although related, are analytically different.

249 See, for example, Farley J. in *Dimples Diapers Inc. v. Paperboard Industries Corp.*, [1992] O.J. No. 1961: ''It is immaterial in establishing abuse of process that the process was properly commenced or founded by the defendants and it does not matter that the process be concluded in the instigator's favour. The improper purpose is the gravamen of liability''. In *M. (A.) v. Matthews* (2003), [2004] 11 W.W.R. 365 (Alta. Q.B.), Veit J. held that the process that allegedly had been abused by the defendant need not even have been concluded before the abuse of process action can be brought. The issue in the tort of abuse of process relates not to whether the proceedings which were brought were justified, but why they were brought in the first place.

250 It has been held that even an omission, for example refusing to provide a mortgage discharge, can amount to an abuse of process. See *Greenspan v. Canadian Imperial Bank of Commerce* (1999), [1999] O.J. No. 1350, 1999 CarswellOnt 1076 (S.C.J.).

251 See, for example, *Metropolitan Separate School Bd. v. Taylor* (1994), 21 C.C.L.T. (2d) 316 (Ont. Gen. Div.). It is not improper to use a libel suit in order to silence a defendant. This is one of the purposes or advantages of the suit itself. It might be improper, however, to use a libel suit not only to silence the defendant, but to intimidate all others who might be tempted to criticize the plaintiff; see *Lee v. Globe & Mail* (2002), [2002] O.J. No. 16, 2002 CarswellOnt 42 (S.C.J.). The advantage must be a collateral advantage not involved in the process itself; e.g. to extort money from the defendant in relation to a completely separate matter. Also see *Toronto Dominion Bank v. Kopman* (2002), 46 O.R. (3d) 773 (Div. Ct.). It has also been held that wrongful motives for bringing the action, such as the desire to injure the defendant, to seek revenge, to damage the defendant's reputation, to cause the defendant financial loss, to antagonize or intimidate, or to induce settlement, are not by themselves sufficiently improper purposes in order to sustain the action. See *Coughlan v. Westminer Can. Ltd.* (1994), 127 N.S.R. (2d) 241, 355 A.P.R. 241 (N.S. C.A.), leave to appeal to S.C.C. refused (1994), 137 N.S.R. (2d) 320 (note), 391 A.P.R. 320 (note) (S.C.C.).

accompanied by an overt act, extraneous to the litigation or process. This requirement of an overt, extraneous act in furtherance of the wrongful purpose has been the stumbling block to establishing a successful claim.[252] The tort is not actionable without proof of damage. However, as held by the British Columbia Court of Appeal in *D.K. Invt. v. S.W.S. Invt. Ltd.*,[253] damages in this tort are "at large." An award is not limited to the actual pecuniary loss that can be specifically proved, and even if specific pecuniary loss cannot be proved, a plaintiff may succeed.[254]

12. MAINTENANCE AND CHAMPERTY

The torts of maintenance and champerty still exist in Canadian tort law.[255] The policy of the law which underlies these torts is to discourage people from traf-

---

252 See, e.g., *Beckingham v. Sparrow* (1977), 2 C.C.L.T. 214 (Ont. H.C.), and *Poulos v. Matovic* (1989), 47 C.C.L.T. 207 (Ont. H.C.). The "two element test", that is (i) proof of an improper purpose and (ii) a definitive act or threat in furtherance of that purpose, was reaffirmed as the law in Ontario in *C.P.I. Freight v. Starber Int.*, above, note 247; and *Dooley v. C.N. Weber Ltd.* (1994), 118 D.L.R. (4th) 750 (Ont. Gen. Div.). A successful Ontario case is *Dimples Diapers v. Paperboard Industries*, [1992] O.J. No. 1961. The two element test has been adopted in Alberta; see, for example, *Rocky Mountain Rail Society v. H & D Hobby Distributing Ltd.* (1995), 24 C.C.L.T. (2d) 97 (Alta. Q.B.), and *Colborne Capital Corp. v. 542775 Alta. Ltd.*, [1995] 7 W.W.R. 671 (Alta. Q.B.), additional reasons at (June 27, 1995), Doc. Calgary 9301-12382, 9301-13674 (Alta. Q.B.), varied [1999] 8 W.W.R. 222 (Alta. C.A.), leave to appeal allowed (1999), 266 A.R. 335 (note) (S.C.C.), additional reasons at (1999), [2000] 2 W.W.R. 715 (Alta. C.A.), and *Ilic v. Calgary Sun*, [1999] 1 W.W.R. 539 (Alta. Q.B.). In *M. (A.) v. Matthews*, above, note 249, Veit J. suggested that the reason the law requires a threat or act in furtherance of the improper purpose is to establish the improper purpose behind the principal proceedings. However, as discussed by Professor Irvine, there are other cases from British Columbia which have found the overt act "in the very pursuit of the impugned process itself", thereby overlooking this requirement. Irvine cites *Glazer v. Kirsch*, [1986] B.C. W.L.D. 159 (Co. Ct.), and *Norton, Stewart, Norton & Scarlett v. Kirsch* (1987), 16 B.C.L.R. (2d) 221 (Co. Ct.), as illustrative of this "trend." See Irvine, above, note 247, at 221-22. Recent cases from British Columbia continue to reflect this approach. See *Walker v. C.R.O.S.*, above, note 247, and *Starbucks Corp. v. Second Cup Ltd.* (1993), 46 C.P.R. (3d) 492 (B.C. S.C.). In the latter case, Donald J. stated that it was "arguable" whether the Ontario requirement of a distinctive overt act applies in British Columbia. Rather, a trial judge may find that the threat or overt act in furtherance of an improper purpose lies within the lawsuit itself. In another B.C. case, however, *Olympic Industries v. McNeill* (1992), 67 B.C.L.R. (2d) 318 (S.C.) Maczko J. approves of the two-part test; reversed (1993), 86 B.C.L.R. (2d) 273 (C.A.). Also see *Office and Professional Employees International Union v. Office and Professional Employees International Union, Local 15* (2006), [2006] B.C.J. No. 1224, where the B.C. case law is reviewed and the two-element test supported.

253 (1986), 6 B.C.L.R. (2d) 291, leave to appeal to S.C.C. refused 75 N.R. 159.

254 See 6 B.C.L.R. (2d) 291 at 305. Irvine, above, note 247, notes that there still is uncertainty whether some pecuniary loss must be proven as a "threshold" requirement.

255 See Rainaldi, ed., *Remedies in Tort*, Chapter 14. In Ontario there is older legislation: the *Act Respecting Champerty Act* R.S.O. 1897, c. 327, raised in *McIntyre Estate v. Ontario (Attorney General)* (2001), 198 D.L.R. (4th) 165 (Ont. S.C.J.), reversed (2002), 218 D.L.R. (4th) 193 (Ont. C.A.), with respect to the validity of contingency fee agreements. In *Galati v. Edwards Estate* (1998), [1998] O.J. No. 4128, 1998 CarswellOnt 4022 (Gen. Div.), Wilkins J. notes that despite the fact that the statute has not been reprinted in the updated revised statutes of Ontario that it is still in force in that province. An excellent history of the Act and the ills that it and the common law tort of champerty were intended to counter is found in *McIntyre Estate v. Ontario (Attorney General)* (2002), 218 D.L.R. (4th) 193 (Ont. C.A.). The Court of Appeal judgment made the point that in interpreting the legislation, regard must be paid to the

ficking in litigation, or from maliciously intermeddling in order to stir up litigation.[256] Maintenance has been defined as the "officious intermeddling with a lawsuit which in no way belongs to one, by assisting either party with money, or otherwise, to prosecute or defend a suit."[257] Champerty "is maintenance together with an agreement to give the maintainer a share in the proceeds or subject-matter of the proceeding, or some other profit."[258]

The essence of the wrong is that the litigation was stirred up without a legitimate motive. As stated in *American Home Assurance v. Brett*,[259] "a person who is not a stranger to an action, one who has a legitimate and genuine business interest in it, has every right to participate in, or maintain, proceedings to protect his or her interests."[260] "It is only when a person has an improper motive which may include,

---

principles of the common law tort. Also see Puri, "Financing of Litigation By Third-Party Investors: A Share of Justice" (1998), 36 Osgoode Hall L.J. 515, where the author discusses maintenance and champerty in relation to the case for third party investor financing of litigation.

256 A leading case frequently referred to is *Fredrickson v. Insurance Corp. of British Columbia* (1986), 28 D.L.R. (4th) 414 (B.C. C.A.), affirmed [1988] 1 S.C.R. 1089. It has been stated that "the fundamental aim of the law of champerty and maintenance has always been to protect the administration of justice from abuse"; see *McIntyre Estate v. Ontario (Attorney General), ibid.,* at para. 32.

257 *Ibid.*, at 14-5, citing *Langtry v. Dumoulin* (1884), 7 O.R. 644 at 661, affirmed 13 S.C.R. 258. In *American Home Assur. Co. v. Brett Pontiac Buick GMC Ltd.* (1992), 96 D.L.R. (4th) 485 at 487 (N.S. C.A.), "maintenance" was defined as the "unjustified interference in a law suit by a stranger to the action, who helps one of the parties, usually by paying or helping to pay the cost."

258 *Ibid.* Also see *American Home Assur., ibid.*: "champerty is when the stranger shares financially in the successful outcome." It has been emphasized that there can be no champerty without maintenance, i.e., the presence of an improper motive; see *McIntyre Estate v. Ontario (Attorney General),* above. Champerty, in other words, "is a subspecies of maintenance." A successful English case of champerty is *Grovewood Holdings plc v. James Capel & Co.*, [1994] 4 All E.R. 417 (Ch. D.). In this case, an arrangement between a liquidator and creditors of the bankrupt that the latter would fund an action brought by the liquidator in return for half of the recoveries from the action was champertous. A related tort that has been mentioned in a few cases is that of "barratry". The difference between the three torts seems to be based on the motives of the defendant. In barratry, the motive of the defendant is to harm the third person. See *McIntyre Estate v. Ontario*, above, note 255 and *Lautec Properties Inc. v. Barzel Windsor (1984) Inc.* (2002), [2002] O.J. No. 4068, 2002 CarswellOnt 3049 (S.C.J. [Commercial List]), where this tort is raised.

259 *Ibid.*

260 *Ibid.* For example, the assignment of a cause of action for breach of contract by a receiver to a purchaser of the assets of the bankrupt was held not to be champertous. The purchaser had a genuine commercial interest in the action. See *NRS Block Bros. Realty Ltd. v. Minerva Technology Inc.* (1997), 145 D.L.R. (4th) 448 (B.C. S.C.). Also see *Graham v. R.* (1997), 151 D.L.R. (4th) 506 (T.C.C.), additional reasons at (1997), [1998] 2 C.T.C. 2117 (T.C.C.). The key question as to whether the assignee, who in this case was petitioning for the debtor's bankruptcy, had a "genuine pre-existing commercial interest" in the litigation, or whether it was only the assignment itself that created the interest was discussed extensively by Brenner J. in *Down, Re* (1999), 178 D.L.R. (4th) 294 (B.C. S.C.), reversed (2001), 196 D.L.R. (4th) 114 (B.C. C.A.), additional reasons at (2001), 198 D.L.R. (4th) 77 (B.C. C.A.), additional reasons at (2001), 2001 CarswellBC 1887 (B.C. C.A.), leave to appeal refused (2002), 2002 CarswellBC 13, 2002 CarswellBC 14 (S.C.C.). The issue of champerty became moot however when the Court of Appeal decided that unless the claims that had been assigned were claims in debt, they could not have supported a petition for bankruptcy at any event. See (2001), 196 D.L.R. (4th) 114 (B.C. C.A.). In *Moore Estate v. Fairview Investments Ltd.* (1999), [1999]

but is not limited to, 'officious intermeddling' or 'stirring up strife' that a person will be found to be a maintainer."[261] Thus, there are a number of "privileges."[262] A common interest between the parties, kinship, and even the charitable desire to assist may justify a person to participate financially in another's law suit.[263] As well, there must be proof of actual loss.[264] Thus, as held in *Oldford v. C.B.C.*, "it is not possible for a party to suffer actual loss as a result of maintenance if the maintained action or defence is successful. An action based on a claim for maintenance cannot be brought until the alleged maintained action or defence has been concluded."[265]

13. INTENTIONAL INFLICTION OF MENTAL SUFFERING: THE TORT IN *WILKINSON v. DOWNTON*

(a) Introduction

In *Wilkinson v. Downton*,[266] the defendant, as a practical joke, told the plaintiff that her husband had been in an accident and had broken both of his legs. The plaintiff was advised to go and get her husband, who purportedly was waiting for

---

N.J. No. 239, 1999 CarswellNfld 226 (T.D.), a person who owned property adjacent to property the title to which was in dispute by two other parties was held to have a legitimate interest in resolving that dispute.

261 *McIntyre Estate v. Ontario (Attorney General)* (2002), [2002] O.J. No. 3417, 2002 CarswellOnt 2880 (C.A.), para. 27.

262 See Fleming, *The Law of Torts*, 9th ed. (1998), at 691.

263 See *S. (J.E.) v. K. (P.)* (1986), 55 O.R. (2d) 111 (Dist. Ct.) — not champertous for Social Services to require mother to seek child support from father. In *American Home Assur. Co. v. Brett*, above, note 255, the Nova Scotia Court of Appeal held that an automobile dealer who encouraged its customers to sue the insurers of a bankrupt administrator of extended warranty contracts could not be sued for maintenance. The dealer was shown in the service contract as a contractor, and the failure of the administrator to honour the service contracts gave the dealer a legitimate and genuine interest in its customers' litigation. In *Ilic v. Calgary Sun*, [1999] 1 W.W.R. 539 (Alta. Q.B.), financial assistance by members of the Calgary Serbian community to the plaintiff with relation to his defamation action against a newspaper was not maintenance. This assistance could be regarded as charitable; in addition there was no evidence that the funders were improperly stirring up litigation. Also see *Margetts (Next Friend of) v. Timmer Estate* (1999), 178 D.L.R. (4th) 577 (Alta. C.A.), where Berger J.A. stated that an assignment of a personal tort is not invariably champertous and will not be struck down when it has been "entered into for the purpose of advancing the cause of justice". In *Laing v. St. Thomas Dragway* (2005), 30 C.C.L.T. (3d) 127 (Ont. S.C.J.), the argument that a municipality's decision to provide secret funding to the plaintiffs in their action for nuisance brought against another private party amounted to maintenance was rejected. As to arguments relating to contingency fee agreements, see *McIntyre Estate v. Ontario (Attorney General)* (2002), [2002] O.J. No. 3417, 2002 CarswellOnt 2880 (C.A.). The Court of Appeal held that contingency fees are not champertous *per se*. Only where the arrangement provides for "unfair" or "unreasonable" fees is it champertous. See Rainaldi, ed., *Remedies in Tort*, Vol. 1, at 14-11, fn. 14, for the various provincial rules relating to contingency fee arrangements. In *Oldford v. Canadian Broadcasting Corp.* (2004), 23 C.C.L.T. (3d) 311 (N.S. S.C.), at 318, Coughlan J. notes the many situations in which third parties legitimately support litigation: "From insurers, professional, trade or business associations, public interest groups, etc., many entities, other than the parties, support litigation."

264 See *Neville v. London Express*, [1919] A.C. 368 (H.L.); Fleming, *The Law of Torts*, 7th ed. (1987), at 594. It is noted, in *obiter*, in *American Home Assur. Co. v. Brett*, above, note 257, that "special damages" other than the costs of defending the action are required.

265 (2004), 23 C.C.L.T. (3d) 311 at 319 (N.S. S.C.).

266 [1897] 2 Q.B. 57.

her at a public-house. These statements were false. The plaintiff sent some people by rail to the public-house to fetch her husband. She also became seriously ill from the shock of the distressing news. She brought action against the defendant for her expenses and for her illness.

What action? The facts did not squarely fit known causes of action. The closest to it was the tort of assault; however, in this case the defendant did not threaten the plaintiff with imminent harm. One must concede that the judgment of Wright J. in maintaining the plaintiff's claim and awarding her damages created a new tort — the tort in *Wilkinson v. Downton*.[267]

The essential ingredients of the tort in *Wilkinson v. Downton* can be derived from the following statement of Wright J.:

> The defendant has, as I assume for the moment, wilfully done an act calculated to cause physical harm to the plaintiff — that is to say, to infringe her legal right to personal safety, and has in fact thereby caused physical harm to her. That proposition without more appears to me to state a good cause of action, there being no justification alleged for the act.[268]

The tort requires (1) an act or statement (2) calculated to produce harm and (3) harm. It clearly did not contemplate actions based on negligence.[269]

(b) An Act or Statement

Although *Wilkinson v. Downton* involved a false statement calculated to produce harm, Wright J.'s decision embraces both statements and acts. In respect of statements, there is nothing in the judgment to suggest that the statement must be a false one in order to be actionable. Where, for example, a person utters a true statement in order to cause anguish to the plaintiff, can this lead to a successful action? The few cases decided on the *Wilkinson v. Downton* principle to date have involved false statements,[270] and although there may be situations where true statements can lead to liability, it is difficult to imagine this arising except in the most unusual circumstances.[271] If the tort in *Wilkinson v. Downton* could be

---

267 Some text writers assert that the tort is an action on the case and not a trespass: see, e.g., Linden and Feldthusen, *Canadian Tort Law*, 8th ed. (20016), at 55; Trindade, Cane and Lunney, *The Law of Torts in Australia*, 4th ed. (2007), at 81 and following. See also Irvine, "Annotation to *Timmermans v. Buelow*" (1987), 38 C.C.L.T. 137. Others have included it in the trespass section of their text: see, e.g., Weir, *A Casebook on Tort*, 7th ed. (1992), at 324; Fleming, *The Law of Torts*, 9th ed. (1998), Chapter 2; Fridman, *The Law of Torts in Canada*, 2nd ed. (2002), Chapter 5. Both classifications raise questions. In *Wilkinson v. Downton* itself, the injury produced, i.e., the illness caused by shock, was the *direct* result of the defendant's conduct. It was not indirectly produced, which is the essence of case. It is clear, however, that the action is not trespass — damages, for example, are required, and the injury can be produced indirectly.

268 [1897] 2 Q.B. 57 at 59.

269 Although as we shall see, mental distress caused negligently has emerged as the more important action. For an interesting commentary on the basis of liability in *Wilkinson v. Downton*, see Denise Réaume, "The Role of Intention in the Tort of *Wilkinson v. Downton*" in Neyers, Pitel, Chamberlain, eds., *Emerging Issues in Tort Law* (2007), Chapter 21. The author discusses the English House of Lords judgment in *Wainwright v. Home Office*, [2004] 2 A.C. 406 (H.L.) and Lord Hoffman's view that "*Wilkinson* was really grounded in negligence and not a separate cause of action at all."

270 *Janvier v. Sweeney*, [1919] 2 K.B. 316 (C.A.); *Bielitski v. Obadiak* (1922), 65 D.L.R. 627 (Sask. C.A.).

271 As we shall see, other tort actions respecting statements, such as negligent mistatement, fraud, deceit, and defamation, also are restricted to false statements.

used where injury has been caused by the malicious publication of a true statement, this would supplement the tort of defamation, where truth is a complete defence notwithstanding the *mala fides* of the defendant.[272] As well, unlike defamation, where the statement must be communicated to a third party, the tort in *Wilkinson v. Downton* does not require publication. There can be a successful action whether the statement is made directly to the plaintiff, or to another who repeats the statement.[273] If the courts wish, therefore, the tort seems to be capable of expansion in order to fill in gaps left by other torts.

Caution must be exercised by the courts when dealing with statements. Freedom of speech must be protected. Not every unpleasant statement should lead to liability. Even the *threat* of liability often is enough to discourage speech. The few successful cases where defendants have been found liable for statements indicate that the speech must be extreme, calculated to cause "terror" or mental anguish.[274] In one case, *Rahemtulla v. Vanfed Credit Union*,[275] the plaintiff bank teller was accused of theft and dismissed from her job. Although her claim for damages for mental distress caused by breach of contract was rejected, the court awarded damages on the basis of *Wilkinson v. Downton*. Conceding that persons cannot be protected "from every practical joke or unkind comment", the court stated that "flagrant and extreme conduct inflicting mental suffering is actionable."[276] The judgment is further proof that the tort can be used as an alternative, or supplement, to other causes of action, such as defamation.[277]

The tort of *Wilkinson v. Downton* also has been applied to acts, as opposed to statements, resulting in mental suffering. In *Purdy v. Woznesensky*,[278] a violent assault made by the defendant upon the plaintiff's husband in the plaintiff's presence caused her nervous shock and illness. Stating that this was an action on the case, the court upheld the plaintiff's claim for damages. As well, the tort of intentional infliction of mental suffering has met with some success in the area of sexual harassment. In *Clark v. Canada*,[279] a female officer in the R.C.M.P. brought a successful action against her employer, the Crown, as a result of a 4-year period of harassment which she suffered at the hands of fellow officers.[280]

---

272 In the United States, there can be liability for truthful statements under what is called the "private facts tort". This involves the publication of private and highly offensive facts that are not of legitimate public concern. See *The Florida Star v. B.J.F.*, 105 L.Ed. (2d) 443 (U.S.S.Ct. 1989). For a discussion of the background and current standing of this tort, see Lorelei Van Wey, "Private Facts Tort: The End Is Here" (1991), 52 Ohio State Law Journal 299. The issue of the publication of a true story damaging to the plaintiff's health was discussed in *Pierre v. Pacific Press Ltd.*, [1994] 7 W.W.R. 579 (B.C. C.A.).

273 For example, *Bielitski v. Obadiak*, above, note 270.

274 See, e.g., *Janvier v. Sweeney*, above, note 270.

275 (1984), 29 C.C.LT. 78 (B.C. S.C.).

276 *Ibid.*, at 94. The case seems to combine acts and statements causing mental distress.

277 Or assault, if one subscribes to the view that an assault cannot be committed by words alone. See Irvine, "Annotation", above, note 267, at 138.

278 [1937] 2 W.W.R. 116 (Sask. C.A.).

279 (1994), 20 C.C.L.T. (2d) 241 (Fed. T.D.).

280 The impugned conduct included physical conduct, e.g. grabbing and kissing, as well as taunting and insulting behaviour, e.g. calling her a "butch", taping plastic breasts to her work station, and showing pornographic movies at work in her presence. Another successful intentional infliction of emotional distress case in the employment context, although not involving sexual harassment, is *Boothman v. Canada* (1993), 49 C.C.E.L. 109 (Fed. T.D.). More recently see *Prinzo v. Baycrest Centre for Geriatric Care* (2002), 215 D.L.R. (4th) 31 (Ont.

Despite some initial judicial success,[281] efforts to apply the *Wilkinson v. Downton* tort to family disputes over the custody and access to children have been rejected. In *Frame v. Smith*,[282] the Supreme Court of Canada decided that tort law cannot be used to deal with the issues of family breakdown, custody and access to children. The court upheld the motion to strike a husband's statement of claim against his estranged wife which alleged that her conduct in frustrating his efforts to have access to his children caused him considerable financial expense, and severe emotional and psychic distress. The majority of the court decided that a breach of the custody order made by virtue of a statutory discretion could not be remedied by means of a civil action.[283]

(c) Calculated to Produce Harm

The requirement that the act or statement must have been calculated to produce harm is vital to a reasonable limiting of the tort. It is this element which will distinguish the tort in *Wilkinson v. Downton* from actions in negligence, or even from offensive, but non-tortious behaviour.

What does "calculated to produce harm" mean? Is it the same as "intention" to produce harm? The judgment in *Wilkinson v. Downton* makes it clear that liability is predicated upon the defendant's intention to cause harm to the plaintiff. In this context, "intention" has the same meaning as when used in other torts based on intention; the defendant must have desired the consequences or realized with substantial certainty that these consequences would ensue. The defendant need not have foreseen the full extent of the injury or the exact impact that the statements would have on the plaintiff, as long as emotional distress or mental suffering was desired or substantially likely to occur.[284] The motive for the defendant's statement or act is not of concern.

The intention element of the tort occasionally has been relaxed, resulting in the merging of this tort with the action for negligence. In those cases, it would have been better to base the action not on *Wilkinson v. Downton*, but on negligence, as for example, where plaintiffs have suffered mental distress as a result of witnessing acts not directed at themselves,[285] or where losses have occurred indirectly as a result of acts undertaken for purposes other than to cause distress to plaintiffs.[286] Often it was the language of negligence and not that of intention which was the basis of judgment.[287]

C.A.) and *Bogden v. Purolator Courier Ltd.* (1996), 19 C.C.E.L. (2d) 77 (Alta. Q.B.), varied (1997), 1997 CarswellAlta 1236 (C.A.) for successful work place harassment actions.

281 See *Cant v. Cant* (1984), 43 R.F.L. (2d) 305 (Ont. Co. Ct.).

282 (1987), 42 C.C.L.T. 1.

283 Wilson J., who dissented on another issue, agreed with the majority's decision to exclude tort law from matters of this kind, finding that the extension of tort law would not be in the best interests of the children.

284 This raises the issue of "remoteness". As we will see, even though the full extent of the injury is not desired or even foreseeable, a defendant, especially in the intentional tort area, still will be held liable. See discussion, below.

285 For example, *Purdy v. Woznesensky*, [1937] 2 W.W.R. 116 (Sask. C.A.).

286 For example, the child custody and access disputes.

287 For example, in *Purdy v. Woznesensky*, [1937] 2 W.W.R. 116 at 119, the following language is more consistent with a negligence claim:

> . . . the defendant must be presumed as a reasonable man to know of the vital concern which

Related to the requirement that the act or statement be calculated to produce harm is the problem of the particularly sensitive victim. In order to prove that the defendant desired or ought to have known with substantial certainty that the plaintiff would suffer emotional distress, the reaction of the victim must have been the ''normal'' one. Unless the defendant knew that the specific plaintiff was unusually susceptible to the act or statement, it will not be possible to show that an abnormal reaction was either desired or substantially certain.[288] This does not mean, however, that the extent of the reaction or degree of injury must have been anticipated, as long as its existence could have been.[289]

> a wife instinctively feels for the safety of her husband and the serious physical reactions which an attack upon him threatening injuries to his person would in all likelihood produce in her. Hence I think he should have foreseen that by causing her to witness such a sudden and violent assault as he made upon her husband he would probably upset her nervous system in such a way as to cause her some physical harm. . . .

See also *Jinks v. Cardwell* (1987), 39 C.C.L.T. 168 (Ont. H.C.), where a doctor was held liable for informing a wife that her husband had committed suicide in the hospital. The court stated that in informing her of this, when he had no valid reason for suggesting suicide, he was at best ''negligent, at worst callous and unfeeling.'' He was held liable although no specific cause of action was identified.

A more recent example is *Lew v. Mount Saint Joseph Hospital Society* (1997), 36 C.C.L.T. (2d) 35 (B.C. S.C. [In Chambers]), leave to appeal refused (1997), 44 B.C.L.R. (3d) 84 (C.A. [In Chambers]). The plaintiff claimed he suffered nervous shock as a result of seeing his wife who suffered a brain injury during an operation. The allegation was that the hospital was negligent for not having prepared him for seeing his wife in this condition. The action was allowed to proceed to trial. Also see *Butler v. Newfoundland (Workers' Compensation Commission)* (1998), 165 Nfld. & P.E.I.R. 84 (Nfld. T.D.), where the tort was made out due to the defendant's reckless disregard of the risk of mental suffering caused to the plaintiffs in the way the plaintiff's worker's compensation claim was handled. Note as well that there is no tort claim for negligent infliction of mental distress flowing from a wrongful dismissal; see *Wallace v. United Grain Growers Ltd.*, [1997] 3 S.C.R. 701 applied in *Cassady v. Wyeth-Ayerst Canada Inc.* (1998), 163 D.L.R. (4th) 1 (B.C. C.A.), additional reasons at (1999), 41 C.C.E.L. (2d) 1 (B.C. C.A.). In *Sulz v. Canada (Attorney General)* (2006), 263 D.L.R. (4th) 58 (B.C. S.C.), affirmed (2006), 2006 CarswellBC 3137 (C.A.), the plaintiff alleged workplace harassment against her commanding officer. Although her action for intentional infliction of mental suffering failed, since the defendant did not "deliberately set out to harass" her, her action for negligent infliction of mental suffering was successful. In *Wainwright v. Home Office*, [2004] 2 A.C. 406 (H.L.), at 425, Lord Hoffmann noted that there might be a reason to maintain a distinctive intentional tort, as opposed to allowing it "to disappear beneath the surface of the law of negligence", where the defendant's actual intention was to cause harm by his unjustifiable act. Perhaps, in that case, mental distress, which falls short of psychiatric illness, could be compensable. This was not found to be the situation on the facts of *Wainwright*. See Denise Réaume, "The Role of Intention in the Tort of *Wilkinson v. Downton*" in Neyers, Pitel, Chamberlain, eds., *Emerging Issues in Tort Law* (2007), Chapter 21. An earlier piece by Réaume is "Indignities: Making a Place for Dignity in Modern Legal Thought" (2002), 28 Queen's L.J. 61.

288 There have been some examples of this. In *Timmermans v. Buelow* (1984), 38 C.C.L.T. 136 (Ont. H.C.), the defendant's liability rested in part on the fact that he knew of the plaintiff's fragile emotional state when he threatened and harassed him. As well, in *Boothman v. Canada*, above, note 280, the defendant was held liable for knowingly exploiting the plaintiff's emotional and mental vulnerability.

289 In *Wilkinson v. Downton*, [1897] 2 Q.B. 57 at 59, Wright J. made this clear when he said:

> It is difficult to imagine that such a statement, made suddenly and with apparent seriousness, could fail to produce grave effects under the circumstances upon any but an exceptionally

(d) Harm

Although it is clear that the tort is not actionable without proof of harm, the type of damage required is by no means a settled issue. The original case dealt with "physical harm" in the nature of "a violent shock to [the plaintiff's] nervous system, producing vomiting and other more serious and permanent physical consequences."[290] This type of physical harm was present in the successful *Wilkinson v. Downton* cases which followed, including *Janvier v. Sweeney*,[291] *Bielitski v. Obadiak*,[292] and *Purdy v. Woznesensky*.[293] This was consistent with the common law resistance to claims based on pure nervous shock, not accompanied by physical illness.[294]

As with the development of claims for nervous shock based on negligence, courts may be relaxing the requirement that mental distress caused intentionally consists of a "visible and provable illness."[295] In *Rahemtulla v. Vanfed Credit Union*,[296] for example, although the court applied previous authority and required a visible and provable illness, the judgment indicates that there was little evidence of one.[297] In *Young v. Borzoni*,[298] Thackray J.A. noted that although "recognizable psychiatric illness, such as are defined in the *Diagnostic and Statistical Manual of Mental Disorders* (DSM-IV) for example, amount to visible and provable illnesses for the purpose of the tort of the intentional infliction of mental suffering. . .emotional stress, mental anguish and despair" are generally not accepted.[299]

---

indifferent person, and therefore an intention to produce such an effect must be imputed, and it is no answer in law to say that more harm was done than was anticipated, for that is commonly the case with all wrongs.

See also Irvine, "Annotation" (1987), 38 C.C.L.T. 137, where this point is elaborated upon.

290 [1897] 2 Q.B. 57 at 58.

291 [1919] 2 K.B. 316 (C.A.).

292 (1922), 65 D.L.R. 627 (Sask. C.A.).

293 [1937] 2 W.W.R. 116 (Sask. C.A.).

294 In *Clark v. Canada*, above, note 279, Dubé J. accepts the view that there must be objective and substantially harmful physical or psychopathological consequences, rather than mere anguish or fright, for the action to succeed. She found that the plaintiff's mental and physical condition satisfied that requirement.

295 See *Radovskis v. Tomn* (1957), 21 W.W.R. 658 (Man. Q.B.).

296 (1984), 29 C.C.L.T. 78 (B.C. S.C.).

297 The plaintiff was humiliated and depressed. She cried a great deal, refused to eat to the point where she fainted, refused to leave the house, and generally displayed symptoms of depression. These were held to satisfy the test of a visible and provable illness, notwithstanding the absence of medical evidence. A similar case is *Tran v. Financial Debt Recovery Ltd.* (2000), 193 D.L.R. (4th) 168 (Ont. S.C.J.). The plaintiff suffered from depression, anxiety, and weight loss, as a result of harassment by a debt collector, but did not see a doctor and did not have a psychiatric condition. The action succeeded at trial but was reversed on other grounds at (October 24, 2001), Doc. 751/00, [2001] O.J. No. 4103 (Div. Ct.). Also see *Nolan v. Mohr* (1996), [1996] O.J. No. 1764, 1996 CarswellOnt 5523 (Small. Cl. Ct.), where the plaintiff's wrongful detention and the manner in which he was treated led to a successful claim for intentional infliction of emotional distress. See, however, *Hasenclever v. Hoskins* (1988), 47 C.C.L.T. 225 (Ont. Div. Ct.), where the action was dismissed because there was no visible or provable illness.

298 (2007), 277 D.L.R. (4th) 685 (B.C. C.A.).

299 *Ibid.*, at 701.

14. INVASION OF PRIVACY

Despite some encouraging suggestions from a few courts,[300] it would be fair to say that Canadian tort law has not generally yet recognized a tort action for invasion of privacy *per se*.[301] Rather, "privacy" rights have been protected under the umbrella of other traditional tort actions,[302] and by legislative interventions.[303]

---

300 See especially *Saccone v. Orr* (1981), 19 C.C.L.T. 37 (Ont. Co. Ct.), and *Capan v. Capan* (1980), 14 C.C.L.T. 191 (Ont. H.C.). In *Roth v. Roth* (1991), 9 C.C.L.T. (2d) 141 (Ont. Gen. Div.), the tort of invasion of privacy was recognized. The trial judge did note, however, that "even if it could be said that there is no remedy for the invasion of privacy," the conduct of the defendants was actionable on other grounds. In *Lipiec v. Borsa* (1996), 31 C.C.L.T. (2d) 294 (Ont. Gen. Div.) at 300, the court stated that "intentional invasion of privacy has been recognized as actionable in Ontario in several cases." The court awarded damages for the unwarranted use of surveillance cameras although it described this conduct as a "trespass and nuisance occasioned by the deliberate invasion of their privacy." In *Somwar v. McDonald's Restaurants of Canada Ltd.* (2006), 263 D.L.R. (4th) 752 (Ont. S.C.J.), at 763, Stinson J. rejected a motion to strike out a statement of claim for invasion of privacy stating that "the time has come to recognize invasion of privacy as a tort in its own right". This is also the view expressed in Bell, "The Tort of Invasion of Privacy – Has its Time Finally Come?" (2004), Annual Review of Civil Litigation 225. Also see *Tran v. Financial Debt Recovery Ltd.*, above, note 297. In *Dyne Holdings Ltd. v. Royal Insurance Co. of Canada* (1996), 135 D.L.R. (4th) 142 (P.E.I. C.A.), leave to appeal refused (1996), [1996] S.C.C.A. No. 344, 139 D.L.R. (4th) vii (note) (S.C.C.), Carruthers C.J. noted the importance that Canadian law places on privacy rights in various contexts. The action was recognized in *Dawe v. Nova Collection Services (Nfld) Ltd.* (1998), 160 Nfld. & P.E.I.R. 266 (Nfld. Prov. Ct.), although it was not successful on the facts of this case. A thorough discussion of this issue, including a comparative review and arguments for creating a common law tort, is provided in J.D.R. Craig's "Invasion of Privacy & Charter Values: The Common Law Tort Awakes" (1997), 42 McGill L.J. 355. The Alberta Law Review published a "Special Issue on Privacy Law" (2006), 43 Alta. Law Review.

301 Some courts explicitly have said so. In *Bingo Ent. Ltd. v. Plaxton* (1986), 26 D.L.R. (4th) 604 at 608 (Man. C.A.), Monnin C.J.M. stated that "it would appear that at common law the tort of violation of privacy in regard to disclosure of private information has not been recognized in Canada." Also see *347202 B.C. Ltd. v. C.I.B.C.*, (1995), [1995] B.C.J. No. 449, 1995 CarswellBC 1821 (S.C. [In Chambers]), additional reasons at (1995), 1995 CarswellBC 1973 (S.C. [In Chambers]), where the court rejected a claim for embarrassment suffered as a result of the service of a process, and *Lord v. McGregor* (2000), 50 C.C.L.T. (2d) 206 (B.C. S.C.). In *Haskett v. Trans Union of Canada Inc.* (2001), 10 C.C.L.T. (3d) 128 (Ont. S.C.J.), reversed in part (2003), 2003 CarswellOnt 692 (Ont. C.A.), additional reasons at (2003), 2003 CarswellOnt 1295 (C.A.), leave to appeal refused (2003), 2003 CarswellOnt 4754, 2003 CarswellOnt 4755 (S.C.C.), Cummings J. rejected a claim for breach of privacy noting that "one cannot assert with confidence that there is a clear recognition by the Canadian common law of the invasion of privacy as a discrete tort."

302 See Gibson, "Common Law Protection of Privacy: What to Do Until the Legislators Arrive", in Klar, ed., *Studies in Canadian Tort Law* (1977); Gibson (ed.), *Aspects of Privacy Law* (1980); and Burns, "The Law and Privacy: The Canadian Experience" (1976), 54 Can. Bar Rev. 1.

303 Several provinces have enacted privacy legislation. See, for example, statutes in Alberta, British Columbia, Manitoba, Newfoundland and Saskatchewan, as well as federal legislation. See Rainaldi, ed., *Remedies in Tort*, Vol. 3 (1988), at 24 and following. A case under the Saskatchewan Act is *Peters-Brown v. Regina District Health Board* (1995), [1996] 1 W.W.R. 337 (Sask. Q.B.), affirmed (1996), 31 C.C.L.T. (2d) 302 (Sask. C.A.). Cases under the B.C. legislation include *Lee v. Jacobson* (1992), 87 D.L.R. (4th) 401 (B.C. S.C.), *Milton v. Savinkoff* (1993), 18 C.C.L.T. (2d) 288 (B.S. S.C.), *Hollinsworth v. BCTV* (1998), 44 C.C.L.T. (2d) 83, [1999] 6 W.W.R. 54 (B.C. C.A.), *F. (J.M.) v. Chappell* (1998), 158 D.L.R. (4th) 430 (B.C.

In Quebec Civil Law, one's right to privacy is specifically protected by the Charter of Human Rights and Freedoms.[304]

Several established torts protect privacy interests. The dignity of one's person is protected by several torts, such as assault, battery, the intentional infliction of emotional distress, and false imprisonment. One's right to be left alone to use and enjoy property is protected by trespass, and nuisance. One's reputation is protected by defamation. The right to the commercial exploitation of one's "personality" and "goodwill" also has received protection. In *Krouse v. Chrysler Can. Ltd.*,[305] the tort of "appropriation of one's personality", fashioned from an action on the case, was recognized by the court.[306] In *Gould Estate v. Stoddart Publishing Co.*,[307] Lederman J. provided a useful analysis of the issues involved in developing such a tort. While the law should protect the commercial exploitation of a celebrity's personality against misappropriation, there are, of course, values of freedom of expression and the public's right to know that must not be ignored. This led to Lederman J.'s distinction between the use of information and other materials relating to celebrities as the subject of an impugned work and its use in order to sell the work. Applied to the case at hand, pictures and interviews of famed Canadian pianist Glen Gould were being used as the subject matter of the defendant's book, and not in order to sell the book; therefore no wrong had occurred.[308]

C.A.), additional reasons at (1998), 1998 CarswellBC 669 (C.A.), leave to appeal refused (1998), 231 N.R. 400 (note) (S.C.C.), *Getejanc v. Brentwood College Assn.* (2001), 6 C.C.L.T. (3d) 261 (B.C. S.C. [In Chambers]) and *Milner v. Manufacturers Life Insurance Co.* (2005), 36 C.C.L.T. (3d) 232 (B.C. S.C.), additional reasons at (2006), 2006 CarswellBC 2615 (S.C.). There has been a spate of legislation dealing with freedom of information issues. For example, Alberta has enacted the Freedom of Information and Protection of Privacy Act, R.S.A. 2000, c. F-25.

304 R.S.Q., c. C-12, s. 5. In *Aubry c. Éditions Vice Versa Inc.* (1998), 157 D.L.R. (4th) 577 (S.C.C.), the Supreme Court held that included in one's right to privacy is a protected right to one's image. This must be balanced however by the public's right to information and freedom of expression. In the case at hand, publishing the plaintiff's photograph, without her consent, was held to outweigh the photographer's right to freedom of expression.

305 (1973), 40 D.L.R. (3d) 15 (Ont. C.A.). See also *Athans v. Can. Adventure Camps Ltd.* (1977), 4 C.C.L.T. 20 (Ont. H.C.); *Racine v. C.J.R.C. Radio Capitale Ltée* (1977), 80 D.L.R. (3d) 441 (Ont. Co. Ct.); and *Heath v. Weist-Barron Sch. of T.V. Ltd.* (1981), 18 C.C.L.T. 129 (Ont. H.C.). See Howell, "The Common Law Appropriation of Personality Tort" (1986), 2 I.P.J. 149; Hylton and Goldson, "The New Tort of Appropriation of Personality: Protecting Bob Marley's Face" (1996), 56 Cambridge L.J. 56; Abramovitch, "Misappropriation of Personality" (2000), Can. Bus. L.J. 230; Eric Singer, "The Development of the Common Law Tort of Appropriation of Personality in Canada" (1998) 15 Cdn. IP Rev. 65; C. Nest, "From ABBA to Gould: A Closer Look at the Development of Personality Rights in Canada" (1999), 5 Appeal 12; and D. Collins, "Age of the Living Dead: Personality Rights of Deceased Celebrities" (2002), 39 Alta. Law Rev. 914.

306 See also *Can. Safeway Ltd. v. Man. Food & Commercial Wkrs., Loc. 832* (1983), 25 C.C.L.T. 1 (Man. C.A.), which also relied on case to protect the plaintiff's rights to its insignia.

307 (1996), 31 C.C.L.T. (2d) 224 (Ont. Gen. Div.), affirmed for other reasons (1998), 161 D.L.R. (4th) 321 (Ont. C.A.).

308 The Court of Appeal affirmed the result of the trial judgment but on the basis of traditional copyright law. No copyright belonging to the plaintiff, Glen Gould's estate, had been infringed by the defendants. Another interesting case is *Horton v. Tim Donut Ltd.* (1997), 45 B.L.R. (2d) 7 (Ont. Gen. Div.), affirmed (1997), 75 C.P.R. (3d) 467 (Ont. C.A.). The action concerned a portrait of hockey star Tim Horton painted by well-known Canadian artist Ken Danby. The painting was commissioned by a charitable foundation linked to the donut chain originally

Another area of growing importance which protects privacy interests is the law relating to liability for breach of confidence.[309]

The issue as to whether a tort of invasion of privacy could form the basis of an injunction to restrain the harassment of women seeking abortions was discussed in an important Ontario case. In *A.G. Ont. v. Dieleman*,[310] Mr. Justice Adams carefully reviewed the case law and literature on privacy, both from Canada and the United States, before concluding that it would be unwise to base the injunction asked for in this case on such an action. He chose instead to rely upon private and public nuisance doctrine. In view of the nature of the complaints in this specific case, free speech interests were critical concerns. On the tort of invasion of privacy in general, Adams J. stated:

> From all the foregoing, it would appear that invasion of privacy in Canadian common law continues to be an inceptive, if not ephemeral, legal concept, primarily operating to extend the margins of existing tort doctrine. One significant explanation for this continuing ''lack of legal profile'' arises from the need to accomodate broad counter privileges associated with free speech and the vast implications of living in a ''crowded society''. . . .[311]

The issue as to whether there should be more adequate protection of privacy rights than currently exists also has been debated in English cases and commentaries. The debate stems from the case of *Kaye v. Robertson*.[312] This concerned the publication of the unauthorized photos of a hospitalized patient. The Court Of Appeal considered four traditional causes of action before they were able to find one — malicious falsehood — which would provide a remedy for the claimant.[313] In *Wainwright v. Home Office*,[314] the English House of Lords firmly closed the door on the recognition of a common law tort of invasion of privacy. Lord Hoffmann, while accepting that privacy may be an important value "which underlies the existence of a rule of law" it should not, because of its breadth and difficulty of definition, become "a principle of law in itself", sufficient to constitute a recognized cause of action.[315]

In view of the alternative remedies which are available, is a separate tort of ''invasion of privacy'' necessary? It is arguable that it is not. The concept of privacy is too ambiguous and broad to be able to be covered adequately in one cause of action.[316] It is more desirable to have the different aspects of privacy

---

established by Tim Horton. The action was dismissed for several reasons including the charitable use of the portrait and the failure to establish any commercial exploitation.

309 See Gibson, ''Common Law Protection of Privacy'', in Klar, ed., *Studies in Canadian Tort Law* (1977), at 363-75.

310 (1994), 117 D.L.R. (4th) 449 (Ont. Gen. Div.), additional reasons at (1995), 22 O.R. (3d) 785 (Gen. Div.), further additional reasons at (1995), 22 O.R. (3d) 785 at 794 (Gen. Div.).

311 *Ibid.*, at 688. Mr. Justice Adams agreed with the view expressed above about the state of the tort of invasion of privacy in Canada stating that ''[l]egally, one cannot speak with confidence of a Canadian tort of invasion of privacy'' (at 680).

312 [1991] FSR 62.

313 See Markesinis, ''Our Patchy Law of Privacy — Time to do Something about It'' (1990), 53 MLR 802; Prescott, ''Kaye v. Robertson — a Reply'' (1991), 54 MLR 451; and Bedingfield, ''Privacy or Publicity? The Enduring Confusion Surrounding the American Tort of Invasion of Privacy'' (1992), 55 MLR 111.

314 [2004] 2 AC 406 (H.L.).

315 *Ibid.*, at 423.

316 See Brown, "Rethinking Privacy: Exclusivity, Private Relation and Tort Law" (2006), 43 Alta. Law Rev. 589, where the author discusses the variety of ways in which the concept of privacy is understood.

protection dealt with in separate torts which more clearly can focus on the interests at hand. Gaps in the law which cannot be filled by extending traditional principles can be dealt with as they arise, either through the expansion of the common law[317] or by legislative intervention.

15. TRESPASS TO CHATTELS

(a) Introduction

The tort of trespass to chattels protects a person's possession of chattels against wrongful interferences. It stems from the writ of trespass *de bonis asportatis*, and encompasses any wrongful taking of chattels, or interference with one's legal possession of chattels.[318] As with the other forms of trespass, it remedies only direct interferences, is actionable without proof of actual damage and, once the *prima facie* case is established, requires that the wrongdoer prove that the trespass was neither intentionally nor negligently caused.

As with compensation for personal injury, claims for property damage largely have been dealt with by the action for negligence, and we have very few reported cases based on the action for trespass to chattels. It nevertheless remains a viable cause of action which arises from time to time.

(b) Intentional Trespass

(i) Intention

An intentional trespass to chattels occurs when the defendant acts desiring to interfere with the possession of the plaintiff's chattels, or in circumstances in which this interference is substantially certain to occur. This does not mean that the defendant must have acted with the intention to commit a wrongful act, or in bad faith. Mistake as to the consequences of one's act is no defence. If the defendant acts voluntarily and with the intention to cause the physical result which occurs, there will be liability if that result should turn out to be tortious.

The difference between intending the physical results of one's act and appreciating the legal consequences of the results can be confusing. For example, in *384238 Ont. Ltd. v. Can.*,[319] the Department of National Revenue mistakenly seized the plaintiff's goods, reasonably believing them to be the goods of a third party against whom a judgment had been obtained. The goods were held for three days, and, when the mistake became known, were returned to the plaintiff. Was this asportation an "intentional trespass"? The judgment of the court indicates the confusion which surrounds the terminology in this area. The court referred to *Cook v. Lewis*,[320] and other cases involving direct trespass which causes injury to persons or damage to property, as authority for the proposition that these torts are

317 By falling back on case, for example.

318 Fleming, *The Law of Torts*, 9th ed. (1998), at 58, notes:

> The earliest cases to attract attention involved total destruction or asportation, and for these wrongs a special writ, known as trespass de bonis asportatis, was created. Much later, it came to be extended to cases of mere damage.

Fleming cites Ames, "History of Trover" (1898), 11 Harv. L. Rev. 277 at 285-86.

319 (1983), 8 D.L.R. (4th) 676 (Fed. C.A.).

320 [1951] S.C.R. 830.

not actionable "without fault." The court, however, held that this principle has not been applied to the wrongful seizure of goods where no physical injury has resulted. Stone J. stated:

> I do not think that the common law in this country has developed to the point where a person who, in execution of process, seizes the goods of another under the honest though mistaken belief that they belonged to his judgment debtor, will escape liability in trespass by proving that his act was neither intentional nor negligent. Liability in trespass for wrongful seizure of chattels has stood on a different footing as a separate and distinct cause of action unlike that which lies when the act consists of a direct act against a person or a chattel resulting in injury. In such a case, the law has viewed inevitable accident as a defence. . . .[321]

The confusion as to the meaning of these terms is evident. The wrongful seizure of the goods in this case was intentional, even though the defendant acted in good faith. The defendant was aware that its act would result in goods being seized. Thus the seizure itself clearly was not accidental. The fact that the defendant was not aware that it had no lawful right to seize the goods was a mistake, which offers no defence.[322]

(ii) Legal Possession

Strictly speaking, a trespass is not an interference with someone's chattel, but with an individual's legal possession of a chattel. The concept of "legal possession" is a fascinating and important one.[323] A person who has both physical control over a chattel and the intention to control it has legal possession of it. Since chattels can be physically controlled in different ways, depending on their size, location, mobility, and so on, the concept of legal possession is a fluid one, which is defined in order to meet the circumstances and conditions of its use. As well, the legal possession of a chattel can be imputed to a person who may not satisfy strictly the requirements of control or intention.[324] The central policy

---

321 8 D.L.R. (4th) 676 at 687-88.

322 An example of an "accidental" trespass may be found in *Everitt v. Martin*, [1953] N.Z.L.R. 298. The plaintiff's coat caught on the dilapidated fender of the defendant's car. Was this contact an actionable trespass by the plaintiff? No — it was an "accidental contact." It was not intended, nor was it even negligent.

323 For an excellent discussion see Harris, "The Concept of Possession in English Law", in Guest (ed.), *Oxford Essays in Jurisprudence* (1961), and Pollock and Wright, *Possession in the Common Law* (1888).

324 This is the central issue in the so-called "finders cases", and the "animal cases", which continue to delight first-year law students. A fascinating case which raises these issues is *A.G. Can. v. Brock* (1993), 82 B.C.L.R. (2d) 1 (B.C. C.A.). The police stopped a person for speeding. When the police became suspicious that the car may have been stolen, the car was searched and a bag containing nearly $300,000 in U.S. cash was found. At first the driver denied all knowledge of the money, but he later claimed it. Before the issue of ownership was resolved, the man died. His estate sued to recover the money. Although the chambers judge held that there was a presumption, which had not been rebutted, that the possessor of the car possessed the bag of money hidden in it, this finding was reversed by the Court of Appeal. Hinkson J.A. stated that the evidence indicated that the owner of the car was unaware that the money was hidden in his car, and that therefore he was not in possession of the money. The money went to the Corporation of the District of West Vancouver. The opposite result occurred in *Neill v. Vancouver Police Department* (2005), [2005] B.C.J. No. 400, 2005 CarswellBC 437 (S.C. [In Chambers]). The police found money stashed in a cognac container in the console of a car. The driver of the car, who was not its owner, denied any knowledge of the money's

behind the common law's adoption of the concept of legal possession and the decision to protect it is to prevent violent or antisocial acts of dispossession, even if this means protecting the legal possession of a wrongful possessor.[325] The concept of legal possession is at the heart of the torts which deal with direct interferences with chattels. The fact that trespass is a direct interference with legal possession means that only the person whose legal possession was interfered with has the right to sue for trespass. An owner of chattels who is out of legal possession of them when an interference occurs does not have the status to bring an action in trespass. That this proposition is true, subject only to a few limited exceptions, was made clear in the classic Australian case of *Penfolds Wines Pty. Ltd. v. Elliott.*[326] The High Court unanimously held[327] that an owner of wine bottles who did not have legal possession of them when they were wrongfully used by the defendant for an improper purpose could not succeed against the wrongdoer in trespass. The only exceptions to this principle apply when there is an interference with the legal possession of chattels which are in the possession of an agent, servant or bailee at will of the claimant who has an immediate right to possession of those goods.

Possession can be abandoned. This results when the possessor abandons the intention to continue in possession, thereby losing all possessory rights in the goods. In *Wicks (Estate) v. Harnett*,[328] for example, the parties disputed the ownership of 2,800 original drawings by well-known Canadian cartoonist Ben Wicks. The drawings were found in plastic garbage bags in the defendant's brother's garage. The house had been purchased by the defendant's brother from Ben Wicks' son. They were in the garage for eight years before the issue of their ownership arose.[329] The defendant claimed that they had been 'abandoned' by the Wicks family. The court found that there had been no intention on the part of the

---

owner. Ultimately, however, the driver brought a replevin application for its return. He was successful. The court found that he was its rightful possessor at the time, based on his control of the console. The fact that he did not know who the money belonged to did not mean he did not possess it.

325 The idea that even a thief can, in theory, sue someone who unlawfully dispossesses him is always met with disbelief. It is nevertheless true. See *Bird v. Fort Frances*, [1949] 2 D.L.R. 791 (Ont. H.C.). What, however, of the concepts *ex turpi causa* or *in pari delicto*? Might they apply to defeat the wrongdoer's claim? In *Baird v. British Columbia* (1992), 77 C.C.C. (3d) 365 (B.C. C.A.), a claim for money and cheques seized from the claimant by the police was defeated by the doctrine of *ex turpi*. Even though the claimant was not convicted of any crime, his admission to the police that the moneys taken had been obtained illegally was sufficient to defeat his claim. See *Newcastle Dist. Fishermen's Co-Op. Soc. v. Neal* (1950), 50 S.R. (N.S.W.) 237, where an illegal transaction prevented a successful claim for conversion. However, in *Gordon v. Chief Commrs. of Metro. Police*, [1910] 2 K.B. 1080 (C.A.), and *Singh v. Ali*, [1960] A.C. 167 (P.C.), claims by wrongful possessors succeeded.

326 (1946), 74 C.L.R. 204 (Aust. H.C.).

327 There were five members on the Bench. Only one equivocated on this point, although he too was sympathetic with the decision of the other four that a trespass had not been committed. See Paton and Sawyer, "Ratio Decidendi and Obiter Dictum" (1947), 63 L.Q.R. 461, for a discussion of the judgment.

328 (2007), 48 C.C.L.T. (3d) 155 (Ont. S.C.J.). Although the action was based on detinue and conversion, the issue of abandonment was at the heart of the dispute.

329 The defendant knew they were in the garage shortly after the house was purchased by his brother, but did not realize that they might be of value until several years later.

Wicks' to abandon the drawings and ordered their return to the Wicks family, in addition to damages for those drawings that had already been sold.[330]

(iii) Directness

As with the other forms of trespass, a trespass to chattels involves a direct interference.[331] The issue of directness raises the same concerns and can be dealt with in the same manner as discussed previously.

(iv) Damage

Whether trespass to chattels is, like other forms of trespass, actionable *per se*, is a somewhat controversial matter. There is no doubt that where there has been a taking of possession, even without actual damage to the chattel, a successful action will lie.[332] There is no authority on whether a mere interference with possession, short of dispossession and without actual damage, is actionable.[333] It is submitted that there is no reason to suggest that this type of trespass differs from other trespasses in this respect. It would be unfortunate if it did. Although people are unlikely to sue for trespasses which do not seriously interfere with their ability to use their chattels and where there has been no damage, a remedy should be available where a person is being harassed or otherwise bothered in the possession of a chattel.[334]

---

330 Another recent case that raised the issue of abandonment is *Air Canada v. West Jet*, [2004] O.J. No. 5627 (Ont. S.C.J.). In that case, shredded documents deposited in a recycling container were held to have been abandoned.

331 See *Covell v. Laming* (1808), 170 E.R. 1034. It was held to be trespass and not case where a ship under the defendant's control ran into the plaintiff's ship.

332 See *384238 Ont. Ltd. v. Can.* (1983), 8 D.L.R. (4th) 676 (Fed. C.A.); *Demers v. Desrosier*, [1929] 3 D.L.R. 401 (Alta. T.D.); *Hudson's Bay Co. v. White* (1997), 32 C.C.L.T. (2d) 163 (Ont. Gen. Div.), varied (1998), 1 C.P.C. (5th) 333 (Ont. Div. Ct.).

333 Trindade, Cane and Lunney, *The Law of Torts in Australia,* 4th ed. (2007), at 206, notes that "the opinion of most writers on the law of torts suggests that it is." Fleming, *The Law of Torts*, 9th ed. (1998), at 59, suggests that it is a "moot" point, although the "meagre authority" which exists points to the requirement of damage. In *Credit Valley Cable v. Peel Condominium* (1980), 107 D.L.R. (3d) 266 (Ont. H.C.), the act of connecting equipment to the plaintiff's cable constituted a trespass to the cable. Although the issue of damage was not discussed, it is clear that the court did not view damage to the cable as a prerequisite for a successful trespass action. Also see *North King Lodge Ltd. v. Gowlland Towing Ltd.*, 2005 BCCA 557 (C.A.). The owner of a vessel sued a towing company for removing its vessel from boom sticks to which it had been anchored. The court found that the vessel had been secured to the boom sticks without the permission of the owner of the boom sticks, and this constituted a trespass to them. Thus the untying of the vessel was a legitimate act.

334 The measure of damages, however, poses a difficulty. In *Hudson's Bay Co. v. White* (1997), 32 C.C.L.T. (2d) 163 (Ont. Gen. Div.), varied (1998), 1 C.P.C. (5th) 333 (Ont. Div. Ct.), a shoplifter was apprehended with five pairs of gloves. The gloves were recovered undamaged. The plaintiff claimed as damages costs that it incurred relating to the prevention of shoplifting. While Lederman J. accepted the principle that there need not be actual losses to succeed in an action based upon trespass, he noted that there are two schools of thought as to the assessment of damages issue. The first is that only "nominal" damages can be awarded in the absence of actual proven losses. The second is that more than nominal damages can be awarded, even in the absence of actual losses, when that is "appropriate in the circumstances" (see *Bank of Nova Scotia v. Dunphy Leasing Enterprises Ltd.* (1991), 120 A.R. 241 (C.A.), affirmed (1994), 18 Alta. L.R. (3d) 2 (S.C.C.)). Lederman J. ultimately awarded only nominal

(c) Negligent Trespass

Canadian courts recognize that a trespass to chattels can be committed negligently, and that this will be treated as an action for trespass and not negligence. In *Bell Can. v. Bannermount Ltd.*,[335] for example, a defendant was held liable for a negligent trespass when it damaged the plaintiff's telephone cables while conducting digging operations. The Ontario Court of Appeal placed the onus of disproving negligence upon the defendant. This was consistent with the Canadian courts' approach to negligent trespass cases.[336] A Manitoba court used a similar approach in *Manitoba Hydro v. Minsky*.[337] The defendant plow operator damaged a transformer owned by the plaintiff. The case was pleaded both in trespass and in negligence and the rule that the onus of disproof for trespass fell upon the defendant was applied.[338]

16. DETINUE

(a) Introduction

The tort of detinue involves the wrongful detention of goods from the person who, *vis-à-vis* the defendant, has the right to the immediate possession of them. There were historically two forms of detinue: detinue sur bailment and detinue sur trover. Detinue sur bailment was considered to be contractual and applied between bailor and bailee. Detinue sur trover was a wrongful detention which applied between strangers, one of whom was allegedly holding the goods of another.[339] In the modern context, there is one action for detinue, which applies equally to defendants who came into possession of the plaintiff's chattels either as bailees or in some other way.

---

damages of $100, which he considered appropriate no matter which of the two approaches prevails. On appeal, the Divisional Court added $300 in punitive damages to the award.

335 (1973), 35 D.LR. (3d) 367 (Ont. C.A.).

336 A similar case is *Bell Can. v. COPE (Sarnia) Ltd.* (1980), 11 C.C.L.T. 170 (Ont.), affirmed (1981), 15 C.C.L.T. 190 (Ont. C.A.). Although the facts supported a negligent trespass, the court also found that the act which damaged the cables was "intentional." Also see *Sleiman v. Dugal*, [1990] O.J. No. 2735, where the court reaffirmed the reverse onus rule of the trespass action, although the case dealt with an intentional and not a negligent trespass to goods. In *London Drugs Ltd. v. Kuehne & Nagel Int. Ltd.* (1990), 2 C.C.L.T. (2d) 161 (B.C. C.A.), affirmed [1993] 1 W.W.R. 1 (S.C.C.), there was a divergence of opinion in the B.C. Court of Appeal concerning the existence of a form of negligent trespass to goods. McEachern C.J.B.C. seemed to approve of the English position, which has subsumed all negligent interferences, whether direct or indirect, into the action for negligence. Southin J.A., on the other hand, held (at 263) that "the modern tort of negligence, all-devouring monster though it is, has not swallowed up the tort of trespass", and that an action for negligent trespass can be pursued. In my respectful opinion, the judgments were misconceived on this point, since the actions of the defendants did not give rise to a trespass, in any event. The defendants were in possession of the object when it was damaged, and thus, the plaintiff's possession was not interfered with. That being the case, no trespass was committed.

337 (1998), [1999] 3 W.W.R. 663 (Man. Q.B.).

338 No negligence was found and the action was dismissed. The court also held that the temporary interference with the plaintiff's easement did not amount to a trespass to land.

339 For a discussion of this historical distinction and its practical implications for the parties see Baker, *An Introduction to English Legal History* (1979), at 325-28; Milsom, *Historical Foundations of the Common Law* (1969), at 228-35. See also Spence J.'s judgment in *Aitken v. Gardiner* (1956), 4 D.L.R. (2d) 119 (Ont. H.C.).

To succeed in an action for detinue, there must be proof that the plaintiff had a better right to the possession of the chattels than did the defendant, and that despite an appropriate demand that the goods be returned, the defendant refused to return the chattels in question to the plaintiff. The plaintiff need not establish "title" to the goods, nor the best rights "in the world" to them. The rights of third parties who are not claiming the goods, and for whom the defendant does not act, are irrelevant to the action. In *Schentag v. Gauthier*,[340] for example, the defendant, who was holding a typewriter which was being claimed by the plaintiff, defended herself on the ground that the typewriter did not belong to the plaintiff but to the trustee in bankruptcy of the plaintiff's company. The court held that whether the plaintiff could "strictly prove his title to the typewriter" was not an element of the plaintiff's claim. The defendant could "only set up the title of a third person where she does so on behalf of and on the express authority of such third person."[341]

Detinue, being an interference with the plaintiff's right to the immediate possession of goods, is, unlike trespass, available to protect an owner who is out of possession when the wrongful act occurs.

(b) Wrongful Detention

In order to constitute a detinue, the defendant's detention of the goods must be wrongful as regards the claimant.

(i) Demand and Refusal

As a general rule, a detinue does not occur until the claimant has demanded that the goods be returned and this demand has been refused. This rule clearly applies where the defendant is holding the goods unaware that the plaintiff is claiming a right to them, and hence not in defiance of the plaintiff's claim.[342] As Fleming explains "the reason for insisting on a prior demand is to ensure that one who came into possession innocently be first informed of the defect in his title and have the opportunity to deliver the property to the true owner."[343] The cases establish that a defendant is not required to comply with a demand immediately but is given a reasonable amount of time to verify the rights of the

---

340 (1972), 27 D.L.R. (3d) 710 (Sask. Dist. Ct.).

341 *Ibid.*, at 716. On this sometimes complex discussion of the right of a defendant to claim a *jus tertii*, see also *Henry Berry & Co. Pty. v. Rushton*, [1937] Q.S.R. 109; *Wilson v. Lombank*, [1963] 1 W.L.R. 1294; Atiyah, "A Re-Examination of the Jus Tertii in Conversion" (1955), 18 Mod. L. Rev. 97; Jolly, "Jus Tertii and the Third Man" (1955), 18 Mod. L. Rev. 371.

342 See, e.g., *Clayton v. Le Roy*, [1911] 2 K.B. 1031 (C.A.), where a jewellery shop received a watch it believed had been stolen originally from the plaintiff. It wrote to the plaintiff and to the purchaser of the watch, who had sent it to the defendant for appraisal, but received no instructions or reply. The plaintiff's solicitors sent a clerk to the defendant's shop, who demanded the watch immediately, and when this was refused, handed the defendant a writ in detinue, which it had taken out two hours previously. The court held that there had been no wrongful refusal on the defendant's part to return the watch before the date of the issue of the writ, and therefore there was no cause of action.

343 Fleming, *The Law of Torts*, 9th ed. (1998), at 65.

claimant.[344] Where the defendant's holding is already wrongful and in defiance of the plaintiff's rights, e.g. where the defendant has stolen the object, no demand for the chattel's return should be necessary.[345] A more difficult issue arises where a plaintiff fails to make a demand for goods held by a defendant who in good faith is resisting the plaintiff's claim. In *Baud Corp., N.V. v. Brook*,[346] the plaintiff failed to make a demand for shares of a company before it sued. The defendant in its defence denied that it was obligated to return these shares. The Alberta Court of Appeal held that:

> where the defence of a defendant shows clearly that if a demand had been made on him for possession of the property, he would have refused delivery, then it should no longer be a defence to an action in detinue that no demand was made.[347]

The mere fact that a defendant cannot return the goods demanded and, therefore, must refuse the request does not in itself establish a wrongful detention. The refusal to return must either be a deliberate rejection of the plaintiff's claim to the goods, or result from the fact that the defendant wrongfully has departed with possession of the goods and thus is unable to comply with the request. Where, for example, a bailee cannot return goods because they have been lost, stolen or destroyed, the refusal to return will constitute a detinue only if the bailee's obligation to take due care of the goods was breached.[348] A person who never had possession of the goods cannot be liable in detinue, but it is no defence to a

---

344 See, e.g., *Clayton v. Le Roy*, above, note 342.

345 In *London Jewellers Ltd. v. Sutton* (1934), 50 T.L.R. 193, Mr. Justice Swift expressed the opinion that if wrongful detention can be established without proving a demand and refusal there is a good action in detinue. This seems to be logical. There is no point in requiring a plaintiff to demand the return of chattels from someone who is aware of the plaintiff's rights but by conduct has repudiated these rights. I must admit, however, that most authorities categorically assert that "demand for delivery up of the chattel was an essential requirement of an action in detinue" without qualification. See, e.g., Diplock L.J. in *Gen. & Fin. Facilities Ltd. v. Cooks Cars*, [1963] 1 W.L.R. 644 at 649 (C.A.).

346 (1973), 40 D.L.R. (3d) 418 (Alta. C.A.), varied (1979), 89 D.L.R. (3d) 1 (S.C.C.), which was varied (1979), 97 D.L.R. (3d) 300 (S.C.C.).

347 40 D.L.R. (3d) 418 at 423. See also Jewers J. in *Anderson Animal Hospital v. Watt* (1991), 72 Man. R. (2d) 225 at 227 (Q.B.): "No demand for delivery up of goods will be required prior to an action, if the defendant would have refused delivery had a demand been made of him", citing in support Fridman, *The Law of Torts of Canada*, Vol 1, at 116. See also *Lomax v. Brower*, [1919] 3 W.W.R. 385 (Alta. T.D.): lack of demand only affects costs. In a case comment at (1975), 53 Can. Bar Rev. 121, Professor Palmer has submitted that the principle in *Baud* should be restricted to cases where the defendant's detention would not have been "honest and reasonable", but "perverse and in bad faith." Palmer suggests that normally those detaining goods should be given the opportunity to consider the plaintiff's claim before a suit is launched. This may discourage litigation and allow the detainer to "come to a more balanced decision as to whether to meet the demand." This view is consistent with my submission that where the detention is knowingly wrongful, a demand ought not to be necessary.

348 See *John F. Goulding Pty. Ltd. v. Victorian Ry. Commrs.* (1932), 48 C.L.R. 157 (Aust. H.C.). This point was affirmed in *Kinsella v. Club "7" Ltd.* (1993), 115 Nfld. & P.E.I.R. 150, 360 A.P.R. 150 (Nfld. T.D.). Puddester J. stated at 170 that even if you sue a bailee in detinue, "it is clear that a defence will exist if the bailee can show on the balance of probabilities that it has exercised reasonable care. In such a case, the bailees' refusal or inability to return the goods will not be 'wrongful' within the requirements necessary to establish a remedy."

detinue that the defendant, who once had possession of the goods, no longer has them.[349]

The fact that a plaintiff can sue in detinue even though some other cause of action, such as breach of bailment, or conversion, also was available, may have implications for the applicable period of limitations. If a detinue arises only when a request and refusal are made, it is possible that the rights of a plaintiff who is out of time to sue for a prior conversion or breach of bailment may be revived, once the plaintiff makes a demand for the goods and sues in detinue.[350] This state of affairs would be unsatisfactory. Where a detinue arises from the breach of a legal obligation the time for suing in detinue ought to be the same as the time for suing on the basis of that breach.

Unless it is a term of the agreement, a person who is holding someone else's goods is under no obligation to redeliver these goods.[351] The defendant merely is required to provide the claimant with reasonable access to the goods.[352]

(c) Remedies

The importance of detinue resides in the fact that, unlike the other torts remedying interferences with chattels, it is possible to sue in detinue to recover the specific chattel which has been withheld. Therefore, although the same conduct can constitute both a detinue and a conversion, it is only by suing in detinue that a claimant can hope to recover the goods.

The case of *Gen. & Fin. Facilities Ltd. v. Cooks Cars*[353] sets out the three forms of judgment which are possible in detinue. Judgment in detinue may be (1) for the value of the chattel as assessed and damages for its detention, (2) for return of the chattel or recovery of its value as assessed and damages for its detention, or (3) for return of the chattel and damages for its detention.[354] Originally the action in detinue did not give the owner of the chattels the right to specific recovery of them, but gave the defendant the choice whether to deliver up the chattels or

---

349 See *Rosenthal v. Alderton & Sons Ltd.*, [1946] K.B. 374 (C.A.); *Gen. & Fin. Facilities Ltd. v. Cooks Cars*, [1963] 1 W.L.R. 644 (C.A.).

350 See *John F. Goulding Pty. Ltd. v. Victorian Ry. Commrs.* (1932), 48 C.L.R. 157 (Aust. H.C.). Let us assume, for example, that a bailee loses possession of a chattel as a result of negligence. The bailor is aware of this but fails to take any action until the time period for suing for breach of bailment has expired. The bailor then makes a demand for the return of the goods, which is refused, and sues in detinue.

351 See *Capital Fin. Co. v. Bray*, [1964] 1 W.L.R. 323 (C.A.).

352 What this means is not altogether clear. In *Metals & Ropes Co. v. Tattersall*, [1966] 3 All E.R. 401, for example, the objects in question were five very large boilers which were not easily moved. The defendant was sued in detinue and was ordered to deliver the goods up to the plaintiffs or pay damages. The defendant did nothing. The goods in fact were not in its possession but were lying in a mill which had been taken over by another company. On an application by the plaintiffs for leave to execute for the value of the boilers, it was held that the defendant minimally ought to have written to the plaintiffs to make it clear that they could have access to the boilers and go and collect them. A related problem involves the case of unsolicited goods. What is the obligation of a person who receives, usually through the mail, goods which have not been ordered and are not wanted? Several jurisdictions have special consumer protection legislation dealing with unsolicited goods.

353 [1963] 1 W.L.R. 644 (C.A.).

354 *Ibid.*, at 650.

pay their assessed value.[355] A claimant who wished to recover goods could have resort to Chancery for such an order. This ultimately was changed by s. 78 of the Common Law Procedure Act, 1854,[356] which gave the court the power to order delivery up of the chattel by the defendant without the option to pay its assessed value.[357] It is, therefore, now possible for a claimant in detinue to ask for the recovery of the specific chattels and it is in the court's, and not the defendant's, discretion to decide whether this request must be complied with. The defendant always has the option, however, of returning the chattels to the claimant, up to the time judgment is rendered.[358] The cases establish that the courts will not order that a chattel be returned where the chattel ''is an ordinary article of commerce'';[359] ''where damages would be adequate compensation'';[360] where the chattels have been improved in value from the effort of the person detaining them, unless the owner is prepared to pay for this increased value;[361] where the claimant has unreasonably delayed the action;[362] or unless it is otherwise just to do so. The ordinary form of judgment will give the defendant the option to return the goods or pay their value as assessed, while maintaining the plaintiff's right to apply to the court to enforce specific restitution. It is also apparently possible, but unusual, for a court to order that the only remedy is a return of the chattel.

The matter of assessing the value of goods detained for the purposes of judgment in detinue raises some problems. A detinue is said to be a continuing wrong which lasts so long as the defendant refuses to give up the chattel, or up to the time of judgment on the plaintiff's action.[363] It therefore has been held that the value of the chattels which have not been returned should be assessed as of the time of judgment.[364] This principle can create difficulties when the value of goods fluctuates significantly, especially when the act which constituted the detinue also can be sued upon as a conversion.[365] In addition to assessing the value of the chattels and awarding this, there also can be consequential damages which arise

---

355 See *Baud Corp., N.V. v. Brook* (1973), 40 D.L.R. (3d) 418 at 424 (Alta. C.A.); *McIntyre v. Brodie*, [1933] 3 D.L.R. 297 at 299 (Man. C.A.).

356 17 & 18 Vict., c. 125.

357 See Diplock L.J.'s judgment in *Gen. & Fin. Facilities Ltd. v. Cooks Cars*, [1963] 1 W.L.R. 644 at 650 (C.A.). This power is now found in the various provincial Rules of Court.

358 In *Gen. & Fin. Facilities Ltd. v. Cooks Cars, ibid.*, Diplock L.J. states that once a judgment is rendered ordering the defendant to pay the value of the chattel as assessed by the court, the plaintiff is entitled to insist upon this, rather than being required to take back the chattel.

359 *Gen. & Fin. Facilities Ltd. v. Cooks Cars, ibid.*

360 *Mayne v. Kidd*, [1951] 2 D.L.R. 652 at 654 (Sask. C.A.), citing Winfield, *The Law of Tort*, 5th ed. (1950), at 353.

361 *Ibid.*, at 655.

362 *Baud Corp., N.V. v. Brook* (1973), 40 D.L.R. (3d) 418 at 425 (Alta. C.A.).

363 See, e.g., Diplock L.J.'s judgment in *Gen. & Fin. Facilities Ltd. v. Cooks Cars*, [1963] 1 W.L.R. 644 at 650 (C.A.).

364 There is some argument whether it is the end of the trial or the time of judgment which is the appropriate time. In *Asamera Oil Corp. Ltd. v. Sea Oil & Gen. Corp.* (1978), 89 D.L.R. (3d) 1 (S.C.C.), which was an appeal of *Baud Corp., N.V. v. Brook,* Estey J. accepted the ''end of trial'' as the decisive time. Note, however, that Estey J. referred to another case, *Metro. Trust Co. of Can. v. Pressure Concrete Services Ltd.* (1973), 37 D.L.R. (3d) 649, affirmed (1975), 60 D.L.R. (3d) 431 (Ont. C.A.), where Holland J. directed the assessment officer to take into account damages incurred beyond the end of trial to the date reserved judgment was delivered.

365 This will be discussed below.

as a result of the detention. For example, in *Middleton v. City Automatic Transmission Ltd.*,[366] the plaintiff was awarded lost profits from its inability to rent a vehicle during the period of detention.

17. CONVERSION

(a) Introduction

A conversion is a positive and intentional act of interference with a person's legal possession or right to the immediate possession of goods.[367] Although conversion, originally known as trover, is of much later origin than either trespass or detinue,[368] it became and remains today the most important of the three torts. It has overtaken the other two torts, and with some exceptions, can be used to satisfy the same objectives.

(b) Who Can Sue?

Conversion does not protect the ownership of chattels, but regulates rights of possession of chattels.[369] A person who has a better right to the possession of a chattel than a wrongdoer who seriously interferes with or deprives that person of that right, can sue for conversion.

That the issue in conversion is not ownership but the right to immediate possession has been demonstrated in many cases. In *F.B.D.B. v. T. & T. Engr. Ltd.*,[370] a plaintiff who had the right to the immediate possession of a ship by virtue of being the mortgagee under two mortgages which were in default had the status to sue in conversion. The plaintiff successfully brought an action against the defendants, one of whom was a co-owner of the ship and had destroyed the chattel. In *Clarke v. Fullerton*,[371] a plaintiff was able to maintain an action in

---

366 (1981), 13 Sask. R. 270 (Q.B.).

367 See Rouleau J.'s definition of conversion in *Shibamoto & Co. v. Western Fish Producers Inc.*, [1991] 3 F.C. 214 at 229 (T.D.), affirmed (1992), 145 N.R. 91 (Fed. C.A.):

> The tort of conversion involves the wrongful taking, using or destroying of goods or the exercise of control over them in a manner that is inconsistent with the title of the owner. It arises when there exists an intentional exercise of control over a chattel which seriously impedes the right of the true owner to control it.

Iacobucci J. defines the tort in much the same way in *Boma Manufacturing Ltd. v. Canadian Imperial Bank of Commerce* (1996), [1997] 2 W.W.R. 153 (S.C.C.) at 168: "The tort of conversion involves a wrongful interference with the goods of another, such as taking, using or destroying these goods in a manner inconsistent with the owner's right of possession."

As with detinue, the tort of conversion does not stem from the writ of trespass and therefore does not require that the legal injury result *directly* from the defendant's conduct. As a practical matter, the legal wrongs sanctioned by detinue and conversion invariably flow directly from the defendant's conduct.

368 See Fleming, *The Law of Torts*, 9th ed. (1998), at 61.

369 See, e.g., *Debor Contr. v. Core Rentals Ltd.* (1982), 40 O.R. (2d) 24 at 29 (H.C.):

> The essence of conversion is not a wrong against the owner in respect of its ownership. It is an infringement of the right of control or the right of possession which is usually an incident of ownership but not always.

370 [1982] 4 W.W.R. 126 (B.C. S.C.).

371 (1871), 8 N.S.R. 348 (C.A.).

conversion even though her title to the chattel may have been defective. The plaintiff had been given a telescope by her father before he died. The defendant, who became the administrator of the deceased's estate and who was also a creditor of the estate, obtained possession of the telescope on the promise that he would return it, which he subsequently refused to do. It was alleged that the gift was fraudulent and therefore void. The court stated that "the plaintiff being in possession of it at the time of taking had, even without title shown, a clear right to maintain the action against the defendant who was a mere wrong-doer."[372] It was not open to the defendant to challenge the validity of the gift; this only could have been done by one of the other creditors of the estate. In a New Zealand case, *Bolwell Fibreglass Pty. Ltd. v. Foley*,[373] the dispute concerned the right to possession of a partially completed yacht. The plaintiffs had ordered and paid for the yacht which was being built by the defendant company. The plaintiffs requested delivery of the yacht before it was finished, but the defendant refused since it was still owed money by the company which had actually contracted with the defendant for the building of the yacht for the plaintiffs. The court held that what is relevant in an action for detinue or conversion is not title or ownership but who has the right to the possession of the chattel in issue. The contract entitled the defendant to retain possession of the chattel until the work on it was completed.[374]

An owner of goods who has given up possession and the right to possession of goods for a term ordinarily lacks the interest to sue in conversion during that period of time. If, however, the act of conversion revives the owner's right to the immediate possession of the goods, the owner can sue. In *Sibley v. Sibley*,[375] for example, the bailee of goods conveyed them absolutely to the defendants. This was held to put an end to the bailment, since it was in violation of the plaintiff's rights as bailor, and the plaintiff had the right to sue the defendants in conversion.[376] A bailee whose possession has been interfered with can sue the wrongdoer in conversion, notwithstanding the bailor's rights of action against the bailee or

---

372 *Ibid.*, at 348-49.

373 [1984] V.R. 97.

374 See also *MacLellan v. Melanson* (1967), 62 D.L.R. (2d) 40 (N.S. C.A.), which confirms that conversion protects possessory rights as opposed to ownership. More recent affirmation of the same point is found in *Rowbotham v. Nave* (1991), 1 P.P.S.A.C. (2d) 206 (Ont. Gen. Div.): "a person can only maintain an action for damages for conversion if at the time of the defendant's act either he or she had ownership and possession of the goods, or possession of them, or an immediate right to possess them." In *889267 Ontario Ltd. v. Norfinch Group Inc.* (1998), [1998] O.J. No. 3850, 1998 CarswellOnt 3696 (Gen. Div.), the issue was whether the right to possession of a defalcating tenant's goods resided in the vendor, under a general security agreement, or in a landlord who was distraining the goods and equipment. The court found in favour of the landlord.

375 (1871), 8 N.S.R. 325 (C.A.).

376 See also *Fed. Savings Credit Union Ltd. v. Centennial Trailer Sales Ltd.* (1973), 37 D.L.R. (3d) 146 (N.S. T.D.); *Battlefords Credit Union Ltd. v. Korpan Tractor & Parts Ltd.* (1983), 28 Sask. R. 215 (Q.B.). A more recent case is *Brule v. Chmilar* (2000), 256 A.R. 168 (Q.B.). The defendant resold hay, which the plaintiff earlier had agreed to buy but had not yet paid for and removed. This ordinarily would not be a conversion because at the time of the resale the plaintiff did not have a right to the immediate possession of it. However, the defendant was characterized as a gratuitous bailee and the resale put an end to the bailment giving the plaintiff the right to sue in conversion, following the *Sibley* case.

the wrongdoer.[377] A plaintiff who sues and recovers judgment in conversion does not lose the right to the immediate possession of the chattel until the judgment is satisfied.[378]

(c) Intention

A conversion is the positive and intentional interference with legal possession or the right to immediate possession. As discussed previously, mistake as to the legal or factual consequences of one's conduct is not a defence if the physical consequences were intended. There have been several cases where well-intentioned defendants were held liable in conversion because their conduct resulted in a denial of the possessory rights of others. In *Can. Laboratory Supplies Ltd. v. Engelhard Indust. of Can. Ltd.*,[379] the plaintiff and defendant were duped by a fraudulent scheme operated by one of the plaintiff's employees. The employee would order platinum from the defendant, allegedly on the plaintiff's behalf. The platinum then would be resold by the employee, using the name of a fictitious customer of the plaintiff, to the defendant as scrap. The plaintiff eventually discovered the scheme and sued the defendant for the conversion of its scrap. Despite the innocent participation of the defendant, it was held to be liable for conversion.[380] Another case of "innocent" conversion is *384238 Ont. Ltd. v. Can.*[381] The defendant seized the plaintiff's goods in the mistaken belief that they belonged to a third party against whom a judgment had been obtained. Although the court held that temporarily detaining a chattel for three days without use does not amount to a conversion, but a trespass, it affirmed the proposition that innocence is no defence if the act constitutes a serious interference with the plaintiff's possessory rights.[382]

---

377 See *Thorne v. MacGregor* (1973), 35 D.L.R. (3d) 687 (Ont. H.C.); *Tanenbaum v. W.J. Bell Paper Co.* (1956), 4 D.L.R. (2d) 177 (Ont. H.C.), which applied *The Winkfield*, [1902] P. 42 (C.A.); *Sask. Brewers Assn. v. Refrigeration Installations* (1985), 38 Sask. R. 269 (Q.B.).

378 Therefore recovery in conversion without satisfaction does not vest the property in the chattel in the defendant, and enables the plaintiff to sue another party who purchases the chattel from the first defendant. See *McArthur v. Clark* (1903), 2 O.W.R. 319 (C.A.).

379 (1979), 97 D.L.R. (3d) 1 (S.C.C.).

380 The main issue in the litigation concerned the defendant's argument that the plaintiff was estopped from denying its employee's authority to sell the platinum back to the defendant. The Supreme Court of Canada held that this defence applied to a part of the transactions.

381 (1983), 8 D.L.R. (4th) 676 (Fed. C.A.).

382 The judgment cited the leading English authorities: *Hollins v. Fowler* (1875), L.R. 7 H.L. 757; *Lancashire & Yorkshire Ry. v. MacNicoll* (1918), 88 L.J.K.B. 601; *Marfani & Co. v. Midland Bank Ltd.*, [1968] 1 W.L.R. 956 (C.A.), among others. Other Canadian cases which affirm this point are: *Simpson v. Gowers* (1981), 121 D.L.R. (3d) 709 (Ont. C.A.) — defendants converted soya beans which had been left in a barn which they purchased, unaware of the plaintiff's interest in the beans; *Battlefords Credit Union Ltd. v. Korpan Tractor & Parts Ltd.* (1983), 28 Sask. R. 215 (Q.B.) — defendants, unaware of the plaintiffs' interest, sold a tractor over which the plaintiffs had a chattel mortgage which was in default; *MacKenzie v. Scotia Lumber Co.* (1913), 11 D.L.R. 729 (N.S. C.A.) — defendant's servants mistakenly took plaintiff's raft for a short period of time thinking that the raft belonged to the defendant; *Mackenzie v. Blindman Valley Co-op. Assn.*, [1947] 2 W.W.R. 443 (Alta. T.D.) — defendant, acting as agent of a thief, sold pigs belonging to the plaintiffs and was liable for conversion even though acting in good faith; *C.I.B.C. v. F.B.D.B.*, [1985] 3 W.W.R. 318 (Alta. Q.B.) — receiver innocently converting assignment of book debts; *Kosczyszyn v. Diamond Towing*

The fact that the law treats those who innocently and in good faith deal with another's goods as converters if their actions constitute a denial of the plaintiff's possessory rights has been criticized.[383] Although some earlier cases have tried to avoid this result, in the case of auctioneers, for example, by holding that the innocent party did not effect a disposition of property but was a mere conduit for the disposition,[384] the correctness of this approach has been doubted.[385]

In order to be actionable, a conversion must result from a positive act of the defendant which denies or seriously interferes with the claimant's possessory rights. A destruction or loss of chattels occurring as a result of the defendant's negligence or passivity is not actionable as a conversion.[386] The defendant's conduct must demonstrate a dominion over the chattels. A bailee cannot be liable in conversion if the goods are lost or destroyed through negligence, although there will be liability if the loss occurred as a result of a positive act, such as a

---

Ltd. (August 14, 2000), Doc. NY18120/99, [2000] O.J. No. 3088 (S.C.J.)—company towing plaintiff's car under mistaken "colour of right" liable for conversion; *Mutungih v. Bokun* (2006), 40 C.C.L.T. (3d) 313 (Ont. S.C.J.) — purchaser of a stolen car liable to owner for conversion, after having significantly altered car, despite the fact that the car had been improved. In the case of *Boma Manufacturing Ltd. v. Canadian Imperial Bank of Commerce* (1996), [1997] 2 W.W.R. 153, 140 D.L.R. (4th) 463 (S.C.C.), Iacobucci J. makes the same point in reference to the "innocent" conversion of cheques by a bank. Iacobucci J. states that "the tort is one of strict liability, and accordingly, it is no defence that the wrongful act was committed in all innocence". Although I would quibble with the characterization of the tort as one of "strict" liability, since in fact intentional conduct is required, Iacobucci J. uses the term not in its technical sense, but to indicate that mistake as to the consequences of one's deliberate act, in this case dealing with cheques on forged endorsements, is no defence to an action for conversion. Also see *Stevenson Estate v. Siewert*, [2001] 10 W.W.R. 401 (Alta. C.A.). A law firm turned over a bank draft to the wrong party. This was done "innocently"; yet the law firm was liable. The Court of Appeal defined conversion as a "strict liability" tort, although as I point out the act of handing over the draft was in fact intentionally done, despite ignorance as to its legal or factual consequences. See *CIT Financial Ltd. v. 1153461 Ontario Inc.* (2004), [2004] O.J. No. 3308, 2004 CarswellOnt 3285 (S.C.J.) where this view of the tort is affirmed by Sutherland J.

383 See Lord Denning's comments in *R. H. Willis & Son v. Br. Car Auctions Ltd.*, [1978] 1 W.L.R. 438 at 442 (C.A.). Lord Denning suggests that the only way for innocent acquirers or handlers to protect themselves is by insurance. Note, however, possible statutory defences. See, for example, *Bartin Pipe & Piling Supply Ltd. v. Western Environment of Oklahoma* (2004), (*sub nom. Epscan Industries Ltd. v. Bartin Pipe & Piling Supply Ltd.*) 236 D.L.R. (4th) 75 (Alta. C.A.), leave to appeal refused (2004), 2004 CarswellAlta 1248 (S.C.C.) re: s. 27(1) of the Sale of Goods Act, R.S.A. 2000, c. S-2 (purchaser in good faith).

384 See *Nat. Mercantile Bank v. Rymill* (1881), 44 L.T.N.S. 767; *Turner v. Hockey* (1887), 56 L.J.Q.B. 301. *Nat. Mercantile Bank* was applied in the case of *Weise v. Douglas*, [1991] S.J. No. 650 (Sask. P. Ct.). Two friends of the defendant, at his request and instructions, transported cattle from one farm to the farm belonging to one of them. They mistakenly believed that the cattle belonged to him. One of the cattle was eventually slaughtered, but the friends had nothing to do with this. The court held that the friends could not be liable in conversion for their roles in the transportation or keeping of the cattle. They were mere "conduit pipes", and bailees without reward, for the limited purposes of transporting and/or keeping the cattle.

385 See *R.H. Willis & Son v. Br. Car Auctions Ltd.*, [1978] 1 W.L.R. 438 (C.A.); and *Irvington Hldg. Ltd. v. Black* (1987), 35 D.L.R. (4th) 641 (Ont. C.A.). One case held that an innocent dealing with goods which have been altered by prior users "stops the chain of liability"; see *Rogers v. Frechette* (1905), 1 W.L.R. 190 (B.C.).

386 See Rouleau J. in *Shibamoto & Co. v. Western Fish Producers Inc.*, [1991] 3 F.C. 214 (T.D.): "...conversion can result only from an intentional act, not from negligent loss or destruction."

misdelivery.[387] Not only must the defendant's act be a positive one, but the conversion must have been intended. It is not sufficient if the loss or destruction resulted from mere carelessness.[388] It must have been substantially certain or desired. In *F.B.D.B. v. T. & T. Engr. Ltd.*,[389] the chattel to which the right of possession attached was a ship which sank. Was the defendant's participation in the sinking a conversion? The court held that the defendant deliberately allowed the ship to sink and that this was, therefore, a conversion.[390] Another borderline case is *Moorgate Mercantile Co. v. Finch.*[391] The defendant used a car, which had been obtained by another person from the plaintiff company on a hire-purchase contract, to smuggle watches across the border. The Customs authorities discovered the crime and seized the car. Could it be said that the defendant converted the car? Did the defendant "intend" that the car be seized? The court held that although the defendant obviously hoped that he would not be found out that "he must be taken to intend the consequences which were likely to happen and which did in fact result in the loss of the car."[392] Unless it could be said that the detection of this crime and seizure of the car were substantially certain consequences, the defendant's conduct ought to have been considered to have been negligent and not a conversion.

(d) Chattels

Conversion involves possessory rights over chattels. Occasionally litigation arises concerning the status of the converted property. There are many cases, for example, concerning the conversion of goods alleged to be fixtures, crops, timber, or minerals, where the court is called upon to determine whether these were

---

387 See *Lovekin v. Podger* (1866), 26 U.C.Q.B. 156 (C.A.); *Joule Ltd. v. Poole* (1924), 24 S.R. (N.S.W.) 387. Note, however, that an "involuntary bailee" who is reasonable in attempting to deliver the goods to the right party will not be held liable, according to Fleming, *The Law Of Torts*, 8th ed. (1992) at 60, cited by Russell J.A. in *Stevenson Estate v. Siewert*, above, note 382, at 533.

388 This passage is quoted with approval in *889267 Ontario Ltd. v. Norfinch Group Inc.* (1998), [1998] O.J. No. 3850, 1998 CarswellOnt 3696 (Gen. Div.). In *Stevenson Estate v. Siewert* (2000), [2001] 2 W.W.R. 517 (Alta. C.A.), additional reasons at [2001] 10 W.W.R. 401 (Alta. C.A.), Russell J.A. cites this passage with reservation. This I believe is due to a misunderstanding of these words. In order to be liable the defendant must act in a positive way, intending to assert dominion over goods. The defendant need not intend that its act will result in denying the true owner's title. Thus when the law firm in this case turned over a bank draft to the wrong party, it was acting in a positive way affecting the dominion over the goods. It knew it was doing this, although it did not know that it was making a mistake. It was appropriately held liable. If on the other hand, the law firm had carelessly left the draft on a desk and it was stolen, it could not be held liable for conversion.

389 [1982] 4 W.W.R. 126 (B.C. S.C.).

390 This finding is somewhat unusual. Unless the evidence shows a deliberate sinking, as opposed to carelessness, or even recklessness, which results in sinking, a conversion ought not to be found.

391 [1962] 1 Q.B. 701 (C.A.).

392 *Ibid.*, at 706.

personalty or realty at the time of the conversion.[393] Although currency cannot generally be converted, money which specifically has been collected and set aside, promissory notes, and cheques can be.[394] Share certificates can be converted.[395] A customer list which was used improperly to obtain business was held to have been converted,[396] as have been accounts receivable.[397] The conversion of artistic creations, knowledge, inventions, and other forms of industrial or intellectual property involves the application of special laws. For example, although knowledge of a secret formula to clean chimneys was held not to be subject to the tort of conversion, this did not rule out other protections which the laws of industrial and intellectual property might offer.[398]

(e) Types of Dealings

The crucial issue in most conversion disputes is whether or not the defendant's dealings with the plaintiff's goods were serious enough to amount to a denial of the plaintiff's possessory rights and hence a conversion. The basic proposition established in early cases[399] is that not every asportation or interference with possession is serious enough to amount to a conversion. As Fleming has stated: "The controlling factor . . . seems to be, not necessarily the defendant's act viewed

---

393 See *Oates v. Cameron* (1850), 7 U.C.Q.B. 228 (C.A.), and *Polson v. Degeer* (1886), 12 O.R. 275 (C.A.), which established that conversion cannot be brought for fixtures. There are, however, many cases allowing conversion for goods which, although normally fixtures, have become chattels. For timber cases, see *McNeill v. Haines* (1889), 17 O.R. 479; *Mann v. English* (1876), 38 U.C.Q.B. 240 (C.A.); *Harshenin v. Bayoff* (1991), 49 C.P.C. (2d) 55 (B.C. S.C.). A crops case is *Duck Lake Feed Processors v. Badowsky* (1983), 26 Sask. R. 46 (Q.B.), varied (1987), 54 Sask. R. 296 (C.A.). There are also cases dealing with dwellings which have been removed from the property. See, e.g., *Reynolds v. Dechman* (1881), 14 N.S.R. 459 (C.A.). See *Kostiuk, Re,* [2002] 8 W.W.R. 457 (B.C. C.A.) for reaffirmation of the point that the tort of conversion does not apply to land.

394 See *Arrow Transfer Co. v. Royal Bank* (1971), 19 D.L.R. (3d) 420 (B.C. C.A.), affirmed (1972), 27 D.L.R. (3d) 81 (S.C.C.); *Eli v. Royal Bank* (1985), 68 B.C.L.R. 353 (S.C.); *Walsh v. Brown* (1868), 18 U.C.C.P. 60 (C.A.); and *373409 Alberta Ltd. (Receiver of) v. Bank of Montreal,* [2001] 7 W.W.R. 638 (Alta. C.A.), leave to appeal allowed (2001), 2001 CarswellAlta 1189, 2001 CarswellAlta 1190 (S.C.C.), reversed (2002), [2003] 2 W.W.R. 1 (S.C.C.). In *Cho Ki Yau Trust (Trustees of) v. Yau Estate* (1999), [1999] O.J. No. 3818, 1999 CarswellOnt 3232 (S.C.J.), it was held that a certificate of deposit is converted where instructions are given to transfer the funds, even if the physical certificate itself is not used to effect the transfer.

395 See, e.g., *Dom. Securities Ltd. v. Glazerman* (1984), 29 C.C.L.T. 194 (Man. C.A.); *Pocklington Foods Inc. v. Alta. (Prov. Treasurer)* (1995), 167 A.R. 300 (Q.B.).

396 *Borden Chem. Co. v. J.G. Beukers Ltd.* (1972), 29 D.L.R. (3d) 37 (B.C. S.C.).

397 *C.I.B.C. v. F.B.D.B.* (1985), 36 Alta. L.R. (2d) 186 (Q.B.).

398 *K.R. Thompson Engr. Ltd. v. Webster* (1980), 31 N.B.R. (2d) 329 (Q.B.). Can "goodwill" be converted? *Brant Avenue Manor Ltd. Partnership v. Transamerica Life Insurance Co. of Canada* (2000), 7 B.L.R. (3d) 94 (Ont. S.C.J.) held yes; *Manina Investments Ltd. v. Regatta Investments Ltd.* (1993), 6 P.P.S.A.C. (2d) 1 (Man. C.A.) held no. In view of the fact that "goodwill" has value, a party who converts it by, for example, transferring it without authority of the owner, ought to be held liable on some basis. Since conversion, however, deals only with property that can be "possessed" it seems to be an inappropriate cause of action for this type of wrongdoing.

399 A leading case in this respect is *Fouldes v. Willoughby* (1841), 151 E.R. 1153.

in isolation, but whether it has *resulted in a substantial interference* with the owner's rights so serious as to warrant a forced sale.''[400] This is a question of fact which depends upon many factors. In his leading article on the subject,[401] Prosser identified the following important factors:

(1) the extent and duration of the exercise of dominion or control;
(2) the intent to assert a right in fact inconsistent with the possessor's rights;
(3) the good faith of the defendant;
(4) the extent and duration of the interference with the right of control;
(5) the harm done to the chattel;
(6) the expense and inconvenience caused.

The temporary detention of a chattel without the intention to exercise dominion over it does not amount to a conversion. In *384238 Ont. Ltd. v. Can.*,[402] for example, the seizure and detention of goods for three days was held not to constitute a dealing with the goods such as would amount to a conversion. It was characterized as merely a ''temporary interference'', which constituted a trespass.[403] In *Dzaman v. Riggs*,[404] the refusal to return a car for a few days was held not to constitute a conversion because the defendant acted without the intention of claiming any interest in it, nor with the intention of keeping it permanently. The detention was held to constitute a detinue for which damages were awarded.[405] In *Robertson v. Stang*,[406] removing the plaintiff's goods from her apartment and placing them in storage did not constitute a conversion since the defendants' purpose in moving them "was not to claim them for their own", but for safety and space concerns. Merely receiving and being in possession of stolen and damaged goods does not amount to conversion, if the party in receipt has not exercised any dominion over them. Thus, in *Regina v. Inland Steel Products*,[407] the defendant scrap metal dealer was not liable for conversion for buying metal signs that had been stolen by the vendors from the city. This was at most a temporary interference that ended when the signs were returned to their owner.

Mere use is not a conversion. In *McDonald v. Stockley*,[408] the mistaken use of a painter's equipment on one occasion by the defendant's employees was said to amount at most to a trivial trespass. If the use is serious, however, demonstrating a dominion over the goods, this is a conversion. In *Can. Orchestraphone Ltd. v. Br. Can. Trust Co.*,[409] the use of sound equipment to carry on the business of a theatre, especially when this use was accompanied by a denial of the plaintiff's ownership and right to possession of the equipment, was regarded as a conversion.

---

400 Fleming, *The Law of Torts*, 9th ed. (1998), at 64.

401 Prosser, ''The Nature of Conversion'' (1957), 42 Cornell L. Rev. 168.

402 (1983), 8 D.L.R. (4th) 676 (Fed. C.A.).

403 Also see *Clow v. Gershman Transport International Ltd.* (2000), 265 A.R. 181 (Q.B.) to the same effect.

404 [1927] 4 D.L.R. 835 (Alta. C.A.).

405 It was significant that the court found that there was a detinue rather than a conversion because the car was destroyed by fire after the detention terminated. Had there been a conversion, the defendant would have been liable for the full value of the car.

406 (1997), 38 C.C.L.T. (2d) 62 (B.C.S.C.).

407 [2007] S.J. No. 595 (Q.B.).

408 (1914), 16 D.L.R. 743 (N.S. C.A.).

409 [1932] 2 W.W.R. 618 (Alta. C.A.)

In *Borden Chemical Co. v. J.G. Beukers Ltd.*,[410] using a list of accounts receivable in order to obtain customers' names and addresses was held to constitute a conversion.[411]

Refusing to return goods without lawful justification after a demand has been made for them is evidence of a conversion. Many conversion actions are determined on the issue of the legitimacy of the refusal, and involve such questions as the availability of a lien, a statutory defence, or some other matter not primarily involved with tort law. Although a demand and refusal may be evidence of conversion, it is not a prerequisite to bringing a successful claim. A refusal to return goods will not be a conversion where the refusal is not based on an intention to convert.[412]

In most cases, the conversion of the plaintiff's goods results directly from the defendant's act. This need not be so, however. In *Iliopoulos v. Gettas*,[413] for example, the defendant committed a conversion when she asked her mother to throw out goods which belonged to the plaintiff.

(f) Remedies

The general rule is that a conversion will result in a "forced sale" requiring the defendant to pay the plaintiff the market value of the goods at the time of the conversion,[414] with the possibility of both consequential and exemplary damages also being awarded.[415] A defendant may return a chattel to its owner after a conversion but prior to an action being instituted and receive credit for its value at the time of restoration, towards any award made to the plaintiff.[416] Where the goods are returned undamaged, the plaintiff is entitled to nominal damages for the technical conversion.[417] Is a plaintiff required to take back chattels which have been converted? According to Fleming, although originally the plaintiff was not bound to accept goods which had been converted, there developed a discretionary

---

410 (1972), 29 D.L.R. (3d) 337 (B.C. S.C.).

411 For an excellent discussion as to when the use of a chattel will amount to a conversion, see *Penfolds Wines Pty. Ltd. v. Elliott* (1946), 74 C.L.R. 204 (Aust. H.C.). See also *Aitken Agencies Ltd. v. Richardson*, [1967] N.Z.L.R. 65 (S.C.), where taking a car for a "joy ride" was held to constitute a conversion. Another example of conversion occurred in *Unisys Canada Inc. v. Imperial Optical Co.* (1998), 43 C.C.L.T. (2d) 286 (Ont. Gen. Div.), affirmed (2000), 49 C.C.L.T. (2d) 237 (Ont. C.A.): vesting in a third party an option to purchase property belonging to the plaintiff.

412 *Dixon v. Spencer* (1951), 4 W.W.R. (N.S.) 222 (B.C. S.C.).

413 (1981), 32 O.R. (2d) 636 (Co. Ct.).

414 See, for example, *Tridont Leasing (Can.) Ltd. v. Saskatoon Market Mall Ltd.*, [1995] 6 W.W.R. 641 at 655 (Sask. C.A.).

415 Where there is no market value, the court has a difficult task in assessing the damages. See *Tom Hopkins Int. Inc. v. Wall & Redekop Realty Ltd.*, [1985] 6 W.W.R. 367 (B.C. C.A.); *Cline v. Don Watt & Assoc. Communications Inc.* (1986), 15 C.C.E.L. 181 (Ont. Dist. Ct.).

416 See *Aitken Agencies Ltd. v. Richardson*, [1967] N.Z.L.R. 65 (S.C.), and *Solloway v. McLaughlin*, [1938] A.C. 247 (P.C.). In *Mutungih v. Bokun* (2006), 40 C.C.L.T. (3d) 313 (Ont. S.C.J.), the defendant actually improved the car before it was returned to its owner. The court conceded that ordinarily the defendant would have been entitled to a fair allowance for the improvements, but due to the facts of this case, no allowance was made. The car had been obtained from a thief in suspicious circumstances and evidence regarding the value of the improvements was unclear.

417 See *MacKenzie v. Scotia Lumber Co.* (1913), 11 D.L.R. 729 (N.S. C.A.).

power in the courts to order that restoration be accepted upon application by the defendant.[418] In *Harbour Equip. Ltd. v. C.N.R.*,[419] this question arose but was not clearly settled. The trial judge stated that although he was prepared to grant an adjournment subject to the consent of all parties at trial, an adjournment would not be granted where there was no evidence regarding the condition of the chattel and where an adjournment could result in considerable delay. The general rule that in conversion the value of the chattel converted is assessed as of the time of the conversion is subject to modification if the value of the chattel has increased from the time of the conversion to the date of trial. A judgment on this issue is *Dom. Securities Ltd. v. Glazerman.*[420] In this decision the Manitoba Court of Appeal, following its earlier decision in *Steiman v. Steiman*,[421] held that the value of goods should be assessed as of the time the plaintiff becomes aware of the loss and reasonably might be expected to replace the goods.[422] This approach, which has not been always followed,[423] raises some difficult questions. First, it raises the possibility that a plaintiff who sues in conversion rather than detinue, when the facts will support either action, will receive different damages for the goods converted than would have been received had the action been framed as a detinue. Since the same wrongful refusal to return is at the gist of both wrongs, this may seem anomalous. Second, it raises problems if the plaintiff was unable to finance a replacement of the converted goods when first becoming aware of the loss.[424] Third, it puts the plaintiff at the risk of having to replace converted goods before being ensured of success in the action or being able to execute on the judgment.[425]

In addition to receiving the value of the converted chattel, the plaintiff may be entitled to additional damages for the loss of use of the chattel,[426] and even for

---

418 Fleming, *The Law of Torts*, 9th ed. (1998), at 80. But see *MacKenzie v. Scotia Lumber Co.* (1913), 11 D.L.R. 729 (N.S. C.A.), where this is described as an "open question."

419 (1976), 25 N.S.R. (2d) 166 (T.D.).

420 (1984), 29 C.C.L.T. 194 (Man. C.A.).

421 (1982), 23 C.C.L.T. 182, leave to appeal to (S.C.C.) granted 52 N.R. 236.

422 This case involved converted shares, whereas *Steiman v. Steiman* involved jewellery.

423 See, e.g., *Asamera Oil Corp. v. Sea Oil & Gen. Corp.*, [1979] 1 S.C.R. 633, and the cases cited therein, which arguably support the position that the plaintiff is entitled to the highest value of the converted goods between the time of conversion and the time of trial. It has been argued that in *Asamera* these observations were *obiter*: See Irvine, "Annotation" (1984), 29 C.C.L.T. 195. For a more recent case, see *Cash v. Georgia Pacific Securities Corp.*, [1990] B.C.J. No. 1315 (B.C. S.C.). In *Stevenson Estate v. Siewert,* [2001] 10 W.W.R. 401 (Alta. C.A.), a bank draft in US funds was converted. The value of the Canadian dollar dropped significantly from the date of the conversion to the date of judgment. It would have cost $116,500 CDN to purchase $100,000 US in 1990 and $149,000 CDN in 2000. The Court of Appeal chose the latter date as the most equitable in this case.

424 See Irvine, *ibid.*, for a discussion of this point.

425 Other cases dealing with this point are: *Grenn v. Brampton Poultry Co.* (1959), 18 D.L.R. (2d) 9, varying 13 D.L.R. (2d) 279, (Ont. C.A.); *Devenish v. Connacher*, [1932] 3 W.W.R. 645 (Alta. C.A.); *Aitken v. Gardiner* (1956), 4 D.L.R. (2d) 119 (Ont. H.C.). *Scobie v. Wing*, [1992] 2 W.W.R. 514 (B.C. C.A.) involved the same issue, but with regard to a negligence claim. The plaintiff's classic car was damaged beyond repair. The car's value rose dramatically between the time of accident and trial, but in that 4 1/2-year period, the plaintiff did not attempt to replace the vehicle. The Court of Appeal held that the plaintiff, not having replaced or ever having tried to replace the car, was entitled only to its value at the time of the accident.

426 See, e.g., *Ford Credit Can. Ltd. v. Russell* (1980), 32 N.B.R. (2d) 612 (C.A.); and *Klewchuk v. Switzer*, [2003] 11 W.W.R. 284 (Alta. C.A.), leave to appeal refused (2004), 2004 CarswellAlta 426 (S.C.C.).

exemplary damages.[427] A bailee whose right to use the bailed object has been interfered with by the defendant's wrongful act can sue for conversion and recover damages for the loss of use of the object even if the wrongdoer has entered into a settlement with the chattel's owner.[428]

18. ACTION ON THE CASE FOR PERMANENT DAMAGE TO REVERSIONARY INTEREST

A person who has given up both legal possession and a right to the immediate possession of chattels is precluded from taking action in trespass, detinue or conversion as long as the right to the possession of the chattels remains suspended. What would happen, however, if during this period of time the chattel over which the person has a reversionary interest were lost or permanently damaged? Is the reversioner required to wait until regaining the right to immediate possession before being allowed to take action against the wrongdoer?

A few cases have recognized a special action on the case for permanent damage to reversionary interest to accommodate this problem. In *Mears v. London & South Western Ry. Co.*,[429] the plaintiff had loaned his barge for a term to another person. Before the term expired, the defendants, through their negligence, seriously damaged the barge. The court held that although an action in conversion was unavailable since the plaintiff did not have the right to the immediate possession of the barge, an action for permanent injury to the barge was available.

This action rarely has been used and thus there are questions concerning its scope. It can be actionable for an intentional or negligent act, which, directly or indirectly, permanently damages the chattel. What constitutes "permanent", as opposed to "temporary", damage or loss is somewhat unclear. It can be hypothesized that where the chattel can be retrieved or restored to its original state prior to the plaintiff regaining the right to the immediate possession of it, the action would not be available. It ought to be restricted to those situations where, due to the seriousness of the damage, the plaintiff's reversionary interest has been permanently affected.

19. REPLEVIN

Replevin is an extraordinary remedy which allows a plaintiff to recover personal property, which allegedly has been taken or detained unlawfully, pending an action to determine the rightful possessor of that property. It is provided for in the provincial Rules of Court which detail the conditions and requirements for a replevin order.[430]

---

427 See, e.g., *Norkan Lodge Co. v. Gillum* (1982), 39 A.R. 597 (N.W.T. S.C.); *Ford Credit Can. Ltd. v. Russell, ibid.*; *Grenn v. Brampton Poultry Co.*, above, note 413.

428 See *Courtenay v. Knutson* (1957), 26 D.L.R. (2d) 768 (B.C. S.C.).

429 (1862), 142 E.R. 1029.

430 Replevin was also an action at common law. See *Littleford v. Loanex Financial Services* (1986), 28 D.L.R. (4th) 613 (Man. C.A.). A useful history of replevin is provided by Twaddle J.A. in *Man. Agricultural Credit Corp. v. Heaman* (1990), 65 Man. R. (2d) 269 (C.A.). Twaddle J.A. emphasizes that the action is limited to claimants who had previous possession of the chattels which they now wish to get back. See Rainaldi, ed., *Remedies in Tort*, Vol. 1, at 4-13, para. 20. The authors note that the common law rules applying to replevin proceedings have been codified in provincial Replevin Acts or in the rules of practice. In *Neill v. Vancouver*

20. TRESPASS TO LAND

(a) Introduction

The tort of trespass to land protects a person's possession of land against wrongful interference. It stems from the writ of trespass *quare clausum fregit* and has the same elements as the other forms of trespass. It involves only direct interferences with the plaintiff's possession of land, is actionable without proof of actual damage, and must be committed either intentionally or negligently in order to be actionable. Once the trespass (i.e., the direct interference with possession) is proven, the defendant has the onus of disproving that it was committed wrongfully.

The action serves several functions. As with the other early actions, it originally ensured that violent disputes would be settled in a peaceable manner, thereby maintaining public order.[431] Later functions, which still remain important today, stem from the tort's primary connection with the laws relating to real property. The action for trespass protects property rights and resolves boundary and title disputes. It can also be used to protect more intangible rights claimed by property owners, such as rights to privacy and the peaceful use of land.

The tort of trespass is now one of several related actions which concern the rights of property owners and occupiers, the principal ones being trespass, nuisance, negligence, and the rule in *Rylands v. Fletcher.* As well, special common law rules and legislation have been developed to regulate the use of water courses, air space, and mines and minerals. Much of this material is outside the scope of this text, although it is important to be aware of the existence of these laws when dealing with disputes related to real property.[432]

(b) Intentional Trespass

(i) Intention

An intentional trespass to land occurs when the defendant acts desiring to interfere with the possession of land, or in circumstances in which this interference was substantially certain to occur. The defendant, of course, need not have known that the land which was being interfered with was, at the time, in the occupation of the plaintiff. The defendant might have acted in good faith, reasonably believing that the interference was justified. Mistake is no defence, however; if an interfer-

---

Police Department (2005), [2005] B.C.J. No. 400, 2005 CarswellBC 437 (S.C. [In Chambers]), Dillon J. noted that in British Columbia, replevin is only an "interim order" for the recovery of property, and that a "final order" must be framed in detinue. In *Richard v. Synak* (2007), 51 C.C.L.T. (3d) 231 (Ont. S.C.J.), G.P. Smith J. noted that in Ontario the remedy for the "recovery of personal property" is provided for in the Courts of Justice Act, R.S.O. 1990, c. C.43, s. 104 and in Rule 44 of the Rules of Civil Procedure. It is limited to the return of property, damages for loss of use, and damages sustained as a result of an interim order requiring security. According to Smith J., damage to the property sustained during the wrongful detainment cannot be compensated in a replevin order.

431 See Fleming, *The Law of Torts*, 9th ed. (1998), at 45.

432 See Ziff, *Principles of Property Law*, 4th ed. (2006), and other texts devoted to property law for comprehensive treatment.

ence occurs as a result of the defendant's voluntary and intentional act, the tort has been made out.[433]

There are many examples of innocent but intentional trespasses in the case law. In *Turner v. Thorne*,[434] for example, parcels mistakenly were delivered to the plaintiff's house and left in his garage. The plaintiff fell over the cartons in the dark and injured himself. The court considered this to have been a trespass, and citing text and case authorities, held that it would be so notwithstanding the innocence of the defendant. Although one might be tempted to describe this trespass as having been ''unintentional'', this would be so only in relation to the defendant's knowledge of wrongdoing. Clearly the trespass was intentional in the legal sense; the defendant was knowingly interfering with the possession of someone. All cases concerning boundary disputes, where two people, in good faith, claim possessory rights over the same piece of land, involve innocent but intentional trespasses, should it turn out that the person who took possession of the land was not legally entitled to do so.[435] Similarly, where an expropriating authority takes possession of a property under the mistaken belief that it had a legal right to do so, an intentional trespass has occurred. As explained by Picard J.A., "a trespass occurs, regardless of consciousness of wrongdoing, if the defendant intends to conduct itself in a certain manner and exercises its volition to do so."[436] Surprisingly, courts occasionally resist the conclusion that innocence does not exonerate a trespassing party.[437] In my opinion, however, this is incorrect. It has been clearly established, and maintained for centuries, that an innocent mistake does not exonerate a trespassing party.[438]

In order to be actionable, trespass to land, like all other torts, must be voluntary. Thus, a defendant who is carried upon the land of the plaintiff cannot be held liable in trespass.[439] Involuntary or accidental trespasses are rare, but they can occur.[440]

---

433 As stated by Rand J. in *East Crest Oil Co. v. R.*, [1945] S.C.R. 191 at 195: ''Trespass does not depend on intention. If I walk upon my neighbour's land, I am a trespasser even though I believe it to be my own . . . .''

434 (1959), 21 D.L.R. (2d) 29 (Ont. H.C.).

435 See, e.g., *Mercer v. Dawe* (1981), 35 Nfld. & P.E.I.R. 352 (Nfld. T.D.); *Wigle v. Vanderkuk* (2005), [2005] O.J. No. 3032, 2005 CarswellOnt 3087 (S.C.J.), additional reasons at (2005), 2005 CarswellOnt 4014 (S.C.J.); and *Sackrider v. Slingerland* (2006), 44 C.C.L.T. (3d) 307 (Ont. S.C.J.).

436 *Costello v. Calgary (City)* (1997), 38 C.C.L.T. (2d) 101 (Alta. C.A.), leave to appeal refused (1998), 212 A.R. 398 (note) (S.C.C.) at 112 [C.C.L.T.].

437 See, e.g., *Henderson v. Volk* (1982), 132 D.L.R. (3d) 690 (Ont. C.A.). The court held that there ''technically'' may have been a trespass when one party mistakenly erected a fence on land subsequently purchased by another party, but it rejected the action for trespass.

438 See, e.g., *Basely v. Clarkson* (1681), 83 E.R. 565.

439 *Smith v. Stone* (1647), 82 E.R. 533.

440 See Trindade, Cane and Lunney, *The Law of Torts in Australia*, 4th ed. (2007), at 138, who cite the case of a defendant who suffered an epileptic fit, falling unconsciously onto the plaintiff's land — *Pub. Tpt. Comm. of N.S.W. v. Perry* (1977), 14 A.L.R. 273 (Aust. H.C.); and the case of defendant who was startled and inadvertently stepped onto the plaintiff's land — *Braithwaite v. South Durham Steel Co.*, [1958] 1 W.L.R. 986.

(ii) Possession of Land

Trespass to land is not concerned with the title or ownership of land, but with the legal possession of it.[441] Although a person who has title to land will be presumed to be in exclusive possession of it and thus entitled to maintain a trespass action,[442] title is not necessary to maintain a trespass action. Possession of land, which entails actual control and the intention to control, gives the possessor property rights which will be protected against those with inferior rights. Even the property rights of wrongdoers will be protected as against other wrongdoers with inferior claims.[443]

Because trespass is an interference with possession, either actual or constructive, a person who is out of possession when the trespass occurs cannot claim in trespass. In *Townsview Properties Ltd. v. Sun Const. & Equip. Co.*,[444] the plaintiffs acquired land which had wrongfully been excavated by the defendant company. The court held that the plaintiffs, after they acquired the land, were not entitled to claim for the prior trespass since "[t]he essence of the action of trespass is a wrongful interference with possession and to succeed the plaintiff must show that he was in possession or in the case of vacant land that he was entitled to enter into possession."[445] If the trespass is a continuing one, the plaintiffs are entitled to claim in trespass once they acquire possessory rights to the land.

The fact that trespass to land involves possessory rights and not proprietorship of land becomes more significant when even those with apparent title fail to succeed in trespass since they have not been in possession of their land. Although title is strong evidence of possession, if contrary evidence can be adduced as to the possessor of the land, the trespass action may fail.[446] As well, where the owner of lands has given up possession temporarily, as in a landlord-tenant situation, there is no right in the owner to maintain an action in trespass. An important contemporary issue concerns the possession by owners of large shopping complexes encompassing private and public areas and the extent to which these owners

---

441 See, however, *Costello v. Calgary (City)* (1995), 23 C.C.L.T. (2d) 125 (Alta. Q.B.), varied (1997), [1998] 1 W.W.R. 222, 38 C.C.L.T. (2d) 101, 152 D.L.R. (4th) 453 (Alta. C.A), leave to appeal refused (1998), 212 A.R. 398 (note) (S.C.C.), with regards to the effect of an expropriation on the right of an owner to sue for trespass. The court held that damages for trespass should begin to flow from the date the City took title of the plaintiff's land as the result of an act of expropriation, which later was declared to be invalid. Rooke J. stated (at 156) that "from that date the Costellos were effectively prevented from exercising the basic rights of ownership and possession. . . ." On the actual facts of the case, however, the plaintiffs only claimed damages for the period commencing shortly before the City physically took over possession of the land. Rookes J. did concede that "[d]amages for trespass normally relate to the taking of possession, not title. . . ."

442 See *Spearwater v. Seaboyer* (1984), 65 N.S.R. (2d) 280 at 284 (T.D.).

443 See, for example, *Jewett v. Bil* (1998), 205 N.B.R. (2d) 300 (Q.B.), affirmed (1999), 210 N.B.R. (2d) 280 (C.A.).

444 (1974), 56 D.L.R. (3d) 330 (Ont. C.A.).

445 *Ibid.*, at 333.

446 See *Patterson v. De Smit*, [1949] 3 D.L.R. 178 (Ont. C.A.). The question of adverse possession is important in this context. This is dealt with fully in texts concerning the law of real property.

have maintained their possessory rights.[447] It does not seem fair that owners of large areas of land which provide recreational and social facilities to the public at large should be permitted to exclude others arbitrarily from coming onto their properties, by using the tort of trespass. Yet the common law of trespass does allow this.[448] This is arguably an instance of tort law failing to accommodate current conditions and failing to reflect contemporary notions of justice.[449]

The general rule that possession of land, even by a wrongdoer without title, is sufficient to maintain an action in trespass, is subject to an exception in the case of Crown land. In the case of Crown land, possession of the land does not give a person a sufficient interest to maintain an action in trepass, unless the person is on the land with the privity or concurrence of the Crown.[450] In all other cases, possession of land gives the possessor the right to maintain an action in trespass. This principle was asserted in *Kastaniuk v. Sarsons*,[451] where it was held:

> It is well settled that trespass to chattels, like trespass to lands, is essentially an injury to possession and not to ownership. As against a wrongdoer, a plaintiff needs to show possession only. Apparently it makes no difference in what manner the plaintiff obtained possession on which he relies. The fact that he has obtained it by his own trespass and has no other title is no defence to his action. A defendant cannot justify his own wrong by invoking the plaintiff's wrong, and he cannot set up against the title of a plaintiff in possession the title of a third person unless he claims under such third person.

Although a person with a right to possession, but without possession, cannot maintain an action in trespass, the doctrine of trespass by relation will allow that person to maintain an action in trespass upon entering into possession, even in relation to prior interferences.[452]

---

447 There are several shopping centre cases. See *Harrison v. Carswell*, [1975] 6 W.W.R. 673 (S.C.C.); *Peters v. R.* (1971), 17 D.L.R. (3d) 128, affirming 16 D.L.R. (3d) 143 (S.C.C.); *Wildwood Mall Ltd. v. Stevens*, [1980] 2 W.W.R. 638 (Sask. Q.B.); and *Grosvenor Park Shopping Centre Ltd. v. Waloshin* (1964), 49 W.W.R. 237. The former two cases maintained the rights of shopping centre owners to sue in trespass; the latter two denied these rights. Although the cases have been distinguished on the basis that the former two cases involved provincial statutes, and the latter two cases the common law, this is a weak distinction. The essence of trespass is the same in both instances and involves the same issue: was the complainant in exclusive possession of the land in question? *Harrison v. Carswell* was affirmed in *281856 B.C. Ltd. v. Kamloops Revelstoke Okanagan Bldg. Trades Union* (1986), 37 C.C.L.T. 262 (B.C. C.A.).

448 See *Russo v. Ont. Jockey Club* (1987), 43 C.C.L.T. 1 (Ont. H.C.). The race track owners were allowed to use the common law of trespass, and the Trespass to Property Act, R.S.O. 1980, c. 511, to prevent a successful bettor from coming into their race tracks. The court upheld the landowner's "absolute right to exclude persons" without regard to the principles of natural justice.

449 See Lisa Loader, "Trespass To Property: Shopping Centres" (1992), 8 Journal of Law and Social Policy 254. In her article, the author discusses the importance of shopping centres to contemporary communal life, and the need for the law to protect public access to them. She discusses the approaches taken in both Canadian and American cases to this concern.

450 See *Boutin v. Boutin* (1985), 23 D.L.R. (4th) 286 (Sask. Q.B.); *Marchischuk v. Lee*, [1954] 2 D.L.R. 484 (Man. Co. Ct.); *Georgian Cottagers' Assn. v. Flos (Twp.)* (1962), 32 D.L.R. (2d) 547 (Ont. H.C.). See, however, *Logan v. Levy* (1975), 20 N.S.R. (2d) 500, 27 A.P.R. 500 (T.D.).

451 [1935] 2 W.W.R. 415 at 417-18 (Alta. Dist. Ct.).

452 See Magnet, "Intentional Interference with Land", in Klar, ed., *Studies in Canadian Tort Law* (1977), Chapter 10 at 304-05, and the cases cited therein.

The types of acts which are sufficient to establish possession of land vary. The Supreme Court of Canada, in *Bentley v. Peppard*,[453] laid down certain fundamental propositions which still remain valid. An owner of land, and similarly a tenant, is presumed to possess all of his or her land. A person who possesses without title and without right legally possesses the ground "which he actually occupies, cultivates and encloses." A person who possesses "under colour of title" constructively possesses the entire area. In *Legere v. Caissie*,[454] the New Brunswick Court of Appeal adopted the following definition of possession:

> Actual possession is a question of fact: it consists of two elements, the intention to possess the land and the exercise of control over land to the exclusion of other persons. The extent of the control which should be exercised in order to constitute possession varies with the nature of the land; possession means possession of that character of which the land is capable.
>
> Any form of possession, so long as it is clear and exclusive and exercised with the intention to possess, is sufficient to support an action of trespass against a wrong-doer. A mere trespasser cannot, however, by the very act of trespass immediately and without acquiescence give himself possession.

In *Shea v. Noseworthy*,[455] it was held that in the case of vacant and unenclosed land which is not capable of cultivation, the "slightest amount of possession is sufficient to entitle the person who is in possession to recover against a trespasser."[456]

(iii) Types of Interferences

In order to be actionable as a trespass, the interference with possession must be direct, positive, and physical.[457] It need not result in damage. In *Boyle v. Rogers*[458] it was stated:

> Under our law every invasion of private property, be it ever so minute, is a trespass. No man can set his foot upon the ground of another without license but he is liable to an action though the damage be nothing; which is proved by every pleading in trespass where the defendant is called upon to answer for bruising the grass and even treading upon soil.

---

453 (1903), 33 S.C.R. 444.

454 (1958), 15 D.L.R. (2d) 424 at 434, citing 33 Hals. (2d) at 11-13.

455 (1975), 25 Nfld. & P.E.I.R. 20 at 34 (Nfld. T.D.).

456 An interesting case is *Hickey v. Walsh* (1997), [1997] N.J. No. 167, 1997 CarswellNfld 112 (T.D.). The plaintiff, although not having "possessory" title to land, occupied and used it over a number of years for different purposes. He stored lumber on it, parked a vehicle on it, extended a deck onto it, planted trees and grass on it and so on. The court held that this constituted sufficient acts of possession to support a trespass action. The action failed, however, based on lack of evidence that the defendant had actually trespassed on this portion of the land or was intending to do so in the future. Although the defendant had trespassed on other disputed land, the plaintiff was unable to establish that he had sufficiently possessed it to allow this part of his trespass action to succeed.

457 See, however, the discussion regarding an invalid expropriation constituting a trespass, even where there has not been a physical interference with the plaintiff's possession, in *Costello v. Calgary (City)* (1995), 23 C.C.L.T. (2d) 125 (Alta. Q.B.), varied (1997), [1998] 1 W.W.R. 222, 38 C.C.L.T. (2d) 101, 152 D.L.R. (4th) 453 (Alta. C.A), leave to appeal refused (1998), 212 A.R. 398 (note) (S.C.C.).

458 [1921] 2 W.W.R. 704 at 706, affirmed [1922] 1 W.W.R. 206 (Man. C.A.).

It has been held that a person in occupation of land "is entitled to refuse permission to enter upon his property for any purpose."[459] There need not be any accommodation, even if this will cause others great costs or inconvenience.[460]

The directness requirement of trespass to land occasionally causes difficulty. In *Mann v. Saulnier*,[461] the defendant's fence, which had originally been built flush with the boundary line of certain land, subsequently encroached a few inches over the adjoining land as a result of accumulation of frost and snow. Did the intruding fence constitute a trespass? The Court of Appeal, relying upon both text and case authorities, held that a trespass to land involved only direct, as opposed to consequential injuries, and that this encroachment, being consequential, at most constituted a nuisance. Analogies were drawn to allowing stones from a ruinous chimney to fall upon premises, or boughs and roots of trees to encroach a neighbour's land.[462] In *Bridges Bros. Ltd. v. Forest Protection Ltd.*,[463] the defendant sprayed insecticide into the air over its forests. The spray drifted to the plaintiff's blueberry fields, killing a number of bees necessary to pollinate the fruit. Was this a trespass? The court, relying on *Mann v. Saulnier*, held that trespass involves direct rather than consequential injuries, and that the injury here, i.e., the spray's effect on pollination, was a consequential injury. One also may refer to *Southport Corp. v. Esso Petroleum Co.*,[464] where oil jettisoned by the defendant into the

---

459 *Austin v. Rescon Const. (1984) Ltd.* (1989), 57 D.L.R. (4th) 591 at 593 (B.C. C.A.).

460 This point was reaffirmed by the B.C. Court of Appeal in *Webb v. Attewell* (1993), 18 C.C.L.T. (2d) 299, additional reasons at (1994), 100 B.C.L.R. (2d) 135 (C.A.). Southin J.A. stated at 18 C.C.L.T. (2d) 322:

> It is also important, and I think requires to be emphasized, that a landowner's right to refuse entry upon his land to a neighbour is absolute and it is no part of a court's function to penalize a refusing landowner for what the court perceives to be unneighbourly behaviour.

The case concerned a defendant who encroached upon the plaintiff's land to facilitate the construction of his new home.

461 (1959), 19 D.L.R. (2d) 130 (N.B. C.A.).

462 See, for example, *Anderson v. Skender* (1993), 17 C.C.L.T. (2d) 160 (B.C. C.A.), varied on reconsideration (1993), 36 B.C.A.C. 79 (C.A.), leave to appeal to S.C.C. refused [1994] 2 W.W.R. lxiv (note) (S.C.C.). The court noted that "border trees" do not trespass; rather it is the party who goes upon the neighbouring land to cut down boughs from these trees who is committing the trespass. In *Bellini Custom Cabinetry Ltd. v. Delight Textiles Ltd.* (2007), 47 C.C.L.T. (3d) 165 (Ont. C.A.), leave to appeal refused (2007) 2007 CarswellOnt 7853 (S.C.C.), affirming (2005), 34 R.P.R. (4th) 93 (Ont. C.A.), the plaintiff sought an injunction for the removal of an encroaching wall. The wall, when originally built by the defendant's predecessor in title, encroached on the land owned by the plaintiff's predecessor in title. A settlement had been entered into by those former owners allowing the encroachment to remain as long as no further encroachment occurred. There was further encroachment leading to the present action. The trial judge held that the initial encroachment was a trespass since the agreement had been breached. The trial judge also held that the further encroachment was a trespass since it was caused by actions of the defendant which put added pressure on the wall. The Court of Appeal held that since the initial encroachment was a trespass, it was unnecessary to decide whether the subsequent encroachment was direct or indirect, and hence constituted a trespass or a nuisance.

463 (1976), 72 D.L.R. (3d) 335 (N.B.Q.B.).

464 [1954] 2 Q.B. 182, reversed on other grounds [1955] 3 All E.R. 864 (H.L.) (the case was determined on the issue of negligence; Lord Tucker agreed that a trespass action would have failed for a lack of directness).

water was carried by the tide to the plaintiff's foreshore. Lord Denning denied this was a trespass, based on the lack of directness. An argument can be made, however, that the interferences in these cases were set in motion by the defendants, assisted only by natural and inevitable forces, and ought to have been treated as sufficiently direct to constitute a trespass.[465] If the results were unexpected, or could not reasonably have been foreseen, this would defeat the claim, not, however, because the injury was not direct, but because it was neither intentional nor negligent.[466]

Trespass involves physical interferences with possession. This can arise as a result of the unauthorized presence of the defendant on the plaintiff's land, or of an object placed or left on the land by the defendant. As long as the object remains on the plaintiff's land without permission, the trespass continues.[467] If a trespass is deemed to be a continuing one, this will allow the plaintiff to sue without regard

---

465 Where a person throws a stone into the sky over the plaintiff's land, and it comes down on the plaintiff's land, one would not deny that a trespass has been committed even though the force of gravity was an important factor in producing the result. Similarly, where one pours oil onto water, sprays a chemical into the air or points a rain spout in the direction of a neighbour's property, and waits for natural forces to produce an invasion of another's land, the results ought to be treated as sufficiently direct. See, however, *Executel Hotel Corp. v. E.B. Eddy Forest Products Ltd.*, [1988] O.J. No. 1905 (Ont. H.C.). The court held that airborne emissions of wood chips and particles from the defendant's pulp and paper mill which settled on the plaintiff's adjoining hotel property did not constitute a trespass, since there was no ''intentional direct interference with the plaintiff's property''. The directness issue also arose in *Hoffman v. Monsanto Canada Inc.* (2005), [2005] S.J. No. 304, 2005 CarswellSask 311 (Q.B.), leave to appeal allowed (2005), 2005 CarswellSask 572 (C.A. [In Chambers]), affirmed [2007] 6 W.W.R. 387 (Sask. C.A.), leave to appeal refused (2007), 2007 CarswellSask 725 (S.C.C.). The action was brought by organic farmers against two defendants who developed and marketed genetically modified seeds. The seeds were planted by some farmers, and made their way into the neighbouring fields of organic farmers. One of the actions brought was trespass. Was the invasion a "direct" interference of the plaintiffs' fields brought about by the defendants? G.A. Smith J. held that even if "the more liberalized requirement for directness" that is suggested here is accepted, it would not have been satisfied in this case. Much more than "natural and inevitable forces" intervened between the marketing of the seeds and their arrival on the plaintiffs' land in this case. The invasion of the seeds was not sufficiently direct to constitute a trespass on the part of those who developed and marketed these seeds. The Court of Appeal agreed with Smith J.'s position.

466 See *Engemoen Hldg. Ltd. v. 100 Mile House*, [1985] 3 W.W.R. 47 (B.C. S.C.), where a break in a water pipe which ran beneath the plaintiff's land caused flooding. The court stated that this was a trespass, without considering the issue of directness. See, however, *Heddinger v. Calgary (City)* (1992), 2 Alta. L.R. (3d) 224 (Q.B.). The court held that the escape of flood water from a ditch is not a trespass, since it is not direct. R.P. Fraser J. was aware of the decision in *Engemoen Hldg. Ltd.* but did not follow it.

467 In *Townsview Properties Ltd. v. Sun Const. & Equip. Co.* (1974), 56 D.L.R. (3d) 330 (Ont. C.A.), the existence of an excavation on the plaintiff's land which previously had been dug by the defendant was held to constitute a continuing trespass. See also *Johnson v. B.C. Hydro & Power Authority* (1981), 16 C.C.L.T. 10 (B.C. S.C.), where hydro transmission lines erected on the plaintiff's land constituted a continuing trespass, and *Austin v. Rescon Const. (1984) Ltd.* (1989), 57 D.L.R. (4th) 591 (B.C. C.A.), where underground rods were considered to be a continuing trespass. But see *Stang v. Kimberley*, [1977] 6 W.W.R. 372 (B.C. Co. Ct.), where a sewer line built across the plaintiff's land without the plaintiff's consent was held not to be of a ''continuing nature.'' The act of trespass was held to be the entering and laying of the line, ''a single act done and over with.'' In the same vein, see *Cameron Invt. & Securities Co. v. Victoria (City)*, [1920] 3 W.W.R. 1043 (B.C. S.C.).

to the limitation period applicable to a single act of trespass.[468] Although a trespass generally results from the unauthorized presence of the defendant on the plaintiff's land, it can also arise when a person, who is authorized to be on the land for one purpose, enters for another unauthorized purpose. Thus a shoplifter or "an individual coming onto property for the purposes of committing theft is engaged in an unauthorised use of land" and hence commits a trespass.[469] In a similar vein, a trespass occurs if a person, who is on land lawfully, refuses to leave once asked to do so.[470]

Non-physical interferences such as vibrations,[471] noise, fumes and odours will not constitute trespasses, although they might amount to actionable nuisances. A trespass also involves a positive act of interference. Therefore, merely allowing a rotten cedar tree to fall upon a neigbour's house will not constitute a trespass.[472] If, however, it was the defendant's initial act which permitted the interference to occur, this will be sufficient.[473]

A person entering land under an authority given by law, who subsequently abuses that authority, will be deemed to be a trespasser *ab initio*.[474]

(iv) ''Land''

According to Blackstone's *Commentaries on the Laws of England*, ''the word 'land' includes not only the face of the earth, but everything under it, or over it.''[475] The issue concerning the true scope of a plaintiff's possession of land occasionally arises in the case law, especially in so far as the question of air space is concerned.[476] The leading Canadian case on this matter, *Lacroix v. R.*,[477] established that Blackstone's definition of land cannot be taken too literally. The case involved the allegation that the defendant had established a flightway over the

468 See *Johnson v. B.C. Hydro & Power Authority* (1981), 16 C.C.L.T. 10 (B.C. S.C.) and more recently *Williams v. Mulgrave (Town)* (2000), 48 C.C.L.T. (2d) 220 (N.S. C.A.).

469 See *Hudson's Bay Co. v. White* (1997), 32 C.C.L.T. (2d) 163 (Gen. Div.), varied (1998), 1 C.P.C. (5th) 333 (Div. Ct.) at 169 [C.C.L.T.].

470 See, for example, *Cottreau v. Rodgerson* (1965), 53 D.L.R. (2d) 549 (N.S.); *Chopra v. T. Eaton Co.* (1999), 70 Alta. L.R. (3d) 90 (Q.B.).

471 *Phillips v. California Standard Co.* (1960), 31 W.W.R. 331 (Alta. T.D.).

472 *Reed v. Smith* (1914), 6 W.W.R. 794 (B.C. C.A.). However, there may be liability under nuisance. See Chapter 18.

473 See, e.g., *Marchischuk v. Lee*, [1954] 2 D.L.R. 484 (Man. Co. Ct.) — defendant liable for trespass when he widened and deepened a natural cut in a ridge, thereby increasing the flow of water onto lower-lying land.

474 *Delta Hotels Ltd. v. Magrum* (1975), 59 D.L.R. (3d) 126 (B.C. S.C.). In *Berscheid v. Ensign* (1999), [1999] B.C.J. No. 1172, 1999 CarswellBC 1111 (S.C.), the court notes that the doctrine applies to positive, wrongful acts and only "when the abuse triggering the trespass is related to and takes away the entire reason for the entry. If the abuse is unrelated to some legitimate and justified reason for the entry" it will not be a trespass *ab initio*.

475 Blackstone, *Commentaries on the Laws of England*, 1st ed., vol. 2, at 16-19, cited by Trindade, Cane and Lunney, *The Law of Torts in Australia*, 4th ed. (2007), at 132.

476 The trespass action can also arise with reference to interferences which occur under the surface of land. See, for example, *Epstein v. Cressey Development Corp.* (1992), 89 D.L.R. (4th) 32 (B.C. C.A.), where the unauthorized insertion of anchor rods into the plaintiff's subsoil constituted a trespass. Also see *Lim v. Titov* (1997), [1998] 5 W.W.R. 495 (Alta. Q.B.), where components of a retaining wall both above and below ground constituted a trespass to land.

477 [1954] 4 D.L.R. 470 (Ex. Ct.).

plaintiff's land. The court, after referring to French civil law, the common law,[478] and American law, concluded that:

> the owner of land has a limited right in the air space over his property; it is limited by what he can possess or occupy for the use and enjoyment of his land. By putting up buildings or other constructions the owner does not take possession of the air but unites or incorporates something to the surface of his land. This which is annexed or incorporated to his land becomes part and parcel of the property.[479]

The plaintiff's claim that the establishment of a flightway over his land was an interference with his property rights was rejected on the basis that the defendant ''could not expropriate that which is not susceptible of possession.''[480]

Subsequent Canadian cases have recognized limited rights over air space. Firing a gun over a farmer's land was deemed to constitute a trespass to the land.[481] As well, when the boom of a sky crane swung over the plaintiff's land, it was considered to be a trespass.[482] The Alberta Court of Appeal in *Didow v. Alta. Power Ltd.*,[483] held that the wires and cross arms of power line poles, which intruded into the plaintiff's air space, constituted a trespass. In a judgment which extensively reviewed the jurisprudence, Haddad J.A. held that a land owner is entitled to freedom from ''permanent structures which in any way impinge upon the actual or potential use and enjoyment of the land.''[484] The court distinguished between intrusions of a permanent nature and transient invasions into the air space of another which are not likely to interfere with the land owner. As well, Haddad J.A. stated that cases of ''encroachment'', for example, where branches of trees grow over a person's land, should be dealt with as nuisance cases and not trespass. Although not identified by His Lordship, it is suggested that the difference between natural encroachments and physical intrusions, the former constituting nuisance and the latter trespass, is explained by the directness requirement of the trespass action.[485]

(v) Remedies

The remedies for trespass to land include nominal, compensatory and punitive damages.[486] As well, in appropriate cases injunctions may be ordered.[487] One also

---

478 The court was assisted greatly by J.E. Richardson, ''Private Property Rights in the Air Space at Common Law'' (1953), 31 Can. Bar Rev. 117.

479 [1954] 4 D.L.R. 470 at 476.

480 *Ibid.*

481 *Dahlberg v. Naydiuk* (1970), 10 D.L.R. (3d) 319 (Man. C.A.).

482 *Lewvest Ltd. v. Scotia Towers Ltd.* (1981), 126 D.L.R. (3d) 239 (Nfld. T.D.). For a comment see Prichard, 19 R.P.R. 193.

483 [1988] 5 W.W.R. 606 (Alta. C.A.), reversing (1986), 37 C.C.L.T. 90 (Alta. Q.B.), leave to appeal to S.C.C. refused 99 N.R. 398n. For a case comment on the trial judgment, see Irvine, ''Some Thoughts on Trespass to Airspace'', 37 C.C.L.T. 99.

484 [1988] 5 W.W.R. 606 at 616.

485 Haddad J.A. referred to the case *Lewvest Ltd. v. Scotia Towers Ltd.* above, note 482, where the court held that an encroaching crane constituted a trespass. Haddad J.A. thought that this should be a nuisance, since it was an ''encroachment'' case. Haddad J.A.'s opinion that a transient interference, such as a swinging crane, should be dealt with as a nuisance, and not a trespass, was adopted by McKeown J. in *Kingsbridge Development Inc. v. Hanson Needler Corp.* (1990), 72 O.R. (2d) 159 (H.C.). In my opinion, as long as an encroachment was directly caused by the defendant, a trespass action should lie, even if that encroachment was transient.

486 For a thorough review of the principles of damage assessment in trespass cases involving an

must have note to various provincial enactments dealing with the issue of trespass and providing for fines or other sanctions for infractions.[488]

(c) Negligent Trespass

Despite the lack of authority, it can be assumed that Canadian law would recognize a trespass to land committed negligently.[489]

---

invalid expropriation, see Picard J.A. in *Costello v. Calgary (City)* (1997), 38 C.C.L.T. (2d) 101 (Alta. C.A.), leave to appeal refused (1998), 212 A.R. 398 (note) (S.C.C.). The issue as to the appropriate measure of damages in cases involving the unauthorized removal of trees arose in *Shewish v. MacMillan Bloedel*, [1991] 1 W.W.R. 27 (B.C. C.A.). The court held that the degree of the defendant's culpability is a relevant factor. Where the trespass and conversion are deliberate, the ''severe'' rule applies. That is, the defendant cannot be recompensed for its expenses in severing the trees, although it can be for the expenses in bringing the product to market. Where the act is innocent, and perhaps even negligent, the ''mild'' rule applies. That is, the defendant is entitled to all of its expenses. See also *Bawa v. Noton*, [1994] B.C.J. No. 1703. An excellent discussion of the law relating to the rights and obligations of land-owners with respect to trees growing on the border of the properties is found in *Koenig v. Goebel*, [1998] 6 W.W.R. 56 (Sask. Q.B.). Punitive damages have frequently been awarded in trespass cases. See, e.g., *Carr-Harris v. Schacter*, [1956] O.R. 994 (H.C.); *Nantel v. Parisien* (1981), 18 C.C.L.T. 79 (Ont. H.C.); *Sulisz v. Flin Flon* (1979), 9 C.C.L.T. 89 (Man. Q.B.); *Pretu v. Donald Tidey Co.* (1965), 53 D.L.R. (2d) 509n (Ont. C.A.); *Austin v. Rescon Const. (1984) Ltd.* (1987), 45 D.L.R. (4th) 559 (B.C. S.C.), varied (1989), 57 D.L.R. (4th) 591 (B.C. C.A.); *Epstein v. Cressey Development Corp.* (1992), 89 D.L.R. (4th) 32 (B.C. C.A.); *Craig v. North Shore Heli Logging Ltd.* (1997), 36 C.C.L.T. (2d) 128 (B.C. S.C.); and *Thee v. Martin* (1998), 41 C.C.L.T. (2d) 86 (B.C. S.C.). In *Craig*, the plaintiff was personally held liable along with his corporation.

487 See, e.g., *Lewvest Ltd. v. Scotia Towers* (1981), 126 D.L.R. (3d) 239 (Nfld. T.D.).

488 See, e.g., the Trespass to Property Act, R.S.O. 1990, c. T-21, s. 12(1), which, in addition to a fine, allows an award of compensation, not exceeding $1,000, to be paid to the person who suffered damage as a result of the trespass. An interesting case involving this legislation is *Davidson v. Toronto Blue Jays Baseball Ltd.* (1999), 170 D.L.R. (4th) 559 (Ont. Gen. Div.). The case concerned the applicability of the legislation to ticket holders at baseball games and other spectacles, who refuse to show their ticket upon demand of the management. It also has been held that legislation regulating hunting does not alter the land owner's common law rights to sue in trespass. See *Gilbert v. Butler* (1986), 29 D.L.R. (4th) 706 (N.B. C.A.).

489 *Bell Can. v. Bannermount* (1973), 35 D.L.R. (3d) 367 (Ont. C.A.), and *Bell Can. v. COPE (Sarnia) Ltd.* (1980), 11 C.C.L.T. 170, affirmed (1981), 15 C.C.L.T. 190 (Ont. C.A.), seem to confirm this, although they deal with trespass to chattels. In *Shewish v. MacMillan Bloedel Ltd.*, [1991] 1 W.W.R. 27 (B.C. C.A.), the defendant company mistakenly logged timber growing on the plaintiff's land. The Court of Appeal described this as a ''negligent trespass.'' It is clear, however, that according to strict legal terminology, the actual trespass in this case, i.e., the logging, was intentional. The negligence related to the knowledge of wrongdoing, which is not an essential element of the intentional torts. I would voice the same objection to Hamilton J.A.'s statement *F. (R.D.) (Litigation Guardian of) v. Co-operators General Insurance Co.* (2004), 246 D.L.R. (4th) 461 (Man. C.A.), at 474 that an interference with land "can be negligent in the sense that the individual is unaware that he is trespassing". This, in my view, would constitute an intentional, though mistaken, trespass. See discussion above. More relevant facts are found in *Manitoba Hydro v. Minsky* (1998), 130 Man. R. (2d) 274 (Q.B.). A front-end loader hit the plaintiff's transformer, which was hidden under snow. The court held that the operator of the loader was not negligent and that the defendant had no reason to suspect the transformer's presence. Thus the trespass was neither intentionally nor negligently committed. Driving one's car carelessly resulting in the car swerving onto the plaintiff's land would be a negligent trespass, for example.

21. REMOTENESS OF DAMAGE

Having found the defendant liable for an intentional tort, the court must consider the extent of the defendant's responsibility. Is a defendant who commits an intentional tort liable for all of the injurious consequences which flow from this act, or is the liability limited?

As we shall later discuss,[490] the common law has devoted considerable attention to determining the extent of liability for those found liable in negligence. Curiously, however, very little attention has been paid to this problem in the area of the intentional torts. The same problems of remoteness which arise in negligence cases can arise with the intentional torts and that some rules to limit defendants' liability are necessary.

It has been held that the ''reasonable foreseeability'' test applied to remoteness questions in negligence actions ''ought not to be imported into the field of intentional torts.''[491] The rationale for this approach is that conduct which is morally reprehensible, as involving acts of deliberate and intentional violence, ought to result in the actor's liability, even for unintended and unforeseeable consequences, rather than requiring the innocent victim to shoulder these losses.[492]

While one can agree that the extent of the defendant's culpability ought to be a factor in determining the extent of that person's liability, it is still necessary that a clear test of remoteness be formulated for the intentional torts. It is one thing, as in *Bettel v. Yim*,[493] to concede that a defendant who batters another ought to be responsible even if the physical injuries caused in that battery are more serious than intended.[494] However, the problem as to how far liability should extend still must be met, especially where unforeseeable events exacerbate injuries suffered

490 Chapter 12.

491 *Bettel v. Yim* (1978), 5 C.C.L.T. 66 at 82-83 (Ont. Co. Ct.).

492 Note, however, that all intentional torts do not involve morally reprehensible behaviour. A doctor is liable for an intentional battery where a patient is treated without consent, despite the best of intentions. Yet, in *Allan v. New Mount Sinai Hosp.* (1980), 109 D.L.R. (3d) 634 (Ont. H.C.), Linden J. applied the *Bettel v. Yim* approach to this situation.

493 Above, note 491.

494 This point was reaffirmed by Iacobucci J. in *Sansalone v. Wawanesa Mutual Insurance Co.* (2000), (*sub nom. Non-Marine Underwriters, Lloyd's of London v. Scalera*) 185 D.L.R. (4th) 1 (S.C.C.) at 41: "...if a tort is intended, it will not matter that the result was more harmful than the actor should, or even could have foreseen."

The remoteness point was not in issue in this case, however, so where to draw the line in intentional torts was not clarified. Also see *Predovich v. Armstrong* (1997), 74 C.P.R. (3d) 351 (Ont. Gen. Div.), additional reasons at (1997), 1997 CarswellOnt 3185 (Gen. Div.), where the same point is made with reference to conversion. In *Aspden v. Maniaci* (2005), [2005] O.J. No. 969, 2005 CarswellOnt 974 (S.C.J.), the plaintiff was arrested and taken to the police station. While her hands were cuffed behind her, she apparently attempted to kick a police officer. She lost her balance, fell and injured herself. Although the court maintained her action for false imprisonment and arrest, it disallowed damages for the injury resulting from the fall. The trial judge stated that the injury did not flow directly from the confinement, utilizing the definition of "directness" provided above.

in the original battery.[495] As stated by McMullin J. in *Mayfair Ltd. v. Pears*,[496] "there are dangers in adopting an absolute rule that an intentional trespasser should be liable for all the consequences of his acts." As are all remoteness questions, it is a matter of judicial and social policy as to where the line between a defendant's wrongdoing and the consequent damages ought to be drawn.

22. PUNITIVE DAMAGES

Although punitive damages[497] can be awarded in any type of tort action,[498] because of their purpose they frequently are awarded in cases involving the intentional torts.

---

495 This will be explored in Chapter 12, within the context of negligence. It is probable that the approaches discussed there would be applied even in the intentional torts. See *Mayfair Ltd. v. Pears*, [1987] 1 N.Z.L.R. 459 (C.A.). A defendant who trespassed by leaving his car in the plaintiff's car park was not liable for a fire subsequently caused by his car. The foreseeability test of remoteness was applied at trial, and the judgment was upheld on appeal, although the reasons of the judges vary. See, re the trial judgment: Todd, "Case and Comment", [1986] N.Z.L.J. 141. See also Williams, "The Risk Principle" (1961), 77 L.Q.R. 179.

496 [1987] 1 N.Z.L.R. 459 at 464.

497 Otherwise known as exemplary damages. One must distinguish punitive or exemplary damages from "aggravated" damages. The latter are awarded in order to compensate victims for injuries which have been aggravated by a defendant's outrageous conduct.

498 An important Supreme Court of Canada judgment on punitive damages is *Whiten v. Pilot Insurance Co.* (2002), 209 D.L.R. (4th) 257 (S.C.C.). The case involved a bad faith claim against an insurance company. The jury awarded $1 million against an insurer who had resisted the payment of a fire insurance claim, alleging arson committed by the insured. The Ontario Court of Appeal reduced the award to $100,000 but the Supreme Court restored the jury's award. In *Whiten*, Binnie J., while recognizing that punitive damages "will largely be restricted to intentional torts or breach of fiduciary duty," affirmed that they can be awarded in contract, and even in negligence or nuisance. The Supreme Court reaffirmed its view that punitive damages can be awarded in bad faith insurance claims in *Fidler v. Sun Life Assurance Co. of Canada*, 2006 SCC 30 (S.C.C.), although in this case an award of punitive damages made by the Court of Appeal was set aside by the Supreme Court. Punitive damages have been awarded in defamation cases, for the business torts, such as deceit or intimidation, and for nuisance. They even have been awarded in the exceptional negligence case; see, e.g., *Robitaille v. Vancouver Hockey Club Ltd.* (1979), 19 B.C.L.R. 158 (S.C.), varied (1981), 30 B.C.L.R. 286 (C.A.); *Vlchek v. Koshel* (1988), 44 C.C.L.T. 314 (B.C. S.C.), affirmed (1988), 52 D.L.R. (4th) 371n (B.C. C.A.); and *Coughlin v. Kuntz* (1987), 42 C.C.L.T. 142 (B.C. S.C.), affirmed [1990] 2 W.W.R. 737 (B.C. C.A.). See, however, *C.N.R. Co. v. di Domenicantonio* (1988), 49 D.LR. (4th) 342 (N.B. C.A.), where it was stated that punitive damages should not be awarded in negligence cases except in the most extreme circumstances. Also see *McBeth v. Boldt* (1998), 164 D.L.R. (4th) 247 (B.C. C.A.), where the Court of Appeal reversed a jury's award of punitive damages against a doctor for negligent malpractice. The issue was carefully canvassed in *McIntyre v. Grigg* (2006), 274 D.L.R. (4th) 28 (Ont. C.A.). The case involved an automobile accident caused by a drunk driver. The majority of the Court of Appeal allowed the jury's award of punitive damages, although it reduced the size of the award. There was one dissent. Both judgments provide a good review of the jurisprudence and principles in issue. In "Innkeeper's Liability for Punitive Damages" (1998), 20 Adv. Q. 1, Professor Berryman reviews the case law with respect to the applicability of punitive damages in negligence cases, and whether punitive damages can be awarded against employers who are vicariously liable for the torts of their employees, among other matters. For a review of the topic, see the Ontario Law Reform Commission, *Report on Exemplary Damages* (1991). For a comparative law symposium on punitive damages, and the basis upon which they are awarded in different jurisdictions see (1995), 17 Loyola of Los Angeles International and

The principal use of punitive damages in Canadian tort law has been to punish defendants for outrageous, antisocial, or illegal behaviour.[499] Although the House of Lords in *Rookes v. Barnard*,[500] limited the circumstances under which punitive damages could be awarded to two situations,[501] Canadian law has rejected this approach.[502] The punishment of outrageous conduct not only allows the court to express society's condemnation of such behaviour, but may serve to deter the specific wrongdoer and others from engaging in this conduct in the future.[503]

A second and less frequently employed use of punitive damages is to prevent a tortfeasor from benefitting from the wrong. Where, for example, a developer who wished to build on land but was prevented from doing so due to the presence of the plaintiff's boutique simply went ahead and demolished the boutique, punitive damages were awarded.[504] If the court had restricted the damage award to reasonable and fair compensation for the plaintiff's boutique, it is clear that the developer would have achieved through its flagrant wrong what it had wanted all along, i.e. the removal of the plaintiff's boutique.[505]

Comparative Law Journal 765. For a comparative examination of the common and civil law approaches, see S. Beaulac, "A Comparative Look At Punitive Damages In Canada" (2002), 17 S.C.L.R. (2d) 351.

499 In *Vorvis v. I.C.B.C.* (1989), 58 D.L.R. (4th) 193 at 201 (S.C.C.), McIntyre J. stated:

> Punitive damages, as the name would indicate, are designed to punish. In this, they constitute an exception to the general common law rule that damages are designed to compensate the injured, not the punish the wrongdoer.

In Whiten, Binnie J. referred to these objectives of punitive damages: punishment, which includes "retribution and denunciation", and deterrence.

500 [1964] All E.R. 367.

501 The first is where there was oppressive, arbitrary or unconstitutional action by servants or governments. The second is where the defendant's conduct was calculated to make a profit which may exceed the compensation payable to the plaintiff. The decision was reaffirmed in *Cassell & Co. v. Broome*, [1972] 1 All E.R. 801 (H.L.). Binnie J. in the *Whiten* judgment notes that these categories have been "somewhat loosened" in recent years and that the House of Lords has "opened up the categories themselves to further evolution" in *Kuddus v. Chief Constable of Leicestershire Constabulary*, [2001] 3 All E.R. 193 (H.L.). In addition to describing the English approach to the issue of punitive damages in some detail, Binnie J. also usefully reviewed the Australian, New Zealand, Irish, and American approaches.

502 See *Vorvis v. I.C.B.C.* (1989), 58 D.L.R. (4th) 193 at 206 (S.C.C.), where McIntyre J. states categorically: "I would conclude that the *Rookes v. Barnard* limitation should not apply in Canada." This was reaffirmed by the court in *Whiten*.

503 Frequently punishment is not possible, but punitive damages will still be awarded with the symbolic and deterrent goals in mind. In *Rollinson v. R.* (1994), 20 C.C.L.T. (2d) 92 (Fed. T.D.), for example, Muldoon J. noted that an award of punitive damages against a public authority really only punishes the tax-paying public. Nevertheless, punitive damages were awarded for deterrence objectives. In *Hill v. Church of Scientology of Toronto* (1994), 20 C.C.L.T. (2d) 129 (Ont. C.A.), affirmed (1995), 126 D.L.R. (4th) 129 (S.C.C.), deterring the defendant from continuing to libel the plaintiff was a major consideration in the $800,000 punitive damages award. The plaintiff was also awarded $300,000 in general damages and $500,000 in aggravated damages.

504 *Nantel v. Parisien* (1981), 18 C.C.L.T. 79 (Ont. H.C.).

505 See also *Claiborne Industries Ltd. v. National Bank of Can.* (1989), 59 D.L.R. (4th) 533 (Ont. C.A.), where punitive damages were awarded in order to make sure that the defendant did not benefit in any way from its tort. See also *Epstein v. Cressey Development Corp.* (1992), 89 D.L.R. (4th) 32 (B.C. C.A.), where Lambert J.A. notes that compensatory damages are assessed

Unlike American tort law,[506] Canadian law does not use punitive damages in order to punish a defendant for systematic misbehaviour or to force industry, through strong economic persuasion, to change their behaviour.[507] Thus, it is extremely unlikely that a plaintiff injured by the negligence of a wealthy defendant will be awarded a huge punitive damage award, as occasionally occurs in the United States. For one thing, punitive damages are very rarely awarded in a negligence action in Canada. As well, despite some contrary authorities,[508] Canadian cases have held that in order to have an award of punitive damages, the tortious conduct complained of must have been directed at the specific plaintiff as the victim.[509] Awards of punitive damages, even for the most outrageous behaviour, have been very moderate in Canadian cases.[510] The guiding principles provided in the *Whiten* judgment strongly indicate that moderation will continue to be the Canadian approach. Binnie J. noted that "rationality" should be promoted by an award. Courts should award "the lowest" amount that would further the objectives of punitive damages, and no more. Courts should take into account "proportionality" by considering the compensatory award plus any other punishment related to the same misconduct in determining the size of the award.[511] Juries should receive guidance and help from trial judges. Appellate courts are "entitled

---

first and then, depending on their quantum, punitive damages may be awarded in order to ensure that the defendant does not retain any benefit from the wrongful act.

506 See the punitive damage symposium, above, note 498. In the *Whiten* case, Binnie J. notes that "the standard of behaviour required to trigger an award of punitive damages in the United States is usually formulated in the epithets (malicious, high-handed, oppressive, outrageous, etc.) familiar to Canadian courts." Nevertheless, I would submit that the only justification for the large size of the awards in the United States is an economic, not a moral, one.

507 In fact, in *Whiten* Binnie J. specifically cautioned against using the defendant's wealth as an excuse for a large award. He stated that it was a factor, but only of "limited importance."

508 Most notably *Vlchek v. Koshel* (1988), 52 D.L.R. (4th) 371 (B.C. S.C.).

509 See, for example, *Kaytor v. Lion's Driving Range* (1962), 35 D.L.R. (2d) 426 (B.C.). Traditionally, cases of punitive damages in Canada involve wrongdoing directed at specific plaintiffs. This factor was noted by Binnie J. In *Whiten*. The plaintiff is not a "private attorney general" who should receive an "excessive windfall" where the plaintiff was "but a minor or peripheral victim." However, with the increased possibility of punitive damages being awarded in negligence actions, e.g., drunk driving cases, this requirement will need to be modified.

510 Prior to the *Whiten* case, there had been only one award over $1,000,000 and that occurred in an unusual case, *Claiborne Industries Ltd. v. National Bank of Can.*, above, note 505. The case involved fraud and the award was calculated based on share prices and the desire to prevent the defendant from recouping some of the damages awarded against it through the purchase and sale of shares. The next highest was $800,000 awarded in a defamation case, *Hill v. Church of Scientology* (1995), 126 D.L.R. (4th) 129 (S.C.C.). In *Colborne Capital Corp. v. 542775 Alberta Ltd.* (1999), 228 A.R. 201 (C.A.), leave to appeal allowed (1999), 266 A.R. 335 (note) (S.C.C.), additional reasons at (1999), 74 Alta. L.R. (3d) 263 (C.A.), a $1 million dollar award made by the trial judge was vacated by the Court of Appeal. Other than for a few other $100,000 plus awards, the rest are well under $100,000 and frequently less than $50,000, even for outrageous sexual wrongdoings.

511 The issue of "proportionality" was stated to be the "key" to determining the quantum of a rational award. The award must be proportional to the blameworthiness of the defendant, the degree of vulnerability of the plaintiff, the degree to which the misconduct was directed at the plaintiff specifically, the need for deterrence, the extent to which the defendant has been punished by other sanctions, and the advantage wrongfully gained by the defendant.

to intervene if the award exceeds the outer boundaries of a rational and measured response to the facts of the case". All of these principles speak to moderation in the size of the award.

Despite the emphasis on punishment of wrongdoers, punitive damages also serve the practical purpose of providing extra compensation to victims. The fact that the punitive damages awarded against defendants go to their victims creates interesting questions.[512] Should courts award punitive damages even if this does not further the punishment objective? In the case of a tort action brought against the estate of a deceased tortfeasor, for example, the punishment objective clearly is irrelevant, although punitive damages have sometimes been awarded.[513] A similar issue arises with respect to an employer's vicarious liability for punitive damages. Where an employer is liable only vicariously, but is otherwise totally innocent of any personal wrongdoing, it does not seem fair or logical to impose vicarious liability on that employer for punitive damages, if punishment and deterrence of wrongdoing are the exclusive objectives of the award. However, if compensation of the victim is an indirect objective or benefit, then vicarious liability for punitive damages makes more sense.[514]

Should punitive damages be denied when defendants have already received punishment through the criminal justice system, on the ground that they should not be punished twice for the same offence? Although courts that have focussed

---

512 Let us recall that the intentional torts are actionable without damage. Thus, punitive damages may be a way of providing the victims with some compensation for their troubles.

513 See *Flame Bar-B-Q Ltd. v. Hoar* (1979), 106 D.L.R. (3d) 438 (N.B. C.A.). Punitive damages were denied, however, in *Breitkreutz v. Pub. Trustee* (1978), 6 C.C.L.T. 76 (Alta. T.D.); and *S. (J.E.) v. M. (P.D.) Estate* (1998), [1998] B.C.J. No. 1461, 1998 CarswellBC 1362 (S.C.). Several provinces have legislation that explicitly or by interpretation prevents an award of punitive damages being made *in favour* of an estate. See, for example, The Survival of Actions Act, R.S.A. 2000, c. S-27, s. 5; the Family Law Act, R.S.O. 1990, c. F3, applied in *Lord (Litigation Guardian of) v. Downer* (1999), 47 C.C.L.T. (2d) 142 (Ont. C.A.), leave to appeal refused (2000), 2000 CarswellOnt 923, 2000 CarswellOnt 924 (S.C.C.); and the Estate Administration Act, R.S.B.C. 1996, c. 122, applied in *Allan Estate v. Co-Operators Life Insurance Co.*, [1999] 8 W.W.R. 328 (B.C. C.A.). The rationale for this is that punitive damages do not represent pecuniary losses of the deceased, and therefore cannot be awarded under our current laws regarding the survival of actions. The rule is not consistent, however, with the rationale of punitive damages—to punish wrongdoers. It is somewhat ironic that wrongdoing that results in the death of the victim cannot be subject to punitive damages, whereas if the victim simply was injured, punitive damages could have been awarded.

514 See *Peeters v. Canada* (1993), 18 C.C.L.T. (2d) 136 (Fed. C.A.) for a discussion of this issue. MacGuigan J.A. notes that, despite objections from authors and commentators, current case law supports the view that vicarious liability does include responsibility for punitive damages. MacGuigan J.A. states, however, that he is "inclined to the view that, for the awarding of punitive damages against an employer, there must have been at least some form or some degree of complicity or blameworthiness on the part of the employer." (18 C.C.L.T. (2d) at 146.) On the facts of the specific case, MacGuigan J.A. affirmed the trial judge's award of punitive damages against the Crown for the misconduct of prison guards in relation to an inmate. Some complicity on the part of the Crown was found, in relation to their procedures and training of staff. This approach is adopted in *A. (M.) v. Canada (Attorney General)* (2001), 212 Sask. R. 241 (Q.B.), varied (2003), 2003 CarswellSask 29 (C.A.), which contains an excellent discussion of the authorities on this point. Also see *A. (T.W.N.) v. Clarke* (2001), 92 B.C.L.R. (3d) 250 (S.C.), additional reasons at (2002), 2002 BCSC 109 (S.C.).

on the punitive aspect of the award have so held,[515] a recent trend has been to admit that this is a question best left up to the trier of fact to be determined in the circumstances of each case.[516] One way to avoid these problems has been to award "aggravated" rather than punitive damages. Aggravated damages have been stated to be compensatory, and not punitive, in nature, and are awarded when the victim's actual injuries have been aggravated by the defendant's behaviour.[517] They are awarded generally in respect of the same type of conduct which would merit an award of punitive damages. They do avoid, however, the conceptual problems involved with punitive damages.

It is impossible to list with certainty those situations which are amenable to an award of punitive damages. It is clear, however, from the adjectives used by the courts in describing these situations, that punitive damages are reserved for cases of serious wrongdoing.[518] Various expressions have been used to describe the necessary degree of wrongdoing. It has been stated that the conduct must "offend the ordinary standards of morality or decent conduct in the community in such marked degree that censure by way of damages is, in the opinion of the Court, warranted."[519] The conduct "may be exemplified by malice, fraud or cruelty as well as other abusive and insolent acts toward the victim."[520] The conduct must demonstrate "high-handedness, maliciousness, contempt of the plaintiff's rights or . . . disregard of every principle of decency."[521] In other words, any misconduct sufficiently serious to warrant the punishment of the offender will qualify for an award of punitive damages. In *Whiten*, Binnie J. noted seven factors that influence the level of blameworthiness underlying a defendant's conduct. These included

515 See, e.g., *Lyth v. Dagg* (1988), 46 C.C.L.T. 25 (B.C. S.C.); *N. (J.L.) v. L. (A.M.)* (1989), 47 C.C.L.T. 65 (Man. Q.B.); among others.

516 Binnie J. in *Whiten* referred to this as the "dominant approach" in Canada. See, for example, *Willington v. Marshall* (1994), 21 C.C.L.T. (2d) 198 (B.C. S.C.); *Joanisse v. Y. (D.)* (1995), 27 C.C.L.T. (2d) 278 (B.C. S.C.); and several other cases cited by Binnie J. at (2002), 209 D.L.R. (4th) 257 (S.C.C.) at 288.

517 See McIntyre J.'s judgment in *Vorvis v. I.C.B.C.* (1989), 58 D.L.R. (4th) 193 at 201-02 (S.C.C). See also *Campbell v. Read* (1987), 43 C.C.L.T. 262 at 267 (B.C. C.A.):

> . . . aggravated damages are the result of the conduct of the wrong-doer which magnifies the harm or injury sustained by the innocent party, and generally includes . . . such matters as humiliation, distress and degradation . . .

518 For example, McIntyre J., in *Vorvis v. I.C.B.C.* (1989), 58 D.L.R. (4th) 193 at 208 (S.C.C.), stated:

> . . . punitive damages may only be awarded in respect of conduct which is of such nature as to be deserving of punishment because of its harsh, vindictive, reprehensible and malicious nature. I do not suggest that I have exhausted the adjectives which could describe the conduct capable of characterizing a punitive award, but in any case where such an award is made the conduct must be extreme in its nature and such that by any reasonable standard it is deserving of full condemnation and punishment.

519 Clement J.A., in *Paragon Properties Ltd. v. Magna Invt. Ltd.* (1972), 24 D.L.R. (3d) 156 at 167 (Alta. C.A.).

520 *Warner v. Arsenault* (1982), 53 N.S.R. (2d) 146 at 152 (C.A.). In the case of *473759 Alta. Ltd. v. Heidelberg Can. Graphic Equip.*, [1995] 5 W.W.R. 214 (Alta. Q.B.), punitive damages were awarded for fraud. The defendant fraudulently sold used equipment as new.

521 *Meyer v. Gordon* (1981), 17 C.C.L.T. 1 at 53 (B.C. S.C.).

the defendant's intent, the defendant's motive, the length of time over which the misconduct persisted, the defendant's effort to conceal or cover up, the defendant's awareness, whether there was profit, and the effect of the misconduct on the plaintiff.

3

Defences to Trespass and Intentional Interferences

1. INTRODUCTION

Litigation concerning many of the torts discussed in Chapter 2 usually involves not whether the plaintiff's *prima facie* case has been made out, but whether there are defences available to defeat it. The essential ingredients of the torts of assault, battery, false imprisonment, and interferences with goods or land are straightforward; proving them is generally not difficult. Ours is a relatively crowded, complex and often violent society; the thresholds for permissible conduct as defined by trespass and other torts of intentional interference are frequently passed. It is in the nature of this type of society, however, that there must be legally recognized defences which allow individuals to engage in conduct which would be tortious in other circumstances. These defences are the subject matter of this chapter.

2. GENERAL COMMENTS

The general rule in civil litigation is that "the person who alleges must prove." The plaintiff has the burden of proving the essential ingredients of the tort and the defendant must prove the defences. As a practical issue, however, the matter is not so clear-cut. First, there may be rules or doctrines which shift the onus of disproving aspects of the cause of action to the defendant. We have seen, for example, that in actions based on trespass the defendant must prove the absence of fault.[1] Second, although the ultimate, or primary, burden of proof, will rest with one party throughout the trial, the secondary, or evidentiary burden, shifts as the evidence introduced tends to favour one side of the case or the other.

Most of the defences that apply to the intentional torts and trespass actions are complete defences. This means that if they are proved, the plaintiff's action is dismissed. This is true of the defence of consent, self-defence, defence of property, defence of others, and lawful authority. The defences of contributory negligence and provocation are partial defences. If successful, they only serve to lessen the

---

1 *Cook v. Lewis*, [1952] 1 D.L.R. 1 (S.C.C.).

plaintiff's damage award. Whether necessity is a defence in a tort action and, if so, what is its effect on the action, is an interesting question and will be explored in this chapter.

3. CONSENT

(a) Introduction

Although the fact that the plaintiff consented to the defendant's conduct effectively negates the argument that a wrong has been committed, consent is treated as a defence which must be established by the defendant.[2] Consent is a useful defence both in relation to the intentional torts, and the action for negligence. It is helpful, however, to distinguish between the defences of consent and *volenti non fit injuria,* since they apply in slightly different ways.[3] When consent is used as a defence in relation to intentional torts, it is argued that the plaintiff consented to the actual interference which constitutes the complaint. For example, when consent is used as a defence to an action for battery, the defendant is alleging that the physical contact in question was one which had been agreed to. *Volenti non fit injuria* used as a defence in negligence actions, including negligent trespass, implies not that the plaintiff agreed to being injured, but that the plaintiff knew that there was a *risk* of injury stemming from the defendant's conduct and accepted that risk.[4] In other words, if the plaintiff agreed to being struck, it is consent, but if the agreement was only to accept the risk of being struck as a result of carelessness, *volenti* is the appropriate defence.[5]

In order to constitute a valid defence, a consent must be free, full, and informed.[6] At common law there is no specific "age of consent." A minor can consent to conduct which might otherwise be considered tortious as long as the child has

---

2 See La Forest J. in *Norberg v. Wynrib*, [1992] 4 W.W.R. 577 (S.C.C.), additional reasons at [1992] 6 W.W.R. 673 (S.C.C.) at 590 [4 W.W.R.]: "Consent, express or implied, is a defence to battery." This was confirmed by McLachlin J., writing for four members of the Supreme Court of Canada in *Sansalone v. Wawanesa Mutual Insurance Co.* (2000), 50 C.C.L.T. (2d) 1 (S.C.C.) at 11: "The burden is then on the defendant to allege and prove his defence. Consent is one such defence." This view was not shared by three members of the Supreme Court who would have put the onus of proof on the plaintiff. See discussion below.

3 Admittedly this distinction is often not made, the term *volenti* being applied equally to intentional and negligent actions in many of the cases. See, however, Trindade, Cane and Lunney, *The Law of Torts in Australia*, 4th ed. (2007) at 109, who also make this distinction.

4 As we will see, the courts have narrowed considerably the defence of *volenti* by requiring not only acceptance of the physical risks of injury, but the legal risks as well. See discussion Chapter 13.

5 See *MacMillan v. Hincks*, [2002] 8 W.W.R. 573 (Alta. Q.B.) where this approach is quoted with approval. The case involved a mutual fight and one of the defences was consent.

6 See Hertz, "Volenti Non Fit Injuria: A Guide" in Klar (ed.), *Studies in Canadian Tort Law* (1977), Chapter 3. As stated by La Forest J. in *Norberg v. Wynrib*, [1992] 4 W.W.R. 577 at 590:

> . . . the consent must be genuine; it must not be obtained by force or threat of force or be given under the influence of drugs. Consent may also be vitiated by fraud or deceit as to the nature of the defendant's conduct.

"sufficient intelligence and understanding to make up his own mind."[7] Thus in *C. (J.S.) v. Wren*,[8] the parents of a 16-year-old were unable to prevent her from undergoing an abortion.[9]

The reality of an apparent consent may be doubted and the "consent" rendered ineffective due to the exploitation of a relationship of unequal power. In *Norberg v. Wynrib*,[10] the Supreme Court of Canada upheld an action for sexual battery brought by a female adult patient against her male doctor. The parties had been involved in a relationship whereby the doctor provided his addicted patient with drugs in return for sexual favours. Whereas the lower courts had dismissed the action based upon the consent of the plaintiff to the impugned activities,[11] La Forest J. held that where it can be shown "that there was such a disparity in the relative positions of the parties that the weaker party was not in a position to choose freely", consent will be considered legally ineffective.[12] This determination is made by proof of (i) inequality between the parties, and (ii) exploitation of that inequality. This is an issue which must be considered on the facts of each case. Applying the test to the circumstances of the *Norberg* case, La Forest J. concluded that there was no meaningful consent.[13]

---

7 See Lord Scarman, in *Gillick v. West Norfolk & Wisbech Area Health Authority*, [1985] 3 All E.R. 402 (H.L.), quoted in *C. (J.S.) v. Wren*, [1987] 2 W.W.R. 669 at 672 (Alta. C.A.). The common law position was reaffirmed in *Ney v. A.G. Can.* (1993), 102 D.L.R. (4th) 136 at 142 (B.C. S.C.):

> . . . where a child has sufficient intelligence and understanding of the nature of proposed health care, he or she is capable at common law of consenting to such treatment. If a child does not meet this test, and as a result is incapable of consenting, the consent of the parents of that child will be required.

The case concerned the constitutionality of the Infants Act, R.S.B.C. 1979, c. 196, s. 16 which in effect codified the common law. The section was held to be constitutional in that it did not infringe the Charter. The judgment also reaffirms the rule that a doctor is not legally required to treat, merely because the patient desires treatment. Also see *Van Mol (Guardian ad litem of) v. Ashmore* (1999), 168 D.L.R. (4th) 637, 44 C.C.L.T. (2d) 228 (B.C. C.A.), leave to appeal refused [2000] 1 S.C.R. vi, additional reasons at (2000), 188 D.L.R. (4th) 327 (B.C. C.A.), where the common law position with respect to a minor's capacity to consent to medical treatment is reaffirmed. See discussion below concerning the court's right to override a minor's decision to refuse medical treatment. It has been held that in so far as sexual acts are concerned, the Criminal Code, R.S.C. 1985, c. C-46, s. 150.1, age of consent of 14, should be applied to tort law. See *Olsen v. Olsen* (2006), 266 D.L.R. (4th) 209 (B.C. S.C), citing *M. (M.) v. M. (P.)* (2000), 82 B.C.L.R. (3d) 125 (S.C.).

8 *Ibid.*

9 As discussed by Picard & Robertson, *Legal Liability of Doctors and Hospitals in Canada*, 4th ed. (2007), Chapter 2, legislation exists in some provinces dealing with the age of consent for medical treatment. See, for example, *Van Mol (Guardian ad litem of) v. Ashmore* (1999), 168 D.L.R. (4th) 637, 44 C.C.L.T. (2d) 228 (B.C. C.A.), leave to appeal refused [2000] 1 S.C.R. vi, additional reasons at (2000), 188 D.L.R. (4th) 327 (B.C. C.A.), where the British Columbia legislation is discussed.

10 [1992] 4 W.W.R. 577 (S.C.C.).

11 [1988] 6 W.W.R. 305, (B.C. S.C.), affirmed [1990] 4 W.W.R. 193 (B.C. C.A.).

12 *Ibid.*, at [1992] 4 W.W.R. 593.

13 Among the factors which led to La Forest J.'s conclusions were the age and education of the plaintiff, her drug dependency, her initial unwillingness to agree to sex, the general nature of the doctor-patient relationship, the doctor's knowledge of the plaintiff's drug dependence, the fact that the suggestion of drugs for sex came from the doctor, and the egregious nature of his

It also has been held that, in some circumstances, the court will not permit, as a matter of public policy, the defence of consent to be raised. In *M. (M.) v. K. (K.)*,[14] it was held that a defendant who was guilty of sexual abuse, criminal misconduct, breach of trust and breach of a duty to act in the best interests of the plaintiff, his foster daughter, could not raise the defence of consent to a civil action arising out of sexual relations with her.[15] In view of the Supreme Court of Canada's approach to this issue in *Norberg v. Wynrib*, it is likely that this pure "public policy" approach will not be necessary to defeat the defence of consent in future cases. A sexual relationship between a minor and a person who is in a position of trust and control bears all the hallmarks of a relationship of inequality and exploitation. Thus, the consent defence in these cases would likely be defeated by the reasoning of the Supreme Court in *Norberg v. Wynrib*.[16]

Consent obtained under duress is not free and hence is invalid. For example, those who agree to submit themselves to questioning or other types of detention have not consented to being imprisoned, if they reasonably believed that their agreement was necessary to avoid embarrassment or actual physical coercion.[17]

---

conduct. McLachlin J. resolved the issue of consent by characterizing the relationship as a fiduciary relationship, and finding the defendant liable for the breach of his fiduciary duty. Sopinka J. dissented. While he recognized that, in certain relationships involving a significant imbalance in power, courts must be careful in assessing the reality of consent, ultimately the issue of consent is a factual one that must be determined in each case. Sopinka J. did not think that the lower court's finding of consent should be disturbed. Sopinka J. did award damages, however, for the doctor's failure to treat. In *T. (L.) v. M. (W.K.)* (1993), 110 D.L.R. (4th) 64 (N.B. Q.B.), the court held that a sexual relationship between a 16-year old girl and a doctor, who was both her counseller and informal foster parent was consensual and thus a battery claim failed. The court did find the defendant liable, however, for breach of fiduciary duty. The judgment indicates that La Forest J.'s test in *Norberg v. Wynrib* must be applied to the facts of each case. Also see *M. (M.) v. M. (P.)* (2000), 82 B.C.L.R. (3d) 125 (S.C.), where a jury's decision that there was genuine consent to sexual activity between a 14-year-old boy and a female teacher was upheld. In *K. (R.) v. A. (J.)* (2000), [2000] N.B.J. No. 498, 2000 CarswellNB 499 (Q.B.), affirmed (2001), [2001] N.B.J. No. 361, 2001 CarswellNB 353 (C.A.), leave to appeal refused (2002), 2002 CarswellNB 209, 2002 CarswellNB 210 (S.C.C.), a sexual relationship between a patient and her doctor was held to be consensual, but still a breach of fiduciary duty.

14 (1989), 50 C.C.L.T. 190 (B.C. S.C.), reversing 39 C.C.L.T. 81 (B.C. C.A.).

15 The trial judge had held that the plaintiff "was possessed of a sufficient degree of intelligence and maturity to understand the nature and consequences of the sexual activity in which she was involved", at 39 C.C.L.T. 81 at 97. See also *Harder v. Brown* (1989), 50 C.C.L.T. 85 (B.C. S.C.), another case involving the sexual assault of a minor, where the consent defence was rejected. See, however, *Lyth v. Dagg* (1988), 46 C.C.L.T. 25 (B.C. S.C.), which involved a consensual sexual relationship between a teacher and a student, where the defence was accepted. As noted above, some courts have held that the Criminal Code age of consent for sexual acts should be applied to tort law cases.

16 See, for example, *B. (J.) v. B. (R.)*, [1994] O.J. No. 324 (Gen. Div.). The plaintiff sued her father for incest. The court held that prior to the age of 14 the plaintiff was unable to consent to the conduct. With relation to the sexual conduct which occurred after the plaintiff was 14, the court noted that this was a well-recognized "power dependency" relationship and exploitation of this relationship occurred. Therefore, there was no legal consent. As noted above, however, this is a question of fact that must be determined on a case-by-case basis.

17 But see *Reynen v. Antonenko* (1975), 54 D.L.R. (3d) 124 (Alta. T.D.). A person suspected of possession of narcotics was taken to a doctor by police where an anal search was conducted. The court held that the plaintiff had co-operated with the doctor in allowing him to perform the treatment, although no actual consent was established. *Nagy v. Canada* (2006), 272 D.L.R.

A patient under sedation who agreed to a spinal anaesthetic in preparation for an operation was held not to have given a full and free consent.[18] Being under the influence of drugs, however, does not in and of itself deprive a person of giving a valid consent. As long as an individual has not been deprived of the ability to reason, consent may be given.[19] Consent which has been obtained as a result of a mistake, or even fraud, seems to raise some difficulties for the courts. A distinction has been made between fraud which goes to the nature of the act objected to, and vitiates consent, and fraud which relates only to a collateral matter, which does not.[20] It is clear from the judgment of the Supreme Court of Canada in *Reibl v. Hughes*[21] that unless the fraud or misrepresentation goes to the very nature of the offensive act, it will not vitiate consent for the purposes of the intentional torts. As well, even where there is a false misrepresentation it must have been made by, or with the knowledge of, the defendant.[22]

A valid consent need not adhere to any specific form. It can be express, either in words or in writing, or it can be implied by conduct.[23] It has been held, however, that although "compliance, or failure to resist or protest, may be evidence of consent"[24] this depends on the circumstances of the case.[25] In the area of trespass to land, "leave and licence" can be implied from the previous conduct and rela-

---

(4th) 601 (Alta. C.A.), additional reasons at (2007), 2007 CarswellAlta 191 (C.A.) came to the opposite conclusion in similar circumstances. See discussion below at note 25.

18 *Beausoleil v. La Communauté des Soeurs de la Charité de la Providence* (1964), 53 D.L.R. (2d) 65 (Que. S.C.).

19 See, e.g., *Norberg v. Wynrib*, [1988] 6 W.W.R. 305 (B.C. S.C.), affirmed [1990] 4 W.W.R. 193 (B.C. C.A.), reversed on another point [1992] 4 W.W.R. 577 (S.C.C.), additional reasons at [1992] 2 S.C.R. 318. In the Supreme Court, La Forest J., although finding the consent invalid, stated that a drug addiction by itself does not render consent legally ineffective.

20 There are only a few cases on point. See *Hegarty v. Shine* (1878), 14 Cox C.C. 145 — failure to communicate that a person has venereal disease does not vitiate the consent to the act of sexual intercourse; *Graham v. Saville*, [1945] O.R. 301 (C.A.) — misrepresenting that a person is single when he is really married and thus inducing another person to enter into a marriage relationship constitutes deceit. In *Bell-Ginsburg v. Ginsburg* (1993), 17 C.C.L.T. (2d) 167 (Ont. Gen. Div.), the plaintiff sued her husband for, among other things, battery. Unknown to the plaintiff, the defendant was a practising bisexual. The plaintiff asserted that had she known this, she would not have agreed to have sex with him. The court refused to strike out the claim for battery, holding that it was possible that the claim could succeed at trial. There are several criminal law cases on this matter, but these are of limited assistance in terms of tort law. Of these, the most important is *R. v. Cuerrier* (1998), 162 D.L.R. (4th) 513 (S.C.C.). The case concerned the criminal offence of sexual assault under the Criminal Code, s. 265(3)(c). This section specifies that "fraud" vitiates consent. The Court held that failing to communicate that you are HIV infected to your sexual partner can constitute fraud, which vitiates consent.

21 [1980] 2 S.C.R. 880.

22 See *Stewart v. Traders Trust Co.*, [1936] 4 D.L.R. 139 (Man. C.A.).

23 See, e.g., *Reynen v. Antonenko* (1975), 54 D.L.R. (3d) 124 (Alta. T.D.), where the fact that the plaintiff "co-operated" by assuming the physical position necessary to permit the physician to conduct a rectal search was taken as consent. Also see *O'Brien v. Cunard S.S. Co.*, 28 N.E. 266 (Mass., 1891); *Nelitz v. Dyck* (2001), 52 O.R. (3d) 458 (C.A.).

24 *Nagy v. Canada* (2006), 272 D.L.R. (4th) 601 at 612 (Alta. C.A.) citing *Norberg v. Wynrib*, above, note 10.

25 The Court of Appeal in *Nagy*, *ibid.*, affirmed the trial judgment (2005 ABQB 26), that a strip search and internal cavity searches were done without the plaintiff's consent although she co-operated when required to do so and even signed a general consent form.

tionship of the parties, which permitted the offensive acts to occur.[26] If, however, the entry onto the land goes beyond the permission given, there is, at least with respect to the excess, no leave and license.[27] The defence of "leave and licence" was thoroughly reviewed by the Saskatchewan Court of Appeal in *Montreal Trust Co. v. Williston Wildcatters Corp.*[28] The case concerned a petroleum and natural gas lease. Although the lease had expired, the defendants had continued to occupy the land and produce the leased substances. The issue was whether they were there with the leave and licence of the plaintiff. Upon reviewing the authorities, Vancise J.A. held that the following indicia have been found to be necessary to establish leave and licence: tacit consent, implied from conduct; an agreement or understanding, or the anticipation of an agreement, for the defendant's presence; trespass over a long period of time; plaintiff's knowledge of the trespass; plaintiff's knowledge of its legal rights; the absence of the plaintiff's reasonable belief that the trespasser thought he had a legal right to be on the land; defendant did not ignore plaintiff; and lack of defiance or contempt in defendant's conduct.[29] The Court of Appeal, in reversing the trial judge,[30] held that, other for a brief period of trespass, the defendants had either an express or implied licence to be on the plaintiffs' land.[31]

As indicated above, the Supreme Court of Canada in *Sansalone v. Wawanesa Mutual Insurance Co.*[32] made it clear that the burden of proving consent falls upon the defendant in all cases.[33] The Supreme Court implied that the defendant can discharge this burden by proving either that the plaintiff did consent, or that it was reasonable for the defendant to have believed that the plaintiff consented. Thus "constructive" consent is a defence in a civil claim.[34]

---

26 See, e.g., *C.P.R. v. R.*, [1931] 2 D.L.R. 386 (P.C.); *De Wurstemberger v. Royalite Oil Co.*, [1935] 2 D.L.R. 177 (Alta. C.A.); *Isitt v. G.T.P. Ry.*, [1918] 3 W.W.R. 500, affirmed 49 D.L.R. 687 (S.C.C.).

27 *Webb v. Attewell* (1993), 18 C.C.L.T. (2d) 299 at 305 (B.C. C.A.), additional reasons at (1994), 100 B.C.L.R. (2d) 135 (C.A.).

28 [2004] S.J. No. 541.

29 *Ibid.*, at para. 36. The court referred to the authorities which have established these factors.

30 [2003] SKQB 360.

31 Also see *Freyberg v. Fletcher Challenge Oil & Gas Inc.*, [2007] 10 W.W.R. 133 (Alta. Q.B.). The case also concerned the validity of oil and gas leases and whether the defendants had leave and license to continue drilling.

32 (2000), 50 C.C.L.T. (2d) 1 (S.C.C.).

33 The dissenting justices argued that while the burden of proving consent in battery ordinarily falls upon the defendant, in sexual battery cases the burden of proving lack of consent ought to fall on the plaintiff. The rationale of Iacobucci J. was that since only non-consensual sexual activity is "harmful or offensive", this must be an element of the plaintiff's case. Iacobucci J. did note however that this burden would be very easily discharged by the plaintiff's simple allegation, absent any evidence by the defendant. I do not agree with the dissenting approach. It is clear, for example, that in medical treatment cases the burden of proof falls upon the defendant doctor, even though only non-consensual treatment is harmful or offensive. There is no justification for a special approach to sexual battery cases.

34 In another case, *Toews (Guardian ad litem of) v. Weisner* (2001), 3 C.C.L.T. (3d) 293 (B.C. S.C.), the defendant was liable in battery for vaccinating a young student against meningitis. The defendant did not know that the parents had not consented to the vaccination, but should have been alerted to the problem when the child objected to being vaccinated. Elizabeth Adjin-Tettey in "Protecting The Dignity and Autonomy of Women: Rethinking the Place of Constructive Consent in the Tort of Sexual Battery" (2006), 39 U.B.C. Law Rev. 3, argues that "sexual

There are two areas where the defence of consent plays a particularly important role: consent to sporting activities and medical treatment. These areas warrant special attention.

(b) Sports

Physical contact sports involve a degree of violence which clearly would not be tolerated in ordinary daily life. Tackling, punching, and body checking are offensive contacts which would constitute batteries were it not for the defence of consent.

The various cases which have dealt with sport injuries have all adhered to the same general principle.[35] Individuals who engage in physical contact sports consent to that degree of physical contact which is part of the game, as it is ordinarily played. Thus, a boxer would agree to being punched,[36] a football player tackled, a wrestler flipped, and so on. Difficulties arise, however, where the contact goes beyond that which is either permitted by the rules, or generally tolerated by the participants. If the contact is contrary to the rules, in the sense that, although it frequently occurs, there is a penalty provided when it does happen, this does not necessarily mean that the defence of consent will fail. It has been recognized that "the leave and licence will include an unintentional injury resulting from one of the frequent infractions of the rules of the game."[37] In other words, an infraction of the rules, when it is within reasonable bounds, will not form the basis of an action in trespass. This in all cases is a matter of the court's judgment, although it is suggested that infractions of the rules intended to inflict serious injury, or

---

battery" should be regarded as a separate tort and that "constructive consent" ought not to be available as a defence. The author submits that "only voluntary and affirmative consent should be accepted as a valid defence to claims of sexual wrongdoing" at 6. Adjin-Tettey is supportive of the use of the tort claim for survivors of sexual abuse and provides a good discussion of the issues.

35 See *Matheson v. Dalhousie* (1983), 25 C.C.L.T. 91 (N.S. T.D.); *Agar v. Canning* (1965), 54 W.W.R. 302 (Man. Q.B.), affirmed (1966), 55 W.W.R. 384 (Man. C.A.); *Pettis v. McNeil* (1979), 8 C.C.LT. 299 (N.S. T.D.); *Martin v. Daigle* (1969), 6 D.L.R. (3d) 634 (N.B. C.A.); *Wright v. McLean* (1956), 7 D.L.R. (2d) 253 (B.C. S.C.); *Colby v. Schmidt* (1986), 37 C.C.L.T. 1 (B.C. S.C.); *Temple v. Hallem* (1989), 58 D.L.R. (4th) 541, leave to appeal to S.C.C. refused 65 Man. R. (2d) 80n; *Gaudet v. Sullivan*, [1992] N.B.J. No. 503. As explained above, these cases deal with the situation where the plaintiff was injured not as a result of an unintended but negligent act, but as a result of intentional contact. See generally Barnes, *Sports and the Law in Canada*, 3rd ed. (1996); Barnes, "Recent Developments in Canadian Sports Law" (1991), 23 Ottawa L. Rev. 623 at 689-94; S.A. Thiele, "Sports and Torts" (2002), 23 Advocates Quarterly 348.

36 See *R. v. Coney* (1882), 8 Q.B.D. 534; *Pallante v. Stadiums Pty. Ltd. (No. 1)*, [1976] V.R. 331 (S.C.); *Bain v. Altoft*, [1967] Qd. R. 32.

37 *Agar v. Canning*, above, note 35, at 304; *Matheson v. Dalhousie*, above, note 35; *Temple v. Hallem*, above, note 35. Also see *Unruh (Guardian ad litem of) v. Webber* (1994), 112 D.L.R. (4th) 83 (B.C. C.A.), leave to appeal refused (1994), 115 D.L.R. (4th) viii (S.C.C.), affirming (1992), 98 D.L.R. (4th) 294 (B.C. S.C.); *Zapf v. Muckalt* (1995), 26 C.C.L.T. (2d) 61 (B.C. S.C.), additional reasons at (1996), 20 B.C.L.R. (3d) 124 (S.C.), varied (1996), 31 C.C.L.T. (2d) 201, [1997] 2 W.W.R. 645 (B.C. C.A.), leave to appeal refused (1997), 223 N.R. 73 (note) (S.C.C.); and *St. Laurent v. Bartley*, [1998] 8 W.W.R. 373 (Man. Q.B.). These cases affirm the proposition that a breach of the rules is an element of what constitutes unreasonable conduct in a game, although it is not conclusive.

committed with a degree of malice or hostility, ought not to be considered to have been consented to by participants in sporting activities.[38]

Occasionally cases involving the direct application of force within a sport are pled as negligence actions and not as batteries. The issue is then characterized as a "standard of care" one, the question being whether the defendant's behaviour was reasonable in view of the rules of the game.[39] This approach can be confusing. If the defendant directly applied physical force to the plaintiff the action is best pled as a battery subject to the defence of consent. Whether there was consent would depend upon the nature of the contact; i.e., was the contact within the rules and expectations of the game? As well, if the contact was neither intended nor negligent, but accidental, the battery action would fail.[40] In addition, issues relating to the severity of the injuries suffered, or the unintended consequences of batteries, properly raise the issue of remoteness of damage.

A related matter concerns consent to violent acts in other contexts, for example, in the case of "mutual fights." The case law supports the proposition that those who engage in fights, even though these activities may be criminal, cannot complain of injuries suffered in the course of the fight, unless the force which is used by one of the combatants is excessive or unnecessary.[41] The dismissal of the plaintiffs' actions in these cases may be grounded either on the basis of the defence of consent or illegality.[42]

The courts must apply the defence of consent with care, in cases of mutual fights. The distinction must be made between those who are fighting in self-defence, or for the defence of others, and those who are fighting consensually. If weapons are used, or the force is otherwise excessive for the occasion, the consent ought not to be held to be valid.[43] The application of the defence of consent for

---

38 See *Agar v. Canning*, above, note 35; *Sexton v. Sutherland*, [1991] O.J. No. 624; and *Gaudet v. Sullivan*, above, note 35. These judgments support the proposition that "injuries inflicted in circumstances which show a definite resolve to cause serious injury to another, even when there is provocation and in the heat of the game, should not fall within the scope of the implied consent"; per Bastin J., at 54 W.W.R. 302 at 304. Another case where there was liability is *Seaton v. Gagnon* (September 30, 1997), Doc. Ottawa 95-CU-95685, 1997 CarswellOnt 3771 (Ont. Gen. Div.).

39 See, for example, *Zapf v. Muckalt* (1996), 31 C.C.L.T. (2d) 201, [1997] 2 W.W.R. 645 (B.C. C.A.), leave to appeal refused (1997), 223 N.R. 73 (note) (S.C.C.); *St. Laurent v. Bartley*, [1998] 8 W.W.R. 373 (Man. Q.B.); and *Wilson v. Haddock*, [1998] 10 W.W.R. 660 (B.C. S.C.), reversed (1999), 129 B.C.A.C. 313 (C.A.).

40 For example, in *Wilson v. Haddock*, *ibid.*, the court dismissed the action because the contact was neither intended nor negligent.

41 See *Wade v. Martin*, [1955] 3 D.L.R. 635 (Nfld. T.D.); *Hartlen v. Chaddock* (1957), 11 D.L.R. (2d) 705 (N.S. T.D.); *Zinck v. Strickland* (1981), 45 N.S.R. (2d) 451, 86 A.P.R. 451 (T.D.); *Mazurkewich v. Ritchot* (1984), 30 Man. R. (2d) 245 (C.A.); *Johnson v. Grandview Branch 179 Royal Can. Legion*, [1986] B.C.W.L.D. 1128, reversed with respect to liability of non-combatant defendants 26 B.C.L.R. (2d) 124 (C.A.); *MacMillan v. Hincks*, [2002] 8 W.W.R. 573 (Alta. Q.B.). Consent also may be withdrawn, due to a change in circumstances. See *Smith v. A.G. B.C.*, [1987] B.C.W.L.D. 2377, affirmed 30 B.C.L.R. (2d) 356 (C.A.).

42 See, e.g., *Dolson v. Hughes* (1979), 107 D.L.R. (3d) 343 (B.C. S.C.). One should keep in mind, however, that the defence of illegality has been severely curtailed as a tort law defence by the Supreme Court of Canada. See Chapter 13 for a full discussion of the defence of illegality. One must also note that the court may disallow the defence of consent in some situations based on public policy, as in *M. (M.) v. K. (K.)* (1989), 50 C.C.L.T. 190 (B.C. C.A.), discussed above.

43 There are apparently even "rules" for fighting. See *Fillipowich v. Nahachewsky* (1969), 3 D.L.R. (3d) 544 (Sask. Q.B.).

the purposes of a criminal prosecution is and ought to be different. Individuals are not entitled to agree to breach the peace, and society has an interest in preserving peace and discouraging illegal acts.[44]

(c) Medical Treatment

The topic of consent to medical treatment is a broad one with many interesting issues.[45] The basic propositions as they relate to tort liability, however, can be clearly stated. Medical treatment which involves any interference with a patient's body is a battery, and subjects the defendant to liability, in the absence of a successful defence, one of which is consent. Let us recall that although a battery involves offensive physical contact, this does not mean that the contact must cause injury to the complainant. The contact need only be one which is out of the ordinary, one which is not generally acceptable as part of everyday living. This has important implications for the law relating to medical treatment, since it preserves the rights of individuals to decide what treatment they will accept or reject without regard to whether the treatment is "good for them" or not.

The right of individuals to determine what medical treatment they will undergo has been consistently upheld in Canadian case law, as illustrated in the following passage:

> While our Courts rightly resist advising the medical profession about how to conduct their practice, our law is clear that the consent of a patient must be obtained before any surgical procedure can be conducted. Without a consent, either written or oral, no surgery may be performed. This is not a mere formality; it is an important individual right to have control over one's own body, even where medical treatment is involved. It is the patient, not the doctor, who decides whether surgery will be performed, where it will be done, when it will be done and by whom it will be done.[46]

---

44 See the Criminal Code, R.S.C. 1985, c. C-46, s. 14, which states that persons cannot consent to have death inflicted upon them for the purpose of affecting criminal responsibility. In *R. v. Jobidon*, [1991] 2 S.C.R. 714, the Supreme Court limited the legal effectiveness of consent with respect to a criminal charge of assault under s. 265 of the Criminal Code. The court held that, at least in so far as fist fights are concerned, consent is vitiated with respect to adults who intentionally apply force causing serious bodily harm or non-trivial bodily harm to each other in the course of the fight. The court noted that fist fights are valueless, may lead to larger brawls and breaches of the peace, and ought to be deterred. Although this judgment does not directly affect tort actions, one can surmise that the policy concerns expressed by the court do have relevance in the civil action as well. The Ontario Court of Appeal applied *Jobidon* to a fist fight between minors at school: see *R. v. W. (G.)* (1994), 18 O.R. (3d) 321 (C.A.). At least one court has applied this to a civil action: see *A. (N.) (Next Friend of) v. J. (M.)* (1997), 208 A.R. 133 (Prov. Ct.). On the issue of the interaction between the Criminal Code and the common law with respect to the defences of consent and self-defence, see Stalker, "Self-Defence And Consent: The Use of Common Law Developments in Canadian *Criminal Code* Analysis" (1994), 32 Alberta L. Rev. 484.

45 See Picard and Robertson, *Legal Liability of Doctors and Hospitals in Canada*, 4th ed. (2007), Chapter 3.

46 Linden J., in *Allan v. New Mount Sinai Hosp.* (1980), 109 D.L.R. (3d) 634 at 642, reversed on a procedural point 125 D.L.R. (3d) 276 (Ont. C.A.). In *Starson v. Swayze* (2003), 225 D.L.R. (4th) 385 (S.C.C.), at 391, McLachlin C.J.C. expressed the principle as follows: "No matter how ill a person, no matter how likely deterioration or death, it is for that person and that person alone to decide whether to accept a proposed medical treatment." See also *Mulloy v. Hop Sang*, [1935] 1 W.W.R. 714 (Alta. C.A.); *Marshall v. Curry*, [1933] 3 D.L.R. 260 (N.S. T.D.); *Reibl v. Hughes* (1980), 14 C.C.L.T. 1 (S.C.C.); *Malette v. Shulman* (1987), 43 C.C.L.T. 62 (Ont. H.C.), affirmed (1990), 2 C.C.L.T. (2d) 1 (Ont. C.A.); *Fleming v. Reid* (1991), 82 D.L.R. (4th) 298 (Ont. C.A.); and *Fortey (Guardian ad litem of) v. Canada (Attorney General)*, [1999] 10

As with consent in other contexts, consent to medical treatment can be in oral or written form, express or implied.[47] It has been suggested that individuals who submit themselves to a doctor for treatment impliedly consent to all necessary procedures.[48] As well, a patient who in some way co-operates with the doctor may be taken as having impliedly consented to the procedure.[49] Where there is consent to a surgical operation, there is an implied consent to procedures, such as the administration of anaesthetics, necessary to carry out the surgery.[50]

Respect for individual autonomy and the right to control one's body also is reflected in the right of an individual to withdraw from treatment which already has been commenced. In *B.(N.) v. Hôtel-Dieu de Québec*,[51] the Quebec court granted the claimant an injunction ordering her hospital and doctor to discontinue life-sustaining treatment. It correctly was seen as logical that if a patient can be treated only with her consent, it follows that the withdrawal of her consent requires the cessation of the treatment.[52] In addition, it must be recognized that although

---

W.W.R. 600 (B.C. C.A.). This right is also enshrined in the Quebec Civil Code, S.Q. 1991, c. 64, s. 10:

> Every person is inviolable and is entitled to the integrity of his person. Except in cases provided for by law, no one may interfere with his person without his free and enlightened consent.

See *Marcoux c. Bouchard* (2001), 204 D.L.R. (4th) 1 (S.C.C.) and *B. (N.) v. Hôtel-Dieu de Québec* (1992), 86 D.L.R. (4th) 385 (Que. S.C.). Exceptions to the patient's right to refuse treatment arise with respect to legislative enactments dealing with public health issues; see Picard & Robertson, *Legal Liability of Doctors and Hospitals in Canada*, 4th ed. (2007), Chapter 2.

47 Subject to legislative provisions which may require written consent. See Picard & Robertson, above, at 50.

48 See *Mulloy v. Hop Sang*, [1935] 1 W.W.R. 714 (Alta. C.A.). See also Robins J.A. in *Malette v. Shulman*, above, note 46.

49 See *Reynen v. Antonenko* (1975), 54 D.L.R. (3d) 124 (Alta. T.D.). But also see *Nagy v. Canada* (2006), 272 D.L.R. (4th) 601 (Alta. C.A.), additional reasons at (2007), 2007 CarswellAlta 191 (C.A.), where co-operation was not seen as consent.

50 See *Villeneuve v. Sisters of St. Joseph* (1971), 18 D.L.R. (3d) 537 (Ont.), reversed in part (1972), 25 D.L.R. (3d) 25 (Ont. C.A.), which was reversed (1974), 47 D.L.R. (3d) 391 (S.C.C.). See also *Brushett v. Cowan* (1990), 69 D.L.R. (4th) 743 (Nfld. C.A.), reversing in part (1987), 42 C.C.L.T. 64 (Nfld. C.A.). Although the plaintiff in this case had not expressly consented to the specific procedure which was performed, Marshall J.A. found that the consent given in the consent form, viewed within the circumstances of the case, was sufficient to establish consent to the treatment. Similar reasoning was applied in *O'Bonsawin v. Paradis* (1993), 15 C.C.L.T. (2d) 188 (Ont. Gen. Div.). The doctor told the patient that two techniques of treatment were possible. The patient expressed preference for the first one, but it was ruled out for medical reasons. During the performance of the second technique, the doctor discovered that the first technique could be done, and he performed it. Under these circumstances, the court found consent to either technique.

51 (1992), 86 D.L.R. (4th) 385 (Que. S.C.).

52 The Supreme Court of Canada implicitly recognized this argument in *Ciarlariello v. Schacter* (1993), 15 C.C.L.T. (2d) 209, in so far as non life-preserving treatment was concerned. The patient, during an angiogram, withdrew her consent to the continuation of the test. After a brief suspension, she then consented to the test's resumption. The court held that this consent was valid and for this reason her battery claim failed. Also see *H. (V.A.) v. Lynch*, [2000] 6 W.W.R. 419 (Alta. C.A.), reconsideration refused (2000), [2001] 1 W.W.R. 83 (Alta. C.A.), additional reasons at [2001] 6 W.W.R. 441 (Alta. C.A.), reconsideration refused [2001] 11 W.W.R. 228 (Alta. C.A.), confirming the right of a patient to withdraw consent. This issue of the right to

a patient has the right to refuse treatment or to discontinue treatment, a doctor does not have a duty to treat merely because the patient requests it. In *Child & Family Services of Central Manitoba v. L. (R.)*,[53] the Manitoba Court of Appeal held that legislation providing for the court to authorize treatment for a child when the child's parents refuse treatment[54] cannot be invoked to require a doctor to recommend that a "Do Not Resuscitate" order be placed on a child's chart, against the parents' wishes. The decision is the doctor's, subject only to the professional standard imposed upon the doctor.

Emergencies which necessitate medical treatment cover a special category of cases. If the patient had not either expressly or impliedly consented to the treatment, prior to the arising of the emergency, but also had not refused the treatment, the treatment can be administered, even though the patient is unable to consent to it. It has been stated that

> where a great emergency which could not be anticipated arises . . . it is the surgeon's duty to act in order to save the life or preserve the health of the patient; and . . . in the honest execution of that duty he [the doctor] should not be exposed to legal liability.[55]

It has been made clear, however, that this principle applies only where the treatment is required in order to save life or preserve health; it must be a question of necessity and not merely convenience.[56] It is important to stress that this rule permitting treatment in cases of emergencies does not apply where the treatment

---

withdraw from treatment becomes more complicated when the patient becomes incompetent and is no longer able to express her will. This raises the question of the validity of "living wills". Even more difficult is assisted suicide, which was the issue in *Rodriguez v. A.G. B.C.* (1993), 82 B.C.L.R. (2d) 273 (S.C.C.).

53 (1997), 154 D.L.R. (4th) 409 (Man. C.A.).

54 In this case the Child and Family Services Act, S.M. 1985-86, c.8, s. 25(3).

55 *Marshall v. Curry*, [1933] 3 D.L.R. 260 at 275 (N.S. T.D.). See also the judgment by Robins J.A. in *Malette v. Shulman* (1990), 2 C.C.L.T. (2d) 1 at 10 (Ont. C.A.). Robins J.A. stated:

> The emergency situation is an exception to the general rule requiring a patient's prior consent. When immediate medical treatment is necessary to save the life or preserve the health of a person who, by reason of unconsciousness or extreme illness, is incapable of either giving or withholding consent, the doctor may proceed without the patient's consent.

56 See Picard & Robertson, *Legal Liability of Doctors and Hospitals in Canada*, 4th ed. (2007) at 50. The authors cite *Murray v. McMurchy*, [1949] 2 D.L.R. 442 (B.C. S.C.), and *Parmley v. Parmley*, [1945] 4 D.L.R. 81 (S.C.C.), where a doctor and a dentist respectively were held liable for proceeding without consent. See also *Brushett v. Cowan* (1987), 42 C.C.L.T. 64 (Nfld. T.D.), reversed in part (1990), 69 D.L.R. (4th) 743 (Nfld. C.A.). At trial, it was held that consent to a muscle biopsy did not entitle the doctor to perform a bone biopsy when he discovered abnormal tissue. The court stated that it was not an emergency, nor was it necessary to preserve the patient's life or health. On appeal, the court held that the consent given for the muscle biopsy was wide enough to encompass the bone biopsy as well. In Alberta, there is legislation permitting treatment without consent: see the Dependent Adults Act, R.S.A. 2000, c. D-11, s. 29. In *F. v. West Berkshire Health Authority*, [1989] 2 All E.R. 545, a much broader test was accepted. Lord Bridge, at 548, stated that a doctor is entitled to treat a patient who cannot, because of "accident, illness or unsoundness of mind" consent to that treatment, as long as the doctor believes that the treatment "is in the patient's best interests", and the doctor acts with "due skill and care." Lord Brandon agreed, stating, at 551, that an operation or other treatment will be considered to be in the best interests of a patient "if it is carried out in order either to save their lives or to ensure improvement or prevent deterioration in their physical or mental health." Not only is a doctor immune from tort liability in such a case, but a doctor would be in breach of a duty to the patient if treatment were withheld.

has been refused.[57] In this respect, a card carried by a Jehovah's Witness refusing blood transfusions has been held to constitute a valid refusal for the purposes of an action in battery.[58] The refusal to be treated must be respected, even if the risks of non-treatment have not been explained to the patient.[59] It must also be kept in mind, however, the patient's right to refuse treatment, depends upon the patient's capacity. A person without capacity cannot consent to, nor refuse, treatment.[60]

Consent to medical treatment must be free, full and informed. Hence, consent given while under sedation may not be valid.[61] Although a valid consent requires that the party who has consented has the requisite capacity, a minor who can understand and appreciate the proposed treatment can give a valid consent.[62]

---

57 See, however, Picard & Robertson, above, at 54, for exceptions to this. Exceptions relate to special cases, such as when the patient has a communicable disease which must be treated, where the patient is under the care and control of others, when the patient is a minor, or when the patient is mentally disabled.

58 See *Malette v. Shulman*, above, note 46.

59 A very interesting case in this respect is *Hobbs v. Robertson* (2006), 265 D.L.R. (4th) 537 (B.C. C.A.), reversing (2004), 243 D.L.R. (4th) 700, 28 C.C.L.T. (3d) 133 (B.C. C.A.). The case involved a direction by a Jehovah's Witness refusing blood and a waiver of any right of action against the doctor. A blood transfusion became necessary during an operation but, because of the directive, no blood was given. The patient died. The issue was whether the waiver applied where the need for the blood arose as a result of the doctor's negligence. The Chambers judge, at [2001] 4 W.W.R. 218 (B.C. S.C.), decided in an application brought by the doctors to dismiss the estate's action against them that the waiver did not apply in this case. The Court of Appeal, at (2002), 13 C.C.L.T. (3d) 109 (B.C. C.A.) held that this issue was a very complex one and should not have been decided by the Chambers judge in an application to dismiss. At trial, the action was dismissed based on the release document. However, the Court of Appeal again remitted the case to trial based on its conclusion that the trial judge was wrong to decide the action on the record that was before him. Thus, despite the fact that almost ten years had passed since the cause of action first arose, the validity, interpretation and application of the Release document had yet to be decided.

60 In *Fortey (Guardian ad litem of) v. Canada (Attorney General)*, [1999] 10 W.W.R. 600 (B.C. C.A.), the police were sued in negligence by a person who had been arrested by them for being intoxicated in a public place. The plaintiff had been injured and the police and ambulance attendance had told the plaintiff that he should be taken to the hospital. The plaintiff refused and was not taken. The plaintiff suffered permanent brain damage as a result of his injury and sued the police for being negligent in not having taken him to the hospital. The issue was whether the plaintiff's refusal was valid. The court held that the police were negligent in not having recognized that the plaintiff was incapable of rational thought due to his intoxication. In effect the plaintiff's intoxication overrode his express refusal to treatment.

61 *Beausoleil v. La Communauté des Soeurs de la Charité de la Providence* (1964), 53 D.L.R. (2d) 65 (Que. S.C.).

62 See *Johnson v. Wellesley Hosp.* (1971), 17 D.L.R. (3d) 139 (Ont. H.C.); *C. (J.S.) v. Wren*, [1987] 2 W.W.R. 669 (Alta. C.A.); *Ney v. A.G. Can.* (1993), 102 D.L.R. (4th) 136 (B.C. S.C.); *D. (T.T.), Re*, [1999] 6 W.W.R. 327 (Sask. Q.B.) and *Van Mol (Guardian ad litem of) v. Ashmore* (1999), 168 D.L.R. (4th) 637, 44 C.C.L.T. (2d) 228 (B.C. C.A.), leave to appeal refused [2000] 1 S.C.R. vi, additional reasons at (2000), 188 D.L.R. (4th) 327 (B.C. C.A.). In the latter case, Lambert J.A. provides an excellent review of the common law and the British Columbia legislative provisions. In *Chmiliar v. Chmiliar*, [2001] 11 W.W.R. 386 (Alta. Q.B.), the court dealt with a 13-year-old girl who was caught in the middle of a dispute between her parents over whether she should be vaccinated against meningitis. The court decided that although the girl normally would have had the maturity to decide for herself, her mother's anti-vaccination arguments had poisoned her mind. The court thus took the decision upon itself and decided not to go along with the father. It refused to order the vaccination, in view of the girl's fears. For a full discussion of this see Picard & Robertson, above, at 81-92. Several provinces

There are also specific rules relating to the capacity of disabled adults.[63]

The question of informed consent as it relates to medical treatment is one which Canadian tort law has examined thoroughly.[64] As a result, the principles which are to be applied in this area are now fairly clear. A valid consent to proposed medical treatment requires that the patient knew what the basic nature of the proposed treatment was and agreed to it. A failure to be informed of the adverse risks associated with the treatment, even if these risks were sufficiently serious to lead a reasonable person to have rejected the treatment, will not vitiate the consent for the purposes of an action in battery. The patient in this situation, however, will have an action in negligence against the doctor for a breach of the duty to disclose.[65] The law was stated by Laskin C.J.C. as follows:

> . . . actions of battery in respect of surgical or other medical treatment should be confined to cases where surgery or treatment has been performed or given to which there has been no consent at all or where, emergency situations aside, surgery or treatment has been performed or given beyond that to which there was consent.[66]

An exception was made for those cases where "there has been misrepresentation or fraud to secure consent to the treatment."[67]

---

have legislation concerning the consent of minors to medical treatment. Minors also can refuse treatment. See *Walker v. Region 2 Hosp. Corp.* (1994), 116 D.L.R. (4th) 477 (N.B. C.A.) where a 15-year-old Jehovah's Witness was allowed to refuse a blood transfusion. The case, however, was decided pursuant to the Medical Consent of Minors Act, S.N.B. 1976, c. M-6.1, which modifies the common law with respect to the minor's right to consent to treatment. A case that came to the opposite conclusion was *H. (B.) (Next Friend of) v. Alberta (Director of Child Welfare)* (2002), [2002] A.J. No. 518, 2002 CarswellAlta 575 (Q.B.), affirmed (2002), [2002] A.J. No. 568, 2002 CarswellAlta 621 (C.A.), leave to appeal refused (2002), 2002 CarswellAlta 862, 2002 CarswellAlta 863 (S.C.C.), additional reasons at (2002), 6 Alta. L.R. (4th) 32 (C.A.), reconsideration refused (2003), 2003 CarswellAlta 24 (C.A.). The case involved a 16-year-old Jehovah's Witness with leukemia who was refusing essential blood transfusions. The girl was an intelligent and capable minor. The court held that despite the fact that the girl was a "mature minor", the Child Welfare Act, R.S.A. 2000, c. C-12 gave the court the ultimate decision regarding her medical treatment. The child's opinion was a factor in this determination but was not conclusive. The court ordered the treatment. The Court of Appeal affirmed the order but interpreted the trial judgment differently. It held that the trial judge had determined that the girl was not a mature minor at the time of the hearing. The patient died before treatment was administered. Also see *U. (C.) (Next friend of) v. Alberta (Director of Child Welfare)*, 2003 ABCA 66 (C.A.), leave to appeal refused (2003), 2003 CarswellAlta 1351, 2003 CarswellAlta 1352 (S.C.C.), reconsideration refused (2004), 2004 CarswellAlta 159, 2004 CarswellAlta 160 (S.C.C.) where the Alberta Court of Appeal reaffirmed that the Child Welfare Act supersedes the right of a mature minor to refuse to consent to essential medical treatment, which in this case was a blood transfusion.

63 See Picard & Robertson, *ibid.* A Supreme Court of Canada case dealing with mentally incompetent persons under the Health Care Consent Act 1996, S.O. 1996, c. 2, is *Starson v. Swayze* (2003), 225 D.L.R. (4th) 385 (S.C.C.).

64 There are numerous cases and legal writing mainly resulting from the two Supreme Court of Canada cases which have led the way in this area: *Hopp v. Lepp*, [1980] 4 W.W.R. 645, and *Reibl v. Hughes* (1980), 14 C.C.L.T. 1. The Supreme Court reaffirmed the basic principles in *Ciarlariello v. Schacter* (1993), 15 C.C.L.T. (2d) 209.

65 See Chapter 10 for a full discussion of this duty.

66 114 D.L.R. (3d) 1 at 10.

67 *Ibid.*, at 11. See *O'Connell v. Gelb*, Ontario H.C., O'Leary J., Doc. No. 262/76, 15th January 1987 (unreported). In *Kita v. Braig* (1992), 71 B.C.L.R. (2d) 135 (C.A.), the plaintiff sued for battery and negligence based upon an alleged misrepresentation concerning the doctor's pre-

As a result of *Reibl v. Hughes,* the battery action has all but been eliminated for failure to inform cases in respect of risks of medical treatment. This has proven not to be of benefit to patients since, as will be discussed, proving a cause of action for failure to inform in negligence is difficult. Battery is still available where there has been no consent at all, or where the treatment itself was misrepresented.[68]

4. SELF-DEFENCE

The right to use force to protect oneself from an actual or threatened attack has long been recognized by the common law.[69] Self-defence frequently arises in battery litigation, and the principles for its application are clear. Self-defence must be proved by the defendant on the balance of probabilities. This burden relates to all aspects of the defence. The defendant must prove that there was a situation of actual or threatened harm which necessitated the use of force, and that the amount of force used was necessary and proportionate to the threat.[70] These are both questions of fact. Clearly where a person is being attacked, or is threatened with imminent attack,[71] and there are no reasonable means of avoiding the danger, self-defence is legitimate.

More problematic is the situation where the defendant has been harassed, threatened or insulted by the plaintiff, but where the defendant can, perhaps with some loss of pride, avoid an altercation. To what extent does the law of torts require a defendant to walk away from a fight? Theoretically, conduct which falls short of a real threat of harm to the defendant does not justify self-defence, but is at most provocation which does not extinguish liability, but may mitigate damage.[72] As a practical matter, the distinction between what is merely provocative and what is truly threatening can present difficulties. In *Wackett v. Calder,*[73] for example, the plaintiff, who was drunk, insulted the defendant and his brother and

---

vious experience. The court held that any misrepresentation made was innocent, and that absent a deliberate misrepresentation made for the purpose of inducing consent, the battery action was not available, although a negligence action for failure to disclose could be pursued. This action also failed.

68 In an earlier case, *Halushka v. Univ. of Sask.* (1965), 52 W.W.R. 608 (Sask. C.A.), a battery action succeeded when a volunteer for a medical experiment was not told the true nature of the treatment to be performed. This type of claim would still be actionable in battery today. An interesting application of battery in a medical case can be seen in *Gerula v. Flores* (1995), 126 D.L.R. (4th) 506 (Ont. C.A.). The doctor operated on the wrong disc. This was a battery. He then altered the hospital records to conceal the mistake, and operated on the correct disc. The Court of Appeal held that since the plaintiff never would have consented to the second operation had he known about the doctor's first mistake, the second operation was also a battery. Moreover, punitive damages were awarded.

69 Fleming, *The Law of Torts*, 9th ed. (1998) at 92, note 75, cites *Chapelyn de Greyes Inne* (1400), Y.B. 2 Hen. IV., 8, pl. 40.

70 See *Miska v. Sivec* (1959), 18 D.L.R. (2d) 363 (Ont. C.A.); *Mann v. Balaban* (1969), 8 D.L.R. (3d) 548 (S.C.C.); *O'Tierney v. Concord Tavern*, [1960] O.W.N. 533 (C.A.); *Cottreau v. Rodgerson* (1965), 53 D.L.R. (2d) 549 (N.S. T.D.); and *MacMillan v. Hincks*, [2002] 8 W.W.R. 573 (Alta. Q.B.).

71 The case law establishes that you are not required to wait for the first blow before you can defend yourself. See, e.g., *Cottreau v. Rodgerson* (1965), 53 D.L.R. (2d) 549 (N.S. T.D.).

72 See below.

73 (1965), 51 D.L.R. (2d) 598 (B.C. C.A.).

invited them to engage in a fight. The defendant took up the plaintiff's invitation and hit him twice, knocking him down and breaking a bone in his cheek. The trial judge found that it must have been obvious to the defendant that the plaintiff's challenge to fight was "alcoholic-induced bravado" and that he posed no real threat. The defendant could have walked away from the fight and called the police. Was he required to do so? The trial judge found that he was. The Court of Appeal, on the other hand, interpreted the facts differently and held that the defendant was being attacked and "not being bound to take a passive defence [was] entitled to return blow for blow."[74]

Another way to approach this issue is from the perspective of the amount of force which can be justified in a hostile, although not necessarily threatening, situation. The less threatening the plaintiff's conduct, and the easier it is for a defendant to avoid harm, the smaller will be the amount of force tolerated.[75] However, because courts do not "measure with complete nicety" the amount of force necessary to repel an attack or an apprehended attack,[76] it is preferable for the issue of self-defence to be resolved on the basis of whether any force at all was legitimate, rather than on how much force was necessary. In *Roundall v. Brodie,*[77] for example, the defendant became annoyed when the plaintiff twice hit his golf ball close to the defendant and his wife. The defendant retaliated by throwing the plaintiff's golf ball, and engaging the plaintiff in a fight, which the defendant cleanly won. Was this attack in self-defence? The court held that although it is lawful to defend oneself or one's spouse, the blows inflicted on this occasion were not proportionate to the threat. It is suggested that the case might have been more satisfactorily dealt with on the basis that no force at all was required. The defendant had not been threatened, and could have avoided injury by stopping play and asking the marshall to remove the plaintiff from the course. The defence of provocation, rather than self-defence, was more apposite on these facts.[78]

Where there has been no threat of force at all, and not even provocatory conduct from which a threat could be implied, the claim of self-defence has failed.[79]

Even where it is necessary to use some force, the force used must be reasonable. This depends on the urgency of the situation and the harm to be prevented. Self-defence cannot be used as an excuse for punishment or retaliation. Thus, where

---

74 *Ibid.*, at 602.

75 See, e.g., *Brake v. Parsons* (1986), 59 Nfld. & P.E.I.R. 330, 178 A.P.R. 330 (Nfld. T.D.).

76 *Wackett v. Calder* (1965), 51 D.L.R. (2d) 598 at 600 (B.C. C.A.).

77 (1972), 7 N.B.R. (2d) 486 (Q.B.).

78 In *Barclay v. Fournier* (1991), 112 N.B.R. (2d) 424, 281 A.P.R. 424 (Q.B.), a 9-year-old girl threw a rock at a 9-year-old boy, allegedly in retaliation for rocks which had been thrown at her. The rock knocked out his four front teeth. The court accepted that the act was done in self-defence, and dismissed the battery action. In *Cyr v. Dubé* (1990), 111 N.B.R. (2d) 218, 277 A.P.R. 218 (Q.B.), a 74-year-old man slapped a 5-year-old child in the face, when the child came onto his property, sprayed the man's car and the man with water, and refused to leave when asked. The court dismissed the action for battery, again on the grounds that the defendant was using reasonable force to defend himself. I would question whether in either of these cases there was the imminent threat of harm which necessitated self-defence. There were other, more reasonable ways, of handling the situation. Provocation was the more appropriate defence.

79 See, e.g., *MacDonald v. Hees* (1974), 46 D.L.R. (3d) 720 (N.S. T.D.); *Harris v. Wong* (1971), 19 D.L.R. (3d) 589 (Sask. Q.B.).

the defendant clearly is physically stronger and more capable than the attacker, only that degree of force required to fend off the attack is permitted.[80] Although a defendant may be justified in using weapons for protection, their use will certainly make the defendant's task of proving that the force used was not excessive more difficult. In *Veinot v. Veinot* it was stated that "it is the exceptional case indeed where the shooting of an unarmed man can be excused or justified on the grounds of self-defence."[81] Where the force used is reasonably necessary, the fact that the damage caused by it is more serious than anticipated will not defeat the defence.[82]

5. DEFENCE OF OTHERS

The same considerations apply to a defendant's contention that force was required in order to defend another person from actual or threatened harm. The courts, however, must exercise a greater degree of caution with this defence. When the defendant is not personally under threat but observes what appears to be a threat to someone else, there exists a greater possibility of error. The defendant is not in the same position as the threatened party to determine the reality and extent of the threat, the reasons for it, and the options to avoid it. As well, the defendant's conduct might be motivated by factors other than a desire to defend — by jealousy, for example.[83] Social policy dictates that, whenever possible, the appropriate authorities should be called upon to provide the necessary protection for those threatened by harm, with private "vigilantism" being discouraged.

There have been very few reported cases where the defence of others has been raised. In *Gambriell v. Caparelli*,[84] the plaintiff and the defendant's 21-year-old son became involved in a fight following a minor traffic accident. The defendant came upon the scene and heard her son screaming and saw him under the plaintiff. Thinking that he was being choked, the defendant struck the plaintiff with a garden rake. The trial judge held that

> where a person in intervening to rescue another person holds an honest (though mistaken) belief that the other person is in imminent danger of injury, he is justified in using force, provided that such force is reasonable; and the necessity for intervention and the reasonableness of the force employed are questions to be decided by the trier of fact.[85]

---

80 See *Cottreau v. Rodgerson* (1965), 53 D.L.R. (2d) 549 (N.S. T.D.); *Cave v. Ritchie Motors Ltd.* (1972), 34 D.L.R. (3d) 141 (B.C. S.C.); *MacDonald v. Hees* (1974), 46 D.L.R. (3d) 720 (N.S. T.D.); *Norman v. Kipps*, [1994] B.C.J. No. 97 (B.C. S.C.); *Dang v. Guiltner* (1999), [1999] B.C.J. No. 1831, 1999 CarswellBC 1775 (S.C.); and *Herman v. Graves* (1998), 42 C.C.L.T. (2d) 250 (Alta. Q.B.).

81 (1977), 81 D.L.R. (3d) 549 at 551 (N.S. C.A.). See also *Organ v. Bell* (1981), 13 Man. R. (2d) 208 (Co. Ct.). See *Hood v. Lemp* (1988), 86 A.R. 315 (Q.B.), where the use of a knife against unarmed attackers was held to have been justified. It may be possible in some circumstances for the defence of assumption of risk or illegality to be employed. See Lord Denning M.R. in *Murphy v. Culhane*, [1976] 3 All E.R. 533 (C.A.).

82 See *Johnson v. Erickson*, [1941] 1 W.W.R. 626, affirmed [1941] 2 W.W.R. 524 (Sask. C.A.); *Bruce v. Dyer*, [1966] 2 O.R. 705, affirmed [1970] 1 O.R. 482 (C.A.).

83 See *Cachay v. Nemeth* (1972), 28 D.L.R. (3d) 603 (Sask. Q.B.). The defendant was "defending" his wife from being kissed by the plaintiff.

84 (1974), 7 O.R. (2d) 205 (Co. Ct.).

85 *Ibid.*, at 210.

Where an individual is under a legal obligation to protect or provide for another, and can be sued or prosecuted for failing to do so, reasonable force exercised to protect the dependent individual is permitted.[86] As well, there are statutory provisions which entitle force to be used to protect others.[87] The more difficult case for the common law arises when someone defends another, despite the absence of a legal duty to do so, a statutory privilege, or a close relationship between the parties. It appears from the *dicta* in a few cases that even here the defence of others can be applied.[88] Thus, in *Defosse v. Wilde*,[89] the defence was applied when the defendant came to the assistance of the plaintiff's sister, although it failed on the basis that the defendant had used excessive force with respect to the plaintiff. The Saskatchewan Court of Appeal confirmed the existence of the defence in relation to the protection of non-family members in *Babiuk v. Trann*.[90] The case involved a rugby player who punched an opponent in the face, breaking his jaw. The trial judge had found that the punch was delivered by the defendant in defence of a team mate who, while lying on the ground, had his face stepped on by the plaintiff. Although the trial judge rejected the defence of consent, on the basis that the punch was not part of the implied consent for playing rugby, she applied the defence of third parties. Sherstobitoff J.A. affirmed the trial judgment, noting that there was no reason in principle that the defence should be restricted to the protection of family members, and no reason why it should not be available to participants in sporting activities. The trial judge's decision that the force was reasonable under the circumstance was upheld by the Court of Appeal.[91]

A related defence is that of stopping a breach of the peace. As with the defence of others, the courts must exercise caution in allowing this defence, so as not to encourage private citizens to "take the law into their own hands." In *Johnston v. Barrett*,[92] a heckler at a political campaign meeting was physically assaulted,

---

86 For example, a parent who is under a Criminal Code obligation (s. 215) to provide for a child is entitled to use reasonable force to protect that child from danger. Similarly, a police officer who is obliged either by statute or by common law to protect citizens is permitted to use reasonable force to do so. In *Prior v. McNab* (1976), 1 C.C.L.T. 137 at 147 (Ont. H.C.), for example, the trial judge stated that "a police officer is not at liberty to shirk his duty. If he does, he may be charged with 'Neglect of Duty', an offence carrying the prospect of severe penalties."

87 Section 37(1) of the Criminal Code provides, for example, that

> every one is justified in using force to defend himself or any one under his protection from assault, if he uses no more force than is necessary to prevent the assault or the repetition of it.

Section 37(2) makes it clear, however, that excessive force cannot be used.

88 The *dicta* in *Gambriell v. Caparelli* (1974), 7 O.R. (2d) 205 (Co. Ct.), do not restrict the defence to family members, although the parties in that case were, in fact, mother and son. See also *Goss v. Nicholas*, [1960] Tas. S.R. 133, cited by Trindade, Cane and Lunney, *The Law of Torts in Australia*, 4th ed. (2007) at 105.

89 [1999] 4 W.W.R. 205 (Sask. Q.B.).

90 [2005] S.J. No. 41, affirming [2003] S.J. No. 614.

91 Both the trial judge and Court of Appeal approved of the argument made in this text that courts must exercise caution in applying this defence. Sherstobitoff J.A. also emphasized that the apprehended harm must be inflicted by "unlawful" means. Although this is not elaborated upon, I assume this means that if the plaintiff had a lawful right to apply physical harm to the third person, the defendant's intervention to protect the third person would not be permissible.

92 (1973), 8 N.B.R. (2d) 499 (Q.B.).

removed from the hall and deposited outside on the sidewalk. The court rejected the defence that the acts were done in order to stop a breach of the peace which had occurred, noting that no breach had been caused by the plaintiff and that his actions at the meeting were a legitimate expression of his democratic rights to freedom of speech. The defence also was rejected in *Smart v. McCarty,*[93] where Dickson J. referred to his judgment in *Johnston v. Barrett* and stated that "mere annoyance or insult to an individual, stopping short of actual personal violence, is not a breach of the peace."[94]

6. DEFENCE OF PROPERTY

One can use reasonable force to defend one's property against wrongful interference. Normally, the defence is applied in relation to real property where there has been an act of trespass followed by a physical ejection of the trespasser. It is questionable whether it is ever legitimate to seriously injure someone who is threatening property.[95] Often, however, intruders pose a threat not only to property but to persons as well, so that self-defence may apply. Since courts are more tolerant of force used to defend life, rather than merely to defend property, the applicability of the defence of self-defence or defence of others to a situation where an intruder has been seriously injured or killed will greatly assist the defendant's case.[96]

---

93 (1980), 33 N.B.R. (2d) 27, 80 A.P.R. 27 (Q.B.).

94 *Ibid.*, at 30. It is readily apparent that there is considerable overlap between the defences of self-defence, defence of others, defence of property, legal authority, and stopping a breach of the peace. Depending on the circumstances, what constitutes a threat to persons or property may also constitute a breach of the peace.

95 The question as to whether one is ever justified in seriously injuring or even killing someone in defence of property has arisen most frequently in criminal as opposed to tort law cases. A recent treatment of this issue can be found in *R. v. Ambroise Joseph McKay* (2006), 211 C.C.C. (3d) 74 (Man. C.A.), reversed [2007] 8 W.W.R. 631 (S.C.C.). The accused, by means of a knife, severely cut the face of a person who had refused to leave his house. He was acquitted at trial of the charge of aggravated assault by virtue of the defence of property section of the Criminal Code, s. 41. The Court of Appeal reversed, stating that "it is never reasonable to apply deadly force intentionally in defence of property, neither is it reasonable to use a weapon against the trespasser solely for that purpose. The case law demonstrates that an intentional killing or intentional use of a weapon will only be justified where self-defence becomes an issue" at para 12. The Criminal Code (s. 34) allows a person to cause death or grievous bodily harm to repel an unlawful assault in some circumstances. Since the Court of Appeal held that self-defence was not available in this case, and since the use of a weapon was not justified under s. 41, the Court of Appeal held that the accused ought to have been convicted. The Supreme Court in a short oral judgment set aside the Court of Appeal decision and ordered a new trial. It agreed with the Court of Appeal that defence of property under s. 41 alone could not justify the commission of the aggravated assault, but it would not endorse the view that defence of property alone will never justify the use of anything more than minor force being used or the intentional use of a weapon. Since the evidence at trial was unclear as to whether the accused intentionally cut the complainant, a new trial was ordered.

96 Although it is often overlooked, it would appear that jurisdictions which have adopted occupiers' liability legislation, which do not distinguish between injuries caused by activities conducted on the premises, as opposed to dangerous conditions on the premises, will be relevant to this issue. See, e.g., *Cullen v. Rice* (1981), 120 D.L.R. (3d) 641 (Alta. C.A.). A 16-year-old youth was injured while being ejected from a restaurant. The Court of Appeal

The right to eject trespassers is subject to reasonable limitations. In *Ball v. Manthorpe*,[97] for example, the court held that although the defendants would have been justified in removing the plaintiff from their premises since he was suspected of being the leader of a disruptive demonstration, they could not confine him in an enclosed space for 20 minutes until the police arrived. The defendants were held liable for a false imprisonment.[98] In some situations, there may exist not only a right to eject trespassers, but a legal duty to do so.[99] Even where there is such a duty to eject disruptive individuals, the courts have held that the forcible removal must be exercised in a reasonable way, with only reasonable force being used.[100]

Where a person's presence is peaceful, and the initial entry was lawful, it is necessary to ask that person to leave, before force can be used.[101] Even a trespasser must be given a reasonable opportunity of leaving, after a request has been made, before force can be used, unless the initial entry was a forceful one.[102]

The use of guns or other weapons to defend property interests raises important policy questions. It is clear that spring guns, or other deadly traps, cannot be set up in order to injure intruders.[103] One is entitled, however, to protect one's property with deterrents, such as guard dogs,[104] or barbed wire fences, as long as these are used to warn intruders not to enter, as opposed to catching them after they have entered, and as long as the methods used are reasonable.[105] It is not permissible

---

held that the force used to eject him was not unreasonable and that s. 13 of the Occupiers' Liability Act, R.S.A. 1980, c. O-3, which imposes a duty on occupiers not to wilfully or recklessly injure trespassers was not breached. For more on occupiers' liability, see Chapter 15.

97 (1970), 15 D.L.R. (3d) 99 (B.C. Co. Ct.).

98 The defence in this case could equally have been stopping a breach of the peace.

99 For example, provisions of the Ontario Liquor Licence Act, R.S.O. 1960, c. 218, s. 53(3), were in issue in the well known case *Jordan House Ltd. v. Menow* (1973), 38 D.L.R. (3d) 105 (S.C.C.). A tavern keeper was held to owe a duty of care to ensure that one of its patrons would not be subject to injury after being ejected from the premises. In *Bruce v. Coliseum Management Ltd.* (1998), [1999] 4 W.W.R. 178, 165 D.L.R. (4th) 472 (B.C. C.A.), the court affirmed the right of a bouncer to physically eject a disruptive patron. The court relied upon provisions of the Liquor Control and Licensing Act, R.S.B.C. 1996, c. 267, s. 46, which allowed licensees to request persons to leave and made it an offence for the disruptive patron to remain. Note, however, that the section does not expressly countenance the use of force or physical ejection.

100 See, e.g., *McKinnon v. DeGroseilliers*, [1946] O.W.N. 110 (H.C.); *O'Tierney v. Concord Tavern Ltd.*, [1960] O.W.N. 533 (C.A.); *Arbeau v. Dalhousie Tavern Ltd.* (1974), 9 N.B.R. (2d) 625 (Q.B.).

101 See, e.g., *Brien v. Astoria Hotels Ltd.*, [1939] 1 W.W.R. 641 (B.C. S.C.); *Green v. Goddard* (1704), 91 E.R. 540.

102 See, e.g., *MacDonald v. Hees* (1974), 46 D.L.R. (3d) 720 (N.S. T.D.).

103 *Bird v. Holbrook* (1828), 130 E.R. 911. It is also a criminal offence: see s. 247 of the Criminal Code.

104 This also may involve legislation. For example, in Ontario the Dog Owners' Liability Act, R.S.O. 1990 c. D-16, s. 3(2), renders a dog owner strictly liable for injuries caused by the dog, but expressly exempts an injury to a person who is on the premises for criminal purposes, "unless the keeping of the dog on the premises was unreasonable for the purpose of the protection of persons or property."

105 See Bohlen and Burns, "The Privilege to Protect Property by Dangerous Barriers and Mechanical Devices" (1926), 35 Yale L.J. 525, cited by Fleming, *The Law of Torts*, 9th ed. (1998), at 97, note 120.

to shoot an intruder who is leaving the premises and no longer poses a threat to persons or property.[106]

Although case law supports the right of an occupier to eject a trespasser so long as reasonable force is used, does this right extend to the removal of trespassing objects? In principle, it should, subject to the same qualification that it be done reasonably. However, in one case, *Cameron v. Morang*,[107] it was held that the defendant could not have a vehicle, parked without authorization on its property, towed away. The trial judge stated that individuals who wish to have other people's property removed must either call the police or use remedies offered by the law. This judgment runs counter to the case law concerning the right of occupiers of land to take steps to protect their property from trespassing animals, which includes killing trespassing animals if necessary.[108] One might distinguish this on the basis that in the case of trespassing animals the damage to the property will increase if immediate steps are not taken to remove the animals.

As a matter of social policy, the right to use force to protect persons or property must be carefully limited. If there is an immediate threat, and the force used is reasonable, the defence should be upheld. If there is the opportunity to avoid violence, for example by calling the police and having the offending person removed, this should be encouraged. It is more likely that a minor incident will erupt into a major one when individuals attempt to resolve the confrontation by themselves.

In certain limited situations, the law will allow a person to commit a trespass to land, or even a battery, in order to recapture chattels wrongfully retained. This right of "self-help" will also be carefully restricted. The law provides other, more appropriate, remedies to those who claim the right to possess chattels.[109]

There are very few reported cases where the right to self-help has been set up as a defence to trespass or battery. The most thorough treatment is in the judgment of the New Brunswick Court of Appeal in *Devoe v. Long*.[110] This decision held that the right to commit a battery in order to recover a chattel detained by another is dependent on two factors: (1) the person withholding the chattel from the person

---

106 See, e.g., *Bigcharles v. Merkel*, [1973] 1 W.W.R. 324 (B.C. S.C.).

107 (1978), 32 N.B.R. (2d) 22 (Co. Ct.).

108 See Fleming, *The Law of Torts*, 9th ed. (1998), at 96. The decision in *Cameron v. Morang* was criticized in *Stewart v. Gustafson* (1998), 171 Sask. R. 27 (Q.B.) as being "inconsistent with numerous authorities that recognize a proprietors' limited right of self-help, including *R. v. Howson* (1966), 55 D.L.R. (2d) 582 (Ont. C.A.)", as well as *Gaudet v. Laviolette*, [1959] Que. S.C. 398 (S.C.). The *Howson* case involved a charge of theft and the defence of "colour of right" with reference to removing a car from the defendant's lot. It is therefore not directly on point. The *Gustafson* case does clearly hold, however, that the defence of self-help allows a party not only to remove chattels from one's premises, but also even to destroy them when it is justifiable on a "cost-benefit" analysis. Also see *Sinclair v. Small* (2007), 2007 CarswellOnt 3555 (S.C.J.) and *Visscher v. Triple Broek Holdings Ltd.*, 2006 ABQB 259 (Alta. Q.B.) to the same effect.

109 Provincial legislation dealing with the seizure of goods provides for the seizing of goods by a sheriff with legal authorization. See, e.g., the Seizures Act, R.S.A. 1980, c. S-11, repealed 1994, c. C-10.5, s. 171, replaced by the Civil Enforcement Act, R.S.A. 2000, c. C-15, and the decision in *Re Can. Accept. Corp. Ltd.* (1977), 2 Alta. L.R. (2d) 377 (Dist. Ct.). See R. Wood, "Enforcement Remedies of Creditors" (1996), 34 Alta. L. Rev. 783.

110 [1951] 1 D.L.R. 203. See also *J.J. Riverside Mfg. Ltd. v. E.J.W. Dev. Co.*, [1981] 5 W.W.R. 607 (Man. Co. Ct.); *Phillips v. Murray*, [1929] 3 D.L.R. 770 (Sask. C.A.).

entitled to it must have initially acquired it wrongfully; and (2) the force used to retake the chattel must be reasonable. A trespass to land can be committed in order to regain possession of a chattel only if: (1) the person withholding the chattel either wrongfully acquired it, or if the possession was initially lawful, a request for its return had been made; and (2) the entry onto the land to retake the chattel can be made peaceably and without committing a breach of the peace.[111]

Similar to the right to recapture chattels by means of self-help is the common law right to enter land and, without using excessive force, to eject a trespasser.[112] Although it is a criminal offence to enter real property in a manner that is likely to cause a breach of the peace,[113] the defence may still be available in relation to a civil action.[114]

7. LEGAL AUTHORITY

The defence of legal authority is the broadest and probably the most frequently raised defence in terms of torts of trespass and other intentional interferences. The gist of the defence is the existence of legislative authority which entitles the defendant to engage in conduct which otherwise would be considered to be tortious and actionable. It usually is seen in cases alleging assault, battery, or false imprisonment, although it also has been raised in relation to trespass to land or chattels.

The defence of legal authority is not one defence with general principles capable of application to a variety of factual disputes, but an umbrella which covers a host of different statutory defences, each of which must be analyzed and interpreted in the context of the legislation in which it appears. In addition to the ordinary rules of statutory interpretation, constitutional and Charter issues also must be considered.[115]

There are numerous statutes, both at the provincial and federal levels, which explicitly or implicitly provide defences to tort claims. Although relevant provisions of the Criminal Code are frequently raised,[116] other statutes may be in issue. One may refer, for example, to cases dealing with the Identification of Criminals

---

111 On what constitutes a breach of the peace, see *Frey v. Fedoruk*, [1949] 2 W.W.R. 604, reversed on other grounds [1950] 3 D.L.R. 513 (S.C.C.).

112 See *Hemmings v. Stoke Poges Golf Club*, [1920] 1 K.B. 720 (C.A.).

113 Criminal Code, R.S.C. 1985, c. C-46, s. 72. See also s. 42.

114 See *Hemmings v. Stoke Poges Golf Club*, above, note 112.

115 Although these statutory provisions are considered in the context of a tort action, generally tort law principles are not in issue. Texts on tort can draw attention to the existence of these statutes but must leave it to other more appropriate sources for a detailed treatment.

116 The most common are ss. 25, 494, and 495.

Act,[117] the Mental Health Act,[118] the Mental Hygiene Act,[119] the Liquor Control Act,[120] and the Narcotic Control Act,[121] among numerous others.

There are several issues which must be considered when statutory provisions are raised as defences in civil actions. If the relevant statute contains an express immunity provision, is it constitutionally valid? As pointed out in Chapter 1, the law of torts is a matter which falls within provincial jurisdiction. Several of the statutes which have been raised in tort cases, however, have been federally enacted. Even with regard to provincial statutes, one must now be concerned with their constitutional validity under the Canadian Charter of Rights and Freedoms. Even if constitutionally valid, the specific provision which allegedly expressly or implicitly justifies tortious conduct must be interpreted according to the rules of statutory interpretation. *Prima facie,* courts ought to be cautious when deciding that statutory provisions deprive victims of compensation for their injuries or deprivation of their rights, especially when a statutory provision affording immunity can be restrictively interpreted.

The Criminal Code provisions relating to the powers of arrest, whether by police officers or private individuals, have been frequently raised to justify seemingly tortious behaviour. Despite the fact that the relevant provisions — ss. 25, 494, and 495 — do not expressly provide an immunity from civil action, they have consistently been applied in this way.[122] One of the more contentious issues relates to the powers of arrest of private citizens, discussed in s. 494 of the Code, and the relationship of this section to s. 25. Section 494(1) restricts the right of arrest of a private citizen to someone the citizen finds committing an indictable offence or to someone he or she believes, on reasonable grounds, has committed

---

117 R.S.C. 1985, c. I-1, raised in *B. v. Baugh*, [1984] 3 W.W.R. 557 (S.C.C.). Charter challenge unsuccessful: *Beare v. R.*, [1989] 1 W.W.R. 97 (S.C.C.).

118 R.S.A. 1980, c. M-13 [now S.A. 1988, c. M-13.1], raised in *Cochlin v. Alta.* (1983), 4 D.L.R. (4th) 763 (Alta. Q.B.), and *Tanner v. Norys*, [1980] 4 W.W.R. 33 (Alta. C.A.); and the Mental Health Act, R.S.B.C. 1979, c. 256, raised in *Ketchum v. Hislop* (1984), 54 B.C.L.R. 327 (S.C.), and more recently in *Mullins v. Levy* (2005), 258 D.L.R. (4th) 460 (B.C. S.C.), varied (2006), 2006 CarswellBC 1145 (B.C. S.C.).

119 R.S.S. 1953, c. 309, raised in *Kozak v. Beatty* (1957), 20 W.W.R. 497, affirmed 13 D.L.R. (2d) 1 (S.C.C.).

120 R.S.A. 1980, L-17, raised in *Rumsey v. R.*, [1984] 5 W.W.R. 585 (Fed. T.D.). See also the Summary Offences Procedure Act, R.S.S. 1978, c. S-63, raised in *Lang v. Burch* (1982), 140 D.L.R. (3d) 325 (Sask. C.A.); Intoxicated Persons Detention Act, R.S.N.B. 1973, c. I-14, raised in *Solomon v. Paul* (1981), 33 N.B.R. (2d) 435, 80 A.P.R. 435 (Q.B.), and in *Barrett v. Lorette* (1979), 27 N.B.R. (2d) 621, 60 A.P.R. 621 (Q.B.); Liquor Control and Licensing Act, S.B.C. 1975, c. 38 [now R.S.B.C. 1979, c. 237], raised in *Besse v. Thom* (1979), 107 D.L.R. (3d) 694 (B.C. C.A.), and *Christopherson v. Saanich (Dist.)*, [1995] 4 W.W.R. 381 (B.C. S.C.).

121 Now R.S.C. 1985, c. N-1, raised in *Schuck v. Stewart*, [1978] 5 W.W.R. 279 (B.C. S.C.).

122 See, among others, *Kennedy v. Tomlinson* (1959), 20 D.L.R. (2d) 273 (Ont. C.A.); *Woodward v. Begbie* (1961), 31 D.L.R. (2d) 22 (Ont. H.C.); *Frey v. Fedoruk*, [1949] 2 W.W.R. 604, reversed on other grounds [1950] S.C.R. 517; *Priestman v. Colangelo and Smythson* (1959), 19 D.L.R. (2d) 1 (S.C.C.); and *Crampton v. Walton*, [2005] 6 W.W.R. 414 (Alta. C.A.). In *Green v. Lawrence*, [1998] 10 W.W.R. 427, 163 D.L.R. (4th) 115 (Man. C.A.), Huband J.A. provides a useful history of s. 25, noting that it is intended to provide a defence against civil and criminal liability with respect to trespass. If, however, the defendant's conduct was negligent, there is no statutory protection.

an indictable offence and is escaping arrest and is freshly pursued by police officers.[123] Section 494(2) is broader and allows an owner or possessor of property or an authorized person of such a person to arrest a person who is found committing any criminal offence on, or in relation to, that property.[124] The question raised is whether s. 25 of the Code expands the right of arrest of private citizens to include someone they, on reasonable grounds, believe has committed an indictable offence, even if it cannot be proved, on the balance of probabilities, that an indictable offence was committed.[125] While some courts have held that the effect of s. 25 is to so expand the private citizen's right of arrest,[126] the majority have held that s. 25 does not alter the requirement of s. 494 that there must be reasonable grounds to detain the suspect *and* proof that an indictable offence in fact has been committed.[127] Complicating this issue is that some cases require proof that it was the actual person detained who committed the indictable offence,[128] whereas others merely require proof that "someone" committed an indictable offence, even if not the person detained. In *Sears Can. Inc. v. Smart,*[129] for example, it was held that the combination of ss. 25 and 494 of the Criminal Code leads to the conclusion that a private person can effect an arrest where that person has reasonable and probable grounds to believe that the suspect has committed an indictable offence,

---

123 This section contrasts with the right of arrest given to peace officers by s. 495. A peace officer may arrest someone who has committed an indictable offence or who, on reasonable grounds, he believes has or is about to commit an indictable offence. Note, however, that the section limits this right in cases where the public interest may be satisfied without arresting the person; see ss. 495(d) and (e), and the cases of *Kucher v. Guasparini* (1998), [1998] B.C.J. No. 582, 1998 CarswellBC 525 (S.C.) and *Walkey (Guardian ad litem of) v. Canada (Attorney General)* (1997), [1997] B.C.J. No. 599, 1997 CarswellBC 603 (S.C.).

124 See *Chopra v. T. Eaton Co.* (1999), 70 Alta. L.R. (3d) 90 (Q.B.). The concept of a citizen's arrest was discussed by Binnie J. in *R. v. Asante-Mensah* (2003), 227 D.L.R. (4th) 75 (S.C.C.). The case concerned the right of arrest given to a police officer, or the occupier, or a person authorized by the occupier under the Trespass to Property Act, R.S.O. 1990, c. T.21, s. 9. Binnie J. noted that in addition to the common law right, a citizen's arrest is authorized by many federal and provincial statutes. The case concerned the amount of force that can be used in executing a citizen's arrest in general, and more specifically, under Ontario's Trespass to Property Act.

125 As noted above, s. 25 is a general section which states:

> Every one who is required or authorized by law to do anything in the administration or enforcement of the law (a) as a private person, . . . is, if he acts on reasonable grounds, justified in doing what he is required or authorized to do and in using as much force as is necessary for that purpose.

126 See, e.g., *Dendekker v. F.W. Woolworth Co.*, [1975] 3 W.W.R. 429 (Alta. T.D.); *Karogiannis v. Poulus* (1976), 72 D.L.R. (3d) 253 (B.C. S.C.); *Lebrun v. High-Low Foods Ltd.* (1968), 69 D.L.R. (2d) 433 (B.C. S.C.).

127 See, for example, *Chopra v. T. Eaton Co.* (1999), 70 Alta. L.R. (3d) 90 (Q.B.), where this approach is discussed and adopted.

128 See, e.g., *Hayward v. F.W. Woolworth Co.* (1979), 8 C.C.L.T. 157 (Nfld. T.D.); *Breau v. K-Mart Can. Ltd.* (1980), 32 N.B.R. (2d) 488, 78 A.P.R. 488 (Q.B.); *Kendall v. Gambles Can. Ltd.*, [1981] 4 W.W.R. 718 (Sask. Q.B.); *Cronk v. F.W. Woolworth Co. (Woolco Dept. Stores)*, [1986] 3 W.W.R. 139 (Sask. Q.B.); *Frey v. Fedoruk*, [1950] S.C.R. 517; *Psathas v. F.W. Woolworth Co.* (1981), 35 Nfld. & P.E.I.R. 1, 99 A.P.R. 1 (Nfld. Dist. Ct.); *Banyasz v. K-Mart Can. Ltd.* (1986), 33 D.L.R. (4th) 474 (Ont. Div. Ct.).

129 (1987), 36 D.L.R. (4th) 756 (Nfld. C.A.).

and there is evidence that an indictable offence has been committed by *someone,* although not necessarily by the person arrested.[130] It has been suggested that *dicta* which seem to require proof that the actual person detained was in fact the person who committed the offence must be interpreted contextually. In those cases, which generally involve suspected shop-lifters, it has been argued that since no-one other than the suspect could have committed the indictable offence, there was no real issue of the offender's identity. If any crime was committed, it was committed by the detainee.[131]

According to either approach, it does not matter that there has not been a criminal conviction, as long as the defendant can prove, utilizing the civil and not the criminal onus,[132] that an indictable offence has been committed.[133] Even the plaintiff's prior acquittal on a criminal charge, does not deprive the defendant of a defence to the false imprisonment claim.[134]

To require both reasonable grounds and proof that an indictable offence has been committed in order to defend oneself against a false imprisonment charge may seem harsh. Courts must weigh the rights of retailers to protect themselves against theft with the rights of shoppers not to be detained and imprisoned by

---

130 See *Eccles v. Bourque* (1974), 50 D.L.R. (3d) 753 (S.C.C.), which was relied upon by the court. This approach was reaffirmed in *Newhook v. K-Mart Can. Ltd.* (1991), 116 Nfld. & P.E.I.R. 102, 363 A.P.R. 102 (Nfld. T.D.) and *Briggs v. Laviolette* (1994), 21 C.C.L.T. (2d) 105 (B.C. S.C.). Also see Puddester J.'s decision in *Maher v. K-Mart Can. Ltd.* (1990), 84 Nfld. & P.E.I.R. 271, 262 A.P.R. 271 (Nfld. T.D.). In this judgment, Puddester J. briefly raises but leaves aside the defendant's contention that in addition to the traditional defences, there is a developing defence that justifies "brief, non-intrusive" detentions by civilians to allow immediate investigation of suspected crimes. Also see *Kovacs v. Ont. Jockey Club* (1995), 126 D.L.R. (4th) 576 (Ont. Gen. Div.), where this "shopkeeper's privilege" is discussed. Cumming J. examines the U.S. law on this developing defence, but declines to import it into Canadian law.

131 See Meiklem J. in *Briggs v. Laviolette* (1994), 21 C.C.L.T. (2d) 105 (B.C. S.C.): "there is usually no proof of a crime committed unless it is proof of the crime committed by the person arrested." Although Meiklem J.'s point is well taken, the *dicta* is confusing on this point, and the issue should be resolved. An excellent treatment of this issue is found in *Kovacs v. Ont. Jockey Club*, above, note 130. Cumming J.'s explanation of the problem is that the wider defence — that is, there must be proof that someone committed an indictable offence — is a common law defence. The narrower defence — that is, there must be proof that the person arrested committed an indictable offence — is the Criminal Code defence. According to Cumming J., the common law defences have not been abrogated by the Code and thus both defences continue to exist. Although rarely utilized, the common law defence is useful when there is more than one potential criminal. This analysis was *obiter* in this case, however, since there was no evidence brought forward by the defendant that someone other than the person who was arrested committed an offence. See also *Chopra v. T. Eaton Co.* (1999), 70 Alta. L.R. (3d) 90 (Q.B.) at 121 and *P. (M.) (Guardian ad litem of) v. Port of Call Holdings Ltd.* (2000), [2000] B.C.J. No. 698, 2000 CarswellBC 729 (S.C.) on this point.

132 See *Frey v. Fedoruk*, [1950] S.C.R. 517. The onus is a heavy one according to this case.

133 In *Banerjee v. K-Mart Can. Ltd.* (1983), 43 Nfld. & P.E.I.R. 252, 127 A.P.R. 252 (Nfld. Dist. Ct.), *prima facie* evidence that a theft had been committed was held to be sufficient.

134 See discussion by Puddester J. in *Newhook v. K-Mart Can. Inc.*, above, note 130. The store owner must prove each of the elements of the criminal offence on the balance of probabilities.

those who are acting primarily in their private, and not, public interest. The balance is admittedly a difficult one to draw.[135]

Section 25 requires that no more force than necessary can be used in conducting an arrest or doing whatever else may be required or authorized by law. The onus of proving that the force used was reasonable lies on the defendant. The question of reasonable force lies at the heart of many of the cases involving Criminal Code defences, especially with regard to the conduct of police officers. In addition, the police must prove that they had reasonable grounds for believing that an offence had been committed.[136]

The power of arrest is dealt with both at common law[137] and by federal and provincial statutes.[138] When one realizes how many federal and provincial statutes,

---

135 Puddester J. in *Newhook v. K-Mart Can. Ltd.*, above, note 130, at 119, justified the current approach as follows:

> . . . it must be remembered that the matter involves the authority of a private citizen to deprive another citizen of his or her liberty, the latter being a concept highly prized under our system of democracy, and recognized and enshrined itself in various rights preserved under the Canadian Charter of Rights and Freedoms insofar as relations between the state and the individual are concerned.

In *Briggs v. Laviolette*, above, note 131, however, Meiklem J. suggested that the recommendations of the Law Reform Commission of Canada's 1986 Report on Arrest, which would apply the reasonable grounds criteria to the private arrest situation, would help simplify the area.

136 See *Koechlin v. Waugh* (1957), 11 D.L.R. (2d) 447 (Ont. C.A.); *Fletcher v. Collins* (1968), 70 D.L.R. (2d) 183 (Ont. H.C.). In *Swansburg v. Royal Canadian Mounted Police* (1996), (*sub nom. Swansburg v. Smith*) 141 D.L.R. (4th) 94 (B.C. C.A.), the British Court of Appeal held that s. 25 cannot be used to protect a police officer from civil liability unless the arrest was lawful, even if the police officer was reasonable in his actions. Also see *Hudson v. Brantford Police Services Board* (2001), 204 D.L.R. (4th) 645 (Ont. C.A), which affirms the point that s. 25 only protects the police in cases where their acts are authorized and not unlawful. The court discusses this issue in depth noting the Supreme Court of Canada judgment in *R. v. Feeney*, [1997] 2 S.C.R. 13, reconsideration granted [1997] 2 S.C.R. 117, dealing with the rights of the police to arrest without warrant. Note that s. 495 formerly required "reasonable and probable" grounds. See *Thornton v. Byers* (1999), (*sub nom. Thornton v. Hamilton (City) Police*) 173 D.L.R. (4th) 568 (Ont. Gen. Div.) and *Lloyd v. Toronto Police Services Board* (2003), 2003 CarswellOnt 58 (S.C.J.). Stinson J. notes that the Supreme Court held, in *Baron v. Canada*, [1993] 1 S.C.R. 416, that there is no analytical difference between the two wordings and that the test for a lawful arrest has not been changed. For a case emphasizing that the police must take all factors into consideration, such as the age of the suspects, the risk that they pose, and the nature of the situation, before arresting without warrant, see *Walkey (Guardian ad litem of) v. Canada (Attorney General)* (1997), [1997] B.C.J. No. 599, 1997 CarswellBC 603 (S.C.). A useful judgment that breaks down the s. 25(1) defence into its three branches is *Crampton v. Walton*, [2005] 6 W.W.R. 414 (Alta. C.A.).

137 The leading case is *Walters v. W.H. Smith & Sons Ltd.*, [1914] 1 K.B. 595. See also *Williams v. Laing* (1923), 55 O.L.R. 26 (C.A.). The question arises whether the common law defences have survived the Criminal Code defences, particularly with respect to the powers of arrest, which are wider at common law. See above, note 131. Also see *Hayward v. F.W. Woolworth Co.* (1979), 8 C.C.L.T. 157 (Nfld. T.D.). See Irvine, "Annotation" (1987), 39 C.C.L.T. 266. In *Chopra v. T. Eaton Co.* (1999), 70 Alta. L.R. (3d) 90 (Q.B.), Brooker J. states that the common law right of arrest of a private citizen still exists at common law.

138 For a comprehensive discussion see Law Reform Commission of Canada, *Arrest*, Working Paper 41, 1985; Report 29, 1986.

in addition to the Criminal Code, provide for arrest powers, one understands the scope of this topic.[139] The right to sue in tort for a false arrest, false imprisonment, battery, or other injury suffered during an arrest or attempted arrest depends upon the legitimacy of the arrest and the propriety of the steps taken to effect it, which in turn depend upon the nature of the legislation which is used to defend the arrest. This is an area where tort, criminal and constitutional law come together.

In addition to the provisions of the Criminal Code dealing with powers of arrest, there are other provisions justifying conduct which normally would be considered tortious. Section 43 of the Code, for example, provides that school teachers, parents, or persons standing in the place of a parent are justified in using force by way of correction toward a pupil or child, providing that the force used does not exceed what is reasonable under the circumstances. This section has its counterpart in the common law of torts which allows parents and teachers the right of disciplining those under their care.[140]

Tort law's approach to the defence of legal authority is in need of a comprehensive rethinking by the courts, particularly with respect to the applicability of the Criminal Code provisions. The Criminal Code is primarily concerned with criminal law, not tort law. The defences and justifications provided for by the Code relate principally to criminal, and not civil, responsibility. Yet certain of the Code provisions, especially those relating to the powers of arrest, have been made an integral part of tort law, even though common law powers of arrest exist. Other provisions of the Code provide different defences and justifications, such as preventing a breach of the peace,[141] suppressing a riot,[142] self-defence,[143] defence of other persons,[144] defence of property,[145] and correction of child by force,[146] but do not seem to carry the same weight in civil suits, the common law defences predominating. Why is there this different treatment? Should not all Criminal Code defences be considered alike in terms of their effect on tort law? In addition to this, it does not appear that the constitutional law issues have been given appropriate thought. Undoubtedly this will change as the Ca-

---

139 See the Law Reform Commission of Canada, Working Paper, *ibid.* The paper discusses the numerous statutes providing for powers of arrest but notes that the most significant ones in terms of actual number of arrests are the Criminal Code arrest powers.

140 See *Murdock v. Richards*, [1954] 1 D.L.R. 766 (N.S. T.D.).

141 Section 30.

142 Section 32. This section was carefully examined in an interesting case involving a "Stanley Cup" riot, which took place in Vancouver. In *Berntt v. Vancouver*, 33 C.C.L.T. (2d) 1, [1997] 4 W.W.R. 505 (S.C.), reversed and new trial ordered (1999), 46 C.C.L.T. (2d) 139, 174 D.L.R. (4th) 403 (B.C. C.A.), additional reasons at (1999), 47 C.C.L.T. (2d) 149, 179 D.L.R. (4th) 380 (B.C. C.A.); new trial dismissing action (2001), 209 D.L.R. (4th) 494 (B.C. S.C.), a participant in the riot sued the police as a result of being hit in the head by a projectile fired at him. The Court of Appeal held that the section provided a defence to a peace officer suppressing a riot if the officer believed in good faith and on reasonable grounds that force was necessary and not excessive. Based on this test the action against the police officer was dismissed.

143 Section 34.

144 Section 37.

145 Sections 38-42.

146 Section 43.

nadian Charter of Rights and Freedoms continues to work its way into existing Canadian law.[147]

8. PROVOCATION

Provocation has been defined as "conduct which caused the defendant to lose his power of self-control, and which occurred at the time of, or shortly before, the tortious act of the defendant."[148] It generally involves insulting or taunting words, or conduct which, although falling short of assault necessitating a defensive reaction, incite the defendant. Because the plaintiff's conduct does not require that the defendant take protective action, but merely provokes an often violent reaction, provocation is not regarded as a complete defence to an intentional tort, nor justification for tortious behaviour.[149] Provocation operates as a type of contributory negligence, mitigating, though not eliminating, the plaintiff's damages.

The current debate concerning provocation relates to whether a successful defence will reduce all of the plaintiff's damages by a certain percentage, as does contributory negligence, or only the portion for punitive damages, if indeed such an award is made. The traditional Canadian position, "supported by a long line of authority stretching back to 1834",[150] was that provocation reduced *all* of the damages. However, two Commonwealth cases, one in 1962,[151] and the other in 1967,[152] rejected this approach and held that provocation can be considered only in terms of the punitive damages award, not compensatory damages. The reasoning of these courts was that once a wrong has been committed by the defendant, the victim has a legal right to be compensated for the injuries caused, notwithstanding the victim's own "misbehaviour." This can only affect the matter of punitive damages.

Notwithstanding the rather fuzzy reasoning of the courts, which focussed exclusively on the defendant's wrongdoing while largely ignoring the plaintiff's, these two judgments subsequently found acceptance in several Canadian cases.

---

147 An interesting Charter case involving aboriginal rights in reference to trespass and intentional torts is *Thomas v. Norris*, [1992] 2 C.N.L.R. 139 (B.C. S.C.). The defendants were sued for false imprisonment and assault and battery occurring in the course of initiation ceremonies on a reserve. Among the defences was that the ceremony was a protected aboriginal right under sections 35 and 52 of the Constitution Act. The defence failed and the action allowed.

148 Atrens, "Intentional Interference with the Person", in Linden (ed.), *Studies in Canadian Tort Law* (1977), Chapter 14 at 414, cited in *Check v. Andrews Hotel Co.* (1974), 56 D.L.R. (3d) 364 at 369 (Man. C.A.).

149 As stated in *Evans v. Bradburn* (1915), 25 D.L.R. 611 at 612 (Alta. C.A.):

> In the absence of statute — in some of the United States, there are such statutes — no words, however opprobrious, disgraceful, annoying or vexatious, will justify an assault or battery, though they may mitigate the punishment.

150 Osborne, "Annotation" (1982), 20 C.C.L.T. 29 at 30, citing, among others, *Short v. Lewis* (1833), 3 O.S. 385 (C.A.); *Miska v. Sivec*, [1959] O.R. 144 (C.A.); *Hartlen v. Chaddock* (1957), 11 D.L.R. (2d) 705 (N.S. T.D.); *Agar v. Canning* (1965), 54 W.W.R. 302 (Man. Q.B.), affirmed (1966) 55 W.W.R. 384 (Man. C.A.); and *Fillipowitch v. Nahachewsky* (1969), 3 D.L.R. (3d) 544 (Sask. Q.B.).

151 *Fontin v. Katapodis* (1962), 108 C.L.R. 177 (Aust. H.C.).

152 *Lane v. Holloway*, [1967] 3 All E.R. 129 (C.A.).

The first was *Check v. Andrews Hotel Co.*,[153] where the Manitoba Court of Appeal thoroughly reviewed the earlier case law and decided to accept the *Fontin v. Katapodis*[154] approach.[155] Complicating the issue somewhat, however, were statements by Lord Denning in *Murphy v. Culhane*[156] which significantly qualified the position taken by the same court in *Lane v. Holloway*.[157] The principle that provocation can be considered only in relation to the matter of punitive damages was restricted to cases "where the conduct of the injured man was trivial — and the conduct of the defendant was savage — entirely out of proportion to the occasion."[158] Lord Denning stated that, in other cases, where the provocative conduct of the plaintiff could be considered to be partly responsible for the damage suffered, this can mitigate *all* of his damages. This approach was soon followed in two Canadian cases: *Rouleau v. Rex Drive-In Theatre (1972) Ltd.*[159] and *Holt v. Verbruggen*.[160] The debate was reviewed in *Hurley v. Moore*.[161] Admitting that the "[l]aw in Canada on the point remains in a befuddled state",[162] the Newfoundland Court of Appeal decided to accept the "traditional" Canadian position and allow the provocative conduct of the plaintiff to reduce the compensatory damages awarded to her.[163]

This matter ought to be clarified and one consistent approach adopted. In principle, provocation should be treated as unreasonable conduct is treated in negligence cases, and go to the reduction of the plaintiff's compensatory damages. To restrict the effect of provocation to punitive damages alone is to render it practically irrelevant, since punitive damages are only to be awarded in extreme cases of defendant misconduct. This degree of misconduct is unlikely to exist where the plaintiff's conduct was provocative, thus causing the defendant to lose self-control. The contention that the purpose of tort law is to compensate, and

153 (1974), 56 D.L.R. (3d) 364.

154 (1962), 108 C.L.R. 177 (Aust. H.C.).

155 Other cases following suit were *Shaw v. Gorter* (1977), 2 C.C.L.T. 111 (Ont. C.A.); *Reeves v. Pollard* (1977), 10 A.R. 349 (T.D.); *Landry v. Patterson* (1978), 7 C.C.LT. 202 (Ont. C.A.); and *Nguyen v. Condello* (1982), 16 Man. R. (2d) 208 (Q.B.). In *Proctor Estate v. Proctor*, [1994] M.J. No. 283 (Master Goldbert), support for *Check v. Andrews*, above, note 153, was reaffirmed although it was suggested that in an action under fatal accidents' legislation, the provocative conduct of the deceased might have a different effect on the damage award. In *Herman v. Graves* (1988), 42 C.C.L.T. (2d) 250 (Alta. Q.B.), the court held that provocation reduces only punitive damages, although no provocation was found in this case.

156 [1976] 3 All E.R. 533 (C.A.).

157 [1967] 3 All E.R. 129 (C.A.).

158 [1976] 3 All E.R. 533 at 535.

159 (1981), 16 C.C.L.T. 218 (B.C. Co. Ct.).

160 (1981), 20 C.C.L.T. 29 (B.C. S.C.).

161 (1993), 18 C.C.L.T. (2d) 78 (Nfld. C.A.).

162 *Ibid.*, at 95.

163 This approach seems to be emerging as the dominant one. See *Norman v. Kipps*, [1994] B.C.J. No. 97 (B.C. S.C.), where the plaintiff's provocative conduct resulted in a 20 per cent reduction of his compensatory damage award; *Defosse v. Wilde* (1998), [1999] 4 W.W.R. 205 (Sask. Q.B.), where damages were reduced by 50 per cent; *Bruce v. Coliseum Management Ltd.* (1998), [1999] 4 W.W.R. 178, 165 D.L.R. (4th) 472 (B.C. C.A.); *Hougen v. Kuehn* (1997), [1997] A.J. No. 982, 1997 CarswellAlta 847 (C.A.); *Chopra v. T. Eaton Co.* (1999), 240 A.R. 201 (Q.B.); *MacMillan v. Hincks*, [2002] 8 W.W.R. 573 (Alta. Q.B.); and *Nichol v. MacKay* (1999), 180 N.S.R. (2d) 76 (C.A.).

thus anything which restricts the right to compensation is to be avoided, overlooks the principle of fault, which is the fundamental prerequisite to liability.

A related issue is the applicability of the defence of contributory negligence to the intentional torts.[164] It has been accepted that contributory negligence can be raised in any action where the fault of the parties is in issue, even if the action is framed as a negligent trespass.[165] Whether the defence applies to torts based on intentional wrongdoing, however, is less certain. Despite earlier reluctance to apply the apportionment legislation to torts other than negligence actions,[166] this attitude seems to be changing. In *Gillen v. Noel*[167] the court considered that the plaintiff's conduct in inviting the defendants to his room to drink and in failing to ask them to leave, which would have avoided the ensuing altercation, was unreasonable conduct constituting contributory negligence.[168] This approach is consistent with the philosophy of apportionment legislation and is a good one. Contributory negligence which does not amount to provocation is unlikely to arise very frequently in the intentional torts, but when it does, and the court feels that the plaintiff contributed to the incident, there should not be a rigid rule excluding apportionment. There is no reason to treat provocation differently from other types of unreasonable behaviour in respect of the possibility of apportioning liability.[169]

---

164 See Chapter 13 for a full discussion of contributory negligence.

165 See *Bell Can. v. COPE (Sarnia) Ltd.* (1980), 11 C.C.L.T. 170, affirmed (1981), 15 C.C.L.T. 190 (Ont. C.A.).

166 See, e.g., *Hollebone v. Barnard*, [1954] 2 D.L.R. 278 (Ont. H.C.).

167 (1984), 50 N.B.R. (2d) 379, 131 A.P.R. 379 (Q.B.).

168 See also *Brushett v. Cowan* (1987), 42 C.C.L.T. 64 (Nfld. T.D.), reversed in part (1990), 69 D.L.R. (4th) 743 (Nfld. C.A.), where contributory negligence was applied to a case of a medical battery. In *Norman v. Kipps*, above, note 159, the plaintiff's provocative conduct was treated as contributory negligence and the apportionment provisions of the B.C. Negligence Act, R.S.B.C. 1979, c. 298, s. 1 were applied. A similar issue is whether apportionment applies between one defendant who is negligent and one who is responsible for an intentional wrong. The trend here is again to interpret "fault" broadly enough to encompass all wrongdoing for the purposes of contribution. See, for example, *Rabideau v. Maddocks* (1992), 12 O.R. (3d) 83 (Ont. Gen. Div.); *Bains v. Hofs* (1992), 76 B.C.L.R. (2d) 98 (S.C.); and *Cragg v. Tone* (2006), 41 C.C.L.T. (3d) 13 (B.C. S.C.), reversed (2007), 285 D.L.R. (4th) 754 (B.C. C.A.), leave to appeal refused (2008), 2008 CarswellBC 241 (S.C.C.), additional reasons at 2008 BCCA 260 (C.A.) — contributory negligence not found, but trial court considering various allegations of lack of reasonable care on the plaintiff's part.

169 In *Wilson v. Bobbie*, [2006] 8 W.W.R. 80, 2006, 263 D.L.R. (4th) 332 (Alta. Q.B.), damages assessed at (2006), 38 C.C.L.T. 169 (Alta. Q.B.), the question whether an initial assault by a plaintiff, which led to a retaliatory assault by a defendant, could be considered as a "fault" under the Contributory Negligence Act, R.S.A. 2000, c. C-27, was considered by Slatter J. Slatter J. concluded that while the initial assault could be considered as a "fault" for the purposes of contributory negligence, that it was not the cause of the defendant's retaliatory assault, and thus the contributory negligence defence was not available. The principle put forward by Slatter J. was that a person who has been convicted of an intentional, criminal act cannot argue that a plaintiff's provocative act constitutes a contributory fault. Having said that, however, Slatter J. did concede that under Alberta law, the defendant can argue that the plaintiff's damages, both compensatory and punitive, can be reduced due to provocation. Slatter J. made it clear that while, as a trial judge (as he then was), he was bound by the Alberta approach, he did not think it was the correct approach. The plaintiff's general and punitive damages were reduced by 20 per cent due to provocation in a separate judgment by Lee J.

9. NECESSITY

The defence of necessity, if reported cases are an accurate indicator, is a fairly obscure and rarely relevant defence to a tort law claim.[170] Yet, the defence has a certain appeal and fascination for tort scholars.[171] This is because the defence focusses on the basic moral and functional objectives of tort laws. Should an individual who acted in order to protect interests which are more important than those which were sacrificed be held liable in tort? Should an individual be required to give up property, health, or even life for the greater good? Who should bear the costs of unavoidable accidents or acts of God? The defence of necessity raises many of the same questions raised in other tort law debates, especially in relation to the objectives and values of fault-based compensation.

What is the defence of necessity and how does it affect an action in tort? Necessity, in a broad sense, is the basis which underlies several of the other defences we have discussed. Self-defence, the defence of persons, and the defence of property, including self-help, are all predicated upon the notion that the defendant's conduct was necessary in order to protect other interests. The statutory provisions constituting the defence of legal authority also apply to situations whereby the law permits certain acts to be done, such as search, arrest and imprisonment, in order to further other interests. As well, the principle that a doctor may act in order to preserve the health or life of the patient, even where there has been no consent to the treatment,[172] is an illustration of a necessity argument. Moreover, necessity is, as we shall see, an important factor in deciding duty of care and standard of care issues in negligence law, when the utility of the

---

170 There are very few direct Canadian or other Commonwealth cases on point. The ones cited most frequently by the texts and articles are: *Southwark London Borough Council v. Williams*, [1971] 2 All E.R. 175 (C.A.); *Sherrin v. Haggerty*, [1953] O.W.N. 962 (Co. Ct.); *Surocco v. Geary*, 3 Cal. 69 (1853); *Dwyer v.Staunton*, [1947] 4 D.L.R. 393 (Alta. Dist. Ct.); *Burmah Oil Co. v. Lord Advocate*, [1965] A.C. 75 (H.L.); *U.S. v. Caltex*, 344 U.S. 149 (1952); *Esso Petroleum v. Southport Corp.*, [1953] 2 All E.R. 1204, reversed [1954] 2 All E.R. 561, which was reversed [1956] A.C. 218; *Manor & Co. v. The Sir John Crosbie* (1965), 52 D.L.R. (2d) 48, affirmed [1967] 1 Ex. C.R. 94 (*sub nom. Munn & Co. v. The Sir John Crosbie*). See Linden and Feldthusen, *Canadian Tort Law*, 8th ed. (2006), at 94-96. There are three important recent criminal law cases which have extensively looked at the defence of necessity from the perspective of criminal law. See *Perka v. R.*, [1984] 2 S.C.R. 233; *Morgentaler v. R.*, [1976] 1 S.C.R. 616; and *R. v. Latimer*, [2001] 1 S.C.R. 3. These have spawned numerous criminal law cases involving the defence of necessity. As well, there is a fascinating civil law case where necessity was argued to be a source of a legal obligation, as well as a defence. See *Lapierre v. P. G. Que.* (1985), 32 C.C.L.T. 233 (S.C.C.).

171 See Williams, "Defence of Necessity" (1953), 6 Current Leg. Prob. 216; Bohlen, "Incomplete Privilege to Inflict Intentional Invasions of Interests of Property and Personality" (1926), 39 Harv. L. Rev. 307; Fuller, "The Case of the Speluncean Explorers" (1949), 62 Harv. L. Rev. 616; Sussman, "The Defence of Private Necessity and the Problem of Compensation" (1967-68), 2 Ottawa L. Rev. 184; Christie, "The Defense of Necessity Considered from the Legal and Moral Points of View" (1999), 48 Duke L.J. 975; as well as the major texts. A substantial treatment of the defence of necessity can be found in a symposium published in *Issues in Legal Scholarship* (Berkeley Electronic Press, 2005). The key note article is Sugarman, "The 'Necessity' Defense and the Failure of Tort Theory". Contributors to the symposium include James Gordley, George Christie, Mark Geistfeld, Gregory Keating, and myself.

172 See above. See *F. v. West Berkshire Health Authority*, [1989] 2 All E.R. 545 (H.L.).

defendant's conduct and the loss sought to be avoided become considerations in whether there should be liability for allegedly negligent conduct. Necessity as a particular defence, however, must be more narrowly construed in order to usefully stand alone.[173]

The defence of necessity need not be considered unless the defendant's conduct has first been found to be tortious and actionable, and there is no other applicable defence, such as legal authority or self-defence. In *Munn & Co. v. The Sir John Crosbie,*[174] for example, the defendant's ship was moored to the plaintiff's wharf, after the ship had discharged a cargo of coal for the plaintiff. During an ensuing storm, the ship pressed against the wharf and damaged it. Although these facts might seem to raise the defence of necessity,[175] the case was decided on the basis of ordinary negligence law principles. The trial court held that the defendant's decision to moor its ship at the dock was a reasonable one. There being no wrongful act, the plaintiff's action failed. This was upheld on appeal to the Exchequer Court. The court held that there was no allegation that the defendant deliberately damaged the dock in order to preserve the ship, and that, therefore, the American case of *Vincent v. Lake Erie Tpt. Co.*[176] and the necessity defence were not relevant to these facts.[177]

The defence of necessity balances the interests of an innocent plaintiff and the greater interests of others.[178] Where the plaintiff is not innocent, but has wrongfully acted in a way which has threatened the interests of others, the defendant's conduct to preserve these others' interests will not be justified on the basis of the necessity defence, but on one of the other defences, such as self-defence. It is this aspect of the case to which the defence of necessity applies — that an *innocent* individual is being asked to bear the burden of others — which distinguishes the defence, and creates philosophical and moral dilemmas.

There have been so few cases which have successfully applied the defence of necessity as a justification for the commission of a tort that it is difficult to define its elements with any certainty. Criminal law cases indicate that, at least in so far as criminal law is concerned, necessity is to be very narrowly restricted. A thorough discussion of the defence occurred in *Perka v. R.,*[179] where Dickson J. described the rationale of the defence as a situation of "normative involuntariness." In other words, necessity applies only where the circumstances are such that the person who committed the crime "had no other viable or reasonable

---

173 As Williams wrote in "Defence of Necessity" (1953), 6 Current Leg. Prob. 216 at 217:

> In a manner of speaking the whole law is based upon social necessity; it is a body of rules devised by the judges and the legislature to provide for what are felt to be reasonable needs. Obviously our present concern is with something narrower than this.

174 [1967] 1 Ex. C.R. 94.

175 Particularly because one of the well-known American cases on the defence of necessity had similar facts; see *Vincent v. Lake Erie Tpt. Co.*, 124 N.W. 221 (Minn., 1910).

176 *Ibid.* The decision in *Vincent* was the focus of the *Issues in Legal Scholarship* symposium, above, note 171.

177 This case is illustrative of the proposition that in its wider sense necessity is an element in standard of care issues in negligence law cases.

178 Occasionally, as shall be discussed, the plaintiff's own competing interests might be in issue.

179 (1984), 13 D.L.R. (4th) 1 (S.C.C.).

choice available; the act was wrong but it is excused because it was realistically unavoidable."[180] According to this approach, "the existence of a reasonable legal alternative" disentitles one to use the defence; "to be involuntary the act must be inevitable, unavoidable and afford no reasonable opportunity for an alternative course of action that does not involve a breach of the law."[181] Dickson J.'s concern was that a less restrictive defence would encourage individuals to decide subjectively whether obedience to the law was in conflict with some higher value which relieved them of the need to obey. As he stated:

> Such a doctrine could well become the last resort of scoundrels and, in the words of Edmund Davies L.J. in *Southwark London Borough Council v. Williams et al.*, [1971] Ch. 734 [at p. 746], it could "very easily become simply a mask for anarchy".[182]

The tort law approach need not be so cautious and timid. Courts in tort cases are not being asked to allow individuals to disregard laws, by excusing ostensibly wrongful conduct on the basis of necessity. Rather, they are being asked to weigh the plaintiff's right to compensation against the defendant's obligation to compensate, where quite legitimate questions as to the wrongfulness and purposes of the defendant's acts must be decided. If an innocent plaintiff is uncompensated this is, by itself, not unique or troublesome to a system of compensation based upon the premise of the defendant's wrongdoing.

In so far as tort law is concerned, it generally is stated that the defence of necessity depends upon there being a situation of great and imminent danger to life or property which can be averted by sacrificing the plaintiff's lesser interests.[183] It applies where the defendant has taken steps which can be considered to have been reasonably necessary in order to avert the threatened harm.[184] The peril which is sought to be avoided may be peril directed at (1) the plaintiff,[185] (2) the defendant,[186] (3) the interests of a third party,[187] or (4) the public's interest.[188]

---

180 *Ibid.*, at 15.

181 *Ibid.*, at 22.

182 *Ibid.*, at 14. Also see the discussion in the *Latimer* case.

183 See *Southwark London Borough Council v. Williams*, [1971] 2 All E.R. 175 (C.A.).

184 See Fleming, *The Law of Torts*, 9th ed. (1998), at 102. Fleming doubts whether necessity ever can justify the infliction of personal injury on an innocent plaintiff, although he speculates that this may be possible where the threatened harm is great and the injury inflicted is only slight.

185 For example, "the forcible feeding of an obdurate suffragette", as in *Leigh v. Gladstone* (1909), 26 T.L.R. 139, cited by Edmund Davies L.J. in *Southwark London Borough Council v. Williams*, [1971] 2 All E.R. 175 (C.A.). Or, *Sherrin v. Haggerty*, [1953] O.W.N. 962 (Co. Ct.), where a defendant trespassed onto the plaintiff's land and moved his cottage back to prevent it from being washed away. There is also the case of treating a person who has not consented to the treatment: see *F. v. West Berkshire Health Authority*, [1989] 2 All E.R. 545 (H.L.).

186 This is the more typical case. For example, *Southwark London Borough Council v. Williams, ibid.* — the defendant trespasses into the plaintiff's house to seek shelter; *Vincent v. Lake Erie Tpt. Co.*, 124 N.W. 221 (Minn., 1910) — the defendant moors its boat onto the plaintiff's dock to prevent it from being destroyed in a storm.

187 For example, where someone's goods are thrown overboard at sea in order to save the lives of the passengers, or the remainder of the cargo. See *Mouse's Case* (1608), 77 E.R. 1341; *Strang, Steel & Co. v. A. Scott & Co.* (1899), 14 App. Cas. 601 (P.C.).

188 See, e.g., *Burmah Oil Co. v. Lord Advocate*, [1965] A.C. 75 (H.L.); *U.S. v. Caltex Inc.*, 344 U.S. 149 (1952) — destruction of private property for the state's benefit during wartime;

Assuming that the test of necessity has been satisfied, i.e., the defendant acted in the face of an imminent and serious peril to avert a greater loss, what should the effect of this defence be? There are two approaches to this question. One approach has been to grant the defendant a complete privilege. That is, once the defence has been successfully established, the plaintiff's action is dismissed without compensation.[189] This is, of course, the effect of other successful defences to a claim in tort; if the defence is upheld, the action is dismissed and no damages are awarded.

A second approach has been to recognize what has been called an incomplete privilege.[190] The rationale of the incomplete privilege is to recognize that, although the defendant acted in a situation of necessity, the innocent plaintiff is still entitled to be compensated for the damages incurred.[191] The legitimacy of the defendant's conduct, however, is recognized and the plaintiff is not entitled to prevent the defendant from acting. If the plaintiff prevents the defendant from exercising his right, and as a result the defendant suffers damages, the plaintiff can be made liable for them.[192]

The incomplete privilege approach is attractive in theory. Where an act is undertaken in order to preserve the defendant's greater interests at the expense of the plaintiff's lesser ones, it is desirable for the law to recognize the legitimacy of the act, to disallow the plaintiff from preventing it, but to require the party who benefited from the act to bear the costs of it.[193] Where the defendant is a public authority which acts in order to preserve the public interest by destroying the plaintiff's property, this also is a loss which should be borne not by the individual plaintiff, but by all members of the public.[194] More difficult, however, is the case where a private individual acts to protect the public's interest or the interests of a third party. Unless there is a mechanism for the parties who benefitted to be required to contribute to the loss, one of the innocent parties, whether plaintiff or defendant, will be required to bear the loss.

Dwyer v. Staunton, [1947] 4 D.L.R. 393 (Alta. Dist. Ct.) — use of plaintiff's property because public highway blocked with snow.

189 See, e.g., *Dwyer v. Staunton, ibid.*; *U.S. v. Caltex Inc., ibid.*; *Cope v. Sharpe (No. 2)*, [1912] 1 K.B. 496 (C.A.). This is the approach favoured by Sugarman, above, note 171. Although his argument is based on several grounds, Sugarman's essential point is that if the defendant's act was reasonable and lawful, there ought to be no legal requirement that the plaintiff be compensated. Sugarman argues that this result is not only consistent with the fault requirement of U.S. tort law, but is also the morally appropriate approach.

190 See Bohlen, "Incomplete Privilege to Inflict Intentional Invasions of Interests of Property and Personality" (1926), 39 Harv. L. Rev. 307. This is the American approach and is discussed by Sussman, "The Defence of Private Necessity and the Problem of Compensation" (1967-68), 2 Ottawa L. Rev. 184. Whether this approach is justified is the topic of the symposium series of articles.

191 The leading case is *Vincent v. Lake Erie Tpt. Co.*, 124 N.W. 221 (Minn., 1910).

192 See *Ploof v. Putnam*, 71 A. 188 (Vt., 1908).

193 This is the view that I argue for in my symposium article. Not only do I consider that the requirement to compensate is dictated by the Canadian law of trespass, which does not excuse a defendant for trespassing even if the trespasser was not morally blameworthy, but I also consider it to be the most practical and efficient answer to a *Vincent*-type dilemma.

194 As in *Burmah Oil Co. v. Lord Advocate*, [1965] A.C. 75 (H.L.). See a contrary decision, *U.S. v. Caltex Inc.*, 344 U.S. 149 (1952).

4

Introduction to Negligence Law

1. THE PLACE OF NEGLIGENCE LAW IN THE LAW OF TORTS

The cause of action in negligence dominates the law of torts, both in terms of number of claims,[1] and theoretical importance. From a tort law which started out as a highly procedural, pigeon-holed series of carefully defined nominative torts, has developed a virtually open-ended, multi-purposive law, which expresses various, and sometimes conflicting, values. As has been written by one author:

> In the law at work, one tort, negligence, quite overshadows the others, driving them into the background, encroaching upon their territory, influencing their rules and sometimes overwhelming them entirely.[2]

The reasons for negligence law's spectacular growth in the years following the landmark decision in *Donoghue v. Stevenson*[3] are easy to identify. Unlike other torts which protect certain well-defined interests from equally well-defined invasions, the action in negligence, at least as it is generally interpreted and applied, has relatively few rigid impediments to continued expansion. Combine this with a society and a judiciary genuinely concerned with the compensation of personal injury victims, and with a system of liability insurance which ensures the compensation of victims without the financial destruction of defendants,[4] and all the ingredients exist for significant growth.

The success of negligence law has generally been greeted with enthusiasm. As Mr. Justice Linden has stated, with unconcealed delight:

> It never ends. And it should never end. A vibrant, growing negligence law should be able to respond to cover new fact situations and new social conditions. With the aid of the neighbour

---

1 It is difficult to know, in actual numbers, how many tort claims are negligence-based and how many are based on other causes of action. It is obvious, however, from the reported cases, and the fact that so many injuries are either automobile- or work-related, that negligence law is dominant. See the reference to the Pearson Report and Professor Sugarman's article, above, Chapter 2, note 2.

2 Millner, *Negligence in Modern Law* (1967), at 6.

3 [1932] A.C. 562 (H.L.).

4 On the effect of liability insurance on tort law, see Fleming, "Accident Compensation Reconsidered: The Impact of Liability Insurance" (1947-48), 57 Yale L.J. 549.

> principle and the inspiration of *Donoghue v. Stevenson,* the law of torts will be forever fresh and supple — able to handle any new problem as it arises with humanity and rationality.[5]

In the mid-1980's, a new factor placing negligence law's continued growth into question emerged. The liability insurance crisis, whereby the cost of liability insurance seemed to suddenly escalate greatly, if it was even available at all, put pressure on negligence law and the courts to slow down the expansion.[6] As it was the presence of liability insurance which allowed, and even encouraged, negligence law's growth, the absence of insurance would be equally instrumental in retarding it.

Two other factors also threaten the domain of negligence law. There are, of course, the persisting philosophical and political arguments which favour the restriction, if not the elimination entirely, of all compensation systems which differentially treat the disabled, based on the cause of disability. There is also the question of equitable access to the legal system, especially because of the high costs of legal services. Small claims, notwithstanding the importance of the rights at stake, are virtually outside of the system already, due to costs. In addition, scarcity of resources, which prevents the speedy determination of disputes, or creates other disincentives for those wishing to avail themselves of the system, reduces the utility and importance of negligence law to many potential users. These issues, while external to the substantive principles of negligence law itself, cannot be ignored, because for those affected, they can be the most critical concerns.

2. THE HISTORY OF NEGLIGENCE LAW

There is little question that the basis of contemporary negligence law is the House of Lords' judgment in *Donoghue v. Stevenson.*[7] However, negligence as a type of wrongful conduct leading to liability was part of the common law of torts hundreds of years before *Donoghue v. Stevenson.* Even as an independent tort, not dependent upon one of the special categories of duty relationships long recognized by the common law, negligence appeared before *Donoghue v. Stevenson.* When Winfield wrote his article on "The History of Negligence in Torts",[8]

---

5 Linden, "The Good Neighbor on Trial: A Fountain of Sparkling Wisdom" (1983), 17 U.B.C.L. Rev. 67, written to honour the 50th anniversary of "the single most important decision in the history of the law of torts: *Donoghue v. Stevenson.*" All, however, are not so sure. Professor Henderson Jr., in a critical exposition of the development of negligence law, argued that the attempt by courts, litigants and scholars to have negligence law decide disputes which are inherently not justiciable by courts of law seriously places in risk negligence law's capacity to survive. Henderson's thesis is that judges cannot decide disputes on the basis of "whim", or on the premise that all they need do is come to a reasonable decision under "all the circumstances of the case." There must be a formalistic process, rules, and most importantly, there must be issues capable of separate resolution. See Henderson, "Expanding the Negligence Concept: Retreat from the Rule of Law" (1976), 51 Ind. L.J. 467. For a counterpoint see Linden, "Reconsidering Tort Law as Ombudsman", in Steel and Rodgers-Magnet (eds.), *Issues in Tort Law* (1983).

6 See Klar, "Negligence — Reactions Against Alleged Excessive Imposition of Liability" (1987), 66 Can. Bar Rev. 159. For a detailed view of the trends in American tort law, see Gary Schwartz, "The Beginnings and the Possible End of the Rise of Modern American Tort Law" (1992), 26 Georgia Law Rev. 601.

7 [1932] A.C. 562 (H.L.).

8 (1926), 42 L.Q.R. 184.

several years before the decision in *Donoghue v. Stevenson* was handed down, the learned author was able to support his thesis that negligence existed as an independent tort by reference to a list of cases going back to *Aston v. Heaven*, decided in 1797.[9] As well, as Linden has noted,[10] at least one Canadian common law case, *Buckley v. Mott,*[11] came to the same decision as did the House of Lords, but 12 years earlier.[12] Nevertheless, *Donoghue v. Stevenson*, because of its high authority and its attractive eloquence, is the inspiration for modern negligence law.[13]

Winfield's research informs us that, until the period commencing about 1825, "the history of negligence is a skein of threads, most of which are fairly distinct, and no matter where we cut the skein we shall get little more than a bundle of frayed ends."[14] The action on the case provided remedies for those injured by negligent conduct in a number of particular instances. Those "who professed competence in certain callings" were apparently among the first exposed to liability based upon their negligence. The innkeeper, the common carrier, the apothecary, the surgeon, and the attorney, are identified by Winfield as those whose callings "had implied in them a duty of carefulness."[15] The law distinguished between "common" or "public" callings and other occupations, the former subject to liability for negligence, the latter not. This liability was based not only on negligent acts, but omissions as well, and applied independently of contract.[16] The principle of negligence was also "concealed" elsewhere; in public office, in bailment, and even in nuisance.[17] Winfield concluded "that in one form or another a fair amount of negligence in the sense of doing what a reasonable man would not do, or not doing what he would do, was covered by medieval law."[18] It was the period from 1825 onwards which Winfield's research indicates as being the most "fruitful" in terms of the development of an independent tort of negligence. Many cases are cited by Winfield to support the proposition that negligence existed as an independent tort, which covered liability for omissions as well as acts of commission. For example, *George v. Skivington*[19] imposed a duty on the vendor and manufacturer of a bottle of hair wash to use "due and ordinary care" to prevent harm to a person who had not purchased the product, but who was

---

9 (1797), 2 Esp. 533 at 535. The list of cases is at 42 L.Q.R. 199.

10 Linden, "The Good Neighbour on Trial" (1983), 17 U.B.C. L. Rev. 67.

11 (1919), 50 D.L.R. 408 (N.S. T.D.).

12 To say nothing of cases based upon the Quebec Civil Code, such as *Ross v. Dunstall* (1921), 62 S.C.R. 393.

13 In the United States this position belongs to *MacPherson v. Buick Motor Co.*, 111 N.E. 1050 (N.Y., 1916).

14 Winfield, "The History of Negligence in Torts", above, note 8, at 185.

15 *Ibid.*, at 186-87.

16 *Ibid.*, at 188. For a discussion of the contract/tort issue as it affected "common callings" see French, "The Contract-Tort Dilemma" (1983), 5 Otago L. Rev. 236, where the author defined "common callings" as a business which displayed two characteristics:

> Its services had to be generally available to the public, and its exercise must have demanded skill. Falling within this category were the carrier, innkeeper, surgeon, apothecary, attorney, veterinary surgeon, smith and barber.

See Le Dain J.'s judgment in *Central Trust Co. v. Rafuse* (1986), 37 C.C.L.T. 117 (S.C.C.).

17 Winfield, above, note 8, at 190.

18 *Ibid.*, at 191.

19 (1869), L.R. 5 Exch. 1.

known by the defendant as the person who was to use the wash. Baron Alderson's statement in *Blyth v. Birmingham Waterworks Co.*[20] that "negligence is the omission to do something which a reasonable man, guided upon those considerations which ordinarily regulate the conduct of human affairs, would do, or doing something which a prudent and reasonable man would not do", still stands as a valid description of the requisite standard of care in a negligence action. In 1883, Brett M.R.'s judgment in *Heaven v. Pender*[21] stated essentially what was hailed 50 years later in *Donoghue v. Stevenson*. The plaintiff, a workman employed by a ship painter who had contracted with a shipowner to paint the latter's ship, fell from defectively constructed staging which had been supplied and put up by the defendant dock owner. In describing the plaintiff's cause of action, Brett M.R. stated:

> Actionable negligence consists in the neglect of the use of ordinary care or skill towards a person to whom the defendant owes the duty of observing ordinary care and skill. . . . The question in this case is whether the defendant owed such a duty to the plaintiff.[22]

The existence of a duty depended upon a proximate relationship between the two parties which was described as follows:

> [W]henever one person is by circumstances placed in such a position with regard to another that every one of ordinary sense who did think would at once recognise that if he did not use ordinary care and skill in his own conduct with regard to those circumstances he would cause danger of injury to the person or property of the other, a duty arises to use ordinary care and skill to avoid such danger.[23]

It was true that Brett M.R.'s general duty principle "proved too radical for the rest of the court, who carefully dissociated themselves from it."[24] The principle, however, is remarkably similar to Lord Atkin's famous declaration in *Donoghue v. Stevenson*. The idea of negligence as a cause of action applying in an open-ended manner, not restricted by narrow and particularized categories, was in the minds of others well before 1932. If the social and economic conditions had been right, and compensation the principal objective of tort law, there certainly existed sufficient *dicta* in nineteenth century judgments to do much earlier what Lord Atkin did in *Donoghue v. Stevenson*.

3. ANALYSIS OF A NEGLIGENCE ACTION

The generality of the negligence principle, although a boon to those who are claiming compensation in novel cases, has proven to be frustrating to those who would like the negligence action to be analyzed in an orderly and logical way. Despite Lord Denning's disapproval of lawyers who would like a clear answer to the question "Where is the line to be drawn?" in limiting liability for negligence,

---

20 (1856), 156 E.R. 1047 at 1049. The case involved an action brought by a homeowner against a waterworks company for damages caused by flooding.

21 (1883), 11 Q.B.D. 503 (C.A.).

22 *Ibid.*, at 507.

23 *Ibid.*, at 509.

24 Millner, *Negligence in Modern Law* (1967), at 12. Brett M.R. himself (then Lord Esher) restricted its application in *Le Lievre v. Gould*, [1893] 1 Q.B. 491 (C.A.), to those in physical proximity to the defendant, to negligent acts but not to negligent words.

in preference to *ad hoc* decision making,[25] a manageable way to study and analyze the negligence action is a necessity.

There are significantly more injuries caused by wrongful conduct which are uncompensated by negligence law than there are those which attract compensation. It is the principal task of lawyers and judges to discriminate between compensable and non-compensable losses. Although in its most general sense, negligence law deals with the compensation of losses caused by unreasonable conduct, this is much too broad a notion to deal effectively with the myriad of issues which must be resolved before a decision as to liability can be reached.[26] Decision-making in negligence actions must be subject to the identification of issues and the consistent application of precedents.

The search for the most comprehensible and useful way to break down the cause of action in negligence has been the preoccupation of all torts writers and teachers. We seek to identify and isolate the elements of a negligence case, so that the issues and the applicable case law which respond to these issues can be known.

One of the most helpful analyses of the negligence action is presented by Professor J.C. Smith.[27] Recognizing that not all losses caused by unreasonable conduct will be eligible for compensation, the following questions must be asked in each case where compensation is demanded:

(1) Does the law impose upon the actor a duty to take care so that the activity in question does not harm the claimant?[28]

(2) Assuming that the answer to (1) is "yes", and, therefore, there is no reason in law to refuse to apply negligence law to the actor or activity in question, do the facts of the case in dispute justify the contention that the actor ought to have taken reasonable care for the plaintiff's protection? In other words, was there "a foreseeable risk of harm" to the plaintiff?

(3) How ought the defendant to have acted in the situation? In other words, did the defendant breach the duty of care by not acting reasonably?

(4) Was this breach a sufficient cause of the plaintiff's injury? Would the injury have occurred even if there had been no breach?

(5) For which of the plaintiff's injuries should the defendant be held liable? Stated technically, which of the injuries are sufficiently proximate in law to the breach to justify the imposition of liability?

---

25 See Lord Denning's judgment in *S.C.M. (U.K.) Ltd. v. W.J. Whittal & Son Ltd.*, [1970] 3 All E.R. 245 at 252 (C.A.).

26 Lord Denning's suggestion that it is "simpler and better to ask the one question: is the consequence within the risk? And to answer it by applying ordinary plain common sense", does not, in my respectful opinion, get us very far. Without breaking the factual dispute down and isolating the legal issues involved, decision-making in negligence law is a hopeless enterprise. See Denning L.J. in *Roe v. Min. of Health*, [1954] 2 Q.B. 66 at 85 (C.A.), cited in *A.G. Ont. v. Crompton* (1976), 1 C.C.L.T. 81 (Ont. H.C.).

27 Smith, *Liability in Negligence* (1984). An important recent book on the law of negligence is Beever, *Rediscovering the Law of Negligence* (Hart Publishing, 2007). As noted in the preface, this book "offers a systematic and theoretical exploration of the law of negligence". It examines its history, the theory that supports it, and its constituent elements.

28 Or, as stated by Professor Smith, does the law of negligence "extend" to cover the particular situation?

(6) Are there any factors in the plaintiff's conduct which justify a reduction, or even an elimination, of the damages which otherwise would have been awarded?

This analysis of a negligence case sufficiently isolates the elements of the cause of action and makes it possible for disputes to be logically approached. While not eliminating the flexibility, or the arbitrary nature of the task, it reveals what factors are in issue.

5

Introduction to Duty of Care

1. THE PURPOSE OF THE DUTY CONCEPT

In its broadest sense, the action for negligence compensates those who have suffered injuries as a result of the unreasonable conduct of others. However, what conduct is negligent from the perspective of the law, as well as which injuries merit compensation, are questions which can only be answered by the application of definitive rules and principles. The function of each of the elements of the negligence action is to direct the decision-maker to an appropriate response by isolating and thereby narrowing the issues presented by every negligence law dispute. This is necessary in order not only to ensure that similar cases will be decided by different courts in fairly similar ways, thus providing an element of certainty and predictability vital for the judicial process, but as well to attempt to achieve negligence law's principal objective; *i.e.*, the correcting of wrongs.

Even before an action in negligence can be decided by the internal rules and principles of negligence law, certain other elements, external to negligence law and designed to satisfy other policies, must be present. First, the defendant must be a person against whom a legal action can be brought, and the plaintiff a person having the status to bring it. A person may be protected from suit for various reasons. At common law, for example, the Crown could not be sued in tort.[1] This has now been changed by provincial and federal statutes which generally allow the Crown to be sued in the same manner as other legal entities.[2] Certain boards

---

1 See Hogg and Monahan, *Liability of the Crown*, 3rd ed. (2000). As the authors note, even the petition of right procedure did not apply to most tort actions insofar as Crown liability was concerned. Thus, although individual Crown servants could be sued, the Crown itself could not be sued. Also see John Law, "Private Law Remedies" in Jones & De Villars, *Principles of Administrative Law* (1999), Chapter 16 at 628-640 and Horsman and Morley, eds., *Government Liability: Law and Practice* (2007).

2 See the various Proceedings Against the Crown Acts. For a good discussion, see Goldenberg, "Tort Actions Against the Crown in Ontario", Spec. Lect. L.S.U.C., *New Developments in the Law of Torts* (1973), at 341; Hogg & Monahan, *Liability Of The Crown*, above, note 1; Lordon, *Crown Law* (1991); Sgayias, Saunders, Rennie and Kinnear, *The Annotated 1995 Crown Liability and Proceedings Act* (Toronto: Carswell, 1994); Horsman and Morley, eds., *Government Liability: Law and Practice*, above, note 1. See Chapter 8, below.

and other bodies are not suable in tort.[3] Foreign sovereigns and diplomats also have some immunities from suit.[4] Certain individuals cannot be plaintiffs in tort actions. For example, most common law provinces had legislation which prevented one spouse from suing the other in tort for personal injuries.[5] There may be other statutory bars, such as workers' compensation schemes, which remove the right to sue for certain parties.[6] As well, even where there are no substantive

3 See, e.g., *B.G. Ranches v. Man. Agricultural Lands Protection Bd.*, [1983] 4 W.W.R. 681 (Man. Q.B.); *Westlake v. R.*, [1971] 3 O.R. 533, affirmed [1972] 2 O.R. 605 (Ont. C.A.), which was affirmed [1973] S.C.R. vii; *Lucas v. Taxicab Bd.*, [1985] 2 W.W.R. 681 (Man. C.A.); *Duggan v. Newfoundland* (1992), 91 D.L.R. (4th) 262 (Nfld. T.D.) — the Welfare Institutions Licensing and Inspection Authority cannot be sued although individual members of the Authority can; *Zundel v. Liberal Party of Canada* (1999), 90 O.T.C. 63 (C.J.) — political parties cannot be sued.

4 See the State Immunity Act, R.S.C. 1985, c. S-18. See *Jaffe v. Miller* (1993), 103 D.L.R. (4th) 315 (Ont. C.A.), leave to appeal to S.C.C. refused (1994), 107 D.L.R. (4th) vii (note) (S.C.C.) — functionaries of the State of Florida entitled to sovereign immunity with respect to an action for conspiracy; *Walker v. Bank of New York Inc.* (1994), 111 D.L.R. (4th) 186 (Ont. C.A.), leave to appeal to S.C.C. refused (1994), 115 D.L.R. (4th) viii (note) (S.C.C.) — foreign state encompasses bank employees acting at the request of U.S. government law enforcement officers. According to s. 6 of the Act, the immunity does not extend to proceedings that relate to death or personal injury, or property damage, that occurs in Canada. *Athabasca Chipewyan First Nation v. Canada (Minister of Indian Affairs & Northern Development)* (2001), 199 D.L.R. (4th) 452 (Alta. C.A.) held that sovereign immunity applies to foreign sovereigns, but does not apply as between provinces within Canada. In *United States v. Friedland* (1999), 182 D.L.R. (4th) 614 (Ont. C.A.), leave to appeal allowed (2000), 141 O.A.C. 199 (note) (S.C.C.) it was held that the personal injury or property damage must be "physical" injury or harm. This would exclude mental distress not related to physical injury or pure economic losses. The Supreme Court of Canada approved of this in *Schreiber v. Canada (Attorney General)* (2002), [2002] S.C.J. No. 63, 2002 CarswellOnt 2921, 2002 CarswellOnt 2922. The court held that a claim for false arrest and detention allegedly resulting in mental distress, denial of liberty, and damage to reputation did not constitute proceedings relating to "death or personal injury". Therefore the section 6 exception to the immunity did not apply.

5 In Alberta, for example, the bar was abolished in 1990. The provision to prevent action was found in the Married Women's Act, R.S.A. 1980, c. M-7, ss. 1, 2 [am. 1990, c. 22, s. 2]. There have been several cases discussing this bar: see *Marr v. Marr Estate*, [1990] 2 W.W.R. 638 (Alta. Q.B.); *Photinopoulos v. Photinopoulos*, [1989] 2 W.W.R. 56 (Alta. C.A.). The statute abolishing this bar is the Gratuitous Passengers and Interspousal Tort Immunity Statutes Amendment Act, S.A. 1990, c. 22.

6 These have been subject to Charter challenge. In *Reference re Workers' Compensation Act, 1983 (Nfld.)* (1989), 56 D.L.R. (4th) 765 (S.C.C.), however, the Supreme Court of Canada upheld the validity of the Newfoundland scheme. See also *Budge v. Alta. (W.C.B.)*, [1987] 6 W.W.R. 217 (Alta. Q.B.), reversed (1991), 77 D.L.R. (4th) 361 (Alta. C.A.). The Supreme Court of Canada discussed the history and reasons behind the immunity in *Pasiechnyk v. Saskatchewan (Workers' Compensation Board)* (1997), 37 C.C.L.T. (2d) 1 (S.C.C.). Another example of tort rights being precluded occurs in the labour relations context. In *Weber v. Ont. Hydro* (1995), 24 C.C.L.T. (2d) 217 (S.C.C.), the Supreme Court of Canada held that, pursuant to the Labour Relations Act, R.S.O. 1990, c. L.2, disputes arising under collective agreements could not be resolved by tort actions, but only through the labour relations' process. The Supreme Court came to the same decision in *New Brunswick v. O'Leary* (1995), 125 D.L.R. (4th) 609 (S.C.C.), a case which arose under the Public Service Labour Relations Act, R.S.N.B. 1973, c. P-25. Also see *Chapman v. 3M Canada Inc.* (1995), 24 C.C.L.T. (2d) 304 (Ont. Gen. Div.), affirmed (1997), 37 C.C.L.T. (2d) 319 (Ont. C.A.); and *Moldowan v. S.G.E.U.*, [1995] 8 W.W.R. 498 (Sask. C.A.), leave to appeal refused [1996] 7 W.W.R. lx (note) (S.C.C.). There are a number of other recent cases on point that affirm that if a dispute falls under a collective agreement, it cannot be resolved through tort litigation. See, for example, *Gillan v. Mount Saint*

bars, the right to sue may be extinguished by the expiration of limitation periods, or for other procedural reasons, such as the failure to give adequate notice of the intention to sue.

These matters aside, the substantive law of negligence imposes its own limits. The action is restricted in terms of (1) those actors who are required to observe a duty of care, (2) those victims who can claim compensation, (3) those activities which can be regulated, and (4) those losses which can be compensated. These are the concerns of negligence law disputes which must be resolved. Although these four matters overlap, they raise separate and distinguishable issues.

The duty of care issue in the negligence action is the first question which must be resolved. It asks whether, in the dispute before the court, the law will impose a duty upon the defendant to take reasonable care for the benefit of the plaintiff. Its existence is predicated upon two fundamental propositions. First, notwithstanding the antisocial, unreasonable or even unlawful nature of the defendant's conduct, tort law will not seek to sanction it by compensating the plaintiff, unless the latter can demonstrate that the defendant's conduct was negligent *vis-à-vis* the plaintiff. Unlike criminal law, tort law does not regulate conduct for the benefit of the State, but only for the benefit of selective victims of that conduct. The second proposition holds that for reasons which, for want of a better term, can be called policy, there must be limitations on the kinds of actors, victims, activities, and injuries which can be dealt with by negligence law. An important limitation device is the duty of care element of the negligence action, although it is not the only restricting device available.

2. THE ELEMENTS OF THE DUTY RELATIONSHIP

(a) Introduction

The establishment of a duty of care has become a much more significant issue in negligence law and the analysis of duty more complex since the Supreme Court of Canada refined its approach to this issue in *Cooper v. Hobart*[7] and *Edwards v. Law Society of Upper Canada*.[8] Although predominantly applied to negligence actions falling into what I would term the 'frontier' areas, namely, the duty to assist others,[9] liability for pure economic losses,[10] and the tort liability of public authorities,[11] the current Canadian approach to establishing a duty of care is becoming increasingly more important in a wide variety of cases. This section will discuss in general terms how a duty of care is established in a negligence

Vincent University (2006), 42 C.C.L.T. (3d) 65 (N.S. S.C.), additional reasons at (2007), 2007 CarswellNS 369 (S.C.), affirmed 2008 NSCA 55 (N.S. C.A.).

7 (2001), 206 D.L.R. (4th) 193, [2002] 1 W.W.R. 221 (S.C.C.).

8 (2001), 206 D.L.R. (4th) 211 (S.C.C.). The new approach has been used by the Supreme Court of Canada in several of its important recent cases, such as *Odhavji Estate v. Woodhouse*, [2003] 3 S.C.R. 263, 233 D.L.R. (4th) 193; *Childs v. Desormeaux*, [2006] 1 S.C.R. 643; *D. (B.) v. Children's Aid Society of Hamilton* (2007), 40 C.C.L.T. (3d) 1; *Hill v. Hamilton-Wentworth (Regional Municipality) Police Services Board* (2007), 50 C.C.L.T. (3d) 1 (S.C.C.); and *Design Services Ltd. v. R.*, 2008 SCC 22 (S.C.C.).

9 See Chapter 6.

10 See Chapter 7.

11 See Chapter 8.

action, leaving to further chapters a closer analysis of the more difficult duty of care areas.

(b) The Leading Cases

(i) Donoghue v. Stevenson: *The Neighbour Principle*

The judgment in *Donoghue v. Stevenson*[12] must clearly be the starting point for any discussion concerning the concept of the duty of care in contemporary negligence law. This judgment is the most celebrated, even revered, negligence law decision.[13]

The critical facts of the case as alleged by the pursuer were as follows. The pursuer and her friend visited a cafe, where the pursuer's friend ordered some ice cream and ginger beer for the pursuer. The ginger beer was served in an opaque bottle, through which the contents could not be seen. After some of the ginger beer had been poured over the ice cream and consumed by the pursuer, more ginger beer was poured, and the pursuer discovered the remains of a decomposed snail as they floated out of the bottle. The pursuer alleged that she suffered both shock and gastroenteritis as a result of seeing the snail and drinking the impure beverage and sued the manufacturer for damages.[14]

At the first hearing, the Lord Ordinary, Lord Moncrieff, found in the pursuer's favour. The judge likened the duty in this case to those who release from their control or maintain in their control instruments of danger, thus staying safely within an already recognized duty category.[15]

On appeal to the Second Division of the Court of Session, this judgment was reversed, the court holding that based on previous authority[16] there was no duty owed in this case. The case then went to the House of Lords, which decided in the pursuer's favour, three for the majority and two dissents.

The stumbling block to the pursuer's action was *Winterbottom v. Wright.*[17] That case had dismissed an action brought by an employee of the postal service, who was injured by a defective coach, against a defendant who had a contract with the postal service to keep the postal carriages in a state of good repair. The judgment seemed to suggest that a person injured as a result of a breach of contract between two other parties could not sue the party in breach even if that breach was a negligent act affecting the plaintiff who did not have privity.[18]

---

12 [1932] A.C. 562 (H.L.).

13 On its 50th anniversary, a symposium was held at the University of British Columbia in honour of the occasion. See the speeches delivered there, at (1983), 17 U.B.C. L. Rev. 59.

14 The suit was initially brought against both the manufacturer of the ginger beer and the cafe's owner, although the action against the latter was dropped at the first stage of the proceedings. The issue came to court as a question of law, the merits of the case to be determined later, i.e., assuming that the facts as alleged were true, did the pursuer have a good cause of action in law?

15 See Linden's account in "The Good Neighbour on Trial: A Fountain of Sparkling Wisdom" (1983), 17 U.B.C. L. Rev. 72.

16 *Mullen v. Barr & Co.*, [1929] S.C. 461.

17 (1842), 152 E.R. 402 (Exch.).

18 See, however, Smith and Burns, "The Good Neighbour on Trial: Good Neighbours Make Bad Law" (1983), 17 U.B.C. L. Rev. 93, where the authors state that this is an erroneous reading of what *Winterbottom v. Wright* actually held. According to the authors, the judgment in *Winterbottom v. Wright* was never intended to be applied to cases of positive acts of negligence, but only to cases of nonfeasance. It was, however, interpreted in that way.

In reversing the appellate court's decision and finding in the pursuer's favour, the House of Lords in *Donoghue v. Stevenson* made two critical contributions to the future development of the law of negligence. First, it unconditionally released the law of negligence from the shackles of the doctrine of 'privity of contract' which had seemingly been placed upon it by *Winterbottom v. Wright.*[19] Second, it established the proposition that the duty of care owed in negligence actions is not confined to a closed list of specific relationships, but is based upon an open-ended and general concept of a relationship of proximity which is capable of extension to new situations. One must recall that long before *Donoghue v. Stevenson,* tort law had recognized special relationships imposing a duty of care on one party for the benefit of another. Even in the area of products liability, for example, it had been established that a non-purchaser injured by a defective product could sue the manufacturer in certain circumstances. If there was a fraudulent misrepresentation as to a chattel's safety,[20] if a chattel could be described as being dangerous *per se,*[21] or if a supplier had knowledge of a defect,[22] a duty of care was owed.[23] What *Donoghue v. Stevenson* did, however, was to state "a general conception of relations giving rise to a duty of care, of which the particular cases found in the books are but instances."[24] This is the so-called "neighbour principle" derived from the following speech by Lord Atkin:

> You must take reasonable care to avoid acts or omissions which you can reasonably foresee would be likely to injure your neighbour. Who, then, in law is my neighbour? The answer seems to be — persons who are so closely and directly affected by my act that I ought reasonably to have them in contemplation as being so affected when I am directing my mind to the acts or omissions which are called in question.[25]

(ii) Anns v. Merton London Borough Council: *The Two-stage Test*

To allow a duty of care to exist whenever it is reasonably foreseeable that negligent conduct is likely to injure the plaintiff, and then to leave it up to the trier of fact to decide whether the conduct of the defendant was negligent or not, would be to extend the judicial process beyond its capacity. The negligence action is only one mechanism of social control; only one vehicle to compensate the disabled, or to redress harms. Tort law must frequently step aside so that other

---

19 Above, note 17.

20 See, e.g., *Langridge v. Levy* (1837), 150 E.R. 863, affirmed 150 E.R. 1458.

21 See, e.g., *Dom. Natural Gas Co. v. Collins,* [1909] A.C. 640 (P.C.).

22 See *Heaven v. Pender* (1883), 11 Q.B.D. 503 (C.A.).

23 See the discussion by Heuston, "Donoghue v. Stevenson in Retrospect" (1957), 20 M.L.R. 1.

24 [1932] A.C. 562 at 580.

25 *Ibid.* The other two majority judges confined their judgments more narrowly. Lords Thankerton and Macmillan stressed the special circumstances of this case, namely that the product in question was placed on the market in a way which intentionally excluded intermediate interference or examination by the consumer. The two dissenting justices, Lord Tomlin and Lord Buckmaster, rejected Lord Atkin's approach. Not only did they consider that the precedents were solidly against it, but they also were supportive of them. As Lord Buckmaster so prophetically asked, if the court were to recognize the duty in this case, why would it not apply to the construction of every article, and even every house? Indeed, "If one step, why not fifty?"! As everyone has seen, the courts have since taken their fifty steps, if not considerably more, in the expansion of the good neighbour principle. After the decision in favour of the pursuer on the preliminary point of law, the case was settled, the pursuer receiving 100 pounds from the defendant's estate. See Linden, "The Good Neighbour on Trial: A Fountain of Sparkling Wisdom" (1983), 17 U.B.C. L. Rev. 67 at 72.

values, policies, and objectives can be promoted. In addition, one must not ignore the fact that "wrongdoing" is not the exclusive prerogative of tort law. Other areas of private law, such as contract or equity, or public law, such as criminal law and legislated schemes, are also involved in dealing with wrongs. The importance of maintaining a duty of care element which must be established as a prerequisite for liability in negligence is to provide the courts with a way to control the expansion of negligence liability by putting it into a larger social and juridical context.

The factual dispute in *Donoghue v. Stevenson* concerned a personal injury caused by a negligently manufactured product. In this context, the Lords held that the principles of English law would be gravely defective if a legal remedy were to be denied to a claimant.[26] In the post-*Donoghue* years, however, it became clear that although sufficient for most cases involving personal injury and property damage caused by acts of negligence the reasonable foreseeability principle alone was not a sufficient condition for the imposition of a duty in other categories of cases.[27] Whether in the area of losses caused by negligent words, by omissions, or by governmental negligence, or where the injuries were of a purely economic or psychological nature, other considerations of judicial and social policy, not relevant to the *Donoghue v. Stevenson* type of dispute, surfaced.[28] It became clear that the relationship of proximity contained more ingredients than that of reasonable foreseeability.[29]

The English House of Lords in *Anns v. Merton London Borough Council*[30] made a significant contribution to the understanding of how a common law duty of care is established by openly taking into account not only *Donoghue v. Stevenson's* 'neighbour' principle, but also policy considerations in the duty of care formula itself. In this judgment, Lord Wilberforce attempted to formulate a general conception of the duty relationship — one single principle that can be applied to all factual disputes. This is, of course, what Lord Atkin attempted to do in

---

26 See Lord Atkin's speech at [1932] A.C. 562 at 582. Of course, the dissenting justices feared that the imposition of a duty would have "outrageous" results, in terms of the difficulties of proof and economic costs which would now be imposed on manufacturers.

27 It must also be noted that initially the neighbour principle did not apply to negligently constructed buildings. The pre-*Donoghue* decision of *Bottomley v. Bannister,* [1932] 1 K.B. 438 (C.A.), was confirmed in *Otto v. Bolton and Norris,* [1936] 2 K.B. 46. Eventually, the duty was applied to buildings, whether built by an owner-builder or a contractor. See the discussion on this point in *Dutton v. Bognor Regis United Bldg. Co.,* [1972] 1 All E.R. 462 (C.A.). See also *Lock v. Stibor,* [1962] O.R. 963 (H.C.), and *Clay v. A.J. Crump & Sons Ltd.,* [1963] 3 All E.R. 687 (C.A.).

28 As we will see with the duty owed to the unborn, even ordinary accident cases involving personal injury can raise policy concerns that will limit the duty of care.

29 This point has been well expressed by Lord Keith in *Hill v. Chief Constable of West Yorkshire,* [1988] 2 All E.R. 238 at 241:

> It has been said almost too frequently to require repetition that foreseeability of likely harm is not in itself a sufficient test of liability in negligence. Some further ingredient is invariably needed to establish the requisite proximity of relationship between the plaintiff and defendant, and all the circumstances of the case must be carefully considered and analysed in order to ascertain whether such an ingredient is present. The nature of the ingredient will be found to vary in a number of different categories of decided cases.

30 (1977), [1978] A.C. 728 (H.L.). This case involved the problem of the tort liability of public authorities and will be examined in detail in Chapter 8.

Donoghue v. Stevenson, to weave the separate categories of duty relationships that had been developed over the years into a unified principle. The heart of the unified principle was a relationship of neighbourhood or proximity between the parties, based on Lord Atkin's concept of reasonable foreseeability. Once this relationship of proximity is found to exist, Lord Wilberforce's principle dictated that a *prima facie* duty of care would arise between the parties, only to be set aside, reduced or limited by policy considerations. This approach, which became known as the "presumptive duty" approach, was explained by Lord Wilberforce in the following terms:

> Through the trilogy of cases in this House — *Donoghue v. Stevenson*, [1932] A.C. 562, *Hedley Byrne & Co. v. Heller & Partners Ltd.*, [1964] A.C. 465, and *Dorset Yacht Co. Ltd. v. Home Office*, [1970] A.C. 1004, the position has now been reached that in order to establish that a duty of care arises in a particular situation, it is not necessary to bring the facts of that situation within those of previous situations in which a duty of care has been held to exist. Rather the question has to be approached in two stages. First one has to ask whether, as between the alleged wrongdoer and the person who has suffered damage there is a sufficient relationship of proximity or neighbourhood such that, in the reasonable contemplation of the former, carelessness on his part may be likely to cause damage to the latter — in which case a *prima facie* duty of care arises. Secondly, if the first question is answered affirmatively, it is necessary to consider whether there are any considerations which ought to negative, or to reduce or limit the scope of the duty or the class of person to whom it is owed or the damages to which a breach of it may give rise.[31]

There were two things that were important about Lord Wilberforce's formula. First, it applied to all factual disputes. Thus, the application of negligence law was not to be confined to personal injury and property damage cases caused by positive acts of negligence, but to all disputes, whether they be for pure economic losses, for losses caused in a commercial or business dispute, or against public authorities. This predictably led to an expansion of liability in those jurisdictions that adopted this approach. Secondly, while recognizing that policy considerations can limit or even negate a duty, these policy considerations became removed from the initial formulation of the *prima facie* duty. Once the *prima facie* duty was found to exist, the burden of "persuasion" was shifted from those who wanted the duty to exist to those who wished to argue that it should not. While it is true that this was not a burden of proof in a legal sense, the recognition of a "presumptive" duty which only can be displaced by policy considerations, changed the nature of the debate.[32] The emphasis was on warmly embracing extensions to negligence law, and seeing resistence to expansion as less desirable.

(iii) The English Courts Retreat From Anns

Arguably due to the expansionist nature of Lord Wilberforce's presumptive duty approach, a cautious English House of Lords soon thereafter retreated from

31 (1977), [1978] A.C. 728 (H.L.), at 751-52. It must be noted that this presumptive duty approach is not solely attributable to Lord Wilberforce. Lord Reid said essentially the same thing in *Home Office v. Dorset Yacht*, [1970] A.C. 1004 at 1026-27.

32 See, however, discussion below concerning the application of the duty formula by the Supreme Court of Canada in *Childs v. Desormeaux*, [2006] 1 S.C.R 643 and *Hill v. Hamilton-Wentworth Regional Police* (2007), 50 C.C.L.T. (3d) 1 (S.C.C.). As will be pointed out, the Supreme Court of Canada seemed to place the evidentiary burden of establishing the policy reasons to negate or limit the *prima facie* duty on the defendant, although the "formal" burden of proving duty rests on the plaintiff.

it, and adopted a new approach. In a series of judgments, commencing in the mid 1980s, the Lords began to reject the concept of a general formula for duty, based upon foreseeability, and only then limited by policy, in favour of a return to a narrower categorization of cases.[33] Fundamental to this rethinking was the view that the so-called first stage of *Anns*, namely, a relationship of proximity between the parties, comprised a good deal more than Lord Atkin's neighbour principle. More specifically, policy considerations which Lord Wilberforce's test had removed from the first stage of the duty test, were introduced back into it. In *Peabody Trust v. Sir Lindsay Parkinson Ltd.*,[34] for example, Lord Keith stated that in determining the scope of a particular duty, there must be consideration of whether it is "just and reasonable" that such a duty should be owed.[35] More pointedly, Lord Keith, in *Yuen Kun-yeu v. A.G. of Hong Kong*,[36] frankly stated that the two stage test for determining the duty of care had been "elevated to a degree of importance greater than it merits, and perhaps greater than its author intended".[37] If there was any doubt about this alternative view of the meaning of the first stage of the test, this was put to rest by Lord Keith:

> [T]he expression of the first stage of the test carries with it a risk of misinterpretation. . . . [T]here are two possible views of what Lord Wilberforce meant. The first view. . .is that he meant to test the sufficiency of proximity simply by the reasonable contemplation of likely harm. The second view. . .is that Lord Wilberforce meant the expression 'proximity of neighbourhood' to be a composite one, importing the whole concept of necessary relationship between plaintiff and

---

33 This approach was well articulated by Lord Bridge in *Caparo Industries plc v. Dickman*, [1990] 1 All E.R. 568 at 574.:

> Whilst recognising, of course, the importance of the underlying general principles common to the whole field of negligence, I think the law has now moved in the direction of attaching greater significance to the more traditional categorisation of distinct and recognisable situations as guides to the existence, the scope and limits of the varied duties of care which the law imposes.

Lord Bridge stated that it was time to recognize the wisdom of the words of Brennan J. in the High Court of Australia in *Sutherland Shire Council v. Heyman* (1985), 60 A.L.R. 1 at 43-44, where he said:

> It is preferable in my view, that the law should develop novel categories of negligence incrementally and by analogy with established categories, rather than by a massive extension of a prima facie duty of care restrained only by indefinable "considerations which ought to negative, or to reduce or limit the scope of the duty or the class of person to whom it is owed."

34 [1985] A.C. 210 (H.L.).

35 *Ibid.*, at 241. What is interesting about this comment is Lord Keith's reference to a quote of Lord Morris in the much earlier case of *Dorset Yacht v. Home Office,* [1970] A.C. 1004, at 1039, that "policy need not be invoked where reason and good sense will at once point the way." The implication is clear; reason and good sense become part of the initial determination of duty. Good sense and consideration of what is fair and reasonable also resulted in the denial of a duty in *Curran v. Northern Ireland Co-ownership Housing Assn. Ltd.*, [1987] 2 All E.R. 13 (H.L.). More interestingly, Lord Bridge noted, at 17, that *Anns* represented the "high-water mark of a trend in the development of the law of negligence by your Lordship's House towards the elevation of the 'neighbourhood' principle. . .into one of general application from which a duty of care may always be derived unless there are clear countervailing considerations to exclude it". This was a trend which Lord Bridge noted was "cogently" criticised by Professors Smith and Burns at (1983), 46 MLR 147, which criticism Lord Bridge evidently supported.

36 [1987] 2 All E.R. 705 (P.C.).

37 *Ibid.*, at 710.

> defendant described by Lord Atkin in *Donoghue v. Stevenson*. . .. In their Lordships' opinion the second view is the correct one. . .it is clear that foreseeability itself does not of itself, and automatically, lead to a duty of care. . .. Foreseeability of harm is a necessary ingredient of such a relationship, but it is not the only one. . ..[38]

In effect, this was an abandonment of the two-stage test. In England, whether a duty of care exists in any given situation would depend upon the category of dispute in issue. Further, proximity would depend upon a variety of factors, foreseeability playing a minor role, especially in the non-conventional dispute.

(iv) Canadian Law's Initial Enthusiasm for the Two-stage Test

Canadian negligence law initially and strongly adopted the *Anns* "two-stage" duty approach. It was first applied by the Supreme Court of Canada in *Nielsen v. Kamloops (City)*,[39] and after that in numerous Supreme Court of Canada decisions.[40] The approach was consistent — the first stage of the duty test was the

---

38 *Ibid.*, at 710. Lord Keith referred extensively to the Australian High Court case of *Sutherland Shire Council v. Heyman* (1985), 60 ALR 1, where this view of the two-stage test was adopted. Lord Keith conceded that on this view of the first stage of the two-stage test, the second stage "is one which will rarely have to be applied", at 712. See also Lord Keith's judgment in *Rowling v. Takaro Properties Ltd.*, [1988] 1 All E.R. 163 (P.C.), *Hill v. Chief Constable of West Yorkshire*, [1988] 2 All E.R. 238 (H.L.), and *Murphy v. Brentwood DC*, [1990] 2 All E.R. 908, at 914. Lord Goff stated essentially the same thing in *Davis v. Radcliffe*, [1990] 1 W.L.R. 821, at 826 (P.C.), as did Lord Bridge in *Caparo Industries plc. v. Dickman*, [1990] 1 All E.R. 568 at 574. In the latter case, three criteria were stated to be part of the *prima facie* duty: foreseeability of damage, proximity of relationship, and reasonableness. Thus a 'three-stage' test was adopted, The third stage, that is the 'just and reasonable' test, has been employed in other House of Lords' cases. See, for example, *Barrett v. Enfield*, [1999] 3 All E.R. 193 (H.L.) regarding the liability of a public authority. The death of *Anns*, not only with respect to its two stage test, but also with respect to the issue of the liability of public authorities, has been much discussed in the literature. See, for example, Howarth, "Negligence After Murphy: Time To Re-Think" (1991), 50 C.L.J. 58, where the author critically notes that the House of Lords has replaced *Anns* two-stage test with a three-stage test, by inserting the vague concept of "proximity" between Lord Wilberforce's original two stages. Also see Brodie, "In Defence of Donoghue" (1997), 2 Juridical Rev. 65 with regard to the 'three-stage' test.

39 [1984] 2 S.C.R. 2, [1984] 5 W.W.R. 1, 29 C.C.L.T. 97, 10 D.L.R. (4th) 641.

40 In *Just v. British Columbia*, [1989] 2 S.C.R. 1228, [1990] 1 W.W.R. 385, 1 C.C.L.T. (2d) 1, at 10 [C.C.L.T.], Cory J. stated that "it is a sound approach to determine first if there is a duty of care owed by the defendant to the plaintiff", and then "to explore two aspects [relating to policy issues concerning liability of public authorities] in order to determine whether liability may be imposed. . .." The first stage involved the reasonably foreseeability of the risk to the plaintiff, the second stage involved looking at the legislation and the policy/operational dichotomy. In *Rothfield v. Manolakos*, [1989] 2 S.C.R. 1259, [1990] 1 W.W.R. 408, 1 C.C.L.T. (2d) 233, at 258 [C.C.L.T.], Cory J. reaffirmed adoption of the test, noting that "the proximity or neighbourhood test familiar to all since *M'Alister (or Donoghue) v. Stevenson*. . .may well establish a *prima facie* duty of care on the part of the public authority." Again the second stage involved looking at the statute involved. In *C.N.R. v. Norsk* (1992), 92 D.L.R. (4th) 289, 11 C.C.L.T. (2d) 1 at 45, Stevenson J. reaffirmed the two-stage test, noting that "at the first stage a *prima facie* duty of care is established by reasonable foreseeability of harm. At the second stage, the *prima facie* duty of care can be negated or reduced in scope by policy considerations." In *London Drugs v. Kuehne & Nagel*, [1993] 1 W.W.R. 1, 97 D.L.R. (4th) 261 at 269, La Forest J. reaffirmed the two-stage test, stating that "the damage in question in this case was reasonably foreseeable and. . .as a result, the first branch of the *Anns* test is satisfied.. . . It is now well established that policy considerations may in fact negate the existence of the duty." In *Hall v.*

relationship of proximity based upon foreseeability, the second stage was consideration of policy to limit or negate the *prima facie* duty. Although it had been argued, especially in judgments from other Commonwealth courts, that stage one of the two-stage test involves not only foreseeability but other factors as well,[41] this was not the Canadian position. This was seemingly made clear by the Supreme Court of Canada in numerous of its judgments, as illustrated by Major J.'s following explanation:

> The first step of the *Anns/Kamloops* presents a relatively low threshold. In order to establish a *prima facie* duty of care, it must be shown that a relationship of "proximity" existed between the parties such that it was reasonably foreseeable that a careless act by the Railways could result in injury to the appellant. The second step of the *Anns/Kamloops* test requires that it be determined whether any factors exist which should eliminate or limit the duty found under the first branch of the test. This approach recognizes that while the test of "proximity" may be met, liability does not necessarily follow. The existence of a duty of care must be considered in light of all relevant circumstances, including any applicable statutes or regulations. Thus, a legislative exemption from liability can negate a duty of care in circumstances where that duty would otherwise exist. The same holds true for immunities created by the courts. A policy decision is made in such cases to prevent the law of negligence from regulating certain relationships or relieving certain injuries, notwithstanding a finding of proximity between the parties. This may reflect the need to shield specific activities from judicial control, or the wish to prevent the "floodgates of litigation" from opening into areas of potentially unlimited liability.[42]

Thus, once it was established that a relationship of proximity based on foreseeability of harm existed, a *prima facie* duty of care, which can be limited or even negated by policy concerns, was created in Canadian tort law.[43]

Hebert (1993), 15 C.C.L.T. (2d) 93 at 120, Cory J. stated that "even if a duty of care is found to exist, the court will have to determine whether, for public policy reasons, that duty should be limited in whole or in part."

41 In *South Pacific Manufacturing Co. Ltd. v. New Zealand Security Consultations and Investigations Ltd.*, [1992] 2 N.Z.L.R. 282, for example, Cooke P. states at 294-295:

> Sometimes it is suggested that a certain formula, for instance that of Lord Wilberforce in *Anns v. Merton London Borough Council* [1978] A.C. 728, 751 - 752, creates a *prima facie* presumption of a duty based on reasonable foresight. I am of the school of thought that has never subscribed to that view, largely because of Lord Wilberforce's reference to a *sufficient* relationship of proximity or neighbourhood. It would be naive, and I believe absurd and dangerous, to assert that a duty of care *prima facie* arises whenever harm is reasonably foreseeable.

42 *Ryan v. City of Victoria* (1999), 168 D.L.R. (4th) 513 at 525. Three other Supreme Court of Canada cases that reaffirmed this approach are *Dobson v. Dobson* (1999), 45 C.C.L.T. (2d) 217 (S.C.C.); *Hercules Managements Ltd. v. Ernst & Young* (1997), 146 D.L.R. (4th) 577; and *Ingles v. Tutkaluk Construction Ltd.* (2000), 49 C.C.L.T. (2d) 1 S.C.C.). In both *Ryan* and *Ingles*, the Justices make the point that, "The first step of the *Anns/Kamloops* test presents a relatively low threshold"; see Bastarache J. at 49 C.C.L.T. (2d) 15. Foreseeability is rarely a contentious issue. Thus, in practical terms if a duty was denied, it was usually on the basis of policy. See Klar, "Judicial Activism in Private Law' (2001), 80 Can. Bar Rev. 215.

43 Although foreseeability of harm or injury, was, prior to the recent refinement of duty, ordinarily the test of proximity, in the negligent statement cases it is the foreseeability of reasonable reliance that creates the duty. See *Hercules Management Ltd. v. Ernst Young, ibid.*, and Chapter 7, below.

(v) Cooper v. Hobart *and* Edwards v. L.S.U.C.*: The Adoption of the Three-stage Test*

In view of Canadian negligence law's long allegiance to the two-stage test, it was surprising to see the Supreme Court of Canada reformulating its approach to the duty issue in two important judgments. In *Cooper v. Hobart*[44] and *Edwards v. Law Society of Upper Canada*,[45] the court altered its analysis and took the opportunity to "highlight and hone the role of policy concerns in determining the scope of liability for negligence".[46] The cases involved negligence actions brought against regulators — in one case a Registrar of Mortgage Brokers and in the other a law society — by investors who believed that their losses were caused in part by the failure of the regulators to reasonably protect them from dishonest third parties. Motions were brought by the defendants to strike out the respective statements of claim on the basis that they disclosed no cause of action.

The Supreme Court struck out the claim in each case on the basis that there was no duty of care owed by the regulators to private individuals for the protection of their interests. Rather, however, than utilizing a simple two-stage duty formula, with foreseeability comprising stage one and policy stage two, the court asserted that stage one of the test is based not only on foreseeability, but also questions of policy. The court put the matter thusly:

> In brief compass, we suggest that at this stage in the evolution of the law, both in Canada and abroad, the *Anns* analysis is best understood as follows. At the first stage of the *Anns* test, two questions arise: (1) was the harm that occurred the reasonably foreseeable consequence of the defendant's act? and (2) are there reasons, notwithstanding the proximity between the parties established in the first part of this test, that tort liability should not be recognized here? The proximity analysis involved at the first stage of the *Anns* test focuses on factors arising from the relationship between the plaintiff and the defendant. These factors include questions of policy, in the broad sense of that word. If foreseeability and proximity are established at the first stage, a *prima facie* duty of care arises. At the second stage of the *Anns* test, the question still remains whether there are residual policy concerns outside the relationship of the parties that may negative the imposition of a duty of care. It may be, as the Privy Council suggests in *Yuen Kun Yeu*, that such considerations will not often prevail. However, we think it useful expressly to ask, before imposing a new duty of care, whether despite foreseeability and proximity of relationship, there are other policy reasons why the duty should not be imposed.[47]

In a nutshell, a new step was added to the formula. At stage one, the courts must consider (i) foreseeability and (ii) policy concerns that arise from the relationship between the parties. If a *prima facie* duty of care based on these factors

---

44 (2001), 206 D.L.R. (4th) 193, [2002] 1 W.W.R. 221 (S.C.C.).

45 (2001), 206 D.L.R. (4th) 211 (S.C.C.).

46 See Klar, "Foreseeability, Proximity and Policy" (2002), 25 Adv. Q. 360 for my analysis of these two judgments. There have been a number of commentaries on this significant development. See, for example, Pitel, "Canada Remakes the *Anns* Test" [2002] Camb. L.J. 252; Rafferty, "Developments in Contract and Tort Law: The 2001-2002 Term" [2002] S.C.L.R. 153; Feldthusen, "The *Anns/Cooper* Approach to Duty of Care" (2002), 18 Constr. L.R. 67; Brown, "Still Crazy After All These Years" (2003), 36 U.B.C. L. Rev. 159; Neyers & Gabie, "Canadian Tort Law since *Cooper v. Hobart* , Parts I and II" (2005), 13 Tort Law J. 302, (2006), 14 Tort Law J. 10; Weinrib, "The Disintegration of Duty" (2006), 31 Advocates' Quarterly 212; and Linden and Feldthusen, *Canadian Tort Law*, 8th ed. (2006) at 288 and following.

47 *Cooper v. Hobart*, above, at para. 30.

arises, the courts can then consider residual policy concerns, extraneous to the relationship between the parties, which can reduce or negate the *prima facie* duty. Based on this analysis, the Supreme Court held that despite the fact that the negligence of regulators could have foreseeably affected the economic interests of private investors, policy concerns prevented there from being a proximate relationship between the regulators and the investors. There was therefore no *prima facie* duty owed.[48]

The Supreme Court has reaffirmed and explained its new duty approach in several recent judgments. In *Odhavji Estate v. Woodhouse*,[49] Iacobucci J. made it clear that in *Cooper* the Supreme Court had chosen a three-stage test for the establishment of a duty which required that the plaintiff prove that the harm complained of was reasonably foreseeable, that there was "sufficient proximity between the parties that it would not be unjust or unfair to impose a duty of care on the defendants", and there exists no policy reasons to negative or otherwise restrict that duty.[50] In *Childs v. Desormeaux*,[51] the three elements of the duty test were re-iterated by the Supreme Court.[52] In *Hill v. Hamilton-Wentworth Regional Police*,[53] the new test was applied to the "tort of negligent police investigation".

The recent Canadian reformulation of *Anns* is therefore clearly very much in line with the English approach. Several questions are raised by the judgments. As with the English approach, the "categorization" of disputes has become an important exercise. It is only when the duty being alleged by the parties is a "new" duty, *i.e.*, when the dispute before the court does not fall into a previously recognized category or "analogous" category, that an analysis of proximity must be undertaken. The difficulty inherent in this analysis is that identifying categories is problematic, especially when the Canadian expansion of negligence law over a 20-year period did not rely on this type of incremental approach. As well, the differentiation between internal policy considerations that go to determining whether there is a relationship of proximity between the parties, and external

---

48 The court examined the scope and purpose of the legislative provisions that established the Registrar of Mortgage Brokers in the *Cooper* case and concluded that to impose a private duty of care would "come at the expense of other important interests, of efficiency and finally at the expense of public confidence in the system as a whole." A similar analysis of the legislation dealing with the Law Society of Upper Canada was undertaken in *Edwards*. The court determined, in other words, that the legislative purpose was not to create a proximate relationship between the defendants and private individuals.

49 [2003] 3 S.C.R. 263, 233 D.L.R. (4th) 193. This judgment is also important for its adoption of a broad view of the tort of misfeasance in a public office. See discussion in Chapter 8.

50 *Ibid.*, at 218 [D.L.R.].

51 [2006] 1 S.C.R. 643 (S.C.C.). The case dealt with "social host" liability. See discussion in Chapter 6.

52 Although it must be noted that McLachlin C.J.C. seems to prefer to characterize the test as a "two stage" test, with stage one having two aspects — foreseeability and other factors that go to the relationship between the parties — which together constitute proximity. This constant rewording has prompted Linden and Feldthusen to note that we have moved from the simple neighbour test of *Donoghue v. Stevenson*, to the two-step test of *Anns*, to the two-step test that includes a two-part first step of *Cooper*, to the three-step test of *Odhavji*, and then back again to the two-step test with a two-part first step. See Linden and Feldthusen, *Canadian Tort Law*, 8th ed. (2006), at 294.

53 (2007), 50 C.C.L.T. (3d) 1 (S.C.C.).

policy considerations that are called into play when deciding whether a *prima facie* duty of care should be negated or reduced, is unclear. Finally, the question of who has the burden of proof with respect to the three elements and how that burden can be discharged must be resolved.

(c) A Closer Look at the Elements: Foreseeability, Proximity, Policy

(i) Foreseeability

To say, as did Lord Atkin, that "you must take reasonable care to avoid acts or omissions which you can reasonably foresee would be likely to injure your neighbour" is to recognize that there is, in virtually all activities, some risk of injury to others, but that one ought not to be blamed should one of these risks eventuate, unless the risk was foreseeable. The notion of foreseeability is critical in the negligence action and is used not only as a factor in determining whether a duty of care was owed, but also whether it was breached, and whether the type of injury which resulted ought to be the defendant's responsibility. It separates liability in negligence from strict liability torts, as well as distinguishing negligence law from the intentional torts.

It has been observed that to base the existence of a duty of care on the foreseeability of harm to the plaintiff should care not be exercised is a superfluous exercise, in view of the fact that foreseeability of an injury is an essential component of the standard of care which must be exercised should a duty be imposed. A well-known Canadian case can best be used to illustrate this point. In *Nova Mink Ltd. v. Trans-Can. Airlines,*[54] the plaintiff, a mink ranch owner, sued the defendant in negligence for damages caused to its mink operation as a result of the noise of low-flying aircraft. The evidence indicated that the defendant did not know, nor did it have reason to know, of the existence of the plaintiff's ranch and the particular susceptibility of the operation with respect to noisy aircraft. Without such knowledge, the reasoning of *Donoghue v. Stevenson* would suggest that there was no duty on the part of the defendant to take reasonable care to prevent injury to the plaintiff, since the parties were not in a sufficiently proximate relationship. This was in fact the approach taken by MacDonald J. in *Nova Mink* when he decided that "in law the defendant owed no duty of care to the plaintiff in respect of the harm of which he complains."[55] It is equally clear, however, that even if the law of negligence recognized a general duty of care owed to all individuals, whether foreseeable or not, rather than a duty owed only to foreseeable victims, the result of *Nova Mink* would have been exactly the same. As conceded by MacDonald J., without knowledge of the existence of the plaintiff's ranch and the particular susceptibility of the operation to the noise caused by aircraft, the defendant could not be considered to have been negligent in failing to take precautions to avoid the injury it caused. In other words, just as the lack of foreseeability of the plaintiff's injury imposed no duty of care on the defendant, it would equally have prevented the defendant's conduct from being considered

54 [1951] 2 D.L.R. 241 (N.S. T.D.).

55 *Ibid.*, at 265.

to have been negligent even if a duty was said to be owed.[56] This is true of all cases in which courts conclude that the plaintiff was an unforeseeable victim of the defendant's conduct and that, therefore, no duty to take care was owed. All such cases could be decided on the basis of no duty, or no negligence.[57]

Why, then, does negligence law require the foreseeability of the victim as an element of the duty of care issue, rather than dealing with foreseeability exclusively as one of the elements of breach? It traditionally was suggested that the main purpose of maintaining a separate duty concept based upon foreseeability, in distinction to foreseeability as one of the components of breach of duty, was to give to the judge "a powerful control over the handling of negligence actions before a jury."[58] Whether a duty of care is said to exist in a particular case is considered to be a question of law, and only where this duty has been found can the finder of fact determine whether this has been breached. However, this explanation is confusing, if not misleading. It is no doubt true that there are elements of the duty of care concept, which are questions of law that only the judge can determine. As we have discussed, notwithstanding the foreseeability of injury to the plaintiff, there may exist reasons based on lack of proximity or external policy, to refuse to impose a duty of care on a defendant, for the benefit of a plaintiff. Where, however, a dispute raises no such proximity or policy issues, is the question of foreseeability one of law or of fact? It is submitted that this decision is one of fact. That is, once the judge decides that as a matter of law there are no impediments to the imposition of a duty of care in the specific case, it is up to the jury to determine whether injury to the plaintiff was foreseeable and what steps would have been appropriate to avert such injury. Failure to see that it is only the proximity and policy aspects, not the foreseeability aspect of the duty question which are questions of law, will encourage judges to usurp the jury's function.[59]

---

56 This is not to say, of course, that had the injury to the plaintiff been foreseeable and a duty to take care therefore owed, the mere failure to prevent the injury would have been negligent. As we will see, the foreseeability of the injury is only one factor to be considered when deciding the standard of care issue.

57 This is why in some judgments one finds some of the judges deciding the case based upon the argument that "no duty was owed", while others state that even if a duty was owed, the defendant's conduct "was not negligent." See, for example, *Bourhill v. Young,* [1943] A.C. 92 (H.L.), an important Scottish case concerning recovery for nervous shock. Lord Thankerton held that the plaintiff was not a foreseeable victim of a motor vehicle accident and, therefore, that no duty of care was owed to her. Lord Macmillan held that although the defendant's conduct might have been negligent *vis-à-vis* some victims it was not negligent in terms of the plaintiff because he could not have foreseen that she would be injured. Whether the law states that you owe a duty to take care to everyone but can only be negligent if the injury to the victim was foreseeable, or that you only owe a duty to take care to foreseeable victims, it amounts to the same thing.

58 Fleming, *The Law of Torts,* 6th ed. (1983), at 130.

59 The clearest case of this occurred in *Wade v. C.N.R.,* [1978] 1 S.C.R. 1064. For a commentary on this see Klar, "A Comment on Wade v. C.N.R." (1977-78), 3 C.C.L.T. 194, and Klar, "Developments in Tort Law: The 1978-79 Term" (1980), 1 Sup. Ct. L. Rev. 311 at 330. Also see McLachlin C.J.C.'s judgment in *Childs v. Desormeaux* (2006), 266 D.L.R. (4th) 257 (S.C.C.). The Chief Justice conceded that the trial judge had found that the defendant social hosts should have foreseen the accident and injury caused by a drunk guest. Yet McLachlin C.J.C. found that since there were no findings that the guest was actually visibly intoxicated, that the injury was not reasonably foreseeable "on the facts established in this case". Hence no duty of care to prevent the guest from leaving the house was owed. Not only is this a puzzling

It is true that judges maintain the power to withhold cases from the jury where the facts suggest that it would be unreasonable to find that a risk of foreseeable injury to the plaintiff existed, but this does not alter the submission that the question itself is a question of fact.[60]

Courts have in the past been able to utilize the foreseeability element of the duty issue to mask what were essentially decisions based on policy, and thus to prevent juries from over-zealously extending tort law. In more recent years, however, it has been frankly admitted that, foreseeability aside, courts retain the power to control the development of negligence law through the devices of proximity and policy. This does not diminish the importance of *Donoghue v. Stevenson* or the requirement of foreseeability. Whether analyzed as a question of duty or as a question of breach, the point still remains that the common law of negligence looks to the conduct of the defendant in relation to the position of the plaintiff when deciding whether or not the plaintiff merits compensation.

The duty of care issue is phrased in terms of the foreseeability of the plaintiff as a potential victim. However, one cannot foresee a victim without foreseeing an injury suffered by that person. In some situations, for example where nervous shock is suffered by a person who, although present at the scene of an accident, was not physically endangered by it, or where pure economic losses are suffered by a person whose person or property were not in actual physical danger, the notion of foreseeability of the victim merges with that of the foreseeability of the injury. In these cases, the victimization of the plaintiff could only have occurred with respect to one type of injury. In most cases, however, there is more than one type of injury that can occur to the victim from the defendant's conduct, and thus, while the victim may have been foreseeable with respect to some injury, the type of injury which did in fact result might not have been. Traditional negligence law analysis, therefore, has kept these concerns separate, designating foreseeability of the plaintiff as a victim of any type of injury as a duty question, and foreseeability of the type of injury itself as one of remoteness.

The proposition that a duty of care is owed when it is reasonably foreseeable that a failure to act reasonably may injure the plaintiff does not mean that the plaintiff as a particular individual need have been contemplated. If the activity

---

conclusion from the point of view of the power of an appellate court judge to reverse a trial judge on findings of fact, absent overriding and palpable error, but it is inconsistent with the way the Supreme Court dealt with a similar issue of foreseeability in *Stewart v. Pettie*, [1995] 1 S.C.R. 131 (S.C.C.). See discussion in Chapter 6.

60 It must be noted that respected authorities assert that "the existence of a duty is a question of law for the court to decide" without distinguishing between the foreseeability, proximity, or policy components. See, for example, Linden and Feldthusen, *Canadian Tort Law*, 8th ed. (2006), at 285, citing Fleming, *The Law of Torts*, 9th ed. (1998). One can perhaps reconcile the different views by arguing that foreseeability, as an aspect of duty, is approached at a general, conceptual level; *i.e.*, is it reasonably foreseeable as a general proposition that the defendant's negligence could harm a person such as the plaintiff? Foreseeability, however, as an aspect of breach would be more specific; i.e., on the facts of this case, ought the defendant have reasonably foreseen that his or her negligent conduct could injure the plaintiff? The former might be seen as a duty issue, and hence a question of law, and the latter as a breach issue, and hence a question of fact. The problem I have with this approach, however, is that foreseeability as a question of law seems to have no content, especially since the policy elements of foreseeability have now been removed from it and are being treated as separate issues.

creates a foreseeable risk of injury to persons in the plaintiff's general class, then a duty to avoid the injury by the exercise of reasonable care is owed to all members of that class.[61]

Although the question as to whether an injury to the plaintiff was foreseeable is to be asked from the perspective of the reasonable person at the time of the activity in question, and not with the aid of 20/20 hindsight after the injury has in fact occurred, as a practical matter, once the defendant's conduct has resulted in injury to the plaintiff, it is relatively infrequently that courts decide that the plaintiff was not reasonably foreseeable.[62] Hence those few cases where it has been decided that a duty of care was not owed due to the actual unforeseeability of the plaintiff, rather than due to policy reasons, best illustrate the nature of the foreseeability requirement.

One of the better known of these cases is *Palsgraf v. Long Island Ry. Co.*[63] A guard who worked for a railway company pushed a passenger who was boarding a car. This caused the passenger to drop a package covered by newspaper and containing fireworks. The fireworks exploded, and the vibrations caused a weigh scale at the other end of the platform to fall, striking the plaintiff. In deciding that the defendant owed no duty of care to the plaintiff, Cardozo J. stated that:

> if no hazard was apparent to the eye of ordinary vigilance, an act innocent and harmless, at least to outward seeming, with reference to her, did not take to itself the quality of a tort because it happened to be a wrong . . . with reference to some one else.[64]

For Cardozo J. the test of duty was measured by what he variously described as "the eye of ordinary vigilance", "the eye of reasonable vigilance", or "the ordinarily prudent eye." Despite the essential ambiguity of these phrases, the message of this classic judgment is clear: one only owes a duty of care to those who, to a reasonable person, would be within the range of danger created by one's act.[65]

In the famous Scottish case, *Bourhill v. Young,*[66] the plaintiff was standing about 45 feet from the point where a motorcyclist collided with a motor-car. Although the plaintiff did not see the accident, she heard the noise of the impact and alleged that she suffered fright resulting in a severe nervous shock. In determining the scope of the duty owed by those who drive motor vehicles to other users of the highway, Lord Thankerton confined the duty to those whose injuries were "within that which the cyclist ought to have reasonably contemplated as the

---

61 For example, it is clearly reasonably foreseeable that careless driving puts at risk passengers, other drivers, and pedestrians. Hence everyone in these classes is owed a duty of care.

62 Weinrib, above, note 46, at 237, illustrates the low threshold for foreseeability in the two-stage test by quoting from *Modbury Triangle Shopping Centre Pty. Ltd. v. Anzil* (2000), 176 ALR 411, at 436 (Australia H.C.):

> In almost every case in which a plaintiff suffers damage it is foreseeable that, if reasonable care is not taken, harm may follow. As Dixon CJ said in *Chapman v. Hearse*, "I cannot understand why any event that does happen is not foreseeable by a person of sufficient imagination and intelligence." Foresight of harm is not sufficient to show that a duty exists.

63 162 N.E. 99 (N.Y.C.A., 1928).

64 *Ibid.*, at 99.

65 Compare this approach with Mr. Justice Andrews' dissent, *ibid.*, at 103. According to Andrews J., "every one owes to the world at large the duty of refraining from those acts that may unreasonably threaten the safety of others." An act which unreasonably threatens A is also a wrong to B, subject to rules of proximate cause.

66 [1943] A.C. 92 (H.L.).

area of potential danger which would arise as the result of his negligence." Applying this test, Lord Thankerton declined to impose a duty on the defendant in favour of the plaintiff who was not even within the range of the defendant's vision.[67] Lord Wright described the principle to be applied in the following terms:

> This general concept of reasonable foresight as the criterion of negligence or breach of duty (strict or otherwise) may be criticized as too vague, but negligence is a fluid principle, which has to be applied to the most diverse conditions and problems of human life. It is a concrete, not an abstract idea. It has to be fitted to the facts of the particular case.[68]

Fitting the principle to the facts of this case, Lord Wright noted that the plaintiff was completely outside the range of the collision and reacted to the collision in a way which no reasonable hypothetical observer could reasonably have foreseen.[69]

(ii) Proximity

The most challenging aspect of the duty formula is determining whether there was sufficient proximity between the plaintiff and defendant to justify the recognition of a *prima facie* duty of care. This is a question of law to be determined by the judge alone.

As a preliminary matter, the Supreme Court in *Cooper* noted that the concept of "proximity" is generally used "to characterize the type of relationship in which a duty of care may arise", and added that these types of sufficiently proximate relationships "are identified through the use of categories."[70] Thus, the first task of a court in determining whether the relationship of the plaintiff and defendant in any specific case is sufficiently proximate to support the existence of a *prima facie* duty of care is to decide whether that relationship constitutes a novel duty category or falls into a recognized category, or into a category analogous to a recognized category. Although the Supreme Court conceded that the categories are not closed and new ones can be introduced, it attempted to illustrate its proposition by identifying those categories in which proximity has been recognized in earlier cases.

---

67 The fact that the plaintiff's injury was nervous shock as opposed to physical injury presented another problem for the courts, even apart from foreseeability. See the discussion in Chapter 12.

68 [1943] A.C. 92 at 107.

69 *Ibid.*, at 111. The role of the "thin skull" plaintiff is of interest here. But as noted by Lord Wright, without first being able to establish the foreseeability of some injury, and hence the existence of a duty, it is unnecessary to consider questions which relate to the extent of the recoverable damage. See the discussion in Chapter 12. Aside from these two well-known cases, there have been relatively few cases that have rejected a duty based upon the unforeseeability of the plaintiff. One case is *D'Aoust v. Lindsay*, [2000] 4 W.W.R. 255 (Alta. Q.B.). The defendant who negligently allowed his dogs to roam freely was held not to have owed a duty to the plaintiff whose deer were mauled by the dogs. This was because the plaintiff lived so far from the defendant that it was not foreseeable that the dogs would travel such a long distance and attack the plaintiff's deer. The plaintiff was therefore "unforeseeable", although had he lived closer he would not have been. Another is *Newton v. Newton*, 2003 BCCA 389 (C.A.). The Court of Appeal held that it was not foreseeable that a small child would jump down stairs into his grandmother, causing her to fall and injure herself. Thus, no duty of care to supervise the child was owed by the child's mother to the child's grandmother. Here again I would question whether this should more appropriately have been dealt with as a breach of duty, rather than a duty, issue.

70 206 D.L.R. 4th 203-204.

The list included some very broad categories of proximate relationships, for example, "where the defendant's act foreseeably causes physical harm to the plaintiff or the plaintiff's property" and some exceedingly narrow and fact specific ones, for example, proximity between a municipality and a prospective purchaser of real estate with respect to the inspection of housing developments. It is clear that the former category encompasses virtually all negligent acts that result in physical damage, and the latter refers to only one type of negligence law dispute.[71] Moreover, the first category is overly broad as there are disputes that fall into it but where there is no duty.[72] It is difficult to ascertain whether a specific factual dispute constitutes its own category or fits into a recognized category or an analogous category.[73] This matter is of no small importance, as the decision as to whether a specific dispute falls into a recognized category of proximity or presents the court with a proposed novel category is a threshold question to the very application of the proximity and policy analysis. It gives trial judges great discretion in defining the issue in a specific dispute as raising a question of proximity and hence law, thereby allowing them to strike out negligence claims on preliminary motions without ever having to decide the case based on its facts.[74]

Another difficulty with the category approach is that, prior to *Cooper v. Hobart*, the determination of duty in Canadian judgments did not use the three-stage foreseeability, proximity, policy formula. Duty was based upon foreseeability limited by policy; the question of whether there was sufficient proximity between the parties to make it just and fair to recognize a duty was not part of the vocabulary of the judgment. Thus, and especially in the public tort liability cases, a *prima facie* duty of care frequently was found without regard to the question as to

---

71 This is commented upon in *755165 Ontario Inc. v. Parsons* (2006), 41 C.C.L.T. (3d) 132 (N.L. T.D.), leave to appeal refused (2006), 273 D.L.R. (4th) 1 (N.L. C.A.). D. Green C.J.T.D. notes that the Supreme Court of Canada in *Cooper* approached the notion of categories in relation to the liability of statutory authorities "as narrower, almost discrete fact-based, situations" in contrast to "other more broadly worded categories, such as foreseeably causing physical harm to a plaintiff or his or her property, which can encompass a wide variety of different situations."

72 For example, no duty is owed by a woman to her child who is born with disabilities as a result of the defendant's pre-natal negligence. See discussion below. Another example is the lack of proximity between a public authority and a plaintiff who is injured or even killed by the authority's neglect of its statutory responsibilities. See discussion in Chapter 8. Both of these cases involve foreseeable physical harm to the plaintiff or the plaintiff's property, yet no duty of care is owed.

73 For example, the dispute between the plaintiffs and the Registrar of Mortgage Brokers in *Cooper* could have been characterized as a dispute falling into the broader, recognized category of proximity between public authorities, such as municipalities or highway maintenance officials, and persons injured by their negligent acts.

74 The idea that there are recognized types of discrete relationships that have attracted a duty of care is elaborated upon in *Hill v. Hamilton-Wentworth (Regional Municipality) Police Services Board* (2007), 50 C.C.L.T. (3d) 1 (S.C.C.) at para. 25. McLachlin C.J.C. identified a number of these relationships; for example, motorist/user of highway, doctor/patient, and solicitor/client. The issue in the case was whether investigating police officer/suspect attracted a duty. This was seen to be a novel category, which according to the majority of the court did attract a duty. The breaking down of the duty of care "into a collection of particular kinds of duties" has been criticized as constituting a return to the pre-*Donoghue v. Stevenson* days, which has "undermined the most notable achievement of negligence law in the twentieth century", namely Lord Atkin's neighbour principle. See Weinrib, above, note 46, at 214.

whether there was proximity between the parties to the dispute, aside from the issue of foreseeability. It is, therefore, somewhat artificial to compare and apply pre-*Cooper* judgments to post-*Cooper* cases, particularly with respect to the question of whether there are recognized "categories" of proximate duty relationships. As I will argue later when dealing with the issue of public tort liability, it is my impression that many of the pre-*Cooper* cases, in which a *prima facie* duty was found, would not survive the more rigorous proximity requirement imposed by *Cooper*. Courts who are opposed to the recognition of proximity and hence a *prima facie* duty in a post-*Cooper* case are therefore now left in the difficult position of having to decide that the earlier judgments that recognized a *prima facie* duty were dealing with a different category, or to frankly admit that the pre-*Cooper* cases are simply not helpful in resolving post-*Cooper* disputes, with regard to the whole question of new categories and proximity.[75]

What have been the factors which the courts have considered in determining the proximity issue? Recall that, in general terms, the issue of proximity asks whether it would be "just and fair"[76] to impose a duty of care on the defendant for the plaintiff's protection, and looks to factors arising from the relationship between the plaintiff and defendant, including questions of policy. These factors include "expectations, representations, reliance and the property or other interests involved."[77]

It has been made clear by the Supreme Court of Canada, especially in its judgment in *Hill v. Hamilton-Wentworth*, that determining the issue of proximity depends upon an examination of the nature of the relationship that existed between the plaintiff and the defendant. As stated by McLachlin C.J.C., "the most basic factor upon which the proximity analysis fixes is whether there is a relationship between the alleged wrongdoer and the victim, usually described by the words 'close and direct.'"[78] Relationships arise through the conduct of the parties; through their interactions, legitimate expectations, or other factors that courts consider sufficient to impose a duty of care on one party for the protection of

---

75 See, for example, *Holstlag v. Alberta* (2006), [2006] A.J. No. 150, 2006 CarswellAlta 164 (C.A.), leave to appeal refused (2006), 2006 CarswellAlta 1190 (S.C.C.), where the Alberta Court of Appeal was forced to distinguish this dispute, an action brought against the Government of Alberta for its negligence in approving untreated pine shakes as roofing material, from a number of pre-*Cooper* cases where governments were held liable in other circumstances. The plaintiffs were arguing that the duty claimed for in *Holstlag* did not represent a novel category. The Court of Appeal held that it was a novel category and dismissed the claim, by distinguishing these earlier cases. Another illustration of the difficulty of using pre-*Cooper* judgments to analyze post-*Cooper* disputes arose in a different way in *Fraser v. Westminer Canada Ltd.* (2003), 228 D.L.R. (4th) 513 (N.S. C.A.), affirming (2001), 199 N.S.R. (2d) 1. The trial judge had determined the issue of duty based on the two-stage pre-*Cooper* test. He therefore did not consider the issue of proximity, as an addition to "foreseeability". *Cooper* was then released by the Supreme Court of Canada. The Court of Appeal had to admit that *Cooper* had changed the analysis and that the trial judge's failure to consider proximity, although understandable, was an error in law. The Court of Appeal then considered the issue of proximity, finding that it was not made out.

76 Or as stated by Iacobucci J. in *Odhavji*, above, note 8 "whether it would not be unjust or unfair".

77 *Cooper*, above, note 7, at para. 34.

78 Above, note 8, at para. 29.

another.[79] There need not be a personal relationship, although "the presence or absence of a personal relationship is an important factor to consider."[80]

In other cases, courts have used expressions such as the physical "propinquity" of the parties, "assumed or imposed obligations", and the closeness of the causal relationship between the act and the harm suffered, as factors in determining proximity.[81] Although these phrases are incapable of precise definition, they do import the sentiment that where defendants should be mindful of the impact of their conduct on the plaintiffs, proximity exists.

In the public tort liability cases, the issue of proximity frequently is resolved by an examination of the statutory provisions that define the duties, powers and responsibilities of the statutory defendants involved in the dispute. As I will discuss in more detail below,[82] this is, in my opinion, an approach that is inconsistent with the principle of Canadian tort law that private law duties of care cannot be based on statutory provisions, but must be based on principles of the common law relating to interactions between parties.[83] Nevertheless, where statutory provisions exist and define the statutory responsibilities of the defendant, the interpretation of these provisions invariably becomes the determining factor in deciding the issue of proximity.[84]

As stated in *Cooper*, in determining the issue of proximity the courts must consider questions of policy, as they relate to the internal relationship between the parties. What these broad issues of policy are and how they differ from the residual policy concerns considered at the final stage of the test is not altogether clear. In *Cooper* itself, for example, it was a consideration of the statutory provisions and how imposing a duty of care on the defendant Registrar of Mortgage Brokers would come "at the expense of other important interests, of efficiency and finally at the expense of public confidence in the system as a whole"[85] which

---

79 See Klar, "Case Comment" (2007), 86 Can. Bar Rev. 343. As stated by McLachlin C.J.C. *ibid.*, at para. 29, whether there is a close and direct relationship "is not concerned with how intimate the plaintiff and defendant were or with their physical proximity, so much as with whether the *actions* of the alleged wrongdoer have a close or direct effect on the victim, such that the wrongdoer ought to have had the victim in mind as a person potentially harmed."

80 *Hill v. Hamilton-Wentworth*, above, at para. 30.

81 See Cromwell J.A.'s judgment in *Fraser v. Westminer Ltd.* above, note 75, at 357. In *Odhavji Estate v. Woodhouse*, [2003] 3 S.C.R. 263, Iacobucci J. considered the "relatively direct causal link between the alleged misconduct and complained of harm", as well as the public's reasonable expectations that the defendant would be mindful of the harm that could result from police misconduct, in deciding that proximity could arise between the parties. Also see Cromwell J.A.'s judgment in *Elliott v. Insurance Crime Prevention Bureau* (2005), 256 D.L.R. (4th) 674 (N.S. C.A.), where the factors outlined in *Fraser* were used to create proximity between an investigator hired by an insurance company to investigate the cause of a fire and the insured. Cromwell J.A. also considered the "vulnerability" of the insured created by his contractual obligation to co-operate with the investigator. These factors were insufficient, however, to create proximity between the insured and the deputy fire marshal.

82 See Chapter 8.

83 See the discussion of *Saskatchewan Wheat Pool v. Canada*, (*sub nom. Saskatchewan v. R.*) [1983] 1 S.C.R. 205, 143 D.L.R. (3d) 9, [1983] 3 W.W.R. 97, in Chapters 8 and 9.

84 As I will discuss, this approach inevitably leads to the conclusion that there is no proximity, since statutes that impose public duties or responsibilities ordinarily cannot be interpreted as creating private law remedies.

85 Above, note 7, at para. 50.

led to a denial of proximity between the parties. In *Childs v. Desormeaux*,[86] it was the common law's concern to not interfere with the autonomy of persons by requiring them to assist others, except in limited circumstances, which led to the Supreme Court's rejection of proximity between a social host and a person injured as a result of drunk driving by a guest. It is questionable whether these types of concerns should be characterized as ones internal to the relationship of the parties themselves or as "residual" policy concerns. This difficulty has been recognized by the Supreme Court. In *D. (B.) v. Children's Aid Society of Hamilton*,[87] Abella J. conceded that there is a possibility of "some blending of policy" considerations between the two stages. In *Hill v. Hamilton-Wentworth*, McLachlin C.J.C. stated as well that "in practice, there may be overlap between stage one and stage two considerations."[88]

(iii) Residual Policy Considerations

Articulating the role of policy considerations in judicial decision-making, with particular reference to the duty of care issue, had always been a matter of ongoing controversy. Some judges sought to de-emphasize the relevance of policy considerations, and to stress the importance of formulating principle, in arriving at judicial decisions.[89] Others favoured an approach that would more clearly bring policy considerations out into the open.[90]

Whatever the former views might have been, it is now clear that policy considerations, relating to the social and economic consequences of recognizing a duty of care, play an open and important role in tort law judgments. The Supreme Court of Canada in *Cooper*, *Edwards*, and its subsequent judgments has clearly dictated that even if a *prima facie* duty of care is found, it can be negated by considering "the effect of recognizing a duty of care on other legal obligations, the legal system and society more generally." Courts can ask whether recognition of a duty would create "the spectre of unlimited liability to an unlimited class",

---

86 Above, note 8.

87 Above, note 8, at para. 33.

88 Above, note 8, at para. 31.

89 Lord Scarman's judgment in *McLoughlin v. O'Brian*, [1982] 2 All E.R. 298 (H.L.), at 310, best exemplifies this approach:

> The distinguishing feature of the common law is this judicial development and formulation of principle. Policy considerations will have to be weighed; but the objective of the judges is the formulation of principle. And, if principle inexorably requires a decision which entails a degree of policy risk, the court's function is to adjudicate according to principle, leaving policy curtailment to the judgment of Parliament. Here lies the true role of the two law-making institutions in our constitution. By concentrating on principle the judges can keep the common law alive, flexible and consistent and can keep the legal system clear of policy problems which neither they, nor the forensic process which is their duty to operate, are equipped to resolve. If principle leads to results which are thought to be socially unacceptable, Parliament can legislate to draw a line or map out a new path.

90 For example, in *McLoughlin v. O'Brian*, *ibid.*, at 303, Lord Wilberforce frankly conceded that "at the margin, the boundaries of a man's responsibility for acts of negligence have to be fixed as a matter of policy." Or, as stated by Lord Edmund-Davies in the same case at 306, quoting from the Court of Appeal, "in any state of society it is ultimately a question of policy to decide the limits of liability."

or whether there are "other reasons of broad policy that suggest the duty of care should not be recognized."[91]

The policy considerations that arise outside of the "garden variety" negligence actions involving physical damage caused by positive acts differ, being peculiar to their context. These will be examined individually in the upcoming chapters of this text. Nevertheless, it may be helpful to identify some of these concerns at this point.

The courts have been fearful of exposing defendants to liability "in an indeterminate amount for an indeterminate time to an indeterminate class",[92] of opening up the "floodgates of litigation", of allowing one step to turn into fifty. Where, either because of the nature of the defendant's conduct, *e.g.*, words rather than deeds, or the nature of the plaintiff's injury, *e.g.*, economic losses or nervous shock as opposed to personal injury or physical damage to property, the potential for the extension of liability is great, these concerns have prompted caution, if not resistance, to the development of the duty of care. Liability that is too great for defendants to bear renders the litigation process meaningless, as when bankrupt defendants are unable to satisfy judgments obtained against them. As well, there is a limitation of resources with respect to the expenses of litigation and to the time and effort that courts have to determine the issues placed before them.

Thus, even where the liability in any one case might not be indeterminate, if an affirmative finding of duty could lead to the opening of liability in a multitude of similar cases, courts are resistant to recognizing a duty.[93]

It has been noted that with respect to the activities of legislative or judicial bodies, liability for negligence may not be appropriate. There are political constraints on the types of decisions courts can make, as well as legitimate questions concerning the ability of judges to weigh and investigate those matters necessary for a proper determination of some public issues. In relation to some actors and activities, such as lawyers, judges and other professionals, there has been the concern that the fear of tort liability will impede their work and result in protracted litigation.

The administrative difficulty of adjudicating certain types of disputes has affected the growth of negligence law. If there are difficult questions of proof, or the possibility exists of fraudulent claims being made, courts have resisted the imposition of tort liability.

A wide category of concerns involves the court's assessment of societal values and needs, and the extent to which these can be furthered or hindered by the imposition of tort liability. Questions concerning the value to be given to concepts such as "individual responsibility" and the "individualistic" nature of society have been raised. As well, the effect that liability might have on social relationships has been a factor. More contemporary issues involving economic factors, such as who is the best loss avoider or cheapest cost bearer, have been argued as being relevant. The wide use of insurance, whether first-party or third-party liability, is

---

91 *Cooper*, above, at para. 37.

92 Cardozo C.J. in *Ultramares Corp. v. Touche,* 174 N.E. 441 at 444 (N.Y.C.A., 1931).

93 This argument was made by the Supreme Court in *Bow Valley Husky (Bermuda) Ltd. v. Saint John Shipbuilding Ltd.*, [1997] 3 S.C.R. 1210, and adopted in *Fraser v. Wesminer Canada*, above, note 75.

said to be important. The availability of liability insurance has been an issue, the suggestion being that an unjustifiably wide extension of tort liability will jeopardize the affordability and obtainability of liability insurance, thereby putting useful activities out of business. The rules of tort law and the availability of a remedy must be seen in the wider juridical context. The courts must ask whether the issue in dispute is best resolved by a private law tort rule, by the use of contract or equity, or by public law or legislative intervention.[94]

(iv) *Burden of Proof*

The question as to who has the burden of proving the elements of the duty formula and, in particular, the residual policy concerns that might negate or limit a *prima facie* duty, has been raised by the Supreme Court in two of its recent judgments. In *Childs v. Desormeaux*,[95] McLachlin C.J. stated that "once the plaintiff establishes a *prima facie* duty of care, the evidentiary burden of showing countervailing policy considerations shifts to the defendant, following the general rule that the party asserting a point should be required to establish it."[96] In *Hill v. Hamilton-Wentworth (Regional Municipality) Police Services Board*,[97] the Chief Justice followed this up by noting that "the plaintiff had the formal onus of establishing the duty of care" and that *Childs* and *Odhavji* "should not be read as changing this fundamental rule."[98] The discussion in the judgment did state, however, that "compelling" reasons must be advanced to negate a duty of care, the policy concerns raised "must be more than speculative", and "a real potential for negative consequences must be apparent."[99] In view of these statements, it will be interesting to see what types of evidence will satisfy the courts that policy concerns should negate a *prima facie* duty. As well, since it seems that the matter of residual policy concerns now must have an evidentiary basis, it is less likely that preliminary motions to strike will be successful prior to trial.[100]

3. A NOTE ON THE LEGAL STATUS OF THE UNBORN

A controversial issue for tort, as for other areas of the law, is the legal status of the "unborn". Is a foetus a foreseeable victim to whom a duty of care is owed?

---

94 A good discussion of these types of factors is found in *Elliott v. Insurance Crime Prevention Bureau*, above, note 81. Despite finding proximity between an insured and an insurance investigator hired by the insurance company to investigate and report back on the cause of a fire, Cromwell J.A. rejected the duty based on policy. Factors considered included the availability of a contractual remedy by the insured against its insurer, and the negative effect of the proposed duty on the legal relationship that existed between the insurer and its investigator, and the insurer and insured. Cromwell J.A. also considered the "legal incoherence" which might be created by the recognition of the duty, with respect to the law of defamation, malicious prosecution, and litigation privilege.

95 [2006] 1 S.C.R. 643.

96 At para. 13.

97 (2007), 50 C.C.L.T. (3d) 1 (S.C.C.).

98 *Ibid.*, at para. 31.

99 *Ibid.*, at para. 48.

100 See *755165 Ontario Inc. v. Parsons* above, note 71, where D. Green C.J.T.D. states at 147 that, "it would be the rare case where the requisite social and economic facts necessary for the court to make an informed decision on the residual policy considerations under the second stage of the *Anns* test will be before the court at that stage."

That "unborn children" or foetuses are, in law, reasonably foreseeable entities that can suffer injury as a result of acts of negligence was first established in *Duval v. Seguin*.[101] This judgment properly held that since pregnant women are reasonably foreseeable persons, the foetuses that they carry are also, by definition, reasonably foreseeable. The issue, however, is not whether foetuses are reasonably foreseeable victims of injury or death occurring as a result of negligent acts, but the legal status of foetuses. That is, if a foetus is not born as a result of a negligent (or deliberate) act, can there be a cause of action brought on its behalf? If it is born with disabilities that it suffered as a result of pre-natal negligent acts affecting it, can the child then sue? If the negligent actor was the child's mother, does the same rule apply?

It has been made clear "that the law of Canada does not recognize the unborn child as a legal or juridical person. Once a child is born, alive and viable, the law may recognize that its existence began before birth for certain limited purposes. But the only right recognized is that of the born person. This is a general proposition, applicable to all aspects of the law, including the law of torts."[102] The absence of a legal status for the unborn child is based not on foreseeability, but on policy. For a host of policy reasons, foremost among them the indivisibility of mother and foetus and the autonomy of the mother, the courts have refused to regard the foetus as a legal person separate in identity from its mother.

Once the foetus is born alive and viable, it has legal status. It is a person.[103] It can sue third parties for disabilities and injuries that it has suffered as the result of negligent acts that took place before it was born, which caused those injuries.[104]

The issue as to whether a child's action against third parties for pre-natal negligent acts extends to its mother was decided by the Supreme Court of Canada in *Dobson (Litigation Guardian of) v. Dobson*.[105] The plaintiff child was born

---

101 [1972] 2 O.R. 686, 26 D.L.R. (3d) 418 (H.C.), affirmed (1973), 1 O.R. (2d) 482 (C.A.).

102 McLachlin J. in *Winnipeg Child & Family Services (Northwest Area) v. G. (D.F.)* (1997), 152 D.L.R. (4th) 193 (S.C.C.). The case concerned an application made by a child welfare agency for an order requiring that a pregnant woman, who was addicted to glue-sniffing, be confined and refrained from her harmful habit until her baby was born. The trial judge granted the order, but the Court of Appeal reversed it. Meanwhile a healthy baby was born. Despite this, the Supreme Court of Canada heard the case. The Supreme Court affirmed the Court of Appeal and refused to grant the order requested. For an excellent collection of case comments on this decision, see (1998), 36 Alta. L. Rev. 707-809.

103 A stillborn child is not a person and has no legal status; see *Gibbons v. Port Hope & District Hospital* (1998), 44 C.C.L.T. (2d) 198 (Ont. Gen. Div.), reversed on another matter (1999), 46 C.C.L.T. (2d) 266 (Ont. C.A.), additional reasons at (1999), 46 C.C.L.T. (2d) 268 (Ont. C.A.).

104 Ontario has legislation, the Family Law Act, R.S.O. 1990, c. F.3, s. 66, which states, "No person is disentitled from recovering damages in respect of injuries for the reason only that the injuries were incurred before his or her birth." The issues of abortion and the rights of the unborn have significant tort law repercussions. See discussion on "wrongful life" and "wrongful birth" below, Chapter 10.

105 (1999), 45 C.C.L.T. (2d) 217 (S.C.C.). See Erin Nelson, "One of These Things Is Not Like The Other: Maternal Legal Duties and the Supreme Court of Canada" (2000), 12 S.C.L.R. (2d) 31, for a case comment. For commentary on the trial judgment and briefly on the Court of Appeal judgment see Foley, "*Dobson v. Dobson:* Tort Liability for Expectant Mothers?" (1998), 61 Sask. L. Rev. 177. Both authors reject the imposition of a duty of care on mothers owed to children for injuries caused by pre-natal accidents. These commentaries provide useful comparative analyses and references to other articles on this topic. One of these is Kerr,

with disabilities as a result of injuries suffered by it when it was a foetus in a traffic accident caused by its mother's negligent driving. The Supreme Court affirmed that a child would have a claim against a third person in such circumstances, but denied its right of action against its mother. This rejection was based not on the unforeseeability of the foetus as a "distinct legal entity" from its mother at the time of the accident,[106] but on policy grounds. According to the majority of the Court, liability of the mother to her child injured in such circumstances would inappropriately violate the privacy and autonomy rights of women. As well, the Court was concerned with the difficulty in "articulating a judicial standard of conduct for pregnant women". The Court rejected arguments that a cause of action could be recognized which was limited in scope. It was suggested, for example, that the duty could be confined to activities which are not "peculiar to parenthood", or that the duty could be owed only in motor vehicle cases, where liability insurance would be triggered.

The dissenting Justices would have allowed this cause of action. Major J. noted that the issue in this case did not involve the legal status of the unborn, or the legal relationship between a pregnant mother and foetus, but the tort rights of a child already born. Major J. argued that to hold a pregnant woman liable to her child for negligent driving would not affect the autonomy of the mother, or her freedom of action, since she was already under a duty to drive with reasonable care.

The dissent is persuasive. It is difficult to see how on the facts of this type of case imposing liability upon a pregnant woman for her negligent driving would interfere with the defendant's autonomy or personal life style choices. It is true that drawing the line between those negligent activities of a pregnant woman which would give rise to liability and those which would not, based on a test that

---

"Pre-Natal Fictions and Post-Partum Actions" (1997), 20 Dal. L.J. 237. Professor Kerr is also critical of the trial court and Court of Appeal judgments and in particular the legal fiction that an unborn child shall for some purposes be treated as if it were born.

106 The Court's wording on this point is, with respect, unfortunate. Cory J. was prepared to assume "that a pregnant woman and her foetus can be treated as distinct legal entities", at 45 C.C.L.T. (2d) 229. That being the case, "a pregnant woman and her foetus are within the closest physical proximity that two 'legal persons' could be in, and a *prima facie* duty of care is owed by the mother to her foetus". The reasoning is flawed since the Supreme Court had earlier clearly decided that a foetus is not a legal entity or legal person: see *Winnipeg Child & Family Services (Northwest Area) v. G. (D.F.)* (1997), 152 D.L.R. (4th) 193 (S.C.C.). What Cory J. arguably meant to say was that it is reasonably foreseeable that a mother could injure her foetus through her negligence, and that a *prima facie* duty of care is owed *to the child* born alive with disabilities as a result of the negligence. This *prima facie* duty is then negated by policy reasons discussed by the Court.

asks whether this activity creates a duty to third parties, might be a difficult exercise in marginal cases.[107] However, drawing lines in tort in marginal cases is not unusual.[108]

---

107 For example, if a pregnant woman injures her foetus in a fall that results from her carelessly running in a crowded area, would she be liable to her child if it were later born with injuries? If she hurt a third person, she would be liable. Would this be an unacceptable intrusion into her life?

108 The Province of Alberta enacted the Maternal Tort Liability Act, S.A. 2005, c. M-7.5, to allow a child who has suffered injuries as a result of his or her mother's negligent driving during her pregnancy to sue her. The judgment is limited to the amount of the mother's automobile liability insurance. The question as to whether a child, although barred from suing his/her mother/driver, can sue the third party/owner of the car under s. 181 of the Highway Traffic Safety Act, R.S.A. 200, c.T-6, was raised in an Alberta case *R. (B.) (Next Friend of) v. R. (L.)* (2004), 236 D.L.R. (4th) 754 (Alta. Q.B.). The motion to strike out the claim was dismissed, although the legal issue was not resolved. As a result of the Maternal Tort Liability Act, this point is now moot in Alberta.

6

The Duty to Assist Others

1. INTRODUCTION

Lord Atkin's proposition in *Donoghue v. Stevenson* that "you must take reasonable care to avoid acts or omissions which you can reasonably foresee would be likely to injure your neighbour" leaves unanswered the question as to whether the common law of torts does, or ought to, impose a duty on individuals to come to the assistance of others who are in peril. Despite the paucity of actual cases, and the lack of any clear evidence that there is in Anglo-American jurisdictions a serious social problem or concern with regard to the Good Samaritan dilemma,[1] this topic fascinates legal scholars and philosophers.[2] This is not surprising. The issue strikes at the very heart of the relationship between law and morality, the functions of law, and the requirements for a successful negligence action. Even if the fact is, as I suspect, that there is not in Canadian society a pressing need for

1 There are occasionally dramatic incidents which stir up the issue. For example, the Kitty Genovese incident, which involved the inaction of 38 witnesses to a brutal murder, was one such case which produced heightened concern.

2 There have been numerous articles and books. See, among others: Weinrib, "The Case for a Duty to Rescue" (1980), 90 Yale L. J. 247: Shapo, *The Duty to Act; Tort Law, Power and Public Policy* (1977); Gray and Sharpe, "Doctors, Samaritans and the Accident Victim" (1973), 11 Osgoode Hall L. J. 1; Ratcliffe (ed.), *The Good Samaritan and the Law* (1966); Smith, *Liability in Negligence* (1984), Chapter 3; Linden, "Rescuers and Good Samaritans" (1971), 34 Mod. L. Rev. 241, reprinted in (1972), 10 Alta. L. Rev. 89; Bohlen, "The Moral Duty to Aid Others as a Basis of Tort Liability" (1908), 56 U. Pa. L. Rev. 217; Rudolph, "The Duty to Act: A Proposed Rule" (1965), 44 Neb. L. Rev. 499; Levmore, "Waiting for Rescue" (1986), 72 Va. L. Rev. 879; D'Amato, "The 'Bad Samaritan' Paradigm" (1975), 70 N.W.U.L. Rev. 798; Heyman, "Foundations of the Duty to Rescue" (1994), 47 Vanderbilt L.Rev. 671; Adler, "Relying Upon The Reasonableness of Strangers . . .", [1991] Wis. L. Rev. 867; Denton, "The Case Against a Duty to Rescue", [1991] Can. J. Law & Juris. 101. Mitchell McInnes has written extensively on the topic: see, McInnes, "The Question of a Duty to Rescue in Canadian Tort Law: An Answer From France" (1990), 13 Dalhousie L.J. 85; "Pyschological Perspectives on Rescue" (1991), 20 Man. L.J. 656; "The Economic Analysis of Rescue Laws" (1992), 21 Man. L.J. 237; "Good Samaritan Statutes: A Summary and Analysis" (1992), 26 U.B.C. L. Rev. 239; and "Protecting the Good Samaritan: Defences for the Rescuer in Anglo-Canadian Criminal Law" (1994), 36 Crim. L.Q. 331. A series of six papers on the topic was published; see "Good Samaritan Symposium" (2000), 4 Santa Clara L. Rev. 957-1103.

the creation of a law requiring individuals to assist others when they can do so with little inconvenience or risk to themselves, the debate is an extremely useful one in that it illuminates much more fundamental issues concerning the relationship of law and morality.

When considering the duty to assist issue,[3] one must carefully define the scope of the discussion. In its narrowest form, the issue is whether the common law of torts does, or should, require an otherwise disinterested bystander, who has in no way participated in the creation of a situation of peril or who has not voluntarily assumed responsibility for an endangered person, to act in order to assist that person. In other words, the issue presents the original dilemma which confronted the priest, the Levite and the Samaritan. The story, as told by Jesus, is as follows.[4] A man was robbed, beaten, and left on the road for dead. A priest passed by, saw him, but merely continued on his way. So did a Levite. However, a Samaritan stopped, rendered medical assistance, took the victim to an inn, and paid for his care. If the victim had not been assisted by the Samaritan, and consequently died, should the law of torts require those who could have easily and successfully prevented his death to compensate the dependants of the deceased?[5]

Apart from the strict case of the disinterested bystander and stranger victim just described, there are, of course, several situations where tort law does presently impose a duty upon one to take affirmative steps to either assist an endangered person, or to prevent another from being put into a situation of peril. These cases are often characterized as exceptions to the general rule that there is in the common law no duty to rescue or to assist. In truth, they are not exceptions at all but different situations altogether — not the case of the imperilled victim and the Good Samaritan, but other relationships which require duties of care. Nevertheless, since these cases do raise similar types of problems, especially as they involve duties to assist or to protect, it is sensible to treat them in this chapter.

2. THE STRICT RULE

There are very few actual decisions, certainly no recent ones, and no Canadian ones of which I am aware, which have dismissed an action brought by an injured victim, or the dependants of a deceased, against an individual who refused to

---

3 By duty to assist I include not only the duty to assist someone who is in danger, or who already has been hurt, but the duty to take preventative steps, such as warnings, to avoid future harm or losses.

4 This story is told in Luke, Chapter 10, by Jesus. See Fingarette, "Some Moral Aspects of Good Samaritanship", in Ratcliffe (ed.), *The Good Samaritan and the Law* (1966), at 213. The biblical story itself is discussed by Waldron, "On The Road: Good Samaritans and Compelling Duties" (2000), 40 Santa Clara L. Rev. 1053. As Professor Waldron notes, the story of the Good Samaritan was told by Jesus to a lawyer, who was asking how he could inherit eternal life. Professor Waldron examines what significance, if any, this gives to the parable.

5 We are now concerned about tort law, which focusses on compensation. Of course, the law can approach the matter from the perspective of criminal law, which is a common European approach. See Rudzunski, "The Duty to Rescue: A Comparative Analysis", in Ratcliffe (ed.), *The Good Samaritan and the Law* (1966), at 91; and Vranken, "Duty to Rescue in Civil Law and Common Law" (1998), I.C.L.Q. 934. This raises some similar issues but also others with important differences. See Law Reform Commission of Canada, *Working Paper on Omissions, Negligence and Endangering*, Working Paper 46, 1985.

render assistance to a stranger in peril.[6] Yet no one doubts the proposition that the modern law of torts imposes no duty to render assistance to those in peril, in the absence of a special relationship, even where assistance can be rendered easily, effectively, and without risk or inconvenience to the rescuer.[7] One of the few cases actually on point is the American case of *Osterlind v. Hill,*[8] where a defendant who rented a canoe to an intoxicated user was allowed to stand by ignoring loud calls for help from the patron after the canoe had overturned. The court stated that these allegations of "willful, wanton or reckless conduct" added nothing to the plaintiff's case since by refusing to help "no legal right of the intestate was infringed."[9] Most of the judgments which have affirmed the common law's refusal to impose a duty to assist on the disinterested bystander, however, were *obiter dicta,* since the mythical "moral monster" who idly stands by while a two-year-old child sits on a railway track about to be crushed by an oncoming train has never actually been sued in a court of law.[10] The *dicta,* however, are clear. In *Buch v. Amory Mfg. Co.*[11] the court stated:

> With purely moral obligations the law does not deal. For example, the priest and Levite who passed by on the other side were not, it is supposed, liable at law for the continued suffering of the man who fell among thieves, which they might, and morally ought to have, prevented or relieved.[12]

In *Gautret v. Egerton,*[13] Willes J. stated that "no action will lie against a spiteful man who, seeing another running into a position of danger, merely omits to warn him."[14] In *Horsley v. MacLaren,*[15] the trial judge stated:

> It is still the modern law of negligence that, there is no general duty to come to the rescue of a person who finds himself in peril from a source completely unrelated to the defendant, even where

---

6 This is apparently also the case in American tort law. Adler, above, note 2, at 868, states that "missed opportunities for easy rescue are rarely the stuff of reported opinions". He also cites Rabin, "Tort Law in Transition" (1988), 23 Val. U.L. Rev. 1, where the simple paradigms of no duty to rescue are described as "little more than an academic exercise".

7 Note that the Quebec Charter of Human Rights And Freedoms, R.S.Q. 1977, c. C-12, states in s. 2:

> Every human being whose life is in peril has a right to assistance.
>
> Every person must come to the aid of anyone whose life is in peril, either personally or calling for aid, by giving him the necessary and immediate physical assistance, unless it involves danger to himself or a third person, or he has another valid reason.

8 160 N.E. 301 (Mass., 1928).

9 *Ibid.,* at 302. See also *Yania v. Bigan,* 155 A. 2d 343 (Pa., 1959), where the defendant refused to help a drowning man, and *Handiboe v. McCarthy,* 114 Ga. App. 541 (1966), where it was held that there is no duty to rescue a drowning child.

10 This example was used to illustrate the no duty proposition in *Buch v. Amory Mfg. Co.,* 69 N.H. 257 (1898). The case actually dealt with a child trespasser who injured himself on the defendant's property.

11 *Ibid.*

12 *Ibid.,* at 310.

13 (1867), L.R. 2 C.P. 371.

14 *Ibid.,* at 373. Of course, again the case did not deal with that situation. A licensee injured himself on the defendant's land without any apparent fault on the defendant's part.

15 [1969] 2 O.R. 137 at 143, reversed [1970] 2 O.R. 487, which was affirmed 22 D.L.R. (3d) 545 (S.C.C.).

> little risk or effort would be involved in assisting: thus a person on a dock can with legal impunity ignore the call for help of a drowning person, even refusing to throw a life ring. The law leaves the remedy to a person's conscience.[16]

Mr. Justice Jessup of the Court of Appeal agreed, stating that "no principle is more deeply rooted in the common law than that there is no duty to take positive action in aid of another no matter how helpless or perilous his position is."[17] Or, as stated more recently by Chief Justice McLachlin, "generally, the mere fact that a person faces danger, or has become a danger to others, does not itself impose any kind of duty on those in a position to become involved." The law "permits third parties witnessing risk to decide not to become rescuers or otherwise intervene."[18] It thus appears that despite the fact that there are few cases actually on point, the courts, through the *obiter* comments of judges, and the writings of scholars, are firmly convinced that the law of torts is not applicable to the plight of the victim left unattended by those who refuse to help.

3. SHOULD THERE BE A DUTY?

The question whether the common law of torts should impose a legal duty on persons to come to the assistance of those in peril, even when there is little inconvenience or risk to the rescuer in doing so, is a controversial one. It is answered according to one's personal views as to what the purposes of liability rules are, and on one's evaluation of how any such rule might actually work out in practice.[19]

Approaching the question on a more abstract or theoretical level, different theories or philosophies of tort provide differing insights into the issue. For example, the law and economics theorists are concerned with liability rules which provide the most efficient solution to tort law disputes. Assuming that there is value in encouraging easy rescues, the economic theorist would ask the following questions: Will making people liable in tort for refusing to rescue or assist encourage more rescues? Might a legal obligation to rescue discourage those who presently offer assistance out of a sense of altruism, rather than legal obligation? Might liability for failure to rescue discourage potential rescuers from coming to

---

16 Of course the case was not concerned with such a person, but with a ship master who allegedly negligently attempted to rescue a drowning passenger and whose obligation to rescue was in fact affirmed by all three levels of courts.

17 [1970] 2 O.R. 487 at 499. Jessup J.A. also stated (at 499) that "despite the moral outrage of the text writers, it appears presently the law that one can, with immunity, smoke a cigarette on the beach while one's neighbour drowns and, without a word of warning, watch a child or blind person walk into certain danger."

18 *Childs v. Desormeaux*, [2006] 1 S.C.R. 643 at para. 31 and para. 29. See discussion of this case below.

19 As McInnes, "The Economic Analysis of Rescue Laws", above, note 2, points out, one can promote rescue by utilizing a tort liability rule, or a compensation rule. A tort liability rule would allow a victim who was not rescued to sue for damages. A compensation rule would allow a person who did rescue and who suffered damage as a result, to sue the person rescued for reimbursement of expenses, or remuneration for services. In this Chapter, tort liability is in issue. As we will see later, tort does provide compensation to those injured during a rescue in certain circumstances. See Chapter 12.

places where the need for rescues may arise?[20] For others, like Richard Epstein, who base liability in tort on a theory of causation,[21] there should be no duty to rescue or assist in tort, since a person who fails to rescue does not cause harm to the person in peril, but merely refuses to confer a gratuitous benefit on that person. Or, as J.C. Smith argues, since imposing legal obligations on individuals limits their freedom of action or free agency, unless a duty to rescue can be justified, one ought not to be imposed.[22] According to Smith, the law must continue to distinguish between what people are obligated to do, as opposed to what they ought to do, and to protect freedom of action. Some do, however, propose the common law's acceptance of a duty to rescue. They do so on theories of morality,[23] or because they believe that the law should reflect morality, should lead rather than follow, should educate and so on.[24]

Tort law, whether based on negligence or strict liability, ordinarily requires that only those individuals who alter the *status quo* to the detriment of others must compensate their victims and restore them to their position prior to the commission of the wrongdoer's act. It is a system of corrective, and not distributive, justice. It is my view that tort law does not, and should not, require individuals to alter the *status quo* for the benefit of others. Despite an understandable disapproval of those who refuse to effect easy rescues, making this conduct tortious is not the appropriate response.[25]

---

20 See Posner, *Economic Analysis of Law*, 2nd ed. at 131; Landes and Posner, "Salvors, Finders, Good Samaritans, and Other Rescuers: An Economic Study of Law and Altruism" (1978), 7 J. Leg. Stud. 83; and Eugene Volokh, "Duties to Rescue and the Anticooperative Effects of Law" (1999), 88 Geo. L.J. 105, cited by Frankin & Ploeger, above, note 2 ("Symposium") at 1004, note 51. An in-depth economic analysis is provided by McInnes, "The Economic Analysis of Rescue Laws", above, note 2. McInnes notes that an economic analysis will construct the most "efficient" rescue law. In this context, an efficient law requiring rescue would ensure that "the dollar value of gains to those who would benefit from the law [presumably the rescuee] would be sufficent to compensate those who would be disadvantaged by the law [the person obliged to effect the rescue], whether or not such compensation was in fact paid," at 240. In his article, McInnes critiques the arguments made by Landes & Posner regarding the possible behavioural effects that a liability rule requiring rescue might have on otherwise potential rescuers. McInnes also talks about the possible behavioural effects that a liability rule requiring rescue might have on potential victims. There is, for example, the possibility that increasing the likelihood of rescue will encourage persons to engage in more hazardous activities and reduce their own self-protection incentives. I can think of the following example. Will parents take more care for the protection of their child if the child is swimming in a pool which is not supervised by a life-guard and less care when the child is in a supervised pool? If so, the advantages of the presence of a lifeguard might be counteracted by the encouragement to more risky behaviour.

21 Epstein, "A Theory of Strict Liability" (1973), 2 J. Leg. Stud. 151; Epstein, "Defences and Subsequent Pleas in a System of Strict Liability" (1974), 3 J. Leg. Stud. 165.

22 Smith, *Liability in Negligence* (1984), Chapter 3.

23 See Weinrib's excellent critique of Epstein's approach, and his own attempt to justify a duty to rescue at common law on the basis of moral theory in "The Case for a Duty to Rescue" (1980), 90 Yale L. J. 247.

24 See, e.g., Honore, "Law, Morals and Rescue", in Ratcliffe (ed.), *The Good Samaritan and the Law* (1966), at 225.

25 See Denton, "The Case Against a Duty to Rescue", above, note 2, where the corrective justice rationale of tort is used to argue for the denial of a duty to rescue. Others who argue against a tort duty to rescue include Franklin & Ploeger "Of Rescue and Report: Should Tort Law Impose a Duty to Help Endangered Persons or Abused Children?" (2000), 40 Santa Clara L. Rev. 991.

The conduct of most people who presently refuse to assist others at no inconvenience or personal risk — if many people such as this even exist[26] — would probably not be altered by the creation of such a duty.[27] As has been observed by others, "the only people who will offer their services to others in distress do not have to be required to do so; and those who will not do it voluntarily pay no attention to official sanctions."[28] Why people who could easily and without risk assist another would refuse to do so must be considered when creating such a legal obligation. If, as has been suggested, one's response to a cry for help is based upon a set of normal human reactions — shock, initial paralysis, guilt and self-justification, rather than a calculated decision to allow others to be harmed — it is questionable whether the imposition of tort liability is the appropriate judicial response.[29] Would it be just and reasonable to hold an individual who refuses to assist out of a sense of fear, cowardliness, or even moral indifference, liable in tort, and accountable to the victim for full compensation? The punishment for refusing to help would be excessively harsh and unfair, were normal principles of damage assessments to be applied to this new tort duty.

Despite the fact that all would agree that tort law does reflect widely held values, there is a point beyond which many people do not want the law to go in enforcing moral dictates. The duty to assist, at least when cast in the strict facts of the Good Samaritan dilemma, falls beyond this point. Laws which require individuals to be righteous, on pain of being mulcted by fines, damages, or even being sent to jail, are incompatible with a society which favours freedom of action, freedom of conscience, and minimal State interference. To the extent that

---

Haberfeld, "*Lowns v. Woods* and the Duty to Rescue" (1998), 6 Tort Law Rev. 56, also argues against a common law tort approach, preferring a legislative solution.

26 Franklin & Ploeger share my skepticism: "There is no evidence that citizens are refusing to make easy rescues. The oft-raised paradigm here is the baby who crawls into a few inches of water in a puddle and might drown. If citizens en masse do not rescue drowning babies, one might well argue that some legal mandate is appropriate. It appears, however, that drowning babies are rescued." *Ibid.* at 1004.

27 See Zeisel, "An International Experiment on the Effects of a Good Samaritan Law", in Ratcliffe, above, note 2, at 209. The author conducted a study of countries with and without Good Samaritan laws and concluded that "it makes no difference in personal behaviour whether or not such a law exists or not." See, however, Brady, "The Duty to Rescue in Tort Law: Implications of Research on Altruism" (1979-80), 55 Ind. L.J. 551, where the author explains how a tort duty to rescue might result in a greater willingness to offer assistance. Also see D'Amato, above, note 2, who submits that a criminal law requiring rescue will produce more rescues, and Franklin, "Vermont Requires Rescue: A Comment" (1972), 25 Stanford L. Rev. 51.

28 Gregory, "The Good Samaritan and the Bad: The Anglo-American Law", in Ratcliffe (ed), *The Good Samaritan and the Law* (1966), at 23, repeating one of Goodhart's observations.

29 See Freedman, "No Response to the Cry for Help", in Ratcliffe, *ibid.*, at 171. The psychology of rescue is discussed in detail in McInnes, "Psychological Perspectives on Rescue", above, note 2. McInnes explores the work of psychologists to help understand "bystander intervention". One of the points of McInnes' article is to demonstrate how a properly devised legal duty to rescue can influence those factors which are conducive to encouraging bystander intervention. See also Radcliffe, "A Duty to Rescue: The Good, the Bad and the Indifferent — the Bystander's Dilemma" (1986), 13 Pepperdine Law Rev. 387. The author also believes that "much of the psychological research to date appears to indicate that the law may be an effective resource in encouraging altruistic behavior", at 404.

laws are unenforceable and run contrary to the public's conception of the function of law, they discredit the whole of the legal system.

On a more pragmatic level, such a tort duty may be difficult to administer. In the extreme case, where an innocent person is killed or injured because many others refused to help, it may be very difficult to discover who the wrongdoers were. Bad Samaritans may be difficult to identify, and it will seem unjust to those who are singled out that many others went undetected.[30] If the duty is predicated on the requirement that the rescue might easily have been carried out, defining the easy rescue will also present practical problems, not only for the defendant who was put into the position of having to decide in an urgent situation whether there was a legal obligation to rescue or not, but for the court later on. No one would suggest that an innocent passerby must assume unreasonable risks in order to rescue; however, to assess a risk when one is confronted with an emergency may be difficult.[31] If it is suggested that the duty will apply only in the most clear-cut case of an easy rescue, where there is absolutely no risk to the rescuer, it can be questioned whether this case even presents a problem which requires attention. As well, the duty to assist or rescue must be set aside the legal system's apparent distaste for vigilantism. This balance may not be an easy one to draw. Although one can in theory easily distinguish between the two situations, as a practical matter the distinction might not be as clear-cut.[32]

Those who argue that the law should impose a duty to rescue do so on the belief that it reflects no credit on the law that "moral monsters" can callously disregard the well-being of others without legal sanction, and that the imposition of a duty might make a positive contribution to society. Opponents of a duty recognize the intrinsic limitations of law in affecting behaviour, especially where the matter pertains to questions of conscience, and fear that not only would such a duty be unworkable, it would serve as an invitation to even greater legal interventions, which would attempt not to reflect current ideas of morality, but to alter them. To some the distinction between requiring individuals to attempt easy rescues, and requiring more from them, such as redistributing their wealth, is not an easy one to draw.[33] In the final analysis, the issue is a political one, which explains why courts have traditionally been reluctant to take a common law tort approach to the question, and have left it for legislators to make the decision.[34]

---

30 Aside from the unfairness of arbitrary or random enforcement, there is also the cost of enforcement, which some suggest would be very high. See Rubin, "Costs and Benefits of a Duty to Rescue" (1986), 6 Int'l Rev. Law & Econ. 273, cited by McInnes, "The Economic Analysis of Rescue Laws", above, note 2, at 242. McInnes questions the correctness of this argument.

31 There have been, of course, incidents of well-intentioned persons who were severely beaten, or even killed, by those who they were attempting to assist. An Alberta Cabinet Minister, for example, was severely beaten when he stopped to assist two men whose car had apparently broken down at the side of the road.

32 Reported incidents occurring in subways and shops where individuals have taken severe measures to assist others or protect themselves highlight this concern.

33 For example, will the duty to assist those in peril lead to a duty to provide food to the hungry, shelter for the homeless, and so forth?

34 One approach has been to encourage Good Samaritanism by reducing the potential liability of those who may injure others while attempting to assist them. See Gray and Sharpe, "Doctors, Samaritans and the Accident Victim" (1973), 11 Osgoode Hall L.J. 1; McInnes, "Good Samaritan Statutes: A Summary and Analysis" (1992), 26 U.B.C. L. Rev. 239. Legislation exists

4. RELATIONSHIPS REQUIRING ASSISTANCE

(a) Introduction

There are several situations in which a special relationship between the parties has allowed the court to conclude that the imposition of a duty of assistance on one for the other's behalf would not be antithetical to the common law's refusal to impose a general duty to assist. Although it is difficult to create a general proposition which would satisfactorily account for all cases, in each the courts have been able to find some element which prevented the parties from being considered to have merely been disinterested strangers. Whether because of previous undertakings, familial relationship, professional relationship, commercial relationship, or because one person had already voluntarily disrupted the *status quo* to another person's detriment, courts have been able to distinguish these cases from that of the Good Samaritan. As well, in some situations legislation has required that there be action on the part of certain professionals, such as the police, or others, for the assistance of those in peril. In these cases, the political decision requiring affirmative action has been taken out of the court's hands.

(b) Relationships of Economic Benefit

(i) Commercial Hosts

Courts have imposed upon individuals who stand to benefit economically from a relationship with another a duty to take affirmative action to assist or to prevent that other person from being injured, within the context of that relationship. While on the surface it only seems fair to require responsible conduct from those who stand to profit from a potentially dangerous activity, and who may in fact require a special permit to operate, whether it is the role of tort law to enforce this type of obligation is a question which must be addressed.

The tort liability of the commercial host is at the forefront of this discussion. The leading case is *Jordan House Ltd. v. Menow.*[35] In this case, the Supreme Court of Canada held a tavern keeper liable for injuries suffered on a highway by a drunk patron after he had been ejected from the defendant's inn. Although several factors in this case were material to the decision,[36] there was, in the court's

---

that reduces the standard of care required of 'Good Samaritans'. See, for example, The Emergency Medical Aid Act, R.S.A. 2000, c. E-7, s. 2; the Volunteers Liability Act, S.P.E.I. 1994, c. 65; and Art. 1471 of the Quebec Civil Code. These provisions require 'gross negligence' in order for liability to be imposed.

35 (1974), 38 D.L.R. (3d) 105. For a good discussion of the leading cases on this topic both from a common and civil law perspective, see Dalphond J., "Duty of Care and the Supply of Alcohol" (2002), 17 S.C.L.R. (2d) 97.

36 For example, there were possible legislative infractions by the tavern keeper, and the parties involved were well known to each other, prompting the defendant to have adopted internal rules about serving liquor to this patron. There is legislation dealing with aspects of this problem as well. See the Liquor Licence Act, R.S.O. 1990, c. L.19, s. 39, which gives an action to the dependants of a deceased against the person who was responsible for the deceased's intoxication. The legislation also gives a cause of action to persons who are injured or whose property is damaged by the intoxicated person. See *Blakely v. 513953 Ont. Ltd.* (1985), 31 M.V.R. 10 (Ont. H.C.). The statutory civil liability provision was considered in *Kauk v. Dickson* (2005), 33 C.C.L.T. (3d) 283 (Ont. S.C.J.), affirmed 2008 ONCA 97 (C.A.). The plaintiff was brutally

judgment, a recognition that the specific relationship in this case involved an economic benefit to the defendant. Laskin J. noted that the parties were in an invitor-invitee relationship, the hotel not merely being "in the position of persons in general who see an intoxicated person who appears to be unable to control his steps."[37]

The tort duty imposed upon commercial hosts was reaffirmed by the Supreme Court in *Stewart v. Pettie*.[38] In this judgment, the duty that a commercial host owes to an intoxicated patron logically was extended for the protection of third parties endangered by the intoxicated person.[39] In *Childs v. Desormeaux*,[40] the Supreme Court, in dismissing an action brought against a social host, justified the imposition of a duty on the commercial host, but not on a social host, by noting the following distinguishing factors. First is the commercial host's advantage in monitoring alcohol consumption. Second is the existence of a regulatory environment in which commercial hosts operate.[41] Third are the legitimate expectations of the public that commercial hosts will regulate alcohol consumption and take affirmative steps to reduce its risks. Fourth is the law's desire to create a disincentive to the commercial host's otherwise profit motivated behaviour. There are numerous Canadian judgments which have imposed a duty on a commercial host with respect to injuries caused to or by intoxicated patrons.[42] In these

---

assaulted and raped by a person who had been drinking at the defendant's bar. The court conceded that a duty was owed by the bar, both by statute and common law, but held that the statutory liability provision was not strict, but required foreseeability. On the facts of the case, foreseeability was absent and hence the action was dismissed. In *McIntyre v. Grigg* (2006), 43 C.C.L.T. (3d) 209 (Ont. C.A.), liability was imposed on a commercial host both at common law and pursuant to the statute. The Court of Appeal held that liability under the statute is not "absolute", but depends upon proof of the "factual conditions provided for therein". Implicit in the Court of Appeal's discussion is that there must be fault, although it must be stated that the section itself does not refer to fault. The court also stated that knowledge of inebriation is not a condition of liability; constructive knowledge will suffice.

37 (1974), 38 D.L.R. (3d) 105 at 111.

38 (1995), 121 D.L.R. (4th) 222.

39 Although recognizing the existence of the duty, the Supreme Court dismissed the action brought by a passenger against the commercial establishment who served the drunk driver. The duty was held not to have been breached, since it was not foreseeable that the drunk patron would leave the bar and drive. The patron was in the company of two sober persons, including the plaintiff, and Major J. held that it was reasonable for the bar to assume that one of them would drive. That being the case, no positive action was required from the bar to prevent the drunk patron from driving. Prior to *Stewart v. Pettie*, several lower courts also had recognized that a commercial host owes a duty not only to the patron, but to third parties as well. See, for example, *Hague v. Billings* (1989), 48 C.C.L.T. 192 (Ont. H.C.), affirmed in part (1993), 15 C.C.L.T. (2d) 264 (Ont. C.A.).

40 [2006] 1 S.C.R. 643.

41 As noted above, statutory civil liability provisions may also exist, apart from a common law duty.

42 See, for example, *Skinner v. Baker Estate* (1991), 8 C.C.L.I. (2d) 154 (Ont. Gen. Div.) — action dismissed due to lack of negligence; *Despres v. Nobleton Lakes Golf Course Ltd.* (1994), 5 M.V.R. (3d) 25 (Ont. Gen. Div.) — tavern liable for fatality caused by drunk patron's driving; *Gouge v. Three Top Invst. Holdings Inc.* (1994), 22 C.C.L.T. (2d) 281 (Ont. Gen. Div.) — hotel 5 per cent liable to drunk motorcyclist; *Lum (Guardian ad litem of) v. McLintock* (1997), 45 B.C.L.R. (3d) 303 (S.C.) — bar 30 per cent liable; and *Laface v. McWilliams* (2005), 29 C.C.L.T. (3d) 219 (B.C. S.C.), additional reasons at (2005), 2005 CarswellBC 3034 (S.C. [In Chambers])), affirmed (2006), 2006 CarswellBC 1200 (C.A.) — hotel equally liable with drunk

cases, an element of particular importance to the courts has been the commercial nature of the relationship.[43]

The economic benefit rationale is at the heart of other Canadian cases which have recognized the duty to assist or to prevent an intoxicated person from injuring himself or others. In another Supreme Court of Canada decision, *Crocker v.*

---

driver for injuries suffered by pedestrians. The duty applies not only with respect to drunk driving, but also to other types of injuries that intoxicated patrons might cause to innocent third parties. See, for example, *Donaldson v. John Doe* (2007), [2007] B.C.J. No. 829, 2007 CarswellBC 851 (S.C.) — injury caused by striking the plaintiff in the eye with a glass mug. The action was dismissed due to lack of foreseeability. In *Holton v. MacKinnon* (2005), [2005] B.C.J. No. 57, 2005 CarswellBC 63 (S.C), three men, including the plaintiff, had been drinking at commercial establishments. They then went to the plaintiff's house without incident. Shortly thereafter they ventured out again. It was then that the accident, which injured the plaintiff, occurred. The court rejected the argument that the defendant commercial host's responsibility had ended, when the plaintiff first arrived home safely after leaving the bar.

43 For example, in *Hague v. Billings* (1989), 48 C.C.L.T. 192 at 211, Granger J. stated:

> . . . when the public through the province licensed the Oasis to sell intoxicants, a special relationship arose between the tavern and motorists, requiring the tavern to take affirmative action to prevent intoxicated patrons from driving on the highway. When the Oasis sold a beer to Billings and thereby made a profit, a duty to take affirmative action arose.
>
> If tavern owners are allowed to sell intoxicating beverages, they must accept, as a price of doing business, a duty to attempt to keep the highways free of drunk drivers.
>
> . . . the public has a right to assume that a person or corporation making a profit from the sale of intoxicants will acknowledge and carry out this duty.

The court held that all tavern keepers owe a special duty to users of highways to take affirmative action to prevent drunk patrons from venturing out onto the highway, even if the patron did not become inebriated in the defendant's tavern. Thus, even though one defendant tavern had sold the already intoxicated patron only one beer, and was not in breach of the Liquor Licence Act, R.S.O. 1980, c. 244, it was held to have breached its duty. It ought to have attempted to prevent the drunk from driving his car, by telephoning the police. The action against this tavern was dismissed, however, since there was no proof that had the police been called, they would have responded to the call in time to stop the patron. The other defendant tavern, which actually sold several beers to the intoxicated patron, was held liable, based both on the common law, and by virtue of the Liquor Licence Act, R.S.O. 1980, c. 244, s. 53, which specifically provides a remedy to those injured by the drunk. On appeal (1993), 15 C.C.L.T. (2d) 264, the finding of liability was affirmed although the apportionment of fault varied. See also *Little Plume v. Weir* (1998), [1999] 3 W.W.R. 348 (Alta. Q.B.). In this case, the defendant bar ejected the patron before he was served any alcoholic beverages because he appeared to be intoxicated. The court held that the bar's conduct in the circumstances was consistent with its statutory duty, and was reasonable. The court conceded that a bar has a duty to act reasonably when ejecting an inebriated patron, even if the bar did not cause the inebriation. One should also note that occupiers' liability law will also apply to injuries sustained by patrons within the commercial establishment itself. See, for example, *Pereira v. Airliner Motor Hotel (1972) Ltd.* (1997), 120 Man. R. (2d) 241 (Q.B.), where there was a fight between two patrons in the defendant bar's parking lot; and *Chartrand v. Gordon Hotels & Motor Inns* (2000), 144 Man. R. (2d) 161 (Master). In *Murphy v. Little Memphis Cabaret Inc.* (1996), 20 O.T.C. 313 (Gen. Div.), affirmed (1998), [1998] O.J. No. 4752, 1998 CarswellOnt 4461 (C.A.), liability was found when a bar ejected a patron who was then involved in a fight with other individuals. As the altercation had commenced in the bar and the subsequent fight was "imminent", the court did not have a problem with applying an occupiers' liability analysis to this case, even though the incident did not actually occur on the premises. See Chapter 15 for a discussion of occupiers' liability.

Sundance Northwest Resorts Ltd,[44] the defendant company, which operated a ski complex, was sued after a competitor in a "tubing" race suffered injuries during the race.[45] The competitor was allowed to enter the race despite the fact that he was clearly intoxicated at the time, part of the drinking having occurred in conjunction with the pre-race activities. The defendant was found liable at trial, but this judgment was reversed by the Court of Appeal, based on the principle that those who willingly take on abnormal and completely unnecessary risks cannot complain of the consequences.[46] In conformity with the *Jordan House* precedent, the Supreme Court of Canada restored the trial judgment. Madame Justice Wilson, after noting the commercial advantages which the defendant hoped to gain from the race, as well as the defendant's knowledge of the dangers of the race in view of the plaintiff's inebriation, held that the jurisprudence inevitably led to the conclusion that there was a duty relationship between the parties. As stated by Her Ladyship:

> . . . when a ski resort establishes a competition in a highly dangerous sport and runs the competition for profit, it owes a duty of care towards visibly intoxicated participants.[47]

Another important case which involved a duty to assist or protect within the context of a commercial enterprise was *Arnold v. Teno*.[48] The Ontario Court of Appeal's decision that the principles enunciated in *Jordan House v. Menow* applied to the situation in which an ice cream vendor deliberately draws children to the street to purchase ice cream was affirmed by the Supreme Court of Canada. The courts held that notwithstanding the common law's general treatment of omissions, a defendant who attracts children to a situation of potential danger has a duty to take reasonable steps to protect them from that danger.

The economic benefit rationale can be used to explain other decisions which seem to represent a departure from the basic 'no duty to assist' principle. The courts have imposed on suppliers of goods[49] and services[50] a duty to ensure that otherwise safe products will not be misused and result in injury to the user or others. While, under traditional analysis, a disinterested observer would not be legally obliged to intervene and prevent someone from unreasonably using a product, but would be entitled to stand by and watch an accident about to happen, there is, in a few cases, the indication that the same is not true of a party who derives an economic benefit from the relationship.

It is legitimate to question whether the economic benefit rationale sufficiently justifies the common law's departure from its 'no duty to assist' principle in the

---

44 (1988), 44 C.C.L.T. 225 (S.C.C.), reversing (1985), 33 C.C.L.T. 73 (Ont. C.A.), which reversed (1983), 25 C.C.L.T. 201 (Ont. H.C.).

45 The competitors went down a mogulled ski hill hanging on to a large tire inner tube.

46 33 C.C.L.T. 73 at 87. For a comment on the trial judgment, see Osborne, "Case Comment" (1983), 25 C.C.L.T. 220. For a critique of the Court of Appeal's judgment, see Klar, "Negligence Law: Reactions Against Alleged Excessive Imposition of Liability" (1987), 66 Can. Bar Rev. 159.

47 44 C.C.L.T. 225 at 236.

48 (1978), 3 C.C.L.T. 272 (S.C.C.).

49 See, e.g., *Good-Wear Treaders Ltd. v. D & B Hldg. Ltd.* (1979), 8 C.C.L.T. 87 (N.S. C.A.).

50 See *Schulz v. Leeside Dev.* (1977), 3 C.C.L.T. 72, reversed 6 C.C.L.T. 248 (B.C. C.A.).

above cases.[51] Undoubtedly there is, especially in activities involving alcohol consumption, a strong public policy desire to ensure responsible behaviour.[52] As well, the desire adequately to compensate the innocent victims of drunk drivers is a major motivating factor. Nevertheless, compensation through tort law is not ordinarily available unless it can be demonstrated that a defendant, through its conduct, detrimentally altered the victim's status quo. In this respect, gaining profit from the sale of liquor or other potentially dangerous commodities should not be the decisive criterion in this determination.[53]

(ii) Do Social Hosts Owe a Duty?

Canadian law's imposition of a duty of care on commercial hosts inevitably led to the question of whether a tort law duty should be imposed on social hosts. Although there had been a number of actions brought against social hosts, none had been successful. It was, therefore, with great interest that the Supreme Court of Canada's judgment in *Childs v. Desormeaux* was awaited.

The defendants hosted a New Year's eve party, to which the guests brought their own alcohol. The inebriation of one of those attending the party led to a serious traffic accident in which the plaintiff, who was a passenger in another car unrelated to the party, became a paraplegic. The trial judge noted that although social hosts had previously been sued in Canada, none had ever been found liable. The court considered this to be a new category of duty and applied the reformulated test of duty as described above in Chapter 5 to this case. Both foreseeability and proximity were said to have existed, and thus a *prima facie* duty at the first stage of the test was created. The court, however, denied the duty based on policy. The court was concerned with the "inordinate burden" that a duty of care would

---

51 In the first edition of this text, I stated that the profit rationale did justify the imposition of such a duty. I must admit to becoming less convinced of that position.

52 In *Childs v. Desormeaux*, above, McLachlin C.J.C. used the profit motive as one of the factors distinguishing the social and commercial host. According to the Chief Justice, because of profit, there is an incentive for commercial hosts "not only to serve many drinks, but to serve too many. Over-consumption is more profitable than responsible consumption. . . .the benefits of over-consumption go to the tavern keeper alone, who enjoys large profit margins from customers whose judgment becomes more impaired the more they consume. This perverse incentive supports the imposition of a duty to monitor alcohol consumption in the interests of the general public." (At para. 22.) Although this argument is somewhat persuasive, it can be countered by noting that it already is an offence to serve liquor to an intoxicated person, and that there may also be non-economic "incentives" that encourage over-consumption in a social host setting. As well, the suggestion that commercial hosts are socially irresponsible, who are willing to sacrifice lives for profit, will no doubt be seen by some to be an unfair assumption.

53 An interesting insight into this issue and the general question of imposing a duty of care on one person to prevent another person from causing injury, is found in Jane Stapleton, "Duty of Care: Peripheral Parties and Alternative Opportunities for Deterrence" (1995), 11 L.Q.R. 301. Stapleton argues that to impose liability on a party whose role in causing injury is only peripheral dilutes "the notions of deterrence and individual responsibility on which the coherence of tort law depends". The author argues that the economic incentives and assertions of moral responsibility, even if they are symbolic, of tort law should be directed at the "principal" wrongdoer. In this context, one may see the commercial host being a peripheral party to the injury actual caused by the drunk person. The same argument would apply to other areas in which tort liability has recently been extended, e.g. the liability of government inspectors. See discussion in Chapter 8.

place on social hosts and was of the view that this was a matter best left to the legislature.

The Court of Appeal affirmed the trial judge's dismissal of the action, but for different reasons.[54] Principal among them was Weiler J.A.'s finding that the trial judge erred in concluding that it was reasonably foreseeable to the defendant social hosts that the guest was not capable of driving when he left the party and thus was putting users of the road at risk.[55] According to Weiler J.A., it was incorrect for the trial judge to have assumed that because the guest had a history of excessive drinking, the hosts should have known that he was intoxicated when he left the party and would be driving home in that state. In the absence of knowledge of inebriation, the defendant social hosts owed no duty of care.[56]

In affirming the dismissal of the action, the Supreme Court of Canada made a number of points that will be important in deciding future social host liability cases in Canada. The actual decision to dismiss the action on the facts of this case was based upon two findings by the court. First, McLachlin C.J. held that because the trial judge did not explicitly find that the hosts knew that the guest was inebriated when he left the party, he erred in concluding that it was reasonably foreseeable to the hosts that the guest was inebriated and hence posed a danger to users of the road. Second, McLachlin C.J. held that even if there was foreseeability, there was no proximity in this case.

In my view, the finding of no foreseeability by the Chief Justice as a factor to deny the existence of a duty of care is puzzling. As discussed earlier in this text, although reasonable foreseeability of harm is, as a matter of law, a requirement for the existence of a duty, whether on the facts of a specific case there was reasonable foreseeability of harm, should best be seen as a question of fact. The trial judge in this case had inferred from the facts that the hosts should have realized that the guest was probably inebriated when he left the party. Although it is certainly open to appellate court judges to disagree with this inferential reasoning, as the Supreme Court itself decided in *Housen v. Nikolaisen*,[57] an appellate court should not reverse findings of fact, *including factual inferences*,

---

54 (2004), 239 D.L.R. (4th) 61, 23 C.C.L.T. (3d) 216 (C.A.), leave to appeal allowed (2005), 2005 CarswellOnt 603 (S.C.C.), affirmed (2006), 2006 CarswellOnt 2710 (S.C.C.).

55 In the trial judge's words, quoted at 23 C.C.L.T. (3d) 230 of the Court of Appeal's judgment:

> Considering Desmond Desormeaux's previous convictions for impaired driving, and other offenses, and Desmond Desormeaux's previous conduct when driving, it is reasonably foreseeable that Desmond Desormeaux was not capable of driving and was putting his passengers and other users of the highway at grave risk.

56 The lack of actual knowledge of inebriation seemed to be used by Weiler J.A. as a factor that denied "proximity"; i.e., it would not be just and fair to impose a duty on the hosts in this situation, as opposed to a factor that denied foreseeability. Even without knowledge of the guest's state when he left the party, proximity might have been found if there was a duty on the social hosts to monitor the guest's consumption, or to control his behaviour. Weiler J.A. held that this duty only arose in limited situations, for example, where there is a statutory duty, a relationship of control or reliance, or where the defendant had been materially implicated in the creation of the risk. None of these were found in this case. Had proximity been established, Weiler J.A. indicated that she would not have necessarily agreed with the trial judge's policy reasons for negating the duty.

57 211 D.L.R. (4th) 577, 10 C.C.L.T. (3d) 157, [2002] 7 W.W.R. 1 (S.C.C.). See discussion below in Chapter 9.

in the absence of "palpable and overriding error". A more orthodox approach to the issue of foreseeability would have been to treat its resolution as a question of breach had a duty of care been found.[58] That it is reasonably foreseeable in a general sense that a social host's negligence in monitoring its guest's alcohol consumption could result in injuries to users of the road seems inarguable and thus the foreseeability aspect of duty in this case should not have been the bar to the recognition of a duty.

The issue of proximity lay at the heart of the Supreme Court's judgment. The court reaffirmed the common law's traditional reluctance to impose a duty of affirmative action on a person unless there is a special relationship or nexus between the parties. Three situations were identified by the courts in which the duty may be imposed. The first is "where a defendant intentionally attracts and invites third parties to an inherent and obvious risk that he or she has created or controls".[59] The second involves paternalistic relationships of control and supervision. The third concerns defendants "who either exercise a public function or engage in a commercial enterprise that includes implied responsibilities to the public at large".[60] Where, however, an individual is not materially implicated in the creation of a risk, or has not assumed responsibility for the safety of others leading to a relationship of reliance, that person can be described as a mere bystander who owes no duty to assist or prevent harm. Since the court did not think that the defendant hosts fell into any of these categories, the degree of proximity required to justify the imposition of a *prima facie* duty of care was not found and the dismissal of the action was affirmed.[61] The court pointedly declined to consider whether any duty, if one were found, should be negated by residual policy concerns.

It is fair to ask where this leaves Canadian law on the question of the tort liability of social hosts. Clearly the possibility of social hosts being found liable is still open. The Supreme Court did state, however, that for there to be liability, more will be required than merely "hosting a party where alcohol is served". There must be "active implication in the creation or enhancement of the risk". Moreover, the court refused to decide whether the fact that a host "continues to serve alcohol to a visibly inebriated person knowing that he or she will be driving home" would be sufficient to implicate the social host in the creation of the risk so as to give rise to a *prima facie* duty. And, as pointed out above, the court did

58 As the Supreme Court did in *Stewart v. Pettie*, above, note 38.

59 Paragraph 35. Under this category, the court included the duty on a captain of a boat to its passengers, on a mobile ice cream vendor to children attracted to the site, and on the organizer of an event that involved the consumption of alcohol to its participants.

60 Paragraph 36. This category included cases where public authorities or commercial enterprises offer services to the public that give rise to risks. The commercial host was identified as falling into this category.

61 To be clear, proximity must exist between the defendant social host and the injured party; not between the social host and the inebriated guest (unless it is the guest who was injured and is the plaintiff). This will arise if the social host was materially implicated in the creation of the risk, if the social host had a relationship of control or supervision over the guest that obligated the host to protect third parties (see Chapter 12), or if the host exercised a public function or commercial enterprise that included implied responsibilities to the public at large. Since none of these three scenarios was found to exist in *Childs*, there was no proximity between the social host defendant and the injured party.

not indicate whether there are policy reasons to negate the duty, even were a presumptive duty to be found.[62]

(c) Relationships of Control or Supervision

(i) Introduction

There are several relationships of control or supervision which require dominant parties to take affirmative steps to either prevent injury to or assist others in vulnerable positions.[63] The hallmark of these relationships is that those who enter into them do so willingly, knowing that situations may develop which will require them to act in order to assist others. Thus the imposition of duties of affirmative action in these cases is not inconsistent with the common law's desire not to interfere unduly with one's freedom of action.[64] As well, concomitant with the duty to assist those who are in one's control is the duty to protect others from being injured by them.

(ii) Parent and Child

The right of parents to make decisions for, and generally bring up, their children is balanced by the obligations of parents to care for and protect them.[65] Implicit in the decision to become a parent is the acceptance of legal obligations to assist and protect the child.[66] Normally, of course, a child will not bring an action against

---

62 In the third edition of this text, I suggested that another approach to social or commercial host liability would be to view all acts of providing alcohol to others as risk-creating activities, which would impose a duty to take reasonable care to prevent injuries arising therefrom on the provider. The resolution of individual cases could be then be determined as a question of breach; i.e., in view of the circumstances of the occasion, the nature of the defendant provider, the characteristics of the person to whom liquor was provided, statutory regulations, among other factors, what steps ought to have been taken to prevent harm? The *Childs v. Desormeaux* approach differs from this suggestion in one important respect. The court refused to acknowledge that the hosting of a party, or even the provision of alcohol at it, were risk-creating activities, and that something "more" would be required. Assuming that the activity was sufficiently risk creating, however, the question of breach would then have to be faced and the factors noted here would be relevant. See the third edition at 182-83.

63 This category was described by McLachlin C.J. in *Childs v. Desormeaux*, above, as "paternalistic relationships of supervision and control". According to the Chief Justice, "the duty in these cases rests on the special vulnerability of the plaintiffs and the formal position of power of the defendants. The law recognizes that the autonomy of some persons may be permissibly violated or restricted, but, in turn, requires that those with power exercise it in light of special duties." (At para. 36.)

64 Although several of the relationships which will be discussed in this section, such as employer-employee, common carrier-passenger, are contractual in nature, and hence, the source of the obligation may be founded in contract, it is my submission that even in the absence of contract, these relationships involve an inherent duty to assist.

65 On the topic generally, see Alexander, *The Family and the Law of Torts* (1979); Bates, "Children's Rights and the Family Unit" (1978), 1 Fam. L. Rev. 242; Drinan, "The Rights of Children in Modern American Family Law" (1962), 2 J. Fam. L. 101; Eekelaar, "What Are Parental Rights?" (1973), 89 L.Q.R. 210. The action can be based in tort or on breach of fiduciary duty.

66 This would also apply to all those in a parenting role, day care parents, for example. See *Lapensée v. Ottawa Day Nursery Inc.* (1986), 35 C.C.L.T. 129, varied (1986), 38 C.C.L.T. 113 (Ont. H.C.). In *S. (C.) (Next friend of) v. Miller*, [2002] 6 W.W.R. 148, 11 C.C.L.T. (3d) 136 (Alta. Q.B.), the duty was applied to a supervisor at a recreational camp for children. The supervisor observed one of the campers being sexually molested by an adult volunteer. Despite

a parent for failing to render assistance or to protect;[67] however, the right to bring such an action exists,[68] and the liability issue may be raised by a third party seeking contribution against the parent co-tortfeasor.[69] In *Arnold v. Teno,*[70] for example, a four-year-old child was struck by a car when she crossed the street, after having purchased ice cream from the defendant company's vending truck. She and her six-year-old brother had been given some money by their mother and

---

the fact that the camper was a non-registered visitor at the camp and the adult who molested him was not an employee of the camp but a friend of the camper's family, the court held that the supervisor had a duty to intervene and take steps to protect the child. The operators of the camp were held vicariously liable for the failure of the supervisor, but not for the assaults committed by the molester. See (2003), [2004] 5 W.W.R. 282 (Q.B.) re: the apportionment of liability decision. The parental duty will also apply to those who may become responsible for the safety of their children's friends — see *G. (J.) (Guardians & Trustees of) v. Strathcona (County)* (2004), [2004] A.J. No. 664, 2004 CarswellAlta 767 (Q.B.). In *B. (K.L.) v. B.C.* (2003), 230 D.L.R. (4th) 513 (S.C.C.), at 521, the standard of care required of those in a parenting role was defined by McLachlin C.J. as "the standard of a prudent parent solicitous for the welfare of his or her child."

67 If insurance is involved, or if a child's welfare has become an issue between disputing parents, it is not inconceivable that an action will be brought. As well, parents' sexual misconduct against their children can result in legal actions. In respect of the duty to protect children from sexual abuse, see *J. (L.A.) v. J. (H.)* (1993), 13 O.R. (3d) 306 (Ont. Gen. Div.). In this case, a plaintiff brought an action for sexual assault and battery against her uncle (whom she had grown up thinking was her father), and an action for breach of fiduciary duty against her mother. The action against her mother was based on the fact that her mother had been aware of the abuse, but did not do anything to protect her daughter from it. The actions were successful. A similar case is *K. (K.) v. G. (K.W.)* (2006), [2006] O.J. No. 2672, 2006 CarswellOnt 4002 (S.C.J.), reversed 2008 ONCA 489 (C.A.). In *M. (M.) v. F. (R.),* [1996] 8 W.W.R. 704 (B.C. S.C.), varied (1997), [1999] 2 W.W.R. 446 (B.C. C.A.), additional reasons at (1998), 48 B.C.L.R. (3d) 360 (C.A.), an action brought by a girl against her foster mother for sexual assaults committed against her by her foster brother was dismissed. One of the contentious issues in this case concerned the appropriate standard of care to be imposed and whether it should be based on a subjective or objective test. The court imposed an objective test, which took into account subjective factors. See discussion below in Chapter 9. See Reaume and Van Praagh, "Family Matters: Mothers as Secondary Defendants in Child Sexual Abuse Actions" (2002), 17 S.C.L.R. (2d) 179; Grace and Vella, "Vesting Mothers With The Power They Do Not Have: The Non-Offending Parent in Civil Sexual Assault Cases" (1994), 7:1 Canadian Journal of Women and the Law 184.

68 That there is no parental tort immunity was confirmed by the Supreme Court of Canada in *Dobson (Litigation Guardian of) v. Dobson* (1999), 45 C.C.L.T. 217 (S.C.C.). This is subject to the immunity that exists between mother and child for pre-natal acts; see discussion in Chapter 5.

69 In *T. (L.) v. T. (R.W.)* (1997), 36 C.C.L.T. (2d) 207 (B.C. S.C.), a father, who was sued for sexual abuse by his daughter, attempted to third party the plaintiff's mother for her failure to protect her child against this abuse. Not only did the court find that there was no breach by the mother but it also appropriately held that that the abuser himself could not claim contribution under these circumstances at any event. In *B. (D.) v. C. (M.),* [2000] 7 W.W.R. 186 (Sask. Q.B.), affirmed [2001] 5 W.W.R. 617 (Sask. C.A.), on the other hand, the court did allow a school board that was being sued as a result of a sexual assault committed on a student by a teacher, to third party the student's parents. In *Bouchard v. Carruthers* (2004), [2005] 2 W.W.R. 227 (Sask. C.A.), however, the court rejected the school board's claim for contribution against the parents since the action against it was based on vicarious liability. The court held that since the abuser herself could not claim contribution from the parents of the abused child, neither could the party who was being held vicariously liable for this abuse. See further discussion of this point in Chapter 13.

70 (1975), 55 D.L.R. (3d) 57 (Ont. H.C.), affirmed (1976), 67 D.L.R. (3d) 9 (Ont. C.A.), which was varied (1978), 3 C.C.L.T. 272 (S.C.C.).

allowed to go and buy ice cream, while their mother was on the telephone. The plaintiff child sued both the motorist and the ice cream vending company, who in turn third-partied the child's mother claiming contribution. None of the judges who heard this case, as it wound its way through the three levels of courts, disputed the principle that parents have a duty to safeguard their children and that a failure to do so reasonably could lead to liability, either to the child directly, or indirectly via third party proceedings for contribution. The point of disagreement concerned only whether the parent in this case was negligent, the trial judge and the majority of the Supreme Court deciding that she had not been, while the Ontario Court of Appeal, and one member of the Supreme Court of Canada, coming to the opposite conclusion. The principle that a duty does exist, however, which recognizes the exceptional role and responsibilities of parents was accepted.[71]

Although parents may be held liable to their children, either directly or indirectly through third party proceedings for contribution, for their failure to reasonably assist or protect them, children are not to be identified with their parents in an action brought by the child against a third party. The notion of imputing the negligence of one person to another, although once part of the common law in reference to parents and children, no longer applies.[72] In *Ducharme v. Davies,*[73] for example, the plaintiff child was injured in a traffic accident. The child was allowed to lie on top of a picnic cooler in the back seat of her mother's car, rather than being properly secured by a seat belt or child restraint system. The child, her mother, and another passenger sued the driver and owner of the other vehicle, who, rather than bringing the mother in as a third party, pleaded the plaintiffs' contributory negligence in failing to wear seat belts. Mr. Justice Cameron made it clear that if the child's mother had been negligent in not ensuring that her daughter was properly restrained in the car, this negligence could not be imputed to the child.[74]

---

71 Mr. Justice Zuber at (1976), 67 D.L.R. (3d) 9 at 19, quoting from *McCallion v. Dood,* [1966] N.Z.L.R. 710 at 712, stated:

> A stranger would render himself liable in negligence only if he had on a particular occasion assumed or accepted the care and charge of the child . . . . Parents are in a somewhat different position, and at all times while present are under a legal duty to exercise reasonable care to protect their child from foreseeable dangers. I do not consider that a parent while present is ever able to shed responsibility for the child's safety. . . .

Also see *Gambino v. DiLeo,* [1971] 2 O.R. 131 (H.C.), which held a parent liable in circumstances similar to the *Teno* case, and *Hache v. Savoie* (1980), 31 N.B.R. (2d) 631, 75 A.P.R. 631 (Q.B.). See *LaPlante (Guardian ad litem of) v. LaPlante* (1995), 26 C.C.L.T. (2d) 32 (B.C. C.A.), where a father was liable for allowing some of his children to accompany him in his car, which another son, an inexperienced driver, was driving. In *Bacon (Litigation Guardian of) v. Ryan* (1995), 27 C.C.L.T. (2d) 308, [1996] 3 W.W.R. 215 (Sask. Q.B.), a mother was successfully third partied for not having taken reasonable care to protect her child from a vicious dog.

72 See *Oliver v. Birmingham & Midland Motor Omnibus Co.,* [1933] 1 K.B. 35; *Kaplan v. Can. Safeway Ltd.* (1968), 68 D.L.R. (2d) 627 (Sask. Q.B.), and *Hudson's Bay Co. v. Wyrzykowski,* [1938] 3 D.L.R. 1 (S.C.C.). See, however, *Tomlinson v. Wurtz* (1982), 16 Man. R. (2d) 145 (Q.B.), where the court, incorrectly in my opinion, reduced a plaintiff child's damages by 10 per cent, to reflect the amount of fault attributed to the child's parents.

73 [1984] 1 W.W.R. 699 (Sask. C.A.).

74 Having said that, the majority of the court refused to consider the question whether the mother should be required to contribute to her daughter's damages, since the defendants had not pleaded this. This would have raised a very interesting question, since, at the time, Saskatchewan required "wilful and wanton" misconduct on the part of a host driver before a guest passenger

The issue of the respective responsibilities of the driver of a motor vehicle, a parent, and a child passenger, came to a head in *Galaske v. O'Donnell.*[75] A collision occurred between two trucks being driven on a highway. In one of the trucks was the driver, an eight-year-old passenger, and the child's father. None of the three occupants of the truck were wearing seat belts and as a result they were all ejected from the vehicle. The accident was caused by the fault of the driver in the other truck. As a result of the accident, the child passenger and host driver were seriously injured and the child's father was killed. In this case, the only issue to be determined was the liability of the host driver to the child passenger, with respect to the fact that the child was not wearing a seat belt. The host driver had breached a provision of the Motor Vehicle Act[76] which obliged him to ensure that the young passenger was wearing his seat belt. Properly applying the Canadian law with respect to breach of statutory duty,[77] all three courts held that although the breach of the statute may be useful evidence of negligence, it did not give rise to a private law duty of care nor a presumption of negligence.

Both the trial court and the Court of Appeal held that in view of the fact that the child was in the presence of his father, the driver of the vehicle owed no duty of care to the child to ensure that the child used his seat belt. The Supreme Court, however, disagreed. Cory J. noted that the driver of a car is in a position of control and responsibility over young passengers in that car, and thus has a duty to act reasonably in exercising that control. The presence of another responsible party, namely the child's parent, does not negate that duty.[78] Relying upon the public policy argument developed in *Jordan House Ltd. v. Menow*[79] and *Crocker v. Sundance Northwest Resorts Ltd.*,[80] the driver accordingly was held liable.[81] While I would agree with the public policy concern for promoting seat belt use, I would question the legitimacy of using tort law to achieve this objective. The decision

---

could recover. See the Vehicles Act, R.S.S. 1978, c. V-3, s. 178(2) [repealed and replaced by S.S. 1983, c. V-3.1, which was repealed S.S. 1986, c. 33, s. 29]. The court would have had to decide whether the mother's liability was based on the driver-passenger relationship, or parent-child relationship, and if the latter, whether this meant that the Vehicles Act would not apply. See Klar, "Recent Developments in Canadian Law: Tort Law" (1985), 17 Ottawa L. Rev. 325 at 381. On the question whether defendants must claim contribution in their pleadings, see also *Sgro v. Verbeek* (1980), 111 D.L.R. (3d) 479 (Ont. H.C.), and *Sample v. Klassen* (1970), 18 D.L.R. (3d) 75 (Man. Q.B.) — rights to contribution and indemnity permitted without a claim.

75 (1994), 112 D.L.R. (4th) 109 (S.C.C.), reversing (1992), 67 B.C.L.R. (2d) 190 (C.A.).

76 R.S.B.C. 1979, c. 288, s. 217(6).

77 See Chapter 9.

78 Although Cory J. conceded that the parent may also be held responsible as a co-wrongdoer.

79 Above, note 35.

80 Above, note 44.

81 Since the action had been dismissed below, Cory J. sent the case back to trial to determine the relative degrees of negligence of the driver of the car, the child, and his father. McLachlin J., dissenting in part, held that the trial judge had dismissed the action based on the absence of a duty, and accordingly, had not gone on to consider the question of breach. Agreeing that a duty was owed, however, McLachlin J. would remit the case to the trial court for consideration of the breach issue. Major J., dissenting, interpreted the trial judgment as finding a duty of care but no breach. That being the case, Major J. would not have interfered with this finding of fact. The judgments illustrate the confusion between duty language, standard of care language, and the respective roles of judge and jury (or in the absence of a jury, a judge as a finder of fact). On this issue, see discussion in Chapter 9.

can be defended, however, based upon the relationship of control and supervision which the driver of the car exercised over his young passenger.[82]

Parents not only have a duty to protect their children from harm; they also have a duty to protect others from being harmed by them. Thus, although parents cannot be held vicariously liable for the torts of their children,[83] they can be held personally liable for their failure to control them. In *Trevison v. Springman*,[84] a troubled teen stole items from the plaintiffs' house and set fire to it. The teen had stolen the key to the plaintiffs' house from his mother who had been given it by the plaintiffs. In an action brought against the teens' parents with respect to the fire, the court held that liability depended on four factors: a mischievous propensity by the teen, knowledge of this by his parents, anticipation by the parents of the harmful act, and reasonable steps that ought to have been taken to prevent it.[85] The court found that, while the defendant mother had been negligent in not ensuring that her son did not steal the key to the plaintiffs' house, the arson was unforeseeable and dismissed the action.[86]

(iii) Teacher and Pupil

As with parent and child, there is inherent in the teacher and pupil relationship an obligation upon teachers to assist and protect those under their care and supervision.[87] As stated by Winnecke C.J., an Australian judge:

> The reason underlying the imposition of the duty would appear to be the need of a child of immature age for protection against the conduct of others, or indeed of himself, which may cause

---

82 In a relationship of control, not only does the controlling party assume responsibility, but the relationship frequently deprives the vulnerable party of means of self-protection and creates in that person a state of reliance on the controlling party. Whether this can be stated to be true in a case such as *Galaske v. O'Donnell* is the problem.

83 See, for example, *B. (D.C.) v. Arkin* (1996), 138 D.L.R. (4th) 309 (Man. Q.B.), leave to appeal refused [1996] 10 W.W.R. 689 (Man. C.A. [In Chambers]). This common law rule has been altered by legislation that makes parents liable for property damage caused by their children in some situations. See, for example, the Parental Responsibility Act, S.M. 1996, c. 61; the Parental Responsibility Act, S.O. 2000, c. 4, s. 2; the Parental Responsibility Act, S.B.C. 2001, c. 45; the School Act, R.S.B.C. 1996, c. 412, s. 10 [re-en. 1997, c. 52, s. 4]. The latter provision was applied in *Coquitlam School District No. 43 v. Clement* (1999), 170 D.L.R. (4th) 107 (B.C. C.A.). The Court of Appeal held that the provision applied to any damage caused by a student to school property, whether or not the student was in attendance at that particular school or whether the damage was caused in the course of a school activity. The parents were potentially liable for $3 million in damages. The Ontario legislation was applied in *Shannon v. Westman (Litigation Guardian of)* (2002), 12 C.C.L.T. (3d) 46 (Ont. S.C.J.). The parents successfully discharged the burden placed upon them to prove that they exercised reasonable supervision and made reasonable efforts to control their child. On this topic, see Elizabeth Adjin-Tettey, "Significance and Consequences of Parental Responsibility Legislation" (2002), 17 S.C.L.R. (2d) 221; Wilson, "Parental Responsibility for the Acts of Children" (2000), 79 Can. Bar Rev. 369.

84 (1995), 28 C.C.L.T. (2d) 292 (B.C. S.C.), affirmed (1997), 1997 CarswellBC 2362 (C.A.).

85 The court relied on *Streifel v. S.* (1957), 25 W.W.R. 182 (B.C. S.C.) at 183.

86 Also see *Coquitlam School District No. 43 v. Clement*, [1999] 11 W.W.R. 605 (B.C.C.A.), where a school board successfully sued student and parents for a school fire. See further discussion on the duty to control and supervise in Chapter 12.

87 On this topic generally see Hoyano, "The 'Prudent Parent': The Elusive Standard of Care" (1984), 18 U.B.C. L. Rev. 1; Barnes, "Tort Liability of School Boards to Pupils", in Klar (ed.), *Studies in Canadian Tort Law* (1977), Chapter 7.

> him injury coupled with the fact that, during school hours the child is beyond the control and protection of his parent and is placed under the control of the schoolmaster who is in a position to exercise authority over him and afford him, in the exercise of reasonable care, protection from injury. . . .[88]

As with parents, teachers and school boards who claim and are given the right to exert authority over those under their supervision must, as a *quid pro quo,* protect their charges from harm.[89] This duty is well accepted,[90] and the considerable amount of litigation between injured pupils and their teachers or school boards generally involves whether or not the required standard of care has been met.[91]

---

88 *Richards v. State of Victoria,* [1969] V.R. 136 at 138-39, cited by Hoyano, *ibid.*, at 2.

89 Although in most cases, a student is a young person, it is not the age of the person which is critical to the duty, but the relationship of teacher-student. Thus, in *Bain v. Calgary Bd. of Education* (1993), 18 C.C.L.T. (2d) 249 (Alta. Q.B.), a 19-year-old student was owed a duty of care. As stated by Virtue J., at 18 C.C.L.T. (2d) 266:

> That right of control carries with it a corresponding duty to take care for the safety of, and to properly supervise the student, whether he or she is a child, an adolescent or an adult.

Also see *Simms v. Conestoga College of Applied Arts & Technology*, [1995] O.J. No. 902 (Ont. Gen. Div.), where the student was a 28-year-old woman taking motorcycle driving lessons; and *Zaba v. Saskatchewan Institute of Applied Science & Technology* (1995), [1996] 1 W.W.R. 534 (Sask. Q.B.), reversed on other grounds [1997] 8 W.W.R. 414, 38 C.C.L.T. (2d) 312 (Sask. C.A.). The legal bases of the duties owed, whether in tort or by statute, and the scope of these duties are fully explored in Barnes, above, note 87.

90 Note, however, legislative provisions that immunize teachers and principals from personal liability. In *Willoughby (Litigation Guardian of) v. Larsen*, [1998] 7 W.W.R. 601 (Sask. Q.B.), the Court applied the provisions of the Saskatchewan Education Act, S.S. 1995, c. E–0.2, s. 232(1), to an action brought by a pupil against her teacher for injuries caused by her negligent driving. The court held that the immunity provision prevailed over the liability provisions of the Highway Traffic Act, S.S. 1986, c. H-3.1. The immunity applies to teachers and principals who are involved in school activities. The court stressed that an action would still lie against the school board. See also *Piercey (Guardian ad litem of) v. Lunenburg (County) District School Board* (1998), 41 C.C.L.T. (2d) 60 (N.S. C.A.), which held that the Nova Scotia Education Act, R.S.N.S. 1989, c. 136 imposes a non-delegable duty on the school board. Also see *Kennedy v. Waterloo (County) Board of Education* (1999), 45 C.C.L.T. (2d) 169 (Ont. C.A.), leave to appeal refused (2000), 2000 CarswellOnt 921, 2000 CarswellOnt 922 (S.C.C.), for an action brought under Ontario's Education Act, R.S.O. 1980, c. 129, for a breach of a duty by a school principal.

91 See, among others: *McKay v. Bd. of Govan Sch. Unit No. 29,* [1968] S.C.R. 589; *Dziwenka v. R.,* [1972] S.C.R. 419; *Thornton v. Prince George Bd. of School Trustees,* (1978), 3 C.C.L.T. 257 (S.C.C.); *Myers v. Peel County Bd. of Educ.* (1981), 17 C.C.L.T. 269 (S.C.C.); *Smith v. Horizon Aero Sports Ltd.* (1981), 19 C.C.L.T. 89 (B.C. S.C.); *Boese v. St. Paul's R.C. Sep. Sch. Dist. No. 20* (1980), 97 D.L.R. (3d) 643 (Sask. Q.B.); *Eaton v. Lasuta* (1977), 2 C.C.L.T. 38 (B.C. S.C.); *Cropp v. Potashville Sch. Unit No. 25* (1977), 4 C.C.L.T. 12 (Sask. Q.B.); *Piszel v. Etobicoke Bd. of Educ.* (1977), 16 O.R. (2d) 22 (Ont. C.A.); *James v. River East Sch. Div. No. 9,* [1976] 2 W.W.R. 577 (Man. C.A.); *Bates (Guardian of) v. Horkoff* (1991), 119 A.R. 270 (Q.B.); *Petersen (Guardian ad litem) v. School District No. 36, Surrey B.C.* (1991), 89 D.L.R. (4th) 517 (B.C. S.C.), affirmed (1993), 104 D.L.R. (4th) 334 (B.C. C.A.); *Bain v. Calgary Bd. of Education* (1993), 18 C.C.L.T. (2d) 249 (Alta. Q.B.); *Madsen v. Mission School District No. 75* (1999), [1999] B.C.J. No. 1716, 1999 CarswellBC 1656 (S.C.); and *Michaluk (Litigation Guardian of) v. Rolling River School Division No. 39*, 5 C.C.L.T. (3d) 1, [2001] 8 W.W.R 34 (Man. C.A.). The latter case dealt with the issue of foreseeability of the injury. For commentaries see Barnes, 2 C.C.L.T. 38, 2 C.C.L.T. 269, 4 C.C.L.T. 12, 5 C.C.L.T. 271, and 17 C.C.L.T. 285.

Although the standard of care which defines the teacher's duty has generally been described as that of the "careful" or "prudent parent",[92] the application of the standard has given rise to difficulties.[93] It has been held, for example, that the standard must be modified to take into account circumstances not ordinarily faced by "careful parents". In *MacCabe v. Westlock Roman Catholic Separate School District No. 110*,[94] the plaintiff was seriously injured during a high school gym class. The trial judge noted that a physical education class involves numerous students engaged in a dangerous activity, thus demanding "*supra* parental expertise". This is of course sensible; when professionals are engaged with children in activities requiring specialized training, experience and knowledge, the standard of care must reflect these conditions.[95]

The duty owed by teachers to protect their pupils applies in a wider setting than that of the traditional class room or school yard. Thus, in *Moddejonge v. Huron County Bd. of Educ.*,[96] a person who acted as the co-ordinator of outdoor educational programmes was found liable when a student drowned during a field trip.[97] In another case, *Smith v. Horizon Aero Sports Ltd.*,[98] a parachute instructor was held liable for failing to properly instruct his student. The prudent and careful parent standard has been applied to a defendant who operated a small day care centre from her home.[99]

---

92 As laid down by Lord Esher in *Williams v. Eady* (1893), 10 T.L.R. 41 (C.A.). This standard was upheld in *Dunbar v. School District No. 71*, [1989] B.C.W.L.D. 1489 (C.A.); and *Plumb (Guardian ad litem of) v. Cowichan School District No. 65* (1993), 83 B.C.L.R. (2d) 161 (C.A.). But see *Hamstra v. B.C. Rugby Union* (1989), 1 C.C.L.T. (2d) 78 (B.C. S.C.), reversed (1995), 4 B.C.L.R. (3d) 127 (C.A.), additional reasons at (1995), 8 B.C.L.R. (3d) 136 (C.A.) — standard is that of reasonable person and not the careful and prudent parent. An interesting issue that arose in the *Hamstra* case was whether the fact that witnesses mentioned that a defendant was covered by liability insurance should lead to an automatic dismissal of the jury. In a judgment reported at (1997), 35 C.C.L.T. (2d) 1, 145 D.L.R. (4th) 193 (S.C.C.), the Supreme Court of Canada held that it is up to the trial judge to determine what should be done in such a case. The judge should consider the possible prejudicial effect of this occurrence, and decide whether instructions to the jury could deal with it, or whether dismissal of the jury is necessary. In this case, the Supreme Court held that the trial judge correctly exercised his discretion in dismissing the jury.

93 See Hoyano, above, note 87.

94 (1998), [1999] 8 W.W.R. 1 (Alta. Q.B.), reversed (2001), [2002] 1 W.W.R. 610, 9 C.C.L.T. (3d) 259 (Alta. C.A.), additional reasons at (2002), 2002 CarswellAlta 1627 (C.A.).

95 The court referred to the four criteria established by the Supreme of Canada in *Thornton v. Prince George Board of Education*, [1978] 2 S.C.R. 267 relating to the suitability of the activity for the student, the lessons provided, the suitability of the equipment, and the supervision provided. Liability was found. The defences of voluntary assumption of risk and contributory negligence were considered and rejected by the trial judge. On appeal, liability was affirmed, but the Court of Appeal held that the plaintiff was 25 per cent contributorily negligent and varied the damage award.

96 [1972] 2 O.R. 437 (H.C.).

97 The accident in *Bain v. Calgary Bd. of Education*, above, note 91, also occurred during a field trip.

98 (1981), 19 C.C.L.T. 89 (B.C. S.C.).

99 *Lapensée v. Ottawa Day Nursery Inc.* (1986), 35 C.C.L.T. 129 (Ont. H.C.), varied on other grounds (1986), 38 C.C.L.T. 113 (Ont. H.C.). In an English case, *Van Oppen v. Bedford Charity Trustees*, [1989] 3 All E.R. 389 (C.A.), the issue of a teacher's duty to pupils was carefully

Whether a civil cause of action can be brought by a pupil against its teacher for failure to educate raises a more novel issue. The Canadian case law to date is not promising in this regard. In *Gould v. Regina (East) School Division No. 77*,[100] the court rejected a claim for 'educational malpractice' noting the difficulties inherent in such a claim. Foremost among these is the ability and appropriateness of courts in establishing reasonable educational standards of conduct, as well as proof that it was a deficient educational experience that caused the student the injuries that allegedly occurred.[101] This reluctance to involve courts in educational malpractice actions is also evident in other jurisdictions.[102]

(iv) Other Relationships

There are several other formal and informal relationships which involve duties of assistance or protection.

One of the clearest examples of a relationship which involves the right of one person to control the behaviour of another is the employer-employee. Concomitant with this right to control is the obligation to protect. Even where the employer-employee relationship is not a formal or contractual one, the element of control will impose a duty of care. Thus, in *Poppe v. Tuttle*,[103] the court held that even when a friend agrees to temporarily and gratuitously assist in the harvesting of grain, the status of master and servant exists. The employer is required to exercise reasonable care to ensure the safety of the employee, whether in relation to the safety of the plant, the premises or the method of work.[104] In *Gies v. Gunwall*,[105]

---

analyzed, the court concluding that it did not extend so far as to ensure that a personal accident policy was obtained for those children who played rugby.

100 (1996), 32 C.C.L.T. (2d) 150, [1997] 3 W.W.R. 117 (Sask. Q.B.).

101 Also see *Rumley v. British Columbia* (1998), [1998] B.C.J. 2588, 1998 CarswellBC 2343 (S.C. [In Chambers]), reversed (1999), 48 C.C.L.T. (2d) 1 (B.C. C.A.), leave to appeal allowed (2000), 2000 CarswellBC 2127, 2000 CarswellBC 2128 (S.C.C.), affirmed (2001), 2001 CarswellBC 1223, 2001 CarswellBC 1224 (S.C.C.), additional reasons at (2001), 10 C.C.L.T. (3d) 1 (S.C.C.). Although the judgment dealt with the certification of a class action by victims of alleged abuse at a residential school, the court in denying a class action for educational malpractice expressed grave reservations about the viability of this claim. The Court of Appeal reversed the trial judgment and allowed the certification of the class action. This was affirmed by the Supreme Court of Canada. A motion to decertify was rejected: see [2003] B.C.J. No. 313.

102 The court cited numerous American cases that have refused to recognize this type of claim.

103 (1980), 14 C.C.L.T. 115 (B.C. S.C.).

104 See *Huba v. Schulze* (1962), 37 W.W.R. 241 (Man. C.A.), and Fleming, *The Law of Torts*, 9th ed. (1998), at 559. The duty was expressed in *Smith v. Baker & Sons*, [1891] A.C. 325, by Lord Herschell. Also see *Wilsons & Clyde Coal Co. v. English*, [1937] 3 All E.R. 628 (H.L.), and *Lochgelly Iron & Coal Co. v. M'Mullan*, [1934] A.C. 1 (H.L.). A Canadian case which affirms and applies the duty is *Schellenberg v. Britton*, [1993] 3 W.W.R. 758 (Sask. Q.B.). In *Currie v. Stirling Fruit Farms Ltd.* (2000), 185 N.S.R. (2d) 359 (S.C.), affirmed (2001), 194 N.S.R. (2d) 60 (C.A.), it was held that while an employer owes a duty of care, it does not warrant the safety of its equipment or assume responsibility for the negligence of others. Thus it was not liable when a ladder, which appeared to be solid and in good shape, broke, causing an injury to the plaintiff who was standing on it while picking apples. If the ladder was defective it was not due to any negligence on the employer's part. In addition to the common law duty, there may also be a statutory one. See *Rudd v. Hamiota Feedlot Ltd.*

the court distinguished between a master-servant relationship and a master-apprentice relationship when considering the scope of the duty owed. It has also been held that the duty owed by an employer to its employees to provide safe working conditions cannot be delegated to third parties.[106]

An interesting case that combines the duty imposed on those who provide others with alcoholic beverages with the duty imposed on employers to provide safe working conditions for their employees is *Jacobsen v. Nike Canada Ltd.*[107] An employer provided its employee with beer during working hours. The employee became impaired and injured himself when he fell asleep at the wheel of his car while driving home. The court recognized the duty that the employer had to his employee to ensure that he was able to go home safely once he had become impaired. The court went further however and held that the act of providing alcohol to the employee in the first place during working hours, with knowledge that the employee had driven to work and was intending to drive home, was in itself a breach of a duty of care. In other words, unlike the traditional commercial host case where the duty and breach do not relate to the serving of the alcohol but to the steps taken by the server once the invitee has become impaired, the duty of care imposed upon an employer is a higher one relating back to the over-serving itself.[108]

Another relationship of control, which involves a duty to assist, is that of passenger-carrier. An example of this occurred in the well known case of *Horsley*

(2006), [2006] M.J. No. 36, 2006 CarswellMan 39 (Q.B.), where the provisions of the Manitoba Workplace Safety and Health Act, C.C.S.M, c. W210, are discussed.

105 (1982), 143 D.L.R. (3d) 126 (B.C. S.C.).

106 See *Marshment v. Borgstrom,* [1942] S.C.R. 374, and *McDermid v. Nash Dredging Ltd.,* [1987] 2 All E.R. 878 (H.L.).

107 (1996), 133 D.L.R. (4th) 377 (B.C. S.C.). For a comment see R.A. Stradiotto, "The Service of Alcohol: The Implications of *Jacobsen v. Nike Canada*" (1997), 166 Advocates' Soc. J., No. 3, 21-28.

108 The court held the employer 75 per cent liable and the employee 25 per cent liable. A similar case is *Hunt (Litigation Guardian of) v. Sutton Group Incentive Realty Inc.* (2001), 196 D.L.R. (4th) 738, 4 C.C.L.T. (3d) 277 (Ont. S.C.J.), reversed and new trial ordered (2002), 215 D.L.R. (4th) 193 (Ont. C.A.). The employer was held liable at trial to an employee who became inebriated at an office party and was injured in a car accident on her way home. A pub that served alcohol to the plaintiff after she left the office party was also held liable. Liability was apportioned 25 per cent to the defendants and 75 per cent to the plaintiff herself. The Court of Appeal reversed the trial judgment and ordered a new trial. The appeal court held that the trial judge erred in discharging the jury and in the manner in which he had dealt with the issue of causation. A case in which the employer was relieved of liability is *John v. Flynn* (2001), 201 D.L.R. (4th) 500 (Ont. C.A.), leave to appeal refused (2002), 210 D.L.R. vi (note) (S.C.C.). The intoxicated employee injured the plaintiff in a traffic accident. The employee had a drinking problem, regularly drank at work in the parking lot, and had been treated for his alcoholism in an employee assistance program. Nevertheless, on this occasion the employee had already safely arrived at home after work, drank some more there, left his house and was involved in the accident. The Court of Appeal noted many factors that distinguished this case from those where there was liability, but foremost among these was the fact that the drinking and the accident in this case had no connection to the workplace. See also *Gartner v. 520631 Alberta Ltd.* (2005), 30 C.C.L.T. (3d) 144 (Alta. Q.B.) — employer not liable, even though there was a breach of the Employment Standards Code, S.A. 1996, c. E-10.3, relating to excessive hours at work.

v. MacLaren.[109] In that case, several friends were out on a pleasure boat when one of them fell overboard. While the owner of the boat was attempting to manoeuvre the boat so as to approach the drowning passenger, a second passenger jumped into the water to assist the first, and he was soon followed by another would-be rescuer. The passenger who fell overboard drowned and the first rescuer died of shock from the cold water. Although the judgments in this case are important from the perspective of the duty owed to rescuers,[110] an essential issue underlying all the actions which resulted from these facts was whether the master of the boat owed a duty to come to the assistance of the passenger who first fell overboard, even though this occurred through no fault of the master. A previous Canadian case, *Vanvalkenburg v. Northern Navigation Co.*[111] had held that although there might be a moral duty to rescue a drowning man who falls overboard, due not to the ship master's negligence but his own, there was no legal duty to do so.[112] This decision was not followed by any of the three courts in *Horsley v. MacLaren,* all of the justices agreeing that a master of a ship has not only a moral duty, but a legal one as well, to come to the assistance of a drowning passenger. Although there were different theories advanced for the creation of this duty, such as statute, and *quasi*-contract, the rationale given by Laskin J. was as follows:

> As owner and operator of a boat on which he was carrying invited guests, he was under a legal duty to take reasonable care for their safety. This was a duty which did not depend on the existence of a contract of carriage, nor on whether he was a common carrier or a private carrier of passengers. Having brought his guests into a relationship with him as passengers on his boat, albeit as social or gratuitous passengers, he was obliged to exercise reasonable care for their safety. That obligation extends, in my opinion, to rescue from perils of the sea where this is consistent with his duty to see to the safety of his other passengers and with concern for his own safety. The duty exists whether the passenger falls overboard accidentally or by reason of his own carelessness.[113]

Having said that, the majority of the Supreme Court did not agree that the defendant had been negligent in attempting to rescue the first passenger and therefore could not be held liable to the other rescuers.[114]

---

109 [1969] 2 O.R. 137 (H.C.), reversed [1970] 2 O.R. 487 (C.A.), which was affirmed (1972), 22 D.L.R. (3d) 545 (S.C.C.). See Binchy, "The Good Samaritan at the Crossroads: A Canadian Signpost" (1974), 25 N.I. Leg. Q. 147, and Alexander, "One Rescuer's Obligation to Another: The 'Ogopogo' Lands in the Supreme Court of Canada" (1972), 22 U.T.L.J. 98.

110 See Chapter 12.

111 (1913), 19 D.L.R. 649 (Ont. C.A.).

112 In 1934 an amendment was enacted to the Canada Shipping Act, R.S.C. 1927, c. 186 [now R.S.C. 1985, c. S-9, s. 451], requiring the master of a ship to render assistance to a person found at sea and in danger of being lost, on pain of a fine not exceeding $1,000.

113 22 D.L.R. (3d) 545 at 559. In *Childs v. Desormeaux*, above, this situation was seen by McLachlin C.J. as an instance where the defendant intentionally attracted and invited a third party to an inherent or obvious risk that he or she created or controlled.

114 Other carriers also have a duty to protect their passengers from harm. See, e.g., *Morgan v. Airwest Airlines Ltd.* (1974), 48 D.L.R. (3d) 62 (B.C. S.C.); and *Johnson Estate v. Pischke,* [1989] 3 W.W.R. 207 (Sask. Q.B.). In addition courts have imposed a high standard of care on public carriers, the leading case being *Day v. Toronto Transportation Commission*, [1940] S.C.R. 433. See *Nice v. Calgary (City)*, 190 D.L.R. (4th) 402, [2000] 10 W.W.R. 40, 2 C.C.L.T. (3d) 86 (Alta. C.A.), leave to appeal refused (2001), 281 A.R. 399 (note) (S.C.C.); and *Horita (Co-Committees of) v. Graham* (1997), [1997] B.C.J. No. 2880, 1997 CarswellBC 2813 (S.C.). See Chapter 9.

The courts have required those who control instruments of danger to intervene to prevent those objects from harming others. Thus, in *Stermer v. Lawson,*[115] a 16-year-old youth was held liable to a 17-year-old friend, for having lent him his motorcycle without having given him sufficient warnings or instruction.[116] As well, in *Hempler v. Todd*[117] and *Ont. Hosp. Services Comm. v. Borsoski,*[118] defendants who allowed incompetent friends to drive their cars were held liable to them and their estates for injuries which they suffered in subsequent accidents.[119] This duty on those who control cars not to permit incompetent persons to drive them was reaffirmed by the Supreme Court of Canada in *Hall v. Hebert.*[120] These cases exhibit a degree of paternalism generally rejected by the traditional position, but can be rationalized on the basis that the defendants did not merely refuse to intervene to confer a benefit on the plaintiffs, but actively altered the status quo to their detriment, by actively putting them into a position perilous to themselves and to others.[121] It must also be stressed that the duty to intervene, in those cases where it is imposed, must always be seen within the context of the requirement of unreasonable conduct. If the defendant's conduct in allowing potentially dangerous instruments to fall into the plaintiff's hands was not unreasonable, the action must be dismissed. Thus in *Schulz v. Leeside Dev. Ltd.,*[122] for example, the British Columbia Court of Appeal held that it was not unreasonable for the defendant to rent a motor boat to an apparently capable and careful 18-year-old.[123]

---

115 (1979), 11 C.C.L.T. 76, varying (1977), 3 C.C.L.T. 57.

116 See Klar, "Case Comment" (1977), 3 C.C.L.T. 57, on the trial judgment.

117 (1970), 14 D.L.R. (3d) 637 (Man. Q.B.).

118 (1973), 54 D.L.R. (3d) 339 (Ont. H.C.).

119 See *Pizzolon v. Pedrosa* (1988), 46 C.C.L.T. 243 (B.C. S.C.), where a similar case was dismissed due to lack of evidence of negligent conduct.

120 [1993] 4 W.W.R. 113 (S.C.C.). The court found a young man partly liable to his friend for an accident caused by his friend's inability to control the former's car. Both persons were intoxicated at the time. They were attempting to "roll start" the car, and the driver lost control of it. The issue of duty was not seriously doubted or debated by the majority of the court. Only the dissenting justice, Sopinka J., saw the issue in terms of an extension of the duty imposed on persons to assist others. He distinguished this case from those where a duty was imposed on commercial operators, and stated "[t]o extend liability [in this case] would not amount to the incremental extension of liability but rather a quantum leap", at 15 C.C.L.T. (2d) 139. Sopinka J. argued that a duty should not be imposed, especially where there was no reasonable expectation on the plaintiff's part that the defendant would owe or assume such an obligation. For a case comment, see Klar, "*Hall v. Hebert* — The Purpose of Negligent Accident Law" (1993), 72 Can. Bar Rev. 553.

121 As discussed above, this is another rationale for explaining *Jordan House Ltd. v. Menow,* above, note 35, and could also have justified the imposition of liability in *Crocker v. Sundance Northwest Resorts Ltd.,* above, note 44, as well as extending a duty to social hosts. What some might find disturbing about this trend in tort law is not that the courts are willing to recognize that a person has a duty to take reasonable care not to put other persons in danger, but that traditional defences, such as voluntary assumption of risk, or illegality, which have in the past been used to deny liability to those who should be held responsible for their own decisions, have been effectively eliminated. Thus, the extension of duty has been accompanied by a reduction of defences, leading to greater liability. See discussion of defences in Chapter 13.

122 (1978), 6 C.C.L.T. 248 (B.C. C.A.).

123 In *Childs v. Desormeaux*, above, at para. 39, McLachlin C.J. stated:

> The law does not impose a duty to eliminate risk. It accepts that competent people have the right to engage in risky activities. Conversely, it permits third parties witnessing risk to

A case in which liability might have been justified on the basis of a duty to assist those under one's supervision, although it was not, is *Robson v. Ashworth.*[124] A claim by the dependants of a man who committed suicide, against the physician who negligently prescribed a dose of barbiturates for him which would be lethal if taken all at once or in combination with other drugs, was dismissed. The trial judge, although conceding duty, breach, and causation, held that the "concept of individual responsibility" required that the suicidal victim, and by extension his dependants, assume the personal responsibility for the patient's sane, conscious and deliberate decision to kill himself. This judgment demonstrated the affinity still held by the common law for the philosophy of individualism which underlies the Good Samaritan issue, although, as I have suggested elsewhere,[125] it was not appropriate in this case, where the defendant's professional duty involved an assumption of responsibility for his patient.

The relationship between those who administer prisons and their inmates is another which requires the former to take care for the safety and protection of the latter.[126] This duty to protect inmates in prisons, applies equally to other kinds of institutions, such as hospitals,[127] and nursing homes.[128] A police officer stands in a special position *vis-à-vis* the protection of the public and has both a common

---

> decide not to become rescuers or otherwise intervene. It is only when these third parties have a special relationship to the person in danger or a material role in the creation or management of the risk that the law may impinge on autonomy. Thus, the operator of a risky sporting activity may be required to prevent a person who is unfit to perform a sport safely from participating or, when a risk materializes, to attempt a rescue. Similarly, the publican may be required to refuse to serve an inebriated patron who may drive, or a teacher be required to take positive action to protect a child who lacks the right or power to make decisions for itself. The autonomy of risk takers or putative rescuers is not absolutely protected, but, at common law, is always respected.

I would suggest that this statement represents a shift in Canadian law's recent expansionist trend, back to a more traditional position regarding the duty to assist.

124 (1985), 33 C.C.L.T. 229 (Ont. H.C.), affirmed (1985), 40 C.C.L.T. 164 (Ont. C.A.).

125 Klar, "Negligence Law: An Important Turning Point?" (1987), 66 Can. Bar Rev. 159.

126 See, e.g., *Howley v. R.* (1973), 36 D.L.R. (3d) 261 (Fed. T.D.); *Ellis v. Home Office,* [1953] 2 All E.R. 149 (C.A.); *Marshall v. Can.* (1985), 57 N.R. 308 (Fed. C.A.), varied (1985), 60 N.R. 180 (Fed. C.A.); *Funk Estate v. Clapp* (1988), 54 D.L.R. (4th) 512 (B.C. C.A.); *Coumont v. Canada* (1994), 77 F.T.R. 253 (Fed. T.D.); *Socha v. Millar,* [1994] O.J. No. 1223 (Ont. Gen. Div.); *Lipscei v. Central Saanich (Dist.),* [1995] 7 W.W.R. 582 (B.C. S.C.); *Gerstel v. Penticton (City),* [1995] 9 W.W.R. 206 (B.C. S.C.); *Eng v. Canada* (1997), 129 F.T.R. 25 (T.D.); *Hodgin v. Canada (Solicitor General)* (1999), [1999] N.B.J. No. 416, 1999 CarswellNB 381 (C.A.); and *Euteneier v. Lee* (2005), 260 D.L.R. (4th) 123 (Ont. C.A.), additional reasons at (2005), 2005 CarswellOnt 6906 (C.A.), leave to appeal refused (2006), 2006 CarswellOnt 2123 (S.C.C.). In *Roy v. Canada (Attorney General)* (2005), 74 D.L.R. (4th) 233 (B.C. C.A.), leave to appeal refused (2005), 2005 CarswellBC 1984 (S.C.C.), Southin J.A. stated that although "a peace officer owes a duty to his prisoner to take reasonable care for the prisoner's safety. . .he is not an insurer." The majority dismissed an action brought by the family members of a person who died in custody as a result of acute alcohol ingestion. The majority found that the police officers involved in the apprehension had not been negligent.

127 See, e.g. (1978), *Lawson v. Wellesley Hosp.* (1975), 61 D.L.R. (3d) 445, affirmed 76 D.L.R. (3d) 688 (S.C.C.); *Koerber v. Kitchener-Waterloo Hosp.* (1987), 62 O.R. (2d) 613 (H.C.); and *Frerotte v. Irwin* (1986), 51 Sask. R. 108 (Q.B.).

128 *Stewart v. Extendicare* (1986), 38 C.C.L.T. 67 (Sask. Q.B.).

law and statutory duty to take affirmative steps for its protection.[129] The police officer's duty is "to protect the life, limb and property of the subject".[130] It can be suggested, however, that due to the nature of the emergencies which police officers frequently face, and the police officer's need to balance conflicting interests and concerns, the courts will be lenient with regards to the standard of care required to discharge this duty. According to some legislative provisions, police officers will be found liable only in extreme cases of negligence.[131]

The duties and liabilities of the police give rise to a variety of different issues. An issue that has received considerable attention recently relates to the police's duty to investigate a crime or a complaint with due care. In *Hill v. Hamilton-Wentworth (Regional Municipality) Police Services Board*,[132] the police were relieved of liability in an action for negligence brought against them by a wrongfully accused suspect. Although the majority of the Supreme Court of Canada held that an investigating police officer owed a duty to a suspect to act reasonably in conducting the investigation, it held that the duty had not been breached in this case.[133] In *Mooney v. British Columbia (Attorney General)*,[134] an action brought

---

129 See *O'Rourke v. Schacht* (1974), 55 D.L.R. (3d) 96 (S.C.C.). In this case a police officer was called to investigate a traffic accident and became aware that a barrier which had been erected to warn highway users of a detour around a culvert under construction had been knocked over by a car. Schroeder J.A., for the Ontario Court of Appeal, stated at (1972), 30 D.L.R. (3d) 641 at 652, that a police officer, both by statute and at common law, has a duty "as an arm of the State to protect the life, limb and property of the subject." The defendant police officer was found liable for having failed to warn oncoming traffic of the obstruction. Although the majority of the Supreme Court of Canada upheld this finding, Spence J., for the majority, focussed on the police officer's statutory duties, leaving aside the common law position. On the use of statutes to create tort duties, see Chapter 9. For an excellent review of the scope of the duties of the police, see Henry J.'s judgment in *Jane Doe v. Police Bd. of Commrs. (Metro. Toronto)* (1989), 48 C.C.L.T. 105 (Ont. H.C.), affirmed (1990), 72 D.L.R. (4th) 580 (Ont. Div. Ct.), leave to appeal to C.A. refused (1991), 1 O.R. (3d) 416 (note) (C.A.).

130 See *Hooey v. Mancini*, [1988] 4 W.W.R. 149 (Man.). The court held that the police officer's duty extended so far as to prevent an intoxicated person from endangering himself by driving. The action was dismissed, however, on the basis of no negligence.

131 Legislative provisions may require "gross negligence", or intentional misconduct before a police officer can be held liable. See, for example, *Doern v. Phillips Estate* (1994), 23 C.C.L.T. (2d) 283 (B.C. S.C.) and *Hodgkin v. Port Alberni (City)*, [1996] 9 W.W.R. 718 (B.C. C.A.) with respect to the Police Act, S.B.C. 1988, c. 53, s. 21. Actions against police officers were dismissed in *Lafleur v. Maryniuk* (1990), 4 C.C.L.T. (2d) 78 (B.C. S.C.); *Edgar v. Richmond (Township)* (1991), 6 C.C.L.T. (2d) 241 (B.C. S.C.); and *Hill v. Hurst* (2001), 203 D.L.R. (4th) 749 (B.C. S.C.). In *Lafleur* the action was dismissed based on a lack of proximity and hence no duty. In Edgar a duty was recognized but there was no negligence. In Hill there was negligence but the statutory immunity protected the police officer from liability. In *Popowich v. Saskatchewan*, [2001] 8 W.W.R. 308 (Sask. Q.B.), affirmed (2001), [2002] 2 W.W.R. 612 (Sask. C.A.), the court held that while the Police Act 1990, S.S. 1990-91, c. P–15.01, s. 10 protected the Police Commission and "people engaged in its work" that the immunity did not apply to police officers in general. The issue of the discretion of the police, and whether they can be sued in negligence for "policy decisions" as opposed to "operations", was the main issue in *Jane Doe v. Police Bd. of Commrs. (Metro. Toronto)*, above, note 129.

132 (2007), 50 C.C.L.T. (3d) 1 (S.C.C.).

133 As discussed in Chapter 5, the majority found that there was proximity between the police and the suspect and no residual policy considerations to negate the duty. The majority held, however, that the standard of care, as defined by the "standard of the reasonable police officer in like circumstances" had not been breached. The dissent held that there was insufficient

by a crime victim against the Attorney General for the failure of the police to adequately investigate a complaint was dismissed based on lack of proof of causation between the failure and subsequent crimes committed by the criminal. That there was a duty owed by the police to the subsequent victims was found by the trial judge.[135] The duty analysis was agreed to by the dissenting judge in the Court of Appeal; the two judges in the majority focused on the issue of causation and dismissed the action on that basis. In *Cragg v. Tone*,[136] an action brought by a victim against the police for failing to respond appropriately to a complaint regarding a threat, although successful at trial, was dismissed on appeal based on a finding that the police had not been negligent.

The duty of police to assist the public arises both from common law and statute. Specific legislative provisions may exist, however, which reduce the standard of care upon which liability is based. Attention must also be paid to the fact that the police, acting pursuant to statute and as public authorities, may be protected from suit by other more general legislative provisions, which provide immunity to such persons.[137] In addition, the common law of negligence itself provides an immunity for decisions taken in good faith by public authorities acting within a discretionary activity.[138] Finally, police actions are subject to the Canadian Charter of Rights and Freedoms, and as we have seen in *Jane Doe v. Metropolitan Toronto (Municipality) Commissioners of Police*,[139] decisions taken by the police can result in the breach of a victim's Charter rights and subject the police to a section 24 Charter remedy.

(d) Creators of Dangerous Situations

Where a person has accidentally created a situation fraught with danger for someone else, there are *dicta* to the effect that the one who created the risk is required to take reasonable steps to avert the potential harm.[140] Since this category of cases, however, frequently overlaps with the others discussed above, the law with regard to this category, standing alone, is far from clear.[141]

---

proximity between the police and the suspect, and residual policy concerns to negate the duty, even if a *prima facie* duty was found.

134 25 C.C.L.T. (3d) 234, [2004] 10 W.W.R. 286 (B.C. C.A.), leave to appeal refused (2005), 2005 CarswellBC 463 (S.C.C.). For a case comment, see Margaret Hall, "Duty, Causation and Third-Party Perpetrators: The Bonnie Mooney Case" (2005), 50 McGill L.J. 597.

135 2001 BCSC 419 (S.C.), additional reasons at (2001), 2001 CarswellBC 1773 (S.C.), affirmed (2004), 2004 CarswellBC 1707 (C.A.), leave to appeal refused (2005), 2005 CarswellBC 463 (S.C.C.).

136 (2006), 41 C.C.L.T. (3d) 13 (B.C. S.C.), reversed (2007), 285 D.L.R. (4th) 754 (B.C. C.A.), leave to appeal refused (2008), 2008 CarswellBC 241 (S.C.C.), additional reasons at (2008), 2008 CarswellBC 1245 (C.A.) reversing (2006), 41 C.C.L.T. (3d) 13 (B.C. S.C.).

137 See, for example, *Boucher v. Milner* (1997), 155 D.L.R. (4th) 106 (N.B. C.A.). Defendant protected by immunity provided for in Protection of Persons Acting Under Statute Act, R.S.N.B. 1973, c. P-20.

138 See discussion below in Chapter 8.

139 (1998), 160 D.L.R. (4th) 697 (Ont. Gen. Div.).

140 If, of course, the dangerous situation was created by the defendant's negligence, there would be no question that the ordinary principles of liability would apply.

141 Several of the cases discussed above, for example, *Menow v. Hornsberger, Hempler v. Todd, Ont. Hosp. Services Comm. v. Borsoski, Stermer v. Lawson,* and *Arnold v. Teno*, can be looked at as cases in which the defendants had created risks of danger for plaintiffs and therefore became responsible for taking reasonable steps to avert these risks.

A good illustration of this situation is *Oke v. Weide Tpt. Ltd.*[142] The defendant truck driver, allegedly while attempting to avoid a collision with another car, collided with a traffic sign which was erected on a strip of land between two lanes. The sign was bent over as a result, but the defendant failed to report this to the police. The next day, the deceased's car was speared by the sign post as the deceased was attempting to pass a truck while travelling in part on the dividing strip. The post penetrated the car's floor board, killing the driver. Assuming that the defendant was not initially negligent in colliding with the post, did he have a duty to report the event to the police so that the sign could be repaired? Although the trial court judge and a dissenting member of the Court of Appeal were prepared to impose such a duty upon the defendant, the majority of the Court of Appeal expressly refused to consider the question, deciding instead that the accident was unforeseeable. Mr. Justice Freedman's dissenting judgment imposed this duty on the defendant since, unlike other passersby, he had "participated in the creation of the hazard."[143]

Where a person has, even accidentally, created a situation of peril for someone else, the law should require that reasonable steps be taken to avert that peril. If the risk of harm emanating from the dangerous situation was reasonably foreseeable and the reasonable person would have taken steps to avert that harm, the failure to do so can lead to liability. This principle is not inconsistent with the reasons traditionally given to support the common law's reluctance to require Good Samaritanism.[144]

(e) Reliance Relationships

There is a wide, and rather ambiguous, category of reliance cases which imposes upon those who, either by their words or conduct, undertake to perform acts for the benefit of others, the legal obligation to do so. What makes this area particularly difficult to analyze is that various legal strands seem to intertwine here; tort, contract, equity, agency, and bailment may all have an impact depending on the facts. As well, the law has distinguished between gratuitous undertakings of

---

142 (1963), 41 D.L.R. (2d) 53, reversing (1963) 38 D.L.R. (2d) 188 (*sub nom. Oke v. Carra*) (Man. C.A.).

143 41 D.L.R. (2d) 53 at 62. Freedman J.A. also noted that the defendant had stopped, removed debris, and resolved to telephone the police, although he ultimately failed to do so. In *O'Rourke v. Schacht* (1974), 55 D.L.R. (3d) 96 at 107 (S.C.C.), Martland J., in an *obiter dictum*, reiterated the common law view that a private individual who becomes aware of a situation of danger on the highway "has no legal duty to do anything."

144 As with the commercial or social host situation, the difficult issue is how far must a person go in preventing harm to others, where, on the surface at least, the initial creation of the dangerous situation by the defendant was itself not negligent. The purist might argue that corrective justice only requires that you restore a person to the state he or she was in before you *wrongfully* injured them. Thus, if you "accidentally" imperil someone, you are no different than everyone else and should have no obligation to assist that person. It is only if your negligence imperiled another that you should have a duty. Although I must admit to being attracted to that argument, it probably takes the principle of corrective justice further than contemporary courts would. Note that in *Childs v. Desormeaux*, above, according to McLachlin C.J. a positive duty to act is owed where a defendant "intentionally attracts and invites third parties to an inherent and obvious risk that he or she has created or controls." In the situation of *Oke v. Weide*, can it be argued that the defendant motorist "intentionally attracted and invited third parties" to the risk that he accidentally created. If not, should a duty be owed?

private defendants and public authorities, with different principles apparently being applied.[145] Moreover, many of the reliance cases typically involve claims for the recovery of purely economic losses, an area which itself raises special problems.[146]

Leaving aside for discussion in later chapters the liability of public authorities for their failure to act, and the law concerning pure economic loss recovery, there are authorities which suggest that once a person who was initially under no legal obligation to assist actually begins to render assistance, a duty to make reasonable efforts to continue to assist arises. Although there are few direct cases on point, there are *dicta* to this effect. In *Zelenko v. Gimbel Bros.*,[147] it was stated that "if a defendant undertakes a task, even if under no duty to undertake it, the defendant must not omit to do what an ordinary man would do in performing the task."[148] The rationale behind the imposition of a legal duty in this type of case must be that by beginning to assist, where this prevents other assistance from being rendered, the actor creates a relationship of reliance or dependence with the victim. Where, on the other hand, an individual who is under no legal obligation to assist neither prevents other help from being offered nor worsens the victim's condition by beginning to assist, liability will not be imposed.[149] This proposition has been expressed in a few cases. For example, in the American case of *H.R. Moch Co. v. Rensselaer Water Co.*,[150] J. Cardozo stated:

> If conduct has gone forward to such a stage that inaction would commonly result, not negatively merely in withholding a benefit, but positively or actively in working an injury, there exists a relation out of which arises a duty to go forward.

As well, both Jessup J.A., and Schroeder J.A., in *Horsley v. MacLaren*,[151] adopted the view that only if a victim's condition is worsened by the intervention of a Good Samaritan should liability attach.

That an undertaking to act can give rise to liability if one does not act with reasonable care is illustrated in an interesting recent case, *Goodwin v. Goodwin.*[152] The defendant was a company that had contracted with the government to provide road maintenance services on certain highways in the province. The company was alerted by the police to a danger caused by black ice on a stretch of road. The defendant's employee said that a crew would be alerted; however, no crew was ever dispatched. The plaintiff was injured in an accident on that road and sued the maintenance company. It turned out that the dangerous road was in an area that did not fall under the contractual responsibility of the defendant. The trial judge summarily dismissed the plaintiff's claim on the basis of lack of proximity.[153] The Court of Appeal reversed, although it is clear from the discussion that the facts of this case did not fit squarely within any of the established jurisprudential principles. The defendant was not a governmental authority that had

145 On the liability of public authorities, see Chapter 8.

146 See Chapter 7.

147 287 N.Y.S. 134 (1935); affirmed 287 N.Y.S. 136 (1936).

148 The case involved a person who was taken ill in the defendant's department store, and was kept in an infirmary without any medical care for six hours.

149 See *East Suffolk Rivers Catchment Bd. v. Kent*, [1940] 4 All E.R. 527 (H.L.).

150 159 N.E. 896 at 898 (N.Y. C.A., 1928).

151 [1970] 2 O.R. 487 (C.A.).

152 (2007), 279 D.L.R. (4th) 227, [2007] 3 W.W.R. 575, 46 C.C.L.T. (3d) 41 (B.C. C.A.).

153 [2006] B.C.J. No. 395 (B.C. S.C.).

assumed responsibility, or was under a statutory responsibility to maintain this road.[154] The defendant had not negligently represented to the plaintiff that it would provide the service.[155] There was no reliance on a direct or indirect undertaking made by the defendant to the plaintiff or for the plaintiff's benefit.[156] It could not be said that the defendant exercised a public function or engaged in a commercial enterprise that included implied responsibilities to the public at large, so as to fit it within the third category of duty to act outlined by McLachlin C.J. in *Childs v. Desormeaux*. Nevertheless, Newbury J.A. held that this case was analogous to the "undertaking" or "assumption of responsibility" cases and that a duty of care was owed.[157]

The issue of the duty to continue to act reasonably when one agrees to act is somewhat problematic. It may admittedly be seen to be unfair to hold someone liable for failing to effect a rescue attempt with due care, when there was no legal obligation to do anything in the first place, unless that attempt prevented other help from being offered to the victim, or in some other way worsened the victim's condition. Why, after all, should a well intentioned, albeit careless person, be treated more harshly than a callous bystander, who stood aside from the outset refusing to do anything? However, the requirement that the victim's condition must have been worsened by the failed rescue attempt will, in many cases, be very difficult to prove. How may one know, or prove in court, that other persons would have rendered assistance, or more effective assistance, had it not been for the interventions of the first rescuer?

The law should require minimum standards of care, even from the volunteer. One who decides to assist ought to be required to act reasonably. The scope of the duty of care, however, will reflect the circumstances of each case. Thus the standard will be lower in the case of an emergency rescue attempt, especially where the person who offers assistance possesses no special skills or expertise.[158]

---

154 Thus distinguishing this case from other cases of negligence in maintaining the safety of roads such as *Just v. British Columbia*, [1989] 2 S.C.R. 1228 (S.C.C.); or *Brown v. British Columbia (Minister of Transportation & Highways)*, [1994] 1 S.C.R. 420 (S.C.C.).

155 Thus distinguishing this from cases such as *Densmore v. Whitehorse (City)*, [1986] 5 W.W.R. 708 (Y.T. S.C.).

156 Thus distinguishing this case from the will beneficiary cases or other cases of pure economic loss recovery. See discussion in Chapter 7.

157 Prowse J.A. wrote a concurring judgment as he disagreed with Newbury J.A.'s characterization of this case as a failure-to-warn case as well as her suggestion that the difference between misfeasance and nonfeasance is of "marginal significance" in current law. He agreed with the result, basing this on the defendant having voluntarily assumed the duty to alleviate the danger caused by the ice. As there had been no determination as to the issues of breach or cause, the action was remitted to trial.

158 See *Stevenson v. Clearview Riverside Resort* (2000), [2000] O.J. No. 4863, 2000 CarswellOnt 4888 (S.C.J.). Two individuals, with no specialized training, were sued for injuries suffered by a person who they were rescuing. The person dove into shallow water and broke his neck. The court noted, "Rescuers must act reasonably. However, placing too high a standard of care on rescuers, particularly trained medical personnel, may be a disincentive to rescue." The rescuers were relieved of liability. This approach has been reflected, in fact, in legislative enactments which have lowered the standard of care required of persons who render medical assistance to victims in emergency situations. See the Emergency Medical Aid Act, R.S.A. 1980, c. E-9, s. 2 [am. 1980, c. H-5.1, s. 34; 1984, c. 53, s. 27]; the Volunteer Services Act, R.S.N.S. 1989, c. 497; the Volunteers Liability Act, S.P.E.I. 1994, c. 65; the Good Samaritan Act, R.S.B.C. 1996, c. 172; the Emergency Medical Aid Act, R.S.S. 1978, c. E-8; the Emergency Medical Aid Act, R.S.N. 1990, c. E-9; the Emergency Medical Aid Act, R.S.N.W.T.

(f) Statutory Duties

There are numerous statutes which require or empower public officials, governmental bodies, municipal corporations and others, to take positive steps to remedy dangerous situations or prevent harm to the public. The extent to which these legislative enactments impose private law duties of care on these bodies, or can be used within the context of a negligence action, will be fully discussed in separate chapters.[159]

(g) Responsibility of Occupiers

In addition to the law of occupiers' liability, which requires an occupier to ensure that premises are reasonably safe, either in respect of their condition, activities conducted thereon, or the conduct of third parties on the premises,[160] there are English cases which have required occupiers of land to take affirmative steps to prevent the operation of natural forces, emanating from their land, from damaging their neighbours' land. These cases can be considered to be exceptions to the normal rules regarding Good Samaritanism, since they do require individuals to assist others, or to prevent harm from occurring to them, even when those individuals have in no way participated in the creation of the situations of peril.

In *Sedleigh-Denfield v. O'Callaghan,*[161] it was established that an occupier of land has a duty to take reasonable steps to abate a nuisance created by the act of a trespasser when the occupier has knowledge or the means of knowledge of its existence. The principle was taken further in *Goldman v. Hargrave,*[162] which established that an occupier's duty of care extends to all hazards on the land, whether natural or man-made, and to the removal or reduction of such hazards, by the exercise of reasonable care in the circumstances.[163] This principle was made part of English law in *Leakey v. Nat. Trust.*[164] Although the principle was reaffirmed by the House of Lords in *Smith v. Littlewoods Organisation Ltd.,*[165] it was done so with circumspection. An owner of an empty theatre was relieved of liability for damage caused to neighbouring properties when children went into the unattended building and started a fire. The Lords held that these events could not have reasonably been foreseen by the defendant. Lord Goff emphasized the common law's traditional refusal to impose a general duty of care on a person to

---

1988, c. E-4; and the Emergency Medical Aid Act, R.S.Y. 1986, c. 52. For a discussion of the statutes, see McInnes, "Good Samaritan Statutes: A Summary and Analysis" (1992), 26 U.B.C. L. Rev. 239. This approach has been rejected both by the Ontario Law Reform Commission, Annual Report, 1971, at 13, and the Manitoba Law Reform Commission, Report No. 11, 1973. On the standard of care issue, see Chapter 9.

159 On public tort duties, see Chapter 8; on the use of statutes in negligence actions, see Chapter 9.

160 This is normally the duty of occupiers under the various legislative enactments. The common law is not as easily stated. See Chapter 15.

161 [1940] A.C. 880 (H.L.). The principle was approved in *McKenzie Barge & Marine Ways Ltd. v. North Vancouver* (1964), 47 W.W.R. 30, reversed on other grounds [1965] S.C.R. 377.

162 [1967] 1 A.C. 645 (P.C.).

163 See Anderson, "*Goldman v. Hargrave*: Liability of a Bad Samaritan for the Natural Condition of his Land" (1967), 3 U.B.C. L. Rev. 211.

164 [1980] Q.B. 485 (C.A.).

165 [1987] 1 All E.R. 710 (H.L.).

prevent third parties from causing damage, even between neighbours, because of the "fundamental reason . . . that the common law does not impose liability for what are called pure omissions."[166] Although *Goldman v. Hargrave* was recognized by Lord Goff as imposing a duty, that duty depends on knowledge or means of knowledge of the deliberate wrongdoing of the third party, coupled with the availability of reasonable steps to prevent the harm.[167]

It is difficult to reconcile this principle with the common law's treatment of Good Samaritanism in general. One explanation might be that the common law has traditionally seen the rights and duties of land owners and occupiers as distinct from the normal rules governing tort. Another might involve the notion of control and the obligations which are inherent in the right to control. Since a land occupier can generally exclude interference with the right to control the land under occupation, it might be seen as justifiable to require occupiers to act reasonably to protect others from dangerous conditions which only the occupier can practically abate.[168]

---

166 *Ibid.*, at 729.

167 See *Wayen Diner Ltd. v. Hong Yick Tong Ltd.* (1987), 39 C.C.L.T. 176 (B.C. S.C.), where the defendant was not liable in nuisance for a leaky pipe since he neither knew nor had reason to know of the breach in the pipe. The reasoning in *Wayen Diner* was applied in *Tremblay v. Lahaie & Sullivan Cornwall Funeral Homes Ltd.* (1988), 44 C.C.L.T. 140 (Ont. Dist. Ct.). Also see *P. Perl (Exporters) Ltd. v. Camden L.B.C.*, [1983] 3 All E.R. 161 (C.A.), where damage caused by thieves who burrowed their way from the defendants' premises into the plaintiffs' premises was considered to be too remote. In *Nicholls v. Hennion* (1989), 49 C.C.L.T. 105 (Ont. H.C.), the application of *Leakey v. Nat. Trust* in Ontario was doubted. In *PPG Can. Inc. v. R.B. Colwell Ltd.* (1991), 7 C.C.L.T. (2d) 31 (N.S. T.D.), the doctrine that a neighbour must take reasonable steps to prevent or minimize a known risk of damage to one's neighbour was accepted and applied to the common law right of support. Also see *Doucette v. Parent* (1996), 31 C.C.L.T. (2d) 190 (Ont. Gen. Div.), where a defendant was relieved of liability for damage done to his neighbour's property by a tree that was blown over by the wind. The court applied a "reasonableness" test to determine the issue. For further discussion regarding liability for the acts of third parties, see below, Chapter 12.

168 This, however, is subject to the point that persons can come onto someone else's land to abate a nuisance. On this topic generally see Goodhart, "Liability for Things Naturally on the Land" (1930), 4 Cambridge L.J. 13.

7
Recovery of Purely Economic Losses

1. INTRODUCTION

Donoghue v. Stevenson gave a remedy in tort to those who suffer property damage or personal injury as a result of the careless acts of others. In the 76 years since that landmark decision was rendered, this extension of tort law has been significant and, with few exceptions, victims of personal injury or property damage now have available to them an action in negligence for compensation.[1] *Donoghue v. Stevenson* is one of the pillars of modern negligence law, the neighbour principle having carved out for itself a vast territory in which to operate. There remain, however, other significant territories left to conquer.

One of the remaining territories concerns claims for the recovery of purely economic losses.[2] Purely economic loss claims arise when individuals who have suffered neither personal injury nor property damage assert that another's negligence has resulted in their financial detriment and, even in the absence of contractual or fiduciary rights, seek compensation. This is generally the area of business and commerce, the traditional bailiwick of contract law. If Lord Atkin's concept of neighbourliness, with its obligation to take care, imposed not by agreement but by the common law, were to be extended here, this would surely be more cataclysmic than *Donoghue v. Stevenson* itself. Tort law's dominance over all of private law would be assured. A duty in tort to take reasonable care to protect the financial interests of foreseeable victims would relegate the law of contracts to protecting those who wished to bargain for more onerous obligations.

The common law with respect to recovery for purely economic losses is complex, the more so because of the diversity of problems which fall under this

---

1 As noted above, no-fault compensation schemes, such as workers' compensation, and no-fault auto plans, may apply, thereby preventing suits.

2 The first frontier is the duty to assist, discussed in the previous chapter. The third frontier is public tort liability, to be discussed in Chapter 8.

general category.[3] A convincing case has been made that, rather than attempting to fashion rules of general application, each class of economic loss dispute merits individual treatment.

As a general proposition it would be true to assert that the common law has not been willing to treat recovery for economic loss on the same basis as it does recovery for physical damages. Where the recovery of purely economic loss has been permitted, it has been on the basis of rules fashioned to meet the concerns of the particular situation.

What in general are these concerns? The major one, which applies in varying degrees to all categories of economic loss claims, is the fear of indeterminate liability. Put simply, the common law has recognized that for both principled and pragmatic reasons, individual defendants, society, and the judicial system should not be overburdened by tort law.[4] Unlike personal injury or property damage, which normally will be confined to a limited number of victims, economic losses following a negligent accident will often spread far and wide.[5] In addition, there is the problem of the accumulation of analogous claims, even where each claim

---

3 The literature on purely economic loss recovery in general, and on specific aspects of the topic, is extensive. It is one of the great challenges of contemporary scholarship to reconcile tort and contract, and to direct the courts as they set out to do this. Of the recent Canadian literature, see especially Feldthusen, *Economic Negligence*, 5th ed. (2008); Smith, *Liability in Negligence* (1984), Chapters 4, 5, 6, and 11; Smillie, "Negligence and Economic Loss" (1982), 32 U.T.L.J. 231; Blom, "Economic Loss: Curbs on the Way Ahead?" (1987), 12 Can. Bus. L.J. 275; Rafferty, "Recovery in Tort for Purely Economic Loss: Contract Law on the Retreat" (1986), 35 U.N.B. L.J. 111; Mactavish, "Tort Recovery For Economic Loss: Recent Developments" (1993), 21 Can. Bus. L.J. 395; Cherniak & How, "Policy and Predictability: Pure Economic Loss in the Supreme Court of Canada" (1999), Can. Bus. L.J. 209; among others. For a recent theoretical examination, see Beever, "A Rights-Based Approach to the Recovery of Economic Loss in Negligence" (2004), 4 Oxford University Commonwealth L.J. 151.

4 The concern that allowing recovery for purely economic losses will lead to "liability in an indeterminate amount for an indeterminate time to an indeterminate class", to quote the famous words of Cardozo J. in *Ultramares Corp. v. Touche*, 255 N.Y Supp. 170 at 179 (C.A., 1931), has and continues to be the principal policy reason given both by courts and commentators for the restriction on this type of claim, especially where relational economic losses are concerned. From Coleridge J.'s judgment in *Lumley v. Gye* (1853), 22 L.J.Q.B. 463 at 479, where the concern was expressed that, although justice might warrant that all those who suffer losses should be compensated, law must be limited to redressing "only the proximate and direct consequences of wrongful acts", to the most recent judicial pronouncements, this concern has consistently prevailed. See, e.g., Thorson J.A.'s judgment in *A.G. Ont. v. Fatehi* (1981), 18 C.C.L.T. 97 (Ont. C.A.); Lord Denning's judgments in *S.C.M. (U.K.) Ltd. v. W.J. Whittall & Son*, [1970] 3 All E.R. 245 (C.A.), and in *Spartan Steel & Alloys Ltd. v. Martin & Co. (Contr.)*, [1972] 3 All E.R. 557 (C.A.); and Wilson J.'s judgment in *Kamloops v. Nielsen* (1984), 29 C.C.L.T. 97 (S.C.C.), where this concern was discussed. In the Supreme Court of Canada's important judgment on pure economic loss recovery, *C.N.R. v. Norsk Pacific Steamship Co.* (1992), 11 C.C.L.T. (2d) 1; *Hercules Management Ltd. v. Ernst & Young*, [1997] 2 S.C.R. 165, 146 D.L.R. (4th) 577; *Bow Valley Husky (Bermuda) Ltd. v. Saint John Shipbuilding Ltd.*, [1997] 3 S.C.R. 1210, 153 D.L.R. (4th) 385; and *Design Services Ltd. v. R.*, 2008 SCC 22 (S.C.C.), this was the principal concern of the judges. In the *Norsk* case, McLachlin J., for example, stated at p. 17: "some limits on the potentially unlimited liability which can theoretically flow from negligence are necessary . . .". See also Stevenson J.'s judgment at pp. 41-43, where this same concern was expressed.

5 See the discussion below on relational economic losses. It is, of course, true that negligent conduct can physically affect numerous victims, as in mass disaster cases, such as the Bhopal tragedy. As well, not all types of economic loss cases result in widespread losses.

taken individually may be relatively confined. If one concedes that a densely populated, urban society creates economic interdependence, where one's fortunes are dictated to a large extent by what happens to others, this problem becomes evident.

Attention has also been paid to the qualitative differences between injuries of a purely economic nature, and physical damage, particularly personal injuries.[6] When one's bodily security or personal integrity has been harmed by the wrongful acts of others, imposing civil sanctions can be justified not only on the basis of the need to compensate the victim, but also on the basis of justice, punishment, deterrence, and education. Interference with an individual's security interests affects not only that individual; it also undermines everyone's sense of well-being, should the offence go unanswered. Since personal injuries can never be fully repaired, even by the payment of monetary damages, it is critical to try to reduce the incidence of these losses, by utilizing the deterrent and educative functions that negligence law provides.[7] Economic losses, which occur generally in a business context, where there is no threat to personal security, do not raise the same concerns. It may be possible to accommodate these losses more adequately by non-tort, non-adversarial, methods. Those who enter into business relations can often protect themselves by means of contract, or by insurance. It is important to ask whether the common law of torts ought to provide protection against business losses, which a claimant might have more efficiently guarded against. As well, accepting that tort obligations essentially restrict freedom of action in a free market society and that the law cannot, even if it should, repair all losses, drawing the line at purely economic losses seems to be a defensible, and not an arbitrary, decision. It is possible that refusing to impose tort liability for purely economic losses may, unless replaced by other deterrent mechanisms, encourage negligent behaviour in certain contexts, but this must be counter-balanced by other concerns.

This chapter will examine the problem of purely economic loss recovery by utilizing the categories suggested by Feldthusen and other writers.[8] Following the

---

6 See Feldthusen, "Economic Loss: Where Are We Going After Junior Books?" (1987), 12 Can. Bus. L.J. 241 at 246:

> A personal injury is *qualitatively* different from a financial loss, it has an entirely different moral significance, and it may entail different policies, deterrence for example. Not only is it difficult to quantify personal injury damages accurately, it is conceptually impossible to do so. Nor is the difference one of quantity or severity alone. There are catastrophic economic losses and minor personal injuries, but they remain qualitatively different.

7 Admittedly, the same is not true of property damage, which can, in most cases, be repaired. Nevertheless, one can justify treating property and personal injury cases together, either because, as a practical matter, the two frequently occur together, or simply on historical grounds. The common law has traditionally placed a high emphasis on property interests, and although it may be too late in the day to change this attitude, it does not justify extending this approach to other purely financial interests.

8 Feldthusen, *Economic Negligence*, 5th ed. (2008). See also Solomon and Feldthusen, "Recovery for Pure Economic Loss: The Exclusionary Rule" in Klar (ed.), *Studies in Canadian Tort Law* (1977), Chapter 6. The same argument has also been made by Blom, "Economic Loss: Curbs on the Way Ahead?" (1987), 12 Can. Bus. L.J. 275 at 278: "Economic loss, unlike physical harm, thus demands to be dealt with in terms of categories, because appropriate criteria for liability must be worked out for each distinct type of case."

suggestion of these academic commentators, the courts have begun to examine the individual disputes by fitting them into discrete classes.[9] This has assisted greatly in the analysis and resolution of disputes which fall into this wide-ranging area.[10]

2. LIABILITY FOR NEGLIGENT STATEMENTS

(a) The Nature of the Problem

Recovery for economic losses resulting from reliance on negligent statements represents the most significant exception to the common law's general rule that purely economic losses caused by negligence are not recoverable in tort. Based on the case of *Hedley Byrne & Co. v. Heller & Partners Ltd.*,[11] a judgment which

---

9 The Supreme Court of Canada adopted the categories approach to pure economic loss in *Winnipeg Condominium Corp. No. 36 v. Bird Construction Co.* (1995), 23 C.C.L.T. (2d) 1 at 13. La Forest J. stated the following:

> . . . the question of recoverability for economic loss must be approached with reference to the unique and distinct policy issues raised in each of these categories. That is because ultimately the issues concerning recovery for economic loss are concerned with determining the proper ambit of the law of tort, an exercise that must take account of the various situations where that question may arise.

This position was reaffirmed in *D'Amato v. Badger* (1996), 137 D.L.R. (4th) 129 (S.C.C.) and is now firmly enshrined in the jurisprudence.

10 In *Martel Building Ltd. v. R.* (2000), 193 D.L.R. (4th) 1 (S.C.C.), the Supreme Court reaffirmed its support of this approach explaining that "the reason for the broader five categories is merely to provide greater structure to a diverse range of factual situations by grouping together cases that raise similar policy concerns". The Court went on to add, however, that, "these categories are merely analytical tools". Thus when the facts of *Martel* could not easily be fitted into one of the recognized categories the Court did not consider this to be an impediment to the imposition of a duty. The case concerned a duty to act in good faith within the tendering process and the Court concluded that there was, on the facts of this case, no duty of care. Also see *Design Services Ltd. v. R.*, 2008 SCC 22, where the Supreme Court rejected a duty of care in another tendering process dispute. Rothstein J. held that a project owner owed no duty of a care to a subcontractor, who, although part of the bidding contractor's design-build team, had not entered into a joint venture contractual agreement with the bidding contractor. Although this case did not fall into any of the recognized economic loss categories, the Supreme Court was prepared to consider whether a new duty category should be recognized based on the *Cooper v. Hobart* formula. The Supreme Court's reformulation of the duty principle in *Cooper v. Hobart* and *Edwards v. Law Society of Upper Canada* gives guidelines as to how "new" categories should now be considered. There have been a number of other cases where novel claims for pure economic losses, which do not "fit" into any of the categories, have been rejected. See *Blacklaws v. 470433 Alberta Ltd.* (2000), 1 C.C.L.T. (3d) 149 (Alta. C.A.), leave to appeal refused (2001), 2001 CarswellAlta 492, 2001 CarswellAlta 493 (S.C.C.). As the Supreme Court did in *Martel*, the Alberta Court of Appeal held that the categories are not closed. However, it denied a duty owed by the manager/director of a company to plaintiffs who lost their investments as a result of the company's failure. Similarly see *Brett-Young Seeds Ltd. v. Assié Industries Ltd.* (2002), 11 C.C.L.T. (3d) 265 (Man. C.A.): application to join the president of a design company as a defendant in an action for defectively designed seeds rejected. Also see *F.W. Hearns / Actes - A Joint Venture v. University of British Columbia* (2000), 6 C.L.R. (3d) 85 (B.C. S.C.), additional reasons at (2001), 11 C.P.C. (5th) 142 (B.C. S.C.): the court acknowledged that the categories were not closed, but rejected a novel claim; and *66295 Manitoba Ltd. v. Imperial Oil Ltd.* (2002), 11 C.C.L.T. (3d) 225 (Man.Q.B.): a claim brought by a purchaser of land against an oil company which had contaminated the land was struck out.

11 [1963] 2 All E.R. 575 (H.L.).

rivals *Donoghue v. Stevenson* in its importance to negligence law, this category has undergone consistent expansion in the relatively few years of its existence, and has had an important spill-over effect into other areas of economic loss recovery.[12]

Prior to *Hedley Byrne*, English common law did not permit recovery for purely economic losses caused by a negligent statement, unless the parties were in a contractual or fiduciary relationship. The common law did, however, impose liability for a misstatement if the plaintiff was able to establish fraud on the part of the defendant.[13] The law was, and still is, less clear with respect to negligent statements which cause either personal injuries or property damages. Despite the opinion of many commentators that even before *Hedley Byrne* there was recovery for physical damages caused by negligent statement, pursuant to the ordinary neighbour principle of *Donoghue v. Stevenson*,[14] judicial statements themselves are equivocal and inconsistent. This question is important. Are physical losses which are caused by negligent statements to be governed by the more restrictive rules of *Hedley Byrne*, or do they fall under the neighbour principle of *Donoghue v. Stevenson*?

Because all of the important judicial pronouncements concerning liability for negligent statements occurred in cases where purely economic losses, and not

---

12 The literature on *Hedley Byrne* and the problem of negligent statements is voluminous. For discussion of the problem of negligent statements pre-*Hedley Byrne*, see Fridman, "Negligence by Words" (1954), 32 Can. Bar Rev. 638, and the articles cited at 638, note 2; Goodhart, "Liability for Negligent Misstatements" (1962), 78 L.Q.R. 107. Of the post-*Hedley Byrne* literature see Weir, "Liability for Syntax", [1963] Cambridge L.J. 216; Gordon, "*Hedley Byrne v. Heller* in the House of Lords" (1964-66), 2 U.B.C. L. Rev. 113; Glasbeek, "Limited Liability for Negligent Misstatement", in Linden (ed.), *Studies in Canadian Tort Law* (1967), at 115; Honore, "*Hedley Byrne v. Heller & Partners*" (1964-65) 8 J. Soc. Pub. Teachers of Law 284; Stevens, "*Hedley Byrne v. Heller*: Judicial Creativity and Doctrinal Possibility" (1964), 27 Mod. L. Rev. 121; Atiyah, "Negligence and Economic Loss" (1967), 83 L.Q.R. 248; Coote, "The Effect of Hedley Byrne" (1966-67), 2 N.Z.U. L. Rev. 263; Rickford, "A Mirage in the Wilderness: Hedley Byrne Considered" (1971), 34 Mod. L. Rev. 328; Harvey, "Economic Losses and Negligence" (1972), 50 Can. Bar Rev. 580; Stevens, "Two Steps Forward and Three Back! Liability for Negligent Words" (1972-73), 5 N.Z.U. L. Rev. 39; "The Law of Tort and Non-Physical Loss," The Ford Foundation Legal Workshop, 12 J. Soc. Pub. Teachers of Law 91; Fridman, "Negligent Misrepresentation" (1976), 22 McGill L.J. 1; Craig, "Negligent Misstatements, Negligent Acts and Economic Loss" (1976), 92 L.Q.R. 213; McLauchlan, "Pre-Contract Negligent Misrepresentation" (1977-80), 4 Otago L. Rev. 23; Cane, "The Metes and Bounds of Hedley Byrne" (1981), 55 A.L.J. 862; Smith, *Liability in Negligence* (1984), Chapter 5; Feldthusen, *Economic Negligence*, 5th ed. (2008), Chapter 2; Smillie, "Negligence and Economic Loss" (1982), 32 U.T.L.J. 231.

13 The leading cases are: *Derry v. Peek* (1889), 14 App. Cas. 337 (H.L.), a case which, although based on an action for deceit, intimated that there could be no liability for a negligent misstatement; *Cann v. Wilson* (1888), 39 Ch. D. 39, a case which, although it recognized liability for negligent statements, was soon overruled by the Court of Appeal in *Le Lievre v. Gould*, [1893] 1 Q.B. 491 (C.A.), which denied liability for negligent statements, and distinguished this area of law from that covered in *Heaven v. Pender* (1883), 11 Q.B.D. 503 (C.A.); *Nocton v. Lord Ashburton*, [1914] A.C. 932 (H.L.), a case based on breach of a fiduciary relationship in which it was suggested by Lord Haldane that liability for negligent statements might exist in special relationships outside of contract, equity, or fraud; *Candler v. Crane, Christmas & Co.*, [1951] 2 K.B. 164 (C.A.), a case which reaffirmed that there was no liability for negligent statements, but which contained a forceful dissenting judgment by Lord Denning. See Feldthusen, *Economic Negligence*, *ibid.*

14 See, e.g., Glasbeek, Craig, and Goodhart, above, note 12, among others.

physical damages, were in issue, it is difficult to determine what the courts' principal concerns were in these cases. It is clear that, for at least some of the judges, negligent words, as opposed to negligent acts, present particular policy problems, notwithstanding the type of damage which results. In *Candler v. Crane, Christmas & Co.*,[15] for example, Lord Asquith stated:

> In the present state of our law different rules seem to apply to the negligent misstatement on the one hand and to the negligent circulation or repair of chattels on the other; and *Donoghue's* case does not seem to have abolished these differences. I am not concerned with defending the existing state of the law or contending that it is strictly logical — it clearly is not. I am merely recording what I think it is.[16]

The Supreme Court of Canada's judgment in another pre-*Hedley Byrne* case, *Guay v. Sun Publishing Co.*[17] also provides evidence that, for at least some judges, words are different from deeds, and must be treated differently in law, no matter what kind of damage results. In that case, the plaintiff suffered nervous shock and physical injuries from a negligently published newspaper report that her immediate family had been killed in a traffic accident. Kerwin J. considered that the law regarding negligent words, whether resulting in physical injuries or not, was not based on *Donoghue v. Stevenson*, but must be considered within the context of *Derry v. Peek*[18] and the subsequent line of negligent statement cases. Locke J. thoroughly canvassed these cases and concluded that he did not think that "the question as to whether a duty exists is to be decided by the nature of the injury claimed to have been sustained."[19] Mr. Justice Locke referred as well to an article written by Lord Wright where the latter stated that although *Donoghue v. Stevenson* has never been applied to economic losses, "perhaps it is more accurate to say that *Donoghue's Case* has never so far been applied to negligence in words."[20]

In *Hedley Byrne* itself there are indications, in some of the speeches, that what essentially distinguishes negligent statement cases from *Donoghue v. Stevenson* lies in the nature of words themselves. According to Lord Pearce: "Words are more volatile than deeds. They travel fast and far afield. They are used without being expended and take effect in combination with innumerable facts and other words."[21] Lord Reid stated that, apart from authority, the law must treat negligent words differently from negligent acts for various reasons. People do not take the same care about expressing opinions as they do when they commit themselves to an act, such as putting goods into circulation. Negligently made articles will generally only cause one accident, whereas words which are easily broadcast, with or without the consent of their speaker, may affect a wide number of "con-

15 Above, note 13.

16 *Ibid.*, at 195. Lord Asquith presented the following hypothetical: if a map maker negligently omitted to indicate on his marine map the existence of a reef, and as a result the captain of the Queen Mary steered into the reef, and lost the ship, would the law impose liability on the map maker? No, suggested Lord Asquith, for who would continue to make maps under this threat of liability? It is clear, therefore, that the fact that the damage caused, in this example would be physical would not allay Lord Asquith's concerns.

17 [1953] 4 D.L.R. 577.

18 Above, note 13.

19 Above, note 17, at 602.

20 Lord Wright, "*Re Polemis*" (1951), 14 Mod. L. Rev. 393 at 401.

21 [1963] 2 All E.R. 575 at 613-14.

sumers." These characteristics of words, which for Lord Reid at least, justify their being treated differently from acts, seemingly apply without regard to the type of damage in question.[22]

There are, on the other hand, equally strong indications in the cases that it is not the difference between words and deeds which lies at the heart of the negligent statement issue, but the difference between physical damages and purely economic losses. The argument is that it is only when the negligent statement results in purely economic losses that special restrictive devices are required. One may refer to Estey J.'s judgment in *Guay v. Sun Publishing Co.*,[23] to Bowen L.J.'s judgment in *Le Lievre v. Gould*,[24] to *Old Gate Estates Ltd. v. Toplis*,[25] and to Lord Hodson's speech in *Hedley Byrne* for examples of this approach. In one case, *Clayton v. Woodman & Son (Bldrs.)*,[26] the court stated directly that *Candler v. Crane, Christmas & Co.*,[27] did not "exclude careless statements causing physical damage from the ambit of *Donoghue v. Stevenson*." Salmon J. stated that he "read the authorities as excluding not all forms of careless misstatement, but only those resulting in financial loss."[28] In *Kripps v. Touche Ross & Co.*,[29] Taylor J.A. affirmed this approach, and stated:

> While *Hedley Byrne* is sometimes referred to as having established a right of recovery in tort for negligent misstatement, it seems more correct to say that it clearly recognized the existence of a right of recovery for pure economic loss *simpliciter*. It seems certain, indeed, that a right of action for negligent misstatement must already have existed in cases in which the misstatement resulted in foreseeable personal injury or physical property damage.[30]

As a matter of policy, should negligent statements resulting in physical losses be treated under the ordinary rules of *Donoghue v. Stevenson*, or are special, more restrictive rules, required? It is unnecessary, and undesirable, to treat negligent

22 See also Lord Diplock's judgment in *Home Office v. Dorset Yacht Co.*, [1970] 2 All E.R. 294 at 326 (H.L.), where the difference between *Hedley Byrne v. Heller*, on the one hand, and *Donoghue v. Stevenson* on the other, is related to the difference between careless words and careless deeds. In some Canadian cases, negligent statements leading to physical losses were analyzed as *Hedley Byrne* cases. See, e.g., *Densmore v. Whitehorse (City)*, [1986] 5 W.W.R. 708 (Y.T. S.C.) — negligent representation that a fire truck would be sent to the scene of a fire led to property damage; *Lyon v. Shelburne* (1981), 130 D.L.R. (3d) 307 (Ont. Co. Ct.) — negligent representation led to flooding; *Gertsen v. Metro. Toronto* (1973), 41 D.L.R. (3d) 646 (Ont. H.C.) — negligent statement led to gas explosion.

23 Above, note 17.

24 Above, note 13.

25 [1939] 3 All E.R. 209 (K.B.).

26 [1962] 2 Q.B. 533 (C.A.).

27 [1951] 2 K.B. 164 (C.A.).

28 Above, note 26, at 545-46. The Manitoba Court of Appeal came to the same conclusion, although in less certain terms. See *Man. Sausage Mfg. Co. v. Winnipeg* (1976), 1 C.C.L.T. 221. See also *Zien v. R.* (1984), 15 D.L.R. (4th) 283 (Fed. T.D.), reversed on other grounds (1986), 26 D.L.R. (4th) 121 (Fed. C.A.).

29 (1992), 94 D.L.R. (4th) 284 (B.C. C.A.), leave to appeal to S.C.C. refused (1993), 78 B.C.L.R. (2d) xxxiv (note) (S.C.C.).

30 *Ibid.*, 94 D.L.R. (4th) at 291. In *Hercules Management Ltd. v. Ernst & Young* (1997), 35 C.C.L.T. (2d) 115 (S.C.C.) at 129, La Forest J. stated that negligent misrepresentation cases "involve special considerations stemming from the fact that recovery is allowed for pure economic loss as opposed to physical damage", thus lending further support to the suggestion that it is the type of loss and not the type of conduct that creates the difficulty in this area of law.

statements causing physical losses differently from negligent acts which result in the same damage. The restrictive rules adopted with regard to negligent statement cases should be reserved for pure economic loss recovery, and in this respect, the negligent statement issue should be viewed as only part of this wider economic loss question. The common law's interest in protecting personal security and property by the use of the principles of negligence law should not discriminate between negligent words and acts. The distinction between words and acts, in any event, is a fine one, since in almost all cases, the defendant's negligence, even where words are in issue, can be re-described in terms of a negligent act.[31] Giving negligent advice regarding the credit-worthiness of a person, for example, can be looked at equally as negligence in the performance of the services which preceded the actual giving of the advice. Distinguishing principles of liability on the basis of words or acts is bound to lead to confusing and artificial results.[32]

The common law's concerns in the area of economic loss recovery relate to the problem of potentially indeterminate liability, and to the qualitative differences between economic losses and physical injuries. The difference between words and acts does not raise these concerns, except when purely economic loss recovery is in issue. Words are generally not different from acts in terms of their ability to cause indeterminate physical losses.[33] This being the case, it is suggested

31 In *Rozenhart v. Skier's Sport Shop (Edmonton) Ltd.*, [2003] 5 W.W.R. 534, 15 C.C.L.T. (3d) 239 (Alta. Q.B.), affirmed (2004), 26 C.C.L.T. (3d) 109 (Alta. C.A.), the plaintiff enrolled in inline skating lessons. The defendant provided the skates and lessons. While waiting for the lesson to begin, the plaintiff fell and broke his hip. His cause of action was based on (i) a product supplier's duty to warn; (ii) an instructor's duty to a student; and (iii) negligent misstatement. The source of the latter claim was a statement made by the defendant that inline skating was similar to ice skating. The trial judge found for the plaintiff only on the negligent misstatement claim, applying the requirements of *Queen v. Cognos Inc.* (1993), 99 D.L.R. (4th) 626 (S.C.C.) The Court of Appeal affirmed the judgment, although it stated it did not agree with certain aspects of the reasoning. In my view, this was a straightforward physical injury case, based on alleged negligence in failing to properly instruct a student on the techniques required for inline skating; the reference to negligent misstatement cases was both confusing and unnecessary. Also see *Walford (Litigation Guardian of) v. Jacuzzi Canada Ltd.* (April 8, 2005), Doc. Hamilton 1722/97 (Ont. S.C.J.), additional reasons at (2005), 2005 CarswellOnt 7742 (Ont. S.C.J.), reversed 2007 CarswellOnt 6736 (Ont. C.A.), leave to appeal refused (2008), 2008 CarswellOnt 1860, 2008 CarswellOnt 1861 (S.C.C.). The plaintiff was seriously injured when she used a slide installed on her parents' above-ground pool. She hit the bottom of the pool and broke her neck. Actions were brought against the slide's manufacturer, a pool store that sold parts to install the slide, the couple who sold the family the used slide, among others. The actions were based on both negligent misrepresentation and product liability. The Court of Appeal held the pool store liable on the basis of the negligent statement requirements laid out in *Queen v. Cognos*.

32 An example given by Lord Devlin in *Hedley Byrne* illustrates this. If A is given a car to overhaul and repair if necessary, it cannot matter in terms of liability if (1) A negligently repairs it and tells the driver it is safe when it is not, (2) A overhauls it and negligently finds it not to be in need of repair and tells the driver it is safe, or (3) A negligently omits to overhaul it and tells the driver it is safe. In all three cases, A acted negligently, and liability should not depend upon whether this was in the form of negligent acts, omissions, or advice.

33 It is true that some types of negligent advice, such as a faulty weather report, or map making, have the potential of causing enormous physical losses. However, some types of negligent acts, such as mass disasters, for example the Bhopal tragedy, have the same ability. If extent of recovery is a problem in these cases, this ought to be dealt with by the ordinary rules of negligence law.

that it is correct to view the negligent statement problem as a particular problem of economic loss recovery.

(b) *Hedley Byrne & Co. v. Heller & Partners Ltd.*

In *Hedley Byrne & Co. v. Heller & Partners*,[34] the House of Lords decided that, in the appropriate circumstances, a duty of care can be imposed on an individual with respect to gratuitous advice which is given to, and relied upon, by another person. This decision, and its break with principle, which has been termed to be "the most radical on record",[35] has led to numerous successful subsequent actions, and opened the door to a wide range of pure economic loss recovery in tort.

The facts of the case are well known. The plaintiff company, which was contemplating extending credit to a customer, asked its bank to inquire into the credit-worthiness of that customer. The plaintiff's bank telephoned, and later wrote to the defendant bank, concerning this matter. The defendant bank, which dealt with the customer, gave satisfactory references, although it disclaimed any responsibility for this advice. The references, which were communicated to and relied upon by the plaintiff, turned out to be inaccurate, and resulted in the loss of the financial investment. The plaintiff's action against the defendant, which had been dismissed both at trial and on appeal, came before the House of Lords on a preliminary point of law. Could there be liability for a negligent statement causing financial loss, outside a contractual or fiduciary relationship?

As has been frequently pointed out, the decision of the House of Lords regarding this general question was *obiter*. There was no liability in this case in view of the disclaimer clause. Despite this, the decision in *Hedley Byrne* has been given considerable weight, and whatever the actual binding effect of the particular decision, its acceptance as good law by subsequent courts of high authority has obviated any defects of the decision itself.[36]

The House of Lords' judgment in *Hedley Byrne* could have been interpreted by subsequent courts in one of two ways. A narrow approach to it would have been to identify a list of specific factors required to establish the reliance relationship giving rise to the duty to take care. A more expansive view would have suggested that, as with *Donoghue v. Stevenson*'s neighbour principle, *Hedley Byrne v. Heller* should be regarded as having established a general principle of liability for negligent speech resulting in financial loss, with no defined limits,

---

34 [1963] 2 All E.R. 575 (H.L.).

35 See Gordon, "*Hedley Byrne v. Heller* in the House of Lords" (1964-66), 2 U.B.C. L. Rev. at 113.

36 In Canada, the Supreme Court of Canada has approved of the *Hedley Byrne* principle on numerous occasions. See, for example, judgments in *Rivtow Marine Ltd. v. Washington Iron Works*, [1973] 6 W.W.R. 692; *The Pas v. Porky Packers Ltd.*, [1976] 3 W.W.R. 138; *Haig v. Bamford*, [1976] 3 W.W.R. 331; *Fletcher v. M.P.I.C.* (1990), 5 C.C.L.T. (2d) 1; *Edgeworth Construction Ltd. v. N.D. Lea & Assoc. Ltd.* (1993), 17 C.C.L.T. (2d) 101; and *Queen v. Cognos Inc.* (1993), 14 C.C.L.T. (2d) 113. In the latter case, at 133, Iacobucci J. stated that the action for negligent statement first recognized in *Hedley Byrne* is "now an established principle of Canadian tort law". Several cases were noted by His Lordship where the Supreme Court has either expressly or tacitly affirmed it. The most recent Supreme Court of Canada elaboration of negligent statement law is *Hercules Management Ltd. v. Ernst & Young* (1997), 35 C.C.L.T. (2d) 115 (S.C.C.). See discussion below.

other than concern for the need of "reasonable and workable limits" to control a potentially wide area of liability.[37] The latter approach has been the one that has generally prevailed. The courts have interpreted *Hedley Byrne*'s importance in terms of its having removed previously impenetrable barriers against recovery for purely economic losses resulting from negligent speech, and have applied it on a case by case basis.[38]

In *Queen v. Cognos Inc.*,[39] Iacobucci J. presented five requirements for a successful *Hedley Byrne* claim. First, there must be a duty of care based upon a special relationship between the parties. Second, the statement or advice given must have been untrue, inaccurate, or misleading. Third, the representor must have acted negligently in making the misrepresentation. Fourth, the representee must have reasonably relied on the misrepresentation. Fifth, the reliance must have resulted in financial detriment.[40] In *Hercules Management Ltd. v. Ernst &*

---

37 See Estey J.'s judgment in *B.D.C. Ltd. v. Hofstrand Farms Ltd.* (1986), 26 D.L.R. (4th) 1 (S.C.C.), relating to pure economic loss recovery in general.

38 This approach was expressed by Bayda J.A. in *Nelson Lumber Co. v. Koch* (1980), 13 C.C.L.T. 201 at 222-23 (Sask. C.A.):

> (1) While it is important to pay heed to the development of the law which followed the enunciation of the *Hedley Byrne* principle it is equally important not to lose sight of the original principle as it was formulated by the five speeches delivered in the case; (2) it is necessary to assess on their own merits the circumstances of the particular situation before the Court; (3) one should determine whether a special relationship between the parties can be found even though the facts do not precisely fall within any one of the tests prescribed in the *Hedley Byrne* case or in any subsequent case: It is enough to determine that the fact situation falls generally within the framework of the *Hedley Byrne* doctrine; (4) broadly speaking one should treat the body of case authority that has developed in this area as a guide or aid and not a series of rigid tests to be met.

Lord Diplock, in *Mut. Life & Citizens Assur. Co. v. Evatt*, [1971] 1 All E.R. 150 at 161, stated:

> As with any other important case in the development of the common law, *Hedley Byrne* should not be regarded as intended to lay down the metes and bounds of the new field of negligence of which the gate is now opened. Those will fall to be ascertained step by step as the facts of particular cases which come before the courts make it necessary to determine them.

See also Iacobucci J.'s judgment in *Queen v. Cognos Inc.*, above, note 36, at 133: "While the doctrine of *Hedley Byrne* . . . is well established in Canada, the exact breadth of its applicability is, like any common law principle, subject to debate and to continuous development."

39 Above, note 36.

40 In the first edition of this text, I noted that there were four requirements, combining the inaccurate and negligent misrepresentation into one. Iacobucci J.'s analysis has separated them into two, which is preferable. As well, Iacobucci J. states in requirement (4), that the reliance must be "reasonable". As we will see, however, this is somewhat redundant, since for the "special relationship" to exist in the first instance, it must be an occasion where reliance would be foreseeable and reasonable. Despite this quibble, however, I would suggest that Iacobucci J.'s analysis of the elements is straightforward and helpful. Note as well Cullity J.'s insightful point in *Transamerica Life Insurance Co. of Canada v. Hutton* (2000), 33 R.P.R. (3d) 1 (Ont. S.C.J.), additional reasons at (2001), 2001 CarswellOnt 6 (S.C.J.), that there is no redundancy since it might be reasonably foreseeable at the time of the statement that the defendant would reasonably rely on it, whereas unreasonable at the time of reliance for the defendant to actually do so. Subsequent events, for example, might make reliance unreasonable. This raises the question as to whether the claim should fail, or there can be a finding of contributory negligence. See the discussion below.

Young,[41] this analysis was refined, although the five requirements maintained. Both of these decisions now form the basis of Canadian negligent statement law.

(c) The Special Relationship and Policy

(i) Introduction

The notion of a special relationship between the parties is at the heart of the *Hedley Byrne* duty. The concept envisages a relationship of proximity which is more restricted than the relationship of proximity based on foreseeability of harm defined by *Donoghue v. Stevenson*, but wider than a relationship of proximity which exists between parties to a contract or parties in a fiduciary relationship. That is, the *Hedley Byrne* relationship seems to occupy some middle ground between the two.

If one has regard to the various speeches of the Law Lords in the judgment, the following conclusion can be drawn with respect to the duty of care which must be established. The duty is based on a relationship of trust or reliance between the parties, in which the maker of the statement knows that the advice being proffered is to be relied upon by its recipient, and where, on objective grounds, such reliance is reasonable. Foreseeable and reasonable reliance is the current which runs through all of the speeches in *Hedley Byrne*. For example, Lord Reid stated that the duty of care would apply to:

> all those relationships where it is plain that the party seeking information or advice was trusting the other to exercise such a degree of care as the circumstances required, where it was reasonable for him to do that, and where the other gave the information or advice when he knew or ought to have known that the inquirer was relying on him.[42]

Foreseeable and reasonable reliance as the basis of the special relationship has generally been the interpretation given to *Hedley Byrne* by subsequent courts and commentators.[43] In *The Pas v. Porky Packers Ltd.*,[44] for example, the Supreme Court of Canada, in approving the principle of *Hedley Byrne*, quoted from *Charlesworth on Negligence*,[45] which adopted the reasonable reliance test.[46] In *Fletcher v. M.P.I.C.*,[47] Wilson J. stated that "[c]ourts in England and Canada have applied the *Hedley Byrne* principle to other relationships where it was foreseeable that one party would reasonably rely on the information or advice given by the other. . . ."[48] It is now fairly common, in the cases, to define the special relationship

---

41 Above, note 30.

42 [1963] 2 All E.R. 575 at 583. See, as well, Lord Morris' imposition of a duty whenever "someone possessed of a special skill undertakes, quite irrespective of contract, to apply that skill for the assistance of another person who relies on such skill", at 594. See also Lord Hodson at 601.

43 Note that this was the *ratio* given to the judgment by the headnote writers, in [1963] 2 All E.R. 575. This was subsequently adopted by the major text books which explained the duty.

44 (1976), 65 D.L.R. (3d) 1 at 9 (S.C.C.).

45 5th ed. (1971), para. 49, p. 32.

46 The Charlesworth quote itself is a slightly modified adoption of the headnote from the All E.R. report of the case.

47 Above, note 36.

48 *Ibid.*, at 18-19. Wilson J. concluded that the defendant would owe a duty of care to the plaintiff if the plaintiff reasonably relied on the information, and the defendant knew or ought to have known that it would so rely. Also see McLachlin J.'s statement in *Edgeworth Construction Ltd. v. N.D. Lea & Assoc. Ltd.*, above, note 36, at 107: "Liability for negligent misrepresentation

in terms of giving advice in a situation where the advisor ought to know that the advice will be relied upon, and where this subsequent reliance is reasonable.[49]

In *Hercules Management Ltd. v. Ernst & Young*,[50] La Forest J., writing for the Supreme Court of Canada, attempted to locate the "special relationship" test within the two-stage duty analysis, which, as we have seen, had consistently been adopted by the Court as the test for duty in a negligence action.[51] La Forest J. wished to avoid creating a "pocket" of negligent misrepresentation cases that determined the issue of "duty" differently from other negligence cases.[52] His Lordship accomplished this by viewing the "special relationship" as constituting stage one of the two-stage test. That is, where the advisor ought reasonably to have foreseen that the advisee would rely on the advice given and where this reliance would be reasonable, a special relationship is created between the parties that satisfies the proximity requirement of stage one of the test. The special relationship so defined creates a *prima facie* duty of care that can then be limited or negated by policy considerations. In the context of *Hercules Management Ltd.*, audited financial statements produced negligently by the defendant auditors allegedly were relied upon by the plaintiff investors in their decision to invest in the audited company. La Forest J. held that since this reliance was both foreseeable and reasonable, a special relationship was created between the parties that created a *prima facie* duty of care.

Moving on to the second stage of the duty test, that of "policy", La Forest J. held that policy reasons dictated that the presumptive duty be negated. As noted above, the major policy concern alluded to by courts in negligent statement cases is that of potentially indeterminate liability. Thus, even though it might have been foreseeable that the plaintiff investors would rely on the audited financial statements in considering their investment decisions, and reasonable for them to do so, a concern for the potentially unlimited liability of auditors should, according to La Forest J., be considered before imposing a duty of care on them owed to the

---

arises where a person makes a representation knowing that another may rely on it, and the plaintiff in fact relies on the representation to its detriment. . .".

49 See, e.g., *Kingu v. Walmar Ventures Ltd.* (1986), 38 C.C.L.T. 51 (B.C. C.A.); *Executive Hldg. v. Swift Current*, [1985] 1 W.W.R. 341 (Sask. Q.B.); *Grand Restaurants of Can. Ltd. v. Toronto* (1981), 123 D.L.R. (3d) 349, affirmed 140 D.L.R. (3d) 191 (Ont. C.A.); *Dorsch v. Weyburn* (1982), 23 Sask. R. 161 (Sask. Q.B.), reversed (1985), 23 D.L.R. (4th) 379 (Sask. C.A.); *Sirois v. Fed. des Enseignants du N.-B.* (1984), 28 C.C.L.T. 280 (N.B. Q.B.); *H.B. Nickerson & Sons Ltd. v. Wooldridge* (1980), 115 D.L.R. (3d) 97 (N.S. C.A.); *Can. Commercial Bank v. Crawford, Smith & Swallow* (1993), 15 C.C.L.T. (2d) 273 (Ont. Gen. Div.), affirmed (1994), 21 C.C.L.T. (2d) 89 (Ont. C.A.), leave to appeal to S.C.C. refused (1994), 21 C.C.L.T. (2d) 89n (S.C.C.); *Dixon v. Deacon Morgan McEwen Easson* (1993), 102 D.L.R. (4th) 1 (B.C. C.A.); and *Hembruff v. Ontario (Municipal Employees Retirement Board)* (2005), 260 D.L.R. (4th) 161 (Ont. C.A.), leave to appeal refused (2006), 2006 CarswellOnt 2357 (S.C.C.), leave to appeal refused (2006), 2006 CarswellOnt 2359 (S.C.C.). All of these judgments base the special relationship on the giving of advice when the giver knows or ought to know that this advice will be relied upon.

50 (1997), 35 C.C.L.T. (2d) 115 (S.C.C.). For commentary, see R. Hollyman, "Hercules Management and the Duty of Care in Negligent Misstatement: How Dispensable is Reliance?" (2001), 34 U.B.C. L. Rev. 515.

51 *Hercules Management Ltd.* was decided before the Supreme Court refined the two-stage test in *Cooper v. Hobart* and *Edwards v. Law Society of Upper Canada*, as discussed above in Chapter 5. As I will discuss below, however, I do not believe that the reformulated two-stage test will affect or alter the *Hercules Management Ltd.* analysis.

52 (1997), 35 C.C.L.T. (2d) 115 (S.C.C.) at 128. La Forest J. cited Stapleton, "Duty of Care and Economic Loss: A Wider Agenda" (1991), 107 L.Q.R. 249.

investors.[53] La Forest J. conceded that indeterminate liability would not necessarily be a problem in some auditor liability cases, for example, where the auditor produced the statement intending that it be used in the specific way in which it was used by the plaintiff. These, however, were not the facts of *Hercules Management Ltd.* La Forest J. concluded that the audited statements were produced for the purpose of allowing the shareholders to oversee the management of the company, and not for the purpose of making individual investment decisions. Thus to impose liability on the auditors would expose them to potentially indeterminate liability and the duty should accordingly not be imposed.[54]

Has La Forest J.'s approach in *Hercules Management Ltd.* altered the law with respect to negligent misrepresentation cases in any practical sense?[55] In my opinion it has not. It has always been understood that liability for economic losses caused by negligent representations must be circumscribed due to the fear of indeterminate liability. This is why the courts have not adopted the ordinary reasonable foreseeability test of *Donoghue v. Stevenson* but articulated instead the more restrictive notion of a "special relationship". It was, in other words, the special relationship that was meant to confine liability in this area to an acceptable limit. The factors that the courts traditionally have examined in order to determine whether a special relationship exists, which will be discussed below, were created with this purpose in mind. What La Forest J. has done, however, is to refine the analysis so that it now fits within the two-stage duty mould. La Forest J.'s analysis allows the court to hold that although relying on advice was foreseeable and reasonable, the duty may still be negated due to the policy concern of indeterminate liability. As a factual matter, it also admits that a plaintiff can be held to have foreseeably and reasonably relied on advice for personal investment decisions even though that advice was not prepared for that purpose and was never intended for that use.[56]

53 Prior to this judgment, the "special relationship" test was the method to curtail indeterminate liability. What La Forest J. effectively decided in *Hercules Management Ltd.* was that even though there is a special relationship between the plaintiff and defendant based upon reasonable and foreseeable reliance, there can still be a problem of indeterminate liability that must be addressed at stage two of the test.

54 This conclusion can usefully be compared with the judgment of the British Columbia Court of Appeal in *Kripps v. Touche Ross & Co.*, [1997] 6 W.W.R. 421, 35 C.C.L.T. (2d) 60 (B.C. C.A.), leave to appeal refused (1997), 102 B.C.A.C. 238 (note) (S.C.C.), which was decided approximately one month earlier. In the *Kripps* case, the plaintiffs were investors who lost a considerable part of their investment when the company whose debentures they had purchased failed. They claimed that they relied upon a negligent auditor's report attached to the prospectus that the company had issued. Both the trial court judgment, reported at (1995), 24 C.C.L.T. (2d) 136 (B.C. S.C.), and the Court of Appeal agreed that the auditor owed the plaintiffs a duty of care since the auditor knew that the audit would be included with the financial statements and the prospectus and was intended for the purpose of facilitating the sale of debentures. The trial court dismissed the action, however, based on lack of proof of reliance. The Court of Appeal reversed on this point and found the auditor liable. Although the new two-stage test was not available to the courts, using the language of *Hercules Management Ltd.* one would conclude that there were no problems of indeterminate liability to negate the *prima facie* duty.

55 By this I mean whether liability for negligent statements has either been made more or less restricted by *Hercules Management Ltd.*

56 This is where I admit to some difficulty with La Forest J.'s new analytical approach. Before *Hercules Management Ltd.*, the court could have come to the same conclusion regarding duty by finding that it was not reasonable and foreseeable for investors to rely on audited financial statements for personal investment decisions and that therefore there was no special relationship

An alternative interpretation of the special relationship favoured by some commentators,[57] as well as by some courts, has been the voluntary assumption of responsibility test. According to this approach, a duty to take reasonable care in giving advice will exist when the circumstances allow the conclusion that, despite the gratuitous nature of the relationship, the defendant assumed responsibility for the advice which was given. This was expressed in several statements in *Hedley Byrne* itself. Lord Reid, for example, stated that "the most natural requirement would be that expressly or by implication from the circumstances the speaker or writer has undertaken some responsibility."[58] Lord Morris related the duty to take care in gratuitous speech to "circumstances in which a duty to exercise care will arise if a service is voluntarily undertaken."[59] Lord Devlin referred to relationships which "are 'equivalent to contract' that is, where there is an assumption of responsibility in circumstances in which, but for the absence of consideration, there would be a contract."[60]

A conclusion that there existed a special relationship between the parties which gave rise to a duty of care rests on the court's conviction that as a matter of judicial policy liability for negligent speech ought to be imposed. Since both tests of reasonable, foreseeable reliance and voluntary assumption of responsibility are legal constructs, it is difficult to envisage cases where characterizing the test in one way or the other will alter the judicial result.[61] In addition, as we have seen

---

created between them in the first place. In other words, the policy concern of indeterminate liability could have been addressed by denying the special relationship. Does the Supreme Court's reformulation of duty in *Cooper v. Hobart* and *Edwards v. Law Society of Upper Canada* affect the analysis presented in *Hercules Management Ltd.*? I do not think so. The reformulation applies to new categories of duties where "proximity" had not previously been found. The negligent statement cases fall into a recognized category where proximity is established by the "special relationship" at stage one. Policy still comes into play at stage two.

57 See especially Feldthusen, *Economic Negligence*, 5th ed. (2008); Harvey, "Economic Losses and Negligence: The Search for a Just Solution" (1972), 50 Can. Bar. Rev. 580; Smillie, "Negligence and Economic Loss" (1982), 32 U.T.L.J. 231.

58 [1963] 2 All E.R. 575 at 581.

59 *Ibid.*, at 589.

60 *Ibid.*, at 610. See also statements in *Kingu v. Walmar Ventures Ltd.*, above, note 49, where the court referred to Blom, "The Evolving Relationship Between Contract and Tort" (1985), 10 Can. Bus. L. J. 257, and the author's argument that the duty should relate to the speaker's "apparent intention to be bound" by his statement. See Goff L.J.'s judgment in *Muirhead v. Indust. Tank Specialities*, [1985] 3 All E.R. 705 at 715 (C.A.), where the voluntary assumption of responsibility test is said to have been the basis of *Hedley Byrne*. Lord Goff has reaffirmed his approval of the "voluntary assumption of responsibility" test as the basis of the *Hedley Byrne* relationship in both *Henderson v. Merrett Syndicates Ltd.*, [1994] 3 W.L.R. 761, and *White v. Jones*, [1995] 2 W.L.R. 187.

61 This point is illustrated by Iacobucci J.'s judgment in *Queen v. Cognos Inc.*, above, at 138. While recognizing that there is a debate as to which is the more appropriate test, Iacobucci J. declined to take part in it, since both tests, in his opinion, would have led to the same result in this case. This is conceded by the proponents of the voluntary assumption of responsibility test as being true for all but the most difficult cases. See, for example, Feldthusen, *Economic Negligence*, 4th ed. (2000), at 48: "The two concepts are very closely related to one another, and in most cases the outcome will be the same regardless of which is employed as the basis of the duty." Feldthusen does argue, however, that in difficult cases, for example when disclaimer clauses are used, the voluntary assumption of responsibility will provide a fairer result. Note, however, Cane, "The Metes and Bounds of *Hedley Byrne*" (1981), 55 A.L.J. 862, where the author notes that the voluntary assumption of responsibility test "expresses nothing not

from *Hercules Management Ltd.* and other Canadian judgments of high authority, the voluntary assumption of responsibility test has clearly given way to the foreseeable and reasonable reliance formula as the basis for the special relationship.[62]

In summary, as a result of the Supreme Court of Canada's judgment in *Hercules Management Ltd.*, the formula for establishing a duty of care in negligent statement cases is as follows.

First, the court has to ask itself whether a *prima facie* duty of care arises between the parties. This *prima facie* duty is based on the concept of the special relationship. A special relationship will exist when the advisor ought to have reasonably foreseen that the advisee would rely on the advice and where that reliance would be reasonable.

Second, the court has to consider policy reasons that might negate or reduce the duty. In the context of negligent statement cases these policy reasons generally relate to the problem of indeterminate liability, should a duty be imposed on the facts of the particular case.[63]

---

captured by the idea of reasonable reliance" and that as a concept it has "suffered a certain eclipse." See also *Haig v. Bamford* (1976), 72 D.L.R. (3d) 68 at 77 (S.C.C.), where Dickson J. states that:

> This "assumption of responsibility" test is an interesting one, although it is no more objective than a foreseeability test. It would allow the Court to narrow the scope of liability from that resulting from a foreseeability test, but it would still require a policy determination as to what should be the scope of liability.

Criticism of the voluntary assumption of responsibility test also came from Lord Griffiths in *Smith v. Eric S. Bush*, [1989] 2 All E.R. 514 (H.L.). His Lordship stated that this test is neither "helpful or realistic" as a test of liability. See also Roth, "Case Comment" (1986-87), 51 Sask. L.R. 317, where a variant of the voluntary assumption of responsibility test is proposed: in making the statement did the defendant know, as a reasonable person, that someone would reasonably believe that the statement was accurate and would reasonably trust, in the circumstances, that the defendant took due care in making it?

62 An interesting issue arises with respect to the effectiveness of disclaimer clauses in a negligent statement scenario. As noted above, it has been argued that using a foreseeable, reasonable reliance test for duty could result in a duty being recognized despite the existence of a disclaimer clause. Under a voluntary assumption of responsibility approach a disclaimer clause would be fatal to a duty. This was fully explored in *Keith Plumbing & Heating Co. v. Newport City Club Ltd.*, [2000] 6 W.W.R. 65 (B.C. C.A.), leave to appeal refused (2000), 152 B.C.A.C. 23 (note) (S.C.C.). The majority held that there was a duty despite the disclaimer clause. The dissent gave effect to the clause and dismissed the claim.

63 Judgments utilizing this two stage approach to negligent statement cases include *Black v. Lakefield (Village)* (1998), 166 D.L.R. (4th) 96 (Ont. C.A.); *NBD Bank, Canada v. Dofasco Inc.* (1999), 47 C.C.L.T. (2d) 213 (Ont. C.A.), leave to appeal refused (2000), 135 O.A.C. 195 (S.C.C.); and *Toronto Dominion Bank v. Forsythe* (2000), 183 D.L.R. (4th) 616 (Ont. C.A.). In the latter case, unsecured creditors claimed that they relied upon representations made by the defendant bank to a loan guarantor. The court denied the duty at stage one of the test by finding that it was neither foreseeable nor reasonable for them to have done so, and thus there was no proximity and *prima facie* duty. This, as I suggested above, is the traditional approach to deny duty in negligent statement cases without the need to break down the analysis of duty into two stages as outlined in *Hercules Management Ltd.* The *NBD Bank* case is an important judgment dealing with the personal liability of directors and officers of companies. The Vice-President of a company was held personally liable for negligent statements made to a bank. The court held that there was a special relationship and no policy reasons to negate the duty. Policy reasons raised by the defendant included the fact that his company could not be sued

In determining stage one of the test, i.e., whether a special relationship exists between parties, the courts have focused on a number of important factors.[64]

(ii) Skill of the Advisor

In determining whether or not a special relationship exists, the courts have considered the status or position of the advisor. While the decision in *Mut. Life Assur. v. Evatt*[65] seemed to restrict the duty of care to those who are in the specific business or profession ordinarily involved with the type of advice being sought,[66] the subsequent case law has not accorded *Mutual Life* this effect. Although the context in which advice is sought and received has certainly been viewed as an important factor in determining whether a special relationship exists between the parties, no rigid rule relating to the advisor's specific status has been adopted. Thus, in two cases where vendors of prefabricated homes advised purchasers regarding the suitability of potential contractors to construct these homes,[67] the courts held the vendors liable on the basis of *Hedley Byrne*.[68] In another case, *Sirois v. Fed. des Enseignants du Nouveau-Brunswick*,[69] a teachers' association was held liable for negligently having provided inaccurate information concerning the eligibility of unemployed teachers for unemployment insurance benefits in its

---

due to protection provided by the Companies Creditors Arrangement Act, R.S.C. 1985, c. C-36, the problem of indeterminate liability, and appropriate risk allocation. The Court of Appeal rejected these arguments. In *Canadian Taxpayers Federation v. Ontario (Minister of Finance)* (2004), 73 O.R. (3d) 621 (S.C.J.), an action based on a campaign promise by the defendant not to raise taxes was appropriately struck out for a number of reasons, including policy.

64 In *Hercules Management Ltd.*, above, at 598, La Forest J., citing Feldthusen, *Economic Negligence*, 3rd ed., at 62, stated that there were five *indicia* of reasonable reliance. These are: (i) the defendant's direct or indirect financial interest in the transaction; (ii) the defendant's skill and knowledge; (iii) the occasion, i.e., business; (iv) advice given deliberately; and (v) advice requested. These are elaborated upon below. As noted by La Forest J., these are not to be regarded as a "strict" test; they are merely factors that judges can take into consideration.

65 [1971] 1 All E.R. 150 (P.C.).

66 Lord Diplock argued that only those persons "who carry on the business or profession of giving advice of the kind sought" are able to appreciate what degree of skill, competence or diligence is required in response to a request for advice, and that even if a person without such skill answers a request knowing that his advice will be relied upon, the law will not hold that he can be held responsible for this. In other words, mere knowledge of reliance is insufficient to create a duty. The dissenting justices rejected this, arguing that the only issue is reasonable reliance, which will be related, of course, to the context in which the advice was given. If the context was a business one, and the reliance was foreseeable on the part of the giver, and reasonable on the part of the recipient, the fact that the advisor was not in the business of giving out that type of advice, or in actual fact had no special skills in relation to it, should not matter.

67 *Beaver Lumber Co. v. McLenaghan* (1982), 23 C.C.L.T. 212 (Sask. C.A.); *Nelson Lumber Co. v. Koch* (1980), 13 C.C.L.T. 201 (Sask. C.A.).

68 In *Nelson Lumber Co. v. Koch, ibid.*, this was so despite the fact that the company, whose business was to sell homes, had a policy not to recommend contractors to their clients. Moreover, the negligent advice related not to the competence of the suggested contractor, but to its financial stability, something which in fact had not been asked about. The judgment prompted one commentator to write: "the present case tends to confirm what many already suspected. *Mutual Life & Citizens Assur. Co. v. Evatt* is dead." See Irvine, 13 C.C.L.T. at 202. Another case cited by Irvine to support this is *Sodd Corp. v. Tessis* (1977), 2 C.C.L.T. 245 (Ont. C.A.).

69 (1984), 28 C.C.L.T. 280 (N.B. Q.B.). For a commentary, see Roth, "Liability for LooseLips . . ." (1986-87), 51 Sask. L. Rev. 317.

news bulletin. Although not discussed, this judgment again shows that *Mut. Life v. Evatt* has not had a restrictive effect on the *Hedley Byrne* special relationship.[70]

Most cases have involved advice given by those in the business or profession of giving advice. Thus property appraisers, accountants and auditors, banks and other financial advisers, realtors, and insurance agents, among others, have been held liable for negligent advice given in the course of conducting their usual business activities.[71] It has been made clear, however, that the duty to use care in giving advice is not limited to those involved in traditional advice-giving professions.[72]

There may be reasons why it would not be reasonable, in view of the status, knowledge, or adverse interest of the advisor, to rely upon an individual. In such cases, the courts have refused to recognize the existence of a special relationship. In *Kingu v. Walmar Ventures Ltd.*,[73] for example, the court held that a purchaser's reliance on statements made by vendors of a hotel concerning the potential profitability of the hotel was unreasonable and did not create a special relationship between the parties. The advisors did not possess the requisite degree of skill or knowledge with regard to the advice volunteered, did not hold themselves out as experts, and in relation to the advisee could not be said to have possessed the degree of "superior skill and knowledge requisite to establishing a duty of care."[74] In another case, *Dorsch v. Weyburn*,[75] the court refused to recognize the existence of a special relationship between the plaintiffs and the solicitor representing the

---

70 In *Mandavia v. Central West Health Care Institutions Board*, [2005] N.J. No. 69 (C.A.), negligent advice regarding the employee's retirement benefits led to a successful negligent misrepresentation action.

71 For reference to a number of these cases, see Chapter 10 below. Although negligent statement cases generally involve advice given within a business or commercial context, *Hedley Byrne* has been applied in other types of cases. *Kelly v. Lundgard*, 202 D.L.R. (4th) 385, [2001] 9 W.W.R. 399 (Alta. C.A.) involved a medical-legal report prepared by a doctor. The report was negligently prepared, failing to inform the plaintiff that her injuries could result in infertility. The plaintiff settled a personal injury lawsuit without this information but later discovered her infertility. She sued the physician who prepared the report. The case raised interesting issues. Was this a case of negligent medical treatment resulting in a special limitation period? Did the full disclosure standard of informed consent apply? The Court of Appeal treated this as a "medical treatment" case for the purposes of the limitation period. The standard applied was the one that applied to negligent statement cases, i.e., professional standard, and not to duty to inform cases; i.e., full disclosure. The case illustrates the difficulties in attempting to apply negligent statement principles to an unorthodox set of facts.

72 See *Blair v. Can. Trust* (1986), 38 C.C.L.T. 300 (B.C. S.C.). Confirmation that this is the approach which is to be adopted in Canadian law comes from Iacobucci J.'s *obiter* comments in *Queen v. Cognos Inc.*, above, note 35, at 139:

> The question of whether a duty of care with respect to representations exists depends on a number of considerations including, but not limited to, the representor's profession. While this factor may provide a good indication as to whether a "special relationship" exists between the parties, it should not be treated in all cases as a threshold requirement. There may be situations where the surrounding circumstances provide sufficient indicia of a duty of care, notwithstanding the representor's profession.

73 (1986), 38 C.C.L.T. 51 (B.C. C.A.).

74 *Ibid.*, at 61.

75 (1985), 23 D.L.R. (4th) 379 (Sask. C.A.).

party who stood in an adverse relationship with the plaintiffs.[76] The rule in all cases is the same: taking into consideration all of the circumstances, would a reasonable person have relied on advice emanating from this advisor?[77]

A variant on the theme that the nature of the advisor is relevant to determining whether it is reasonable to rely on that person may be found in the case of *Schilling v. Certified General Accountants Assn. (British Columbia).*[78]

In this case, the plaintiffs lost money that had been placed with an accountant for investment. The accountant held himself out as a "Certified General Accountant" even though the defendant association that had originally certified him had earlier disciplined him. The accountant had promised to resign from the Association but he did not do so. Did the Association have a duty to notify the public about the de-certification? Would it be reasonable for the plaintiff to have relied on the certification? The Court of Appeal held that the certification related to the member's skill as an accountant, and not as an investment advisor. There was, in effect, no special relationship created between the plaintiffs and the defendant association with respect to the plaintiffs' reliance on the certification for this type of activity.[79]

(iii) Skill of the Advisee

Another factor which is relevant when determining whether or not a special relationship exists between the parties is the apparent skill or knowledge of the person to whom the advice is being given. While it might be legitimate to hold that an advisor who is giving advice to a person without particular knowledge of the subject matter ought to foresee that this advice will be relied upon, or ought to assume responsibility for that advice, the same may not prevail when the advisee

---

76 See also *Andronyk v. Williams* (1985), 35 C.C.L.T. 38 (Man. C.A.); *Boulderwood Dev. Co. v. Edwards* (1984), 30 C.C.L.T. 223 (N.S. C.A.).

77 Now that a *Hedley Byrne* claim is available for pre-contractual misrepresentations, the issue as to the reasonableness of relying on a party with an adverse interest, is becoming tricky. To what extent, short of not being fraudulent, is a party responsible for representations made in pre-contractual negotiations? There are a growing number of judicial decisions in this area. In *J.R.K. Car Wash Ltd. v. Gulf Can. Ltd.*, (1992), 46 C.P.R. (3d) 525 (Ont. Gen. Div.), the court held that the defendant who leased a gas station to the plaintiff, was liable to him both in contract and in tort for inaccurate estimates as to the throughput of the station. In *Brar v. Mutti*, [1994] B.C.J. No. 2426 (B.C. S.C.), a vendor, although not liable for a fraudulent misrepresentation, was liable in negligence for failing to disclose the existence of restrictive covenants on lots which were being sold. In *Sergius v. Janax Design & Drafting Services Ltd.* (1992), 9 C.C.L.T. (2d) 257 (B.C. S.C.), a vendor, who had acted as his own contractor and builder, was liable for negligent misrepresentations concerning the structural soundness of the house. The main conclusions which one can draw from the jurisprudence is that although *Hedley Byrne* clearly has enlarged the legal responsibilities of vendors and others to those with whom they are dealing, a "special" relationship founded upon foreseeable and "reasonable" reliance must be established based on the specific facts of each case. The duty imposed on vendors to disclose latent defects is discussed below in Chapter 17.

78 (1996), 29 C.C.L.T. (2d) 44, 135 D.L.R. (4th) 669 (B.C. C.A.), leave to appeal refused (1997), 89 B.C.A.C. 92 (note) (S.C.C.), reversing (1994), 23 C.C.L.T. (2d) 70, [1995] 2 W.W.R. 115 (B.C. S.C.).

79 Note that this case is similar to *Cooper v. Hobart* and *Edwards v. Law Society of Upper Canada*, above, and in view of the Supreme Court's approach in those cases, could now be analyzed as a "no duty" case based on lack of "proximity".

is skilled in the subject matter. As was stated in one case, "the comparative knowledge, skill and judgment of the respective parties in regard to the particular matter" is of importance when applying the principle of *Hedley Byrne*.[80] *Hedley Byrne* does not impose a duty of care with respect to speech unless it is foreseeable that this speech will influence the conduct of its recipient. This will not be so when the recipient's own knowledge or experience makes reliance unreasonable and hence unforeseeable. An important judgment which illustrates this is *The Pas v. Porky Packers Ltd.*[81] The Supreme Court of Canada held that "it is a requisite for liability under the *Hedley Byrne* principle that the representations be made to a person who has not expert knowledge himself by a person whom the representee believes has a particular skill or judgment in the matter."[82]

(iv) Nature of the Occasion

Another factor which goes to the issue of the special relationship is the nature of the occasion during which the advice was offered. As conceded in *Hedley Byrne* itself, there is an important difference between advice given on a social or informal occasion and that given as part of a professional or business relationship.[83] Although there are no rigid rules, there is no question that the seriousness of the occasion is an important factor in determining the special relationship issue. Advice given during an informal, social, or non-business occasion will likely not give rise to a duty on the part of the advisor.[84]

(v) Request

Although ordinarily advice will be offered as a result of a specific request or inquiry, it is not necessary that there be a request in order to impose a duty of care. This matter is of considerable importance, however, since without the re-

---

80 See *John Bosworth Ltd. v. Pro. Syndicated Dev. Ltd.* (1979), 97 D.L.R. (3d) 112 at 122-23 (Ont. H.C.). Since, however, the question of the skill of the advisee is also relevant to the issue of causation, i.e., was there in fact reliance on the advice, as well as contributory negligence, i.e., was the advisee partly at fault for having followed the advice, it is often not dealt with as an aspect of the duty of care issue.

81 (1976), 65 D.L.R. (3d) 1 (S.C.C.).

82 *Ibid.*, at 13.

83 As with the other factors relating to the reasonableness of the reliance, this can also be looked at as a matter which goes to the question of causation or contributory negligence.

84 See, e.g., *John Bosworth Ltd. v. Pro. Syndicated Dev. Ltd.* (1980), 97 D.L.R. (3d) 112 (Ont. H.C.). In *Howard Marine v. Ogden & Sons*, [1978] Q.B. 574 at 591 (C.A.), Lord Denning stated that "representations made during a casual conversation in the street; or in a railway carriage; or an impromptu opinion given offhand; or 'off the cuff' on the telephone" are excluded from the principle of *Hedley Byrne*. The issue is whether it appears that the information given is "unconsidered" and would not reasonably be relied upon. In *Ruffolo v. Mulroney*, Ont. Prov. Ct., Doc. York 363/88, Thomson Prov. J., June 28th 1988, an action based on reliance on election promises was struck out. The trial judge held that even most gullible of voters would be foolish to rely solely on candidates' statements! In *Shirlyn Fishing Co. v. Pumps & Power Ltd.* (1990), 3 C.C.L.T. (2d) 304, the B.C. Court of Appeal held that an enquiry made over the telephone by a caller, who did not identify himself, to an employee, who also was unidentified, concerning the capacity of a pump, owned by the caller, was insufficient to give rise to a duty. As stated by Macdonald J.A., at 316: "a 'reasonably prudent and skeptical person' would not think that this information, given to an unidentified enquirer, carried a conviction of any legal weight."

quirement of a request or inquiry specifically responded to by the advisor, there is the danger of extending liability beyond desirable limits.

The matter has arisen in two contexts. First, advice may be offered even though no one asked for it. This issue was dealt with in *392980 Ont. Ltd. v. Welland.*[85] Although the parties disputed the fact, the court found that the defendant city, through its solicitor, sent zoning information to a developer, even though this information had not been previously sought. The court, cautioning that "ordinary prudence would make it rare for persons to give information or advice . . unless requested to do so",[86] nevertheless held that where the advice is given to someone whom the representor knows or ought to know will rely on it, and assuming that the other requirements of *Hedley Byrne* are met, a duty to take care will arise.[87] This approach is sensible. Where the reasonable person knows or ought to know that advice will be relied upon, the fact that the advice was not specifically requested ought to be of no importance.

More problematic is the situation where the advice offered has either been used by persons or for purposes other than those for which it was prepared. It is in these situations where the concern for indeterminate liability is most obvious. Where advice is used by a person who did not request it, or for a purpose other than the one for which it was prepared, it will be more difficult to establish a relationship based either upon reasonable reliance or voluntary assumption of responsibility.[88]

The leading Canadian case is *Haig v. Bamford*,[89] where a financial statement prepared for a company to be used primarily in order to obtain a loan from a governmental institution was shown to other investors who relied upon it. The Supreme Court of Canada decided that, as long as there was foreseeable reliance on the statement by a "limited class" of persons actually known to the defendant, any person within that class, whether individually known or not by the advisor,

---

85 (1984), 6 D.L.R. (4th) 151 (Ont. H.C.).

86 *Ibid.*, at 159.

87 See also *Foster Advertising Ltd. v. Keenberg* (1987), 38 C.C.L.T. 309 (Man. C.A.), reversing (1986), 27 D.L.R. (4th) 141 (Man. Q.B.) — chairman of a race track not liable for statements made during a press conference called to alleviate concerns about the future of the track; *Executive Hldg. Ltd. v. Swift Current*, [1985] 1 W.W.R. 341 (Sask. Q.B.) — public statements concerning downtown development schemes giving rise to a special relationship with those who would reasonably rely on such statements; *Sirois v. Fed. des Enseignants du N.-B.* (1984), 28 C.C.L.T. 280 (N.B. Q.B.) — advice in news bulletin regarding eligibility for unemployment insurance benefits giving rise to special relationship; *Dixon v. Deacon Morgan McEwen Easson* (1993), 102 D.L.R. (4th) 1 (B.C. C.A.) — press release presenting a false picture of the company giving rise to liability to a person who relied upon it. *Cf. Dorsch v. Weyburn* (1985), 23 D.L.R. (4th) 379 (Sask. C.A.).

88 Note, however, the approach of the Supreme Court in *Hercules Management Ltd.*, as discussed above. Despite the fact that the investors used the audited financial statement for a purpose other than the one for which it was prepared, the Supreme Court held that their reliance was both reasonable and foreseeable. Thus, the issue of indeterminate liability had to be resolved at stage two of the test.

89 (1977), 72 D.L.R. (3d) 68 (S.C.C.). This judgment should now be compared with the Court's judgment in *Hercules Management*.

would be owed a duty of care.[90] The Supreme Court reaffirmed this principle, within the context of the provision of engineering services, in *Edgeworth Construction Ltd. v. N.D. Lea & Associates Ltd.*[91] In this case, an engineering firm which negligently had prepared a tender package which it knew would be relied upon by a definable group of persons, i.e. tenderers, was liable to one of them for losses which it suffered.[92]

Where advice is given without it being reasonably foreseeable that it would be relied upon by that plaintiff, or for the purpose of that transaction, the duty does not arise. In *Clarkson Co. v. Penny & Keenleyside Appraisals Ltd.*,[93] for example, the court held that a reasonable person contemplating lending money on the security of property would not rely on an appraisal of that property prepared not for that purpose, but for purposes of possible development.[94] As well, in *Can. Commercial Bank v. Crawford, Smith & Swallow*,[95] the court held that financial statements prepared for the use of a company and the company's institutional lender could not become the basis for a cause of action brought against the accountants by a second bank, which took over from the original lending bank. The concern of the court was that since the accountants did not know that its client had switched banks, or that it was even contemplating such a move, it would be unfair to saddle them with the larger potential loss that a new bank could suffer if there was an error with the financial statements.[96] It is arguable

---

90 This was followed in *Snow v. Cumby* (1986), 31 D.L.R. (4th) 192 (Nfld. C.A.), where a property appraisal was undertaken pursuant to an application to insure a mortgage loan. The defendant knew that this property appraisal report would be relied upon by both the mortgagor and mortgagee to determine the property's value and the deficiencies in the property which required repair, in assessing the size of the loan and in determining the proper purchase price for the property.

91 (1993), 17 C.C.L.T. (2d) 101 (S.C.C.).

92 The more interesting aspect of the decision was the Supreme Court's decision not to hold the individual engineers liable, and the manner in which the court dealt with the contract/tort interface. See discussion later. A case where engineers were relieved of liability because it was not foreseeable that their report would be used by the plaintiff or persons in the plaintiff's position is *327973 B.C. Ltd. v. HBT Agra Ltd.* (1994), 120 D.L.R. (4th) 726 (B.C. C.A.).

93 [1985] 5 W.W.R. 538 (B.C. S.C.).

94 See also *Foster Advertising Ltd. v. Keenberg*, above, note 87. In *B. Cusano Contracting Inc. v. Bank of Montreal* (2006), [2006] B.C.J. No. 217, 2006 CarswellBC 230 (C.A.), affirming (2004), [2004] B.C.J. No. 2219, 2004 CarswellBC 2488 (S.C.), a bank employee made a representation to a bonding company concerning the financial means of the bank's client who was embarking on a construction project. The bond was required by a contractor. It was obtained and the project was commenced. When the owner ceased to make payments, the contractor sued the bank. The court dismissed the claim, finding that the bank owed no duty to the contractor. The bank could not foresee that the letter which it provided to the bonding company would be shown to the contractor. The Court of Appeal affirmed the trial judgment.

95 (1993), 15 C.C.L.T. (2d) 273 (Ont. Gen. Div.), affirmed (1994), 21 C.C.L.T. (2d) 89 (Ont. C.A.), leave to appeal to S.C.C. refused (1994), 21 C.C.L.T. (2d) 89n (S.C.C.).

96 The trial judge held, at 15 C.C.L.T. (2d) 283-84, that there was no duty either under the *Haig v. Bamford* test, i.e. actual knowledge of the limited class of which the plaintiff was a part, or the *Caparo Industries Plc. v. Dickman*, [1990] 2 A.C. 605 (H.L.) test, i.e. being a member of an identifiable class specifically in connection with a particular transaction or transactions of a particular kind. See also *Roynat Inc. v. Dunwoody & Co.* (1993), 18 C.C.L.T. (2d) 43 (B.C. S.C.), where, on motion for summary judgment, an action brought by a lender against accountants for allegedly negligently prepared annual reports was dismissed, on the basis of the test in

that as a result of the approach followed by the Supreme Court of Canada in *Hercules Management*, another way of now resolving these types of cases would be by utilizing stage two of the duty test. Where statements are used by persons other than those for whom the statements were prepared, or for purposes for which they were not prepared, the issue of indeterminate liability arises.

(vi) Nature of Advice

It has been held that the duty to take care in giving advice relates solely to statements of fact, as opposed to opinion or forecasting. In *Andronyk v. Williams*,[97] the Manitoba Court of Appeal held that statements describing land as "improved land" amounted to an opinion concerning the quality of the land, and hence, were not covered by *Hedley Byrne*.[98] The issue as to whether opinions or statements relating to future events or expectations can form the basis of a *Hedley Byrne* claim was also discussed, without resolution, by Iacobucci J. in *Queen v. Cognos*. It was unnecessary to decide the point because the relevant misrepresentations in the case dealt with existing facts.

I would suggest that it would be unwise to state categorically that opinions or statements about future events cannot form the basis of a *Hedley Byrne* claim. Opinions or speculations about the future generally are based upon one's assertion or implication about existing facts, which, of course, can form the bases of a claim.[99] It would seem that any effort to clearly distinguish between statements that qualify as fact, as contrasted with opinion, would be so fraught with difficulty that it would best be avoided. The distinction has not been raised in the vast majority of *Hedley Byrne* cases, and it is well to recall that the judgment in *Hedley*

Haig v. Bamford. As well in *Rangen Inc. v. Deloitte & Touche* (1994), 21 C.C.L.T. (2d) 92 (B.C. C.A.), a claim by a creditor who extended credit based upon reliance on audited financial statements was struck out. It thus appears that the courts will be restrictive as to the class of persons who will be permitted to rely on financial statements. A more unusual claim arose in *Kovacvich v. Ortho Pharmaceuticals (Can.) Ltd.* (1995), 25 C.C.L.T. (2d) 295 (B.C. S.C.), additional reasons at (August 29, 1995), Doc. Rossland 2324 (B.C. S.C.). The biological father claimed that a special relationship arose between himself and his partner's doctor concerning birth control advice which his partner received. The court dismissed the action, the trial judge finding that there was no reliance relationship between the doctor and his patient's partner.

97 (1985), 35 C.C.L.T. 38 (Man. C.A.).

98 O'Sullivan J.A. did concede that some statements concerning the quality of goods, if intermingled with facts, might be covered.

99 See Alberta Court of Appeal's judgments in *Kelly v. Lundgard* (2001), 202 D.L.R. (4th) 385 (Alta. C.A.), where the point is made that merely because a medical-legal report makes a prognostication about a patient's future medical condition does not mean that it is not subject to an action for negligent statement. The prognosis is made based upon an assessment of existing facts, which can be done negligently. As stated by Conrad J.A.: "a prediction which misstates or implies an existing fact can be a misrepresentation". Also see *Hayes v. Schimpf* (2005), 36 C.C.L.T. (3d) 203 (B.C. C.A), affirming (2004), 24 R.P.R. (4th) 235 (B.C. S.C.), where a vendor's inaccurate projections about the profitability of an Echinacea farm led to a successful negligent misrepresentation claim. The court's judgment seems to be based on the inaccurate representations as to the knowledge and experience of the vendor, rather than on the mere fact that the projections were inaccurate. A similar point is made in *Ismail v. Treats Inc.* (2004), 21 C.C.L.T. (3d) 279 (N.S. S.C.).

Byrne itself dealt with statements of information or advice about the credit worthiness of a third party.[100]

The cases illustrate the difficulty inherent in such a distinction. Some, relying on the principle that speculation or opinion on future events cannot form the basis of a negligent statement claim, have dismissed the action.[101] Others, however, have recognized that merely because the representation relates to the future does not automatically exclude a *Hedley Byrne* claim.[102] Nevertheless, the point raised by the Manitoba Court of Appeal in *Andronyk* has validity if seen as simply an additional factor in determining the existence of a duty. One can agree that the more arguable or speculative a statement is, and the less it is based on an assessment of ascertainable facts, the less reasonable reliance on this statement will be, to the point that any reliance at all might legitimately be considered as unreasonable.

An interesting case is *David v. Halifax (Regional Municipality)*.[103] The plaintiffs, a group of property owners, sued the general manager of a regional water commission, as well as the commission itself. The community members were told by the defendant that if they gave their approval for a proposal to extend water service to their community, money would be returned to them in the form of reduced frontage fees, if the project's cost came in under budget. On the basis of this representation, the plaintiffs approved the project.[104] Ultimately, however,

---

100 See Irvine's annotation on *Andronyk v. Williams* at 35 C.C.L.T. 38.

101 See for example *Freedman v. Brodzik* (2001), [2001] O.J. No. 4714, 2001 CarswellOnt 4268 (S.C.J.); *Bhairo v. Westfair Foods Ltd.* (1997), 115 Man. R. (2d) 234 (C.A.), additional reasons at (1997), 118 Man. R. (2d) 172 (C.A.); and *Canadian Community Reading Plan Inc. v. Quality Service Programs Inc.* (1999), 50 B.L.R. (2d) 303 (Ont. S.C.J.), reversed (2001), 10 B.L.R. (3d) 45 (Ont. C.A.), additional reasons at (2001), 2001 CarswellOnt 853 (C.A.).

102 See, for example, *Apex Mountain Resort Ltd. v. British Columbia* (2000), 50 C.C.L.T. (2d) 123 (B.C. S.C.), additional reasons at (2001), 2001 CarswellBC 600 (S.C.), affirmed (2001), 6 C.C.L.T. (3d) 157 (B.C. C.A.); *Beenham v. Rigel Oil & Gas Ltd.* (1998), [1999] 6 W.W.R. 28 (Alta. Q.B.), additional reasons at (1998), 240 A.R. 122 (Q.B.), as well as other cases discussed in this section. In *Smith v. Union of Icelandic Fish Producers Ltd. (S.I.F.)* (2005), 34 C.C.L.T. (3d) 167 (N.S. C.A.), reversing in part (2004), 2004 CarswellNS 300, 224 N.S.R. (2d) 358 (S.C.), the plaintiff relied on a statement that there was a job for him with the defendant company. This statement was made within the context of negotiations for the sale of the plaintiff's company to the defendant. The plaintiff never received employment. Conceding that "the distinction between representations as to future events and those relating to present facts can be elusive", Cromwell J.A. held that this statement was actionable. It implied that at the time the statement was made, the defendant's intention was to employ the plaintiff in the future. This was found to be an inaccurate, untrue, or misleading statement, since the defendant never did have the intention to employ the plaintiff. See also *Kerr v. Danier Leather Inc.* (2004), 23 C.C.L.T. (3d) 77 (Ont. S.C.J.), at 93-94, where the above text is quoted with approval. This case is interesting because it deals not only with the common law, but also with provisions of the Securities Act, R.S.O. 1990, c. S.5, which provide for statutory civil liability for negligent misrepresentations contained in a prospectus. The Court of Appeal found that the trial judge had misinterpreted the disclosure requirements and this was affirmed by the Supreme Court of Canada. See *Kerr v. Danier Leather Inc.* (2007), [2007] S.C.J. No. 44, 2007 CarswellOnt 6445 (S.C.C.), affirming (2005), 77 O.R. (3d) 321 (C.A.).

103 (2004), 27 C.C.L.T. (3d) 213 (N.S. C.A.), leave to appeal refused (2005), 2005 CarswellNS 187 (S.C.C.), reversing in part (2003), 41 M.P.L.R. (3d) 30, 216 N.S.R. (2d) 325 (N.S. C.A.).

104 The community's approval also resulted in the provincial government's release of money to the local authority for the project.

the excess funds were not returned by the public authority, but were used for the purpose of extending water service to another community. The action for negligent misstatement was successful both at trial and on appeal. Although the trial judge conceded that "political promises" are unenforceable and cannot be made the subject of enforcement by the court, the defendant's statement that frontage fees would be reduced from excess funds was a representation as to the policy or practice of the public authority. This was found to be an inaccurate, untrue or misleading representation of an existing fact, since there was no such policy or practice. The defendant commission was liable vicariously for its manager's misrepresentation. One can see from this case that the distinction between a statement of an existing fact, which has implications for the future, and speculative comments about what will happen in the future, can be a fine one.

(d) Inaccurate or Misleading Statement

Once having established the special relationship, the plaintiff has to prove that the defendant's statement was inaccurate or misleading. Though not often in issue in the cases, this requirement must not be overlooked.[105]

The accuracy of the statement must be assessed as of the time it was made. A statement which, although accurate at the time, becomes inaccurate due to subsequent developments, does not satisfy the requirement of inaccuracy. Thus, there was no liability when a defendant school board induced the plaintiff to leave a previous job to come and work for it, assuring the plaintiff that despite the possibility of a grievance being filed by a union relating to the hiring, he had "nothing to worry about." Based on past experience, this prediction about what would happen in the future concerning the grievance could not be said to have been inaccurate.[106] Similarly, public statements concerning a proposed downtown redevelopment scheme which resulted in financial losses to the plaintiff were not adjudged to have been inaccurate or misleading merely because the development never ultimately occurred.[107] If there is a change in circumstances, however, an obligation to communicate these changes can arise. In *De Groot v. St. Boniface General Hospital*,[108] for example, the defendant was held liable, not for an initial

---

105 The two issues of whether it was reasonable for the defendant to have relied upon the statement and whether the statement was inaccurate can overlap, when it comes to dealing with opinions or forecasts. As discussed above, although opinions about the future are not in themselves actionable, if they imply existing facts or intentions, these can be. Thus, judgments dealing with the actionability of negligent opinions or forecasts can focus in on the question of reasonable reliance; i.e., is it reasonable to rely on an opinion? Or on inaccuracy; i.e., can an opinion be inaccurate? Liability for a statement that is truly only an opinion and does not imply an existing state of facts can be denied either because it is not reasonable to rely on it or it cannot, by its nature, be seen as inaccurate.

106 See *Williams v. Saanich Sch. Dist. 63* (1986), 37 C.C.L.T. 203 (B.C. S.C.), affirmed 14 B.C.L.R. (2d) 141 (B.C. C.A.). Perhaps it would be better to explain this case by conceding that although the statement turned out to be inaccurate, there was no negligence on the part of the representor in making it. See the discussion in *Queen v. Cognos Inc.*, above, concerning "negligence".

107 *Executive Hldg. Ltd. v. Swift Current*, [1985] 1 W.W.R. 341 (Sask. Q.B.).

108 (1993), 15 C.C.L.T. (2d) 287 (Man. Q.B.), varied as to damages [1994] 6 W.W.R. 541 (Man. C.A.).

representation concerning the plaintiff's job prospects, but for failing to advise him when there was a significant change in those prospects.[109]

The requirement of inaccuracy explains why it is difficult to base an action upon opinions as opposed to statements of fact. Statements of opinion or forecasting cannot be shown to be inaccurate at the time they were made, although one may be liable for the implications of fact upon which these opinions are based.[110]

A statement which is accurate on its surface may become actionable if it leads to a misinterpretation reasonably drawn from it. Thus, information concerning the zoning of certain land parcels, although accurate as to these, is actionable if the informant knows or ought to realize that the recipient of the information will reasonably interpret the information as applicable to other differently zoned parcels of land as well.[111] It has also been held that the misrepresentation need not occur as a result of an expressed statement. The misrepresentation may occur "by implication from circumstances."[112] Thus, a failure to warn of a dangerous situation has been held to be an implicit misrepresentation of safety.[113] In *Queen v. Cognos Inc.*, Iacobucci J. rejected the submission that "representations which depend on implications or inferences cannot give rise to actionable negligence under the *Hedley Byrne* doctrine".[114] Rather, a "flexible" approach was held to

---

109 The need to advise of a change of course must depend upon the facts. In this case, the plaintiff wrote to the defendant concerning his proposed position, after the defendant already knew that the circumstances concerning the scope of the position had changed. In a reply letter to the plaintiff, the defendant did not mention the changes. Thus, the court held that the failure to communicate the changes misled the plaintiff into believing that things were still as he expected. Also see *Brar v. Mutti*, [1994] B.C.J. No. 2426 (B.C. S.C.) — although the initial representations made by the advisor represented the true extent of his knowledge at the time, once he became aware of different conditions, he was obliged to communicate this information to the advisee. See also *Raypath Resources Ltd. v. Toronto Dominion Bank* (1995), 170 A.R. 109, 1995 CarswellAlta 655 (Q.B.), affirmed (1996), 135 D.L.R. (4th) 261 (Alta. C.A.) — bank liable for negligent statement for failing to advise plaintiff of its internal decision to reduce the plaintiff's credit limit.

110 In *Petro-Can. Inc. v. Capot-Blanc* (1992), 95 D.L.R. (4th) 69 (B.C. S.C.), a complicated issue arose as to whether a sale of gasoline and diesel fuel to an Indian band was exempt from taxes. The plaintiff sold the fuel based on the representation given to it by the band that it was exempt, but the company later paid these taxes to the appropriate governments. It sued the band. The action was dismissed on a variety of grounds, including the fact that the representation was an opinion of law and not a statement of fact, was not false, and was not relied upon.

111 See *392980 Ont. Ltd. v. Welland* (1984), 6 D.L.R. (4th) 151 (Ont. H.C.). In *Yaholnitsky v. Canada (Min. of Employment & Immigration)* (1993), 65 F.T.R. 83 (Fed. T.D.), the plaintiff's argument that she was misled by a letter sent to her concerning the assessment of her maternity benefits was rejected. The court held that the information which she was given was accurate and any misinterpretation of it by the plaintiff was of her own doing.

112 See *Doherty v. Allen* (1988), 55 D.L.R. (4th) 746 at 752 (N.B. C.A.), where this phrase, used by Lord Reid in *Hedley Byrne*, is quoted with approval.

113 *Doherty v. Allen, ibid.*

114 Above, at 148.

be preferable, whereby, "in appropriate circumstances, implied misrepresentations can, and often do, give rise to actionable negligence".[115]

(e) Negligence

An advisor does not guarantee the accuracy of the statement made, but is only required to exercise reasonable care with respect to it.[116] As with the issue of standard of care in negligence in general, this is a question of fact which must be determined according to the circumstances of the case. Taking into account the nature of the occasion, the purpose for which the statement was made, the foreseeable use of the statement, the probable damage which will result from an inaccurate statement, the status of the advisor and the level of competence generally observed by others similarly placed, the trier of fact will determine whether the advisor was negligent.[117]

The issue of the appropriate standard of care required by advisors, although a matter frequently ignored in the case law, was discussed by Mr. Justice Iacobucci in *Queen v. Cognos Inc.* Iacobucci J. noted that the standard is higher than one

---

115 *Ibid.* In *Opron Construction Co. v. Alberta* (1994), 151 A.R. 241 (Q.B.), Feehan J. suggested the following test: would a reasonable person in the same circumstances have drawn the same inference as did the plaintiff? Note that a "statement" need not necessarily be in the form of words. In *Birchwood Pontiac Buick Ltd. v. Hasid* (1997), 35 C.C.L.T. (2d) 54 (Man. Q.B.), a replacement odometer that did not correctly describe a car's mileage led to liability. In addition, the representation need not be a positive statement. It has been held that a failure to divulge information, or to give full information, may be as misleading as a positive misstatement. See *Spinks v. R.* (1996), 134 D.L.R. (4th) 223 (Fed. C.A.); and *Deraps v. Labourer's Pension Fund of Central & Eastern Canada (Trustees of)* (1999), 179 D.L.R. (4th) 168 (Ont. C.A.). In *Hembruff v. Ontario Municipal Employees Retirement Board* (2005), 260 D.L.R. (4th) 161 (Ont. C.A.), leave to appeal refused (2006), 2006 CarswellOnt 2357 (S.C.C.), an action brought by retired employees against pension plan administrators for their failure to inform them of possible future changes to the plan was dismissed. The court held that although there was a duty relationship, the information given to them when they were deciding whether to retire was not untrue, inaccurate or misleading. The Board had no obligation to disclose this type of speculative information.

116 As has been pointed out, this, and not the statement's accuracy, is what the plaintiff is relying upon. See Blom, "Economic Loss: Curbs on the Way Ahead" (1987), 12 Can. Bus. L.J. 275.

117 This paragraph was quoted with approval by Iacobucci J. in *Queen v. Cognos Inc.*, above, at 142. See *Hodgins v. Hydro-Elec. Comm. of Nepean* (1975), 60 D.L.R. (3d) 1 (S.C.C.); *Bell v. Sarnia (City)* (1987), 37 D.L.R. (4th) 438 (Ont. H.C.). Also see *Barrett v. Reynolds* (1998), 170 N.S.R. (2d) 201 (C.A.), leave to appeal refused (1999), 183 N.S.R. (2d) 198 (note) (S.C.C.), where these factors are applied by Cromwell J.A. in determining that a bank employee's advice to a customer was negligently given. The issue of the standard of care required of professional advisors is an important one that will be discussed below in Chapter 9. The case law, such as *ter Neuzen v. Korn* (1995), 127 D.L.R. (4th) 577 (S.C.C.) and *Kripps v. Touche Ross & Co.*, 35 C.C.L.T. (2d) 60, [1997] 6 W.W.R. 421 (B.C. C.A.), leave to appeal refused (1997), 102 B.C.A.C. 238 (note) (S.C.C.), indicates that generally approved practise will be accorded great weight unless the matter to be judged is one capable of being determined by the ordinary person. In *Kripps*, the B.C. Court of Appeal held that 'generally approved auditing practises' will not insulate an auditor from liability where the auditor knows that although financial statements were prepared in accordance with 'gaap', they misrepresented the financial position of the company. Also see *Kelly v. Lundgard*, above, note 99, where the issue of the standard of care required of a physician in preparing a medical-legal report was extensively explored.

of common honesty. This must be so; otherwise only deliberately dishonest statements, which at any event probably would lead to an action in fraud, could be the basis of liability. It is an objective standard based on the hypothetical "reasonable person".[118] It is not sufficient that the advisor reasonably believed in the accuracy of the advice, or lived up to his or her own standards.[119]

(f) Reliance

Under the traditional application of *Hedley Byrne*, a defendant will not be held liable for negligent speech, even where there is a duty to take care, unless the plaintiff can prove actual reliance on the misrepresentation which caused the damage. In the absence of reliance, the plaintiff is normally unable to prove that losses were caused by the defendant's negligence.[120]

Although the burden of proving reliance falls upon the plaintiff, the court can infer reliance from facts of the case where appropriate. Thus in *Kripps v. Touche Ross & Co.*,[121] the British Columbia Court of Appeal held that where a statement was calculated or where it would naturally tend to induce the plaintiff to rely on it, an inference of reliance may be drawn by the court.[122]

There also have been indications in a few cases that the principle of *Hedley Byrne* can be extended to non-reliance situations. Thus, in *Whittingham v. Crease & Co.*,[123] a solicitor who negligently drafted a will was held liable to a plaintiff whose bequest under that will was invalid. The principle of *Hedley Byrne* was applied to this case, and the concept of reliance significantly relaxed in order to provide compensation to the plaintiff.[124] More significantly, similar subsequent cases have acknowledged the absence of reliance on the part of a potential

---

118 See discussion in Chapter 9.

119 For an excellent analysis of the standard of care required by an owner to a tenderer, with respect to tender documents, see Feehan J.'s judgment in *Opron Construction v. Alberta*, above, note 115.

120 See, e.g., *Hanas v. Molnar*, [1985] 2 W.W.R. 475 (Sask. Q.B.); *Excellon Indust. v. Dunwoody Ltd./Dunwoody Ltée* (1985), 33 Man. R. (2d) 117 (Q.B.). In *Loof v. Thompson*, [1994] B.C.J. No. 475, the plaintiff made an offer to purchase a property which had been advertised as zoned for a hotel. This was incorrect; hotel use was not permitted. The plaintiff sued. The court found that as the plaintiff had never intended to operate a hotel, the misrepresentation was not relevant to his decision to purchase the property, and the action was dismissed. In *Howael Ventures (1984) Inc. v. Arthur Andersen & Co.*, [1996] 7 W.W.R. 382 (Man. Q.B.), additional reasons at [1997] 3 W.W.R. 256 (Man. Q.B.), an action by a lender against accountants was dismissed because there was no proof that the lender had relied on financial statements in deciding to advance the loan. In *Carom v. Bre-X Minerals Ltd.* (1998), 43 C.C.L.T. (2d) 310 (Ont. Gen. Div.), it was held that Canadian tort law did not recognize a "fraud on the market" theory that would create a rebuttable presumption of reliance by plaintiffs on misrepresentations affecting the price of a company's shares.

121 (1997), 35 C.C.L.T. (2d) 60 (B.C. C.A.), leave to appeal refused (1997), 102 B.C.A.C. 238 (note) (S.C.C.), reversing (1995), 24 C.C.L.T. (2d) 135 (B.C. S.C.).

122 Also see *Chan v. GMS Datalink International Corp.* (1998), [1998] B.C.J. No. 1550, 1998 CarswellBC 1445 (S.C.). Note that proving reliance is essentially proving causation, and as with other cases of proving cause, courts can infer it from direct or indirect evidence, or can adjust the plaintiff's burden of proof. See discussion on cause in Chapter 11 below.

123 (1978), 6 C.C.L.T. 1 (B.C. S.C.).

124 For a criticism, see Klar, "A Comment on Whittingham v. Crease" (1978), 6 C.C.L.T. 311.

beneficiary to a negligently drafted will, but have, nevertheless, upheld the liability of solicitors in these situations.[125]

It is submitted that a relationship of reliance and actual reliance are necessary elements of a *Hedley Byrne* claim. On the other hand, it is clear that courts have been willing to extend negligence liability for purely economic losses in non-*Hedley Byrne* relationships where this has appeared to be sound policy. *Hedley Byrne* has been used by these courts as illustrative of the common law's willingness to extend purely economic loss recovery for a variety of relationships which do not raise problems of indeterminate liability.[126]

(g) Damage Caused by the Reliance

As with other actions based on negligence, it must be proved by the plaintiff that it suffered damage as a result of the defendant's breach of its duty.[127] Generally this has not proved to be a problem in the negligent statement area. However, if a plaintiff fails to show that it suffered damage as a result of its reliance on the defendant's statement, its action will fail.[128]

---

125 See especially *White v. Jones*, [1995] 2 W.L.R. 187 (H.L.); *Ross v. Caunters*, [1979] 3 All E.R. 580 (Ch. D.). In *Yorkshire Trust Co. v. Empire Accept. Corp. Ltd. (Receiver of)* (1986), 24 D.L.R. (4th) 410 (B.C. S.C.), McLachlin J. held that reliance is an unnecessary element of a negligence action based upon the performance of a service, which in this case was property appraisal for mortgage purposes, where other factors in the case establish the necessary relationship of proximity and causal connection in order to attract liability. See, however, *Kamahap Ent. Ltd. v. Chu's Central Market Ltd.*, [1990] 1 W.W.R. 632 (B.C. C.A.), where Taylor J.A. reaffirmed the traditional approach that, absent reliance or some other reason for imposing a duty, there will be no recovery merely because the economic loss suffered by the plaintiff as a result of the defendant solicitor's negligence was foreseeable. The "disappointed beneficiary" cases are discussed below.

126 See discussion on "liability for negligent performance of services", below.

127 While they overlap, the issues of reliance and damages caused by the reliance raise different concerns. The plaintiff must first prove that it relied on the advice, i.e., acted upon it, and second, that this reliance caused it financial damage. Thus where the plaintiff would have done the same thing even if the advice that had been given was accurate, the plaintiff cannot establish reliance on the negligent advice. Where, on the other hand, the plaintiff can establish that the decision to act was based on the negligent advice, but cannot establish that his or her financial position would have been better had he/she not acted upon it, the plaintiff has been unable to establish damage. See discussion below.

128 See, for example, *Roncato v. Caverly* (1991), 84 D.L.R. (4th) 303 (Ont. C.A.). The plaintiff sued its accountants for advising it that a person would be a reliable bookkeeper. The person was dishonest and stole money from the plaintiff. The company went bankrupt. The Court of Appeal held that the plaintiff was unable to prove that the cause of its bankruptcy was due to the bookeeper's minor thefts, and dismissed the action. In *Green v. Royal Bank* (1996), 135 D.L.R. (4th) 337 (Ont. Gen. Div.), the plaintiff sued a bank for negligently misrepresenting that an insurer had provided life insurance on her husband's life, relating to a mortgage loan. The husband died uninsured. The court awarded only nominal damages for breach of contract, since there was no proof that that the husband could have obtained insurance from another insurer. Also see *Blais v. Royal Bank* (January 31, 1997), Doc. 1291/92, [1997] O.J. No. 2288 (Gen. Div.). In *Stasiuk v. Sun Life Assurance Co. of Canada,* [2001] 6 W.W.R. 339 (Alta. Q.B.), affirmed 2003 CarswellAlta 425, 2003 ABCA 95 (C.A.), on the other hand, the plaintiff believed that she was the beneficiary of $43,368 of insurance on her husband's life. In fact, the insurance was only $3,368; the Certificate of Insurance was in error. The couple relied on this Certificate for 18 years. The court upheld the claim based on negligent misrepresentation and in the absence of any evidence as to what the couple would have done had they known

(h) Contributory Negligence

The *Hedley Byrne* special relationship is defined as one in which an advisor gives advice to a person who will foreseeably and reasonably rely upon it. This raises the interesting question as to whether the defence of contributory negligence has any role in a *Hedley Byrne* case.

In *Grand Restaurants of Can. Ltd. v. Toronto*,[129] it was held that "there is a distinction at law between reasonable reliance as a necessary prerequisite to ground liability, to constitute the cause of action under *Hedley Byrne*, and reliance in the context of contributory negligence as simply a factor going to the *extent* of the damages suffered." In this case, a purchaser of a restaurant business was incorrectly informed by the city, prior to the purchase, that there were no outstanding work orders or building violations with respect to the property. This led to economic losses suffered by the plaintiff when he later rescinded the sale and vacated the premises. The court held that the extent of the plaintiff's reliance on the city's information was unreasonable, and that if he had done what he ought to have done, i.e., made further investigations or more specific inquiries, he would have been alerted to the true information prior to closing the transaction. Nevertheless, the court did not ignore the defendant city's negligence and, pursuant to the Negligence Act,[130] apportioned liability between the parties.[131]

It is difficult to justify this approach. If the plaintiff's reliance was unreasonable, then despite the defendant's negligence, a special relationship between the parties

---

earlier that they only had $3,368 in insurance, the court awarded the plaintiff $10,000 minus the insurance that they did have. Another difficult case is *Webster v. Ernst & Young* (2000), 184 D.L.R. (4th) 619 (B.C. C.A.), leave to appeal refused (2001), 153 B.C.A.C. 160 (note) (S.C.C.). The plaintiffs proved all of the elements of the tort including reliance on the defendants' advice. The plaintiffs were lawyers who had left a law fim based on a Departure Agreement that was drafted based on tax advice given to them by the defendants. The advice was wrong and the plaintiffs' tax liabilities were greater than they had anticipated. The defendants were arguing that the plaintiffs would not have been better off even if they had received correct advice and as a result decided to pursue their original plan of action, which was to leave the firm under the terms of the Partnership Agreement. In the first trial, the action was dismissed on the basis that no damages were proved. The Court of Appeal held, however, that the onus of proving that the plaintiffs were no worse off because of the advice was on the defendants, and it remitted the case to a trial judge. The trial judge again found that no damages were proved; see (2001), 199 D.L.R. (4th) 763 (B.C. S.C.). On a further appeal, however, the Court of Appeal held that the plaintiffs had suffered foreseeable damages as a result of the negligent advice and calculated these damages: (2003), 2003 CarswellBC 334 (C.A.). Another decision placing the burden of proof on the defendant to establish what the plaintiff would have done had the negligent advice not been given is *Gauthier v. Canada (Attorney General)* (2000), 185 D.L.R. (4th) 660 (N.B. C.A.). In this case, the court held that if the defendants were alleging that the plaintiff would have done the same thing—in this case retire—even if he had received correct advice as to the financial effects on him, they had the onus of proving this. Also see discussion of *Rainbow Industrial Caterers v. C.N.R.*, below, note 135.

129 (1981), 123 D.L.R. (3d) 349 at 367 (Ont. H.C.), affirmed (1982), 140 D.L.R. (3d) 191 (Ont. C.A.).

130 R.S.O. 1980, c. 315.

131 There have been several other similar decisions. See, e.g., *Sirois v. Fédération des enseignants du N.-B.* (1984), 28 C.C.L.T. 280 (N.B. Q.B.); *H.B. Nickerson & Sons Ltd. v. Wooldridge* (1980), 115 D.L.R. (3d) 97 (N.S. C.A.); *Spiewak v. 251268 Ont. Ltd.* (1987), 43 D.L.R. (4th) 554 (Ont. H.C.); and *Gallant v. Central Credit Union Ltd.* (1994), 22 C.C.L.T. (2d) 251 (P.E.I. T.D.), additional reasons at (1995), 127 Nfld. & P.E.I.R. 101, 396 A.P.R. 101 (P.E.I. T.D.).

did not exist. We must recall that one of the requirements of a successful *Hedley Byrne* claim, as stated by Iacobucci J. in *Queen v. Cognos Inc.*,[132] is that the representee relied "in a reasonable manner" on the negligent misrepresentation. It is, in my opinion, a contradiction to hold that a plaintiff can be considered to have been reasonable in relying on advice for the purposes of the establishment of a successful claim, but unreasonable for having relied upon it for the purposes of contributory negligence.[133] Only where the plaintiff acts unreasonably in failing

---

132 Above, at 134.

133 This view seems to be supported by Taylor J.A. in *Betker v. Williams*, [1992] 2 W.W.R. 534 (B.C. C.A.). In reference to the contention that plaintiffs who relied upon a realtor's statement were contributorily negligent, Taylor J.A. stated at 541:

> . . . if, as seems clear, they [i.e. the plaintiffs] acted reasonably in relying upon representations made by Mr. Klinkhamer, a matter which I have already dealt with, it cannot, in my view, be said that they ought to have made inquiries to ensure that those representations were reliable.

Also see Lowry J.'s comment in *Kripps v. Touche Ross & Co.* (1998), [1999] 3 W.W.R. 629 (B.C. S.C.) at 633:

> It is not very often that a successful plea of contributory negligence in an answer to an allegation of negligent misstatement can be made. That is because the reliance on the statement, an element essential to found liability, must itself be reasonable. It cannot be said that a person relied reasonably on the statement yet acted unreasonably in relying on it.

Lowry J. conceded that courts do nevertheless apply contributory negligent in negligent statement cases, although he declined to do so in the instant case. The contributory negligence issue is also discussed by Cullity J. in *Transamerica Life Insurance Co. of Canada v. Hutton* (2000), 33 R.P.R. (3d) 1 (Ont. S.C.J.), additional reasons at (2001), 2001 CarswellOnt 6 (S.C.J.). Cullity J. disagrees with the view that a finding of contributory negligence is inconsistent with the existence of reasonable reliance for the establishment of duty. He notes that while reliance can be reasonable for the purpose of duty, it may be excessive in the circumstances or it may not account fully for the plaintiff's behaviour, in which case contributory negligence is a legitimate finding. Also see the Ontario Court of Appeal's decision in *Avco Financial Services Realty Ltd. v. Norman* (2003), 2003 CarswellOnt 1300 (C.A.), leave to appeal refused (2003), 2003 CarswellOnt 5189, 2003 CarswellOnt 5190 (S.C.C.). The trial judge (reported at (2001), 19 B.L.R. (3d) 174) (Ont. S.C.J.)) had found the defendant liable for a negligent misrepresentation but reduced the plaintiff's award by 50 per cent for its own contributory negligence. The plaintiff appealed, arguing that since the trial judge had found reasonable reliance for the purpose of the defendant's liability, it should not have found unreasonable reliance for the purpose of contributory negligence. The plaintiff relied on *Perry v. Clintar Ltd.* (1996), 41 C.B.R. (3d) 90 (Ont. C.A.). The Court of Appeal in *Avco* held that a finding of reasonable reliance for the purpose of duty precludes a finding of contributory negligence only where the plaintiff's alleged negligence relates to the same event that the duty itself relates to; i.e., reliance on the representation. If the plaintiff's negligence relates to another event, for example, something that the plaintiff should have done after the statement was made, but before the plaintiff acted upon it, then contributory negligence can be found. On the facts of *Avco*, the Court of Appeal found that the plaintiff's negligence related to its actual reliance on the representation, which in this case was an omission to explain the conditions of an insurance policy. The Court of Appeal accordingly would not have held the defendant liable in the first place, since there was no reasonable reliance. Since the defendant had not appealed the matter of its own liability, however, the trial judgment stood. See *Mikealice Management Corp. v. De Thomas Financial Corp.* (2003), [2003] O.J. No. 2896, 2003 CarswellOnt 2751 (S.C.), where contributory negligence was found. Also see *Chapeskie v. Canadian Imperial Bank of Commerce* (2004), [2004] B.C.J. No. 523, 2004 CarswellBC 581 (C.A.), where the B.C. Court of Appeal approves of *Avco* although it did not find contributory negligence in this case.

to mitigate damages caused by the breach of a duty should the argument that there ought to be a reduction in damages succeed.[134]

(i) Pre- and Post-Contractual Negligent Misrepresentations

Although the judgments in *Hedley Byrne* seemed to limit the tort duty and special relationship to parties who are not in a contractual relationship, subsequent case law has given *Hedley Byrne* an important role in the area of pre- and post-contractual negligent misrepresentation. It is now clear that a party who claims financial losses resulting from reliance on a negligent statement is not barred from pursuing a claim in tort under *Hedley Byrne* merely because the representations occurred in either a pre- or post-contractual context.[135]

The Supreme Court of Canada has paid particular attention to the problem of negligent misrepresentations made in a pre-contractual setting. The possibility that a contracting party can sue in tort for a negligent misrepresentation leading to the formation of the contract was opened up by the Supreme Court of Canada in its judgment in *Central & Eastern Trust Co. v. Rafuse*.[136] This decision firmly and finally laid to rest any objections to imposing a tort law duty of care to parties in a sufficiently proximate relationship, merely because the parties were also parties in a contractual relationship. The court held, per Le Dain J., that subject to the qualification that "a concurrent or alternative liability in tort will not be admitted if its effect would be to permit the plaintiff to circumvent or escape a contractual exclusion or limitation of liability for the act or omission that would constitute the tort",[137] the plaintiff will be allowed to base a claim on either contract

134 For example, in *Vanderburgh v. ScotiaMcleod Inc.*, [1992] 6 W.W.R. 673 (Alta. Q.B.), the court held that once the plaintiff became aware of the defendant's error it had a duty to mitigate its damages by selling its shares.

135 There have been many cases and commentaries. See, among others, *BG Checo International Ltd. v. B.C. Hydro & Power Authority* (1993), 14 C.C.L.T. (2d) 233 (S.C.C.), application for re-hearing refused (1993), 14 C.C.L.T. (2d) 233n (S.C.C.); *Queen v. Cognos Inc.* (1993), 14 C.C.L.T. (2d) 113 (S.C.C.); *Edgeworth Construction Ltd. v. N.D. Lea & Associates Ltd.* (1993), 17 C.C.L.T. (2d) 101 (S.C.C.); *Rainbow Industrial Caterers Ltd. v. C.N.R.* (1991), 8 C.C.L.T. (2d) 225 (S.C.C.); *Opron Construction Co. v. Alberta* (1994), 151 A.R. 241 (Q.B.); *Kingu v. Walmar Ventures Ltd.* (1986), 38 C.C.L.T. 51 (B.C. C.A.); *Esso Petroleum Co. v. Mardon*, [1976] 2 All E.R. 5 (C.A.); *Sodd Corp. v. Tessis* (1977), 2 C.C.L.T. 245 (Ont. C.A.); *Andronyk v. Williams* (1985), 35 C.C.L.T. 38 (Man. C.A.); *Boulderwood Dev. Co. v. Edwards* (1984), 30 C.C.L.T. 223 (N.S. C.A.); *Herrington v. Kenco Mtge. & Invt. Ltd.* (1981), 125 D.L.R. (3d) 377 (B.C. S.C.); *Hyndman v. Jenkins* (1981), 16 C.C.L.T. 296 (P.E.I. S.C.); *H.B. Nickerson & Sons Ltd. v. Wooldridge* (1980), 115 D.L.R. (3d) 97 (N.S. C.A.); *Nelson Lumber Co. v. Koch* (1980), 13 C.C.L.T. 201 (Sask. C.A.); *Roberts v. Montex Dev. Corp.* (1979), 100 D.L.R. (3d) 660 (B.C. S.C.); *Ronald Elwyn Lister Ltd. v. Dunlop Can. Ltd.* (1978), 19 O.R. (2d) 380, reversed 27 O.R. (2d) 168, which was reversed 41 C.B.R. (N.S.) 272 (S.C.C.); *Friesen v. Berta* (1979), 100 D.L.R. (3d) 91 (B.C. S.C.); *Komarniski v. Marien* (1979), 100 D.L.R. (3d) 81 (Sask. Q.B.); *Sealand of the Pac. Ltd. v. Ocean Cement Ltd.*, [1973] 3 W.W.R. 60, varied (*sub nom. Sealand of the Pac. Ltd. v. Robert C. McHaffie Ltd.*) [1974] 6 W.W.R. 724 (B.C. C.A.). For academic analysis see Rafferty, "Liability for Pre-Contractual Misstatements" (1984), 14 Man. L.J. 63; Schwartz, "Hedley Byrne and Pre-Contractual Misrepresentations: Tort Law to the Aid of Contract?" (1978), 10 Ottawa L. Rev. 581; McLauchlan, "Pre-Contract Negligent Misrepresentation" (1977), 4 Otago L. Rev. 23; Feldthusen, *Economic Negligence*, 5th ed. (2008).

136 (1986), 37 C.C.L.T. 117.

137 *Ibid.*, at 166.

or tort where liability in both exists.[138] Thus, in the context of a pre-contractual negligent representation made between parties who would be considered to be in a *Hedley Byrne* special relationship, unless the terms of the contract preclude it, a breach of the duty can lead to liability in tort.[139]

The consequences of the acceptance of the concurrent liability approach have been explored in recent cases. It has been advantageous for plaintiffs to ignore their contractual remedies and sue in tort for a variety of reasons. One of these has been the advantage which a tort action can give to plaintiffs with respect to the running of their limitation period for bringing the claim.[140]

Another advantage has been the possibility of a more favourable assessment of damages.[141] This was in issue in *Rainbow Industrial Caterers Ltd. v. C.N.R.*[142] In this case, the plaintiff bid on a food catering contract based upon a representation concerning the quantity of meals which would be required. The plaintiff's bid was successful and it entered into the contract. It transpired that the estimate was incorrect and as a result the plaintiff's losses were significant. The plaintiff could have sued in contract, since the representation as to the estimate of meals was a term of the contract, but chose to sue in tort. It did so because the tort measure of damages arguably offered the plaintiff a higher assessment than did the contract measure. The Supreme Court of Canada held that according to the tort measure, the plaintiff was entitled to be put back into the position in which it would have been in had the misrepresentation concerning the estimate of meals not been made. In this case, the court accepted that the plaintiff would not have entered into the contract at all had it been aware of the correct estimate.[143] That being the case, the plaintiff was entitled to all of the losses which it suffered as a result of having entered into the contract. Sopinka J. held, for the majority, that

---

138 The decision clarified *dicta* by Pigeon J. in the earlier case of *J. Nunes Diamonds Ltd. v. Dom. Elec. Protection Co.* (1972), 26 D.L.R. (3d) 699 (S.C.C.), that in order for a contractual party to be able to sue in tort, the tort duty must be "independent" of the contract. The nature of this independence was a source of confusion.

139 The concurrent liability approach also was adopted by the House of Lords in *Henderson v. Merritt Syndicates Ltd.*, [1994] 3 W.L.R. 761, along the lines suggested by Mr. Justice Le Dain in *Central & Eastern Trust v. Rafuse*, above, note 136.

140 This was the problem in *Central & Eastern Trust Co. v. Rafuse*, above, note 136. The tort action against the negligent solicitor commenced running 6 years from the time that the damage caused by the solicitor's negligence became reasonably discoverable. The action in contract arguably arose from the date of the breach itself, which had occurred at a much earlier point in time.

141 On this somewhat complicated question, see McLauchlan, "Assessment of Damages For Misrepresentation Inducing Contracts" (1987), 6 Otago L. Rev. 370; Blom, "Remedies In Tort And Contract: What Is The Difference?", in Berryman, ed., *Remedies: Issues and Perspectives* (1991), Chapter 16.

142 Above, note 135.

143 Sopinka J. did concede that a defendant could attempt to prove that the plaintiff would have entered into the contract had the correct representations been made. It is unclear how easy it would be to discharge this burden. Compare this with the damage assessment in *BG Checo International Ltd. v. British Columbia Hydro & Power Authority* (1994), 109 D.L.R. (4th) 1 (B.C. S.C.), affirmed (1995), 126 D.L.R. (4th) 127 (B.C. C.A.). In this case the court assumed that the contractor would have still entered the contract had the representations been accurate, although it would have adjusted its bid. The damages in tort were therefore based on the losses flowing from the misrepresentation, and not from having entered into the contract in the first place.

this included even those losses which were not caused by the actual misrepresentation.[144] The plaintiff, in other words, was entitled to avoid all of the deleterious consequences of what proved to be a "bad bargain". On a contract measure, however, the plaintiff only would have been entitled to be put back into the position it would have been in had the estimate of meals as represented, been true. Thus, losses not related to the misrepresentation would not have been recoverable.[145]

A basic requirement of the concurrent liability approach is that a tort action cannot be used in order to circumvent a term of a contract. This issue arose, but was easily dealt with, by the Supreme Court of Canada in *Queen v. Cognos Inc.*[146] In this case, the plaintiff was induced to terminate his existing employment, and move to another city, in order to take up a job with the defendant. The inducement was a representation concerning the general nature of the job, and the favourable prospects which it offered for the plaintiff. The representations turned out to be inaccurate, and the plaintiff's new job subsequently was terminated, according to the terms of the contract. As there was no breach of contract, the plaintiff's only recourse was to sue in tort for negligent misrepresentation. The question was whether the terms of the contract dealing with notice, termination, and job security, could be interpreted as implicitly disclaiming any pre-contractual misrepresentations upon which a tort action could be based. The Supreme Court found that these representations dealt with matters separate from the contractual terms relating to job security. As explained by Iacobucci J., it was "the existence, or reality, of the job being interviewed for, not the extent of the appellant's involvement therein"[147] which was at the heart of the tort misrepresentations. These were not items covered by the terms of the contract.[148]

---

144 The plaintiff could have lost money on the contract even if the meal estimate was correct, from such things as employee misconduct, market forces, its own poor performance, or acts of third parties. In other words, it may have been a "bad bargain" for the plaintiff, misrepresentation aside.

145 McLachlin J. dissented. She held that if the defendant could show that some of the losses were not foreseeable or caused by reliance on the misrepresentation, these losses would not be recoverable, either in tort or in contract.

146 (1993), 14 C.C.L.T. (2d) 113 (S.C.C.).

147 *Ibid.*, at 137.

148 Iacobucci J. examined specific terms of the contract which were argued to be disclaimers, and held that these clauses did not disclaim liability for representations made in the pre-contractual negotiations. They dealt with matters relating to the rights and obligations of the parties in the event of job termination or transfer, and not with the type of representations upon which the plaintiff had relied in deciding to join the defendant company. See discussion at 14 C.C.L.T. (2d) 149-56. Although the argument is subtle, it is persuasive. The plaintiff was given inaccurate information about his new job prospects, and relying upon them he signed a new employment contract. Although the contract itself contained no job security protections for the plaintiff, the plaintiff felt confident that, based upon the pre-contractual representations, these were risks which he could reasonably assume. A similar Alberta case in which a contractual exemption clause was held not to bar a tort action for pre-contractual misrepresentations which induced the plaintiff to enter into the employment contract is *Beenham v. Rigel Oil & Gas Ltd.* (1998), [1999] 6 W.W.R. 28 (Alta. Q.B.), additional reasons at (1998), 240 A.R. 122 (Q.B.). A case in which a contract did successfully exclude liability for a negligent pre-contractual misrepresentation is *Monette v. Tramer*, [1999] 9 W.W.R. 467 (Man. Q.B.). The case involved the sale of a house. The vendor had represented that the gas fireplaces were in working order. This was not true. The court however upheld a clause in the contract

The Supreme Court of Canada also has held that the fact that a pre-contractual representation becomes an express term of a contract is not a bar to suing in tort. In *BG Checo International v. B.C. Hydro & Power Authority*,[149] La Forest and McLachlin JJ. held that, as with implied terms, where an express term of a contract is co-extensive with a pre-contractual misrepresentation, the plaintiff has the option of suing in either tort or contract.[150]

Although the leading cases have dealt with pre-contractual misrepresentations, the principles apply equally to post-contractual misrepresentations. A contracting party can sue in negligence for a post-contractual misrepresentation, as long as the elements of the *Hedley Byrne* relationship are established, and the tort action is not being used in order to circumvent a term of the contract.

To summarize the principles emerging from the recent Supreme Court of Canada judgments, one can fairly conclude the following:

(1) A common law duty of care in tort will arise as a result of a relationship of sufficient proximity and it is unimportant in this regard whether the relationship arises in a contractual or non-contractual setting.
(2) A plaintiff can sue a co-contractant in tort for a pre-contractual negligent misrepresentation unless the terms of the contract limit, modify or negate the duty which otherwise would have been owed.
(3) A plaintiff can sue a co-contractant in tort for a pre-contractual negligent misrepresentation, even if the representation being relied upon as the basis of the tort claim, has become an express (or implied) term of the contract.
(4) A party suing in tort for a negligent misrepresentation which also consists of a breach of the contract will benefit from those advantages offered by the tort claim, for example, the applicable limitation period or the manner of assessing the plaintiff's damages.
(5) The same principles apply, where appropriate, to post-contractual misrepresentations.

---

that excluded liability for any representations not specifically noted in the agreement. Also see *Intrawest Corp. v. No. 2002 Taurus Ventures Ltd.*, 281 D.L.R. (4th) 420, 46 C.C.L.T. (3d) 1, [2007] 11 W.W.R. 85 (B.C. C.A.). The Court of Appeal held that "an entire agreement clause" precluded the plaintiff from making a tort claim based on an alleged negligent misrepresentation leading to the contract. Levine J.A. held that although the issue is not an easy one, the circumstances of the case, the entire agreement, the nature of the parties, and other factors must be examined to determine whether the contract alone was intended to govern the relationship between the parties.

149 Above, note 135.

150 The case involved a pre-contractual representation which became an express term of the contract. The term was breached. The issue involved the assessment of damages. Unlike its conclusion in *Queen v. Cognos Inc.*, above, note 136, the court agreed that the contract would have been entered into even if the correct representation had been made. There was a dissenting judgment by Iacobucci J., concurred in by Sopinka J., with reference to the availability of a tort action. According to the dissent, at 14 C.C.L.T. (2d) 275: "If the parties to a contract choose to define a specific duty as an express term of the contract, then the consequences of a breach of that duty ought to be determined by the law of contract, not by tort law." The rule, however, would be open to modification if there were policy concerns, such as unequal bargaining power, or if a non-commercial contract were involved. The result of the judgment was that the case was remitted to trial for assessment of damages, although the dissent would have restricted the assessment based on breach of contract alone.

(j) The Employee's Duty

The concurrent liability thesis, which allows a contracting party to sue either in tort or contract, gives rise to the following interesting question. Can an employee who has negligently performed a contractual obligation undertaken by its employer for the benefit of a client, be sued in tort personally by that client for losses which flow from this negligence?[151]

In order to answer this question, one must look first to the Supreme Court of Canada's judgment in *London Drugs Ltd. v. Kuehne & Nagel International Ltd.*[152] The plaintiff company entered into a contract with the defendant company for the storage of an expensive piece of equipment. The storage contract limited the liability of the defendant company to $40 for damage to the equipment. Two employees of the defendant company negligently damaged the equipment while moving it. The plaintiff brought contract and tort claims against the defendant company, and a tort claim against the employees.

The defendant company's liability, whether based in contract or tort, was subject to the $40 limitation clause. This is consistent with the principle noted above that a tort claim cannot be used in order to circumvent a contractual limitation. The tort liability of the employees, however, raised different issues. First, the Supreme Court was called upon to decide whether, in the circumstances of this case, the employees owed a duty in tort to the plaintiff company. Second, if a tort duty was owed, was it limited by the clause in the contract?

The majority of the court, per Iacobucci J., had little difficulty with the first question.[153] The employees were held "unquestionably" to have owed a duty of care in tort based on the reasonable foreseeability test of *Donoghue v. Stevenson.* The fact that the employees' obligation to take care was related to their own employment duties, as well as to their employer's contractual obligations, did not negate, in the majority's view, the tort duty in the circumstances of this type of case.[154] Having determined that matter, the remainder of the majority's decision dealt with the application of the limitation of liability clause to the employees' tort duty. The court held that the contractual limitation should be extended to limit their tort liability. The court reasoned that (1) where the limitation of liability clause either expressly or impliedly extends its benefit to the employees and (2) where the employees were acting in the course of their employment *and* performing the very services contracted for between the employer and the customer when the loss occurred, the clause ought to be extended to protect the employees.[155]

There was one forceful dissent. La Forest J. emphasized that this case concerned the allocation of the risk of loss in a contractual context. Relying on various policy

151 See C. Gosnell, "The Personal Liability of Corporate Agents: Who Should Bear Pure Economic Loss?" (1997), 55 U.T. Fac. L. Rev. 77, for a broad discussion of this general issue.

152 (1993), 97 D.L.R. (4th) 261 (S.C.C.). Although the case dealt with property damages caused by negligence, the principle which it established has relevance for this discussion on negligent statement and economic losses.

153 The lower courts both held that the employees owed a tort duty, but disagreed as to the effect of the limitation of liability clause. See B.C. Court of Appeal decision at [1990] 4 W.W.R. 289, and the trial decision at [1986] 4 W.W.R. 183.

154 The majority conceded that this was an ordinary type of negligence case. It was not, in other words, one of the "frontier" areas.

155 See discussion at 97 D.L.R. (4th) 366-67.

reasons relating to such things as an employee's capacity to bear a loss, insurance, and economic efficiency, La Forest J. concluded that employees should be immunized from tort liability in cases such as *London Drugs*. For La Forest J., what was important was not the nature of the damage caused, i.e. property damage or economic loss, but that the negligent conduct and the loss occurred within a commercial context in which the allocation of the risk had been agreed to by the parties.[156]

Somewhat complicating the existing state of Canadian law relating to an employee's tort duty in the contractual setting, however, is the Supreme Court of Canada's second judgment on this matter, *Edgeworth Construction Ltd. v. N.D. Lea & Associates Ltd.*[157] In this case, the plaintiff contractor sued an engineering firm and engineers personally for negligence in the preparation of design work and specifications for a highway project. The work was contracted for by another party, the Crown, but it was intended for use by the bidding contractors. The contract documents between the contractor and the Crown also ultimately incorporated these plans. While the Supreme Court of Canada allowed the contractor's tort claim for negligent misrepresentation against the engineering firm,[158] it disallowed the tort claim against the individual engineers who had prepared the documents. Without much discussion, and no reference to *London Drugs* on this specific point, the court merely concluded that there was no duty of care between the individual engineers who prepared the documents and the contracting company.[159]

156 La Forest J.'s doctrine of "vicarious immunity" would not apply to all employees' torts. Thus, where the employees' negligence arises independently from the work for which they were hired, they would remain liable. La Forest J.'s dissent is very far ranging in its discussion. McLachlin J. wrote a judgment concurring with the majority result, but she based her reasoning on the doctrine of voluntary assumption of responsibility. La Forest J.'s approach of restricting the employee's liability for torts committed during the course of employment was favoured by the Ontario Court of Appeal in *Douglas v. Kinger (Litigation Guardian of)*, 2008 ONCA 452 (Ont. C.A.), affirming 2006 CarswellOnt 8695 (Ont. S.C.J.). Unlike *London Drugs*, however, the case did not involve a client's action against the employee, but a claim by the employer himself, for the benefit of his insurer, against the employee. The employee, a 13-year-old boy, had negligently burned down the employer's boat house and contents. Lang J.A. applied a duty analysis and held that there was no proximity between the employee and employer to support a duty, and there were policy reasons to negate one. Lang J.A. noted that the result could be different if the employee committed an intentional tort, a "wilful misconduct", or perhaps gross negligence. The trial judge had dismissed the plaintiff's claim based on the distinction between skilled and unskilled employees; liability attaching in the former case but not in the latter. The question as to whether an employer who is vicariously liable for the tort of its employee should be able to seek indemnity from that employee, was not in issue in this case. Lang J.A.'s reasoning, however, was supportive of La Forest J.'s dissent in *London Drugs*.

157 (1993), 17 C.C.L.T. (2d) 101.

158 The firm argued that the contract entered into between the contractor and the Crown limiting or excluding the liability of the Crown for any misrepresentation in the tender documents, protected the firm as well. The court was not prepared to hold, as it did in *London Drugs*, that the contract impliedly extended its protection to anyone other than the direct contracting party.

159 McLachlin J., who wrote the judgment, stated that "[t]he affixation of a seal, without more, is insufficient to found liability for negligent misrepresentation", at 17 C.C.L.T. (2d) 112. Only La Forest J., at 113, in a concurring judgment, focussed on the issue. Reverting back to his own dissenting judgment in *London Drugs*, he noted that while the majority in that case "was unwilling to absolve ordinary workers from liability flowing from their negligence . . .", they were willing to absolve "professional employees" in this case. La Forest J., of course,

As a result of this judgment, the law concerning the liability of an employee of a firm for a negligent misrepresentation made during the course of his or her employment is somewhat unclear. It is clear from *London Drugs* that in ordinary negligence claims employees will bear personal liability for their negligence, as long as a duty of care based on *Donoghue v. Stevenson* can be established. On principle, the same should apply to employees who are in a *Hedley Byrne* relationship with their employer's customers. Although the employees in *Edgeworth Construction* were relieved of liability, this ought not, in my opinion, to be taken for the proposition that in negligent statement cases reliance on employees sufficient to establish a special relationship cannot be made out. Where the facts indicate a special relationship between employees and their employer's clients, based upon foreseeable and reasonable reliance on their skill,[160] a duty ought to be owed.[161]

3. LIABILITY FOR NEGLIGENT PERFORMANCE OF SERVICES

(a) Direct Undertakings to Perform a Gratuitous Service

There is a wide, and rather ambiguous, category of cases, similar to the negligent statement cases, wherein a duty can be imposed on an individual to take reasonable care to perform a gratuitous service. The crux of this duty is the defendant's voluntary undertaking to carefully perform a service for the plaintiff's benefit, coupled with the plaintiff's detrimental reliance on this undertaking. In this situation, the fact that the plaintiff's loss is purely economic is not a bar to recovery once the necessary relationship has been found to exist.

This category of cases is problematic not because of the fear of indeterminate liability, but because of other difficult legal and policy issues. The suggestion that a person can be found legally responsible for failing to perform a gratuitous promise certainly must be viewed as problematic for a jurisprudence which traditionally has stressed the unenforceability of gratuitous undertakings. The common law's decision, in *Donoghue v. Stevenson*, to impose legal obligations on individuals to protect the personal and property rights of non-privity plaintiffs was the first major step. This can be justified on the basis that the interests which are being protected are of such importance, both to individual victims and to

---

was satisfied with the result in this case, because it was consistent with his dissenting judgment in *London Drugs* that the duty was owed by the firm, and not by its individual employees. There was no reliance on individual persons within the firm.

160 And not on their "pocket books", as La Forest J.'s test requires.

161 I do not believe, in other words, that *Edgeworth Const.* can be taken as affirmation of the B.C. Court of Appeal's judgment in *Sealand of the Pacific Ltd. v. Robert C. McHaffie Ltd.*, [1974] 6 W.W.R. 724, where a contractual claim against Robert McHaffie's architecture firm succeeded, while the tort claim against Robert McHaffie, personally, failed. Where reliance on an individual can be established, a duty ought to be owed by that individual. It is important to stress, however, that absent a special relationship or other basis upon which to create a tort duty, an employee will not be held liable. See, for example, *Blacklaws v. Morrow* (2000), 1 C.C.L.T. (3d) 149 (Alta. C.A.), leave to appeal refused (2001), 270 N.R. 197 (note) (S.C.C.). The Court of Appeal held that a director/manager of a company is ordinarily not liable for economic losses suffered by the company's contractual clients. Barring special circumstances, the duties and rights are between the company and its co-contractants; not between the officers or employees of the company and those with whom the company interacts.

society, that the protection offered by tort law is one that need not be bargained for. However, it is questionable whether tort law should intrude into the world of business and commerce in the same way. Where purely economic losses are in issue, and where protection from losses can be more efficiently provided for by appropriate contractual or insurance arrangements, liability in tort is expensive and unnecessary. The common law has been justifiably cautious to avoid extending tort liability in this area too far.

Several of the successful reliance cases have concerned the relationship between insurance agent and prospective client. Disputes frequently have arisen when an undertaking on the part of an agent to obtain insurance for its client has not been carried through, leaving the client uninsured when a loss later arises. In these cases, alternate bases of liability have been contemplated by the courts. The duty on the insurance agent to procure insurance for its customer, once the agent has undertaken to do so, has been based on the general law of contract,[162] in equity,[163] on special duties relating to insurance agents,[164] and in tort, on reliance relationships.[165] In most of these cases, the choice of the cause of action was not important, the court applying the one which best suited the facts. However, where issues of contributory negligence,[166] limitation periods, or damage assessments[167] arise, the basis of liability, which may have different consequences for the parties, can be important.[168]

That courts will be hesitant in creating legal obligations based upon a plaintiff's reliance on a gratuitous undertaking is clear from the decision in *Maxey v. Can. Permanent Trust Co.*[169] In this case, the plaintiff mortgagor was informed by a

---

162 See, e.g., *Cosyns v. Smith* (1983), 25 C.C.L.T. 54 (Ont. C.A.).

163 See, e.g. Estey J.'s judgment in *Fine's Flowers v. Gen. Accident Assur. Co.* (1977), 81 D.L.R. (3d) 139 (Ont. C.A.).

164 See, e.g., *Fine's Flowers v. Gen. Accident Assur. Co., ibid.; Truman v. Sparling Real Estate Ltd.* (1977), 3 C.C.L.T. 205 (B.C.S.C.); *G.K.N. Keller Can. v. Hartford Fire Ins. Co.* (1983), 27 C.C.L.T. 61, reversed as to insurer's liability 4 C.C.L.I. xxxvii (Ont. C.A.).

165 See, e.g., *Fletcher v. M.P.I.C.* (1990), 5 C.C.L.T. (2d) 1 (S.C.C.); *Grove Service Ltd. v. Lenhart Agencies Ltd.* (1979), 10 C.C.L.T. 101 (B.C. S.C.); *Morash v. Lockhart & Ritchie Ltd.* (1978), 95 D.L.R. (3d) 647 (N.B. C.A.); and *Milroy v. Toronto Dominion Bank* (1997), 35 C.C.L.T. (2d) 37 (Ont. Gen. Div.). In these cases, there were no specific undertakings, but a relationship of "habitual" reliance based on "past conduct." See, however, *Edmond Vienneau Assur. Ltée v. Roy* (1986), 35 C.C.L.T. 249, where the New Brunswick Court of Appeal held that there had been no undertakings or previous course of conduct which permitted the plaintiff to rely on the automatic renewal of his policies. In *Fletcher v. M.P.I.C.*, the duty was based on *Hedley Byrne*, Wilson J. stating, at 5 C.C.L.T. (2d) 21:

> . . . the sale of automobile insurance is a business in the course of which information is routinely provided to prospective customers in the expectation that they will rely on it and who do, in fact, reasonably rely on it.

Wilson J. concluded that the plaintiff was within the class of persons who would rely. The main issue in the case was the scope of the duty and whether there was the same duty for public and private insurers. The duty owed by public insurers was held to be less onerous than that owed by private insurers.

166 See *Cosyns v. Smith*, above, note 162.

167 See *B.D.C. Ltd. v. Hofstrand Farms Ltd.* (1986), 36 C.C.L.T. 87 (S.C.C.).

168 This is less likely to arise now that the concurrent liability approach of *Central & Eastern Trust* has been accepted.

169 (1983), 26 C.C.L.T. 148 (Man. Q.B.), reversed (1984), 27 C.C.L.T. 238 (Man. C.A.).

letter sent to him by the defendant mortgagee that he had failed to insure his house, as required by the mortgage agreement, and that if he did not insure within a short period the mortgagee would "have no alternative but to place insurance and charge the premium" to the mortgage. The plaintiff understood by this letter that if he did not do anything, insurance would be placed on his house, which would cover not only the mortgagee's interest, but the plaintiff's equity as well. He was mistaken in this assumption. The mortgagee insured only its interest, and only for a period of one year. The next year, the uninsured house burned down, and the plaintiff sued the mortgagee.

In rejecting the plaintiff's claim, the Court of Appeal tightened the elements of a relationship of reliance which would turn a gratuitous undertaking into an enforceable promise.[170] Philp J.A. stated that the undertaking to perform the voluntary act and the fact that steps had been taken to perform it were not sufficient to create a legal obligation. His Lordship stated that "there must be something more. The relationship between the parties must be such as to create a trust or other duty which the person has assumed and which he has miscarried."[171] The court identified other relationships which have in previous cases justified the imposition of such a duty, such as bailor/bailee,[172] or principal/agent,[173] but noted that in other less structured relationships where duties have been imposed there were circumstances, not present in this case, which created "a trust" or "other duty."[174] Missing in this case was a sufficient relationship of reliance, based upon a clear promise, adequate communication, and knowledge of the parties' beliefs or intentions.[175]

Outside the insurance agency context, there have been relatively few decisions which have imposed tort duties of affirmative action on those who create a reliance relationship based upon gratuitous promises or undertakings. In principle, however, the law governing cases concerned with reliance on gratuitous undertakings to act for the benefit of others should be no different from the law relating to reliance upon negligent advice. Where the parties have created a relationship whereby one party has voluntarily undertaken to act for the benefit of the other,

---

170 The Court of Appeal reversed the trial judge, who, relying on an earlier Manitoba decision, *Campbell v. Can. Co-op. Invt. Co.* (1906), 16 Man. R. 464 (K.B.), held that by its letter the defendant had induced the plaintiff to believe that it would insure his property and protect his interest, and that "it was negligent of the company to proceed in an entirely different manner without notice to the exposed plaintiff", at 26 C.C.L.T. 148 at 162.

171 (1984), 27 C.C.L.T. 238 at 242.

172 The leading case being *Coggs v. Bernard* (1703), 92 E.R. 107 (K.B.).

173 E.g., *Baxter & Co. v. Jones* (1903), 6 O.L.R. 360 (C.A.).

174 The court cited *Campbell v. Can. Co-op. Invt. Co.*, above, note 170, and *Kostiuk v. Union Accept. Corp.* (1969), 66 D.L.R. (2d) 430 (Sask. Q.B.).

175 See Irvine's "Annotation" to the trial judgment at 26 C.C.L.T. 150. Although Irvine thought that the trial judgment seemed "to produce a perfectly fair and just result", he points out the problems with trying to use promissory estoppel, or other theories, to create this result. The Court of Appeal's judgment has not really alleviated these concerns. For a similar case which came to a different conclusion see *Twardy v. Humboldt Credit Union Ltd.* (1985), 34 C.C.L.T. 140 (Sask. Q.B.). In that case, the defendant credit union was held liable for having undertaken to insure the plaintiff's husband's life to the extent of the outstanding balance of the mortgage, and for subsequently changing this practice without notifying the plaintiff.

and reliance was both foreseeable and reasonable, a duty to act in furtherance of this undertaking ought to be imposed.[176]

(b) Indirect Undertakings to Perform a Service

An analogous class of cases wherein purely economic losses may be recovered are those in which a plaintiff has relied upon the careful performance of a service which, while undertaken for the plaintiff's benefit, was in the context of a contractual relationship between the defendant and a third party. As with the former category, although the imposition of a tort duty will not give rise to a problem of indeterminate liability, since the duty, if owed, will be confined to a small class of known claimants, there are other policy concerns. The law must determine to what extent non-privity claimants are entitled to legal protection for their economic expectations, especially when they themselves might have governed their own affairs to prevent foreseeable losses. Further complicating matters is the fact that a third party, direct beneficiary of the service will be involved, and the law must avoid placing the rights and obligations of the three parties in a position of conflict.

An important case which illustrates these problems is *B.D.C. Ltd. v. Hofstrand Farms Ltd.*[177] In this case a land developer sued a private courier, hired by a third party (the Crown), for negligently failing to deliver important documents on time, resulting in economic losses to the plaintiff developer. The British Columbia Court of Appeal held that, based on the presumptive duty approach of *Anns v. Merton London Borough Council*,[178] the courier would be liable in damages in tort if he could reasonably foresee that damage would occur "to a known limited class of persons" if he failed to act carefully. Taken on its face, this proposition must be considered too broad. If liability for purely economic losses were to be based merely on their foreseeability to a limited class, without the need for a special relationship based either upon reliance or a voluntary assumption of responsibility, this would be an untenable extension of the tort law duty.

The Supreme Court of Canada dismissed the action. Estey J. noted the problem "of circumscribing . . . what otherwise might be an unending chain of liability in an incalculable amount"[179] were recovery permitted for losses of this nature. There was in this case neither a sufficient relationship of proximity between the parties to create even a presumption of liability, according to His Lordship, nor was there a relationship of reliance.[180]

---

176 See *Hejduk v. R.*, [1981] 4 W.W.R. 122 (B.C. S.C.), affirmed [1984] 4 W.W.R. 283 (B.C. C.A.). An undertaking to act for the plaintiff's benefit which was not relied upon by the plaintiff did not create a legal duty of care.

177 (1986), 36 C.C.L.T. 87 (S.C.C.), reversing (1982), 20 C.C.L.T. 146 (B.C. C.A.), which reversed (1980), 114 D.L.R. (3d) 347 (B.C. S.C.). For an excellent commentary, see Blom, "Slow Courier in the Supreme Court" (1986-87), 12 Can. Bus. L.J. 43.

178 [1977] 2 All E.R. 492 (H.L.).

179 36 C.C.L.T. 87 at 94.

180 Blom, above, note 177, argues that where, as in this case, a plaintiff enters into a contractual relationship able to foresee that by the terms of its contract it places itself at risk if a third party acts carelessly, it should be required to arrange its own affairs appropriately. Tort law should not enlarge the defendant's contractual obligations to the third party. Nor should it save the plaintiff from the adverse financial consequences which its arrangement made pos-

The result in *B.D.C. Ltd. v. Hofstrand Farms Ltd.* may be compared with the earlier, well-known House of Lords decision in *Junior Books Ltd. v. Veitchi Co.*[181] In this case, the plaintiff had engaged a general contractor to construct a factory, and the general contractor had in turn engaged the services of a flooring subcontractor. When the negligence of the subcontractor resulted in economic losses to the plaintiff, the plaintiff chose to sue the subcontractor in tort, rather than pursuing the more expected contractual recourse against the general contractor. The House of Lords considered that the relationship between the plaintiff and the subcontractor was sufficiently proximate to create a presumptive duty relationship,[182] and could find no reasons of policy or precedent to negative a duty of care in this case. Lord Brandon, in dissent, agreed that the relationship was sufficiently proximate, but disagreed that either policy or precedent favoured the plaintiff's contentions. Foremost among Lord Brandon's concerns was that the creation of a tort duty between non-privity parties such as these, when each had governed its relationship with respect to the activity by contract with another party, creates serious practical problems.[183]

Junior Books was not met with much enthusiasm. Not only was it specifically rejected by other Commonwealth courts,[184] but even the English courts have attempted to restrict its application.[185] It was held to be inapplicable to cases where a party suffers economic loss because a contract with a third party was rendered

---

sible. Also see Blom, "Tort, Contract and the Allocation of Risk" (2002), 17 S.C.L.R. (2d) 289, for a broader discussion of this thesis.

181 [1982] 3 All E.R. 201. This case will also be considered under the heading "Liability for Economic Losses Caused by Defective Products or Buildings", to be discussed below.

182 Lord Roskill, for example, noted that the subcontractors had been nominated, they knew what was required by the plaintiff, the plaintiff had relied on their skill, etc. In fact, according to Lord Roskill, "the relationship between the parties was as close as it could be short of actual privity of contract" (*ibid.*, at 214).

183 For example, is the subcontractor's duty to be defined by the terms of its contract with the main contractor? Is the plaintiff to be bound by exemption clauses, or other terms which limit the subcontractor's liability to the main contractor? Why, except perhaps for convenience, give the plaintiff a recourse against the subcontractor when it presumably would have a perfectly adequate contractual recourse against the general contractor? And what of the legal precedents in this area, which generally exclude recovery for purely economic losses when there is no damage, or threat of damage, to person or property? There have been many commentaries on *Junior Books*. See Cohen, "Bleeding Hearts and Peeling Floors: Recovery of Economic Loss at the House of Lords" (1984), 18 U.B.C. L. Rev. 289; Waddams, "Tort Liability for Economic Loss: *Junior Books v. Veitchi*" (1983-84), 8 Can. Bus. L. J. 101; Holyoak, "Tort and Contract After Junior Books" (1983), 99 L.Q.R. 590; Feldthusen, "Economic Loss: Where Are We Going After *Junior Books*?" (1987), 12 Can. Bus. L.J. 241.

184 See, e.g., *Buthmann v. Balzer* (1983), 25 C.C.L.T. 273 (Alta. Q.B.). See, however, *Univ. of Regina v. Pettick* (1986), 38 C.C.L.T. 230 (Sask. Q.B.), reversed (1991), 6 C.C.L.T. (2d) 1 (Sask. C.A.), where the court followed *Junior Books*, but dismissed the claim against the subcontractor since negligence was not shown.

185 See *Candlewood Navigation Corp. v. Mitsui OSK Lines*, [1986] A.C. 1 (P.C.); *Leigh & Sillavan Ltd. v. Aliakmon Shipping Co.*, [1986] 2 All E.R. 145 (H.L.); *Muirhead v. Indust. Tank Specialities*, [1985] 3 All E.R. 705 (C.A.); *Simaan Gen. Contr. Co. v. Pilkington Glass Ltd.*, [1988] 1 All E.R. 791 (C.A.); *D. & F. Estates Ltd. v. Church Commrs. for England*, [1988] 2 All E.R. 992 (H.L.). Professor Blom has concluded that both *Anns v. Merton* and *Junior Books* are now "spent" forces in England, having been denied the seminal status in the law of negligence that for a while they appeared to be assuming. See Blom, "Slow Courier in the Supreme Court" (1986-87), 12 Can. Bus. L.J. 43.

less profitable due to the defendant's negligence.[186] It even was rationalized on the ground that the plaintiff in *Junior Books* had a proprietary interest in the defective floor which was the cause of the economic losses,[187] and, in another case, on the ground that the parties in *Junior Books* were in a reliance relationship.[188]

An area of greater success for the claimant who alleges that economic fortunes have been detrimentally affected by the defendant's careless performance of a contract with a third party is the will beneficiary case. In British Columbia, a disappointed beneficiary of an invalid bequest, executed carelessly by the defendant solicitor, was able to recover his damages on the basis of the *Hedley Byrne* reliance relationship.[189] A more realistic approach was adopted in *Ross v. Caunters.*[190] In this case, a disappointed beneficiary was able to recover her economic losses, not because she relied upon the solicitor's services, but because there was a sufficient degree of proximity between herself and the solicitor to create a duty of care, and no reasons of policy to negate it.[191]

The House of Lords considered the liability of a solicitor to a disappointed beneficiary in *White v. Jones.*[192] In this case, despite the testator's instructions to solicitors to draft a new will leaving bequests to the testator's two daughters, whom he had left out of an earlier will, the will was not prepared. The testator died before a new will was executed, and the daughters were disinherited. They sued the solicitors in negligence for their failure to execute the new will. While the majority judgment, per Lord Goff, was not prepared to accept the broad reasoning upon which *Ross v. Caunters* was decided, the Lords did find liability in this case, on a principle more limited than "reliance". The condition upon which liability in this case was based was that the solicitors' failure to properly execute the testator's instructions arose in circumstances such that neither the testator nor the testator's estate were in a position to remedy it. If the defect had come to light before the testator's death, no remedy would have been extended to the daughters, since the testator could have remedied the defect, had he been so inclined. The logic underlying Lord Goff's approach was that the law should provide a remedy to beneficiaries where there otherwise could have been no recourse available.[193]

---

186 *Candlewood Navigation Corp. v. Mitsui OSK Lines, ibid.*

187 *Leigh & Sillavan v. Aliakmon Shipping Co.*, above, note 185.

188 *Muirhead v. Indust. Tank Specialities*, above, note 185.

189 *Whittingham v. Crease & Co.* (1978), 6 C.C.L.T. 1 (B.C. S.C.). For a criticism see Klar, "A Comment on Whittingham v. Crease" (1979), 6 C.C.L.T. 311.

190 [1979] 3 All E.R. 580 (Ch. D.).

191 For a contrary decision, see *Seale v. Perry*, [1982] V.R. 193 (S.C.). See generally Litman and Robertson, "Solicitor's Liability for Failure to Substantiate Testamentary Capacity" (1984), 62 Can. Bar Rev. 457; Rawlins, "Liability of a Lawyer for Negligence in the Drafting and Execution of a Will" (1983), 6 Estates & Trusts Q. 117; Kay, "The Liability of Solicitors in Tort" (1984), 100 L.Q.R. 680; Luntz, "Solicitors' Liability to Third Parties" (1983), 3 Oxford J. Leg. Stud. 284.

192 [1995] 2 W.L.R. 187. See Benson, "Should *White v. Jones* Represent Canadian Law: A Return to First Principles" in Neyers, Pitel, Chamberlain, eds., *Emerging Issues in Tort Law* (2007), Chapter 6.

193 As stated by Lord Goff, at [1995] 2 W.L.R. 199, if a duty is not recognized to the beneficiaries in this type of case, "the only persons who might have a valid claim (i.e. the testator and his estate) have suffered no loss, and the only person who has suffered a loss (i.e. the disappointed beneficiary) has no claim". Lord Browne-Wilkinson supported liability based upon the voluntary assumption of responsibility test. Lord Keith and Lord Mustill dissented. Lord Mustill's

The majority approach in *White v. Jones* was followed in *Earl v. Wilhelm.*[194] This involved not an invalidly executed will, but a will in which certain beneficiaries did not receive their bequests because of problems related to estate planning. In effect, land transfers undertaken to avoid taxes and land title fees resulted in the testator bequeathing property that was not beneficially owned by him. The disappointed beneficiaries were successful in suing the lawyers responsible for the will and deficient estate planning.[195]

Graham v. Bonnycastle[196] indicates the difficulties courts face when they are asked by a third party to intervene in the relationship between a lawyer and its client. The testator executed a will, married, and then executed a second will, leaving bequests to the two children of his first marriage and the residue of his estate to his sister and new wife. This resulted in a decrease in his children's inheritance. The children contested the validity of the marriage and of the second will, alleging the testator's incapacity. Ultimately, the interested parties settled, leaving the issues of the validity of the marriage and the second will unresolved. The children sued the lawyers who drafted the second will, alleging their negligence in allowing a person without testamentary capacity to execute a will. They sought as damages the difference between what they received in the settlement and what they would have received had there been no second will.

The problems with this type of claim are evident. First, and foremost, it places the lawyer in a conflict with its own client. Should the lawyer allow a will to be executed, there is a threat of a law suit against the lawyer from a third party, who loses out because of the second will. However, the lawyer's duty should exclusively be to act competently in the best interests of the client, according to the terms of the retainer. The interests and desires of third parties should not play any

---

dissent was forceful and unequivocal. He argued that the existing authorities did not support the duty proposition in this case, and concluded, at [1995] 2 W.L.R. 228, that "to hold that a duty exists, even *prima facie*, in such a situation would be to go far beyond anything so far contemplated by the law of negligence."

194 (1997), [1998] 2 W.W.R. 522, 40 C.C.L.T. (2d) 117 (Sask. Q.B.), additional reasons at [1998] 5 W.W.R. 509 (Sask. Q.B.), additional reasons at (1998), [1999] 3 W.W.R. 524 (Sask. Q.B.), reversed [2000] 4 W.W.R. 363, 183 D.L.R. (4th) 45 (Sask. C.A.), affirmed [2000] 9 W.W.R. 196 (Sask. C.A.), leave to appeal refused (2000), 213 Sask. R. 156 (note) (S.C.C.). Other cases finding lawyers or notaries liable to beneficiaries include *Crowe (Committees of) v. Bollong* (1998), 42 C.C.L.T. (2d) 1 (B.C. S.C.). In two other cases, namely *Wakeford v. Arnold* (2001), 41 E.T.R. (2d) 309 (Alta. Q.B.) and *Rosenberg Estate v. Black* (2001), [2001] O.J. No. 5051, 2001 CarswellOnt 4504 (S.C.J.), duties were found but the actions were dismissed for other reasons. For a useful commentary on Wilhelm and the broader issue, see J.R. McJannett, "Wilhelm v. Hickson: The Canadian Tort Approach to the Disappointed Beneficiary" (2001), 64 Sask. LR. 113.

195 The trial judge held the testator himself negligent for having failed to properly instruct his solicitor and accordingly held his estate 25 per cent contributorily negligent. This effectively would have meant that a testator has a duty to take reasonable care to ensure that his own bequests are valid! This is a troubling finding which indicates the difficulties that the courts create when they permit third party beneficiaries to interfere in the contractual relationship between a solicitor and client. The Court of Appeal, however, overturned the trial judge's finding of contributory negligence. Also see *Makhan v. McCawley* (1998), 158 D.L.R. (4th) 164 (Ont. Gen. Div.), where the lawsuit alleged not only the negligent failure to draft a will in a timely fashion, but negligence in failing to take steps to increase the size of the testator's estate during her life time.

196 (2004), [2005] 4 W.W.R. 205, 243 D.L.R. (4th) 617 (Alta. C.A.), leave to appeal refused (2005), 2005 CarswellAlta 493 (S.C.C.).

part in the lawyer's considerations.[197] Second, it allows the parties and the courts to avoid the real issues in the case. The issues were the validity of the marriage and the will; these could have been determined. Rather than resolving those matters, and living with the consequences of the decisions, the parties thought that a better result for them would be to have the lawyer pay damages, allowing them all to receive full testamentary benefits, even though in truth, the testator clearly did not intend that result.[198] The Court of Appeal affirmed the decision of the trial judge and dismissed the negligence action.[199]

There are important policy considerations in the "disappointed beneficiary" cases. Courts must not place a solicitor's primary duty to a client into a position of conflict with a duty to third parties.[200] As well, there must not be a circumvention of the policy of wills legislation which requires that a will be the product of a free and capable testator, unaffected by either fraud or undue influence, in order for it

---

197 Whether a lawyer can refuse to act for a client even if the lawyer believes that the client has testamentary capacity was discussed in *Hall v. Bennett Estate* (2003), 15 C.C.L.T. (3d) 315 (Ont. C.A.). The court suggested that there is no legal obligation to act, absent reliance or some other circumstances. However, refusing to act might give rise to "a serious question of professional conduct and, depending on all the circumstances, could form the basis of disciplinary proceedings" (at 330).

198 The testator either wanted the first will or the second will – not both. He also did not have a large enough estate for both.

199 As pointed out by the Court of Appeal, the marriage, assuming it was valid, revoked the first will in any event. Thus the beneficiaries could not let the marriage stand and still claim benefits from the first will. The Court of Appeal did not rule out all actions brought by beneficiaries in all circumstances. If there was no other remedy available and if the interests of the beneficiaries were congruent with those of the testator, the court conceded that the jurisprudence supported a claim.

200 This has been made clear even in the cases that recognize the duty. The solicitor's duty is primarily to its client to carry out its instructions. The beneficiaries' cause of action is dependent upon this not having been done. The solicitor has no duty to advance the case of a beneficiary to the testator or to encourage the testator to benefit any particular person. See, for example, *Korpiel v. Sanguinetti* (1999), 26 E.T.R. (2d) 147 (B.C. S.C.), additional reasons at (1999), 1999 CarswellBC 1864 (S.C.), varied on reconsideration (1999), 1999 CarswellBC 2694 (S.C.). The difficulty with this reasoning, however, is that in the absence of a valid will and a living testator it might not be clear what the testator's true intentions were. This is made more difficult due to the confidential relationship between solicitor and client. Also see *Smolinski v. Mitchell*, [1995] 10 W.W.R. 68 (B.C. S.C.). The solicitor did not promptly execute a new will for his client, as he was concerned that his client obtain independent legal advice concerning the intended bequest to the solicitor himself. The new will was not executed, the testator dying before that could happen. A disappointed beneficiary sued. The court dismissed the action, affirming the proposition "that the court will not impose a duty on a solicitor to a third party when that duty conflicts with his duty to his client, the testator", at [1995] 10 W.W.R. 68 (B.C. S.C.) at 87. See *Abacus Cities Ltd. (Trustee of) v. Bank of Montreal* (1986), 39 C.C.L.T. 7 (Alta. Q.B.), affirmed (1987), 44 C.C.L.T. 199 (Alta. C.A.), leave to appeal refused (1988), 58 Alta. L.R. (2d) xlix (S.C.C.), and *Midland Mortgage Corp. v. Jawl & Bundon*, [1999] 8 W.W.R. 535 (B.C. C.A.), additional reasons at (1999), 64 B.C.L.R. (3d) 1 (C.A.), leave to appeal refused (2000), 260 N.R. 392 (note) (S.C.C.) for further discussion on this issue of placing the solicitor or other professional in a conflict of interest position with its own client by imposing upon the solicitor a duty to third parties.

to be valid.[201] There are, in my opinion, convincing reasons to reject a solicitor's liability to disappointed beneficiaries, and I prefer the dissenting judgments in *White v. Jones*.[202] With every extension of the duty of care in tort,[203] analogous claims must be considered. There are many situations where financial services will be provided to one party in order to benefit others, for example, estate planning or tax advice, and the limits of the professionals' legal duties to these others will have to be considered.[204] The common law will have to determine the limits of the legal responsibilities of those who are either directly or indirectly providing gratuitous services to others, and the obligations on these others to take adequate precautions for their own protection.[205]

---

201 Where the invalidity of a will resides in the fact that the witness was one of the will's beneficiaries, strong evidence will have to be led that this did not unduly influence the bequest for damages in the tort action against the solicitor to be recovered. What in effect is happening in some of the tort cases is that courts are accepting that a testator's intention was to confer a benefit on someone, based on proof which is much less stringent than that which ordinarily is required by wills' legislation.

202 I discussed some of my objections in Klar, "A Comment on *Whittingham v. Crease*" (1978-79), 6 C.C.L.T. 311. In *White v. Jones*, above, note 192, other objections were raised, even by some of the Lords who were in favour of liability on the condition imposed. Among these were the inconsistency between contract and tort principles if a duty were owed, the absence of reliance, the absence of any existing financial interest of the plaintiffs' actually damaged, the potential indeterminacy of such a duty (would it apply for example to ineffective *inter vivos* transactions?), and precedent. As I argued in my earlier case comment, the solution to the disappointed beneficiary case is to allow courts, by legislation if necessary, to give effect to the "true" intentions of the testator, if the court is persuaded that the testator's intentions have been frustrated. The solution is not to enlarge the testator's estate by allowing all parties, even those presumably not intended to be benefitted by the testator, to benefit through a tort remedy. For a contrary view on this issue, see J.R. McJannet's Commentary above, note 194.

203 One must recall that the law regarding the solicitor's duties to those who are not clients had been well settled. Prior to *Whittingham v. Crease*, it had been accepted that a solicitor's only duty is to the client, no duty in tort being owed to third parties. See discussion in Chapter 10.

204 See *Linsley v. Kirstiuk* (1986), 28 D.L.R. (4th) 495 (B.C. S.C.) — beneficiaries of a trust allowed to sue lawyers who were advising estate's trustees; *Philp v. Woods* (1985), 34 C.C.L.T. 66 (B.C. S.C.) — solicitor not liable to executor of an estate for litigation costs surrounding testator's testamentary capacity.

205 For example, in *Tracy v. Atkins* (1979), 11 C.C.L.T. 57 (B.C. C.A.), a lawyer hired by the purchaser of property was held liable for failing to take reasonable care to protect the vendor's interests. Why should the law not require the vendor to hire a lawyer to safeguard its own interests? Should a solicitor be required to provide gratuitous services when the parties have chosen not to pay for them? Or see *Clarke v. Bruce Lance & Co.*, [1988] 1 All E.R. 364 (C.A.), where a beneficiary of a will sued the solicitor since he was unhappy with the way the solicitor advised the testator concerning a transaction involving one of the properties left in the will. The action was properly dismissed. Or see *Kamahap Ent. Ltd. v. Chu's Central Market Ltd.*, [1990] 1 W.W.R. 632 (B.C. C.A.), where the court correctly dismissed an action brought by a potential purchaser of property against the vendor's solicitor. The purchaser argued that the solicitor was negligent in advising the vendor, and that as a result the transaction was frustrated, causing the purchaser financial losses. Also see *Esser v. Brown*, [2004] 10 W.W.R. 205 (B.C. C.A.) and *Elms v. Laurentian Bank of Canada* (2006), 37 C.C.L.T. (3d) 213 (B.C. C.A.). For further discussion of the solicitor's liability to third parties, see Chapter 10. A more unusual case is *Kovacvich v. Ortho Pharmaceutical (Canada) Ltd.* (1995), 25 C.C.L.T. (2d) 295 (B.C. S.C.), additional reasons at (August 29, 1995), Doc. Rossland 2324 (B.C. S.C.). A father of an illegitimate child who was required to make monthly child support payments sued the mother's doctor for his negligence in misprescribing oral contraceptive pills. Although the doctor was held liable to the mother, he was held to have owed no duty to

4. LIABILITY FOR RELATIONAL ECONOMIC LOSSES

(a) Economic Losses Consequent on Property Damage Suffered by a Third Party

The fear of imposing excessive burdens on negligent defendants, as well as overloading the judicial system, were all reasonably foreseeable economic losses resulting from careless acts to be recoverable, is nowhere more real than in the area of relational economic losses.[206] It is in this area where one can most clearly see how the interdependence of members of society, where an injury to one person will detrimentally affect the financial situation of others, requires the imposition of practical limitations on the liability of negligent actors.[207]

One may confidently state that as a general rule a person cannot claim recovery for relational economic losses based solely on a test of reasonable foreseeability. Recovery for these losses has been permitted only when the courts' concerns for indeterminate liability have been allayed.[208]

There are two views regarding recovery for relational economic losses. The first is that, other than the practical need to restrict recovery for what are potentially

---

the child's father. Similarly in *Freeman v. Sutter* (1996), 29 C.C.L.T. (2d) 215 (Man. C.A.), the biological father of a child unsuccessfully sued a doctor whose negligence in performing an abortion led to the birth of the child.

206 This term is used by Feldthusen, *Economic Negligence*, 5th ed. (2008), Chapter 5. It refers to losses which relate to personal injuries or property damages caused not to the economic loss claimant but to a third party. For a recent discussion, see Brown, "The Impossibility of Recoverable Relational Economic Loss" (2006), 5 Oxford University Commonwealth L.J. 25.

207 This reasoning has prevailed at least since *Cattle v. Stockton Waterworks Co.* (1875), L.R. 10 Q.B. 453, where Blackburn J. dismissed an action brought by a contractor for economic losses suffered by him when a tunnel he was digging on land belonging to a third party became flooded by the defendant's negligence. Blackburn J. noted that when a mine is flooded, not only the owners of the mine, but its workmen and others lose wages because of its closure. A perfect law might give all of these persons compensation, but a wise approach dictates that there must be practical limits. Also see Lord Penzance's judgment in *Simpson v. Thomson* (1877), 3 App. Cas. 279 (H.L.); and Hamilton J.'s judgment in *Société Anonyme de Remorquage à Hélice v. Bennetts*, [1911] 1 K.B. 243. See Addy J.'s judgment in *C.N.R. v. Norsk S.S. Co.* (1989), 49 C.C.L.T. 1 (Fed. T.D.), affirmed (1990), 65 D.L.R. (4th) 321 (Fed. C.A.), affirmed (1992), 11 C.C.L.T. (2d) 1 (S.C.C.), application for re-hearing refused (July 23, 1992), Doc. 21838 (S.C.C.), for an excellent review of this issue.

208 There are numerous cases which one might cite in support of this. Of the important ones, see *Weller & Co. v. Foot & Mouth Disease Research Institute*, [1965] 3 All E.R. 560 (Q.B.D.); *Electrochrome Ltd. v. Welsh Plastics*, [1968] 2 All E.R. 205; *Margarine Union v. Cambay Prince S.S. Co.*, [1967] 3 All E.R. 775 (Q.B.D.); *S.C.M. (U.K.) Ltd. v. W.J. Whittal & Son Ltd.*, [1970] 3 All E.R. 245 (C.A.); *Spartan Steel & Alloys Ltd. v. Martin & Co. (Contr.) Ltd.*, [1972] 3 All E.R. 557 (C.A.); *Hunt v. T.W. Johnstone Co.* (1976), 69 D.L.R. (3d) 639 (Ont. H.C.); *Gypsum Carrier Inc. v. R.; C.N.R. v. The Harry Lundeberg* (1977), 78 D.L.R. (3d) 175 (Fed. T.D.); *Bethlehem Steel Corp. v. St. Lawrence Seaway Authority* (1977), 79 D.L.R. (3d) 522 (Fed. T.D.); *C.N.R. v. Norsk Pac. S.S. Co.* (1989), 49 C.C.L.T. 1 (Fed. T.D.), affirmed (1990), 65 D.L.R. (4th) 321 (Fed. C.A.); affirmed (1992), 11 C.C.L.T. (2d) 1 (S.C.C.), application for re-hearing refused (July 23, 1992), Doc. 21838 (S.C.C.); and *Bow Valley Husky (Bermuda) Ltd. v. Saint John Shipbuilding Ltd.* (1997), 40 C.C.L.T. (2d) 235 (S.C.C.). An excellent review of the earlier jurisprudence may be found in the various judgments in *Caltex Oil (Australia) Pty. Ltd. v. The Dredge "Willemstad"* (1977), 136 C.L.R. 529 (Aust. H.C.).

enormous losses, there are no other reasons to distinguish between economic losses consequent upon personal injuries or property damage suffered by a claimant, and relational economic losses suffered in the absence of physical damage to the claimant. In both cases, justice, the need to compensate, punish, deter, and educate, dictate that the victim of the loss be entitled to recover. If one adopts this view, and can articulate a restrictive test which would limit otherwise excessive burdens for defendants or the judicial system, recovery should be allowed. The implicit adoption of this approach has resulted in a variety of such restrictive devices, adopted solely to narrow the ambit of recovery.[209] The second view asserts that although indeterminate liability is frequently a problem of relational economic loss recovery, it is not the only concern; thus, even if losses could be narrowed by some restrictive test, such losses still ought not to be recoverable in every case. The thrust of this approach is that purely economic losses are qualitatively different from injuries to persons or property, do not involve the same moral or symbolic issues, may be more efficiently distributed by other methods, such as insurance, and hence should not be the subject of expensive, litigious processes.[210]

The leading Canadian cases on the recovery of relational economic losses are *C.N.R. v. Norsk*[211] and *Bow Valley Husky (Bermuda) Ltd. v. Saint John Shipbuilding Ltd.*[212] The essential facts of *C.N.R. v. Norsk* are as follows. A tug boat operator towing a barge down the river negligently allowed the barge to collide with a railroad bridge owned by the Crown. In addition to the Crown's claim for damage caused to the bridge, three railway companies, who had a contractual right to use the bridge, sued the owner of the tug for the economic losses which they suffered as a result of not being able to use it.[213] The lower courts allowed these claims, and the case went to the Supreme Court of Canada.

McLachlin J., writing for three Justices of the Court, allowed the claim.[214] Her judgment recognized that the principle policy problem associated with this type of relational economic loss claim is the fear of indeterminate and unlimited liability. In McLachlin J.'s opinion the solution to this concern was to ensure a close proximity between the defendant's negligent act and the plaintiff's loss, before a duty of care to prevent relational economic losses can be owed. According

---

209 As we shall discuss, this was essentially the view of four members of the Supreme Court in *C.N.R. v. Norsk*, above, note 208.

210 This was essentially the view of the three dissenting members of the Supreme Court in *C.N.R. v. Norsk*, above, note 208. See especially Feldthusen, *Economic Negligence*, 5th ed. (2008), for an articulation of these and other arguments.

211 Above, note 208.

212 Above, note 208.

213 The principal user of the bridge was the C.N.R. It was agreed that only its claim would proceed and the claims of the other two smaller railway users would depend upon the result of the C.N.R. action.

214 There were three judgments in the case. McLachlin J. wrote one, concurred in by L'Heureux-Dubé and Cory JJ., dismissing the appeal. Stevenson J. wrote a separate judgment also dismissing the appeal. La Forest J. wrote a dissenting judgment, concurred in by Sopinka and Iacobucci JJ. See MacGuigan J., "The *Jervis Crown* Case: A Jurisprudential Analysis" (1993), 25 Ottawa L. Rev. 61, where the author examines the judgments. One of his conclusions is that there was in this case no majority view; rather there was a majority against every view.

to McLachlin J., proximity was "the controlling concept which avoids the spectre of unlimited liability."[215] Although proximity is, according to this approach, a necessary requirement which is determined differently in different contexts,[216] it is not a sufficient indicator of a duty, and can be negated by policy. Having established this framework, McLachlin J. considered that the facts of this case established the relationship of proximity, and she rejected all policy arguments put forth to negate the duty.[217] If one were to attempt to summarize this approach, one is tempted to conclude that McLachlin J.'s prime motive was her consideration that it would be just to compensate the plaintiff. As has been typical of this area, she then was able to identify characteristics of the plaintiff which factually distinguished this plaintiff from other potential claimants, thereby avoiding the spectre of unlimited liability.[218]

La Forest J.'s dissenting judgment took a very different tact. Indeterminate or unlimited liability, and finding a way to deal with it, would not solve the issue in this case. Rather, it was whether this type of claim, which La Forest J. termed a "contractual relational economic loss", should, on economic and social policy grounds, be permitted to succeed.[219] It was based on this type of analysis that La Forest J. decided that policy dictated that there ought to be no recovery, the indeterminate liability issue aside.[220]

---

215 Above, note 208, at 27.

216 For example, in negligent statement cases proximity is determined by reliance on an undertaking.

217 Proximity factors were that (i) the plaintiff users of the bridge were parties physically threatened by the tugboat owner's negligence, being frequent users of the bridge; (ii) the plaintiff's property was in close proximity to the bridge; (iii) the plaintiff could not enjoy its property without the bridge; (iv) the plaintiff had certain maintenance responsibilities with respect to the bridge; (v) the plaintiff was the main user of the bridge. Policy factors were that recovery here would be fair, and practical, without fear of unlimited liability. McLachlin J. stated that this was similar to a case of "joint venture". She also rejected economic policy arguments raised by the dissenting Justice, La Forest J.

218 As raised by the dissenting judgment, although the plaintiff was able to determine its "uniqueness", was this uniqueness relevant to the issue whether there should be a duty owed to it? Stevenson J.'s approach was similar to McLachlin J.'s, although his proximity test was significantly more specific and confined. According to Stevenson J., proximity in this case was made out by the fact that the defendant actually could have foreseen the plaintiff as the specific party which would be injured by damage to the bridge. This "known plaintiff" test thus effectively eliminated the concern for indeterminate liability, which according to Stevenson J. was *the* concern in these types of cases.

219 A "contractual relational economic loss" claim is where a plaintiff's contractual relationship with a third party is affected by the negligence of the defendant. On the facts of this case, the plaintiff had a contractual right to use the third party's bridge, but was prevented from doing so by the tug boat operator's negligence.

220 The judgment is quite lengthy, and it is impossible in this text, to discuss it in too much detail. It contained a jurisprudential and comparative review. At the risk of overly simplifying a complex judgment, it ultimately came down to this: there were no strong policy reasons to depart from the general exclusionary rule and allow recovery; liability would not lead to greater deterrence of the defendant, since it clearly would remain liable to the bridge's owner, even if it were not liable to the bridge's user; the proximity factors noted by other members of the court were generally unpersuasive in terms of justifying why this plaintiff should succeed, while others, not so physically placed, would not; moreover, policy factors in fact supported the exclusionary rule, from a cost avoidance, insurance, administration, and pre-

The Supreme Court of Canada revisited the issue of contractual relational economic loss in *Bow Valley Husky (Bermuda) Ltd. v. Saint John Shipbuilding Ltd.*[221] In this case, the plaintiff companies suffered economic losses when an oil rig was damaged by fire. The plaintiffs had a contract with the rig's owners that allowed them to use the rig.[222] The contract obliged them to pay day rates for the use of the rig even when it was out of service. The plaintiffs sued to recover the day rates and for other expenses which they incurred relating to the rig.[223]

Unlike the duty in *C.N.R. v. Norsk*, which was a simple duty not to damage the bridge by its negligence, the defendants' duty in *Bow Valley* was a duty to inform the rig's owner of the fact that a cladding used as a component part of the rig was flammable. An appropriate warning would have alerted the rig's owner of the need to install a ground fault breaker system that would have prevented a fire started by an electrical fault. It was the spread of this fire that led to the rig's damage. Applying the two-stage test of duty, the Supreme Court of Canada held that users of the rig such as the plaintiffs were foreseeable victims if a fire damaged the rig, and thus were owed a *prima facie* duty of care. Moving on to the second stage, that of policy, the Court held that to impose a duty on the defendants to warn the plaintiffs would be to create a problem of an indeterminate liability. The Court rejected arguments that indeterminate liability could be countered by restricting the duty to "known plaintiffs", to users of the rig only, or to users relying on the product's quality. The Court rejected the plaintiffs' argument that the duty, being only a "duty to warn", was in itself a sufficient restrictive device. Thus, ultimately the *prima facie* duty was negated at the second stage of the two-stage test due to policy concerns relating to indeterminate liability.[224]

---

dictability, perspective. Feldthusen's book, *Economic Negligence*, 5th ed. (2008), discusses these arguments in considerable detail.

221 (1997), 40 C.C.L.T. (2d) 235 (S.C.C.).

222 The rig's owner was in fact a company incorporated by the plaintiffs specifically for the purpose of owning the rig. This strategy was adopted in order to secure better financing arrangements.

223 The Newfoundland Court of Appeal [(1995), 126 D.L.R. (4th) 1 (Nfld. C.A.)] had rejected the claim for purely economic losses based on a lack of proximity argument. It also extensively dealt with the issue as to whether a "joint venture" existed between the owner of the rig and its users. The Court of Appeal rejected this argument of joint venture, and the Supreme Court of Canada upheld this aspect of the judgment. Although it was not discussed as such, a fact situation which might be seen as a "joint venture" and allowed the non-proprietary party to recover economic losses is *Tri-Line Expressways v. Ansari*, [1997] 5 W.W.R. 342, 143 D.L.R. (4th) 100 (B.C. C.A.). A tractor owned by one party was damaged. It hauled a trailer owned by the plaintiff. The tractor carried the markings of the plaintiff company, was under exclusive contract to haul only the cargo belonging to the plaintiff, the licenses were registered in the plaintiff's name, and the revenues generated were divided between the parties.

224 Professor Feldthusen, while in agreement with the result in *Bow Valley Husky (Bermuda) Ltd.*, is critical of the reasoning that led to it. Professor Feldthusen argues that the case should have been resolved at stage one of the two-stage test. The duty to warn of the flammability of the rig was owed only to its owner, who was the party capable of taking preventive measures to avert the fire hazard. There was, according to Feldthusen, no *prima facie* duty to warn users. See Feldthusen, "Liability for Pure Economic Loss: Yes, But Why?" (1999), U.W.A. L. Rev. In support of the Supreme Court of Canada's approach, however, I would argue that the question was not whether the defendants owed a duty to warn the plaintiffs, but whether the duty to warn the rig's owners could be extended so as to protect other users as well. In

The approach of the majority judgment in *C.N.R. v. Norsk* and *Bow Valley Huskey* is characteristic of the way in which courts traditionally have approached the issue of relational economic losses. Courts which have conceded that purely economic losses should in theory be recoverable as long as they are not too attenuated and can, for practical reasons, be confined within tolerable limits have adopted, in previous cases, a variety of restrictive devices, including the following:

(1) If a duty to take care based on reasonably foreseeable personal injury or property damage can be established, all economic losses which are reasonably foreseeable can be recovered, even if the threatened physical damages did not occur.[225]
(2) Where a claimant has suffered actual physical damage, all economic losses which also resulted from the negligent act may be recovered, even those that were not related to the physical damages.[226]
(3) Where a plaintiff has suffered actual expenditures, i.e., positive outlays of money as opposed to merely lost opportunities to earn money, these are not too remote and may be recovered.[227]
(4) Courts have attempted to narrow the range of recovery for purely economic losses by limiting recovery to only those losses which are both the direct and foreseeable consequences of the defendant's negligence.[228]

---

other words, McLachlin J.'s argument is that the owners had a *prima facie* duty of care to all foreseeable victims to either manufacture the rig competently, or to issue warnings to the appropriate persons, and that these foreseeable victims included the rig's users. This *prima facie* duty however is then negated by the problem of indeterminate liability.

225 This is put forth in *Weller & Co. v. Foot & Mouth Disease Research Inst.*, [1965] 3 All E.R. 560 (Q.B.D.). An auctioneer who suffered economic losses as a result of an outbreak of foot and mouth disease was unable to recover, since neither he nor his property was threatened.

226 *Seaway Hotels Ltd. v. Gragg (Can.) Ltd.*, [1959] O.R. 177, affirmed [1959] O.R. 581 (C.A.). Electricity was cut off to the plaintiff's hotel when the defendant damaged the electric company's line. Economic losses not consequential upon physical damages were held to be recoverable. These damages have been termed "parasitic." This approach was rejected by Lord Denning in *Spartan Steel & Alloys Ltd. v. Martin & Co. (Contr.) Ltd.*, above, note 208, and by Gibbs J. in *Caltex Oil v. The Dredge "Willemstad"* above, note 208, where it was termed "entirely irrational."

227 See *Dom. Tape of Can. Ltd. v. L.R. McDonald & Sons Ltd.*, [1971] 3 O.R. 627 (Co. Ct.). The defendants negligently damaged a hydro pole, interrupting electricity to the plaintiff's manufacturing plant. Lost profits were not recoverable; however, wages paid to employees during the time which they were unable to work were. But see *MacMillan Bloedel Ltd. v. Foundation Co.* (1977), 1 C.C.L.T. 358 (B.C. S.C. [In Chambers]), where recovery was denied for similar economic losses. Also see *Seaboard Life Ins. Co. v. Babich*, [1995] 10 W.W.R. 756 (B.C. S.C.), where this type of distinction was rejected. The case concerned a power outage which resulted in a loss to the plaintiff of computer data and loss of profit. An interesting aspect of the case was whether the loss of computer data constituted a property damage or an economic loss. The court considered it as a pure economic loss.

228 See, e.g., *Gypsum Carrier Inc. v. R.; C.N.R. v. The Harry Lundeberg* (1977), 78 D.L.R. (3d) 175 (Fed. T.D.); *Interocean Shipping Co. v. M/V Atl. Splendour* (1983), 26 C.C.L.T. 189 (Fed. T.D.); *Gold v. DeHavilland Aircraft of Can. Ltd.* (1983), 25 C.C.L.T. 180 (B.C. S.C.); and *Trappa Hldg. Ltd. v. Surrey (Dist.)* (1978), 95 D.L.R. (3d) 107 (B.C. S.C.). Also see Edmund Davies L.J.'s dissent in *Spartan Steel*, above, note 208.

(5) Purely economic losses ought to be recovered as a matter of policy considering the particular facts of each case.[229]

C.N.R. v. Norsk and *Bow Valley Huskey (Bermuda) Ltd. v. Saint John Shipbuilding Ltd.* provide other illustrations of the principle underlying these earlier cases. If the problem of indeterminacy can be solved due to a particular set of facts, and the court is not convinced that policy factors militate against a duty, a duty of care will be imposed.[230]

(b) Economic Losses Consequent on Personal Injuries Suffered by a Third Party

(i) Introduction

As with property damage, a personal injury suffered by one individual may affect the financial well-being of others. Relatives, colleagues at work, creditors, and all others who are in any way economically linked to the immediate victim, stand to suffer economic losses. Thus, for the same reasons which have led to the common law's resistance to economic loss claims related to another person's property damage, the common law has restricted claims for economic losses consequent on personal injuries suffered by others.[231]

There are three areas where recovery for this category of relational economic losses is permitted. First, there is the action for loss of consortium and services which may be brought by one spouse for losses caused as a result of personal injuries suffered by the other. Second, there is the action for loss of services which may be brought by an employer for economic losses caused as a result of personal injuries suffered by an employee. Third, there is the action under provincial legislation which may be brought by dependants of those killed, and, in some

---

229 This approach was adopted by Lord Denning in *Spartan Steel & Alloys Ltd. v. Martin & Co. (Contr.) Ltd.*, above, note 208, a case involving physical and economic losses caused by an electrical power failure. Lord Denning stated that these policy considerations included such things as the nature of the services affected by the outage, whether the claimant might have avoided the losses in other ways, whether there was the possibility of inflated or fraudulent claims if this one were to be permitted, and so forth. Ultimately, Lord Denning dismissed the plaintiff's economic loss claims.

230 The recent Supreme Count judgements did not specifically overrule any of these earlier tests. I might note, however, that the "parasitic" damages approach, or the positive outlay of money approach, have not attracted much favour. However, the "threatened physical" damage approach might still prove to be attractive. See discussion below relating to Defective Products and Buildings. A case very similar on its facts to *C.N.R. v. Norsk*, is *Caltex Oil (Australia) Pty. Ltd. v. The Dredge "Willemstad"* (1977), 136 C.L.R. 529 (Aust. H.C.). It also involved economic losses suffered by a plaintiff as a result of damage to property which it had a contractual right to use. A duty was established essentially based on "proximity" factors. The judgments in this case are very worthy of consideration, and contain many ideas similar to those raised in *C.N.R. v. Norsk*.

231 For a general discussion of relational losses, looking at it from both the common and civil law, see Van Praagh, "Who Lost What? Relationship and Relational Loss" (2002), 17 S.C.L.R. (2d) 269.

provinces, injured, for loss of support, or for expenses incurred as a result of the death, or injury, of their relative.[232]

(ii) Loss of Consortium[233]

The action *per quod consortium amisit* was, at common law, an action brought by a husband for a wrong done to his wife which resulted in a loss of her services to him. It has a long history, and originates in a society whose approach to the relationship between husband and wife would clearly be repugnant to us today.[234] Nevertheless, in some jurisdictions the action still survives, changed however by public policies and legislative enactments which have attempted to achieve sexual equality with respect to it.[235] It also must be noted that provincial statutes now provide for a wide range of compensation to relatives of those injured or killed by the torts of others, which render the common law actions unnecessary.[236]

Several features of the common law claim are worth noting. First, claims for unintentionally caused loss of consortium[237] are restricted to husbands.[238] Second,

---

232 This topic, which basically relates to assessment of damages, is thoroughly canvassed in Cooper-Stephenson *Personal Injury Damages in Canada*, 2nd ed. (1996) and will not be dealt with in this text.

233 See Risely, "Sex, Housework and the Law" (1980-81), 7 Adelaide L. Rev. 421; Bailey, "A Married Woman's Right of Action for Loss of Consortium in Alberta" (1979), 17 Alta. L. Rev. 513; Popescul, "Action Per Quod Consortium Amisit" (1979), 43 Sask. L. Rev. 27; West, "*Per Quod Consortium Amisit:* New Life for an Old Tort?" (1975), 33 U. of T. Fac. L. Rev. 76.

234 See Popescul, "Action Per Quod Consortium Amisit", *ibid.*, where the history of the action is traced. The author notes that it was a case in 1585 which first recognized the husband's separate right to sue in respect of an injury to his wife.

235 The action has been abolished in British Columbia by the Family Relations Act, R.S.B.C. 1996, c. 128, s. 123, in Ontario, by the Family Law Reform Act, R.S.O. 1980, c. 152, s. 69(3), in New Brunswick, by An Act Respecting Compliance of the Laws of the Province with the Canadian Charter of Rights and Freedoms, 1985, S.N.B. 1985, c. 41, s. 3, in Manitoba by the Equality of Status Act, C.C.S.M., c. E130, s. 1(1)(c), and in Saskatchewan by the Equality of Status of Married Persons Act, S.S. 1984-85-86, c. E-10.3, s. 6. It has been extended to wives in Alberta by the Tort-Feasors Act, R.S.A. 2000, c. T-5, s. 2.1(1). It has been extended to wives by the application of the Charter of Rights and Freedoms in *Power v. Moss* (1986), 38 C.C.L.T. 31 (Nfld. T.D.). One must also note that even provinces which have abolished it, for example, Ontario, may provide damages to a spouse whose relationship with an injured spouse has suffered. See, for example, *Sutton v. Pelley*, [1993] O.J. No. 2429.

236 Compensation is now frequently provided, for example, for the loss of care, guidance and companionship, of relatives injured or killed in accidents. In the case of *Ordon Estate v. Grail*, [1998] 3 S.C.R. 437, the Supreme Court extended the common law action for loss of consortium and services to provide for similar compensation to relatives of those injured or killed in boating accidents, which is not governed by the provincial statutes but by maritime common law. The judgment indicates the willingness of the court to modify the stricter common law to accommodate changing conditions. It has also been held, however, that in the absence of a specific statutory provision, a child cannot claim for the loss of consortium of its injured parent. See *Springer v. Thiede* (2001), 296 A.R. 154 (Q.B.). The court was unwilling to extend the Supreme Court's judgment in *Ordon Estate v. Grail* to provide for this type of claim in Alberta, where there is no statutory provision allowing for it.

237 As opposed to loss of consortium caused by deliberate acts, such as enticement.

238 The leading case is *Best v. Samuel Fox & Co.*, [1952] A.C. 716 (H.L.). This case was considered by the Supreme Court, with the implication that the action should not be extended, in *Montreal Tramways Co. v. Deeks*, [1953] 2 S.C.R. 404. As well, in *Woelk v. Halvorson* (1980), 14

there is considerable disagreement concerning the nature of the losses which make up a loss of consortium claim. One may look at loss of consortium and services as comprising two distinct elements — a material and a sentimental side.[239] The material side comprises various degrees of domestic services and assistance normally provided by one spouse for the other. The sentimental side involves the company, affection, and companionship of one spouse for the other. One line of authority suggests that a successful loss of consortium claim requires that there be a loss of services, the law not recognizing a claim for the loss of the intangible elements of the relationship.[240] The other point of view is that the action is available for any of the heads which fall under the rubric of consortium, be they services or comfort.[241] A second aspect of the disagreement concerns the extent of the required loss: must it be a total loss, either for a permanent or temporary period, or is a mere impairment of the consortium sufficient? On this as well, there was division in *Best v. Samuel Fox & Co.*, Lords Porter and Goddard thinking that a total loss was required, Lords Reid and Oaksey holding that a mere impairment would suffice. These differences of opinion have been seen in Canadian cases, some courts opting for the narrower view, others for the broader.[242] Another aspect of the common law action which ought to be noted is that it applies

---

C.C.L.T. 181 (S.C.C.), McIntyre J. stated that Canadian courts have tended to follow *Best v. Samuel Fox & Co. Ltd.*, and that it would be "fair . . . to say that a review of the authorities on the common law action leads to the conclusion that judicial opinion in this country has been, on balance, that the remedy is open to husbands only (though there are cases to the contrary)", at 14 C.C.L.T. 188. See, for example, *Perdicaris v. Kuntz* (1985), 45 Sask. R. 78 (Q.B.); and cases cited by West, above, note 233, at notes 57 and 84. Common law actions for enticement are apparently also restricted to husbands: see, e.g., *Davenport v. Miller* (1990), 70 D.L.R. (4th) 181 (N.B. Q.B.), additional reasons at (1990), 70 D.L.R. (4th) 181 at 187 (N.B. Q.B.).

239 See Popescul, above, note 233.

240 In *Best v. Samuel Fox & Co.*, above, note 238, at 733-34, Lord Goddard stated that "the only loss the law can recognize is the loss of that part of the consortium that is called servitium, the loss of service." The action per quod is distinct from a claim that an injured person can bring for his or her inability to continue to perform household services. There are numerous cases on this type of damage; see, for example, *Fobel v. Dean* (1991), 83 D.L.R. (4th) 385 (Sask. C.A.), leave to appeal to S.C.C. refused [1992] 2 W.W.R. lxxii (note) (S.C.C.); *Knoblauch v. Biwer Estate*, [1992] 5 W.W.R. 725 (Sask. Q.B.); and *McLaren v. Schwalbe* (1994), 16 Alta. L.R. (3d) 108 (Q.B.). In *Fobel v. Dean*, Vancise J. noted that this approach of compensating injured wives for the loss of their homemaking capacity is preferable to the "antiquated if not sexist" action for loss of consortium. As I noted above, however, the action for loss of consortium still exists in some jurisdictions. As well, one must keep in mind that although the action per quod claim is distinct from the action of the injured person to claim in her own right, double compensation must be avoided. The value of household services presumably cannot be awarded twice over. This is recognized by McLachlin J. in a more general context in *Ratych v. Bloomer* (1990), 3 C.C.L.T. (2d) 1 at 24 (S.C.C.).

241 See Lord Reid's judgment in *Best v. Samuel Fox & Co.*, above, note 238. The Supreme Court of Canada's judgement in *Ordon Estate v. Grail* above, note 236, supports this more generous approach.

242 See the articles by Popescul and West, above, note 233, where the Canadian cases are discussed. See *Stein v. Sobczak* (1981), 16 C.C.L.T. 262 (Man. C.A.), where the jurisprudence is reviewed, the court ultimately holding that an impairment of consortium was sufficient to justify a claim. Also see *Woelk v. Halvorson* (1980), 14 C.C.L.T. 181 (S.C.C.), where McIntyre J. stated that on balance the Canadian view has been that "an impairment, as distinct from a destruction of the consortium, should suffice to found the action", at 14 C.C.L.T. 188.

only to cases of personal injury. A spouse is unable to bring a claim for loss of consortium as a result of the death of the other spouse, a state of affairs which is difficult to justify.[243] Finally, one must recognize that at common law, even where an action for loss of consortium succeeds, the amount of damages awarded is very moderate.[244]

Although the action for loss of consortium seems, in most provinces, to be somewhat inconsequential, if not having been eliminated altogether, in Alberta it has been given new life. The Supreme Court of Canada, in *Woelk v. Halvorson*,[245] upheld an award of $10,000 given by the trial judge to a wife for the loss of consortium of her injured husband.[246] The decision was based on Alberta's Domestic Relations Act,[247] which extended the common law action to women, and was interpreted by the Supreme Court as having created a right of action which was not to be treated as "trivial and deserving of only token awards."[248] The judgment has accordingly revitalized the Alberta claim, not only for women, but presumably for men as well.[249]

---

243 See Popescul, above, note 233, who notes that this rule emanates from *Baker v. Bolton* (1808), 170 E.R. 1033, and seems to still be good law. But see *McGinn v. All-Pave*, [1987] 1 W.W.R. 160 (Alta. Q.B.), where the court, without even apparently considering the rule, awarded damages for loss of consortium of a deceased husband. One must also keep in mind that the expansion of fatal accident legislation can mitigate this position.

244 See McIntyre J.'s judgment in *Woelk v. Halvorson*, above, note 238, where he sums up the common law position by stating that the awards have generally been "modest."

245 (1980), 14 C.C.L.T. 181. See Klar, "Developments in Tort Law: The 1980-81 Term" (1982), 3 Sup. Ct. L. Rev. 399.

246 The amount had been reduced to $100 by the Alberta Court of Appeal at (1979), 11 C.C.L.T. 152 (C.A.).

247 R.S.A. 1970, c. 113, s. 35 (am. 1973, c. 61, s. 5(16)) [now R.S.A. 2000, c. D-14, s. 46]. The section reads:

> (1) Where a person has, either intentionally or by neglect of some duty existing independently of contract, inflicted physical harm upon a married person and thereby deprived the spouse of that married person of the society and comfort of that married person, the person who inflicted the physical harm is liable to an action for damages by the married person in respect of the deprivation.
>
> (2) The right of a married person to bring the action referred to in subsection (1) is in addition to, and independent of, any right of action the spouse has, or any action that the married person in the name of the spouse has, for injury inflicted upon the spouse.

A literal reading of the section implies that the injured spouse (i.e. the "married person") takes the action. This cannot be what was intended, and it has not been the interpretation given to the section by the courts. The action for loss of consortium is taken by the spouse who has lost the consortium, and not the injured spouse. This specifically was decided in *Logozar v. Golder* (1992), 136 A.R. 363, affirmed (1994), 157 A.R. 102 (C.A.), leave to appeal to S.C.C. refused (1995), 27 Alta. L.R. (3d) xlviii (S.C.C.). The loss of consortium provision is now found in the Tort-Feasors Act, R.S.A. 2000, c. T-5, s. 2.1(1).

248 [1981] 1 W.W.R. 289 at 296.

249 The amendment applies to both men and women who have been deprived of the "society and comfort" of their spouse. There have been several successful claims. See, for example, *Labonte v. Sowers* (1994) 158 A.R. 350 (Q.B.); and *Lawrence v. Smith* (1991), 124 A.R. 288 (Q.B.). See, however, *Joyce v. C.P. Hotels Corp.* (1994), 161 A.R. 53 (Q.B.), where it was held that the claim was for loss of comfort and support and not loss of service. In *Madge v. Meyer* (1999), [2000] 5 W.W.R. 38 (Alta. Q.B.), additional reasons at [2000] 6 W.W.R. 272 (Alta. Q.B.), affirmed [2001] 7 W.W.R. 635 (Alta. C.A.), additional reasons at [2002] 5 W.W.R. 50

(iii) *Loss of Services*[250]

As with the action for loss of consortium, the action for the loss of an employee's services has a long history, stemming from a period of time in which a master was thought to have a proprietary right in the servants he employed. When these servants were injured, the loss of their services was an economic loss, which was recoverable from the tortfeasor by the employer, thus constituting another exception to the exclusionary rule for relational economic losses. Despite the very different nature of employment relations today, the action still survives.[251]

In considering the action today, several important questions need to be answered. The first entails the action's scope. What sort of master-servant relationship is contemplated by the action *per quod servitium amisit*? As is discussed elsewhere,[252] there are inconsistent answers to this question. One view has it that the action is only available where the injured servant is a menial domestic servant.[253] A second view has been that it applies to all master-servant relationships, except the relationship between the government and public employees, such as army and police.[254] The third view, which is the one generally accepted in Canada,

---

(Alta. C.A.), the court rejected an argument that the $10,000 awarded in *Woelk* should be viewed as a type of "upper limit" and awarded $30,000. Twenty-thousand dollars was awarded in *Vespa v. Dynes* (2002), [2002] A.J. No. 644, 2002 CarswellAlta 644 (Q.B.) and *Semeniuk v. Cox* (2000), 258 A.R. 73 (Q.B.). An unusual case is *Martin v. Mineral Springs Hospital* (2001), 283 A.R. 178 (Q.B.). Due to medical negligence, a mother gave birth to a stillborn child. Both parents suffered psychologically. The husband's claim for the loss of consortium of his wife was allowed because she had suffered physical harm. The wife's claim, however, was denied because her husband had suffered no physical harm, as required by the Alberta statute.

250 See Hansen and Mullan, "Private Corporations in Canada: Principles of Recovery for the Tortious Disablement of Shareholders/Employees" in Klar (ed.), *Studies in Canadian Tort Law* (1977), Chapter 8; Irvine, "The Action Per Quod Servitium Amisit in Canada" (1980), 11 C.C.L.T. 241; Jones, "Per Quod Servitium Amisit" (1958), 74 L.Q.R. 39.

251 Although it is said to be "in a sorry state of dishevelment." See Irvine, *ibid.* See also Dickson J.'s judgment in *R. v. Buchinsky* (1983), 24 C.C.L.T. 266 (S.C.C.), where the notion that a master has a type of proprietary interest in his servant as a chattel is said to be "plainly offensive in today's society." See Klar, "Developments in Tort Law: The 1982-83 Term" (1984), 6 Sup. Ct. L. Rev. 325. The action has been abolished in British Columbia and New Brunswick. See the Law and Equity Act, R.S.B.C. 1979, c. 224, s. 59 [en. 1988, c. 42, s. 4]; and the Law Reform Act, S.N.B. 1993, c. L-1.2, s. 1 (1). This action also applies for a parent's loss of services of a child. See *dicta* in *Ordon Estate v. Grail*, [1998] 3 S.C.R. 437. Whether the action exists in Alberta was in issue in *Canada (Attorney General) v. Livingstone* (2004), 24 C.C.L.T. (3d) 320 (C.A.), reversing (2003), [2003] A.J. No. 1638, 2003 CarswellAlta 1962 (Alta. C.A.). The motions judge held that the action should be recognized as a new category of recoverable pure relational economic loss. The Court of Appeal reversed, holding that since the motions judge did not consider the duty formula of *Cooper v. Hobart* in his judgment, the matter should be sent back to Queen's Bench to be reconsidered on a *de novo* basis.

252 See Irvine, *ibid.*; Hansen and Mullan, above, note 250.

253 This is the English view: see Irvine, *ibid.*, at 245. The leading English case is *Inland Revenue Commrs. v. Hambrook*, [1956] 3 All E.R. 338 (C.A.).

254 This is the Australian approach, stemming from *The Commonwealth v. Quince* (1944), 68 C.L.R. 227 (Aust. H.C.); *A.G. N.S.W. v. Perpetual Trustee Co.* (1952), 85 C.L.R. 237, affirmed [1955] 1 All E.R. 846 (P.C.); and *Commr. for Rys. (N.S.W.) v. Scott* (1959), 102 C.L.R. 392 (Aust. H.C.).

is that it applies to all servants, menial or not, with no exception made to exclude the Crown.[255]

A second question concerning an employer's right to launch an action *per quod* relates to the status of the injured employee after the time of the injury. Must the employment relationship be continued to warrant the bringing of the claim, or can an employer sue even though the injured person is no longer an employee? It appears, both from the authors,[256] and the case law,[257] that the action is dependent upon a continuing relationship between the employer and employee, although, as is well noted, this position raises a number of unsettled questions.[258]

The third, and probably most difficult, aspect of the action *per quod* relates to the assessment of the claimant's damages. Although it is clear that damages are required for a successful *per quod* claim, what the damages are for is far from clear. As discussed by Irvine, there are a variety of possible claims which an employer might want to make as a result of an injury to an employee: such things as medical and hospital expenses, wages paid while the employee was unable to work, wages paid to hire a substitute, or loss of profits and income to the enterprise as a result of the loss of the employee's services. The surveys provided by the authors who have written in this area indicate the inconsistency prevalent in the case law. Some courts have allowed a loss of profits claim,[259] while others have rejected it, restricting recovery to wages and medical expenses paid to or on behalf of the injured employee.[260] Both of these approaches,

---

255 The most recent authoritative decision is *R. v. Buchinsky*, above, note 251, which expressly reaffirmed the Crown's right to the action when an injury occurred to a member of the armed forces, and implicity, held that it applies generally to all servants. For other cases supporting this, see *A.G. Can. v. Szaniszlo* (1985), 25 D.L.R. (4th) 606 (B.C. S.C.); *Davidson v. Pun* (1982), 21 C.C.L.T. 1 (B.C. S.C.), reversed on other grounds (1984), 30 C.C.L.T. 316 (B.C. C.A.); *Racicot v. Saunders* (1979), 11 C.C.L.T. 228 (Ont. H.C.); *Canada (Attorney General) v. Kerr* (1997), 36 O.R. (3d) 71 (Div. Ct.), leave to appeal refused (1997), 1997 CarswellOnt 3040 (C.A.); and *Nugent v. Rosetown Sch. Bd.* (1977), 2 C.C.L.T. 325 (Sask. C.A.), where the authorities are cited. There are, as noted by Irvine, above, note 250, contrary lower court decisions in Manitoba and Nova Scotia.

256 See especially Hansen and Mullan, above, note 250, at 223-24.

257 Hansen and Mullan, *ibid.*, cite *Swift Can. Ltd. v. Bolduc* (1961), 29 D.L.R. (2d) 651 (N.S. T.D.); and *Pagan v. Leifer* (1969), 6 D.L.R. (3d) 714 (Man. Q.B.).

258 See Hansen and Mullan, *ibid.*, at 224.

259 Cases cited by Hansen and Mullan, *ibid.*, include *Kneeshaw v. Latendorff* (1965), 54 D.L.R. (2d) 84 (Alta. T.D.); *Bermann v. Occhipinti*, [1954] 1 D.L.R. 560 (Ont. H.C.).

260 See cases cited by Hansen and Mullan, *ibid.*, including *Genereux v. Peterson Howell & Heather (Can.) Ltd.* (1972), 34 D.L.R. (3d) 614 (Ont. C.A.), and the trial judgment in *Nugent v. Rosetown Sch. Bd.* (1975), 60 D.L.R. (3d) 357 (Sask. Q.B.). The latter case was upheld on appeal at (1977), 2 C.C.L.T. 325. See Annotation by Mullan at 2 C.C.L.T. 325. This view was supported in *Everett v. King* (1981), 20 C.C.L.T. 1 (B.S. S.C.), affirmed (1983), 53 B.C.L.R. 144 (C.A.) (see accompanying Annotation by Mullan 20 C.C.L.T. at 2). Also see *Racicot v. Saunders* (1979), 11 C.C.L.T. 228 (Ont. H.C.). In *Vaccaro v. Giruzzi* (1992), 93 D.L.R. (4th) 180 (Ont. Gen. Div.), it was held that loss of profits are not recoverable, even in a one man company. Another way of approaching the issue of lost profits in a "one man company" seems to be for the injured plaintiff to sue in his or her own name for loss of profits which the "company" suffered as a result of the plaintiff's injuries. See, for example, *Webster v. Blair*, [1989] N.S.J. No. 396. A similar approach was taken in *Delange v. Parkinson Estate* (1997), 46 C.C.L.I. (2d) 56 (Ont. Gen. Div.), where the sole director and shareholder of a

however, give rise to several difficult further dilemmas, yet to be resolved by the courts.[261]

In *D'Amato v. Badger*,[262] a claim was made by a company for the loss of profits that it suffered as a result of an injury suffered by one of its two principal shareholders and employees. Although this type of claim would normally have been advanced as an action *per quod servitium amisit*, this had been abolished by statute in British Columbia. Thus the claim proceeded simply as a relational economic loss claim. Utilizing the jurisprudence that had been developed with regard to relational economic loss claims, the Supreme Court of Canada, per Major J., dismissed the company's claim. The Court held that due either to lack of proximity or based on policy concerns regarding indeterminate liability, the claim should fail.[263] It is curious that the claim should have been permitted to proceed at all. This was essentially a claim for the loss of services of an employee, which had been for policy reasons statutorily abolished in British Columbia. Allowing the claim to be resurrected through ordinary negligence law principles seems to run counter to the legislative intent in abolishing the action in the first place.[264]

5. LIABILITY FOR ECONOMIC LOSSES CAUSED BY DEFECTIVE PRODUCTS OR BUILDINGS

A final category of cases wherein recovery of purely economic losses has occasionally been permitted comprises economic losses suffered by non-privity users of defective products or buildings. While *Donoghue v. Stevenson* swept

---

company was allowed to personally claim for losses that the company did and would incur as a result of his injury. An interesting issue arose in *Schittone v. George Minkensky Ltd.* (1997), 36 O.R. (3d) 75 (Gen. Div.). The employee was injured in a motor vehicle accident. The employer continued to pay the employee's wages while it was not at work. Despite the fact that legislation prevented the employee from suing, this did not preclude the employer from recovering the wages paid through the *per quod* action for loss of services. See *Canada (Attorney General) v. Kerr* (1997), 36 O.R. (3d) 71 (Gen. Div.), leave to appeal refused (1997), 1997 CarswellOnt 3040 (C.A.) to the same affect.

261 See Hansen and Mullen, *ibid.*, and Irvine, above, note 250.

262 31 C.C.L.T. (2d) 1, 137 D.L.R. (4th) 129, [1996] 8 W.W.R. 390 (S.C.C.).

263 The trial court had allowed the claim at (April 7, 1993), Doc. Vancouver B893510, [1993] B.C.J. No. 764 (S.C.). The trial judge held that there was proximity. The Court of Appeal held that there was insufficient proximity between the defendants' negligence in injuring the employee and the company's loss of profits. The Court of Appeal, however, applied the *alter ego* principle and allowed the employee himself to recover 50 per cent of the profits lost. See [1994] 10 W.W.R. 141 (B.C. C.A.). The Supreme Court of Canada questioned the rationale for the *alter ego* principle but since it was not a subject of appeal allowed the award to stand. The *alter ego* principle was explained by the Court of Appeal as permitting a recovery "by an individual plaintiff who is the owner of all of the shares or virtually all of the shares of a limited company for a loss which he suffers through the loss which the company suffers"; see [1994] 10 W.W.R.141 (B.C. C.A.) at 149.

264 As noted above, the Alberta Court of Appeal in *Canada (Attorney General) v. Livingstone*, above, note 251, held that the existence of the action should be determined by an application of the duty formula of *Cooper v. Hobart*. Thus, although the action *per quod* has not been statutorily abolished in Alberta, the implication of the judgment is that if it exists, it must be justified by the new duty test.

away the requirement of privity for persons physically damaged by negligently manufactured goods and buildings,[265] it did not do so in respect of the purely economic losses suffered by these users.[266] Negligence law certainly allows recovery for physical damages and personal injuries caused to foreseeable victims by defective products or structures. It even may allow recovery for physical damage caused to one part of a structure as a result of a defect in another part.[267] It may allow the recovery of money expended in order to avert a threatened accident.[268] It does not allow, however, a user of a product or owner/occupant of a structure to sue the manufacturer or builder, in tort, for economic losses associated merely with the poor performance or quality of the product or structure. In the latter case, the common law has confined the complainants to either their contractual recourse against the seller or builder, or to whatever statutory protection might be available.

The first important Canadian case on recovery of economic losses suffered by a non-privity user of a defective product was *Rivtow Marine Ltd. v. Washington Iron Works.*[269] The plaintiff, in its logging business, used a special type of crane which had been designed and manufactured by the defendant. Because of a crack which developed in the crane, the plaintiff was forced to remove the crane from service during the peak of the logging season, in order to have it repaired. The crane, in its defective state, presented the threat of danger, and in fact, a similar crane had already collapsed, killing its operator. The defendant knew of the defect, but failed to warn the plaintiff of it for several months. The plaintiff sued the defendant for the costs of repairing the crane and for the loss of profits it suffered while the crane was idle.

Although on the surface, *Rivtow Marine* might look like an ordinary damage to property case, it clearly was not. The plaintiff's claim was not that the defendant's negligence damaged its property, but that the defendant's negligence supplied it with defective property. As well, the plaintiff could not allege that the

---

265 That *Donoghue v. Stevenson* applies to builder/owners, at least in so far as physical damages are concerned, although initially questioned, has now been accepted. See, e.g., Lord Denning's judgment in *Dutton v. Bognor Regis United Bldg. Co.*, [1972] 1 All E.R. 462 at 471-72 (C.A.), where His Lordship rejected the immunity given to builder/owners by *Bottomley v. Bannister*, [1932] 1 K.B. 458 (C.A.).

266 The focus is on a "pure" economic loss — a loss that is suffered by the user of a product, or an owner/occupant of a structure, without that person, or anyone else, suffering any actual physical damage or personal injury caused by the defective product or structure. Where the defect manifests itself in physical damage to the product or structure itself, e.g., a defective toaster blows up or parts of a building collapse, this is still a pure economic loss since the toaster or building has not damaged any other property. The defect also can manifest itself in the fact that the toaster simply does not work; e.g., it will not toast bread or the heating system of the building will not work. These are also pure economic losses, quantified by the costs of repairing or replacing the product or structure. If, however, the defect causes physical damage to other property or personal injury, e.g., the toaster blows up and burns down the house or the building collapses and injures someone, this is not a case of pure economic loss.

267 This is the "complex structure" problem, to be discussed below.

268 This is discussed in detail below.

269 (1973), 40 D.L.R. (3d) 530 (S.C.C.). See Harvey, "Case Comment to *Rivtow Marine*" (1974), 9 U.B.C. L. Rev. 170; Waddams, "Case Comment to *Rivtow Marine*" (1974), 52 Can. Bar Rev. 96; Binchy, "Negligence and Economic Loss: The Canadian *Tabula Rasa*" (1974), 90 L.Q.R. 181.

defective property caused an accident resulting in physical damages, in which case ordinary negligence principles would have applied. It could only allege that the property was defective and needed to be repaired, involving not only the direct costs of repair, but indirect costs as well, such as loss of profits. It could also show, however, that the defect in the property was dangerous, and could have resulted in personal injury or property damage if the property had not been repaired.[270]

The majority judgment in *Rivtow Marine* upheld a part of the plaintiff's claim. The plaintiff was able to recover the difference between the loss of profits it suffered as a result of being forced to repair the crane during peak logging season and what would have been lost if the crane had been repaired during the off-season. The majority judgment disallowed the claim for the cost of repairs. The court did not apply the ordinary duty of care principles based on foreseeability of damage, to this case, but imposed a special duty on the defendant to have warned the plaintiff, at the earliest opportunity, of the defect in the crane, so that the repairs could have been effected earlier. The duty was imposed because of the particular relationship of the parties to this case, which involved the defendant's knowledge of the plaintiff, and the plaintiff's reliance on the defendant's expertise with respect to this rather specialized product. Put in these terms, the majority's decision, while permitting some economic loss recovery and thereby signalling the common law's readiness to consider novel economic loss claims, can be interpreted relatively narrowly.[271] The majority judgment, delivered by Ritchie J., was in fact quite careful to make it clear that the ordinary principles of negligence law were not applicable to cases of pure economic losses suffered by non-privity users of defective products.

Laskin J.'s dissenting judgment went considerably further. He disagreed with the majority's holding that the defendant manufacturer of the crane could only be held liable for its failure to warn, and found that it was also liable for its negligence in having produced the defective crane in the first place. Ordinarily, a breach of the manufacturer's duty would make it liable for foreseeable physical harm, and

---

270 In *Strandquist v. Coneco Equipment* (1999), 48 C.C.L.T. (2d) 209 (Alta. C.A.), additional reasons at (2000), 2000 CarswellAlta 443 (C.A.), logging equipment purchased and used by the plaintiffs caught fire and was destroyed. The action against the manufacturer of the equipment was upheld based on its negligence in designing the equipment. The court did not take note of the fact that this was a pure economic loss case and not a property damage one, and the issues of liability in tort for pure economic losses were accordingly not discussed. In my opinion, this was not the correct approach. As discussed in this section, a manufacturer of goods is ordinarily not responsible in tort to the consumer if the goods are defective but do not cause injury or property damage.

271 It is interesting to note that some courts have construed *Rivtow Marine* as creating a broad principle permitting recovery of pure economic losses — for example, see *Maughan v. Int. Harvester Co. of Can.* (1980), 112 D.L.R. (3d) 243 (N.S. C.A.); *Gold v. DeHavilland Aircraft of Can. Ltd.* (1983), 25 C.C.L.T. 180 (B.C. S.C.); *Smith v. Melancon*, [1976] 4 W.W.R. 9 (B.C.S.C.) — while others have construed it narrowly, limiting economic loss recovery — for example, see *Langille v. Scotia Gold Co-op. Ltd.* (1978), 33 N.S.R. (2d) 157 (T.D.); *Ital-Can. Invt. Ltd. v. North Shore Plumbing & Heating Co.*, [1978] 4 W.W.R. 289 (B.C. S.C.); *Buthmann v. Balzer* (1983), 25 C.C.L.T. 273 (Alta. Q.B.); *Bethlehem Steel Corp. v. St. Lawrence Seaway Authority* (1978), 79 D.L.R. (3d) 522 (Fed. T.D.); *Marigold Hldg. Ltd. v. Norem Const. Ltd.*, [1988] 5 W.W.R. 710 (Alta. Q.B.) *Logan Lake (Dist.) v. Rivtow Indust. Ltd.*, [1990] 5 W.W.R. 525 (B.C. C.A.).

according to Laskin J., that same rationale "should equally support such recovery in the case where, as here, there is a threat of physical harm and the plaintiff is in the class of those who are foreseeably so threatened."[272] Thus, where a manufacturer's negligence in producing a dangerous product either results in physical damages, or economic losses expended to avert physical damages, there will be recovery. The dissent would have awarded the plaintiff not only the full loss of profits suffered while the crane was out of service for repairs, but the costs of these repairs as well.[273]

Over two decades later, the Supreme Court of Canada revisited the issue of pure economic losses caused by dangerous defects, this time in reference to a building. In *Winnipeg Condominium Corp. No. 36 v. Bird Construction Co.*[274] a non-privity purchaser of a building sued the builders for negligence.[275] The building developed a problem with its exterior cladding, pieces of which fell to the ground.[276] The owner of the building replaced the cladding and sued the builder for its considerable costs. A motion to strike out the claim was allowed by the Court of Appeal,[277] and the case went to the Supreme Court.

The result of the Supreme Court of Canada's judgment was the virtual acceptance of Laskin J.'s dissenting judgment in *Rivtow Marine.* Mr. Justice La Forest held, for a unanimous court, that a duty of care arises in tort between a builder and a subsequent user or occupant of a building when it is reasonably foreseeable that a defect in the construction poses a risk of danger to those persons or their property. It was the threatened personal injury or property damage, the cornerstone

---

272 40 D.L.R. (3d) 530 at 549.

273 Although these were permitted on the theory that they were expended to mitigate damages for the physical losses which would have been caused had the repairs not been done. In *Murphy v. Brentwood Dist. Council*, [1990] 2 All E.R. 908, the House of Lords rejected Laskin C.J.C.'s approach, expressing approval instead for the majority's reasoning. Although the case concerned a defective building, Lord Keith argued that in the case of chattels, it would be wrong to distinguish between a useless chattel and one which is dangerous due to a defect. In either case, once the defect is discovered, the costs of remedying it are purely economic ones, which are not recoverable in tort. Lord Bridge also argued that in the absence of a special relationship of proximity imposing on the tortfeasor a duty to safeguard the plaintiff from such an economic loss, these damages are not recoverable in tort. Lord Oliver termed the distinction between defective chattels which are not dangerous and those which are a fallacious one. It thus appears that for English courts at least, Laskin C.J.C.'s dissent in *Rivtow* is unacceptable.

274 (1995), 23 C.C.L.T. (2d) 1 (S.C.C.). For articles suggesting non-tort approaches to the *Winnipeg Condomium* problem see M. Moran, "Rethinking *Winnipeg Condo:* Restitution, Economic Loss.I.I." (1997), 47 U.T.L.J. 115 and N. Siebrasse, "The Choice Between Implied Warranty & Tort Liability for Recovery of Pure Economic Loss" (1996), 19 Dal. L.J. 247. Recent articles on recovery of pure economic losses in tort for defective products or structures include Brown, "Assumption of Responsibility and Loss of Bargain in Tort Law" (2006), 29 Dal. L.J. 345; Todd, "Policy Issues in Defective Property Cases" in Neyers, Pitel, Chamberlain, eds., *Emerging Issues in Tort Law* (2007), Chapter 8, Partlett, "Defective Structures and Economic Loss in the United States" in Neyers, Pitel, Chamberlain, eds., *Emerging Issues in Tort Law* (2007), Chapter 9.

275 The building was completed in 1974. The plaintiff in this action became the registered owner in 1978.

276 A potential problem with the cladding developed in 1982, 8 years after completion of the building. Inspections revealed no problems. However, 7 years later, in 1989, cladding fell.

277 (1993), 15 C.C.L.T. (2d) 1.

of Laskin J.'s dissent in *Rivtow*, which is the *ratio* of the decision in *Winnipeg Condominium*.[278]

The Supreme Court's decision clearly put Canadian tort law in this area on a different path than has been followed by the English House of Lords. In *D. & F. Estates Ltd. v. Church Commrs. for England*,[279] plaintiffs, who were lessees and occupiers of a flat built 15 years previously, sued the builders, among others, for the costs of remedial work to repair loose wall plaster. The initial work had been carried out negligently by subcontractors who had been hired by the builder. The action was rejected by the House of Lords. Lord Bridge held that if a chattel is defective, but causes no property damage or personal injury, the costs of remedying the defect ought to be treated as purely economic and ought not to be recoverable in tort. This is so even if the defect is dangerous to life or property. The same principle, according to Lord Bridge, is applicable to defective and dangerous structures, at least in so far as simple structures are concerned.

In its later judgment in *Murphy v. Brentwood Dist. Council*,[280] the House of Lords further elaborated on its approach. The case concerned the liability of a public authority for failing to properly oversee the construction of a defective building. The defect, which posed an imminent risk to health and safety, was discovered by the plaintiff, a purchaser of the building. Since the plaintiff was unable to repair the defective structure, he sold it, subject to its defects, and suffered a financial loss. He sued the council. The House of Lords rejected the claim. In the absence of a special relationship of proximity, created, for example, by reliance, there was no duty of care owed, either by public authorities or builders, even if the defective structure posed a threat of physical harm.[281] The general exclusionary rule, which prevents the recovery of purely economic losses was reaffirmed.

---

278 The threatened harm issue is repeated throughout the judgment. It is encapsulated in the following paragraph at 23 C.C.L.T. (2d) 26-27:

> In my view, the reasonable likelihood that a defect in a building will cause injury to its inhabitants is also sufficient to ground a contractor's duty in tort to subsequent purchasers of the building for the cost of repairing the defect if that defect is discovered prior to any injury and if it poses a real and substantial danger to the inhabitants of the building. In coming to this conclusion, I adopt the reasoning of Laskin J. in *Rivtow*, which I find highly persuasive. If a contractor can be held liable in tort where he or she constructs a building negligently and, as a result of that negligence, the building causes damage to persons or property, it follows that the contractor should also be held liable in cases where the dangerous defect is discovered and the owner of the building wishes to mitigate the danger by fixing the defect and putting the building back into a non-dangerous state. In both cases, the duty in tort serves to protect the bodily integrity and property interests of the inhabitants of the building.

279 [1988] 2 All E.R. 992 (H.L.).

280 Above, note 273.

281 Although the case concerned the liability of a public authority, the Lords maintained that this issue logically was inseparable from the issue of the builder's liability. The authority could not be held liable for failing to prevent the builder from doing something which could not result in the builder's own liability. Also see Lord Oliver's judgment for a detailed elaboration on why the public authority could not be in a more vulnerable position than the builder. In *Dept. of Environment v. Thomas Bates & Son Ltd.*, [1990] 2 All E.R. 943, the Lords briefly dealt with a builder's liability in tort for a defective structure.

In both *Winnipeg Condominium* and *Murphy v. Brentwood*, the "complex structure" theory was rejected. The argument, which first was suggested in *D. & F. Estates,* is that recovery for economic losses suffered as a result of a defective structure may be permitted when damage results to one part of a complex structure as a result of a defect in another part. In essence, the argument attempts to convert an economic loss case into one involving property damage. In *Murphy,* Lords Bridge and Jauncey found that "the complex structure theory" was artificial, and did not allow for economic loss recovery under the guise that the damage caused was physical.[282] In *Winnipeg Condominium,* Mr. Justice La Forest agreed, stating that the theory "serves mainly to circumvent and obscure the underlying policy questions".[283]

Difficult questions arise from *Winnipeg Condominium*. The most important is whether there can be liability for economic costs to repair structures which *do not pose a danger to persons or property*? Although it certainly appears from the judgment that a duty in this case would be unlikely, one must note that La Forest J. expressly declined to rule out a duty in such a case.[284] Cases decided subsequent to *Winnipeg Condominium* have required a real and substantial danger in order for a manufacturer to be liable for defective products.[285] Thus, in *M. Hasegawa*

---

282 It was conceded that if the defective chattel was truly separate from the rest of the structure, and not integral to the structure's integrity, the argument could succeed. Thus, if a defective boiler exploded and damaged a part of the building, the damage caused could be considered as physical, thus not raising economic loss concerns. Also see *Simaan Gen. Contr. Co. v. Pilkington Glass Ltd.*, [1988] 1 All E.R. 791 (C.A.), where the court carefully considered *Junior Books* and did not apply it to a similar case.

283 23 C.C.L.T. (2d) 15.

284 His Lordship stated that "[g]iven the clear presence of a real and substantial danger in this case, I do not find it necessary to consider whether contractors should also in principle be held to owe a duty to subsequent purchasers for the cost of repairing non-dangerous defects in buildings", at 23 C.C.L.T. (2d) 29. La Forest J. pointed out that while some other jurisdictions do allow for this, Dickson J.'s reasons in *Fraser-Reid v. Droumtsekas*, [1980] 1 S.C.R. 720 are "cool" to this idea.

285 The issue as to whether a defective, but non-dangerous motor home, could lead to tort liability was raised in *Del Harder v. Denny Andrews Ford Sales Inc.*, [1995] 9 W.W.R. 439 (Alta. Master) at 445. Master Funduk refused to dismiss the plaintiff's action on the defendant's motion for summary judgment, but he did lament the fact that "[a]bout all that can safely be said at this time is that the present state of Canadian law on this point is chaos." In *Privest Properties Ltd. v. Foundation Co. of Canada Ltd.*, [1995] 10 W.W.R. 385 (B.C. S.C.), affirmed (1997), 143 D.L.R. (4th) 635 (B.C. C.A.), additional reasons at (1997), 145 D.L.R. (4th) 729 (B.C. C.A.), leave to appeal refused (1997), 149 D.L.R. (4th) vii (S.C.C.) at 441 [W.W.R.], the principle of *Winnipeg Condominium* was stated to apply to buildings, and products incorporated into buildings, "if that product is later found to be dangerously defective in that it poses a 'real and substantial danger' of causing injury to persons or property." The court found that a fireproofing material containing asbestos did not pose a danger to the occupants of the building. In *Cook v. Bowen Island Realty Ltd.* (1997), 38 C.C.L.T. (2d) 217, [1998] 1 W.W.R. 647 (B.C. S.C.), additional reasons at (1998), 19 C.P.C. (4th) 148 (B.C. S.C.), *Winnipeg Condominium* was applied and an engineer of a defectively constructed water and sewage system was successfully sued. The water was undrinkable and the sewage system did not function. The court did not specifically address the issue of 'imminent danger'. There has been discussion in a few cases as to whether the danger must be an "imminent" one. This might have particular relevance for limitation periods; i.e., when does the cause of action arise? The Saskatchewan Court of Appeal in *Roy v. Thiessen* (2005), 252 D.L.R. (4th) 475, [2005] 7 W.W.R. 199 (Sask. C.A.), held that the risk need not be imminent. Other cases have suggested that there must be an imminent risk, although it is not altogether clear whether this

& Co. v. Pepsi Bottling Group (Canada) Co.,[286] a supplier of bottled water was not held liable to a purchaser in tort when it was discovered that some of the water was contaminated and that the entire shipment accordingly had to be destroyed. The Court of Appeal upheld the trial judge in concluding that this was not a property damage case but a pure economic loss one. It also agreed that the product had not caused any injury nor did it pose a real and substantial danger to consumers.[287] In view of this, the Court of Appeal agreed that there could be no liability.[288] As well, it is unclear to what extent an owner is entitled to be compensated. While the theory is that the owner is entitled to recover the reasonable cost of putting the building into a non-dangerous state, it still must be determined what this means.[289] The distinction between a "dangerous" and "non-dangerous" defect also might raise questions. Although heavy cladding which falls is certainly dangerous, the matter may not be so clear in other cases; leaky roofs, and cracked foundations, for example.[290] One must also not neglect the fact that the negligence

---

phrase was being used as being synonymous with "real and substantial" as opposed to implying a timeliness element. See *Blacklaws v. 470433 Alberta Ltd.*, [2000] 11 W.W.R. 476 (Alta. C.A.), leave to appeal refused 2001 CarswellAlta 492, 2001 CarswellAlta 493, [2001] S.C.R. vii (S.C.C.) and *Sentinel Self-Storage Corp. v. Dyregrov*, [2004] 11 W.W.R. 454 (Man. C.A.).

286 213 D.L.R. (4th) 663, 11 C.C.L.T. (3d) 249, [2002] 7 W.W.R. 600 (B.C. C.A.).

287 This obviously was a contentious issue. The Court of Appeal upheld the trial judge's finding that based on the evidence, the contaminated water posed no health risk.

288 The Court rejected the plaintiff's attempts to re-categorize this case as one of negligent services, and as well rejected the argument that a special rule should be adopted for defective food products as opposed to other types of goods. In dismissing the claim, the Court held that finding liability in tort for defective but non-dangerous goods would "create an implied warranty of product quality for the sale of commercial products in the absence of contract." Not only would this result in indeterminate liability, but also the Court agreed that the law of contract and sale of goods already adequately allocates risks for goods of poor quality and that tort law should accordingly not interfere. Also see *Edmonton (City) v. Lovat Tunnel Equipment Inc.* (2000), [2001] 4 W.W.R. 490, 3 C.C.L.T. (3d) 78 (Alta. Q.B.), which rejected a tort claim for a defective product that posed no imminent danger, after thoroughly canvassing the policy issues and jurisprudence. Also see *Zidaric v. Toshiba of Canada Ltd.* (2001), 5 C.C.L.T. (3d) 61 (Ont. S.C.J.), where a tort claim for a defective computer was struck out. In *Clare v. I.J. Manufacturing Ltd.* (2003), 16 C.C.L.T. (3d) 272 (B.C. S.C.), additional reasons at (2003), 2003 CarswellBC 2081 (S.C.), a tort claim for defective windows was dismissed on the basis that the defect posed no real and substantial danger to personal health and safety. In *Sentinel Self-Storage Corp. v. Dyregrov* (2003), 21 C.C.L.T. (3d) 1 (Man. C.A.), at 24, Steel J.A. re-iterated that "Canadian law does not allow redress *in tort* for non-dangerous deficiencies."

289 For example, one can make the building safe by removing all the exterior cladding. Is the builder also entitled to the costs of putting up all new cladding, and if so, of what quality? The principle that all that the plaintiff is entitled to receive as damages are the reasonable costs necessary to put the structure back into a non-dangerous state was reaffirmed by the Ontario Court of Appeal in *Mariani v. Lemstra* (2004), 246 D.L.R. (4th) 489, 27 C.C.L.T. (3d) 261 (Ont. C.A.), leave to appeal refused (2005), 2005 CarswellOnt 90 (S.C.C.). Also see *North Sydney Associates (Receiver of) v. United Dominion Industries* (2006), 268 D.L.R. (4th) 491 (N.S. C.A.), leave to appeal refused (2006), 2006 CarswellNS 536 (S.C.C.) to the same effect.

290 Does a smoke detector that does not alert an occupant of a fire in time for the occupant to escape pose an imminent danger? The occupant cannot be harmed by the detector; but can be harmed by unduly relying on it. This interesting question was in issue in *Hughes v. Sunbeam Corp. (Canada)* (2002), [2002] O.J. No. 3457, 2002 CarswellOnt 2919 (C.A), reversing (2000), 11 B.L.R. (3d) 236 (Ont. S.C.J.). The Court of Appeal reversed a trial judgment and refused to strike out the statement of claim for a proposed class action. The claimant sued for

of the contractor leading to the defect must be established. This means that normal wear and tear will be acceptable. More serious, however, is the problem that the tort duty ought not, in principle, be defined by the duty in contract. Thus, where a contractor competently constructs a building according to a contract which calls for poor quality materials, which might pose a greater danger to persons or property than better materials, will this be considered to be negligent?[291]

The Canadian Supreme Court has charted its own course in the area of economic loss recovery. It has broken down barriers between tort and contract, to an extent that no other jurisdiction has, and given tort law a very large role to play in settling commercial disputes. Whether this is the right course to follow remains to be seen.[292]

---

the replacement costs of a $20 smoke detector claiming that the detector was inadequate. The Court of Appeal acknowledged that this was a borderline case and hence allowed it to proceed. Laskin J.A. pointed out the difficulties inherent in allowing tort to be used as a product warranty mechanism.

291 The issue of negligence was not decided in *Winnipeg Condominium*, and was remitted to trial for consideration. Prior to this judgment, Canadian lower courts had followed various approaches. Some had followed *Junior Books v. Veitchi*, above, note 182 and allowed a duty based on a close proximate relationship. See, for example, *SEDCO v. William Kelly Hldg. Ltd.*,[1988] 4 W.W.R. 221 (Sask. Q.B.), varied [1990] 4 W.W.R. 134 (Sask. C.A.), where a tenant of a building whose cooling system was defective as a result of the negligence of an engineer was successfully able to sue. The court followed the authority of *Junior Books*, and other pure economic loss cases which allow recovery in "appropriate circumstances", and "especially in circumstances where the breach constitutes a foreseeable danger to the health or safety of a person." In *Strike v. Ciro Roofing Products U.S.A. Inc.*, (1988), 46 C.C.L.T. 209 (B.C. S.C.), the court quoted extensively from *Junior Books* in allowing a claim brought by a project owner against a roofing subcontractor for a defective roof. As well, in *Univ. of Regina v. Pettick* (1986), 38 C.C.L.T. 230 (Sask. Q.B.), reversed (1991), 6 C.C.L.T. (2d) 1 (Sask. C.A.), a subcontractor was held to have breached a duty of care owed to the non-privity plaintiff. However, in *Buthmann v. Balzer* (1983), 25 C.C.L.T. 273 (Alta. Q.B.), the court rejected the claim of purchasers of a defective house, brought against the builder/vendor, for the costs of repairing the defects found in the house. The court held that the claim in tort required proof of either personal injury or consequential property damage.

292 In its most recent pure economic loss judgment, *Design Services Ltd. v. R.*, 2008 SCC 22, the Supreme Court rejected a claim for pure economic losses suffered by sub-contractors. The sub-contractors were associated with a contractor who had submitted a bid for a construction project. The contract for the project was awarded to a non-compliant bidder. The contractor settled its claim with the project owner. Rothstein J. held that the sub-contractors could have protected themselves by joining with the contractor in the bid, thereby creating contractual relations with the project owner. Having deliberately failed to do so, Rothstein J. held that it was not appropriate to allow the parties to use tort law to avoid the consequences of their decision. This judgment heralds a return to a more traditional approach to respecting the boundaries between tort and contract.

8

The Duty of Care of Public Authorities

1. INTRODUCTION

The duty of care owed by public authorities[1] is the third major area of refinement of Lord Atkin's neighbour principle. As with the duty to assist and the duty to prevent purely economic losses, the extent to which the common law of negligence ought to permit private actions for injuries caused by the activities of public authorities has challenged both the judiciary and the academic commentator.[2] The common law faces here, as it does in the other two areas, the same dilemma: should unreasonable conduct in the face of foreseeable injury necessarily result in a private cause of action or do overriding policy concerns prevent the imposition of a duty of care? Public tort liability raises complex issues which have certainly not been clearly resolved as of yet.

2. CROWN LIABILITY

As this chapter is concerned with the substantive rules of negligence law which apply to public authorities, the issue of proceedings against the Crown will only

---

1 This term is intended to comprise all those persons and bodies, from the Crown down through to municipal corporations, other local authorities, and their employees, who are elected, appointed or employed in the public sector. Litigation generally involves the Crown, local governments, and their employees, i.e., civil servants.

2 The literature on this topic is extensive. In addition to the many articles on the topic cited in prior editions of this text, recent articles and books include: Feldthusen, *Economic Negligence*, 5th ed. (2008), Chapter 6; Linden and Feldthusen, *Canadian Tort Law*, 8th ed (2006), Chapter 17; M. Randall, "Sex Discrimination, Accountability of Public Authorities and the Public/Private Divide in Tort Law" (2001), 26 Queen's L.J. 451; Doyle & Redwood, "The Common Law Liability of Public Authorities: The Interface between Public & Private Law" 7 Tort Law Rev. 30; Bailey & Bowman, "Public Authority Negligence Revisited" (2000), 59 Camb. L.J. 85. There have been as well a number of comments on specific cases. The Bailey & Bowman article is particularly useful as it comments on three House of Lords judgments on the issue of public tort liability; namely, *X (minors) v. Bedfordshire County Council*, [1995] 2 A.C. 633 (U.K. H.L.); *Stovin v. Wise*, [1996] A.C. 923 (U.K. H.L.); and *Barrett v. Enfield London Borough Council*, [1999] 3 W.L.R. 79 (U.K. H.L.).

be briefly addressed.[3] Although under our system of government and law, "every official, from the Prime Minister down to a constable or a collector of taxes, is under the same responsibility for every act done without legal justification as any other citizen,"[4] the Crown itself, as opposed to its servants and agents, could not be sued at common law.[5] One could only sue the Crown by way of the procedure known as "petition of right", whereby one asked the Crown for permission for it to be sued, subject to a number of other prerogative Crown privileges.[6] This situation has been changed and now the federal government and all provinces

---

3 On this topic see Horsman and Morley, eds., *Government Liability: Law and Practice.* (2007); Hogg and Monahan, *Liability of the Crown*, 3rd ed. (2000); Goldenberg, "Tort Actions Against the Crown in Ontario", Spec. Lect. L.S.U.C., *New Developments in the Law of Torts* (1973), at 341; Kennedy, "Suits by and Against the Crown" (1928), 6 Can. Bar Rev. 373; Cairns, *The Law of Tort in Local Government*, 2nd ed. (1969); Cohen and Smith, "Entitlement and the Body Politic: Rethinking Negligence in Public Law" (1986), 64 Can. Bar Rev. 1; Jack, "Suing the Crown and the Application of the Charter" (1986), 7 Advocates' Q. 277; Rainaldi (ed.), *Remedies in Tort* (1988), Vol. 4, Chapter 28; Law Reform Commission of B.C., "Civil Rights — Legal Position of the Crown"; Lordon, *Crown Law* (1991).

4 Dicey, *Law of the Constitution*, 10th ed. at 193, cited by Martland J. in *Nat. Harbours Bd. v. Langelier* (1968), 2 D.L.R. (3d) 81 at 84 (S.C.C.). In *Decock v. Alberta* (2000), 186 D.L.R. (4th) 265 (Alta. C.A.), leave to appeal allowed (2000), 293 A.R. 388 (note) (S.C.C.), the Court noted that the liability of Crown servants is first and foremost a personal liability, and thus defendants should be named personally. In this case the Court held that it was proper to name Premier Ralph Klein and Health Minister Shirley McClellan personally as defendants in a case concerning inadequate health care services. Moreover, the Premier of Alberta was held not to be a suable entity since it is not an office or role specifically recognized in law. The Premier and Minister of Health could be named as representatives of the Crown. The suit was subsequently settled.

5 This has been expressed in the maxim that "the King could do no wrong." See Goldenberg, above, note 3, at 345, for a list of cases supporting the proposition. For a judgment discussing the principles, see *Re Air India* (1987), 44 D.L.R. (4th) 317 (Ont. H.C.). Also see *Bank of B.C. v. C.B.C.*, [1992] 3 W.W.R. 183 at 188 (B.C. C.A.):

> The decision in *Langelier* finally established that in this country, as in the United Kingdom, Crown privilege or immunity, while it protects the Crown and property and revenues of the Crown, does not at common law protect Crown servants, or individual or corporate agents of the Crown, in respect of claims in tort for acts committed by them, even though committed in the course of carrying out their functions.

The court decided that the Crown Liability Act, R.S.C. 1970, c. C-38, s. 10(1) requirement of 90 days' notice did not apply to a defamation action brought against the C.B.C., since this action was one brought pursuant to the common law. In *Botting v. British Columbia* (1996), 33 C.C.L.T. (2d) 294 (B.C. S.C.), the Crown was sued for an accident occurring on a bridge. The bridge was built before the enactment of the Crown Proceedings Act, S.B.C. 1974, c. 24 although the accident occurred many years later. In deciding that the Crown could be sued, Shaw J. made the point that the pre-legislation bar to suing the Crown was a procedural and not a substantive one. In other words, the Crown could do wrong—it just could not be sued. In *B. (K.L.) v. British Columbia* (1999), 46 C.C.L.T. (2d) 237 (B.C. C.A.), leave to appeal refused (2000), 256 N.R. 395 (note) (S.C.C.), actions were brought against the Crown for sexual assaults committed at a foster care facility prior to the enactment of the Crown Proceedings Act. The Court of Appeal held, with one dissent, that the "reasonable discoverability" rule applied to the act for the purpose of determining when the cause of action arose. Also see *Arishenkoff v. British Columbia*, 215 D.L.R. (4th) 744, [2002] 10 W.W.R. 130 (B.C. S.C. [In Chambers]) on the same point.

6 Professor Hogg notes that the petition of right procedure did not apply to most tort actions, and thus the Crown was virtually immune from tort suit. See Hogg & Monahan, *Liability of the Crown*, 3rd ed. (2000) at 6-7.

have legislation permitting legal proceedings to be brought against the Crown.[7] Although the various acts are not identical,[8] and are certainly not simply analyzed or explained,[9] their effect is to allow the Crown to be sued in tort, as if it were an ordinary person, with respect to its liabilities for the torts of its servants or agents, as an employer, as an owner, occupier, or possessor of property, or by virtue of statute.[10] In this context, the Crown refers to the executive governments of Canada and the ten provinces,[11] acting through the Governor General in Council and the ten Lieutenants Governor in Council.[12] The Crown can be sued either directly, or

---

7 See Crown Proceeding Act, R.S.B.C. 1996, c. 89; Proceedings Against the Crown Act, R.S.A. 2000, c. P-25; Proceedings Against the Crown Act, R.S.S. 1978, c. P-27 (as amended S.S. 2000, c. L-5.1, s. 3, S.S. 2000, c. I-2.01, s. 3); Proceedings Against the Crown Act, R.S.M. 1987, c. P140 (as amended); Proceedings Against the Crown Act, R.S.O. 1990, c. P.27 (as amended); Proceedings Against the Crown Act, R.S.N.B. 1973, c. P-18; Proceedings Against the Crown Act, R.S.N.S. 1989, c. 360 (as amended); Crown Proceedings Act, R.S.P.E.I. 1988, c. C-32; Proceedings Against the Crown Act, R.S.N. 1990, c. P.26 (as amended); Crown Liability and Proceedings Act, R.S.C. 1985, c. C-50 (as amended S.C. 2001, c. 4). In Quebec, see Special Procedure Act, R.S.Q. 1977, c. P-27, s. 1, repealed by An Act to Amend and Repeal Certain Legislation; Code of Civil Procedure, R.S.Q. 2000, c. C-25, s. 94. Note that prior to the passage of the Federal Crown Liability Act, the Exchequer Court Act, R.S.C. 1927, c. 34, s. 19, provided for negligence actions to be brought against the Federal Crown in certain circumstances. See *Kaiswatum v. Canada (Attorney General)*, [2003] 5 W.W.R. 558 (Sask. Q.B.) where this is discussed.

8 Hogg & Monahan, *Liability of the Crown*, 3rd ed. (2000), at 88, notes that a uniform provision was enacted by all provinces, excepting British Columbia and Quebec, and the federal government.

9 Goldenberg, above, note 3, at 352, makes this perfectly clear when he states:

> Any successful claim against the Crown will have to make its way through a minefield of statutory preconditions; at any moment, a sudden sweep of the procedural scythe can cut the plaintiff off at the knees.

10 There are some variations with respect to these liabilities. Readers are advised to refer to the particular legislation governing the case. On the question of the applicability of provincial statutes to the Federal Crown, see *Stuart v. Can.*, [1988] 6 W.W.R. 211 (Fed. T.D.), with respect to Alberta's Occupiers' Liability Act, R.S.A. 2000, c. 0-4; and *Hood v. Canada* (1998), 162 F.T.R. 167 (T.D.)—Crown bound by Manitoba's Fatal Accidents Act, R.S.M. 1987, c. F 50, s. 3.

11 Including their ministries, departments, boards, commissions and corporations. See *Remedies In Tort*, above, note 3.

12 For example, Crown proceedings legislation was invoked when the federal Department of Consumer and Corporate Affairs was sued for its alleged negligence with relation to inadequate legislation governing the safety of baby cribs — *Mahoney v. R.* (1986), 38 C.C.L.T. 21 (Fed. T.D.); when the Nova Scotia Department of Health was sued for the alleged negligence of the officers of the Department with respect to the suitability of a lot for a sewage disposal system — *A.G. N.S. v. Aza Avramovitch Assoc. Ltd.* (1984), 11 D.L.R. (4th) 588 (N.S. C.A.); and when the Alberta Gas Protection Branch and its employees were sued for their alleged negligence with respect to the regulation and inspection of gas furnaces — *Kwong v. R.* (1978), 8 C.C.L.T. 1 (Alta. C.A.), affirmed (1979), 12 C.C.L.T. 297 (S.C.C.). As discussed elsewhere in this text, several recent actions against the Crown involve allegations of sexual or physical abuse suffered by residents of schools and those in foster or other supervised care. These have been based on theories of negligence, vicarious liability, breaches of non-delegable duties, and breaches of fiduciary duties.

vicariously for the torts of its servants or agents.[13] It is important to note, however, that although the Crown can be sued vicariously for the torts of its servants, and its servants can be sued personally, government officials cannot be sued by title alone. Thus, in *M. (M.) v. K. (K.)*[14] actions brought against "the Superintendent of Family and Child Service", and "the Ministry of Human Resources", in their official, and not personal, capacities, were thrown out.[15]

Once having determined that the Crown or its agent is suable, either directly, or vicariously, other matters must concern the claimants.[16] Over and above the substantive law of negligence which might prevent there being a successful suit,

---

13 See, however, discussion by Goldenberg, above, note 3, regarding Ontario, as to the liability of the Crown when agents or Crown corporations are involved. Despite ambiguity in the legislation itself, Goldenberg's conclusion is that the Crown will usually be able to be sued vicariously for the torts of all its servants, corporate and natural, superior and subordinate, as well as for the torts which originate in the activities of statutory agencies. There may be situations, however, where only the Crown agency can be sued. See Goldenberg, at 364. On what is an agent of the Crown see *Lucas v. Taxicab Bd.*, [1985] 2 W.W.R. 681 (Man. C.A.); *Westeel-Rosco Ltd. v. Bd. of Gov. of South Sask. Hosp. Centre*, [1977] 2 S.C.R. 238; *R. v. Ont. Lab. Rel. Bd.*, [1963] 2 O.R. 91 (C.A.); *Nor. Pipeline Agency v. Perehinec*, [1983] 2 S.C.R. 513; and *Robb Estate v. Canadian Red Cross Society*, [2000] O.T.C. 23 (S.C.J.), additional reasons at (2001), 2001 CarswellOnt 545 (S.C.J.), reversed (2001), 9 C.C.L.T. (3d) 131 (Ont. C.A.), additional reasons at (2002), 9 C.C.L.T. (3d) 193 (Ont. C.A.), leave to appeal refused (2002), 2002 CarswellOnt 2839, 2002 CarswellOnt 2840 (S.C.C.). On who is a servant, see Le Dain J. in *Baird v. R.* (1983), 148 D.L.R. (3d) 1 (Fed. C.A.). See Hogg & Monahan, above, note 3, at 11. Also note that in *Munro v. Canada* (1992), 98 D.L.R. (4th) 662 (Ont. Gen. Div.), it was held that the proper defendant was the Attorney-General of Canada and not Her Majesty the Queen in Right of Canada. The distinction between the direct or vicarious liability of the Crown, and the related issue of whether claimants must identify the particular employee or agent who committed the tort has been raised in recent cases. See in particular Cullity J.'s decision in *Williams v. Canada (Attorney General)* (2005), 257 D.L.R. (4th) 704, 34 C.C.L.T. (3d) 213 (Ont. S.C.J.), where this issue is fully explored. The conclusion of Cullity J.'s review seems to be that the line between the direct and vicarious liability of the Crown has become blurred, if not ignored, by courts, and that a plaintiff is able to sue the Crown without the requirement of identifying who it actually was that owed the plaintiff a duty and breached it. See also Lori Sterling, "Limiting Governmental Liability in Tort", a paper prepared for the Third Conference on Crown Liability, Osgoode Professional Development Centre (2006); Horsman and Morley, above, note 3, at 1.50(10)1.

14 (1987), 39 C.C.L.T. 81 (B.C. S.C.), reversed in part on other grounds (1989), 50 C.C.L.T. 190 (B.C. C.A.).

15 Also see *Re Air India*, above, note 5; and *Decock v. Alberta*, above, note 4.

16 On the suability of statutory agencies or boards, see *Westlake v. R.* (1971), 21 D.L.R. (3d) 129 (Ont. H.C.), affirmed (1972), 26 D.L.R. (3d) 273 (Ont. C.A.), which was affirmed (1973), 33 D.L.R. (3d) 256n (S.C.C.); *B.G. Ranches v. Man. (Agricultural Lands Protection Bd.)*, [1983] 4 W.W.R. 681 (Man. Q.B.); *Duggan v. Newfoundland* (1992), 91 D.L.R. (4th) 262 (Nfld. T.D.); *Trosin v. Sikora* (2000), 272 A.R. 137 (Q.B.)—Alberta Securities Commission is capable of being sued; *Smith v. New Brunswick (Human Rights Commission)* (1997), 143 D.L.R. (4th) 251 (N.B. C.A.), leave to appeal refused (1997), 192 N.B.R. (2d) 198 (note) (S.C.C.)—Human Rights Commission not a suable entity; among others. See discussion of this point in Horsman and Morley, above, note 3, at 1.50.10(1).

specific statutory immunities from suit might exist.[17] As well, special limitation periods and notice requirements must also be observed.[18]

In addition to tort actions brought against the Crown, its agents, servants, or other bodies, either based on common law torts or specific statutory torts, much of the activity in public negligence law relates to litigation brought against municipal corporations and their officials. These bodies and officials were not subject to immunity from suit at common law,[19] and thus, aside from the question of suability based on their status and statutory foundation,[20] do not raise the same concerns associated with proceedings against the Crown. They are, however, political bodies, and it is within the substantive rules of negligence law that their real immunities are found.

3. THE DUTY OF CARE OF PUBLIC AUTHORITIES

(a) Introduction

For many of their activities, public authorities are judged according to the ordinary principles of negligence law. Public officials who drive cars in the course of their employment, who give out advice upon which others rely, or public authorities which own, occupy or construct buildings, for example, owe a private law duty of care and are expected to live up to the same standards of care for the protection of their neighbours as is everyone else. There remains, however, an area of political activity which is not as vulnerable to a private law suit for damages, and which courts are reluctant to assess according to the ordinary standards of negligence law. It is the dividing line between the activities of government which are subject to the ordinary principles of negligence law and those which are not which has provoked considerable judicial and scholarly interest.

Several reasons why the judiciary has been reluctant to expose certain of the activities of public authorities to the scrutiny of negligence law and its sanctions can be put forward. The most significant one relates to the notion that those who engage in certain types of political activities should be exclusively accountable, with respect to their performance, to the citizenry which elects them. The quality

---

17 Goldenberg gives the example of the Cancer Remedies Act, R.S.O. 1990, c. C.2 (repealed by Government Process Simplification Act, R.S.O. 1997, c. 15, s. 17) and the Securities Act, R.S.O. 1990, c. S.5 (as amended), which contain immunity provisions. See Goldenberg, above, note 3, at 388.

18 To say nothing of the effect of the Canadian Charter of Rights and Freedoms on this whole question! See, e.g., *Mirhadizadeh v. Ont.* (1986), 33 D.L.R. (4th) 314 (Ont. H.C.), affirmed (1989), 60 D.L.R. (4th) 597 (Ont. C.A.); *Streng v. Winchester (Twp.)* (1986), 37 C.C.L.T. 296 (Ont. H.C.). There is also the issue of the immunity of the Crown from execution of judgments. See Law Reform Commission of Canada, *Immunity from Execution*, Working Paper 40, 1987. A case raising this issue is *Hislop v. Canada (Attorney General)* (2002), [2002] O.J. No. 2799, 2002 CarswellOnt 2344 (S.C.J.).

19 Cohen and Smith, "Entitlement and the Body Politic: Rethinking Negligence in Public Law" (1986), 64 Can. Bar Rev. 1, note that suits against municipal corporations and other incorporated public authorities for physical injuries or property damage, either based in nuisance or negligence arising out of the breach of statutory duties, were successful beginning in the late eighteenth century.

20 Discussed in such cases as *Westlake v. R.*, above, note 16.

and wisdom of some political decisions ought not to be second-guessed by the judiciary. Public authorities are required to assess what is in the public's interest, and in this process, decisions may harm private interests. One can readily see, for example, that decisions relating to land use regulation, taxation policies, expenditures of public funds and the like will harm the interests of some, and may even, by any standard, be considered unreasonable. One would not suggest that these activities *cannot* be assessed according to the standards of the negligence action, but that they *ought* not to be.

Other concerns are more pragmatic or administrative in nature. Since many governmental activities involve difficult decision-making, the balancing of conflicting interests and the weighing of competing claims of efficiency and thrift, which in turn demand access to, and the analysis of information by those with special backgrounds and expertise, courts are naturally frequently reluctant to get involved. Judges cannot spend their time acting like city councillors, examining impact studies, listening to special interest groups, and poring over city budgets. Finally, if tort law review of political decisions were possible, there is the fear that this would lead to a flood of suits, the intimidation of decision-makers, and the opening up of old, and seemingly already decided, disputes.

Whereas negligence actions brought against public authorities seemed to have had a fairly good chance of success in the decades of the 1980s and 1990s, the tide has recently turned. *Cooper v. Hobart*[21] has, as we have seen, introduced a new factor into the duty formula, that of proximity. This has proven to be a major obstacle for plaintiffs in their efforts to establish the existence of a duty of care relationship between themselves and government.

(b) Express Statutory Liability

A significant number of the private law claims for damages instituted against public authorities stem from specific statutory enactments which require the authorities to perform public functions, such as the maintenance and repair of roads, and which provide civil liability for their failure to do so. Although these cases clearly require courts to assess the competence of public bodies as they carry out their statutory responsibilities, and thus to determine the reasonableness of both planning and operational activities, this is a task that the courts cannot avoid. They have been directed by the legislatures to assess the quality of the authorities' works, in the context of a private cause of action.

That courts are not reluctant, and seem quite capable, in assessing the conduct of public bodies, whether it be in the decision-making or operational stages of their activity, when a statutory duty of care is imposed, is evident from the leading case of *R. v. Cote.*[22] This case involved the statutory duty to maintain and keep a highway in repair imposed on the Crown by the Highway Improvement Act.[23] The alleged act of negligence was the Department of Highways' failure to remove or warn of the hazard of ice or snow on one of its highways. The trial judge held

21 (2001), 206 D.L.R. (4th) 193 (S.C.C.).

22 (1974), 51 D.L.R. (3d) 244 (S.C.C.), affirming as to the Crown's liability (*sub nom. Millette v. Cote; Dennery v. Cote*) (1972), 27 D.L.R. (3d) 676 (Ont. C.A.), which affirmed (1970), 17 D.L.R. (3d) 247 (Ont. H.C.).

23 R.S.O. 1960, c. 171, s. 33(1).

the Department liable for negligence, stating that it ought to have known of the dangerous condition on its road; that it failed to perform reasonable inspections of its highway; and that it failed to take reasonable steps to reduce the dangers or warn the public regarding them.[24] The fact that the defendant was a public body, performing functions both at the planning and operational stages for the public's benefit, did not prevent the courts from assessing the competence of its performance once the duty was statutorily imposed.[25]

There have been several other cases where, pursuant to express statutory duties, the activities of public bodies have been judicially reviewed, both at their planning and operational stages, without much apparent difficulty. The Alberta case of *Berezowski v. Edmonton*[26] well illustrates the point that the courts will review both the policy and operational activities of governmental bodies, under legislation imposing an express statutory duty. The plaintiff was involved in a traffic accident allegedly caused by the absence of a traffic control sign. The majority of the court held that the statutory duty imposed on the defendant municipality

---

24 These findings were confirmed by both the Court of Appeal and Supreme Court of Canada. Because the defendant did not call evidence regarding its system of inspection, and other policies adopted to maintain the road in question, the courts were unable to assess the reasonableness of its programs.

25 There have been several other failure to salt or sand cases, which have followed *R. v. Cote*. See *McAlpine v. Mahovlich* (1979), 9 C.C.L.T. 241 (Ont. C.A.); *Gould v. Perth (County)* (1984), 12 D.L.R. (4th) 763 (Ont. C.A.), affirming (1983), 149 D.L.R. (3d) 443 (Ont. H.C.); *Landriault v. Pinard* (1976), 1 C.C.L.T. 216 (Ont. C.A.); *Simms v. Toronto* (1978), 4 C.C.L.T. 214 (Ont. C.A.), affirming (1976), 74 D.L.R. (3d) 533 (Ont. H.C.); *Rydzik v. Edwards* (1982), 23 C.C.L.T. 23 (Ont. H.C.); *Peddle (Litigation Guardian of) v. Ontario (Minister of Transportation)* (1997), 30 O.T.C. 85 (Gen. Div.), additional reasons at (1997), 36 O.T.C. 43 (Gen. Div.), additional reasons at (1997), 1997 CarswellOnt 3697 (Gen. Div.), affirmed (1998), 117 O.A.C. 379 (C.A.); and *Bisoukis v. Brampton (City)* (1999), 180 D.L.R. (4th) 577 (Ont. C.A.), leave to appeal refused (2000), 141 O.A.C. 200 (note) (S.C.C.). They confirm the argument made above. For example, in *Gould v. Perth County*, a positive decision not to salt or sand due to high winds, but to postpone operations until the next morning, coupled with the fact that there was no practicable or financial impediment to sanding, led to liability under the statute. Query: if there was not an express statutory duty, would the court have reviewed this decision? See *Barratt v. North Vancouver (Dist.)* (1980), 14 C.C.L.T. 169 (S.C.C.), and discussion below. In *Roberts v. Montana* (1997), 38 C.C.L.T. (2d) 1 (Ont. Gen. Div.), additional reasons at (1997), 37 O.R. (3d) 333 (Gen. Div.), additional reasons at (1997), 37 O.R. (3d) 333 at 342 (Gen. Div.), additional reasons at (1998), 37 O.R. (3d) 333 at 353 (Gen. Div.), affirmed (2000), 2 C.C.L.T. (3d) 247 (Ont. C.A.), affirmed (2000), 2 C.C.L.T. (3d) 248 (Ont. C.A.), the court considered but rejected the argument that decisions regarding sanding the highway were "policy" decisions as contemplated in *Just v. British Columbia*, discussed below. The issue has also arisen with respect to a public authority's duty under occupiers' liability legislation. In *Kennedy v. Waterloo (County) Board of Education* (1999), 45 C.C.L.T. (2d) 169 (Ont. C.A.), leave to appeal refused (2000), 134 O.A.C. 397 (note) (S.C.C.), the court held that the policy/operational dichotomy is not applicable to the express statutory duty. The fact that the defendant is a public authority operating under restraints can be a factor in establishing the standard of care, but the authority cannot make a "policy" decision to exempt itself from its duty. Also see *Restoule v. Strong (Township)* (1999), 4 M.P.L.R. (3d) 163 (Ont. C.A.) to the same effect—a "policy" decision cannot be used by a public authority to exempt itself from a statutory duty. For commentaries see J. Mascarin, "Annotation: *Kennedy v. Waterloo*" 6 M.P.L.R. (3d) 2; M.R. O'Conner & D.G. White, "Annotation: *Bisoukis v. Brampton*" 7 M.P.L.R. (3d) 2; G. Smith, "Statutory Duties and Policy Decisions" (2001), 24 Adv. Q. 121. For further discussion of this point as it relates to occupiers' liability, see Chapter 15.

26 (1986), 38 C.C.L.T. 96 (Alta. C.A.).

by the Municipal Government Act[27] to maintain the roads and streets within its limits required the defendant to adopt a system of inspections of its streets sufficient to enable it to discharge its statutory responsibilities. The statute required the defendant city to prove that it was not aware of the fact that the traffic control sign was absent. The defendant failed to establish this by proving the adequacy of its system of street inspections.[28] It has also been held that where a municipality has followed a policy of not taking any systematic or regular action to observe its statutory duty, the onus of proof is on it, once an injury has resulted from the breach of the duty, to show that the injury would have resulted even if it had adopted a policy to comply with its duty.[29]

In sum, where there is an express statutory duty of care, coupled with a civil liability provision, courts have generally assessed all aspects of the governmental activity, whether in the planning or operational stages, to determine whether or not this duty has been breached. It is suggested, however, that even with statutory provisions which impose civil liability on public authorities with respect to a breach of their statutory duties, courts cannot avoid the issue of the legitimacy of judicial review of policy decisions. When the public authority's failure relates to the legitimate exercise of its discretion rather than the negligent implementation

27 R.S.A. 1980, c. M-26, s. 184; now Municipal Government Act, R.S.A. 2000, c. M-26, s. 532. The section imposes a duty on the municipality to keep its roads in a reasonable state of repair and specifically provides for civil liability for damage caused by its breach. Note, however, the immunity provided for in s. 530 with respect to systems of inspection and maintenance. The Act contains a number of other provisions restricting the liability of the municipality; for example, with respect to snow on roads, repair of roads, traffic control devices, things on roads and so on.

28 In *Housen v. Nikolaisen* (1997), [1998] 5 W.W.R. 523 (Sask. Q.B.), reversed [2000] 4 W.W.R. 173 (Sask. C.A.), leave to appeal allowed (2000), 217 Sask. R. 320 (note) (S.C.C.), reversed (2002), 211 D.L.R. (4th) 577, 10 C.C.L.T. (3d) 157 (S.C.C.), the issue was whether the Rural Municipality ought to have erected warning signs in light of a curve in the road that was dangerous and hidden. The trial judge held that it should have and found it partly liable for an accident. The discussion focused solely on the express statutory duty, the issue on appeal being whether the trial judge's findings were on fact or law and the appropriate standard of appellate court review. See discussion on this question in Chapter 9. Compare this decision with *Barratt v. North Vancouver (Dist.)*, above, note 25, where the courts held that in the absence of an express statutory duty, the courts were not qualified to assess this exercise of discretion. There are a large number of cases, many of which were cited in previous editions of this text. Some of the more recent cases where liability has been found due to unsafe road or sidewalk conditions include *Bras v. Winnipeg* (2004), 2004 CarswellMan 491 (Q.B.); *Epifano v. Hamilton (City)* (2005), [2005] O.J. No. 3010, 2005 CarswellOnt 3078 (S.C.J.), additional reasons at (2005), 2005 CarswellOnt 4010 (S.C.J.); *McNulty v. Brampton (City)* (2004), [2004] O.J. No. 3240, 2004 CarswellOnt 3190 (S.C.J.); and *Yovanovich v. Windsor* (2007), [2007] O.J. No. 2134, 2007 CarswellOnt 3390 (S.C.J.). There are also recent cases where actions have been dismissed based on findings of no negligence. See, for example, *Slater v. Toronto (City)* (2004), [2004] O.J. No. 4919, 2004 CarswellOnt 5061 (S.C.J.); and *Ledrew v. Cornerbrook* (2004), [2004] N.J. No. 143, 2004 CarswellNfld 100 (Prov. Ct.).

29 See *Dorschell v. Cambridge (City)* (1980), 14 C.C.L.T. 233 (Ont. C.A.). See also *Nicholls v. Hennion* (1989), 49 C.C.L.T. 105 (Ont. H.C.), where it was held that once non-repair has been shown, the onus of proving reasonable care shifts to defendant.

of its decisions, the issue of the standard of care to be imposed on the authority arises.[30]

(c) The Negligent Statement Cases

Since the decision in *Hedley Byrne & Co. v. Heller & Partners Ltd.*,[31] the courts have generally treated liability for negligent advice given by public officials no differently than negligent advice rendered in the private sphere. That is, public officials who render advice as part of the performance of their public duties must take reasonable care to ensure that this advice is given with due care.[32]

In some ways, the readiness of courts to impose liability on public authorities under the *Hedley Byrne* principle is curious. Public officials, unlike those in the private sphere, frequently do not have the choice whether to give out the requested information or refrain from doing so. They are expected to give out advice in furtherance of their public responsibilities. As well, the negligent statement cases often involve the same practical problems which are faced by public authorities in the performance of their other activities. Public authorities operate with scarce resources, limited staff, and face the same pressures in relation to their advice giving functions as they do with respect to their other activities.

Two Canadian cases in particular demonstrate that resort to the *Hedley Byrne* principle can conceal legitimate policy concerns which the courts might have paid attention to had the issues not been framed in terms of negligent statement. In *Dubnick v. Winnipegosis*,[33] a city council was sued for advising the plaintiff that he could not dig a private well, but was required to purchase his water from the public system. This advice was the result of a conscious policy decision taken by the council, for reasons of public health and economy, that private wells were not to be permitted. It subsequently became evident, however, that the council's decision not to allow private wells was invalid, since the council had failed to

---

30 One can refer to *Gosselin v. Moose Jaw (City)* (1997), 155 D.L.R. (4th) 374 (Sask. C.A.). The Urban Municpality Act, 1984 S.S. 1984, c. U-11, imposed a duty on the municipality to maintain their streets in a good state of repair, a failure of which would lead to civil liability. The city adopted a program of visual inspection whereby one-third of the sidewalks would be inspected annually. The plaintiff was injured when she fell due to a large sidewalk crack. The Court of Appeal reversed the trial judge's finding of liability by holding that the decision to inspect in this manner was a policy decision and not an operational one. Thus the policy/operational dichotomy was used even though this was an express statutory liability case.

31 [1963] 2 All E.R. 575 (H.L.). See Chapter 7.

32 See *Densmore v. Whitehorse (City)*, [1986] 5 W.W.R. 708 (Y.T. S.C.); *Sharadan Builders Inc. v. Mahler* (1977), 79 D.L.R. (3d) 439 (Ont. H.C.), reversed (1978), 93 D.L.R. (3d) 480 (Ont. C.A.); *Jung v. Burnaby (Dist.)* (1978), 7 C.C.L.T. 113 (B.C. S.C.); *392980 Ont. Ltd. v. Welland* (1984), 6 D.L.R. (4th) 151 (Ont. H.C.); *Man. Sausage Mfg. Co. v. Winnipeg* (1976), 1 C.C.L.T. 221 (Man. C.A.); *Grand Restaurants of Can. Ltd. v. Toronto* (1981), 123 D.L.R. (3d) 349 (Ont. H.C.), affirmed (1982), 140 D.L.R. (3d) 191 (Ont. C.A.); *Lyon v. Shelburne* (1981), 130 D.L.R. (3d) 307 (Ont. Co. Ct.); *Sevidal v. Chopra* (1987), 41 C.C.L.T. 179 (Ont. H.C.); *Merritt v. New Brunswick (Minister of Municipal Affairs & Environment)* (1990), 108 N.B.R. (2d) 107 (Q.B.); *Serendipity Ventures Ltd. v. White Rock (City)* (1990), 43 B.C.L.R. (2d) 90 (C.A.); *Black v. Lakefield (Village)* (1998), 166 D.L.R. (4th) 96 (Ont. C.A.); *Granitile v. R.* (1998), 41 C.L.R. (2d) 115 (Ont. Gen. Div.); *Northern Goose Processors Ltd. v. Canadian Food Inspection Agency* (2006), [2006] M.J. No. 298, 2006 CarswellMan 292 (Q.B.); among others.

33 [1985] 2 W.W.R. 437 (Man. Q.B.), affirmed [1985] 5 W.W.R. 758 (Man. C.A.).

enact the required by-law. The plaintiff sued for the extra costs which he had incurred in purchasing the city's water. The court considered the council's refusal to permit the private well as a negligent misrepresentation concerning the plaintiff's legal rights, upon which he relied to his detriment, and applied *Hedley Byrne* in maintaining his claim for damages. One can see, however, how this characterization strained the facts of the case, and overlooked the principles at stake. The defendant council had in fact been found liable not for a negligent statement, but for negligence in the manner in which it had attempted to promulgate a policy decision. It is suggested that had the issues been framed in this way, the result may have been different.

In the case of *Windsor Motors Ltd. v. Powell River (Dist.)*,[34] the principle of *Hedley Byrne* was also used to assess the competence of the performance of what appeared to be a discretionary decision. The case concerned the negligence of a licence inspector, who issued a business licence to operate a used car business in an area not zoned for that purpose. The inspector was required by his statutory mandate to ensure that the business complied with all relevant by-laws, presumably including zoning, before he issued a licence. The court interpreted the issuance of the licence as a representation to the licensee that his proposed business was legitimate. When this turned out not to be the case, to the financial detriment of the licensee, he was permitted to succeed in his damage action, under the *Hedley Byrne* principle. Once again, however, this characterization of the issue made it possible for the court to ignore both the principled and practical objections to allowing public law responsibilities to be assessed according to private law principles.[35]

In short, although it is submitted that the negligent statement cases may raise the same difficult issues of policy discussed in many of the other public tort liability cases, the attractiveness and utility of the *Hedley Byrne* principle has served to isolate this area.

(d) Establishing a *Prima Facie* Duty of Care

Where there is no express statutory duty imposed on the public authority for the plaintiff's protection, or the existence of a *Hedley Byrne* reliance relationship, Canadian tort law utilizes the reformulated two-stage test to resolve the duty issue. As we have discussed, the first step involves foreseeability and proximity, and the second policy. Assuming there is foreseeability and the plaintiff and the public authority are in a proximate relationship, a *prima facie* duty of care arises. This duty can then be mitigated by policy considerations.

Canadian jurisprudence increasingly is making it clear that one should not automatically assume that every failure on the part of public authorities, which

---

34 (1967), 4 D.L.R. (3d) 155 (B.C. C.A.).

35 See also *Gadutsis v. Milne*, (1973), 34 D.L.R. (3d) 455 (Ont. H.C.); and *Bell v. Sarnia (City)* (1987), 37 D.L.R. (4th) 438 (Ont. H.C.). In *Moin v. Blue Mountains (Town)* (2000), 13 M.P.L.R. (3d) 1 (Ont. C.A.), the Reeve of a township made assurances during a council meeting that a road would be rebuilt. The plaintiff relied upon this in proceeding with a development. The road was not rebuilt and the plaintiff lost money. The Court of Appeal stated that while the decision to build the road was a legislative or policy decision, the statements concerning it were operational and could form the basis of a successful negligent misstatement claim. The municipality was held liable for the representations of its Reeve.

injures private interests, will form the basis of a *prima* facie duty of care. For one thing, we must recall that in the absence of an express legislative provision, there is no tort of breach of statutory duty in Canada.[36] Thus merely because a public authority failed to live up to its statutory duties does not mean that an individual whose interests have been damaged can sue for compensation. That individual must establish that a duty of care based on common law principles was owed.

The plaintiff must establish that there was proximity between the parties. Looking for proximity within the terms of the statutory provisions that empower a public authority was the approach adopted by the Supreme Court of Canada in *Cooper v. Hobart*[37] and *Edwards v. Law Society of Upper Canada*.[38] The Supreme Court examined the statutory provisions in question and concluded that their purpose was not to protect the interests of private persons. It accordingly decided that there was no proximate relationship between the parties and hence no *prima facie* duty of care. This made consideration of the policy/operational doctrine unnecessary.[39]

---

36 See *Saskatchewan Wheat Pool v. Canada*, [1983] 1 S.C.R. 205, [1983] 3 W.W.R. 97 and the discussion in Chapter 9.

37 (2001), 206 D.L.R. (4th) 193, [2002] 1 W.W.R. 221 (S.C.C.).

38 (2001), 206 D.L.R. (4th) 211 (S.C.C.).

39 The "statutory purpose" approach had been adopted in a number of other Canadian judgments, even before the *Cooper* and *Edwards* judgments. See, for example, *Birchard v. Alberta (Securities Commission)*, [1987] 6 W.W.R. 536 (Alta. Q.B.), where it was held that the Legal Profession Act, S.A. 1966, c. 46, was not enacted in order to protect the public who did not entrust their money with lawyers in their capacity as barristers and solicitors. As well, it was held that the Securities Act, R.S.A. 1980, c. S-6, did not impose a duty of care upon the Securities Commission in favour of potential depositors and investors. See also *Gutek v. Sunshine Village Corp.* (1990), 65 D.L.R. (4th) 406 (Alta. Q.B.), where it was held that the Elevator and Fixed Conveyances Act, R.S.A. 1980, c. E-7, was enacted in order to protect users of ski-chair lifts, and did not impose a duty upon the government with respect to the owners and operators of such equipment. In *M-Jay Farms Enterprises Ltd. v. Canadian Wheat Board* (1997), [1998] 2 W.W.R. 48 (Man. C.A.), leave to appeal refused (1998), 126 Man. R. (2d) 154 (note) (S.C.C.), reconsideration refused (August 6, 1998), Doc. 26346 (S.C.C.), the Manitoba Court of Appeal reversed a lower court decision and held that wheat producers could not sue the Canadian Wheat Board. The Court did not refer to the operational/policy dichotomy but held that as a matter of policy the Canadian Wheat Board did not owe a duty of care to producers. In *CSL Group Inc. v. Canada* (1998), 163 D.L.R. (4th) 307 (Fed. C.A.), leave to appeal refused (1999), 236 N.R. 194 (note) (S.C.C.), the failure of the Treasury Board to designate employees who would be required to work during a strike did not lead to liability to those who suffered economic detriment as the result of the strike. Whether the failure to act was a policy decision or even the result of negligence was irrelevant in the opinion of Marceau J., who viewed the Crown's obligations as public duties not owed to private claimants. A similar approach was adopted by McQuaid J.A. in *Lewis v. Prince Edward Island* (1998), 157 D.L.R. (4th) 277 (P.E.I. C.A.), leave to appeal refused (1998), 235 N.R. 394 (note), 176 Nfld. & P.E.I.R. 162 (note), 540 A.P.R. 162 (note) (S.C.C.). The plaintiff's potato crop was detrimentally affected by spraying, which had been ordered by an inspector pursuant to statute. The trial judge found in favour of the plaintiff on the basis that the order to spray with a specific chemical was negligence within the operational sphere and that the defendant was not protected by a statutory immunity provision. The majority of the Court of Appeal disagreed with the finding that the "good faith" statutory immunity provision did not apply. Moreover, McQuaid J.A. held that even if the order to spray was operational and not policy that where an operational act carried out in order to protect the public interests conflicts with the plaintiff's private interests, the public interest must take precedence. In other words, the defendant's duty was owed to the public and not to the plaintiff.

It is therefore understandable that *post-Cooper v. Hobart* judgments have primarily relied upon the interpretation of statutory provisions to determine whether there was proximity between the parties sufficient to give rise to a *prima facie* duty of care. In the vast majority of these cases, a *prima facie* duty has been denied based on this approach.

A series of Ontario judgments dealing with law suits against public authorities relating to the outbreaks of West Nile Virus and Severe Acute Respiratory Syndrome (SARS) in the province are illustrative of this approach.[40] In addition, actions against statutory authorities involving the protection of children,[41] the education of children with special needs,[42] the public tendering process,[43] the approval of untreated pine shakes as roofing material,[44] the inadequacy of health care funding,[45] the regulation of schools,[46] the approval and licensing of irrigation projects,[47] the regulation of medical devices,[48] and the closing of a pulp mill[49] have been decided by courts by their examination of statutory provisions to determine the existence of proximity. As noted above, most plaintiffs have failed to establish the *prima facie* duty of care.[50]

---

40 The judgments include *Eliopoulos Estate v. Ontario (Minister of Health and Long Term Care)* (2006), 276 D.L.R. (4th) 411 (Ont. C.A.), leave to appeal refused (2007), 2007 CarswellOnt 3256 (S.C.C.); *Williams v. Canada (Attorney General)* (2005), 257 D.L.R. (4th) 704, 76 O.R. (3d) 763, 34 C.C.L.T. (3d) 213 (S.C.J.); *Laroza v. Ontario* (2005), 257 D.L.R. (4th) 761, 34 C.C.L.T. (3d) 264 (Ont. S.C.J.), leave to appeal allowed (2007), 2007 CarswellOnt 4774 (Div. Ct.); *Arbaquez v. Ontario* (2005), 257 D.L.R. (4th) 745, 34 C.C.L.T. (3d) 249 (Ont. S.C.J.); *Jamal Estate (Trustee of) v. Scarborough Hospital* (2005), 34 C.C.L.T. (3d) 271 (Ont. S.C.J.); and *Henry Estate (Trustee of) v. Scarborough Hospital* (2005), 34 C.C.L.T. (3d) 278 (Ont. S.C.J.). See Klar, "Tort Liability of the Crown: Back to *Canada v. Saskatchewan Wheat Pool*" (2007), 32 Advocates' Quarterly 293.

41 *D. (B.) v. Children's Aid Society of Halton (Region)* (2007), 49 C.C.L.T. (3d) 1 (S.C.C.) See Klar, Case Comment (2007), 86 Can. Bar Rev. 337.

42 *L. (A.) v. Ontario Ministry of Community and Social Services)* (2006), 274 D.L.R. (4th) 431 (Ont. C.A.), leave to appeal refused (2007), 2007 CarswellOnt 3059 (S.C.C.); and *Wynberg v. Ontario* (2006), 269 D.L.R. (4th) 435, 40 C.C.L.T. (3d) 176 (Ont. C.A.), leave to appeal refused (2007), 2007 CarswellOnt 2148 (S.C.C.).

43 *Exploits Valley Air Services Ltd. v. College of the North Atlantic* (2005), 258 D.L.R. (4th) 66, 33 C.C.L.T. (3d) 138 (Nfld. C.A.), leave to appeal refused (2006), 2006 CarswellNfld 83 (S.C.C.).

44 *Holstag v. Alberta* (2004), [2005] 1 W.W.R. 504 (Q.B.), affirmed 37 C.C.L.T. (3d) 216, [2006] 4 W.W.R. 637, 265 D.L.R. (4th) 518 (Alta. C.A.), leave to appeal refused (2006), 2006 CarswellAlta 1190 (S.C.C.). Also see *Kimpton v. Canada (Attorney General)* (2004), 236 D.L.R. (4th) 324 (B.C. C.A.), which also involved a Building Code issue.

45 *Mitchell Estate v. Ontario* (2004), 242 D.L.R. (4th) 560 (Ont. Div. Ct.).

46 *Wilson v. R.*, 2007 SKQB 141 (Q.B.).

47 *Nelson v. Saskatchewan* (2003), [2004] 3 W.W.R. 89 (Sask. Q.B.).

48 *Klein v. American Medical Systems Inc.* (2006), 278 D.L.R. (4th) 722 (Ont. Div. Ct.); *Taylor v. Canada (Minister of Health)* (2007), 2007 CarswellOnt 5541 (S.C.J.), leave to appeal refused (2007), 2007 CarswellOnt 8122 (Div. Ct.); *Attis v. Canada (Minister of Health)* (2007), [2007] O.J. No. 1744, 2007 CarswellOnt 2786 (S.C.J.), additional reasons at (2007), 2007 CarswellOnt 4258 (S.C.J.).

49 *James v. British Columbia* (2005), 30 C.C.L.T. (3d) 30 (B.C. C.A).

50 Although plaintiffs have had limited success, for the most part actions have failed. Clear rejections of a *prima facie* duty occurred in *D.(B.), Mitchell, Eliopoulos, L.(A.), Wynberg, Exploits Valley, Holstag, Wilson, Attis* and *Kimpton.* Plaintiffs had mixed success in the SARS cases, due to possible negligence in operational activities that created a duty of care. The action was allowed to proceed in *James v. B.C.* In *Sauer v. Canada* (2007), 49 C.C.L.T. (3d) 161

As I have argued elsewhere,[51] looking for proximity within the provisions of statutes is problematic for various reasons. There is no tort of breach of statutory duty in Canada. Breach of a statute can be useful evidence of negligent conduct, but only once a common law duty of care has been established.[52] Although it has been argued that "civil courts are still free to extend tort duties by relying on penal legislation"[53] and thus "advance the policy" underlying statutes "by providing a civil remedy",[54] there is, in my respectful opinion, no logical difference between construing a statute to create a private law duty, which under Canadian law is not permitted, and adopting a statutory duty by converting it into a private law duty. In the absence of a common law duty relationship between the parties, which must exist apart from the construction of a statutory duty, there can be no private law tort remedy.

Furthermore, as held in *Childs v. Desormeaux*,[55] in the absence of a special relationship based on the active creation of a risk, the invitation of a person to a situation of risk controlled by the defendant, or a paternalistic relationship of control or supervision, there is no duty imposed on one person to prevent harm being suffered by another. Many of the actions brought against public authorities allege the failure of government defendants to confer statutory benefits; e.g., funds for schools or health care, licenses, or contracts; or their failure to prevent harm from risks not created by the public authority defendants; e.g., the spread of contagious diseases, the dishonest activities of third parties, harmful medical devices, or the inadequacy of other consumer products. The common law would ordinarily not impose a duty on a defendant with respect to such omissions.[56] As conceded by McLachlin C.J. in *Cooper*, the only source of a public authority's duty with respect to such matters is statutory.[57] The dilemma is obvious. If there

---

(Ont. C.A.), affirming (2006), 36 C.C.L.T. (3d) 296 (Ont. C.A.), leave to appeal refused 2008 CarswellOnt 4315, 2008 CarswellOnt 4316 (S.C.C.), the Court of Appeal allowed an action brought against the government relating to the regulation of the importation of cattle feed to proceed. There was no discussion of the legislative provisions relevant to this matter with respect to the nature of the relationship that existed between cattle farmers and the government.

51 See Klar, "Tort Liability of the Crown", above note 40, and "Case Comment," above, note 41.

52 This was well stated by Cameron J.A. in *Exploits Valley Air Services*, at 33 C.C.L.T. (3d) 150:

> The appellant submits that the *Public Tender Act* determines whether proximity is established. It is clear that in Canada the breach of the statute of itself does not ground liability in tort (*Saskatchewan Wheat Pool v. Canada*, [1983] 1 S.C.R. 205 (S.C.C.)), except of course if the statute so provides. That is, there is no nominate tort of statutory breach. Neither does the existence of a statutory duty create a presumption of a private law duty of care. Consequently, the plaintiff must establish a common law duty which corresponds to the statutory duty. A court may, however, rely on legislative standards when determining the applicable standard of care, though "the two are not necessarily coextensive" (*Ryan v. Victoria (City)*, [1999] 1 S.C.R. 201 (S.C.C.), para. 29).

53 Linden & Feldthusen, *Canadian Tort Law*, 8th ed. (2006), at 232.

54 *Ibid* at 333.

55 [2006] 1 S.C.R. 643.

56 This problem was identified and discussed by M.K. Woodall, "Private Law Liability of Public Authorities for Negligent Inspection and Regulation" (1992), 37 McGill L.J. 83. It is an important point that is frequently neglected in the jurisprudence dealing with this issue.

57 As stated with regard to the Registrar of Mortgage Brokers: "The statute is the only source of his duties, private or public. Apart from that statute, he is no different than the ordinary man or woman in the street. If a duty to investors with regulated mortgage brokers is to be found, it must be in the statute." (*Cooper v. Hobart*, above, at para. 43.)

is no common law duty relationship between the parties, and courts cannot construe statutory duties to create common law duties, how can proximity be found within the provisions of statutes?

The solution that I have suggested to the creation of proximity between statutory defendants and private parties is to look to the actual relationship that existed between the parties. Based on the application of common law principles, proximity might very well be found there. As stated by the Supreme Court of Canada itself in *Cooper* "defining the relationship may involve looking at expectations, representations, reliance and the property or other interests involved".[58] Proximity will be found where statutory authorities have done something which if done by private persons would give rise to a *prima facie* duty. The statutory environment will provide the context to the relationship and explain the interactions, but it will be the relationship and interactions themselves that will have to provide the source of the common law duty.[59]

(e) Policy Reasons to Limit the *Prima Facie* Duty: The Policy/ Operational Dichotomy

If foreseeability and proximity between a public authority and a private claimant are established, a *prima facie* duty of care is owed. This can be mitigated by policy concerns. The principal policy concerns that arise in the area of public authority liability are those relating to the legitimacy and competency of courts second-guessing the political decisions of public authorities. This rationale for limiting or denying a public authority's *prima facie* duty of care requires courts to distinguish between the political and non-political activities of government and has given rise to the policy/operational dichotomy.[60]

The thesis has been that if a complaint is raised relating to the authority's lack of due care in determining policy matters, for example, deciding whether and how to implement a program, then negligence law review, at least on an ordinary foreseeability of harm and standard of care analysis, is not appropriate. As long as the authority's exercise of discretion in formulating policy was conscientious

---

58 *Cooper*, above, at para. 34. The fact that proximity is based on relationships was emphasized repeatedly by the Supreme Court in *Hill v. Hamilton-Wentworth (Regional Municipality) Police Services Board* (2007), 50 C.C.L.T. (3d) 1 (S.C.C.). See discussion in Chapter Five.

59 This point is made by Cullity J. in his judgments dealing with the SARS litigation. For example, in *Williams v. Canada*, above, note 40, at 245 C.C.L.T., Cullity J. states "although. . .private law duties may not have arisen solely from the provisions of statutes, it does not follow that proximity between the Provincial Crown and the class members could not arise from the manner in which policy decisions made pursuant to the statutory powers were implemented." The same point is made in *Jamal Estate*, above, note 40, at 276 C.C.L.T.

60 See *Dorman Timber Ltd. v. British Columbia* (1997), 152 D.L.R. (4th) 271 (B.C. C.A.) for a clear articulation of this approach. Finch J.A. notes that once a presumptive duty based on foreseeability is established the duty can be limited by the policy/operational dichotomy, by a statutory or common law protection or exemption, or by considerations of justice. The case concerned a "good faith" statutory exemption. As we have discussed, the Supreme Court of Canada in *Edwards v. Law Society of Upper Canada* (2001), 206 D.L.R. (4th) 211 (S.C.C.) and *Cooper v. Hobart* (2001), 206 D.L.R. (4th) 193 (S.C.C.) refined the analysis. Stage one now includes proximity, which takes into account policy considerations, some of which would formerly have been considered in stage two.

and in good faith,[61] the authority is immune from liability in tort. Where, however, the alleged negligence relates to something done during the operational or implementational stages of an activity, especially when the injury causing event was neither planned nor anticipated, then ordinary negligence law principles can be applied. This dichotomy provides a valuable insight into the public tort liability dilemma, responding, as it does, directly to the policy concerns which underlie this area.

The policy/operational dichotomy, as the touchstone of the duty issue, was articulated by Lord Wilberforce in *Anns v. Merton London Borough Council*.[62] Lord Wilberforce observed that statutory provisions relating to public authorities prescribe, or at least presuppose, two areas of responsibilities. The first area is that of "discretion." A discretionary decision is one for the authority and not the court to make. The second task of public authorities is the practical execution of policy, i.e. the operational area. With respect to the exercise of discretion, the authority must act *bona fide*, or in good faith. With respect to operations, a standard of reasonable care can be imposed. Although a convenient framework, Lord Wilberforce admitted that the distinction between policy and operations is one of degree, with some elements of discretion contained within operational activities.

The leading Canadian case which first adopted this approach was *Kamloops (City) v. Nielsen*.[63] In this case, the defendant municipality was sued by a purchaser of a house which had been built on foundations that were not in accordance with the approved building plans. The municipality had the statutory authority to regulate the construction of buildings and the power to pass by-laws with respect thereto. It had passed a by-law prohibiting construction of buildings without a permit, providing for an inspection system, prohibiting occupancy of buildings without a permit, and requiring its building inspectors to enforce these by-laws. Inspectors had the power to issue stop-work orders on buildings which were not in compliance with the requirements and to withhold occupancy permits. The municipality could go further and enforce these orders by court proceedings, or even by demolishing the offending structure. On the facts of *Kamloops*, the building under construction had not been built according to the approved plans

---

61 See *Anns v. Merton London Borough Council*, [1977] 2 All E.R. 492 (H.L.); *Kamloops (City) v. Nielsen* (1984), 29 C.C.L.T. 97 (S.C.C.); *Just v. British Columbia* (1989), 1 C.C.L.T. (2d) 1 (S.C.C.); *Swinamer v. A.G. N.S.* (1994), 112 D.L.R. (4th) 18 (S.C.C.); and *Brown v. British Columbia (Min. of Transportation & Highways)*, [1994] 4 W.W.R. 194 (S.C.C.).

62 *Ibid.*

63 (1984), 29 C.C.L.T. 97 (S.C.C.). There have been several case comments. See Bilson, "Should City Hall Be Worried? *City of Kamloops v. Nielsen*" (1984-85), 49 Sask. L. Rev. 345; Feldthusen, "*City of Kamloops v. Nielsen*: A Comment on the Supreme Court's Modest Clarification of Colonial Tort Law" (1984-85), 30 McGill L.J. 539; Horton, "*Kamloops v. Nielsen*: Municipal Liability for Community Planning Negligence" (1986), 44 U. of T. Fac. L. Rev. 109; Elder, "*Kamloops v. Nielsen* — Good Result, Unclear Law" (1986), 24 Alta. L. Rev. 540; Irvine, "Case Comment" (1984), 29 C.C.L.T. 185; Perell, "Common Law Negligence and the Liability of Governments and Public Authorities (No. 2)" (1985-86), 6 Advocates' Q. 312; Gibson, "Developments in Tort Law: The 1983-84 Term" (1985), 7 Sup. Ct. L. Rev. 387; Klar, "Recent Developments in Canadian Law: Tort Law" (1985), 17 Ottawa L. Rev. 325; Thomas, "*Kamloops v. Nielsen*: A Flickering Light in the Dark Tunnel Surrounding the Liability of Public Authorities" (1987), 7 Advocates' Q. 501.

and was subjected to two stop-work orders. Despite this, the builder, to the inspector's knowledge, completed the house. Although an occupancy permit was never obtained, the house's owner, a city alderman and the builder's father, moved in. He subsequently sold the house to the plaintiff, an unwitting purchaser, who discovered its defects and sued the city.

Madame Justice Wilson's majority judgment recognized, as did Lord Wilberforce's in *Anns*, that the policy/operational dichotomy, although useful, is not the complete answer to the public tort liability question. Her Ladyship held the defendant council liable for its failure to give serious consideration to what it should do, if anything, to deal with the infractions committed by the builder. Its inaction, for what were most likely improper reasons,[64] was not "a policy decision taken in the *bona fide* exercise of discretion."[65]

The policy/operational dichotomy was refined further in the Supreme Court of Canada's decision in *Just v. British Columbia*.[66] The appellant and his daughter were stopped in a line of traffic by a rocky slope on a major highway in British Columbia. A boulder from a slope above the highway became dislodged and came crashing down upon the appellant's car, seriously injuring the appellant and killing his daughter. The appellant sued the provincial Crown, alleging negligence in its system of monitoring the situation and dealing with potential hazards. At trial,[67] McLachlin J. decided that the decisions which had been made by the defendant Crown in this case fell within its area of policy, and could not be reviewed by the court. The Court of Appeal agreed with this characterization.[68] The majority of the Supreme Court of Canada, however, in a judgment delivered by Cory J., held that the allegations of negligence which were raised in this case with respect to the manner and quality of the defendant's inspection system fell clearly within the operational aspects of the activity. Cory J. conceded that public authorities ought not to be restricted in making decisions based upon "social, political or economic factors", by having these "true policy decisions" subjected to tort law claims. However, His Lordship viewed the dividing line between the policy and operational activities of government quite differently than had the lower courts, and in the end very narrowly construed the policy aspects of governmental activity. Policy was restricted to what may be called threshold deci-

---

64 The suggestion was that nothing was done because the problem involved one of the city's aldermen.

65 29 C.C.L.T. 97 at 119. While not disagreeing with the proposition that where there is a failure to exercise discretion there can be civil liability if there is evidence of corruption, bad faith, or some other factor which makes the decision making *ultra vires*, the dissenting justices held that there had been no such evidence adduced in this case. Another case along the same lines is *Oosthoek v. Thunder Bay (City)* (1996), 139 D.L.R. (4th) 611 (Ont. C.A.), leave to appeal refused (1997), 104 O.A.C. 240 (note) (S.C.C.). The city failed to enforce a by-law that required residents to disconnect leaders that drained rainwater into the house connections and ultimately into the sewer. The court held that this failure to enforce was "operational" because the city did not give consideration to the issue of enforcement. The question is whether this is "operational" or a failure to exercise discretion. I would suggest that it can only be the latter and bad faith need be shown.

66 (1989), 1 C.C.L.T. (2d) 1 (S.C.C.).

67 (1985), 33 C.C.L.T. 49 (B.C. S.C.).

68 (1986), 40 C.C.L.T. 160 (B.C. C.A.).

sions, i.e., the initial decision as to whether something will or will not be done.[69] These decisions which formulate policy are made by those in high levels of authority, and will involve such considerations as budgetary allocation or other political matters. Once made, however, the details regarding the manner and characteristics of a program which relate to its implementation fall into the operational aspects of the activity. This is so notwithstanding that the formulation of these details also involve decision-making relating to the allocation of resources or other discretionary matters. Cory J. did concede, however, that in determining the reasonableness of operational decisions, i.e., the question of the standard of care, the nature of the defendant, and the financial and political constraints under which it operated, must be considered.[70]

The Supreme Court revisited the issue of the policy/operational dichotomy in *Swinamer v. A.G. N.S.*[71], *Brown v. British Columbia (Min. of Transportation & Highways)*[72] and in *Ingles v. Tutkaluk Construction Ltd.*[73] The facts of *Swinamer* bore a close resemblance to those in *Just*. A tree, growing alongside a highway, became diseased and fell onto the plaintiff's truck. The province had initiated a limited program of identifying, flagging and removing dangerous trees. One of the issues in the action brought by the injured plaintiff against the province was whether its tree removal program was subject to negligence law review.[74] The trial judge had decided that, based on *Just*, the activities of the department relating to its tree removal program were reviewable operational activities and the court found the department negligent in the manner in which it conducted them.[75] The Court of Appeal reversed, largely, however, for reasons resting on matters other than the policy/operational dichotomy.[76]

Cory J., for a unanimous Supreme Court, also dismissed the action, but for different reasons. Cory J. held that certain aspects of the departmental planning for the tree removal program involved policy and could not be reviewed.[77] In

---

69 As will be discussed below, Cory J. rejects this as a correct characterization of what he decided in his later judgment in *Brown v. British Columbia (Min. of Transportation & Highways)*, [1994] 4 W.W.R. 194 (S.C.C.).

70 See also *Laurentide Motels Ltd. v. Beauport (City)*, [1989] 1 S.C.R. 705, where the court applied the same approach to a public tort case under the Quebec Civil Code. Sopinka J. dissented in *Just*, precisely because he disagreed with the majority's characterization of what constitutes policy. According to Sopinka J., policy involves not only the question of whether to do something, but as well, the time, manner and technique of doing it.

71 (1994), 112 D.L.R. (4th) 18 (S.C.C.).

72 [1994] 4 W.W.R. 194.

73 (2000), 49 C.C.L.T. (2d) 1 (S.C.C.).

74 There were numerous other issues involving the applicable legislation, whether the Crown could enter private land to remove trees, and whether the Crown had a duty to maintain roads or was exempt from liability by statute. See Klar, "Case Comment: Falling Boulders, Falling Trees and Icy Highways: The Policy/Operational Test Revisited" (1994), 33 Alta. Law Rev. 167.

75 (1991), 6 C.C.L.T. (2d) 270 (N.S. T.D.).

76 (1992), 10 C.C.L.T. (2d) 207 (N.S. C.A.). The court held that the provisions exempted the Minister from a duty to maintain highways, questioned the Minister's right to go onto private lands to remove trees, and concluded that it had adopted no program with respect to diseased, as opposed to dead, trees.

77 More specifically, the decision to survey the trees could not be reviewed.

terms of the program itself, however, Cory J. held that the decisions which the department made were prudent, in view of the constraints under which the department operated.[78]

The facts of the second recent case, *Brown*, were quite different. The accident involved a classic Canadian winter dilemma, snow and ice on highways. The defendant highways department had instituted a program to deal with this danger, but unfortunately on this occasion the arrival of a sanding crew came too late to prevent the plaintiff's accident. The trial judge dismissed the action based on a lack of negligence.[79] The Court of Appeal affirmed.[80]

In the Supreme Court, Cory J. revisited the policy/operational dichotomy by focussing on one aspect of the road maintenance program, the decision to have two work schedules, one for summer and another for winter.[81] Cory J. characterized this as a policy decision, which was immune from ordinary tort law review. It was, according to Cory J., "truly a governmental decision involving social, political and economic factors."[82] It therefore only could be attacked on the ground that it "was not *bona fide* or was so irrational or unreasonable as to constitute an improper exercise of governmental discretion."[83] In arriving at his decision, Cory J. expressly rejected the interpretation of the *Just* decision articulated above. The argument that policy decisions are limited to threshold decisions, that is to say, "broad initial decisions as to whether something will or will not be done" was stated as being "contrary to the principles set out in *Just*..."[84] Having concluded that the decision to have the two schedules was a non-reviewable matter of policy, Cory J. then subjected the manner in which the sanding was carried out under the summer schedule to negligence law review. He concluded that the plaintiff had failed to show that there was negligence in the manner in which the system had been operated, and the action was accordingly dismissed.

Ingles v. Tutkaluk Construction Ltd.[85] involved negligent building inspection. The Supreme Court reaffirmed its earlier judgments in similar cases,[86] holding that where a municipality has been given the statutory power to inspect it has to first exhibit good faith in exercising its discretion whether to create an inspection

---

78 In the final analysis, it is my opinion that Cory J.'s approach here was similar to his approach in *Just*, with one major exception. In *Just*, the decision as to the reasonableness of the program was remitted to the trial judge. In *Swinamer*, Cory J. decided that the program was reasonably carried out, *despite the fact* that the trial judge had decided that it was not.

79 (1989), 17 M.V.R. (2d) 69 (B.C. S.C.).

80 (1992), 10 C.C.L.T. (2d) 188 (B.C. C.A.).

81 The accident occurred during the last week of the summer schedule. The summer schedule provided for a lighter operations.

82 (1994), 19 C.C.L.T. (2d) 268 at 285.

83 *Ibid.*, at 280.

84 *Ibid.* Although the portion of this text was not referred to as the source of this, the wording is virtually identical.

85 (2000), 183 D.L.R. (4th) 193, 49 C.C.L.T. (2d) 1 (S.C.C.). For commentary see J. Levitt, "Municipal Building Department Liability" (2000), 5 Digest M. & P.L. 287; Marr & Juliano, "Liability of Public Bodies Regarding Private Construction Projects" (2001), 10 C.L.R. (3d) 53; N. Rafferty, "Developments in Contract and Tort Law" (2000), 13 Sup. Ct. L. Rev. (2d) 125.

86 *City of Kamloops v. Nielsen*, [1984] 2 S.C.R. 2; *Rothfield v. Manolakos*, [1989] 2 S.C.R. 1259.

scheme or not, and second, if it makes the decision to inspect, it "must exercise the standard of care in its inspection that would be expected of an ordinary, reasonable and prudent person in the same circumstances". In this case, the defendant municipality, while not required to do so, made the decision to inspect and enforce safety standards even after the building's construction had commenced. This was a policy decision. Once it decided to implement the decision and to send an inspector out, the inspection must be carried out reasonably. It is interesting to note that the city could have made the policy decision not to inspect after a permit was issued and construction was commenced, as long as this decision was made in good faith and was consistent with the purpose of the legislative provisions.[87]

(f) Critique of the Policy/Operational Dichotomy

Despite its attractive simplicity, the policy/operational dichotomy has proven to be very difficult for courts to apply. This has produced a mass of inconsistent and seemingly irreconcilable judgments. This is attributable to the fact that one cannot clearly separate the policy or discretionary stages of an activity from its operational or implementational stages. The two are intermeshed, with most activities containing elements of both in varying degrees.[88] Numerous operational activities occur during the policy stages of governmental activity.[89] Similarly, during the operational stages of an activity, matters of policy or discretion will invariably arise.[90] Although there has been general agreement on those factors which incline specific conduct towards either the policy or operational end of the

87 There were other interesting aspects of this judgment. The Supreme Court held that the authority owes a duty of care to owner-builders even where the owner-builders themselves have been negligent and have, for example, commenced the building's construction before obtaining a building permit. It is only where the owner-builder's conduct has been so extreme in "flouting" the by-law so as to make it impossible for the inspectors to do their jobs that the owner-builder will be solely responsible for the consequences. This will be raised as a defence by the public authority and not as an issue that goes to the existence of the duty. Secondly, the Supreme Court upheld the approach that under Ontario's Negligence Act, R.S.O. 1990, c. N.1, even where a plaintiff is contributorily negligent the defendants will remain jointly and severally liable for the balance.

88 As stated by Lord Wilberforce in *Anns v. Merton London Borough Council*, [1977] 2 All E.R. 492 at 500:

> Although this distinction between the policy area and the operational area is convenient, and illuminating, it is probably a distinction of degree; many "operational" powers or duties have in them some element of "discretion."

Or, as stated by McLachlin J., "the distinction between a policy decision and an operational function of a government body or agent is often difficult to draw in a given situation, however easily it may be stated", in the trial judgment of *Just v. British Columbia* (1985), 33 C.C.L.T. 49 at 53 (B.C. S.C.).

89 In formulating a policy, or passing a by-law, for example, a city council may be required to follow certain procedures, give notice, hear certain evidence, obtain approvals, and so forth, procedures which are not matters of policy, nor subject to the exercise of their discretion.

90 When an inspector inspects a building under construction to determine if it conforms to the approved plans, for example, "on the job" decisions regarding how much time should be spent, how thorough the inspection should be, whether extra costs should be incurred, and so on — all matters of discretion — will need to be made.

scale,[91] the fact that all activities contain elements of both has caused great difficulties for the courts.[92]

One may illustrate the use of the policy/operational dichotomy, and the inherent problems with it, by reference to those judgments in which the dichotomy has prominently figured. If one looks, for example, at the judgments in *Just, Swinamer,* and *Brown* themselves, one can see that while some judges thought that certain activities or decisions were operational, others considered the same matters to be issues of policy.[93] As well, as I have suggested elsewhere,[94] Mr. Justice Cory's own statements in the above cases reflect an uncertainty as to what is policy and what is operations.[95]

Judgments decided before *Just* also reflected the uncertainty. In *Barratt v. North Vancouver (Dist.)*,[96] for example, the defendant municipality was sued by a cyclist for the municipality's alleged negligence in maintaining its roads. The plaintiff was seriously injured when he drove over a concealed pothole. The municipality had a statutory power to maintain roads and, pursuant to this authority, had instituted a system of road inspection and repairs. Martland J., adopting the policy/operational dichotomy, held that although the municipality might be liable in tort for the negligent implementation of its policies, it could not be held to be negligent because it formulated one policy of operation rather than

---

91 In the trial judgment of *Just v. British Columbia* (1985), 33 C.C.L.T. 49 at 53 (B.C. S.C.), McLachlin J. noted that one can identify the characteristics of policy decisions in general terms. They involve planning, the allocation of resources, balancing factors such as efficiency or thrift, a greater degree of discretion, and the absence of standards.

92 See *Atlantic Leasing Ltd. v. Newfoundland* (1998), 162 D.L.R. (4th) 54 (Nfld. C.A.) at 83 where Green J.A. considers this argument and the suggestion that the policy/operational dichotomy be abandoned. The policy/operational dichotomy has been abandoned in England; see Bailey and Bowman, above, note 2.

93 In *Just*, the trial judge, the Court of Appeal and one of the Supreme Court justices felt that the activities were matters of policy. The majority of the Supreme Court in that case thought they were operational. In *Swinamer*, the trial judge thought the activity was operational, the Court of Appeal dealt with the case on another basis, and the Supreme Court held that certain activities were policy and others operational. In *Brown*, the trial judge dealt with the main complaint as a question of operations, the Court of Appeal dealt with one of the activities by assuming that it was either policy or operations and the Supreme Court again viewed some of the activities as policy and others as operational.

94 See Klar, "Case Comment: Falling Boulders", above, note 74.

95 In *Just*, Mr. Justice Cory asserted that a "system of inspections" can be assessed in terms of reasonableness, and that "the manner and quality of an inspection system is clearly part of the operational aspect of a governmental activity and falls to be assessed in the consideration of the standard of care issue", at (1989), 1 C.C.L.T. (2d) 18. However, he also argued, for purposes of illustration, that a system of inspection at an aircrafts parts manufacturing plant, which called for periodic spot checks as opposed to checks of all parts manufactured during a specific period, was a "policy" decision that could not be attacked. As I pointed out in my Case Comment, the characterizations seem contradictory. In *Holbrook (Guardian ad litem of) v. Argo Road Maintenance Inc.* (1996), 31 C.C.L.T. (2d) 70 (B.C. S.C.), the Court suggested that if the level of maintenance of a road is a "policy" decision, a public authority can purposely control its liability by setting the standard for the frequency of inspections lower than would be reasonably acceptable under a private law test. The real issue is whether the frequency of inspections is a policy or operational matter and this is where the confusion lies.

96 (1980), 14 C.C.L.T. 169 (S.C.C.), affirming (1978), 5 C.C.L.T. 303 (B.C. C.A.), which reversed (1977), 2 C.C.L.T. 157 (B.C. S.C.).

another.[97] And, in this respect, "the determination of the method by which the Municipality decided to exercise its power to maintain the highway, including its inspection system, was a matter of policy or planning."[98]

Compare this decision, however, to the one in *Malat v. Bjornson (No. 2)*.[99] In this case, the Crown was sued, also for its alleged negligence in the exercise of its power to maintain roads. The Department of Highways had erected 18-inch median rails in 1961, despite their knowledge that there were risks associated with them. They designed and adopted safer median barriers in 1965, but had not installed them by 1974 when an accident occurred. The evidence indicated that the accident would not have occurred had the safer barrier been erected. Did the failure to erect the safer barrier more expeditiously relate to policy or to operations?[100] The Court of Appeal held that the failure of the district engineer to install the barrier within a reasonable time after it had become available for installation on the section of highway concerned was negligence at the operational stage, and subjected the Crown to tort liability.[101]

If one reviews the numerous judgments involving the liability of public authorities which have relied upon the operational/policy dichotomy, one important point emerges. *There is no apparent pattern in the judgments or any way to predict whether a court will decide that a specific governmental activity is a matter of policy or operations.* For example, all of the following activities and

---

97 14 C.C.L.T. 169 at 179.

98 *Ibid.*, at 180. It is interesting to note that this specific quote was raised by the defendant in *Just* to support its argument that its system of inspections could not be attacked, as constituting a "policy" matter. Cory J. rejected this submission, at 1 C.C.L.T. (2d) 13, by noting that:

> This statement [i.e., Martland J.'s statement] was not necessary to the decision, as it had already been determined that the system of inspection established by the municipality was eminently reasonable. . . . With the greatest respect, I am of the view that the portion of the reasons relied on by the respondent went farther than was necessary to the decision or appropriate as a statement of principle.

To further confuse matters, however, Cory J. later suggested that it was open to a litigant to attack the "policy" to inspect as not "having been adopted in a *bona fide* exercise of discretion and to demonstrate that in all the circumstances, including budgetary restraints, it is appropriate for a court to make a finding on the issue." One must recall that in *Just*, Cory J. specifically stated that the "manner and quality" of an inspection system was a matter of operations. In *Stovin v. Wise*, [1996] A.C. 923 (U.K. H.L.) at 955, Lord Hoffmann specifically referred to *Barratt*, *Just*, and *Brown* and concluded "that these cases seem to me to illustrate the inadequacy of the concepts of policy and operations to provide a convincing criterion for deciding when a duty of care should exist. The distinctions which they draw are hardly visible to the naked eye."

99 (1978), 6 C.C.L.T. 142 (B.C. S.C.), affirmed (*sub nom. Malat v. R.*) (1980), 14 C.C.L.T. 206 (B.C. C.A.).

100 There was no evidence as to why a decision taken several months before the accident occurred to install the safer barrier had not been implemented by the time the accident occurred.

101 Under *Just*, as elaborated upon in *Brown*, would the failure to erect the barriers more expeditiously be considered a "policy" decision or a question of "operations"? One might also refer to the case of *A.G. N.S. v. Aza Avramovitch Assoc. Ltd.* (1984), 11 D.L.R. (4th) 588 (N.S. C.A.), where the decision of the Department of Health officers not to order percolation test holes to be dug was declared to be negligent, even though the court admitted that the officers had wide discretion. Is this decision, under the *Just* approach, a policy decision made by a lower level official or a matter of operations?

decisions were characterized by courts as policy decisions, and therefore were not subjected to ordinary negligence law review:

(1) a statutory conservation authority's policies regarding flood control measures;[102]
(2) the adoption and implementation of an elk feeding program by the Minister of the Environment, to increase the elk population;[103]
(3) the standard of care adopted by the city in its street maintenance program;[104]
(4) a decision not to inspect traffic control devices but to rely upon public complaints;[105]
(5) a decision not to grant a temporary pass to an inmate;[106]
(6) a decision not to upgrade water supply for fire fighting services;[107]
(7) a municipality's failure to enforce provisions of a restrictive covenant;[108]
(8) the decision by a provincial licensing body to adopt a certain procedure in certifying and licensing guide-outfitters;[109]
(9) decision by municipality to visually inspect only one-third of sidewalks annually;[110]
(10) the failure on the part of provincial Cabinet Ministers to take actions to protect the environment;[111]

102 *Scarborough Golf & Country Club v. Scarborough (City)* (1986), 28 D.L.R. (4th) 321 (Ont. H.C.), additional reasons at (1986), 32 D.L.R. (4th) 732 (Ont. H.C.), varied (1988), 54 D.L.R. (4th) 1 (Ont. C.A.), leave to appeal to S.C.C. refused (1989), 37 O.A.C. 91n (S.C.C.).

103 *Diversified Holdings Ltd. v. R.* (1982), 20 C.C.L.T. 202 (B.C. S.C.), affirmed (1982), 23 C.C.L.T. 156 (B.C. C.A.).

104 *Hugh v. Vancouver (City)*, [1981] 5 W.W.R. 250 (B.C. S.C.).

105 *Thornhill v. Martineau* (1987), 39 C.C.L.T. 293 (B.C. S.C.).

106 *Toews v. Mackenzie* (1980), 12 C.C.L.T. 263 (B.C. C.A.).

107 *Riverscourt Farms Ltd. v. Niagara-on-the-Lake (Town)* (1992), 9 C.C.L.T. (2d) 231 (Ont. Gen. Div.).

108 *Century Holdings Ltd. v. Delta*, [1994] 5 W.W.R. 229 (B.C. C.A.).

109 *Lake v. Callison Outfitters Ltd.* (1991), 7 C.C.L.T. (2d) 274 (B.C. S.C.). The judgment indicates the difficulty in distinguishing between policy and operations. For example, the regional manager made the decision to randomly check guide-outfitters with respect to whether they had public liability insurance. Is this policy or operations? Melnick J. stated that it appeared to "be more in the nature of a policy than an operational decision", but was prepared to deal with it as either.

110 *Gosselin v. Moose Jaw (City)* (1997), 155 D.L.R. (4th) 374 (Sask. C.A.).

111 *Tottrup v. Alberta (Minister of Environment)* (2000), 186 D.L.R. (4th) 226 (Alta. C.A.). The actions were struck out. Note that in a companion case, *Decock v. Alberta* (2000), 186 D.L.R. (4th) 265 (Alta. C.A.), leave to appeal allowed (2000), 293 A.R. 388 (note) (S.C.C.), actions of negligence brought against the Premier of Alberta and the Minister of Health were not struck out. The distinction between the two judgments appears to be the Court of Appeal's determination that in *Tottrup v. Alberta (Minister of Environment)*, the allegations related to breaches of statutory duties, for which no action could lie, whereas the allegations in *Decock v. Alberta* related to common law actions for negligence, which could lie. Russell J.A. dissented in *Tottrup* on the basis that the Statement of Claim did allege negligence actions, as in *Decock*. Also see *Paron v. Alberta (Minister of Environmental Protection)*, [2000] 9 W.W.R. 727 (Alta. Q.B.), where an action brought against the Minister was not struck out.

(11) a decision by a municipality to scale down its inspection of playgrounds at a certain time of the year;[112]
(12) decisions taken with respect to mitigating the hazard posed by falling rocks;[113]
(13) a decision as to the funding of special programs for children with autism;[114]
(14) a municipality's decision not to enforce unsightly premises legislation;[115] and
(15) Superintendent of Motor Vehicle's failure to establish and implement procedures to determine the fitness of all licensed drivers.[116]

The following activities, however, were characterized as operational in nature and were subjected to a negligence law standard of care:

(1) an irrigation district's decision to shut off water;[117]
(2) the Department of Transport's failure to respond to complaints and reports concerning safety infractions by an airline operator;[118]

---

112 *Pritchett (Guardian ad litem of) v. Gander (Town)* (2001), 205 Nfld. & P.E.I.R. 45 (Nfld. C.A.). There was a lengthy discussion of the policy/operational dichotomy. The Court of Appeal ultimately concluded that the decision not to inspect would have been a policy decision. It found, however, that the evidence supported the conclusion that the municipality had in fact decided to continue with its daily inspections but did not carry out that policy. This was operational negligence and hence subject to review.

113 *Gobin (Guardian ad litem of) v. British Columbia* (2002), 214 D.L.R. (4th) 328 (B.C. C.A.), leave to appeal refused (2002), 2002 CarswellBC 3158, 2002 CarswellBC 3159 (S.C.C.), reversing (2001), 5 C.C.L.T. (3d) 221 (B.C. S.C.). The case is another illustration of the difficulty in delineating between operations and policy. The trial judge had determined that there was liability based on negligence in operations. The Court of Appeal reversed the finding that decisions based on budgetary considerations and dealing with such matters as the scheduling of operations were policy decisions.

114 *Wynberg v. Ontario* (2006), 269 D.L.R. (4th) 435 (Ont. C.A.), leave to appeal refused (2007), 2007 CarswellOnt 2148 (S.C.C.).

115 *Homburg Canada Inc. v. Halifax* (2003), 228 D.L.R. (4th) 646, 16 C.C.L.T. (3d) 178 (N.S. C.A.).

116 *McMurray v. Marshall*, [2005] B.C.J. No. 1456.

117 *Hunt v. Westbank Irrigation District*, [1991] 6 W.W.R. 549 (B.C. S.C.), affirmed [1994] 6 W.W.R. 107 (B.C. C.A.). The judgments in this case provide an excellent illustration of the confusion which surrounds the policy/operational dichotomy. The trial judge, basing his judgment on *Just*, stated that the decisions of the Westbank Irrigation District to regulate water supply were "a manifestation of the policy decision to provide the water and are operational in nature,": [1991] 6 W.W.R. at 562. He also stated that the defendant acted in a fair and reasonable manner, and in good faith. The Court of Appeal upheld the judgment, Lambert J.A. rejecting the argument that the wrong test was applied by Oliver J. Lambert J.A.'s conclusion was that good faith was the standard which Oliver J. applied to the policy decision to adopt the water supply system, and reasonableness in relation to the operation of the system.

118 *Swanson Estate v. R.* (1991), 7 C.C.L.T. (2d) 186 (Fed. C.A.). The department regulated airlines in terms of safety. The decision was based on an interpretation of *Just* which confined policy decisions to generally high level decisions. The Regional Director's task of enforcing decisions was stated to be clearly operational. Linden J.A. distinguished between the "governing" role and "servicing" role of governments. The negligence was stated to lie in the department's failure to enforce the regulations, and specifically, its failure to ground the airline.

(3) the Canadian Grain Commission's failure adequately to monitor the level of security posted by licensed grain dealers;[119]

(4) the Minister of Fisheries' decision to withdraw his previous authorization to grant new lobster licenses;[120]

(5) a municipality's decision to issue a residential building permit even though it offended the by-law;[121]

(6) a municipality's decision to issue a building permit and its failure to detect deficiencies in construction;[122]

---

119 *Brewer Brothers v. A.G. Can.* (1991), 8 C.C.L.T. (2d) 45 (Fed. C.A.). The negligence related to decisions taken with respect to the implementation of a new system of verification, and the system's failure with respect to a specific operator. Also see *Layden v. A.G. Can.* (1991), 8 C.C.L.T. (2d) 41 (Fed. C.A.); *Devloo v. R.* (1991), 8 C.C.L.T. (2d) 93 (Fed. C.A.); and *Comte v. R.* (1991), 8 C.C.L.T. (2d) 90 (Fed. C.A.).

120 *Comeau's Sea Foods Ltd. v. Canada (Minister of Fisheries & Oceans)* (1992), 11 C.C.L.T. (2d) 241 (Fed. T.D.), reversed (1995), 24 C.C.L.T. (2d) 1 (Fed. C.A.), leave to appeal allowed (1995), 127 D.L.R. (4th) vii (S.C.C.), affirmed [1997] 1 S.C.R. 12. The judgments in this case again demonstrate, probably more than any other recent judgment, the enormous difficulties with this dichotomy. The trial judge held that having authorized the licence, the Minister's decision to revoke the authorization was *ultra vires*. Conceding that the decision to authorize the issuance of the licence was "policy", Strayer J. suggested that the failure to implement the policy, by routinely issuing the licence, was now a matter of operations, to which a duty of care would attach. In the Federal Court of Appeal, Stone J.A. held that since the decision to retract was *ultra vires*, it was neither policy nor operations. According to Stone J.A., a duty was owed by the Minister, but it was negated because the plaintiff had alternative, more expeditious and effective administrative law remedies. According to Robertson J.A.'s approach, the policy/operational dichotomy was very subtle. Robertson J.A. held that the decision whether to revoke the licence was a matter of policy. However, the manner in which the decision was made (whether to revoke) was a question of operations. Thus, while one could not subject the actual decision to revoke to ordinary negligence law, one could subject the *manner in which the decision was made* to negligence law. And in this respect, Robertson J.A. held that it was not established by the plaintiff that the Minister's decision to revoke the licence was made as a result of negligent conduct. Linden J.A. dissented. His view was that the decision to withdraw the authorization for the licence was not a policy decision. It was without statutory authorization, and similar to Strayer J.'s approach, it was treated as negligence at the operational stage. The Supreme Court of Canada, per Major J., upheld the Court of Appeal's judgment. Major J. held that the Minister exercised his statutory authority appropriately and accordingly did not breach his duty of care in ascertaining the scope of his statutory authority. For comment, see W.D. Vern, "Case Comment: *Comeau's Sea Foods*" (1997), 76 Can. Bar Rev. 253. Compare this case with *Keeping v. Canada (Attorney General)* (2003), 16 C.C.L.T. (3d) 250 (Nfld. C.A.), where the refusal by the Ministry to grant a fishing license, due to negligence by an employee in determining the size of the applicant's boat, led to liability. The court held that the error was one of operations, and that had the proper measurements been taken, the license would have been issued.

121 *Tarjan v. Rocky View No. 44 (Municipal Dist.)* (1992), 3 Alta. L.R. (3d) 216 (Q.B.), reversed on other grounds (1993), 13 Alta. L.R. (3d) 220 (C.A.).

122 *Mortimer v. Cameron* (1994), 111 D.L.R. (4th) 428 (Ont. C.A.). See also *Rothfield v. Manolakos*, [1989] 2 S.C.R. 1259. A similar case dealing with granting a permit for a sewage disposal system and deficiencies in inspection is *Cook v. Bowen Island Realty Ltd.* (1997), 38 C.C.L.T. (2d) 217, [1998] 1 W.W.R. 647 (B.C. S.C.), additional reasons at (1998), 19 C.P.C. (4th) 148 (B.C. S.C.). Also see: *Strata Plan NW 3341 v. Canlan Ice Sports*, [2001] 10 W.W.R. 214, 7 C.C.L.T. (3d) 111 (B.C. S.C.), additional reasons at (2001), [2002] 2 W.W.R. 456 (B.C. S.C.), affirmed [2002] 11 W.W.R. 37 (B.C. C.A.), where a municipality was held liable for failing to enforce provisions of the provincial Building Code, having by by-law adopted responsibility for enforcement; and *Gibbs v. Edmonton (City)* (2001), 6 C.C.L.T. (3d) 277

(7) Crown's failure to adequately inspect and maintain a highway;[123]
(8) a municipality's failure to enforce a by-law requiring residents to disconnect their rain pipes from the city storm sewer;[124]
(9) Crown's failure to safely design and construct new railway bridge;[125]
(10) Cabinet's failure to deal with the renewal of a lease in a timely and appropriate manner;[126]
(11) a local authority's failure to take action regarding dangerous dogs despite the fact that it had adopted a policy with respect to this danger;[127]
(12) the Corrections Branch's decision to transfer a violent inmate to a minimum security prison;[128] and
(13) Crown's failure to implement a judicial decision.[129]

Close examination of these two sets of cases reveals the difficulty and unpredictability inherent in the policy/operational dichotomy.[130]

(g) Conclusion

Cooper v. Hobart and *Edwards v. Law Society of Upper Canada* have altered the way Canadian courts are currently approaching the issue of the negligence liability of public authorities. Rather than simply finding a *prima facie* duty of care based on the foreseeability of harm, the more onerous requirement of proximity has allowed courts to deny a *prima facie* duty at "stage one" of the test, and thereby avoid the need to characterize the public authority's activity as either one of policy or one of operations at stage two.

(Alta. Q.B.), where a municipality was liable for negligently approving a subdivision. Also see *Bowes v. Edmonton (City)* (2005), [2006] 4 W.W.R. 112 (Alta. Q.B.), additional reasons at (2005), 2005 CarswellAlta 1557 (Alta. Q.B.), affirmed (2007), [2007] A.J. No. 1500, 2007 CarswellAlta 1851 (Alta. C.A.), where a city's decision to issue development and building permits was held to be operational in nature.

123 *Lewis (Guardian ad litem of) v. British Columbia* (1997), 153 D.L.R. (4th) 594, 40 C.C.L.T. 153 (S.C.C.). This case was similar to *Just*. Having adopted a program to stabilize the rock slope adjacent to a highway, the manner in which the authority carried this out was stated to be operational. The independent contractor who was hired was negligent. The issue in the case was whether the Crown was liable for this negligence. The Supreme Court held that the Crown's duty was "non-delegable" and hence the Crown was liable. See also *Mochinski v. Trendline Industries Ltd.* (1997), 154 D.L.R. (4th) 212 (S.C.C.), which was a companion case dealing with falling ice. See a discussion of this point in Chapter 16. For commentary on *Lewis* see Rafferty & Rowbotham, "Developments in Contract and Tort Law: the 1997-98 Term" (1999), 10 Sup. Ct. L. Rev. 169.

124 *Oosthoek v. Thuder Bay (City)* (1996), 139 D.L.R. (4th) 611 (Ont. C.A.), leave to appeal refused (1997), 104 O.A.C. 240 (note) (S.C.C.).

125 *Botting v. British Columbia* (1996), 33 C.C.L.T. (2d) 294 (B.C. S.C.).

126 *Atlantic Leasing Ltd. v. Newfoundland* (1998), 162 D.L.R. (4th) 54 (Nfld. C.A.).

127 *Young v. Cumberland House Local Community Authority No. 3* (1999), 50 C.C.L.T. (2d) 186 (Sask. Q.B.).

128 *Pete v. Axworthy* (2005), [2006] 5 W.W.R. 581 (B.C. C.A.), leave to appeal refused (2006), 2006 CarswellBC 279 (S.C.C.).

129 *Holland v. Saskatchewan (Minister of Agriculture, Food & Rural Revitalization)*, 2008 SCC 42 (S.C.C.).

130 Now that proximity must be established before the courts are required to characterize the activity as policy or operations, there have been far fewer judgments utilizing this difficult dichotomy.

Although this way of analyzing the question is relatively new in Canadian jurisprudence,[131] it had for a long time been the English approach to the question of public tort liability. Unlike in Canada, the judiciary's reaction in England was to quickly retreat from *Anns* and to restrict the tort liability of public authorities. The courts cautioned against a "too literal application" of Lord Wilberforce's judgment and noted that several relevant considerations must be taken into account in determining whether a public authority has breached a private law duty of care.[132] Moreover, in *Murphy v. Brentwood Dist. Council*,[133] *Anns* was explicitly overruled, at least in so far as it imposed a duty on public authorities with respect to purely economic losses, resulting from their negligent supervision of building construction. While concentrating on issues relating to economic loss recovery, rather than on the question of public tort liability in general, some of the *dicta* went so far as to express doubts about the liability of public authorities in their supervision of compliance with building regulations, even with respect to personal injury claims.[134]

Approaching the issue of the negligence liability of statutory authorities by seeking to find proximity within the terms of a statute, invariably leads to the dismissal of actions brought against public authorities. Public law statutes do not create civil law remedies, unless they do so expressly. Proximity can be established, however, where the interactions between governments and private persons create common law duties of care. Not only is this approach consistent with Canadian law concerning the interaction between statutory breaches and tort law, but it is a more flexible and logical approach that can be more easily understood and applied by the courts.

Failing adequate common law approaches, legislative interventions provide a possible solution. Legislators, who have conferred the powers or expanded the duties of public authorities in the first instance, might consider adopting specific

131 See discussion above. Although several lower courts were approaching the matter in this way, it was in *Cooper v. Hobart* and *Edwards v. Law Society of Upper Canada* that the Supreme Court first decided to take this route.

132 See Lord Keith's judgment in *Rowling v. Takaro Properties Ltd.*, [1988] 1 All E.R. 163 at 172 (P.C.). Lord Keith wrote reasons in four important judgments, emphasizing the point in each case that various considerations must be taken into account, depending upon the circumstances, before the courts will impose a duty of care. In addition to his judgment in *Rowling v. Takaro Properties*, see Lord Keith's judgments in *Hill v. Chief Constable of West Yorkshire*, [1988] 2 All E.R. 238 (H.L.)—police do not owe a duty of care to individual members of the public to identify and apprehend criminals; *Yuen Kunyeu v. A.G. Hong Kong*, [1987] 2 All E.R. 705 (P.C.)—Commissioner of Deposit-taking Companies owed no duty of care to would-be depositors; *Peabody Donation Fund Governors v. Sir Lindsay Parkinson & Co.*, [1985] A.C. 210 (H.L.)—local building authority owed no duty of care to developers. In *Murphy v. Brentwood Dist. Council*, [1990] 2 All E.R. 908, the Lords categorically rejected a claim against a public authority for purely economic losses suffered as a result of a defective structure. These judgments, and particularly *Yuen Kun-yeu*, were particularly influential in the Supreme Court's thinking in *Cooper v. Hobart* and *Edwards v. Law Society of Upper Canada*. Note that despite its rejection of the operation/policy approach and its analysis of public tort liability cases by relying on a number of considerations, the English jurisprudence is itself in a confused state. Bowman & Bailey's concluding remarks after a lengthy article examining English law, although hopeful, indicate the problem. The authors state that "the ingredients are available for the courts to bring some order into an area that has threatened to descend into chaos", at [2000] 59 Camb. L.J. 132.

133 *Ibid.*

134 See Lord Mackay, at [1990] 2 All E.R. 912, and Lord Keith at 917, for example.

liability provisions. Since the resistence to imposing liability on public authorities is policy or politically driven, the solution might better come from legislatures and not courts.[135] Legislative protections from suit are routinely enacted in order to lessen the liability of public authorities as they carry out their public functions.

(h) Legislative and Judicial Immunity

Two areas of public tort liability likely to be unaffected by the above developments are negligence in the exercise of purely legislative or judicial functions.

In *Welbridge Hldg. Ltd. v. Winnipeg*,[136] the Supreme Court of Canada established that a public authority cannot be held accountable in tort for acts at the legislative or quasi-judicial level, even if these acts are beyond the authority's powers. In this case, there was negligence in the passing of a by-law, which was subsequently declared invalid, resulting in economic losses to the plaintiff. This principle was later applied by the Alberta Court of Appeal in *Kwong v. R.*,[137] where it was held that a government department cannot be sued for its failure to pass regulations which might have prevented a tragic accident from occurring. That this position has remained unchanged despite the influence of *Anns* and *Kamloops* can be seen in the case of *Mahoney v. R.*,[138] where the court struck out an action brought against the Crown for its failure to pass safety regulations concerning the design of baby cribs.[139] The effect of *Cooper v. Hobart* has only been to reinforce this resistance to imposing common law duties on legislative bodies for the protection of private interests. Both the lack of proximity between government authorities and private citizens and policy concerns provide strong reasons to deny the existence of private law duties of care.[140]

The courts must be careful, however, to avoid unduly extending the immunity protection offered to legislative acts to situations which may not warrant it. In *Bowen v. Edmonton*,[141] allegations of negligence were brought against the defen-

---

135 The confusing state of the case law has also prompted one judge to state: "In matters of this kind, legislation is better than litigation". See Southin J.A. in *Gobin v. British Columbia*, [2002] BCCA 373 (C.A.).

136 [1971] S.C.R. 957.

137 [1979] 2 W.W.R. 1 (Alta. C.A.), affirmed [1979] 6 W.W.R. 573 (S.C.C.).

138 (1986), 38 C.C.L.T. 21 (Fed. T.D.).

139 A similar case is *Kirkpatrick v. Ford Motor Co. of Canada* (2001), [2001] O.J. No. 4387, 2001 CarswellOnt 4031 (S.C.J.), where an action against the Crown for failing to regulate motor vehicle airbags was struck out. The same approach pertains under Quebec civil law. See *Entreprises Sibeca Inc. v. Frelighsburg (Municipality)*, [2004] 3 S.C.R. 304 (S.C.C.). The rationale is explained by Deschamps J. at para. 24:

> Municipalities perform functions that require them to take multiple and sometimes conflicting interests into consideration. Where no constitutional issues are in play, it would be inconceivable for the courts to interfere in this process and set themselves up as arbitrators to dictate that any particular interest be taken into consideration. They may intervene only if there is bad faith. The onerous and complex nature of the functions that are inherent in the exercise of a regulatory power justify incorporating a form of protection both in civil law and common law.

140 See, for example, *Granite Power Corp. v. Ontario* (2004), 72 O.R. (3d) 194 (C.A.), leave to appeal refused (2005), 2005 CarswellOnt 793 (S.C.C.), and the myriad of other recent judgments discussed above that have dismissed actions brought by private citizens against governmental authorities based on a lack of proximity argument.

141 (1977), 4 C.C.L.T. 105 (Alta. T.D.). See Laux, "A Comment on *Bowen v. Edmonton*" (1978), 4 C.C.L.T. 132.

dant city with respect to its decision to grant approval to a replotting scheme permitting residential use on land which was later shown to be unstable and hence unsuitable for residential purposes. In approving the scheme, the city failed in its statutory duty to ensure that the land was suited to the subdivision purpose. It had ignored advice to conduct studies before the replotting, despite the fact that it was aware of the hazard of soil instability. The court applied *Welbridge Holdings* and considered the approval of the scheme to be legislative in nature. It is arguable, however, that the allegations of negligence related not to the city's legislative decision, but to acts taken outside its *bona fide* area of discretion. The city was required to assure itself that the replotting scheme met the statutory standards, and its failure to do so ought not to have been regarded as a political decision.[142] For example, in the more recent case of *Bowes v. Edmonton (City)*,[143] the city was again sued for its negligence in issuing building permits on unstable land. In this case, the trial judge held that the city owed and breached its duty to exercise reasonable care in its review of development applications leading to its decision regarding the issuance of building permits.[144]

The tort liability of judges and others who are performing judicial activities also raises difficult issues.[145] This topic involves not only the common law, but

---

142 In many respects, this case parallels *Windsor Motors Ltd. v. Powell River (Municipality)* (1969), 4 D.L.R. (3d) 155 (B.C. C.A.) and not *Welbridge Holdings*. The public official or body failed to do something which it was required to do in arriving at its legislative decision. See also *Birch Builders Ltd. v. Esquimalt (Township)* (1992), 90 D.L.R. (4th) 665 (B.C. C.A.), leave to appeal refused [1992] 3 S.C.R. v (note). In this case, the plaintiff sought and obtained rezoning. Pursuant to the rezoning, the plaintiff then applied for a development permit. The development permit was issued. Unfortunately for the plaintiff, however, a court challenge later revealed that the permit had not been properly issued due to a technical defect. The plaintiff was never successful in obtaining a new permit and sued. The Court of Appeal characterized the municipality's negligence as occurring in a legislative function, i.e., the failure to pass a proper resolution, and, based on *Welbridge*, dismissed the action. Query: would the plaintiff have had a better chance by framing the action in negligent statement, or by suing the appropriate municipal employee in negligence for not ensuring that the proper resolution was put before the council? Should this case have been argued along the lines of *Windsor Motors*? Also see *Woestenburg v. Kamloops (City)* (2001), 18 M.P.L.R. (3d) 257 (B.C. S.C.), which followed *Birch* and held that even if a municipality passed a by-law enacting an official community plan based on negligent advice and interpretation of the law, a party injured as a consequence did not have an action, as the approval of the plan was a legislative activity. Compare this with *Becze v. Edmonton (City)* (1996), [1996] A.J. No. 754, 1996 CarswellAlta 703 (Q.B.), where actions done by a city employee after building plans had been approved led to a successful action against the city. Also see *Prince George (City) v. Rahn Bros. Logging Ltd.* (2001), 203 D.L.R. (4th) 499 (B.C. S.C.), varied (2003), 2003 CarswellBC 61 (C.A.), where the city was held liable for negligently issuing a building permit in contravention of its by-law. The distinction between negligence in operational activities and in legislative functions becomes blurred in these types of cases.

143 [2006] W.W.R. 112 (Alta. Q.B.), additional reasons at (2005), 2005 CarswellAlta 1557 (Q.B.), affirmed (2007), [2007] A.J. No. 1500, 2007 CarswellAlta 1851 (C.A.).

144 The action failed, however, due to the ten-year ultimate limitation period contained in the Limitations Act, S.A. 1996, c. L-15.1. The Court of Appeal affirmed the trial judgment, although it varied the award for costs. There was a strong dissent by Cote J.A. on the matter of the city's liability for negligence, although the Court of Appeal unanimously agreed that the limitation period had expired.

145 See Glenn, "La responsabilité des juges" (1983), 28 McGill L.J. 238; Gibson, "Developments in Tort Law: The 1985-86 Term" (1987), 9 Sup. Ct. L. Rev. 455 at 459ff; and J.M. Law, "A Tale of Two Immunities: Judicial and Prosecutorial Immunities in Canada" (1990), 28 Alta. L. Rev. 468.

the interpretation of statutes which define the liability of judges.[146] Further, there may be a distinction based upon the level of the judge concerned. The few cases which have dealt with this issue evidence the uncertainty which is attached to it.[147]

The immunity which tort law provides to judges, or others performing judicial functions, for their negligence in the performance of their duties, pertains not to the judges in their personal capacities but to the judicial activity being performed.[148] The difficulty arises, however, in determining the scope of the immunity afforded to judges for negligence occurring in the performance of the judicial activity. Can judges perform judicial functions negligently, or even maliciously and corruptly, without fear of civil suit? According to early cases, it appeared that the immunity extended this far.[149] This view was reaffirmed by Lord Denning in *Sirros v. Moore.*[150] His Lordship noted that a judge will be immune from civil suit while acting within jurisdiction, even though that judge has acted "under some gross error or ignorance, or was actuated by envy, hatred and malice, and all uncharitableness", even if it appears that the judge "has accepted bribes, or been in the least degree corrupt, or has perverted the course of justice."[151] What, however, is the scope of the requirement that the judge be acting within jurisdiction? And further, are judges strictly liable for all acts which are outside their jurisdiction, or is wrongfulness required? These are the critical questions, for it is here that the immunity of judges begins to break down.

In terms of "acts without jurisdiction", Lord Denning noted an important distinction between judges of inferior and superior courts. The former were subject to civil action in the case of all acts outside jurisdiction, even where due to an innocent mistake of law.[152] In so far as the superior courts are concerned, however,

146 For example, see the various Provincial Court statutes, such as the Provincial Court Act, R.S.M. 1987, c. C275 (also C.C.S.M. c. C275), and the Public Authorities Protection Act, R.S.O. 1990, c. P.38. See *Shaw v. Trudel Prov. J.* (1988), 44 C.C.L.T. 194 (Man. Q.B.), affirmed [1989] 1 W.W.R. 377 (Man. C.A.); and *Kramer v. Forgrave* (1989), 68 O.R. (2d) 414 (H.C.). *Koita v. Toronto Police Services Board*, [2000] O.T.C. 897 (S.C.J.), reversed (2001), 151 O.A.C. 360 (Div. Ct.), dealt with the immunity provided to Justices of the Peace under the Justices of the Peace Act, R.S.O. 1990, c. J.4. The legislation provides Justices of the Peace with the same immunity possessed by Superior Court Justices. Also see *Nova Scotia (Labour Relations Board) v. Future Inns Canada Inc.* (1999), 178 D.L.R. (4th) 202 (N.S. C.A.). The Public Inquiries Act, R.S.N.S. 1989, c. 372 provided members of the Labour Relations Board with the same immunities as judges of the Supreme Court.

147 See especially *Morier v. Rivard*, [1985] 2 S.C.R. 716; *Sirros v. Moore*, [1975] 1 Q.B. 118 (C.A.), and *McC. v. Mullan*, [1984] 3 All E.R. 908 (H.L.). See also *Romaniuk v. Alta.* (1988), 44 C.C.L.T. 148 (Alta. Q.B.); *Royer v. Mignault* (1988), 50 D.L.R. (4th) 345 (Que. C.A.).

148 Thus "the judge who defamed someone in private correspondence, for example, or in the course of an entirely unauthorized attempt to adjudicate a curbside dispute between motorists, would be fully liable in tort." See Gibson, above, note 145, at 460.

149 See, e.g., *Fray v. Blackburn* (1863), 122 E.R. 217, and *Royal Aquarium & Winter Garden Soc. Ltd. v. Parkinson*, [1892] 1 Q.B. 431, cited by Chouinard J. in *Morier v. Rivard*, [1985] 2 S.C.R. 716 at 738. Also cited in support of this position was *Halsbury's Laws of England*, 4th ed., vol. 1 (1973), at 197 and Brun and Tremblay, *Droit constitutionnel* (1982), at 514. See also Law, above, note 145, at 481: "it is clear that the immunity extends to the malicious actions of a judge." Professor Law's own view, however, is that judicial immunity should not extend to the malicious acts or decisions of judges.

150 [1975] 1 Q.B. 118 (C.A.).

151 *Ibid.*, at 132.

152 Lord Denning M.R. cited the *Marshalsea Case* (1613), 10 Co. Rep. 68b.

a judge is immune from liability for acts done even without jurisdiction while acting "in the *bona fide* exercise of his office and under the belief that he has jurisdiction, though he may be mistaken in that belief and may not in truth have any jurisdiction."[153] His Lordship could find no valid reason for maintaining the distinction between superior and inferior court judges, and stated that they were both liable to civil suit for acts done without jurisdiction, unless they honestly believed that these acts were within their jurisdiction.

What does the term "jurisdiction" mean for the purpose of this immunity rule? Does it refer only to the situation wherein a judge acts completely outside the given boundaries, in the broad sense of the word,[154] or as well to the case where the subject is within the judge's limits but the judge improperly exercises judicial powers?[155]

In *McC. v. Mullan*,[156] Lord Bridge suggested that acts outside a judge's jurisdiction are not confined to cases where the acts themselves are not subject to jurisdiction at all, but can entail misconduct of such a magnitude in terms of *how* jurisdiction was exercised.[157] Lord Bridge conceded, however, that some procedural irregularities or even breaches of the rule of natural justice might be more narrow and technical in nature, not necessarily exposing justices to liability in damages.

As discussed by Gibson,[158] there were thus three questions for the Supreme Court of Canada in *Morier v. Rivard.*[159] First, what types of misconduct amount to sufficient excesses of jurisdiction and are thus not protected by an absolute immunity? Second, if a judge acts outside of jurisdiction, as defined, is Lord Denning's "honest belief" defence applicable? Third, are inferior court and superior court judges to be treated alike? The majority of the Supreme Court, per Chouinard J., held that the issue of immunity, in the instant case, fell to be decided by the relevant statutory law, which protected those in the defendant's position for acts done "in the execution of their duty", with no distinction made between acts within or without their jurisdiction. On this basis, the immunity was upheld. Although discussed by Chouinard J., the basic questions went unanswered. La Forest J., in dissent, accepted Lord Bridge's contention that between clear cases of excess of jurisdiction *ab initio* and mere technical jurisdictional errors there

---

153 [1975] 1 Q.B. 118 at 135.

154 For example, using Gibson's example, adjudicating a dispute between two people quarrelling on the street. The judge has no jurisdiction *ab initio* in this case.

155 For example, a judge refuses to accept a jury's verdict and orders an accused imprisoned. The court has jurisdiction over the case, but in the exercise of the jurisdiction the judge makes a mistake. As stated by Lord Bridge in *McC. v. Mullan*, above, note 147, at 912, concerning the term "jurisdiction":

> There are many words in common usage in the law which have no precise or constant meaning. But few, I think, have been used with so many different shades of meaning in different contexts or have so freely acquired new meanings with the development of the law as the word 'jurisdiction'.

156 *Ibid.*

157 For example, "gross and obvious irregularity of procedure, as for example if one justice absented himself for part of the hearing and relied on another to tell him what had happened during his absence", *ibid.*, at 920.

158 Above, note 145.

159 Above, note 147.

lies "a vast area in which the law is less clear." In this area, serious and obvious errors also oust jurisdiction and hence remove the immunity. On this basis, the dissent argued that serious errors were made in the instant case, to deprive the defendant of its immunity.

In *Prefontaine v. Gosman*,[160] the immunity afforded to judges was stated in the broadest possible terms. The court stated that "a judge acting in his or her judicial capacity will not be civilly liable for any actions done in such judicial capacity whether the judge was acting within or outside of his or her jurisdiction, and even if the judge was acting out of hatred, envy or malice, if the judge believed that he or she was acting with jurisdiction and in the course of his or her judicial duties."[161] Questions arise, however, even with regard to the scope of this protection. If the judge is not acting in good faith can he or she be stated to be acting judicially? Can a judge who is acting maliciously in order to harm a litigant be acting in the "honest" belief that he or she has jurisdiction? Honest belief and good faith seem to be a prerequisite to judicial conduct.[162]

Immunity for negligence actions is provided not only to judges, but to all those involved in the judicial proceedings, such as the actual litigants or their witnesses.[163] It has been held, for example, that a litigant does not owe a duty of care to another litigant regarding the manner in which the litigation is conducted.[164] A civil action cannot be brought against someone based on the latter's false evidence.[165]

---

160 [2000] 6 W.W.R. 530 (Alta. Q.B.), affirmed [2002] 11 W.W.R. 45 (Alta. C.A.).

161 *Ibid.*, at 545. In *Taylor v. Canada (Attorney General)* (2000), 184 D.L.R. (4th) 706 (Fed. C.A.), leave to appeal refused (2000), 263 N.R. 399 (note) (S.C.C.), a party complained to the Human Rights Commission as a result of the actions of a judge. The judge had barred the complainant from his court unless he removed his religious headgear. The commission decided that it lacked jurisdiction to hear the complaint because of the principle of judicial immunity. The Federal Court of Appeal accepted that the principle of immunity applies unless the judge knowingly acted beyond his jurisdiction. Not only did this not occur in this case, but also the judge did in fact have jurisdiction to do what he did. The "bad faith" exception to judicial immunity was discussed and reference made to M.L. Friedland, "A Place Apart: Judicial Independence and Accountability in Canada" (Ottawa: Canadian Judicial Council, 1995). Complaints were also made to the Canadian Judicial Council. For a judgment concerning the C.J.C.'s treatment of this complaint, see *Taylor v. Canada (Attorney General)* (2001), 207 D.L.R. (4th) 552 (Fed. T.D.), affirmed (2003), 2003 CarswellNat 219 (C.A.).

162 Judicial immunity is defended on the ground that it is not for judges' protection but for the public's protection. Judges should be able to act independently and fearlessly without threat of lawsuit by disappointed litigants. This rationale is understandable. It does not, however, justify extending the immunity to judges who act maliciously in order to harm claimants.

163 There have been a number of recent cases affirming the witness immunity rule. See, for example, *Robinson v. Gulder*, [2007] O.J. No. 2718; *Howatt v. Klassen*, [2005] O.J. No. 1381; and *Elliott v. Insurance Crime Prevention Bureau*, [2005] N.S.J No. 322. In *Robinson*, an action brought against witness for negligently or intentionally misrepresenting evidence in a Competition Tribunal hearing was struck out. In *Howatt*, an action brought against a defendant relating to a psychiatric assessment report which he prepared was struck out. In *Elliott*, fire investigators for an insurer who were witnesses at the insurance trial were protected from suit, although other investigators who were not witnesses were not.

164 *Bus. Computers Int. Ltd. v. Reg. of Companies*, [1987] 3 All E.R. 465 (Ch. D.).

165 See *Marrinan v. Vibart*, [1962] 3 All E.R. 380 (C.A.); *Cabassi v. Vila* (1940), 64 C.L.R. 130 (Aust. H.C.). Also see *Horn Abbot Ltd. v. Reeves* (2000), 189 D.L.R. (4th) 644 (N.S. C.A.) and *Smith (Next Friend of) v. Kneier* (2001), 288 A.R. 144 (Q.B.).

4. MISFEASANCE IN A PUBLIC OFFICE

Although most actions brought against public authorities arise from allegations of negligence in the performance of their duties, there have been a rising number of claims alleging misconduct of a much more serious nature. The tort of misfeasance in a public office, or abuse of public office,[166] can be brought for intentional acts of wrongdoing by public officials that have harmed the economic or other interests of private persons.[167]

As discussed by Professor Irvine, while the tort of misfeasance in a public office requires "willful, conscious misconduct" and not "mere carelessness, indolence or ineptitude", the degree of misconduct required and more specifically the nature of the defendant's state of mind has been an issue of debate in the recent jurisprudence.

The requirements of the tort are as follows:

(a) the actor must be a public official;
(b) the public official must have engaged in wrongful conduct in his or her capacity as a public officer; and
(c) the wrongdoing must be intentional.

(a) Public Official

The tort is committed by those who hold public office or act under statutory authority. In *Uni-Jet Industrial Pipe Ltd. v. Canada (Attorney General),*[168] for example, the tort applied to a peace officer who was a member of the RCMP. He was subject to the Royal Canadian Mounted Police Act[169] and his act, which in this case was to divulge information to the media prematurely, was held to be a

166 In *Uni-Jet Industrial Pipe Ltd. v. Canada (Attorney General)* (2001), 9 C.C.L.T. (3d) 1 (Man. C.A.), Kroft J.A. notes that the following terminology seems to be used to describe the tort: abuse of public authority, abuse of statutory authority, abuse of public office, and misfeasance in public office. As stated by Kroft J.A., "nothing really turns on this point" and he accepts that the descriptions can be used interchangeably.

167 The leading Canadian judgment on the elements of the tort is *Odhavji Estate v. Woodhouse*, [2003] 3 S.C.R. 263, 233 D.L.R. (4th) 193, 19 C.C.C.L.T. (3d) 163. For commentary on the resurgence of this tort and a broad discussion of the key issues involved see John Irvine, "Misfeasance in Public Office: Reflections on Some Recent Developments" (2002), 9 C.C.L.T. (3d) 26. Also see Phegan, "Damages for Improper Exercise of Statutory Powers" (1980-82), 9 Sydney L. Rev. 93; Shibley, "The Personal Liability of Members of Municipal, Provincial and Federal Governments" (1985), 1 Admin. L.J. 56. An especially good discussion on the tort of "misfeasance in a public office" is found in Robert Sadler, "Liability for Misfeasance in a Public Office" (1992), 14 Sydney L. Rev. 137. For commentary post-*Odhavji*, see Bodner, "The *Odhavji* Decision: Old Ghosts and New Confusion in Canadian Courts" (2005, 42 Alta. L. Rev. 1061; Erika Chamberlain, "Misfeasance in a Public Office: In Defence of the Power/Duty Distinction", a paper prepared for "Emerging Issues in Tort Law Conference", Faculty of Law, University of Western Ontario, 2006; and Horsman and Morley, eds., *Government Liability: Law and Practice* (2007), Chapter 7.

168 Above, note 166.

169 R.S.C. 1985, c. R-10.

violation of his statutory authority.[170] The definition of public office is wide and generally has not posed a problem.[171]

An interesting case is *Freeman-Maloy v. York University*.[172] The defendant was the President of a public university. She was sued by a student who had been suspended for his participation in campus demonstrations. Although the motions judge had struck out the claim on the basis that the defendant, although a statutory officer, was not a public officer subject to governmental control and hence the Charter, the Court of Appeal held that it was not plain and obvious that the claim could not succeed. Although not subject to governmental control, the plaintiff was subject "to the regime of public law", and her activity in this case, i.e., suspending a student, was subject to "judicial review".[173] Thus, it has been suggested that the test for public office is "an administrative law-based test. If the impugned action involves the exercise of statutory power, and is reviewable on the application of judicial review, it is also (at least arguably) subject to liability under the tort of misfeasance in public office".[174]

(b) Wrongful Conduct in the Defendant's Capacity as a Public Officer

The nature of the wrongful conduct which is required in order to constitute the tort of misfeasance in a public office has been in issue in recent cases and was the primary issue in the *Odhavji* case.

The traditional misfeasance case involved a public official who maliciously exercised a power or authority which the official actually had. The example given of this by Iacobucci J. in *Odhavji* was *Ashby v. White*.[175] An elections officer who had the power to deprive certain persons from voting, exercised this power maliciously and fraudulently to deprive the plaintiff of his voting right.

Similar to this is where a public official commits a wrongful act in the purported exercise of a power which he or she knowingly does not have. Thus, for example, a Premier and Attorney General who ordered that a person's liquor license be cancelled can be used to illustrate this type of wrongdoing.[176] The Premier did not actually have the power to cancel the plaintiff's license, but used his authority to prevail upon the person who had the power to do so. Thus, either abusing a

---

170 The court considered the Criminal Code provisions relating to search warrants in determining that the release of details concerning searches prior to the execution of the warrant and before the Return to the Judge had been filed was in violation of the Code. The court held, however, that violation of operational or policy manuals that do not have statutory authority cannot form the basis of this tort.

171 Actions have been brought against a mayor, other municipal officials, the Premier and Attorney General of a province, a member of the R.C.M.P., police officers, a Cabinet Ministry, superintendents of hospitals, among others.

172 (2006), 267 D.L.R. (4th) 37 (Ont. C.A.), leave to appeal refused (2006), 2006 CarswellOnt 5558 (S.C.C.), reversing in part (2005), 253 D.L.R. (4th) 37 (Ont. C.A.).

173 Whether this will be the minimum requirement remains to be seen. As noted by Chamberlain, above, note 167, there seems to be a trend towards a "looser definition of public office", and the law on this point remains unsettled.

174 See Horsman and Morley, above, note 167, at 7.20.10(1).

175 (1703), 2 Ld. Raym. 938, 92 E.E. 126 (Eng. K.B.).

176 *Roncarelli v. Duplessis*, [1959] S.C.R. 121.

power which one actually has or knowingly exceeding one's powers are activities that can constitute the tort of abuse of power.[177]

More difficult to rationalize as a tort of misfeasance in a public office are those cases where public officials breach their statutory duties, but are not, at least in the traditional sense, abusing their powers. It is here where the recent cases have made their most significant extension to the tort.

The leading Canadian case is *Odhavji Estate v. Woodhouse*.[178] The plaintiffs sued the defendant police officers alleging that they intentionally breached their statutory duties under the *Police Services Act*.[179] The statute imposed a duty on the defendants to co-operate with a Special Investigations Unit established to investigate the fatal police shooting of the plaintiffs' relative. The police officers' failure to co-operate allegedly caused the family of the deceased mental distress.

At the Court of Appeal,[180] Borins J.A., for the majority of the court, distinguished between breaching a statutory duty, for which a negligence action, for example, might lie, and the improper exercise or the abuse of an administrative or legislative power. According to Borins J.A., it is only the latter wrongdoing which can form the basis of the tort of misfeasance in a public office. In this respect, the Court of Appeal held that the police officers' failure to co-operate in the investigation, while perhaps a breach of a statutory duty imposed on them, did not constitute an improper exercise of their power or authority.

The dissenting judge, Feldman J.A., held that the tort could be made out by proving that the defendants deliberately breached their statutory duties to co-operate, if they knew or were recklessly indifferent to the fact, that the plaintiff would likely be injured. In other words, the tort should not be confined to the abuse of an administrative or legislative power.

The Supreme Court of Canada adopted the broader approach of Feldman J.A. According to Iacobucci J., the essence of the tort is deliberate *unlawful or wrongful conduct* by a public official, where the plaintiff's injury is either intended or likely to occur. The wrongful conduct can consist of the unlawful exercise of a statutory or prerogative power, *or* the intentional breach of a statutory duty. In coming to this conclusion, Iacobucci J. referred to other Commonwealth cases that have moved the tort forward in this direction.[181] In addition, this broader view of the

---

177 In essence, in both cases the public official is exercising a power that he or she does not have, since one can assume that in democratic societies public officials are not granted powers for the sole purpose of harming others.

178 [2003] 3 S.C.R. 263.

179 R.S.O. 1990, c. P.15.

180 (2000), 194 D.L.R. (4th) 577, 3 C.C.L.T. (3d) 171 (Ont. C.A.), additional reasons at (2001), 2001 CarswellOnt 476 (C.A.), leave to appeal allowed (2001), 2001 CarswellOnt 3081 (S.C.C.), reversed (2003), 2003 CarswellOnt 4851 (S.C.C.).

181 Cases referred to include *Northern Territory of Australia v. Mengel* (1995), 129 A.L.R. 1 (Austalia H.C.); *Garrett v. New Zealand (Attorney General)*, [1997] 2 N.Z.L.R. 332 (New Zealand C.A.); and *Three Rivers District Council v. Bank of England (No. 3)*, [2000] 2 W.L.R. 1220 (U.K. H.L.).

nature of the wrongful conduct necessary for the commission of the tort had been accepted in earlier Canadian cases cited by Iacobucci J.[182]

There is the danger that an over-extension of the tort of misfeasance in a public office can clash with Canadian law's refusal to recognize a tort of breach of statutory duty and its restrictive attitude to negligence claims against public authorities. As discussed above, many negligence actions against public authorities for beaching statutory duties have failed for want of proximity. Statutory provisions have invariably been construed as creating duties of care owed only to the public. The tort of misfeasance in a public office seems now to provide an alternative and perhaps more easily proved remedy to plaintiffs.[183]

(c) Intentional Wrongdoing

It is this element of the tort that has received the most attention from the recent jurisprudence. What constitutes intentional wrongdoing sufficient to establish the tort of misfeasance in a public office?

It is recognized that there are two forms of the tort. First, where a public official acts, even within its statutory authority or power, for an improper purpose, namely to specifically injure the plaintiff,[184] the tort is made out. Second, and alternatively, where a public official acts, knowing that it lacked the authority to do so, and knowing that this act would probably injure the plaintiff, the tort is also made out.[185]

---

182 Cited were *Alberta (Minister of Public Works, Supply & Services) v. Nilsson* (1999), 46 C.C.L.T. (2d) 158, [199] 9 W.W.R. 203 (Alta. Q.B.), leave to appeal allowed (1999), 1999 CarswellAlta 1119 (C.A.), affirmed (2002), 2002 CarswellAlta 1491 (C.A.), additional reasons at (2003), 2003 CarswellAlta 565 (C.A.), leave to appeal refused (2003), 2003 CarswellAlta 1050 (S.C.C.); *Uni-Jet Industrial Pipe Ltd. v. Canada (Attorney General)* (2001), 9 C.C.L.T. (3d) 1 (Man. C.A.); and *Powder Mountain Resorts Ltd. v. British Columbia* (2001), 94 B.C.L.R. (3d) 14 (C.A.).

183 Others have also commented negatively on the broadening of the tort. Erika Chamberlain, "Misfeasance in a Public Office: In Defence of the Power/Duty Distinction", above, note 167, writes:

> . . .the tort has undergone rapid expansion in the last few decades, and threatens to shed its "exceptional" character if current trends persist. There has been a relaxation of the elements necessary to prove the claim: a looser definition of public office; a watering down of the requisite malicious state of mind; and an erosion of the necessary proximity between the public officer and the plaintiff. . . . The effect of this trend is that a public officer can now be sued for misfeasance in a public office for breach of duty that is not directed at anyone in particular, and without any vindictive purpose. In the author's view, this trend offends the exceptional nature of the tort, and provides the potential for misfeasance in a public office to overtake negligence in the sphere of authority liability.

184 Whether other types of improper purposes will satisfy this tort remains unclear. See discussion below.

185 See Irvine, above, note 167. Irvine explains these two forms or varieties of the tort. Category A: using actual statutory authority or power for an improper purpose; i.e., to injure the plaintiff. Category B: acting knowing that one has no authority and that this act would "probably" injure the plaintiff. This analysis is the one articulated by the House of Lords in *Three Rivers District Council v. Bank of England (No. 3)*, [2000] 3 All E.R. 1 (H.L.), discussed below. Cases supporting the two category approach prior to *Three Rivers*, which are frequently referred to in recent cases, include *Bourgoin SA v. Ministry of Agriculture, Fisheries & Food*

The leading Canadian authority on the first form of this tort, i.e., "targeted malice", is *Roncarelli v. Duplessis*.[186] In this case, the Supreme Court of Canada found the defendant, who was Premier and Attorney General of the Province of Quebec, personally liable for ordering the Commission that regulated liquor licensing in Quebec to cancel the plaintiff's liquor license. The majority of the Court held that the defendant acted with the deliberate intention to injure the plaintiff and to punish him for his support of a religious sect that the defendant found objectionable. The Court also held that the defendant acted knowing that he did not have the authority to do so. In this type of case where there are acts that are outside of the official's authority, where the official is aware of this, and where the act is done in order to injure the plaintiff, the tort is clearly made out.

In *Three Rivers District Council v. Bank of England (No. 3)*,[187] the English House of Lords reviewed the history of the tort and laid down its ingredients.[188] It confirmed that exercising public power or authority for an improper purpose or ulterior motive, i.e., in order to injure a person, is tortious. This is the classical view of the tort and has been widely referred to as a case of "targeted malice".[189] In addition, and in the absence of targeted malice, acting with actual knowledge that one's act is unlawful and that damage to the plaintiff is probable is also tortious.[190] The Lords went further, however, and held that either reckless indifference as to the legality of one's act or to its probable consequences satisfies the above requirements of intentional misconduct.[191] The Lords rejected the argument that mere foreseeability of the damaging consequences is sufficient to establish liability, even where the defendant acted with knowledge that its acts were unlawful.

The Supreme Court of Canada adopted this approach in *Odhavji*. According to Iacobucci J., the nature of the tort requires intentional and unlawful conduct, coupled with the knowledge that the conduct is unlawful and likely to harm the plaintiff. Where the intention to injure is present, i.e., targeted malice, both elements are automatically proven. This is because a public official does not have

---

(1984), [1985] 3 All E.R. 585, [1986] Q.B. 716, [1985] 3 W.L.R. 1027 (Q.B.), *Chhabra v. R.* (1989), 89 D.T.C. 5310 (Fed. T.D.) and *Francoeur v. R.* (1994), 78 F.T.R. 109 (T.D.), affirmed (1996), 110 F.T.R. 321 (note) (C.A.).

186 [1959] S.C.R. 121. The case emanated from Quebec and was based on the Civil Code. The principle it established, however, would apply to common law jurisdictions as well and has been used as the basis of the common law cases.

187 Above, note 181.

188 Separate judgments on the tort of misfeasance in public office were written by Lord Steyn, Lord Hutton, Lord Millett and Lord Hobhouse. There were some differences in the way the tort was explained, although all agreed with the basic principles.

189 It can be explained on the basis that since it is obvious that the statute was not enacted with the purpose of injuring a specific person, a public official who is using the statute to specifically target someone is clearly acting without the honest belief that he is acting lawfully. See Lord Hobhouse's judgment in *Three Rivers*.

190 This can be termed "untargeted malice". Note, however, that malice in the narrow sense of intending to injure the plaintiff, or acting out of spite or ulterior motive is not required in this form of the tort.

191 Lord Hobhouse in *Three Rivers* called this "reckless untargeted malice". As Newbury J.A. noted in *Powder Mountain Resorts Ltd. v. British Columbia* (2001), 8 C.C.L.T. (3d) 170 (B.C. C.A), this is "subjective" recklessness. The defendant must have been reckless in its disregard of the legality of its acts or its probable consequences.

the authority to deliberately set out to injure a specific person, and one who does so clearly knows this and realizes that the plaintiff will be injured by the abuse. Where there is no intention to injure, the two elements must be proven separately. Not only must it be shown that the official knew or was recklessly indifferent to the fact that he or she was acting unlawfully, but in addition it must be shown that the official knew or was recklessly indifferent to the fact that harm to the plaintiff was likely. The allegations in *Odhavji* were directed to the second form of the tort; that is, the police officers knew that they were not acting lawfully in refusing to co-operate and that this would likely injure the plaintiffs.

Several Canadian cases have considered the tort both before and after the House of Lords decision in *Three Rivers*. In a detailed review of the action, Marceau J. in *Alberta (Minister of Public Works, Supply & Services) v. Nilsson*[192] found the Crown liable for the second form of the tort. The Crown abused its statutory authority to create a Restricted Development Area by creating an RDA for an improper purpose.[193] The court held that although the evidence did not allow for the conclusion that the Crown actually knew that its act was illegal, it was "recklessly indifferent as to whether or not it was acting illegally". This was done with knowledge that damage would occur to the claimant, whose land was affected by the order, and thus the action was made out.[194]

---

192 [1999] 9 W.W.R. 203, 46 C.C.L.T. (2d) 158 (Alta. Q.B.), leave to appeal allowed (1999), [2000] 2 W.W.R. 688 (Alta. C.A.), affirmed (2002), [2003] 2 W.W.R. 215 (Alta. C.A.).

193 The issue arose in a land-use planning context under The Department of the Environment Act, S.A. 1971, c. 24. Restricted Development Areas could be created pursuant to statute for environmental purposes, e.g., creating a green belt. The Crown used it in this case for the goal of eventual highway development. The Court held that this purpose was invalid.

194 The decision went into further details on this matter. Essentially, the plaintiff's use of his land was restricted, a specific development proposal was turned down, and the government failed to purchase it from him at fair market value within a reasonable time. The Court of Appeal agreed with the trial judge's approach. Although the tort cannot be used for the "merely negligent exercise of power" it can be invoked in a case of "willful blindness to the lack of statutory authority to act." Moreover, foresight of the risk of the type of harm suffices, even if the defendant did not foresee the specific harm actually suffered. In *Longley v. Minister of National Revenue* (1999), 176 D.L.R. (4th) 445 (B.C. S.C.), affirmed (2000), 184 D.L.R. (4th) 590 (B.C. C.A.), leave to appeal refused (2000), 152 B.C.A.C. 320 (note) (S.C.C.), the Minister of National Revenue was liable for the tort when officials in its department knowingly misled the plaintiff by refusing to acknowledge the legality of a tax avoidance scheme that the plaintiff had concocted. The court held that the defendant had therefore knowingly acted outside of its statutory authority where damage to the plaintiff was probable satisfying the second form of the tort. In *E. (D.) (Guardian ad litem of) v. British Columbia* (2004), 28 C.C.L.T. (3d) 283 (B.C. C.A), reconsideration refused (2005), 2005 CarswellBC 1220 (C.A.), the court allowed actions to proceed against Superintendents of medical hospitals who recommended sterilization procedures on patients in cases where the Superintendents ought to have known that the procedures were not justified by the provisions of the statute. In *O'Dwyer v. Ontario Racing Commission*, 2008 ONCA 446 (Ont. C.A.), the Ontario Racing Commission was held liable for refusing to acknowledge that it had made an adverse decision with respect to the plaintiff, thereby depriving him of his statutory right to challenge that decision. A case where the action was dismissed based on a lack of intentional wrongdoing is *CADNET Productions Inc. v. R.* (2004), 25 C.C.L.T. (3d) 297 (Fed. C.A.), leave to appeal refused (2004), 2004 CarswellNat 2946 (S.C.C.). Also see *Mitchell Estate v. Ontario* (2004), 242 D.L.R. (4th) 560 (Ont. Div. Ct.); and *Windset Greenhouses (Ladner) Ltd. v. Delta (Corp.)*, [2007] 8 W.W.R. 503 (B.C. C.A.), affirming (2006), [2006] B.C.J. No. 459, 2006 CarswellBC 494 (B.C. C.A.).

Another case that dealt with the "targeted malice" form of the tort is *First National Properties Ltd. v. Highlands (District)*.[195] The case involved an action brought by a property developer against a mayor and other municipal officials who frustrated the developer's efforts in terms of the property's development. Newbury J.A. reaffirmed the two forms of the tort; i.e., abusing one's office by using one's authority in order to cause harm to an individual, or abusing one's office by knowingly acting without authority where such act would cause probable injury to an individual. Since the actor's motive can turn a lawful act into an unlawful one in this action,[196] Newbury J.A. advised "judicial caution" in imputing bad faith to elected officials. Newbury J.A. concluded that the defendants' motive in this case was not to injure the plaintiffs but to further its political agenda of preserving natural lands in an undeveloped state and on this ground, as well as others, found that the tort had not been committed.[197]

In addition to the above elements, the plaintiff must establish a causal connection between the wrongdoing and the injuries suffered. The type of injuries suffered must be compensable. In *Odhavji*, the plaintiffs were claiming that they suffered mental distress as a result of the defendants' misconduct. The Supreme Court affirmed that while under Canadian law damages for grief or emotional distress are not recoverable, psychiatric damages resulting from a "visible or provable illness" or "recognizable physical or psychopathological harm" are.[198]

5. CONCLUSION

Delineating the principles of public tort liability continues to challenge the courts, not only in Canada but also across the Commonwealth. The Supreme

---

195 (2001), 198 D.L.R. (4th) 443, 9 C.C.L.T. (3d) 34 (B.C. C.A.), leave to appeal refused (2001), 169 B.C.A.C. 320 (note) (S.C.C.), reversing (1999), 48 C.C.L.T. (2d) 94, 178 D.L.R. (4th) 505 (B.C. S.C.). The Court of Appeal judgment was decided after the House of Lords decided *Three Rivers* and provides a good review of the jurisprudence.

196 Therefore being "an exception to the general rule that, if conduct is presumptively unlawful, a good motive will not exonerate the defendant, and that, if conduct is lawful apart from motive, a bad motive will not make him liable"—Newbury J.A. at (2001), 9 C.C.L.T. (3d) 34 (B.C. C.A.) at 52, quoting from Lord Steyn in *Three Rivers*. Newbury J.A. reiterated that caution must be exercised in imputing bad motives to public officials in *Powder Mountain Resorts Ltd. v. British Columbia* (2001), 8 C.C.L.T. (3d) 170 (B.C. C.A.).

197 Newbury J.A. implies that the wish to injure another is one type of targeted malice, but that the improper motive can also be the desire to advance one's interests, or even to advance a private purpose that is "foreign" to the purposes for which the powers are granted; at 62-63 C.C.L.T. This expands "targeted malice" and raises the question as to what a specific claimant who is harmed by this improper motive must show in order to succeed in a claim. Newbury J.A. also disagreed with the trial judge's conclusion on the matter of a causal link between the defendants' actions and the failure of the development as well as with regard to the assessment of damages. Also see Newbury J.A.'s judgment in *Powder Mountain Resorts Ltd. v. British Columbia* (2001), 8 C.C.L.T. (3d) 170 (B.C. C.A.). An action for abuse of public office against the Premier and other officials was brought based on a developer's failure to win a government contract for developing a ski resort. In dismissing the action, Newbury J.A. held that the plaintiff had failed to show that the province had acted in order to injure it as opposed to acting in the province's best interests. In addition, there were no abuses of statutory authorities or powers. As she had done in earlier cases, Newbury J.A. cautioned against an unwarranted extension of this tort.

198 19 C.C.L.T. (3d) at 189 (S.C.C.). This is also the position taken with reference to this tort by the House of Lords. See *Watkins v. Home Office*, [2006] UKHL 17.

Court of Canada, the House of Lords, and authoritative courts elsewhere have devoted a considerable amount of their time in recent years in attempting to clarify this area.

There are two conflicting and legitimate points of view that create the disharmony. On the one hand it is believed that public authorities, like individuals in the private sector, ought to be required to conduct themselves reasonably and lawfully in furtherance of their statutory mandates, with due regard to the interests of others who are foreseeable victims of their misbehaviour. If they fail to do so, they ought to be subject to liability. On the other hand, public authorities are not like private persons. They are meant to act not in their own interests, but in the public interest. They do not operate for profit or for the furtherance of their own goals. They must weigh and balance conflicting interests in determining what is in the public good. They are, in many cases, answerable to the electorate.

Despite the confusing terminology, and the tortured attempts to rationalize individual decisions, the common law has been taking these factors into consideration in determining the tort liability of public authorities. A duty to take reasonable care can be imposed on the public authority defendant in the appropriate case. Its conduct will be measured within the context of its statutory purposes and the realistic pressures and constraints under which public authorities operate. Where claimants have been able to convince courts that the activities of public defendants have gone beyond the reasonable limits that an inherently flexible negligence law will permit, liability has been imposed. If, after taking into account the special circumstances of the defendant, the evidence has failed to indicate that there has been unacceptable conduct or conduct that is legitimately justiciable, liability has been rejected. Where the impugned conduct of the defendant related not to conduct that can logically be described as being reasonable or unreasonable, but rather to activities that involved political choices and value judgments, then tort law has correctly been seen as an inappropriate vehicle of opposition or dissent.

It is of course true that here, as elsewhere, there will be grey areas: did the conduct fall into a legitimate exercise of political discretion, or was it carried out so inappropriately that it ought not to be allowed to go unsanctioned? The resolution of this area is unlikely to be assisted by the adoption of labels, but must ultimately reflect the judgment of the court and the extent to which it is believed that negligence law can and should remedy the wrong.

9
The Standard of Care

1. INTRODUCTION

The essence of the cause of action in negligence is the defendant's duty to take reasonable care in order to avoid a risk of foreseeable injury to the plaintiff. Negligence law does not require actors to guarantee the safety of their conduct, nor does it admonish only those who deliberately set out to injure others. It covers a large middle ground, within which most actions in tort fall.

Whether a defendant's conduct can be termed negligent is a question of fact left to the best judgment of judge or jury. As with all elements of the negligence action, however, there are of course important considerations of law that are brought into play. How one defines the standard, and what factors must be considered by the fact finder in applying it to the facts of each case are questions of law. Thus this issue, as with most issues, can perhaps better be described as a question of "mixed law and fact".[1] Ultimately, however, it is the fact finder who is called upon to apply the rules and decide whether the standard of care has been met.

The negligence issue is, at least in theory, a difficult one. It is impossible to describe what negligence is, except by using vague generalities which invariably tend merely to rephrase the issue. It is generally an issue not subject to hard and fast rules. Yet, at the same time, the standard of care element is one of negligence law's most attractive features. It permits the common law to reflect the opinions and values of society, as well as to lead and forge ahead when necessary. It is inherently fluid and flexible. Unlike legislated standards, which can easily become outdated and rigid, the common law standard of care can keep abreast of new developments and advances in science, technology, and in human relations. Missing are the inertia and politics which can impede legislative action. Courts, for example, when deciding whether those who drive in cars ought to wear seat belts, do not have to worry about political "fall-out." It is, of course, true that with this freedom and absence of political accountability comes the danger that courts will go too far, or not far enough, and use negligence law to achieve goals which may

---

1 See discussion below on *Housen v. Nikolaisen* (2002), 211 D.L.R. (4th) 577, 10 C.C.L.T. (3d) 157 (S.C.C.).

not be desirable or popular. One must always recall, however, that when all is said and done, the legislative branch of government has the last say, and can steer its own path.

This chapter will discuss how the standard of care question is generally treated in negligence law. It will suggest that although in the abstract the question whether the defendant breached the duty of care by failing to act reasonably seems to be intolerably open-ended, in reality there are sufficient specific guidelines available to the fact-finder which make the task easier. In routine cases, such as motor vehicle accident litigation, for example, the question of negligence has been well defined by numerous statutory provisions, the use of fault charts, and the vast number of previously decided, similar cases. In other areas, such as professional negligence or product liability, the use of experts and reliance on customary behaviour greatly assist the courts in deciding the negligence issue. In the end, there are probably not many negligence cases where deciding whether the parties acted reasonably has presented the court with an unmanageable task.

2. THE NEGLIGENCE ISSUE: THE ROLES OF JUDGE AND JURY

It is generally stated that whether or not the common law will impose a private law duty of care on the defendant for the protection of the plaintiff is a question of law for a judge to decide. Whether the duty of care has been breached, however, is said to be a question for the trier of fact. What do these statements imply?

A judge must determine, as a question of law, whether the facts of a case can reasonably support a finding that the parties were in a relationship of sufficient proximity to support a duty relationship, and whether there are reasons of policy or precedent to limit or negate the duty. Once all legal obstacles to the imposition of a duty are removed, however, the existence of a specific duty relationship will be a question of fact for the jury, or single judge sitting alone.[2] By this division of responsibilities, the court can prevent an overly zealous trier of fact from turning a remote relationship into a proximate one, or from extending the common law of negligence into areas generally considered to be out of bounds.[3]

To state that the facts of a case are governed by a common law duty of care is merely to open the door to the resolution of the dispute before the court. As important will be the determination of what the scope of the duty is, and whether it was breached — in other words, what the specific things were that the defendant

---

2 That is, once it is decided that there are no legal barriers to the imposition of a duty of care, the actual findings and inferences to be derived therefrom must be left to the trier of fact. See Fleming, *The Law of Torts*, 9th ed. (1998), at 117 ff. See, however, Trindade, Cane and Lunney, *The Law of Torts in Australia*, 4th ed. (2007), at 451, who submit that the judge must decide whether the plaintiff was "foreseeable for the purposes of deciding whether a duty existed", while the jury must consider the foreseeability aspect of the breach of duty issue. The authors concede, however, that "the question of foreseeability is one that can only be decided on the basis of particular facts." As argued in Chapter 5, the foreseeability question is the same in both duty and breach, and it is confusing to state that foreseeability of a specific plaintiff is either a question of fact or of law, depending on whether duty or breach is being considered.

3 This assumes, of course, that the civil trial is judged by judge and jury, something which is infrequent in most Canadian provinces. Where there is only a judge, who then must decide both questions of law and fact, the distinction becomes much less significant, except for the purpose of appeals.

should have done, or should not have done, in the fulfilment of this duty of care. It is these *specific* duties which will dictate whether the duty of care, as a general concept, was observed and, accordingly, whether there will be liability in negligence. This is a question of fact for the jury, or for the single judge.[4]

By confusing the question "does negligence law impose a duty of care in this case?" with "what does the observance of the duty of care require in this case?", the duty and breach issues are merged, and the function of the jury emasculated. Courts must be careful to avoid this.[5] A Supreme Court of Canada judgment illustrates my concern. In *Wade v. C.N.R.*,[6] the defendant railway was sued by a young child who was injured while attempting to mount a moving freight train. The case was tried by a jury which decided that the defendant had been negligent in various respects. It had inadequately fenced its property, failed to have proper signs, failed to remove allurements, and failed to better arrange its trains so as to increase visibility. Liability was found and affirmed on appeal, but when the case reached the Supreme Court of Canada the decision was reversed. Rather than challenging the reasonableness of the jury's fact-finding,[7] the majority of the court characterized the issues before it as questions of law. The court held that whether the plaintiff was within the range of reasonable foreseeability and therefore owed a duty of care, and how this duty ought to have been fulfilled, were questions of law. This removed from the jury its function of determining what the defendant ought to have foreseen and guarded against, and how it ought to have done this. It allowed the appeal court not only to judge whether the parties were in a recognized duty relationship, as a question of law, but to prescribe the specifics of this duty. As I have argued elsewhere,[8] this approach was incorrect, and not consistent with the authorities.[9] The question whether the plaintiff was

---

4 As stated by Fleming, *The Law of Torts*, 9th ed. (1998), at 118:

> It is for the court to determine the existence of a duty relationship and to lay down in general terms the standard of care by which to measure the defendant's conduct; it is for the jury to translate the general into a particular standard suitable for the case in hand and to decide whether that standard has been attained.

See also Bohlen, "Mixed Questions of Law and Fact" (1923-24), 72 U. Pa. L. Rev. 111:

> The common law does not profess to lay down a minute code of definite standards by which the conduct of mankind is to be judged in every combination of circumstances which may possibly arise. It recognizes the futility of any attempt to fix such standards, and often contents itself with announcing broad general principles which give the material and general directions for the construction of the standard to be applied in each specific case as it may arise.

See discussion below on *Housen v. Nikolaisen* (2002), 211 D.L.R. (4th) 577 (S.C.C.).

5 See *Gosling v. Roper* (2002), [2002] A.J. No. 347, 2002 CarswellAlta 344 (C.A.), for a discussion of this point as well as a review of the principles underlying standard of care issue in general.

6 (1978), 3 C.C.L.T. 173 (S.C.C.). See Klar, "Developments in Tort Law: The 1978-79 Term" (1980), 1 Sup. Ct. L. Rev. 311.

7 Which an appeal court can do when the findings are perverse or there was "palpable and overriding error": see Klar, *ibid.*

8 *Ibid.*

9 See, e.g., *C.N.R. v. Vincent*, [1979] 1 S.C.R. 364, involving a similar fact pattern from Quebec. Referring to *Metro. Ry. Co. v. Jackson* (1877), 3 App. Cas. 193 (H.L.), Pratte J. stated, at 376:

> The role of the jury then is not merely to establish the facts; it must also say whether the conduct of the defendant was that of a prudent and reasonable person which necessarily

foreseeable and what the defendant ought to have done to prevent the harm were issues which were properly determined by the jury, once it had been decided that, as a matter of law, the relationship of the parties gave rise to a duty to take reasonable care.[10]

The tendency to confuse the duty question, i.e. "does a duty of care exist?", with the breach question, i.e. "what were the specific things that a reasonable person would or would not have done to live up to the duty?", is evident in another Supreme Court of Canada judgment — *Galaske v. O'Donnell.*[11] The case concerned the liability of a driver of a truck to a child passenger who was not wearing a seat belt. The trial judge had decided that since the child's father was with him in the truck, the driver had no obligation to see to it that the child was wearing a seat belt. Did this mean that the driver's duty to take reasonable care with respect to his passenger had not been breached in these circumstances, i.e. a breach issue, or that the driver owed no duty of care to this child, i.e. a duty issue?

The majority on the Supreme Court held that the trial judge had dismissed the plaintiff's action based on a "no duty" analysis. Since the duty issue is a question of law, it is legitimate to reverse it on appeal, if erroneous. The majority on the Supreme Court thought the trial judge was in error on this matter and accordingly reversed the trial judgment. As well, based on this interpretation, the trial judge did not consider the issue of breach, no duty having been found. Thus the Supreme Court remitted the issue of breach to trial to decide whether the duty had been breached, and to determine the respective degrees of fault of the various parties.[12]

The dissenting judges, however, read the trial judgment differently. Major J. held that the trial judge had decided that there was a duty of care, but that in the circumstances, the duty had not been breached. That being the case, and in view of the fact that there was no "palpable and overriding error", the dissent would not have reversed the trial judgment.

> implies that the jury must determine how, in the circumstances of a given case a prudent and reasonable person would have acted; it must translate this objective and theoretical criterion into concrete terms.

See also *McKay v. Bd. of Govan Sch. Unit No. 29* (1968), 64 W.W.R. 301 (S.C.C.).

10 This view of *Wade v. C.N.R.* was approved of by Mr. Justice Major writing for the Supreme Court of Canada in *Ryan v. Victoria (City)* (1999), 168 D.L.R. (4th) 513 (S.C.C.). Major J., referring to *Wade*, noted that "while the distinction [between duty and breach] is obvious, courts from time to time seem to lose sight of that principle", at 525. The question of whether a duty exists, in what circumstances, and on which principles is a question of law. The content of the duty, i.e., what conduct is required to meet it, is a question of breach or standard. Judicial policy can limit the existence of a duty; i.e., it may only apply in certain situations. Legislative or judicial policies may also dictate the scope or content of the duty; for example, legislative standards may exist with regard to this type of activity. Major J. conceded that while "both formulations go to reducing a defendant's exposure to liability, and in most cases the outcome will be the same under either approach", he added that "as a matter of analytical coherence. . .the distinction is important", at 526.

11 (1994), 112 D.L.R. (4th) 109 (S.C.C.).

12 Among the judges interpreting the trial judgment as residing on a question of "duty", there were different approaches. Cory J. held that there was a duty, and strongly implied that it was not discharged merely because the child's parent was in the car. Thus, in this case, where the driver did nothing to ensure that the child was buckled in, Cory J. effectively also was holding that the duty was breached. This was also the view of La Forest J.. McLachlin J., on the other hand, was willing to concede that a trial judge could find that the duty was not breached, even in this case.

The dissenting judgment is, in my opinion, more persuasive. It is implausible that the trial judge would have held that there was no duty relationship between the driver of the truck and his passenger. They were in a relationship of sufficient proximity and there were no policy reasons to negate the duty. However, according to the trial judge, no positive steps were required to discharge the duty, since in the circumstances, the driver of the truck was entitled to defer to the father's judgment. While one might disagree with this finding, it went to the issue of negligence, and not to the issue of duty. The majority on the Supreme Court might well have been justified in holding that the trial judge's finding on this matter of breach was perverse, but it is only on this basis that the judgment could have been reversed.

Once it is determined that a defendant owed the plaintiff a duty to take reasonable care, whether reasonable care was taken must be decided. As noted above, this can be described as a question of mixed law and fact. The judge must decide, as a matter of law, the rules determining how the standard of care applicable to the specific case should be defined.[13] The jury or judge then must decide, as a question of fact, whether based on these rules, the defendant was negligent or not.

The Supreme Court of Canada thoroughly reviewed this issue in *Housen v. Nikolaisen*.[14] In this case a trial judge had held that a municipality was partly responsible, along with the plaintiff passenger and the driver of a truck, for injuries suffered by the plaintiff when the driver was involved in a single vehicle accident.[15] The Court of Appeal reversed the finding of the municipality's negligence.[16] The issue for the Supreme Court was whether the Court of Appeal's reversal could be sustained.

The majority of the Supreme Court[17] in restoring the trial judgment laid down the following propositions. First, an appellate court is free to replace the opinion of a trial judge with its own opinion on pure questions of law.[18] Second, findings of fact are not to be reversed by appellate courts unless it can be established that the trial judge made a "palpable and overriding error". Third, this standard of review applies to both findings of fact and factual inferences that are made by the triers of fact. Fourth, where the question is one of mixed law and fact, the standard of correctness applies to the question of law and the more stringent standard of palpable and overriding error applies to the finding of fact, *if the issues of law*

---

13 See *Kripps v. Touche Ross & Co.* (1997), 35 C.C.L.T. (2d) 60 (B.C. C.A.), leave to appeal refused (1997), 102 B.C.A.C. 238 (note) (S.C.C.), at 80 [C.C.L.T.], where Finch J.A. states that the "selection of the appropriate standard of care is a question of law". Finch J.A. quotes from *Canadian National Railway v. Vincent,* [1979] 1 S.C.R. 364 at 375: "It is up to the judge to law down the criterion that will be used to determine whether there has been fault; this is undoubtedly a question of law. . .". Also see *Hammond v. Wabana (Town)* (1998), 44 C.C.L.T. (2d) 101 (Nfld. C.A), leave to appeal refused (1999), 184 Nfld. & P.E.I.R. 180 (note) (S.C.C.), where defining the appropriate standard of care to be imposed on an untrained, non-compensated, volunteer fire department was seen as a question of law.

14 211 D.L.R. (4th) 577, 10 C.C.L.T. (3d) 157, [2002] 7 W.W.R. 1 (S.C.C.).

15 (1997), [1998] 5 W.W.R. 523 (Sask. Q.B.). The driver lost control of the truck while attempting to negotiate a steep curve in the road. The driver was impaired and the plaintiff passenger was aware of this. The municipality's negligence related to its statutory obligation to maintain the road in a reasonable state of repair.

16 [2000] 4 W.W.R. 173 (Sask. C.A.).

17 The Court was divided 5-4, indicating the difficulty of this issue.

18 This was described as a standard of "correctness".

can be extricated from the findings of fact. Otherwise the more stringent standard, i.e., palpable and overriding error, applies.

The majority conceded that it can be extremely difficult in questions of mixed law and fact to draw the line between the two, i.e., "to extricate a purely legal question from what appears to be a question of mixed fact and law".[19] Nevertheless, findings of negligence, or no negligence, are questions of fact, assuming that the correct legal standards were applied. The majority summed up its position in the following way:

> a finding of negligence by a trial judge involves applying a legal standard to a set of facts, and this is a question of mixed fact and law. Matters of mixed fact and lie along a spectrum. Where, for instance, an error with respect to a finding of negligence can be attributed to the application of an incorrect standard, a failure to consider a required element of a legal test, or similar error in principle, such an error can be characterized as an error of law, subject to a standard of correctness. Appellate courts must be cautious, however, in finding that a trial judge erred in law in his or her determination of negligence, as it is often difficult to extricate the legal questions from the factual. It is for this reason that these matters are referred to as questions of "mixed law and fact". Where the legal principle is not readily extricable, then the matter is one of "mixed law and fact" and is subject to a more stringent standard. The general rules, as stated in *Jaegli Enterprises,* is that, where the issue on appeal involves the trial judge's interpretation of the evidence as a whole, it should not be overturned absent palpable and overriding error.[20]

Although the decision as to whether a defendant's conduct was negligent is to be determined on the facts of the case, and is not to be used as a precedent for other cases, the fact that most civil trials are tried by judge alone is significant. Judges tend to articulate rules of behaviour which they apply to the cases before them, and these rules become guides to future similar cases. This occurs particularly in routine cases, such as highway traffic accidents, where what is reasonable conduct for drivers becomes fairly fixed, over time.[21] The concern has been expressed that, as judges' reasons for their findings in individual negligence cases

19 (2002), 211 D.L.R. (4th) 577 (S.C.C.) at 594.

20 (2002), 211 D.L.R. (4th) 577 (S.C.C.) at 594. Based on this test, the majority found that the trial judge did not make any errors of law or palpable and overriding errors of fact. The judgment carefully reviewed the various findings of the trial judge in coming to this conclusion. The dissenting justices, in an equally detailed review, concluded that there were both errors of law; e.g., failing to apply correct standards, failing to consider essential requirements before liability could be imposed, and failing to put the onus of proof on the correct party, as well as errors of fact; e.g., misapprehending evidence, drawing erroneous conclusions, and ignoring relevant evidence. More significantly, the dissenting justices disagreed as to the roles of appellate courts in reviewing findings of trial judges on mixed questions of fact and law. The dissent was more inclined to view findings that involved policy or normative judgments as questions of law subject only to a standard of correctness. It is impossible in this text to review the detailed arguments of both sides of the deeply divided Court on this issue. In *L. (H.) v. Canada (Attorney General)*, [2005] 1 S.C.R. 401, the Supreme Court reaffirmed *Housen v. Nikolaisen* and rejected the Saskatchewan Court of Appeal's argument ([2002] S.J. No. 702 and [2002] S.J. No. 499) that the powers of the Saskatchewan Court of Appeal under the statutory framework are much broader than those suggested in *Housen* and the normally accepted principles of appellate review.

21 See, e.g., *Kosinski v. Snaith* (1983), 25 Sask. R. 73 at 76 (C.A.), where the court lists the "clear and well defined standard of care imposed upon the driver of a vehicle which follows another" in terms of quite specific duties.

become treated as law, "the precedent system will die from a surfeit of authorities."[22]

3. THE REASONABLE PERSON

(a) Introduction

The duty in negligence law is one of reasonable care. From whose perspective is this to be judged, however? In other words, reasonable according to whom?

The common law's traditional answer has been that the defendant's conduct must be assessed from the perspective of the reasonable and prudent person.[23] This person's role in deciding the negligence issue was explained by Alderson B. in *Blyth v. Birmingham Waterworks Co.*:

> Negligence is the omission to do something which a reasonable man, guided upon those considerations which ordinarily regulate the conduct of human affairs, would do, or doing something which a prudent and reasonable man would not do.[24]

The reasonable man was articulately described by Laidlaw J.A. in *Arland v. Taylor*:

> The standard of care by which a jury is to judge the conduct of parties in a case of the kind under consideration is the care that would have been taken in the circumstances by "a reasonable and prudent man". I shall not attempt to formulate a comprehensive definition of "a reasonable man" of whom we speak so frequently in negligence cases. I simply say he is a mythical creature of the law whose conduct is the standard by which the Courts measure the conduct of all other persons and find it to be proper or improper in particular circumstances as they may exist from time to time. He is not an extraordinary or unusual creature; he is not superhuman; he is not required to display the highest skill of which anyone is capable; he is not a genius who can perform uncommon feats, nor is he possessed of unusual powers of foresight. He is a person of normal intelligence who makes prudence a guide to his conduct. He does nothing that a prudent man would not do and does not omit to do anything a prudent man would do. He acts in accord with general and approved practice. His conduct is guided by considerations which ordinarily regulate the conduct of human affairs. His conduct is the standard "adopted in the community by persons of ordinary intelligence and prudence."[25]

---

22 See Lord Somervell in *Qualcast (Wolverhampton) Ltd. v. Haynes*, [1959] A.C. 743 (H.L.). See also Windeyer J. in *Teubner v. Humble* (1962-63), 108 C.L.R. 491 at 503 (Aust. H.C.), where he stated:

> Observations made by judges in the course of deciding issues of fact ought not to be treated as laying down rules of law. Reports should not be ransacked and sentences apt to the facts of one case extracted from their context and treated as propositions of universal application. . . . That would lead to the substitution of a number of rigid and particular criteria for the essentially flexible and general concept of negligence.

See Trindade, Cane and Lunney, above, note 2, at 452.

23 This person has been described in a variety of ways and until recently was generally called the "reasonable man." See Linden and Feldthusen, *Canadian Tort Law*, 8th ed. (2006), at 140; Fleming James Jr., "The Qualities of the Reasonable Man in Negligence Cases" (1951), 16 Mo. L. Rev. 1; Seavey, "Negligence — Subjective or Objective?" (1927-28), 41 Harv. L. Rev. 1; Green, "The Reasonable Man: Legal Fiction or Psychological Reality?" (1967-68), 2 L. & Soc. Rev. 241; and Green, *Judge and Jury* (1930). A scholarly treatment of the "reasonable person" standard is provided by Mayo Moran, *Rethinking the Reasonable Person: An Egalitarian Reconstruction of the Objective Standard* (Oxford University Press, 2003).

24 (1856), 156 E.R. 1047 at 1049.

25 [1955] O.R. 131 at 141-42 (C.A.).

The reasonable person concept is more useful for its role in telling triers of fact how *not* to assess the reasonableness of the defendant's conduct than it is for what it can say about how to make this determination. It directs fact-finders not to assess the conduct by examining what the particular defendant honestly thought was reasonable.[26] "Doing one's best", for example, ought not to be a sufficient test of whether one met the required standard of care, if doing one's best departs from what the reasonable person would have done in like circumstances.[27] Nor are they to assess the defendant's conduct according to what the witnesses, or the triers themselves, thought was reasonable.[28] The reasonable person test directs the triers of fact not to judge the case on the basis of what any specific person might have done in the defendant's circumstances, but on their assessment of what *ought* to have been done. The court must consider the views of the parties and their witnesses, but ultimately will have to set its own standard of reasonableness.

It is generally stated that because what is reasonable is decided not on the basis of the defendant's characteristics and abilities, but on those of the reasonable person in like circumstances, the test for negligence is an objective rather than a subjective one.[29] To what extent, however, will the reasonable person be given the intellect, knowledge, experience, age, moral qualities, physical and mental abilities or other personal characteristics of the defendant? The answer to this is central to the whole notion of an objective reasonable person test. It is also one of the most serious dilemmas of a fault-based accident compensation law, which must constantly balance the goal of affording compensation to victims of accidents with the need to remain faithful to its underlying premise that it is a system of compensation based on the defendant's fault.

(b) Intellect, Knowledge and Experience

The starting point for assessing the defendant's conduct is the assumption that the defendant's intellect, knowledge and experience were those of the "man of ordinary prudence."[30]

For most cases, this assumption poses no difficulties. In regulated activities, such as driving motor vehicles, there must be a basic amount of knowledge and experience before permission to engage in that activity will be granted. Where individuals engage in activities for which they lack sufficient knowledge or

---

26 That is, negligence is not a state of mind, but a type of conduct. See *Sullivan v. Oshawa Ry.* (1925), 28 O.W.N. 184, where it was held that evidence of what the defendant thought he should have done was irrelevant.

27 See discussion below relating to the standards required of volunteer fire departments, and whether "doing one's best" is sufficient.

28 See *Kralj v. Murray*, [1954] O.W.N. 58 (C.A.); *Arland v. Taylor*, above, note 25; *Eyers v. Gillis & Warren Ltd.*, [1940] 3 W.W.R. 390 (Man. C.A.).

29 As stated by Lord Macmillan in *Glasgow Corp. v. Muir*, [1943] A.C. 448 at 457 (H.L.):

> The standard of foresight of the reasonable man is, in one sense, an impersonal test. It eliminates the personal equation and is independent of the idiosyncrasies of the particular person whose conduct is in question.

30 *Vaughan v. Menlove* (1837), 132 E.R. 490.

experience, they will be at fault, not so much for their inability to properly carry out the activity, but for their decision to attempt the activity without having accounted for their deficiencies. Individuals are expected to ask questions, or to seek help, when they go beyond their depth. Further, in some cases where inexperienced or ignorant people engage in risky activities, there will be other defendants who ought to have used reasonable care in controlling the inexperienced actors, and who will be held legally responsible for having failed to do so.[31] Thus, the question whether the inexperienced or ignorant will be required to have experience or knowledge which they do not in fact have, will often be an unnecessary inquiry. The difficult case may arise, of course, where none of these alternative arguments for imposing liability will be available. In this situation, the court should strictly adhere to the principle that the inexperienced defendant ought to have acted with the knowledge and experience of the ordinary prudent person, even if this means that a morally blameless individual will be liable in negligence.[32] Conversely, those with greater skill or experience than normally possessed by the ordinary person must live up to a higher standard of care.[33] Those who hold themselves as having particular skills and experience must live up to the standards possessed by persons of reasonable skill and experience in that calling.[34]

The position regarding the intellectual and emotional characteristics of the defendant is similar. Assuming absence of a debilitating condition so extreme as

---

31 See, e.g., *Gale v. Box* (1987), 50 Man. R. (2d) 3 (Q.B.) — experienced plumber negligent for allowing inexperienced worker to complete job without supervision.

32 See, however, *Prasad v. Frandsen* (1985), 60 B.C.L.R. 343 (S.C.). The plaintiffs were excused of contributory negligence for failing to wear seat belts partly because they had just arrived from England and had no knowledge that B.C. law required the use of seat belts. There was also no evidence that the plaintiffs were aware of the safety value of seat belts. This is inconsistent with the objective, reasonable person test, and the decision most likely would have been different had the inexperienced parties been defendants and not claimants. In *Hammond v. Wabana (Town)* (1998), 44 C.C.L.T. (2d) 101 (Nfld. C.A.), leave to appeal refused (1999), 184 Nfld. & P.E.I.R. 180 (note) (S.C.C.), the defendants were volunteer firefighters. They had relatively little training or experience, and they received little compensation. The trial judge declined to impose a standard of "due care" of the "ordinary volunteer firefighter" replacing it with the requirement that they "will do their best to put the fire out", taking into account the resources available to them. The Court of Appeal essentially agreed with this flexible approach, and lowering the standard to reflect the lack of training, experience, and professional skills of a volunteer, non-compensated, fire department. The dissent found that even based on the lower standards of a volunteer, non-professional fire department, the conduct of the defendants was wanting. The Alberta court in *Killip's Television Service Ltd. v. Stony Plain (Town)*, [2000] 3 W.W.R. 702, 48 C.C.L.T. (2d) 250 (Alta. Q.B.) was less receptive to the "doing one's best" standard for a volunteer fire department although it recognized that the standard must be based on a reasonable fire department in similar circumstances and with like resources.

33 See, for example, *Davidson v. British Columbia* (1995), [1996] 1 W.W.R. 137 (B.C. S.C.) at 144:

> A person must exercise reasonable care and skill in his actions towards others and the more skill he has, the higher will be the expected standard of care.

34 This is true whether or not the vocation is recognized as a "profession" or is subject to regulation as such. See *T. (S.) v. Gaskell* (1997), 147 D.L.R. (4th) 730 (Ont. Gen. Div.), additional reasons at (1999), 1999 CarswellOnt 3749 (S.C.J.), additional reasons at (2000), 2000 CarswellOnt 9 (S.C.J.). See Chapter 10 below regarding the liability of professionals.

to render the act involuntary,[35] the defendant is required to possess the mental ability of the reasonable person. This is certainly true with regard to variations in human temperament, for instance with respect to such emotional states as anger, nervousness, courage, performance under stress, and so on. The effect of actual medical illness on the standard of care question is, however, more controversial.[36] Since there are relatively few cases where mentally ill individuals are sued in negligence, the common law position is not altogether clear. It seems to depend upon the degree of the illness, and how the issue has been defined, i.e., one of volition, capacity, or merely standard of care. Where, for example, a defendant is so severely ill as to be unable to refrain from engaging in the act which produces the harm, an action will fail based on the lack of volition. It is not that such an individual is not required to observe the standard of care of the reasonable person, but that there has been no voluntary act at all.[37] In *Boomer v. Penn*,[38] for example, the defendant alleged that an insulin reaction caused him to lose control of his vehicle. Evans J. reaffirmed the common law position:

> The test to be applied is whether the faculties of judgment of the driver became impaired to such a degree that a reasonable person could not regard his operation of the motor vehicle in the manner complained of as the conscious act of his will. . . . The evidence must disclose the probability that the driver's acts and omissions were not conscious acts of his volition and that what he did or failed to do was not done or omitted by him as a conscious being.[39]

Although these statements are clear and seem to restrict the defence of insanity in negligence to situations equivalent to a total lack of volition, other *dicta* seem

---

35 See discussion in Chapter 2, and the cases and articles noted therein.

36 There is a problem of terminology and a proper understanding of the medical input. Various terms are used by legal commentators when discussing this problem, which probably mean different things to those whose expertise is in medicine, not law. Terms such as "mentally impaired", "mentally incompetent", "mental illness", "mental disability", "insanity", and "lunacy" are used. The failure to carefully define and distinguish these terms probably accounts for some of the confusion. See Picher, "The Tortious Liability of the Insane in Canada" (1975), 13 Osgoode Hall L.J. 193. The author states that "no agreed upon medical definition exists, nor an agreed upon legal definition", and that "the term [insanity] has been indiscriminately used in tort cases." The author cites several articles in reference to this position. For a good discussion concerning the meaning of the concept of "mental illness", see Alexander and Szasz, "Mental Illness as an Excuse for Civil Wrongs" (1967-68), 43 Notre Dame Lawyer 24. See Robertson, *Mental Disability and the Law in Canada*, 2nd ed. (1994), Chapter 10.

37 See, e.g., *Buckley v. Smith Tpt. Ltd.*, [1946] O.R. 798 (C.A.) — action dismissed against a driver of a truck who drove into an intersection because he was labouring under the delusion that the truck was operated by remote control and could not be stopped. See also *dicta* in *Slattery v. Haley*, [1923] 3 D.L.R. 156 at 160 (Ont. C.A.):

> I think that it may now be regarded as settled law that to create liability for an act which is not wilful and intentional but merely negligent it must be shewn to have been the conscious act of the defendant's volition. He must have done that which he ought not to have done, or omitted that which he ought to have done, as a conscious being.

It has been held, however, that "one cannot accept as exculpation anything less than total loss of consciousness": see *Roberts v. Ramsbottom*, [1980] 1 All E.R. 7 at 15 (Q.B.D.) — impaired consciousness while driving a car will not relieve the driver from observing ordinary standard of care. Nothing short of "automatism" will suffice.

38 (1965), 52 D.L.R. (2d) 673 (Ont. H.C.).

39 *Ibid.*, at 677.

to suggest that the defence may be broader than that. In *Buckley v. Smith Tpt. Ltd.*,[40] Roach J.A. stated that the test was whether or not the defendant "understood and appreciated the duty upon him to take care, and whether he was disabled, as a result of any delusion, from discharging that duty."[41] This suggests that something less than a total lack of volition will suffice, although as noted above, the actual facts of the case are consistent with the narrower defence.[42] The more permissive interpretation of *Buckley v. Smith* was followed in *Hutchings v. Nevin*.[43] A driver of an automobile suffering through a "manic episode" and, labouring under the delusion that he was a son of God, travelling to see God, was relieved of tort liability to a passenger injured when the driver lost control of the car. The court held that the driver was not able to understand and appreciate the duty of care which he owed, and if he was, that he was disabled from discharging that duty due to his mental disorder.

The Alberta Court of Appeal adopted this approach in *Fiala v. Cechmanek*.[44] The defendant was out jogging when he suffered a severe manic episode. He apparently believed that he was God and was seeking to inform others of his ideas. He jumped on the roof of a stationary car, broke through the sunroof, and started choking the driver. The driver involuntarily accelerated and hit another car injuring its occupants.[45] The injured plaintiffs sued both the driver and her attacker.[46] The action against the defendant attacker was dismissed at trial based on the defence of insanity and this was upheld by the Court of Appeal. In a thorough review of the jurisprudence and periodic literature,[47] the Court held that where a person is suddenly and without warning afflicted with a mental illness, and can prove on a balance of probability either an absence of capacity to understand or appreciate the duty of care, or an inability to discharge the duty due to a lack of ability to control his or her actions, there can be no tort liability. The Court emphasized that tort law requires fault on the part of the wrongdoer and that in the absence of either of these two elements, fault is not present.[48]

---

40 Above, note 37.

41 *Ibid.*, at 806.

42 See also *A.G. Can. v. Connolly* (1989), 64 D.L.R. (4th) 84 (B.C. S.C.), where the court held that the defendant's inability to foresee the consequences of his act due to mental illness relieved him of liability for negligence, although he was held liable for battery. This decision is questionable, since the ability to foresee consequences is as important in the intentional torts as it is in negligence.

43 (1992), 9 O.R. (3d) 776 (Gen. Div.).

44 201 D.L.R. (4th) 680, [2001] 9 W.W.R. 1 (Alta. C.A.), affirming (1999), 246 A.R. 120 (Q.B.).

45 The court noted that although this case was argued in negligence, trespass might have been more appropriate.

46 The action against the driver was dismissed based on her lack of negligence.

47 The court cited E.J. Goldstein, "Asking the Impossible: The Negligence Liability of the Mentally Ill" (1995), 12 J. of Contemp. Health L. & Pol'y 67; Harry Korrell, "The Liability of Mentally Disabled Tort Defendants" (1995), 19 L. & Psych. Rev. 1; Grant Morris, "Requiring Sound Judgments of Unsound Minds: Tort Liability and the Limits of Therapeutic Jurisprudence" (1994), 46 SMU L. Rev. 1837; among others.

48 The court referred to Klar, "The Role of Fault and Policy in Negligence Law" (1996), 35 Alta. L. Rev. 24 and my argument that "there ought to be an element of moral blame in all conduct which tort law deems as negligent". The court also discussed the earlier Alberta case of *Wenden v. Trikha* (1991), 116 A.R. 81, 8 C.C.L.T. (2d) 138 (Q.B.), additional reasons at (1992), 124

Should the law of negligence relax the standard of care for the mentally disabled? Four reasons have been given to support the common law's position that short of lack of volition, a mentally disabled person must conform to the reasonable person test.[49] First, as between the innocent victim and the defendant who caused the injury, the law ought to favour compensating the victim. Second, if mental illness is accepted as justification for lowering the standard of care, problems of proof, especially in relation to distinguishing between legitimate and fraudulent cases, will arise. Third, if mentally ill persons are held liable for their acts, there will be a greater incentive for those who are responsible for caring for them to exercise care in their supervision. Fourth, once the door is opened to a relaxed standard for mental illness, it will be hard to identify what qualifies as such, and to distinguish mental illness from other less serious personality problems. The stricter standard has also been supported by those who believe that this will facilitate the integration of the mentally ill into the community, as opposed to their institutionalization.[50] The stricter standard will minimize the burden on the community of accidents caused by the disabled, will foster community acceptance, and will encourage self-sufficiency. It has also been argued that to treat the mentally ill as people who cannot be held responsible for the consequences of their acts is to "diminish, or even deny, [their] status as a full-fledged human being", with its attendant consequences.[51] There are others, however, who reject the common law's refusal to treat the mentally ill more leniently.[52] In addition to discounting the reasons generally used to support the objective standard, the principal argument for a subjective standard which will reflect the diminished capacity of the mentally ill is the unfairness in imposing fault-based liability upon individuals who were, due to illness, unable to live up to the standard of the reasonable person. As well, it is seen as discriminatory to test the conduct of the

---

A.R. 1 (Q.B.), affirmed (1993), 14 C.C.L.T. (2d) 225 (Alta. C.A.), leave to appeal refused (1993), 17 C.C.L.T. (2d) 285 (note) (S.C.C.). In this case, a driver, while operating under an insane delusion, crashed his motor vehicle. The driver, believing that his soul was being taken away by a comet, and this his car was a time machine, had been attempting to retrieve his spirit from the spaceship in the sky. While conceding that the driver of the car may not have appreciated the nature and quality of his acts, Murray J. nevertheless found him liable for negligent driving. Nothing less than proof that the defendant's actions while driving were not "conscious acts of his own volition" would relieve the driver of his liability. The Court of Appeal affirmed the trial judgment, but was less clear on the question of the insanity defence. The Court held that even if the driver could prove that he was too insane at the time of the accident to be found negligent, that he would still have to prove that he was not negligent in deciding to drive in the first place, when he was not insane. As well, there seemed to be a question in the Court's mind as to the credibility of the plaintiff's story. Finally, there was a question of reversing findings of fact.

49 See Splane, "Tort Liability of the Mentally Ill in Negligence Actions" (1983-84), 93 Yale L.J. 153, where these are outlined.

50 *Ibid.*

51 Alexander and Szasz, above, note 36, at 35.

52 See, e.g., Bohlen, "Liability in Torts of Infants and Insane Persons" (1924-25), 23 Mich. L. Rev. 9; Curran, "Tort Liability of the Mentally Ill and Mentally Deficient" (1960), 21 Ohio State L.J. 52; Ellis, "Tort Responsibility of Mentally Disabled Persons (1981), 4 Am. B. Found. Res. J. 1079; Seidelson, "Reasonable Expectations and Subjective Standards in Negligence Law: The Minor, the Mentally Impaired, and the Mentally Incompetent" (1981), 50 Geo. Wash. L. Rev. 17; as well as the articles cited in *Fiala v. Cechmanek*, above note 44.

mentally disabled on the basis of an objective standard of care, while relaxing the standard for children and the physically disabled.[53]

The paucity of negligence cases involving the mentally disabled indicates that the dilemma, in theory a difficult one, rarely presents itself. There are without question character traits, personality quirks, and differences in backgrounds, experience, and education, which lead some people to be involved in more accidents than others.[54] In order to assure compensation to accident victims where socially acceptable standards of conduct have not been observed, it is obvious that legal fault and moral fault cannot be expected to be synonymous concepts. Nevertheless, the case law indicates that it is very rare for a totally innocent mentally disabled person to be held liable in negligence, despite the theoretical rigidity of the common law's position.[55]

The common law does modify its reasonable person standard for those who are graced with superior knowledge, intellect or experience and who can accordingly do better than the reasonable person.[56] This is so especially with regard to professionals or others who are expected to possess superior skills and training.[57] This, unlike the situation regarding the standard applied to those who are disadvantaged, has never been argued to be an objectionable deviation from the objective test.[58]

(c) Physical Abilities

It has been stated that "[n]egligence law has departed from its objective standard in its treatment of physical disabilities; it has made the standard of care partially subjective in order to take them into account."[59] Illustrations used to support this statement refer to the deaf, the lame, and the blind, although as with the standard

---

53 The arguments pro and con are discussed in *Fiala v. Cechmanek*, above note 44.

54 See Fleming James Jr., "The Qualities of the Reasonable Man in Negligence Cases" (1951), 16 Mo. L. Rev. 1; James and Dickinson, "Accident Proneness and Accident Law" (1950), 63 Harv. L. Rev. 769. Authors note that studies indicate that a fairly small group of accident-prone people cause most of the accidents. See, e.g., Bristol, "Medical Aspects of Accident Control" (1936), 107 A.M.A.J. 653 — 10 per cent of working population may be responsible for 75 per cent of accidents; Blain, "The Automobile Accident — A Medical Problem" (1941), 3 J. Crim. Psychopathology 37 — 4 per cent of all drivers account for 33 per cent of automobile accidents.

55 The position taken in *Wenden v. Trikha*, and supported by authors, such as Professor Robertson, above, note 36, that mental incapacity, no matter how extreme, is not a defence in tort is essentially founded on the notion that the law of negligence is about compensating victims of "objectively" sub-standard behaviour, and not about "moral culpability". While this is to some extent true, it is, in my opinion, an overstatement to deny that moral culpability is a part of the *raison d'être* of negligence law. After all, the principal justifications for fault-based compensation, as opposed to "no fault" insurance, reside on issues of morality. What is satisfying to me about negligence law is my observation that in most cases defendants who are found liable are in fact those who should have known and could have done better.

56 See, e.g., *Smith v. Inglis Ltd.* (1978), 83 D.L.R. (3d) 215 (N.S. C.A.), where the plaintiff who was described as "a knowledgeable and experienced builder" was held contributorily negligent for failing to check the electrical plug on his refrigerator.

57 See Chapter 10.

58 It can, of course, easily be justified on the argument that a reasonably prudent person would not disregard superior knowledge, intellect or experience when engaged in a relevant activity.

59 Linden and Feldthusen, *Canadian Tort Law*, 8th ed. (2006), at 149.

which will be applied to the mentally disabled, there are so few cases directly on point that it is difficult to predict what a court might decide in a truly difficult case.[60]

It is not altogether clear what constitutes a physical disability for the purposes of the more subjective standard. If one accepts the studies which indicate that accident-prone individuals cause more accidents than ordinary people as a result of their physical characteristics, such as poor vision, and psychomotor characteristics,[61] but yet one recognizes that these characteristics will not be deemed to be acceptable excuses for negligent behaviour, then it is clear that there is a subjective standard for very few physical disabilities. As well, even where a physical disability is sufficiently severe to qualify for special treatment, liability can be imposed on the defendant for not having acted in a way which accounted for the disability. The case law demonstrates that the burden of proof on a defendant who relies on the defence of "inevitable accident" in relation to a sudden loss of consciousness while driving an automobile, for example, is very onerous.[62] Where a driver relies upon the defence of "inevitable accident", and there are no external factors which explain the accident, the driver must prove that the accident "could not have been prevented by reasonable care on his part."[63] Further, the cases in which defendants have been exonerated from liability due to a sudden loss of consciousness from a physical illness can better be justified on the basis of lack

---

60 For example, *South Australian Ambulance Tpt. Inc. v. Walheim* (1948), 77 C.L.R. 215 (Aust. H.C.), is cited as a case supporting the point that a deaf person is not required to hear. In actual fact the plaintiff who was slightly deaf was found contributorily negligent for failing to keep a proper lookout. Although *Haley v. London Elec. Bd.* [1965] A.C. 778 (H.L.), supports the point that the law does not expect the blind to be able to see, the case concerned not a blind defendant, but the duty owed to blind pedestrians by those who create dangers for them. See also *Carroll v. Chicken Palace Ltd.*, [1955] O.R. 798 (C.A.), which dismissed an action brought by a blind person against a restauranteur for injuries suffered during a fall down a stairway. In *Carper v. Oakway Holdings Ltd.*, [1991] B.C.J. No. 3851 (S.C.), a hotel was held partially liable to a 78-year-old frail plaintiff who fell while leaving the premises. The court held that while the plaintiff, knowing of her condition, ought to have taken more care, the defendant, knowing that elderly and handicapped persons frequented its establishment, ought to have made their walkway safer.

61 Other causes of accident-proneness are habits and skills, mental characteristics and attitudes, age and experience. See James and Dickinson, above, note 54.

62 See *Dobbs v. Mayer* (1985), 32 C.C.L.T. 191 (Ont. Div. Ct.); *Gordon v. Wallace* (1973), 2 O.R. (2d) 202 (H.C.); *Telfer v. Wright* (1978), 95 D.L.R. (3d) 188 (Ont. C.A.); *Boomer v. Penn* (1965), 52 D.L.R. (2d) 673 (Ont. H.C.); *Turner's Transfer Ltd. v. Anderson* (1962), 37 D.L.R. (2d) 399 (N.S. C.A.); *Conn v. Conn*, [1992] B.C.J. No. 2925 (S.C.); *Calvert v. Gauthier*, [1991] B.C.J. No. 150 (S.C.); *Spillane (Litigation Guardian of) v. Wasserman* (1992), 13 C.C.L.T. (2d) 267, varied (1998), 41 C.C.L.T. (2d) 292 (Ont. C.A.); *Perry v. Banno* (1993), 15 C.C.L.T. (2d) 199 (B.C. S.C.); and *Whitmore v. Arens* (1999), [1999] B.C.J. No. 313, 1999 CarswellBC 274 (S.C.). The defence failed in each of these cases. For successful defences see *Slattery v. Haley*, [1923] 3 D.L.R. 156 (Ont. C.A.); *Gootson v. R.*, [1947] 4 D.L.R. 568 (Ex. Ct.), affirmed [1948] 4 D.L.R. 33 (S.C.C.); *Dessaint v. Carriere* (1958), 17 D.L.R. (2d) 222 (Ont. C.A.); *MacPherson v. Mallabon* (1958), 11 D.L.R. (2d) 350 (Ont. C.A.); *Sheldon v. Gray* (1989), 20 M.V.R. (2d) 80 (Ont. H.C.), affirmed (1994), 8 M.V.R. (3d) 62 (Ont. C.A.); and *Liberty Mutual Insurance Co. v. Scott*, [1990] O.J. No. 2713 (Gen. Div.).

63 See *Perry v. Banno*, above, note 62, and *Sheldon v. Gray*, above, note 62. The point is made that a driver who crashes his car into another car on that other car's side of the road need merely offer an explanation which is consistent with due care. Where "inevitable accident" caused by a physical disability is raised, however, the burden of proof is more onerous. See discussion below, under heading "Emergencies."

of volition, rather than a reduced standard of care. As with excuses based on intellectual, emotional or mental characteristics, the courts must be wary not to allow the physical disabilities of the defendant to be too readily accepted as justifying a departure from the objective standard of reasonable care.

(d) Age

The one characteristic of the defendant which the common law clearly takes into account is youth. Negligence law does not expect young children to possess the common sense, intelligence, and knowledge of the reasonable adult and has fashioned a standard suitable to children.

It must be noted, however, that young children are very rarely sued for their allegedly negligent conduct. This is probably a result of the small likelihood that a judgment against a child can be satisfied from the child's assets, combined with the absence of liability insurance.[64] Undoubtedly, another factor is the tolerance that victims of negligent children might have towards them, as well as the victims' knowledge that suits against children will be difficult to win as a result of the common law's indulgence. Be that as it may, the result is that the law's relaxed standard towards children is most often displayed in cases where the child is not a defendant but a plaintiff, in reference to a claim that the child was contributorily negligent. Although in theory the standard of reasonable conduct should be the same whether it is being applied to a defendant or to a plaintiff, in practice this may not be the case. The consequence of applying a low standard of care in the case of a child defendant is to risk leaving an injured plaintiff without compensation, a result which may seem harsh, especially where insurance is involved. Conversely, the consequence of applying a high standard of care to a child plaintiff might be to deprive the victim of needed compensation, which will be paid for, in many cases, by an insurer. The pressure thus clearly exists to relax the standard for child plaintiffs, but not to do so for child defendants.[65]

---

64 It would usually be better to sue the negligent child's parents. Although parents are not vicariously liable for the torts of their children, they may be found liable personally for their failure to properly supervise them, or for permitting them to have access to dangerous objects without proper training or preparation. See, e.g., *Floyd v. Bowers* (1978), 6 C.C.L.T. 65 (Ont. H.C.), affirmed (1979), 106 D.L.R. (3d) 702 (Ont. C.A.); *Ryan v. Hickson* (1974), 55 D.L.R. (3d) 196 (Ont. H.C.); and *Pasheri v. Beharriell* (1987), 61 O.R. (2d) 183 (Dist. Ct.). In *Trevison v. Springman* (1995), 28 C.C.L.T. (2d) 292 (B.C. S.C.), affirmed (1997), [1997] B.C.J. No. 2557, 1997 CarswellBC 2362 (C.A.), the principles were discussed and parents held not liable for a fire set by their son. In *Robertson v. Butler* (1985), 32 C.C.L.T. 208 (N.S. T.D.), the parents of a 15-year-old were held partly responsible for injuries suffered by another youth while riding a motor bike belonging to the former. The court held that there was a failure to properly supervise and control their child's use of his bike. The court also held, at 217, that "a parent may be vicariously liable for negligent acts committed by his or her child with the knowledge or consent of the parent." This principle was neither explained nor backed by authority and is contrary to accepted principle. See further discussion on the responsibility of parents for acts of their children in Chapters 6 and 12.

65 Professor Moran, above, note 23, at 24, notes that the more subjective standard applied to children does not vary depending upon whether the child is a defendant or plaintiff and this has been made explicitly clear in American case law. While I do not disagree with that observation, the fact that children are more frequently plaintiffs than they are defendants might have influenced the courts in their decision to adopt a more "child friendly" standard. In addition, as we will see, the "adult activities" doctrine has been developed in order to raise the standard

The leading Canadian case which established the standard of care to be applied to children is *McEllistrum v. Etches*.[66] The case concerned a six-year-old who died from injuries suffered as a result of being struck by a vehicle, and his alleged contributory negligence. Kerwin C.J.C. stated the principle which has been followed in Canada ever since:

> It should now be laid down that where the age is not such as to make a discussion of contributory negligence absurd, it is a question for the jury in each case whether the infant exercised the care to be expected from a child of like age, intelligence and experience.[67]

The test suggested by Kerwin C.J.C. involved two stages. This was more fully explained in *Heisler v. Moke*.[68] Addy J. explained that there were two questions to be considered when dealing with children:

> The first one is whether the child, having regard to his age, his intelligence, his experience, his general knowledge and his alertness is capable of being found negligent at law in the circumstances under investigation. In other words, we consider here the particular child. As has been stated frequently, there is no absolute rule as to age in order to determine this question. Age is merely one of the factors, although the age of seven is often regarded as the crucial or critical age where normally a child may be expected to begin to assume responsibility for his actions.[69]

Assuming that on this very subjective test the child is considered to be capable of negligence, the second question is then to be asked. What would a reasonable child of like age, intelligence, and experience have foreseen and done in the circumstances?[70]

---

of care for children defendants. Professor Moran also notes the law's more generous treatment of children as contrasted with its approach towards the "developmentally disabled".

66 (1956), 6 D.L.R. (2d) 1 (S.C.C.).

67 *Ibid.*, at 6-7.

68 (1971), 25 D.L.R. (3d) 670 (Ont. H.C.). Again, this was a child plaintiff.

69 *Ibid.*, at 672. See *Bouvier v. Fee*, [1932] S.C.R. 118, where Anglin C.J.C. strongly hinted that a child under the age of eight could never be held responsible for alleged carelessness. Also see *Acadia Coal Co. v. MacNeil*, [1927] S.C.R. 497 at 504, where it was stated that "children aged seven and nine years have by the common law the benefit of something in the nature of a presumption that they have not sufficient capacity to know that they are doing wrong." Note, however, that in *McEllistrum v. Etches* itself, the plaintiff who was found contributorily negligent was only just six years old at the time of his accident. In *Weaver v. Buckle* (1982), 42 A.R. 241 (C.A.), a plaintiff, not yet seven years old at the time of his accident, was found negligent when he ran out from behind a parked car and was struck by the defendant's vehicle. The action against the defendant was dismissed.

70 Addy J. preferred a more objective test which would consider only what a reasonable child of that age would have done. See *McHale v. Watson* (1966), 39 A.L.J.R. 459 (Aust. H.C.), where this is used. He felt bound however by *McEllistrum v. Etches* and the more subjective approach. There have been numerous cases that have considered the issue of contributory negligence cases as applied to children. See earlier editions of this text where several of these are referenced. Some of the more recent cases include *Farrell (Litigation Guardian of) v. 1151400 Ontario Inc.* (1999), [1999] O.J. No. 4580, 1999 CarswellOnt 3961 (S.C.J.), affirmed (2001), [2001] O.J. No. 1349, 2001 CarswellOnt 1259 (C.A.), additional reasons at (2001), 2001 CarswellOnt 2939 (S.C.J.)—6-year-old not contributorily negligent; *Pritchett (Guardian ad litem of) v. Gander (Town)* (2001), 205 Nfld. & P.E.I.R. 45 (Nfld. C.A.)—10-year-old found contributorily negligent; *Rice v. Chan Estate* (1998), 62 B.C.L.R. (3d) 113 (S.C.)—16-year-old not contributorily negligent; *Gordon (Next Friend of) v. Harmon* (1999), 246 A.R. 305 (Q.B.), additional reasons at (1999), 246 A.R. 305 at 335 (Q.B.)—7-year-old not contributorily negligent; and *Bartosek (Litigation Guardian of) v. Turret Realties Inc.* (2001), [2001] O.J. No. 4735, 2001

A principle which has some jurisprudental basis in raising the standard of care which is to be applied to children is the "adult activities" doctrine.[71] According to the leading American case which applied this principle, *Dellwo v. Pearson*,[72] minors who operate automobiles, airplanes, or powerboats will be held to the same standard of care as would adults in similar circumstances. Several reasons may be behind this approach. One is that victims of accidents involving motorized vehicles should be entitled to expect ordinary prudence from the drivers of such vehicles, especially since these activities are ordinarily adult activities. There is, as well, the probability that such accidents will be covered by liability insurance, and the recognition of the inherent dangers involved in these types of activities. The doctrine has been criticized, however, as being vague and difficult to apply;[73] what, after all, is an adult activity? As well, its appropriateness in cases where the minor is a plaintiff, and not a defendant, has rightly been questioned.[74] It has nevertheless been applied in Canada, although infrequently and arguably without making much practical difference to the outcome of the case.[75] An example is *McErlean v. Sarel*,[76] where the standard which was applied to a child plaintiff injured while riding a trail bike was that of an adult engaged in the same activity. The Ontario Court of Appeal's judgment stated that "it would be unfair, and indeed, dangerous to the public to permit [teenagers] in the operation of these power-driven vehicles to observe any lesser standard than that required of all

---

CarswellOnt 4292 (S.C.J.)—6-year-old found contributorily negligent. There are also cases where the test has been applied to children as *defendants*. See *Strehlke v. Camenzind*, [1980] 4 W.W.R. 464 (Alta. Q.B.); *Yorkton Agricultural & Indust. Exhibition Assn. v. Morley* (1967), 57 W.W.R. 97, affirmed 62 W.W.R. 340 (Sask. C.A.); *Serediak v. Farraway*, Alta. Dist. Ct., Calgary No. D 12843, Kerans A.C.J., 3rd March 1976 (unreported); and *Belzile v. Dumais* (1986), 69 N.B.R. (2d) 142 (Q.B.). In *Nespolon v. Alford* (1998), 40 O.R. (3d) 355 (C.A.), leave to appeal refused (1999), 122 O.A.C. 200 (note) (S.C.C.), the Ontario Court of Appeal reversed a trial judgment and relieved two 16-year-olds and one 14-year-old from liability for the death of a friend and the nervous shock suffered by the driver as a result of a car accident. The 16-year-old boys dropped off the inebriated 14-year-old from their car. He was subsequently killed by the plaintiff driver, who then sued the boys for nervous shock. The Court of Appeal dismissed the claim for a variety of reasons including the ages of the boys.

71 See Binchy, "The Adult Activities Doctrine in Negligence Law" (1985), 11 William Mitchell L. Rev. 733.

72 107 N.W. 859 (Minn., 1961).

73 See Binchy, above, note 71.

74 See Irvine's annotation to *Robertson v. Butler* (1985), 32 C.C.L.T. 208 at 209 (N.S. T.D.). The doctrine was applied to a plaintiff who injured himself on his friend's defective motor bike.

75 See *Ryan v. Hickson*, above, note 64, and *Robertson v. Butler, ibid.* In both cases the minors were probably foolish, even from the perspective of others their age. See also *Mont v. Reid* (1988), 83 N.S.R. (2d) 407 (T.D.). The doctrine was not applied in *Christie v. Slevinsky* (1981), 12 M.V.R. 67 (Alta. Q.B.), where in fact it might have made a difference. The case concerned an 11-year-old defendant who struck the plaintiff with a dune buggy. The court stated that had the defendant been an adult, liability would have been imposed, but in view of the relaxed standard for children the action was dismissed. The doctrine was not discussed in the judgment. In *Pope v. RCG Management Inc.* (2002), [2002] A.J. No. 1229, 2002 CarswellAlta 1231 (Q.B.), it was held that golf is an adult activity. A 12-year-old golfer whose ball hit the plaintiff in the mouth was sued for negligence. The court held that the boy was not negligent, even based on this higher standard of care.

76 (1987), 42 C.C.L.T. 78 (Ont. C.A.).

other drivers of such vehicles. The circumstances of contemporary life require a single standard of care with respect to such activities."[77]

Although the law of negligence takes into account a young defendant's age, it apparently does not consider old age as warranting special consideration.[78] This has been strongly criticized as being unjust, especially when one considers that the infirmities of old age are just as debilitating to defendants accused of negligence as are the weaknesses of youth.[79] Although the balance between justice to the defendant and the need to compensate the plaintiff is, as always, a difficult one to make, the argument that there is no good reason to treat the elderly more harshly than the young is persuasive.[80]

---

77 *Ibid.*, at 98-99. In view of the fact, however, that the plaintiff was a 15-year-old, experienced rider with a "detailed knowledge" of the trail in question, whose conduct was characterized as "reckless in the extreme", it is highly unlikely that the adoption of the "adult standard" affected the actual result of the case. Nevertheless, the court's clear approval of the doctrine, especially with regard to a child plaintiff, firmly implants it into Canadian law. Note that in *Lutley (Guardian ad litem of) v. Jarvis Estate* (1992), 113 N.S.R. (2d) 201 (T.D.), Nova Scotia court declined to apply the "adult activities" doctrine to a 12-year-old trail bike rider. The judge stated that a trail bike is a "non-adult" vehicle, especially when being driven where it should not have been, i.e. on a paved highway. The youth was found to have been negligent nevertheless. In *Nespolon v. Alford* (1998), 41 C.C.L.T. (2d) 258 (Ont. C.A.), leave to appeal refused (1999), 122 O.A.C. 200 (note) (S.C.C.), the Court held that while driving might be an adult activity, the decision by teenagers to let a drunk teen out of their car was not. Thus they were not to be judged according to adult standards with respect to this activity. A variant on the "adult activities" doctrine is found in *Parrill v. Genge* (1994), 125 Nfld. & P.E.I.R. 27 (Nfld. T.D.). In this case, the court held that the experience of a 15-year-old snowmobile operator was equivalent to that of an adult. This was the case with all 15-year-olds in the community, where snowmobiles were viewed as an essential means of transportation. That being the case, a reasonable 15-year-old would act and be expected to live up to the same standard as a responsible adult. The court, in the alternative, also adopted the "adult activities" doctrine to justify the imposition of the adult standard. The judgment was affirmed (1997), 148 Nfld. & P.E.I.R. 91 (Nfld. C.A.), leave to appeal refused (1997), 165 Nfld. & P.E.I.R. 149 (note) (S.C.C.).

78 In *McKee (Guardian ad litem of) v. McCoy* (2001), 9 C.C.L.T. (3d) 294 (B.C. S.C.), the Court rejected a lower standard of care for an 81-year-old driver. Since the defendant was engaged, however, in an "adult activity" one would assume that even if courts did accept a lower standard for the elderly, as it does with youth, it would not apply to those engaged in adult activities. This was in fact the reason for rejecting a lower standard in this case.

79 See Barrett, "Negligence and the Elderly: A Proposal for a Relaxed Standard of Care" (1984), 17 John Marshall L. Rev. 873. The author notes that the unavoidable infirmities of old age are memory loss, loss of strength, impairment of hearing, impairment of vision, diminished perception, loss of reflexes.

80 Cases such as *Carper v. Oakway Holdings Ltd.*, [1991] B.C.J. No. 3851, where a court allowed the claim of a 78-year-old frail and arthritic plaintiff against a hotel, suggest that courts do take into account old age in determining both negligence and duty. The plaintiff's fall was entirely due to her ill health and age, yet the court found the hotel negligent for not having installed a handrail. The plaintiff was found to have been contributorily negligent for not being more careful. See also *Mills v. Moberg* (1996), 34 C.C.L.T. (2d) 103 (B.C. S.C.). An elderly woman walking with the aid of a walker collided with a 30-year-old delivery man. The court noted that this appeared to be the first Canadian case involving a collision between two pedestrians. Without specifically giving any legal significance to the fact that the pedestrian was elderly, the court assigned 90 per cent of the blame for the collision to the young man and 10 per cent to the plaintiff.

4. REASONABLE AND UNREASONABLE RISKS

(a) Introduction

One way of thinking about whether the defendant's conduct was reasonable or not is to think in terms of reasonable and unreasonable risks of injury. Much of what we do involves some risk of injury to ourselves or to others. Not clearing the sidewalk of snow immediately after a snowfall, playing in a game of ice hockey, or manufacturing products which are not accident-proof, all involve a foreseeable risk of injury to ourselves or to others. This does not mean, however, that those who engage in these activities will be branded as negligent. It is only when the defendant has decided to undertake a risk which the reasonable person would not have undertaken because it was unreasonable that the defendant can be considered to have been negligent. What factors does the reasonable person consider in making this decision?

(b) The "Learned Hand" Formula

A useful way of weighing those factors a reasonable person ought to consider when deciding upon a course of conduct has been attributed to the American judge Learned Hand. In *Conway v. O'Brien*,[81] Learned Hand stated:

> The degree of care demanded of a person by an occasion is the resultant of three factors: the likelihood that his conduct will injure others, taken with the seriousness of the injury if it happens, and balanced against the interest which he must sacrifice to avoid the risk.[82]

In his later and better known case, *U.S. v. Carroll Towing Co.*,[83] Learned Hand expressed these three variables in algebraic terms, suggesting that the formula provided some perspective on the unreasonable risk concept:

> If the probability be called P; the injury, L; and the burden, B; liability depends upon whether B is less than L multiplied by P: i.e., whether $B<PL$.[84]

This formula has provided us with an economic analysis of the negligence concept. Stated in words, a reasonable risk, i.e., one which can, without fear of liability, be assumed, is one whose cost of avoidance is greater than the probability of the injury multiplied by its severity, should it occur. An unreasonable risk, on the other hand, is one whose cost of avoidance is less than the probability of the injury multiplied by its severity, should it occur. It would not, for example, be reasonable for a defendant to spend $1,000 to avoid a risk of injury whose cost, i.e., probability multiplied by gravity, is less than that amount. Only if the cost of the injury were greater than the $1,000 would it be reasonable to expend that amount.

The Learned Hand formula is useful as a theoretical approach to the standard of care issue. However, as conceded by Learned Hand himself in *Conway v. O'Brien*:

> The three factors are practically not susceptible of any quantitative estimate, and the second two (i.e. the gravity of the injury and its probability) are generally not so, even theoretically. For this

---

81 111 F. 2d 611 (C.A., 2nd Cir., 1940).

82 *Ibid.*, at 612.

83 169 F. 2d 169 (C.A., 2nd Cir., 1947).

84 *Ibid.*, at 173.

> reason a solution always involves some preference, or choice between incommensurables, and it is consigned to a jury because their decision is thought most likely to accord with commonly accepted standards, real or fancied.[85]

Despite this, however, there is no doubt that breaking down the notion of unreasonable risk into components does assist courts and others in thinking about what should be considered by reasonable individuals when they embark upon activities. Let us examine these elements more closely.

(i) Likelihood of Injury

The element of the likelihood, or probability, of injury, i.e., the risk factor, is essentially a question of statistical fact. The reasonable person will always consider what the likelihood of an injury is before undertaking a specific activity. The statistical probability of an injury, when weighed with its seriousness and the cost of its avoidance, will help the reasonable person decide whether or not to undertake a risk.[86]

One must distinguish between the ability of the reasonable person to have foreseen the injury, and the statistical likelihood of the injury occurring. Merely that an injury was in fact a probable or likely result of an activity does not mean that it was reasonably foreseeable.[87] The reasonable person's ability to have foreseen the risk depends not only on its statistical probability, but on the state of knowledge which existed at the time the activity was undertaken. Although it can be stated that, as a general rule, the greater the risk of injury the more likely it will be that it ought to have been foreseen, there may be cases where probable, or even certain, injuries could not reasonably have been foreseen.[88] Conversely, even quite remote risks can be foreseeable.[89]

---

85 111 F. 2d 611 at 612. These concerns were restated by Learned Hand in *Moisan v. Loftus*, 178 F. 2d 148 at 149 (1949):

> It is indeed possible to state an equation for negligence in the form, C\rP\9D, in which the C is the care required to avoid risk, D, the possible injuries, and P, the probability that the injuries will occur, if the requisite care is not taken. But of these factors care is the only one ever susceptible of quantitative estimate, and often that is not. The injuries are always variable within limits, which do not admit of even approximate ascertainment: and, although probability might theoretically be estimated, if any statistics were available, they never are; and, besides, probability varies with the severity of the injuries. It follows that all such attempts are illusory, and, if serviceable at all, are so only to center attention upon which one of the factors may be determinative in any given situation.

See Epstein, "Theory of Strict Liability" (1973) 2 J. Leg. Stud. 151, for a further critique of this theory.

86 A reasonable person, for example, will not ignore even a very small risk of a serious injury where the risk can be eliminated at small cost or inconvenience.

87 I use the term "reasonably foreseeable" here in its narrow, factual sense, i.e., would the reasonable person have perceived the existence of the risk? It is also used in a much broader sense, i.e., to express the court's view that, taking into account all questions of fact and law, the plaintiff was reasonably foreseeable, and was therefore owed a duty of care.

88 This can occur, for example, in product liability or professional negligence cases, where the state of knowledge at the time did not indicate the link, later discovered, between the product or treatment and serious consequences.

89 For example, in the classic case of *Bolton v. Stone*, [1951] 1 All. E.R. 1078 (H.L.), the plaintiff was injured by a cricket ball which was hit from the defendant's cricket club. Although the

(ii) Gravity of the Injury

The second factor that a reasonable person will take into account in deciding whether it is reasonable to run the risk of injury associated with a proposed activity is the gravity of the injuries which might occur. The more grave the possible injuries, the more cautious the actor must be.

This factor was considered in *Paris v. Stepney Borough Council*,[90] where the House of Lords held an employer liable for failing to provide protective goggles to a workman who only had one eye, although it would not have required such care with respect to ordinary employees. In so deciding, the majority of the Lords rejected the Court of Appeal's contention that in determining liability only the probability of injury was relevant, and not its gravity. Referring to several authorities,[91] Lord Normand expressed no doubt that a reasonable and prudent person would be influenced not only by the greater or lesser probability of an accident occurring, but also by the gravity of the consequences should an accident occur.[92]

(iii) Cost of Avoidance

All risks of injury can be significantly decreased, if not entirely eliminated, if the actor is prepared to absorb certain economic costs, or alter the proposed activity in some other way. When one considers the burden of eliminating a risk as a factor in determining whether a risk of injury is reasonable or not, both economic and non-economic concerns must be taken into account.

It may be possible to make a proposed activity safer by merely expending some costs, without altering the activity in any significant way. For example, in *Ware's Taxi Ltd. v. Gilliham*,[93] transporting children in a taxi-cab would have been made safer had the alleged tortfeasor installed safety devices which were available for about $10. In this type of case, the decision not to expend the extra costs, assuming of course that the tortfeasor knew or ought to have known that these safety devices were available, can be adjudged reasonable or not based on economic considerations. Courts must of course remember that the defendants are not required to guarantee the safety of plaintiffs but to take reasonable steps to make them safer.[94]

The more difficult case involves the situation where the activity can be made safer only by altering it in some significant way and thereby risking the loss of, or in fact losing, a valuable objective of the activity. In this case it must be decided

---

occurrence was described as "readily foreseeable", it certainly was not a statistical probability or likelihood. Only six balls at most had ever left the cricket grounds in about 30 years.

90 [1951] 1 All E.R. 42 (H.L.).

91 *Mackintosh v. Mackintosh* (1864), 2 Macph. (Ct. of Sess.) 1357; *Northwestern Utilities Ltd. v. London Guar. & Accident Co.*, [1936] A.C. 108 (P.C.); and *Salmond on Torts*, 10th ed. (1945), at 438.

92 See also *Glasgow Corp. v. Muir*, [1943] A.C. 448 at 456 (H.L.), where Lord Macmillan stated: "There is no absolute standard, but it may be said generally that the degree of care required varies directly with the risk involved." Or as stated in a case involving an injury caused by a gun shot: "the more dangerous the act the greater is the care that must be taken in performing it"; see Ryan J. in *Anderson v. Williams* (1997), 36 C.C.L.T. (2d) 1 (N.B. C.A.) at 9 referring to Dickson J.A.'s judgment in another gun accident case, *Dahlberg v. Naydiuk* (1969), 72 W.W.R. 210 (Man. C.A.).

93 [1949] S.C.R. 637.

94 In the *Ware's* case, the transportation company was held liable.

whether the value of the activity warrants assuming greater risks.[95] For example, traffic accidents would be reduced if everyone drove much more slowly. This would mean, however, that people would either arrive at places late, or be forced to leave for them much earlier.[96] This factor, i.e., the utility of an activity, has been the main issue in several negligence law cases, particularly where the activities of police officers have been concerned[97] or others who are acting in the public interest during a situation of urgency.[98] It also has been recognized by legislative provisions which either reduce the standard of care or permit otherwise unlawful conduct when emergencies or other highly-valued activities are involved.[99]

---

95 In *Kendal v. St. Paul's Roman Catholic Separate School Division No. 20*, 2003 CarswellSask 329, [2003] S.J. No. 330 (Sask. Q.B.) at para. 22, affirmed (2004), 25 C.C.L.T. (3d) 25 (Sask. C.A.), the trial judge expressed this principle as follows: "The degree of risk that a reasonable person might tolerate will vary in direct proportion to the worthiness of the undertaking. The more highly valued the societal interest in the undertaking, the greater will be the acceptable risk." The case involved an injury inflicted upon a teacher by a student with special needs. One of the factors that the judge took into consideration in exonerating the school was the high social value of the program.

96 See *Daborn v. Bath Tramways Motor Co.*, [1946] 2 All E.R. 333 at 336 (C.A.), where Asquith L.J. stated:

> In determining whether a party is negligent . . . a relevant circumstance . . . may be the importance of the end to be served by behaving in this way or that. As has often been pointed out, if all the trains in this country were restricted to a speed of 5 miles an hour there would be fewer accidents, but our national life would be intolerably slowed down. . . .

This was quoted with approval in *Bittner v. Tait-Gibson Optometrists Ltd.* (1964), 44 D.L.R. (2d) 113 (Ont. C.A.).

97 See, e.g., *Priestman v. Colangelo and Smythson*, [1959] S.C.R. 615; *Beim v. Goyer* (1966), 57 D.L.R. (2d) 253 (S.C.C.); *Woodward v. Begbie*, [1962] O.R. 60 (H.C.); *Poupart v. Lafortune* (1974), 41 D.L.R. (3d) 720 (S.C.C.); *Hambley v. Shepley* (1967), 63 D.L.R. (2d) 94 (Ont. C.A.); *Bittner v. Tait-Gibson Optometrists Ltd.* (1964), 44 D.L.R. (2d) 113 (Ont. C.A.); *Pepper v. Hoover* (1976), 71 D.L.R. (3d) 129 (Alta. T.D.); *O'Reilly v. C.*, [1978] 3 W.W.R. 145 (Man. Q.B.), affirmed [1979] 3 W.W.R. 124 (Man. C.A.).

98 See *Daborn v. Bath Tramways Motor Co.*, [1946] 2 All E.R. 333 (C.A.); *Watt v. Hertfordshire County Council*, [1954] 2 All E.R. 368 (C.A.); *Coderre v. Ethier* (1978), 85 D.L.R. (3d) 621 (Ont. H.C.); *W.C.B. v. Giesbrecht*, [1980] 4 W.W.R. 350 (Man. Q.B.).

99 See, for example, *Doern v. Phillips Estate* (1994), 23 C.C.L.T. (2d) 283 (B.C. S.C.). The plaintiff was injured by a police car which was involved in a high speed police chase. The police car sped through a red light and collided with the plaintiff's car. The court considered provisions of the Motor Vehicle Act, R.S.B.C. 1996, c. 318, which allows emergency vehicles to depart from normal traffic rules in certain circumstances, the police department's own pursuit policies, and the Police Act, R.S.B.C. 1996, c. 367, s. 21, which requires proof of gross negligence on the part of a police officer, in deciding the plaintiff's action. Although the city and its police department were found liable, the action against the police officer personally was dismissed. In *Burbank v. B. (R.T.)* (2005), 259 D.L.R. (4th) 754 (B.C. S.C.), affirmed (2007), 47 C.C.L.T. (3d) 25 (B.C. C.A), leave to appeal refused (2007), 2007 CarswellBC 2745 (S.C.C.), the court considered regulations passed by the B.C. government to limit high-speed police chases, as well as written R.C.M.P. pursuit policies. The constable in this case was found partly at fault for causing an accident as a result of such a chase. The Court of Appeal affirmed the trial judgment, with one dissent. Also see *Radke v. S. (M.) (Litigation Guardian of)* (2007), 47 C.C.L.T. (3d) 75 (B.C. C.A.), which reached the same result. One issue in both cases was whether expert evidence as to the standard of care required was necessary. The Court of Appeal

(c) Emergencies

In deciding whether the defendant acted reasonably or not, the fact that a sudden emergency arose which was not of the defendant's own making will be relevant.[100] As stated in *C.P. Ltd. v. Gill*,[101] "it is trite law that faced with a sudden emergency for the creation of which the driver is not responsible, he cannot be held to a standard of conduct which one sitting in the calmness of a courtroom later might determine was the best course."[102]

The sudden emergency, "agony of collision", or "agony of the moment" doctrine, illustrates the basic proposition that the standard of care is that degree of care which would have been taken by the reasonable person *in like circumstances.* Since negligence law does not guarantee the safety of others, but only assures them that they will be compensated for injuries caused by unreasonable conduct, errors in judgment which do not qualify as being negligent are permitted. The significance of the sudden emergency doctrine is that it will permit a person who is faced with a sudden emergency to make a choice which would not have been acceptable in a non-emergency situation, and in retrospect, was not the best choice of those available. Since this will, in some cases, throw the unfortunate consequences of the emergency onto the shoulders of an innocent victim, the courts will not lightly recognize the sudden emergency doctrine as a defence in a negligence suit. The doctrine will not apply if the party's negligence brought about or contributed to the creation of the emergency in the first place.[103] As well, the emergency must have been one which could not have reasonably been antici-

---

decided that it was not as this was a matter well within the knowledge and competence of the trial judge. For a case under the emergency vehicles provisions in the Highway Traffic Act, R.S.A. 2000, c. H-8, s. 68.2, see *Murphy v. Hollingshead* (1991), 84 Alta. L.R. (2d) 312 (Q.B.). See also *Van Paassen v. Burch*, [1995] 1 W.W.R. 462 (Alta. Q.B.), reversed in part (1995), 35 Alta. L.R. (3d) 14 (C.A.), which dealt with special legislative provisions relating to funeral processions.

100 See Reynolds Jr., "Put Yourself in an Emergency — How Will You Be Judged?" (1973-74), 62 Ky. L.J. 366; Wise, "The Sudden Emergency Doctrine as Applied in South Carolina" (1968), 20 S.C.L. Rev. 408; Note, "The Sudden Emergency Doctrine" (1965), 36 Miss. L.J. 392.

101 [1973] S.C.R. 654.

102 *Ibid.*, at 665. Also see *Babineau v. MacDonald* (1974), 8 N.B.R. (2d) 520 (Q.B.), varied on other grounds (1975), 10 N.B.R. (2d) 715 (C.A.); *Gauthier & Co. v. R.*, [1945] S.C.R. 143; *Spratt v. Edmonton*, [1942] 2 W.W.R. 456 (Alta. T.D.); *Laplante (Guardian ad litem of) v. Laplante* (1992), 93 D.L.R. (4th) 249 (B.C. S.C.), affirmed (1995), 8 B.C.L.R. (3d) 119 (C.A.); *Bisheimer v. Bryce*, [1991] 2 W.W.R. 738 (Sask. C.A.); among others. As stated by Perry J. in *Loyie Estate v. Erikson Estate*, [1991] B.C.J. No. 2625 (S.C.): "The courts recognize that a person who is confronted with an emergency is not to be held to the same standard of conduct normally applied to one who is not in such a situation."

103 See *Spratt v. Edmonton*, [1942] 2 W.W.R. 456 at 457 (Alta. T.D.); *C.P. Ltd. v. Gill*, [1973] S.C.R. 654; *Swanson v. Hanneson* (1972), 26 D.L.R. (3d) 201 (Man. Q.B.), affirmed (1973), 42 D.L.R. (3d) 688 (Man. C.A.); *Orser v. Mireault* (1914), 8 Alta. L.R. 117 (C.A.). The doctrine can apply to plaintiffs with respect to an allegation of contributory negligence. See, for example, *Lloyd v. Fox*, [1991] 6 W.W.R. 100 (B.C. C.A.). In this case, the "agony of collision" doctrine did not relieve the plaintiff of contributory negligence, since the court held that his negligence contributed to the sudden emergent situation.

pated.[104] Assuming that these conditions are met and a true emergency existed,[105] the doctrine will apply.[106] Where, for example, a driver risks the safety of passengers, or others, to preserve the life of an animal on the road, the courts have held that this choice was not reasonable.[107] If, however, the animal is large, and thus threatens the safety of the occupants of a vehicle, the choice not to hit the animal, but to attempt to avoid it either by braking or swerving the vehicle, may be excused.[108]

Closely related to the sudden emergency doctrine is the so-called defence of inevitable accident.[109] The defence has arisen in those cases where the facts themselves raise a *prima facie* inference of the defendant's negligence, generally in motor vehicle accident cases.[110] For example, where one vehicle strikes the

---

104 See, e.g., *Gellie v. Naylor* (1986), 28 D.L.R. (4th) 762 (Ont. C.A.), where the court held that the defendant motorist should have foreseen that the plaintiff might act foolishly and create a dangerous situation. See also *MacIsaac v. Reg. of Motor Vehicles* (1986), 45 M.V.R. 102 (N.S. T.D.), affirmed (1987), 79 N.S.R. (2d) 125 (C.A.) — agony of collision doctrine not applied when cyclist had ample time to ascertain if there was a danger.

105 It has been stated that an emergency must have actually or apparently existed, and that there was no time for reflective judgment. See Wise, "The Sudden Emergency Doctrine as Applied in South Carolina" (1968), 20 S. C. L. Rev. 408.

106 One of the earliest applications occurred in *Jones v. Boyce* (1816), 171 E.R. 540, where the plaintiff jumped from a coach which was out of control, breaking his leg. Had he not jumped, he would not have been injured since the coach did not overturn. The jury found that the plaintiff's actions were not rash and imprudent in the circumstances. For other examples see *Phillips v. Dooks* (1958), 14 D.L.R. (2d) 401 (N.S. T.D.); *Rowan v. Toronto Ry. Co.* (1899), 29 S.C.R. 717; *Corothers v. Slobodian*, [1975] 2 S.C.R. 633; *Klapischuk v. C.P.R.*, [1932] 1 W.W.R. 528 (Sask. C.A.); *Moore v. B.C. Elec. Ry.* (1916), 10 W.W.R. 631 (B.C. S.C.), affirmed [1917] 2 W.W.R. 729 (B.C. C.A.); *Ricketts v. Sydney & Glace Bay Ry. Co.* (1905), 37 N.S.R. 270 (C.A.), among others. More recent cases include *Stevenson v. Clearview Riverside Resort* (2000), [2000] O.J. No. 4863, 2000 CarswellOnt 4888 (S.C.J.)—inexperienced rescuers saving drowning man excused for their actions in view of the emergency; and *Ferguson Estate v. MacLeod* (2000), 187 Nfld. & P.E.I.E.R. 54 (P.E.I. T.D.)—actions of driver when faced with slow snowmobile attempting to cross highway reasonable in circumstances.

107 See *Molson v. Squamish Transfer Ltd.* (1969), 7 D.L.R. (3d) 553 (B.C. S.C.).

108 See *Hogan v. McEwan* (1975), 64 D.L.R. (3d) 37 (Ont. H.C.).

109 The two doctrines often are used interchangeably although they can be distinguished. With "agony of the moment" the argument is that the defendant made a choice, which in retrospect might seem unreasonable but in view of the emergency existing at the time was reasonable. With "inevitable accident" the argument is that the defendant acted reasonably and could not have avoided the accident.

110 It has been argued that one must distinguish between the "defence of explanation" and the "defence of inevitable accident". The defence of explanation refers to the case where an inference of negligence can be explained away by the defendant showing that in view of external factors, such as road conditions, the defendant's conduct was not negligent. The defence of inevitable accident refers to the case where due to factors "under the exclusive control or wholly within the defendant himself" the accident was inevitable. See Brenner J. in *Perry v. Banno* (1993), 15 C.C.L.T. (2d) 199 (B.C. S.C.), discussed in *MacLean (Litigation Guardian of) v. Thomson* (1999), 171 Nfld. & P.E.I.R. 98 (P.E.I. T.D.). Most cases where the defence is raised fall into the first category. Two recent cases of the defence of inevitable accident are *Barron v. Barron* (2003), 16 C.C.L.T. (3d) 93 (N.S. S.C.) and *Codner v. Gosse* (2003), 16 C.C.L.T. (3d) 120 (Nfld. T.D.). See Robert Currie, "Putting Inevitable Accident to Rest" 16 C.C.L.T. (3d) 171.

rear end of a vehicle which is in front of it,[111] or a car leaves its lane of traffic and collides with a vehicle in the oncoming lane,[112] there is *prima facie* evidence that the driver of the offending vehicle was negligent. If the defendant can prove, however, that despite the accident, reasonable care was exercised, which did not, and could not have, prevented the accident, the inference of negligence will be negated.[113] Although it has been held by some authorities that the defence of inevitable accident requires not merely proof of reasonable care, but of "the greatest care and skill",[114] Canadian authorities have not imposed this high standard of care on defendants.[115] Thus, in *A.G. Can. v. Stewart*,[116] the defendant driver was relieved of liability for an automobile accident which resulted when a partridge flew into the open window of his car and struck him on the temple. The defendant lost control of the car, crossed over into the other side of the highway, and collided with the plaintiff's motorcycle. The court found that the defendant had demonstrated that he had taken reasonable care and dismissed the action.[117]

Even if the immediate cause of an accident relates to a condition over which the defendant had no control, the defence of inevitable accident will not succeed

---

111 See, e.g., *Goveia v. Lalonde* (1977), 1 C.C.L.T. 273 (Ont. C.A.). Also see *Elliott v. Hill Bros. Expressways Ltd.* (1998), 221 A.R. 277 (Q.B.), affirmed (1999), [1999] A.J. No. 184, 1999 CarswellAlta 138 (C.A.), additional reasons at (1999), 240 A.R. 371 (Q.B.)—driver acted reasonably when faced with overturned vehicle on highway; *Parsons v. Rose* (1998), 164 Nfld. & P.E.I.R. 162 (Nfld. T.D.)—drivers in multi-party collision all acted reasonably; *Deveau v. Fournier* (1997), [1997] N.B.J. No. 441, 1997 CarswellNB 447 (Q.B.)—driver could not have avoided colliding with car that entered road from parking lot.

112 See, e.g., *A.G. Can. v. Stewart* (1989), 50 C.C.L.T. 77 (N.B. C.A.). Also see *Insurance Corp. of British Columbia v. Vancouver (City)* (1997), [1997] B.C.J. No. 1272, 1997 CarswellBC 1448 (S.C.).

113 The question arises as to the nature of the burden of proof imposed upon the defendant. Is it a primary or secondary burden? In other words, does the defendant have to demonstrate, on the balance of probabilities, that despite the fact that his or her car was on the wrong side of the road, there was no negligence, or merely provide a reasonable explanation which negates the inference? The approach that all that is required is a "reasonable explanation" was applied in *Masztalar v. Wiens*, [1994] B.C.J. No. 744 (S.C.); *Smith v. Hartson* (1993), 108 Nfld. & P.E.I.R. 147 (Nfld. T.D). In the latter case, Green J. explained that the burden of proof always rests on the plaintiff, and the plea of "inevitable accident" is merely a denial of negligence. The defendant need not prove the absence of negligence. This is the defence of explanation. Where, however, the defence is that due to an "internal" factor, such as a medical condition, the driver lost control of his or her car, it appears that the burden of proof is heavier. In *Perry v. Banno* (1993), 15 C.C.L.T. (2d) 199 (B.C. S.C.), Brenner J. held that in the latter case the defendant must prove that "the [collision] could not have been prevented by reasonable care on his part": 15 C.C.L.T. (2d) at 204. Also see *Sheldon v. Gray* (1989), 20 M.V.R. (2d) 80 (Ont. H.C.), affirmed (1994), 8 M.V.R. (3d) 62 (Ont. C.A.), which supports this heavier burden approach. This is the defence of inevitable accident.

114 See Lord Esher M.R. in *The Schwan*, [1892] P. 419 (C.A.).

115 See *Rintoul v. X-Ray & Radium Indust. Ltd.*, [1956] S.C.R. 674 (S.C.C.); and *Aubrey v. Harris; Drabik v. Harris*, [1957] O.W.N. 133 (C.A.). See Klar, "Annotation" (1976-77), 1 C.C.L.T. 273. The Supreme Court of Canada's decision in *Rintoul* is admittedly somewhat ambiguous since the court refers approvingly to cases that apply the more onerous standard, but the judgment actually applies "the exercise of reasonable care" standard. The heavier standard was recently applied in *Codner v. Gosse* above, note 110.

116 Above, note 112.

117 This is an example of the "defence of explanation" as discussed above.

if the defendant had reasonable grounds to know that this could happen. Thus, in *Barron v. Barron*,[118] the fact that the defendant had a coughing fit that led him to blackout while driving his car was no defence. The coughing fit occurred as a result of drinking coffee and the defendant, based on previous experience, knew that this could happen to him.[119]

The suggestion by Professor Currie that the Supreme Court of Canada should, as it did with *res ipsa*, clarify the law regarding the defence of inevitable accident is a good one. The defendant's argument that the accident was caused by a condition or circumstance over which he or she had no control is essentially an argument that the defendant was not negligent. To elevate this to a named defence and suggest that it in some way alters the normal rules relating to the burden of proof is to cause needless confusion for judges and juries.

5. GENERAL PRACTICE

A very useful factor in determining whether a person's conduct was reasonable or not is the general practice of those engaged in a similar activity.[120] Although it is true that what is reasonable conduct depends upon what the trier of fact thinks ought to have been done in the situation, and not what is usually done by average individuals, there is no denying that the latter will be an extremely significant matter, especially in cases which involve matters beyond the experience and competence of the trier of fact.[121]

Evidence of general practice will be given more or less weight depending on the circumstances. There are no specific requirements to establish a generally approved practice. Although the number of individuals who conduct themselves as did the defendant or plaintiff, and the length of time of this practice, are clearly relevant considerations in deciding the negligence issue, there are no minimum requirements. It is up to the court to determine whether the evidence indicates that sufficient numbers of others followed the same conduct for a sufficient period

---

118 Above, note 110.

119 The court also considered an "alternative" argument. The fact that the defendant's car ended up in a ditch was by itself *prima facie* evidence of negligence. As pointed out by Currie, above, note 110, this is in essence a *res ipsa loquitur* argument, and as shall be discussed below in Chapter 14, may be treated as circumstantial evidence of negligence. The effect of either argument is the same — the defendant must negate the inference of negligence by his own evidence. And, in this respect, the coughing fit does not accomplish that because the defendant was negligent in drinking coffee while driving.

120 This is frequently called custom, by both courts and commentators. Since, however, the term custom does have a technical meaning as a source of law, as well as meanings in sociology and related disciplines, I prefer the term general practice. See Linden, "Custom in Negligence Law" (1968), 11 Can. Bar Rev. 151; Morris, "Custom and Negligence" (1942), 42 Colum. L. Rev. 1147; Fricke, "General Practice in Industry" (1960), 23 Mod. L. Rev. 653; Weiler, "Groping Towards a Canadian Tort Law" (1971), 21 U.T.L.J. 267 at 318-21; Epstein, "The Path to the *T.J. Hooper*: The Theory and History of Custom in the Law of Tort" (1992), 21 J. of Leg. Studies 1.

121 See the discussion of custom as it relates to professional negligence in Chapter 10.

of time to influence the standard of care decision.[122] The burden of proving that a custom exists is on the person so alleging, and "only in the rarest and most patently obvious cases will the Courts take judicial notice of a custom."[123] Under the previous, but now discredited, theory that evidence of general and approved practice was conclusive proof that the defendant acted reasonably,[124] it was of course important to have a fixed idea of what constituted general practice. Under the current, more realistic, approach that what others do is only a relevant factor in deciding what is reasonable, the weight of which varies depending on the circumstances, it is unnecessary to attempt to define the elements of a general practice with precision.[125]

Cases which have involved evidence of general practice bear out the point that the weight assigned to this evidence is determined by the extent to which the courts have been persuaded that such practices as relied upon by the parties did in fact exist. In a leading case, *Anderson v. Chasney*,[126] the defendant doctor was sued for his failure to adopt a system to ensure that all of the sponges which were used during an operation were removed. The court rejected the defence that his procedure was consistent with the general practice at this specific hospital. Not only was the issue in this case one which the ordinary person was competent to judge, but further it was held that "no modern, approved practice followed by surgeons generally" had been established.[127]

---

122 For example, in *Ware's Taxi Ltd. v. Gilliham*, [1949] S.C.R. 637 at 642, Estey J. stated: "It is true that evidence of established practice or custom may be adduced for the purpose of rebutting an allegation of negligence but in order to establish such it must have been a practice over a long period of years." Establishing thresholds such as "a long period of years" is unhelpful. Not only is it extremely vague, but it makes it appear that general practice or custom is a definite thing which either exists or does not rather than treating it merely as evidence that other individuals conducted themselves in a similar way. See also *Rothschild v. The Royal Mail Steam Packet Co.* (1852), 18 L.T.R. 334, where the term "for a great number of years" is used. One court was even specific, requiring a period of 20 years; see *Hart v. Lancashire Ry. Co.* (1869), 21 L.T.R. 261.

123 Iacobucci J. in *Waldick v. Malcolm* (1991), 8 C.C.L.T. (2d) 1 at 15 (S.C.C.). Iacobucci J. agreed with Linden, above, note 120, at 167, that taking judicial notice of a custom is a "dangerous practice" for courts.

124 See *Vancouver Gen. Hosp. v. McDaniel*, [1934] 4 D.L.R. 593 at 597 (P.C.): "a defendant charged with negligence can clear his feet if he shows that he has acted in accord with general and approved practice." This was followed in *MacLeod v. Roe*, [1947] S.C.R. 420; *London & Lancashire Guar. & Accident Co. of Can. v. La Cie F.X. Drolet*, [1944] S.C.R. 82; *Karderas v. Clow*, [1973] 1 O.R. 730 (H.C.).

125 See discussion, however, of generally approved practice as it relates to professionals in Chapter 10.

126 [1949] 4 D.L.R. 71 (Man. C.A.), affirmed [1950] 4 D.L.R. 223 (S.C.C.). This case is discussed further in Chapter 10, in so far as professionals are concerned.

127 *Ibid.*, at 82. There have been several other cases as well, where the courts' rejection of the defence of general practice can at least partly be explained by the defendants' failure to convince the courts that the practice argued for actually was sufficiently common and widespread to have any real weight. See, e.g., *Ware's Taxi Ltd. v. Gilliham*, [1949] S.C.R. 637; *King v. Stolberg* (1968), 70 D.L.R. (2d) 473 (B.C. S.C.), reversed in part on other grounds (1969), 8 D.L.R. (3d) 362 (B.C. C.A.); and *James v. River East Sch. Div. No. 9* (1975), 64 D.L.R. (3d) 338 (Man. C.A.). Even where the court is convinced that there is a general practice, however, they can still reject it. See, for example, *Rast v. Killoran*, [1995] B.C.J. No. 1354 (S.C.); *Plasway v. Abraham*, [1993] B.C.J. No. 172 (S.C.).

Several reasons can be given to explain the courts' interest in evidence of general practice as an important factor in a negligence action. Most basic to these is the assumption that "what is reasonable in a world not wholly composed of wise men and women must depend on what people presumed to be reasonable, constantly do."[128] It also can be suggested that general practice is not evidence of reasonableness merely because it is commonly done by most people, but, rather, it has become general practice because it is reasonable. It is fair to assume that unreasonable behaviour is unlikely to become generally approved.

There are other reasons for giving considerable importance to general practice in reference to the standard of care. For example, it assists in "crystallizing", with some precision, the standard which should be adhered to, which can then be learned and utilized.[129] Further, it will definitely assist the triers of fact, and will not unfairly label as negligent, conduct which the defendant would have followed naturally. And finally, it will act as a guard against findings which may prove to be economically unrealistic.[130] All of these reasons point to the requirement that the practice relied upon was truly a general one, consciously and deliberately adopted. Thus, where a defendant's failure to take precautions is justified on the ground that others, in a similar situation, have also acted that way, the trier must determine whether this conduct was a deliberate practice, or merely an unthinking omission by everyone.[131]

It is almost universally conceded that evidence of general practice can never, as a matter of law, settle the negligence issue.[132] Thus whether the evidence is that of the plaintiff, i.e., that the defendant failed to adhere to general practice, or of the defendant, i.e., that the defendant was adhering to general practice, the evidentiary effect is the same. This may raise an inference of negligence, or of reasonable care, or may in fact raise a *prima facie* case, but will not be conclusive

---

128 *Marshall v. Lindsey County Council*, [1935] 1 K.B. 516 at 540. This was approved in *Moss v. Ferguson* (1979), 35 N.S.R. (2d) 181 (T.D.).

129 See Iacobucci J. in *Waldick v. Malcolm* [1991] 2 S.C.R. 4, at para. 31 quoting from Linden, above, note 120.

130 See Weiler, Linden, and Morris, above, note 120. These arguments are those advanced in support of the use of custom as evidence of reasonableness.

131 In terms of proof of general practice, therefore, it might be relevant whether there is evidence that the party adopted a practice actually utilized by many others, as opposed to merely being as lackadaisical as everyone else in failing to take extra care.

132 See McK. Norrie, "Common Practice and the Standard of Care in Medical Negligence" (1984-85), 30 Juridical Rev. 145. The author discusses Scottish and English law with regards to the effect of evidence of common practice in medical negligence cases, and concludes that, despite contrary indications, both jurisdictions recognize that evidence of common practice does not prevent the court from deciding what ought to have been done by the reasonable doctor, even if this differs from what is commonly done. See discussion, however, in Chapter 10 below as regards professional standards of care and the judgment in *ter Neuzen v. Korn*, [1995] 3 S.C.R. 674. A Supreme Court of Canada reaffirmation of the evidentiary weight of custom, in a non-professional context, is found in the occupier's liability case, *Waldick v. Malcolm* (1991), 8 C.C.L.T. (2d) 1 (S.C.C.). Iacobucci J. stated that "no amount of general community compliance will render negligent conduct 'reasonable . . . in all the circumstances' ": 8 C.C.L.T. (2d) at 16. Also see *Barnfield v. Westfair Foods Ltd.* (2000), 258 A.R. 183 (Q.B.).

proof.[133] As indicated above, the weight given to the evidence will vary depending upon the extent to which a generally approved practice has been established.[134]

6. BREACH OF STATUTORY STANDARDS

Prior to 1983, Canadian tort law was vexed with two difficult questions. First, when a statute imposes a duty and prescribes a penalty for its breach, but is silent with respect to the effect of this breach on a civil remedy, can a person injured by this breach sue in tort? Second, when a statute lays down standards of conduct for the purpose of statutory duties, can these standards be used in a negligence action in determining the issue of reasonable care?

In *R. v. Sask. Wheat Pool*,[135] the Supreme Court of Canada, in large measure, answered these questions. The case concerned a breach of the Canada Grain Act[136] which resulted in the plaintiff's economic losses. The plaintiff did not allege that the defendant owed it a common law duty to take reasonable care, which it breached, but based its claim on the breach of the statutory duty. The breach, which involved the delivery of infested grain out of a terminal elevator, was penalized under the statute, but there was no provision for a civil action by a person injured by the breach.

After considering the various approaches taken in Great Britain and in the United States to actions for damages involving breaches of statutory duties, Dickson J. adopted the following propositions to be followed in Canadian tort cases. First, there is no tort of breach of statutory duty in Canada. Where a statute is silent about the creation of a litigable civil duty in addition to a penal offence, courts ought not to interpret the statute's intent in such a way as to create a private

---

133 The leading case is *Cavanagh v. Ulster Weaving Co.*, [1960] A.C. 145 (H.L.). In it, Viscount Simonds stated that adopting a general practice would be "at least a *prima facie* defence to an action for negligence." Lord Tucker agreed with statements in previous cases that evidence of the practice "weighs heavily in the scale on the side of the defendant and the burden of establishing negligence which the plaintiff has to discharge is a heavy one." In *Moss v. Ferguson*, above, note 128, it was held that trade custom was "prima facie proof of a standard of reasonable care." See, however, the discussion on this point as it relates to professional negligence cases in Chapter 10.

134 In *Warren v. Camrose (City)*, [1989] 3 W.W.R. 172 at 179 (Alta. C.A.), Côté J.A. stated:

> The court can override expert evidence and brand a universal practice as negligent only in a strong case; the experts' thinking or the profession or trade's practice, properly understood, must offend logic or common sense, or flow from a gross error in weight.

135 (1983), 23 C.C.L.T. 121 (S.C.C.). For case commentaries see Mahoney, "Civil Causes of Action Bases on Breach of Statute: *Herman v. Saskatchewan Wheat Pool*" (1983), 4 Advocates' Q. 359; Brudner, "Case Comment" (1984), 62 Can. Bar Rev. 668; Klar, "Developments in Tort Law: The 1982-83 Term" (1984), 6 Sup. Ct. L. Rev. 309 at 310; Fridman, "Civil Liability for Criminal Conduct" (1984), 16 Ottawa L. Rev. 34. For more recent commentaries see C. Forell, "Statutes and Torts: Comparing the United States to Australia, Canada, and England" (2000), 36 Willamette L. Rev. 865, and Klar "Breach of Statute and Tort Law" in Neyers, Pitel, Chamberlain, eds., *Emerging Issues in Tort Law* (Hart Publishing, 2007), Chapter 2.

136 S.C. 1970-71-72, c. 7 [now R.S.C. 1985, G-10].

law remedy.[137] Second, where there is a common law duty of care, courts may have regard to statutory standards as useful evidence of the standard required of the parties. The weight to be ascribed to the breach is a matter of discretion for the triers of fact. Third, there remains a possible exception for breaches of industrial, penal legislation, although the nature of this was not in issue in *Sask. Wheat Pool*, and awaits further elaboration.

Applying these principles to the case at hand, the Supreme Court rejected the plaintiff's action. The plaintiff did not allege a breach of a common law duty of care, and having relied exclusively on a breach of the Canada Grain Act, which did not expressly provide a civil remedy, it followed that the plaintiff did not have a cause of action.[138]

As a result of this decision, the effect of statutory breach in tort has been significantly simplified. Where a plaintiff sues in negligence, basing the claim on a well-recognized common law duty of care, the effect of the breach of a statutory duty which relates to the same matter, and which was both a factual and proximate

---

137 Several statutes expressly provide for civil remedies based upon a statutory breach. In this case, the courts must interpret the statutes in order to determine whether the duty is absolute, or merely one of reasonable care, and to decide whether it has been breached. See, e.g., *Parisian v. C.P. Ltd.* (1983), 25 C.C.L.T. 105 (Sask. Q.B.), which dealt with an alleged breach of the Railway Act, R.S.C. 1970, c. R-2 [repealed by Canada Transportation Act, S.C. 1996, c. 10, s. 185]. As we have discussed, statutes impose duties on public authorities and frequently provide for civil liability. There are some judgments where courts have recognized private rights of action based on breaches of statutory duties which did not expressly provide for civil liability. In *Roth v. Roth* (1991), 9 C.C.L.T. (2d) 141 (Ont. Gen. Div.), a breach of the Road Access Act, R.S.O. 1980, c. 457 was stated to give rise to a civil cause of action. In *Whistler Cable Television Ltd. v. Ipec Canada Inc.* (1992), 17 C.C.L.T. (2d) 16 (B.C. S.C.), the court stated that while there is no tort of breach of statutory duty in Canada, there remains a "tort of statutory breach, distinct from any issue of negligence." The case concerned a breach of the Broadcasting Act, S.C. 1991, c. 11, and specifically, a violation of the plaintiff's exclusive broadcasting rights under the Act. The court distinguished this type of breach from the normal breach of statutory duty case and allowed the action to proceed to trial. In this case, the court reasoned that the issue was whether a statutory right specifically given to the plaintiff could be enforced by a civil action for damages. Also see *Canada Post Corp. v. G3 Worldwide (Canada) Inc.*, 2007 ONCA 348 (C.A.), leave to appeal refused (2007), 2007 CarswellOnt 7026, 2007 CarswellOnt 7027 (S.C.C.), dealing with the plaintiff's exclusive statutory right to deliver the mail, to the same effect. The distinction is subtle, and in my opinion, inconsistent with the judgment and reasoning in *Saskatchewan Wheat Pool*. As discussed above in Chapters 5 and 8, the current post-*Cooper* approach is to examine statutes to see whether they give rise to "proximity", which can then be used to support the creation of a common law duty of care.

138 The Supreme Court reaffirmed its position with regards to the effect of a statutory breach on civil liability in *Galaske v. O'Donnell* (1994), 112 D.L.R. (4th) 109 (S.C.C.). The case concerned the seat belt issue, and Cory J. noted how the seat belt legislation provided further support for the conclusion that the driver of the car was liable to the child passenger. In its most recent judgment on this matter, *Holland v. Saskatchewan (Minister of Agriculture, Food & Rural Revitalization)*, 2008 SCC 42, the Supreme Court reaffirmed that Canadian law does not recognize an action for "negligent breach of statutory duty", and that "a mere breach of statutory duty does not constitute negligence." The court did hold, however, that while the government cannot be sued for "negligently acting outside the law, or breach of statutory duty", it could be held liable for negligently failing "to implement an adjudicative degree." The case came before the court on a motion to strike, and the question as to whether the facts and the law supported the plaintiffs' claims in this instance was sent back to trial.

cause of the plaintiff's injury,[139] will clearly be relevant and useful evidence. If the purpose of the statutory duty was to protect a class of persons and interests which correspond to the plaintiff's position, it is likely that this breach will weigh heavily in the court's determination of the standard of care issue.[140] For example, drivers who breach highway traffic rules established for the protection of persons such as the plaintiff will most certainly be required to explain how despite these infractions they were not in breach of their common law duty of care.[141] In most situations, this will be difficult to do.[142] Prior to the decision in *R. v. Sask. Wheat Pool* it had generally been agreed, based on the Supreme Court's earlier decision in *Sterling Trusts Corp. v. Postma*[143] and the Ontario Court of Appeal's decision in *Queensway Tank Lines Ltd. v. Moise*,[144] that breaches of such legislation, which regulated activities ordinarily covered by common law duties of care, created

---

139 Causation must be established for the statutory breach to have any possible relevance. See, e.g., *McKay v. C.P. Ltd.*, [1988] 1 W.W.R. 170 (Man. Q.B.), affirmed [1988] 4 W.W.R. 288 (Man. C.A.), where the trial judge held that the statutory breach was not an effective cause of the accident. Also see *Gamblin v. O'Donnell* (2001), 207 D.L.R. (4th) 469 (N.B. C.A.). The plaintiff was a passenger in the defendant's truck. The truck did not have its headlights on. This arguably was a violation of the Motor Vehicles Act, R.S.N.B. 1973, c. M-17, which required headlights on at night time, defined as 30 minutes before sunset. It was 30 minutes before sunset. The truck was plainly visible. The plaintiff was injured when a bullet fired by a hunter who allegedly mistook the truck for an animal hit him. The court held that the violation was at most technical and secondly was not causally related to the injury. Thus, the driver of the truck was relieved of liability. Also see *Day & Ross Inc. v. Randall* (2001), 236 N.B.R. (2d) 317 (C.A.)—speeding not causally connected to the accident. A more recent example is *Gartner v. 520631 Alberta Ltd.* (2005), [2005] A.J. No. 194, 2005 CarswellAlta 244 (Q.B.). The court found that there was no causal link between the fact that an employee was allowed to work beyond the statutory maximum set by the Employment Standards Code, S.A. 1996, c. E-10.3 and his subsequent car accident. The court also held that despite the fact that the Code was breached, there was no negligence on the employer's part.

140 See, for example, *Hildebrandt v. W.F. Botkin Construction Ltd.*, [1998] 7 W.W.R. 418 (Sask. Q.B.), where a breach of the Occupational Health and Safety Regulations, R.R.S. c. O-1.1, Reg. 1, s. 156 was used as evidence of negligence.

141 See Linden, "Automobile Equipment Legislation and Tort Liability" (1967), 5 Western L. Rev. 76. For a very thorough discussion of the effect of highway traffic legislation on negligence actions, see Linden, *Canadian Tort Law*, 3rd ed. (1982), at 212-35.

142 In *Dubreuil v. Sawyer* (1981), 12 M.V.R. 206 (Ont. H.C.), however, a driver was able to establish that despite a breach of the Highway Traffic Act, R.S.O. 1970, c. 202, relating to his duty to maintain his vehicle and its equipment in safe condition and in compliance with the regulations, he acted as a reasonable and prudent person. Failures to comply with provincial seat belt legislation have been excused as not necessarily constituting negligent conduct: see *Prasad v. Frandsen* (1985), 60 B.C.L.R. 343 (S.C.); and *Rinas v. Regina (City)* (1983), 26 Sask. R. 132 (Q.B.). It has also been held that a plea of guilty to an offence under the Saskatchewan Vehicles Act, R.S.S. 1978, c. V-3 [now Highway Traffic Act, S.S. 1986, c. H-3.1, repealed by the Highway Traffic Act, S.S. 1996, c. H-3.2, s. 141] relating to the accident which is the subject of tort litigation does not mean that the defendant was guilty of negligence causing or contributing to the accident: see *Belair v. Thiessen* (1983), 24 M.V.R. 251 (Sask. Q.B.).

143 [1965] S.C.R. 324.

144 [1970] 1 O.R. 535 (C.A.).

presumptions of negligence which must be rebutted by defendants.[145] This approach has been rejected by the Supreme Court of Canada. A trial judge is free to give whatever weight seems appropriate to evidence of statutory breach. This may result in requiring an explanation from the defendant, but this is a matter for the discretion of the trier of fact. It is clear, however, that trial judges will not be able to find defendants liable for negligence merely because statutory standards were breached, where the court is not convinced that the breach is evidence of unreasonable conduct.[146]

A second important aspect of the judgment in *Sask. Wheat Pool* was the Supreme Court's decision that statutory duties do not, in and of themselves, give rise to common law duties of care. Prior to the decision, courts frequently created common law duties in areas not generally recognized as giving rise to civil law remedies, due to the presence of statutory duties. As discussed in Chapter 6, for example, the common law has generally not recognized the duty to take affirmative action to assist others except in limited situations. Where, however, statutory duties to assist existed, courts were more willing to recognize concomitant tort duties. This occurred with reference to governmental employees who have specific safety obligations,[147] to police officers,[148] and to municipalities.[149] Although the recognition of duties in these cases was, at least on the surface, an extension of the common law not dependent upon the fact that statutory duties existed, it is clear that the existence of the statutory duties led directly to this recognition. This possibility was of course not precluded by *Sask. Wheat Pool*, although it is suggested that the judgment must be interpreted as cautioning against it. In fact, many of the cases decided subsequent to *Sask. Wheat Pool* indicated that statutory duties were having a less persuasive effect on courts in tort law cases.[150]

---

145 See, e.g, Linden, *Canadian Tort Law*, 3rd ed. (1982), at 206:

> The second way a statutory violation may be handled is as *prima facie* evidence of negligence or as a presumption of negligence. This is currently the method most widely used by Canadian courts. According to this technique, proof of a penal violation entitles a plaintiff to judgment if the defendant offers no explanation of his breach. In order to escape responsibility, the violator must satisfy the court that he was not negligent. In short, the onus of proof of lack of negligence is shifted to the defendant by this treatment.

146 As occasionally occurred prior to *Sask. Wheat Pool*. See, e.g., *Unsworth v. Mogk* (1979), 107 D.L.R. (3d) 454 (Ont. H.C.). The trial judge, having conceded that failing to have a guardrail on scaffolding would not constitute common law negligence, nevertheless found for the plaintiff, since this was a breach of a statute designed for the safety of the plaintiff.

147 For example, a provincial gas inspector was held liable for failing to carry out his statutory duties under the Gas Protection Act, R.S.A. 1955, c. 129 [repealed by Safety Codes Act, R.S.A. 2000, c. s-1, s. 73(3)], in *Ostash v. Sonnenberg; Ostash v. Aiello* (1968), 63 W.W.R. 257 (Alta. C.A.).

148 In *O'Rourke v. Schacht*, [1976] 1 S.C.R. 53, a police officer was held liable for the breach of a duty to maintain a traffic patrol, pursuant to the Police Act, R.S.O. 1970, c. 351, s. 3(3) [repealed by An Act to Revise the Police Act and Amend the Law Relating to Police Services, S.O. 1990, c. 10, s. 148(1)].

149 See Chapter 8.

150 See, e.g., *Belmont Hotel Ltd. v. Atl. Speedy Propane Ltd.* (1985), 64 N.B.R. (2d) 271 (C.A.) — no liability for breach of National Fire Code; *Ryan v. W.C.B.* (1984), 6 O.A.C. 33 (Div. Ct.) — the Occupational Health and Safety Act, R.S.O. 1990, c. O.1, as am., did not give rise to tort remedies in addition to the remedies statutorily provided; *Palmer v. N.S. Forest Indust.*

After *Cooper v. Hobart*, however, the situation has become more complicated. For, as I discussed above, although Canadian courts have not abandoned the position that there is no nominate tort of breach of statutory duty, a new issue has emerged. Courts have been looking for proximity, which is at the core of the new common law duty formulation, within the terms of statutory provisions. Although I believe that this is a misguided approach, which in spirit runs counter to *Saskatchewan Wheat Pool*, there is no doubt that it is the approach sanctioned by the Supreme Court of Canada and faithfully followed by lower courts. Notwithstanding this, the experience to date has indicated that in the vast majority of cases, courts have not been willing to find proximity between public authority defendants and private parties within the provisions of public interest statutes. Thus, private law duties of care have been rejected. This has effectively in result, even if not in approach, reaffirmed the message of *Saskatchewan Wheat Pool*.[151]

Normally, the existence of statutory duties is used in a tort case by a plaintiff in order to strengthen a claim. Statutes may, however, be utilized by defendants in order to assist them as well. Just as breach of a statute may be used as evidence of negligence, compliance with a statutory standard can be evidence of reasonable care. In *Ryan v. Victoria (City)*,[152] Major J., writing for the Supreme Court of Canada, confirmed that "statutory standards can. . .be highly relevant to the assessment of reasonable conduct in a particular case, and in fact may render reasonable an act or omission which would otherwise appear to be negligent."[153] As with statutory breach, however, this depends on the facts of the case and is a matter for the trier of fact to consider when determining the negligence issue. As stated by Major J., "one cannot avoid the underlying obligation of reasonable

(1983), 2 D.L.R. (4th) 397 (N.S. T.D.) — breach of Fisheries Act, R.S.C. 1985, c. F-14, did not give rise to a cause of action; *Murray v. Canada* (1983), 47 N.R. 299 (Fed. C.A.) — breach of Public Service Employment Act, R.S.C. 1985, c. P-33, did not give rise to tort action; *McGeek Enterprises Ltd. v. Shell (Canada)*, [1991] O.J. No. 2078 — breach of the Gasoline Handling Act, R.S.O. 1990, c. G.4, repealed by S.O. 2000, c.16, s.45, not establishing negligent conduct; *Chong v. Flynn*, [1999] 10 W.W.R. 671 (Alta. Q.B.) and *Bongiardina v. City of Vaughan* (2000), 189 D.L.R. (4th) 658 (Ont. C.A.) — breach of municipal by-law requiring homeowner to clear snow-covered city sidewalk did not give rise to a civil action on behalf of injured pedestrian; *Laing Property v. All Seasons Display Inc.* (2000), 190 D.L.R. (4th) 1 (B.C. C.A.) — breach of construction by-laws did not give rise to liability to city. The snow clearing cases were followed in *Kluane v. Chasse* (2001), [2001] A.J. No. 384, although the court did concede that "there may be special circumstances which create an unusual risk which can lead to a duty of care on an abutting landowner". See also *R. (L.) v. Nyp* (1995), 25 C.C.L.T. (2d) 309 (Ont. Gen. Div.), where the breach of a court order banning publication of the details of an assault case led to a successful tort action for negligence causing emotional distress. Although the court justified the duty based on the common law, it is arguable that the court order was, in reality, the basis of the duty.

151 See Klar, "The Tort Liability of the Crown: Back to *Canada v. Saskatchewan Wheat Pool*" (2007), 32 Adv Q. 293. My research indicated that out of approximately 70 post-*Cooper* cases in which plaintiffs argued that proximity existed within statutory provisions, 40 were summarily dismissed, and 3 failed at trial. Only a handful actually succeeded after a trial on their merits.

152 (1999), 168 D.L.R. (4th) 513 (S.C.C.).

153 *Ibid.* at 527.

care simply by discharging statutory duties."[154] Whether or not a defendant's compliance with a statute will satisfy its obligation of reasonable care will depend upon a variety of factors noted by Major J. Where the statutory standard was directed at the event and accident in question, where it is a specific standard, where there is little discretion in the manner of performance, it is more likely that compliance will constitute reasonable care. Where, on the other hand, the statute is general, permits discretion, or where the circumstances of the event or accident are unusual, the statute will be given less weight. On the facts of the case itself, Major J. held that compliance with regulatory orders did not satisfy the defendant railway's duty of care in the circumstances of this case.[155]

The existence of a statutory scheme can, in exceptional cases, be used by a defendant to preclude a plaintiff's common law tort claim, even where the statute is silent as to its effect on civil remedies. In *Seneca College of Applied Arts & Technology Bd. of Gov. v. Bhadauria,*[156] the Supreme Court of Canada held that the development of a common law tort of discrimination in Ontario was precluded due to the existence of a comprehensive scheme provided in the Ontario Human Rights Code.[157] In *Frame v. Smith,*[158] the Supreme Court held that breaches of custody and access orders made pursuant to child welfare legislation could not give rise to tort claims for damages, but must be remedied by the statutory scheme. In these cases, therefore, not only did the court reaffirm the point of *Sask. Wheat Pool* that statutory breaches *per se* cannot be used in a tort law claim for damages to create a remedy, but it went further by declaring that in some instances, the statutory duty may even preclude the growth of the common law of torts into that area.[159]

---

154 *Ibid.* The case concerned whether compliance by a railway with its statutory obligations discharged its duty of care. Major J. noted that in this regard a "special rule" relating to railways had been developed by the common law. Railways were under no obligation — "absent extraordinary circumstances" — to be more prudent than their statutes, regulations and administrative orders dictated. See *Paskivski v. C.P. Ltd.* (1975), 57 D.L.R. (3d) 280, [1976] 1 S.C.R. 687. In *Ryan v. Victoria*, this special privilege was overruled and railways are now subject to the same rule as all other defendants.

155 A similar Ontario case that followed *Ryan* is *Danco v. Thunder Bay (City)* (2000), 13 M.P.L.R. (3d) 130 (Ont. S.C.J.), affirmed (2001), 21 M.P.L.R. (3d) 18 (Ont. C.A.).

156 [1981] 2 S.C.R. 181.

157 R.S.O. 1990, c. H.19.

158 (1987), 42 C.C.L.T. 1 (S.C.C.).

159 For commentary on *Seneca College v. Bhadauria*, see Klar, "Developments in Tort Law: The 1980-81 Term" (1982), 3 Sup. Ct. L. Rev. 388. See also *Chapman v. 3M Canada Inc.* (1995), 24 C.C.L.T. (2d) 304 (Ont. Gen. Div.) which applied *Seneca College*. A similar action is *Allen v. C.F.P.L. Broadcasting Ltd.* (1995), 24 C.C.L.T. (2d) 297 (Ont. Gen. Div.). The court held that the plaintiff's complaint for sexual harassment was precluded by the Canadian Human Rights Act, R.S.C. 1985, c. H-6. Also see *Ayangma v. Eastern School Board* (2000), 187 D.L.R. (4th) 304 (P.E.I. C.A.) applying *Seneca College* to the tort of discrimination. *Seneca College*, however, has not been interpreted to apply to all common law actions. For example, in *Lehman v. Davis* (1993), 16 O.R. (3d) 338 (Gen. Div.), the plaintiff was allowed to proceed with a wrongful dismissal action even though she also had filed a complaint against the employer under the Human Rights Code, R.S.O. 1990, c. H.19. Also see *Sargeant v. Patterson Dental Canada Inc.* (January 9, 1998), Doc. 97-CU-116745, [1998] O.J. No. 82 (Div. Ct.), affirming (1997), [1997] O.J. No. 4775, 1997 CarswellOnt 5455 (Gen. Div.). In *Chapman*, the court distinguished *Lehman* on the basis that the plaintiff in *Lehman* was suing for wrongful dismissal, and not for a breach of the Human Rights Code. In *Lajoie v. Kelly*, [1997] 3 W.W.R.

7. DEGREES OF NEGLIGENCE

Negligence law requires the defendant to display that degree of care exhibited by the reasonable person in like circumstances, the standard varying according to the risk and gravity of the injury weighed against the costs necessary to avoid such a risk. It is, therefore, a concept which inherently recognizes that there will be degrees of care. On occasion, however, legislators have deemed it necessary to intrude into the assessment process and to notify courts that defendants engaged in certain types of activities ought to be given less onerous responsibilities. That is to say, because of factors peculiar to the activity, the balance ought to be tilted in the defendant's favour, making it more difficult for a victim to show that the defendant's conduct ought to result in legal liability. This has been done by imposing liability only when conduct can be characterized as grossly negligent. Thus, for example, the Alberta Emergency Medical Aid Act[160] directs that doctors and others who render emergency first aid assistance under certain circumstances are not to be held liable for damages for injuries to, or the death of, a person unless it can be established that these injuries or the death were caused by the gross negligence of those rendering the assistance. As well, until recently the highway traffic legislation of several provinces directed that those who gratuitously gave other people rides in their cars were not to be held liable to them for injuries caused in a traffic accident unless the accident was caused by the gross negligence or wilful and wanton misconduct of the host drivers.[161] Other examples can be found in Municipal Government Acts[162] which relieve municipalities of liability for injuries caused to persons or property as a result of slippery sidewalks, unless the gross negligence of these defendants can be proved.[163]

Legislation requiring that gross negligence be proved in order for a defendant to be held liable for injuries caused has been criticized. It is clear that the phrase

---

181, 32 C.C.L.T. (2d) 115 (Man. Q.B.), the Court allowed an action based on the tort of "sexual harassment" even though the Human Rights Code, S.M. 1987-88, c. 45, s. 19(1) provided a remedy for harassment. Smith J. stated that the plaintiff's "appropriate remedy" would have been to lay a complaint under the Code, but concluded that the Code was not given "exclusive jurisdiction" for such complaints.

160 R.S.A. 2000, c. E-7, s. 1.

161 The legislation varied slightly. Most stated that there was no liability unless there was "gross negligence or wilful and wanton misconduct." The guest passenger discrimination provisions have now been repealed.

162 For example, Alberta's Municipal Government Act, S.A. 2000, c. M-26, s. 531. There are numerous other legislative provisions establishing "gross negligence" as the standard of care, for example, in relation to the activities of police, civil servants, and so on. See, for example, the Police Act, R.S.B.C. 1996, c. 367, s. 21 applied in *Doern v. Phillips Estate* (1994), 23 C.C.L.T. (2d) 283, affirmed (1997), 43 B.C.L.R. (3d) 53 (C.A.), *Noel (Committee of) v. Royal Canadian Mounted Police* (1995), [1995] B.C.J. No. 1184, 1995 CarswellBC 342 (S.C.), and *Insurance Corp. of British Columbia v. Vancouver (City)* (1997), 38 C.C.L.T. (2d) 271 (B.C. S.C.), affirmed (2000), 182 D.L.R. (4th) 366 (B.C. C.A.).

163 See, e.g., *Ancvirs v. London (City)* (1987), 48 D.L.R. (4th) 252 (Ont. H.C.). In *Bannon v. Thunder Bay (City)* (2000), 48 O.R. (3d) 1 (C.A.), leave to appeal allowed (2001), 149 O.A.C. 198 (note) (S.C.C.), reversed (2002), 210 D.L.R. (4th) 62 (S.C.C.), the Court of Appeal upheld the finding of the trial judge that the City's failure to plough or sand the sidewalk for one month constituted "gross negligence" as required by the statute. The trial judge allowed the claim, but the Court of Appeal reversed based on the plaintiff's failure to give the required notice. The Supreme Court of Canada restored the trial judgment.

'gross negligence' itself is not susceptible of a clear definition to assist courts in deciding whether it has been shown.[164] It has frequently been defined in terms which merely replace the words "gross negligence" with other equally ambiguous words, without actually clarifying the concept.[165] It has, for example, been described as "very great negligence",[166] as being the same thing as negligence with the addition of a "vituperative epithet",[167] or as "conduct in which, if there is not conscious wrong doing, there is a very marked departure from the standards by which responsible and competent people . . . habitually govern themselves."[168] One writer has described the doctrine of different degrees of care as "an untested invention of fancy" which does not spring from the common law.[169] Others have argued that it is meaningless to suggest that there can even be degrees of negligence, for "a man is either guilty of negligence or he is not."[170] The Chief Justice of Manitoba conceded that "the term is not susceptible of definition and, consequently, judges have found gross negligence where none existed and where at most plain, ordinary negligence existed but nothing else."[171] It has been agreed,

---

164 This was recognized by Anglin C.J.C. in *Holland v. Toronto* (1925), 59 O.L.R. 628 at 634 (S.C.C.), where the Chief Justice stated: "The term 'gross negligence' . . . is not susceptible of definition." See MacArthur, "Gross Negligence and the Guest Passenger" (1960), 38 Can. Bar Rev. 47 at 50.

165 Locke J. in *Cowper v. Studer*, [1951] S.C.R. 450, regretted that the term was used instead of a "more definite term."

166 For example, Wilson J. in *Dahl v. Saydack* (1970), 73 W.W.R. 133 (Man. Q.B.).

167 Dean Wright, in his S.J.D. Thesis on Gross Negligence, written in 1927 and and published in (1983), 33 U.T.L.J. 184, notes that Baron Rolfe used this expression to describe gross negligence in *Wilson v. Brett* (1843), 152 E.R. 737.

168 Duff C.J.C. in *McCulloch v. Murray*, [1942] S.C.R. 141 at 145. This phrase has been very popular in many of the cases. See, e.g., *Dahl v. Saydack* (1970), 73 W.W.R. 133 (Man. Q.B.), and cases discussed in the literature, especially Singleton, "Gross Negligence and the Guest Passenger" (1973), 11 Alta. L. Rev. 165. There are dozens of cases which have applied the term under the various legislative enactments which have used it. In *Marino v. Marino* (1981), 13 Man. R. (2d) 169 (Q.B.), it was noted that the Supreme Court of Canada has been called upon to decide the gross negligence issue in *McCulloch v. Murray*, [1942] S.C.R. 141; *Studer v. Cowper*, [1951] S.C.R. 450; *Burke v. Perry*, [1963] S.C.R. 329; and *Walker v. Coates*, [1968] S.C.R. 599.

169 Green, "High Care and Gross Negligence" (1928), 23 Ill. L. Rev. 4, cited by Pierce in a paper delivered to the 1965 meeting of the Canadian Bar Association. For a thorough historical account see Wright, "Gross Negligence", 1927 S.J.D. Thesis, published in (1983), 33 U. T.L.J. 184. Note that the common law did apply a rule of gross negligence in certain situations. See, e.g., *Nightingale v. Union Colliery of B.C.* (1905), 35 S.C.R. 65; cf. *Armand v. Carr*, [1926] S.C.R. 575. The phrase gross negligence is said to have first been introduced in the bailment case of *Coggs v. Bernard* (1703), 92 E.R. 107 (K.B.).

170 Lynskey J. in *Pentecost v. London Dist. Auditor*, [1951] 2 K.B. 759, cited by MacArthur, above, note 164. MacArthur also cites others who share this view that there are no degrees of negligence, although the author himself did not agree that the term is meaningless.

171 Monnin C.J.M. in *Occhino v. Winnipeg (City)* (1988), 51 D.L.R. (4th) 546 at 548 (Man. C.A.). A similar sentiment was expressed by Chief Justice Hickman in *Andrews v. Leger* (1981), 30 Nfld. & P.E.I.R. 258 at 263 (Nfld. T.D.), quoted by Green J. in *Mayo v. Harding* (1993), 111 Nfld. & P.E.I.R. 271 (Nfld. T.D.):

> The courts, over many years, have wrestled with the problem of defining that invisible juridical line which separates ordinary negligence from gross negligence. It is not a fixed line or one that is forever straight but one which has been bent and positioned as the

however, that despite these objections, whether there has been gross negligence or not is a question of fact depending entirely upon the circumstances of the case.[172] It also has been argued that as with the concept of ordinary negligence itself, there is no rigid definition of gross negligence, the standard varying according to the type of activity in issue.[173] It has been generally held that the requirements for gross negligence are less than for criminal negligence,[174] and that gross negligence can be proved by cumulating the effect of several acts, each of which taken alone might only be considered as being ordinary negligence.[175]

Despite the difficulty involved in defining the term gross negligence, that the intention of its use has been to lighten the legal liability of defendants engaged in certain activities. The legislators have decided that for a variety of reasons, it ought to be more difficult for victims of accidents caused by some defendants to succeed in a negligence claim. It is this aspect of the legislators' use of the phrase gross negligence, especially in relation to the now repealed guest passenger discrimination, which has been the subject of most of the criticism.[176] The argument that some victims of accidents caused by the negligence of others should be denied compensation except in cases of extreme misconduct by defendants, has not been popular to a compensation-oriented tort law. It has become evident that a sufficiently flexible negligence law is able to accommodate legitimate policy considerations in determining the liability of defendants, and thus has little need for the notion of gross negligence.

8. PRODUCT LIABILITY

(a) Introduction

Product liability law in Canada is governed both by the law of contract and the law of tort.[177] In the regime of contract, persons who purchase goods from sellers

---

exigencies and justice of the cause persuaded the trial judge or jury was necessary to ensure that justice be done.

172 See, e.g., *Gordon v. Nutbean*, [1969] 2 O.R. 420 (H.C.); *McCulloch v. Murray*, above, note 168; *Studer v. Cowper*, above, note 168; *Remmers v. Lipinski* (2000), 262 A.R. 295 (Q.B.), affirmed (2001), 203 D.L.R. (4th) 367 (Alta. C.A.), leave to appeal refused (2002), 2002 CarswellAlta 784, 2002 CarswellAlta 785 (S.C.C.). Nevertheless, certain conduct, such as falling asleep at the wheel, has been held to amount to gross negligence, almost as a matter of law. See Dickson J. in *Power v. Roussel* (1978), 23 N.B.R. (2d) 298 (Q.B.). This view was contradicted in *Steeves v. Lutes* (1982), 43 N.B.R. (2d) 338 (Q.B.), affirmed (1983), 51 N.B.R. (2d) 105 (C.A.).

173 See *Doern v. Phillips*, above, note 162.

174 See, e.g., *Marino v. Marino* (1981), 13 Man. R. (2d) 169 (Q.B.).

175 See, e.g., *Ogwa v. Alli* (1972), 4 N.B.R. (2d) 423 (C.A.); *Jones v. Green*, [1995] 4 W.W.R. 118 (Alta. C.A.). It has also been held that *res ipsa loquitur* can be used to assist in establishing gross negligence. See *Genik v. Ewanylo* (1980), 12 C.C.L.T. 121 (Man. C.A.).

176 See, e.g., Gibson, "Guest Passenger Discrimination" (1968), 6 Alta. L. Rev. 211. The Alberta legislation was subject to an unsuccessful Charter challenge: see *Mohr v. Scoffield* (1991), 83 Alta. L.R. (2d) 1 (C.A.), reversing (1990), 77 Alta. L.R. (2d) 68 (Q.B.), leave to appeal to S.C.C. refused (1992), 12 A.R. 398 (note) (S.C.C.).

177 Recent texts on product liability include S.M. Waddams, *Products Liability*, 4th ed. (2002); D.F. Edgell, *Product Liability Law in Canada* (Markham: Butterworths, 2000); Jane Stapleton, *Product Liability* (1994). There are numerous articles and books on specific aspects of this

and who are unhappy with their product, or who are injured by it, may be able to utilize the warranties provided for by legislation.[178] For these complainants, who can base their actions in contract, there is a major advantage. Assuming that they can satisfy the requirements of the legislation, liability for their injuries is strict. Negligence need not be proved.[179]

In a tort/contract borderline case on the subject of contractual warranties, *ter Neuzen v. Korn*,[180] the Supreme Court of Canada reviewed the elements of the contractual warranty. The case involved the artificial insemination of semen which was contaminated with the HIV virus. Sopinka J. noted that the warranty under the Sale of Goods Act[181] applies to contracts whose primary purpose was the sale of goods, as opposed to the provision of services. Sopinka J. agreed with the lower court's finding that the contract in this case was primarily one for the provision of medical services and not one for the sale of semen.[182] Thus the Sale of Goods Act warranties did not apply with respect to the product provided.

This, however, was not the end of the question. Apart from the statutory warranties, there are implied warranties at common law with respect to certain contracts for the provision of work and materials. These warranties are similar to the statutory warranties, i.e., that the goods provided are of merchantable quality and fit for their intended purpose. Noting, however, that there are important policy differences between contracts for the provision of goods and services in the commercial context and in the context of the provision of blood or semen for medical services,[183] Sopinka J. agreed with the Court of Appeal's decision not to

---

area of the law. As well, chapters in major tort texts also deal with product liability; see, for example, Fleming, *The Law of Torts*, 9th ed. (1998), Chapter 23, and Linden and Feldthusen, *Canadian Tort Law*, 8th ed. (2006), Chapter 16.

178 The warranties are embodied in Sale of Goods statutes. There are two warranties. First, that the goods purchased are reasonably fit for their purpose. Second, that the goods purchased are of merchantable quality. For a case on the latter see *Strandquist v. Coneco Equipment* (1999), 48 C.C.L.T. (2d) 209 (Alta. C.A.), additional reasons at (2002), 2000 CarswellAlta 443 (C.A.), affirming (1996), 32 C.C.L.T. (2d) 287 (Alta. Q.B.). Also see *Morse v. Cott Beverages West Ltd.* (2001), [2002] 4 W.W.R. 281 (Sask. Q.B.), an action for personal injury brought pursuant to the Consumer Products Warranties Act, R.S.S. 1978, c. C-30.

179 Typically, the contract action arises between the seller of the product and its buyer. However, as Linden and Feldthusen, above, note 177 at 616 notes, the courts and legislatures have, in some contexts, been able to "stretch the operation of these warranties to third persons." Thus, in some cases, those who are not the buyers can come under the protection of the warranties, and those who are not the sellers can come under the obligations imposed by them.

180 (1995), 127 D.L.R. (4th) 577 (S.C.C.).

181 In this case it was the Sale of Goods Act, R.S.B.C. 1979, c. 370.

182 Although Sopinka J. expressed uncertainty that this issue of characterization ought to have been left to the jury.

183 One important distinction is that in commercial contracts, even if the provider of the service is strictly liable for defective goods used, that supplier will have an equivalent remedy against the manufacturer of the goods. This would not be the case in the blood or semen donation context. There have been a number of important "tainted blood" cases that deal with issues of product liability, professional negligence, and causation. See especially *Walker Estate v. York-Finch General Hospital* (2001), 198 D.L.R. (4th) 193, 6 C.C.L.T. (3d) 1 (S.C.C.) and *Robb Estate v. Canadian Red Cross Society*, [2000] O.T.C. 23 (S.C.J.), additional reasons at (2001), 2001 CarswellOnt 545 (S.C.J.), reversed (2001), 9 C.C.L.T. (3d) 131 (Ont. C.A.), additional reasons at (2002), 9 C.C.L.T. (3d) 193 (Ont. C.A.), leave to appeal refused (2002), 2002 CarswellOnt 2839, 2002 CarswellOnt 2840 (S.C.C.).

apply the implied contractual warranties to the semen provided in this case.[184]

Outside of contract law, tort law has become an important vehicle to remedy injuries suffered by victims of manufacturers' negligence during the past century.[185] It is, of course, *Donoghue v. Stevenson*[186] which is credited as opening the doors not only to product liability claims but to all of negligence law.[187] The elements of a negligence action for a product liability claim are the same as the elements of any negligence claim, and are discussed throughout this text in other chapters. However, as with topics such as "professional negligence", the law of negligence has developed to accommodate the particular characteristics and issues raised in product liability cases. It is therefore useful to focus briefly on some of the distinctive features of product liability tort actions in this section.[188]

(b) Duty of Care: To Whom is it Owed?

As *Donoghue v. Stevenson* established, a duty of care is owed to all reasonably foreseeable victims of the defendants' negligent conduct, subject to policy concerns which may limit or negate the duty. In reference to product liability claims, this duty naturally extends to all purchasers and other foreseeable users and consumers of a product, whether they purchased it or not. For example, the fact that women who received defective breast implants were not the purchasers of these implants, since they were sold only to doctors and to medical establishments and not directly to the public, did not mean that a duty was not owed to these women.[189] It also is clear that a duty will be owed to third parties who are injured by the malfunctioning of a defective product. It is, in fact, difficult to envisage a

---

184 Another extensive discussion concerning the suitability of applying contractual warranties to the "sale" of bodily fluids, this time blood, can be found in Lang J.'s judgment in *Pittman Estate v. Bain* (1994), 112 D.L.R. (4th) 257 (Ont. Gen. Div.). As did Sopinka J., Lang J. found that it was inappropriate to apply either the statutory or common law warranties to the medical services provided in this case.

185 I refer here to personal injuries or property damage; not purely economic losses. Liability for purely economic losses caused by a poor quality product raises entirely different issues, as discussed in Chapter 7.

186 [1932] A.C. 562 (H.L.). See discussion in Chapter 5.

187 Although as Linden notes there were Canadian cases which beat *Donoghue v. Stevenson* to the punch. Linden cites *Ross v. Dunstall* (1921), 62 S.C.R. 393, and *Buckley v. Mott* (1919), 50 D.L.R. 408 (N.S. S.C.). See Linden, *Canadian Tort Law*, 5th ed. (1993), at 548-49.

188 A very interesting development is the use of "waiver of tort" as an alternative cause of action to tort claims in product liability suits. The plaintiffs essentially claim for an accounting for a disgorgement of profits based on equitable remedies. See, for example, *Serhan Estate v. Johnson & Johnson* [2006] O.J. No. 2421 (Ont. Div. Ct.), leave to appeal to S.C.C. denied [2006] S.C.C.A. No. 494; and *Heward v. Eli Lilly & Co.* (2007), 47 C.C.L.T. (3d) 114 (Ont. S.C.J.), leave to appeal allowed (2007), 51 C.C.L.T. (3d) 167 (Ont. S.C.J.), affirmed (July 2, 2008), Doc. Toronto 181/07, 2008 CarswellOnt 3837 (Ont. Div. Ct.). The nature of this equitable claim is outside the scope of this text, but this is certainly a development worth following as it will bear directly on the use of tort in future claims.

189 See *Hollis v. Birch* (1993), 103 D.L.R. (4th) 520 (B.C. C.A.), affirmed (1995), 14 B.C.L.R. (3d) 1 (S.C.C.).

circumstance where a manufacturer of a product will not be liable to a person injured by that product, due to the absence of a duty of care.[190]

(c) Standard of Care

The standard of care imposed upon manufacturers, or distributors,[191] of products is based upon ordinary negligence law principles. As we have discussed in this chapter, the standard is an objective one, and is influenced by such factors as general practice,[192] statutes and other codes of performance, and the consideration of costs of avoidance and acceptable levels of risk.

The duty of care extends to three general areas: (i) design, (ii) manufacture, and (iii) marketing.

(i) Design

A manufacturer of a product can be held liable for negligence for its design of the product.[193] The interesting aspect of negligent design is the fact that each product manufactured according to the design will suffer from the same defect. This has significant liability implications for the product's manufacturer.

There are a number of negligent design cases. In *Baker v. Suzuki Motor Co.*,[194] the plaintiff was injured in a fire which resulted when his motorcycle was involved in a collision with another vehicle. The plaintiff alleged that the fire occurred because of a design defect in the cycle's gas cap. The trial judge affirmed that negligent design can lead to a successful product liability claim, but she rejected the plaintiff's contention that there was negligence in design in this case. She accepted that there are trade-offs in a manufacturer's design decision, and that one must consider the risks in alternative designs. She also affirmed that weight must be given to evidence of industry standards. The burden of proving negligent design rests on the plaintiff, and is not shifted merely because the plaintiff is able

---

190 Although one must keep in mind that liability might be defeated for a variety of other reasons; e.g. no breach, no cause, too remote and so on. It is rarely defeated, however, on the basis of "no duty."

191 For a case dealing with the liability of manufacturers and distributors, see *McEvoy v. Ford Motor Co.*, [1989] B.C.J. No. 1639. Note that the distributor's participation in the product will differ from the manufacturer's. Thus, its liability will relate to negligence in the marketing of the product, rather than negligence in its design or manufacture. A leading authority establishing that a distributor has a duty of care is *Watson v. Buckley, Osborne, Garrett & Co.*, [1940] 1 All E.R. 174 (K.B.). A recent case involving the duty of a distributor is *Moran v. Wyeth-Ayerst Canada Inc.* (2004), [2005] 1 W.W.R. 716 (Alta. Q.B.).

192 Or, in the context of product liability cases, "industry standards." See discussion in *Meisel v. Tolko Industries Ltd.*, [1991] B.C.J. No. 105 (S.C.); and *Piche v. Lecours Lumber Co.*, [1993] O.J. No. 1686 (Gen. Div.). This is sometimes referred to as the "state of the art" defence; that is, as long as the product complied with the state of the art at the time of its manufacture, the required standard has been met. See, for example, *Holt v. P.P.G. Industries Canada Ltd.* (1983), 25 C.C.L.T. 253 (Alta. Q.B.).

193 A case frequently cited in support of this proposition is *Phillips v. Ford Motor Co.* (1970), 12 D.L.R. (3d) 28 (Ont. H.C.). Another frequently cited case is Linden J.'s judgment in *Gallant v. Beitz* (1983), 42 O.R. (2d) 86 (H.C.). A useful discussion of negligent design is found in S. Gordon McKee, "Liability for Negligent Design" (1993), 11 Can. J. of Ins. L. 51 and "Is Your Product 'State of the Art' and What Difference Does it Make" (1994), 12 Can. J. of Ins. L. 3.

194 (1993), 17 C.C.L.T. (2d) 241 (Alta. Q.B.).

to show that his injuries were caused by the way the vehicle was designed. There must be proof that it was designed negligently.[195]

A design defect case which was successful is *Nicholson v. John Deere Ltd.*[196] The case involved a riding lawn-mower which caught on fire. The fire was caused due to the fact that the mower's gas tank and battery were positioned in such a way that a spark could be created under certain conditions. The court held that this design presented a serious risk and hazard to the knowledge of the product's manufacturer. It also held that there were alternative designs which were safer. This was critical to the court's decision. In a case where a manufacturer knowingly creates a product with a negligent design, a warning to the consumer of that danger will not exonerate the manufacturer of liability. If knowledge of the danger only reaches the manufacturer after the product is marketed, warnings or other steps to prevent the risk from occurring may relieve the manufacturer of liability, but the standard of care required is very high.[197]

In determining whether a manufacturer's design was negligent, several factors ought to be considered. As discussed in *McEvoy v. Ford Motor Co.*,[198] these include the following:

(1) the utility of the product to the public as a whole and to the consumer;
(2) the likelihood of harm;
(3) the availability of a safer design;
(4) the costs, both in terms of functionality and price, of the safer design;
(5) the ability of the consumer to avoid harm by careful use of the product;
(6) the ability of the consumer to become aware of the risks;

---

195 The view that liability for a design defect ought to be strict, and not based on negligence, has been expressed. See, for example, Henry J.'s judgment in *Biancale v. Petro-lon Canada Ltd.*, unreported, March 19, 1986, discussed by McKee, "Liability for Negligent Design", above, note 193, at 52. As McKee notes, Henry J.'s statement was in *obiter*, as no design defect was found in the case, and his stance is not in accordance with the prevailing legal position. An excellent discussion of whether product liability in Ontario should be "strict" is found in *Andersen v. St. Jude Medical Inc.*, [2002] O.T.C. 53 (S.C.J.). The court struck out pleadings arguing for strict liability for injuries caused by implanted heart valves. The judge concluded that despite arguments in favour of strict liability, it was clear that in Ontario product liability is based on negligence law. Also see Borins J.'s judgment in *Walker Estate v. York-Finch General Hospital* (1997), 39 C.C.L.T. (2d) 1 (Ont. Gen. Div.), additional reasons at (1998), 1998 CarswellOnt 2319 (S.C.J.), leave to appeal refused (1998), 1998 CarswellOnt 4293 (C.A.), reversed (1999), 44 C.C.L.T. (2d) 205 (C.A.), leave to appeal allowed (1999), 137 O.A.C. 398 (note) (S.C.C.), leave to appeal allowed (1999), 137 O.A.C. 399 (note) (S.C.C.), affirmed [2001] 1 S.C.R. 647, rejecting strict liability in the provision of tainted blood.

196 (1986), 58 O.R. (2d) 53 (H.C.), affirmed (1989), 68 O.R. (2d) 191 (C.A.).

197 The court stated that the manufacturer "had a duty to devise a programme that left nothing to chance", at 34 D.L.R. (4th) 549. See Boivin, "Negligence, Strict Liability, and Manufacturer Failure to Warn: On Fitting Round Pegs in a Square Hole" (1993), 16 Dal. L.J. 299. This case, among others, is used to support the author's thesis that, despite the rhetoric to the contrary, the differences between Canadian and American approaches to product liability are not as large as one imagines. Both use a "compound" standard of liability which combines both negligence and strict liability elements.

198 [1989] B.C.J. No. 1639. In this case, the manufacturer was found liable for a design defect. The factors cited stem from American case law and articles. See, for example, Jasen J.'s judgment in *Voss v. Black & Decker Manufacturing Co.*, 450 N.E. 2d 204 (N.Y.C.A. 1983), and the articles cited therein.

(7) the manufacturer's ability to spread the costs related to improving the safety of the design.

This approach has been termed the "risk-utility" approach.[199] One compares the risks of injury posed by the product and compares these risks with the cost of avoiding them. It is essentially the "Learned Hand" formula.[200] In *Rentway Canada v. Laidlaw*,[201] for example, application of this analysis led to the conclusion that the manufacturer's design was negligent. The potential risks of the design far outweighed its utility.[202] One must keep in mind that, as with the Learned Hand formula, the risk-utility approach, although useful as a general abstraction, should not be seen exclusively in terms of economics or efficiency. Injury to persons or their property should be avoided where reasonably possible, notwithstanding the "profitability" of such avoidance measures.[203]

(ii) Manufacture

Unlike a design defect which affects an entire product line, a manufacturing defect occurs when one product is manufactured improperly and a defect occurs. As stated by Waddams,[204] and agreed to by the courts,[205] where a product has been manufactured with a defect, and this defect has resulted in the plaintiff's injuries, "the inference of negligence is practically irresistible." This inference is

---

199 See Granger J.'s judgment in *Rentway Can. Ltd./Ltée v. Laidlaw Transport Ltd.* (1989), 49 C.C.L.T. 150 (Ont. H.C.), affirmed (January 13, 1994), Doc. CA 16/90, C9877 (Ont. C.A.).

200 See discussion above.

201 Above, note 199.

202 The case dealt with whether the electrical circuit for a truck's headlights should have been designed so that the two lights were not on the same circuit. The court held that in view of the risks as compared to the costs of redesign, the system should have been redesigned. The action against the manufacturer was dismissed, however, due to lack of evidence of a causal connection between the negligent design and the accident. Also see *Tabrizi v. Whallon Machine Inc.* (1996), 29 C.C.L.T. (2d) 176 (B.C. S.C.), additional reasons at (1996), 4 C.P.C. (4th) 72 (B.C. S.C.), where a similar finding of liability was made based on a risk-utility analysis. Liability was also found in *Mayburry v. Ontario (Liquor Control Board)*, [2001] O.T.C. 271 (S.C.J.), affirmed (2002), [2002] O.J. No. 1177, 2002 CarswellOnt 1298 (C.A.). In this case, a beverage manufacturer was held liable for failing to design a bottle that would not be so explosive when dropped. The Court seemed particularly concerned that the defendant had not apparently expended any effort in attempting to reduce the risk. The defendant noted the rarity of the plaintiff's injury (only one in 9,000,000 sales). The plaintiff who dropped the bottle was held 60 per cent at fault.

203 A thorough discussion of the "risk-utility" approach is found in *Ragoonanan Estate v. Imperial Tobacco Canada Ltd.* (2001), 4 C.C.L.T. (3d) 132 (Ont. S.C.J.). This was a class action case against cigarette manufacturers alleging negligence in their failure to design a "fire safe cigarette"; i.e., cigarettes that were less likely to cause fires if left unattended. The court considered the factors that go into the risk-utility analysis and concluded that while a consumer's knowledge of the risks is an important factor in determining whether a manufacturer should be liable for a design defect, it is not the determinative factor. The court was not prepared to decide, in an application to dismiss the statement of claim, that a product is not defective merely because there is a known risk and the product would not be dangerous to a reasonably careful consumer. These factors did, however, certainly suggest no liability.

204 Waddams, *Products Liability*, 4th ed. (2002), at 67.

205 See, for example, *Meisel v. Tolko Industries Ltd.*, [1991] B.C.J. No. 105.

predicated upon proof that the defect was in the product when it left the manufacturer.[206]

Case law has held that a manufacturer of a product which uses a component part supplied by a third party remains responsible for a defect in that component.[207]

The issue of "intermediate examination" warrants attention. Where a product is used by the consumer without there having been the possibility of intermediate examination, liability of the manufacturer will readily follow.[208] What, however, of the case where the user could have examined the product before use, or even worse, where the user did examine the product, discovered the defect, but still decided to use it? It is suggested that the ordinary rules of negligence law are applicable to these cases. Thus, where the user's conduct was negligent, according to the standards of the reasonable consumer, contributory negligence should apply.[209] In more extreme cases, a plaintiff's conduct might be considered a new intervening act severing the chain of causation between the manufacturer's negligence and the ultimate injury.[210] It has also been held that the anticipated inspection and adaptation of a component part by an intermediary will exonerate the manufacturer of the component party from any liability to the ultimate user

---

206 See *Pacific Lumber & Shipping Co. v. Western Stevedoring Co.*, [1995] B.C.J. No. 866 (S.C.), a recent judgment which affirms this point. Edwards J. cites a leading Commonwealth authority: *Grant v. Australia Knitting Mills Ltd.*, [1936] A.C. 85 (P.C.). Also cited is *McMorran v. Dominion Stores Ltd.* (1977), 74 D.L.R. (3d) 186 (Ont. H.C.).

207 See *Farro v. Nutone Electrical Ltd.* (1990), 68 D.L.R. (4th) 268 (Ont. C.A.); and *Pacific Lumber & Shipping Co. v. Western Stevedoring Co.,* [1995] B.C.J. No. 866. See David, Draper, and Bawolska, "Tort Liability for Defective Components" (2007), Advocates' Quarterly 152. The authors argue that since product liability in Canada is based on negligence principles, a manufacturer should not be held liable for a defective component used in its product, unless there was fault on the manufacturer, with respect to its use of that defective part. This, for example, could be in terms of its selection of the supplier, its knowledge of the danger, or its duty to inspect the final product. Arguments that the manufacturer should be vicariously liable for the negligence of the supplier of the defective component, or that the duty on the manufacturer to reasonably manufacture a safe product should be a non-delegable one, are rejected by the authors. In principle, the authors are correct in arguing that Canadian product liability law is based on negligence. In practical terms, however, requiring a plaintiff to prove which component of the product was defective, who supplied it, and that its supplier was negligent, can be very onerous. As long as the plaintiff can prove that the product itself was defective, was negligently made, and put into circulation by its manufacturer in that state, should the manufacturer not be held responsible for it? It can then attempt to recover its damages from suppliers, presumably either through contract or tort.

208 A leading case on this point is *Smith v. Inglis Ltd.* (1978), 83 D.L.R. (3d) 215 (N.S. C.A.).

209 See, for example, *McCain Foods Ltd. v. Grand Falls Industries Ltd.* (1991), 80 D.L.R. (4th) 252 (N.B. C.A.). The court held that the user of a second hand truck with a crane ought to have made a reasonable inspection of the vehicle before using it. The inspection would have disclosed the defects. Rather than exonerating the manufacturer, the court apportioned the fault between the parties.

210 The case of *Saunders v. Bitz*, [1989] B.C.J. No. 1846 (S.C.) illustrates the point. The defendant purchased a "kit car", put it together, and raced it for two years. He then sold it to the plaintiff. It was clear that the plaintiff was going to work on the car, and adapt it for his own use as a "hot rod", for highway use. After conversion of the car, a problem with the rear suspension caused an accident. Even assuming that this was the result of a defect in a part which the defendant had installed originally, the court placed full responsibility for seeing that the car was safe onto the plaintiff.

of the final product. The Alberta Court of Appeal held that in this case there is no duty owed by the manufacturer of the component part to the ultimate consumer since it is not reasonably foreseeable that the consumer will use the part without prior inspection and adaptation if necessary.[211] It must be underlined, however, that there ought to be no mystique to the concept of "intermediate examination" in product liability cases.

(iii) Marketing

Even if due care was exercised in the design and manufacture of a product, a manufacturer can be held liable for failing to adequately warn the consumer of the appropriate use of the product or the risks associated with its use. This duty is stated to be a basic one involved in the manufacture of a product, stemming from *Donoghue v. Stevenson*.[212] The duty to warn is owed to "all those who may reasonably be affected by potentially dangerous products. . .even those persons who are not party to the contract of sale".[213]

The duty to warn of risks extends not only to dangers which are inherent in the ordinary, intended use of a product, but to risks which flow from the foreseeable

---

211 *Viridian Inc. v. Dresser Canada Inc.* (2002), 216 D.L.R. (4th) 122, 12 C.C.L.T. (3d) 135 (Alta. C.A.).

212 See *Buchan v. Ortho Pharmaceutical (Can.) Ltd.* (1986), 35 C.C.L.T. 1 at 12 (Ont. C.A.). Another case affirming the duty to warn of risks is *Chase v. Goodyear Tire & Rubber Co.* (1991), 115 N.B.R. (2d) 181 (Q.B.). The leading Canadian authority on the duty to warn is the Supreme Court of Canada's judgment in *Lambert v. Lastoplex Chemicals Co.*, [1972] S.C.R. 569 at 574-75:

> Where manufactured products are put on the market for ultimate purchase and use by the general public and carry danger (in this case, by reason of high inflammability), although put to the use for which they are intended, the manufacturer, knowing of their hazardous nature, has a duty to specify the attendant dangers, which it must be taken to appreciate in a detail not known to the ordinary consumer or user.

The Supreme Court extensively dealt with the duty to inform of risks in *Hollis v. Birch*, [1996] 2 W.W.R. 77 and *Bow Valley Husky (Bermuda) Ltd. v. Saint John Shipbuilding Ltd.* (1997), 153 D.L.R. (4th) 385 (S.C.C.). The duty to warn was imposed upon a fishing lodge with respect to problems its guests were encountering with boats provided to them by the lodge, in *Cuppen v. Queen Charlotte Lodge Ltd.* (2005), 32 C.C.L.T. (3d) 103 (B.C. S.C.), affirmed. (2006), 43 C.C.L.T. (3d) 254 (B.C. C.A.). Although the defendant was not the manufacturer of the boats, the duty imposed by the court was drawn from the product liability jurisprudence. Alternative theories of liability arguably existed such as contract, innkeeper's liability, or occupier's liability. The court also considered provisions of the Marine Liability Act, S.C. 2001, c. 6.

213 McLachlin J. in *Bow Valley Husky (Bermuda) Ltd. v. Saint John Shipbuilding Ltd.* (1997), 153 D.L.R. (4th) 385 (S.C.C.) at 397. McLachlin J. noted that as long as the potential user was "reasonably foreseeable", a duty to warn exists. For an interesting Quebec case on the duty to warn see *Létourneau c. Impérial Tobacco Ltée* (1998), 162 D.L.R. (4th) 734 (C.Q.). An action brought by a smoker against a cigarette manufacturer for failing to warn of the danger of addiction to cigarettes was dismissed. The Court reviewed the legal basis for the duty to warn under Quebec law.

use of the product, even if these uses were not intended by the manufacturer.[214] There need not be warnings, however, of a risk of danger which is "so obvious and apparent that anyone would be aware of it."[215] Thus, for example, the dangers posed by moving feed rolls which drew into them any objects with which they came into contact, was so evident to any user of the machine, that a warning was unnecessary.[216]

The question has been raised as to whether the user's knowledge of the risks should be seen in the context of a factor which negates the manufacturer's duty to warn, or in the context of a defence to the action, in the form of *volenti*. In *Bow Valley Huskey (Bermuda) Ltd. v. Saint John Shipbuilding Ltd.*,[217] it was suggested by the Newfoundland Court of Appeal and confirmed by the Supreme Court of Canada that the matter should be treated as one of *volenti*.[218] I would suggest that this must depend upon the nature of the risk. If the risk would be so obvious to the user that no reasonable manufacturer would warn of it, there ought to be no duty to warn.[219] For risks, however, which are not so readily obvious, there ought to be a duty. Liability of the manufacturer could then be reduced, however, by

---

214 See Lacourcière J.A.'s judgment in *Deshane v. Deere & Co.* (1993), 17 C.C.L.T. (2d) 130 (Ont. C.A.). Although Lacourcière J.A. was dissenting, the majority of the Court of Appeal agreed with the principles enunciated in his judgment. On the duty to warn of risks emanating from unintended uses of a product, Galligan J.A. stated at 17 C.C.L.T. (2d) 149: "I do not doubt that cases could arise where a manufacturer's knowledge of the use of a product in a fashion for which it had not been designed would call for a warning about the danger posed by such a use." For a recent case that applied this principle, see *Holowaty v. Bourgault Industries Ltd.*, [2007] 5 W.W.R. 638 (Sask. Q.B.).

215 *Deshane v. Deere & Co.* (1993), 17 C.C.L.T. (2d) 130 at 147, per Galligan J.A. for the majority. Also see *Piche v. Lecours Lumber Co.*, [1993] O.J. No. 1686 (Gen. Div.); *Tabrizi v. Whallon Machine Inc.* (1996), 29 C.C.L.T. (2d) 176 (B.C. S.C.), additional reasons at (1996), 4 C.P.C. (4th) 72 (B.C. S.C.); *Thomson v. Cosgrove* (1998), [1998] B.C.J. No. 789; and *Rozenhart v. Skier's Sport Shop (Edmonton) Ltd.* (2002), [2003] 5 W.W.R. 534 (Alta. Q.B.), affirmed [2004] 9 W.W.R. 527 (Alta. C.A.).

216 See *Deshane v. Deere*, above, note 214.

217 (1997), 40 C.C.L.T. (2d) 235 (S.C.C.), affirming as to this point (1995), 126 D.L.R. (4th) 1 (Nfld. C.A.).

218 According to McLachlin J.:

> Liability for failure to warn is based not merely on a knowledge imbalance. It is based primarily on the manufacture or supply of products intended for the use of others and the reliance that consumers reasonably place on the manufacturer and supplier. Unless the consumer's knowledge negates reasonable reliance, the manufacturer or supplier remains liable. This occurs where the consumer has so much knowledge that a reasonable person would conclude that the consumer fully appreciated and willingly assumed the risk posed by the use of the product, making the maxim *volenti non fit injuria* applicable. ((1997), 40 C.C.L.T. (2d) 235 (S.C.C.) at 248.)

This was not found to be the case on the facts.

219 This argument is accepted by the Court of Appeal itself in *Bow Valley*, *ibid.*, at 26, when it is stated in the judgment that "this case does not fall into that category of cases where the dangers of use or misuse are so apparent or well known to the ordinary prudent person that a warning is unnecessary in law".

the plaintiff's own negligence in using the product, despite its knowledge of the risks,[220] or even negated altogether by the defence of *volenti*.[221]

The duty to warn has been termed a "continuing one" which can be "triggered by information that became known after the product had been in use."[222] It has been stated that this duty is owed not only by a manufacturer of goods, but may extend to others, such as distributors, installers and repairers.[223] The duty is predicated upon the requirement that the defendant knew or ought to have known of the dangers associated with the product.[224] The warning "must be reasonably communicated, and must clearly describe any specific dangers that arise from the ordinary use of the product. . . ."[225] Where warnings are given by means of labels, it has been stated that the test of their adequacy is whether they were "fair and

---

220 In *Bow Valley*, the plaintiff was held contributorily negligent. The contributory negligence did not relate, however, to its use of the product in disregard of the specific risks of its flammability, of which it was unaware, but due to its failure to have installed a ground fault circuit breaker.

221 See discussion of defences in Chapter 13. As will be discussed, *volenti* is very difficult to establish. Thus to impose a duty on manufacturers to warn of all risks, even those that are obvious, and to force the manufacturer to rely on the defence of *volenti* would, in my opinion, be unreasonably onerous.

222 See *Bow Valley Huskey (Bermuda) Ltd. v. Saint John Shipbuilding Ltd.*, above, note 217, at 24. Also see La Forest J. in *Hollis v. Birch*, above, note 212:

> The duty to warn is a continuing duty, requiring manufacturers to warn not only of dangers known at the time of sale, but also of dangers discovered after the product has been sold and delivered. . . .

In *Walford (Litigation Guardian of) v. Jacuzzi Canada Inc.* (2005), [2005] O.J. No. 1376, 2005 CarswellOnt 1392 (S.C.J.), additional reasons at (2005), 2005 CarswellOnt 7742 (S.C.J.), reversed (2007), [2007] O.J. No. 4053, 2007 CarswellOnt 6736 (Ont. C.A.), leave to appeal refused (2008), 2008 CarswellOnt 1860 (S.C.C.), the continuing duty was said to embrace warning label requirements that only came into effect after the product was manufactured and sold. The court held that the manufacturer had a duty to ensure that products, in this case water slides, manufactured before the new regulations came into effect were retrofitted with the new labels. The action was dismissed, however, based on lack of causation. The plaintiff also sued the pool store that sold her some parts needed to install the slide, which had been purchased elsewhere. The plaintiff alleged that the store's employee was negligent in misrepresenting that it was "okay" to use the slide on her pool. The trial judge dismissed this claim as well, on the basis that this was not a negligent statement. It was truthful and not misleading or inaccurate. The Court of Appeal allowed an appeal by the plaintiff against the store. Feldman J.A. for the majority found that the pool employee's statement was misleading and was negligently made. Rouleau J.A. dissented. Not only was he not prepared to reverse the trial judge on findings of fact, but he noted that the standard to be applied to a vendor of replacement parts for a product which it neither manufactured nor sold was a lower standard of care.

223 See *Bow Valley Huskey v. Saint John Shipbuilding*, above, note 217, at 24, and the numerous cases cited therein.

224 Thus, for example, in *Moore v. Cooper Can. Ltd.* (1990), 2 C.C.L.T. (2d) 57 (Ont. H.C.), the action was dismissed since the defendant, a manufacturer of hockey helmets, neither knew of the danger nor could reasonably have been expected to know of it. An opposite conclusion was reached in *Smithson v. Saskem Chemicals Ltd.* (1985), 34 C.C.L.T. 195 (Sask. Q.B.) where the court held that the defendants ought to have realized the risks.

225 La Forest J., in *Hollis v. Birch*, above, note 212. La Forest J. further held that the degree of specificity of the warning depends upon the significance of the dangers at risk. The case dealt with a breast implant, which, similar to other medical products that are either ingested or implanted, involves substantial risks to their users.

reasonable in the circumstances."[226] This means that although "warnings are not required to be perfect", they "are required to address dangers that are inherent, or arise from the use of the product in certain circumstances."[227] Warnings need not be given of "the possibility of injury that is remote."[228]

In the case of products which are sold or otherwise conveyed to consumers by means of a doctor, or other intermediary, the "learned intermediary" rule applies. This happens, for example, with relation to prescription drugs, or breast implants. There have been two significant Canadian cases on the "learned intermediary" defence as it relates to medical products. The first is *Buchan v. Ortho Pharmaceutical (Can.) Ltd.*[229] This case involved a commonly prescribed drug — the birth control pill. The plaintiff suffered from one of the risks of the pill, and sued the drug's manufacturer for having failed to warn her of these risks. The case for failure to inform proceeded along two alternative theories. The first was that the warning should have been given directly to the consumer, notwithstanding the fact that the drug could only be obtained by prescription. The second was that the learned intermediary rule applied, and that, accordingly, as long as adequate advice and information was given to the prescribing doctor, it could be assumed by the manufacturer that the information would be passed on to the consumer.

Robins J.A. noted the characteristics of the duty to warn of risks. The warning must be clear and understandable as to the nature and extent of the risk. The adequacy of the warning is commensurate with the gravity of the risk of danger. The warning must not be neutralized or negated by collateral efforts by the manufacturer.[230] The duty to warn continues after the product is sold, and extends to new dangers later discovered.[231]

Robins J.A. applied the learned intermediary rule to this case. Since prescription drugs cannot be purchased independently by a consumer, the law allows a manufacturer to assume that the information concerning the product which it conveys to the intermediary will be communicated to the consumer by the intermediary. Thus, an adequate warning or other information given to the intermediary will satisfy the manufacturer's duty to the ultimate consumer. In the case of *Ortho Pharmaceutical*, however, Robins J.A. concluded that the warning and information given to physicians was inadequate and the company was held negligent.[232]

---

226 *Moran v. Wyeth-Ayerst Canada Inc.* (2004), [2005] 1 W.W.R. 716 (Alta. Q.B.), citing several authorities for this proposition. The case concerned warnings concerning the use of pesticides on crops. Liability was found for inadequate warnings.

227 *Ibid.*

228 *Ibid.*

229 (1986), 25 D.L.R. (4th) 658 (Ont. C.A.).

230 Robins J.A. quoted Laskin J. from *Lambert v. Lastoplex Chemicals Co.*, [1972] S.C.R. 569, a leading authority on the duty to warn of the attendant dangers of a product.

231 *Rivtow Marine Ltd. v. Washington Iron Works*, [1974] S.C.R. 1189 was cited as authority for this proposition. One must recall, however, that *Rivtow Marine* involved a highly specialized product, with few users, all of whom were known to the manufacturer and distributor.

232 In *obiter*, Robins J.A. considered whether the learned intermediary rule, while applicable to most prescription drugs, should apply to birth control pills. He concluded that birth control pills differ in certain important respects from other prescription drugs, and that information concerning them should be provided directly to women. Patient involvement in choosing to take birth control pills is high, and it is both feasible and desirable to provide information

The Supreme Court of Canada dealt extensively with the learned intermediary rule in *Hollis v. Birch*.[233] The defendant manufacturer was sued for failing to warn the plaintiff of the risk that her silicone breast implant could rupture.[234] The Court of Appeal had applied the "learned intermediary" rule in this case, found that inadequate information had been provided to the physician by the manufacturer, and that the duty was breached.[235] The manufacturer appealed to the Supreme Court.

La Forest J., writing for the majority of the court, stated that the learned intermediary rule is applied either where a product "is highly technical in nature and is intended to be used only under the supervision of experts, or where the nature of the product is such that the consumer will not realistically receive a direct warning from the manufacturer before using the product."[236] In this case, the manufacturer can discharge its duty to inform the consumer by informing the learned intermediary. La Forest J. held, as had the Court of Appeal, that adequate information had not been given to the learned intermediary in this case.[237]

As will be discussed in Chapter 11, causation is a major element of a successful negligence claim. A negligent defendant cannot be held liable and be required to compensate a plaintiff for injuries which were not caused by the defendant's wrongdoing. Put into the context of the duty to inform or warn of risks, where a duty to inform of risks has been breached, the plaintiff must prove that had the information been given, the injury would have been avoided. In the context of the doctor's duty to disclose the risks of treatment, for example, the plaintiff must prove that had there been disclosure, the plaintiff, acting as a "reasonable patient", would have declined the treatment.[238] Where the defendant has a duty to inform

---

directly to them. The action against the manufacturer succeeded in this case. Unlike failure to inform in medical treatment cases, where an objective test of causation is used, Robins J.A. applied a subjective test of causation. It concluded that the trial judge was correct in finding that the plaintiff herself would not have taken the pill had she been informed of its risks. Also see discussion below in relation to *Hollis v. Birch*.

233 Above, note 212. For a subsequent case dealing with a class action application for injuries caused by breast implants, see *Harrington v. Dow Corning Corp.* (1996), 31 C.C.L.T. (2d) 48 (B.C. S.C.), affirmed (2000), 2 C.C.L.T. (3d) 157 (B.C. C.A.), leave to appeal refused (2001), 276 N.R. 200 (note) (S.C.C.). The Court developed a list of questions common to all plaintiffs in this type of action and granted the application for a class action.

234 The plaintiff had alleged as well that the manufacture of the implant was negligent. This was accepted at trial, but reversed on appeal, and did not form part of the appeal to the Supreme Court.

235 The Court of Appeal did not follow *Buchan v. Ortho Pharmaceutical* on the test of causation, and applied the objective test. Even on this basis, however, causation was made out.

236 [1996] 2 W.W.R. 77, 1995 CarswellBC 967, 1995 CarswellBC 1152 (S.C.C.) at 95 [W.W.R.].

237 Also see the Supreme Court of Canada's decision in *Bow Valley Husky (Bermuda) Ltd. v. Saint John Shipbuilding Ltd.* (1997), 153 D.L.R. (4th) 385 (S.C.C.). The defendant supplier argued that it had fulfilled its duty to warn the owner of an oilrig of the flammability of a component of the rig, by warning the rig builder. The rig builder was knowledgeable about this matter and could have advised the owner of the danger or have taken steps to deal with the problem. McLachlin J. rejected this "learned intermediary" defence finding that the product in question was not a highly technical product, that there was direct contact between the supplier and the owner, and that it was not unrealistic to expect the supplier to have advised the owner directly.

238 See discussion in Chapter 10, below.

users of a product of the risks posed by the product, the plaintiff has to prove that had these risks been known, the plaintiff would have avoided the accident.[239]

What the test of causation is with respect to the learned intermediary rule was very much in issue in *Hollis v. Birch*. The majority of the court, per La Forest J., held that where a manufacturer is in breach of its duty to inform the consumer of the risks of a product, by failing to inform the learned intermediary, the plaintiff proves that injury resulted from the breach, by establishing, on a *subjective* test, that the product would not have been used had the warnings been disclosed to the learned intermediary. This departs from the ordinary "reasonable patient" test, applicable in failure to inform cases against doctors.[240]

An additional causation issue arises in the learned intermediary situation. Must the plaintiff prove that, had the information been communicated by the manufacturer to the learned intermediary, that the learned intermediary would have passed along the information to the plaintiff? The majority of the Supreme Court answered "no". La Forest J. held that disclosure to the intermediary will irrefutably be presumed to be disclosure to the consumer.[241]

Sopinka J. disagreed. Emphasizing the importance of the causation element for a successful negligence action, Sopinka J. held that where the evidence establishes that the learned intermediary would not have communicated the information to the patient, even if the manufacturer had adequately disclosed it to the learned intermediary, there is no causal connection between the manufacturer's negligence and the plaintiff's injury, and the action against the manufacturer must accordingly be dismissed.

The causation issue raised in the Supreme Court's judgment is intriguing. There is a difficulty with both the majority and minority judgments, if traditional causation language or standards of proof are applied to the case. The problem with the majority judgment is that a manufacturer can be held liable for damage which it did not factually cause, where there is evidence that the learned intermediary

---

239 This has not been an issue in any of the recent cases. However, in *Bow Valley Husky (Bermuda) Ltd. v. Saint John Shipbuilding Ltd.* (1997), 153 D.L.R. (4th) 385 (S.C.C.), the defendants' duty to the plaintiffs, who were the users but not the owners of an oil rig, was to warn them of the flammability of the product. The unstated assumption in the case was that had the plaintiffs known of these risks, they would have been able to take steps to avoid the fire. It is unclear, however, what exactly the plaintiffs would or could have done had they been advised of the risk of fire.

240 See discussion in Chapter 10. Sopinka J., concurred in by McLachlin J., dissented. Sopinka J. supported the use of the objective test in failure to inform cases against doctors, and could see no reason to use a different test in actions against manufacturers. See D.W. Boivin, "Factual Causation in the Law of Manufacturer Failure to Warn" (1998-99), 30 Ottawa L. Rev. 47. In his article, Professor Boivin distinguishes between "injury causation", i.e., was the injury caused by the defendant's product, and "decision causation", i.e., was the plaintiff's decision to use the product influenced by what the defendant said or failed to say about it. Although the article focuses on *Hollis*, it offers a broad discussion on "decision causation". Another insightful article on decision causation is Vaughan Black, "Decision Causation: Pandora's Tool-Box" in Neyers, Pitel, Chamberlain, eds., *Emerging Issues in Tort Law* (2007), Chapter 12.

241 La Forest J. made it clear that even the "probability" that the learned intermediary would not have advised the patient of the warnings, does not absolve the manufacturer of its responsibility. There could be apportionment of fault between them.

would not have communicated the information to the patient, even if the learned intermediary was informed of it.[242] The difficulty with the minority approach is that a plaintiff will fail in both its action against the manufacturer and against the doctor, where there is evidence that the manufacturer failed to provide adequate information to the learned intermediary, but that the learned intermediary would not have passed along the information, even if informed. The action against the manufacturer will fail due to lack of proof of causation. The action against the learned intermediary will fail due to lack of proof of negligence.[243] Thus, an innocent plaintiff will "fall between the cracks." As we will discuss in Chapter 11, the solution in this type of case is to alter the language of causation, or the manner of proving it, in order to provide justice to the victim.[244]

(d) Problems of Proof

In addition to proving duty and breach, a plaintiff in a product liability case must prove that damage was caused. As will be discussed in Chapter 14, and as we have just seen in relation to the "learned intermediary" rule, product liability cases may present difficult challenges in this respect. In recognition of this fact, evidentiary techniques, such as the doctrine of *res ipsa loquitur*,[245] frequently have been employed in product liability actions.

(e) Economic Losses

The ordinary product liability action involves personal injury or property damage suffered by a user or foreseeable third party as a result of a defective product. As we have seen, however, negligence law has made some inroads into the area of recovery of economic losses suffered by purchasers of shoddy products. This area was discussed above in Chapter 7.

---

242 See the discussion of the "but for" test in Chapter 11. If the learned intermediary would not have communicated the warning to the consumer even if it had the information, the manufacturer's negligence in not informing the learned intermediary is causally unconnected to the patient's decision to use the product.

243 After all, the learned intermediary cannot be negligent for failing to pass on information which it did not have.

244 For example, by arguing that the manufacturer's failure to inform "increased the risk" that the plaintiff would not be informed. Or, by drawing a strong inference that the plaintiff would have been informed. In *Walker Estate v. York-Finch General Hospital* (2001), 198 D.L.R. (4th) 193 (S.C.C.), one of the issues was whether a blood donor, whose blood was infected with the AIDS virus, would have donated blood had different screening measures been used. The trial judge [(1997), 39 C.C.L.T. (2d) 1 (Ont. Gen. Div.)] decided that the donor would still have given blood. The Court of Appeal [(1999) 169 D.L.R. (4th) 689 (Ont. C.A.)] disagreed and held that there was an irrefutable presumption that the donor would not have given blood. The Supreme Court of Canada decided that the failure to have better screening measures "materially contributed" to the fact that the donor gave blood. It is obvious that this issue is complicated. See discussion in Chapter 11. For useful commentary, see V. Black, "Case Comment: *Walker Estate v. York-Finch General Hospital*" (2001), 24 Advocates' Q. 478.

245 See the discussion on the status of this doctrine in Canada in Chapter 14.

10
Professional Negligence

1. INTRODUCTION

The law relating to the liability of professionals for injuries caused by them in the course of their practices gives rise to numerous issues.[1] This chapter will look at the topic of professional malpractice as it relates to the action in negligence, and more particularly, the standard of care issue, and will highlight some of the current issues which have been debated in the cases.

2. CONCURRENT LIABILITY

Prior to 1986, the nature of the action which a client could bring against certain kinds of professionals was a controversial question in Canadian law.[2] It was clear that a client's action against certain types of professionals, for example doctors and dentists, could be based either in contract or in tort,[3] for the negligent perfor-

---

1 There have been several textbooks on the subject. See, e.g., Jackson and Powell, *Professional Negligence*, 4th ed. (1997); Partlett, *Professional Negligence* (1985); Dugdale and Stanton, *Professional Negligence*, 3rd ed. (1998); Picard and Robertson, *Legal Liability of Doctors and Hospitals in Canada*, 4th ed. (2007); Grant and Rothstein, *Lawyers' Professional Liability*, 2d ed. (1998); and Knoppers (ed.), *Professional Liability in Canada* (1988).

2 The great number of cases and academic commentary indicated the extent of the debate. See Rafferty, "The Tortious Liability of Professionals to Their Contractual Clients", in Steel and Rodgers-Magnet (eds.), *Issues in Tort Law* (1983), at 243, for a good list of cases and articles on the topic.

3 The issue of whether an action against a doctor can be brought either in contract or tort and the implications of this has been raised in the cases. In *de la Giroday v. Brough,* [1997] 6 W.W.R. 585 (B.C. C.A.), leave to appeal refused (1997), 102 B.C.A.C. 238 (note) (S.C.C.), the Court held that since an action against a doctor could be based in contract, damages for loss of an opportunity to avoid an injury might be recoverable, even if they cannot be recoverable in tort. In a subsequent judgment, *Oliver (Guardian ad litem of) v. Ellison*, [2001] 7 W.W.R. 677 (B.C. C.A.), leave to appeal refused (2001), 170 B.C.A.C. 320 (note) (S.C.C.), the issue was also raised, again in relation to damage assessment. A mother whose child was born with disabilities as a result of medical negligence during the pregnancy and delivery process was claiming, among other heads, damages for her mental distress. The trial judge disallowed the claim for mental distress. The majority of the Court of Appeal affirmed, holding that these damages were not recoverable in tort. The majority also refused to consider whether a contract claim would produce a different result, since contract had not been argued at trial. The dissenting judge, Southin J.A.,

mance of their professional services. Curiously, however, a client's action against other professionals, notably solicitors, accountants, architects and engineers, was, in the opinion of many courts, restricted to contract.[4] This position had been taken in England, for example in relation to solicitors, in the case of *Groom v. Crocker*,[5] and it persisted even after *Hedley Byrne* gave a claim in tort to those who stood in no contractual relationship with a solicitor.[6] This approach was followed by many Canadian courts. For example, in *Schwebel v. Telekes*,[7] it was held that an action against a notary public could be founded in contract alone.[8] At the same

---

provided a detailed and scholarly historical review of the liability of doctors and other professionals, founded either in *assumpsit* or case. She agreed that the action could be based in contract and would have awarded damages for mental distress. Let us also recall that a fiduciary relationship may also exist between doctor and patient. See, e.g., *Norberg v. Wynrib* (1990), 66 D.L.R. (4th) 553, affirming 44 C.C.L.T. 184 (B.C. C.A.). In *Chaster (Guardian ad litem of) v. LeBlanc* (2007), 51 C.C.L.T. (3d) 131 (B.C. S.C.), additional reasons at (2008), 2008 CarswellBC 60 (S.C.), although a tort action against a lawyer was dismissed due to lack of damage, the contract action was upheld with an award of $1,000.

4 There may also be a breach of a fiduciary duty. There have been numerous solicitor-client cases involving breach of fiduciary duty. See Viscount Haldane's judgment in *Nocton v. Lord Ashburton*, [1914] A.C. 932 (H.L.) and the Supreme Court of Canada's judgments in *Canson Enterprises v. Boughton* (1991), 85 D.L.R. (4th) 129, 9 C.C.L.T. (2d) 1 (S.C.C.) and *3464920 Canada Inc. v. Strother* (2007), 48 C.C.L.T. (3d) 1 (S.C.C.). Cases of breach of fiduciary duty between solicitor and client include *Martin v. Goldfarb* (1997), 31 B.L.R. (2d) 265 (Ont. Gen. Div.), reversed (1998), 41 O.R. (3d) 161 (C.A.), leave to appeal refused (1999), 123 O.A.C. 199 (note) (S.C.C.); and *Lemieux v. Gibney-McCullough* (2001), 55 O.R. (3d) 520 (S.C.J.); but see *Girardet v. Crease* (1987), 11 B.C.L.R. (2d) 361 (S.C.) In *Girardet*, Southin J., at 362, condemned the casual use of the concept of fiduciary relationships, noting that not every breach by a solicitor constitutes a breach of fiduciary duty. There must be "the stench of dishonesty—if not of deceit, then of constructive fraud." A discussion of this matter is found in *Stewart v. Canadian Broadcasting Corp.* (1997), 150 D.L.R. (4th) 24 (Ont. Gen. Div.), additional reasons at (1997), 152 D.L.R. (4th) 102 (Ont. Gen. Div.). Also see *Fraser Park South Estates Ltd. v. Lang Michener Lawrence & Shaw* (1999), [1999] B.C.J. No. 150, 1999 CarswellBC 130 (S.C.), affirmed (2001), 84 B.C.L.R. (3d) 65 (C.A.), leave to appeal refused (2001), 161 B.C.A.C. 320 (note) (S.C.C.), where there was negligence but it did not amount to a breach of a fiduciary duty; and *Threemor Enterprises Ltd. v. Parente, Borean*, [2000] O.T.C. 282 (S.C.J.), where the court stresses that not every breach of contract or negligence will amount to a breach of fiduciary duty. In *Barrett v. Reynolds* (1998), 170 N.S.R. (2d) 201 (C.A.), leave to appeal refused (1999), 183 N.S.R. (2d) 198 (note) (S.C.C.), the Court of Appeal considered *Giradet v. Crease* but concluded that a solicitor who acted for both sides of a real estate transaction breached a fiduciary duty owed to the vendors despite the fact that there was no fraudulent or dishonest conduct on his part. Attempting to represent both vendor and purchaser ultimately led to his breaching a fiduciary duty that he owed to them. Also see *Hussey v. Parsons* (1997), [1997] N.J. No. 99, 1996 CarswellNfld 324 (T.D.). See L.I. Rotman, "Balancing the Scales of Justice: Fiduciary Obligations & *Stewart v. C.B.C.*" (1999), 78 Can. Bar. Rev. 445 for an excellent discussion of the principles of fiduciary law as they relate to professional negligence cases.

5 [1939] 1 K.B. 194 (C.A.).

6 Rafferty, above, note 2, cites other cases such as *Clark v. Kirby-Smith*, [1964] Ch. 506; and *Bagot v. Stevens Scanlan & Co.*, [1966] 1 Q.B. 197.

7 [1967] 1 O.R. 541 (C.A.).

8 There have been several judgments which have taken the contract only approach. For those regarding solicitors, see *Banks v. Reid* (1974), 6 O.R. (2d) 404 (H.C.), reversed on other grounds (1977), 4 C.C.L.T. 1 (C.A.); *Gouzenko v. Harris* (1976), 13 O.R. (2d) 730 (H.C.); *Messineo v. Beale* (1978), 5 C.C.L.T. 235 (Ont. C.A.); *Royal Bank v. Clark* (1978), 88 D.L.R. (3d) 76 (N.B. C.A.), affirmed 105 D.L.R. (3d) 85 (S.C.C.); *Melanson v. Leger* (1978), 24 N.B.R. (2d) 632 (Q.B.). For cases regarding architects and engineers, see *Bagot v. Stevens Scanlan & Co.*, above,

time, however, there were a significant, and growing, number of judgments which accepted a concurrent liability approach to the question of professional malpractice. Accordingly, a claimant's action could be based on either tort or contract, whichever was to the claimant's advantage. This occurred primarily in relation to solicitors,[9] and in relation to other professionals as well.[10]

The historical basis for the debate over the concurrent liability issue has been well analyzed by others.[11] Judicial developments in both Canada and England have now settled the issue and have adopted the concurrent liability approach.[12]

It was in England where the position that a client could sue a professional either in tort or in contract was first firmly accepted. The case of *Midland Bank Trust Co. v. Hett, Stubbs & Kemp*[13] concerned the applicable limitation period for a negligence action brought by a client against a solicitor.[14] In a decision which thoroughly reviewed the jurisprudence on the question of concurrent liability, Oliver J. decided that, whatever was the correct law before the House of Lords decided *Hedley Byrne*, it is clear that since *Hedley Byrne*, tort liability will arise from a relationship created by the assumption of responsibility, regardless of whether that relationship arose in a contractual context or not. Oliver J. held further that this is so not only in relation to the negligent misrepresentation cases, but where any service is undertaken, and is performed carelessly or not at all. Although this reasoning was certainly sufficient to dispose of *Groom v. Crocker*,[15] and other pre-*Hedley Byrne* decisions, Oliver J. was forced to contend with the post-*Hedley Byrne* judgments which continued to follow *Groom v. Crocker*.[16] Mr. Justice Oliver refused to follow these cases, and justified this approach by reference primarily to the Court of Appeal's decision in *Esso Petroleum Co. v.*

---

note 6; *Terrace Sch. Dist. No. 53 v. Berwick* (1963), 42 W.W.R. 25 (B.C. S.C.). The contract only approach is in a large measure attributable in Canada, to Pigeon J., who strongly presented this view in *J. Nunes Diamonds Ltd. v. Dom. Elec. Protection Co.*, [1972] S.C.R. 769, and reaffirmed it in *Smith v. McInnis* (1978), 4 C.C.L.T. 154 (S.C.C.).

9 See, e.g., *Jacobson Ford-Mercury Sales Ltd. v. Sivertz* (1979), 10 C.C.L.T. 274 (B.C. S.C.); *Power v. Halley* (1978), 88 D.L.R. (3d) 381 (Nfld. T.D.); *Doiron v. Caisse Populaire d'Inkerman Ltée* (1985), 17 D.L.R. (4th) 660 (N.B. C.A.); *Ferris v. Rusnak* (1983), 9 D.L.R. (4th) 183 (Alta. Q.B.); *Bank of N.S. v. Terry* (1982), 141 D.L.R. (3d) 438 (Ont. H.C.), reversed on other grounds (1984), 9 D.L.R. (4th) 101 (Ont. C.A.); *Nielsen v. Watson* (1981), 125 D.L.R. (3d) 326 (Ont. H.C.).

10 See, e.g., re engineers and architects, *Consumers Glass Co. v. Foundation Co. of Can.* (1985), 33 C.C.L.T. 104 (Ont. C.A.); *John Maryon Int. Ltd. v. N.B. Tel. Co.* (1982), 141 D.L.R. (3d) 193 (N.B. C.A.); *Dabous v. Zuliani* (1976), 68 D.L.R. (3d) 414 (Ont. C.A.); and *Dom. Chain Co. v. Eastern Const. Co.* (1976), 68 D.L.R. (3d) 385 (Ont. C.A.), affirmed (1978), 4 C.C.L.T. 143 (*sub nom. Giffels Assoc. Ltd. v. Eastern Const. Co.*) (S.C.C.).

11 See Rafferty, above, note 2, and the many articles cited by him. A very useful article is Kaye, "The Liability of Solicitors in Tort" (1984), 100 L.Q.R. 680.

12 As stated by one commentator, the perennial debate concerning concurrent liability has "at long last" been laid to rest. The concurrent liability thesis "has conclusively triumphed." See Irvine, "Annotation" (1986), 37 C.C.L.T. 119.

13 [1979] Ch. 384.

14 The issue of concurrent liability is generally raised when a limitation issue, a damage issue, or a contributory negligence/contribution issue is involved, since, otherwise, it will generally not matter whether the client's action is in tort or contract.

15 Above, note 5.

16 For example, *Clark v. Kirby-Smith*, [1964] Ch. 506; and *Bagot v. Stevens Scanlan & Co.*, [1966] 1 Q.B. 197.

Mardon,[17] a judgment which, according to Oliver J., clearly accepted the concurrent liability thesis.[18] This view has since been followed in England,[19] and thus the concurrent liability approach prevails.[20]

The law in Canada remained unsettled until 1986, when the Supreme Court rendered its judgment in *Central & Eastern Trust Co. v. Rafuse*.[21] As with *Midland Bank*, the issue concerned the applicable limitation period in a client's negligence action against a solicitor. In a thorough judgment, which comprehensively reviewed the previous authorities, Mr. Justice Le Dain came to the following conclusions. First, a common law duty of care in tort will arise as a result of a sufficient relationship of sufficent proximity, as defined by the cases,[22] and it is unimportant whether this relationship arises in a contractual or non-contractual setting. Second, the scope of the duty of care in tort must not depend on the specific contractual obligations. Third, liability in tort will not be permitted if its effect would be to allow the plaintiff to circumvent or escape a contractual exclusion or limitation of liability clause with respect to the act or omission which also constitutes the tort. In this respect, issues of contributory negligence, damage assessments, or statutory limitation periods will not be considered to be contractual exclusions or limitations of contractual liability which forbid the use of tort law, even though they might operate differently in the two causes of action.[23] If, however, the contract contains express terms relating to these matters, the plaintiff will be bound by them.[24] Mr. Justice Le Dain made it clear that this principle of

17 [1976] Q.B. 801.

18 Oliver J. also referred to *Arenson v. Casson Beckman, Rutley & Co.*, [1977] A.C. 405 (H.L.), and *Batty v. Metro. Property Realisations*, [1978] 2 All E.R. 445 (C.A.). The latter case clearly supported Oliver J. although it was not reported at the time Oliver J. wrote his judgment and did not have an overt influence on Oliver J.'s judgment.

19 For example, in *Ross v. Caunters*, [1980] Ch. 297.

20 In *Henderson v. Merrett Syndicates Ltd.*, [1994] 3 W.L.R. 761, the English House of Lords, per Lord Goff, finally laid to rest any lingering doubts. Oliver J.'s judgment in *Midland Bank Trust Co.* was accepted, and the concurrent liability approach adopted. The action was brought by underwriting members against underwriting agents. Lord Goff extensively reviewed the authorities in England, France, Canada and elsewhere, as well as Oliver J.'s judgment, and the criticisms against it, particularly by Kaye, above, note 11, in arriving at his decision.

21 (1986), 37 C.C.L.T. 117 (S.C.C.). See Charles, "Torts and Contract — Merging Areas?" (1987), 8 Advocates' Q. 222; Caplan and Schein, "Caught in a Cross-Fire: The Erring Employee in the Borderland of Contract and Tort" (1987), 8 Advocates' Q. 243; and case comments by Blom (1987), 21 U.B.C. L. Rev. 429, and Rafferty (1989), 63 Alta. L.R. (2d) 396.

22 Of course, there must be a duty of care based in tort before the issue of concurrent liability can ever arise. Not all contractual or professional services imply a tort law duty of care. See, e.g., *Moss v. Richardson Greenshields of Can. Ltd.*, [1989] 3 W.W.R. 50 (Man. C.A.), where the breach of a term of an Options Trading Agreement was held not to give rise to a duty of care in tort between the individual stockbroker and his client.

23 Usually it is the plaintiff who is attempting to use tort to gain an advantage. However, the defendant might wish to plead the plaintiff's contributory negligence, which arguably can only be used in a tort context. Can the plaintiff avoid this by insisting on proceeding in contract, notwithstanding concurrent liability in tort? See Chapter 13 on the defence of contributory negligence.

24 Note, however, that the exempting or limiting clause might be held to be applicable only in favour of the employer who contracted for it, and not in favour of an employee who committed a tort. In this case, it has been held that the employee can be fully liable. See *Katz v. Thompson Horse Van Lines Ltd.*, [1988] 4 W.W.R. 356 (B.C. S.C.). As noted above in Chapter 7, the Supreme Court of Canada in *London Drugs Ltd. v. Kuehne & Nagel International Ltd.*, [1993]

concurrent liability applies not only to solicitors, but to all professionals, and is based, in the case of solicitors, on a client's right to recover purely financial losses pursuant to the relationship of proximity outlined in *Hedley Byrne*. This principle is not restricted to professional advice but applies to any act or omission in the performance of the solicitor's services.

As discussed above in Chapter 7, the concurrent liability thesis has been reaffirmed by the Supreme Court of Canada on several occasions. In *Queen v. Cognos Inc.*[25] and *BG Checo International Ltd. v. B.C. Hydro & Power Authority*,[26] plaintiffs were permitted to sue co-contractants in tort.[27] As held in the latter case, the concurrent liability approach applies even where the misrepresentation being relied upon as the basis of the tort claim, has become an express term of the contract.[28]

3. GENERAL PRINCIPLES

Although different considerations apply to the various professional groups which are vulnerable to negligence law claims, there are certain general principles which are applicable to them all.

(a) The Standard of Care

The care required of the professional person is that degree of care which is shown by the reasonably prudent practitioner operating in like circumstances.[29] As stated by Mr. Justice Le Dain of the Supreme Court of Canada, in reference to the duty of solicitors, "the requisite standard of care has been variously referred to as that of the reasonably competent solicitor, the ordinary competent solicitor and the ordinary prudent solicitor."[30] As well, Lord Edmund-Davies has reaffirmed this view, in *Whitehouse v. Jordan*,[31] when he stated that "the test is the

---

1 W.W.R. 1 allowed employees to rely on a limitation of liability clause contained in the contract between their employer and a third party.

25 (1993), 14 C.C.L.T. (2d) 113 (S.C.C.).

26 [1993] 2 W.W.R. 321 (S.C.C.).

27 The concurrent liability approach was reaffirmed by the Supreme Court in *Martel Building Ltd. v. Canada*, [2000] 2 S.C.R. 860.

28 See discussion above, Chapter 7.

29 There are numerous quotes in cases and commentaries which can be used to illustrate this basic proposition. Tindal C.J.'s statement in *Lamphier v. Phipos* (1838), 8 Car. & P. 475 at 479, is often cited:

> Every person who enters into a learned profession undertakes to bring to the exercise of it a reasonable degree of care and skill. He does not undertake if he is an attorney, that at all events you shall gain your case, nor does a surgeon undertake that he will perform a cure; nor does he undertake to use the highest possible degree of skill. There may be persons who have higher education and greater advantages than he has, but he undertakes to bring a fair, reasonable, and competent degree of skill.

See Glos, "Commentary" (1963), 41 Can. Bar Rev. 140.

30 *Central & Eastern Trust Co. v. Rafuse* (1986), 31 D.L.R. (4th) 481 at 523. See also Sopinka J.'s statement with respect to doctors in *ter Neuzen v. Korn* (1995), 127 D.L.R. (4th) 577 at 588:

> It is well settled that physicians have a duty to conduct their practice in accordance with the conduct of a prudent and diligent doctor in the same circumstances.

31 [1981] 1 W.L.R. 246 (C.A.).

standard of the ordinary skilled man exercising and professing to have that special skill."[32] It also is important to emphasize that the standard must be judged in relation to the state of knowledge which existed at the time of the allegedly negligent act, and not from the vantage of hindsight.[33]

The requirement that a professional's conduct conform to that of the ordinarily competent, or prudent, practitioner raises an interesting question concerning the weight to be given to evidence of custom or general practice in professional malpractice cases. As previously discussed,[34] it is now generally conceded that the standard of the reasonable person allows the court to give considerable weight to evidence of general practice, without requiring it to be conclusively bound by what the experts say. What of the professional negligence cases, however? Is the standard required of the reasonable professional only that of the ordinary prudent practitioner, or can courts disregard evidence of generally approved professional practice in finding a defendant professional liable in an action for negligence?[35]

To argue that a professional must only conform to the standards of the ordinary prudent practitioner in like circumstances, but that evidence of general practice is never to be regarded as conclusive evidence of reasonable care, seems to be contradictory. Yet this is the prevalent approach. One can find many Canadian decisions which have clearly accepted the ordinarily prudent practitioner test as constituting the standard of care required of professionals,[36] standing alongside other judgments which have asserted that evidence of commonly accepted practice is not conclusive evidence of reasonable care.[37] How can this apparent contradiction be explained?

The Supreme Court of Canada decision in *ter Neuzen v. Korn*[38] has answered this question. The case involved a medical practitioner who was found negligent at trial by a jury with respect to the manner in which he conducted an artificial insemination (AI) program. The plaintiff contracted HIV as a result of infected semen. The allegation was that the defendant's recruitment and screening pro-

---

32 *Ibid.*, at 258, quoting from the judgment of McNair J. in *Bolam v. Friern Hosp. Mgmt. Ctee.*, [1957] 1 W.L.R. 582. The same standard of care applies to professionals under Quebec Civil Law. See, e.g., *Lapointe v. Hôpital Le Gardeur* (1992), 90 D.L.R. (4th) 7 (S.C.C.).

33 See Sopinka J.'s comment to this effect in *ter Neuzen v. Korn*, above, note 30, at 589.

34 Chapter 9.

35 On this topic, see especially McK. Norrie, "Common Practice and the Standard of Care in Medical Negligence" (1984-85), 30 Juridical Rev. 145; Mahoney, "Lawyers — Negligence — Standard of Care" (1985), 63 Can. Bar Rev. 221; Rice, "Is Custom a Defence for a Lawyer in a Professional Negligence Suit?" (1987), 8 Advocates' Q. 452.

36 See, e.g., *Aaroe v. Seymour* (1956), 6 D.L.R. (2d) 100 at 101-102 (Ont. H.C.), affirmed (1957), 7 D.L.R. (2d) 676 (Ont. C.A.), where the standard of care is stated to be that of "a normal prudent practitioner of the same experience and standing", and several other cases cited by Mahoney, *ibid.*, at 224, n. 15. See *Grover Hldg. Ltd. v. Weir*, [1987] 3 W.W.R. 465 (Sask. Q.B.): "the standard is that of a normal prudent practitioner."

37 See, e.g., *Anderson v. Chasney*, [1949] 4 D.L.R. 71 (Man. C.A.), affirmed [1950] 4 D.L.R. 223 (S.C.C.), and other cases cited by Linden, *Canadian Tort Law*, 4th ed. (1988), at 164. In a Supreme Court of Canada decision emanating from Quebec dealing with the liability of a notary, *Roberge v. Bolduc* (1991), 78 D.L.R. (4th) 666 (S.C.C.), L'Heureux-Dubé J. made this point clear. A professional who follows general practice will not be cleared of negligence, unless the practice followed is "demonstrably reasonable." And in this respect, a generally followed practice in not determinative of reasonable care.

38 (1995), 127 D.L.R. (4th) 577 (S.C.C.).

grams were negligent with respect to HIV transmission, and that the defendant was negligent for failing to warn of this risk. The evidence indicated, however, that the defendant was not aware of the possibility of transmission of HIV until after the plaintiff had already become infected, and moreover, that the defendant's practice of recruitment and screening of donors was in accordance with generally approved practice. In other words, the evidence established that the defendant's conduct in continuing with an AI program, and in not warning of the risks of HIV transmission through semen, if judged by the generally approved practice at the time, was not negligent. Thus, *unless it was open to the jury to disregard general practice and in effect to decide that the general practice itself was negligent,* the jury could not find the defendant to have been negligent. Was such a decision open to the jury?

Sopinka J. decided that it was not, and his judgment significantly clarified Canadian law with respect to the effect of general practice in professional negligence cases. Sopinka J. stated that "it is generally accepted that when a doctor acts in accordance with a recognized and respectable practice of the profession, he or she will not be found to be negligent."[39] This principle is subject to a limited exception. When the allegedly negligent act is one which is so "fraught with obvious risks,"[40] that "anyone is capable of finding it negligent, without the necessity of judging matters requiring diagnostic or clinical expertise,"[41] then, and only then, can the standard practice be adjudged to be negligent. In other words, it is only when the issue in dispute is not one requiring professional expertise, knowledge, or skill, but is a matter of common sense, that finders of fact can exercise their own judgment.[42] In the actual case, it was unclear from the jury's decision whether it found that there was a general practice but disregarded it, which would have been erroneous, or whether it found that no general practice had been established. If the latter were true, the jury could establish its own standard, but with the same qualification, as above. That is, the issue must have been on a matter which was within the jury's competence to judge. If it was a

---

39 *Ibid.*, at 590.

40 Sopinka J. quoted from Fleming, *The Law of Torts*, 7th ed. (1987), at 109.

41 Above, note 38, at 591.

42 There are numerous passages in Sopinka J.'s judgment which express this point. For example, at 127 D.L.R. (4th) 592:

> The question that remains is under what circumstances will a professional standard practice be judged negligent? It seems that it is only where the practice does not conform with basic care which is easily understood by the ordinary person who has no particular expertise in the practices of the profession.

Also at 127 D.L.R. (4th) 592:

> Courts and juries do not have the necessary expertise to assess technical matters relating to the diagnosis or treatment of patients. Where a common and accepted course of conduct is adopted based on the specialized and technical expertise of professionals, it is unsatisfactory for a finder of fact to conclude that such a standard was inherently negligent.

Or at 127 D.L.R. (4th) 595:

> . . . as a general rule, where a procedure involves difficult or uncertain questions of medical treatment or complex, scientific or highly technical matters that are beyond the ordinary experience and understanding of a judge or jury, it will not be open to find a standard medical practice negligent.

matter of professional skill, the jury could not decide it, in the absence of expert evidence.[43]

The decision of the Supreme Court in *ter Neuzen v. Korn* is consistent with earlier decisions on this point, both in Canada and in England. One may refer, for example, to the House of Lords decision in *Maynard v. West Midlands Regional Health Authority*.[44] In this case, the House of Lords held that it is an error of law for a judge to hold a professional liable for negligence where it has been shown that there is a body of competent, professional opinion which supports the impugned conduct of the defendant. This is so even where there exists a competing body of professional, and equally competent, opinion which would consider that the decision taken by the defendant was wrong. In other words, where there is evidence of generally approved practice, according to qualified and skilled professionals, compliance with this practice must be regarded as reasonable.[45] This view had also been adopted in several Canadian cases. In *McLean v. Weir*,[46] for example, Gould J. stated:

---

43 The Supreme Court decided that the question of the defendant's knowledge of HIV and whether he should have discontinued AI or warned of HIV transmission, was a question which the jury could not determine in the absence of expert evidence. The question of the type of recruitment and screening which should have been followed, however, was a matter within the jury's competence which could be determined without experts. Thus, a new trial had to be ordered on this point. Contrast this judgment with the Supreme Court's decision in *Walker Estate v. York-Finch General Hospital* (2001), [2001] S.C.J. No. 24, 2001 CarswellOnt 1209, 2001 CarswellOnt 1210. The case involved blood infected with HIV. One of the issues was whether the questionnaire provided by the defendant to potential blood donors was adequate to warn those in high-risk categories about the dangers of HIV transmission. Two medical experts testified that the question asked was an adequate alternative to a more symptom-specific question. The trial judge disagreed with their opinion. Both the Court of Appeal and the Supreme Court of Canada concluded that this was not a "complex scientific or highly technical matter" where deference to the view of the experts was required. The issue was how a layperson would respond to the questionnaire, not how experts would.

44 [1984] 1 W.L.R. 634.

45 As stated by Lord Scarman, "a doctor who professes a special skill must exercise the ordinary skill of his specialty", *ibid.*, at 638. Although this approach adopted in *Maynard v. West Midlands* was subsequently unsuccessful in the Canadian case *Brain v. Mador* (1985), 32 C.C.L.T. 157 (Ont. C.A.), this was based not on a rejection of the principle, but on the court's decision that on the fundamental issue of the case, there were not two camps of respectable opinion. See Irvine, "Annotation" (1985), 32 C.C.L.T. 158. See also *Quintal v. Datta*, [1988] 6 W.W.R. 481 (Sask. C.A.), where *Maynard v. West Midlands* was cited with approval.

46 [1977] 5 W.W.R. 609 at 620 (B.C. S.C.), affirmed [1980] 4 W.W.R. 330 (B.C. C.A.). See also Walker J.'s judgment in *Haughian v. Paine* (1986), 36 C.C.L.T. 242 at 250 (Sask. Q.B.), reversed on other grounds (1987), 40 C.C.L.T. 13 (Sask. C.A.):

> A surgeon is not liable for an error of judgment if he applies ordinary and reasonable skill and care or keeps within recognized and approved methods. Accordingly, where there is more than one recognized and approved method of treatment applicable to the case, a surgeon is not liable for an honest mistake of judgment in selecting a method.

Further, in *Quintal v. Datta, ibid.*, at 498, the court held:

> Except in those unusual medical negligence cases where the standard of care is a matter of common knowledge, the jury must determine the standard of professional learning, skill and care required of a defendant physician only from the opinions of physicians (including a defendant physician) who have testified as expert witnesses as to such standard. The jury are not at liberty to formulate their own standard of care and must be instructed that the

> . . . in technical matters, unlike in lay matters within the traditional intellectual competence of the court, [the court] cannot substitute its own medical opinion for that of qualified experts. The court has no status whatsoever to come to a medical conclusion contrary to unanimous medical evidence before it even if it wanted to . . . There is an evidentiary bar to opinion evidence on technical subjects from non-qualified witnesses, and an equally rigid bar against judges coming to conclusions on technical matters (other than domestic and constitutional law) founded on their own opinions rather than on evidence from qualified witnesses.[47]

Cases such as *Anderson v. Chasney,*[48] and *Roberge v. Bolduc,*[49] are not necessarily inconsistent with this view and can be explained in two ways. First, a court may not actually be convinced that there is a commonly accepted professional practice. Mere evidence that, in the opinion of some experts, the defendant's conduct was reasonable does not necessarily establish a sufficiently authoritative practice.[50] The fact that some professionals do one thing, and others do another, in fact works against such a presumption. Second, even if there is evidence of general practice, as clearly pointed out by Sopinka J. in *ter Neuzen v. Korn,* the issue in dispute must relate to a matter which is exclusively within the professional domain,[51] and not within the trier of fact's own competence. Thus, where the issue is one which can be judged by the reasonable non-professional person, since it is a matter of common sense and not one of technical detail, evidence of general, professional practice clearly ought not to be treated as conclusive.[52] In addition,

---

> standard of care is to be determined by weighing and considering the expert evidence proffered on this issue.

See also *Belknap v. Meakes* (1989), 64 D.L.R. (4th) 452 (B.C. C.A.); *285614 Alberta Ltd. v. Burnet, Duckworth & Palmer*, [1993] 4 W.W.R. 374 (Alta. Q.B.); *Goodwin v. Brady* (1991), 7 C.C.L.T. (2d) 319 (B.C. S.C.), affirmed (1994), 89 B.C.L.R. (2d) 27 (C.A.); *Kaban v. Sett*, [1994] 1 W.W.R. 476 (Man. Q.B.), affirmed [1994] 10 W.W.R. 620 (Man. C.A.).

47 Thus it has been held "that the failure of a plaintiff to adduce the evidence of an expert witness usually entitles a defendant to succeed in cases alleging professional negligence except where the alleged negligence is so evident that the trier of fact can determine the issue on the basis of common sense". See *Gerelus v. Lim* (2006), 43 C.C.L.T. (3d) 256 (Man. Q.B.), affirmed 2008 MBCA 89 (Man. C.A.), at 268 [C.C.L.T.], citing *ter Neuzen v. Korn*, [1995] 3 S.C.R. 674; and *Palmer-Johnson v. Tochor* (2003), [2004] 6 W.W.R. 130 (Sask. Q.B.).

48 Above, note 37.

49 Above, note 37.

50 See *285614 Alberta Ltd. v. Burnet, Duckworth & Palmer*, [1993] 4 W.W.R. 374 at 382 (Alta. Q.B.), where Russell J. cites this statement with approval.

51 See Mahoney, above, note 35.

52 In *ter Neuzen v. Korn* (1995), 127 D.L.R. (4th) 577 at 594, Sopinka J. considered *Anderson v. Chasney* in some detail. He concluded from the court's judgment in that case that the issue in dispute there did not involve any matters of "scientific or highly technical character" but "simply a matter of whether obvious and simple precautions, easily understood by ordinary individuals, were required to be taken": [1995] 10 W.W.R. at 20. See also, *Hajgato v. London Health Assn.* (1982), 36 O.R. (2d) 669 at 693 (H.C.), where Callaghan J., in rejecting the proposition that evidence of general practice is conclusive, stated:

> I accept that the evidence of approved practice is most helpful and persuasive and I fully recognize an absence of expertise in medical matters on the part of the Court. In my view, however, a court has a right to strike down substandard approved practice when common sense dictates such a result.

Another similar case, this time dealing with lawyers, is *Edward Wong Fin. Co. v. Johnson, Stokes & Master*, [1984] 2 W.L.R. 1 (P.C.). The solicitor was sued for negligence, although she was following the standard Hong Kong practice for real estate completions. In agreeing with the dissent of the Court of Appeal, and finding in the plaintiff's favour, the Privy Council

a trial judge is free to weigh conflicting evidence from competent experts and to prefer one over the other.[53] Further, in those cases such as *Roberge v. Bolduc*, where the judges' own experience and backgrounds make them less reliant on the evidence of experts, evidence of usual legal practice will carry less weight.[54]

---

judgment quoted from the dissent, part of which stated (at 7):

> As a reasonable person of ordinary prudence she should or ought to have foreseen the risk of parting with the money before obtaining the property one bought in any ordinary transaction. It was not her skill that was put to test. It was her *common sense, her prudence of any ordinary person* that is put to test. [Emphasis added.]

In other words, the issue did not involve professional skill and judgment. It has also been held that where the issue is one of common sense, for example, the need for accountants to comply with filing deadlines, expert evidence is not necessary; see *Dyck v. F.M.A. Farm Management Associates Ltd.*, [1996] 3 W.W.R. 509 (Sask. Q.B.). Also see *Comeau v. Saint John Regional Hospital* (2001), 9 C.C.L.T. (3d) 223 (N.B. C.A.), varying (1999), 221 N.B.R. (2d) 201 (Q.B.), where the Court of Appeal affirmed a finding of negligence despite the fact that the practice of the doctors to discharge a patient without consulting with the referring doctor was one commonly followed in Canadian hospitals. In *Rupert v. Toth* (2006), 38 C.C.L.T. (3d) 261 (Ont. S.C.J.), the trial judge held that an issue of "communications management", i.e., the manner in which a doctor follows up with a patient regarding the patient's condition and treatment, is not a "matter of medical science" over which doctors have a "monopoly or particular expertise". Negligence was found in this case.

53 See *Crawford (Litigation Guardian of) v. Penney* (2003), 14 C.C.L.T. (3d) 60 (S.C.J.), affirmed (2004), 26 C.C.L.T. (3d) 246 (Ont. C.A.), leave to appeal refused (2005), 2005 CarswellOnt 280 (S.C.C.); *Houlihan v. Caskey* (2006), 42 C.C.L.T. (3d) 86 (Ont. S.C.J.); *Sanger (Litigation Guardian of) v. Stoffman* (2006), [2006] O.J. No. 49, 2006 CarswellOnt 49 (S.C.J.); *Maynard v. West Midlands* and *Brain v. Mador,* above, note 45. This approach is admittedly difficult to reconcile with the proposition that where two schools of thought are supported by competent, professional opinion, it is an error to find a professional negligent for preferring one over the other. A possible answer to this apparent inconsistency is that in determining whether there are two competent but opposing schools of thought, a trial judge must consider factors such as the credibility of the experts, the consistency of their testimony, their objectivity, and how their testimony relates to the facts of the case, in weighing their evidence. These factors might influence the judge's decision to prefer one expert over the other.

54 In *Roberge v. Bolduc*, above, note 37, L'Heureux-Dubé J. found that the defendant notary made a clear error of law on a non-controversial matter. The fact that other notaries made the same mistake and adopted the same "casual" attitude to the issue, left her unconvinced that this was a reasonable practice. As we will discuss later, it is rare for lawyers to be cleared of negligence when they fail to properly understand the law. Also see *Shute v. Premier Trust Co.* (1993), 35 R.P.R. (2d) 141 (Ont. Gen. Div.), another legal malpractice case where the court was prepared to find the solicitor's conduct negligent even if it were in accordance with general and approved practice. The issue arose in a different context in *Palmer-Johnson v. Tochor* (2003), [2004] 6 W.W.R. 130 (Sask. Q.B.). The plaintiff, a self-represented litigant, sued her lawyers for their alleged negligence in unsuccessfully defending her against charges that she had engaged in the unauthorized practice of medicine. In the civil action, before judge and jury, the plaintiff did not call any experts to support her allegations. The defendants' motion for a non-suit was granted. The court held that in the absence of expert testimony, the jury could not find that the lawyers had been negligent in their conduct of the plaintiff's defence, and if so, that this was the cause of her having been found guilty of the charges brought against her. These issues were beyond the competence of the jury to decide by using ordinary common sense. Compare with *Van de Geer Estate v. Penner* (2004), [2005] 2 W.W.R. 310 (Sask. Q.B.), reversed (2006), 2006 CarswellSask 45 (C.A.), where a trial judge held that the defendant solicitor was negligent, even though the plaintiff did not call any expert evidence. See also *Zink v. Adrian*, [2005] 4 W.W.R. 420 (B.C. C.A). Here again the trial judge found the solicitor negligent in the absence

In most cases, however, where there is evidence of a clear, general practice relating to a matter which requires professional knowledge, courts ought not to, and will most likely not,[55] find this practice to have been negligent.[56]

One final point can be noted. It has been argued that "in the professional cases, the contractual undertaking made is only to employ customary treatment methods."[57] A tort law duty which would depart from the standard of customary treatment would impose a higher burden on practitioners, thus creating a conflict between the duties required by tort and contract. This being the case, it is arguable that as a result of the Supreme Court of Canada's judgment in *Central & Eastern Trust Co. v. Rafuse*,[58] the contractual standard must prevail between parties in a

---

of expert evidence. Although the Court of Appeal affirmed the trial judgment, Southin J.A. did state that judges should only "rarely make such a finding in the absence of expert evidence as to the standard of a competent solicitor conducting the business in question" (at 433). The case must raise "nontechnical matters or those of which an ordinary person may be expected to have knowledge" (citing *Anderson v. Chasney*, [1949] 2 W.W.R 337 (Man. C.A.), at 341). Southin J.A. argued that the parties have the opportunity to cross-examine experts, an opportunity that they do not have with judges.

55 See, e.g., *Winrob v. Street* (1959), 28 W.W.R. 118 (B.C. S.C.), where the court exonerated a solicitor who adhered to general practice although it accepted that if this practice was "inconsistent with provident precautions against a known risk" it would not be a sufficient justification.

56 As stated by one author:

> A stricter view which would require the individual practitioner to go beyond the practices sanctioned by his compatriots would be an unrealistic and wistful approach. It is difficult enough for today's busy practitioner to keep up with developments in his profession. To expect and demand a continual individual judging of these developments, and a consequential innovation beyond current standards should a suspicion of negligence be raised, is to demand the unattainable.

Mahoney, above, note 35, at 225. See also *Sceptre Resources Ltd. v. Deloitte Haskins & Sells* (1991), 83 Alta. L.R. (2d) 157 at 165-166 (C.A.), where Côté J.A. states:

> Acting in concert with an opinion or practice held by a significant fraction of the profession, is almost always a defence to a suit for malpractice. . . . The only exception arises where the practice of the profession is totally unreasonable.

Côté J.A. went on to say (at 166) that "a court should be slow to tell a sizeable portion of the accounting profession that it does not know how to speak its own language." In *Girard v. General Hospital of Port Arthur* (1998), [1998] O.J. No. 6137, 1998 CarswellOnt 4118 (Div. Ct.), leave to appeal refused (1998), 1998 CarswellOnt 4117 (C.A.), reversing (1997), [1997] O.J. No. 2666, 1997 CarswellOnt 5879 (Gen. Div.), a decision by a trial judge to find doctors negligent despite having followed generally approved practice was reversed. The Court held that it was not open to the trial judge to replace the doctors' assessment of the plaintiff's condition with his own in determining whether special precautions ought to have been taken in this instance to protect the patient from falling down. To the same effect is *Emmonds v. Makarewicz* (2000), 81 B.C.L.R. (3d) 75 (C.A.), varying (1999), [1999] B.C.J. No. 1513, 1999 CarswellBC 1475 (S.C.), where the Court of Appeal, applying *ter Neuzen*, held that the trial judge erred in finding the defendant doctor negligent in the face of evidence of generally approved practice in a matter requiring clinical expertise. Also see *Vescio v. Garfield* (2007), 50 C.C.L.T. (3d) 279 (Ont. S.C.J.). An apparently contrary decision is *McKinnon v. Grand River Hospital* (2007), 50 C.C.L.T. (3d) 244 (Ont. S.C.J.), at 271, where the trial judge stated that "experts are ultimately just like every other witness in a case. We can accept all, some, or none of what they say."

57 See Linden, "The Negligent Doctor" (1973), 11 Osgoode Hall L.J. 31.

58 (1986), 37 C.C.L.T. 117 (S.C.C.).

contractual relationship. Where a professional person contractually undertakes to follow customary practices in rendering the professional service, it would be wrong for the court to hold the professional liable for failing to do more than what was promised.

(b) The Locality Rule

It has occasionally been suggested that the standard of care demanded of professionals will vary according to the community or locality in which they practise, the implication usually being that those who work in rural areas are not expected to perform to the same high levels of their urban colleagues. The Supreme Court of Canada has lent respectability to this thesis,[59] and it is one which has received approval in other cases.[60] It has now been generally recognized that the locality rule is merely illustrative of the well-accepted proposition that the conduct of a defendant must be judged on the basis of the conduct exhibited by a reasonable person "in like circumstances," and that accordingly, the location of the service *might* be one of these relevant circumstances. If, for example, the service was performed in an area which had limited access to facilities, equipment, and specialists, the defendant can only be asked to do what the reasonable person so limited would have done.[61] It may very well be, however, that the location did not limit the quality of the service's performance, and if so, it is not a relevant

---

59 See *Wilson v. Swanson*, [1956] S.C.R. 804; *McCormick v. Marcotte* (1971), 20 D.L.R. (3d) 345 (S.C.C.).

60 See, e.g., *Davidson v. Connaught Laboratories* (1980), 14 C.C.L.T. 251 (Ont. H.C.); *Layden v. Cope* (1984), 28 C.C.L.T. 140 (Alta. Q.B.); *Haughian v. Paine* (1986), 36 C.C.L.T. 242 (Sask. Q.B.), reversed without considering this point [1987] 4 W.W.R. 97 (Sask. C.A.); *Pierre (Next Friend of) v. Marshall*, [1994] 8 W.W.R. 478 at 488 (Alta. Q.B.): "he is expected to meet the standard of care reasonably expected of the normal, prudent general practitioner practicing obstetrics in communities similar to Calgary"; *Fleury (Next Friend of) v. Woolgar*, [1996] 5 W.W.R. 721 (Alta. Q.B.) at 724; and *Elofson v. Davis* (1997), 34 C.C.L.T. (2d) 283 (Alta. Q.B.) at 304. In the latter case, Binder J. suggested that without the rule that imposes a lower standard on rural practitioners, it might even be more difficult for rural communities to attract doctors. In *Phillips v. Central Cariboo Chilcotin Council* (2002), [2002] B.C.J. No. 1245, 2002 CarswellBC 1329 (S.C.), the locality rule was recognized but did not have an effect on the outcome of the case. The doctor's negligence did not relate to a lack of equipment, resources or specialists. Although these cases involved doctors, the locality rule has been applied to other professionals, for example, lawyers: *Grima v. MacMillan* (1972), 27 D.L.R. (3d) 666 (Ont. H.C.); and *Hauck v. Dixon* (1975), 64 D.L.R. (3d) 201 (Ont. H.C.). See discussion by Rice, above, note 35, at 457-59.

61 See, e.g., *St. Jules v. Chen*, [1990] B.C.W.L.D. 341 (S.C.) — acceptable practice considering the facilities in town. See *Bateman v. Doiron* (1991), 8 C.C.L.T. (2d) 284 (N.B. Q.B.), affirmed (1993), 18 C.C.L.T. (2d) 1 (N.B. C.A.), with relation to standard required of hospital. The court took into account problems created by unavailability of trained personnel, and resources, in setting the standard required. In *Smith v. Liwanpo* (2007), [2007] O.J. No. 1542, 2007 CarswellOnt 2492 (S.C.J.), the court rejected the locality rule, and noted that even if the procedure required was not available in the local hospital, the patient could have been referred to another hospital.

consideration.[62] It was stated in one case that "the locality is merely one circumstance and is not an absolute limit on the care and skill required."[63] If seen in this way, the locality rule is a sensible one, which will not necessarily demand less of the rural practitioner.[64]

A different type of locality issue arises if it is argued that the expert evidence introduced at trial should come from professionals in the community in which the defendant practices. Thus, according to this view, expert testimony from a professional whose experience is from elsewhere in Canada should be not be relevant. This argument was rejected in *Rupert v. Toth*,[65] the court holding that since there was "no demonstrated difference in the qualifications, level of skill, or access to facilities and repositories of knowledge" as between the urban Ontario doctor and one practising in Nova Scotia, the expert's evidence was accepted as being "insightful and compelling".[66]

(c) Generalists and Specialists

In judging the conduct of the defendant practitioner, the courts will consider whether the defendant was a general practitioner or a specialist in the field. That this is so in relation to the medical profession, where specialists have educational qualifications different from those of the general practitioner, has long been recognized.[67] Although more arguable in relation to professional groups without

---

62 In *Marbel Developments Ltd. v. Pirani* (1994), 18 C.C.L.T. (2d) 229 (B.C. S.C.), the court rejected the contention that the standard should vary based on the geographical location and type of legal practice. The court stated that the standard is based on the work undertaken, and not the "particular circumstances" of the practitioner. Also see *Wilcox v. Johnston* (2001), 238 N.B.R. (2d) 325 (Q.B.), where the Court, referring to the fact that all lawyers practicing in New Brunswick have to pass the same Bar examinations, rejected that locality within New Brunswick should affect the standard of care imposed upon solicitors. Although this is so, there is still the issue of generally approved practice, discussed above. Locality might affect the customs that are followed by lawyers in different communities.

63 *Haughian v. Paine* (1986), 36 C.C.L.T. 242 at 250 (Sask. Q.B.), per Walker J.

64 It might even demand more, if, for example, rural practitioners ought to be more familiar with the matter at hand than their urban counterparts. The notion that there is a lower standard of care expected of rural doctors was strongly rejected in an Alberta case, *Skeels Estate v. Iwashkiw*, [2006] 11 W.W.R. 632 (Alta. Q.B.) at 646. Germain J. stated that "patients, where ever they are in Alberta, are entitled to receive the same standard of care, both in terms of currency and competency, whether they go to a doctor in a city, town, village, or farm community. There may still be differences — those that flow from facilities, equipment, and availability to consult — but conceptually a family practitioner providing, as here, a delivery service, should be performing at the same level, all other things being equal, anywhere in Alberta."

65 (2006), 38 C.C.L.T. (3d) 261 (Ont. S.C.J.).

66 *Ibid.* at 281. I would suggest, however, that as with competing schools of reputable thought on professional matters, if professionals from two communities have different ways of doing things, each way being reasonable, a professional from one community should not be held negligent for failing to follow the other community's practice.

67 See Picard and Robertson, above, note 1. Some of the leading Canadian cases noted by Picard are *Crits v. Sylvester* (1955), 1 D.L.R. (2d) 502 (Ont. C.A.), affirmed [1956] S.C.R. 991; and *Wilson v. Swanson* (1956), 5 D.L.R. (2d) 113 (S.C.C.). Reaffirmation of this point is provided by Sopinka J. in *ter Neuzen v. Korn*, above, note 38, at 588-89:

> In the case of a specialist, such as a gynaecologist and obstetrician, the doctor's behaviour must be assessed in light of the conduct of other ordinary specialists, who possess a

de jure specialization, it is becoming accepted that where a professional person is known to specialize, that person is expected to perform at a higher level. This was recognized in relation to lawyers in *Central & Eastern Trust Co. v. Rafuse*.[68] The defendants were lawyers who acted for clients in a corporate lending transaction. Although they had extensive experience with small commercial transactions and property and mortgage transactions, they did not have expertise, nor did they hold themselves out as having expertise, in corporate transactions. They made an error which the reasonable specialist would not have made. The trial court held that the standard demanded of the defendants in this case depended upon what the reasonably competent general practitioner would have done, and not what the specialist would have done. If the defendants were, or had held themselves out as, specialists, it is evident that the trial judge would have exposed them to a higher standard. In the Supreme Court of Canada, the trial judge's decision to distinguish between generalist and specialist lawyers was noted without disapproval, although ultimately Mr. Justice Le Dain found, as did the Court of Appeal, that even as general practitioners, the defendants were liable for their error.[69]

The issue was met squarely, and discussed in greater detail, in *Elcano Accept. Ltd. v. Richmond, Richmond, Stambler & Mills*.[70] The case concerned lawyers who failed to take into account a stipulation in the Interest Act[71] which prohibited monthly rates of interest in promissory notes such as those which the defendants had drafted for their clients. The trial judge held that, as with the locality rule, the reason for demanding a higher standard of care from specialists than from general practitioners is based upon the expectations of clients. More is expected of, and hence more should be demanded of, those who profess to be specialists in certain areas of law.[72] It has also been argued that to demand a higher standard of care

---

reasonable level of knowledge, competence and skill expected of professionals in Canada, in that field. A specialist, such as the respondent, who holds himself out as possessing a special degree of skill and knowledge, must exercise the degree of skill of an average specialist in his field.

68 Above, note 21.

69 One must also keep in mind that a general practitioner, although not required to live up to the same level of competence as a specialist, will be negligent for undertaking work in circumstances where the reasonable general practitioner would have sought the assistance of specialists. See, for example, *Dillon v. LeRoux*, [1994] 6 W.W.R. 280 (B.C. C.A.): family doctor without specialty in emergency medicine or cardiology should have sought specialist's help. See also *Fleury (Next Friend of) v. Woolgar*, [1996] 5 W.W.R. 721 (Alta. Q.B.) at 724: general practitioner with a special interest in obstetrics must use "the skill, knowledge and judgment of a family practitioner engaging in a significant practise in obstetrics", and while "not expected to possess the same degree of expertise as an obstetrician [is] required to know when the circumstances required a consultation with or referral to an obstetrician". Also see *Jaglowska v. Kreml* (2003), 23 C.C.L.T. (3d) 248, [2005] 3 W.W.R. 485 (Man. C.A.), reversing (2002), [2003] 1 W.W.R. 711 (Man. Q.B.). The Court of Appeal held that the trial judge erred in finding a g.p. negligent for failing to refer, since the evidence supported the finding that the doctor's approach of "watchful waiting" was also acceptable.

70 (1985), 31 C.C.L.T. 201 (Ont. H.C.), reversed on other grounds (1986), 9 C.P.C. (2d) 260 (Ont. C.A.).

71 R.S.C. 1970, c. I-18 [now R.S.C. 1985, c. I-15].

72 Having said this, the court found that either as a general practitioner or a specialist, the defendants should have been aware of the Interest Act and its effect on their clients' notes.

from specialists is justified with respect to the terms of the contract of retainer which one may have with the professional. As stated by Megarry J.:

> If the client engages an expert, and doubtless expects to pay commensurate fees, is he not entitled to expect something more than the standard of the reasonably competent? . . . The essence of the contract of retainer, it may be said, is that the client is retaining the particular solicitor or firm in question, and he is therefore entitled to expect from that solicitor or firm a standard of care and skill commensurate with the skill and experience which that solicitor or firm has.[73]

This approach is certainly consistent with the general formulation of the standard of care, based as it is on the reasonably competent practitioner in like circumstances.[74]

(d) Beginners

It has been stated that the standard of care required of the professional person is that of "a normal prudent practitioner of the same experience and standing."[75] Does this mean, therefore, that beginners are not required to live up to the same standards as those with average experience in their field?

Despite the obvious disparity with the above statement, the few courts which have considered this issue have held that lack of experience is not an answer to a claim of negligence brought against a professional. Thus, in *Dale v. Munthali*,[76] R.E. Holland J. argued that the statement in *Crits v. Sylvester*[77] by Schroeder J.A. that every medical practitioner "is bound to exercise that degree of care and skill which could reasonably be expected of a normal, prudent practitioner of the same experience and standing" was unsupported by the authorities in so far as beginners were concerned. His Lordship held that a standard should not be lowered as a result of the inexperience of the practitioner.[78]

This issue was dealt with in *Wilsher v. Essex Area Health Authority*.[79] Mustill L.J., while supporting the traditionally accepted view that the standard of care ought not to be tailored to the experience of the individual defendant, held that it can be related to the post occupied by the defendant practitioner. Thus, if a post in a hospital unit offering a highly specialized service is occupied by less experienced practitioners, the duty on those who occupy the post must be based on

73 *Duchess of Argyll v. Beuselinck*, [1972] 2 Lloyd's Rep. 172 at 183.

74 In *Harela v. Powell* (1998), 163 D.L.R. (4th) 365 (Ont. Gen. Div.) at 376, the standard imposed upon the defendant lawyer was expressed as that of a "reasonably competent lawyer practising in the real estate area at the time of this transaction", again illustrative of a notion of *de facto* specialization. In *Côté c. Rancourt*, 2004 SCC 58, the Supreme Court of Canada held that a criminal defence lawyer fulfilled his duty to provide competent advice to his client by acknowledging his lack of qualifications in civil matters and advising him to consult a lawyer specializing in that area.

75 Mahoney, above, note 35, at 224.

76 (1977), 16 O.R. (2d) 532 (H.C.), affirmed (1978), 21 O.R. (2d) 554 (C.A.).

77 [1956] O.R. 132 at 143 (C.A.), affirmed [1956] S.C.R. 991.

78 See also *McKeachie v. Alvarez* (1970), 17 D.L.R. (3d) 87 (B.C. S.C.); *Wills v. Saunders*, [1989] 2 W.W.R. 715 (Alta. Q.B.); *Cohen v. Ostry* (1992), 5 C.L.R. (2d) 11 (B.C. S.C.), varied (1994), 89 B.C.L.R. (2d) 231 (C.A.); *Miles v. Judges* (1997), 37 C.C.L.T. (2d) 160 (Ont. Gen. Div.); *Bearden v. Lee*, [2003] O.J. No. 1261, 2003 CarswellOnt 1178 (S.C.J.), additional reasons at (2003), 2003 CarswellOnt 2024 (S.C.J.); and *Sharp v. Hurlbert*, [2007] 9 W.W.R. 657 (Alta. Q.B.).

79 [1986] 3 All E.R. 801 (C.A.), reversed on other grounds [1988] 1 All E.R. 871 (H.L.).

the competence of those who ordinarily fill this post. Sir Nicholas Browne-Wilkinson V.C., in dissent, would have gone much further. His Lordship would require that beginners who accept posts at hospitals in order to gain experience live up to the standards of which they are capable, and not the standards of more experienced practitioners. According to His Lordship, a system based on "personal fault" must not distort this principle in order to compensate plaintiffs and thereby "conceal the real social issues which arise."[80]

The debate concerning the standard that is to be demanded of beginners is no different from the debate about other personal characteristics of defendants which negligence law does, or does not, take into account when determining liability.[81] It balances the desire to compensate with the need to remain faithful to a fault principle. As with other disabling characteristics, however, the problem is often more theoretical than real. Negligence law requires beginners to appreciate their own limitations, by seeking specialist help or referrals, and requires their supervisors to take into account the inexperience of these beginners.[82] Liability can be imposed in these cases, therefore, without sacrificing the integrity of the fault principle.[83]

(e) Errors of Judgment

Professionals do not guarantee results nor promise perfection. This is recognized in the law's distinction between actionable negligence, and mere "errors of judgment." Although errors of judgment are mistakes, they are mistakes which

---

80 *Ibid.*, at 834.

81 See Chapter 9.

82 In *Brown (Next Friend of) v. University of Alberta Hospital* (1997), 33 C.C.L.T. (2d) 113 (Alta. Q.B.), Marceau J. noted that the medical profession acts as a team and in this respect exonerated one of the doctors, a first-year surgery resident, doing a two-month rotation in surgery, from liability. The resident had met the standard required of a person in his position. In *Chow (Litigation Guardian of) v. Wellesley Hospital* (1999), [1999] O.J. No. 279, 1999 CarswellOnt 349 (Gen. Div.), on the other hand, a second-year resident was held liable along with the principal obstetrician for negligence in the delivery of a baby. Plaintiffs argued that the resident was subject to the same standard as an ordinary doctor. The court found the resident negligent although no specific reference was made to this issue by the trial judge. Fault was apportioned 75 per cent to the principal doctor and 25 per cent to the resident. In *Aldana v. March* (1999), 44 C.C.L.T. (2d) 164 (B.C. S.C.), the standard imposed on an intern was that of the reasonable intern, not doctor. The court noted that an intern is in fact not a doctor but a graduate medical student training in order to become qualified as a doctor. In *Adair Estate v. Hamilton Health Sciences Corp.* (2005), 32 C.C.L.T. (3d) 283 (Ont. S.C.J.), the court distinguished *Aldana* by noting that in that case the interns were working under licensed doctors, dealt with the patient briefly, and their diagnosis was not relied upon. The court favoured imposing the same standard of care on residents as is imposed on fully licensed doctors.

83 The obligation to "call for help" when confronting an emergency situation which the professional cannot deal with was front and centre in *Skeels Estate v. Iwashkiw*, [2006] 11 W.W.R. 632 (Alta. Q.B.). This tragic case involved the death of a baby shortly after its delivery as a result of an undue delay in its delivery caused by the medical staff's inability to deal with the urgent situation. The need to balance the respective responsibilities of doctors and nurses in confronting an emergency was one of the issues in this case.

even a reasonably competent professional might have made.[84] The Supreme Court has recognized this in several cases, for example, in *Lapointe v. Hôpital Le Gardeur*.[85] Although the distinction is usually applied in the context of medical negligence cases, there is no reason to limit it in this way.[86]

4. SPECIFIC PROFESSIONAL GROUPS

In addition to the above general principles, there are specialized rules applicable to the individual professional groups, which take into account their different concerns and characteristics. A detailed account of these rules is not possible in a general text such as this. The following sections will discuss, however, some of the more important cases and issues relating to those professions which are most often involved in litigation.

(a) Lawyers

(i) The Immunity Question

Canadian lawyers, whether acting as solicitors or as barristers, cannot claim an immunity from suit. This was first clearly established in the Ontario case of *Demarco v. Ungaro*,[87] where Mr. Justice Krever decided not to follow the House of Lords decision in *Rondel v. Worsley*,[88] as modified by *Saif Ali v. Sydney Mitchell & Co.*,[89] and not to grant Ontario barristers an immunity from suit. This decision was followed in numerous other Canadian cases.[90]

---

84 In *Ahmed v. Stefaniu* (2006), 275 D.L.R. (4th) 101 (Ont. C.A.), leave to appeal refused (2007), 2007 CarswellOnt 2152 (S.C.C.), at 111 [D.L.R.], Armstrong J.A. conceded that "there is often a fine line between a mere error in judgment and a failure to meet the professional standard of care". The case concerned a psychiatrist's decision to change the status of a patient from involuntary to voluntary. The patient subsequently murdered the plaintiff's wife. The jury decided that the decision was negligent and the Court of Appeal affirmed.

85 (1992), 90 D.L.R. (4th) 7.

86 It has been applied, for example, to legal malpractice cases. See *Pelky v. Hudson Bay Insurance Co.* (1981), 35 O.R. (2d) 97 (H.C.); *Grand Anse Contracting Ltd. v. MacKinnon* (1993), 121 N.S.R. (2d) 423 (T.D.) and *Greig v. Waldock (Trustee of)* (1997), [1997] B.C.J. No. 2217, 1997 CarswellBC 2091 (S.C.).

87 (1979), 8 C.C.L.T. 207 (Ont. H.C.).

88 [1967] 3 All E.R. 993 (H.L.).

89 [1978] 3 All E.R. 1033 (H.L.).

90 In Ontario, see *Karpenko v. Paroian, Courey, Cohen & Houston* (1980), 117 D.L.R. (3d) 383 (Ont. H.C.); *Wechsel v. Stutz* (1980), 15 C.C.L.T. 132 (Ont. Co. Ct.); and *Deshpande v. Siskind, Cromarty & Ritchie* (1987), 24 O.A.C. 311 (Div. Ct.). In Saskatchewan, see *Garrant v. Moskal*, [1985] 2 W.W.R. 80 (Sask. Q.B.). The decision as to liability was affirmed on appeal, [1985] 6 W.W.R. 31 (Sask. C.A.), although it must be noted that as to the question of immunity from suit, Wakeling J.A. expressed strong sympathy with the then English position. See also *Stevenson v. Stanek*, [1980] 4 W.W.R. 239 (Sask. Q.B.); and most recently *Henderson v. Hagblom*, 2003 CarswellSask 283, 2003 SKCA 40 (C.A.), leave to appeal refused (2004), 2004 CarswellSask 5, 2004 CarswellSask 6 (S.C.C.). In Alberta, see *Romaniuk v. Alta.* (1988), 58 Alta. L.R. (2d) 114 (Q.B.) and *Sherman v. Ward*, [1998] 10 W.W.R. 765 (Alta. Q.B.). In New Brunswick, see *Guardian Ins. Co. of Can. v. McCullogh* (1988), 87 N.B.R. (2d) 210 (Q.B.), affirmed (1988), 95 N.B.R. (2d) 88 (C.A.). On this matter see Smith, "Liability for the Negligent Conduct of Litigation: The Legacy of *Rondel v. Worsley*" (1982-83), 47 Sask. L. Rev. 211;

Prior to the House of Lords decision in *Arthur J S Hall & Co. v. Simons*,[91] English law recognized an immunity from suit for the negligence committed by barristers in the conduct of either civil or criminal proceedings. Several reasons were advanced to justify this protection, unique among professionals. The immunity was said to be important because: (1) a barrister is an independent officer of the court and has a duty not only to a client, but to the administration of justice; (2) abolishing the immunity would result in problems caused by the need to retry litigation; (3) a barrister must maintain the right to control the conduct of the litigation; and (4) the immunity's abolition would expose the barrister to liability for errors of judgment.[92] In *Hall v. Simons*, the House of Lords carefully considered these arguments and ultimately concluded that they no longer justified the continuation of an immunity. In arriving at this decision, the Canadian experience, and in particular the judgment of Krever J. in *Demarco v. Ungaro*, proved to be persuasive to the Lords.[93]

As has been argued, if courts continue to believe that the nature of a barrister's work and responsibilities warrant according the barrister special considerations, even if the rule of an absolute immunity from suit is rejected, it may only be an illusory victory for dissatisfied clients.[94] For, while a lawsuit might technically be available, winning it might well prove to be exceptionally difficult.[95]

Catzman, "Comment" (1968), 46 Can. Bar Rev. 505; Fera, "*Harris v. Quain and Quain*: A Comment" (1978), 24 McGill L.J. 303; Klar, "Annotation" (1978), 4 C.C.L.T. 2; among others.

91 [2000] 3 All E.R. 673 (Eng. H.L.) [hereinafter *Hall v. Simons*].

92 These reasons and others are discussed in the *Hall v. Simons* judgment. Another is the so-called 'cab rank' rule that requires barristers "to accept instructions from anyone who wishes to engage their services in an area of law which they practised". See [2000] 3 All E.R. 678.

93 The Lords were unanimous in their decision not to follow *Rondel v. Worsley* in so far as an immunity from suit for negligence in the conduct of civil proceedings was concerned. The dissenting Lords, however, wished to maintain the immunity for negligence in the conduct of criminal proceedings.

94 See Smith, above, note 90.

95 See, e.g., *Hunter v. Roe*, 1990 CarswellSask 176, [1990] 6 W.W.R. 85 (Sask. Q.B.), where the court, while agreeing that there is no immunity, held that only in a case of an egregious or clear error could a lawyer be held liable. Also see *Grand Anse Contracting Ltd. v. MacKinnon*, above, note 90, and *Henderson v. Hagblom,* 2000 CarswellSask 228, [2000] 7 W.W.R. 357 (Q.B.), reversed 2003 CarswellSask 283, 2003 SKCA 40 (C.A.), leave to appeal refused (2004), 2004 CarswellSask 5, 2004 CarswellSask 6 (S.C.C.). In *Henderson,* the Court of Appeal reversed a trial judgment that had accepted the "clear and egregious error" standard, holding that the standard was one of "reasonable care, skill and knowledge". Since the action involved trial preparation and not negligence within the course of the trial itself, Jackson J.A. did not conclusively hold that the standard for barristers for conduct within the course of the trial should be no different. Justice Jackson was inclined, however, to the view that the standard should be the same in either case. The Ontario Court of Appeal firmly rejected the argument that the standard of care for barrister's work should be any different than the reasonably competent lawyer standard, in *Folland v. Reardon* (2005), 28 C.C.L.T. (3d) 1 (Ont. C.A.). The case involved an action against a barrister for his alleged negligence in defending a client in a criminal law matter, and the Court of Appeal held that the motion judge was in error in applying the "egregious error" standard. This was reaffirmed by the Court in *Ristimaki v. Cooper* (2006), 268 D.L.R. 155 (4th) (Ont. C.A.). In an earlier case, *Boudreau v. Benaiah* (1998), 1998 CarswellOnt 119, 154 D.L.R. (4th) 650 (Ont. Gen. Div.), varied (2000), 2000 CarswellOnt 250, 182 D.L.R. (4th) 569 (Ont. C.A.), a barrister representing an accused charged with abduction relating to a family law dispute was found negligent and liable for damages. The

Another way of looking at the immunity issue is by asking whether a negligence suit brought against a lawyer by a disappointed client can be struck out as an abuse of process. The English courts have held that absent special circumstances (fraud or fresh evidence) attempting to challenge a final criminal conviction by a collateral attack on the competence of the lawyer representing the accused may be treated as an abuse of process.[96] Concerns about the possibility of inconsistent final judgments by two competent courts, the impossibility of retrying cases, and the importance of finality in litigation, have led English courts to treat lawsuits brought against lawyers in order to challenge criminal convictions as an abuse of process.[97] Courts are also concerned about the countervailing concerns; e.g., accountability of lawyers, fairness to litigants, standards for lawyers, and the public perception, and hence there is no broad "abuse of process" bar to suing lawyers.[98]

The Saskatchewan Court of Appeal in *Fischer v. Halyk*,[99] after a careful review of both Canadian and English authorities,[100] came down on the side of the English

---

trial judge stressed that the plaintiff was not being held liable for merely errors in judgment in conducting his defence but for a series of negligent acts including failing to communicate with his client, failing to keep appointments, discharging witnesses without consulting his client, failing to follow his client's instructions, among others. Although this negligence did not affect the outcome of the case, it did cause the accused mental distress for which he was compensated.

96 This is fully discussed by Doherty J.A. in *Wernikowski v. Kirkland, Murphy & Ain* (1999), 1999 CarswellOnt 4139, 50 O.R. (3d) 124 (Ont. C.A.), additional reasons at (2000), 2000 CarswellOnt 464, 181 D.L.R. (4th) 625 at 642 (Ont. C.A.), leave to appeal refused (2000), 2000 CarswellOnt 4190, 2000 CarswellOnt 4191, 145 O.A.C. 398 (note) (S.C.C.). The Ontario Court of Appeal reversed a trial judgment that granted a motion to strike out an action brought by a plaintiff against a lawyer who represented him in an unsuccessful defence to criminal charges. The English authorities referred to by Doherty J.A. include *Smith v. Linskills*, [1996] 2 All E.R. 353 (Eng. C.A.) and the Court of Appeal judgment in *Arthur J.S. Hall & Co. v. Simons* (1998), [1999] 3 W.L.R. 873 (Eng. C.A.). In the House of Lords decision in *Hall*, the "abuse of process" principle that was enunciated in *McIlkenny v. Chief Constable of the West Midlands* (1981), (*sub nom. Hunter v. Chief Constable of West Midlands*) [1982] A.C. 529, [1981] 3 All E.R. 727 (U.K. H.L.) was reaffirmed, despite the fact that the barrister's immunity from suit rule was abolished. As pointed out by Lord Hobhouse, the *Hunter* case did not involve a lawsuit brought against a lawyer, but a claim for assault brought against the police by persons convicted of a terrorist offence. The plaintiffs argued that their confessions to the police were involuntary as they had resulted from police beatings. Since this argument was rejected at trial in the criminal case, the civil action was struck out as constituting a collateral attack on the trial judge's finding and the jury's verdict.

97 As discussed in *Arthur J.S. Hall & Co. v. Simons*, [2000] 3 All E.R. 673 (H.L.), this rule is not inflexible. Thus, if the criminal conviction has been set aside on any ground prior to the civil trial, the action would not be barred. The bar will only apply where it would be "manifestly unfair" to a party that the action proceed or where the action "would bring the administration of justice into disrepute"; [2000] 3 All E.R. 703.

98 The House of Lords made it clear that the abuse of process rule is not to be automatically applied in all cases. For criticism of the Canadian position see P. Calarco, "The Ontario C.A. Gives Green Light to Relitigate Criminal Convictions By Suing Your Lawyer (2000), 31 C.R. (5th) 129.

99 (2003), 229 D.L.R. (4th) 67, 18 C.C.L.T. (3d) 56, [2004] 1 W.W.R. 412 (Sask. C.A.), leave to appeal refused (2004), 2004 CarswellSask 242 (S.C.C.).

100 The court considered not only the English cases of *Hall v. Simons* and *McIleny v. Chief Constable of the West Midlands* (the *Hunter* case) above, note 96, and the Ontario Court of Appeal judgment in *Wernikowski*, above, note 96, but also the Ontario Court of Appeal's

House of Lords, holding that in the usual case it is an abuse of process to relitigate a criminal conviction by challenging it in a negligence action brought against the lawyer who acted for the accused.[101]

(ii) The "Trial Within a Trial"

Where a plaintiff sues a lawyer for the latter's negligence in the conduct of litigation, the plaintiff must establish that had the lawyer acted with reasonable care the results would have been more favourable. This issue, which is one of proof of damages, is problematic. First, there is the suggestion in the case law that not only must the plaintiff prove that the lawyer's negligence resulted in a less favourable outcome, but that the outcome which was reached was actually unjust.[102] As pointed out by Smith,[103] this requirement is a departure from ordinary negligence law principles, as applied to other professional malpractice claims. Second, there is the issue of what must be proved in order to recover damages, where, due to the solicitor's negligence, the plaintiff's first case was never tried. Two views prevail here. One is that the plaintiff in the malpractice case must prove, on a balance of probabilities, that had the original action been tried, it would have been successful. If this is shown, recovery would be for the full amount of the lost claim, and, conversely, if this is not proven, the claimant is entitled to nothing.[104] The second view is that as long as the plaintiff can show that there was some chance of success in the original claim, recovery would be for that portion of the lost claim represented by this chance of success.[105] It has been suggested that the loss of a chance approach is inconsistent with the position that plaintiffs should not recover damages for unmeritorious claims, and that it only applies, at any event, to cases where it is impossible to properly determine the merits of a plaintiff's cause of action because of the passage of time, unavail-

---

judgment in *Toronto (City) v. C.U.P.E., Local 79* (2001), 2001 CarswellOnt 2760, 55 O.R. (3d) 541 (C.A.), leave to appeal allowed (2002), 2002 CarswellOnt 1093 (S.C.C.), affirmed (2003), 2003 CarswellOnt 4328 (S.C.C.), among others.

101 The court conceded that there may be exceptions that will be developed through subsequent case law. For example, if due to the negligence of the lawyer in conducting the defence, the plaintiff suffered mental distress, damages may be awarded even if the outcome of the case would have been the same had there been no negligence. See *Boudreau v. Benaiah* above, note 95.

102 See, e.g., *Saif Ali v. Sydney Mitchell & Co.*, [1980] A.C. 198 at 222 (H.L.), discussed by Smith, above, note 85. As Lord Diplock stated: "The client cannot be heard to complain that the barrister's lack of skill or care prevented him from obtaining a wrong decision in his favour from a court of justice."

103 Above, note 90.

104 See *Fyk v. Millar* (1973), 2 O.R. (2d) 39 (H.C.); *Banks v. Reid* (1974), 6 O.R. (2d) 404 (H.C.), reversed on other grounds (1977), 18 O.R. (2d) 148 (C.A.); *Davies v. Fiddes* (1989), 34 B.C.L.R. (2d) 137 (C.A.); and *Bueckert v. Mattison* (1996), [1997] 1 W.W.R. 430 (Sask. Q.B.).

105 See *Kitchen v. Royal Air Force Assn.*, [1958] 2 All E.R. 241 (C.A.); *Cook v. S.*, [1967] 1 All E.R. 299 (C.A.); *Gouzenko v. Harris* (1976), 1 C.C.L.T. 37 (Ont. H.C.); *Prior v. McNab* (1976), 1 C.C.L.T. 137 (Ont. H.C.).

ability of evidence and so on.[106] Otherwise, the courts ought to determine the merits of the plaintiff's claim, and if, on a balance of probabilities, they are convinced that the claim was meritorious, award full damages. Despite comments in Canadian cases which approve of the loss of a chance approach, it has been suggested that in practice Canadian courts award "all or nothing," except where the merits of the lost cause are impossible to determine.[107]

Another issue raised in the cases relates to the "collectibility" of the judgment which would have been awarded in the lost action. Even assuming that the plaintiff in the malpractice action can prove that it would have succeeded in the lost cause, does it have to go further and prove that the judgment which would have been awarded, would have been collectible? In *Alberta (Workers' Compensation Board) v. Riggins*,[108] the Alberta Court of Appeal decided that although the burden of proving collectibility rests with the plaintiff, proof of collectibility only arises when the defendant places the issue in doubt. Although this burden on the defendant is slight, there must be some evidence of uncollectibility which satisfies the trial judge that the issue has been fairly raised. At that point, the plaintiff would only be entitled to recover the amount of damages that it could prove was collectible.[109] In *Bueckert v. Mattison*,[110] the plaintiff received only 50 per cent of

---

106 See Smith, above, note 90. In *Fisher v. Knibbe* (1992), 3 Alta. L.R. (3d) 97 (C.A.), varying [1989] 6 W.W.R. 130 (Alta. Q.B.), the Court of Appeal held that where it is found that the plaintiff would not have been successful, only "nominal" damages can be awarded. It is only where the "trial within a trial" is impossible due to the passage of time, that the lost opportunity calculation is to be employed. The court awarded the plaintiff $100 as nominal damages, reducing the $28,000 award which had been made by the trial judge. Also see *Stealth Enterprises Ltd. v. Hoffman Dorchik*, [2000] 7 W.W.R. 692 (Alta. Q.B.), affirmed 2003 ABCA 58 (C.A.), which applied *Fisher* and awarded only nominal damages. In *Henderson v. Hagblom*, above, note 95, Jackson J.A. carefully reviewed the authorities and concluded that the "loss of a chance" approach should be applied even in cases where the plaintiff has proved its loss on the balance of probabilities. The lawyer's negligence in the original trial was in his failure to consult with an expert. The Court of Appeal decided that had he done so, his client, the then defendant, had a 75 per cent chance of successfully defending a negligence suit that had been brought against him. The plaintiff in the second trial was awarded 75 per cent of his damages, which included the amount and costs of the first judgment.

107 See Smith, *ibid.*; also see Klar, "Annotation" (1976), 1 C.C.L.T. 137. Although in *obiter*, Doherty J.A. discussed the arguments *pro* and *con* the "loss of a chance" doctrine, in *Folland v. Reardon*, above, note 95. The case involved an allegedly negligent defence in a criminal trial. Doherty J.A. concluded that the loss of a chance argument was inappropriate in such circumstances and the "but for" balance of probabilities approach was the correct one. This issue is closely related to the problem of proving cause when it is "impossible" for the plaintiff to do so, and whether, in such a case, an alternate test of causation should be applied. See discussion in Chapter 11.

108 (1992), 95 D.L.R. (4th) 279 (Alta. C.A.).

109 On the facts of the case, the Court of Appeal held that the defendants had failed to adduce sufficient evidence of uncollectibility. Also see an earlier case, *Doiron v. Caisse populaire d'Inkerman Ltée* (1985), 17 D.L.R. (4th) 660 (N.B. C.A.), where La Forest J.A. (as he then was) held that the burden of proving collectibility is on the plaintiff, where the issue was in doubt. Since there was a "possibility" of collectibility, only a portion of the judgment which would have been obtained was awarded. See also *Page v. A Solicitor* (1971), 20 D.L.R. (3d) 532 (N.B. C.A.), affirmed (1972), 29 D.L.R. (3d) 386n (S.C.C.), applied in *Aikmac Holdings v. Loewen* (1993), 86 Man. R. (2d) 56 (Q.B.). *Alberta v. Riggins* involved negligence in settling a claim for too little. The issue of settlement was raised in *Rose v. Mitton* (1994), 111

his lost judgment upon a finding that the wrongdoer would have declared bankruptcy and would probably have been required to pay a sum equivalent to approximately one-half of what he owed. In *Valness v. MacLowich*,[111] the court was required to decide whether the wrongdoer's liability judgment would have been covered by insurance. The court determined that the insurance applied and that the claim would have therefore been collectible by the plaintiff.

(iii) The Lawyer's Duty to Third Parties

The fact that a lawyer's legal obligations can stem from contract, tort, or equity substantially broadens the range of potential plaintiffs who can complain about a lawyer's negligent work. Litigation against lawyers initiated by those who were not their clients is the most important recent development in the area of lawyers' liability.[112]

As discussed in Chapter 7, one of the more important and interesting areas has involved actions brought by disappointed beneficiaries against lawyers who negligently failed to execute valid bequests in their favour. It is now clear that when acting for testators in preparing or drafting wills, or even with respect to matters of estate planning, lawyers must keep the beneficiaries of these transactions in mind. A tort duty of care owed to these third parties is now fairly widely accepted by Canadian courts.[113]

Although it is unlikely to occur in the typical solicitor-testator-beneficiary relationship, a potential conflict between the solicitor's contractual duty to its client and to the third party is one of the principal policy objections to the recognition of tort duties owed to third parties.[114] Those who have legal rights, or wish to protect their interests, ought to be required to do so themselves, by entering into their own contractual relationships. Courts are increasingly recognizing that while a solicitor may owe a duty of care to third persons in some limited circum-

---

D.L.R. (4th) 217 (N.S. C.A.). Where the negligence is in settling a claim for too little, how are damages assessed: by determining (1) what a court would have awarded at the date of the settlement, (2) what a court would have awarded at the date of the malpractice action, or (3) what a reasonable settlement would have been at the date of the actual settlement? In *Rose v. Mitton*, the court accepted the first option, although Hallett J.A. suggested that the third option might be more appropriate. This would eliminate the need to have a "trial within a trial" as was done in *Alberta v. Riggins*.

110 (1996), [1997] 1 W.W.R. 430 (Sask. Q.B.).

111 (1997), [1998] 3 W.W.R. 754 (Sask. Q.B.), affirmed (1998), 7 C.C.L.I. (3d) 302 (Sask. C.A.).

112 See Debra Rolph, "Solicitors' Liability To Non-Clients In Negligence" (1993), 15 Advocates Quarterly 129, for a good discussion of the topic and the cases.

113 See extensive discussion on this matter in Chapter 7.

114 See *Abacus Cities Ltd. (Trustee of) v. Bank of Montreal* (1986), 39 C.C.L.T. 7 (Alta. Q.B.), affirmed (1987), 44 C.C.L.T. 199 (Alta. C.A.), leave to appeal refused (1988), 58 Alta. L.R. (2d) xlix (S.C.C.) and *Kamahap Enterprises Ltd. v. Chu's Central Market Ltd.* (1989), [1990] 1 W.W.R. 632 (B.C. C.A.). In *Abacus*, a debtor company was put into receivership partly as a result of advice given to the creditor company by its solicitors. Mr. Justice McDonald refused to recognize a duty owed by the solicitors to the debtor. *Kamahap Enterprises* has been followed in British Columbia in *Esser v. Brown*, [2004] 10 W.W.R. 205, 25 C.C.L.T. (3d) 1 (B.C. C.A.) and *Elms v. Laurentian Bank of Canada* (2004), 27 C.C.L.T. (3d) 145 (B.C. S.C.), affirmed (2006), 37 C.C.L.T. (3d) 213 (B.C. C.A.).

stances,[115] that as a general proposition a solicitor's duty is one that is owed to a client alone.[116]

Unlike the typical solicitor/beneficiary relationship where the two parties are not in personal and direct contact, there are examples where solicitors do advise, or informally act for, others who are not actually their clients. This occurs, for example, where one party to a land transaction retains a lawyer, while the other does not, but the lawyer prepares all of the documents for the transaction and

---

115 For example, where the transaction was for the benefit of the third party (e.g., the will beneficiary case), or where the solicitor voluntarily assumed responsibility for the third party (e.g., the reliance case). See *Granville Savings & Mortgage Corp. v. Slevin* (1993), [1994] 1 W.W.R. 257, 108 D.L.R. (4th) 383 (S.C.C.), reversing [1992] 5 W.W.R. 1, 12 C.C.L.T. (2d) 275 (Man. C.A.), reversing (1990), 68 Man. R. (2d) 241 (Q.B.). The Supreme Court of Canada, in a brief judgment, affirmed a trial judgment that imposed a duty on solicitors acting for a mortgagor, to the mortgagee. Cory J. held that there was a special relationship between the solicitors and the mortgagee based on reliance. The Court of Appeal had denied the duty, stating that the solicitors had been retained by the mortgagor, to the knowledge of the mortgagee, in circumstances in which the mortgagee knew that the parties' interests might conflict. Although the solicitors were negligent in the way they handled the transaction, this is precisely why, according to Huband J.A, the mortgagee should have retained its own lawyer to better protect its interests.

116 In *Seaway Trust Co. v. Markle* (1991), 7 C.C.L.T. (2d) 83 (Ont.), the court held that in the absence of an undertaking or reliance, there is no duty on a solicitor to inform the opposite party of a fraud being perpetrated on it by the solicitor's client. The solicitor can be sued, of course, for participating in the fraud. In *Jensen v. McGregor* (1992), 89 D.L.R. (4th) 68, [1992] 4 W.W.R. 320 (B.C.), the court struck out a statement of claim brought by the plaintiff against the solicitor of his estranged wife. The plaintiff, who brought the action on his own and his children's behalf, alleged that due to the advice given by his wife's solicitors to her, that he and the children had been damaged. Also see *Mantella v. Mantella* (2006), 267 D.L.R. (4th) 532 (Ont. S.C.J.), additional reasons at (2006), 2006 CarswellOnt 3176 (S.C.J.), which again involved an unsuccessful claim brought by a husband against the lawyer for his estranged wife. A frequently referred to case is *Kamahap Enterprises Ltd. v. Chu's Central Market Ltd.* (1989), [1990] 1 W.W.R. 632 (B.C. C.A.), which held that in the absence of special circumstances a solicitor's duty is not owed to those who are in a contractual relationship with the solicitor's client. It is a duty owed only to the client. This is particularly so when a potential duty to the third party would conflict with the solicitor's duty to its client. As noted above, the reasoning in *Kamahap* has been followed in subsequent B.C. cases. Maczko J. in *Elms v. Laurentian Bank of Canada* (2004), 27 C.C.L.T. (3d) 145 (B.C. S.C.), affirmed (2006), 2006 CarswellBC 525 (C.A.), at 157 [C.C.L.T.] explained that "Lawyers have duties to their clients. Except where the Law Society permits, lawyers cannot have divided loyalties. If that were so, no client would feel secure that his or her lawyer is acting in his best interest and will keep confidences." Also see *J.A. Industries (Canada) Ltd. v. Highfield Development Ltd.* (1998), 230 A.R. 71 (Master), where Master Funduk dismissed as an abuse of process an action brought by one party to a dispute against the solicitors for the adverse party. The interests of the parties must be protected by their own counsel; not by the counsel for the opposing party. Also see *Baypark Investments Inc. v. Royal Bank* (2002), 57 O.R. (3d) 528 (S.C.J.), affirmed (2002), 2002 CarswellOnt 4023 (C.A.) to the same effect; and *Dubé c. Dionne* (1998), 201 N.B.R. (2d) 387 (C.A.). In *D'Amore Construction (Windsor) Ltd. v. Lawyers Professional Indemnity Co.* (2005), 30 C.C.L.T. (3d) 191 (Ont. Div. Ct.), an action brought against a lawyer by a non-client for allegedly negligent advice which that lawyer gave to the plaintiff's lawyer was struck out. Pierce J.A. held that the ultimate responsibility for the plaintiff's case was on his own lawyer. If, as a professional courtesy, a lawyer gives his advice on the matter to the plaintiff's lawyer, this does not create a proximate relationship between that other lawyer and the plaintiff.

advises both parties.[117] In this case the lawyer has undertaken to perform a service for the benefit of both parties, and based on *Hedley Byrne*, owes both a duty of care. For example, a plaintiff who invested money in a company which had retained the defendant lawyer was able to sue the lawyer in tort when her investment was lost. The court held that the lawyer had acted to reassure the plaintiff concerning the soundness of the investment and thus was in a duty relationship with her.[118] In another case, *Bowles v. Johnston, Oliphant, Van Buekenhout & Deans*,[119] the court went even further and imposed a duty on a solicitor to prevent a sale between the solicitor's own client and purchasers. The solicitor's client, a real estate agent, was "flipping" land, and the solicitor was completing the real estate conveyances. The court, applying both *Anns v. Merton London Borough Council*[120] and *Home Office v. Dorset Yacht Co.*,[121] held that there was a sufficient relationship of proximity between the parties to require a duty of care.[122]

Another way in which some courts have dealt with the relationship between a solicitor and a person who has not retained that solicitor has been through the laws relating to fiduciaries. In *Jacques v. Seabrook*,[123] for example, the court held that a fiduciary relationship was created between the plaintiff mortgagor and the defendant solicitor for the mortgagees. The relationship was created by the act of the defendant in undertaking to look into some legal matters for the plaintiff's

---

117 See, e.g., *Clarence Const. Ltd. v. Lavallee* (1980), 111 D.L.R. (3d) 582 (B.C. S.C.), affirmed (1982), 132 D.L.R. (3d) 153 (B.C. C.A.). Also see *Heath v. Ivens* (1991), 6 C.C.L.T. (3d) 311, [1991] 6 W.W.R. 201 (B.C.), where a solicitor, who was retained by one family member to protect his interests in property, was held to owe a duty to siblings with similar interests. The solicitor had met with them all, and had informally undertaken to act for them. The court also held that the contract of retainer contained an undertaking to protect the interests of all of the family members. Also see *347671 B.C. Ltd. v. Heenan Blaikie* (2002), 10 C.C.L.T. (3d) 306 (B.C. C.A.), affirming (2000), 2 C.C.L.T. (3d) 290 (B.C. S.C.), where personal assurances and representations made by a lawyer to third parties involved in a transaction with his client led to a successful third-party claim based on negligent misrepresentation. In *Midland Mortgage Corp. v. Jawl & Bundon* (1997), 33 C.C.L.T. (2d) 248 (B.C. S.C.), additional reasons at (1997), 9 C.P.C. (4th) 236 (B.C. S.C.), reversed (1999), [1999] B.C.J. No. 665, 1999 CarswellBC 617 (C.A.), additional reasons at (1999), [1999] B.C.J. No. 1766, 1999 CarswellBC 1708 (C.A.), leave to appeal refused (2000), 146 B.C.A.C. 73 (note) (S.C.C.), reliance was used by the trial judge as the basis for creating a duty of care owed by solicitors to investors who were not their clients. The Court of Appeal reversed, finding that the defendant solicitors had not been negligent in the performance of their duties to their client. Also see *Szelazek Investments Ltd. v. Orzech* (1997), 23 O.T.C. 53 (Gen. Div.).

118 *Klingspon v. Ramsay*, [1985] 5 W.W.R. 411 (B.C. S.C.). See also *Begusic v. Clark, Wilson & Co.* (1992), 92 D.L.R. (4th) 273 (B.C. S.C.). An unusual case is *Al-Kandari v. J.R. Brown & Co.*, [1988] 1 All E.R. 833 (C.A.). The court held that although solicitors generally owe no duty to the opposing party in hostile litigation, they may step outside their role as solicitor for their clients and accept responsibilities towards their client's opponent. In this case, the solicitor undertook not to release a passport to his client. This undertaking made him liable in tort to the opposing party when it was breached.

119 [1988] 4 W.W.R. 242 (Man. Q.B.).

120 [1978] A.C. 728 (H.L.).

121 [1970] A.C. 1004 (H.L.).

122 This is a clear example of a solicitor's duty to a client being in direct conflict with the duty to a third party. This is arguably a matter not for tort, but for disciplinary proceedings, if called for.

123 [1982] 4 W.W.R. 167 (B.C. Co. Ct.).

protection. As with the *Hedley Byrne* cases, the relationship arises due to the solicitor's gratuitous undertaking to act with care for the plaintiff's protection.[124]

(iv) The Effect of a Retainer

The tort standard of care which ordinarily applies between parties in a *Donoghue v. Stevenson* relationship can be displaced, or supplemented, by more stringent obligations which the parties accept pursuant to contract. In this respect, the terms of a solicitor's retainer with a client can impose more onerous, and additional, responsibilities on the solicitor than a simple duty to take reasonable care would imply.[125] If a solicitor, or any other professional, undertakes to provide a specific service, and guarantees a result, the court will require strict performance.

There is, however, the danger that an overly literal interpretation of the contractual undertaking of a solicitor will improperly lead to the imposition of strict liability and the displacement of the traditionally accepted reasonable care standard. This is what occurred in *Polischuk v. Hagarty*.[126] A solicitor was found liable, in contract, for failing to complete a contract of purchase and sale on behalf of clients, according to its terms. In a controversial decision,[127] the court replaced the standard of the reasonably competent professional by what amounted to a standard of strict liability by finding that when a solicitor undertakes to do something, it must be done, and it is no excuse that the failure to do it was not the result of negligence. This decision has the effect of constituting the solicitor an insurer for legal services. Unless a solicitor specifically agrees to guarantee a result or to act in a certain defined way, it is suggested that it would be preferable

---

124 Other similar cases where courts have created a fiduciary relationship between a solicitor and those who although not clients were relying upon the solicitor for protection are *Dorndorf v. Hoeter* (1981), 122 D.L.R. (3d) 758 (B.C. S.C.) — notary public; *Tracy v. Atkins* (1977), 83 D.L.R. (3d) 46 (B.C. S.C.), affirmed (1979), 105 D.L.R. (3d) 632 (B.C. C.A.); *Lapierre v. Young* (1980), 117 D.L.R. (3d) 643 (Ont. H.C.); *Commerce Capital Trust v. Berk* (1989), 68 O.R. (2d) 257 (C.A.); *Hongkong Bank of Canada v. Phillips* (1997), 39 C.C.L.T. (2d) 301 (Man. Q.B.), varied as to costs [1997] 8 W.W.R. 212 (Man. Q.B.); among others.

125 There have been several expressions of this point in the case law. See especially Oliver J.'s judgment in *Midland Bank Trust Co. v. Hett, Stubbs & Kemp*, [1979] Ch. 384 at 434: "A contract gives rise to a complex of rights and duties of which the duty to exercise reasonable care and skill is but one." This was applied in *Bank of N.S. v. Omni Const. Co.*, [1983] 4 W.W.R. 577 (Sask. C.A.). In *3464920 Canada Inc. v. Strother* (2007), 48 C.C.L.T. (3d) 1 (S.C.C.), at 29, Binnie J. made the point that although "the scope of the retainer is governed by the contract" the "relationship thus created is however overlaid with certain fiduciary responsibilities, which are imposed as a matter of law." McLachlin C.J.C. asserted, however, that the fiduciary duties "are molded" by the retainer. The majority, per Binnie J., held that the solicitor breached his fiduciary duty of loyalty to his client by taking on a personal pecuniary interest in one of his client's competitors. This placed his personal interests in conflict with his client's interests.

126 (1983), 149 D.L.R. (3d) 65 (Ont. H.C.), varied as to damages (1984), 14 D.L.R. (4th) 446 (Ont. C.A.).

127 See Mahoney, "Lawyers — Negligence — Standard of Care" (1985), 63 Can. Bar Rev. 221.

to adhere to the traditional view that in carrying out the terms of a retainer a solicitor agrees to do so with the prudence of a competent practitioner.[128]

The terms of a retainer can also be used to limit a solicitor's responsibilities. Thus, in *Smith v. McInnis*,[129] for example, the Supreme Court of Canada agreed with lower court findings that the terms of a solicitor's retainer were limited, and in the circumstances had been fulfilled, even though a broader view of why the solicitor was retained might have resulted in liability.[130] As well, in *Spence v. Bell*,[131] the majority of the court excused the defendant solicitor from liability in view of the limited scope of the retainer.[132]

(v) *Examples of Legal Malpractice*

Lawyers have been found liable in negligence for a wide range of breaches.[133] Although it is not intended, in a general text such as this, to provide an encyclopedic review of these cases, a brief reference to some of the more recent judgments will indicate how the general principles of liability have been applied.[134]

---

128 The argument that by using contract a professional's duty can be made more onerous was raised and rejected in relation to a doctor. In *Grey v. Webster* (1984), 14 D.L.R. (4th) 706 at 713 (N.B. Q.B.), the court held that in the absence of "further undertakings" the doctor's duty is to exercise reasonable care in providing services.

129 (1978), 4 C.C.L.T. 154 (S.C.C.).

130 As found by the dissenting judge, Pigeon J.

131 [1982] 6 W.W.R. 385 (Alta. C.A.).

132 See also *Wekherlien v. McCord*, [1993] 4 W.W.R. 313 (Alta. Q.B.), affirmed [1995] 6 W.W.R. 266 (Alta. C.A.), where the solicitor's duty was defined by the role which it had agreed to play in the transaction. Note, however, *Marbel Developments v. Pirani* (1994), 18 C.C.L.T. (2d) 229 (B.C. S.C.), where the court, while agreeing that the scope of the retainer is important in defining the lawyer's duties, held that the lawyer must not be permitted to allow the client to define the retainer "unilaterally," in ignorance of material risks. That is, the lawyer has a duty to inform the client of the material risks surrounding the transaction. Several cases discussing the importance of retainers in defining the scope and nature of a solicitor's duties are *Wilcox v. Johnston* (2001), 238 N.B.R. (2d) 325 (Q.B.); *Fasken Campbell Godfrey v. Seven-Up Canada Ltd.* (1997), 142 D.L.R. (4th) 456 (Ont. Gen. Div.), affirmed (2000), 47 O.R. (3d) 15 (C.A.), leave to appeal refused (2000), 143 O.A.C. 396 (note) (S.C.C.); *Watts v. Wakerich* (2002), [2002] A.J. No. 750, 2002 CarswellAlta 777 (Q.B.); *Coughlin v. Comery* (1996), [1996] O.J. No. 822, 1996 CarswellOnt 686 (Gen. Div.), additional reasons at (1996), 1996 CarswellOnt 2816 (Gen. Div. [In Chambers]), affirmed (1998), [1998] O.J. No. 4066, 1998 CarswellOnt 3958 (C.A.), leave to appeal refused (1999), 125 O.A.C. 399 (note) (S.C.C.); and *Lenz v. Broadhurst Main* (2004), [2004] O.J. No. 288, 2004 CarswellOnt 333 (S.C.J.), affirmed (2005), 2005 CarswellOnt 4416 (C.A.). In *Lenz*, Himel J. discusses the importance of the retainer in defining the lawyer's duty in conjunction with the broader duty to protect the interests of the client more generally. As well, the legal implications attached to a lawyer signing a certificate of "independent legal advice" are considered. In *Hall v. Bennett Estate* (May 14, 2003), Doc. CA C37163 (Ont. C.A.), the court noted that "the retainer is usually the very basis of a relationship between a solicitor and client" and in the absence of one there would usually be no duty owed by the solicitor to the client. A reliance relationship could create a duty in the appropriate case.

133 See Rainaldi, ed., *Remedies in Tort* (1987), Chapter 16.

134 A useful statement of the scope of a lawyer's obligations is the following from Riley J. in *Tiffin Hldg. Ltd. v. Millican* (1964), 49 D.L.R. (2d) 216 at 219 (Alta. T.D.):

(1) To be skilful and careful.

(2) To advise his client on all matters relevant to his retainer, so far as may be reasonably

In *Central & Eastern Trust Co. v. Rafuse*,[135] the Supreme Court of Canada, while holding that a solicitor need not have a "working knowledge" of all the law applicable to the service being performed, held that "he must have a sufficient knowledge of the fundamental issues or principles of law applicable to the particular work he has undertaken to enable him to perceive the need to ascertain the law on relevant points."[136] Put simply, it appears that, in almost any case where a solicitor failed to know the law, there will be liability for either a lack of knowledge or a lack of research.[137] It is possible that a lawyer will be forgiven for not knowing or researching an old and obscure principle,[138] but even here the Supreme Court of Canada, per Le Dain J., has suggested that there must be other extenuating circumstances for not having researched the law. Where the law is unclear, a lawyer who gives carefully formed advice will not be held liable should it subsequently transpire that this advice was wrong.[139] Depending upon the circumstances, however, the lawyer may be found negligent for failing to warn a client that the advice may be later found to be wrong. Where the uncertainty relates to a critical matter, such as the applicability of a short limitation period, a lawyer ought to take a cautious approach. Thus, a lawyer was held negligent for having missed a limitation period, even though at the time most lawyers would have considered that the short limitation period did not apply to that type of case.[140]

---

necessary.

(3) To protect the interests of his client.

(4) To carry out his instructions by all proper means.

(5) To consult with his client on all questions of doubt which do not fall within the express or implied discretion left to him.

(6) To keep his client informed to such an extent as may be reasonably necessary, according to the same criteria.

This was applied in *Couture v. Lamontagne* (1996), [1997] 5 W.W.R. 23 (Sask. Q.B.), reversed (1997), [1998] 6 W.W.R. 481 (Sask. C.A.), leave to appeal refused (1998), 168 Sask. R. 319 (note) (S.C.C.), where a lawyer was held liable at trial for failing to fully and carefully inform his client of the possible risks of signing a personal guarantee. The Court of Appeal reversed, finding that the trial judge had made an error in rejecting testimony that established that the client had indeed understood the risks. In *Chaster (Guardian ad litem of) v. LeBlanc* (2007), 51 C.C.L.T. (3d) 131 (B.C. S.C.), additional reasons at (2008), 2008 CarswellBC 60 (S.C.), the plaintiff was a lawyer who was injured in a motor vehicle accident. He retained a lawyer to represent him in his action against the driver of the other motor vehicle. The case was settled. The plaintiff then sued his lawyer for his negligence in preparing the case leading to the settlement. The court identified various acts of negligence; for example, failing to locate and interview a witness, to obtain medical records, and to adequately discuss the case with his client. Ultimately, however, the court found that the plaintiff himself had decided to settle the case and would have done so even had his lawyer's preparatory work not been done negligently.

135 (1986), 37 C.C.L.T. 117 (S.C.C.).

136 *Ibid.*, at 167.

137 See also *Elcano Accept. Ltd. v. Richmond, Richmond, Stambler & Mills* (1989), 68 O.R. (2d) 165 (H.C.), additional reasons at (1989), 68 O.R. (2d) 641 (H.C.), affirmed (1991), 3 O.R. (3d) 123 (C.A.).

138 See *Bannerman Brydone Folster & Co. v. Murray*, [1972] N.Z.L.R. 411 (C.A.), cited by Le Dain J. at 37 C.C.L.T. 168. See also *B & R Farms Ltd. v. Ulmer* (1987), 55 Sask. R. 309 (Q.B.).

139 See *Ormindale Hldg. Ltd. v. Ray, Wolfe, Connell, Lightbody & Reynolds* (1980), 116 D.L.R. (3d) 346 (B.C. S.C.), affirmed (1982), 135 D.L.R. (3d) 577 (B.C. C.A.).

140 *Boros v. Bodnar, Wanhella & Courtney*, [1988] 6 W.W.R. 645 (Sask. Q.B.).

The question of a lawyer's responsibility for settlements has also been dealt with. In *Karpenko v. Paroian, Courey, Cohen & Houston*,[141] the court stressed the public policy interest in discouraging law suits and encouraging settlements, and recognized that the solicitor's decision whether to accept a settlement or proceed to trial is a subjective decision based on experience and knowledge. It would therefore only be in the face of an "egregious" error that the court would hold a solicitor liable with respect to the settlement decision.[142]

The case law confirms that allegations of legal malpractice frequently arise when lawyers act for more than one of the parties involved in a transaction. Although not always successful, these cases ought to strike a cautionary note for lawyers, who by acting for both parties may place themselves in a "conflict of interest" position.[143]

The obligations of lawyers who represent clients in real estate transactions have also been the focus of case law and commentary. It has been suggested that some case law has imposed unreasonably onerous obligations on real estate lawyers.[144]

---

141 (1980), 117 D.L.R. (3d) 383 (Ont. H.C.).

142 There have been a number of cases alleging negligence relating to settlements. Actions have invariably failed: see *Startup v. Blake* (2001), [2001] B.C.J. No. 16, 2001 CarswellBC 15 (S.C.); *Spadaccini v. Rogers* (2000), [2000] O.J. No. 779, 2000 CarswellOnt 772 (S.C.J.); *Grieg v. Waldock (Trustee of)* (1997), [1997] B.C.J. No. 2217, 1997 CarswellBC 2091 (S.C.); *Simanek v. Lamourie* (2001), [2001] O.J. No. 3957, 2001 CarswellOnt 3559 (S.C.J.), affirmed (2002), 2002 CarswellOnt 2472 (C.A.); *Huberman Cristall Hutchinson v. Chu* (1996), 1996 CarswellBC 2159 (C.A.), leave to appeal refused (1997), 94 B.C.A.C. 320 (note) (S.C.C.), reconsideration refused (June 19, 1997), Doc. 25681 (S.C.C.); and *Kaslik v. Futerman* (2004), [2004] O.J. No. 4640, 2004 CarswellOnt 4675 (C.A.). It will be interesting to see whether the case law discussed above, which has rejected the "egregious error" standard for lawyers, in favour of the reasonably competent lawyer standard, will be applied to cases involving negligent settlements. See, for example, *Rivait v. Monforton* (2005), [2005] O.J. No. 4698, 2005 CarswellOnt 5898 (S.C.J.), affirmed 2007 ONCA 829 (C.A.). The trial judge, while acknowledging the Ontario Court of Appeal's rejection of the "egregious error" standard in *Folland v. Reardon* (2005), 74 O.R. (3d) 688 (C.A.), stated that the concerns expressed in *Karpenko v. Paroian* remain valid. The court rejected the plaintiff's contention that the settlement amount agreed to was too low. The "egregious" error standard was applied in *Forbes v. Siskind, Cromarty, Ivey & Dowler LLP* (2003), 20 C.C.L.T. (3d) 87 (Ont. S.C.J.), additional reasons at (2003), 2003 CarswellOnt 5059 (S.C.J.). The case involved alleged negligence in representing a client in an arbitration procedure. This also must now be considered in doubt in view of the Ontario Court of Appeal's rejection of this lower standard of care for lawyers.

143 Cases include: *Grand Anse Contracting Ltd. v. MacKinnon*, above, note 86; *Shute v. Premier Trust Co.* (1993), 35 R.P.R. (2d) 141 (Ont. Gen. Div.); and *McKitterick v. Duco, Geist & Chodos*, [1993] O.J. No. 648. An interesting judgment which helps identify the factors which determine whether a lawyer was acting as a lawyer or as a businessman when dealing with investors' money in his own company is *Yang v. Overseas Investments (1986) Ltd.*, [1995] 4 W.W.R. 231 (Alta. Q.B.).

144 The two cases in issue are *Vaz-Oxlade v. Volkenstein* (1998), 22 R.P.R. (3d) 159 (Ont. Gen. Div.), reversed (2000), 35 R.P.R. (3d) 165 (Ont. C.A.); and *Wong v. 407527 Ontario Ltd.* (1999), 26 R.P.R. (3d) 262 (Ont. C.A.), additional reasons at (2000), 2000 CarswellOnt 3701 (C.A.). One should note that in both cases although lawyers were found liable at trial, their liability was reversed on appeal. See T.B. Rotenberg, "The Real Estate Lawyer as Superman" in (1999), 22 R.P.R. (3d) 176, and (2000), 29 R.P.R. (3d) 289; Lem & White, "Annotation" (1999), 26 R.P.R. (3d) 264 and (2000), 30 R.P.R. (3d) 163. A strange issue that was litigated is the lawyer's responsibility to ensure that those who profess to be certain persons are in fact

The obligations of lawyers with respect to determining a person's testamentary capacity before agreeing to prepare a will was in issue in *Hall v. Bennett Estate*.[145] The Court held that a solicitor has a duty to decline a retainer to prepare a will where the solicitor has concluded that the testator lacks capacity. Whether the solicitor has an obligation to accept the retainer where there is testamentary capacity, once having agreed to meet with the prospective client, was doubted, although the question was left open.

(b) Doctors

If the reported cases are a true indicator, no professional is subject to as much malpractice litigation as is the medical practitioner. The subject of medical malpractice is a large one, and there are numerous recent books and articles on the topic.[146] This section will discuss some of the more interesting and important recent developments.[147]

(i) The Duty to Disclose

The growing number of reported medical negligence cases can largely be attributed to the duty to inform requirement. Doctors have long been expected to provide their patients with due diligence and skill with respect to the treatment

---

not impostors. In *Yamada v. Mock* (1996), 136 D.L.R. (4th) 124 (Ont. Gen. Div.), a lawyer retained by a mortgagee to act on his behalf with respect to a mortgage was duped by an impostor claiming to be the mortgagor with title to the home. The court held that lawyers must take reasonable steps to ensure that those who are professing to be certain individuals are in fact not impostors.

145 (2003), 15 C.C.L.T. (3d) 315 (Ont. C.A.). Also see *Slobodianik v. Podlasiewicz* (2003), 228 D.L.R. (4th) 610 (Man. C.A.).

146 In addition to the textbooks, several judgments in the area have also provided an extensive review of the authorities and general principles. See, for example, *Bauer (Litigation Guardian of) v. Seager*, [2000] 11 W.W.R. 621 (Man. Q.B.).

147 It is also interesting to note that this is an area where judicial unhappiness with the tort litigation process seems particularly pronounced. See, e.g., comments by Krever J. in *Ferguson v. Hamilton Civic Hosps.* (1983), 40 O.R. (2d) 577 at 618-19 (H.C.); by Cavanagh A.C.J.H.C. in *Koerber v. Kitchener-Waterloo Hosp.* (1987), 62 O.R. (2d) 613 at 632 (H.C.); and by the Saskatchewan Court of Appeal in *Quintal v. Datta*, [1988] 6 W.W.R. 481. For recent academic criticism of tort litigation in the medical field, see R.L. Akazaki, "Medical Malpractice in Crisis" (1999), 21 Advocates' Q. 163. An emerging issue in the medical negligence field is the effect of budget cutbacks and cost containment objectives on a doctor's standard of care. This was commented on by Lofchik J. in *De Vos v. Robertson* (2000), 48 C.C.L.T. (2d) 172 (Ont. S.C.J.). Lofchik J. stated that "if it comes to a choice between the physician's responsibility to his or her individual patient and his or her responsibility to the medical care system overall, the former must take precedence in a case such as this". The case concerned the choice of anaesthetic for a day surgery. See John Irvine, "Case Comment" (1994), 21 C.C.L.T. (2d) 266, written concerning *Law Estate v. Simice* (1994), 21 C.C.L.T. (2d) 228 (B.C. S.C.), affirmed (December 12, 1995), Doc. CA018888 (B.C. C.A.); John Irvine, "The Physician's Duty in the Age of Cost Containment" (1994), 22 M.L.J. 345; T. Caulfield, "Health Care Reform: Can Tort Law Meet The Challenge?" (1994), 32 Alta. L. Rev. 685; J.T. Curry, "Are Cuts to Health Care Funding Changing the Legal Standard of Care?" (2000), 22 Advocates' Q. 337; and Robert-Jean Chenier, "Resource Allocation and the Standard of Care of Physicians" (2004), 83 Can. Bar Rev. 1.

aspects of the medical service.[148] Thus, when diagnosing illnesses, deciding upon treatment, treating, and taking care of a patient after treatment, doctors must live up to those standards applied to all professionals as defined by the general law of negligence.[149] A relatively recent development, however, has occurred with respect to the doctor's duty to inform the patient[150] concerning the nature, gravity, and risks inherent in medical treatment, and the patient's right to make an informed choice concerning what treatment will be performed. Today, medical malpractice litigation is not confined only to those cases where unhappy results of treatment have occurred due to the alleged incompetence of defendant doctors. It also extends to the large number of instances where less than perfect or hoped-for results have occurred despite the competence of the defendant doctor, through the avenue of the breach of the doctor's duty to inform.[151]

In Canada, it was the well-known cases of *Reibl v. Hughes*[152] and *Hopp v. Lepp*[153] which introduced the patient's right to be fully informed of all material, special and unusual risks of treatment and which started a veritable flood of failure to inform cases.[154] These two cases decided the following:

---

148 In *Erkelens v. Ledger* (1996), 34 C.C.L.T. (2d) 209 (Man. Q.B.), the court held that a doctor's advice as to whether a private disability policy covers an anxiety disorder "does not come within even the broadest definition of medical practice" and is thus not subject to the limitation period provided for by the Medical Act, R.S.M. 1987, c. M90. In *Branco v. Sunybrook & Women's College Health Sciences Centre* (2003), [2003] O.J. No. 3287 (S.C.J.), the court held that a doctor conducting a medical examination of the plaintiff at the request of the plaintiff's employer owes no duty to the employee other than the duty not to harm him in the course of the examination.

149 In *Brown (Next Friend of) v. University of Alberta Hospital* (1997), 33 C.C.L.T. (2d) 113 (Alta. Q.B.), the court held that the duty to diagnose extended beyond "pure diagnosis" and required a radiologist to report suspected child abuse to the authorities. The court found that had this been done further child abuse that caused serious injury to the child would have been avoided.

150 Or the patient's guardian. See, e.g., *Rayner v. Knickle* (1988), 47 C.C.L.T. 141 (P.E.I. T.D.), reversed in part (1991), 88 Nfld. & P.E.I.J. 214 (P.E.I. C.A.).

151 The doctor's duty to inform is also extensively dealt with in Ontario by the Health Care Consent Act, 1996, S.O., c. 2, Sch. A. As noted by Doherty J.A. in *Van Dyke v. Grey Bruce Regional Health Centre* (2005), 33 C.C.L.T. (3d) 1 (Ont. C.A.), the statutory definition of informed consent in the Act contains many of the same principles found in the common law. Wilson J. in *Ross v. Welsh* (2003), 18 C.C.L.T. (3d) 107 at 123 (Ont. S.C.J.) notes that the legislation and its predecessor, the Consent to Treatment Act, S.O. 1992, c. 31, "were intended as a codification of the common law aimed at promoting consistency in information provided to patients." Picard and Robertson, *Legal Liability of Doctors and Hospitals in Canada*, 3rd ed. (1996) at 130 was cited in support of this proposition.

152 (1980), 14 C.C.L.T. 1 (S.C.C.).

153 (1980), 13 C.C.L.T. 66 (S.C.C.).

154 There have been dozens of reported cases since those judgments, too numerous to note here. The reader can refer to the several commentaries on this topic which discuss the more important of these cases. See, e.g., Robertson, "Overcoming the Causation Hurdle in Informed Consent Cases: The Principle in *McGhee v. N.C.B.*" (1984), 22 U.W.O.L. Rev. 75; Picard, "Consent to Medical Treatment in Canada" (1981), 19 Osgoode Hall L.J. 140; Sanda Rodgers-Magnet, "Recent Developments in the Doctrine of Informed Consent to Medical Treatment" (1980-81), 14 C.C.L.T. 61; Osborne, "Causation and the Emerging Canadian Doctrine of Informed Consent to Medical Treatment" (1985), 33 C.C.L.T. 131; Somerville, "Structuring the Issues in Informed Consent" (1981), 26 McGill L.J. 673; Klar, "Recent Developments in Canadian

(1) A failure on the part of a doctor to fully inform the patient of the risks of a proposed treatment will generally be dealt with by negligence law, and not by battery. It is only when a doctor has acted without an informed consent going to the basic nature of the treatment that a battery action will be appropriate.[155]

(2) A doctor's duty to inform relates to all the material, special or unusual risks of treatment.[156] In this respect, what is material is determined by what the reasonable patient would want to know, and not by what the reasonable doctor would like to disclose.[157] Material risks have been defined as "significant risks that pose a real threat to the patients' life, health or comfort."[158] Special or unusual risks are risks that "are not ordinary, common, everyday matters" which are known to occur occasionally.[159] There is some confusion about the status of "unusual"

Law: Tort Law" (1985), 17 Ottawa L. Rev. 325; Picard and Robertson, *Legal Liability of Doctors and Hospitals in Canada*, 4th ed. (2007).

155 As a result, virtually all reported cases dealing with the failure to inform, since the two judgments, have been in negligence. See Linden J.'s judgment in *White v. Turner* (1981), 15 C.C.L.T. 81 at 97 (Ont. H.C.), affirmed (1982), 12 D.L.R. (4th) 319 (Ont. C.A.), for the types of failure to inform cases which could still be actionable in battery, for example, proceeding with anaesthetic when a patient objected. It has also been held that a failure to obtain consent is actionable not only in battery, but in negligence as well. See *Adan v. Davis* (1998), 43 C.C.L.T. (2d) 262 (Ont. Gen. Div.). In *Gerelus v. Lim* (2006), 43 C.C.L.T. (3d) 256 (Man. Q.B.), affirmed 2008 MBCA 89 (Man. C.A.), the plaintiff sued for battery alleging that she had specifically asked that "no interns" participate in the delivery of her baby. The defendant doctor was a resident. The court rejected the claim holding that the defendant was not an intern and that the plaintiff knew about and consented to the doctor's participation. The allegations of negligent treatment and failing to inform of risks were also rejected. The trial judgment was affirmed on appeal.

156 This includes the risks of leaving the ailment untreated and the alternative treatments. See *Haughian v. Paine* (1987), 40 C.C.L.T. 13 (Sask. C.A.).

157 It has been held that in regard to elective treatment the doctor fulfills the duty by disclosing the risks of the treatment, without necessarily advising the plaintiff whether to undergo the treatment or not. It is up to the patient to weigh the benefits and risks of elective treatment and decide what is "best" for him or her. See *Zamparo v. Brisson* (1981), 16 C.C.L.T. 66 (Ont. C.A.). It should also be noted that the full disclosure standard has not been accepted in England, where the professional disclosure standard is retained. See *Sidaway v. Bethlem Royal Hosp. Govs.*, [1985] 1 All E.R. 643 (H.L.). The Supreme Court of Canada's commitment to the right of the patient to know was reaffirmed in *Arndt v. Smith*, 35 C.C.L.T. (2d) 233, [1997] 8 W.W.R. 303, 148 D.L.R. (4th) 48 (S.C.C.). As stated in this case by Cory J.: "*Reibl v. Hughes* is a very significant and leading authority. It marks the rejection of the paternalistic approach to determining how much information should be given to patients. It emphasizes the patient's right to know and ensures that patients will have the benefit of a high standard of disclosure", at (1997), 35 C.C.L.T. (2d) 233 (S.C.C.) at 245.

158 Linden J. in *White v. Turner* (1981), 120 D.L.R. (3d) 269 at 284 (Ont. H.C.), affirmed (1982), 12 D.L.R. (4th) 319 (Ont. C.A.).

159 *Ibid.*, at 285. Also see *Kitchen v. McMullen* (1989), 62 D.L.R. (4th) 481 (N.B. C.A.). A very useful summary of the scope of the duty of disclosure is found in *Rohde v. Steinhoff* (1995), 25 C.C.L.T. (2d) 62 (B.C. S.C.). Among the points made by Murphy J. are the following, at 73-74:

(i) common everyday risks, such as that an incision will cause bleeding, some pain, may result in a scar, and might become infected, do not have to be revealed;
(ii) what the specific patient would want to know should be taken into consideration;
(iii) in evaluating risks, a court should consider not only their probability, but their gravity should they occur.

risks. If a risk is unusual in the sense that it is rare, must it be disclosed? This issue was dealt with by Mandel J. in *Leung v. Campbell.*[160] The rarity of a risk must be measured alongside its potential severity to determine whether a reasonable patient would want to know about it. The fact that a risk is either common or rare is only one factor to consider. I would suggest that in cases of doubt, the wise doctor would err on the side of more rather than less information.[161]

(3) The duty to inform will be more onerous should the patient ask specific questions, or should the doctor know in some other way that the patient desires a fuller explanation.[162]

(4) There may be situations where, due to the plaintiff's inability to understand or cope with the information, information can legitimately be withheld. This has been termed the therapeutic privilege.[163]

(5) Where the duty to disclose has been breached, the patient will have to prove that damages were caused by this breach. In this respect, it will be necessary to establish that had the required information been communicated, the patient, as a reasonable patient, would have declined the treatment. The court, in deciding

---

160 (1995), 24 C.C.L.T. (2d) 63 (Ont. Gen. Div.).

161 In *Painter v. Rae*, [1998] 8 W.W.R. 717 (Man. Q.B.), the court held that although the risk of a bowel injury during a postpartum tubal ligation was less than one-tenth of one per cent it had to be disclosed in view of the gravity of the consequences if the risk materializes. See also *Berezowski-Aitken v. McGregor*, [1998] 8 W.W.R. 322 (Man. Q.B.), affirmed [1999] 9 W.W.R. 94 (Man. C.A.). A case that came to an opposite conclusion was *DeFerrari v. Neville* (1998), 42 C.C.L.T. (2d) 327 (Ont. Gen. Div.), additional reasons at (1998), 1998 CarswellOnt 4259 (Gen. Div.). The risk of permanent numbness due to local anaesthetic was one in 800,000. It was not a serious enough risk to warrant disclosure. In *Koller v. Colcleugh* (1999), 47 C.C.L.T. (2d) 193 (Ont. S.C.J.), the risk was held to be very remote and the fact that the surgery was elective was held not to affect the standard of disclosure. An extensive discussion of the duty to disclose is found in *Rhine v. Millan,* [2000] 7 W.W.R. 136, 49 C.C.L.T. (2d) 256 (Alta. Q.B.). Particularly useful is the point that the duty to disclose of risks is a continuing one throughout the course of treatment. The case involved the prescription of drugs.

162 See, for example, *Hartjes v. Carman* (2004), [2004] O.J. No. 5597, 2004 CarswellOnt 9807 (Div. Ct.). It has also been held that where the treatment is purely for the purposes of scientific experimentation, all known risks, even if they are rare, must be disclosed. See *Weiss v. Solomon* (1989), 48 C.C.L.T. 280 (Que. S.C.).

163 See e.g., *Haughian v. Paine* (1987), 40 C.C.L.T. 13 at 41 (Sask. C.A.); *Hajgato v. London Health Assn.* (1982), 36 O.R. (2d) 669 (H.C.), affirmed (1983), 44 O.R. (2d) 264 (C.A.). The therapeutic privilege is essentially inconsistent with a plaintiff's right to self-determination and hence will be difficult to establish. See *Pittman Estate v. Bain* (1994), 19 C.C.L.T. (2d) 1 (Ont. Gen. Div.), where a doctor's failure to inform his patient that he had been transfused with HIV infected blood was held to be negligent. The court stated that "while information about one's bad health is clearly 'bad news', a patient is entitled to know that that is his or her prognosis, absent clear indication that he or she does not want to receive that news," 19 C.C.L.T. (2d) at 144. One trial judge has gone so far as to state that the therapeutic privilege exception does not and should not form part of Canadian law. See Maloney J. in *Meyer Estate v. Rogers* (1991), 2 O.R. (3d) 356 (Gen. Div.). According to Maloney J., Laskin C.J.C.'s comments about therapeutic privilege in *Reibl v. Hughes* were equivocal, and *obiter*.

what the reasonable patient would have done, can take into account the circumstances of the particular patient.[164]

As has been commented upon by others,[165] the causation hurdle has been an extremely difficult one for patients to overcome. There is a good reason for this. Where a court has decided that a doctor's decision to treat a patient in a specific manner, despite inherent risks of adverse effects, was a reasonable decision, it is highly unlikely that this same court will then decide that a reasonable patient, having been properly informed of the risks, would have declined the treatment. In most situations, the factors which led the court to find that the doctor's decision to pursue a risky treatment was the right and reasonable one will also persuade the court that a reasonable patient would have accepted the treatment. This has been the experience from the cases.[166] Where the methods of treatment themselves have been found to be unreasonable,[167] plaintiffs have been able to satisfy the objective test of causation in a failure to inform claim. In the few other cases of successful claims,[168] although the recommended treatment was apparently rea-

---

164 See *Currie c. Blundell* (1992), 10 C.C.L.T. (2d) 288 (C.S. Qué.), a case of informed consent from Quebec. The question arose whether the objective or subjective test of causation applies in Quebec law. Despite authorities which suggested a subjective test, the court held that on either test, the plaintiff had established causation. In *Drolet c. Parenteau* (1994), 26 C.C.L.T. (2d) 168 (Que. C.A.), the court applied a subjective test of causation, while noting that this must be evaluated in light of what a reasonable patient in the plaintiff's circumstances would have done.

165 See Robertson, Picard, and Osborne, above, note 154.

166 This paragraph was quoted with approval in *Van Dyke v. Grey Bruce Regional Health Centre* (2005), 33 C.C.L.T. (3d) 1 at 22 (Ont. C.A.). The court found that although the defendant doctor failed in his duty of disclosure, causation was not made out. As stated by Doherty J.A. "Absent any factors particular to the individual patient, I cannot see why a reasonable person in the patient's position would not take the medically reasonable advice offered by the treating physician."

167 See, e.g., *Reynard v. Carr* (1983), 30 C.C.L.T. 42 (B.C. S.C.), affirmed as to liability (1986), 38 C.C.L.T. 217 (B.C. C.A.); *Graham v. Persyko* (1984), 30 C.C.L.T. 85 (Ont. H.C.), affirmed (1986), 27 D.L.R. (4th) 699 (Ont. C.A.); *Coughlin v. Kuntz* (1987), 42 C.C.L.T. 142 (B.C. S.C.), affirmed (1989), 2 C.C.L.T. (2d) 42 (B.C. C.A.); *Schanczl v. Singh*, [1988] 2 W.W.R. 465 (Alta. Q.B.); *Mann v. Jugdeo*, [1993] 4 W.W.R. 760 (Sask. Q.B.); *Semeniuk v. Cox*, [2000] 4 W.W.R. 310, 48 C.C.L.T. (2d) 286 (Alta. Q.B.); *Lyne v. McClarty*, [2001] 8 W.W.R. 453 (Man. Q.B.), reversed (2003), 2003 CarswellMan 33 (C.A.) (liability was affirmed, although damages were varied). In *Christie v. Jason* (2004), [2005] 5 W.W.R. 163 (Man. Q.B.), the trial judge found in the plaintiff's favour on the issue of cause. Although not specifically stating that the treatment was unreasonable, Duval J. stated that he "cannot conceive that a reasonable person in the plaintiff's circumstances would have agreed to this elective surgery" if informed of the risks.

168 E.g., *Rawlings v. Lindsay* (1982), 20 C.C.L.T. 301 (B.C. S.C.); *Montaron v. Wagner* (1988), 43 C.C.L.T. 233 (Alta. Q.B.), varied as to costs (1989), 70 Alta. L.R. (2d) 86 (C.A.); *Bryan v. Hicks* [1995] 10 W.W.R. 145 (B.C. C.A.), affirming [1993] B.C.W.L.D. 1076; *De Vos v. Robertson* (2000), 48 C.C.L.T. (2d) 172 (Ont. S.C.J.). In *Huisman v. MacDonald* (2007), 280 D.L.R. (4th) 1 (Ont. C.A.), leave to appeal refused (2007), 2007 CarswellOnt 7855 (S.C.C.), affirming (2007), 2005 CarswellOnt 2302 (S.C.C.), the Court of Appeal affirmed liability in a failure to inform case. The treatment prescribed was reasonable. The trial judge seemed influenced on the question of causation by the fact that the plaintiff had raised a question concerning the risk. Armstrong J.A. affirmed essentially because the decision as to cause was a question of fact and there was no palpable and overriding error in the trial judge's conclusion.

sonable, the courts have considered that the patient's personal circumstances, combined with the fact that the treatment was not urgent, would have led the reasonable patient to decline the treatment.[169]

The nature of the test of causation that patients must meet in failure to inform cases was revisited by the Supreme Court of Canada in *Arndt v. Smith*.[170] The case involved a doctor's duty to disclose to a pregnant woman that her chicken pox entailed risks of serious birth defects for her unborn child. The plaintiff gave birth to a child who was disabled as a result of the chicken pox, and argued that had she been informed of the risks that she would have terminated her pregnancy. Would she have? The issue was the appropriate test of causation. Does the plaintiff have to prove on an objective or subjective test that had she been aware of the risks that she would have terminated the pregnancy?

The trial judge applied a modified objective test of causation and found that a reasonable woman in the plaintiff's position would have continued with the pregnancy to term despite the risks. That being so, causation was not proved and the plaintiff's action was dismissed.[171]

The Court of Appeal disagreed with the trial judgment. It applied a modified objective test of causation but found that there were factual errors in the determination made by the trial judge, and hence ordered a new trial.[172]

The Supreme Court of Canada affirmed its support for a modified objective test of causation in failure to inform cases brought by patients against doctors. In so doing, Cory J. for the majority of the Court elaborated upon the nature of the subjective factors that a court should consider as part of this modified objective test. These factors include "objectively ascertainable circumstances such as plaintiff's age, income, marital status and other factors".[173] They also include "the patient's reasonable beliefs, fears, desires and expectations", as well as the pa-

---

169 Do plaintiffs have to give specific evidence as to what they would have done had they been informed of the risks? In *Jaskiewicz v. Humber River Regional Hospital* (2001), 4 C.C.L.T. (3d) 98 (Ont. S.C.J.), the plaintiff took the stand but did not testify as to what she would have done had she been informed of the risk. Wilkins J., *in obiter*, held that the failure of a plaintiff to testify regarding this matter, in cases where the plaintiff is able to testify, is virtually fatal to her failure to inform claim. The court must be able to evaluate what the plaintiff says she would have done by looking at her circumstances objectively. The matter was *obiter* since the trial judge held that even if she had testified on this point he would have concluded that, based on the modified objective test, she would have consented. See *contra Hartjes v. Carman* (2003), 20 C.C.L.T. (3d) 31 (Ont. S.C.J.), at 41, affirmed (2004), [2004] O.J. No. 5597, 2004 CarswellOnt 9807 (Div. Ct.). Gans J. held that "the mere asking of a self-serving question" is not the "only way to prove the causation issue on a balance of probabilities." Thus, despite the fact that the plaintiff was not asked whether she would have consented to the procedure, the evidence suggested that she would not have. The trial judgment was affirmed on appeal.

170 35 C.C.L.T. 233, [1997] 8 W.W.R. 303, 148 D.L.R. (4th) 48 (S.C.C.), reversing [1995] 7 W.W.R. 378 (B.C. C.A.), reversing [1994] 8 W.W.R. 568, 21 C.C.L.T. (2d) 66 (B.C. S.C.). There have been a number of commentaries: see M. Crow, "Confusion Over Causation: A Journey Through *Arndt v. Smith*" (1998), 7 Health L. Rev. 3; Flood, "Conundrums in Causation & Informed Medical Consent" (2000), 23 Advocates' Q. 217; Nelson & Caulfield, "You Can't Get There from Here: A Case Comment on *Arndt v. Smith*" (1998), 32 U.B.C. L. Rev. 353.

171 [1994] 8 W.W.R. 568, 21 C.C.L.T. (2d) 66 (B.C. S.C.).

172 [1995] 7 W.W.R. 378 (B.C. C.A.).

173 (1997), 35 C.C.L.T. (2d) 233 (S.C.C.) at 242.

tient's "state of mind".[174] Excluded from the court's consideration, however, are the "honestly held but idiosyncratic and unreasonable or irrational beliefs of the patient."[175]

It is difficult to know whether the Supreme Court's relaxation of the objective test of causation and its willingness to modify it by accounting for so many of the patient's particular circumstances and beliefs will assist plaintiffs.[176] There is little doubt that the objective test of causation has prevented the vast majority of failure to inform cases from succeeding, and that hence the plaintiff's legal right to know has proven to be largely illusory. On the other hand, allowing disappointed patients to establish too easily that had they known of the risks of treatment they would have refused it, will merely add to the already significant number of failure to inform cases. As well, the patient's right to know must be balanced by other policy concerns. Where a patient has been informed of and has consented to the basic nature of the treatment, in a situation where the treatment suggested was reasonable and competently performed, how far ought a fault-based law to go in order to compensate that patient for the adverse, but statistically inevitable, results of that treatment? The right to know, if not carefully defined and restricted, may incrementally turn negligence law into a no-fault compensation scheme for those who have suffered adversely from competent but risky medical treatment.

There are two other factors which have not received adequate attention, however, which can help address these concerns. First, courts ought to treat the duty to inform as being one not of strict liability, but of reasonable care. Not every failure to inform ought to lead to liability. Where a doctor has acted reasonably in attempting to inform a patient fully, keeping in mind the type of treatment proposed, its urgency, the nature of the risks, the nature of the patient, and so on, the duty is not breached. In this respect, the courts will have to determine whether

---

174 *Ibid.*

175 *Ibid.* at 245. The court affirmed the trial judge's decision to dismiss the plaintiff's action. McLachlin J. wrote a concurring judgment. She favoured a subjective test, which "incorporates elements of objectivity; the plaintiff's subjective belief at trial that she would have followed a certain course stands to be tested by the circumstances and attitudes at the time the decision would have been made as well as medical advice she would have received at the time", (1997), 35 C.C.L.T. (2d) 233 (S.C.C.) at 254. There seems to be no real practical difference between the majority's test and McLachlin J.'s test. One is a "modified objective test", the other is a "modified subjective test". Depending upon how much each are "modified", they may amount to the same thing.

176 That it might ease the plaintiff's burden is perhaps illustrated by a post-*Arndt* case: *Painter v. Rae*, [1998] 8 W.W.R. 717 (Man. Q.B.). Although the risk was only .1 per cent, the court took into account the plaintiff's cautious attitude towards surgery, and her distrust of statistics, in finding that she would have opted for an alternative form of birth control. Also see *Webster v. Morcos* (1998), [1999] 3 W.W.R. 417 (Alta. Q.B.), where the court considered the patient's personal circumstances in finding that the objective text of causation had been met. In *Dumais v. Hamilton* (1998), 219 A.R. 63 (C.A.), affirming (January 28, 1997), Doc. 9001-03513, [1997] A.J. No. 159 (Q.B.), the court considered the vanity of the patient in determining that she would have declined the treatment had she been informed of the remote risk of disfigurement. In another post-*Arndt* case, dealing with whether the plaintiff would have had an abortion or not if informed of the abnormality of her fetus, the court stated that a reasonable person in her position would not have chosen an abortion; see *Mickle v. Salvation Army Grace Hospital, Windsor* (1998), 166 D.L.R. (4th) 743 (Ont. Gen. Div.). In *Lue v. St. Michael's Hospital* (1999), 46 C.C.L.T. (2d) 153 (Ont. C.A.), the modified objective test also did not assist the plaintiff in establishing causation.

the approaches adopted by doctors to provide information to their patients are sufficient to satisfy the test of reasonableness. Is it, for example, sufficient for a surgeon to rely on the fact that a resident has fully informed the patient concerning the risks of treatment prior to obtaining the patient's consent?[177] Is it reasonable for a referring doctor to leave the matter of disclosure of risks to the patient to the doctor who will perform the treatment?[178] Is it reasonable for a doctor to refuse to disclose to the patient a possible alternative treatment where the doctor reasonably believes that the alternative treatment is not satisfactory in the circumstances?[179] It has been held that it is not reasonable for a patient to be informed while under the influence of a sedative, and while in the anteroom of the operating room awaiting the procedure.[180] If a patient has difficulty comprehending the information, due, for example, to a language problem,[181] even greater care must be taken. Where the information regarding the treatment is given to the patient through literature and a video, there is a special burden on the doctor to ascertain whether the patient has comprehended the disclosure.[182] As well, it must be

177 See *Considine v. Camp Hill Hosp.* (1982), 133 D.L.R. (3d) 11 (N.S. T.D.). The court, although critical of the way in which the surgeon and his resident approached their duty to disclose, calling it a "case of loose practice," concluded that "it was not a breach of duty of sufficient degree that it can be found to be the cause of the loss."

178 See *Ferguson v. Hamilton Civic Hosps.* (1983), 23 C.C.L.T. 254 (Ont. H.C.), affirmed (1985), 33 C.C.L.T. 56 (Ont. C.A.). Krever J. held that it did not matter which of the doctors informed the patient, as long as one of them did. The requesting doctor could leave the task to the performing doctor in some cases, but not where the former knows that the latter does not have the qualifications to do so. See also *Davidson v. Connaught Laboratories* (1980), 14 C.C.L.T. 251 (Ont. H.C.); *MacDuff v. Vrabec* (1982), 24 C.C.L.T. 239 (B.C. S.C.); Picard, "Informed Consent Takes Shape" (1983), 24 C.C.L.T. 250. In *Rayner v. Knickle* (1988), 47 C.C.L.T. 141 (P.E.I. T.D.), reversed on other grounds (1991), 88 Nfld. & P.E.I.R. 214 (Nfld. C.A.), the trial court held the doctor who administered an amniocentesis test negligent for having wrongly relied on the fact that the doctor who had ordered the test had already informed the patient of the details of the test.

179 See *Bucknam v. Kostiuk* (1983), 3 D.L.R. (4th) 99 (Ont. H.C.), affirmed (1986), 55 O.R. (2d) 187 (C.A.), Krever J. suggested that it is an unreasonable requirement to impose upon a doctor to disclose an alternative treatment which the doctor does not think is in the patient's interest. Also see *Oliver-Rogers v. Bhatia* (1998), 43 C.C.L.T. (2d) 73 (Ont. Gen. Div.); *Baksh-White v. Cochen* (2001), 7 C.C.L.T. (3d) 138 (Ont. S.C.J.); and *Thibault v. Fewer* (2001), [2002] 1 W.W.R. 204 (Man. Q.B.). See, however, the Ontario Court of Appeal's decision in *Van Dyke v. Grey Bruce Regional Health Centre* (2005), 33 C.C.L.T. (3d) 1 (C.A.), leave to appeal refused (2005), 2005 CarswellOnt 7439 (S.C.C.), where the court favoured the view that all reasonably appropriate alternatives must be disclosed, even if the physician does not agree that they are appropriate for this patient. See further discussion below.

180 *Bucknam v. Kostiuk, ibid.*

181 See, e.g., *Schanczl v. Singh*, [1988] 2 W.W.R. 465 (Alta. Q.B.). In *Adan v. Davis* (1998), 43 C.C.L.T. (2d) 262 (Ont. Gen. Div.) at 281, the court held that where the information is being transmitted to the patient through an interpreter, "the physician must be attentive to the language ability of the interpreter. The physician must ensure that the patient is returning reasonable and responsive replies. If the patient is silent and asks no questions. . .it is the responsibility of the physician to ask appropriate questions so as to be satisfied that the information has been understood."

182 See *Byciuk v. Hollingsworth* (2004), 27 C.C.L.T. (3d) 116 (Alta. Q.B.). In order to save time, a video explaining the proposed "gastroplasty" was sent to the patient. The court said that "a physician must, at the least, take reasonable steps to determine whether his or her patient understood the information provided", at 27 C.C.L.T. (3d) 125. The action failed ultimately due to lack of proof of causation. It has been held that the burden of proving that the patient

recalled that the duty is to inform a patient of all material risks, that is, those risks which the reasonable patient would consider relevant. If the doctor acts reasonably in attempting to determine what risks will qualify as being material and, hence, what risks must be disclosed, and these risks are disclosed, this should satisfy the duty. The reasonable doctor test is still the standard which defines the duty of care,[183] even if it does not define the scope of the disclosure requirement.

Second, the issue of damages must be more carefully looked at. The courts must consider not only what the effects of the treatment were, but as well, what likely would have happened had the treatment been declined. If the patient would have suffered equally serious, or more serious, complications with no treatment, or with other treatment, this must be taken into account when assessing damages for the failure to inform. Thus, in *Strachan v. Simpson*,[184] although the court found that the plaintiff would have declined the treatment had he been informed of the risks of paralysis, his damages were limited by the fact that without the surgery, he would have become paraplegic in one year. A similar issue arose in *Seney v. Crooks.*[185] The defendant doctor was found negligent for having failed to inform his patient of an alternative treatment. The question then arose as to whether the alternative treatment would have provided the plaintiff with a better result. The majority of the Court of Appeal found that the evidence did support this conclusion and hence awarded the plaintiff her damages.[186] In *Tremblay v. McLauchlan*,[187] the plaintiff suffered nerve damage during surgery. The trial judge held that the doctor had failed to disclose this specific risk, it was a material risk, and that the reasonable person in the plaintiff's position would have opted not to have the surgery done by this doctor had the risk been disclosed.[188] The judge accordingly awarded the plaintiff damages resulting from the nerve damage. The Court of Appeal, although affirming the trial judgment on all findings regarding liability, held that the burden of proving damages fell upon the plaintiff. In this respect,

---

understood the doctor's explanation of the risks is on the doctor. See *Lacroix (Litigation Guardian of) v. Dominique*, [1999] 12 W.W.R. 38 (Man. Q.B.), affirmed [2001] 9 W.W.R. 261, 6 C.C.L.T. (3d) 212 (Man. C.A.), leave to appeal refused (2002), 163 Man. R. (2d) 247 (note) (S.C.C.). The court referred to *Ciarlariello v. Schacter*, [1993] 2 S.C.R. 119.

183 In *White v. Turner* (1981), 15 C.C.L.T. 81 at 100 (Ont. H.C.), Linden J. stated:

> In most cases, the courts will probably continue to accept as reasonable the customary practices of the profession as to disclosure, since they are, after all, based on experience, common sense and what doctors honestly perceive their patients wish to know.

See also *Schinz v. Dickinson* (1984), 31 C.C.L.T. 313 (B.C. C.A.), where the court conceded that evidence of what other dentists did, although not conclusive, was an important element in the duty to inform.

184 (1979), 10 C.C.L.T. 145 (B.C. S.C.).

185 (1998), 166 D.L.R. (4th) 337 (Alta. C.A.).

186 There was an issue as to the burden of proof. Having proved that the doctor failed to inform of the alternative treatment and that the plaintiff would have agreed to it had she been informed, who has the burden of proving that the alternative treatment would or would not have made a difference? The majority of the court was inclined to the view that the doctor should have the burden of proof. The dissenting judge held that there was no evidence on a balance of probabilities that the alternative treatment would have made a difference and would have dismissed the action.

187 (1999), 47 C.C.L.T. (2d) 177 (B.C. S.C.), reversed (2001), 6 C.C.L.T. (3d) 238 (B.C. C.A.).

188 The court held that the patient would have sought a second opinion from a specialist in a larger city and had the surgery done there.

the plaintiff had the burden of proving that had another doctor performed the surgery, the nerve damage would not have occurred. Since the trial judge found there was no evidence of this,[189] the Court of Appeal held the plaintiff failed to prove its case for damages.[190] This is a troublesome finding for plaintiffs, since in the absence of negligent treatment, proving that the adverse result probably would have been avoided had the operation been done by some other doctor, could be a difficult task.[191]

A similar question is raised if the plaintiff's case is that although the plaintiff would have had the treatment, it would have been postponed until a more opportune time. Assuming that the risk of adverse effects remains the same, no matter when the treatment is performed, traditional causation principles dictate that the plaintiff's damages should be limited to those that arose due to the earlier than later treatment.[192] What the plaintiff has lost in this case was not the choice to avoid the treatment altogether, but the right to choose the best time for having it. Thus arguably all that the plaintiff should be entitled to receive are the damages, if any, caused by that loss of timing choice.[193] This argument has not, however, been favourably received by the courts. It was specifically rejected in *Martin v. Capital Health Authority*.[194] Wilson J. held that as long as the plaintiff could establish that he would not have agreed to have the surgery at that time, he was entitled to recover in full for the damages which he suffered.[195] The English House of Lords in *Chester v. Afshar*[196] also rejected it, although even the majority agreed that to allow recovery in cases where a patient cannot prove that the treatment

---

189 The trial judge apparently required the doctor to prove that the nerve damage probably would have occurred even had the operation been performed by another doctor. The Court of Appeal held this put the burden on the wrong party. Moreover, since the trial judge found that the operation had been "meticulously" performed, the Court of Appeal reasoned that there was no proof that another doctor would have avoided the injury.

190 The Court of Appeal did allow for some damages. The court held that the plaintiff probably would have postponed surgery to ensure that he was covered by disability benefits.

191 Unless courts use pure statistical evidence and argue that if the risk is, for example, one in one hundred, the probability is that in another operation the risk would not have eventuated. Under this reasoning, the issue disappears and the plaintiff will always succeed (unless the risk is over 50 per cent).

192 For example, in *Reibl v. Hughes*, the decision to have the treatment a year before retirement led to a decrease in pension benefits. Thus, in this case, the timing of the surgery was relevant.

193 In *Felde v. Vein & Laser Medical Centre* (2003), 21 C.C.L.T. (3d) 81 (Ont. C.A.), affirming (2002), 14 C.C.L.T. (3d) 246 (Ont. S.C.J.), the trial judge stated that the plaintiff would not have had the surgery "that day" if properly informed. It is not clear whether she would ever have had it, or would merely have postponed her decision. She was awarded damages as if the treatment never would have been performed.

194 [2007] 8 W.W.R. 328 (Alta. Q.B.), reversed 2008 CarswellAlta 559, 2008 ABCA 161 (Alta. C.A.).

195 The Court of Appeal reversed the trial judgment on the issue of the standard of the disclosure which was required. The trial judge had held that the defendant had failed to meet his duty of disclosure because he did not specifically tell the plaintiff that the operation involved the risk of a "stroke". The Court of Appeal held, however, that the risks of the operation were adequately disclosed even if the word "stroke" was not used. In other words, there was an informed consent. The question of cause and damage was not discussed by the Court of Appeal.

196 2004 UKHL 41 (H.L.).

would not have been performed at a later date, is inconsistent with traditional causation principles. It is a decision made for purposes of policy.[197]

The fact that a patient has signed a standard consent form in which it is acknowledged that the nature of the operation has been explained does not necessarily prove that the duty to inform has been observed. It has been held that "the existence of such a consent does not protect the doctor from liability unless the patient has been informed to the satisfaction of the Court."[198] Or, as stated in another judgment, "a consent form is only as good as the degree of material disclosure".[199]

(ii) Extensions of the Duty to Disclose

The duty to inform of risks of treatment originated from the desire to give patients control over their own medical choices. It was premised on the argument that in the absence of material information about the risks of treatment, a patient's right to self-determination was compromised.

Case law has extended the duty to inform of risks into a requirement for much broader types of disclosure. Now well recognized, for example, is the duty to inform a patient of the results of treatment or tests.[200] As with the duty to inform of risks, however, liability for a failure to inform a patient of the results of treatment depends upon proof that the duty's breach caused the plaintiff's damages. Thus, where a dentist did not tell his patient that a piece of the drill bit broke during treatment and became incorporated into the filling, no liability was found

---

197 There were two dissents in *Chester*. The judgment referred extensively to an Australian case on the same point, *Chappel v. Hart* (1998), 195 C.L.R. 232 (Australia H.C.), which was equally contentious, but ultimately came to the same conclusion. A number of articles are also referred to. For commentary see Jane Stapleton, "Occam's Razor Reveals an Orthodox Basis for *Chester v. Afshar*" (2006), 122 L.Q.R. 426.

198 *Bickford v. Stiles* (1981), 128 D.L.R. (3d) 516 at 520 (N.B. Q.B.). See also *Hajgato v. London Health Assn.* (1982), 36 O.R. (2d) 669 (H.C.), affirmed (1983), 44 O.R. (2d) 264 (C.A.); *Casey v. Provan* (1984), 30 C.C.L.T. 169 (Ont. H.C.); *Pridham v. Nash* (1986), 33 D.L.R. (4th) 304 (Ont. H.C.). When faced with a "form of authorization" used by a dentist, one judge has even gone so far as to state: "I place no reliance upon this writing. It begs the question. From the dentist's point of view it would be much better to make a note of any warning actually given, and to make such note contemporaneously with the warning." See McEachern C.J.S.C. in *Diack v. Bardsley* (1983), 25 C.C.L.T. 159 at 164 (B.C. S.C.), affirmed (1984) 31 C.C.L.T. 308 (B.C. C.A.). See, however, *Brushett v. Cowan* (1990), 69 D.L.R. (4th) 743 (Nfld. C.A.), where it was held that the formal consent form cannot be interpreted too narrowly, but must be viewed within the context of the case. Here, consent was established, despite the fact that the form did not refer specifically to the procedure which was performed.

199 *Tremblay v. MacLauchlan* (2001), 6 C.C.L.T. (3d) 238 (B.C. C.A.).

200 See *Stamos v. Davies* (1985), 33 C.C.L.T. 1 (Ont. H.C.); *Kueper v. McMullin* (1986), 37 C.C.L.T. 318 (N.B. C.A.). A Quebec case that found a doctor liable for failing to inform his patient of risks arising during the post-operative stage of treatment is *Drolet c. Parenteau* (1994), 26 C.C.L.T. (2d) 168 (Que. C.A.). The doctor's duty to follow up with the patient and ensure that the patient realizes what the results are and what further treatment may be necessary was extensively discussed in *Rupert v. Toth* (2006), 38 C.C.L.T. (3d) 261 (Ont. S.C.J.). This can be seen as part of the duty to inform or, more generally, as part of the doctor's duty of care in treatment and post-operative care. In this case, both the doctor and the patient were held at fault for the doctor's failure in communicating the patient's circumstances to him.

because the reasonable patient would not have done anything about this matter.[201] An interesting variant of the duty to disclose treatment results arose in *Kelly v. Lundgard*.[202] A doctor was held liable for failing to advise the plaintiff through her lawyers that as a result of injuries suffered in a motor vehicle accident that she might be infertile. The plaintiff accordingly settled her motor vehicle claim for an amount that did not take this risk into consideration. The trial judge applied the informed consent standard to the preparation of medical-legal reports dealing with prognosis. The Court of Appeal, however, disagreed and held that the appropriate standard is that of the reasonable and diligent doctor in the same circumstances.

An interesting issue can be raised concerning the standard of disclosure with regard to the duty to disclose the results of treatment. Is it, as is the duty to disclose risks, a full disclosure or a professional disclosure standard? In other words, must a doctor disclose all those results about which the reasonable patient would want to know, or only those results which the reasonable doctor would disclose? In principle, the full disclosure standard, which protects the autonomy of the patient, and respects the right of patients to determine their own medical choices, should apply. In one important case, however, *Pittman Estate v. Bain*,[203] the court, without overtly considering the issue of which standard applies, applied the professional disclosure standard. The case concerned a doctor's decision not to inform his patient that blood products which had been transfused into him in an earlier surgery, were contaminated with HIV. The doctor's decision to conceal this information from his patient was a deliberate one, made taking into account his patient's heart condition, and the doctor's belief that there was no danger of his patient passing on the disease to his wife. In actions brought by the estate of the deceased patient, and his widow, against the doctor, the court considered the standard of disclosure of other practitioners, in determining that the doctor's failure to inform was negligent. Arguably, the court ought to have considered the reasonable patient standard in coming to this decision, in recognition of the patient's right to know. While one might see the doctor's duty to disclose results as merely part of the doctor's general duty to treat a patient with reasonable care, i.e. a professional standard, once the information affects a patient's medical or life style choices, the patient's autonomy is the paramount issue and hence the full disclosure standard ought to apply.[204]

---

201 *Kueper v. McMullin, ibid.*

202 (1996), 29 C.C.L.T. (2d) 113 (Alta. Q.B.), reversed (2001), 202 D.L.R. (4th) 385 (Alta. C.A.).

203 (1994), 112 D.L.R. (4th) 257 (Ont. Gen. Div.).

204 Also see *Lawson c. Laferrière* (1991), 6 C.C.L.T. (2d) 119 (S.C.C.), a case which concerned a doctor's failure to inform his patient that she had cancer. The courts recognized that this was a breach, without considering the scope of disclosure. The paramount issue in the case was whether damages were caused by the breach. See discussion in Chapter 11. Another judgment that applied a professional disclosure standard, without overtly considering the issue, is *McCann v. Hyndman* (2003), [2004] 2 W.W.R. 353 (Alta. Q.B.), affirmed [2004] 11 W.W.R. 216 (Alta. C.A.). The court held that the doctor's failure to inform his patient following surgery that matter from earlier treatments remained in his body and could result in later problems was negligent. This and the fact that the doctor did not monitor the situation were held to be a breach of the doctor's post-operative duties of care. One could argue that

The duty to disclose risks has been extended to other areas of information as well. In *Rayner v. Knickle*,[205] the trial judge described the duty to disclose as encompassing disclosures regarding (1) how the procedure is carried out, (2) the benefits of having the procedure done,[206] (3) the material or special or unusual risks of having the procedure done or of forgoing the procedure, (4) any alternatives to the procedure,[207] and (5) the risks associated with the alternatives.[208] The obligation to inform a patient of alternative treatments was discussed in *Van Dyke v. Grey Bruce Regional Health Centre*.[209] The interesting issue raised by the court was the scope of this duty. Is the doctor obliged to disclose all reasonable medical alternatives or is the duty limited to only those alternatives which the doctor, acting reasonably, considers appropriate for that patient? The Court of Appeal conceded that this is an issue of some controversy, but favoured the broader duty that respects the patients' right to make their own choices from a range of reasonable alternatives.[210] In *Snider v. Henniger*,[211] the court held that a doctor had a duty to inform his patient that if the treatment performed did not work, a hysterectomy probably would have to be done. The court held that the failure to

---

the full disclosure standard should have applied so that the patient could have known what risks were present and participated in the decision as to how to deal with them.

205 (1988), 47 C.C.L.T. 141 (P.E.I. T.D.), reversed in part (1991), 88 Nfld. & P.E.I.R. 214 (P.E.I. C.A.).

206 In *Ross v. Welsh* (2003), 18 C.C.L.T. (3d) 107 (Ont. S.C.J.), additional reasons at (2003), 2003 CarswellOnt 4603 (S.C.J.), the court held that the doctor was obliged to disclose the statistical likelihood of the treatment improving the plaintiff's condition (50%), of having no effect (35%), or of worsening it (15%). The court found that if informed, it would have been reasonable for the plaintiff to have at minimum postponed the treatment and tried more conservative approaches.

207 Also see *Seney v. Crooks* (1998), 166 D.L.R. (4th) 337 (Alta. C.A.) and *Semeniuk v. Cox*, [2000] 4 W.W.R. 310, 48 C.C.L.T. (2d) 286 (Alta. Q.B.). In *Van Mol (Guardian ad litem of) v. Ashmore* (1999), 168 D.L.R. (4th) 637, 44 C.C.L.T. (2d) 228 (B.C. C.A.), leave to appeal refused (1999), 138 B.C.A.C. 269 (S.C.C.), additional reasons at (2000), 188 D.L.R. (4th) 327 (B.C. C.A.), the court held that where it is the minor who has the capacity to consent, the informed consent must come from the minor. This involved informing the patient of alternative ways of performing the treatment. In *Oliver-Rogers v. Bhatia* (1998), 43 C.C.L.T. (2d) 73 (Ont. Gen. Div.), it was held that discussing other options is not necessary when the treatment prescribed is the reasonable one in the circumstances and the options do not present fewer risks to the patient.

208 The Court of Appeal, although not disagreeing with this characterization, reversed the trial judgment on the issue of the duty to inform. The court made the point that before determining whether the doctor had a duty to inform, the court first has to decide what risk is in issue. In other words, what risk eventuated? The Court of Appeal decided that the risk which occurred here, an amniocentesis needle striking the umbilical vein and causing a haematoma which in turn caused partial asphyxiation during an amniocentesis procedure, was so rare that there was no duty to disclose it. The Court of Appeal also decided that even if the risk ought to have been disclosed, the judgment at trial that the plaintiff would have refused the treatment, was also wrong.

209 (2005), 33 C.C.L.T. (3d) 1 (Ont. C.A.), leave to appeal refused (2005), 2005 CarswellOnt 7439 (S.C.C.). The case concerned which antibiotics should be used by the patient.

210 Thus, under this approach, even if the doctor's opinion as to what is appropriate for the patient is a reasonable one, the doctor must disclose other appropriate alternatives. The doctor must also advise the patient of the risks and benefits inherent in the use of these alternatives.

211 (1992), 96 D.L.R. (4th) 367 (B.C. S.C.).

inform her of this made her less prepared for the hysterectomy which ultimately was needed, adding to her psychological distress. In *Shobridge v. Thomas*,[212] the duty to disclose was applied to errors made by the doctor during the operation. Concealing an error, which resulted in adverse consequences, was held to be a breach of the doctor's fiduciary duty.[213] In *Skeels Estate v. Iwashkiw*,[214] the duty to disclose was applied to the choice of hospital location for the treatment. The doctor was held to have an obligation to inform his patient of the risks involved if she elected to have her baby delivered in a Level 1 hospital in a smaller city rather than at a large city hospital better equipped to deal with high-risk deliveries.[215]

Another extension of the duty to disclose can be seen in the case of *Arndt v. Smith*.[216] The court held that a doctor has a duty to disclose to a pregnant patient that her chicken pox entailed a risk of serious birth defects for her unborn child.[217] In another case, *Joshi (Guardian ad litem of) v. Woolley*,[218] the duty to disclose was extended to disclosure that a tubal ligation to prevent conception might not work.[219] In *Joyal v. Starreveld*,[220] the duty to disclose extended to the increased risks of day time seizures due to a reduction in the dosage of the plaintiff's medication. Whether a doctor has a duty to disclose that he has epilepsy was the issue in *Halkyard v. Mathew*.[221] The court held that he need not make that disclosure. The doctor's performance in the operating room was unaffected by his medical condition and thus any risk that his epilepsy presented did not materialize.[222]

(iii) Wrongful Life and Wrongful Birth

A new type of claim that persons in the medical profession are confronting is that for wrongful life or wrongful birth.[223] As defined by Lax J. in *Kealey v.*

---

212 (1999), 47 C.C.L.T. (2d) 73 (B.C. S.C.), additional reasons at (1999), 1999 CarswellBC 2185 (S.C. [In Chambers]).

213 The doctor left a large piece of gauze in the patient's abdomen. This caused an infection, necessitating further surgical interventions. Damages were awarded not only for the negligence in leaving the gauze there in the first place, but for the emotional effect that the concealment and breach of trust had on the patient. Aggravated and punitive damages were also awarded.

214 [2006] 11 W.W.R. 632 (Alta. Q.B.).

215 This aspect of the claim failed, however, on the causation issue.

216 [1997] 2 S.C.R. 539.

217 As discussed above, the Supreme Court of Canada upheld the trial judgment that dismissed the plaintiff's action on the issue of causation.

218 (1995), 4 B.C.L.R. (3d) 208 (S.C.).

219 There was a 1 in 200 chance of failure. The plaintiff, a mother who became pregnant and had a child, successfully sued. If she had been informed of the risks of failure, she might, as a reasonable woman, have taken other precautions against pregnancy.

220 [1996] 4 W.W.R. 707 (Alta. Q.B.).

221 (1998), 43 C.C.L.T. (2d) 171 (Alta. Q.B.), affirmed (2001), 4 C.C.L.T. (3d) 271 (Alta. C.A.).

222 The Court of Appeal left open the question whether there would have been liability had the patient's death following her surgery been caused in some way by the doctor's epilepsy. One presumes that there could have been liability for failure to disclose or even for negligence in the treatment phase itself if this had happened.

223 See Picard & Robertson, *Legal Liability of Doctors and Hospitals In Canada*, 4th ed. at 260 *et seq.*; Gibson, "Annotation to *Kealey v. Berezowski*" (1996), 31 C.C.L.T. (2d) 143. This has

Berezowski, a wrongful birth action normally is brought by the parents of a child who is born with birth defects following a planned pregnancy.[224] It can arise, however, in a broader context. Whenever parents claim that the birth of their child ought not to have occurred, and would not have occurred had it not been for the defendant's negligence, a wrongful birth action arises.[225] A wrongful life action is one that is brought by a child, who is claiming that its life ought not to have occurred and would not have had it not been for the defendant doctor's negligence. As with wrongful birth, the negligence could have been with respect to a failed abortion, a failure to warn of risks of injury to a foetus, or a failure to carry out genetic testing.

In *Krangle (Guardian ad litem of) v. Brisco*,[226] Low J. identified four categories of cases involving unwanted children or children injured in the womb:

(1) unwanted conception following a failed medical sterilization procedure;[227]
(2) unwanted birth following a failed medical abortion;[228]
(3) loss of opportunity to have an abortion following failure to be provided with the necessary medical information or advice;[229] and

---

been a difficult claim for the courts to deal with, and as indicated below, courts in Canada, the United States, England, and Australia have written interesting and lengthy judgments to justify the decisions they have taken. Readers should consult the case law and commentaries to get a better understanding of the complexities that this issue presents.

224 (1996), 31 C.C.L.T. (2d) 143 (Ont. Gen. Div.) at 166.

225 As noted by Picard and Robertson, above note 223, a wrongful birth can be the result of negligence in birth control or abortion, genetic counseling, or any act that deprived the woman of the option of terminating a pregnancy. In other words, the birth would not have occurred had the doctor not been negligent in some way.

226 (1997), 154 D.L.R. (4th) 707 (B.C. S.C.), additional reasons at (1998), 25 C.P.C. (4th) 134 (B.C. S.C.), reversed (2000), 184 D.L.R. (4th) 251 (B.C. C.A.), leave to appeal allowed (2000), 152 B.C.A.C. 318 (note) (S.C.C.), reversed (2002), 208 D.L.R. (4th) 193 (S.C.C.). The case went to the Court of Appeal and to the Supreme Court of Canada on the issue of the appropriate measure of damages. See (2002), 208 D.L.R. (4th) 193 (S.C.C.), reversing (2000), 184 D.L.R. (4th) 251 (B.C. C.A.).

227 Cases cited included *Cataford c. Moreau* (1978), 114 D.L.R. (3d) 585 (Que. S.C.); *Udale v. Bloomsbury Area Health Authority*, [1983] 2 All E.R. 522 (Q.B.); *Thake v. Maurice*, [1984] 2 All E.R. 513 (Q.B.); *Emeh v. Kensington*, [1984] 3 All E.R. 1044 (C.A.); and *Kealey v. Berezowski* (1996), 30 O.R. (3d) 37, 136 D.L.R. (4th) 708 (Ont. Gen. Div.). Also see *S. (M.) v. Baker* (2001), [2002] 4 W.W.R. 487 (Alta. Q.B.); *Y. (M.) v. Boutros*, [2002] 6 W.W.R. 463, 11 C.C.L.T. (3d) 271 (Alta. Q.B.). The latter judgment makes extensive reference to the House of Lords' judgment in *McFarlane v. Tayside Health Board (Scotland)* (1999), [2000] 2 A.C. 59 (U.K. H.L.). Recent cases include *Bevilacqua v. Altenkirk* (2004), 27 C.C.L.T. (3d) 75 (B.C. S.C.) — conception following a failed vasectomy; *Chasse v. Evenson*, [2006] 9 W.W.R. 233 (Alta. Q.B.) — conception following a failed tubal ligation. See the House of Lord's decision in *Rees v. Darlington Memorial Hospital NHS Trust*, [2003] UKHL 52, [2004] 1 A.C. 309 (H.L.), which also involved conception following a failed sterilization. An Australian High Court judgment on the same matter is *Cattanach v. Melchior* (2003), [2003] H.C.A. 38, 77 A.L.J.R. 1312 (Australia H.C.).

228 Cases cited included *Fredette v. Wiebe* (1986), 29 D.L.R. (4th) 534 (B.C. S.C.). A more recent case involving a birth following a failed abortion is *Roe v. Dabbs* (2004), 26 C.C.L.T. (3d) 115 (B.C. S.C.).

229 Cases cited included *H. (R.) v. Hunter* (1996), 32 C.C.L.T. (2d) 44 (Ont. Gen. Div.). This was the category into which *Krangle (Guardian ad litem of) v. Brisco* fell. Also see *Mickle v. Salvation Army Grace Hospital, Windsor* (1998), 166 D.L.R. (4th) 743 (Ont. Gen. Div.).

(4) physical damage to the foetus as a result of a medical procedure during gestation.[230]

Kealey v. Berezowski[231] is an example of a successful wrongful birth claim, in the nature of a wrongful pregnancy. The doctor's negligence in failing to competently perform a sterilization procedure led to the plaintiff's pregnancy and consequent birth of a healthy baby. While recognizing the validity of the plaintiff's action, the difficult issue for the court was the assessment of damages. What damages are caused to parents as a result of the birth of an unplanned healthy baby? After a careful analysis of the authorities, including American and British cases, as well as the policies and principles underlying this determination, Lax J. awarded the plaintiff general damages relating to her pregnancy, labour and delivery, as well as loss of income, but no damages for child rearing costs.[232]

Where a child is born with disabilities as a result of a doctor's negligence with respect to failure to inform of risks,[233] or a negligently performed abortion,[234] the policy issue as to whether the courts should be awarding damages to the parents for the birth of a healthy child does not arise. In these cases, the courts view the matter more as an issue of prenatal negligence leading to physical injuries, rather than as wrongful life or birth, and are therefore willing to award damages.[235] An example of such a case is *H. (R.) v. Hunter*.[236] The parents of two sons born with

---

230 *Cherry (Guardian ad litem of) v. Borsman* (1992), 94 D.L.R. (4th) 487 (B.C. C.A.), leave to appeal refused (1993), 99 D.L.R. (4th) vii (S.C.C.).

231 (1996), 31 C.C.L.T. (2d) 143 (Ont. Gen. Div.).

232 In *S. (M.) v. Baker* (2001), [2002] 4 W.W.R. 487 (Alta. Q.B.) the trial judge would have awarded child-rearing costs. The action was dismissed, however, based on lack of proof of negligence with respect to the failed sterilization. The court noted that where financial considerations were the reason for the parents to seek sterilization, this type of award could be made. See, however, *Y. (M.) v. Boutros*, above, note 227, where in a similar case the court stated that it would not have awarded child-rearing costs, even if the doctor had been negligent. In this case Rawlins J. explicitly stated, "the benefits a child brings to a family outweigh the costs of that child to a family". A good discussion of this issue is found in *Roe v. Dabbs* (2004), 26 C.C.L.T. (3d) 115 (B.C. S.C.). Parrett J. commented on the four approaches considered in the authorities to damage assessment where the birth of a healthy child is concerned: (i) no recovery; (ii) total recovery, including full cost of child raising; (iii) offset/benefits; and (iv) limited damages relating to things such as costs of pregnancy and childbirth. Parrett J. made an award under the heading of "non-pecuniary" damages of $55,000. The four approaches were also extensively discussed by Groberman J. in *Bevilacqua v. Altenkirk* (2004), 27 C.C.L.T. (3d) 75 (B.C. S.C.). Groberman J. also ultimately classified the loss as a "non-pecuniary" one, and taking into consideration the circumstances of the parents, and their reasons for not having wanted another child, awarded the mother $30,000 and the father $20,000.

233 See, for example, *Arndt v. Smith*, above 216.

234 See, for example, *Cherry (Guardian ad litem of) v. Borsman* (1992), 94 D.L.R. (4th) 487 (B.C. C.A.), leave to appeal refused (1993), 99 D.L.R. (4th) vii (S.C.C.).

235 As Picard and Robertson point out, however, since the plaintiffs are arguing that the child's life is wrongful in that it should have been terminated by a successful abortion, these actions have "the classic hallmark of a wrongful life claim" and present the court with difficult moral issues. See Picard & Robertson, above, at 269. See further discussion below.

236 (1996), 32 C.C.L.T. (2d) 44 (Ont. Gen. Div.).

a genetically transmitted degenerative disease sued the doctors. The plaintiffs alleged that the doctors were negligent for having failed to provide appropriate genetic counselling that could have resulted in the parents preventing the births by way of abortion or contraceptive precautions. Both parents were awarded general damages.[237] In addition, the plaintiff mother was awarded damages for her future loss of income as well as substantial damages for the cost of caring for her two sons.[238]

The issue is more difficult however where it is the child itself who is claiming that its birth was wrongful, and that it ought to have been prevented. In *Lacroix (Litigation Guardian of) v. Dominique*,[239] a child was born with disabilities as a result of an anti-epileptic drug that its pregnant mother had taken. The allegations of negligence against the doctor by both the parents (for wrongful birth) and the child (for wrongful life), were based on the doctor's failure to have advised the mother of the risks to the fóetus if she became pregnant while taking the drug. Although the action by the parents would have succeeded but for the expiration of a limitation period,[240] the action for wrongful life by the child was rejected. The court noted the dilemma in assessing the child's damages for wrongful life. Had the doctor not been negligent, the child would not have been conceived.[241]

---

237 The parents had separated and one of the issues was whether the father should also be entitled to general damages.

238 Also see *Krangle (Guardian ad litem of) v. Brisco*, above, note 226, where the negligence was a failure to advise the 36-year-old pregnant woman to have amniocentesis. The child was born with Down's Syndrome. Full costs of future care were awarded, in addition to non-pecuniary loss to both parents. In *Zhang v. Kan*, 2003 CarswellBC 145, 2003 BCSC 5 (S.C.), although the doctor was found liable, the plaintiff mother was held 50 per cent contributorily negligent for not having pursued the possibility of amniocentesis despite her doctor's advice against having one.

239 [1999] 12 W.W.R. 18 (Man. Q.B.), affirmed [2001] 9 W.W.R. 261, 6 C.C.L.T. (3d) 212 (Man. C.A.), leave to appeal refused (2002), [2001] S.C.C.A. No. 477, 2002 CarswellMan 89, 2002 CarswellMan 90.

240 The court accepted that the doctor had failed in his duty to warn the plaintiff of the risks of becoming pregnant while taking the drug, and that had she been warned, she would not have become pregnant.

241 It was assumed that had the mother been warned of the risks she would not have become pregnant. The option of stopping the drug against epilepsy and becoming pregnant was considered not to have been viable since the risks to the foetus if its mother had an epileptic seizure during pregnancy were significant. *Bosard v. Davey*, [2006] 5 W.W.R. 320 (Man. Q.B.) also involved wrongful life and wrongful birth claims. A child was born with disabilities allegedly due to the fact that his parents were first cousins. The suits were based on the doctor's duty to inform the couple of the risks to children born in such circumstances. McKelvey J. rejected the child's claim on the basis that Canadian law does not recognize wrongful life claims. The parents' claim for wrongful birth was rejected on the basis that the doctors did not know that the couple were cousins, were not negligent in not knowing, and even had they known and advised the couple of the risks involved, the couple still would have gone ahead with the birth.

That being the case, how does a court compare the child's "non-existence" with its existing life in assessing its damages?[242]

This dilemma presented itself to the Ontario Court of Appeal in *Bovingdon (Litigation Guardian of) v. Hergott*.[243] An action for damages was brought by several members of a family, including twins who were born disabled, as a result of the fact that the plaintiff mother took a fertility drug in order to become pregnant. The mother's action was based on the doctor's failure to inform her of the risk of giving birth to twins if a fertility drug were taken. The drug increased the risk of premature births, and disabilities suffered by the babies. There was no dispute that the mother had a right to bring this claim. The defendants argued, however, that the twins' claim was one for "wrongful life" and could not be brought. The trial disagreed, ruling that it was not a wrongful life claim.

On appeal, Feldman J.A. carefully reviewed the authorities, particularly the Manitoba Court of Appeal's decision in *Lacroix*.[244] Twaddle J.A., in his judgment in *Lacroix*, distinguished between two types of cases. The first is where a child is born with abnormalities caused as a result of a doctor's pre-natal negligence. The second is where a child is born *because of* a doctor's pre-natal negligence. Cases that fall into the first category are compensable; cases that fall into the second category are not. As Feldman J.A. observed, however, the two-category approach fails to provide "a coherent theory that can assist courts in making the difficult decision of when a child should be able to recover damages from a doctor for being born with disabilities."[245] This is because negligence on the part of a doctor can result in a child being born with disabilities, where if reasonable care had been taken, the child would not have been born at all.[246] Feldman J.A. held that if the two-category approach were to be applied in the case before her, she would find that the case fell into the second "wrongful life" category. She preferred, however, to reject the category approach and to apply normal duty of care principles to this case. She found that the doctor's duty to inform his patient of the risks of the fertility drug was a duty owed to her alone. There was no co-

---

242 The court was faced with the dilemma that the doctor's negligence was not in prescribing the drug to the mother, but in not warning her against becoming pregnant. Had the doctor's negligence actually injured the child, the case would have been more like *Cherry (Guardian ad litem of) v. Borsman*, above, note 205; i.e., the negligent abortion that injured the child. It should be stated, however, that the issues are not dissimilar, since in the latter case if the abortion had not been negligently performed, the child also would not have been born.

243 (2008), [2008] O.J. No. 11, 2008 CarswellOnt 15 (C.A.), leave to appeal refused (2008), 2008 CarswellOnt 3167 (S.C.C.), reversing (2006), 2006 CarswellOnt 7459 (Ont. S.C.J.).

244 Above, note 239.

245 Above, note 243, at para. 55.

246 Feldman J.A. refers to *Cherry v. Borsman*, above, note 234. A negligently performed abortion results in a child being born with disabilities, whereas a competently performed abortion prevents the child from being born at all. Or, as in *Lacroix*, negligently failing to inform a pregnant woman that her foetus is in danger of being born with disabilities, where the mother would have aborted had she been told, results in a child being born with disabilities as opposed to the child not having been born at all.

extensive duty owed to the twins and it was on this basis that the Court of Appeal rejected their claim.[247]

The wrongful birth and life cases are presenting tort law with difficult moral issues. Advances in medical knowledge and testing techniques do present opportunities for detecting genetic abnormalities as well as for preventing births of children with disabilities. The extent to which society wishes to utilize this information and the role that tort law ought to play in this arena is still very much an open question.

(c) Engineers and Architects

As with other professionals whose roles frequently require that they provide advice to persons who are not in contractual relationships with them, the potential liability of engineers and architects has been significantly increased by the tort duty created in *Hedley Byrne*, and subsequently extended by the courts to other cases of pure economic losses. When engineers and architects, pursuant to their contractual undertaking with project owners, give advice and assistance to consultants and contractors, they place themselves in a sufficiently close special relationship with the latter so as to owe them a duty of care. In addition, the jurisprudence dealing with other categories of pure economic loss claims, such as direct or indirect undertakings to provide services, or liability for losses caused by defective buildings, expands the potential liability of engineers and architects. These duties are, of course, in addition to the ordinary duty of care owed by engineers and architects to victims of foreseeable personal injury or property damage.[248]

There have been numerous cases which highlight this tort vulnerability of architects and engineers. In *Cardinal Const. Ltd. v. Brockville*,[249] for example, a consulting engineer was held liable in tort to a general contractor who relied upon the engineer's drawings in the preparation of a tender. The relationship between the two was governed by *Hedley Byrne v. Heller*, and therefore provisions in the contract entered into between the project owner and the contractor could not be invoked in the engineer's defence. In another case, *Trident Const. Ltd. v. W.L. Wardrop & Assoc. Ltd.*,[250] a consulting engineer was held liable to a general contractor for failure to adequately supervise and approve the work of a subcontractor, and for design defects which were relied upon by the general contractor and the subcontractor. Liability existed despite the fact that the project owner, who had retained the engineer, had an immunity clause written into the contract it had with the general contractor.

---

247 Feldman J.A. pointedly noted that although she felt that the claim, if characterized as suggested in *Lacroix*, was a wrongful life claim, she was not deciding that there is no such claim possible in Ontario. This remained "undecided". In addition, she noted that in failure to inform claims, the test of causation is based on what the plaintiff asserts she would have done, tested as to its reasonableness by the "hypothetical reasonable person".

248 See Chapter 7, where the leading recent cases have been discussed. They include three Supreme Court of Canada decisions: *Edgeworth Construction v. N.D. Lea* (1993), 17 C.C.L.T. (2d) 101, 107 D.L.R. (4th) 169 (S.C.C.); *Auto Concrete Curb Ltd. v. South Nation River Conservation Authority* (1993), 17 C.C.L.T. (2d) 123, 105 D.L.R. (4th) 382 (S.C.C.); and *Winnipeg Condominium Corp. No. 36 v. Bird Construction Co.* (1995), 23 C.C.L.T. (2d) 1 (S.C.C.).

249 (1984), 4 C.L.R. 149 (Ont. H.C.).

250 [1979] 6 W.W.R. 481 (Man. Q.B.).

One of the more interesting developments on the liability of engineers is the Supreme Court of Canada's decision in *Edgeworth Construction Ltd. v. N.D. Lea & Associates Ltd.*[251] As discussed above in Chapter 7, the Supreme Court, while finding an engineering firm liable in tort to non-privity contractors for negligence in the preparation of tender documents, exonerated the individual engineers in their personal capacities. The court held that the affixing of a seal to documents by an engineer merely attests that a qualified engineer prepared the drawing. It does not guarantee accuracy, nor does it establish liability for a negligent misrepresentation.[252]

(d) Other Professionals

In addition to the above, several other professional groups are vulnerable to tort and contract liability as a result of the negligent performance of their professional responsibilities. In general, the principles of negligence law canvassed above apply equally to them, although the nature of their responsibilities varies of course with their roles.[253]

---

251 (1993), 17 C.C.L.T. (2d) 101 (S.C.C.).

252 The Supreme Court also exonerated engineers from liability in *Auto Concrete Curb Ltd. v. South Nation River Conservation Authority* (1993), 17 C.C.L.T. (2d) 123. The court held that engineers are not responsible for advising potential contractors of the need to obtain permits, nor for advising contractors on the method to employ in their work. Other litigation involving engineers include *Sergius v. Janax Design & Drafting Services Ltd.* (1992), 9 C.C.L.T. (2d) 257 (B.C. S.C.); *B.C. Hydro & Power Authority v. N.D. Lea Associates Ltd.* (1992), 92 D.L.R. (4th) 403 (B.C. S.C.); *ACA Cooperative Assn. Ltd. v. Associated Freezers of Can. Inc.* (1992), 93 D.L.R. (4th) 559 (N.S. C.A.); *British Columbia v. R.B.O. Architecture Inc.*, [1994] 9 W.W.R. 317 (B.C. C.A.); *British Columbia v. R.B.O. Architecture Inc.*, [1995] 6 W.W.R. 679 (B.C. S.C.); *327973 B.C. Ltd. v. HBT Agra Ltd.* (1994), 120 D.L.R. (4th) 726 (B.C. C.A.); *Opron Construction Co. v. Alberta* (1994), 151 A.R. 241 (Q.B.); *Foyer Valade Inc. v. Red River Construction Co.* (1997), [1998] 3 W.W.R. 89 (Man. Q.B.), additional reasons at [1998] 5 W.W.R. 491 (Man. Q.B.), reversed [1999] 9 W.W.R. 576 (Man. C.A.); *Trizec Equities Ltd. v. Ellis-Don Management Services Ltd.* (1998), [1999] 5 W.W.R. 1 (Alta. Q.B.), additional reasons at (1999), 251 A.R. 101 (Q.B.), affirmed (1999), [2000] 2 W.W.R. 371 (Alta. C.A.); *606346 Alberta Ltd. v. Abugov*, [2000] 5 W.W.R. 623 (Alta. Q.B.), affirmed (2003), 2003 CarswellAlta 229 (C.A.); among others. For commentary see L. Rochester, "Professional Engineers: Does a Higher Risk Imply a Higher Standard of Care?" (2000), 50 C.L.R. (2d) 199. As with other areas of professional malpractice, although the general principles apply to each profession, there have specific duties and standards. These are dealt with in specialized texts on the topics.

253 An interesting recent case dealt with the standard of care required of nursing staff when they are assisting a doctor. In *Skeels Estate v. Iwashkiw*, [2006] 11 W.W.R. 632 (Alta. Q.B.), Germain J. held that subordinate health care workers are not expected to second-guess or take control of a deteriorating situation when assisting a doctor. Should, however, the situation become critical and it is clear that the doctor is unable to deal with it, it is a breach of the nursing staff's duty to fail to call for help. Another recent case dealing with the standard of care demanded of nurses is *Gemoto v. Calgary Regional Health Authority* (2006), [2006] A.J. No. 1278, 2006 CarswellAlta 1315 (Q.B.).

Cases have been brought against accountants and auditors,[254] bankers and other financial advisors,[255] insurers and their agents,[256] and realtors.[257]

---

254 These include, of course, *Hercules Management Ltd. v. Ernst & Young* (1997), 35 C.C.L.T. (2d) 115 (S.C.C.) and other important cases on recovery of pure economic loss discussed in Chapter 7. Also see *Ranjoy Sales & Leasing Ltd. v. Deloitte, Haskins & Sells*, [1984] 4 W.W.R. 706 (Man. Q.B.), affirmed [1985] 2 W.W.R. 534 (Man. C.A.); *Revelstoke Credit Union v. Miller* (1984), 28 C.C.L.T. 17 (B.C. S.C.); *H.E. Kane Agencies Ltd. v. Coopers & Lybrand* (1983), 23 C.C.L.T. 233 (N.B. Q.B.), affirmed as to auditor's liability (1985) 32 C.C.L.T. 1 (N.B. C.A.); *Sceptre Resourses v. Deloitte, Haskins & Sells* (1991), 83 Alta. L.R. (2d) 157 (C.A.); *Bloor Italian Gifts Ltd. v. Dixon* (2000), 2000 CarswellOnt 1781, 187 D.L.R. (4th) 64 (Ont. C.A.); and *Hart Building Supplies Ltd. v. Deloitte & Touche* (2004), 41 C.C.L.T. (3d) 240 (B.C. S.C. [In Chambers]). For academic analysis, see Bruce Chapman, "Limited Auditors' Liability: Economic Analysis and the Theory of Tort Law" (1992), 20 Can. Bus. L.J. 180; and Ivan Ivankovich, "Accountants And Third-Party Liability — Back To The Future" (1991), 23 Ottawa Law Rev. 505. The *Hart Building Supplies* case dealt with the identification doctrine, which arises when the act of a senior manager of a company is attributed to the company itself. See Darcy MacPherson's "Annotation" on this matter at 41 C.C.L.T. (3d) 240. For an analysis of auditors' liability from a comparative law perspective, see L. Khoury, "Liability of Auditors Beyond their Clients" (2001), 46 McGill L.J. 413. Also see J. Blackier & Paskell-Mede, "Auditor Liability in Canada" (1999), 48 U.N.B. L.J. 65, and Trakman and Trainor, "The Rights and Responsibilities of Auditors to Third Parties: A Call for a Principled Approach" (2005), 31 Queens L.J. 148.

255 See, e.g., *Blair v. Can. Trust Co.* (1986), 38 C.C.L.T. 300 (B.C. S.C.); *Twardy v. Humboldt Credit Union Ltd.* (1985), 34 C.C.L.T. 140 (Sask. Q.B.); *V.K. Mason Const. Ltd. v. Bank of N.S.* (1985), 16 D.L.R. (4th) 598 (S.C.C.); *Hayward v. Bank of N.S.* (1985), 32 C.C.L.T. 286 (Ont. C.A.), *Labreche v. Harasymiw* (1992), 89 D.L.R. (4th) 95 (Ont. Gen. Div.); *Vita Health Co. (1985) Ltd. v. T.D. Bank*, [1993] 7 W.W.R. 242 (Man. Q.B.), varied [1994] 9 W.W.R. 360 (Man. C.A.); *Vanderburgh v. ScotiaMcLeod Inc.*, [1992] 6 W.W.R. 673 (Alta. Q.B.); *Milroy v. Toronto Dominion Bank* (1997), 35 C.C.L.T. (2d) 37 (Ont. Gen. Div.); *Alvin's Auto Service Ltd. v. Clew Holdings Ltd.* (1997), 37 C.C.L.T. (2d) 135 (Sask. Q.B.); *Keith Plumbing & Heating Co. v. Newport City Club Ltd.*, [2000] 6 W.W.R. 65 (B.C. C.A.), leave to appeal refused (2000), 152 B.C.A.C. 23 (note) (S.C.C.); *Quantum Financial Services (Canada) Ltd. v. Yip* (1998), 168 D.L.R. (4th) 155 (B.C. S.C.), additional reasons at (1999), 173 D.L.R. (4th) 366 (B.C. S.C.); *Davis v. Orion Securities Inc.* (2006), 41 C.C.L.T. (3d) 302 (Ont. S.C.J.); *Baldwin v. Daubney* (2006), 275 D.L.R. (4th) 762 (Ont. C.A.), leave to appeal refused (2007), 2007 CarswellOnt 2853 (S.C.C.); among others. What is significant in many of these cases, of course, is the *Hedley Byrne* relationship. Also see Kligman, "Stockbroker's Liability" (1987), 41 C.C.L.T. 82.

256 See, e.g., *Edmond Vienneau Assurance Ltée v. Roy* (1986), 35 C.C.L.T. 249 (N.B. C.A.); *G.K.N. Keller Can. Ltd. v. Hartford Fire Ins. Co.* (1983), 27 C.C.L.T. 61 (Ont. H.C.), reversed in part (1984), 4 C.C.L.I. xxxvii (Ont. C.A.); *Random Ford Mercury Sales Ltd. v. Noseworthy* (1992), 95 D.L.R. (4th) 168 (Nfld. T.D.); *Miller v. Guardian Insurance Co. of Canada* (1995), [1996] 1 W.W.R. 228 (Alta. Q.B.), reversed [1997] 9 W.W.R. 225 (Alta. C.A.), leave to appeal refused (1998), 216 A.R. 200 (note) (S.C.C.); *Clark v. D.A. Hargreaves Ins. Ltd.* (2007), 51 C.C.L.T. (3d) 86 (Alta. Q.B.); among others. See Chapter 7. One of the more important liability issues affecting insurers is their duty to act in good faith. See *Whiten v. Pilot Insurance Co.*, [2002] 1 S.C.R. 595; *Walsh v. Nicholls* (2004), 25 C.C.L.T. (3d) 33 (N.B. C.A.); and *Fidler v. Sun Life Assurance Co. of Canada*, [2006] 8 W.W.R. 1 (S.C.C.).

257 See, e.g., *Scholl v. Royal Trust Corp. of Can.* (1986), 40 C.C.L.T. 113 (Ont. H.C.); *Semkuley v. Clay* (1982), 140 D.L.R. (3d) 489 (Alta. Q.B.); *Betker v. Williams*, [1992] 2 W.W.R. 534 (B.C. C.A.); *Can. Trust Co. v. Sorkos* (1992), 90 D.L.R. (4th) 265 (Ont. Gen. Div.); *Wong v. 407527 Ontario Ltd.* (1999), 179 D.L.R. (4th) 38 (Ont. C.A.), additional reasons at (2000), 2000 CarswellOnt 3701 (C.A.); *Johnston v. Re/Max Real Estate (Edmonton) Ltd.* (2004), 25 C.C.L.T. (3d) 75 (Alta. Q.B.), additional reasons at (2000), 2000 CarswellOnt 3701 (C.A.); among others.

11

Causal Connection

1. INTRODUCTION

The third major element of the cause of action in negligence is the requirement that the defendant's breach of duty be causally connected to the plaintiff's injury.

The theoretical importance of the issue of causal connection in a fault-based compensation process cannot be overstated. In contrast to no-fault compensation programs, negligence law must focus on the causal inquiry. For negligence law, it is the infliction of injury through the wrongdoing of another that entitles a person to full compensation, which must be provided by the wrongdoer who caused the injury.[1] The corrective justice underpinning of fault-based compensation is predicated not only upon the defendant's wrong, but upon its causal connection to the plaintiff's harm. Although the issue of causation can be ignored by compensation programs which consider the fact of a disability as being a sufficient reason to compensate a claimant, or which consider the responsibility to compensate as one belonging to the community,[2] it must be addressed by negligence law.

Academic debate concerning the nature of the causation inquiry is intense.[3] Disagreement centres around the extent to which the causation issue is factual

---

1 Although other arrangements for payment, such as liability insurance, can be made by the wrongdoer.

2 Such as the New Zealand Accident Compensation program. Although it must be noted that even here causation cannot be ignored, since the program only compensates those whose injuries arose as a result of an accident, and not a disease.

3 The topic has engaged many notable scholars. See Hart and Honore, *Causation in the Law*, 2nd ed. (1985); Green, "The Causal Relation Issue in Negligence Law" (1962), 60 Mich. L. Rev. 543; Malone, "Ruminations on Cause-In-Fact" (1956), 9 Stan. L. Rev. 60; Williams, "Causation in the Law", [1961] Cambridge L.J. 62; Weinrib, "A Step Forward in Factual Causation" (1975), 38 Mod. L. Rev. 518; Wright, "Causation in Tort Law" (1985), 73 Calif. L. Rev. 1737; Epstein, "A Theory of Strict Liability" (1973), 2 J. Leg. Stud. 151; Pincus, "Progress on the Causal Chain Gang: Some Approaches to Causation in Tort Law and Steps Toward a Linguistic Analysis" (1986), 24 Osgoode Hall L. J. 961; McInnis, "Causation in Tort Law: Back to Basics at the Supreme Court of Canada" (1997), 35 Alta. L.R. 1013; Beever, "Cause-in-fact: Two Steps Out of the Mire" (2001), 51 U.T.L.J. 327; among many others. Pincus and Wright, in their respective articles, provide excellent critical reviews of much of the writing in this area. David Cheiftez

and objective, or subjective and policy laden.[4] Various theories of causation have been put forward, especially in an effort to provide rational solutions to intriguing causation dilemmas which seem not to be readily amenable to easy answers.[5] Despite the jurisprudential furore, however, courts, in the vast majority of tort cases, seem to have very little difficulty in determining the issue of cause. In their view at least, whether a defendant's alleged misconduct is sufficiently causally connected to a plaintiff's harm is an issue which usually is not too difficult to resolve.[6] Recent jurisprudence both in Canada and elsewhere illustrate, however, how the "difficult" causation cases present judges with extremely complex issues and tough choices.

There are two aspects to the inquiry into causal connection. The first is the issue of "cause-in-fact". That is, before a defendant can be held accountable to the plaintiff, it must be established by the plaintiff that the defendant's alleged misconduct was, as a matter of fact, causally connected to the harm suffered. Negligence law does not concern itself with unreasonable conduct in the abstract. It is only because the conduct has resulted in the consequences complained of that it is of concern in a private right of action for damages.[7] Factual causation is

---

has written several articles on this topic, which will be referenced throughout this chapter. I am indebted to David for his assistance in reviewing this chapter; although, of course, the responsibility for all of its failings remains mine.

4 The traditional approach is that the causation inquiry is basically a factual one, which is policy-neutral. See Fleming, *The Law of Torts*, 9th ed. (1998), at 218:

> The first [inquiry] involves the "factual" question whether the relation between the defendant's breach of duty and the plaintiff's injury is one of cause and effect in accordance with "scientific" or "objective" notions of physical sequence.

Green, *ibid.* at 549 states that: "Causal relation is a neutral issue, blind to right and wrong . . . Conduct is a factual concept; the victim's hurt is a factual concept; causal relation is a factual concept." See also Wright, "The Law of Torts: 1923-1947" (1948), 26 Can. Bar Rev. 46; R.W. Wright, "Causation in Tort Law", *ibid.* Others believe that policy and value judgments are relevant and influence the decisions regarding causal connections. "Policy may often be a factor when the issue of cause-in-fact is presented sharply for decision, much as it is when questions of proximate cause are before the court.": see Malone, "Ruminations on Cause-In-Fact", *ibid.* Pincus, *ibid.*, at 978, states:

> Determining whether there is causation in a particular case is not a matter of drawing a cut-off point at the *next* link in a simple causal chain, but drawing the bounds around the *nearest* impinging forces in a dense causal web. . . . [N]ot only is the process of drawing these causal bounds influenced by policy considerations, but the very web of events itself is value-laden. Political, social, economic, cultural, and philosophical perceptions and prejudices are entangled and embedded within it.

5 See, e.g., the ten causal problems presented by Pincus, *ibid.*, at 971-73. Beever examines 15 fact patterns that he asserts present all of "the logical patterns into which the world falls, no more and no less"; above, note 3, at 329.

6 Whether this is due to the fact that the truly difficult case rarely arises and that in most cases causation is a question of "common sense", or to the fact that the court decides the issue of the defendant's liability without regard to causation, and then uses causal language to justify and support the desired result, is another point of disagreement. The causal "maximalists", such as Epstein, above, note 3, place a lot of importance on the causal inquiry, whereas the causal "minimalists", such as Malone, state that the causation inquiry actually explains very little about why courts find liability.

7 See Rutherford J. in *Mitchell Estate v. Low*, (1995), [1995] O.J. No. 621, 1995 CarswellOnt 2649 (Gen. Div.), affirmed (1998), 1998 CarswellOnt 936 (C.A.), at 25, where this passage is quoted with approval.

the subject matter of this chapter. The second aspect of the causal connection is proximate cause, or "cause-in-law". Having determined that the defendant's conduct was, as a matter of fact, causally connected to the plaintiff's harm, the court must then determine the limits of the defendant's liability.[8]

2. ESTABLISHING THE CAUSAL CONNECTION

(a) Introduction

However it is explained or rationalized, negligence law requires that the defendant's misconduct be causally connected to the plaintiff's harm, in order for the defendant to be liable to the plaintiff. There must be a reason to single out the defendant from other actors, and this reason ought to accord with negligence law's goals.[9] How the causal connection is established and explained will reveal what the liability decision in the specific case is meant to achieve.[10]

The case law reveals that there is no single test or approach which has been used to establish the causal requirement. Courts have been prepared to be flexible in their approaches, in an effort to reach decisions which accord with their sense of what the just or right result in the case would be.

(b) The "But For" Test

In most negligence cases, the causal connection between the defendant's negligent conduct and the plaintiff's injury is established by the application of the so-called "but for" test. If it can be proved, on the balance of probabilities, that the plaintiff's injury would not have occurred but for the defendant's negli-

---

8 This will be the focus of Chapter 12 — Remoteness. The Ontario Court of Appeal has held that a trial court first must determine what caused the plaintiff's injury before it can decide whether the defendant was negligent; see *Grass (Litigation Guardian of) v. Women's College Hospital* (2001), 5 C.C.L.T. (3d) 180 (Ont. C.A.), leave to appeal refused (2002), 293 N.R. 194 (note) (S.C.C.), where the Court of Appeal approved of its earlier decision in *Meringolo v. Oshawa General Hospital* (1991), 46 O.A.C. 260 (C.A.), leave to appeal refused (1991), 50 O.A.C. 159 (note) (S.C.C.). What the court means by this is somewhat unclear. A plaintiff must prove that a defendant was negligent and that it was this negligence that caused the plaintiff's injury. If the plaintiff cannot prove that the defendant was negligent in any respect, the action must be dismissed, even if it is not clear what caused the injury. If the plaintiff proves that the defendant was negligent, but cannot prove that it was this that caused the injury, the action must also be dismissed. See the Ontario Court of Appeal's most recent judgment on this point in *Locke v. Smith* (2002), 11 C.C.L.T. (3d) 245 (Ont. C.A.), where it held that a trial judge was *not* in error in dismissing a plaintiff's action even though the exact cause of the medical mishap was not known. See also Picard J.A.'s judgment in *McArdle Estate v. Cox*, 2003 CarswellAlta 435, 2003 ABCA 106 (C.A.), where the argument that the issue of cause must be determined before negligence was rejected. This suggestion, according to Picard J.A., "truly is putting the cart before the horse."

9 This was stated by Sopinka J. in *Snell v. Farrell* (1990), 72 D.L.R. (4th) 289 at 298-99 (S.C.C.), in the following way: "Causation is an expression of the relationship that must be found to exist between the tortious act of the wrongdoer and the injury to the victim in order to justify compensation of the latter out of the pocket of the former."

10 For example, to impose liability on a defendant because the defendant's misconduct actually damaged the plaintiff is to support negligence law's traditional corrective justice goals. To find a defendant liable, however, because the defendant was rich and the victim poor, or because the defendant could best absorb or redistribute the loss, may be defensible, but does not accord with the objectives of fault-based compensation.

gent conduct, the causal connection is established. Stated in other words, if the defendant's conduct can be shown to have been a necessary cause of the plaintiff's harm, conduct which made a difference to the plaintiff's *status quo ante*, the "but for" test is satisfied.[11] Conversely, if the plaintiff fails to prove this on the balance of probabilities, the causal connection has not been established.[12] Despite the considerable litigation and confusion over the use of the "but for" test in some difficult cases,[13] it is clear that the "but for" still remains "the primary test for causation in negligence actions"[14] in Canada.[15]

Lord Denning's statement in *Cork v. Kirby Maclean Ltd.*[16] explains the test:

> If you can say that the damage would not have happened but for a particular fault, then that fault is in fact a cause of the damage; but if you can say that the damage would have happened just the same, fault or no fault, then the fault is not a cause of the damage.

Thus, in *Matthews v. MacLaren*,[17] the defendant was relieved of liability with respect to a passenger who died as a result of falling into the cold water from the defendant's boat, since it could not be established that the defendant's negligent rescue attempt of the deceased was a factual cause of death. The deceased may have died of shock immediately or shortly after his plunge into the water. If it

---

11 As will be discussed below, the "but for" test does not work in "overdetermined" causation cases; i.e., cases in which two or more factors each alone would have been sufficient to produce the injury, so that not one of them was a necessary condition for the injury. The NESS test has been used to deal with this. That is, if the factor was a "Necessary Element of a Set of antecedent actual conditions that was Sufficient for the occurrence of the consequence" factual causation has been satisfied. See Wright, note 3, at 1774 *et seq.* for a complete discussion of NESS. For a more recent account, see Wright, "Acts and Omissions as Positive and Negative Causes" in *Emerging Issues in Tort Law*, Neyers, Chamberlain, and Pitel, eds. (2007, Hart Publishing), Chapter 11.

12 Difficulty arises where it is impossible for the plaintiff to satisfy the "but for" test, due to the existing state of knowledge or to the manner in which the plaintiff's injury occurred. The issue in these cases is whether the tests should be relaxed or jettisoned altogether in order to allow the plaintiff to be compensated. It must be stressed, however, that the orthodox approach to causation dictates that the plaintiff should fail where the causal connection based on the "but for" is not made out. It is important to underscore the fact that many tort actions are dismissed on this basis. See below.

13 See discussion below.

14 To quote from McLachlin C.J. in *Resurfice Corp. v. Hanke*, [2007] 1 S.C.R. 333 at para. 22.

15 The debate concerning when the "but for" test should be relaxed or even abandoned demonstrates that strong differences of opinion exist. The more traditional approach is a strict adherence to the test. As expressed by Smith J.A. in *Mooney v. British Columbia (Attorney General)* (2004), 25 C.C.L.T. (3d) 234 (B.C. C.A.), leave to appeal refused (2005), 2005 CarswellBC 463 (S.C.C.), at 286 [C.C.L.T.], "the elimination of causation as an element of negligence is a radical step." Smith J.A. further stated that "the causal connection is the lynchpin of liability in negligence." In another appellate court decision, *Aristorenas v. Comcare Health Services* (2006), 42 C.C.L.T. (3d) 220 (Ont. C.A.), additional reasons at (2006), 2006 CarswellOnt 7257 (C.A.), additional reasons at (2007), 2007 CarswellOnt 742 (C.A.), leave to appeal refused (2007), 2007 CarswellOnt 1878 (S.C.C.) at 232 [C.C.L.T.], Rouleau J.A. affirmed the "but for" test as "the standard for establishing causation in most negligence cases." See discussion below on when courts might depart from it.

16 [1952] 2 All E.R. 402 at 407 (C.A.). Cited in *Matthews v. MacLaren* (1969), 4 D.L.R. (3d) 557 at 566 (Ont. H.C.). See Cooper-Stephenson and Saunders, *Personal Injury Damages in Canada*, 2nd ed. (1996), Chapter 13 at 761.

17 (1969), 4 D.L.R. (3d) 557 (Ont. H.C.), reversed on another point [1970] 2 O.R. 487 (C.A.), which was affirmed [1972] S.C.R. 441.

could have been shown that a reasonably conducted rescue probably would have saved the deceased, the causal connection would have been established.[18]

The "but for" test is evaluative and speculative. It requires the trier of fact to predict what would have happened to the plaintiff had the defendant not acted unreasonably. Thus, again using *Matthews v. MacLaren*[19] as an illustration, the

18 There are many cases where the plaintiff's failure to prove causation on the "but for" test has led to the dismissal of the action. See, for example, *Michalchuk v. Yorkton (City)* (1987), 54 Sask. R. 74 (Q.B.)—although fire fighters arrived late and without equipment, the plaintiff failed to show on the balance of probabilities that this failure caused the destruction of the plaintiff's home; *Zaba v. Saskatchewan Institute of Applied Science & Technology,* [1997] 8 W.W.R. 414 (Sask. C.A.), reversing (1995), [1996] 1 W.W.R. 534 (Sask. Q.B.)—although the instructor failed to give adequate instructions to the student, this would not have prevented the accident in view of the student's own experience and training; *Stefanyshyn v. Rubin* (1996), [1997] 2 W.W.R. 298 (Man. C.A.)—although the doctor did not wear prescription glasses during a surgical procedure, this would not have prevented the medical misadventure that occurred; *Sohal v. Brar* (1998), [1999] 3 W.W.R. 553 (Alta. Q.B.), affirmed (1998), [1999] 7 W.W.R. 345 (Alta. C.A.)—although the doctor's negligence delayed the plaintiff's admission to the hospital, no proof that this would have prevented the need for the plaintiff's leg to be amputated; *Hagan v. Dalkon Shield Claimants Trust* (1998), 43 C.C.L.T. (2d) 11 (Alta. Q.B.)—although I.U.D.s were linked to a disease that sometimes resulted in infertility, not proved in this case that the plaintiff's infertility was caused this way; *Kirschenbaum-Green c. Surchin* (1997), 44 C.C.L.T. (2d) 68 (Que. C.A.), leave to appeal refused (1997), 223 N.R. 396 (note) (S.C.C.), affirming (1993), [1993] Q.J. No. 1865, 1993 CarswellQue 137 (C.A.)—although the doctor was negligent for not having accompanied the boy to the hospital, no proof that this would have prevented or delayed the cardiac arrest that the boy suffered en route; *Hammond v. Wabana (Town)* (1998), 44 C.C.L.T. (2d) 101 (Nfld. C.A.), leave to appeal refused (1999), 184 Nfld. & P.E.I.R. 180 (note) (S.C.C.)—even if volunteer the fire department was negligent, no proof that the other steps that could have been taken would have prevented the spread of the fire to the plaintiff's house; *Meloche v. Hotel Dieu Grace Hospital / Villa Marie* (1999), 179 D.L.R. (4th) 77 (Ont. C.A.), reversing (1998), [1998] O.J. No. 1549, 1998 CarswellOnt 1555 (Gen. Div.)—although the doctor was negligent in delaying the diagnosis of an eye infection, not proved that this caused the loss of the plaintiff's eyesight; *Bigcharles v. Dawson Creek & District Health Care Society* (2001), 5 C.C.L.T. (3d) 157 (B.C. C.A.), leave to appeal refused (2002), 171 B.C.A.C. 160 (note) (S.C.C.), affirming (1999), [1999] B.C.J. No. 1795, 1999 CarswellBC 1735 (S.C.)—despite negligence of doctors in diagnosing and treating, no proof that this caused the plaintiff's injury; *Montgomery v. Luoma* (2001), 92 B.C.L.R. (3d) 195 (C.A.)—although the doctor was negligent in failing to diagnose fluid in lungs, not proved that early diagnosis would have prevented the need for a subsequent operation; *Cottrelle v. Gerrard* (2003), 20 C.C.L.T. (3d) 1 (Ont. C.A.), leave to appeal refused (2004), 2004 CarswellOnt 1622 (S.C.C.)—although doctor was negligent with respect to treatment of plaintiff's foot, not proved that more effective treatment would have prevented the spread of an infection; *Mooney v. British Columbia (Attorney General)* (2004), 25 C.C.L.T. (3d) 234 (B.C. C.A.), leave to appeal refused (2005), 2005 CarswellBC 463 (S.C.C.)—although police negligent in failing to conduct a more thorough investigation of an earlier incident, no causal connection between that failure and a subsequent very serious incidence of violence; *Sabourin Estate v. Watterodt Estate* (2005), 34 C.C.L.T. (3d) 193 (B.C. C.A.), leave to appeal refused (2006), 2006 CarswellBC 125 (S.C.C.), leave to appeal refused (2006), 2006 CarswellBC 125 (S.C.C.), reconsideration refused (2006), 2006 CarswellBC 2772 (S.C.C.), affirming (2004), [2004] B.C.J. No. 326, 2004 CarswellBC 356 (S.C.)—although a "flight service specialist" was negligent in not repeating a warning to a pilot, not proved that the pilot who was responsible for a mid-air collision would have changed his course; among many others. All of these cases pre-date *Resurfice Corp. v. Hanke* (2007), 278 D.L.R. (4th) 643 (S.C.C.), which will be discussed below. Whether *Resurfice* now has made proving causation an easier task for plaintiffs will be considered below.

19 Above, note 17.

trier of fact was required to decide whether, if there had not been a negligent rescue attempt, the death would have been avoided. Since a court cannot repeat a past event, controlling some conditions while altering others to see what results, the issue is necessarily speculative.[20] The court must guess at what would have occurred, using its best judgment, intuition, common sense, experiences, expert evidence, and whatever else might be of assistance.

A principal objection to the use of the "but for" test is that it is simply too all-encompassing to be very useful. All causes which can be shown to have been necessary in order to produce the plaintiff's injury are, at least initially, candidates for liability. It is, of course, true that there are literally countless causes or events which must have occurred in order for the plaintiff's injury to have happened, and it would be preposterous to suggest that each ought to be investigated as a source of responsibility and compensation for the victim.[21] This, however, is not a serious objection. For one thing, most of these causes will immediately be eliminated from consideration, not, however, because they were not causally linked, but for other reasons. There might not have been a duty owed, the acts might not have been negligent, or the injuries might have been too remote. It must always be remembered that factual causation is only one of the requirements for a successful negligence claim. If anything, the contention that the "but for" test allows too many causal factors in for consideration might be a positive attribute of the test. It is worthwhile to consider, at least initially, many factors which may be linked to the plaintiff's injury, so as to not to eliminate too easily those, which although not obvious, might in fact be implicated in responsibility for the injury.[22] It must at least be conceded that certain possibilities will be excluded by the application of the but for test, and that this will be important in some cases.[23]

---

20 And therefore subject to being manipulated in order to reach the preferred result. See Malone, above, note 3, where the author shows how the judge can control the jury's decision by the manner in which the causal question is phrased. Or, as conceded by Fleming, *The Law of Torts*, 8th ed. (1992) at 194:

> Though factual in the sense of [being] dependent on the evidence available, it offers a certain latitude which may occasionally be exploited by judge or jury to introduce a policy tilt into what is ordinarily regarded as a policy neutral issue.

21 For example, a two car collision occurs. There are thousands of causal factors which could be considered — the fact that the cars were built, that they were sold, that the drivers were born, that they were licensed to drive, that roads were built, and so on. As Williams, above, note 3, at 64, asks: "What is the use of defining 'cause' so widely that it goes back to the primeval slime?"

22 For example, although one immediately blames a collision on one or both of the drivers, consider other possibilities. Perhaps one can inculpate the car manufacturer, the motor vehicle repairer, the designer or maintainer of the highway, the person who owned and lent the car to the driver, a tavern keeper, or the passengers. Keeping one's eyes open to all the realistic possibilities under the element of causal connection might well broaden the number of liable parties.

23 For example, as the negligent rescue attempt was excluded in *Matthews v. MacLaren*, above, note 17. Note, however, Cooper-Stephenson's caution that merely because the "but for" test excludes a cause does not necessarily mean that this is the right conclusion. The test will not work in some types of cases (multiple sufficient causes, for example) and other approaches might have to be adopted to achieve a just result. See Cooper-Stephenson, *Personal Injury Damages in Canada*, 2nd ed. (1996) at 752.

It must also be recalled that the issue of causation in tort arises not as a matter of philosophical inquiry or academic exercise, but within the context of a litigated dispute between a victim and a defendant. The court need not discover and list all of the causal factors which resulted in the plaintiff's injury. The court is only interested in the plaintiff's contention that the defendant's conduct was one of those responsible factors.[24] In this respect, the fact that others may be responsible for the plaintiff's harm is irrelevant to the plaintiff's contention that the defendant was responsible, unless the contribution of others in some way negated, superseded, supplemented or in some other way altered, in a legally relevant way, the defendant's role. These are contentions which the parties are free to raise and establish, and unless they do, they are of no concern to the court. Triers of fact are interested in the allegations made and the evidence presented to support them, and need not go on fact-finding missions of their own. In addition, determining that the defendant's misconduct was a cause of the plaintiff's injury, although speculative in nature, is a decision which need not be made with absolute confidence or certainty.[25] The trier of fact is afforded a margin of error, since all that is required is the establishment of a probable connection. As well, the judge or jury can well take comfort in the knowledge that its best judgment is probably as good as anyone else's, and that once the determination is made, it is unlikely to ever be proved to have been incorrect.[26]

3. ALTERNATIVE APPROACHES: ESTABLISHING CAUSE IN THE DIFFICULT CASE

(a) *Athey v. Leonati:*[27] The Basic Propositions

Proving that the defendant's negligence was a necessary cause of the plaintiff's injury, on the balance of probabilities, can be very difficult if there were many

---

24 As Williams, above, note 3, at 63, states:

> Factual causation is important in assessing legal responsibility because it does something to limit the field of legally relevant events. The court does not, of course, have to compile an exhaustive list of the causes of an item of damage in respect of which the litigation arises. The question is a specific one: was the act or omission of the defendant (or of one for whom he is responsible) a cause of the damage?

25 Or, as stated by Sopinka J., in *Snell v. Farrell*, above, note 9: "Causation need not be determined by scientific precision."

26 Recall that causation is a question of fact and a finding can only be overturned if there was "overriding and palpable error". Also note, however, that as with the standard of care issue, the determination of which test must be applied to answer the factual question is a question of law. See *Housen v. Nikolaisen*, 211 D.L.R. (4th) 577, 10 C.C.L.T. (3d) 157, [2002] 7 W.W.R. 1 (S.C.C.), where the Supreme Court was divided on whether to overturn the trial judge's findings regarding causation.

27 (1996), 140 D.L.R. (4th) 235, [1997] 1 W.W.R. 97, 31 C.C.L.T. (2d) 113 (S.C.C.).

other possible causes of the injury.[28] *Athey v. Leonati* was arguably one such case.[29]

The plaintiff had a history of back problems over a great number of years. He was injured in a motor vehicle accident and experienced pain and stiffness in his back. He began treatment and was recovering when he was involved in a second car accident. He did not appear to be seriously injured, continued to be treated, and again appeared to be on the road to recovery. While exercising several months later, he suffered a herniated disc, which required surgery.

The plaintiff sued the drivers who caused the accidents alleging that the herniated disc was caused by the injuries suffered in the accidents.[30] The defendants admitted liability for the car accidents but argued that the herniated disc was not caused by them, but by the exercise and the plaintiff's pre-existing weakness in his back. The trial judge held that the accidents contributed to "some degree to the herniation", but were "a minor contributing factor" and awarded the plaintiff 25 per cent of his damages from the defendants.[31] The Court of Appeal dismissed the plaintiff's appeal for 100 per cent compensation.[32] On further appeal to the Supreme Court of Canada, the Court held that the trial judge erred and that the plaintiff was entitled to full damages.

In arriving at its decision, the Supreme Court of Canada articulated the general principles applicable in tort to issues of causation. Many courts have adopted these principles since *Athey* as fundamental to resolving causation questions. What are these principles?

First, the Court reaffirmed that the "but for" test, proved on a balance of probabilities, is the general test for causation.

Second, the Court noted that the "but for" test does not require that the defendant's negligence be the only condition necessary to cause the plaintiff's injury. There will always in fact be other necessary causes that were conditions of the injury occurring. Defendants whose acts were necessary parts of the causal sequence will be fully liable for the injuries.[33] Where the other causes were non-tortious, the defendants will bear the entire burden. Where the other causes were

---

28 These difficult cases seem to be arising more frequently. Professor Richard Wright's insight that "advances in science combined with mass production and distribution of products have created an expanding number of risks and harms, which, however, are often difficult to attribute to specific actors" is a sound explanation for this development (see Wright, "Acts and Omissions as Positive and Negative Causes" above, note 11, at 307). The more we know about how injuries *might have occurred*, the less certain we can be about how they actually did occur in any specific case. This might truly be an area where "ignorance is bliss" — at least in so far as the law is concerned.

29 See Klimchuk and Black, "A Comment on *Athey v. Leonati*: Causation, Damages and Thin Skulls" (1997), 31 U.B.C. L. Rev. 163.

30 Since the same insurer insured both drivers, both car accidents and drivers were treated as one. This obviated the need to deal with another complication, the need to distinguish between the separate effects of each of the accidents.

31 (December 29, 1993), Doc. Vancouver C921241 (B.C. S.C.).

32 (March 10, 1995), Doc. CA018227, CA018228, [1995] B.C.J. No. 666 (C.A.). The appellant argued that the "material contribution" test would allow 100 per cent recovery. The Court of Appeal held that it would not consider this test because it had not been argued at trial.

33 Subject to rules of "remoteness", which may limit a defendant's liability for injuries even where the defendant's negligence was factually connected to them. See discussion in Chapter 12.

tortious, there can be apportionment between defendants, although in most jurisdictions each defendant will remain fully liable to the plaintiff.[34] Where the other cause was the plaintiff's own fault, the rules of contributory negligence will apply.[35]

Third, defendants are only liable for those injuries that were caused by their negligent acts. Thus, for example, if the plaintiff's injuries are divisible, some being caused by one defendant, and others by another party, defendants remain liable only for the injuries that they caused. As we will see, this does not mean that defendants cannot be held liable for subsequent injuries suffered by a plaintiff that flow from the defendant's initial negligent act and the immediate injuries. This issue, however, does not raise an issue of factual cause but a problem of remoteness or proximate cause that will be discussed in the next chapter.

Fourth, the Court confirmed that a defendant is liable for the full extent of a plaintiff's injuries, even if they are more serious due to a pre-existing susceptibility or vulnerability of the plaintiff. This is the "thin skull" rule, which arises as a question not of factual but of legal cause.[36]

Fifth, the Court recognized the "crumbling skull" scenario. A defendant is liable only for the injuries and losses that the plaintiff suffered as a result of the defendant's negligence. If the plaintiff would have suffered some of the same consequences anyway, due to an on-going degenerative process that might have eventually caused them, this must also be taken into consideration.[37]

Based on these principles, the Supreme Court held that the trial judge erred in awarding the plaintiff only 25 per cent of its damages. If the defendants' negligence was one of the necessary conditions, along with non-tortious conditions, required to bring about the plaintiff's injury, i.e., a herniated disc, then the defendants should have been held fully liable for this injury. This is how the Supreme Court interpreted the trial judge's findings of fact, and hence it awarded the plaintiff full compensation.[38]

---

34 For a discussion of apportionment, see Chapter 13.

35 For a discussion of contributory negligence, see Chapter 13.

36 It is in other words a remoteness issue that will be discussed in Chapter 12. In these cases, there is no question that the defendant's negligence was a factual cause of the plaintiff's extreme injury. The only question is whether the defendant should, on a proximate cause analysis, be liable for it.

37 In *A. (T.W.N.) v. Clarke*, 2003 BCCA 670 (C.A.) at para. 28, Smith J.A. points out that the pre-existing condition can be either "quiescent or active". This assimilates a "crumbling" skull with a "thin" skull, something which Justice Smith thinks is a good idea, since in either case the plaintiff's damages can be reduced. Although this is so, the reduction is based on two different ideas. In crumbling skull cases, where the injury was already occurring or likely to occur, the defendant is only liable for the accelerated or exacerbated damages; i.e., the additional damages that the defendant caused. In "thin skull" cases, the defendant is fully liable, but damages can be reduced by a contingencies reduction. See discussion in Chapter 12.

38 The problem with many of the cases in this area is that the evidence and what it shows is frequently confusing. In *Athey v. Leonati* itself, for example, the trial judge was faced with contradictory and unclear evidence as to the extent of the contribution of the car accidents to the herniated disc. The trial judge was prepared to attribute "little weight to those injuries in terms of overall causation", and awarded the plaintiff only 25 per cent of its damages. It is unclear what the trial judge meant by this award. It is possible that the trial judge felt that there was only a 25 per cent chance that the car accidents were one of the necessary contributing

In addition to determining whether a defendant's negligence caused a plaintiff's injuries, which is the threshold liability question, the court must determine as well what losses flowed from, i.e., were caused by, the injuries that the plaintiff suffered. This is the assessment of loss issue. Both are equally important to the plaintiff's case, and both raise the same types of causation issues. Although the "but for" test is fundamental to both questions of liability and assessment of loss, it is useful to keep these two stages of the causal inquiry distinct. They focus on different matters and for analytical clarity, if for no other reason, it is helpful to separately identify them.[39] Although this chapter and the leading cases that will be discussed below mainly deal with questions of factual causation of injury for liability purposes, causation questions for the purpose of assessing losses invariably are raised by the cases and will also be addressed.

(b) Making it Easier for Plaintiffs: Alternatives to the "But For" Test

Difficulties for a plaintiff arise where a plaintiff can establish that it has been injured, the defendant was negligent, and the injuries were quite possibly caused by the negligence, but it cannot be proved on the balance of probabilities that the defendant's negligence was in fact one of the necessary causes of the injuries. In other words, there were several possible causes, including the defendant's negligence, but no probable ones. What should a court do then? Should it dismiss the plaintiff's action? Should it abandon the "but for" test? Should it change the burden of proof? Should it redefine the nature of the plaintiff's injury?

In resolving this problem, courts must keep in mind that there have been and will continue to be *many cases* where plaintiffs find it very difficult, if not impossible, to prove causation on traditional principles and where actions ac-

---

factors to the herniation. In this case, the action should have been dismissed. Or the trial judge might have meant that there were several contributing causes of the herniation, one of them being the injuries resulting from the car accidents. In this case, the defendant would be 100 per cent liable. This is indeed what the Supreme Court of Canada held the trial judge meant.

39 In *Blackwater v. Plint* (2005), 258 D.L.R. (4th) 275 (S.C.C.), at 296, McLachlin C.J.C. explained the distinction as follows:

> It is important to distinguish causation as the source of the loss and the rules of damage assessment in tort. The rules of causation consider generally whether "but for" the defendant's acts, the plaintiff's damages would have been incurred on a balance of probabilities. Even though there may be several tortious and non-tortious causes of injury, so long as the defendant's act is a cause of the plaintiff's damage, the defendant is fully liable for that damage. The rules of damages then consider what the original position of the plaintiff would have been. The governing principle is that the defendant need not put the plaintiff in a better position than his original position and should not compensate the plaintiff for any damages he would have suffered anyway: *Athey*.

I would suggest that for the purposes of clarity, the first question focuses on the cause of the plaintiff's injury, and the second on the cause of the plaintiff's losses. Also see Smith J.A.'s statement in *A. (T.W.N.) v. Clarke*, 2003 BCCA 670 at para 16: "Determining the cause of loss and damage must be kept separate from the assessment of damages to compensate for that loss and damage, since different principles govern the two questions."

cordingly have been, and continue to be, dismissed for this reason.[40] If courts are willing to jettison the "but for" test for some difficult cases, but not for others, what are the essential elements that must be established in these aberrational cases to justify applying these alternative tests? As discussed above, establishing a causal connection between a defendant's negligent act and a plaintiff's injury is essential in a system of corrective justice, a system based on fault causing harm. Where defendants are held liable for injuries that, at least on the application of normal principles of tort law, they did not in fact cause, other persuasive rationales need to be advanced to explain this. These things must be kept in mind by courts as they develop alternative tests to the traditional "but for" approach.[41]

(c) The "Material Contribution" Test: What is it and When Does it Apply?

(i) Introduction

An expression which courts have used which seems to lighten a plaintiff's burden of proving that the defendant's negligence was, on the balance of probabilities, a cause of the plaintiff's injuries is that of "material contribution". As stated by Major J. in *Athey v. Leonati*,[42] "the 'but for' test is unworkable in some circumstances, so the courts have recognized that causation is established where the defendant's negligence 'materially contributed' to the occurrence of the injury". What does this expression mean and when should the courts apply this alternative test? These have proven to be difficult questions to answer; the ex-

40 See above, note 18, for a listing of a number of these cases. The extensive list is provided in order to illustrate the proposition that it is not unusual for actions of injured plaintiffs to be dismissed against negligent defendants because the plaintiffs fail to prove cause using the traditional "but for" approach.

41 The difficult causation cases have challenged not only the courts but also academics as well. There has been extensive commentary. See J. Stapleton, "Lords a'leaping Evidentiary Gaps" (2002), 10 Tort L. Rev. 276; J. Stapleton, "Legal Cause: Cause-in-Fact and the Scope of Liability for Consequences" (2001), 54 Vand. L. Rev. 941; J. Stapleton, "Unpacking Causation" in Cane and Gardner, eds., *Relating to Responsibility* (Oxford: Hart Publishing, 2001); V. Black, "A Farewell to Causation" (2001), 24 Advocates' Q. 478; G. Demeyere, "The Material Contribution Test: An Immaterial Contribution to Tort Law" (2000), 34 U.B.C. L. Rev. 317; Klimchuk and Black, "Causation, Damages & Thin Skulls" (1997), 31 U.B.C. L. Rev. 163; Black, "The Transformation of Causation in the Supreme Court: Dilution and Policyization" in Archibald and Cochrane, eds., *Annual Review of Civil Litigation* (2002), at 187. The more recent writings include Cheifetz, "Materially Increasing the Risk of Injury as Factual Cause of Injury: *Fairchild v. Glenhaven Funeral Services Ltd.* in Canada" (2004), The Advocates' Q. 253; Cheifetz, "The Snell Inference and Material Contribution: Defining the Indefinable and Hunting the Causative Snark" (2005), The Advocates' Q. 1; Cheifetz and Black, "Material Contribution and Quantum Uncertainty: *Hanke v. Resurfice Corp.*" (2006), 43 Can. Bus. L.J. 155; Brown, "Material Contribution's Expanding Hegemony: Causation after *Hanke*" (2007), Can. Bus. L.J.; Black and Cheifetz "Through the Looking Glass, Darkly: *Resurfice Corp. v. Hanke* (2007), 45 Alta. L. Rev. 1; Black, "Decision Causation: Pandora's Tool Box" in Neyers, Pitel, Chamberlain, eds., *Emerging Issues in Tort Law* (Hart Publishing, 2007), Chapter 12; Khoury, *Uncertain Causation in Medical Liability* (2006); and Cheifetz, "Risk As Legal Causation: Causation in Tort in Canadian Common Law After *Resurfice Corp v. Hanke*" (2008), Special Lectures Law Society of Upper Canada.

42 (1996), 31 C.C.L.T. (2d) 113 (S.C.C.) at 120.

pression "material contribution" as a test of causation has been used by courts in different ways and applied under different circumstances.[43]

(ii) The Defendant's Negligence was one of Several Necessary Causes

The expression "material contribution" has been used by some judges simply as a way of illustrating the application of the "but for" test to an injury which has more than one cause. In other words, the defendant's negligence was a material factor contributing, along with other necessary factors, to producing the plaintiff's injury. Used in this way, the material contribution test is merely the application of the "but for" test to injuries which have multiple causes.

It should be recognized that in all cases the defendant's misconduct was only one of several necessary factors required to produce the plaintiff's injury, each one of which was not sufficient in itself to cause the harm. There is, in other words, never a single necessary and sufficient cause of an injury, but numerous factors which together contributed to the result.[44] To satisfy the requirements of causation, the plaintiff is only required to prove that the defendant's negligence "materially contributed" to the injury; that is, it was one of several necessary causes in leading to the plaintiff's injury. Used in this limited sense, a material contribution is equivalent to a cause for the purpose of applying the "but for" test. In the leading English case, *Bonnington Castings Ltd. v. Wardlaw*,[45] Lord Reid defined a "material contribution" as any contribution which does not qualify within the exception *de minimis non curat lex*. In other words, as long as the plaintiff can prove, on the balance of probabilities, that the defendant's negligence, although not exclusively responsible for the injury, was one of the material factors contributing to it, the "but for" test is met.[46]

In *Myers v. Peel County Bd. of Educ.*,[47] the Supreme Court of Canada accepted the trial judge's finding that the defendant's negligence was causally connected

43 This point is made abundantly clear by the academic writing in this area. See especially Cheifetz, "The Snell Inference. . .", above, note 41. Also see Ken Cooper-Stephenson, "Justice in Saskatchewan Robes: The Bayda Tort Legacy" (2007), 70 Sask. L. Rev. 269 at 293, where the author notes the meaning of the phrase "material contribution" is nowhere to be found.

44 Where only one of these factors is wrongful, it is of course the only legally relevant cause. It is not, however, the only cause.

45 [1956] 1 All E.R. 615 (H.L.).

46 The words "material contribution" used in this way have proved to be helpful in medical negligence cases particularly. See, for example, *Rhine v. Millan*, [2000] 7 W.W.R. 136 (Alta. Q.B.), where despite contrary theories, the judge accepted the plaintiff's argument that her disease was caused or "materially contributed to" by the drugs that had been inappropriately prescribed. Also see *Elofson v. Davis* (1997), 144 D.L.R. (4th) 143 (Alta. Q.B.), another case involving drugs. The court in that case concluded that continuing to prescribe a drug after a certain time was negligent and materially contributed to the plaintiff's injury. In *Sam v. Wilson*, 2007 BCCA 622 (C.A.), Smith J.A. observed that the phrase "material contribution" used in this way is synonymous with the phrase "substantial connection". It indicates that "the indivisible damage would not have occurred but for the combination of multiple tortious causes". Thus it is simply the "but for" test applied to multiple necessary causes. Smith J.A. went on to remark that this use of the phrase material contribution should not be confused with the "material contribution test", which is an exception to the "but for" test and "is not a test of causation at all: rather it is a rule based on policy." In my view, these remarks are insightful, and explain some of the confusion in this area. See discussion below.

47 (1981), 123 D.L.R. (3d) 1 (S.C.C.).

to the plaintiff's injury upon proof that it "probably contributed" to it. Mr. Justice McIntyre stated:

> It is not, in my view, incumbent upon the plaintiff in a case such as this to prove positively that the presence of the crash mat would have prevented the injury. The plaintiff is bound to prove, according to a balance of probabilities, that the failure of the school authorities to provide more adequate matting and insist upon its use contributed to the accident.[48]

The court stated that although it could not be proved that the existence of the crash mats would have prevented the injury, proof that their absence was probably one of the factors involved in the accident was sufficient.[49]

Used in this limited sense, the expression "material contribution" is not an alternative to the "but for" test, but an application of it. As others have pointed out,[50] the "but for" test is workable when there are multiple independent causes, including the defendant's negligence, which can be proved to be necessary causes of the plaintiff's injury. This is what happened in *Athey v. Leonati*. This is the typical case.[51]

(iii) The "But For" Test is Unworkable

The true difficulty arises when the "but for" test is unworkable. This happens when it is impossible for the plaintiff to establish on the balance of probabilities that the defendant's negligence was a necessary cause of the injuries which the plaintiff suffered. It is for these types of cases that Major J. suggested, in *Athey*, that alternate tests might need to be considered.[52]

As emphasized above, there have been and will continue to be many cases where plaintiffs are not able to prove, on the balance of probabilities, that the defendants' negligence was in fact one of the necessary causes of their injuries.

---

48 *Ibid.*, at 12.

49 See also Wilson J.A.'s judgment in *Cotic v. Gray* (1981), 124 D.L.R. (3d) 641 at 673 (Ont. C.A.), affirmed (1983), 1 D.L.R. (4th) 187 (S.C.C.), where Wilson J.A. concedes that the introduction of the words "contributed to" into the causation question put to the jury "substantially increased the likelihood of a 'Yes' answer. The jury did not have to face the bald alternative of whether the accident caused the deceased's death or whether something else caused it."

50 See Cheifetz and Black, "Material Contribution and Quantum Uncertainty", above, note 41.

51 This is what the Alberta Court of Appeal overlooked in *Resurfice Corp. v. Hanke* (2005), 53 Alta. L.R. (4th) 219 (C.A.), additional reasons at (2006), 2006 CarswellAlta 417 (C.A.), leave to appeal allowed (2006), 2006 CarswellAlta 482 (S.C.C.), reversed (2007), 2007 CarswellAlta 130 (S.C.C.). Merely because there was more than one potential wrongful cause of the plaintiff's injury, the Court of Appeal held that the "but for" test was unworkable, and that the "material contribution" test should have been used. *Walker Estate v. York-Finch General Hospital* (2001), 198 D.L.R. (4th) 193 (S.C.C.) was referenced. McLachlin C.J. corrected this in *Resurfice Corp. v. Hanke* (2007), 278 D.L.R. (4th) 643 (S.C.C.), at para. 19:

> The Court of Appeal erred in suggesting that, where there is more than one potential cause of an injury, the "material contribution" test must be used. To accept this conclusion is to do away with the "but for" test altogether, given that there is more than one potential cause in virtually all litigated cases of negligence.

As stated by McLachlin C.J. "the basic test for determining causation remains the 'but for' test" and "this applies to multi-cause injuries", at para. 21. Also see McLachlin C.J.'s reaffirmation of this in *Hill v. Hamilton-Wentworth* (2007), 50 C.C.L.T. (3d) 1 (S.C.C.) at para. 94.

52 It should be recalled that Sopinka J. said somewhat the same thing in *Snell v. Farrell* (1990), 72 D.L.R. (4th) 289 (S.C.C.), at 299. See discussion below.

In the vast majority of these instances, the plaintiffs' actions are dismissed, and rightly so, if the "but for" test is faithfully applied. For these unsuccessful plaintiffs, the "but for" test does not work. No one would suggest, however, that in all cases where plaintiffs cannot prove that the defendants' negligent acts resulted in their injuries, an alternative, easier test should be applied. There must, therefore, be something special about a case, other than the mere fact that the plaintiff cannot satisfy the "but for" test, which will justify a court in abandoning it, for a more 'plaintiff-friendly' one. In other words, the "but for" test must be unworkable, not merely because the plaintiff is unable to satisfy it, but for very particular and restricted reasons. When, therefore, is the "but for" test so unworkable that it must be jettisoned?[53]

(iv) Walker Estate v. York Finch General Hospital

An important Supreme Court of Canada case which was one of the first to suggest that the "material contribution" test represents an alternative to the "but for" test is *Walker Estate v. York Finch General Hospital*.[54] The plaintiffs contracted HIV due to infected blood supplied by the defendant. They alleged that had the defendant used a more effective blood screening process that the donors who had given the infected blood would not have done so. The trial judge disagreed, finding that the evidence did not support this conclusion and he dismissed the action.[55] The Court of Appeal reversed the trial judge, finding that there was a presumption that had he been informed, the donor would not have given blood.[56]

Major J., writing for the Supreme Court of Canada, held that in some cases the "but for" test is "unworkable" because it is "difficult or impossible" to apply. In these cases, the "material contribution" test was suggested. In defining this test, Major J. referred to the Court's earlier judgment in *Athey v. Leonati* where it was stated, "a contributing factor is material if it falls outside the *de minimis* range".[57] Unfortunately, apart from this brief reference, the Court did not further clarify the meaning of this test or when it is applicable. Major J. ultimately concluded that "the strict but-for test" applied on the facts of *Walker* and thus the discussion was ultimately *obiter*.[58]

---

53 David Cheifetz in "The Snell Inference and Material Contribution", above, note 41, at 83-84, has suggested that the ambiguity of the term "unworkable" is evident in the fact that courts have defined it in a number of different ways. It is, therefore, difficult to know what the term precisely means and when an alternate test to "but for" is legitimate. The best we can do is to examine under what circumstances the courts have relaxed the causation requirement for plaintiffs as guidance for future cases.

54 (2001), 198 D.L.R. (4th) 193 (S.C.C.).

55 (1997), 39 C.C.L.T. (2d) 1 (Ont. Gen. Div.).

56 (1999), 169 D.L.R. (4th) 689 (Ont. C.A.). The Court of Appeal applied the Supreme Court of Canada's judgment in *Hollis v. Birch*, [1995] 4 S.C.R. 634, discussed in Chapter 9. According to the Court of Appeal, the presumption could not be rebutted by the defendant absent evidence of "extraneous conduct" on the part of the donor, which would have made the failure to adequately screen irrelevant.

57 (2001), 198 D.L.R. (4th) 193 (S.C.C.) at 215, citing *Athey v. Leonati*, [1996] 3 S.C.R. 458.

58 The Supreme Court disagreed with the Court of Appeal's decision to create a presumptive causal link in this case. Major J. restricted the *Hollis* approach to a case where there is a learned intermediary, and *Walker* was not such a case. See Black, " A Farewell To Causation" (2001), 24 Advocates' Q. 478 for a critique of the Supreme Court's judgment.

Nonetheless, reaffirmation by Major J. that courts can jettison the "but for" test in cases where it is difficult or impossible to apply was an important start.[59]

(v) *Materially Increasing the Risk of Injury:* McGhee v. National Coal Board

In some cases, the courts have held that the defendant's negligence caused the plaintiff's injury by materially increasing the risk that the injury would occur. This is a radical departure from the way the law normally connects the defendant's negligence to the plaintiff's injury, since it focuses on the defendant's negligence contributing to a risk of injury rather than to the injury itself.

The classic problem arose in *McGhee v. Nat. Coal Bd.*,[60] a case which illustrates the difficulties a plaintiff can face in proving, on a balance of probabilities, that the defendant's negligence was one of the necessary causes of harm, where there were a number of possible other causes which, even in the absence of the defendant's fault, might have produced the same result. The pursuer, an employee at the defender's brick works, contracted dermatitis. The pursuer established that the defender's failure to provide washing facilities for the employees' use was negligent, but was unable to show, upon a balance of probabilities, that this was a necessary factor in causing the dermatitis. Dermatitis might have occurred even had the proper washing facilities been provided.[61] There was evidence, however, that the lack of washing facilities "materially increased the risk" of the pursuer contracting dermatitis.[62]

In finding in favour of the pursuers on the basis of this evidence, Lords Simon, Kilbrandon, and Salmon redefined the concept of cause itself. The majority of the House of Lords decided that negligent conduct which materially increased a risk of injury can be held to have caused an injury which occurs within that risk, thus satisfying the test of causation and entitling a claimant to full compensation.[63]

Lord Wilberforce followed a different approach. He held that the evidence in *McGhee* created a presumption of causation which required the defender to show, if it could,[64] that its negligence was causally unrelated to the injury. This was in

---

59 There is, of course, a difference between the words "difficult" and "impossible". As we will see, McLachlin C.J. in *Resurfice Corp. v. Hanke* stated that the important factor in *Walker* that would have justified the departure from the "but for" test, was that the plaintiff was required to prove "what a particular person in the causal chain would have done had the defendant not committed a negligent act or omission." The argument is that this might be impossible to do, especially where, as in *Walker*, this other person is deceased.

60 [1972] 3 All E.R. 1008 (H.L.). See Weinrib, "A Step Forward in Factual Causation" (1975), 38 Mod. L. Rev. 518; Robertson, "Overcoming the Causation Hurdle in Informed Consent Cases" (1984), 22 U.W.O. L. Rev. 75.

61 The dermatitis might have happened anyway due to the fact that the pursuer was covered in dust while at work.

62 The longer the person was covered in dust before washing it off, the greater the risk of getting dermatitis.

63 The Lords equated "materially increasing a risk" with "materially contributing to the injury." See, e.g., Lord Reid, above, note 60, at 1011:

> From a broad and practical viewpoint I can see no substantial difference between saying that what the respondents did materially increased the risk of injury to the appellant and saying that what the respondents did made a material contribution to his injury.

64 Which of course it could not, due to the very nature of the evidentiary problem which provoked this innovative treatment of causation in the first place.

effect to leave the concept of cause unchanged, but to alleviate the plaintiff's burden of proving it.

Taken at face value, the judgment in *McGhee* involved a radical proposition. Since, by definition, all negligent conduct involves the creation of an unreasonable risk of injury,[65] the assumption that an injury which occurs within that risk will be deemed to have been caused by the unreasonable conduct, effectively eliminates proof of causation from the negligence action.[66] It is thus clear that unless constrained by certain conditions, *McGhee* would significantly change how causation is established.

In England, the House of Lords seemed to at first retreat from the full significance of the *McGhee* principle, although in a somewhat equivocal manner. In *Wilsher v. Essex Area Health Authority*,[67] the Lords suggested that the *McGhee* principle went too far, although, due to the unclear evidence in the case, the Lords could not clearly resolve the issue. The case involved an infant plaintiff who was born prematurely and developed an incurable eye condition. The lower courts had decided that one of the possible causes of the plaintiff's condition was the excessive oxygen which the defendants had negligently administered to the plaintiff. Applying the principle of *McGhee*, Mustill L.J., in the Court of Appeal, held:

> If it is an established fact that conduct of a particular kind creates a risk that injury will be caused to another or increases an existing risk that injury will ensue, and if the two parties stand in such a relationship that the one party owes a duty not to conduct himself in that way, and if one party does conduct himself in that way, and if the other party does suffer injury of the kind to which the injury related, then the first party is taken to have caused the injury by his breach of duty, even though the existence and extent of the contribution made by the breach cannot be ascertained.[68]

On appeal to the House of Lords, Lord Bridge held that the lower courts had misapprehended the evidence. It had not been established that the excess oxygen which had been administered to the plaintiff was capable of having caused or materially contributed to the plaintiff's disease. Nevertheless, Lord Bridge held that even assuming that the excess oxygen was one of the possible causes of the disease, the principle in *McGhee* could not assist the plaintiff's case. Lord Bridge warned that the principle in *McGhee* should not be interpreted too broadly and stated:

> *McGhee v. National Coal Board* laid down no new principle of law whatever. On the contrary, it affirmed the principle that the onus of proving causation lies on the pursuer or plaintiff. Adopting a robust and pragmatic approach to the undisputed primary facts of the case, the majority concluded that it was a legitimate inference of fact that the defenders' negligence had materially contributed to the pursuer's injury. The decision, in my opinion, is of no greater significance than that and the attempt to extract from it some esoteric principle which in some way modifies, as a matter of law, the nature of the burden of proof of causation which a plaintiff or pursuer must discharge once he has established a relevant breach of duty is a fruitless one.[69]

---

65 See discussion in Chapter 9.

66 Subject to the defendant's right to prove that the injury was probably caused in some other way.

67 [1988] 1 All E.R. 871 (H.L.).

68 [1986] 3 All E.R. 801 at 829 (C.A.).

69 [1988] 1 All E.R. 871 at 881-82. See *Westco Storage v. Inter-City Gas Utilities Ltd.*, [1989] 4 W.W.R. 289 (Man. C.A.), and *Couillard v. Waschulewski Estate*, [1988] 4 W.W.R. 642 (Alta. Q.B.), where approval is given to the *Wilsher* approach.

In other words, merely being a possible cause of the plaintiff's injury was neither sufficient to establish causation nor to shift the burden of disproof to the defendant.

In *Fairchild v. Glenhaven Funeral* Services,[70] the Lords revisited and revitalized the *McGhee* principle. The facts are as follows. Employees worked for more than one employer at different times and for differing periods.[71] The employees were exposed to asbestos dust at their places of work. The employees developed a fatal disease, mesothelioma, as a result of their asbestos exposure(s), and died. The employers owed a duty of care to the employees not to expose them to asbestos dust, and they breached the duty. The exposures to the asbestos occurred only at work and the mesothelioma could not have been caused as a result of non-work exposure.

What was not provable, however, due to inadequate medical knowledge, was which exposure or exposures triggered the mesothelioma. Did the disease originate due to the exposure to the asbestos at employer one's workplace, at employer two's workplace, or as a result of exposures at both workplaces? By the nature of the disease, it could be caused by a single exposure to one single asbestos fibre, to a few fibres, or to many fibres. The greater the exposure to asbestos, the greater the odds of contracting mesothelioma, but the disease is not necessarily or even probably the result of an extended exposure as opposed to a single one. In other words, mesothelioma is not caused by an accumulation of asbestos on the skin.[72] Thus, on the facts of this type of case, it was impossible to say with any degree of probability where the employees contracted the disease. Because of this, the lower courts had dismissed the employees' claims against their employers.[73] The employees appealed to the House of Lords.

In a lengthy set of judgments,[74] the Lords allowed the appeal. Several important points, made by the various Lords in their judgments should be noted. First, the Lords made it clear that Lord Bridge's comment in *Wilsher* that *McGhee* laid down no new principle of law but was decided based on an inference from the evidence was wrong. There was no factual inference that could be drawn from the evidence in *McGhee* to permit the conclusion that the defendant's negligence caused, on a "but for" approach, the pursuer's dermatitis. The Lords in *McGhee* had indeed created a new principle of law.[75] Second, the Lords agreed, that despite this error, *Wilsher* was correctly decided since it was unlike *McGhee* on the facts. In *McGhee*, there was only one causal agent, dust at work, from one wrongdoer, which could have caused the pursuer's dermatitis. In *Wilsher*, there were a number of factors that could have caused the plaintiff's blindness. Third, based on the

70 [2002] 3 W.L.R. 89, [2002] 3 All E.R. 305 (H.L.). See Stapleton, "Lords a'leaping Evidentiary Gaps", above, note 41.

71 There were three claims made by the estates of different employees against different employers.

72 This is a critical fact, which distinguishes this case from other cases, such as *Bonnington Castings Ltd. v. Wardlaw*, [1956] 1 All E.R. 615 (H.L.).

73 The Court of Appeal judgment is reported at [2002] 1 W.L.R. 1052 (Eng. C.A.).

74 Five judgments were written.

75 See Lord Bingham at [2002] 3 All E.R. 305 (H.L.) at 326. Lord Nicholls at [2002] 3 All E.R. 305 (H.L.) at 338; Lord Hoffman at [2002] 3 All E.R. 305 (H.L.) at 344; Lord Rodger at [2002] 3 All E.R. 305 (H.L.) at 376. Lord Hutton disagreed, holding that *McGhee* could be explained as a case of drawing in inference to establish causation. See [2002] 3 All E.R. 305 (H.L.) at 357.

circumstances of this case, and despite the absence of proof of a probable causal connection based on the "but for" test, the Lords agreed that justice required that the plaintiffs be able to recover full compensation from the defendants and the appeals were unanimously maintained.[76]

It is difficult to generalize from the five separate judgments in order to conclusively outline the factors or conditions that are necessary to establish causation based on a "material increase in risk" approach. Certain essentials are clear. The case must be one in which the defendant breached a duty of care to the plaintiff thereby exposing the plaintiff to a risk of injury. The injury, as defined by that risk, must have occurred. The case must be one where it is impossible for the plaintiff to prove that the defendant's negligence was a cause of the injury due to inadequate scientific or medical knowledge.

A very important factor in *Fairchild* was that the claimants were definitely injured by the negligence of one of their employers.[77] There were no alternative innocent possibilities.[78] Thus, if the wrongdoers did not compensate the plaintiffs, an injustice would certainly have been created. As with other similar cases,[79] courts will strive to fashion a just solution in this type of case to allow a wronged plaintiff to recover. Courts will not allow wronged plaintiffs to fall between the cracks due to the formal requirements of proving cause.

Although this factor, that there were no innocent possible causes of the plaintiffs' injuries, was true about *Fairchild*, it was not true about *McGhee*. In *McGhee*, the claimant's dermatitis could have been caused by an *innocent* possibility, as he could have contracted the disease before he showered, even had there been available showers. Thus, in *McGhee*, it could not be said with certainty that the pursuer was wronged *and* one of those who had wronged him was the cause of the injury. Despite this missing feature, the Lords in *Fairchild* did not consider that *McGhee* had been wrongly decided.

The key question left unanswered by combining *McGhee* with *Fairchild* is what were the essential common features of the two cases that allowed for the material increase in risk approach to be adopted in each? Was it that, in both cases, the plaintiffs' injuries were caused by only one type of substance or agent? Was it that, in both cases, the exposures occurred at work? Although there were non-tortious possibilities in *McGhee* that could have caused the dermatitis, did the fact that all of the non-tortious factors were under the control of the same defendant make up for this deficiency? In both *McGhee* and *Fairchild* the courts were dealing with diseases from exposure to dangerous agents where it could be

76 Lord Bingham conceded that contribution between defendants was a possibility. He also stated that it did not matter if all negligent employers were all sued; the same principles would apply.

77 In the previous edition of this text, I stated that the claimants were definitely injured by "one of the defendants", at p. 400. As Cheifetz and Black, above, note 41, at 161 correctly point out, not all wrongdoing employers were in fact sued. The important point, however, is that all of the employers who were sued were wrongdoers and there was no innocent explanation which could have accounted for the plaintiffs' illnesses. As stated by Lord Bingham, at para. 34, the fact that all not wrongdoing employees are before the court does not affect the decision to hold liable the wrongdoing employer who is before the court.

78 This is because the court discounted the possibility that the claimants might have been exposed to the fibres that cause the disease anywhere but at work. The fact that there were several innocent possibilities in *Wilsher* that could have caused the plaintiff's blindness was critical to the Lords' conclusion that *Wilsher* was a different type of case and was correctly decided.

79 See, for example, *Cook v. Lewis*, [1951] S.C.R. 830 (S.C.C.).

said that the greater the exposure the more significant the risk.[80] In *McGhee*, the damaging agent (dust) only came from one source. Where the agent comes from different sources, as it did in *Fairchild*, how significant do each of the defendants' contributions to the whole risk have to be before those defendants will be liable on a material increase in the risk approach? Will a defendant with a minor contribution be responsible for the full amount of the plaintiff's loss? Will contribution or apportionment be possible, and if so, on what basis?[81]

Barker v. Corus (UK) Plc[82] provided the House of Lords with the opportunity to answer some of these questions. As in *Fairchild*, persons who had been exposed to asbestos at workplaces, contracted mesothelioma and subsequently died. In the case of one employee, the exposures occurred not only at two workplaces, but also when the employee was self-employed. In the case of the others, exposures occurred at several workplaces, but some of these employers were now insolvent. The Lords held that the liability principle of *Fairchild* was based on a material increase in risk approach. Unlike *Fairchild*, however, the facts in *Barker* did not support the contention that all the exposures to asbestos were wrongful. Did *Fairchild* still apply? The House of Lords held that it did. Lord Hoffman, for example, affirmed that it was "irrelevant whether the other exposure was tortious or non-tortious, by natural causes or human agency or by the claimant himself."[83] In order to prevent the "material increase in risk approach" from becoming too widespread as an alternative to "but for", however, the Lords did insist upon the requirement that the exposures which increased the risk of injury must have all emanated from the same agent or from agents which operated in the same way.[84] The Lords also decided that, although the defendants in a case like *Barker* would be held liable based on a material increase in risk approach, their liability would be several. Each defendant would accordingly be liable only for its own share of contribution to the risk.[85]

---

80 It must be emphasized, however, that these were not cases where the conditions were caused by an accumulation of exposures that then triggered the condition. If that were the situation, the problem would have been easily resolved since each tortfeasor who contributed to the accumulation would be responsible for the total damage. In *Fairchild* and *McGhee* even one single exposure might have caused the diseases.

81 As there were five separate judgments it is difficult to answer these questions. The fact, for example, that the only source of the disease was the defendants' wrongful exposures was an important point for Lord Bingham. Lord Rodger, on the other hand, would apply the principle if the other sources were lawful, but under the control of the same defendant (*McGhee*). He would even leave open the possibility that it would apply to other similar and lawful sources emanating from other persons or due to natural occurrences. Lord Nicholls noted that in order for a defendant to be liable on this test, its contribution to the whole risk must have been "significant". Professor Stapleton in "Lords a'leaping Evidentiary Gaps", above, note 41, discusses the judgments and looks at these questions and at the issue of contribution or apportionment.

82 [2006] UKHL 20 (H.L.).

83 *Ibid.*, at para. 17.

84 *Ibid.*, at para. 24, per Lord Hoffman. This ensured that cases like *Gregg v. Scott*, [2005] UKHL 2 (H.L.) and *Wilsher v. Essex* above, note 67, where the material increase in risk approach was rejected, could continue as good law.

85 Although how this was to be determined was not in issue in the judgments, it was suggested that factors such as the intensity of the exposure and the type of asbestos involved would be relevant. See Lord Hoffman's judgment at para. 48, and Lord Scott's judgment at para. 62. Lord Rodger dissented on this point and would have applied the usual rule of liability in *solidum*, at para. 91. The United Kingdom Parliament has enacted the Compensation Act 2006.

The Supreme Court of Canada also took the opportunity to consider the applicability of *McGhee*, with less than conclusive results. In *Snell v. Farrell*,[86] the plaintiff underwent an eye operation to remove cataracts. Some months after the surgery, it was discovered that the plaintiff was blind in the eye which had been operated on. One of the possible causes of the blindness was bleeding which had occurred during the surgery. The trial judge, having found that the defendant was negligent and that the bleeding was one of the possible causes of the plaintiff's condition, applied *McGhee* and shifted the onus of disproving causation to the defendant. The decision to apply *McGhee* was affirmed by the Court of Appeal. Sopinka J., in the Supreme Court's decision, noted that since the judgments in *McGhee* and *Wilsher*, Canadian courts have adopted either the *McGhee* reverse onus approach or the *Wilsher* inferential reasoning approach.[87] While not totally discounting the usefulness or legitimacy of either of these alternative approaches,[88] Sopinka J.'s general conclusion was that ordinary causation principles properly applied were adequate to the task of dealing with the facts of *Snell*, and by implication, most seemingly difficult proof of causation problems. Significantly, however, these principles were cast in very flexible terms. Sopinka J. noted, for example, that the principles of proof must not be applied too rigidly and that causation was a practical question of fact which can best be answered by ordinary common sense rather than abstract metaphysical theory.[89] Sopinka J. emphasized the principle that where the facts of a case lie particularly within the knowledge of the defendant, very little affirmative evidence on the plaintiff's part will justify the drawing of an inference of causation in the absence of evidence to the contrary. Having said all of this, it is not surprising that Sopinka J. found that the evidence in *Snell* supported the inference that it was the defendant's negligence which caused the plaintiff's injury. In sum, while rejecting the bold principle of *McGhee*, Sopinka J. adopted its spirit, and upheld the plaintiff's claim.[90]

The effect of *Snell v. Farrell* on proving causation in cases where the scientific and expert evidence cannot establish a probable connection between a defendant's

---

Section 3 provides that with respect to mesothelioma, those responsible shall be fully liable, but may seek contribution from other responsible persons. The extent of contribution shall be based on the relative lengths of exposure unless the parties agree otherwise or the court thinks there is a more appropriate measure in a particular case.

86 (1990), 72 D.L.R. (4th) 289 (S.C.C.), affirming (1988), 84 N.B.R. (2d) 401 (C.A.), which affirmed (1986), 40 C.C.L.T. 298 (N.B. Q.B.).

87 In other words, Sopinka J. accepted the argument put forth in *Wilsher* that the Lords, other than Lord Wilberforce, had found for the pursuer in *McGhee*, on the basis of a common sense inference that the defender's negligence had probably contributed to the pursuer's injury. Prior to *Snell v. Farrell* courts took various approaches. Some supported the "inferential reasoning" approach: see, for example, *Haag v. Marshall* (1989), 61 D.L.R. (4th) 371 (B.C. C.A.). Others supported *McGhee*: see, for example *Nowsco Well Service Ltd. v. Can. Propane Gas & Oil Ltd.* (1981), 16 C.C.L.T. 23 (Sask. C.A.). Some rejected *McGhee*: see, for example, *Wilkinson Estate v. Shannon* (1986), 37 C.C.L.T. 181 (Ont. H.C.).

88 Sopinka J. stated (at 299) that if he "were convinced that defendants who have a substantial connection to the injury were escaping liability because plaintiffs cannot prove causation under currently applied principles, [he] would not hesitate to adopt one of these alternatives."

89 Citing Lord Salmon in *Alphacell Ltd. v. Woodward*, [1972] 2 All E.R. 475 (H.L.).

90 The principles established in *Snell v. Farrell* were reaffirmed by the Supreme Court, per Gonthier J., in *Laferrière c. Lawson* (1991), 78 D.L.R. (4th) 609 (S.C.C.).

negligence and a plaintiff's injury has been significant.[91] To allow an inference of cause to be drawn even where there is no scientific evidence of a probable connection between negligence and injury is in effect to accept the essential principle of *McGhee* via a different route.

(vi) Resurfice Corp. v. Hanke: *A Revival of* McGhee*?*

The Supreme Court of Canada elaborated upon the material contribution test in *Resurfice Corp. v. Hanke*.[92] In its discussion, the court arguably has revived, and perhaps even extended, *McGhee*.

The facts of the case itself did not raise a difficult causation issue, at least from a theoretical perspective. The plaintiff was seriously injured in an explosion. The explosion was caused due to the fact that water was mistakenly put into the gasoline tank of an ice-surfacing machine. This caused vaporizing gasoline to be released into the air, which then ignited. The defendants, who were the machine's manufacturer and distributor, argued that the accident was caused by operator error. The plaintiff alleged that the machine was defectively designed with respect to the positioning of the water and gasoline tanks. The trial judge accepted the defendant's version, rejected allegations of design defect and dismissed the ac-

---

91 Cases decided after *Snell v. Farrell* indicated this more liberal and relaxed approach. There were several cases, especially in the medical malpractice area, where despite the absence of scientific evidence of a probable connection between negligence and injury, an inference of causation was accepted. See, for example, *Lankenau v. Dutton* (1991), 7 C.C.L.T. (2d) 42 (B.C. C.A.) — evidence uncertain; however, "a robust and pragmatic approach to the facts" allows plaintiff to succeed; *Levitt v. Carr*, [1992] 4 W.W.R. 160 (B.C. C.A.) — it was open to the trial judge to infer that negligence caused a material increase in risk of injury and that this was a contributing cause of the injury; *Scott (Crick) v. Mohan* (1993), 142 A.R. 281 (Q.B.) — despite the fact that no statistical studies could provide a clear link to the causation issue, appropriate to draw "adverse inference" suggestive of a causative link, according to "common sense, having regard to the parties, their respective knowledge and information, in all of the surrounding circumstances;" *Taylor v. Hogan* (1994), 119 Nfld. & P.E.I.R. 37 (Nfld. C.A.) — Court of Appeal rejected trial judge's findings on causation stating that his "rigid application of the traditional approach to causation was made without regard to the recent developments in the law which provide for 'a less onerous burden' on a plaintiff in a case of medical malpractice." Court of Appeal applied a "material risk of injury" approach. In *Webster v. Chapman* (1997), 155 D.L.R. (4th) 82 (Man. C.A.), leave to appeal refused (1998), 129 Man. R. (2d) 158 (note) (S.C.C.), the Court of Appeal applied the "material increase in risk" approach to a drug case. The evidence could not establish whether harm to a foetus occurred before the doctor negligently prescribed a drug, or after. Despite this, the Court concluded that continued use of the drug during a critical period "materially increased the risk of damage". Also see *Robinson v. Sydenham District Hospital Corp.* (1998), [1998] O.J. No. 3844, 1998 CarswellOnt 3782 (Gen. Div.)—trial judge accepted "material increase in risk" approach. Although the Court of Appeal stated that this was wrong, it affirmed liability based on the broader inference approach: (2000), 130 O.A.C. 109 (C.A.). In *Crotin v. National Post, Southam Publications* (2003), 20 C.C.L.T. (3d) 316 (Ont. S.C.J.), the court held that it was "a matter of common sense speculation" that the accumulation of newspapers at the front of the house was the reason that the unoccupied house was broken into.

92 (2007), 278 D.L.R. (4th) 643 (S.C.C.). The case involved two potential wrongful acts contributing to the plaintiff's injury. The "but for" test was workable in this case, so the discussion of alternative tests was unnecessary. Nevertheless, as the issue was raised by the Alberta Court of Appeal, the Supreme Court took the opportunity to comment on it.

tion.[93] The Court of Appeal set aside the trial judgment and ordered a new trial.[94] It held that since multiple causes of the accident were alleged, the "but for" test was unworkable, and the trial judge erred in not using the material contribution test. The defendants appealed to the Supreme Court of Canada.

The Supreme Court agreed with the trial judge's use of the "but for" test, despite the fact that multiple causes of the accident were alleged. As McLachlin C.J. stated "there is more than one potential cause in virtually all litigated cases of negligence"[95] and the "but for" test applies to multi-cause injuries.[96] It is the "primary test" for proving cause.

Having said that and thus dispensed with the appeal, McLachlin C.J. *in obiter* affirmed that the "material contribution test" is indeed an exception to the "but for" test, which is to be applied in "special circumstances". The Chief Justice noted that "broadly speaking, the cases in which the 'material contribution' test is properly applied involve two requirements."[97] The first is where it is "impossible" for the plaintiff to prove cause by using the "but for" test. This impossibility "must be due to factors that are outside of the plaintiff's control; for example, current limits of scientific knowledge."[98] Thus, mere difficulty in proving "but for" is arguably not enough. The second requirement is that the defendant was negligent, exposed the plaintiff to an unreasonable risk of injury, and that form of injury occurred. If these two conditions are met, "liability may be imposed, because it would offend basic notions of fairness and justice to deny liability by applying a 'but for' approach."[99]

*(vii) Post-*Hanke *Fall Out*

The two requirements laid out by McLachlin C.J., in support of material contribution as an alternative to the "but for" test, resemble those of *McGhee.* Can it be taken, therefore, that *McGhee* has been revived, or even extended, in Canadian law?[100] If so, under what circumstances can a court replace the basic "but for" test with the material contribution test?

---

93 (2003), 333 A.R. 371 (Q.B.), additional reasons at (2004), 2004 CarswellAlta 226 (Q.B.).

94 (2005), 53 Alta. L.R. (4th) 219 (C.A.), additional reasons at (2006), 2006 CarswellAlta 417 (C.A.), leave to appeal allowed (2006), 2006 CarswellAlta 482 (S.C.C.), reversed (2007), 2007 CarswellAlta 130 (S.C.C.).

95 Above, note 92, at para. 19.

96 *Ibid.*, at para. 21.

97 *Ibid.*, at para. 24.

98 *Ibid.*, at para. 25.

99 *Ibid.* McLachlin C.J. went on to illustrate the application of these principles. The first reference was to the case of *Cook v. Lewis*, [1951] S.C.R. 830. I will discuss this case below. The second reference was to the type of situation that occurred in *Walker Estate v. York Finch*, discussed above.

100 *Hanke* has generated substantial academic commentary. See Brown, "Material Contribution's Expanding Hegemony: Causation After *Hanke*", above, note 41; Black and Cheifetz, "Through the Looking Glass, Darkly", above, note 41; among others. Brown states, for example, that "*Hanke* appears to represent the evolution of 'material contribution' into a generic and comprehensive alternative applicable to *all* cases where the plaintiff cannot demonstrate probable causation under the but-for test." Cheifetz has written an extensive article on *Hanke* and its impact on Canadian case law entitled "Scraping the Surface: *Resurfice Corp. v. Hanke* [2007] SCC 7", which may be found on the website of the law firm of Bennett Best Burn LLP.

Since the discussion of the material contribution test in *Hanke* was in *obiter*, and the Supreme Court was not applying the test to an actual set of facts, it is difficult to know under what circumstances the material contribution test, as defined by the Supreme Court in *Hanke*, can be used. I think, however, it is safe to assert the following. First, it is to be reserved for exceptional cases, involving special circumstances. The Supreme Court has emphasized that the "but for" test remains the basic and primary test for proving cause. Canadian case law is replete with examples of cases where, due to lack of scientific knowledge or other types of gaps in the evidence, plaintiffs could not prove, upon a balance of probabilities, a "but for" causal connection between defendants' negligent acts and their injuries. As a result of this deficiency, most of these plaintiffs have lost their negligence claims.[101] This is particularly true of medical negligence cases. In all of these failed cases, the defendants' negligence acts exposed plaintiffs to increased risks of injuries, which injuries did occur. Yet the "but for" test was applied and was not satisfied.

Second, proving causation on the "but for" test must not merely be difficult; it must be impossible. It is in the definition of "impossible" that the key for unlocking the meaning of *Hanke* lies.[102]

Third, there must be proof of negligent conduct that materially increased the risk of the injury, which injury did in fact occur.

Cases decided since *Hanke* support the view that the material contribution test will not be too readily applied.[103] In *Barker v. Montfort Hospital*,[104] Rouleau J.A. rejected the test in a medical negligence case because the plaintiffs did not show "that it was impossible to prove" that a delay in carrying out an operation caused the injury on a balance of probabilities.[105] In *Jackson v. Kelowna General Hospital*,[106] Levine J.A. rejected the material contribution test stating that it only

---

101 See above, note 18.

102 An excellent discussion of this issue is found in Smith J.A.'s judgment in a pre-*Hanke* case — *Mooney v. British Columbia (Attorney General)* (2004), 25 C.C.L.T. (3d) 234 (B.C. C.A.), leave to appeal refused (2004), 2005 CarswellBC 463 (S.C.C.). Justice Smith recognized that the *McGhee* risk principle dispenses with the need to prove causation and hence must be applied in the "rare" case. There must be the scientific impossibility to establish the "but for" test and it must be clear that the harm was caused by the tortious acts of several defendants or by one defendant, who controlled all the possible agents of the harm. Justice Smith reviewed the leading cases dealing with this matter. The material increase in risk approach was not adopted. This was also the position taken by the Ontario Court of Appeal in *Aristoneras v. Comcare Health Services* (2006), 42 C.C.L.T. (3d) 220 (Ont. C.A.), additional reasons at (2006), 2006 CarswellOnt 7257 (C.A.), additional reasons at (2007), 2007 CarswellOnt 742 (C.A.), leave to appeal refused (2007), 2007 CarswellOnt 1878 (S.C.C.). Rouleau J.A. expressly rejected loss of a chance or increase in risk as acceptable tests of causation under Canadian law.

103 A full list of cases is found in Cheifetz's article "Scraping the Surface", above, note 100.

104 (2007), 278 D.L.R. (4th) 215 (Ont. C.A.), leave to appeal refused (2007), 2007 CarswellOnt 6323 (S.C.C.).

105 Rouleau J.A. noted that experts were not asked about this. Weiler J.A. dissented. She held that the trial judge had inferred cause from the evidence and was entitled to do so. She also would have applied the material contribution test based on *Hanke*.

106 (2007), 277 D.L.R. (4th) 385 (B.C. C.A.), leave to appeal refused (2007), 2007 CarswellBC 2083 (S.C.C.).

applies "to cases where it is truly impossible to say what caused the injury."[107] In *B.S.A. Investors Ltd. v. Mosly*,[108] Ryan J.A. rejected the use of the test, noting that it is confined to "rare cases".[109] In *Seatle (Guardian ad litem of) v. Purvis*,[110] Kirkpatrick J.A. rejected the use of the test, noting that there was no "scientific gap" preventing the plaintiff from proving its case on the ordinary "but for" test.[111] In *Fullowka v. Royal Oak Ventures Inc.*, the Northwest Territories Court of Appeal rejected the use of the material contribution test even in those cases "where the hypothetical question requires prediction of human reaction."[112] Thus all indications are that the *Resurfice v. Hanke* test has not had much of an impact on the case law, at least not as of yet.[113]

---

107 *Ibid.* at para. 22. Levine J.A. noted that the experts were not asked the hypothetical questions which might have provided the required evidence.

108 [2007] 9 W.W.R. 193 (B.C. C.A.), additional reasons at (2007), 2007 CarswellBC 2729 (C.A.), leave to appeal refused (2008), 2008 CarswellBC 124 (S.C.C.).

109 The issue was whether a fraudster would have been able to carry out his fraud had the defendant lawyer not been negligent in failing to require a second signature on a mortgage document. Ryan J.A. noted, at para. 41 that this inquiry "did not involve principles of causation unknown to modern science." Although there was no direct evidence on point, the trial judge was able to use the available circumstantial evidence in order to decide the point. As Ryan J.A. stated, at para. 43, "there is an important difference between drawing an inference as to causation from circumstantial evidence, which is often done, and drawing an inference as to causation from no relevant evidence at all." Ryan J.A. noted that the plaintiffs could have led evidence; the fraudster himself could have been called to testify as to what he would have done, had a second signature been asked for.

110 (2007), 47 C.C.L.T. (3d) 179 (B.C. C.A.), leave to appeal refused (2008), 2008 CarswellBC 81 (S.C.C.), affirming (2005), 38 C.C.L.T. (3d) 125 (B.C. C.A).

111 The case was another medical negligence one. The trial judge dismissed the action finding that neither the "but for" test nor the material contribution test of *Athey* could be made out. The Court of Appeal affirmed, finding that *Hanke*, which was released after the trial judgment, was not helpful to the plaintiff's case.

112 2008 NWTCA 04, at para. 201.

113 There are post-*Hanke* cases in which "the material contribution to the risk approach" was applied in order to establish causation. See, for example, *Bowes v. Edmonton (City)*, 2007 ABCA 347 (C.A.). In this case, Ross J., as an *ad hoc* member of the Alberta Court of Appeal, held that the *Hanke* "material contribution" approach allows a plaintiff to prove causation when it is "impossible" for the plaintiff to prove causation using the "but for" test and when the injury which occurred was within a risk of injury which the defendant's negligence had materially increased. The issue in the case was whether the defendant City's negligence in failing to order a soil report led to the plaintiffs' decision to build homes on land that turned out to be unstable. Since the report was never ordered, it was unknown what recommendation it would have made and what the City or plaintiffs would have done based on it. Since the failure to have the report was outside of the plaintiff's control, the "impossibility" requirement of *Hanke* was held to have been satisfied. Ross J. also concluded that the risk which the report would have addressed was the type of risk which occurred; namely, a "deep-seated bed rock slide". Ross J. was satisfied that proof of causation was established. The finding was *obiter*, since the action was dismissed based on the expiration of a ten-year ultimate limitation period. The judgment conflates the *Athey* "material contribution to the injury" test with the *Hanke* "material contribution to the risk of injury" test and has been criticized on that basis. See Cheifetz, "Risk as Legal Causation", above, note 41. It must also be noted that despite the fact that the *Hanke* approach has generally been unsuccessful in assisting plaintiffs, it has become a "talking point" in a large number of judgments. See Cheifetz, above, note 100, for a discussion of many of them.

(d) Redefining "Injury": Increasing the Risk of Adverse Results is an Injury in Itself

Where the causal connection, however defined, between negligence and injury has been established on the balance of probabilities, a plaintiff should be able to recover full compensation.[114] Where the plaintiff, however, can establish only that a defendant's negligence increased the possibility of an injury, but did not "probably" cause it, traditional definitions of cause and the standard of proof dictate that the plaintiff's action should fail. As discussed above, the desire to compensate plaintiffs even in such cases has resulted in a fudging of the standard of proof in difficult cases. Are there other solutions which are compatible with traditional tort principles?

An attractive approach suggested by some commentators,[115] but not recognized by Canadian law,[116] is to redefine the very nature of the plaintiff's injury itself. The argument is that a negligent act which increases the possibility of an injury occurring effectively deprives the plaintiff of a chance of avoiding the injury. This "loss of a chance" could be seen as an injury in itself, caused by the defendant's negligence, and the plaintiff could be awarded compensation for it.

The Quebec case of *Laferrière c. Lawson*[117] illustrates the problem. The defendant doctor failed to inform his patient that a tumour removed from her breast in 1971 was malignant. In 1975, the patient's health deteriorated and it was determined that she had generalized cancer. The patient sued her doctor for his negligence in not advising her of the cancer in 1971. The patient died in 1978, and the suit was continued by her estate. Conceding that the doctor's failure to disclose

---

114 This is the normal rule; it is of course subject to a reduction for a plaintiff's contributory negligence. See Chapter 13. It also should be noted that if a "causal connection" is determined by an increase in risk approach, courts might choose to alter the way defendants should bear responsibility for that loss, as the House of Lords did in *Barker v. Corus*, above, note 82.

115 See Wright, above, note 3; Fleming, "Probabilistic Causation in Tort Law" (1989), 68 Can. Bar Rev. 661; Mirandola, "Lost Chances, Cause-in-fact, and Rationality in Medical Negligence" (1992), 50 U. T. Fac. L. Rev. 258.

116 The Supreme Court has rejected this approach in the Quebec case of *Laferrière c. Lawson* (1991), 78 D.L.R. (4th) 609. Prior to *Laferrière*, the loss of a chance approach received both judicial approval and rejection in the common law. It was accepted by the B.C. Supreme Court in *Seyfert v. Burnaby Hosp. Soc.* (1986), 36 C.C.L.T. 224. It has also been rejected in B.C., however, in *Smith v. Moscovich* (1989), 40 B.C.L.R. (2d) 49 at 53. Gibbs J.A., sitting as a Supreme Court Justice, stated:

> Risk is not injury. There is no cause of action for risk whether material or not. It is only when the risk leads to injury that there is a claim, the claim being founded upon the negligence implicit in creating the risk, and even then the claim can only be maintained if the causal link is proven.

In an interesting twist on this topic, the B.C. Court of Appeal has held that while loss of a chance is not recoverable in tort, it is in contract. Thus, since an action against a doctor can be based in contract, damages can be recoverable for loss of a chance. See *de la Giroday v. Brough*, [1997] 6 W.W.R. 585 (B.C. C.A.), leave to appeal refused (1997), 102 B.C.A.C. 238 (note) (S.C.C.). The proposition that if you can re-characterize the action as a breach of contract claim you can recover for loss of a chance was rejected by the Ontario Court of Appeal in a solicitor's negligence case, *Folland v. Reardon* (2005), 249 D.L.R. (4th) 167 (Ont. C.A.).

117 *Ibid.*

was negligent, the issue of damages arose. What damages were caused by the breach?

The evidence indicated that had the plaintiff been informed of her cancer at the earliest opportunity, she would have undergone treatment which possibly, but not probably, could have cured her cancer or extended her life. Thus on this evidence the doctor's negligence did not probably cause the patient's death, and a traditional approach to cause, standard of proof, and definition of injury would result in the dismissal of the plaintiff's claim. If, however, the injury suffered by the plaintiff were redefined as the "loss of a chance" to avoid death or extend life, the plaintiff would, on traditional principles, be able to succeed in recovering some damages.

The Supreme Court rejected the "loss of a chance" approach to this case.[118] After a thorough review of the authors, the civil law jurisprudence, and the various arguments, Gonthier J.'s view was that the traditional approach to cause, proof and injury was preferable to the "loss of a chance" approach. Where an injury, in this case death, had occurred prior to trial, the plaintiff must prove on the balance of probabilities the causal connection between the negligence and the injury. Otherwise the action must fail, and on this reasoning the plaintiff's claim was denied.[119]

The "loss of a chance" approach in cases where scientific or medical evidence can only ever establish "possibilities" and not "probabilities" is in my opinion meritorious. It is particularly compelling in those cases where the defendant's duty is specifically related to providing the plaintiff with the chance of avoiding

---

118 The argument had been accepted by the Quebec Court of Appeal, at [1989] R.Q.J. 27.

119 Some damages were permitted for psychological anguish, frustration, and the loss in quality of life, resulting from the failure to inform. For a critical analysis of the judgment, see Mirandola, "Lost Chances, Cause-in-Fact, and Rationality in Medical Negligence", above, note 115. The author raises arguments for and against adoption of the approach, but ultimately favours it. Compare this case with *Stell v. Obedkoff*, [2000] O.T.C. 742 (S.C.J.). This involved the failure to detect cancer at an earlier stage. The court rejected the "loss of a chance" approach but decided based on the evidence that early detection would have increased the patient's life expectancy and decreased her suffering. Note, however, that the court reduced the damages by 30 per cent to reflect the "contingency" that the treatment would not have had these positive effects. *Query:* is this merely not another way of applying the "loss of chance" approach? In *Saint-Clair v. Spiegel* (2001), 31 C.C.L.T. (3d) 119 (Ont. S.C.J.), the defendant negligently failed to diagnose breast cancer. The cancer was discovered one year later. The cancer subsequently spread. The plaintiff sued, claiming that the defendant's negligence materially contributed to her cancer spreading. The court found that the delay in diagnosis increased the plaintiff's risk of relapse and the suffering which accompanied it, and awarded the plaintiff damages. In effect, the court defined the injury as an "increased risk of relapse" which was contributed to by the delay in diagnosis and treatment. The "loss of a chance" doctrine was expressly rejected by the Ontario Court of Appeal in *Cottrelle v. Gerrard* (2003), 20 C.C.L.T. (3d) 1 (Ont. C.A.), leave to appeal refused (2004), 2004 CarswellOnt 1622 (S.C.C.). In *Gregg v. Scott*, [2005] UKHL 2 (H.L.), the "loss of a chance" doctrine was rejected by the House of Lords in another case involving a delayed diagnosis of cancer. The issues and authorities were thoroughly canvassed, and there were two dissenting Lords who would have awarded damages.

an adverse result.[120] It maintains the common law's traditional approach to questions of cause and standard of proof, while recognizing that depriving a person of a chance of good results is in fact harmful to that person. It is also more intellectually honest than the inference approach discussed above, which frequently tends to award damages, nominally based on a balance of probabilities test, but where in truth only possibilities have been and can be shown.[121]

As with the "material increase in risk" approach, however, courts must carefully define its applicability.[122]

(e) The Failure of the "But For" Test in Other Contexts

Interesting conceptual difficulties arise where due to a peculiar sequence of events, wrongdoers seem capable of escaping through the causal net, if the ordinary language of causation and the "but for" test were applied. In these instances, courts have willingly modified their approaches in order to provide results that appear to them to be just. Due to the extensive and excellent literature analyzing

---

120 Taking *Laferriere v. Lawson* as an example, the doctor's duty was specifically to determine whether the plaintiff had a malignant tumor, in order to do something about it if she did. It was, in other words, a duty to ensure that the plaintiff had the best opportunity to get well. The doctor's failure to inform the patient that she had cancer deprived her of the opportunity to seek treatment. The doctor's negligence resulted in the very injury that his duty was meant to avoid and it seems just therefore that the plaintiff should be compensated for it. The same rationale can be used for other loss of a chance cases such as *McGhee v. National Coal Board*.

121 Should the "loss of a chance" doctrine be utilized when the plaintiff establishes causation based on a balance of probabilities in order to reduce the compensation awarded? For example, if there is a 70 per cent probability that the plaintiff's injury was caused by the defendant's negligence, should the damages be set at only 70 per cent? Some authors would go that far, others would limit the doctrine only to cases where probabilities cannot be shown. I favour the latter approach. As I discuss below, proving that the defendant's negligence caused the plaintiff's injury is an "all or nothing" proposition. See *Cabral v. Gupta*, [1993] 1 W.W.R. 648 (Man. C.A.), where the Court of Appeal rejected "loss of a chance" to reduce full compensation. The trial judge had reduced the plaintiff's award by 30 per cent to reflect the 30 per cent possibility that his injury would have been caused even without negligence. This was erroneous. It would have been legitimate, however, to reduce the damage awards by a "contingency" deduction arising from other possible sources, once the proof of an injury has been established if the evidence had merited it.

122 The "loss of a chance approach" and "material increase in risk" approach are two facets of the same problem. In a sense, every negligent act that increases a risk of injury creates a loss of a chance for the plaintiff to avoid the injury. Thus, as in *Fairchild*, the courts must decide whether justice would be served if a plaintiff were denied compensation for the loss of a chance to avoid an injury due to the defendant's negligence. See Cooper-Stephenson's discussion of "loss of a chance" approach, above, note 23, at 767-776. Among the several points made by Cooper-Stephenson is that if the of "loss of a chance" question is seen not as one which goes to establishing the defendant's liability, but one that goes to the assessment of the plaintiff's losses as a result of negligent conduct, loss of a chance doctrine is acceptable. That is because damages are assessed based on simple probability, and not upon an all or nothing approach. Cooper-Stephenson suggests that the loss of a chance approach is appropriate whenever "the uncertainty relates to past hypothetical events or future events rather than past events"; at 768.

these problems, only a brief reference to some of the more well-known scenarios will be attempted here.[123]

(i) Additional Causes

This problem arises where two acts are sufficient in themselves to have caused the plaintiff's injury, and each would have been necessary to do so, had the other act not occurred.

The two acts can occur simultaneously. For example, two culpable persons shoot at and hit the plaintiff at the same time, killing him. Each bullet was sufficient to produce the fatality by itself. As it turned out, each was unnecessary, however, since the plaintiff would have been killed by either bullet. Thus the "but for" test, if applied, would exonerate both actors. All agree that, in this case, both actors will be held jointly liable for the plaintiff's injury. The plaintiff's death was caused by wrongdoing and those who caused the death, or would have had the other wrongdoer not also been involved, are held liable.[124]

Where the plaintiff's fault, or another non-culpable condition, is one of the additional causes, however, different reasoning prevails. For example, assume that the plaintiff and a wrongdoer approach a room full of gas at the same time, each carrying a lighted candle. The gas explodes and the plaintiff is burned. Should both parties be held jointly liable for the plaintiff's burns?

It is argued in this case that the defendant did not cause an injury to the plaintiff and thus should not be held liable. The defendant did not alter the plaintiff's "normal" existence, since the explosion and consequent injury would have occurred anyway from non-tortious causes.[125] Although at first sight it may seem unjust that of two negligent parties, only one, in this case the plaintiff, will be required to bear responsibility for the injury, this result is in fact consistent with negligence law principles. Tort law only compensates plaintiffs for losses arising from injuries caused by wrongdoers, and in this respect injuries suffered by the

---

123 Hart and Honore's classic text, above, note 3, details some of the scenarios. Also see Beever, "Cause-in-Fact: Two Steps Out of the Mire", above, note 3, for a discussion of 15 possible fact patterns, and McInnes, above, note 3. See Cooper-Stephenson, *Personal Injury Damages in Canada,* 2nd ed. (1996), Chapter 13, for an excellent discussion of these issues.

124 See Fleming, *The Law of Torts*, 9th ed. (1998) at 222; Cooper-Stephenson, *ibid.* at 786-808. Cooper-Stephenson cites *Kingston v. Chicago & N.W. Railway*, 211 N.W. 913 (1927) as the leading authority. Beever, *ibid.,* agrees that both should be liable, but not for the reasons usually offered by other commentators. Beever's theory in a nutshell is that a wrongful defendant should be required to restore the plaintiff to his or her pre-accident state. In this respect, the defendant can harm a plaintiff either by actually injuring him or her, or by making it impossible for the plaintiff to recover his or her damages from someone else. In addition, the law should treat defendants in the same position alike. Putting these points together, if each defendant in the above case were able to use the "but for" test to escape liability, the plaintiff would not be compensated for his injury. This would be because each defendant acted wrongfully in a way that had prevented this compensation from taking place. Thus, each defendant should be required to compensate the plaintiff. For a full discussion see Beever, *ibid.* at 351 *et seq.*

125 See Cooper-Stephenson, above, note 123, at 805, and Hart and Honore, above, note 3, at 237.

plaintiff as a result of non-actionable factors determine the loss that was caused to the plaintiff as a result of a defendant's misconduct.[126]

(ii) Alternative Causes

An alternative cause "is one which would have operated to cause the plaintiff injury or detriment had the defendant's tort not done so."[127] For example, if two wrongdoers fire at a plaintiff at approximately the same time but the first wrongdoer's bullet strikes and kills the plaintiff seconds before the other wrongdoer's bullet hits, who should be liable? It is suggested here that where a defendant's tortious conduct actually harms the plaintiff, the fact that a second wrongful act would have done so anyway, had the first not occurred, is no excuse to the first actor. Thus, only the first wrongdoer is held liable for the death. The second wrongdoer is responsible only if its act caused further injury to the plaintiff. The issue then becomes one of assessment of loss. As we will discuss below, the court must determine how the second act should affect the losses that must be assessed against both parties.[128]

(f) The Rule in *Cook v. Lewis*

A problem of proof worthy of mention arose in the curious case of *Cook v. Lewis*.[129] The case concerned a hunting accident in which the plaintiff was injured by a gun shot fired by one of the two defendants. The two defendants fired at the same time; the birdshot from one of their guns struck the plaintiff. The jury found that both parties were negligent in firing when they did, but could not determine which one of them caused the plaintiff's injury.[130] What could be done in a case such as this?

It is interesting to first note what could not be done to assist the plaintiff in his action. Although the injury was caused by a trespass, the rule, which was reaf-

126 It is important to distinguish this from *Athey*. In *Athey*, the court was not dealing with tortious and non-tortious causes that were sufficient in themselves to produce the injury. The court was dealing with tortious and non-tortious causes that were necessary to produce the injury but which were not sufficient in themselves. Thus, this allowed the court to ascribe full liability to the tortious cause.

127 Cooper-Stephenson, above, note 123, at 800.

128 This is why I feel it is analytically sensible to separate liability issues from damage assessment issues. First we ask: who of the two wrongdoers should be held liable? A person who does not cause an injury cannot be held liable and should immediately be eliminated from further consideration. Second we ask: assuming liability, for what losses should the parties be responsible?

129 (1951), [1952] 1 D.L.R. 1 (S.C.C.).

130 Cheifetz points out that the jury did not decide that both hunters negligently shot in the direction of the plaintiff; this was one of the facts in dispute. The case was sent back to trial so that the jury could decide which of the two hunters shot in the direction of the plaintiff. Once the jury decided who it was, the issue of cause would be resolved. Nevertheless, the importance of the Supreme Court of Canada's judgment is that it discusses what the law would be if the jury decided that they both negligently shot in the plaintiff's direction, the pellets from only one of the guns hit the plaintiff, but it could not be determined from which defendant's gun the pellet came. This raises the dilemma and gives rise to the "rule in *Cook v. Lewis*". See Cheifetz's discussion in "Risk as Legal Causation", above, note 41.

firmed in *Cook v. Lewis*, that there is a burden on a defendant in a trespass action to disprove intentional or negligent conduct, was of no use to this plaintiff. The plaintiff could not prove which of the defendants had caused the trespass. The argument that the parties were joint tortfeasors and thus each responsible for each other's acts also did not work. Cartwright J. held that the defendants were not joint tortfeasors. *Res ipsa loquitur* was also not relevant. The exact cause of the accident was known, although who did it was not, and negligence was not in issue. No theory seemed to be available to assist.

It was in this situation that the Supreme Court formulated a novel approach, which has come to be known as the rule in *Cook v. Lewis*. Rand J. held that where the plaintiff is injured by one of two parties, where they were both negligent, and where the plaintiff's difficulties of proof arose because of the defendants' negligence, the onus of disproving the causal link must shift to the defendants. As Rand J. explained, each defendant in this situation has "violated not only the victim's substantive right to security, but he has also culpably impaired the latter's remedial right of establishing liability."[131]

Due to the unusual features of the case, and the requirements of the rule, it is not surprising that the application of *Cook v. Lewis* has been infrequent. Although it has been applied in one case,[132] in another case similar to *Cook v. Lewis*, the court refused to apply the rule on account of the plaintiff's own negligence.[133] In *Hollis v. Birch*,[134] the principle of *Cook v. Lewis* was reaffirmed, although the facts of the case bore no resemblance to those in *Cook v. Lewis*. The important point for the majority of the Court, however, was the principle that when a plaintiff is seriously disadvantaged in proving her case, through no fault of her own, the penalty should fall on the negligent defendant who created the problem.[135]

4. SUMMARY

It is fair to say that the tests for proving causation under current Canadian law, and in other common law jurisdictions, provide the parties and the courts with a

---

131 Above, note 130, at 4. In *Resurfice v. Hanke*, McLachlin C.J. used *Cook v. Lewis* as an example of the failure of the "but for" test and its legitimate replacement by her "material contribution" test. According to the Chief Justice, in *Cook v. Lewis* it was impossible to apply the "but for" test, both parties negligently created an unreasonable risk of injury, and the injury occurred. *Cook v. Lewis* is a unique type of case, which has little in common with most other difficult causation cases. As noted above, not only were the defendants in *Cook v. Lewis* negligent, but also their mode of negligence arguably made it impossible for the plaintiff to succeed against either of the parties.

132 See *Woodward v. Begbie* (1961), [1962] O.R. 60 (H.C.).

133 See *Lange v. Bennett* (1963), [1964] 1 O.R. 233 (H.C.). As well, in *Kolesar v. Jeffries* (1977), 2 C.C.L.T. 170 (S.C.C.), the Supreme Court of Canada rejected its application to a medical negligence action. Its application was also rejected in *Apex Realty Properties Ltd. v. Leslie* (1988), 54 Man. R. (2d) 194 (Q.B.).

134 (1995), [1995] S.C.J. No. 104, 1995 CarswellBC 967, 1995 CarswellBC 1152.

135 As discussed previously in Chapter 9, the majority of the court held that if a manufacturer negligently fails to inform a doctor of the risks of a product, the patient should not have to prove that had the doctor been informed, the information would have been passed on to the patient. Sopinka J. dissented. He argued that the key to *Cook v. Lewis* was that the negligent defendants had "essentially removed the means of proof of causation from the plaintiff", a factor that was absent from the *Hollis* case.

confusing array of choices. This is due to the occasional efforts by courts to relax the more scientifically based "but for" test, proved upon a balance of probabilities standard, and to adopt a more generous, pro-plaintiff approach. Well-intentioned though this may be, it has led to uncertainty and ambiguity in the law. It is useful therefore to summarize the choice of causation tests, which seems to be available to litigants and judges, presented to them by the current case law.

First, it is clear that the predominant test is the "but for" test and the onus of proof is upon the balance of probabilities. In the vast majority of cases, if the plaintiff cannot satisfy this requirement, the action will be dismissed. Under this approach, it does not matter that the defendant was negligent and that this negligence was a possible cause of the plaintiff's injury. It does not matter that the negligence increased the risk of the plaintiff's injury, or deprived the plaintiff of a chance to avoid the injury.

Second, the "but for" test applies to cases involving multiple cause injuries, since all injuries are the result of multiple causes. *Athey v. Leonati* explains this and lays out the framework for dealing with injuries that have multiple causes, whether tortious or non-tortious.

Third, courts can be persuaded to jettison the "but for" test and accept a more plaintiff-oriented approach in rare cases. Although the Supreme Court of Canada has acknowledged this, it is interesting to note that it has never actually done so.[136]

Despite *dicta* in *Snell v. Farrell, Walker v. York Finch*, and *Resurfice Corp. v. Hanke* to this effect, the "but for" test was applied in each of these cases. The English House of Lords has, on the other hand, accepted a material increase in the risk approach in three cases, *McGhee*, *Fairchild*, and *Barker*.

5. CAUSATION AND LOSSES

In order for there to be liability, a defendant's negligence must have caused the plaintiff some injury or damage. Once a defendant is found liable, the extent of its responsibility to the plaintiff for its losses must be determined.[137] Although there is the tendency to treat both of these issues together as part of one causation inquiry, it is useful to keep them distinct and thereby to avoid confusion.

Harm or damage is the gist of the action for negligence. In order for the defendant to be held liable in negligence, the defendant's negligence must have injured the plaintiff, thereby violating the plaintiff's right to the integrity of its person or property.[138] It is the fact that the defendant caused damage to the plaintiff that gives rise to the defendant's liability. It creates the obligation falling on a specific defendant to compensate an individual plaintiff for that injury. The

136 Other than for *Cook v. Lewis*, which as I argue above, is a very unique case, involving not an abandonment of the "but for" test but a shift in the onus of proof.

137 Although it is true, as stated by Lord Reid in *Baker v. Willoughby* (1969), [1970] A.C. 467 (U.K. H.L.) at 492, cited by McInnes, "Causation In Tort Law" above, note 3, at 1027, that tort law compensates plaintiffs for losses and not for injuries, the plaintiff obviously must have suffered some injury or damage from which the losses ensued. This can be personal injury, physical harm, or even a purely economic loss. The defendant must have caused that injury or damage in order to be responsible for the losses. Thus, there are two aspects to the causation question.

138 Including, as in the recoverable pure economic loss cases, the defendant's wealth.

inquiry is basically an historical one. It looks at what happened. As well, once it is proved, on the "but for" or a modified test, that there was a causal connection, this is accepted as a given fact. Conversely, if it is not proved, it is taken that there was no connection. There is no middle ground. It is an all or nothing issue.

The purpose of the principle that a defendant is only liable for the losses that flow from the injury is the compensation goal of tort law. The plaintiff is entitled to be put back into the same position it was in before the tort occurred. The plaintiff is not required to accept a worsened state. Similarly, the defendant is not required to put the plaintiff into a better position. Thus, the plaintiff's losses must be assessed as precisely as possible. This, however, is not a matter that is approached on an "all or nothing upon a balance of probabilities" way. Courts must not only look at what actually happened to the plaintiff as a result of the tort and other non-related factors up to the time of trial, but also must speculate as to what might happen to the plaintiff in the future after trial. Speculation regarding future possibilities is not only permitted in the assessment stage, it is demanded. In this assessment, courts must be concerned not only with tortious causes, but also non-tortious causes as well.

Cases such as *Athey*, *Snell*, *McGhee*, and *Fairchild* were dealing with the first part of the causation inquiry; i.e., did the defendants' negligence cause the injuries suffered by the plaintiffs in those cases (disc herniation, blindness, dermatitis, mesothelioma). It was because these questions required a "yes" or "no" answer, as opposed to a "maybe", that the courts had difficulties. The principles enunciated in those cases were constructed to deal with the liability/injury issue and not the assessment issue. Courts in dealing with assessment issues must keep this distinction in mind.[139]

In determining a plaintiff's losses, courts must consider what actually happened to the plaintiff before the trial that had an effect on the losses being claimed from the defendant. In *Penner v. Mitchell*,[140] for example, the plaintiff was injured by a tortious act and as a result was required to be absent from work for a period of 13 months. During these 13 months, the plaintiff became ill from a cause totally unrelated to the defendant's tort, which would have necessitated three months

---

139 This distinction between the injury issue and assessment issue was articulated in *W.R.B. v. Plint*, [2001] B.C.J. No. 1446, at para. 363, by Brenner C.J.B.C.:

> Once a sexual assault has been proven the court must consider (a) the extent to which the act has caused plaintiff an injury and further, (b) whether that injury has caused plaintiff a loss. The former is concerned with establishing the existence of liability, the latter with the extent of that liability.

Brenner C.J. went on to explain that the injury refers to the physical or mental impairment of the plaintiff's person and loss to the pecuniary or non-pecuniary consequences of that impairment. The case involved sexual assault victims. The court noted the "daunting" task of "unraveling the question of causation" when victims come to court with problems arising not only from torts that occurred long ago, but who also have other problems, such as post-traumatic stress disorder, depression, substance abuse, and other psychological conditions. In *Gregg v. Scott*, [2005] UKHL 2 (H.L.) at para. 69, Lord Hoffman referred to an early Canadian case, *Kranz v. M'Cutcheon* (1920), 18 Ontario Weekly Notes 395, to support his argument that courts must distinguish between the question as to whether damage is attributable to the defendant and, if so, how that damage is to be quantified. Also see Cooper-Stephenson, above, note 123, at 750-751 for his discussion regarding the distinction between questions of factual causation as they relate to liability issues and damages issues.

140 (1978), 6 C.C.L.T. 132 (Alta. C.A.).

absence from work. Was the plaintiff still entitled to receive compensation for 13 months' loss of work from the defendant? The Court of Appeal, reversing the trial judge, held that to award the plaintiff 13 months' loss of income, when three months of that loss of income would have been suffered by the plaintiff anyway notwithstanding the tort, would be to overcompensate the plaintiff. Only ten months' loss of income was therefore awarded. Using the terminology noted above, this is a case of an "additional non-culpable" cause. And, as indicated above, where a plaintiff's normal situation has not been affected by the defendant's wrongful act, the plaintiff is not entitled to compensation.[141]

A Supreme Court of Canada case that adopted a contrary approach to *Penner* is *Sunrise Co. v. "Lake Winnipeg" (The)*.[142] In this case, the plaintiff's ship was damaged by the defendant's negligence, necessitating 27 days of repairs in dry dock and consequent loss of profits. Before the repairs could begin, however, the ship was damaged in a non-tortious incident that was unconnected to the first one. The repairs for the second incident ordinarily would have taken 14 days. They were completed however in the same 27-day period required for the other repairs. The issue was whether due to this subsequent event the defendant's original obligation to compensate the plaintiff for 27 days loss of profits should be reduced and if so by how much.[143]

The majority of the Supreme Court allowed the plaintiff to recover for the full 27 days' loss of profit. The dissent would have allowed full recovery for the days caused by the defendant's fault and would have apportioned responsibility for the overlapping days between the parties that caused them. Both of these solutions are inconsistent with the principle discussed above and the *Jobling* and *Penner* cases.[144] It seems to me incorrect to ignore what actually happened to the plaintiff's ship after the first incident occurred as a result of a non-tortious incident.

---

141 Also see *Jobling v. Associated Dairies Ltd.*, [1981] 2 All E.R. 752 (H.L.), which applied the *Penner v. Michell* approach to a case involving a tortious event followed by a non-tortious one. Where the plaintiff dies before judgment, this is obviously something that the court must take into account; see *Lankenau v. Dutton* (1991), 7 C.C.L.T. (2d) 42 (B.C. C.A.), leave to appeal refused (1991), 10 C.C.L.T. (2d) 314 (note) (S.C.C.). In *Smith v. Shade*, [1996] 6 W.W.R. 52 (B.C. C.A.), the *Penner* approach was accepted although the finding of the trial judge that the losses from the non-tortious incidents did not overlap with the losses from the tort was upheld. The tort injury caused more loss than did the non-tortious injuries alone. Note that in reviewing the causation principles, Major J. in *Athey* referred approvingly to both *Penner* and *Jobling*. According to Major J., these cases illustrate the principle that the victim is to be put back into its "original" position, absent the tort, and not placed in a "better" position. See [1996] 3 S.C.R. 458 at 472.

142 [1991] 1 S.C.R. 3. This case is discussed by Beever, "Cause-in-Fact: Two Steps Out of the Mire", above, note 3, at 333, and McInnes, "Causation in Tort Law: Back to Basics at the Supreme Court of Canada", above, note 3, at 1023, n. 43.

143 The Federal Court of Appeal [(1998), 96 N.R. 310 (Fed. C.A.)] had awarded the plaintiff only 13 days' loss of income based on the argument that this was what was lost because of the defendant's negligence. This is the *Penner* and *Jobling* approach.

144 One might attempt to draw a distinction between the *Sunrise* case and the personal injury cases. First, *Sunrise* was a maritime law case and the jurisprudence that the court reviewed were shipping accident cases. Second, it was a property damage case and it has been suggested that since losses from property damages occur immediately upon the tort, damages should be assessed at that time notwithstanding future developments. See McInnes, "Causation In Tort Law", above, note 3, at 1023, n. 43, citing Cooper-Stephenson, *Personal Injury Damages in Canada*, 2nd ed. (1996) at 789, 792-793. Cooper-Stephenson's point is that once the property damage has occurred, there is an "instant devaluation" that renders irrelevant "a subsequent

An exception is made to the *Jobling* and *Penner* principle when its application will cause injustice to the plaintiff. This can occur where successive *wrongs* produce the same loss, i.e., additional culpable causes. Consider the classic case of *Baker v. Willoughby*.[145] The plaintiff's leg was injured in an accident caused by the defendant's negligent driving. The injury was permanent and would cause the plaintiff life-long pain, loss of amenities and so forth. Prior to trial, the plaintiff's leg was shot in a robbery and as a result it was amputated. The first wrongdoer, i.e., the negligent driver, was sued. The issue was how the effects of the second tort, which effectively pre-empted the effects from the first tort, should affect the defendant's liability. In other words, how should losses be apportioned as between two wrongdoers, who cause different injuries but overlapping losses?

Lord Pearson illustrated the dilemma presented by this type of case.[146] Assume that prior to the first tort, the plaintiff was earning $100 per week. The damage to the plaintiff's leg caused by the tort reduced the plaintiff's earning capacity to $50 per week. Had nothing further occurred, this is what the plaintiff would have been entitled to receive from defendant 1 for the remainder of his life. Assume, however, that prior to the trial relating to the first tort, a second tort occurred and the leg needed to be amputated. As a result, the plaintiff's wages were reduced by an additional $25 a week. Assume that this consequence (the second tort and the amputation) had nothing to do with the first tort and would have occurred even had the first tort not occurred.

If the second tort and its effects on the plaintiff's earning capacity are permitted to be taken into account in assessing the damages against the first wrongdoer, an injustice might arise. The first wrongdoer would argue that its liability should be limited only to the losses that the injury caused. This is the decrease in the plaintiff's earning capacity prior to the occurrence of the second tort. This is because the second tort overtook the effects of the first tort, and eliminated any further consequence arising from it. If the second wrongdoer is then sued, this wrongdoer might claim that "one takes one's victim as one finds him or her", and that accordingly its liability should be limited to the reduction caused to the plaintiff's earning capacity by the tort; i.e., $25 per week. A gap is created. Rather than the plaintiff receiving $50 a week for period 1, and $75 a week for the remainder of his life, which were the damages he actually suffered as a result of being injured by two wrongdoers, he would only receive $50 a week for period 1, and $25 a week thereafter. He would in other words receive less compensation than he would have had he been injured by the first wrongdoer alone.

Several approaches have been suggested to solve this dilemma. The first approach is to treat both actors as jointly responsible for the plaintiff's continuing injury, as would be done if the acts occurred simultaneously.[147] The second has

cause that would have been sufficient also to devaluate the property". Note that Major J. in *Athey* quoted *Penner* and *Jobling* with approval and did not comment on *Sunrise*.

145 (1969), [1970] A.C. 467 (U.K. H.L.).

146 (1969), [1970] A.C. 467 (U.K. H.L.) at 495. While Lord Pearson used a formula to illustrate the dilemma, I will use hypothetical amounts.

147 This approach is defended by Cooper-Stephenson, above, note 123, at 798-799. In *Bourque v. Wells* (1991), 82 D.L.R. (4th) 574 (N.B. C.A.), leave to appeal refused (1992), 87 D.L.R. (4th) vii (S.C.C.), the injury was attributed to two successive wrongdoers and responsibility for it was apportioned between them. I assume that the joint liability would apply only to that portion of the loss actually caused by both tortfeasors, i.e., $50 a week. The additional $25 added on by the second wrongdoer would remain its sole responsibility.

been to argue that the second tort has overtaken the first, so that the first tortfeasor is responsible only for the plaintiff's loss up to the time of the second tort, and the second tortfeasor is responsible for the loss thereafter.[148] The third approach has been to hold the first tortfeasor liable for all of the plaintiff's losses that resulted from the first tort, and to hold the second tortfeasor liable only for whatever additional losses may have flowed from the second. Canadian courts have favoured the third approach with respect to successive tortfeasors.[149] Courts assess the losses from the first tort as if the action for this tort had been tried immediately before the second tort occurred.[150]

As with actual events that occurred before trial that affected a plaintiff's loss arising from the defendant's wrong, courts must also consider future possible events arising after trial. That is, courts are entitled to take into consideration factors that indicate that the plaintiff's losses might have occurred anyway, due to realistic possible contingencies. These factors do not need to be established on a balance of probabilities as things that will happen. They can be established as possibilities and if the court is satisfied that they are "real" possibilities, the court can discount the damage award to reflect them. The fact that these possible events are non-tortious does not mean that they cannot be considered.[151] As discussed above, in order to properly assess a defendant's losses, courts cannot ignore additional, non-culpable factors that have caused the same loss, or which might in the future do so.

An interesting issue that has been raised in some cases relates to the appropriate standard of proof for assessing the plaintiff's losses suffered between the time of the accident and the trial. As pointed out above, in assessing the future losses that the plaintiff will incur as a result of the injury, courts must consider realistic possibilities, even if they are not probabilities. Damages will be assessed according to the likelihood of these future losses occurring. How, however, are pre-trial hypothetical losses to be determined? For example, if the plaintiff argues that as

---

148 As discussed by Fleming, *The Law of Torts*, 9th ed. (1998) at 223, this only works if the second tortfeasor is not allowed to discount the claim based on an argument that you take your victim as you find him or her. The second tortfeasor must be liable for the full continuing loss. Thus, in the above example, assuming there was a tort action against the robber, it would be liable for the $75 reduction in earning capacity.

149 See, e.g., *Masson v. Rowan*, [1988] 4 W.W.R. 430 (Man. Q.B.); *Long v. Thiessen* (1968), 65 W.W.R. 577 (B.C. C.A.); *Paziuk v. Ewbank*, [1987] 5 W.W.R. 307 (Man. C.A.); *Hicks v. Cooper* (1973), 1 O.R. (2d) 221 (C.A.); *Gilson v. Lekach*, [1996] 6 W.W.R. 90 (Sask. Q.B.); among others. This was the approach adopted by the House of Lords in *Baker v. Willoughby*, [1969] 3 All E.R. 1528 (H.L.).

150 Thus, in the above example the first defendant would remain liable for a $50 per week reduction and the second wrongdoer for the additional $25. What if the second tort eliminates losses caused by the first tort? Assume, for example, that the second tort results in the death of the injured plaintiff. In this case, principle dictates that losses that flowed from the first tort such as pain and suffering, or costs of future care, would no longer be recoverable from the first tortfeasor. See Cooper-Stephenson, above, note 123, at 800 who refers to *Stene v. Evans* (1958), 14 D.L.R. (2d) 73 (Alta. C.A.).

151 In fact, the court can *only* consider contingencies that are non-tortious in reducing the damages payable by the defendant. The court cannot consider possible subsequent torts as contingencies for the same reason it cannot allow a second tort that actually occurs before trial to result in the plaintiff's under-compensation. *Penner* and *Jobling* make it clear that a second tort cannot reduce the damages payable by the defendant who caused the first tort. This would apply even more so to a possible future tort that has not even actually occurred.

result of his or her injury, income was lost prior to trial, must this be established on the balance of probabilities or will the mere possibility of losses suffice?

There is inconsistency in the jurisprudence concerning this matter. In *Smith v. Knudsen*,[152] the British Columbia Court of Appeal held that the proof of past losses resulting from a plaintiff's injuries is to be treated in the same way as is the proof of future hypothetical losses. The plaintiff need only show that there was a real possibility that had he not been injured, his past income would have been higher than it actually turned out to be. The plaintiff would be entitled to damages which represented that possibility.[153] Other judgments from British Columbia, however, have held that all pre-trial losses, whether real or speculative, must be proved on the balance of probabilities.[154]

---

152 (2004), [2004] B.C.J. No. 2509, 2004 CarswellBC 2835 (C.A.), additional reasons at (2005), 2005 CarswellBC 1483 (C.A.).

153 In a subsequent judgment, the trial court in *Smith v. Knudsen* found that there was a 50 per cent likelihood that the plaintiff's past income was detrimentally affected by his injury and an amount representing that degree of likelihood was awarded to him. See 2007 BCSC 1270 (S.C.). The "possibility" approach for page wage loss also was applied in *Naidu v. Mann* (2008), 53 C.C.L.T. (3d) 1 (B.C. S.C.).

154 See, for example, *Sales v. Clark* (1998), [1998] B.C.J. No. 2334, 1998 CarswellBC 2165 (B.C. C.A), affirming (1996), [1996] B.C.J. No. 2190, 1996 CarswellBC 2323 (S.C.). The plaintiff was injured and subsequently was dismissed from his employment as a salesman because he made no sales. At trial, the plaintiff argued that his lack of performance was attributable to his injuries and that he should be compensated for loss of income. The trial judge rejected this claim. On appeal, the plaintiff argued that the trial judge should have recognized the possibility that the plaintiff's lack of income was due to his injuries and awarded him some damages. This would be consistent with the approach taken with regard to losses after trial. The Court of Appeal, referring to passages from *Athey*, rejected the plaintiff's argument. In *Athey*, Major J. stated that "hypothetical events (such as how the plaintiff's life would have proceeded without the tortious injury) or future events need not be proven on a balance of probabilities. Instead, they are simply given weight according to their relative likelihood. . . . By contrast, past events must be proven and once proven they are treated as certainties"; at [1996] 3 S.C.R. 470-471. The Court of Appeal interpreted this to apply to all past events, whether to prove injury or loss. Major J.'s statement was *obiter* and not entirely clear on this point. See Cooper-Stephenson, above, note 122, on this point at 759-760. Cooper-Stephenson agrees that all past hypothetical events, whether relating to proving injuries or losses, are to be resolved on a balance of probabilities, all or nothing, standard. I, on the other hand, find the possibility approach for future *and* past losses attractive. Once the threshold test of liability for an injury is satisfied, using a balance of probabilities approach, why should the more precise "possibility" approach not be used for assessing losses? After all, the purpose of compensation is to attempt to restore the plaintiff to its pre-tort position as precisely as possible. To ignore real possible losses, even if they occurred prior to trial, fails to do that. Another distinction between injuries and losses arises with respect to remoteness rules. Although the "reasonable foreseeability" test limits a defendant's liability with respect to injuries, this limiting device has not been applied to losses. A plaintiff is entitled to full compensation for the pecuniary losses which it suffers as a result of its injuries, whether these pecuniary losses were reasonably foreseeable or not. See discussion in Chapter 12.

Although the Court of Appeal in *Smith v. Knudsen* was aware of these earlier cases, it distinguished them from the case at bar,[155] or refused to follow them.[156] While I favour the *Smith v. Knudsen* approach, due to the inconsistent judgments on this point, clarity is required.

6. SUCCESSIVE ACCIDENT CASES

Sorting out which injuries ought to be attributed to which causal events, as well as which losses flowed from which injuries, can be a nightmare for courts when dealing with a plaintiff who has been involved in a series of successive culpable accidents or non-tortious conditions prior to trial. The principles enunciated by the Supreme Court of Canada in *Athey v. Leonati*, and by courts in other cases, seem to be fairly straightforward. Difficulties arise however when the principles are not properly applied or where the evidence seems to frustrate the application of these principles.[157]

Kozak v. Funk[158] is illustrative of one of these nightmarish cases.[159] The plaintiff was involved in car accident 1 in 1986. As a result of this accident, he suffered a whiplash injury. The accident was defendant 1's fault. The plaintiff experienced a variety of symptoms, and missed several months of work. In 1987, the plaintiff

---

155 For example, the court held that the issue in *Sales*, *ibid.*, was not whether the defendant's negligence caused the plaintiff's losses, but whether it caused the plaintiff's impairment, which resulted in the plaintiff's losses. Although I do not agree that the issue in *Sales* was different than the issue in *Smith v. Knudsen*, I do favour the approach which the Court of Appeal followed in *Smith v. Knudsen*. As explained by Rowles J.A. at para. 29: "What would have happened in the past but for the injury is no more "knowable" than what will happen in the future and therefore it is appropriate to assess the likelihood of hypothetical and future events rather than applying the balance of probability test that is applied with respect to past actual events."

156 For example, *Schellak v. Barr* (2003), 8 B.C.L.R. (4th) 245 (C.A.), leave to appeal to S.C.C. refused (2003), [2003] S.C.C.A. No. 91, 2003 CarswellBC 2229 (S.C.C.).

157 One must again distinguish between successive accidents or events which contribute to the same injury from successive accidents or events which result in the same losses. The principles of *Athey v. Leonati* apply to the former situation. Thus in *G. (E.D.) v. Hammer* (2003), 230 D.L.R. (4th) 554 (S.C.C.), the fact that the plaintiff's psychological injuries caused by sexual assaults were also contributed to by other factors in her life did not relieve the wrongdoer of full responsibility for these injuries. Also see *Hutchings v. Dow*, 2007 BCCA 148 (C.A.), leave to appeal refused (2007), 2007 CarswellBC 2328 (S.C.C.). In this case, the plaintiff was injured in a motor vehicle accident and in a subsequent assault. He suffered from depression. The court held that the depression was a result of both incidents and thus the defendant responsible for the accident should be held fully liable for it. This was an application of *Athey*. The Court of Appeal affirmed, finding that the depression was indivisible. It could not be divided between the two incidents. The plaintiff would not have suffered from depression as a result of the assault had the accident not also contributed to it. Also see *Ashcroft v. Dhaliwal* (2007), 47 C.C.L.T. (3d) 294 (B.C. S.C.) to the same effect. Cases such as *Baker v. Willoughby*, [1969] 3 All E.R. 1528 (H.L.) and *Long v. Thiessen* (1968), 65 W.W.R. 577 (B.C. C.A.), discussed above, apply to where successive accidents result in overlapping losses and involve different principles.

158 (1995), 28 C.C.L.T. (2d) 53, [1996] 1 W.W.R. 79 (Sask. Q.B.), varied (1997), [1998] 5 W.W.R. 232 (Sask. C.A.).

159 Unfortunately there seem to be many such cases and other illustrations might have been used. See for example *Dushynski v. Rumsey*, [2001] 9 W.W.R. 327 (Alta. Q.B.). The plaintiff was involved in four successive car accidents, none of them being her fault.

injured his neck and shoulders in an accident at work, caused by his own negligence. The injury was diagnosed as a recurrence of the injury suffered in the prior car accident. A disc herniation was subsequently diagnosed. In 1988, the plaintiff was involved in car accident 2, caused by defendant 2's fault. He suffered a soft tissue injury with renewed pain. After accident 2, the plaintiff was laid off from work for unrelated reasons; his pain symptoms and depression worsened. He was diagnosed as having "chronic pain syndrome". The plaintiff sued defendant 1 and 2.

In determining liability for the injuries and responsibility for the plaintiff's losses in a case such as this the following principles must be applied:

(i) A defendant should be liable only for the injuries that he caused the plaintiff. In this case, defendant 1 clearly caused the whiplash injury. As well, if any of the subsequent injuries suffered by the plaintiff, e.g., the disc herniation, the soft tissue injury, or the chronic pain syndrome, fell within the risk set in motion by the defendant's negligence, the defendant's liability would extend to them.[160] If these subsequent injuries were unrelated to the injuries suffered due to the defendant's negligent driving, the defendant should not be liable for them. In this case, these subsequent injuries seem not to have been related in this way.[161]

(ii) If the injury suffered in any accident is more severe than what ordinarily would have resulted due to a latent vulnerability or susceptibility of the plaintiff, the defendant remains liable for the more severe injury. This is known as a "thin skull" case.[162]

(iii) If the injury suffered in an accident is an exacerbation of a manifest, on-going pre-existing injury, or the acceleration of an existing degenerative process, the defendant should only be liable for the "new" injury. This is known as a "crumbling skull" case.

(iv) Keeping these above points in mind, defendant 1 should have been responsible to compensate the plaintiff for any of the losses that flowed from the whiplash injury that he caused. In this case, this would clearly have included loss of work, and pain and suffering.

(v) If the subsequent non-tortious events, for example, the work place accident, or the dismissal from work, would have created the *same* losses that the plaintiff was suffering from as a result of the injuries suffered in car accident 1, even if that accident had not occurred, they would extinguish defendant

---

160 This is an issue of proximate cause that will be discussed in Chapter 12.

161 The same principle applies to injuries which the plaintiff suffered prior to the injury caused by the defendant. Thus, in *Blackwater v. Plint* (2005), 258 D.L.R. (4th) 275 (S.C.C.), the Supreme Court held that the trial judge did not err in taking into account trauma suffered by the plaintiff as a result of abuse which occurred prior to the sexual assault committed against him in an Aboriginal residential school. These acts of prior abuse were independent from the abuse suffered at the school and produced their own serious psychological difficulties. Even though McLachlin C.J.C. conceded that "untangling the different sources of damage and loss may be nigh impossible. . .yet the law requires that it be done, since at law a plaintiff is only entitled to be compensated for *loss caused by the actionable wrong*" at para. 74.

162 This will be discussed in Chapter 12 as it raises an issue of remoteness.

1's continuing responsibility for these losses.[163] To the extent that subsequent non-tortious events did not overlap with the original losses, and the original losses continued, defendant 1 would remain responsible for them.[164]

(vi) If the subsequent tortious events, for example, car accident 2, would have created the *same* losses that the plaintiff was suffering from as a result of car accident 1, even if that first car accident had not occurred, the court must decide which of the three options discussed above it preferred. This is the *Baker v. Willoughby* dilemma. It could hold both defendants liable jointly for the continuing losses, it could hold defendant 1 liable for the losses occurring up to the time of the second tort and defendant 2 liable for all of the continuing losses occurring thereafter, or it could hold defendant 1 liable for the continuing losses and defendant 2 liable only to the extent that its negligence exacerbated those losses.

(vii) Finally, in assessing the damages recoverable from defendant 1, the court is entitled to consider non-tortious contingencies that might affect the plaintiff's future well being. Thus, for example, plaintiffs with "thin skulls" might have their damages reduced due to their heightened susceptibility to future injuries.

The same principles apply in determining the damages recoverable from defendant 2 or any subsequent wrongdoer. Defendants will be liable for any new losses that the plaintiff suffered as a result of the injuries that they caused. They also might be responsible for the continuing losses caused by both accidents, as discussed above.

---

163 This is the *Penner* approach discussed above. It goes without saying that if the plaintiff's losses are found to have been caused by injuries that the defendant is not factually and legally responsible for, there can be no recovery for these from the defendant. *Bell v. Tilden Car Rental Inc.* (1996), [1997] 1 W.W.R. 356 (Alta. C.A.), additional reasons at (1997), 47 Alta. L.R. (3d) 251 (C.A.) and *Edgar v. Freedman* (1997), [1998] 4 W.W.R. 473 (B.C. C.A.) are examples of this type of case.

164 This was a major issue in *Kozak*. The trial judge apportioned liability for the losses flowing from the work place accident 90 per cent to the plaintiff, whose own recklessness caused the injury, and 10 per cent to defendant 1. This can only be justifiable on the basis that 90 per cent of the losses following the workplace injury were overlapping losses caused by the plaintiff's fault, and 10 per cent of the losses were different ones continuing from the first car accident.

Resolution of the successive accident cases depends upon the applicability of these principles to what is frequently very confusing, if not contradictory evidence. It is therefore not surprising that these cases are very difficult to resolve.[165]

165 In *Kozak v. Funk*itself the trial judge and the Court of Appeal came out with significantly different interpretations of the evidence and calculations of damages. In general, the Court of Appeal thought that the trial judge erred in ascribing too much of the responsibility for the plaintiff's condition on defendant 2, ignoring the effect that the prior incidents had on the plaintiff's continuing losses. Other successive accident cases that can be consulted for guidance as to how these cases might be approached include: *Gilson v. Lekach*, [1996] 6 W.W.R. 90 (Sask. Q.B.); *Smith v. Shade,* [1996] 6 W.W.R. 52 (B.C. C.A.); *Cipriano v. Cipriano,* [1996] 8 W.W.R. 574 (B.C. C.A.); *Bell v. Tilden Car Rental Inc.* (1996), [1997] 1 W.W.R. 356 (Alta. C.A.), additional reasons at (1997), 47 Alta. L.R. (3d) 251 (C.A.); *Santoro v. Raban,* [2000] 7 W.W.R. 668 (Alta. Q.B.); and *Dushynski v. Rumsey*, [2001] 9 W.W.R. 327 (Alta. Q.B.); among others. *Baillargeon v. Murray* (2001), 52 O.R. (3d) 278 (S.C.J.) was a particularly difficult case as it not only involved three successive motor vehicle accidents but also in addition the court was required to decide whether the injuries suffered by the plaintiff in each of the accidents met the threshold requirements of Ontario's automobile accident legislation.

12

Remoteness

1. INTRODUCTION

As with the question of duty of care, the remoteness or proximate cause aspect of the negligence action allows judges to control the use of the negligence action and to limit a defendant's responsibility to compensate injured victims. Duty asks the question: is this defendant obligated to take reasonable care for the protection of this plaintiff? Remoteness asks the question: even if there is an obligation to take reasonable care and it was breached, how far will the legal liability of the defendant stretch?

As this chapter will indicate, the courts and commentators have endeavoured to formulate tests or formulae which can be applied to solve remoteness problems.[1] Although these have been helpful, especially in relation to particular remoteness issues which, due to their recurrence, can now benefit from the existence of a substantial body of law, ultimately all remoteness questions will be decided by the application of common sense, pragmatics and politics.[2] How far a tortfeasor's financial responsibility ought to extend will depend upon the current state of negligence law and the courts' respective views as to its functions and its roles.

Remoteness questions deal with how far liability should extend in reference to injuries caused to the plaintiff, once a duty relationship and negligent behaviour have been established. As we shall see, however, because foreseeability is the cornerstone of remoteness analysis, as it is with duty and breach, these elements

---

1 See Linden and Feldthusen, *Canadian Tort Law*, 8th ed. (2006), Chapter 10; Fleming, *The Law of Torts*, 9th ed. (1998), Chapter 9; Cooper-Stephenson, *Personal Injury Damages in Canada*, 2nd ed. (1996), Chapter 14; Seidelson, "Some Reflections on Proximate Cause" (1980), 19 Duquesne L. Rev. 1; Coval, Smith and Rush, "Out of the Maze: Towards a 'Clear Understanding' of the Test for Remoteness of Damages in Negligence" (1983), 61 Can. Bar Rev. 559, among many others.

2 This was best stated by Andrews J. in *Palsgraf v. Long Island Ry. Co.*, 162 N.E. 99 at 103 (N.Y.C.A., 1928):

> A cause, but not the proximate cause. What we do mean by the word "proximate" is that, because of convenience, of public policy, of a rough sense of justice, the law arbitrarily declines to trace a series of events beyond a certain point. This is not logic. It is practical politics.

frequently overlap, merge together, and in some instances even coincide. Where the plaintiff, as a foreseeable victim, was subject to different possible injuries, whether foreseeable or not, then the duty and remoteness issues are distinct. Where, however, the plaintiff can be defined as a foreseeable victim because of vulnerability to only one type of injury, the elements coincide. Thus, in the famous American case of *Palsgraf v. Long Island Ry. Co.*,[3] or the equally well-known Scottish case, *Hay (or Bourhill) v. Young*,[4] the plaintiffs could only be foreseen and defined as victims by reference to the foreseeability of peculiar and narrow injuries. This allowed the judges hearing these cases to approach them from the perspective either of duty or remoteness. As well, as was previously pointed out in reference to duty,[5] if no injury was reasonably foreseeable at all, the negligence action can fail on grounds of lack of duty, negligent conduct, or remoteness of harm.[6] This may be disturbing to those who would prefer more clearly defined categories.[7] However, one must recall that in many cases duty, breach and remoteness do deal with separate territories, both from the point of view of factual analysis, and legal, including policy, orientation.[8]

---

3 *Ibid.*

4 [1942] 2 All E.R. 396 (H.L.).

5 See Chapter 5.

6 The overlap between duty and remoteness was highlighted in an interesting English case, *Meah v. McCreamer*, [1986] 1 All E.R. 943 (Q.B.D.). The plaintiff's personality was changed as a result of a car accident. This personality disorder led him to sexually assault two women. He was sentenced to prison for these assaults and, as well, was sued by his victims. He then sued the driver responsible for the car accident claiming as damages the judgment awarded against him in the civil assault actions. Was this too remote? The court observed that this question was the same as asking whether the two women could sue the initial negligent driver. If it was reasonably foreseeable that the plaintiff might sexually assault others and suffer adversely as a result, then the assault victims must in turn have been reasonably foreseeable victims of the car accident and would thus have been owed a duty by the negligent driver. The trial judge stated that the foreseeability test for duty is "almost identical to the test that is applied whether damages are too remote." This is because in this instance the damages resulting from the assault judgment were predicated upon the existence of assault victims. The damages were considered too remote.

7 See, e.g., Denning L.J.'s views in *Roe v. Min. of Health*, [1954] 2 Q.B. 66 at 85 (C.A.), or Clement J.A.'s statement in *Abbott v. Kasza*, [1976] 4 W.W.R. 20 at 29 (Alta. C.A.). In the latter case, Clement J.A. stated:

> The question raised is whether in cases such as the present there is an appreciable difference in law in the projection of the reasonably foreseeable between remoteness of damage and duty and causation. For myself, I think that the law does not compel any distinction to be drawn and that the interests of a workable jurisdiction militate against it. As Denning L.J. points out, each component of liability is only a facet of the whole, and judgment must be based on the entirety, not piecemeal on refractions from each facet.

8 The fact that foreseeability of harm is a component of duty, breach and proximate cause and thus can create analytical confusion is illustrated in *Resurfice Corp. v. Hanke*, [2007] 1 S.C.R. 333, reversing (2005), 53 Alta. L.R. (4th) 219 (C.A.), affirming (2003), 333 A.R. 371. The trial judge found that the risk that an operator of an ice resurfacing machine could confuse the water and gasoline tanks was not foreseeable; hence the manufacturer of the machine was not negligent in its design of the machine. This is an issue of breach. The Court of Appeal, on the other hand, saw the issue of foreseeability of the risk of harm as one relating to proximate cause, and applied the jurisprudence relating to that issue. I would agree with the trial judge's approach; the issue was one relating to breach.

As with the resolution of duty issues, remoteness raises issues of both fact and law. It is up to the court to determine whether, as a matter of law, the common law of torts can accommodate recovery in the plaintiff's circumstances. If there are legal obstacles to recovery,[9] then the court must not permit a fact-finder to award damages to the plaintiff merely on a reasonable foreseeability test. Or, if the facts are such that the court determines that no reasonable fact-finder could find that the damages are proximate, and thus such a finding would be perverse, the question must not be left with a jury. Absent these situations, however, the determination of remoteness is a question of fact for the jury.[10]

2. TESTS FOR PROXIMATE CAUSE

(a) Introduction

The remoteness or proximate cause issue can be illustrated by the case of *Falkenham v. Zwicker.*[11]

The defendant was driving her car in excess of the posted speed limit on an extremely slippery highway. A cat ran onto the road, and the defendant braked, swerving to avoid the cat. The defendant lost control of her car and crashed into the plaintiff farmer's fence, shearing off five or six fence posts at ground level. Fence staples were scattered about. Several months later, the farmer's cows ingested these staples. Some cows became ill, other cows died.

Negligence law principles, ordinarily applied, would lead to the conclusion that the defendant owed the farmer, a land owner adjacent to the highway and thus a reasonably foreseeable victim of either personal injury or property damage, a duty to take reasonable care in driving along the highway. Reasonable care was not taken. Damage resulted.

The issue of remoteness asks: how far ought a negligent defendant's legal liability, and hence financial responsibility, to extend? All of the harmful results of negligent conduct cannot be laid at the feet of the actor who is factually responsible for these results. The notion of proximate cause indicates that after some point, a defendant's negligent conduct will no longer be considered a legal cause of the plaintiff's injuries. Whether the defendant driver's conduct in *Falkenham v. Zwicker* was the legal cause of all of the plaintiff's losses raised a question of remoteness.[12]

Over the past decades, the courts have articulated various tests to determine such remoteness issues. It is clear that, although vague and hence difficult to apply, these tests do correlate with judicial views as to the appropriateness of the negligence action as a response to the plaintiff's claims. No test is better than any other in terms of logic or ease of application. All ultimately require subjective

9 For example, policy rules restricting recovery for nervous shock, grief, sorrow, economic losses, or suicide.

10 See, e.g., *Barnard v. Carnegie* (1924), 26 O.W.N. 264 (C.A.); *Cotic v. Gray* (1981), 17 C.C.L.T. 138 at 171 (Ont. C.A.), affirmed (1983), 26 C.C.L.T. 163 (S.C.C.).

11 (1978), 93 D.L.R. (3d) 289 (N.S. T.D.).

12 The result of the case was that the defendant was held liable, although the damages were reduced because of the plaintiff's failure to mitigate his losses.

judgment, based on policy. One can, however, see in the general formulations the desire to expand or restrict tort law, according to prevailing judicial attitudes.

(b) The Directness Test of *Re Polemis*

The English Court of Appeal, in the well-known case of *Re Polemis and Furness, Withy & Co.*,[13] decided that once having proved negligence,[14] a claimant is entitled to compensation for all damages "directly traceable to the negligent act, and not due to the operation of independent causes having no connection with the negligent act, except that they could not avoid its results."[15] In thus adopting the directness test of remoteness, the Justices decided between two competing views which were then current. They rejected the first, which held that liability for negligence extended to only those consequences which were "intended", "natural and probable", or those which "might reasonably be expected to result."[16] The test they adopted was that the anticipation of the reasonable person went only to the initial question of negligence. Once an act is considered negligent, because damage of some kind would have been anticipated and avoided by the reasonable person, all the damage that flows directly from it is recoverable.[17]

What was meant by directness in *Polemis* is of course not clear.[18] The context of the case, however, clearly indicated that the court had enlarged the ambit of a defendant's liability by accepting directness and rejecting foreseeability.

(c) The Reasonable Foreseeability Test of *Wagon Mound No. 1*[19]

It was negligent conduct within the context of another charter relationship which led to the reversal of the *Polemis* directness rule of remoteness and the adoption of the test of reasonable foreseeability. In *Overseas Tankship (U.K.) Ltd. v. Mort's Dock & Engr. Co.*, otherwise known as *Wagon Mound No. 1*, bunker oil was carelessly discharged into the bay surrounding the Port of Sydney. It spread to the foreshore and wharf where ship repairs were being conducted by the owners of the dock. A spark from welding operations ignited a rag which was floating in the water, and this in turn set the oil on fire. The fire destroyed the plaintiffs' wharf and the ship's charterers were sued.

The trial judge found that the defendants did not know and could not reasonably be expected to have known that oil was capable of being set on fire when floating

---

13 [1921] 3 K.B. 560.

14 The dispute concerned the terms of a charter agreement for a ship. Neither duty nor negligence was in issue. The issue was: absent an exclusion, is a charterer responsible for all consequences of its negligent act?

15 [1921] 3 K.B. 560 at 577, per Scrutton L.J.

16 Cases cited to support this included *Greenland v. Chaplin* (1850), 5 Ex. 243; *Rigby v. Hewitt* (1850), 5 Ex. 240; and *Cory & Son Ltd. v. France, Fenwick & Co.*, [1911] 1 K.B. 114 (C.A.).

17 Cases cited to support this included *Smith v. London & South Western Ry.* (1870), L.R. 6 C.P. 14 (Ex. Ch.); *Weld-Blundell v. Stephens*, [1920] A.C. 956. It is interesting to note that the defendant's junior counsel argued specifically for a test which would admit liability for damages the extent of which could not be anticipated, as long as the type of damage could reasonably have been foreseen. The court rejected this argument.

18 See earlier discussions in Chapter 2 concerning the difficulties involved in attempting to distinguish between direct and indirect consequences of torts based on trespass.

19 [1961] A.C. 388 (P.C.).

on water. Since discharging bunker oil in water surrounding a port would foreseeably cause some damage, namely polluting the foreshore and interfering with port operations, it was a negligent act. The critical remoteness question thus presented itself: once having found duty, breach and factual causation, what was the extent of the defendants' liability?

The Privy Council explicitly rejected the *Polemis* test. Viscount Simonds, who delivered the judgment of the court, noted that the notion that foreseeability went only to culpability, and not to compensation, had not been accepted in the years since *Polemis* in several noteworthy Scottish cases.[20] It was now time to declare that *Re Polemis* "should no longer be regarded as good law."[21] Viscount Simonds declared:

> For it does not seem consonant with current ideas of justice or morality that for an act of negligence, however slight or venial, which results in some trivial foreseeable damage the actor should be liable for all consequences however unforeseeable and however grave, so long as they can be said to be "direct". It is a principle of civil liability, subject only to qualifications which have no present relevance, that a man must be considered to be responsible for the probable consequences of his act. To demand more of him is too harsh a rule, to demand less is to ignore that civilised order requires the observance of a minimum standard of behaviour.[22]

The reasonable foreseeability test of *Wagon Mound No. 1* was based on the principle that it would be wrong, unjust, and out of step with the moral basis of negligence law to hold a defendant liable for damages which were unforeseeable, and thus unpreventable. Its focus was particularly narrow, ignoring as it did the relative positions of the plaintiff and defendant, and the loss distribution function of modern negligence law.[23] In addition, it must be conceded that the reasonable foreseeability test itself was no more clearly defined by the court than had been the directness test, and thus no easier to apply. However, a new sentiment was expressed. The extent of legal responsibility should in a rough way accord with the extent of blameworthiness, and this, at least from a broad perspective, was to be a guide to the courts to limit recovery. How precisely this was to operate as a limiting device would be left to future courts. This led to the retreat from *Wagon Mound No. 1*.[24]

(d) The Scope of Foreseeability

(i) Hughes v. Lord Advocate — *The Type of Injury*

Two years after the decision in *Wagon Mound No. 1* the House of Lords significantly broadened the reasonable foreseeability test of remoteness. In *Hughes v. Lord Advocate*,[25] the Post Office was found to have been negligent in

---

20 For example, *Glasgow Corp. v. Muir*, [1943] 2 All E.R. 44 (H.L.); *Bourhill v. Young*, [1943] A.C. 92 (H.L.).

21 [1961] A.C. 388 at 422.

22 *Ibid.*, at 422-23.

23 See Fleming, "The Passing of Polemis" (1961), 39 Can. Bar Rev. 489.

24 Canadian courts have clearly accepted the *Wagon Mound No. 1* test. See, e.g., *Price v. Milawski* (1977), 82 D.L.R. (3d) 130 at 140 (Ont. C.A.), where Arnup J.A. states that "there is no doubt the principle is now part of the common law of Canada," and cites the following case law: *Child v. Vancouver Gen. Hosp.*, [1970] S.C.R. 477 at 488; *Moran v. Pyle Nat. (Can.) Ltd.*, [1975] 1 S.C.R. 393 at 405; and *R. v. Côté*, [1976] 1 S.C.R. 595.

25 [1963] 1 All E.R. 705 (H.L.).

leaving a manhole shelter and paraffin lamps unattended. The child plaintiff entered the shelter and either knocked or lowered one of the lamps into the manhole opening. This caused a chain of events which was totally unforeseeable. Paraffin escaped from the lamp, vaporized, and the explosive mixture thus created was detonated by the lamp. The explosion shot a flame up the manhole, causing the plaintiff to fall into the opening. The plaintiff suffered serious burns.

In determining the extent of the defendant's liability, the Lords held that the reasonable foreseeability test required neither foreseeability of the extent of a plaintiff's injuries, nor even of the manner of their occurrence, as long as the type of injuries which occurred was foreseeable. Since it was reasonably foreseeable that easily accessible lamps would create dangers of burning, the test of remoteness had been satisfied in this case.

One could argue that the judgment in *Hughes v. Lord Advocate* was an abandonment of the principle of *Wagon Mound No. 1* that there is only liability for the reasonably foreseeable consequences of one's acts. That the child plaintiff suffered burns from the explosion, rather than being injured in some other way, such as being thrown into the path of an oncoming car, was merely fortuitous. On the reasoning of the Lords, there would not be liability for the latter occurrence. The negligence of the defendant in failing to adequately guard the lamps related to the foreseeable risk that the lamps would burn the hands of a curious child. The reasoning of *Wagon Mound No. 1* would suggest that the extent of liability should, therefore, have rested only with such injuries. *Hughes v. Lord Advocate* shows, however, that the principle of *Wagon Mound No. 1*, taken too literally, ran afoul of contemporary notions of compensation and loss distribution and simply could not stand the test of time.

The liberal test of *Hughes v. Lord Advocate* has generally found favour with the courts. In *Assiniboine South Sch. Div. No. 3 v. Greater Winnipeg Gas Co.*,[26] for example, the Manitoba Court of Appeal, per Dickson J.A., applied the principle of *Hughes v. Lord Advocate* to a rather strange snowmobile accident. The snowmobile, being driven by a 14-year-old, ran out of control and fractured a gas-riser pipe. The gas escaped, entered a building, and exploded. Mr. Justice Dickson held that:

> It is enough to fix liability if one could foresee in a general way the sort of thing that happened. The extent of the damage and its manner of incidence need not be foreseeable if physical damage of the kind which in fact ensues is foreseeable.[27]

This approval of the principle of *Hughes v. Lord Advocate* was reaffirmed by Mr. Justice Dickson, who was by then a member of the Supreme Court of Canada, in *R. v. Côté*[28] and more recently by McLachlin J. in *Bow Valley Husky (Bermuda) Ltd. v. Saint John Shipbuilding Ltd.*[29] Numerous other Canadian judgments as well have supported this approach.[30]

---

26 [1971] 4 W.W.R. 746 (Man. C.A.), affirmed (*sub nom. Hoffer v. Assiniboine South Sch. Div.*) [1973] 6 W.W.R. 765 (S.C.C.).

27 [1971] 4 W.W.R. 746 at 752. This was referred to with approval in *Falkenham v. Zwicker*, above, note 11.

28 [1976] 1 S.C.R. 595.

29 (1997), 40 C.C.L.T. (2d) 235 (S.C.C.) at 264.

30 See, e.g., *R. (G.B.). v. Hollett* (1996), 30 C.C.L.T. (2d) 215 (N.S. C.A.), leave to appeal refused (1997), 160 N.S.R. (2d) 80 (note) (S.C.C.); *C.N.R. v. Sask. Wheat Pool*, [1986] 4 W.W.R. 371

Merely requiring foreseeability of the type of damage, rather than the kind of occurrence or accident which produced it, has greatly diminished the importance of *Wagon Mound No. 1*, and has narrowed, if not entirely closed, the gap between it and *Re Polemis*.

(ii) Wagon Mound No. 2 — *The Possibility of Injury*

The same accident which gave rise to the claim in *Wagon Mound No. 1* resulted in *Wagon Mound No. 2*.[31] This time, however, the claimants were not the owners of the wharf which had been damaged by the fire, but the owners of other vessels. The finding of the trial judge who heard this case, moreover, was that although the defendants' employees would regard the ignition of the oil as a rare occurrence, it was, in their experience, a "possibility."[32] Since it was a remote possibility, the trial judge held that it could not be considered to have been a reasonably foreseeable occurrence, and he accordingly dismissed the negligence action.[33]

On appeal to the Privy Council, Lord Reid significantly diminished the importance of *Wagon Mound No. 1*. Lord Reid held that although remote, the possibility of a fire was a "real" risk, which would, under the circumstances, not have been ignored by the reasonable person. The risk was a serious one, and the steps needed to eliminate it were minor. It was, therefore, negligent of the defendants to have ignored it, and they were held liable when it eventuated.

Stated in this way, the issue of remoteness was superfluous to the decision in *Wagon Mound No. 2*. Having defined the defendants' negligence in reference to the possibility of a fire if the defendants failed to take reasonable care, it went without saying that the fire, once it had occurred, would be considered to have

---

(Sask. Q.B.); *Lauritzen v. Barstead* (1965), 53 D.L.R. (2d) 267 (Alta. T.D.); *Weiner v. Zoratti* (1970), 11 D.L.R. (3d) 598 (Man. Q.B.); *Prasad v. Prasad* (1974), 54 D.L.R. (3d) 451 (B.C. S.C.); and *Bow Valley Husky (Bermuda) Ltd. v. Saint John Shipbuilding Ltd.* (1995), 126 D.L.R. (4th) 1 (Nfld. C.A.). See, however, *Grant Estate v. Mathers* (1991), 100 N.S.R. (2d) 363 (T.D.). The deceased was bitten by the defendants' dog. His wound became infected from a very rare bacterium and caused his death. The evidence indicated that the bacterium was practically unknown to medical practitioners and to dog owners. It was described as one of those "one in a million" occurrences. The court held that the death of the victim from this disease was "of a different class or character from the injuries which were reasonably foreseeable" from dog bites, and was too remote. Another case where the action was dismissed because the "means and type of the injury caused to the plaintiffs was of a totally different type" is *Trevison v. Springman* (1995), 28 C.C.L.T. (2d) 292 (B.C. S.C.), affirmed (1997), 1997 CarswellBC 2362 (C.A.). Although it was foreseeable that the defendant's son could break into the plaintiff's home, it was not foreseeable that he would deliberately burn down the house.

31 [1966] 2 All E.R. 709 (P.C.).

32 A difference in evidence at the two trials can be explained on the following basis. In *Wagon Mound No. 1* if a fire was a foreseeable occurrence in these circumstances, it was foreseeable by both plaintiffs and defendants. Since the plaintiffs' employees were the ones actually using the welding equipment, they may have been considered to have been contributorily negligent for continuing to weld despite the foreseeable risks. This was not evidence that the plaintiffs wished to lead, since contributory negligence would have been a complete defence. In *Wagon Mound No. 2*, the plaintiffs were not involved in the welding operations. Thus it was in their interest to prove that the risk of the fire was foreseeable. See [1966] 2 All E.R. 709 at 717.

33 The case was also pursued in nuisance, and the trial judge found for the plaintiff on this branch of the action. He held that foreseeability of damage was not a necessary requirement in a nuisance claim.

been within the risk created by the defendants' negligent conduct.[34] The decision was not at all consistent with the statement in *Wagon Mound No. 1* that "a man must be considered to be responsible for the probable consequences of his act." It was, in fact, more consistent with *Re Polemis* and the sentiment that a negligent actor ought to be responsible for all direct consequences of the act, whether foreseeable or not.[35]

3. WHERE TO DRAW THE LINE? — A QUESTION OF POLICY

In recent years, the courts have been frank in admitting that the reasonable foreseeability test, whether defined in terms of probable or possible risks, has been a useful shield, behind which the judicial policies dictating the resolution of remoteness questions can be hidden. Should an individual who negligently caused a motor vehicle accident be held responsible for the suicide of someone injured in the accident? Should liability attach if negligent medical intervention, or a second accident, exacerbates a victim's original injuries? Should a defendant be liable to those who suffer injuries while rescuing a person imperiled by the defendant's negligence? These are not issues which will be solved merely by asking whether these consequences were reasonably foreseeable.

One can refer to several cases in which courts have frankly recognized the policy content of the remoteness question. In *Spagnolo v. Margesson's Sports Ltd.*,[36] for example, the court was called upon to decide whether a defendant who negligently failed to provide security at a car park lot ought to be held responsible when a stolen car was involved in a collision with the plaintiff's vehicle. The accident occurred six days after the theft. In exonerating the defendant, Zuber J.A. stated that "the term 'reasonably foreseeable' contains more policy than fact

---

34 A case that illustrates this point is *Michaluk (Litigation Guardian of) v. Rolling River School Division No. 39* (2001), 5 C.C.L.T. (3d) 1 (Man. C.A.). A student lost his eyesight when he was struck in an eye by a coat hanger that he was using in an art project at school. The teacher was found to have been negligent for failing to have given better safety instructions and for not having provided the students with safety goggles. The trial applied the "possibility" of injury rather than the "probability" of injury test to the question of foreseeability. The Court of Appeal conceded that although the possibility test is applicable to "inherently dangerous" activities it is not the test for only "potentially dangerous" activities. In this respect, bending the wire hanger was only potentially dangerous. Nevertheless, the Court of Appeal held that since there was a real or substantial risk of possible injury that was foreseen by the teacher that he should be held liable. The Court of Appeal also applied the "type of damage" test discussed above in finding that the injury was foreseeable. One can see that once the court decided the negligence issue, i.e., the teacher was negligent for not guarding against the possibility of injuries caused by the coat hanger, the remoteness question became superfluous with relation to those types of injuries. The "possibility" test was accepted by Linden J. in *Gallant v. Beitz* (1983), 148 D.L.R. (3d) 522 (Ont. H.C.).

35 *Wagon Mound No. 2* was declared to have struck a "mortal blow" to *Wagon Mound No. 1*. See J.C. Smith, "Comment" (1967), 45 Can. Bar Rev. 336. See also Glasbeek, "*Wagon Mound II — Re Polemis* Revived; Nuisance Revised" (1967), 6 U.W.O. L. Rev. 192.

36 (1983), 145 D.L.R. (3d) 381 (Ont. C.A.).

as courts struggle with the issue of remoteness of damage . . ."[37] Since the court was not persuaded that a risk of an accident which occurred six days after the theft of the vehicle was within the risk created by failing to prevent the theft, the action was dismissed.[38]

Lord Denning has been particularly open in stressing the importance of policy in deciding issues of duty, cause and remoteness in negligence actions. In *Lamb v. London Borough of Camden*,[39] for example, Lord Denning M.R. held that as a question of policy, the plaintiff could not fix the responsibility for damage caused to her property by squatters on the council whose initial negligent act led to the house becoming vacant.[40] Watkins L.J., in the same judgment, argued that "a robust and sensible approach to this very important area of the study of remoteness will more often than not produce . . . an instinctive feeling that the event or act being weighed in the balance is too remote to sound in damages for the plaintiff."[41] Basing himself on his "instinctive feeling", Watkins L.J. held that the plaintiff's damages were too remote.[42]

It is clear that "instinct" and "intuition" are not satisfactory tests of remoteness. Certainty and predictability surely require that courts do better than that in articulating those factors which direct them to the resolution of remoteness problems. There are numerous factors which undoubtedly play a role. Clearly, factors such as the foreseeability of the injuries, their probability, their seriousness, the nature

---

37 *Ibid.*, at 383. Zuber J.A. referred to one of his earlier judgments, *Kienzle v. Stringer* (1981), 130 D.L.R. (3d) 272 at 277 (Ont. C.A.), where he stated that "in using the terms 'reasonably foreseeable' or 'within the contemplation of the parties' Courts are often not concerned with what the parties, in fact, foresaw or contemplated." It was "a matter to be determined by a Court", which contained "more policy than fact." Also see Cameron J.A.'s judgment in *Bow Valley Husky v. Saint John Shipbuilding* above, note 29: "Proximate cause is concerned with the extent of liability of the defendant for the loss which his conduct has caused. This involves matters of law and policy."

38 The trial judge had found that there was "a sufficient relationship between the culpability and the damage caused, to justify, in terms of public morality and policy, the shifting of the loss" from plaintiff to defendant. See 127 D.L.R. (3d) 339 at 345. Other similar cases where liability was not found are *Hollett v. Coca-Cola Ltd.* (1980), 11 C.C.L.T. 281 (N.S. T.D.); *O'Reilly v. C.*, [1978] 3 W.W.R. 145 (Man. Q.B.), affirmed (1979), 8 C.C.L.T. 188 (Man. C.A.); and *Werbeniuk v. Maynard*, [1994] 7 W.W.R. 704 (Man. Q.B.). A case where liability was found is *Cairns v. General Accident Assurance Co. of Canada*, [1992] O.J. No. 1432 (Gen. Div.). The court was particularly concerned with the fact that car keys were stolen from the defendant automobile dealer's lot, but despite its knowledge of this, the defendant did nothing to prevent the eventual theft of the car itself.

39 [1981] 2 All E.R. 408 (C.A.).

40 It is unclear what policy concerns dictated this result, other than Lord Denning's assumption that the plaintiff had insurance which would cover her losses. Even this reason loses its force when Lord Denning concedes that if the plaintiff did not have insurance, that would be her "misfortune." Also see Lord Denning's judgments in *Dutton v. Bognor Regis United Bldg. Co.*, [1972] 1 All E.R. 462 (C.A.), and in *Spartan Steel & Alloys Ltd. v. Martin & Co. (Contr.) Ltd.*, [1972] 3 All E.R. 557 (C.A.).

41 [1981] 2 All E.R. 408 at 421.

42 He came to this conclusion even though he believed the squatter's antisocial and criminal behaviour to have been reasonably foreseeable. In a similar case, *Ward v. Cannock Chase Dist. Council*, [1985] 3 All E.R. 537 (Ch. D.), the defendant council was held liable for the damages caused to the plaintiff's vacant property by vandals. Also see *Meah v. McCreamer*, [1986] 1 All E.R. 943 (Q.B.D.). In this case, Woolf J., basing himself on his "intellectual and instinctive response," held that the plaintiff's damages were too remote.

and degree of the defendant's misconduct, the relative financial positions of the parties,[43] and the behaviour of the plaintiff in response to the defendant's conduct or the initial injuries are important in considering whether it would be consistent with negligence law's general values and objectives to compensate the plaintiff for the losses in issue.[44]

4. SPECIFIC REMOTENESS PROBLEMS

There has developed around certain remoteness problems a substantial body of law, which can be used to resolve disputes in these recurring areas. This has greatly assisted courts and litigants by providing them with some guidance.

(a) Recovery for Nervous Shock and Purely Economic Losses

Historically, the common law has had substantial difficulties with claimants' demands for damages for nervous shock and purely economic losses.[45] Due to the complexity of the law relating to recovery for purely economic losses, this topic has been dealt with independently in Chapter 7. Fortunately, the law relating to the recovery of damages for nervous shock is much simpler and can be dealt with briefly.

---

43 In *Resurfice v. Hanke*, above, note 8, at para. 21, the Court of Appeal was critical of the trial judgment for failing to consider the potential seriousness of the injury and the relative financial positions of the parties as factors in determining whether a risk of harm was too remote. The court made reference to the statement in the text above. As noted before, the trial judge was approaching the issue not from the perspective of proximate cause, but from breach. The Supreme Court stated, in reference to the Court of Appeal judgment, that it erred in suggesting that these factors were relevant to foreseeability. As stated by McLachlin C.J.C. at para. 11, "Foreseeability depends on what a reasonable person would anticipate, not on the seriousness of the plaintiff's injuries (as in this case) or the depth of the defendant's pockets." McLachlin C.J.C. referred to an earlier case, *Haida Nation v. British Columbia (Minister of Forests)* [2004] 3 S.C.R. 511, at para. 55, where she stated that "we cannot sue a rich person, simply because the person has deep pockets or can provide a desired result." While I agree that such factors will normally not be overtly considered by courts in determining foreseeability and hence liability, it is certainly arguable that courts may be more inclined to find proximity where the plaintiff suffered a serious injury as a result of the negligence of a defendant, who was in a better position than the plaintiff to absorb its costs. One cannot deny that insurance and the relative financial ability of the parties to bear a loss has and will continue to influence tort law judgments.

44 Coval, Smith and Rush, "Out of the Maze: Towards a Clear Understanding of the Test for Remoteness of Damages in Negligence" (1983), 61 Can. Bar Rev. 559, suggest the following tests for remoteness. Recovery should be granted for all damages which fall within a "reasonably foreseeable as probable" class of damages, even though the actual damage which resulted was not reasonably foreseeable as probable. The more dangerous an activity the broader the class of injuries. Although the authors claim that this test successfully explains the outcome of approximately 90 per cent of all decided remoteness cases, it still leaves the basic question unanswered. How is it decided which injuries are reasonably foreseeable as "probable" and whether the actual injury fits within that class as a foreseeable "possibility"?

45 These issues raise both duty and remoteness problems, since they frequently involve claimants whose foreseeability as victims can only be defined with respect to the foreseeability of their specific injuries.

Despite initial misgivings,[46] nervous shock claims are presently viewed by the courts in the same way as are other damage claims, with some qualifications. Nervous shock is treated as a type of damage,[47] recoverability for which is based on the ordinary reasonable foreseeability test.[48] In this respect, of course, the language of reasonable foreseeability has been used to control the limits of recoverability for nervous shock claims, due to the common law's reticence with regards to them. As the justice of these claims has become more obvious, an increasingly confident judiciary has broadened the reasonable foreseeability test, and accordingly now affords greater scope for recovery.

The courts distinguish between nervous shock,[49] which is recoverable, and sorrow, grief, and emotional distress, which are not.[50] This has led to the require-

---

46 See Linden and Feldthusen, *Canadian Tort Law*, 8th ed. (2006), at 422-423, for a discussion of the common law's traditional fears concerning nervous shock recovery. Briefly, these concerns included the usual floodgates argument, problems of proof, and cynicism concerning the merits of damage claims based on mental illness. Many articles were written concerning this problem, but as the courts gradually reconciled themselves to the recoverability of these losses, academic writing in the area has diminished. For recent literature, see Mullany & Handford, *Tort Liability for Psychiatric Damage: The Law of Nervous Shock* (1993); Mullany, "Negligently Inflicted Psychiatric Injury and the Means of Communication of Trauma-Should it Matter?" in Mullany & Linden, eds., *Torts Tomorrow: A Tribute to John Fleming* (1998), Chapter 11; Belanger-Hardy, "Nervous Shock, Nervous Courts: The *Anns/Kamloops* Test to the Rescue" (1999), 37 Alta. L. Rev. 553; Trindade, "The Principles Governing the Recovery of Damages for Negligently Caused Nervous Shock" (1986), 45 Cambridge L.J. 476; among others.

47 See *Turton v. Buttler* (1987), 42 C.C.L.T. 74 (Alta. Master), and *Anderson v. St. Pierre*, [1988] 1 W.W.R. 712 (Man. Q.B.), where the courts quite correctly rejected the notion that a claim for nervous shock is a "substantive tort", rather than merely being a head of damage in a traditional negligence action. The suggestion that nervous shock is a substantive tort was raised in an earlier case, *Abramzik v. Brenner* (1967), 65 D.L.R. (2d) 651 (Sask. C.A.). It has been generally agreed that this is an unhelpful and puzzling characterization of the issue. See, e.g., *Marshall v. Lionel Ent. Inc.*, [1972] 2 O.R. 177 at 185 (H.C.), where Haines J. states that "nervous shock is nothing more than a particular type of damage which may be suffered by a plaintiff."

48 See, e.g., *Marshall v. Lionel Ent. Inc., ibid.* The jurisprudence is reviewed by McEachern C.J.B.C. in *Devji v. Burnaby (District)* (1999), 180 D.L.R. (4th) 205 (B.C. C.A.), leave to appeal refused (2000), 145 B.C.A.C. 320 (note) (S.C.C.) at 213 [D.L.R.] *et seq.* His Lordship notes the evolution from a starting position of no recovery without physical injuries to the foreseeability test. Also see Blair J.A.'s judgment in *Mustapha v. Culligan of Canada Ltd.* (2006), 275 D.L.R. (4th) 473 (Ont. C.A.), additional reasons at (2007), 2007 CarswellOnt 318 (C.A.), leave to appeal allowed (2007), [2007] S.C.C.A. No. 109, 2007 CarswellOnt 4075 (S.C.C.), affirmed (2008), 2008 CarswellOnt 2824 (S.C.C.).

49 It has been suggested that "nervous shock" is a "misleading and inaccurate expression", and that a more suitable term is "psychiatric damage", which includes all relevant forms of mental illness, neurosis and personality change. See Bingham L.J. in *Attia v. Br. Gas plc.*, [1987] 3 All E.R. 455 at 462 (C.A.). This point is well taken, since many of the contemporary cases deal more with these latter types of disorders, and less with typical reactions of shock. Brennan J., in the same case, stressed that claims for nervous shock must involve two elements. There is firstly the shock, i.e., "the sudden sensory perception" of a distressing thing, and secondly, the psychiatric illness, which the shock produces. This is useful in understanding why sorrow, distress or grief which everyone suffers when unhappy events occur does not fit within the definition of nervous shock. The issue was gone into in some depth in the excellent judgment of the British Columbia Court of Appeal in *Devji v. Burnaby (District)* (1999), 180 D.L.R.

ment that the nervous shock be accompanied by a recognizable physical or psychological illness,[51] presumably because it is thought that these accompanying disorders will verify the reality of the trauma, and make it easier to distinguish trauma from sorrow.[52] One must also concede that to allow recovery for nervous shock as opposed to sorrow is not so much a matter of logic or principle as it is a practical way to limit recoverability for a type of damage which courts justifiably fear can extend too far.

The courts also require that the plaintiff be of normal susceptibility, although this qualification is one which is invariably satisfied.[53] How far should recovery

---

(4th) 205 (B.C. C.A.), leave to appeal refused (2000), 145 B.C.A.C. 320 (note) (S.C.C.). MacKenzie J.A. noted that modern medicine distinguishes between psychiatric injury or illness caused by a 'severe reaction to bereavement or similar trauma' and 'ordinary grief or distress'. The law is concerned with the former. Unfortunately it is in practice a difficult distinction to make. His Lordship also agreed that the term 'nervous shock' is not a medical term; psychiatric illness would be more appropriate. Also see MacKenzie J.A.'s article "'Oh, What A Tangled Web We Weave': Liability in Negligence for Nervous Shock" (2002), 17 S.C.L.R. (2d) 125.

50 There are many cases which affirm this. See, e.g., *Heighington v. Ont.* (1987), 41 C.C.L.T. 230 (Ont. H.C.), additional reasons at (1987), 41 C.C.L.T. 230 at 248, affirmed (1989), 50 C.C.L.T. 1 (Ont. C.A.); *Beaulieu v. Sutherland* (1986), 35 C.C.L.T. 237 (B.C. S.C.); *Montgomery v. Murphy* (1982), 136 D.L.R. (3d) 525 (Ont. H.C.); *Cox v. Fleming* (1993), 13 C.C.L.T. (2d) 305 (B.C. S.C.), additional reasons at (1994), 96 B.C.L.R. (2d) 393 (S.C.), reversed in part (November 9, 1995), Doc. CA016770 (B.C. C.A.). In *Mustapha v. Culligan of Canada Ltd.*, 2008 SCC 27 at para. 9, MacLachlin C.J. stated that "compensable injury . . . must be serious and prolonged and rise above the ordinary annoyances, anxieties and fears that people living in society routinely, if sometimes reluctantly, accept."

51 See *Heighington v. Ont., ibid.*; *Mount Isa Mines v. Pusey* (1971), 45 A.L.J.R. 88; *Hinz v. Berry*, [1970] 1 All E.R. 1074 (C.A.). But see *McDermott v. Ramadanovic Estate* (1988), 44 C.C.L.T. 249 (B.C. S.C.), where Southin J. held that emotional pain caused by seeing one's parents killed is compensable, even though there has been no "recognizable psychiatric illness." This was followed in a breach of bailment case, involving the loss of a loved one's ashes; see *Mason v. Westside Cemeteries Ltd.* (1996), 135 D.L.R. (4th) 361 (Ont. Gen. Div.). The requirement of a recognizable psychiatric illness was affirmed by the B.C. Court of Appeal in *Graham v. MacMillan*, 2003 CarswellBC 360, 10 B.C.L.R. (4th) 397 (B.C. C.A.).

52 Note, however, the concern that this distinction made by lawyers and judges has no medical basis. If one views psychiatric illness as harm to the central nervous system, there is no distinction between physical and psychiatric harm. See MacKenzie J.A. in *Devji v. Burnaby (District)* (1999), 180 D.L.R. (4th) 205 (B.C. C.A.), leave to appeal refused (2000), 145 B.C.A.C. 320 (note) (S.C.C.) at 237 [D.L.R.], citing Lord Steyn's judgment in *White v. Chief Constable of South Yorkshire Police* (1998), [1999] 1 All E.R. 1 (H.L.).

53 See *Jaensch v. Coffey* (1984), 54 A.L.R. 417 (Aust. H.C.); *Bourhill v. Young*, [1943] A.C. 92 at 110 (H.L.). In *Bechard v. Haliburton Estate* (1991), 10 C.C.L.T. (2d) 156 (Ont. C.A.), the plaintiff, who was involved in a car accident, suffered nervous shock when one of the victims of the initial accident was run over by a second driver. Her claim for nervous shock was allowed, even though she was not related to the victim. It was reasonably foreseeable that the accident would upset "the average sensitive byestander." Thus, even assuming that the plaintiff was suffering from a pre-existing condition which made her more vulnerable to the psychological illness which resulted, she was entitled to recover, since some shock was foreseeable to the average witness. The "thin skull" rule could then be applied to allow her to recover for her more extensive illness due to her unusual susceptibility. See discussion on "thin skull" below. A case where the requirement of normal susceptibility was not satisfied is *Vanek v. Great Atlantic & Pacific Co. of Canada* (1999), 180 D.L.R. (4th) 748 (Ont. C.A.), leave to appeal refused (2000), 145 O.A.C. 200 (note) (S.C.C.), reconsideration refused (2001), 2001 CarswellOnt 958, 2001 CarswellOnt 959 (S.C.C.). The Ontario Court of Appeal found that parents who became 'obsessed' with the fact that their daughter had consumed contaminated

for nervous shock go? The common law started from the position that all nervous shock standing by itself without physical injury was too remote.[54] It then permitted recovery for nervous shock caused due to fear for one's own personal safety.[55] Later the courts allowed parents who suffered nervous shock caused by fear for the safety of their children to recover.[56] Recovery for nervous shock caused by witnessing an accident or its immediate aftermath was soon permitted.[57]

New situations have faced the courts, which have tested the applicability of the above principles and the limits of nervous shock recovery. In *McLoughlin v. O'Brian*,[58] the House of Lords dealt with the following facts. After hearing about a car accident involving her husband and three children, the plaintiff went to the hospital, saw her injured family members, and learned that one of her children had died. Was her nervous shock recoverable? The lower courts had said that it was not, since it was not foreseeable. She had not been present at the scene of the accident itself, and up to this point in time, the courts seemed to draw the line at that point. The House of Lords extended the boundaries for recovery. They held that the mother's shock was reasonably foreseeable and hence recoverable. The Lords did recognize, however, that this was the expression of a policy decision which dictated recovery in this type of case.[59] Similar facts presented themselves to the Australian High Court in *Jaensch v. Coffey*,[60] and the decision in *McLoughlin v. O'Brian* was followed. The court generally agreed that the test for the recoverability of nervous shock is the reasonable foreseeability of such shock, tempered by the pragmatic concerns which accompany this issue. Factors such as the relationship of the parties, the proximity of the victims of shock to the accident which produced it, and the nature of the shock-producing event must be

---

juice 'were not acting like the average concerned parent' and thus their 'highly unusual reaction and the psychiatric damage that flowed from it' were not foreseeable. Another unusual case is *Mustapha v. Culligan of Canada Ltd.* (2006), 275 D.L.R. (4th) 473 (Ont. C.A.), additional reasons at (2007), 2007 CarswellOnt 318 (C.A.), leave to appeal allowed (2007), [2007] S.C.C.A. No. 109, 2007 CarswellOnt 4075 (S.C.C.), affirmed (2008), 2008 CarswellOnt 2824 (S.C.C.). See discussion of this case below.

54 *Victorian Ry. Commrs. v. Coultas* (1888), 13 App. Cas. 222 (P.C.).

55 *Dulieu v. White & Sons*, [1901] 2 K.B. 669.

56 *Hambrook v. Stokes Bros.*, [1925] 1 K.B. 141 (C.A.).

57 *Pollard v. Makarchuk* (1958), 16 D.L.R. (2d) 225 (Alta. T.D.); *Marshall v. Lionel Ent. Inc.*, [1972] 2 O.R. 177 (H.C.); *Hinz v. Berry*, [1970] 2 Q.B. 40 (C.A.). The trend has been toward the steady extension of recovery.

58 [1982] 2 All E.R. 298 (H.L.).

59 See, e.g., Lord Wilberforce's judgment: "the statement that there is a 'duty of care' denotes a conclusion into the forming of which considerations of policy have entered." Only Lord Scarman argued that "the policy issue where to draw the line is not justiciable." For an extensive review of what each of the five Law Lords said in relation to the issue, see Taggart J.A.'s judgment in *Beecham v. Hughes*, [1988] 6 W.W.R. 33 (B.C. C.A.). A similar, Canadian case where nervous shock suffered by a father who saw his badly injured son in hospital was recoverable is *Cox v. Fleming* (1993), 13 C.C.L.T. (2d) 305 (B.C. S.C.), reversed in part as to damages (November 9, 1995), Doc. CA016770 (B.C. C.A.). An Ontario case which disallowed recovery in similar circumstances is *Dube (Litigation Guardian of) v. Penlon Ltd.* (1994), 21 C.C.L.T. (2d) 268 (Ont. Gen. Div.). The parents saw their child in hospital following minor surgery which produced devastating disabilities for the child. The court held that the parents' pyschological illness was produced not by the shock of the events, but from depression and grief.

60 Above, note 53.

considered. Mr. Justice Brennan held that since claims for nervous shock require both the reasonable foreseeability of the traumatic event as well as the illness produced by it, and a sufficient causal connection between the two, it becomes more difficult to establish these elements the more distant, spatially and temporally, the victim is from the immediate accident. These were considered to raise questions of fact, however, and not principle. As stated by His Lordship, "the exigencies of proof of the elements of the cause of action impose the appropriate limits upon the scope of the remedy."[61] An extension of the limits of recoverability for nervous shock occurred in *Attia v. British Gas plc.*[62] In this case, the court decided that as a matter of law damages for nervous shock were not restricted to accidents involving personal injuries, but could include nervous shock suffered by witnessing the destruction of one's personal property. The test was again stated to be one of reasonable foreseeability.

The House of Lords revisited the issue of the recoverability for nervous shock in the fascinating case, *Alcock v. Chief Constable of South Yorkshire Police.*[63] The litigation stemmed from a soccer tragedy which occurred in England in 1989. Ninety-five people were killed and over 400 injured due to overcrowding in one part of the stadium. The Chief Constable of South Yorkshire admitted liability in negligence and the issue arose as to whether relatives of the victims, who were not present in the area of the disaster, but who were present in other parts of the stadium, or were outside of the stadium, or heard about the tragedy from friends, or saw it on television, or listened to the radio reports, could recover for nervous shock.

In rejecting the appeals of ten unsuccessful plaintiffs, the House of Lords, in several judgments, made some important points. Lord Keith noted that the duty, while based on the relationship between the immediate victim of the tragedy and the nervous shock claimant, and the temporal and spatial proximity between the claimant and the tragedy, should not be restricted to relatives, but could be owed to anyone closely tied to the victim.[64] Lord Ackner emphasized the "shock" aspect of the claim, and the need for there to be a physical injury or illness accompanying the shock. Lord Ackner also approved restricting nervous shock claimants to those who either directly saw or heard the accident occur, although he was not willing to rule out claims by persons who witnessed the event on simultaneous broadcasts of the disaster. Lord Oliver emphasized the need for proximity, based upon the immediacy of the shock, closeness of time and space, and direct visual or aural perception.[65] All of their Lordships clearly recognized the extreme difficulty inherent in attempting to draw a line beyond which recovery is not permitted, and the infusion of policy concerns into this issue.[66]

---

61 (1984), 54 A.L.R. 417 at 434.

62 [1987] 3 All E.R. 455 (C.A.).

63 [1991] 4 All E.R. 907 (H.L.).

64 Lord Ackner admitted the possibility that even a stranger could claim, in circumstances where "a reasonably strong-nerved person would have been so shocked", [1991] 4 All E.R. at 919.

65 Lord Oliver would not rule out visual perception by simultaneous television, although he expressed reservations about this mode of perception.

66 Following the judgment, the Court of Appeal heard an appeal from the trial judgment in *Ravenscroft v. Rederiaktiebolaget Transatlantic*, [1991] 3 All E.R. 73. The trial judge had allowed a claim for nervous shock brought by a mother, arising from the death of her son. The mother was not present at the site of the accident, but was called to the hospital and was told

The same soccer tragedy gave rise to *White v. Chief Constable of South Yorkshire Police*.[67] The plaintiffs in this case were some of the police officers who were on duty at the scene and were claiming damages for post-traumatic stress disorder, which they suffered as a consequence of their involvement. The action was brought against their employer, the chief constable, whose liability for the tragedy itself was, as in *Alcock*, not in issue. The question was whether the fact that the claimants were employees who suffered the shock, and perhaps even rescuers at the time, should permit them to recover, even though other bystanders could not.

The majority of the Lords was not persuaded that these new factors made any difference to the outcome of their claims. Reaffirming the need to distinguish between physical harm and psychiatric harm and hence to develop more restrictive tests for the latter,[68] the Lords reversed the Court of Appeal's decision to allow these claims, and restored the trial judge's rejection of them.[69] Lord Steyn reaffirmed the *Alcock* requirements that in order for a bystander to recover there must be a close tie of love and affection with the person killed, injured or imperiled, there must be a close temporal and spatial connection to the incident, and the incident must have been directly perceived, as opposed to having, for example, merely being heard about.[70] The fact that the claimants were either employees on duty at the tragedy or rescuers who were not themselves in any danger did not justify treating them any differently than other bystanders.[71]

---

that her son had died. The mother's reaction was in the nature of grief and depression. In the appeal, a brief Note at [1992] 2 All E.R. 470 (C.A.), indicates that in view of the House of Lords' judgment in *Alcock v. Chief Constable of the South Yorkshire Police,* the trial judgment was incorrect and should be reversed. The mother's shock, not arising through the sight or hearing of the accident or its immediate aftermath, was not recoverable.The Court of Appeal also refused the plaintiff leave to appeal to the House of Lords. A similar Canadian case is *Strong v. Moon* (1992), 13 C.C.L.T. (2d) 296 (B.C. S.C.). The court refused the nervous shock claim of an 11-year-old girl who was told by her friends at school that her mother had been in a car accident and was "road pizza."

67 (1998), [1999] 1 All E.R. 1 (H.L.).

68 Lord Steyn noted four factors. First, the evidentiary difficulty in distinguishing between recoverable psychiatric injury and non-recoverable grief; second, the potential of a larger number of psychiatric injuries if compensation were available as a result of the unconscious desire to be compensated (i.e., "compensation neurosis"); third, the expansion of claims to bystanders in a growing number of situations, i.e., the class of claimants would increase; and fourth, the consequent onerous burden that would fall on defendants, which might be disproportionate to their degree of fault.

69 Court of Appeal's judgment reported at [1997] 1 All E.R. 540, [1997] 3 W.L.R. 1194 (C.A.).

70 (1998), [1999] 1 All E.R. 1 (H.L.) at 35. In terms of this last requirement, I assume the "incident" need not be the actual accident itself; it could be its aftermath, as in *McLoughlin v. O'Brian.* Lord Hoffmann confirms this at (1998), [1999] 1 All E.R. 1 (H.L.) at 41.

71 As with other House of Lords' decisions, they are several judgments, making it difficult to generalize about the reasons for the judgments. Lord Steyn saw no connection between the employer's duty to take reasonable care to prevent physical harm to employees as a result of unreasonable working conditions and psychiatric injury caused to an employee while at work in the circumstances of this case. In terms of rescue, Lord Steyn held that since there was no exposure to danger, real or perceived, there could be no recovery even for a rescuer. Lord Hoffman wrote the other majority judgment and agreed with these reasons. Lord Browne-Wilkinson concurred in the result and the reasons expressed in both judgments. Lord Griffiths and Lord Goff dissented. Lord Griffiths would have allowed the actions for the police who were acting as rescuers, although not simply as employees. Lord Goff would have allowed all the claims based on the fact that the claimants were employees involved in the incident or its

One other House of Lords judgment on nervous shock is particularly noteworthy. In *Page v. Smith*,[72] the plaintiff, who was involved in a car accident caused by the defendant's fault, suffered a psychiatric illness. The plaintiff was physically unhurt in the accident, but the trauma of the accident triggered the onset of a latent psychiatric illness that the plaintiff had had for about 20 years.[73] Although a plaintiff can clearly recover for psychiatric damage that flows from physical injuries, or for foreseeable psychiatric illness that is suffered as a result of being involved in a car accident (even if there is no physical injury), can a plaintiff involved in a car accident and who is unhurt recover for *an unforeseeable* psychiatric illness that is suffered as a result of the accident? Do the ordinary rules that govern liability for the recovery of nervous shock, i.e., that the nervous shock must have been foreseeable and the plaintiff must have been of normal susceptibility, apply to these "primary" victims of an accident?[74]

The majority of the House of Lords held that the plaintiff could recover for his damages, thereby reversing the Court of Appeal's dismissal of his claim.[75] Lord Lloyd emphasized the distinction between primary and secondary victims. In the case of primary victims, as long as some physical injury was foreseeable, it is not necessary that the psychiatric illness suffered also was foreseeable. A primary victim can recover for this illness, even if it was unforeseeable and caused as a result of the plaintiff's unusual susceptibility to it. The psychiatric illness is compensable even if no physical injury actually resulted. In terms of secondary victims, however, the psychiatric injury must have been reasonably foreseeable to a person of normal fortitude.[76]

---

aftermath. In *Joudrey v. Swiss Transport Co.* (2004), [2004] N.S.J. No. 268, 2004 CarswellNS 275 (S.C.), the plaintiff, a member of the Canadian Armed Forces, was involved in recovering dead bodies following the Swiss Air crash. He suffered psychological injuries. He sued Swiss Air. The action was dismissed. The court held that he was not a "rescuer", but a "recoverer". The *Anns* duty test was applied. The court held that his injuries were not reasonably foreseeable, there was no proximity between the parties, and policy reasons dictated against compensation.The court's approach in this case was somewhat unusual for nervous shock cases. The trial judge separated foreseeability from the factors going to proximity. Ordinarily, in nervous shock analysis, the proximity factors are what determine foreseeability.

72 [1995] 2 All E.R. 736 (H.L.).

73 The condition was described in various terms, such as chronic fatigue syndrome.

74 In *Alcock*, Lord Oliver described two categories of claimants. The first category comprises those involved as participants in the traumatic incident—primary victims. The second category comprises those who merely witness the incident or its aftermath—secondary victims. These categories have frequently been raised in the case law.

75 [1994] 4 All E.R. 522 (C.A.).

76 Lord Keith and Lord Jauncey dissented. They would have maintained the same requirements for both primary and secondary victims. In *White v. Chief Constable of South Yorkshire Police*, above, note 67, Lord Goff is very critical of the majority approach in *Page*, and makes reference to several scholarly critiques of Lord Lloyd's judgment. See (1998), [1999] 1 All E.R 1 (H.L.) at 14-21. The House of Lords reconsidered the matter in *Grieves v. F.T. Everard*, [2007] UKHL 39 (H.L.). While not abandoning the distinction between primary and secondary victims, the Lords noted that it should not be interpreted too broadly and they refused to apply it in the case before them. See discussion concerning this case below. The distinction between primary and secondary victims was recognized in *Sant v. Jack Andrews Kirkfield Pharmacy Ltd.* (2002), 161 Man. R. (2d) 121 (Q.B.), additional reasons at (2002), 162 Man. R. (2d) 193 (Q.B.), although on the facts of this case the plaintiff did suffer some physical consequences from exposure to a toxic substance and the psychiatric damage was held to have been foreseeable. In *Falbo v. Coutts Estate* (2000), [2000] B.C.J. No. 504, 2000 CarswellBC 548 (S.C.), the plaintiff's car was rear-ended by a motorcycle. The motorcyclist was killed. The plaintiff saw

The distinction between "primary" and "secondary" victims, although perhaps useful as a description of how persons may suffer psychiatric harm, becomes problematic if used in order to justify different legal rules. For one thing, the categories are not clear cut.[77] In addition, to state that psychiatric injury can be recovered by a primary victim even if that type of injury was not reasonably foreseeable runs counter to years of jurisprudence based on the *Wagon Mound* test. Finally, it is highly likely that in most cases involving primary victims, i.e., active participants in traumatic incidents, an argument can be made that once physical injury was reasonably foreseeable, psychiatric damage was as well. That a more serious traumatic injury occurred, as in *Page*, can be accounted for by the law's existing principles relating to "thin" and "crumbling skulls".

The criticisms leveled against the primary/secondary victim dichotomy led the Ontario Court of Appeal to reject it in *Mustapha v. Culligan of Canada Ltd.*[78] The plaintiff suffered a recognizable psychiatric illness, a major depressive disorder, as a result of seeing a dead fly floating in a sealed bottle of drinking water.[79] He was awarded damages at trial, but this decision was reversed on appeal. The Court of Appeal rejected the argument that as he was a participant in the shock-producing event that he was a primary victim, and could recover even if his psychiatric injury was not reasonably foreseeable.[80] The court held that the test in Ontario for recovery for nervous shock is whether this type of injury was a reasonably foreseeable injury to a person of normal fortitude. The test of foreseeability which Blair J.A. applied, however, was reasonably foreseeable as "prob-

---

the motorcyclist being thrown from his bike onto the road. She may have seen blood. She was told the next day that the motorcyclist had been killed. She suffered moderate soft tissue injuries but significant post-traumatic stress disorder. She sued the estate of the motorcyclist. The court accepted the distinction between primary and secondary victims as discussed by Lord Lloyd in *Page*. In this case, however, the plaintiff was both a primary victim, i.e., involved as a participant in the accident, and a secondary one, i.e., a witness to the post-accident aftermath. Using Lord Lloyd's approach, the plaintiff was entitled to be compensated under both categories as she satisfied the requirements of both.

77 Are people who are "rescuers" primary or secondary victims? Are bystanders who witness the accident, but who could have been hurt by it, primary or secondary victims? Can a person be both a primary and secondary victim, as in *Falbo v. Coutts Estate*, *ibid.*? In *White v. Chief Constable of South Yorkshire Police* (1998), [1999] 1 All E.R. 1 (H.L.), Lord Steyn and Lord Hoffman, in their majority judgments, held that unless a rescuer was in foreseeable physical danger, the rescuer should be treated as a bystander in respect to compensation for psychiatric injury, *Chadwick v. British Railways Commission*, [1967] 2 All E.R. 945 (Q.B.) notwithstanding. Lord Goff and Lord Griffiths, in dissent, held that rescuers, whether in foreseeable physical danger or not, should be viewed as primary victims and thereby entitled to recover for foreseeable psychiatric damage, even if ordinary bystanders could not. See discussion below on rescuers.

78 (2006), 275 D.L.R. (4th) 473 (Ont. C.A.), additional reasons at (2007), 2007 CarswellOnt 318 (C.A.), leave to appeal allowed (2007), [2007] S.C.C.A. No. 109, 2007 CarswellOnt 4075 (S.C.C.), affirmed (2008), 2008 CarswellOnt 2824 (S.C.C.).

79 The plaintiff's wife also saw the fly and sued. The trial judge held, however, that she did not suffer a "recognizable psychological injury" and dismissed her action, which went no further. See (2005), 32 C.C.L.T. (3d) 123 (S.C.J.), additional reasons at (2006), 2006 CarswellOnt 2385 (S.C.J.), reversed (2006), 275 D.L.R. (4th) 473 (Ont. C.A.), additional reasons at (2007), 2007 CarswellOnt 318 (C.A.), leave to appeal allowed (2007), [2007] S.C.C.A. No. 109, 2007 CarswellOnt 4075 (S.C.C.), affirmed (2008), 2008 CarswellOnt 2824 (S.C.C.).

80 Of course, as the court correctly pointed out there was no foreseeable physical injury from merely seeing the dead fly. He never drank the water. If anyone suffered physical injury from seeing the fly, it was the plaintiff's wife who vomited and had stomach cramps.

able" or "likely"; not reasonably foreseeable as merely "possible". The court decided that the psychiatric injury was not reasonably foreseeable in this case and dismissed the action. The Supreme Court of Canada affirmed the Court of Appeal's judgment and dismissed the plaintiff's action, but for different reasons. Characterizing the terms "probable" and "possible" as "misleading", in so far as they can define the standard necessary to satisfy the reasonable foreseeability test, Chief Justice McLachlin preferred instead to see risks as either "real" or "far-fetched".[81] In so far as mental injury claims are concerned, only those injuries which "would occur in a person of ordinary fortitude" will be considered by the law to be "reasonably foreseeable"; "unusual or extreme reactions to events caused by negligence are imaginable but not reasonably foreseeable."[82] As the evidence in *Mustapha* failed to establish that the plaintiff's reaction was one which foreseeably would have resulted in a person of "ordinary fortitude", the Supreme Court reversed the trial judgment and dismissed the action.[83]

The nervous shock issue was thoroughly reviewed by the British Columbia Court of Appeal in *Beecham v. Hughes*.[84] In that case, the plaintiff suffered a "reactive depression" following a car accident which severely injured his common law wife. Taggart J.A., although conceding that this depression was a reasonably foreseeable result of the event, dismissed the plaintiff's claim on the basis of a test of "causal proximity." Lambert J.A. dismissed the action based on a composite test which considered "foreseeability, proximity, causation and remoteness." It is, however, clear from this judgment, as well as the others noted above, that courts are struggling, with little success, to find words which can clearly explain why, on the basis of arbitrary *policy* choices, certain types of claims seem to be too remote and uncompensable.[85]

Although the typical nervous shock claim arises when bystanders, or relatives of those killed or injured in accidents, suffer psychiatric illness from seeing the victims or being present in the immediate aftermath of the accident, claims can

---

81 McLachlin C.J. referred approvingly to *The Wagon Mound (No.2)*, above, note 31, where these terms are used.

82 Above, note 78, at para. 15.

83 With respect to the court, the judgment avoided the question as to what degree of probability would be sufficient to conclude that a person of ordinary fortitude foreseeably would have suffered Mr. Mustapha's particular reaction. Clearly "highly unusual" reactions fail to meet the threshold. How "highly" unusual, however, was left undetermined. The Supreme Court also did not deal with the "primary" and "secondary" victim dichotomy, or the matter of what constitutes "ordinary" fortitude.

84 [1988] 6 W.W.R. 33 (B.C. C.A.).

85 See also *Rhodes v. C.N.R.*, (1989) 49 C.C.L.T. 64 (B.C. S.C.), reversed (1990), 5 C.C.L.T. (2d) 118 (B.C. C.A.), where this notion of "causal proximity" is further discussed. The trial judge left open the possibility that a mother who was not at the scene of a train accident which killed her son could recover for the nervous shock which she suffered. The Court of Appeal reversed the trial judgment and dismissed the claim for nervous shock, on the basis of a lack of proximity. Also see the very thorough judgment of the B.C. Court of Appeal in *Devji v. Burnaby (District)* (1999), 180 D.L.R. (4th) 205 (B.C. C.A.), leave to appeal refused (2000), 145 B.C.A.C. 320 (note) (S.C.C.), where relatives who viewed the deceased body at the hospital were unable to recover. A B.C. case where recovery was allowed is *Bruneau v. Bruneau* (1997), 32 B.C.L.R. (3d) 317 (S.C.). A mother came upon the accident scene very shortly after it happened. She saw the wrecked vehicle with her children still inside it.

arise from more unusual circumstances. *Mustapha v. Culligan*[86] is obviously one such case, but there have been others. In *Lew v. Mount Saint Joseph Hospital Society*,[87] the plaintiff claimed shock as a result of seeing his wife in a brain-injured state following an operation. The claim was not that the negligence of the doctor in treating the wife caused her the brain injury. The allegation was that the hospital had failed to properly prepare the husband and forewarn him of his wife's condition before he was allowed in to see her. The claim was allowed to proceed to trial. In another unusual case, *Nespolon v. Alford*,[88] the plaintiff driver suffered nervous shock as a result of killing a teen in a motor vehicle accident. The plaintiff sued the estate of the teen and two other teens who he claimed were negligent and responsible for the accident. The action was dismissed. In *Anderson v. Wilson*,[89] plaintiffs claimed that a notice that they received informing them that they should be tested for possible hepatitis B infection resulted in nervous shock. The claim was allowed to proceed as part of a class action brought by those who actually contracted the disease. In *Martin v. Mineral Springs Hospital*,[90] a woman whose baby was born stillborn was able to recover for the psychological damage that this caused her, although her husband was not allowed to recover for his sorrow.[91]

In *Grieves v. F.T. Everard & Sons*,[92] workers who had been negligently exposed to asbestos developed "pleural plaques" on the membranes surrounding their lungs. The existence of these plaques caused no damage to the workers, nor did their existence increase the risk that an asbestos related disease would later develop. They sued for the anxiety and stress which they allegedly suffered as a result of the plaques' existence. The House of Lords rejected their claims. The anxiety that they suffered did not constitute actionable damage. One of the workers suffered a recognizable psychiatric illness; clinical depression. Even his action was dismissed, however, on the basis that this illness was not a reasonably foreseeable injury which would be suffered by a person of "ordinary fortitude" in the circumstances of this case.[93] These cases indicate that nervous shock may

86 Above, note 78.

87 (1997), 36 C.C.L.T. (2d) 35 (B.C. S.C. [In Chambers]), leave to appeal refused (1997), 44 B.C.L.R. (3d) 84 (C.A. [In Chambers]).

88 (1998), 41 C.C.L.T. (2d) 258 (Ont. C.A.), leave to appeal refused (1999), 122 O.A.C. 200 (note) (S.C.C.).

89 (1999), 175 D.L.R. (4th) 409 (Ont. C.A.), leave to appeal refused (2000), 138 O.A.C. 200 (note) (S.C.C.).

90 (2001), 283 A.R. 178 (Q.B.).

91 It seems that had the husband been suffering from a recognizable psychiatric illness he would have been able to recover. The husband was at his wife's side during the delivery. Using the terminology of primary and secondary victims, into which categories would these two claimants fall? Compare this case with *Webb v. Motta* (1998), 233 A.R. 9 (Q.B.), where a husband was allowed to be compensated for stress that he suffered as a result of the negligent medical treatment that his wife received.

92 Above, note 76.

93 The Lords rejected the argument that this worker was a "primary victim"; i.e., he was in danger of physical harm from asbestos exposure, and thus he should be entitled to recover for psychiatric injury, even if that type of injury was not foreseeable.

be a compensable injury if it arises from the negligence of others in a variety of contexts, as long as the requirements for recoverability are satisfied.[94]

Despite the contention by some, that reasonable foreseeability provides a satisfactory limiting device for nervous shock claims, combined with the other requirements for a successful action, it seems evident that the rapid growth of this area can only be explained by the courts' increased willingness to accommodate these actions. There has been a clear shift in policy. Nervous shock damages are viewed with less skepticism, and negligence law seems better able to handle these actions, without causing undue administrative or economic harms.

(b) The "Thin Skull" Problem

Shortly after the Privy Council's judgment in *Wagon Mound No. 1* was handed down, the decision in *Smith v. Leech Brain & Co.*[95] reaffirmed what is known as the "thin skull" rule. The case concerned the claim of a widow whose husband died of cancer. The deceased had suffered a burn on his lip caused by a piece of molten metal, and this injury ultimately led to the cancer. The court held that the reasonable foreseeability test of *Wagon Mound No. 1* had not altered what "has always been the law of this country that a tortfeasor takes his victim as he finds him."[96]

What is the thin skull rule? As we have seen, *Hughes v. Lord Advocate*[97] clearly established that the reasonable foreseeability test of *Wagon Mound No. 1* required only that there be foreseeability of the *type* of injury, and not its *extent* or the *manner of its occurrence*. Thus, if one were to apply this to the facts of *Smith v. Leech Brain*, since the deceased's burn was reasonably foreseeable, the fact that its effect was more serious than one would have expected ought to be of no particular consequence. Parker C.J. in fact affirmed this view when he stated:

> The test is not whether these defendants could reasonably have foreseen that a burn would cause cancer and that Mr. Smith would die. The question is whether these defendants could reasonably foresee the type of injury he suffered, namely, the burn. What, in the particular case, is the amount

---

94 Also see *Peters-Brown v. Regina District Health Board* (1995), 26 C.C.L.T. (2d) 316 (Q.B.) affirmed (1996), 31 C.C.L.T. (2d) 302 (Sask. C.A.) — plaintiff recovered for mental distress caused as a result of inappropriate circulation of list containing names of persons with infectious diseases. In *McLoughlin v. Arbor Memorial Services Inc.* (2004), 36 C.C.L.T. (3d) 158 (Ont. S.C.J.), the family of the deceased sued a crematorium in both tort and contract for the mental distress they suffered as a result of a mix-up over the deceased's ashes. Due to the crematorium's error, the family believed that the wrong ashes may have been put in an urn. Although this turned out not to be so, it caused upset to the family. The tort action was dismissed based on lack of reasonable foreseeability, although the breach of contract action succeeded. In *McPhee v. C.U.P.E., Local 2094* (2007), 46 C.C.L.T. (3d) 269 (S.C.), the plaintiffs sued for psychiatric damage allegedly resulting from the use of harsh language during a labour grievance. The action was dismissed due in part to the absence of a traumatic event giving rise to the injury.

95 [1961] 3 All E.R. 1159.

96 *Ibid.*, at 1161. Lord Parker C.J. referred to a passage in *Dulieu v. White & Sons*, [1901] 2 K.B. 669 at 679, which enunciated this principle. It is a "rule" which has been applied in Canadian cases. See, e.g., the Supreme Court of Canada's affirmation of it in *Corrie v. Gilbert*, [1965] S.C.R. 457.

97 Above, note 25.

of damage which he suffers as a result of that burn, depends on the characteristics and constitution of the victim.[98]

One must also agree that the actual physical consequences of an accident for any individual are always unpredictable, and depend upon so many variables that it would be wrong to presume that the reasonable foreseeability test ever required foreseeability of the plaintiff's specific injury.[99] Understood in this way, the thin skull rule was merely reaffirmation of the point made in *Hughes v. Lord Advocate*. A defendant will be held liable for the full extent of a plaintiff's injuries, notwithstanding that they were more serious due to a pre-existing condition, or the increased vulnerability of the plaintiff, as long as the initial injuries were of a kind that was reasonably foreseeable.[100]

The typical thin skull problem which has appeared in the case law is adequately accommodated for by this narrow interpretation of the rule. Where complexities do enter into the equation, however, is in the damage assessment calculation for a person with a "thin skull."

The classic thin skull case arises where a plaintiff's injury is of the kind that was foreseeable, but becomes more serious because of a pre-existing condition. In other words, the plaintiff, in these cases, has an inherent weakness or susceptibility which results in a more serious injury. In this case, there is no question that the plaintiff is entitled to full compensation for the results caused by the defendant's negligence.[101]

The principle should also be applied to cases where the plaintiff's injury becomes more serious because of unexpected complications, or a susceptibility to further problems. On the basis of this reasoning, one can be critical of the decision in *Grant Estate v. Mathers*.[102] As discussed above, the victim was bitten by a dog and due to a very rare and unknown bacterium, the victim's wound became infected and he died. The court held that this result was not reasonably foreseeable and dismissed the claim. One could argue that all that was required for liability in this circumstance was the foreseeability of the type of injury, i.e. a dog bite,

---

98 [1961] 3 All E.R. 1159 at 1162.

99 See *Negretto v. Sayers*, [1963] S.A.S.R. 313, where it is stated that the "consequences of even the simplest accident are unpredictable."

100 For a good discussion and review of the cases which support this, see *Stephenson v. Waite Tileman Ltd.*, [1973] 1 N.Z.L.R. 152 (C.A.).

101 Several cases illustrate this. In *Smith v. Maximovitch* (1968), 68 D.L.R. (2d) 244 (Sask. Q.B.), an injury to the plaintiff's teeth was more serious because of their poor condition. The defendant still was held fully liable, although the damage assessment for the teeth which had to be removed reflected their lower value to the plaintiff. In *Bishop v. Arts & Letters Club of Toronto* (1978), 83 D.L.R. (3d) 107 (Ont. H.C.), that the plaintiff's recovery from a fracture was more extended since he was a haemophiliac was not a factor in reducing the plaintiff's damages. In *Sawchuck v. Novak*, [1992] B.C.J. No. 326, a mild trauma, which ordinarily would not have amounted to much, caused a serious disability to a plaintiff who had an unusually inflexible and rigid spine. The thin skull rule was applied. In *Davies v. Chouinard* (1995), 166 A.R. 363 (Q.B.), the trial judge appropriately accepted the theory that a person can have an "emotional" thin skull, which makes the person vulnerable to more serious emotional damage from an accident. Thus if an accident triggers this vulnerability, the tortfeasor should be fully liable.

102 (1991), 100 N.S.R. (2d) 363 (T.D.).

and that its actual effect on the victim's health need not have been foreseen. The court considered the thin skull authorities but concluded that this was not the "type" of injury which could have been foreseen.[103] It is my opinion that the weight of authorities could have supported liability in this case.

Cases in which plaintiffs' pre-existing conditions are either aggravated or activated by an accident frequently arise. Where a plaintiff has a pre-existing condition which is latent and inactive at the time of the accident, but becomes triggered by it, the courts appropriately treat this as a thin skull case. The plaintiff is entitled to full compensation.[104] Where, however, the plaintiff is suffering from an active and existing condition at the time of the accident, which is aggravated by the accident, courts will assign only partial responsibility for the plaintiff's injuries to the defendant. The defendant's responsibility will depend upon the extent to which the accident aggravated the plaintiff's existing condition.[105] Finally, a third category of cases has been suggested. A case may arise where the plaintiff has an asymptomatic, degenerative condition at the time of the accident which ultimately would have resulted in the type of injury suffered by the plaintiff in the accident. The accident accelerates the process of degeneration. This has been called a "crumbling skull," with the plaintiff entitled only to the damages corresponding to the effect of the accident on the degenerative process.[106] In principle, this category of cases raises the same issue as raised by cases where plaintiffs are suffering from existing conditions which become aggravated by the defendant's negligence, and should be treated in a similar way.[107]

---

103 The court applied such cases as *Tremain v. Pike*, [1969] 3 All E.R. 1303. The plaintiff contracted a very rare disease from rats. The court held that the foreseeable injuries from rats were bites or food poisoning, and *in obiter* held that the plaintiff's disease was too remote.

104 See, for example, *Montgomery v. Gasoff*, [1993] B.C.J. No. 184.

105 There are numerous cases which illustrate this situation. See, for example, *Pryor v. Bains* (1986), 69 B.C.L.R. 395 (C.A.); *Lee v. O'Farrell* (1988), 43 C.C.L.T. 269, additional reasons at (1988), 30 B.C.L.R. (2d) 130 (S.C.); *Finch v. Herzberger*, [1993] 4 W.W.R. 179 (Sask. Q.B.); and *Hunter v. Manning*, [1993] 5 W.W.R. 738 (Sask. Q.B.).

106 See, for example, *Price v. Garcha* (1988), 44 C.C.L.T. 1 (B.C. S.C.), affirmed (1989), 2 C.C.L.T. (2d) 265 (B.C. C.A.); and Hutcheon J.A.'s judgment in *Pesonen v. Melnyk*, [1993] 6 W.W.R. 578 (B.C. C.A.). In *Zacharias v. Leys* (2005), 36 C.C.L.T. (3d) 93 (C.A.), the B.C. Court of Appeal also affirmed that a crumbling skull need not be "already manifest and presently disabling" for the principle to be applied. The distinction between "thin" skulls and "crumbling" skulls is also discussed in *Thomson v. Juliana's Cabaret Ltd.*, [1993] B.C.J. No. 340, which cites several other B.C. cases.

107 The difficulty arises in attempting to distinguish between (i) latent and inactive conditions that become triggered by an accident; (ii) manifest, active conditions that become accelerated by an accident; and (iii) asymptomatic degenerative conditions, which would have continued on their degenerative process, notwithstanding the accident. I would suggest that (i) is a thin skull problem, whereas (ii) and (iii) are crumbling skulls. The problem is even more acute when the court is considering a psychological, as opposed to a physical condition, since "there is no x-ray for emotional susceptibility". See Veit J. in *Davies v. Chouinard* (1995), 166 A.R. 363 (Q.B.), and Paperny J. in *Whitfield v. Calhoun* (1999), 242 A.R. 201 (Q.B.). In the latter case, Paperny J. found that the plaintiff had pre-existing "personality traits" that were predictive of the physical and psychological reactions experienced by him following his involvement in a motor vehicle accident. Although he had kept these traits "in check" prior to the accident, he was classified as a "crumbling skull" victim. Damages were accordingly reduced to account for this. Another approach would have been to classify the plaintiff as having an "egg shell

The thin skull rule as applied to the above cases merely illustrates that although the type of injury must be reasonably foreseeable, the extent of the injury need not be. Is the thin skull rule more significant than this, however? Can it be used to extend the doctrine of reasonable foreseeability, or even to ignore it altogether? This would be so if the rule permitted recovery for injuries which, due to a victim's abnormal susceptibilities, are not only more serious, but different in kind from those which might have been foreseen.[108] At least one eminent Canadian jurist, Madam Justice Bertha Wilson, has interpreted the rule in this broader way. In *Cotic v. Gray*,[109] Her Ladyship stated:

> I think that the main issue . . . is whether or to what extent the reasonable foreseeability test for the recovery of damages is applicable in a thin skull case. In my view, it has little, if any, application once it is recognized that some personal injury may be reasonably foreseen to the victim of a motor vehicle accident. Beyond that, it seems to me that reasonable foreseeability does not afford a useful tool for the resolution of remoteness problems in a thin skull context. Both the type of injury suffered and the extent of the injury suffered will be conditioned by the type of thin skull the victim has and the degree to which he has it. Neither the class or kind nor the extent of the injury, it seems to me, can be reasonably foreseen in the case of a thin skull victim.

The extended scope of the thin skull rule can be tested by examining how courts have approached cases where plaintiffs have suffered new injuries which are not merely an exacerbation of foreseeable injuries. The suicide cases illustrate this problem. If a plaintiff is involved in an accident, and as a result becomes depressed and commits suicide, is the defendant whose negligence caused the accident liable for the suicide?[110]

This problem has been discussed in a few cases. In *Cotic v. Gray*,[111] Lacourcière J.A. extensively reviewed the jurisprudence on this question. One approach followed in the case law is to distinguish between suicides committed by sane as opposed to legally insane persons. Where a suicide is committed by a sane person, it is considered to be too remote, and, hence, not the responsibility of the defendant. If, however, the initial injuries suffered by the deceased lead to a situation of insanity which then results in suicide, the suicide itself is considered to be

---

personality" (i.e., a "thin skull") and discounting the award for contingencies. Compare *Whitfield* to *Dushynski v. Rumsey* (2001), 295 A.R. 309 (Q.B.), where there was no reduction even though the plaintiff's psychological condition before her accident (the fourth successive one) was "likely fragile". The court concluded that the condition (chronic pain syndrome) and the consequent inability of the plaintiff to ever return to work *would not have* occurred had it not been for the defendant's negligence; i.e., a "thin skull" case.

108 In considering the thin skull problem, one must be careful to distinguish between two matters. The thin skull problem properly relates only to the question of the defendant's liability for the injuries suffered by the plaintiff. It is not concerned with the damage assessment process, that is, the financial impact of the injuries on the plaintiff. Thus, if you punch a person with a "glass jaw" and as a result the jaw totally disintegrates, this is a thin skull problem. If it turns out that the plaintiff was an opera singer who now can never perform again, this is a damage assessment issue. Principles of remoteness apply only to the former issue, and not to the latter. The damage assessment process is covered by its own rules. See discussion in Chapter 11 where this distinction is made.

109 (1981), 17 C.C.L.T. 138 at 178 (Ont. C.A.), affirmed (1983), 26 C.C.L.T. 163 (S.C.C.).

110 The suicide issue is further discussed below, under *novus actus interveniens*.

111 Above, note 109.

within the risk created by the wrongdoing defendant.[112] In *Swami v. Lo*,[113] the court used this distinction to reject a claim under the Families' Compensation Act[114] which arose out of the suicide of the plaintiff's husband. The trial judge distinguished between a suicide brought about directly by the plaintiff's injuries, for example, an injury to a head which renders the defendant subject to irrational acts, such as suicide, and suicide brought about by a condition which is extraneous to the injuries. This distinction may be justified on the basis of a narrow interpretation of the thin skull rule. Where the plaintiff's mental disturbance is caused by an accident, the suicide can be argued to be merely a more extensive, but similar injury. Where the accident does not result in insanity, however, and the plaintiff commits suicide not directly as a result of the injuries, the suicide can be seen as a different type of injury, and hence too remote.[115] In *Costello v. Blakeson,*[116] the court used the thin skull approach to allow partial recovery for an attempted suicide. The plaintiff had attempted suicide three months prior to a car accident. Approximately three years later, she attempted suicide again, and suffered injuries as a result. The court held that the plaintiff was in a fragile emotional state before the accident, which was exacerbated by the accident. This was, in other words, a case of a pre-existing susceptibility to suicide being aggravated by the defendant's negligence, and according to a thin skull approach, the defendant was held liable for a portion of the ensuing damage.[117]

A second approach has been to permit recovery for suicide, whether committed by a sane or insane person, as long as it is related to the original accident.[118] This represents the more expansive view of the thin skull rule, since it permits recovery of injuries which are not only more serious than what was foreseeable, but also

---

112 See *Murdoch v. Br. Israel World Fed.*, [1942] N.Z.L.R. 600 (C.A.); *McFarland v. Stewart* (1900), 19 N.Z.L.R. 22 (C.A.).

113 (1979), 11 C.C.L.T. 210 (B.C. S.C.).

114 R.S.B.C. 1960, c. 138, s. 3.

115 See also *Robson v. Ashworth* (1985), 33 C.C.L.T. 229 (Ont. H.C.), affirmed (1987), 40 C.C.L.T. 164 (Ont. C.A.). Although this was not a thin skull case, the court refused to allow the dependants of a sane man to sue for suicide, even when it was clearly caused by the doctor's negligence in prescribing barbiturates to the suicidal patient. For a criticism, see Klar, "Comment" (1987), 66 Can. Bar Rev. 159 at 162.

116 [1993] 2 W.W.R. 562 (B.C. S.C.).

117 In *Hauk Estate v. Hudson* (1997), 50 C.C.L.I. (2d) 159 (Ont. Gen. Div.), the deceased suffered from depression prior to the motor vehicle accident. After the accident, which resulted in disabling injuries, the deceased committed suicide. The court applied *Athey* and held that since the suicide was caused by both the accident and the deceased's own mental health, the defendant should be liable for the full financial consequences (funeral expenses) of the suicide. Based on this reasoning, one could argue that the same result should have applied in *Costello* and full damages awarded, subject perhaps to a contingency reduction, as discussed in Chapter 11.

118 See *Pigney v. Pointers Tpt. Services Ltd.*, [1957] 1 W.L.R. 1121; *Cotic v. Gray*, above, note 107. Also see *Hayes v. Green* (1983), 30 Sask. R. 166 (Q.B.). In *Wright Estate v. Davidson* (1989), 49 C.C.L.T. 116 (B.C. S.C.), reversed (1992), 88 D.L.R. (4th) 698 (B.C. C.A.), the trial judge applied the *Hayes* decision and allowed recovery for a suicide committed by a sane person. The Court of Appeal reversed, noting that when the suicide is a conscious decision of a sane person, there is no recovery. Merely because the victim suffered a head injury in the accident did not mean that she was suffering from a disabling mental illness when she made the decision to take her life.

different. The leading authorities which have supported this approach, however, are not strong. One, *Pigney v. Pointers Tpt. Services Ltd.*,[119] was decided on the basis of *Re Polemis*,[120] and prior to *Wagon Mound No. 1*.[121] It was also based on a statutory provision which predicated recovery upon causation, without additional qualification. In the second, *Cotic v. Gray*,[122] the courts merely upheld a jury's finding that the defendant caused the deceased's suicide, without delving further into the question of proximate cause.[123]

The uncertainty concerning the extent of the thin skull rule is reflected in the suicide cases. Since it is not yet clear whether the thin skull rule extends *Hughes v. Lord Advocate*,[124] or merely restates it, it is also not clear whether suicide not occurring due to a mental state caused by the accident should be recoverable.[125]

(c) The Problem of *Novus Actus Interveniens*

(i) Introduction

Where the act of a third party, or a subsequent act of the plaintiff, intervenes between the defendant's conduct and the plaintiff's injury, several difficult issues in negligence law are raised. Depending on the circumstances, the courts will be called upon to settle questions of duty, breach, or proximate cause. Unfortunately, these three questions are not always kept distinct in this area, and the jurisprudence is somewhat confused. One must be careful to distinguish between two situations. In the first, the defendant breaches a duty of care and injures the plaintiff. Subsequently, the act of a stranger, or even the plaintiff, exacerbates the initial injury.

---

119 *Ibid.*

120 [1921] 3 K.B. 560.

121 [1961] A.C. 388 (P.C.).

122 Above, note 109.

123 For a commentary see Gibson, "Developments in Tort Law: The 1983-84 Term" (1985), 7 Sup. Ct. L. Rev. 387; Klar, "Recent Developments in Canadian Law: Tort Law" (1985), 17 Ottawa L. Rev. 325 at 372.

124 [1963] 1 All E.R. 705 (H.L.).

125 The recovery of damages by the dependents of a suicide victim was considered by the House of Lords in *Corr v. IBC Vehicles*, [2008] UKHL 13. The deceased had been seriously injured at work. His injuries brought on post-traumatic stress disorder, nightmares, mood changes and so on. He became depressed and ultimately committed suicide. All of the Lords agreed that damages were recoverable. Lord Bingham found that although the deceased was not insane when he decided to commit suicide, unlike the deceased in *Wright v. Davidson*, above, note 118, "the suicide was not a voluntary, informed decision taken by him as an adult of sound mind making and giving effect to a personal decision about his future." (At para.15.) In essence, the Lords felt that since the deceased's physical injuries were foreseeable, his psychiatric injuries were compensable, and the fact that this led to suicide should not be considered a *novus actus interveniens*. The controversial issue was whether there should be a reduction for contributory negligence. The majority held that there should not be a reduction, based either on principle, or because the matter had not been adequately raised and dealt with by the parties in the courts below. Another useful House of Lords decision dealing with remoteness principles and their application to a person who suffered from a depressive illness following an accident at work is *Simmons v. British Steel plc.*, [2004] UKHL 20.

In this case, a true remoteness issue arises.[126] The question for the court is whether the second act, with its injurious results, should be considered to be within the risk set into motion by the defendant, and thus remain the defendant's responsibility, or whether the act should be seen as a *novus actus interveniens* severing the causal connection.

A second type of problem, which is incorrectly seen as a *novus actus* problem, is entirely different. It goes to the heart of the defendant's duty itself, and asks whether a defendant can be responsible for the misconduct of third parties, based on a duty to take reasonable care to have prevented this misconduct from occurring. This issue is initially not one of remoteness, but of duty. Having determined the duty question, the issue of liability for the acts of the third party will be resolved based on whether the duty was breached and whether this breach, i.e., failing to control the thirdy party, was both the factual and proximate cause of the plaintiff's injury. Since courts do, however, frequently regard this problem in the context of *novus actus interveniens*, it will be briefly discussed here.[127]

(ii) Responsibility for the Acts of Third Parties

A. Injuries Caused by Persons under One's Control and Supervision

As a starting proposition, the common law takes the view that an individual ought not to be held responsible for the acts of another person. This was stated by an Australian judge, Mr. Justice Dixon, in *Smith v. Leurs*:

> It is, however, exceptional to find in the law a duty to control another's actions to prevent harm to strangers. The general rule is that one man is under no duty of controlling another man to prevent his doing damage to a third.[128]

One can suggest several reasons for this position. The principal one relates to the common law's refusal to recognize a duty to assist those who stand in no special relationship with the defendant.[129] A defendant who stands in no special relationship with a stranger will be considered as a disinterested bystander, in so far as the duty to assist is concerned. The victim will not be able to rely on the defendant to control the conduct of a third party.

---

126 Let us recall that remoteness is concerned with how far the defendant's liability should extend, once duty, breach and cause-in-fact have been established. As stated by Mr. Justice Linden, the function of the concept of remoteness is "to draw the appropriate line between the *additional* consequences for which an admittedly negligent defendant will be liable, and those for which he will escape liability." See *Gallant v. Beitz* (1983), 148 D.L.R. (3d) 522 at 526 (Ont. H.C.).

127 In *Fullowka v. Royal Oak Ventures Inc.*, 2008 NWTCA 4 (C.A.), the Court of Appeal agreed with this analysis and held that responsibility for the acts of third parties raises a duty issue. The case concerned the legal responsibility of a number of defendants for the deaths of replacement workers, who were killed in a bomb explosion. The bomb had been set by a striking miner, during the course of a protracted and violent labour grievance. The trial judge found several of the defendants liable, but this decision was reversed by the appellate court. See discussion of this case below. A useful recent article on liability with respect to the acts of third parties and the duty to protect others is Hall, "Duty to Protect, Duty to Control and the Duty to Warn" (2003), 82 Can. Bar Rev. 645.

128 (1945), 70 C.L.R. 256 at 262 (Aust. H.C.).

129 See Chapter 6.

A second reason for the common law's reluctance to impose liability on one party for the tortious acts of another relates to the element of control. Responsibility for the acts of an individual implies a right to control that individual. The liberty of a person who is under control is limited to the extent of the control. This is antithetical to the individualistic ethic of the common law and to the rights of competent individuals to do what they want without interference from others.

A third reason suggested in the jurisprudence relates to the unpredictability of human behaviour. To require a defendant to be responsible for the acts of another assumes a degree of predictability of behaviour, enabling the responsible individual to anticipate dangerous behaviour and to protect others from it. Some deny that there is this predictability, and allege that a duty to control unpredictable behaviour would be unfair.

There are, of course, clearly defined relationships which require a supervising party to control the activities of a supervisee. As we have previously seen,[130] parents are required to take reasonable steps to control their children.[131] As well, those who have custodial care over individuals, in such places as prisons, hospitals, or schools, are required to protect others in these institutions, whether they be inmates, patients, students, employees, or visitors, from harm.[132] The duty to prevent persons who are under one's care or treatment from harming others, or even themselves,[133] also extends to incidents occurring outside of the institutional environment.[134] It is quite clear in these types of cases that the fact that the

---

130 Chapter 6.

131 See Alexander, "Tort Responsibility of Parents and Teachers for Damage Caused by Children" (1965), 16 U.T. L.J. 165. For a decision which discusses in some detail the scope of a parent's duty, see *Segstro v. McLean*, [1990] B.C.J. No. 2477 (S.C.). The court reaffirms that there is no vicarious liability of a parent for a child. Whether the parent can be personally negligent depends upon such factors as the age of the child, the propensity of the child to act destructively, and whether the child is in possession of dangerous goods. The duty is greater with younger children, and children with known propensities to act destructively. In this case, parents were held liable.

132 In *Coumont v. R.*, [1994] F.C.J. No. 655 (T.D.), for example, the duty of a correctional service to take reasonable steps to protect an inmate from fellow inmates was affirmed, although the action was dismissed based upon lack of negligence.

133 One has a duty in some cases to protect individuals from *themselves*. In *Shackleton v. Knittle* (1999), 46 C.C.L.T. (2d) 300 (Alta. Q.B.), the defendant ambulance drivers were taking a schizophrenic patient to hospital. They allowed him to sit in the front seat. While there, the patient became delusional and grabbed the steering wheel. He caused a fatal motor vehicle accident. He was charged with murder and criminal negligence, but was found not guilty by reason of insanity. He sued the ambulance drivers for all of the losses and expenses that flowed from this episode. Fraser C.J.A approached the issue from the perspective of duty and breach. She found that the decision to allow the patient to drive in the front was not negligent. The fact that the instrumentality of the harm was the act of another person, in this case the plaintiff himself, did not raise any special issues of *novus actus*.

134 The leading case which discusses these principles is *Home Office v. Dorset Yacht Co.*, [1970] 2 All E.R. 294 (H.L.). For a B.C. case, see *MacAlpine v. H. (T.)*, [1991] 5 W.W.R. 699 (B.C. C.A.), reversing (1988), 48 C.C.L.T. 80 (B.C. S.C.). Two youths, under the supervision of "special care parents," destroyed property and burned down a cabin belonging to neighbours. The special care parent and the Superintendent of Family and Child Services were sued by those neighbours who suffered damage. Although recognizing the duty relationship between the defendants and the plaintiffs, the Court of Appeal dismissed the claim against the Superintendent due to the immunity provision provided for in the Family and Child Service Act, S.B.C. 1980, c. 11. Although the special care parent was not protected by the Act, the action

immediate instrumentality of the plaintiff's injury was not the act of the defendant but a third party is no defence. The defendant had a duty to control the third party. The only questions that remain are whether there was negligence with respect to that control, and whether the injuries suffered were both factually and proximately caused by that negligence.[135]

The case of *Williams v. Saint John*[136] illustrates this point. Injuries were caused to inmates of a prison when one of the inmates deliberately set fire to his cell. The prison authorities were sued by relatives of those killed. In response to the defendant's argument that the actions of the prisoner in setting the fire were intervening acts which severed the causal connection, the trial judge relied on Greer J.'s proposition in *Haynes v. Harwood*:

> If what is relied upon as a *novus actus interveniens* is the very kind of thing which is likely to happen if the want of care which is alleged takes place, the principle embodied in the maxim is no defence . . .[137]

Having found that the prison authorities owed a duty to take reasonable care to protect its inmates from other inmates, only two questions remained. Was reasonable care exercised? Were the type of misconduct and the injuries caused reasonably foreseeable?[138]

Other situations which impose a duty on a defendant to protect the plaintiff from the acts of third parties arise with respect to occupier's liability and nuisance.

---

against him was dismissed based on the finding that he had not been negligent in his supervision of the boys. For another judgment relieving a social worker of liability relating to the placement of a foster child, see *D. (B.) v. British Columbia* (1995), [1996] 1 W.W.R. 581 (B.C. S.C.), reversed [1997] 4 W.W.R. 484 (B.C. C.A.), leave to appeal refused (1997), 97 B.C.A.C. 80 (note) (S.C.C.). Also see *S. (J.) v. Clement* (1995), 22 O.R. (3d) 495 (Gen. Div.), where a government correctional service was held liable to a victim of a sexual assault by an escaped offender. The negligence resided in the defendant's failure to promptly notify the police when the inmate was first suspected to be missing. In *Wenden v. Trikha* (1991), 8 C.C.L.T. (2d) 138 (Alta. Q.B.), affirmed (1993), 14 C.C.L.T. (2d) 225 (Alta. C.A.), the court recognized the duty which a hospital owes to its patients to take reasonable care to prevent them from being injured by other patients. The trial judge was prepared to extend this duty to persons outside of the institution when harm was foreseeable and there was the "requisite proximity of relationship" based upon the third party's exposure to a particular risk of danger due to the nature of the patient. The trial judge, although elaborating upon the duty issue, resolved the case by finding that there was no negligence by the hospital staff. This made it unnecessary to decide whether the plaintiff, who was the victim of a car accident caused by a psychiatric patient, was in the class of persons to whom a duty was owed. The Court of Appeal also agreed that there was no negligence. For a case where liability was found, see *Spillane (Litigation Guardian of) v. Wasserman* (1992), 13 C.C.L.T. (2d) 267, varied as to apportionment (1998), 41 C.C.L.T. (2d) 292 (Ont. C.A.), where doctors who were treating a patient with epilepsy were held partly responsible to victims of a car accident caused when the patient suffered an epileptic seizure while driving.

135 The commercial host/social host liability cases, discussed in Chapter 6, illustrate the point. The fact that the immediate instrumentality of a car accident is the drunk driver and not the inn that over-served, does not shield the host from liability once it has been decided that the host had a duty to prevent the patron from drinking to excess and driving.

136 (1983), 27 C.C.L.T. 247 (N.B. Q.B.), additional reasons at (1984) 66 N.B.R. (2d) 43 (Q.B.), varied as to costs (*sub nom. Williams v. N.B.*) (1985), 34 C.C.L.T. 299 (N.B. C.A.).

137 [1935] 1 K.B. 146 at 156 (C.A.).

138 A similar case is *Hodgin v. Canada (Solicitor General)* (1999), 218 N.B.R. (2d) 164 (C.A.). A prisoner was set on fire by other inmates. The trial judge dismissed an action brought against the prison authorities. The trial judge found that there was no negligence. The Court of Appeal affirmed the decision.

As we have seen,[139] an occupier has a duty to protect others from damage caused by trespassers in certain situations. One may also be held liable in nuisance for damages emanating from one's land as a result of the acts of others. The fact that these duties relate to the conduct of third parties raises the concerns discussed above.[140] Once a duty is recognized, however, the ordinary elements of the cause of action for negligence must be applied.

B. Responsibility for Injuries Caused by Strangers

In addition to these defined relationships, an issue of duty which has presented the courts with some difficulty arises in those cases where the defendant's wrongful conduct has afforded a *stranger* the opportunity or means to injure the plaintiff. Under what circumstances does an individual owe a duty to protect third parties from being harmed by strangers; i.e., by persons who are in no antecedent relationship with the defendant?

This problem is illustrated by the case of *Stansbie v. Troman*.[141] A decorator, hired by a householder, left the house unlocked when he went out to purchase some material. While he was gone, a thief entered the house and stole some goods. The decorator sued the householder for the cost of his services, and the householder counterclaimed for the value of the stolen articles.

The court held that the contractual relationship between the parties "imposed a duty on the plaintiff to take reasonable care with regard to the state of the premises if he left them during the performance of his work."[142] Having established the duty, the court held that the house was left unlocked for an unreasonable length of time. These findings naturally led to the conclusion that the damage caused by the thief, though the criminal act of an independent party, was the direct result of the decorator's breach and thus his responsibility. Though the court made reference to the problem of *novus actus interveniens* and the statement by Lord Sumner in *Weld-Blundell v. Stephens*[143] that "even though A. is in fault, he is not responsible for injury to C., which B., a stranger to him, deliberately chooses to do," the court quite correctly reasoned that this could not apply to the case where "the very act of negligence itself consisted in the failure to take reasonable care to guard against the very thing that in fact happened." It is quite clear that the policy problem which was in issue in the case, i.e., whether a person can be held responsible for the deliberate acts of a stranger, had been resolved at the duty stage, by applying a contractual responsibility to the decorator. Having decided this, there were no further policy issues, merely factual ones, to resolve.

The same principle was applied in *Canphoto Ltd. v. Aetna Roofing (1965) Ltd.*[144] The plaintiff's property was damaged in an explosion and fire which started from propane equipment owned by the defendants. On the assumption that the

---

139 Chapter 6.

140 Another example is bailment. A bailee has a duty to take reasonable care of the bailor's goods, the standard of care required depending upon the type of bailment. The fact that the goods are damaged or stolen by a third party does not raise a defence of *novus actus*. The issue is simply whether reasonable care was taken in relation to the type of damage that could reasonably have been foreseen. See *Robertson v. Stang* (1987), 38 C.C.L.T. (2d) 62 (B.C. S.C.).

141 [1948] 1 All E.R. 599 (C.A.).

142 *Ibid.*, at 600.

143 [1920] A.C. 956.

144 [1971] 3 W.W.R. 116 (Man. Q.B.).

fire was caused as a result of a stranger meddling with the equipment, could the defendants be held liable? The defence was *novus actus*, but the court correctly rejected it. Where there is a duty to take precautions against the interventions of a third party, there is no issue of *novus actus*. The issue is resolved at the level of duty and breach in these cases, not on the issue of remoteness.[145]

Another illustration of this problem is found in the cases concerning damage caused by drivers of stolen vehicles. Does an owner of a car have a duty to victims of traffic accidents not to allow a criminal to steal the vehicle, which subsequently becomes involved in a traffic accident? If there is a duty, in which circumstances is it breached? Stated in this way, it can be seen that these cases raise problems not of remoteness, but of duty and reasonable care. In *Moore v. Fanning*,[146] for example, the defendant police officer, who left his keys in his police cruiser, was found not liable to victims of an accident involving his stolen vehicle, on the basis that the accident was not reasonably foreseeable. Although not expressed in this way, these victims could be described as unforeseeable, to whom no duty of care was owed. Moreover, the court held that there was no negligence in leaving the keys, since this was in conformity with the orders the defendant had received.[147]

There has been a series of English decisions which have debated the duty issue as it relates to the liability of the defendant for acts of third parties. What is the standard of foreseeability which is required before one can conclude that a duty to take reasonable care to prevent the third party's misconduct was owed? What must be reasonably foreseen?[148]

The debate stems from *dicta* by Lord Reid in *Home Office v. Dorset Yacht Co.*[149] which suggest a more onerous standard of foreseeability in cases where the duty relates to activities of strangers. Lord Reid stated:

---

145 Unless of course the type of injury caused by the stranger was different than the type that could reasonably have been foreseen. Remoteness principles would then apply to cut off the defendant's liability.

146 (1987), 41 C.C.L.T. 67 (Ont. H.C.).

147 The absence of reasonable foreseeability, and hence a duty of care, has exonerated defendants in other cases in which stolen cars have led to losses by plaintiffs. See *A.G. Can. v. LaFlamme*, [1983] 3 W.W.R. 350 (B.C. Co. Ct.) — the defendant owed no duty of care to the plaintiff; *Hewson v. Red Deer* (1977), 146 D.L.R. (3d) 32 (Alta. C.A.) — action dismissed due to lack of reasonable foreseeability; *Spagnolo v. Margesson's Sports Ltd.* (1983), 145 D.L.R. (3d) 381 (Ont. C.A.) — action dismissed as a result of lack of reasonable foreseeability, although the issue was characterized as one of remoteness; *Tong v. Bedwell*, [2002] 6 W.W.R. 327 (Alta. Q.B.)—action dismissed based on lack of negligence and reasonable foreseeability. See also *Hollett v. Coca-Cola Ltd.* (1980), 11 C.C.L.T. 281 (N.S. T.D.), *O'Reilly v. C.*, [1978] 3 W.W.R. 145 (Man. Q.B.), affirmed (1979), 8 C.C.L.T. 188 (Man. C.A.), and *Werbeniuk v. Maynard*, [1994] 7 W.W.R. 704 (Man. Q.C.) for similar results. In *Campiou Estate v. Gladue* (2002), [2003] 4 W.W.R. 536 (Alta. Q.B.), the action was dismissed based on policy, which negated any duty of care owed by the owner of a truck to a passenger injured in a stolen vehicle. One case where liability was found is *Cairns v. General Accident Assurance Co. of Canada*, [1992] O.J. No. 1432 (Gen. Div.).

148 As with the "nervous shock" cases, these cases can be analyzed from either the perspective of duty or remoteness. The duty question, i.e., was the plaintiff a reasonably foreseeable victim of the defendant's negligence, is the same as the remoteness question, i.e., was the type of injury that the plaintiff suffered reasonably foreseeable. That is because in these cases the plaintiff's foreseeability as a victim was defined by only one type of injury. If, on the other hand, the third party could cause different types of harm to the plaintiff, some foreseeable and others not, it would be more useful to break the issues down into two—duty and remoteness.

149 [1970] 2 All E.R. 294 (H.L.).

> . . . where human action forms one of the links between the original wrongdoing of the defendant and the loss suffered by the plaintiff, that action must at least have been something very likely to happen if it is not to be regarded as a novus actus interveniens breaking the chain of causation. I do not think that a mere foreseeable possibility is or should be sufficient, for then the intervening human action can more properly be regarded as a new cause than as a consequence of the original wrongdoing. But if the intervening action was likely to happen I do not think it can matter whether the action was innocent or tortious or criminal.[150]

These *dicta* have been interpreted by some as suggesting that a duty to take care in reference to the acts of other parties can only extend to activities of those parties which were "very likely" to occur.

The first important decision to adopt this interpretation was *Lamb v. London Borough of Camden*.[151] The case concerned damage done to the plaintiff's unoccupied house by squatters. The house became unoccupied because of the defendant council's negligence in replacing water pipes, which resulted in water damage to the foundation of the house. The trial judge held that the damage done by the squatters, although reasonably foreseeable, was not likely, and the action was dismissed.

Different views as to the meaning of Lord Reid's *dicta* in *Home Office* were presented when the case went to the Court of Appeal. Lord Denning rejected both standards of "reasonable foreseeability" and "likely to occur" as being too wide, and held that as a matter of policy, the plaintiff ought to have been required to protect herself from the squatters' damage by purchasing insurance. Oliver L.J.'s view was that "likelihood" was also insufficient and that there may be some circumstances in which "the courts would require a degree of likelihood amounting almost to inevitability before it fixes a defendant with responsibility for the act of a third party over whom he has and can have no control."[152]

The issue came before the Court of Appeal again in *P. Perl (Exporters) Ltd. v. Camden London Borough Council*.[153] The plaintiffs complained that the defendants' negligence allowed strangers to break into their premises and steal their property. Waller L.J., in dismissing the plaintiffs' cases, stated that he agreed with Oliver L.J.'s judgment in *Lamb* that "the foreseeability required to impose a liability for the acts of some independent third party requires a very high degree of foreseeability."[154] Oliver L.J. approached the issue from the perspective of duty and asked, "in what circumstances is a defendant to be held responsible at common law for the independent act of a third person which he knows or ought to know may injure his neighbour?"[155] His Lordship's conclusion was that there is "apart from special relationships, no general duty to avoid or inhibit conduct of third parties which foreseeably may lead to damage."[156] Goff L.J. also approached the issue from the perspective of duty, and agreed that, apart from special situations, there is no duty. One of these special categories includes cases "where the defen-

150 *Ibid.*, at 300. I would reject Lord Reid's characterization of this issue as being one of *novus actus*.
151 [1981] 2 All E.R. 408 (C.A.).
152 *Ibid.*, at 419.
153 [1983] 3 All E.R. 161 (C.A.). See Highley, "Comment" (1985), 43 U. of T. Fac. L. Rev. 136.
154 [1983] 3 All E.R. 161 at 166.
155 *Ibid.*, at 167.
156 *Ibid.*, at 168.

dant presents the wrongdoer with the means to commit the wrong, in circumstances where it is obvious or very likely that he will do so."[157]

The same issue came before the House of Lords in *Smith v. Littlewoods Organisation Ltd.*[158] A fire was started in the defendants' unoccupied cinema and the neighbouring properties were seriously damaged. The Lords again approached the issue from the duty perspective, although there was no consensus on the standard of foreseeability required.[159] The action was dismissed on the basis that a lack of foreseeability prevented there being a duty owed to the plaintiffs.[160]

The view that a higher degree of foreseeability is required when dealing with the acts of third parties was adopted in a British Columbia case, *Robertson v. A. (A.).*[161] A mentally disabled adult who lived in a group home attacked a shopper during an outing at a store. He was with two care workers at the time. The victim of the attack sued the operator of the group home. The court held that when dealing with liability for the acts of a third person "a mere foreseeable possibility of risk is insufficient to render a person liable".[162] Rather, there must be "a reasonable foreseeability of a likely risk of harm".[163] Based on this test the operator of the group home was relieved of liability.[164]

This decision illustrates the court's concern when one is being sued for the acts of a third person. I would suggest, however, that in this case this worry was misplaced and developing a different test of foreseeability for it was unnecessary. Unlike the English cases discussed above, the defendant was under an existing

157 *Ibid.*, at 172.

158 [1987] 1 All E.R. 710 (H.L.).

159 Lord Brandon stated that it must be "reasonably foreseeable." Lord Mackay agreed that a high degree of likelihood was necessary in these cases. Lord Goff reiterated the comments he earlier expressed as a member of the Court of Appeal in *P. Perl (Exporters) Ltd. v. Camden London Borough Council*, above, note 153, insisting that there was no general duty.

160 For other cases which discuss the standard of foreseeability where the acts of a third party are involved, see *Knightley v. Johns*, [1982] 1 All E.R. 851 (C.A.); *Ward v. Cannock Chase Dist. Council*, [1985] 3 All E.R. 537 (Ch. D.). In *Bowles v. Johnston, Oliphant, Van Buekenhout & Deans*, [1988] 4 W.W.R. 242 (Man. Q.B.), the court imposed a duty on a solicitor to protect a purchaser of real estate from being defrauded by a scheme of the solicitor's own client. In *Okanagan Exteriors Inc. v. Perth Developments Inc.*, [2002] 3 W.W.R. 224, 10 C.C.L.T. (3d) 298 (B.C. C.A.), additional reasons at (2002), 99 B.C.L.R. (3d) 44 (C.A.), the Court of Appeal affirmed a trial judgment holding the defendant developers liable for a fire started by an unknown third party on their property. The Court of Appeal stated that for a defendant to be liable in such circumstances it must have known that there was a "real" risk of harm that "may" result. The court conceded that this test is "perhaps somewhat more rigorous than the usual test of foreseeability in cases of negligence".

161 (2000), 2 C.C.L.T. (3d) 120 (B.C. S.C.).

162 *Ibid.*, at 130.

163 *Ibid.*

164 The court also held that there was no duty, nor negligent conduct. Also see *C. (C.L.) v. Lions Gate Hospital* (2001), 95 B.C.L.R. (3d) 347 (S.C.), additional reasons at (2002), 2002 CarswellBC 3265 (S.C.), which followed and applied *Robertson*. Another case that applied the requirement of a higher degree of foreseeability is *Harrington (Guardian ad Litem of) v. Harrington* (1998), 55 B.C.L.R. (3d) 305 (S.C.). A young child suffered a brain injury in a daycare facility presumably as a result of being assaulted by someone there. The public trustee, on behalf of the child, sued the child's mother for having left the child in that facility. In addition to finding that the mother was not negligent with respect to her decision to place the child in that facility, the court held that the risk in this case was neither "highly probable nor very likely".

duty to prevent the supervisee from injuring others. The supervisee was not a stranger. The only question was whether the defendant was negligent and the injury that he caused was reasonably foreseeable; i.e., not too remote. In my opinion, the ordinary tests of breach and remoteness were sufficient to deal with the matter.[165]

The issue of the liability for the acts of third parties was highlighted in the case of *Fullowka v. Royal Oak Ventures Inc.*[166] A disturbed person, Roger Warren, murdered nine miners, by setting off a bomb in an underground mine. The incident took place during a protracted and bitter strike. The killed miners were replacement workers. The families of the deceased miners sued a host of parties, including the corporate owner of the mine and several of its officers, the security company hired to provide protection, government officials as well as the government itself, unions, and individual miners. Although the trial judge attributed liability to eight different defendants, the actions against the union, the government, the security company, and one of the striking miners were dismissed by the Court of Appeal.[167] Applying the duty analysis of *Cooper* to the facts of this case, the court held that even if the foreseeability and proximity elements of the duty test were met, policy reasons negated the duty. These policy reasons included the principle of individual autonomy and the general principle that one is only liable for one's own acts.[168] In the absence of a special relationship between the defendants and the deceased miners, which required the defendants to protect them, or a relationship of control between the defendants and the immediate tortfeasor, the court held that an "ancillary" tortfeasor should not be held responsible for the intentional tort of an "immediate" tortfeasor. Since the facts of this case did not support either of those relationships, the actions were dismissed.[169]

(iii) Exacerbation of Original Injuries

The real question of *novus actus interveniens*, as a problem of remoteness, arises in those cases where a breach of a duty of care causes the plaintiff's original injuries, but these injuries are exacerbated by subsequent events involving the plaintiff's conduct, or that of a third party. The issue here is not whether the defendant owed a duty to prevent these subsequent events, but whether by virtue of the original wrongdoing these increased injuries ought to be the defendant's responsibility.

---

165 The defendant's negligence ought to have been judged by the ordinary tests discussed in Chapter 9. In view of the risk of harm and the gravity of the injury, were the steps taken by the defendant to prevent the risk reasonable or not? If not, was the type of injury that was caused by failing to appropriately supervise the third party "reasonably foreseeable", as defined by *Wagon Mound* and subsequent case law?

166 [2005] 5 W.W.R. 420 (N.W.T. S.C.), reversed 2008 NWTCA 4 (N.W.T. C.A.).

167 One of the defendants, namely the owners of the mine, settled with the plaintiffs and abandoned its appeal.

168 Another policy reason raised by the court was that to allow the defendants to be held liable for not having closed down the mine due to threats of violence would be to encourage those threatened to yield to threats and intimidation. As this was not an issue raised by the parties themselves, the court refrained from stating whether it should be a factor in these types of cases.

169 The union had also been held vicariously liable by the trial judge. This decision was reversed as well. See Chapter 16.

This issue has arisen in the case law in a few situations.

A. The "Second Accident" Case

One type of *novus actus* case arises when a plaintiff's injury is exacerbated by what may be called a second accident. The defendant has breached a duty of care owed to the plaintiff, resulting in injury. Further harm is then caused to the plaintiff in a second accident. A true remoteness issue arises: having proved duty, breach and cause, how far should a defendant's liability extend?[170]

In general, the test of *Wagon Mound No. 1*, as modified by the subsequent case law, will be applied to the second accident situation. The question "was the second accident within the risk of harm set into motion by the defendant?" will be approached from the perspective of the test of "reasonable foreseeability."

In *Bradford v. Kanellos*,[171] the defendant, the operator of a restaurant, was sued by a customer who was injured following a fire in the restaurant. The fire was negligently started by an employee, and a fire extinguisher was used to put it out. The fire extinguisher emitted a hissing noise, which one of the other customers mistook for escaping gas. When that customer panicked and shouted out, he caused a stampede in the restaurant which injured the plaintiff. The question whether the defendant ought to be held liable for the injuries caused by the second accident, which in this case was the conduct of the third party which resulted in the stampede, was one of remoteness.[172] The Court of Appeal and the Supreme Court of Canada considered the conduct of the customer which created the second accident as a *novus actus interveniens*. It was an event which could not have been reasonably anticipated, nor fairly to be regarded "as within the risk created by the respondent's negligence." The judges were no doubt concerned with not wanting to penalize the defendant for having utilized one of the best fire extinguishers available by holding him liable for damages caused by the system.[173] As well, the

---

170 Second accident cases also may involve difficult issues of assessment of damages. In this section, we are discussing whether the second accident is legally to be considered as the result of the defendant's wrongdoing. If it is, the defendant is liable for all damages which flow from the second accident, based upon ordinary damage assessment principles. However, the matter may not end there. Even if the second accident is not attributable to the defendant, the court will have to determine how the effects of the second accident affect how the damages from the first accident should be assessed. See, for example, *Dudek v. Li*, [2000] 6 W.W.R. 209 (B.C. C.A.). The fact that the plaintiff was involved in a second motor vehicle accident that was not related to a earlier accident does not mean that the defendant who was responsible for the first accident is no longer liable for the plaintiff's injuries. The court must determine what injuries caused in the first accident persisted even after the second accident. See discussion in Chapter 11.

171 (1971), 18 D.L.R. (3d) 60 (Ont. C.A.), affirmed (1973), 40 D.L.R. (3d) 578 (S.C.C.).

172 It is true that in this case the defendant's negligence did not initially cause any harm to the plaintiff. This does not, however, alter the issue involved in the case. The question in issue is the same: having breached the duty of care owed to his customer by causing the fire, how will his liability be affected by subsequent events over which the defendant had no control?

173 Although it must be emphasized that the negligence and responsibility relate to the fire. If, for example, water used to put out the fire damaged property, liability would follow, despite the reasonableness of this measure.

courts considered the customer's conduct as "idiotic", and thus they decided that it was too remote.[174]

This type of *novus actus* problem also arose in *Beutler v. Beutler*.[175] The defendant motorist negligently drove into a gas meter, which caused a major escape of gas. As a result of the negligently inadequate emergency response by the utilities company, the gas subsequently exploded and caused extensive damage. Was this negligence a *novus actus interveniens*, or was it within the risk of injury set into motion by the defendant motorist's original negligence? The trial judge applied the test of reasonable anticipation and held that the negligence of the utilities company was within the risk of harm set into motion by the defendant motorist.[176]

The same reasoning applies to those cases where the worsening of the plaintiff's original injury is caused by an act of the plaintiff. If the plaintiff's conduct was within the risk set into motion by the defendant, that is, if it was reasonably foreseeable, the defendant will be held responsible for it.[177] Thus, in *Wieland v. Cyril Lord Carpets Ltd.*,[178] the plaintiff's original neck injury made it difficult for her to see properly through her bifocals. As a result she fell while descending stairs and suffered further injuries. The court's principal reason for allowing the plaintiff to recover for these injuries was that they were merely consequences of the foreseeable injuries initially suffered, and thus, as with the extent of injuries, need not have been reasonably foreseeable themselves. The court conceded, however, that if reasonable foreseeability was the test of recovery for these latter injuries, it was foreseeable that the original injury could affect the plaintiff's ability to cope with the vicissitudes of life.[179] The opposite conclusion was reached in *McKew v. Holland*.[180] In this case, where the plaintiff's initial injuries were worsened by his own "unreasonable conduct", the court held that this was a *novus actus interveniens*. Interestingly, Lord Reid did not consider it unforeseeable that a person who suffered from a disability would worsen his condition by acting

174 The dissenting Supreme Court justice, Spence J., considered the conduct to have been "very human," "usual," "utterly foreseeable," and "part of the natural consequence of events leading inevitably to the plaintiff's injury," and therefore not too remote. See 40 D.L.R. (3d) 578 at 582.

175 (1983), 26 C.C.L.T. 229 (Ont. H.C.).

176 Both were held equally at fault for the damages caused in the explosion.

177 The plaintiff may of course be held contributorily negligent.

178 [1969] 3 All E.R. 1006 (Q.B.D.).

179 Difficult issues of proof may arise in these cases. The plaintiff will have to prove the causal connection on the balance of probabilities. If the plaintiff can only show that the initial injuries increased the risk of further complications, but that these might have occurred anyway, the court will either have to dismiss the action or award the plaintiff damages for the increased vulnerability. A similar "second accident" case is *Pauluik v. Paraiso*, [1995] 2 W.W.R. 61 (Man. Q.B.), affirmed [1996] 2 W.W.R. 57 (Man. C.A.). The plaintiff's automobile accident occurred in 1984. In 1988, the plaintiff jarred his neck when he crossed over railway tracks. This aggravated injuries suffered in the first accident, but was not seen by the court as a *novus actus interveniens*. It was a normal part of his job, and not an "unusual or hazardous" activity. Also see *Mills v. Moberg* (1996), 34 C.C.L.T. (2d) 103 (B.C. S.C.).

180 [1969] 3 All E.R. 1621 (H.L.).

unreasonably. However, as a matter of judicial policy, Lord Reid did not think that this should remain the legal responsibility of the original wrongdoer.[181]

B. The Suicide Cases

In addition to being seen as a thin skull problem, the suicide cases have also been analyzed as a problem of *novus actus interveniens*. Where the plaintiff has been injured by the defendant's negligence, can the plaintiff's decision to commit suicide due to an inability to cope with these initial injuries be considered a *novus actus interveniens*?

As discussed above, one approach to the suicide cases has been to distinguish between a suicide directly caused by the wrongdoer's act, in the sense that the accident actually affected the victim's sanity and ability to rationally consider the suicide option, and a suicide which was the deliberate decision of a sane individual. It is evident that, in this area, the policy concerns of the common law with respect to allowing dependants of suicide victims to recover damages frequently have overridden arguments about the reasonable foreseeability of suicides.

It is suggested that where a suicide is the very risk which the careful conduct of the defendant ought to have prevented, the use of *novus actus interveniens* to deny recovery is inappropriate.[182] If the claims of the dependents of suicide victims are to be rejected in these cases, this can only be based upon a frank admission that to allow such claims would be contrary to judicial policy.[183] As I have argued

---

181 This decision is questionable, and certainly, in view of contributory negligence legislation, is not consistent with those other cases which hold that despite the negligence of other parties, an original wrongdoer can still be found liable, as a co-tortfeasor, for subsequent injuries. See, e.g., *Beutler v. Beutler*, above, note 175. A similar case is *Penno v. Stephanian* (2002), [2002] B.C.J. No. 362, 2002 CarswellBC 372 (S.C.), although in this case the court also held that there was no connection between the plaintiff's initial injuries and her subsequent accident. In *Larsen v. Wilson* (2007), 49 C.C.L.T. (3d) 88 (B.C. S.C.), the plaintiff was injured in a motor vehicle accident. While involved in a rehabilitation exercise program, the plaintiff injured herself. Her injury was not connected in any way to the injuries originally suffered. Despite this, the trial court held that she could recover from the defendant motorist. The rehabilitation program and hence the injury suffered in it "was a foreseeable consequence of the motor vehicle accident", according to the trial judge.

182 See *Funk v. Clapp* (1986), 68 D.L.R. (4th) 229 (B.C. C.A.). Seaton J.A. concluded that where a suicide was within the risks created by the defendant's negligence, the doctrine of *novus actus interveniens* cannot assist the defendant. The deceased committed suicide while being held in prison. His widow sued the prison authorities. At trial, reported at (1984), 12 D.L.R. (4th) 62 (B.C. S.C.), a nonsuit was granted. This was reversed by the Court of Appeal, and a new trial was ordered at (1986), 68 D.L.R. (4th) 229. The action was dismissed when it again went to trial, and the dismissal was upheld by the Court of Appeal at (1988), 54 D.L.R. (4th) 512. See discussion of *novus actus* in relation to suicide claims in *Corr v. IBC Vehicles*, [2008] UKHL 13 (H.L.).

183 See, e.g., *Robson v. Ashworth* (1985), 33 C.C.L.T. 229 (Ont. H.C.), affirmed (1985), 40 C.C.L.T. 164 (Ont. C.A.). The court rejected a suicide claim on the policy ground that the deceased ought to be considered personally responsible for his own act. In *Holan Estate v. Stanton Regional Health Board* (2002), 11 C.C.L.T. (3d) 34 (N.W.T. S.C.), an action brought by the relatives of a psychiatric patient who committed suicide against the hospital was dismissed due to lack of negligence on the hospital's part. This is of course a perfectly legitimate finding. Negligence of course must be established, but once it is the fact that the injury was a suicide should not disentitle the claimants.

elsewhere,[184] where a suicide was fairly within the risk created by a defendant's negligence, there are no justifiable reasons of policy to exonerate the negligent defendant and to deprive the beneficiaries of the suicide victim of their compensation.

C. Subsequent Medical Treatment

Whether medical treatment which exacerbates an original injury ought to be considered as a *novus actus interveniens* is an issue which has arisen in several cases. The problem arises when a plaintiff who has been injured in a first accident claims that these injuries have been worsened as a result of medical interventions. Is the defendant who caused the original injuries liable for this additional damage? The traditional approach is illustrated in the case of *Mercer v. Gray*.[185] This case held that medical treatment which is so negligent as to be actionable against the doctor, as opposed to mere medical complications, misadventure or *bona fide* medical error, is a *novus actus interveniens*. The court held that if a person injured in an accident uses reasonable care to employ a competent physician, and the results of that treatment are unsuccessful, even though by an error, that the increased damages are a proper head of damages. The court did not explain why the case would be different with treatment which was so negligent as to be actionable. This decision was upheld by the Ontario Court of Appeal in *Papp v. Leclerc*,[186] although the court held that the burden of proving that the intervening medical act was negligent, and hence was a *novus actus interveniens*, fell on the original wrongdoer.

The *Mercer v. Gray* approach is out of step with the modern approach to apportion when there are several concurrent acts of negligence and not to relieve one wrongdoer of liability merely because other wrongdoers are involved. Since the original wrongdoer will have the opportunity to collect contribution from the negligent doctor, even if initially required to compensate the plaintiff in full, no injustice would result by discarding the *Mercer v. Gray* approach and considering all errors of treatment, whether actionable against the doctor or not, as falling within the risk of injury set into motion by the first defendant. As well, the argument that medical errors which fall short of negligence are reasonably foreseeable risks, but that negligent acts are not, is not a persuasive one. This is particularly so when one considers that the negligent acts of other intervening actors, who are not doctors, have frequently been regarded to be within the original wrongdoer's responsibility. These factors seem to be leading to an abandonment of the *Mercer v. Gray* approach. In *Katzman v. Yaeck*,[187] the Ontario Court of Appeal reversed the decision of the trial judge, who had struck out a third party

---

184 See Klar, "Negligence — Reactions Against Alleged Excessive Imposition of Liability — A Turning Point" (1987), 66 Can. Bar Rev. 159 at 162.

185 [1941] 3 D.L.R. 564 (Ont. C.A.). See also *David v. Toronto Transit Comm.* (1976), 77 D.L.R. (3d) 717 (Ont. C.A.).

186 (1977), 77 D.L.R. (2d) 536. Also see *Thompson v. Toorenburgh* (1972), 29 D.L.R. (3d) 608 (B.C. S.C.), affirmed (1973), 50 D.L.R. (3d) 717 (B.C. C.A.), which was affirmed (1973), 50 D.L.R. (3d) 717n (S.C.C.).

187 (1982), 136 D.L.R. (3d) 536 (Ont. C.A.).

notice brought by a defendant motorist against a dentist. The defendant alleged that the dentist's negligence had exacerbated the plaintiff's original injuries. The trial judge had followed *Mercer v. Gray* and held that if the dentist had been negligent, this would in law constitute a *novus actus* and the defendant motorist would not be responsible for these aggravated injuries.[188] The Court of Appeal held that the law was "far from clear with respect to this matter"[189] and sent the issue back to trial. As I have argued elsewhere,[190] this decision means that, as a matter of law, negligent intervening medical treatment is no longer to be treated as *novus actus interveniens*.[191]

There is no reason to treat negligent medical acts differently than other intervening acts of negligence. The *Mercer v. Gray* approach ought to be abandoned.

5. THE DUTY TO RESCUERS

An issue which is frequently treated as one of remoteness[192] is the liability of a tortfeasor for injuries suffered by a rescuer. If a negligent individual is either personally imperilled, or imperils someone else, and as a result a third person attempts a rescue and is injured, is the negligent individual liable to the rescuer for these injuries?

The authorities are clear that a rescue attempt is a reasonably foreseeable occurrence in a perilous situation and that, therefore, an injured rescuer has a right to sue the person who created the peril.[193] There are a few important quali-

---

188 If the dentist, on the other hand, was not negligent, the indemnity claim would also fail. Thus, whether the dentist was negligent or not, the logic of *Mercer v. Gray* was to disallow the third party notice.

189 (1982), 136 D.L.R. (3d) 536 at 541.

190 Klar, "Recent Developments in Canadian Law: Tort Law" (1985), 17 Ottawa L. Rev. 325 at 374.

191 It is still, of course, open to the courts to find, based on the facts, that specific intervening medical treatment is a *novus actus interveniens*. Earlier cases which either questioned or departed from the *Mercer v. Gray* approach are *Watson v. Grant* (1970), 72 W.W.R. 665 (B.C. S.C.); *Kolesar v. Jeffries* (1974), 9 O.R. (2d) 41 (H.C.), varied (1976), 12 O.R. (2d) 142 (C.A.), which was affirmed (*sub nom. Joseph Brant Memorial Hosp. v. Koziol*) (1978), 2 C.C.L.T. 170 (S.C.C.), and *Price v. Milawski* (1977), 82 D.L.R. (3d) 130 (Ont. C.A.). These cases did not deal directly with the problem. In *Watson v. Grant*, the issue was left open. In *Kolesar v. Jeffries*, the court stated that it was following *Mercer v. Gray*, although the actual decision was inconsistent with it. In *Price v.Milawski*, the court was dealing with a sequence of negligent acts by defendant doctors. See also *Law Estate v. Simice* (1994), 21 C.C.L.T. (2d) 228 (B.C. S.C.), affirmed (December 12, 1995), Doc. CA018888 (B.C. C.A.), where several negligent doctors were held liable. The issue of whether subsequent negligent treatment should relieve earlier negligent treatment of liability is not discussed in these types of cases.

192 Although it is probably better seen as a duty question.

193 The leading authorities are *Videan v. Br. Tpt. Comm.*, [1963] 2 Q.B. 650 (C.A.); *Horsley v. MacLaren*, [1972] S.C.R. 441; *Moddejong v. Huron County Bd. of Educ.*, [1972] 2 O.R. 437 (H.C.); *Corothers v. Slobodian*, [1975] 2 S.C.R. 633; and *Wagner v. Int. Ry. Co.*, 133 N.E. 437 (N.Y., 1921), among others. The general principles were reaffirmed in *White v. Chief Constable of South Yorkshire Police*, [1997] 1 All E.R. 540 (H.L.). *Corothers v. Slobodian* was applied in *Roberts v. Morana* (1997), 38 C.C.L.T. (2d) 1 (Ont. Gen. Div.), additional reasons at (1997), 37 O.R. (3d) 333 (Gen. Div.), additional reasons at (1997), 37 O.R. (3d) 333 at 342 (Gen. Div.), additional reasons at (1998), 37 O.R. (3d) 333 at 353 (Gen. Div.), affirmed (2000), 2 C.C.L.T. (3d) 247 (Ont. C.A.), affirmed (2000), 2 C.C.L.T. (3d) 248 (Ont. C.A.). In *Dufault v. Excelsior Mortgage Corp.* (2002), [2002] A.J. No. 453, 310 A.R. 117

fications. The first is that the situation of peril must have been brought about as a result of the defendant's negligence. This was a critical issue in the leading Canadian case on rescue, *Horsley v. MacLaren.*[194] When one of the guests on a pleasure craft fell overboard, the host operator attempted to rescue him. Since the rescue manoeuvre seemed inept, a second guest dove into the water to try to rescue the first. This was followed by yet another rescue attempt, when a third guest dove into the cold waters to rescue the previous one. In the end, both the original guest and the first rescuer were drowned. In the action brought by the first rescuer's estate against the boat operator, the decisive issue was whether the boat operator had a duty to rescue the first passenger, who fell overboard, and if so whether this duty had been negligently performed. The majority of the Supreme Court conceded that the defendant had a duty to rescue the passenger, but did not agree with the trial judge, or the dissenting judges, that this duty had been negligently performed. Thus the subsequent rescue attempts, not having been induced by the defendant's negligence, were not his responsibility.

Although the rescue attempt must have been induced by the defendant's negligence in creating the peril, this does not mean that the victim who is the object of the rescue need also have a viable cause of action against the defendant. There may be no cause of action due to an available defence,[195] there may have been no duty owed,[196] or, in the most obvious case, the object of the rescue may be the negligent person.[197] In *C.N.R. v. Bakty*,[198] for example, the defendant motorist, who was injured when he negligently drove his car into a train, was liable to the conductor on the train for the back injury which the latter suffered while assisting the injured defendant.

The cases have outlined the characteristics of a suitable rescue attempt. It need not necessarily be successful; in fact, it may have been futile from the outset.[199] As long as the rescue attempt was not "reckless and foolhardy",[200] it remains within the risk set into motion by the wrongdoer. There must, however, be a situation of peril; i.e., a real risk of injury to potential victims or an effort to assist those who have already been hurt. Thus, pushing a vehicle which has run out of gas from stationary traffic to the side of the road has been held not to

---

(Q.B.), affirmed (2003), 17 C.C.L.T. (3d) 280 (Alta. C.A.), leave to appeal refused (2003), 2003 CarswellAlta 1779 (S.C.C.), the plaintiff, who was a guest at the defendant's hotel, was injured in a fight with a gang of youths. The youths had been threatening the desk clerk and the plaintiff intervened to protect him. The court held that the security provisions in place by the hotel to guard against such incidents were inadequate. Murray J. held that the hotel was in breach of its duties to the plaintiff under the Occupiers Liability Act, R.S.A. 1980, c. 0-3. In addition, its negligence placed its desk clerk in peril and the plaintiff was a rescuer who was entitled to be compensated for his injuries as such. There was neither willing assumption of risk nor contributory negligence on the plaintiff's part. The judgment was affirmed by the Alberta Court of Appeal, with one dissent.

194 *Ibid.*

195 Such as *volenti*, which might have been possible in *Horsley v. MacLaren* had the original victim's estate sued.

196 For example, in *Videan v. Br. Tpt. Comm.*, above, note 193, where the victim was a trespasser.

197 This is stated by Laskin J. in his dissent in *Horsley v. MacLaren*, although it of course was *obiter*.

198 (1977), 18 O.R. (2d) 481 (Co. Ct.).

199 For example, in *Horsley v. MacLaren*, the victim probably died on impact with the cold water.

200 See the judgment of Linden J. in *Cleary v. Hansen* (1981), 18 C.C.L.T. 147 at 155 (Ont. H.C.).

constitute a rescue since the vehicle was posing no danger or imminent peril to users of the road.[201] More troublesome is the question of contributory negligence. Can a rescue attempt be sufficiently unreasonable so as to allow a finding of contributory negligence on the rescuer's part, but not so unreasonable as to qualify as being reckless and foolhardy? In *Cleary v. Hansen*,[202] a rescuer was found to be contributorily negligent in the way in which the rescue attempt was managed.[203]

An interesting question relates to the right of the professional rescuer. Should a fire fighter, police officer, or other person whose job it is to rescue, have a right to sue the negligent party responsible for the initial emergency? In *Ogwo v. Taylor*,[204] Lord Bridge rejected the argument that a professional fireman should not be entitled to sue a tortfeasor who was responsible for setting the fire, unless his injuries arose from an exceptional or unusual risk. As long as the fireman was exercising his proper duties and acting skillfully, his remedy would be the same as for all other rescuers. Their Lordships rejected the so-called "fireman's rule", adopted in some American cases,[205] which would, for policy reasons, deny an action to firemen or other professional rescuers.[206] Numerous reasons are given in the American jurisprudence in support of the rule. The main one is based on the principle of voluntary assumption of risk, although this by itself is insufficient to distinguish the professional rescuer from the pure volunteer. More important is the fact that professional rescuers are paid from public funds to confront known hazards. Presumably, their wage level reflects the hazards of their occupation and takes into account the possibility of an injury. Further, they may be entitled to more than normal compensation and other benefits should they be injured in the line of duty.[207] Although there are no Canadian authorities directly on point, it has been held that the defence of voluntary assumption of risk does not apply to police and other professionals who are injured on the job.[208] The argument,

---

201 See *Smith v. Tucker* (2007), 47 C.C.L.T. (3d) 150 (B.C. S.C.) The plaintiff was injured while pushing the vehicle.

202 *Ibid.*

203 Linden J. noted other cases where self-rescuers, i.e., people trying to save themselves or their property, were found to have been contributorily negligent. See *Sayers v. Harlow Urban Dist. Council*, [1958] 2 All E.R. 342 (C.A.); *Holomis v. Dubuc* (1974), 56 D.L.R. (3d) 351 (B.C. S.C.), and *Toy v. Argenti*, [1980] 3 W.W.R. 276 (B.C. S.C.).

204 [1987] 3 All E.R. 961 (H.L.).

205 See *Krauth v. Geller*, 157 A. 2d 129 (N.J., 1960); *Walters v. Sloan*, 20 Cal. 3d 199 (1977). There have been many commentaries on the "fireman's rule." See, for example, Peltz, "The Transformation of the 'Fireman's Rule'." (1987), 17 Stetson L. Rev. 137; Cahill and Zeeb, "Abolishing Tort Immunities in Oregon . . ." (1985), 21 Willamette L. Rev. 349; Lovell, "Fireman's Rule" (1985-86), 34 Drake L. Rev. 1109; Brown, "Oregon Abolishes the Fireman's Rule" (1985), 19 Suffolk U.L. Rev. 957; Werner, "The Fireman's Rule Burns Police Officers" (1984-85), 37 Rutgers L. Rev. 195.

206 This position was reaffirmed by the House of Lords in *White v. Chief Constable of South Yorkshire Police* (1998), [1999] 1 All E.R. 1 (H.L.). The Lords made it clear that it was rejecting the claims of the police for psychiatric damage not because of the "fireman's rule" but because they did not qualify for compensation on the application of the ordinary principles.

207 For a refutation of these arguments, see Tobriner J.'s dissenting judgment in *Walters v. Sloan*, above, note 205.

208 See, e.g., *Hambley v. Shepley* (1967), 63 D.L.R. (2d) 94 (Ont. C.A.). This case concerned the deliberate injuring of a policeman by the defendant, who was attempting to escape arrest. This is clearly different from the typical rescue problem.

however, that tort litigation is not an appropriate economic response to the problem of compensation for public rescuers is, in my opinion, persuasive.

The common law's indulgence of rescuers[209] illustrates its curious ambivalence towards the values of individual and communal responsibility. Although there is no duty to assist or rescue, since the law believes that an individual is free to choose, there is liability to rescuers, since "peril invites rescue." The fact that consent is not a defence in actions brought by rescuers, on the ground that the rescuer had really no choice, is somewhat inconsistent with the common law's insistence that everyone does have a free choice whether to assist or not. One may also contrast the common law's different attitudes towards rescuers and suicide victims. Although suicides which are the deliberate acts of sane persons are seen as the individual responsibility of the victim, and not the responsibility of those who negligently precipitated the decision, the deliberate acts of rescuers are treated differently. One can readily see how policy and the courts' attitudes towards these events are shaping the laws in these areas.

---

209 It is interesting to note how liberally this word is defined. In *Urbanski v. Patel* (1978), 84 D.L.R. (3d) 650 (Man. Q.B.), for example, a father who donated his kidney to his daughter was treated as a rescuer for the purpose of compensation from the wrongdoer. In *Bechard v. Haliburton Estate* (1991), 10 C.C.L.T. (2d) 156 (Ont. C.A.), a person who was attempting to warn an oncoming driver that a motorcyclist lay injured on the road was considered to be analogous to a rescuer. She was able to recover for her nervous shock caused when the oncoming driver ignored her warnings and ran over the motorcyclist. In *Bridge v. Jo* (1998), [1999] 3 W.W.R. 167 (B.C. S.C.), a plaintiff who slipped on icy pavement while returning to her house from the scene of an accident in order to phone "911" was held to be a rescuer. In *Schlink v. Blackburn* (1993), 18 C.C.L.T. (2d) 173 (B.C. C.A.), reversing [1992] 4 W.W.R. 251 (B.C. S.C.), however, a man, who upon hearing that his wife had been involved in an accident, ran down the stairs, fell, and broke a bone, was denied recovery by the Court of Appeal. The court disagreed with the Chambers Judge's decision that the man had been a rescuer. In *Saccone v. Fandrakis* (2002), 11 C.C.L.T. (3d) 151 (B.C. S.C.), the plaintiff saw, from a distance, that his parked car might have been hit by a van. He thought that the driver of the van was going to leave the scene. He accordingly ran down the street to the car but injured his leg on the way. The plaintiff apparently was concerned that if the driver left the scene, his insurance recovery would be affected. The court dismissed the plaintiff's claim that he should be compensated for his leg injury as a rescuer of his property. It referred to previous cases where persons were injured in emergencies while trying to protect property, but distinguished this case from them. A most unusual case is *Turvey v. Wilkins*, [1994] O.J. No. 3074 (Small Claims Ct.). The plaintiff, a drunk owner of a truck, asked the defendant, his friend, to drive him home. The defendant drove negligently and damaged the truck. The plaintiff sued for damages. The court conceded that while the defendant was partly responsible for the damage, the defendant, by driving the plaintiff home, was "rescuing" the plaintiff and should be partly reimbursed for the costs of the rescue, i.e. the judgment obtained against him for his negligent driving!

13

Defences to the Negligence Action and Apportionment Issues

1. INTRODUCTION

Having established the required elements of a negligence action, the plaintiff will be entitled to full compensation for the injuries suffered, unless the defendant can succeed in establishing one of the few available defences. In this respect, there is no doubt that the partial defence of contributory negligence is the most significant. Two other defences to the negligence action can be raised; they are the defence of *volenti non fit injuria* and the defence of illegality, otherwise known as *ex turpi causa non oritur actio*. These, however, have a limited use. This chapter will examine these three defences.

Topics related to the defence of contributory negligence are those of multiple wrongdoing and apportionment of liability. These will also be examined in this chapter.

2. CONTRIBUTORY NEGLIGENCE[1]

(a) Contributory Negligence Defined

Contributory negligence can be defined as unreasonable conduct on the part of a victim which, along with the negligence of others, has in law contributed to the victim's own injuries.[2] It is based on the principle that one has a duty not only to take reasonable care to prevent injury to others, but to oneself as well.

---

1 See generally Glanville Williams, *Joint Torts and Contributory Negligence* (1951); Cheifetz, *Apportionment of Fault in Tort* (1981); Klar, "Contributory Negligence and Contribution Between Tortfeasors", Chapter 5, in Klar (ed.), *Studies in Canadian Tort Law* (1977); Alberta Institute of Law Research, *Contributory Negligence and Concurrent Wrongdoers*, Report No. 31, 1979; Ontario Law Reform Commission, *Report on Contribution Among Wrongdoers and Contributory Negligence*, 1988; New Zealand Law Commission, *Apportionment of Civil Liability*, No. 47, 1998.

2 For a good discussion of what contributory negligence is, see Gravells, "Three Heads of Contributory Negligence" (1977), 93 L.Q.R. 581.

Although this principle seems simple and sound, certain basic propositions ought to be emphasized, since they have occasionally been misunderstood. When considering the defence of contributory negligence, it is not correct to think in terms of a duty of care owed by a victim to a wrongdoer. Victims owe no duty to wrongdoers to prevent the latter from causing them injury; rather, victims owe the duty to themselves.[3] In *Froom v. Butcher*,[4] Lord Denning M.R. stated this clearly:

> Negligence depends on breach of duty, whereas contributory negligence does not. Negligence is a man's carelessness in breach of duty to *others*. Contributory negligence is a man's carelessness in looking after *his own* safety. He is guilty of *contributory* negligence if he ought reasonably to have foreseen that, if he did not act as a reasonably prudent man, he might hurt himself . . .[5]

The reasons why the common law of torts imposes such a duty of care on plaintiffs themselves parallel the reasons why defendants must take reasonable care for the protection of others. Justice, deterrence, and education goals are thought to be achieved or fostered through this defence. The existence of the defence also clearly indicates that tort law's principal objective is not to compensate disabled victims as would a social insurance or welfare program. Compensation is the remedy available when the fault components have been satisfied.

Having accepted that tort law imposes a duty of care on plaintiffs for their own protection, what standard of care will be required in order for them to discharge it? In theory, the standard will be set on the same bases as it is for the duty owed by defendants to plaintiffs.[6] Thus, concepts such as the reasonable person, unreasonable risk, sudden emergencies, general practice, and statutory breach which, as we have seen, are relevant in considering the nature of the duty owed by defendants will be equally important here.

In practice, however, the courts tend to take a more forgiving attitude towards the faults of plaintiffs. This can be explained primarily by considering the effects of a finding of contributory negligence. A finding of contributory negligence will reduce the plaintiff's compensation, and will thus work against the compensation and loss distribution goals of contemporary negligence law. Since liability, rather than first party, insurance is more common, finding a plaintiff contributorily negligent will not only reduce the immediate compensation benefits, but as well, it will be unlikely that these losses will be made up by insurance benefits. Another factor underlying a lenient attitude towards plaintiffs may be the individualistic orientation of some common law courts. It is one thing to demand appropriate behaviour from defendants in view of the dangers that careless individuals present to innocent others. To require that plaintiffs take care for their own protection, and to set the standard at too high a level, suggests to some courts an unwarranted

---

3 As held in *Milroy v. Toronto Dominion Bank* (1997), 35 C.C.L.T. (2d) 37 (Ont. Gen. Div.), a plaintiff does not have a duty to ensure that the defendant does his duty. There will be a duty to mitigate damages, but this is separate from the defence of contributory negligence.

4 [1975] 3 W.L.R. 379 (C.A.).

5 *Ibid.*, at 383. Also see Linden J., in *Bell Can. v. COPE (Sarnia) Ltd.* (1980), 11 C.C.L.T. 170 at 179 (Ont. H.C.), affirmed (1981), 15 C.C.L.T. 190 (Ont. C.A.). For an apparently contrary view see Mr. Justice Ritchie's judgment in *Carl B. Potter Ltd. v. Mercantile Bank of Can.* (1980), 112 D.L.R. (3d) 88 (S.C.C.). For a case comment see Klar, "Developments in Tort Law: The 1979-80 Term" (1981), 2 Sup. Ct. L. Rev. 342.

6 See Chapter 9.

intervention in the freedom of action of individuals. This sentiment is, however, misplaced. The defence of contributory negligence does not require plaintiffs to do anything that they do not want to do, provided of course that they are prepared to assume part of the responsibility for the adverse results of their decisions.

It must also be stressed that in considering the defence of contributory negligence, either at common law or by statute, what is relevant is whether the plaintiff's negligence contributed to the injuries, and not whether it contributed to the original accident. As pointed out by one commentator,[7] this can happen in one of three ways. The plaintiff's negligence may (1) contribute to the accident itself, (2) consist in the plaintiff's self-exposure to a risk of involvement in an accident,[8] or (3) consist in the failure to take precautions to prevent or minimize possible injuries should an accident occur.[9] All three examples of a plaintiff's carelessness can lead to a defence of contributory negligence.[10]

(b) Contributory Negligence at Common Law

At common law if a plaintiff was found negligent, however slightly, and this negligence was a proximate cause of the injury, there was no recourse against a negligent defendant. This rule was expressed in *Butterfield v. Forrester*,[11] by Lord Ellenborough C.J.:

> One person being in fault will not dispose with another's using ordinary care for himself. Two things must concur to support this action, an obstruction in the road by the fault of the defendant, and no want of ordinary care to avoid it on the part of the plaintiff.[12]

Underlying the rule was the refusal of the courts to come to the assistance of wrongdoers by allowing the common law of torts to relieve them from consequences caused in part by themselves.

The harshness of the common law rule was ameliorated by another rule, that of "last clear chance." Stemming from the case of *Davies v. Mann*,[13] this had the effect of allowing a negligent victim recovery, as long as it could be shown that the defendant might have by the exercise of reasonable care, avoided causing the injury.

Both common law rules were wanting. The "stalemate solution"[14] excessively punished a negligent plaintiff, and too generously treated the negligent defen-

---

7 Gravells, above, note 2.

8 For example, going into a car with a drunk driver — *Robinson v. Williams Estate* (2005), 34 C.C.L.T. (3d) 131 (Alta. Q.B.), additional reasons at (2005), 39 C.C.L.T. (3d) 213 (Alta. Q.B.), affirmed (2007), 44 C.C.L.T. (3d) 1 (Alta. C.A.); or driving with a person who was drinking coffee, knowing that he frequently coughed and choked on his coffee — *Barron v. Barron* (2003), 16 C.C.L.T. (3d) 93 (N.S. S.C.).

9 For example, failing to wear a seat belt. See discussion below.

10 This is generally accepted by the courts. Occasionally, however, judges have held that in order to be contributory negligence, the negligent conduct must have contributed to the accident. See, e.g., Angers J.A.'s judgment in *Bulmer v. Horsman* (1987), 42 C.C.L.T. 220 (N.B. C.A.). This is incorrect. Negligence law focuses not on accidents, but injuries caused by accidents.

11 (1809), 103 E.R. 926 (K.B.).

12 *Ibid.*, at 927. The case involved a plaintiff who was injured when he was thrown off his horse, as a result of an obstruction left on the road by the defendant. The jury dismissed the action because the plaintiff had been negligent in the manner in which he had been riding his horse.

13 (1842), 152 E.R. 588.

14 See Fleming, *The Law of Torts*, 9th ed. (1998), at 303.

dant.[15] The "last clear chance" doctrine forced a court into a hopeless causal inquiry in order to counter the contributory negligence bar.

Every common law province in Canada has adopted contributory negligence apportionment legislation which has replaced the common law.[16] Although this legislation has brought with it many new problems, at least one thing is clear. The common law's all or nothing approach is now only of historical interest.[17]

(c) Contributory Negligence Legislation

(i) Introduction

Despite differences in wording, every common law province has adopted some form of contributory negligence legislation which performs one principal function. Plaintiffs are entitled to recover damages from wrongdoers who have injured them, despite the victims' own negligence in contributing to their injuries. The "stalemate solution" has been replaced by the principle of apportionment of liability based upon fault.

The legislative provisions which permit the defence of contributory negligence, and the consequent apportionment between plaintiff and defendant(s), are found in contributory negligence statutes.[18] Although the wording of these statutes varies somewhat, the intention of all provisions is the same. In Alberta, for example, the relevant section is found in s. 1(1) of the Contributory Negligence Act,[19] which states:

> When by fault of 2 or more persons damage or loss is caused to one of them, the liability to make good the damage or loss is in proportion to the degree in which each person was at fault but if, having regard to all the circumstances of the case, it is not possible to establish different degrees of fault, the liability shall be apportioned equally.

The Ontario provisions, on the other hand, found in the Negligence Act,[20] ss. 3 and 4, state:

---

15 In *Bow Valley Husky (Bermuda) Ltd. v. Saint John Shipbuilding Ltd.* (1997), 153 D.L.R. (4th) 385 (S.C.C.), McLachlin J. used a causation rationale to explain the bar. The tortfeasor could not be said to have caused the damage where it was partly due to the plaintiff's own fault. The case involved maritime law to which the contributory negligence legislation did not apply. The Supreme Court decided to overrule the common law stalemate rule and apportion even in maritime cases. This change was deemed appropriate in view of "the modern view of fairness and justice", which underlines apportionment. The court also held that contrary to the old common law rule there can, for the same reasons, be contribution between tortfeasors.

16 Contributory Negligence Act, R.S.A. 2000, c. C-27; Negligence Act, R.S.B.C. 1996, c. 333; Contributory Negligence Act, R.S.N. 1990, c. C-33; Contributory Negligence Act, R.S.P.E.I. 1988, c. C-21; Contributory Negligence Act, R.S.S. 1978, c. C-31; Negligence Act, R.S.O. 1990, c. N.1; Tortfeasors and Contributory Negligence Act, R.S.M. 1987, c. T90 (also C.C.S.M., c. T90); Contributory Negligence Act, R.S.N.S. 1989, c. 95; Contributory Negligence Act, R.S.N.B. 1973, c. C-19. There is also legislation in the territories; see the Contributory Negligence Act, R.S.N.W.T. 1988, c. C-18; Contributory Negligence Act, R.S.Y. 1986, c. 32 (s. 7, repealed by Spousal Tort Immunity Abolition Act, S.Y. 1998, c. 25, s. 2).

17 Equally in maritime cases; see note 15 above.

18 Six of the provinces have one statute dealing with both contributory negligence and contribution between tortfeasors. Three provinces — Alberta, New Brunswick, and Nova Scotia — have two statutes, one dealing primarily with contributory negligence, and the other with contribution between wrongdoers. See Tort-Feasors Act, R.S.A. 2000, c. T-5; Tortfeasors Act, R.S.N.B. 1973, c. T-8; Tortfeasors Act, R.S.N.S. 1989, c. 471.

19 R.S.A. 2000, c. C-27.

20 R.S.O. 1990, c. N.1.

3. In any action for damages that is founded upon the fault or negligence of the defendant if fault or negligence is found on the part of the plaintiff that contributed to the damages, the court shall apportion the damages in proportion to the degree of fault or negligence found against the parties respectively.

4. If it is not practicable to determine the respective degree of fault or negligence as between any parties to an action, such parties shall be deemed to be equally at fault or negligent.

These provisions are comparable to those found in the other common law provinces.[21]

The courts and commentators have raised several questions with respect to these provincial statutes.

(ii) Scope of the Statutory Defence

One of the interesting problems of interpretation of the contributory negligence provisions has been determining their scope.[22] Ordinarily, the defence of contributory negligence is raised in the context of an action for negligence. Can a defendant, however, who has not been sued for negligence, but for some other tort, or even for some other cause of action, such as breach of contract or breach of trust, utilize the contributory negligence legislation in defence?

The source of the problem is both terminological and conceptual. As noted above, the legislative provisions use the terms fault, or negligence, to determine when there shall be apportionment, without, however, defining these terms. Do these terms restrict the defence of contributory negligence to the action for negligence? As a matter of policy, should these words be broadly interpreted, allowing the defence of contributory negligence even in those actions which do not have an equivalent common law defence?

To restrict the contributory negligence defence to actions in negligence and exclude it from other tort actions which are based on a defendant's negligent conduct would be to place too narrow an interpretation on the legislation, and has rightly been resisted. The defence of contributory negligence has been applied, on several occasions, to the negligent forms of trespass.[23] It has also been applied

---

21 The Alberta-type wording is found in the legislation of British Columbia, New Brunswick, Newfoundland, Nova Scotia, Prince Edward Island, and Saskatchewan. Manitoba's wording is slightly different. Section 4 reads:

> Contributory negligence by a plaintiff is not a bar to the recovery of damages by him and in any action for damages that is founded upon the negligence of the defendant, if negligence is found on the part of the plaintiff which contributed to the damages, the court shall apportion the damages in proportion to the degree of negligence found against the plaintiff and defendant respectively.

22 See Crocker, "Apportionment of Liability and the Intentional Torts: The Time Is Right for Change" (1982), 7 Dalhousie L.J. 172; Sullivan, "Trespass to the Person in Canada: A Defence of the Traditional Approach" (1987), 19 Ottawa L. Rev. 533.

23 See, e.g., *Verbrugge v. Bush*, [1976] W.W.D. 79 (B.C. S.C.); *Teece v. Honeybourn* (1974), 54 D.L.R. (3d) 549 (B.C. S.C.); and *Bell Canada v. COPE (Sarnia) Ltd.* (1980), 11 C.C.L.T. 170 (Ont. H.C.), affirmed (1981), 15 C.C.L.T. 190 (Ont. C.A.). See also *Rabideau v. Maddocks* (1992), 12 O.R. (3d) 83 (Gen. Div.) where the term "fault" was interpreted to include negligence and intentional torts. See *contra, Hollebone v. Barnard*, [1954] O.R. 236 (H.C.). Wells J.'s judgment in *Hollebone v. Barnard*, which denied the applicability of the Ontario Negligence Act to even negligent trespassess, was the stumbling block to a wider use of the defence for many years. For a criticism of the reasons in the judgment, see Sullivan, above, note 22. One of the arguments made by Sullivan is that the assumption that contributory negligence was not

to an action in nuisance, where the gist of the defendant's liability was its negligent conduct.[24] These decisions are correct. The statutes do not restrict apportionment to the action in negligence, but even on a literal reading are broader than that.[25]

Where the plaintiff's tort action is based not on the fault or negligence of the defendant, but on intentional or deliberate wrongdoing, the issue of the defence's applicability becomes more difficult. In these cases, not only must the courts construe the words "fault" or "negligence" to include intentional wrongs, but they must also be satisfied that on policy grounds it would be acceptable to reduce the damages awarded against deliberate wrongdoers. However, even here, there are answers to these objections which would argue for the application of the statutes in some cases of intentional wrongdoing. From the perspective of statutory interpretation, the word "fault," as used in the statutes, does not exclude intentional wrongdoing. One might assume that if the defence of contributory negligence were meant to be restricted to actions based only on negligence, the statutes would have used these latter words.[26] Further, a statute such as Ontario's uses both words, "fault or negligence," thus suggesting that the word "fault" encompasses more than merely negligent conduct. This approach was adopted by Mr. Justice Linden in *Bell Canada v. COPE (Sarnia) Ltd.*,[27] where His Lordship stated:

> Fault and negligence, as these words are used in the statute, are not the same thing. Fault certainly includes negligence, but it is much broader than that. Fault incorporates all intentional wrongdoing, as well as other types of substandard conduct. In this case, both intentional and negligent wrongdoing were satisfactorily proved.[28]

Even when the defendant is liable on account of intentional wrongdoing, apportionment, by way of the contributory negligence defence, ought to be an option available to the courts. Whether it will be exercised will depend on the circumstances of the case. In *Berntt v. Vancouver (City)*,[29] for example, a trial court judge found the defendant police officer liable for intentionally firing an anti-riot

---

a defence to trespass actions at common law was a wrong one. As authority she cites *Knapp v. Salsbury* (1810), 170 E.R. 1231. See, however, Hudson, "Contributory Negligence as a Defence to Battery" (1984), 4 Leg. Stud. 332, for the view that contributory negligence was not available at common law as a defence to a battery.

24 *Koch Indust. Ltd. v. Vancouver*, [1982] 4 W.W.R. 92 (B.C. S.C.).

25 The court may not recognize that the action is one of negligent trespass. In *Finnie v. Ropponen* (1987), 40 C.C.L.T. 155 (B.C. S.C.), the court found the defendant golfer negligent for hitting another golfer. The plaintiff was held to have been contributorily negligent for standing where he was and not warning the defendant. The fact that the action was a negligent trespass was not recognized in the judgment.

26 As does, for example, the Manitoba Act, where this argument would accordingly not apply. See *Caners v. Eli Lilly Canada Inc.*, [1996] 5 W.W.R. 381 (Man. C.A.), where based on the fact that the Manitoba act uses the word negligence alone, the Court of Appeal held that the legislation was inapplicable to claims founded on breach of contract.

27 (1980), 11 C.C.L.T. 170 at 180 (Ont. H.C.). Despite the clear *dicta*, it is arguable that the defendant's wrongdoing in this case was not deliberate, but only negligent, thus weakening the strength of this authority. Nevertheless, the statement itself is strong support for a broad application of the defence. The judgment was affirmed on appeal: see (1981), 15 C.C.L.T. 190 (Ont. C.A.).

28 (1980), 11 C.C.L.T. 170 (Ont. H.C.).

29 [1997] 4 W.W.R. 505, 33 C.C.L.T. (2d) 1 (S.C.), reversed (1999), 46 C.C.L.T. (2d) 139 (B.C. C.A.), additional reasons at (1999), [1999] B.C.J. No. 2219, 1999 CarswellBC 2167 (C.A.), action dismissed in new trial (2001), [2001] B.C.J. No. 2658, 2001 CarswellBC 2946 (S.C.).

weapon at the plaintiff's back during a Stanley Cup riot. The plaintiff, however, was held contributorily negligent for having incited the crowd and having been a ringleader in the riot.[30] Further, we must recall that the intentional torts do not necessarily involve morally reprehensible conduct on the part of defendants, since a well-intentioned defendant can be liable for an intentional tort.[31]

Where the defendant acts with the intention to cause harm to the plaintiff, the case for apportionment is more difficult. There has been great reluctance to accept the contributory negligence defence in this type of case. However, even here contributory negligence ought to be an option. As we have seen, the courts have accepted the defence of provocation in the intentional torts, with the result that a plaintiff's damages can be reduced despite a defendant's own turpitude.[32] Provocation can be seen as a specific type of contributory negligence, and there is no reason why other examples of unreasonable behaviour on a plaintiff's part ought not to be considered. In the case of *Bettel v. Yim*,[33] for example, a defendant was liable in battery to a plaintiff who had initiated the incident by throwing a lighted match into the defendant's store, causing a small fire. Although contributory negligence was not raised in the case, this was the type of incident where it might have received a sympathetic hearing.[34] In *Gillen v. Noel*,[35] contributory negligence in fact was applied in a case of intentional wrongdoing. The plaintiff, who was kicked in a scuffle, was found contributorily negligent for having put himself in the situation which led to the incident.[36] Contributory negligence ought to be an available defence in all tort actions.[37] There may be situations in which the wrongdoing of the defendant is so serious, and that of the plaintiff so trivial in

---

30 The degree of the plaintiff's fault was set at 75 per cent. *C. (T.L.) v. Vancouver (City)* (1995), 13 B.C.L.R. (3d) 201 (S.C.) was cited in support of the proposition that in British Columbia, contributory negligence is a defence to intentional torts. The action was subsequently dismissed however after an appeal and new trial, based on a defence under s. 32 of the Criminal Code. See Chapter 3 above.

31 See Chapter 2. In *Brushett v. Cowan* (1987), 40 D.L.R. (4th) 488 (Nfld. T.D.), reversed in part (1990), 69 D.L.R. (4th) 743 (Nfld. C.A.), the trial judge applied the defence of contributory negligence to a medical battery action, on the basis that there were "no policy reasons why the Contributory Negligence Act should not apply to a battery in which 'there was no intent to cause harm' " (at 496). The battery action was subsequently dismissed by the Court of Appeal on the basis of consent, although the doctor was held liable for negligence in post-operative care, and the patient held contributorily negligent with respect to her own conduct.

32 See Chapter 2. As discussed, there is the debate as to whether provocation reduces all damages or merely punitive damages.

33 (1978), 5 C.C.L.T. 66 (Ont. Co. Ct.).

34 See Klar, "Annotation", 5 C.C.L.T. 66.

35 (1984), 50 N.B.R. (2d) 379 (Q.B.).

36 See also *Anderson v. Stevens*, [1981] 5 W.W.R. 550 (B.C. S.C.). Although the case concerned contribution between defendant tortfeasors, one whose liability was based in negligence, and the other for fraud, the court stated that the word "fault" encompasses both intentional and negligent torts.

37 In strict liability torts, the fault of the plaintiff is an established defence. See Chapter 16. Note, however, the Supreme Court of Canada's decision in *Boma Manufacturing Ltd. v. Canadian Imperial Bank of Commerce*, [1996] 3 S.C.R. 727 that contributory negligence is not an available defence in conversion. The case involved fraudulently drawn cheques that were honoured by the defendant bank. See also *Cash v. Georgia Pacific Securities Corp.* (June 7, 1990), Doc. Vancouver C881459, [1990] B.C.J. No. 1315 (S.C.), where the defence was said to be inapplicable to conversion.

comparison, that the court will choose not to apportion.[38] This, however, ought to be a choice which is available.[39]

Whether the apportionment legislation applies to other causes of action, especially breach of contract, has been raised in numerous cases.[40] Prior to the decision of the Supreme Court in *Central & Eastern Trust Co. v. Rafuse*,[41] this issue was of interest from the perspective of tort law, since it related to the concurrent liability debate. Even if the courts decided that the apportionment legislation was inapplicable to actions in contract, they could decide that contract actions could also be framed in tort, thus making the legislation applicable. Now that the concurrent liability approach has been adopted, contract and tort actions based

---

38 In *Wilson v. Bobbie*, [2006] 8 W.W.R. 80 (Alta. Q.B.), Slatter J. held that a defendant who has been convicted of a crime for which the *mens rea* was intention, cannot avail himself of the defence of contributory negligence, alleging that his victim provoked him to commit the crime. Slatter J. did concede, however, that Alberta law does allow for provocation as a defence to reduce damages, despite the several objections which he voiced in respect of this position. In a subsequent judgment dealing with damages, reported at (2006), 38 C.C.L.T. (3d) 169 (Alta. Q.B.), the plaintiff's compensatory and punitive damages were reduced by 20 per cent due to provocation.

39 There is wide agreement that the defence ought not to be restricted to certain types of tort actions. See, e.g., Crocker, above, note 22; Sullivan, above, note 22; and Cheifetz, above, note 21. This is also the recommendation of reform groups. For example, the Uniform Contribution Fault Act, s. 1, Uniform Law Conference of Canada, 1984, defines "fault" as:

(a) a tort,
(b) a breach of statutory duty that creates a liability for damages,
(c) a breach of duty of care arising from a contract that creates a liability for damages, or
(d) a failure of a person to take reasonable care of his own person, property or economic interest, whether or not it is intentional.

40 For reference to some of the earlier cases, see prior editions of this text. More recent cases include *Seaboard Life Insurance Co. v. Bank of Montreal* (2002), [2002] B.C.J. No. 599, 2002 CarswellBC 630 (C.A.); *Crown West Steel Fabricators v. Capri Insurance Services Ltd.* (2002), 214 D.L.R. (4th) 577 (B.C. C.A.); *Intrawest Corp. v. Hart* (2002), 100 B.C.L.R. (3d) 173 (S.C.), additional reasons at (2002), 2002 CarswellBC 3259 (S.C.); *Treaty Group Inc. v. Drake International Inc.* (2005), 36 C.C.L.T. (3d) 265 (S.C.J.), additional reasons at (2006), 2006 CarswellOnt 2332 (S.C.J.), affirmed (2007), 51 C.C.L.T. (3d) 5 (Ont. C.A.), additional reasons at (2007), 2007 CarswellOnt 5108 (C.A.); among others. See Weinrib, "Contribution in a Contractual Setting" (1976), 54 Can. Bar Rev. 338; Swanton, "Contributory Negligence as a Defence to Actions for Breach of Contract" (1981), 55 A.L.J. 278; Chandler, "Contributory Negligence and Contract: Some Underlying Disparities" (1989), 40 N.I. Leg. Q. 152; Logie, "Contributory Negligence in Contract and Tort" (1987), 131 Sol. J. 929; Taylor, "Contributory Negligence — A Defence to Breach of Contract" (1986), 49 Mod. L. Rev. 102; and Law Commission (U.K.), "Contributory Negligence as a Defence in Contract", 1989; s. Elliott, "Contributory Fault in British Columbia Contract Law" (1998), 56 The Advocate 731; and J. Blom, "Contributory Negligence & Contract—A Canadian View of *Astley v. Austrust* (2000), 8 Tort L. Rev. 70. Regarding breach of trust, see *Carl B. Potter Ltd. v. Mercantile Bank of Can.* (1980), 112 D.L.R. (3d) 88 (S.C.C.), and *United Services Funds (Trustees of) v. Richardson Greenshields of Can. Ltd.* (1988), 48 D.L.R. (4th) 98 (B.C. S.C.). In the latter case, Southin J. examines this question in considerable detail. It was decided that the Act does not create a contributory negligence defence where none had existed prior to the legislation, and that the defence was not applicable to cases of fraud. For a contrary judgment which did apply the defence to an action for fraudulent misrepresentation, see *Laird Group Inc. v. Astral Bellevue Pathe Inc.*, [1990] O.J. No. 47 (Dist. Ct.).

41 (1986), 37 C.C.L.T. 117 (S.C.C.). See the discussion in Chapter 10.

on a similar duty of care ought to be both subject to the contribution provisions.[42] Whether the defence of contributory negligence ought to be available in contract actions where there is no concurrent tort liability is a disputed matter which must be resolved as a matter of contract law.[43]

(iii) Problems of Imputed Fault

In the ordinary case, the defence of contributory negligence relates to the personal fault of the plaintiff which contributed to the injuries sustained. Since, however, the legislative provisions do not define the terms fault or negligence, the question has been raised as to whether these terms include the notion of imputed fault.

Imputed fault refers to the situation whereby the fault of another person is imputed to the innocent plaintiff for the purposes of the contributory negligence provisions. Can a plaintiff's damages be reduced pursuant to the legislation on account of the fault of another party?

The question of imputed fault in general is rather clouded. It has been suggested by commentators that the terms fault or negligence as used in the legislation are not restricted to cases of personal fault and thus, that in certain relationships, fault may be imputed to one party as a result of the negligence of another.[44] It is thus argued that in cases of vicarious liability, whether between master and servant, principal and agent, or owner and driver, not only will the former parties be liable for the negligence of the latter, but if injured, will also have their damages reduced, if these were partly caused by the latter persons' fault.[45] This, however, is not an issue which has been clearly settled in the case law. Not only are there very few actual decisions on point, but those that exist deal with different legislative

---

42 Although one must keep in mind that the Supreme Court of Canada gave a plaintiff the choice of suing in tort if that was advantageous. Can a defendant treat a contract action as a tort action, in order to raise the defence of contributory negligence? Note that the Uniform Contributory Fault Act specifically defines "fault" to include breach of contractual duties of care. In *Crown West Steel Fabricators v. Capri Insurance Services Ltd.*, above, note 40, it was held that where the breach of contract is concurrent with tort liability for negligence, and there is nothing in the contract to stipulate otherwise, a plaintiff cannot avoid the defence of contributory negligence by pleading only in contract.

43 See Fleming, *The Law of Torts*, 9th ed. (1998), at 317, and articles cited therein. See also *Fuerst v. St. Adolphe Co-Op Parc Inc.*, [1990] 3 W.W.R. 466 (Man. C.A.), where it was held that the defence applies to all breach of duty cases, whether in contract or tort. Also see *Northern Rock Products Ltd. v. British Columbia* (1994), 16 C.L.R. (2d) 44 (B.C. S.C.), for a similar view. In *Treaty Group Inc. v. Drake International Inc.* (2005), 36 C.C.L.T. (3d) 265 (S.C.J.), additional reasons at (2006), 2006 CarswellOnt 2332 (S.C.J.), affirmed (2007), 51 C.C.L.T. (3d) 5 (Ont. C.A.), additional reasons at (2007), 2007 CarswellOnt 5108 (C.A.), the trial judge decided that although the tort defence of contributory negligence did not apply to breach of contract actions, "contributory fault" could reduce a plaintiff's damages.

44 See Williams, above, note 1, at 432; Fleming, *The Law of Torts*, 9th ed. (1998), at 323 ff.; Cheifetz, above, note 1, at 212.

45 This is called the "both ways" test. As Fleming puts it, "identification is co-extensive with vicarious liability."

provisions, where policy concerns might dictate different results.[46] Where vicarious liability does not exist, there is, of course, no identification. Thus, there is no identification between parents and children,[47] or between spouses, for example.[48]

Another area of imputed fault for the purposes of contributory negligence involves actions by relatives for damages they suffer as a result of injuries to family members. Although not free from doubt, it has generally been agreed that in the action for loss of *consortium* and *servitium*, the negligence of the injured party will be imputed to the plaintiff.[49] The same identification will apply to claims under fatal accidents legislation.[50]

(iv) Rule of Last Clear Chance

Prior to the introduction of apportionment legislation, the courts were able to avoid the contributory negligence bar, by finding that despite the plaintiff's negligence, the defendant had the last clear chance to avoid the accident. In this case, the plaintiff was entitled to full recovery. With apportionment legislation and the ability of the courts to divide liability among those parties at fault, a decision had to be made concerning the status of the rule of last clear chance. Was it a rule that could, or should, survive?

Whether or not the rule of last clear chance has survived the introduction of apportionment legislation depends upon one's interpretation of the rule itself. It can be seen either as a rule dealing with causation, or as one dealing with comparative fault.

From the point of view of causation, one can argue that the intention of the rule was to permit the court to ignore the plaintiff's unreasonable conduct, when it was not a proximate cause of the injury suffered. Thus, by utilizing this approach, the courts were able to avoid the contributory negligence bar to the plaintiff's recovery. Looked at in this way, the rule is still clearly a part of negligence law, although it is not necessary, and no doubt confusing, to call it the rule of last clear

---

46 See, e.g., *Hilburn v. Lynn* (1955), 17 W.W.R. 15 (Alta. T.D.), dealing with the meaning of "fault" for the purpose of a claim for contribution, where fault was restricted to personal fault; *Flamant v. Knelson*, [1971] 4 W.W.R. 454 (B.C. S.C.), dealing with the meaning of "fault" for the purposes of a guest passenger defence, where fault was defined as including imputed fault; *Iliuk v. Stein*, [1940] 2 W.W.R. 646 (Alta. T.D.), dealing with the meaning of "fault" for purposes of contributory negligence defence, where the fault of a driver of a car was imputed to the injured plaintiff, who was the car's owner.

47 See, e.g., *Sgro v. Verbeek* (1980), 111 D.L.R. (3d) 479 at 485 (Ont. H.C.).

48 Prior to the repeal of interspousal tort immunity and guest passenger legislation, the contributory negligence legislation ensured that (i) an injured spouse could not recover the portion of damages represented by the negligence of the other spouse; and that (ii) a guest passenger could not recover the portion of damages caused by the host driver, unless the host driver was also liable to the passenger, on the basis of gross negligence. These sections have become unnecessary, now that spouses and guest passengers have no special status in tort actions.

49 See *Enridge v. Copp* (1966), 57 D.L.R. (2d) 239 (B.C. S.C.); *Young v. Otto*, [1947] 2 W.W.R. 950 (Alta. T.D.).

50 Some statutes specifically state this: see, e.g., the Family Law Act, R.S.O. 1990, c. F.3, s. 61(3). A case which makes it clear that an action under fatal accident legislation is derivative and not independent is *Jaman Estate v. Hussain*, [1995] 7 W.W.R. 258 (Man. C.A.).

chance.[51] Whether a party's negligent conduct should be described as proximate or remote in view of the intervening act of negligence of a subsequent party cannot be resolved on the basis of who had the last clear chance to avoid the injury. It is clear, however, that where a party's conduct has not been a factual and proximate cause of the injuries in question, it is by definition not contributory and hence not relevant to the issue of apportionment.[52] Thus, if the rule of last clear chance is seen as a rule of proximate causation, it is already provided for in the legislation and by the application of causation principles.[53]

The causation approach has been followed in a few of the cases. In *Brooks v. Ward*,[54] for example, the Supreme Court of Canada, per Taschereau J., exonerated the owner of a parked truck of all liability for a collision which occurred when a driver of a car, in an attempt to avoid the truck, swerved and hit an oncoming car. Taschereau J., citing an earlier Supreme Court case,[55] stated:

> I do not believe that the appellant can be charged with negligence which contributed to the accident . . . . where a clear line can be drawn between the negligence of a plaintiff and defendant, it is not a case of contributory negligence at all. When a driver sees a car in his path, and has plenty of opportunity to avoid it but fails to do so, there is no contributory negligence and he must bear the full responsibility. Or if, by his own negligence, he disables himself from becoming aware of a danger and cannot therefore avoid the accident, he is the only party to blame. . . .[56]

In another case, *Boulay v. Rousselle*,[57] the deceased carelessly drove his car into the rear of a tractor-trailer which negligently had been parked on the highway. The tractor-trailer had its headlights, tail-lights and warning flashers on, and the court held that a driver with normal perception and ability to react would have been able to avoid the collision. The trial judge, interpreting the doctrine of last clear chance as a matter of causation, found that the deceased was the effective cause of the accident and dismissed the claim.[58]

---

51 It is sometimes called the rule of "ultimate negligence", or the "last opportunity" rule.

52 This is made explicit in some of the legislation. For example, the Contributory Negligence Act, R.S.A. 1980, c. C-23, s. 1(2), states that: "Nothing in this section operates to render a person liable for damage or loss to which the person's fault has not contributed." See *Lillos v. Tilden Rent-a-Car Co.* (1987), 50 M.V.R. 280 (Alta. Q.B.).

53 See Klar, "Annotation to *MacKay v. MacLellan*" (1976-77), 1 C.C.L.T. 310, where this argument is amplified. Proximate cause does not depend upon last clear chance, ultimate negligence or last opportunity. The use of these terms to make what is a proximate cause argument thus only serves to confuse. As stated by Stevenson J., "There is no magic in the words 'last chance'. The issue always comes down to which party or parties caused the damage or loss." See *C.N.R. Co. v. di Domenicantonio* (1988), 49 D.L.R. (4th) 342 at 356 (N.B. C.A.).

54 (1956), 4 D.L.R. (2d) 597 (S.C.C.).

55 *McKee and Taylor v. Malenfant*, [1954] 4 D.L.R. 785 (S.C.C.).

56 Above, note 54, at 599.

57 (1984), 30 C.C.L.T. 149 (N.B. Q.B.).

58 See also *Hunter v. Briere*, [1989] 3 W.W.R. 528 (Man. Q.B.), where a motorcyclist collided with the rear of a car which had run out of gas and been left on a bridge. The trial judge held that despite the defendant's negligence in having run out of gas, the plaintiff "had ample opportunity to avoid the effect of any negligence" and was hence fully to blame for the accident. A similar case is *Haydu v. Calgary (City)* (1991), 81 Alta. L.R. (2d) 106 (Q.B.). A plaintiff who struck a stationary truck which was partially obstructing a lane of traffic was held 100 per cent at fault. The then "last clear chance" section of the Contributory Negligence Act, R.S.A. 1980, c. C-23, s. 7 (since repealed) applied. See also *Halford (Guardian at litem of) v. Maradi*

If last clear chance is looked at as a rule of comparative fault,[59] it is clearly inconsistent with apportionment legislation. It is no longer necessary to use the rule to avoid the stalemate solution of the earlier common law. Notions of comparative fault leading to an all or nothing approach are inconsistent with apportionment laws.

Despite these arguments, the rule, as a separate doctrine, has not disappeared. Some of the apportionment statutes have even expressly adopted it, in a modified form.[60] Up until its recent repeal, a provision of the Alberta legislation, for example, directed a judge, or a jury, not to consider the question of last clear chance unless the evidence indicates that the act or omission of one party "was so clearly subsequent to and severable from the act or omission" of another so as not to be "substantially contemporaneous with it."[61] It has been applied even in those provinces whose apportionment legislation does not contain any reference to the rule.[62] In three jurisdictions, the rule has expressly been abolished.[63]

(1991), 8 C.C.L.T. (2d) 129 (B.C. S.C.), where a 10-year-old bicyclist who rode his bike into a stationary truck was held 100 per cent at fault. In *Wickberg v. Patterson* (1997), 33 C.C.L.T. (2d) 231 (Alta. C.A,), involving a motorcyclist running into the rear of a parked vehicle, Justice Picard overturned a trial judgment that applied "last clear chance". Justice Picard held that both parties were negligent and caused the accident. It was accordingly incorrect to apply the doctrine to hold the motorcyclist fully responsible. Her Ladyship agreed with the views expressed in this text that the doctrine is amply taken care of by the application of ordinary principles of factual and legal cause and need not exist as a separate doctrine. In *Crackel v. Miller* (2003), [2004] 3 W.W.R. 684 (Alta. Q.B.), affirmed (2004), [2005] 3 W.W.R. 593 (Alta. C.A.), the plaintiff, who had been drinking, drove his car into the back of the defendant's truck and trailer, which had broken down on the side of the road. The court apportioned 25 per cent of the liability to the plaintiff and 75 per cent to the defendant.

59 That is, you compare the plaintiff's fault with that of the defendant's. If the plaintiff's fault is trivial, you conclude that the defendant had the last clear chance to avoid the accident. This enabled the court, prior to the apportionment legislation, to award the plaintiff compensation, thus avoiding the stalemate solution.

60 See the legislative provisions of Saskatchewan, Newfoundland, the Northwest Territories, and the Yukon. For an excellent review of the history and the debate see Bowker, "Ten More Years Under the Contributory Negligence Acts" (1965), 2 U.B.C. L. Rev. 198.

61 R.S.A. 1980, c. C-23, s. 6. See *Meyer v. Hall*, [1972] 2 W.W.R. 481 (Alta. C.A.), where the court suggested that the rule survived as a question of proximate cause, citing Viscount Simon in *Boy Andrew (Owners) v. St. Rognvald (Owners)*, [1948] A.C. 140 at 148-49 (H.L.). Sections 6 and 7 of the Act were repealed by the Justice Statutes Amendment Act, S.A. 2000, c. 20, s. 72. The Act now provides (s. 31) that "This Act applies if caused or contributed to by the act or commission of a person, whether or not another person had the opportunity of avoiding the consequences of that act or omission and failed to do so."

62 Nova Scotia, New Brunswick, Manitoba, and Ontario. For a discussion of the Ontario cases, see Cheifetz, above, note 1, at 201-04. The cases are not in agreement. The Supreme Court of Canada, in a Manitoba case, *Hartman v. Fisette* (1976), 66 D.L.R. (3d) 516, expressed the "gravest doubt" about the survival of the rule in Manitoba. This passage was approved in two recent Nova Scotia cases, *A.C.A. Co-operative Assn. v. Associated Freezers of Canada Inc.*, (1992), 93 D.L.R. (4th) 559 (N.S. C.A.); and *Gaudet v. Doucet* (1991), 101 N.S.R. (2d) 309 (T.D.). See, however, *Keough v. Royal Can. Legion, Henderson Highway Branch 215*, [1978] 6 W.W.R. 335 (Man. C.A.); *Holian v. United Grain Growers Ltd.* (1980), 11 C.C.L.T. 184 (Man. Q.B.), varied (1980), 13 C.C.L.T. 269 (Man. C.A.).

63 The British Columbia Negligence Act, R.S.B.C. 1996, c. 333, s. 8, states: "This Act applies to all cases where damage is caused or contributed to by the act of a person even if another person had the opportunity of avoiding the consequences of that act and negligently or carelessly failed

In practice, the rule of last clear chance is rarely applied, even in those jurisdictions which have statutorily maintained it in its modified form. Most would agree that its existence as a separate doctrine is unnecessary.[64] As a rule of causation, it is sufficiently taken care of by existing negligence law theory, and made explicit in the statutes.[65] As an "all or nothing" rule, it is antithetical to the apportionment process.[66]

(v) Basis of Apportionment

For contributory negligence to be a relevant defence, the defendant must prove that the plaintiff was negligent and that this negligence caused or contributed to the injuries which were sustained. The contributory fault must, of course, relate to the same injuries as those caused by the other wrongdoers.[67] Once this is shown, the fact-finder must apportion the liability for these injuries among those found at fault. How is this apportionment to be done?

The legislation directs that each person's liability is to be "in proportion to the degree in which each person was at fault but if, having regard to all the circumstances of the case, it is not possible to establish different degrees of fault, the

---

to do so." See also the Contributory Negligence Act, R.S.P.E.I. 1988, c. C-21, s. 4 and the recent amendment to the Alberta Act, above, note 61.

64 The 1984 Uniform Contributory Fault Act recommended its abolition, as did the Alberta Institute of Law Research and Reform and the Ontario Law Reform Commission.

65 A case that illustrates this is *Lawrence v. Prince Rupert (City)*, [2005] B.C.J. No. 2522 (B.C. C.A.). The plaintiff tripped over a pole that had been left unattended on the sidewalk by the defendant. The trial judge found that both parties had been negligent, but that the defendant's conduct was not an effective cause of the accident, since the plaintiff had ample opportunity to avoid the pole. The majority of the Court of Appeal agreed with the trial judge's decision that the defendant's negligence was not a proximate cause of the accident. This finding could be made despite the explicit abolition of the last clear chance rule in the B.C. legislation. Esson J.A. dissented, holding that to relieve the defendant of all responsibility for the accident, even though negligence was found against it, was to effectively ignore the statutory provision which abolished last clear chance. As noted in Chapter 12, to decide that although negligent, the defendant's act was not a proximate cause of the plaintiff's fall, is a difficult call to make. In that respect, Esson J.A.'s dissent is quite supportable. The issue is also discussed in a subsequent case, *Dyke v. British Columbia Amateur Softball Assn.* (2008), 54 C.C.L.T. (3d) 142 (B.C. C.A.), where Donald J.A. states at para. 27: "I wish to say in the strongest terms that the doctrine [i.e., last clear chance] is extinct and occupies no place in the law of torts in this jurisdiction."

66 For an excellent discussion of "last clear chance," its historical basis, its status, the legislation, and the case law see D.G. Casswell, "Avoiding Last Clear Chance" (1990), 69 Can. Bar Rev. 129. Professor Casswell's view is that the rule is "obsolete and courts in all provinces and territories should and can avoid its application." In *Wickberg v. Patterson* (1997), 33 C.C.L.T. (2d) 231 (Alta. C.A.), Justice Ellen Picard, after an extensive review, concluded that the rule serves no purpose and urged the government to repeal the statutory provisions that have maintained it. As we have discussed above, the Alberta government has now done just that.

67 In *Sorenson v. Abrametz*, [1988] 1 W.W.R. 609 (Sask. C.A.), for example, a solicitor's negligence which resulted in a missed limitation period and a driver's negligence which led to the victim's injuries were not contributory, since they did not lead to the same damages. Thus the solicitor who was sued by his client, the injured party in the car accident, for the lost action, could not claim contribution from the person who would have been the defendant in the action for the automobile accident. This is also a problem, as we shall see, in the seat belt cases, where it must be shown that the failure to wear the seat belt contributed to the injuries suffered in the car accident.

liability shall be apportioned equally."[68] Although the courts have not clearly explained how each person's degree of fault is to be determined, their task is basically to determine the relative degrees of blameworthiness of the concerned parties. The courts consider all the circumstances of the parties' misconduct to determine their relative negligence. Although it has also been suggested that the apportionment decision also relates to questions of causation,[69] ultimately the question must come down to an assessment of relative misconduct from the perspective of departures from standards of reasonable care.[70] In *Heller v. Martens*,[71] Fruman J.A. thoroughly canvassed this issue and concluded that the comparative blameworthiness approach was the correct approach for a variety of reasons. In determining comparative blameworthiness, Fruman J.A. suggested that the following factors are relevant: the nature of the duty owed by the defendant, the number of acts of fault committed by each party, the sequence (timing) of the negligent acts, the nature of the misconduct, and the extent to which statutory breach was involved.[72]

The process of apportioning liability based upon relative degrees of fault can be difficult, as is illustrated in the case of *Ottosen v. Kasper*.[73] This case involved a defendant bus driver and his employer, a defendant adult motorist, and an 11-year-old plaintiff. The plaintiff crossed in front of the bus and was struck by the passing car. Since the apportionment of liability in all cases must add up to 100

---

68 This is the Alberta-type wording. See R.S.A. 2000, c. C-27, s. 1(1). Wording in other statutes is similar.

69 For example, whose negligence was more immediate, who had the best chance to avoid the accident, etc. See *Street On Torts*, Brazier (ed.), 9th ed. (1993), at 275.

70 A good discussion of this issue can be found in *Clyke v. Blenkhorn* (1958), 13 D.L.R. (2d) 293 (N.S. C.A.). Although conceding that some decisions and textual authorities support the position that both culpability and causation must be considered when apportioning blame, MacDonald J. considered this to be wrong. According to MacDonald J., at 304, "the prevailing Canadian practice is to look at such causative conduct in terms of *relative or comparative blameworthiness or culpability, i.e.*, to see in what degrees the parties departed from the norm of reasonable conduct. . .". Numerous judgments now support this approach. See, for example, *Cempel v. Harrison Hot Springs Hotel Ltd.* (1997), 43 B.C.L.R. (3d) 219 (C.A.); *Alberta Wheat Pool v. Northwest Pile Driving Ltd.* (2000), 2 C.C.L.T. (3d) 53 (B.C. C.A.), additional reasons at (2000), 2 C.P.C. (5th) 12 (B.C. C.A.); and *British Columbia v. Canadian Forest Products Ltd.* (2002), 11 C.C.L.T. (3d) 1 (B.C. C.A.), additional reasons at (2002), 2002 CarswellBC 1267 (C.A.), leave to appeal allowed (2003), 2003 CarswellBC 130, 2003 CarswellBC 131 (S.C.C.); *Refco Futures (Canada) Ltd. - Refco Valeurs Mobilieres (Canada) Ltée v. SYB Holdings Corp.* (2004), 21 C.C.L.T. (3d) 127 (B.C. C.A.); *Chow v. Chan* (2007), 46 C.C.L.T. (3d) 249 (B.C. S.C.); *Robinson v. Williams Estate* (2007), 44 C.C.L.T. (3d) 1 (Alta. C.A.); and *Rizzi v. Marvos* (2008), [2008] O.J. No. 935, 2008 ONCA 172 (Ont. C.A.), additional reasons at (2008), 2008 CarswellOnt 2968 (C.A.); among others.

71 (2002), 213 D.L.R. (4th) 124 (Alta. C.A.). The case involved failing to wear a seat belt. The trial judge had assessed 25 per cent as the degree of fault for failing to wear a seat belt in a vehicle that was not equipped with one. The majority of the Court of Appeal affirmed this; the dissent would have increased it to 50 per cent.

72 Fruman J.A. cited cases that have raised these as factors. The Court of Appeal reaffirmed this approach in *Chae v. Min*, [2005] 9 W.W.R. 10 (C.A.). The cases involved the failure to wear a seat belt. See discussion, below.

73 (1986), 37 C.C.L.T. 270 (B.C. C.A.).

per cent,[74] the assessment for each of the parties must take into account everyone else's negligence.[75] In assessing the plaintiff child's degree of fault, the court kept in mind the age of the plaintiff and the degree of care which he, as compared with other children, ought to have exercised. The defendants submitted, however, that their degrees of negligence ought to be the same whether or not the plaintiff who was injured was a child or an adult. This argument misapprehended the relativity of the assessment process. If the plaintiff child was only slightly negligent, taking into account the standard of care demanded of children, and the adult defendants were ordinarily negligent, taking into account the standard of care demanded of adult motorists, then it would be appropriate that they would bear a larger portion of the liability than would the plaintiff. The court also rejected the argument that the assessment of liability considers matters of causation. As stated by Lambert J.A.:

> The words used are the words of fault. The question that affects apportionment, therefore, is the weight of fault that should be attributed to each of the parties, not the weight of causation. In many cases they would be the same thing but, particularly in the case of a young child, the weight of

---

74 This is basic. See, however, *Houle v. B.C. Hydro & Power Authority* (1972), 29 D.L.R. (3d) 510 (B.C. S.C.), where a jury attributed 10 per cent of the blame to the defendant, 15 per cent to one of the plaintiffs and 75 per cent to no one. The effect of this, of course, is to reduce the plaintiffs' recovery by this unattributed blame. In *Wells v. McBrine*, [1989] 2 W.W.R. 695, the B.C. Court of Appeal upheld a jury's finding which attributed 40 per cent of the fault for the plaintiff's injuries to persons who were not parties, either as defendants or third parties, in the action. Esson J.A. stated that although a jury must apportion the whole of the 100 per cent, it need not apportion the whole against persons who are parties to the action. See also *Reekie v. Messervey* (1989), 36 B.C.L.R. (2d) 316 (C.A.), *Busby (Guardian ad litem of) v. Cartier*, [1993] 3 W.W.R. 58 (B.C. S.C.) and *Hall v. Pinette*, 2004 BCSC 1367 (S.C.), where this approach was reaffirmed. This has serious consequences for a plaintiff in light of the position taken by the B.C. courts that a plaintiff who is contributorily negligent has only several judgments against each of the parties at fault for the injuries. When the joint and several judgment method is used, the burden of absorbing the fault of parties, neither sued nor third-partied, falls, not on the plaintiff, but on the defendants. See discussion below. Where the fault of the unknown third party becomes the responsibility of another party, such as occurs in statutory schemes for unidentified or uninsured drivers, that party can be sued. See, for example, *Watkins v. Goode*, [1995] 7 W.W.R. 523 (Alta. Q.B.). In *Martin v. Listowel Memorial Hospital* (2000), 192 D.L.R. (4th) 250 (Ont. C.A.), the Court of Appeal held that under the Ontario legislation fault could only be apportioned to parties to the action. The action was complicated by the effect that a "secret settlement" entered into between the plaintiffs and some of the defendants would have on the other defendants. In *M. (J.) v Bradley* (2004), 240 D.L.R. (4th) 435 (Ont. C.A.), the Court held that the degrees of fault of non-parties could be determined in some circumstances. In *Bradley*, the "non-parties" were sued, they settled, the actions against them were accordingly dismissed, the settlement was public, and the liability of the non-settling defendants was agreed to be limited to their respective degrees of fault. The issue of the "absent tortfeasor" and how courts in Ontario should deal with apportionment when all potential parties who were at fault are not sued is extensively dealt with by Cheifetz, who has written several articles on recent Ontario developments. See "Allocating Financial Responsibility Among Solvent Concurrent Wrongdoers" (2004), 28 Advocates' Quarterly 138; "PostScript: The Retreat Begins" (2004), 28 Advocates' Q. 389; "PostScript # 2: The Retreat Continues" (2007), 29 Advocates' Quarterly 276; and "For Whom the Bell Tolled" (2007), 48 Advocates' Quarterly 46.

75 Thus if everyone's negligence is slight or gross their shares of the liability will not necessarily be small or large. It will depend upon how many persons are sharing the 100 per cent.

> fault may well be less than the weight that would be attributed if causation were the basis of the balancing.[76]

The statutes also provide, however, that where it is not "possible"[77] or "practicable"[78] to establish different degrees of fault, the liability shall be apportioned equally.

(vi) Effect of a Finding of Contributory Negligence

When a plaintiff is found to have been contributorily negligent, the defendant's liability is reduced according to the plaintiff's degree of fault. A difficult issue, however, involves the effect of a finding of contributory negligence in an action by a plaintiff against two or more negligent defendants. In this case, is the plaintiff's degree of fault determined by considering the fault of each defendant *individually* or by grouping the defendants together? As well, ought the plaintiff to be awarded a joint and several judgment against each defendant for the total of the damages, as reduced, or is the contributorily negligent plaintiff entitled only to a several judgment?

In determining these issues, one must recall that the various legislative provisions dealing with contributory negligence and apportionment are not the same, and thus judicial precedents from one jurisdiction may not be satisfactory for another. The legislative provisions themselves are ambiguous, making interpretation difficult. Various approaches have been suggested to resolve these questions, but none is completely satisfactory.[79] The English case of *Fitzgerald v. Lane*,[80] decided by the House of Lords, illustrates these difficulties. The plaintiff pedestrian was injured in a motor vehicle accident which involved two defendant drivers. The plaintiff was first struck by one car, and then by the other. Assuming that all of the plaintiff's injuries were legally attributable to the fault of both drivers and the plaintiff,[81] how ought the parties' liabilities to be determined, and what form of judgment ought to be awarded?

The trial judge found that all three parties were to blame for the injuries, and that it was impossible to distinguish among their degrees of fault. That being the case, he gave the plaintiff a joint and several judgment for two-thirds of his damages against each of the defendants. In the Court of Appeal,[82] it was held that the plaintiff's position ought to be considered in relation to each defendant separately, and therefore, since the plaintiff and each of the defendants were *equally* at fault, the plaintiff would be entitled to a joint and several judgment against each for 50 per cent of his damages. Sir Edward Eveleigh reasoned that awarding

---

76 (1986), 37 C.C.L.T. 270 (B.C. C.A.), at 277. See also *Parker (Guardian ad litem of) v. Hehr*, [1993] B.C.J. No. 2821 (S.C.).

77 The Alberta-type wording.

78 The Ontario and Manitoba wording.

79 The New South Wales case of *Barisic v. Devenport*, [1978] 2 N.S.W.L.R. 111 (C.A.), presents an excellent, in-depth discussion of the issues.

80 [1988] 3 W.L.R. 356 (H.L.).

81 This is an important assumption. If the plaintiff's injuries were separable, some caused in the first accident, and others in the second, we would not be dealing with the same issues.

82 [1987] 2 All E.R. 455 (C.A.).

the plaintiff a two-thirds judgment against a defendant who was equally at fault with him would be to award that plaintiff twice as much as he deserved.[83]

In the House of Lords, Lord Ackner stressed that there are two distinct and different stages in a case such as was before him. In the first stage, the court must determine whether the defendants are legally liable to the plaintiff for the alleged damages, whether the plaintiff was contributorily negligent, and to what extent the plaintiff's damages ought to be reduced. In the second stage, the defendants' rights to contribution *inter se* must be determined. In stage one, the court must consider the fault of the plaintiff on the one hand, and that of the defendants *jointly* on the other.[84] Lord Ackner held that the Court of Appeal was incorrect in attributing 50 per cent of the responsibility for the damages to the plaintiff if the trial judge's finding that the three parties were equally at fault was to be accepted. According to Lord Ackner, however, the trial judge himself had erred in having failed to keep the two distinct stages separate and finding the three parties equally at fault. This being the case, the House of Lords dismissed the plaintiff's appeal and affirmed the Court of Appeal's 50/50 split. In effect, the trial judge's finding that the three parties were equally at fault was replaced by a finding that the plaintiff was 50 per cent at fault, and the defendant's negligent acts taken together were responsible for the other 50 per cent.

The House of Lords' approach is consistent with the Canadian legislative provisions. The plaintiff's damages are to be reduced by the degree of his or her contributory negligence, which is to be determined by comparing the plaintiff's conduct with that of the other parties taken together. If the three parties are equally at fault, the plaintiff's damages ought to be reduced by one-third only.

As in *Fitzgerald v. Lane*, the traditional approach in most common law provinces has been to award a joint and several judgment, not only in favour of innocent plaintiffs, but in favour of contributorily negligent plaintiffs as well.[85] This means

---

83 The rest of the court agreed. See Slade L.J., for example, at 474. On the other hand, of course, the effect of the Court of Appeal's approach was that the plaintiff would bear 50 per cent of the damages, and each defendant only 25 per cent, after contribution between them. This would result in a supposedly equally blameworthy plaintiff carrying twice the burden of each of the defendants.

84 See *Barisic v. Devenport*, above, note 79, and particularly the judgment of Samuels J.A. for a discussion of this approach. After an extensive review of the authorities, including Canadian authorities, Samuels J.A. agreed that the clear practice in Australia, England and Canada is the "joint or unit basis of apportionment." The plaintiff's negligence is compared with the defendants' negligence, taken together. Samuels J.A. conceded, however, that how this is to be done is a difficult issue. Also see *Renaissance Leisure Group Inc. v. Frazer* (2001), 197 D.L.R. (4th) 336 (Ont. S.C.J.), reversed (2004), 242 D.L.R. (4th) 229 (Ont. C.A.), where the plaintiff's negligence was reduced according to its relative culpability of the other wrongdoers taken as a unit (even if they are not part of the action). The issue for the Court of Appeal was whether a separate action for contribution against a tortfeasor who was not sued in the principal action should reflect the apportionment of blame determined in the principal action. The Court of Appeal held that it should. This case is discussed further below.

85 See, e.g., *Menow v. Honsberger Ltd.*, [1970] 1 O.R. 54 (H.C.), affirmed (1970), 14 D.L.R. (3d) 545 (Ont. C.A.), which was affirmed (*sub nom. Jordan House Ltd. v. Menow*) (1973), 38 D.L.R. (3d) 105 (S.C.C.). This approach was confirmed by the Alberta Court of Appeal in *Campbell Estate v. Calgary Power Ltd.*, [1989] 1 W.W.R. 36. Côté J.A. supported this approach on the basis that it is supported by the judicial authorities, it is in line with the statutory construction,

that once a damage award has been reduced by the plaintiff's degree of fault, the judgment can be executed in full from any of the defendants who are found liable. In British Columbia, however, the courts have used a several judgment method of apportionment when contributorily negligent plaintiffs are involved. The British Columbia Court of Appeal has held that s. 4 of the Negligence Act,[86] which dictates a joint judgment, applies to innocent plaintiffs, whereas ss. 1 and 2, which dictate a several judgment, apply to contributorily negligent plaintiffs.[87]

There are persuasive arguments on both sides of this question. A joint and several judgment method, even in cases of contributorily negligent plaintiffs, is in line with negligence law's emphasis on compensation and loss distribution, since it assures that victims will receive maximum compensation, once their damages have been reduced by their own degree of fault. To adopt a joint judgment method for innocent plaintiffs, but a several judgment method for contributorily negligent ones, is to penalize contributorily negligent plaintiffs twice. Not only will their damages be reduced, but the advantages of the joint judgment method will be lost. There are, on the other hand, reasons for the adoption of the several judgment method in cases of contributorily negligent plaintiffs. Not only does it appear more equitable to treat all wrongdoers alike, whether they be plaintiffs or defendants, but it avoids mathematical calculations which can become quite complex.[88]

(d) Special Cases

The defence of contributory negligence can be applied to virtually any type of negligence case.[89] One can identify, however, certain types of contributory negligence cases which frequently come before the courts.

---

it is simpler, and it is no less fair than the several judgment method. A Saskatchewan case that affirms the joint judgment approach is *Housen v. Nikolaisen* (1997), [1998] 5 W.W.R. 523 (Sask. Q.B.), reversed [2000] 4 W.W.R. 173 (Sask. C.A.), leave to appeal allowed (2000), 217 Sask. R. 320 (note) (S.C.C.), reversed (2002), 211 D.L.R. (4th) 577 (S.C.C.), affirming the trial judgment, although this matter was not in issue. In *Ingles v. Tutkaluk Construction Ltd.* (2000), 183 D.L.R. (4th) 193 (S.C.C.), the Supreme Court of Canada affirmed the joint judgment approach in the context of an Ontario case.

86 R.S.B.C. 1996, c. 333.

87 See *Leischner v. West Kootenay Power & Light Co.*, [1986] 3 W.W.R. 97 (B.C. C.A.); *Cominco Ltd. v. C.G.E. Co.* (1983), 4 D.L.R. (4th) 186 (B.C. C.A.); and *Wells v. McBrine*, [1989] 2 W.W.R. 695 (B.C. C.A.). There is also a Nova Scotia Court of Appeal judgment to the same effect: *Inglis Ltd. v. South Shore Sales & Service Ltd.* (1979), 104 D.L.R. (3d) 507. Note, however, that where there is no contributory negligence, the joint judgment method applies; see *Piercey (Guardian ad litem of) v. Lunenburg (County) District School Board* (1998), 41 C.C.L.T. (2d) 60 (N.S. C.A.). The Saskatchewan Contributory Negligence Act, R.S.S. 1978, c. C-31, s. 3.1(1), provides that if a person's share of the damage is uncollectable, that amount is apportioned among the other persons who are found at fault according to their respective degrees of fault.

88 See Williams, *Joint Torts and Contributory Negligence* (1951). But see Côté J.A. in *Campbell Estate v. Calgary Power Ltd.*, above, note 85.

89 See Rainaldi (ed.), *Remedies in Tort*, Vol. 2 (1987), Chapter 16 (Part II), for a detailed listing of the types of cases in which the defence has been raised.

(i) Children

As discussed previously,[90] children are more usually parties to negligence actions as plaintiffs than as defendants. As plaintiffs, it is not unusual for children to be faced with the defence of contributory negligence.[91] In determining the contributory negligence issue with regard to children, one must recall that the standard of care which will be applied is a significantly relaxed one. The court will first consider the child's capacity, and will apply a subjective test to that child. It is only if that child is capable of being negligent that the child's conduct in the particular case will be examined. Even here, however, the test is only partly objective, as the court will compare the child to a child of like age, intelligence and experience.[92] One also must recall that in determining the degree of fault to be attributed, the court must take into account the different standard of care which is required of children.[93]

Although a parent's negligence which has contributed to a child's injuries will not be imputed to that child for the purposes of contributory negligence, a child's damages can be indirectly affected by the parent's negligence. A defendant can third-party the child's parent and seek contribution from that parent, if it can be shown that the parent was negligent and either was liable to the child or would, if sued, have been found liable.[94] In this case, unless the parent's contribution to the defendant will be covered by liability insurance, the result will be a diminution in the family's assets, which will, of course, normally work to the disadvantage of the injured child.

(ii) Failure to Use a Safety Device

A plaintiff's failure to use a safety device, particularly a car's seat belt, has been raised by defendants as an item of contributory negligence on numerous occasions. The essence of the argument is that the plaintiff's failure to employ the device was unreasonable, and that this unreasonable conduct was a contributing cause of the plaintiff's injuries. As noted above, the fact that the failure did

---

90 Chapter 9.

91 See Rainaldi (ed.), *Remedies in Tort*, Vol. 2 (1987), Chapter 16 (Part II), at 22 ff, for a detailed list of cases.

92 See *McEllistrum v. Etches* (1956), 6 D.L.R. (2d) 1 (S.C.C.), and the cases discussed in Chapter 9.

93 See *Ottosen v. Kasper* (1986), 37 C.C.L.T. 270 (B.C. C.A.) and cases discussed above. For a recent application of this principle, see *Hixon v. Roberts*, 2004 BCCA 335 (C.A.).

94 See below re contribution between wrongdoers. There have been several cases in which defendants have third-partied parents alleging their negligence. See, e.g., *Teno v. Arnold*, [1978] 2 S.C.R. 287; *Ducharme v. Davies*, [1984] 1 W.W.R. 699 (Sask. C.A.); *Gambino v. DiLeo*, [1971] 2 O.R. 131 (H.C.); *Peter v. Anchor Transit Ltd.*, [1979] 4 W.W.R. 150 (B.C. C.A.); *Migliore v. Gerard* (1987), 42 D.L.R. (4th) 626 (Ont. H.C.); and *Pelletier v. Olson* (1987), 42 C.C.L.T. 129 (Sask. Q.B.). Where the parent cannot be held liable to the child, the parent cannot be third partied. Thus *Preston v. Chow* (2002), 211 D.L.R. (4th) 758, 10 C.C.L.T. (3d) 145 (Man. C.A.) held that a mother whose prenatal negligence allegedly contributed to the injuries of her child could not be third partied as she owed no duty to her child, as per *Dobson (Litigation Guardian of) v. Dobson* (1999), 45 C.C.L.T. (2d) 217 (S.C.C.).

not contribute to the accident itself is not relevant in so far as the defence of contributory negligence is concerned.[95]

One can summarize the following conclusions which emerge from the numerous seat belt cases:

(1) A plaintiff's failure to employ a seat belt may or may not be unreasonable, depending upon the circumstances. Although it is generally held to be unreasonable conduct not to wear an available seat belt,[96] or not to use a seat belt or other safety device in the appropriate way,[97] this is not always the case. Some judges continue to reject the seat belt defence based on the philosophy that it is the negligent driver and not the passenger who ought to bear full responsibility for the accident and the consequent injuries.[98] Other courts, while not denying the theoretical validity of the argument, reject the defence because of a lack of evidence that the plaintiff's injuries were actually worsened by the failure to employ a seat belt.[99] One must also recall that the failure to employ the safety device must have been *unreasonable*. Excuses are permitted, although it has been held by one court that once a defendant has proved that the plaintiff failed to wear a seat belt and that this failure was a contributing factor to the injuries, the onus

---

95 That a failure to wear a seat belt constitutes contributory negligence was reaffirmed by the Supreme Court of Canada in *Galaske v. O'Donnell* (1994), 112 D.L.R. (4th) 109. As discussed above in Chapter 6, the case concerned the duty of a driver to ensure that a young passenger was safely buckled up. In *Philip v. Hironaka* (1997), [1998] 3 W.W.R. 703 (Alta. Q.B.), Girgulis J. argues that technically, since failing to wear a seat belt does not cause or contribute to an injury, but may only fail to prevent an injury, it does not fall within the wording of the contributory negligence legislation. He does concede, however, that it falls within the "spirit and intention" of the legislation. This point was also raised in *Snushall v. Fulsang* (2005), 258 D.L.R. (4th) 425 (Ont. C.A.), leave to appeal refused (2006), 2006 CarswellOnt 1366 (S.C.C.), at 432 [D.L.R.]. Juriansz J.A. noted that while negligent driving causes an accident, "the failure to wear a seat belt 'causes' injuries in the sense that the failure to use a prophylactic 'causes' pregnancy". Nevertheless, the Ontario Court of Appeal conceded that it is an aspect of contributory negligence which does reduce the damage award.

96 See, e.g., *Stamp v. Ont.; Stamp v. Bacon* (1984), 47 O.R. (2d) 214 (C.A.); *Yuan v. Farstad* (1967), 66 D.L.R. (2d) 295 (B.C. S.C.); *Gagnon v. Beaulieu*, [1977] 1 W.W.R. 702 (B.C. S.C.); *Mandzuk v. Vieira* (1986), 28 D.L.R. (4th) 677 (B.C. C.A.), affirmed (1988), 47 C.C.L.T. 63 (S.C.C.); *Gervais v. Richard* (1984), 30 C.C.L.T. 105 (Ont. H.C.); *Berge v. Langlois* (1984), 6 D.L.R. (4th) 766 (Ont. C.A.); *Wallace v. Berrigan* (1988), 47 D.L.R. (4th) 752 (N.S. C.A.); and *Pelletier v. Olson* (1987), 42 C.C.L.T. 129 (Sask. Q.B.), among many others.

97 See, for example, *Vargas v. Leung*, [1992] B.C.J. No. 827: plaintiff contributorily negligent for having removed the "head rest" from the back of her seat, because she considered that it was uncomfortable; *Streichert v. Lautard*, [1993] B.C.J. No. 1809: plaintiff contributorily negligent for having removed shoulder portion of the seat belt; *Korpela v. March* (1993), 138 A.R. 179 (Q.B.): plaintiff contributorily negligent for having altered her seat belt so she could sleep, which substantially reduced effectiveness of the device.

98 See, e.g., Mr. Justice Angers' comments in *Bulmer v. Horsman* (1987), 42 C.C.L.T. 220 at 223 (N.B. C.A.).

99 See, e.g., *Harrison v. Brown*, [1987] 1 W.W.R. 212 (B.C. S.C.); *Colborne v. Llewellyn* (1982), 133 D.L.R. (3d) 284 (N.S. T.D.); *Webber v. Crawford* (1988), 46 C.C.L.T. 1 (B.C. S.C.); *Rogers v. Pierson Estate*, [1993] 4 W.W.R. 583 (Y.T. C.A.); and *Hooiveld v. Van Biert*, [1994] 4 W.W.R. 143 (B.C. C.A.).

of establishing an acceptable excuse falls upon the plaintiff.[100] The courts have accepted as excuses the fact that a plaintiff was an asthmatic who believed that wearing a seat belt would detrimentally affect her asthma,[101] the fact it was a "fine day for driving," "the road was straight and in good condition for driving," "traffic was not heavy," and the driver was "cautious,"[102] the fact that it was a short drive and the plaintiff did not foresee the risk,[103] and the fact that the plaintiff found the shoulder part of the belt uncomfortable.[104]

An interesting issue which has arisen in the cases involves persons injured in vehicles which are not equipped with seat belts. Can a plaintiff be contributorily negligent for not having worn a seat belt, when in fact there was none available in the vehicle? One case, *Nye v. Hogan*,[105] involved a 1964 car which was manufactured without seat belts. The vehicle had been restored by its owner, but seat belts were not installed. The owner was killed in a traffic accident involving the vehicle. In finding that the deceased was contributorily negligent, the judge observed that it is negligent to drive an older ill-equipped vehicle on roads designed for modern vehicles and heavy traffic, or a vehicle not equipped with modern standard safety equipment. Plaintiff passengers in vehicles owned by others and not equipped with seat belts available for their use also have been found negligent for having agreed to ride in such vehicles.[106] These cases dem-

---

100 *Reekie v. Messervey* (1986), 4 B.C.L.R. (2d) 194 (S.C.), additional reasons at (1986), 10 B.C.L.R. (2d) 231 (S.C.), affirmed (1989), 48 C.C.L.T. 217 (B.C. C.A.), leave to appeal to S.C.C. refused (1989), 40 B.C.L.R. (2d) xxxiii (note) (S.C.C.), leave to appeal reversed in part [1990] 3 W.W.R. 673 (S.C.C.).

101 *Ibid.*

102 Huband J.A. in *Genik v. Ewanylo* (1980), 12 C.C.L.T. 121 (Man. C.A.).

103 *Holohan v. Dunfield* (1982), 133 D.L.R. (3d) 267 (N.B. Q.B.).

104 *Anderson v. Davis* (1979), 10 C.C.L.T. 120 (B.C. S.C.), affirmed (1980), 15 C.C.L.T. 192 (B.C. C.A.).

105 [1992] O.J. No. 1490 (Gen. Div.).

106 See, for example, *Watson v. Kang* (1994), 4 B.C.L.R. (3d) 60 (C.A.) — passenger negligent for agreeing to go on a pleasure trip with her boss and his wife, when vehicle did not have seat belt available for her; *Stranden v. Le,* [1994] A.J. No. 428 (Q.B.) — plaintiff passenger, her two children, and driver drove in truck equipped with only two belts. Driver used one, two children strapped in other, plaintiff unbuckled; plaintiff contributorily negligent — should have taken her own car; *Goglin v. Lightheart*, [1992] B.C.J. No. 2416 (S.C.) — plaintiff contributorily negligent for going in car with no available seat belt — should have taken her own car; *Heller v. Martens* (1999), [2000] A.J. No. 1678, 1999 CarswellAlta 1513 (Q.B.), affirmed on another point (2002), 213 D.L.R. (4th) 124 (Alta. C.A.) — driver/employee negligent for driving in a milk van not equipped with seat belts. There are decisions going the other way: see, for example, *Fennellow v. Falez*, [1993] B.C.J. No. 2445 (S.C.), and *Woodgate v. Watson* (1995), 59 B.C.A.C. 226, 1995 CarswellBC 502 (C.A.), leave to appeal refused (1996), 82 B.C.A.C. 240 (note) (S.C.C.), where plaintiffs were found not to have been contributorily negligent, despite the fact that they went into vehicles without available seat belts for them. In the *Fennellow* case, the plaintiff was not found negligent despite the fact that he rode in the open back of a pickup truck. In *Rewcastle v. Sieben,* [2001] 10 W.W.R. 700 (Alta. Q.B.), reconsideration refused [2002] 7 W.W.R. 196 (Alta. C.A.), no contributory negligence was assessed against a passenger who rode in a vehicle without an available seat belt for her use. In *Ford v. Henderson*, 2005 BCSC 609 (S.C.), the seat belt defence was unsuccessful because the trial judge found that the defendant failed to prove that the seat belt was functioning properly. The trial judge conceded that since the car was a newer model, it undoubtedly was equipped with a seat belt.

onstrate the increased willingness on the part of courts to recognize the importance of seat belt use and the significantly greater role of the seat belt defence in negligence cases.

(2) The failure to employ the safety device must have been a causal factor in the plaintiff's injuries.[107] Although theoretically courts ought to isolate the injuries that the plaintiff would have received even had a seat belt been worn from those that were contributed to by the plaintiff's failure to have worn a seat belt, and only then apply the plaintiff's contributory negligence reduction to the latter injuries, as a practical matter this is a difficult task. Courts simplify the matter by applying a percentage reduction to the plaintiff's global damage award.[108] As with the increased willingness on the judiciary's part to accept the seat belt defence, there appears also to have been a gradual, but significant, increase in the degree of fault being assigned to contributorily negligent plaintiffs.[109] It has been suggested that courts adopt, as a matter of judicial policy, a fixed upper limit of a 25 per cent reduction in seat belt cases,[110] but this is as yet not the practice.

---

107 In *MacDonald v. MacInnis* (1993), 126 N.S.R. (2d) 54 (T.D.) a judge was prepared to take "judicial notice" of the probability of reduced injury by wearing a restraining device. This type of ruling, however, is not the norm. Evidence must be led to prove this. See, for example, *Mezzomo v. Mezzomo* (1995), 57 B.C.A.C. 315 (C.A.); *Koopman v. Fehr* (1993), 81 B.C.L.R. (2d) 145 (C.A.); *Bishop (Litigation Guardian of) v. Sexsmith*, [1995] 6 W.W.R. 385 (Sask. Q.B.); *Terracciano (Guardian ad litem of) v. Etheridge* (1997), 36 C.C.L.T. (2d) 92 (B.C. S.C.); and *Madge v. Meyer* (1999), [2000] 5 W.W.R. 38 (Alta. Q.B.), additional reasons at [2000] 6 W.W.R. 272 (Alta. Q.B.), affirmed [2001] 7 W.W.R. 635 (Alta. C.A.), additional reasons at [2002] 5 W.W.R. 50 (Alta. C.A.). In *Labbee v. Peters* (1999), 237 A.R. 382 (C.A.), additional reasons at (2000), 86 Alta. L.R. (3d) 67 (C.A.), affirming (1997), 201 A.R. 241 (Q.B.), the Court of Appeal made the point that the failure to wear a seat belt must have contributed to the "damage or loss", not necessarily to the "injury". Thus if other equally serious injuries resulting in the same losses would have occurred even had a seat belt been worn, there is no reduction.

108 The Saskatchewan Court of Appeal makes this point in *Vigoren v. Nyusten* (2006), 266 D.L.R. (4th) 634 (C.A.), leave to appeal refused (2006), 2006 CarswellSask 715 (S.C.C.), at 664 [D.L.R.], although ultimately it also applied a reduction to the global award.

109 In the first edition, I noted that the degree of fault attributed to the seat belt defence was quite modest — in the range of 10 - 15 per cent. In *Galaske v. O'Donnell*, above, note 92, Cory J. suggested that the range has been between 5 - 25 per cent. Recent case law indicates, however, that reductions of 25 to 35 per cent are not uncommon. It even has been as high as 50 per cent, for example, *Palek v. Hansen* (1997), [1998] 1 W.W.R. 475 (Alta. C.A.); and 75 per cent, see *Chae v. Min* (2001), [2002] 4 W.W.R. 179 (Alta. Q.B.). In *Chae v. Min* (2001), [2002] 4 W.W.R. 179 (Q.B.), the trial judge found the plaintiff 75 per cent liable, but this was reduced to 25 per cent by the Court of Appeal at [2005] 9 W.W.R. 10.

110 Girgulis J. in *Chamberland v. Fleming* (1984), 29 C.C.L.T. 213 (Alta. Q.B.). Justice Girgulis re-iterated this view in *Philip v. Hironaka* (1997), [1998] 3 W.W.R. 703 (Alta. Q.B.), stating that this would be a sensible and appropriate limit in the vast majority of cases. In *Fowler v. Schneider National Carriers Ltd.* (2001), 193 N.S.R. (2d) 206 (C.A.), the Court of Appeal reduced a jury's apportionment of 42.5 per cent for failure to wear a seat belt to 15 per cent. More interestingly, the court, per Freeman J.A., considered 25 per cent to be a cap on the reduction, one "deeply embedded" in the jurisprudence. Freeman J.A. referred to Cory J.'s judgment in *Galaske v. O'Donnell*, [1994] 1 S.C.R. 670, where numerous cases were noted of reductions, none exceeding 25 per cent. Freeman J.A. also referred to the New Brunswick Insurance Act, R.S.N.B. 1973, c. I-12, which in 1996 legislated a 25 per cent cap. Although Freeman J.A. stated that he was not aware of any reductions higher than 25 per cent in Canadian cases, there have been several, as indicated above. Juriansz J.A. in *Snushall v.*

The seat belt defence has been successful in both personal injury and fatal accident cases. Its use in fatal accident cases raises an interesting point. Since damages for serious personal injuries are generally higher than damages awarded in the case of death, should the courts continue to reduce fatal accident awards for the deceased's failure to wear a seat belt? Had the seat belt been worn and the deceased not died, the personal injuries sustained might have resulted in a greater financial responsibility for the negligent defendants.[111]

(3) The fact that the plaintiff's failure to employ a safety device was, or was not, in breach of a legislative provision cannot conclusively determine the contributory negligence issue.[112] There are obviously many unreasonable acts which courts consider to constitute contributory negligence which are not legislatively prohibited. It is thus clearly incorrect for a court to decide that since the failure to employ the safety device was not a statutory offence, it cannot constitute contributory negligence.[113] As discussed previously, however, a statutory duty to wear a seat belt creates a useful standard of conduct which courts may adopt in setting a standard of reasonable care in tort actions.[114] Since all Canadian provinces have legislation requiring the use of seat belts in certain conditions, it is now even more likely that the failure to employ them will constitute contributory negligence.

Fulsang, above, note 95, also held that in no case should the reduction be greater than 25 per cent. The 25 per cent reduction should be made only where all the damages could have been avoided by wearing a seat belt. The Ontario Court of Appeal reduced the jury's reduction, which was 35 per cent, to 5 per cent. This approach was adopted by the Saskatchewan Court of Appeal as well in *Vigoren v. Nyusten* (2006), 266 D.L.R. (4th) 634 (C.A.), leave to appeal refused (2006), 2006 CarswellSask 715 (S.C.C.). Richards J.A. rejected the Alberta Court of Appeal's approach in *Heller v. Martens*, [2002] 9 W.W.R. 71 (C.A.), which looked to the comparative blameworthiness of the parties in allocating responsibility. While not denying that the percentages should be based on comparative fault in theory, the practical difficulties in deciding this led Richards J.A. to adopt the formulaic approach of 0 – 25 per cent, depending upon how much of the injury would have been prevented by seat belt use. Newfoundland and Labrador has legislated a mandatory 25 per cent reduction in damages for the plaintiff's failure to wear a seat belt, unless that person can prove that there was no causal link between the failure and the injuries. See Automobile Insurance Act, R.S.N.L. 1990, c. A-22, s. 28.1; am. 2004 c. 27, s. 7.

111 This point is made by Thornicroft, "Contributory Negligence and the Seat Belt Law" (1984), 42 Advocate 29. My answer to this is that death is the more serious injury, notwithstanding the peculiarities of the damage assessment process. In *Labbee v. Peters,* above, note 107, the court seems to implicitly support Thornicroft's point because it held that what is relevant to the contributory negligence issue is whether the negligence contributed to the "damage or loss", i.e., the "compensable consequences of the injury" and not to the injury itself. The issue in the case, however, did not deal with Thornicroft's point. The question in that case was whether an equally serious different type of injury would have occurred even had a seat belt been worn.

112 See *Migliore v. Gerard* (1987), 42 D.L.R. (4th) 619 (Ont. H.C.). Cases in which plaintiffs were found to have been contributorily negligent even though legislative provisions did not require them to wear a seat belt include *Wallace v. Berrigan* (1988), 47 D.L.R. (4th) 752 (N.S. C.A.); *Shaw v. Roemer* (1982), 134 D.L.R. (3d) 590 (N.S. C.A.); *Jaswal v. Tait* (1987), 15 B.C.L.R. (2d) 232 (S.C.); *MacDonald v. MacInnis*, above, note 107; and *Heller v. Martens*, above, note 110.

113 As some courts have indeed decided. See, e.g., *Shkwarchuk v. Hansen* (1984), 30 C.C.L.T. 121 (Sask. Q.B.).

114 *Sask. Wheat Pool v. Canada* [1983] 1 S.C.R. 205.

(4) The failure of parents or drivers to ensure that young children are secured in a seat belt or car seat may be negligent conduct.[115] This may be so whether or not there is legislation requiring drivers or parents to ensure that young passengers are properly protected.[116] A parent or driver can be third-partied by other defendants involved in the accident, and be required to contribute to the injured child's damages. In *Migliore v. Gerard*,[117] the court, while accepting the argument, relieved the parents of liability on the basis of the accepted standard of care by parents generally in the community in 1981.

3. VOLUNTARY ASSUMPTION OF RISK

(a) Basis of the Defence

Although the defence of voluntary assumption of risk, otherwise known as the defence of consent or *volenti non fit injuria*, has declined in importance, far overshadowed by the more frequently successful defence of contributory negligence, it can still be, at least in theory, a relevant consideration in certain types of negligence cases.[118] Furthermore, its theoretical basis continues to interest courts and commentators.[119]

If successfully pleaded, the defence of voluntary assumption of risk will completely exonerate a defendant from liability for the plaintiff's injuries. Why is this so? What is the basis of the defence?

The defence as it relates to an action for negligence[120] arises when there is an agreement between two or more parties that they will participate in an activity which involves a risk of injury, and will give up their right to sue in the event that one of these risks eventuates. The agreement, whether made expressly by words,

---

115 This point was affirmed by the Supreme Court of Canada in *Galaske v. O'Donnell*, [1994] 1 S.C.R. 670, discussed above in Chapter 6. As noted there, the driver of a truck was found negligent for not having ensured that his young passenger was in a seat belt, despite the fact that the child's father was in the truck at the time. In *Parker v. Merkel*, [1994] B.C.J. No. 1175 (S.C.), the court held that there is a duty on the driver to inform passengers of the location of seat belts when they are not readily available.

116 See *Migliore v. Gerard*, above, note 112. However, in *Pelletier v. Olson* (1987), 42 C.C.L.T. 129 (Sask. Q.B.), the court relieved a parent of liability based upon the fact that there was no statutory provision requiring seat belts for children under the age of five.

117 *Ibid.*

118 Although it is interesting to note that in the six years that have passed since I wrote the last edition of this text, I have not been able to find one case in which the defence has been successful. In view of this, its continued relevance seems to be somewhat questionable.

119 See, among others, Jaffey, "*Volenti Non Fit Injuria*", [1985] Cambridge L.J. 87; Ingman, "A History of the Defence of *Volenti Non Fit Injuria*" (1981), 26 Juridical Rev. 1; Gaetanos, "Assumption of Risk: Casuistry in the Law of Negligence" (1980-81), 83 W. V. L. Rev. 471; Hertz, "*Volenti Non Fit Injuria*: A Guide", in Klar (ed.), *Studies in Canadian Tort Law* (1977), Chapter 3; and S.D. Sugarman, "Assumption of Risk" (1997), 31 Valpraiso U.L. Rev. 833.

120 Consent in the intentional tort context differs from consent in the negligence context. Consent as a defence to intentional torts applies when the plaintiff agreed to the very conduct which constituted the tort. For example, a boxer consents to contact which in the absence of consent would have been an actionable battery. In negligence law, consent goes not to the acceptance of tortious conduct, but to the risks of injury which might occur as a result of negligent conduct. Since there is no action in negligence unless damage occurs, you do not consent to the tort, but to the risk of injury.

or implicitly by conduct, is entered into before the activity commences.[121] It was described by Estey J. in the following way:

> Thus, *volenti* will arise only where the circumstances are such that it is clear that the plaintiff, knowing of the virtually certain risk of harm, in essence bargained away his right to sue for injuries incurred as a result of any negligence on the defendant's part. The acceptance of the risk may be express or may arise by necessary implication from the conduct of the parties, but it will arise. . . only where there can truly be said to be an understanding on the part of both parties that the defendant assumed no responsibility to take due care for the safety of the plaintiff, and the plaintiff did not expect him to.[122]

Voluntary assumption of risk is a complete defence to the plaintiff's action. Its place in the negligence action can be explained in one of three ways. First, it has been suggested that the defence goes to the very existence of the duty relationship. The basic proposition is that there is no duty to one who consents.[123] Thus, an agreement that the defendant will not be held legally accountable to the plaintiff for the consequences of unreasonable conduct will relieve the defendant of an otherwise existing legal duty to take reasonable care for the plaintiff's protection. This no duty explanation of the defence has strong support in both case law and textual authorities. In *Lehnert v. Stein*,[124] for example, Cartwright J. quoted with approval the following passage from *Salmond On Torts*:[125]

> The true question in every case is: did the plaintiff give a real consent to the assumption of risk without compensation; did the consent really absolve the defendant from the duty to take care?[126]

The no duty approach was clearly articulated by Asquith J. in *Dann v. Hamilton*,[127] in the following terms:

> As a matter of strict pleading it seems that the plea *volenti* is a denial of any duty at all, and, therefore, of any breach of duty, and an admission of negligence cannot strictly be combined with the plea.

The defence has also been explained in relation to the breach of duty aspect of the negligence suit. The substance of this suggestion is that the effect of a plaintiff's consent, or voluntary assumption of risk, is to qualify the nature of a defendant's duty to take reasonable care. In other words, in determining the scope of the defendant's duty, the facts that the plaintiff knew of the risks and the nature of the proposed activity, and agreed to assume these risks, are considered to be critical in considering the question of breach. Put simply, it is argued that a defendant cannot be found negligent for acting in the way which was contemplated and agreed to by the participants. This no negligence approach also has some

---

121 If the negligent act and damage have already occurred, the defence of consent is not available to assist the defendant. As noted by Jaffey, above, note 119, this would be an agreement to release the defendant from its liability, and would have to be contractually valid.

122 *Dubé v. Labar* (1986), 36 C.C.L.T. 105 at 114 (S.C.C.).

123 Which is roughly what *volenti non fit injuria* means.

124 (1962), 36 D.L.R. (2d) 159 (S.C.C.).

125 13th ed. (1961), at 44.

126 This language has been used in several cases. See, e.g., Taylor J. in *Mack v. Enns* (1981), 17 C.C.L.T. 291 at 305 (B.C. S.C.), "Did the plaintiff, then, convey to the defendant an intention to relieve the defendant of any legal duty of care towards him?"

127 [1939] 1 All E.R. 59 at 60.

support in the authorities.[128] One may, for example, explain the case of *Hagerman v. Niagara Falls (City)*[129] on this basis. The plaintiff spectator was hit in the eye by a puck during a hockey game played in the defendant's arena. The defendant had taken some steps to protect spectators, but these of course were not foolproof, and the puck went into the stands. The court held that the defendant owed the plaintiff a duty to take reasonable steps for her protection. Whether, however, this duty was satisfied depended in part on the plaintiff's knowledge and acceptance of the risks associated with the activity. In this case, in view of the plaintiff's knowledge and acceptance of the ordinary risks of the event, reasonable steps had been taken, and the defendant accordingly was found not negligent. Although the trial judge argued that *volenti* was not relevant to the case, since there was no negligence, it can be seen that the finding of no negligence in fact depended in part upon the consent concept itself.

Finally, it is also argued by some that it is useful to see the defence as not relating, in the first instance, to either the notion of duty or breach, but strictly as a defence. In other words, the defence is relevant only where both a duty relationship and a breach of duty have been proved.[130] According to this approach, the defence does not alter the defendant's ordinary obligation owed to all neighbours, but relieves the defendant from liability in this case, because of the nature of the plaintiff's conduct. In *Thompson v. Steinbring*,[131] for example, the court upheld the defence and stated that the defendant should not be held liable "because of the plaintiff's own conduct and not because of a lack of duty owed to the plaintiff." The gist of this argument is that the defence of consent is only relevant once duty and breach have otherwise first been proven. It is hoped that by framing the issue in this way, courts will not introduce into the already difficult duty and breach concepts this additional complicating issue.

In the final analysis, it is unimportant how the defence is seen within the context of the negligence action as long as two points are remembered. The burden of proving the allegation that the plaintiff voluntarily assumed the risk of injury is a primary burden which falls upon the defendant. As well, the question is one of fact, to be tried not by the judge but by the fact-finder or jury.[132]

It is also instructive to inquire as to what the common law's objectives are in giving recognition to and upholding the defence of voluntary assumption of risk. Differing views as to the function of the defence may lead to differences in the way it is applied by the courts. As well, justification for the defence must be persuasive in view of the serious consequences of its successful pleading. Not only will the defence deprive an injured person of any compensation for the injuries which were suffered, but it also may encourage unreasonably dangerous conduct which endangers not only the immediate parties, but innocent strangers as well.

---

128 See Payne, "Assumption of Risk and Negligence" (1957), 35 Can. Bar Rev. 950, where some of the leading proponents of this view are noted.

129 (1980), 114 D.L.R. (3d) 184 (Ont. H.C.).

130 See, e.g., Linden and Feldthusen, *Canadian Tort Law*, 8th ed. (2006), at 509.

131 (1986), 46 Sask. R. 119 at 121 (Q.B.).

132 See, e.g., *Dubé v. Labar*, above, note 122.

One may suggest different functions. The first is a purely moralistic one. Many of the cases in which the defence has been successfully pleaded involved joint participation in unreasonably dangerous activities, which often involved criminal wrongdoing. The courts did not want to lend their assistance to these wrongdoing victims by relieving them of the consequences of their wrongdoing.[133] Second, there is the element of fairness to defendants. In some situations, it may only have been because of the prior consent of the plaintiff to assume the risks of injury that the defendant agreed to allow the plaintiff to participate in the activity in the first place. It seemed only fair, therefore, that the defendant's legitimate expectations and reliance be respected by the court. As well, for certain types of arrangements it may be economically efficient to permit the parties to allocate the financial responsibility for the injuries which may result from the proposed activity in the manner they consider to be best. Finally, it has been suggested that the defence reflects "the stout individualism of the early common law" which allows every one to work out his or her own destiny.[134]

(b) Express Agreements

An agreement to accept the risks of unreasonable conduct can be made expressly or implicitly.[135]

An express agreement to accept the risks of injury stemming from the defendant's unreasonable conduct can be entered into as part of a contractual arrangement with the defendant. In these cases, the validity of these exemption clauses, or waivers of liability, will be determined as a matter of contract law. In *Dyck v. Man. Snowmobile Assn. Inc.*,[136] for example, the plaintiff paid $25 in consideration for the privilege of competing in the defendant association's snowmobile race. As part of the contractual relationship, the plaintiff expressly agreed to hold "harmless" the association, and its officials, servants and representatives, from all legal claims for damages stemming from the negligence of the parties. When the plaintiff was injured as a result of the negligence of one of the employees administering the race, the determinative issue was the validity of the release, especially in terms of its applicability to the employee. The courts held that the clause was effective in protecting both the association and its employees from liability and dismissed the action. The legal precedents relied upon by the courts in coming to this conclusion were contract law cases, and more particularly, cases dealing with the rights of third parties to benefit from exemption clauses in

---

133 What makes this argument unconvincing, however, is the fact that by refusing to assist the victim in any way, the court was thereby assisting the defendant, and relieving that party from the consequences of the wrongdoing.

134 See Linden and Feldthusen, *Canadian Tort Law*, 8th ed. (2006), at 508.

135 The Supreme Court of Canada has stated this in several of its *volenti* judgments. See, e.g., *Dubé v. Labar*, above, note 122; *Car & Gen. Ins. Corp. v. Seymour* (1956), 2 D.L.R. (2d) 369 (S.C.C.); *Miller v. Decker* (1957), 9 D.L.R. (2d) 1 (S.C.C.), among others. For an article discussing express disclaimer clauses, see Jeffrey J. Neumann, "Disclaimer Clauses And Personal Injury" (1991), 55 Sask. L. Rev. 312.

136 (1981), 17 C.C.L.T. 225 (Man. Q.B.), affirmed (1982), 21 C.C.L.T. 38 (Man. C.A.), which was affirmed (1985), 32 C.C.L.T. 153 (S.C.C.).

contracts to which they were not privy.[137] The tort defence of consent was effectively overcome by the contractual exemption clause.[138] In *Crocker v. Sundance Northwest Resorts Ltd.*,[139] on the other hand, the Supreme Court of Canada, affirming the trial court's decision, refused to uphold a contractual exemption clause. The Supreme Court found that since the clause had not been drawn to the plaintiff's attention, had not been read by him, and was not otherwise known to him, it could not be relied upon.[140]

A plaintiff can expressly agree to exempt a defendant from liability outside the terms of a contract. This can occur in the context of gratuitous relationships, as in allowing others to come onto your premises, or agreeing to give them a lift in your car.[141] It might also transpire that an express disclaimer clause which is part of a contractual relationship is invalid for lack of consideration or for some other reason based on contract law principles. In this case, there is no reason why the tort defence of consent, based on an express assumption of risk, ought not to be available to the defendant. This can occur through either verbal or written notice, the terms of which are made clear to and agreed to by the plaintiff. As with contractual exemption clauses, these express agreements will be interpreted strictly. They must be clear, brought to the parties' attention, adequate for the purpose for which they are intended, and agreed to by the parties.

---

137 For example, *Scruttons Ltd. v. Midland Silicones Ltd.*, [1962] 1 All E.R. 1 (H.L.); *Greenwood Shopping Plaza Ltd. v. Beattie* (1980), 111 D.L.R. (3d) 257 (S.C.C.), among others.

138 A similar case is *Delaney v. Cascade River Holidays Ltd.* (1981), 19 C.C.L.T. 78 (B.C. S.C.), affirmed (1983), 24 C.C.L.T. 6 (B.C. C.A.). The deceased was a paying passenger on a white-water rafting excursion. He signed a standard liability release and an agreement to assume all risks. This release was upheld, on the basis of contract law, by the trial judge and was affirmed on appeal, with one dissent. The contract defence in essence overtook the need to show consent in tort. The same result was arrived at in *Wurban v. Lipak* (1982), 23 C.C.L.T. 37 (Alta. Q.B.). A waiver and indemnity agreement signed by a participant in a motorcar race was upheld by the court. See also *Karroll v. Silver Star Mountain Resorts Ltd.* (1988), 47 C.C.L.T. 269 (B.C. S.C.); *Ocsko v. Cypress Bowl Recreations* (1992), 95 D.L.R. (4th) 701 (B.C. C.A.); *Schuster v. Blackcomb Skiing Enterprises Limited Partnership*, [1995] 3 W.W.R. 443 (B.C. S.C.); and *Goodspeed v. Tyax Mountain Lake Resort Ltd.*, 2005 BCSC 1577 (S.C.).

139 (1983), 150 D.L.R. (3d) 478 (Ont. H.C.), reversed (1985), 20 D.L.R. (4th) 552 (Ont. C.A.), which was reversed (1988), 44 C.C.L.T. 225 (S.C.C.).

140 See also *Smith v. Horizon Aero Sports Ltd.* (1981), 19 C.C.L.T. 89 (B.C. S.C.). The case concerned an injury suffered by the plaintiff during a parachute jump. As part of their contractual relationship, the parties had agreed to a "hold harmless" agreement. The court strictly construed the agreement and held that it did not apply to injuries resulting from the defendants' negligence. See also *Greeven v. Blackcomb Skiing Enterprises Ltd.* (1994), 22 C.C.L.T. (2d) 265 (B.C. S.C.). The court held that there is an onus on the party relying upon the exemption clause to prove that reasonable measures had been taken to bring it to the attention of the plaintiff. The defendant failed to discharge the onus in this case. A case where a release was upheld is *Dixon v. Kamloops Exhibition Assn.*, 2003 CarswellBC 769, 2003 BCCA 174 (B.C. C.A.). Also see *Parker v. Ingalls*, 2006 BCSC 942 (S.C.).

141 Fleming, *The Law of Torts*, 9th ed. (1998), at 328. See, e.g., *Birch v. Thomas*, [1972] 1 All E.R. 905 (C.A.), where an uninsured driver allowed his friends to drive with him on the express condition that they do so on their own risk and waiving their rights to make claims against him.

(c) Implied Agreements

More relevant from the perspective of tort law, and certainly more difficult to understand and apply, are cases of implied voluntary assumption of risk. It is clear law that even where there has been no express waiver of liability or exemption clause, a trier of fact may imply from the parties' conduct an agreement that, in the event of injury from negligent behaviour, no law suit would be brought. When a court will do this is difficult to predict with certainty, although one can identify factors which provide helpful guides. It is also important to keep in mind two points which weigh heavily against this finding. Since the defence of voluntary assumption of risk will completely deprive the victim of any compensation while exonerating a negligent defendant, the courts will naturally resist it. As well, where there has been no express agreement, the fiction of implying the agreement, especially where its consequences are so significant to the parties, is too artificial a finding for most courts to make.[142]

The area in which the defence of implied voluntary assumption of risk most often arose was the "drunk driver/willing passenger" situation.[143] It was here that the courts have struggled to provide acceptable rationales for the application of the defence. In particular, the Supreme Court of Canada, in a series of three drunk driver/willing passenger cases,[144] and one sober driver/drunk passenger case,[145] provided the tests and rationale for the defence which have since formed the basis of Canadian tort law in this area.

In the first of the Supreme Court cases, *Car & Gen. Ins. Corp. v. Seymour*,[146] the plaintiff was seriously injured in an automobile accident caused by the drunk driver of the car in which she was riding. Although the plaintiff knew of the condition of the driver, she did not approve of it, and had in fact attempted to have someone else drive the car.[147] The Supreme Court, rather than focussing primarily on the passenger's conduct alone, emphasized the bilateral situation, and more particularly the agreement aspect of the parties' relationship. Could one legitimately infer from the conduct *of both parties* that the plaintiff had impliedly agreed to waive the defendant's legal responsibility for injuries which might result from his drunk driving? The implicit terms of the plaintiff's and defendant's activity became critical to the success of the defence. Did the defendant require, as part of the activity, that the plaintiff assume the risks of the activity? Did the plaintiff agree to assume these risks? The notion that the defence involved a

142 It is becoming increasingly rare to find cases where the *volenti* defence has been successfully invoked based upon an "implied" agreement. Discussion of the defence is thus quickly becoming a matter of historical interest.

143 Sport injuries also provide many cases, although these most typically involve intentional torts. As well, the liability issue in sport cases based on negligence is frequently resolved at the level of either duty or breach.

144 *Car & Gen. Ins. Corp. v. Seymour* (1956), 2 D.L.R. (2d) 369 (S.C.C.); *Miller v. Decker* (1957), 9 D.L.R. (2d) 1 (S.C.C.); and *Lehnert v. Stein* (1962), 36 D.L.R. (2d) 157 (S.C.C.).

145 *Eid v. Dumas* (1969), 5 D.L.R. (3d) 561 (S.C.C.).

146 Above, note 144.

147 Several other factors were noted by Rand J. The plaintiff was a young woman, not terribly sophisticated, unfamiliar with her surroundings, and possibly intimidated by the event. The defendant was dominating and aggressive.

unilateral decision on the part of the plaintiff to take a chance was replaced by the requirement of a bilateral arrangement, whose implicit terms must have been agreed to by both parties in order for it to be valid. The court found that the facts of the case did not support the inference that the joint activity agreed to allowed for a reduced level of care on the defendant's part, and rejected the defence.

In the second case, *Miller v. Decker*,[148] the conduct of all of the parties was more questionable. The case involved three men, all of whom were involved in a "common purpose," which involved an evening of "beering." The majority of the court found that "the drinking of each was an encouragement to the same act in others."[149] Although the court did not abandon the reasoning of its judgment in *Car & Gen. Ins. Corp. v. Seymour*, it is interesting to note that on the facts of *Miller v. Decker*, the majority of the court emphasized the plaintiff's own offensive conduct in finding the implied agreement to accept the responsibility for the evening's results.[150]

The facts of the third case, *Lehnert v. Stein*,[151] resembled closely the facts of *Car & Gen. Ins. Corp. v. Seymour*, with the same legal resolution. The plaintiff was a young woman, had not been actively participating in the drinking, and was not confident of her position.[152] On these facts, the majority emphasized the agreement aspect of the defence. Cartwright J. adopted the distinction advanced by Professor Williams[153] between the physical risks of an activity and its legal risks, stating that for the defence of consent to succeed, there must be an acceptance of both.[154]

In the fourth case, *Eid v. Dumas*,[155] the consent defence was rejected. As with the earlier cases, the court focussed on the interaction between the parties. The passenger had not "actively contributed" to the accident and "was merely a passive victim and not responsible for the way the car was driven."[156] The common purpose and active encouragement which gave rise to the implied agreement in *Miller v. Decker* was not present in this case.

One may make several observations regarding the defence of implied consent as a result of these Supreme Court of Canada judgments. There is no doubt that on at least the theoretical level, the success of the defence depends upon the ability of a court to find an implied waiver of legal liability. This, all would agree, sets a standard which, if taken seriously, will rarely be met. It is not realistic to impose this implied agreement upon parties who are frequently unaware of the legal niceties surrounding these types of events, and who are not deliberating upon the

---

148 Above, note 144.

149 9 D.L.R. (2d) 1 at 3.

150 One must note, however, the dissenting judgment of Abbott J., *ibid.*, at 9, with its emphasis on "the express or implied bargain between the parties whereby the plaintiff gave up his right of action."

151 Above, note 144.

152 As stated by Cartwright J., 36 D.L.R. (2d) 157 at 164, "she went with him because he urged her to do so and she lacked the resolution to refuse."

153 Williams, *Joint Torts and Contributory Negligence* (1951), at 308.

154 Physical risk is the risk of damage; legal risk is the risk of damage for which there will be no legal redress.

155 Above, note 145.

156 (1969), 5 D.L.R. (3d) 561 at 567.

physical or legal risks of dangerous conduct.[157] Where parties, however, have jointly engaged in reckless conduct, with the active participation of all, a new factor may enter the equation. Courts may be reluctant, on the basis of the moral issues discussed above, to allow compensation in such circumstances. Thus the desire to punish, or to set down moral principles, may incline the court to find the implied agreement. Although one may argue that the more actively involved the plaintiff was in the reckless activity which produced the injuries, the more likely it is that there was an implied agreement to assume the legal risks of this activity, this is an argument which I do not find persuasive. It is my assessment that since the Supreme Court judgments, the success of the consent defence in individual negligence actions can be explained by the interplay between the bilateral agreement requirement and the use of the defence to condemn an unworthy plaintiff.

One of the strongest affirmations of the bilateral agreement approach was articulated by a Nova Scotia trial court, and by its Court of Appeal, in *Crossan v. Gillis*.[158] The case involved a drunk driver and two passengers, one of whom was drunk, and the other sober. Applying the case law which stressed the need for an express or implied bargain between the parties, whereby the plaintiff gave up his right of action,[159] the trial judge held that a drunk passenger was unable, due to his condition, to make this bargain, and therefore the defence could not apply to his case.[160] The sober passenger, however, was not disabled in this respect, and the defence was held to be applicable. It is therefore clear that in the interplay between the bargain requirement and the moral statement, in so far as this court was concerned the former was predominant, so much so that a less worthy claimant was treated better than was a more innocent one.[161]

In the Court of Appeal, MacKeigan C.J.N.S. strongly affirmed the bilateral agreement approach, finding that the evidence indicated that neither passenger impliedly agreed to give up their legal right of action. The Nova Scotia Chief Justice stated:

---

157 This passage was quoted with approval by Mackenzie J.A. in *Joe v. Paradis* (2008), [2008] B.C.J. No. 198, 2008 CarswellBC 226 (C.A.), at para. 16. Although the jury had applied the defence, the Court of Appeal reversed the decision. As stated by Mackenzie J.A. at para. 20, "*volenti* should not be invoked unless there is evidence that the parties put their minds to the question of legal liability and expressly or tacitly made an agreement to waive liability that could be supported on basic contract law principles." As noted above, even express, contractual agreements are frequently ignored by courts. This certainly makes it unlikely that implied agreements will be upheld.

158 (1979), 7 C.C.L.T. 269 (N.S. C.A.), reversing in part (1977), 4 C.C.L.T. 184 (N.S. T.D.).

159 In addition to the Supreme Court of Canada decisions noted above, the trial judge also referred to *MacDonald v. Flynn*, N.S.T.D., 1973 (unreported).

160 There are contrary decisions, which do not allow the fact that the party was drunk to work advantageously in this way. See, e.g., *Priestly v. Gilbert* (1973), 40 D.L.R. (3d) 349 (Ont. C.A.), and *Tomlinson v. Harrison* (1972), 24 D.L.R. (3d) 26 (Ont. H.C.). See, however, *Dore v. Clark* (1988), 9 M.V.R. (2d) 222 (N.B. C.A.), where the plaintiff's condition was a factor in the defence's rejection.

161 For a criticism see Klar, "Annotation" (1977), 4 C.C.L.T. 185. One of the questions I ask is this: how could the drunk driver set the terms of the undertaking, in view of his own inebriation? See Hertz, "*Volenti Non Fit Injuria:* A Guide", above, note 119, for a discussion of the possibility of a unilateral undertaking on the passenger's part.

> . . . Canadian law now requires proof that a bilateral bargain was actually made, expressly or by necessary implication from the facts, with the onus on the defendant to advance such proof, a burden especially difficult to discharge in passenger gross negligence cases.[162]

His Lordship stressed that the evidence must *necessarily* infer such a bargain, it not being sufficient to prove mere knowledge and acceptance of the risks of injury. There must have been "an actual bargain" — not merely "an imaginary interchange which did not take place and which it is difficult to imagine ever taking place."[163] His Lordship conceded that this emphasis on agreement and waiver makes the possibility of ever proving the defence of consent in drunk driving cases very remote.[164]

In the most recent Supreme Court of Canada judgment dealing with the defence, *Dubé v. Labar*,[165] this approach was reaffirmed. Estey J. conceded that the defence will "necessarily be inapplicable in the great majority of drunken driver/willing passenger cases."[166] Wilson J. stated that "it was not enough for the jury to find that the plaintiff had voluntarily assumed the risk of harm. They had to go on and determine whether or not the plaintiff had agreed to absolve the defendant either expressly or by necessary implication from any liability for negligence."[167]

In view of this strong resistence to the application of the *volenti* defence from authoritative courts, it is highly unlikely that the defence will be successful in a

---

162 7 C.C.L.T. 269 at 277-78.

163 *Ibid.*, at 282.

164 MacKeigan C.J.N.S. stresses in several parts of his judgment the unlikelihood of ever succeeding on the consent defence in automobile passenger cases except where there has been an express waiver. Contributory negligence, however, should be a viable defence. See, however, *Gosling v. Roper*, [2002] 5 W.W.R. 79 (Alta. C.A.), affirming (1999), [1999] A.J. No. 704, [1999] A.J. No. 704 (Q.B.). The Court of Appeal affirmed a trial judgment that rejected the contributory negligence defence. Despite the fact that all the parties had been drinking, the passenger herself was impaired, the driver had smoked marijuana, and the plaintiff passenger was aware of all of this, no contributory negligence was found. According to the trial court, there was insufficient action in encouraging the drinking and driving, and insufficient awareness of the impairment to justify finding the plaintiff at fault. This should be compared with the later decision in *Robinson v. Williams Estate* (2005), 34 C.C.L.T. (3d) 131 (Alta. Q.B.), additional reasons at (2005), 2005 CarswellAlta 1972 (Q.B.), affirmed (2007), 44 C.C.L.T. (3d) 1 (Alta. C.A.). In this case, the plaintiff was found 25 per cent contributorily negligent for going into a car with a drunk driver. The trial judge held that in view of the comparative blameworthiness approach adopted by the Court of Appeal in *Heller v. Martens*, [2002] 9 W.W.R. 71 (C.A.), *Gosling* should not be followed. Moreover, the two cases were distinguished on their facts.

165 (1986), 36 C.C.L.T. 105 (S.C.C.).

166 *Ibid.*, at 115.

167 *Ibid.*, at 119. The Supreme Court also discussed the *volenti* defence, albeit *in obiter*, in *Hall v. Hebert*, [1993] 2 S.C.R. 159. As will be discussed below, the case involved the application of the *ex turpi* defence in a car accident scenario. *Volenti* itself was not raised as a defence. However, Cory J. referred to it in his judgment, noting that it still applies to tort cases for damages caused by negligence or intentional torts, is based on consent to the legal risks of injury, is rarely accepted, has been severely limited by the courts, and will be applicable only in a narrow range of cases. As I discussed in my case comment at (1993), 72 Can. Bar Rev. 553, the *Hall v. Hebert* decision does not bode well for the future of *volenti* in Canada. The court's emphasis on the compensatory function of negligence law, and the corresponding de-emphasis of the morality of tort, is a bad sign for a defence which to a large extent is based on the notion that wrongdoers should not be compensated for the consequences of their own wrongdoing.

negligence action. While it is true that the defence has succeeded in the past,[168] the trend in recent years has clearly been to reject it.[169] It may be opportune for the Supreme Court of Canada to eliminate the defence of implied consent from negligence law, as it has effectively done with the defence of illegality, in order to erase any uncertainty which may exist concerning its current viability.

4. ILLEGALITY

(a) Introduction

One of the most obscure, yet intriguing, defences to an action in negligence is that of illegality, or *ex turpi causa non oritur actio*. The defence has been of interest to numerous commentators,[170] and despite criticism, it even seemed for a while that *ex turpi* was encountering a rebirth in Canadian tort law.[171] This rebirth

---

168 See, for example, *Quinlin v. Steffens* (1980), 12 C.C.L.T. 162 (Ont. H.C.); *Henderson v. Pearson Forest Prod. Ltd.* (1979), 10 C.C.L.T. 209 (Ont. H.C.); *Cherrey v. Steinke* (1979), 9 C.C.L.T. 276 (Man. Q.B.), affirmed [1980] 6 W.W.R. 298 (Man. C.A.); *Boulay v. Wild* (1971), [1972] 2 W.W.R. 234 (Alta. C.A.); *Tallow v. Tailfeathers*, [1973] 6 W.W.R. 732 (Alta. C.A.); *Tomlinson v. Harrison* (1971), [1972] 1 O.R. 670 (H.C.); *Kinney v. Haveman* (1976), 1 C.C.L.T. 229 (B.C. S.C.); and *Dallibar v. Gillies* (November 6, 1991), Doc. Grand Forks Registry 26/88, [1991] B.C.J. No. 3421 (S.C.).

169 Aside from the recent cases discussed above, see *Mongovius v. Marchand* (1988), 44 C.C.L.T. 18 (B.C. S.C.); *Baumeister v. Drake* (1986), 38 C.C.L.T. 1 (B.C. S.C.); *Poirier v. Murphy* (1986), 36 C.C.L.T. 160 (B.C. S.C.); *Schmidt v. Sharpe* (1983), 27 C.C.L.T. 1 (Ont. H.C.); *Schill v. Weimer* (1980), 5 Sask. R. 112 (Q.B.), varied on other grounds (1981), 132 D.L.R. (3d) 25 (Sask. C.A.); *Schanuel v. Hoglund*, [1980] 3 W.W.R. 544 (Alta. C.A.); *Court v. Schwartz* (1994), [1994] B.C.J. No. 2164, 1994 CarswellBC 2520 (S.C.), additional reasons at (1995), 1995 CarswellBC 2281 (S.C.); *Nielsen v. Brunet Estate* (1994), 95 B.C.L.R. (2d) 303 (C.A.); *Clarance v. Kerr*, [2000] O.T.C. 832, 2000 CarswellOnt 4563 (S.C.J.); among others. The defence was recently applied in *Laws v. Wright*, [2000] 5 W.W.R. 325 (Alta. Q.B.). A rider was bitten by a horse. She approached the horse to feed it despite the fact that she had been warned not to. The case was dismissed based on assumption of risk and also due to lack of foreseeability. There was also consideration of the Occupiers' Liability Act, R.S.A. 1980, c. O-3, s. 9, which deals specifically with warnings. Thus, there were several reasons in this case to deny the plaintiff's claim, aside from the *volenti* defence.

170 See, e.g., Fridman, "The Wrongdoing Plaintiff" (1972), 18 McGill L.J. 275; Weinrib, "Illegality as a Tort Defence" (1976), 26 U.T.L.J. 28; Gibson, "Illegality of Plaintiff's Conduct as a Defence" (1969), 47 Can. Bar Rev. 89; Swanton, "Plaintiff a Wrongdoer: Joint Complicity in an Illegal Enterprise as a Defence to Negligence" (1980-82), 9 Sydney L. Rev. 304; Ford, "Tort and Illegality: The *Ex Turpi Causa* Defence in Negligence Law" (1977-78), 11 Melbourne U. L. Rev. 32, 164; DeBattista, "*Ex Turpi Causa* Returns to the English Law of Torts: Taking Advantage of a Wrong Way Out" (1984), 13 Anglo-Am. L. Rev. 15; Crago, "The Defence of Illegality in Negligence Actions" (1964), 4 Melbourne U. L. Rev. 534; R. Glotcheski, "Plaintiff's Illegality as a Bar to Recovery of Personal Injury Damages (1999), 19 L.S. 6.

171 See Linden, *Canadian Tort Law*, 5th ed. (1993), at 473: "There has been a rebirth of an old, harsh doctrine of the common law — *ex turpi causa non oritur actio*, or what may be called the illegality defence." According to the case law, Linden was right. In recent years, there had been at least three new cases where the defence had been successfully employed: *Norberg v. Wynrib* (1988), 44 C.C.L.T. 184 (B.C. S.C.), affirmed (1990), 66 D.L.R. (4th) 553 (B.C. C.A.), reversed [1992] 4 W.W.R. 577 (S.C.C.); *Mongovius v. Marchand* (1988), 44 C.C.L.T. 18 (B.C. S.C.); and *Johnson v. Grandview Royal Can. Legion Branch 179*, [1988] 5 W.W.R. 267 (B.C. C.A.). In another case, *Zickefoose (Next Friend of) v. Barotto Sports Ltd.* (1992), 91 D.L.R. (4th) 116 (Alta. Q.B.), reversed (1992), 99 D.L.R. (4th) 57 (Alta. C.A.), Chief

was short-lived. In *Hall v. Hebert*,[172] the Supreme Court of Canada restricted the applicability of the illegality defence in tort claims, virtually eliminating it from personal injury actions for compensation.

(b) *Hall v. Hebert*

In *Hall v. Hebert*, two young men went to a party, and after a long night of drinking, were involved in a car accident. The driver of the car at the time was Hall; the car belonged to Hebert, his friend. The accident occurred when Hall lost control of the car and it overturned in a ditch. Although no serious injuries were apparent at the time, it was later discovered that Hall had suffered head injuries in the accident. He sued his friend Hebert, alleging negligence in allowing him to drive the car, despite the fact that he was drunk.

Among the various issues which arose in the case was that of the applicability of the illegality defence. The British Columbia Court of Appeal accepted it as one of the reasons to dismiss the plaintiff's claim.[173] Gibbs J.A. viewed the defence as being available in tort claims "wherever the conduct of the plaintiff giving rise to the claim is so tainted with criminality or culpable immorality that as a matter of public policy the Court will not assist him to recover."[174] Based on the facts of this case, Gibbs J.A.'s conclusion was that "fair-minded, right-thinking people would be outraged if the Court lent its assistance to this drunk driver to recover damages from his drunk passenger."[175]

The Supreme Court of Canada reversed the appeal judgment, based both on its disagreement with Gibbs J.A.'s view of public sentiment as expressed above, but more importantly, on the role of *ex turpi* and its viability in tort cases. Whereas existing case law had suggested several objectives which were thought to be served by the illegality defence,[176] the majority of the Supreme Court, per McLachlin J., viewed the objectives of the defence very narrowly. Its purposes are to prevent a person from profiting from an illegal or wrongful act or from evading a criminal penalty by means of securing tort damages. According to McLachlin

---

Justice Moore stated that the Supreme Court's judgment in *Can. Cement LaFarge v. B.C. Lightweight Aggregate* (1983), 145 D.L.R. (3d) 385, certainly indicated that "*ex turpi* is alive and well in Canada." The Chief Justice granted a summary motion to dismiss a claim brought by a youth injured by an exploding pipe bomb against the boys who had made the bomb and the supplier of the gunpowder. While the Supreme Court rejected the application of *ex turpi* in *Norberg v. Wynrib*, [1992] 4 W.W.R. 577, it did not reject the defence's applicability in tort claims. On the contrary, the Justices seemed to approve of the defence's use where public policy could not countenance the plaintiff's compensation. Little could we know that a short time later the court would deal the *ex turpi* defence a fatal blow in *Hall v. Hebert*, [1993] 2 S.C.R. 159. See discussion below.

172 Above, note 171.

173 (1991), 6 C.C.L.T. (2d) 294.

174 6 C.C.L.T. (2d) at 302.

175 *Ibid.*, at 306.

176 These were discussed in some detail in the first edition of this text. They are briefly:

(i) to defend the integrity of the legal system, by not allowing it to be used in the aid of a wrongdoer seeking compensation for injuries;
(ii) to prevent a wrongdoer from profiting from the wrong;
(iii) to reinforce the criminal law; and
(iv) to satisfy the intention of certain statutes.

J., compensation for personal injuries caused in an accident is neither profit, nor a rebate for a criminal penalty, and therefore cannot be precluded by the wrongdoing of a plaintiff.

The majority of the court also reduced the possibility that the illegality defence could re-enter the negligence action through an alternative route. In some cases, courts, although denying the applicability of the defence of illegality to negligence actions, have allowed the wrongdoing of the victim to influence the duty, breach or causal elements of the action. Thus, for example, Windeyer J. in *Smith v. Jenkins*,[177] although rejecting the defence of illegality, still dismissed the action brought by a passenger against the negligent driver of the car, on the basis of the parties' wrongdoing. The car had been stolen and the parties had been drinking prior to the accident. Windeyer J. held there was no right of action in this case because there was no duty of care owed by the wrongdoing defendant to his "companion in crime." It also has been argued that there is no appropriate standard of care by which to judge the conduct of a wrongdoer, or that the "cause" of a wrongdoer's injury is not the negligence of a co-wrongdoer but the victim's own wrongdoing.[178] In this way, the wrongdoing of the victim, although not a defence, has effectively precluded a successful claim for compensation.

In *Hall v. Hebert*, McLachlin J. stated that to allow the illegality defence to bar a plaintiff's claim by denying a duty of care owed to the plaintiff, or to refuse to impose a standard of care on the defendant, would be to avoid the fundamental problem, and merely to trade one label for another. McLachlin J., writing for the majority of the court, was opposed to this. McLachlin J.'s view was that the illegality of the plaintiff's conduct as a factor in denying the plaintiff compensation should be seen exclusively as a defence to a claim, should be restricted, as noted above, and should not be re-introduced into the negligence claim as a factor in one of the other elements of the action.[179]

The effect of *Hall v. Hebert* on the defence of illegality in Canadian negligence actions has been immediate and significant. Whereas prior to the decision, several courts had employed the defence to prevent plaintiffs involved in extreme wrongdoing from succeeding in claims for compensation for injuries caused in the course of the wrongdoing,[180] the defence virtually disappeared from personal injury cases for compensation after the court's judgment.[181]

---

177 [1970] A.L.R. 519 (Aust. H.C.).

178 See, for example, *Johnson v. Grandview Royal Can. Legion Branch 179*, [1988] 5 W.W.R. 267 (B.C. C.A.).

179 Cory J., while agreeing that the defence of illegality should not be applied to tort actions for compensation, seemed to leave open the possibility that the wrongdoing of the plaintiff could be considered as a public policy factor going to the issue of duty. McLachlin J. specifically rejected this. Both Gonthier J. and Sopinka J. were willing to allow the illegality defence to be applied in tort cases when lending assistance to a plaintiff involved in serious criminal activity would reflect adversely on the administration of justice. Neither was of the opinion, however, that this would qualify as such a case.

180 These cases were discussed in the first edition of this text. See, for example, *Mack v. Enns* (1981), 17 C.C.L.T. 291 (B.C. S.C.), varied in part (1983), 25 C.C.L.T. 134 (B.C. C.A.); *Tallow v. Tailfeathers* (1973), 44 D.L.R. (3d) 55 (Alta. C.A.); and *Mongovius v. Marchand* (1988), 44 C.C.L.T. 18 (B.C. S.C.).

181 See, for example, *Court v. Schwartz*, [1994] B.C.J. No. 2164 (S.C.). Whereas British Columbia courts, in particular, had been willing to employ the illegality defence to plaintiffs injured

The Supreme Court of Canada re-visited the *ex turpi* defence in *British Columbia v. Zastowny*.[182] The plaintiff, while in prison, was sexually assaulted by a prison official. After his release, he became addicted to heroin. He became a repeat offender and spent 12 of the next 15 years in prison. He sued the government for its vicarious liability relating to the sexual assaults which had been committed against him by its employee, the prison official. The allegation was that the sexual assaults had contributed to the plaintiff's subsequent difficulties; i.e., his drug addiction and personality and employment problems. The trial judge found that this causal link existed and this finding was not disputed on appeal.

The contentious issue in the case was whether the plaintiff was able to recover for the loss of income which he incurred during his lengthy periods of incarceration. The trial judge found that the long period of time that the plaintiff spent in prison was caused in part by the sexual assaults committed against him and consequently the judge made an award for loss of income for that period of time.[183] The Court of Appeal reversed this judgment, with one dissent.[184]

---

during a course of criminal wrongdoing with a defendant, in this case the court simply concluded that since the plaintiff was not attempting to profit from his behaviour or to evade criminal consequences, the defence was inapplicable. The defence was considered in a different context in *Beljanski (Guardian ad litem of) v. Smithwick* (2006), 42 C.C.L.T. (3d) 264 (B.C. C.A.). The issue was whether the dependants of a person, described by the trial judge as a "career criminal", could sue for damages for loss of companionship, support and inheritance under the Family Compensation Act, R.S.B.C. 1996, c. 126. The deceased was killed in a motor vehicle accident. The trial judge disallowed the claims because the money that would have been used to support the children would have been obtained from crime. The Court of Appeal agreed that there could be no recovery for loss of support, due to *ex turpi*, although an award could be made for loss of inheritance and parental guidance. The dissenting judge, Newbury J.A., would have awarded damages under all three heads. Another recent *ex turpi* case is *Watts v. Klaemt*, [2007] 11 W.W.R. 146 (B.C. S.C.). The plaintiff succeeded on a claim for breach of privacy under the B.C. Privacy Act, R.S.B.C. 1996, c. 373. The defendant had secretly monitored her telephone conversations, recorded them and forwarded their contents to the plaintiff's employer. Despite the fact that these conversations revealed the fact that the plaintiff had committed wrongdoings for which she was dismissed from her job, the defence of *ex turpi* did not bar her claim for breach of privacy damages.

182 2008 SCC 4.

183 *X v. M. (R.D.)*, 2004 BCSC 1273 (S.C.). The trial judge found that the plaintiff spent more time in prison for his crimes than he otherwise would have due to his attitude towards authority, his motivation, and his anger, all the result of the sexual abuse he suffered. The trial judge extensively considered the matter of judicial policy and *ex turpi*, but rejected these as reasons not to award the plaintiff loss of income for his periods of incarceration.

184 (2006), 269 D.L.R. (4th) 510 (B.C. C.A.), leave to appeal allowed (2007), 2007 CarswellBC 272 (S.C.C.), reversed (2008), 2008 CarswellBC 214 (S.C.C.). Justice Saunders recognized that although *ex turpi* barred the plaintiff from recovering loss of wages for time spent in prison which was not causally connected to the sexual assaults, the "extra" time spent due to the sexual assaults, having affected the plaintiff's behaviour, should be recovered. Justice Smith held that the issue was not one of *ex turpi*, but of *novus actus interveniens* and that the crimes which led to the imprisonment broke the chain of causation between the sexual assaults and loss of income while in prison. Thus he would have awarded no loss of income award for this time. He agreed, however, with Justice Saunders' resolution in order to be able to decide the case. Chief Justice Finch dissented, distinguishing this case from *H.L. v Canada*, [2005] 1 S.C.R. 401. He argued that since there was a causal connection in this case between the prison time and the sexual assaults, loss of income, as determined by the trial judge, should be awarded.

In its judgment, the Supreme Court of Canada unanimously held that allowing any recovery for loss of income suffered while the plaintiff was in prison "would constitute a rebate of the natural consequence of the penalty provided by the criminal law" and hence recovery was disallowed due to the defence of *ex turpi*.[185] The court applied this reasoning to both the "core" time that the plaintiff spent in prison due to his crimes, as well as to the "extra" time which he spent there due to the effect that the sexual assaults had on his behaviour. In addition, Rothstein J. rejected the argument that the criminal conviction was a *novus actus* which broke the chain of causation between the sexual assaults and the prison time. Rothstein J. conceded that there was a factual connection between the sexual assaults, the criminal convictions and the prison time, but despite this the *ex turpi* defence barred recovery.[186]

(c) Conclusion

In view of *Hall v. Herbert*, it is now very unlikely that the defence of illegality can be successfully used in personal injury cases to deny compensation to a wrongdoing plaintiff. While some judges on the Supreme Court were prepared to allow a limited role for *ex turpi* even in compensation claims, this was a minority view. It is still possible for a wrongdoing plaintiff to fail in a negligence claim due to arguments based on duty, breach or cause, but courts must keep in mind McLachlin J.'s admonition not to allow the illegality defence to affect claims for compensation, by replacing one label with another. *British Columbia v. Zastowny*, on the other hand, illustrates how the *ex turpi* defence can be used in tort to deny compensation in rare circumstances.

5. CONTRIBUTION BETWEEN WRONGDOERS

(a) The Common Law

(i) Joint and Several, Concurrent Tortfeasors

A person may be injured by the joint act of two or more joint tortfeasors or by the independent acts of several, concurrent tortfeasors.[187]

A joint tort will arise in two general areas. The first is where one person is vicariously liable for the torts committed by another. This occurs as between master and servant, and principal and agent. Vicarious liability may also be imposed by statute, the most common example being the deemed agency provi-

185 Rothstein J. at para. 22. Rothstein relied on *H.L. v. Canada, ibid.*, finding that in that case the loss of income for time spent in prison was denied not only because the evidence did not support a causal connection between the sexual assaults and the prison time, but because of the judicial policy underlying the defence of *ex turpi*.

186 Rothstein J. recognized that the Supreme Court in *H.L. v. Canada* opened the door to recovery of wage loss while in prison in "exceptional circumstances", but held that no such circumstances existed in this case. He gave a wrongful conviction as an example of an exceptional circumstance which might allow for recovery of loss of income during a period of incarceration.

187 See generally Glanville Williams, *Joint Torts and Contributory Negligence* (1951); and Cheifetz, *Apportionment of Fault in Tort* (1981).

sions of provincial motor vehicle statutes, which state that owners of vehicles are liable for the negligent acts of those driving their cars with the owners' consent.[188] In all of these cases, the tortfeasor and the person who is vicariously liable for the former's acts are joint tortfeasors.[189]

A joint tort will also arise when two or more persons act together in furtherance of a common design or plan, during the course of which a tortious act is committed. Although it is not altogether clear,[190] it appears from the case law that the common design or plan must either be unlawful in itself, or at least involve the reasonable likelihood that one or more of its participants will engage in unlawful behaviour.[191]

Many of the reported cases dealing with joint tortfeasors involve common plans which were, in themselves, unlawful. In *Bushell v. Hamilton*,[192] for example, two men who broke into the plaintiffs' house, and stole some goods were joint tortfeasors. They were accordingly each responsible for the fire which was caused by one of them during the course of their tortious joint venture. A similar case was *Newcastle (Town) v. Mattatall*.[193] Three youths broke into the town rink with the intention of committing theft. During the course of this venture, one of the three negligently started two fires. The court found that it was reasonably foreseeable that a negligently set fire might be part of a theft attempt, and thus that all three were jointly liable for the fires that were set. In upholding the trial judgment, Hoyt J.A. argued that there is "a distinction to be made when two or more persons engage in a common action for a wrongful purpose as contrasted with those who engage in a common action for lawful purposes."[194] Where the joint venture is wrongful, an act done by one party to further it implicates all the actors. In *Harpe v. Lefebvre*,[195] for example, two men who were towing a van

---

188 For example, the Highway Traffic Act, R.S.O. 1990, c. H.8, s. 192(1):

> The owner of a motor vehicle or street car is liable for loss or damage sustained by any person by reason of negligence in the operation of the motor vehicle or street car on a highway unless the motor vehicle or street car was without the owner's consent in the possession of some person other than the owner or the owner's chauffeur.

Subsection (6) states that "the driver, owner, lessee and operator that are liable under this section are jointly and severally liable".

There are numerous cases which have interpreted these sections.

189 See *Lee v. Tremblay* (1993), 144 A.R. 301 (Q.B.), which reaffirms the point that a person vicariously liable for the tort of another is a joint tortfeasor.

190 See, e.g., Fleming, *The Law of Torts*, 9th ed. (1998), at 288, where a joint tort is described as "concerted action to a common end . . . though it is probably not necessary that they should realise they are committing a tort." Fleming concedes that "the requisite degree of participation has not been precisely defined in modern decisions. . . ."

191 See, e.g., Prosser, *The Law of Torts*, 5th ed. at 323:

> All those who, in pursuance of a common plan or design to commit a tortious act, actively take part in it, or further it by cooperation or request, or who lend aid or encouragement to the wrongdoer, or ratify and adopt the wrongdoer's acts done for their benefit, are equally liable.

Also see Cheifetz, *Apportionment of Fault in Tort* (1981), at 5-7, cited with approval in *Reeves v. Arsenault*, [1995] P.E.I.J. No. 159 (T.D.).

192 (1980), 113 D.L.R. (3d) 498 (N.S. C.A.).

193 (1987), 37 D.L.R. (4th) 528 (N.B. Q.B.), affirmed (1988), 52 D.L.R. (4th) 356 (N.B. C.A.).

194 52 D.L.R. (4th) 356 at 367.

195 (1976), 1 C.C.L.T. 331 (Alta. Dist. Ct.).

belonging to one of them behind a truck belonging to the other were held to be joint tortfeasors, and thus each was responsible for negligent acts committed by either during the course of this adventure.[196] Where the common venture is not unlawful, and there is no reasonable likelihood that unlawful acts will be committed during its course, participants involved in that activity will not be considered to be joint tortfeasors. Thus, in *Keough v. Royal Can. Legion Henderson Highway Branch 215*,[197] the contention that all participants in a snowmobile race were joint tortfeasors and therefore responsible for the negligent design of the race track or the negligence of one of the drivers was rejected. Merely participating in the race, a lawful pursuit, did not implicate all drivers in the wrongful acts of some drivers or the race's organizers.[198] Where, however, the "race" is unlawful

---

196 See Klar, "Annotation" (1976), 1 C.C.L.T. 332. Also see *Bains v. Hofs* (1992), 76 B.C.L.R. (2d) 98 (S.C.). The defendant L. drove defendants D. and H. to the plaintiff's barn. D. and H. were intending to burn down the barn. The defendant L. knew in general terms of the plan, attempted to dissuade D. and H. from carrying through with it, and did not participate in the crime. He did, however, wait for them in his car and drove them away after the fire was set. The court held that in these circumstances, L. was a joint tortfeasor with D. and H. In *Raywalt Construction Co. v. Bencic*, [2006] 8 W.W.R. 440 (Alta. Q.B.), four youths were held to be joint tortfeasors and hence responsible for a fire which one of them set. They were involved in the mischievous activity and the argument that some of them might have lost interest in trying to ignite diesel fuel before one of them successfully ignited it was rejected by the court.

197 (1978), 7 C.C.L.T. 146 (Man. C.A.).

198 See Klar, "Annotation" (1979), 7 C.C.L.T. 146. Even drinking and driving together does not seem to constitute the parties as joint tortfeasors. For example, in *Crossan v. Gillis* (1979), 7 C.C.L.T. 269 (N.S. C.A.), MacKeigan C.J.N.S. rejected the contention that three men who were involved in a drinking and driving accident were jointly responsible for the accident. They did not participate jointly in the negligent driving of the van. They would have had to control or direct the driver, or have done something to encourage him to drink and drive. Also see *Martin v. Martin* (1995), 159 N.B.R. (2d) 81 (Q.B.), reversed (1996), [1996] N.B.J. No. 83, 1996 CarswellNB 239 (C.A.). The case involved two main protagonists to a fight. Several other persons were present at the time of the fight, but they did not actually take part in it. They did, however, side with the defendant. Were they joint tortfeasors? The court considered the participation of each of them, and concluded that since they did not do anything to aid or assist the fighter they were not joint tortfeasors. The blows struck were the "independent actions" of the defendant. The judgment was reversed on appeal. The Court of Appeal emphasized that the parties were all trespassers and aggressors, and looking at the whole sequence of events, found them to be joint tortfeasors. A case with the same result is *Chow v. Hiscock* (2005), 41 C.C.L.T. (3d) 155 (B.C. S.C.). The plaintiff was severely injured as a result of being punched in the head by one of the defendants, causing him to fall to the ground unconscious. One of the other defendants had taunted the plaintiff; another kicked him when he was down. All three were joint tortfeasors. They had acted as "aiders and abetters of each other". See also *Brown v. Cole* (1995), [1996] 2 W.W.R. 567 (B.C. C.A.) and *Insurance Corp. of British Columbia v. Vancouver (City)* (2000), 182 D.L.R. (4th) 366 (B.C. C.A), reversing (1997), 38 C.C.L.T. (2d) 271 (B.C. S.C.). In this latter case, two police officers acted together in implementing a dangerous manoeuvre to arrest an apparent car thief. During the course of this, one of the officers negligently shot the plaintiff. Although the trial court considered the parties joint tortfeasors, the Court of Appeal disagreed. The parties were not carrying out an unlawful act and the negligence of one was not imputable to the other party. A contrary judgment is *Osborne v. Pavlick* (2000), 49 C.C.L.T. (2d) 239 (B.C. C.A). A married couple sold a business to the plaintiff based on the wife's fraudulent misrepresentations. The husband was not party to the deceit. Despite this, the parties were found jointly liable. This judgment goes against the authorities unless it could be found that the husband knew or ought to have known of the fraud and did nothing.

and dangerous, all of those who participate in it are joint tortfeasors.[199] In *Horvath v. Thring*,[200] the plaintiff, an R.C.M.P. motorcyclist, was injured as a result of the negligence of other R.C.M.P. officers in controlling traffic and the negligence of the driver of another vehicle. The fact that the defendant officers had given the defendant driver permission to drive in an area that had been closed to regular traffic, leading to the collision with the plaintiff, did not make them "joint tortfeasors". The acts of negligence were separate; there was no common design or common intention leading to the accident.

Two or more persons are classified as several, concurrent tortfeasors where they cause the same injury to another as a result of their separate tortious acts. This is the more common situation, and occurs, for example, whenever two motorists are negligent, cause an accident, and injuries result.[201] In the usual case of several, concurrent tortfeasors there is only one injury caused. Even where there are successive injuries caused, however, parties remain several, concurrent tortfeasors, as long as the negligence of each is both a factual and proximate cause of each injury. Thus, where one party negligently caused a fire and because of a second party's negligence the fire spread, as long as the subsequent fire was causally connected, both factually and legally, to the first and second person's fault, both are several, concurrent wrongdoers with respect to it.[202]

(ii) Consequences of Joint Liability

The classification of two or more wrongdoers as joint tortfeasors had, and in some areas continues to have, important practical consequences.

Foremost is its effect on resolving difficult issues of causation. When two or more persons are joint tortfeasors, each is responsible for the injuries caused by everyone else. In cases, therefore, where it is impossible for a plaintiff to prove which of several actors actually caused the injury, a finding that the parties were joint tortfeasors will resolve the plaintiff's difficulties. The leading Canadian case on this matter is *Cook v. Lewis*.[203] The plaintiff was injured in a hunting accident, having been shot by one of two defendants. Due to the sequence of events, it was impossible for the plaintiff to establish which of the defendants' bullets actually

---

199 See *Chow v. Chan* (2007), 46 C.C.L.T. (3d) 249 (B.C. S.C.) and other cases cited therein. The case involved street racing by six motorcyclists. The motorcycles were speeding across both lanes of traffic. All defendants were held liable for a collision involving one of the motorcycles and the plaintiff. The trial judge agreed that in order to constitute the parties as joint tortfeasors, the common activity must be engaged in for an unlawful purpose.

200 (2005), 30 C.C.L.T. (3d) 19 (B.C. C.A.).

201 As we will discuss, several concurrent tortfeasors are "jointly and severally" liable for the damage which their acts cause or to which their acts contribute. This, however, does not make them "joint tortfeasors," in the sense in which this term is used in this section. See, for example, *Tucker (Public Trustee of) v. Asleson*, [1993] 6 W.W.R. 45 (B.C. C.A.), where Southin J.A. notes that it is incorrect to call several, concurrent tortfeasors "joint tortfeasors" where all that is meant is that their liability is joint and several. There are important differences between joint tortfeasors and several, concurrent tortfeasors.

202 See *Economy Foods & Hardware Ltd. v. Klassen* (2001), 196 D.L.R. (4th) 413 (Man. C.A.).

203 [1951] S.C.R. 830.

hit him.[204] The Supreme Court of Canada rejected the plaintiff's submission that the two defendants were joint tortfeasors. According to Cartwright J. merely hunting together without more did not convert the "lawful pursuit" into a joint tort. Nevertheless, it was clear from the decision that had the parties been joint tortfeasors, each would have been responsible for the other's act, and the causation difficulty would have been resolved.

There were as well procedural consequences flowing from the joint tort relationship. The liability of joint tortfeasors is derived from one cause of action. Therefore, at common law, once one joint tortfeasor was sued and judgment was entered, the plaintiff could not institute another action against one of the other joint tortfeasors.[205] This was based on the principle of *transit in rem judicatam*. If the plaintiff failed to sue all of the joint tortfeasors, and could not execute in full against the ones who were sued, the judgment could not be satisfied. This did not apply to several, concurrent tortfeasors, since the plaintiff's cause of action against each was separate. Legislation has now changed the one judgment rule in relation to joint tortfeasors.[206]

Releases also presented a problem for joint tortfeasors. Because there is only one cause of action against joint tortfeasors, the plaintiff's agreement to settle with, and release from further liability, one joint tortfeasor could result in all joint tortfeasors being released.[207] This did not apply to several, concurrent tortfeasors. Nor did it apply in the joint tort situation, where the plaintiff merely agreed not to sue one of the joint tortfeasors, as opposed to entering into a release.[208] The

---

204 As discussed in Chapter 11, note 127, as Cheifetz points out, it was not clear from the jury's findings at trial whether both hunters did in fact negligently shoot in the direction of the plaintiff. This had to be determined. The rule in *Cook v. Lewis* is predicated upon that assumption.

205 See *Wah Tat Bank v. Chan Cheng Kum*, [1975] 2 All E.R. 257 (P.C.), for a discussion of this common law rule. The early cases cited in support of it include *King v. Hoare* (1844), 13 M. & W. 494 at 504, and *Brinsmead v. Harrison* (1872), L.R. 7 C.P. 547 at 553.

206 See, e.g., *Scarmar Const. Ltd. v. Geddes Contr. Ltd.* (1989), 61 D.L.R. (4th) 328 (B.C. C.A.), with respect to the Law and Equity Act, R.S.B.C. 1979, c. 224, s. 48. The Court of Appeal, reversing the trial judgment, held that the common law rule was altered by the statute, but only when both joint tortfeasors have been sued in the same proceeding. Thus where the plaintiff sued B. in one proceeding, entered into a settlement agreement with him, obtained judgment, but failed to satisfy it, he could not then obtain a judgment against the joint tortfeasor G. who had been sued in a separate proceeding. The "judgment bar rule" is dealt with in other Canadian statutes; see, for example, the Courts of Justice Act, R.S.O. 1990, c. C.43, s. 139(1); the Tortfeasors Act, R.S.N.S. 1989, c. 471, s. (3)(a); the Contributory Negligence Act, R.S.S. 1978, c. C-31, s. 7.1(1), the Tortfeasors Act, R.S.N.B. 1973, c. T-8, s. 2(a); and the Contributory Negligence Act, R.S.P.E.I. 1988, c. C-21, s. 7(1).

207 See *Dodsworth v. Holt* (1964), 44 D.L.R. (2d) 480 (Alta. T.D.); *Duck v. Mayeu*, [1892] 2 Q.B. 511 (C.A.); *London Assn. for Protection of Trade v. Greenlands Ltd.*, [1916] 2 A.C. 15 (H.L.); *Brinsmead v. Harrison* (1872), L.R. 7 C.P. 547. For a recent illustration, see *Long v. Brown*, [1996] 1 W.W.R. 280 (Sask. Q.B.) and *Skalicky v. Baraniski* (1997), [1998] 2 W.W.R. 175 (Sask. C.A.). This is called the "release bar rule". See The Final Report, "Joint Tortfeasors and the Common Law 'Release Bar Rule'" (Nova Scotia, July 2002), where this issue is reported on.

208 See *Cutler v. McPhail*, [1962] 2 All E.R. 474; *Dixon v. R.* (1979), 99 D.L.R. (3d) 652 (B.C. S.C.), affirmed (1980), 128 D.L.R. (3d) 389 (B.C. C.A.). This has been called "an arid and technical distinction without any merits. It is a trap into which the unwary fall but which the clever avoid." See Lord Denning in *Bryanston Fin. Ltd. v. de Vries*, [1975] 2 All E.R. 609 at 619 (C.A.).

rule regarding releases has also been changed by legislation in some jurisdictions.[209]

(iii) No Contribution Between Wrongdoers

At common law there could be no contribution between wrongdoers, whether joint or several, concurrent tortfeasors.[210] When an innocent victim[211] suffered an injury as a result of a joint or several, concurrent tort, each tortfeasor was liable to the plaintiff for the whole of the loss, and there was no right in the wrongdoer who paid the full amount to recover any portion of it back from the other wrongdoers. The courts were unwilling to allow a wrongdoer to come into court and seek relief from the consequences of proven wrongdoing. The first case which laid down this principle was that of *Merryweather v. Nixan*.[212] The principle established there was that "if A recover in tort against two defendants, and levy the whole damages on one, that one cannot recover a moiety against the other for his contribution."[213] As with the rule forbidding contributorily negligent victims from recovering any damages, the no contribution rule was manifestly unfair. The entire burden of a plaintiff's losses was imposed on only one of those responsible for these losses. This inequity led to a relaxation of this bar.[214] Ultimately, as with the contributory negligence bar, the no contribution rule was changed by legislation.

(b) Contribution Legislation

(i) Introduction

Every common law province has enacted contribution legislation whose primary purpose is to repeal the common law rule of no contribution between wrongdoers.[215] As with the contributory negligence provisions, although the

---

209 See, e.g., *North York v. Kert Chem. Indust.* (1985), 33 C.C.L.T. 184 (Ont. H.C.), applying s. 149(1) of the Courts of Justice Act, S.O. 1984, c. 11. Also see the Contributory Negligence Act, R.S.P.E.I. 1988, c. C-21, s. 7(1)(b) and the other provincial provisions, above, note 206. The Nova Scotia Report, above, note 207, has recommended the abolition of the rule as well. At common law there were as well other procedural consequences of joint liability. See Law Reform Commission of B.C., *Report on Shared Liability*, 1986, at 10. See also Fleming, *The Law of Torts*, 9th ed. (1998), at 292. Joint tortfeasors could be sued in one, or several proceedings. Several tortfeasors could not be sued together. As well, with the death of one of those jointly liable, the liability passed not to the estate, but to the survivors.

210 Unless there was an express or implied contractual right to indemnity or contribution, as in vicarious liability relationships. See Law Reform Commission of B.C., *Report on Shared Liability*, at 25.

211 As we have seen, a contributorily negligent victim was barred from any recovery.

212 (1799), 101 E.R. 1337.

213 *Ibid.*

214 Glanville Williams argued that the rule applied only to those tortfeasors whose acts were malicious, wilful, or intentional and not to those liable only in negligence. See Williams, *Joint Torts and Contributory Negligence* (1951), at 83.

215 In British Columbia, Saskatchewan, Manitoba, Ontario, Prince Edward Island, and Newfoundland, these provisions are found in the same Act which deals with contributory negligence. See above, note 16. In Alberta, New Brunswick and Nova Scotia they are contained in separate statutes, namely, Tort-Feasors Act, R.S.A. 2000, c. T-5, Tortfeasors Act, R.S.N.B. 1973, c. T-8, Tortfeasors Act, R.S.N.S. 1989, c. 471, although there is a confusing overlap between

wording of these provisions differs, the intent of all provincial statutes is the same — to allow contribution between tortfeasors.[216]

In the Alberta-type statute,[217] contribution between tortfeasors is provided for in the following terms:

> When damage is suffered by any person as a result of a tort, whether a crime or not . . .
>
> . . . any tort-feasor liable in respect of that damage may recover contribution from any other tort-feasor who is or would, if sued, have been liable in respect of the same damage, whether as a joint tort-feasor or otherwise . . . .
>
> . . . the amount of the contribution recoverable from any person shall be an amount that the court finds to be just and equitable having regard to the extent of that person's responsibility for the damage.

In the Ontario-type statute,[218] the provision is as follows:

> . . . where two or more persons are found at fault or negligent, they are jointly and severally liable to the person suffering loss or damage for such fault or negligence, but as between themselves, in the absence of any contract express or implied, each is liable to make contribution and indemnify each other in the degree in which they are respectively found at fault or negligent.

Despite their apparent simplicity, these legislative provisions have given rise to a number of perplexing questions.

(ii) Scope of the Contribution Provisions

As with the defence of contributory negligence, a question raised by the wording of the contribution provisions relates to their scope. Is the right of contribution limited to tortfeasors who are liable in negligence, or can it be extended to all tort actions? As well, do the statutes apply to defendants whose liabilities are based in contract and other non-tort causes of action?

The Alberta-type wording specifically refers to "tort-feasors" and to damage suffered as a result of a "tort."[219] Thus it would appear that the right of wrongdoers to seek contribution under these statutes is confined to actions in tort. Accordingly,

---

the two separate statutes. For a excellent account of these legislative provisions see Kutner, "Contribution Among Tortfeasors: Liability Issues in Contribution Law" (1985), 63 Can. Bar Rev. 1. David Cheifetz has written extensively on these issues, especially as they relate to the Ontario legislation. See above, note 74.

216 In *Coquitlam School District No. 43 v. Clement* (1999), 173 D.L.R. (4th) 348 (B.C. C.A.), a tortfeasor who was allegedly responsible for fire damage to a school sought to third party a municipality alleging that its failure to ensure that the school had complied with fire regulations contributed to the plaintiff's damage. Southin J.A. questioned the right of the tortfeasor to do so, stating that the law does not permit a tortfeasor to argue that if a third party had done its duty to the plaintiff, the damage caused by the tortfeasor to the plaintiff would be less. With respect to Southin J.A. this is precisely what contribution legislation permits tortfeasors to do. For example, in *Economy Foods & Hardware Ltd. v. Klassen*, [1999] 11 W.W.R. 433 (Man. Q.B.), affirmed 196 D.L.R. (4th) 413, [2001] 6 W.W.R. 104 (Man. C.A.), a florist who had negligently left a candle burning and a renovator who had negligently removed a fire sprinkler head were both responsible for damages caused by a fire that started in the florist's washroom and subsequently spread in a mall. The parties had full contribution rights *inter se*.

217 See Tort-Feasors Act, R.S.A. 2000, c. T-5, s. 3. Also used in Manitoba, New Brunswick and Nova Scotia.

218 Negligence Act, R.S.O. 1990, c. N.1, s. 1. Also in British Columbia, Saskatchewan, Prince Edward Island, and Newfoundland.

219 Let us also note that it is called the Tort-Feasors Act.

if one defendant has been found liable to the plaintiff in tort, and a second defendant has been found liable for breach of contract, the provisions would not apply. The issue, of course, is significantly less serious since the adoption of the concurrent liability approach.[220] Where the liability of either defendant can be based either in tort or in contract, the courts will be entitled to treat them as tortfeasors for the purpose of the contribution provisions.[221]

In statutes where the words "fault or negligent" are used, and not the words "tort" or "tortfeasor", the applicability of the contribution provision to non-tort actions is more arguable. Nevertheless, in Ontario, the case law has restricted the right to seek contribution under the legislation to tortfeasors.[222] This has not been the case in British Columbia, where courts have interpreted the word fault to include breach of contract cases, as well as tort.[223]

In the provinces which have tortfeasors legislation,[224] the wording of the contribution provision is broad enough to allow contribution among all tortfeasors, and is not restricted to actions based on negligence. In those provinces which base the right to seek contribution on fault or negligence,[225] the issue is more arguable, although even here the courts are prepared to extend the right to seek contribution to all tortfeasors. An example of this is found in *Siegl v. Sylvester*,[226] where the court apportioned liability between an intentional tortfeasor and one whose liability was based in negligence.[227]

(iii) Right to Seek Contribution

In those provinces which use the wording of tortfeasor legislation, the right to seek contribution is given to "any tortfeasor liable in respect of" the victim's damages. Negligence statutes give this right to persons "who are found at fault or negligent."

In most of the provincial legislation, there is no provision which specifically entitles those who have settled with victims to make a claim for contribution.[228]

---

220 *Central & Eastern Trust Co. v. Rafuse* (1986), 37 C.C.L.T. 117 (S.C.C.). See Chapter 10.

221 See, e.g., *A.G. N.S. v. Aza Avramovitch Assoc. Ltd.* (1984), 11 D.L.R. (4th) 588 (N.S. C.A.), where this was done.

222 See, e.g., *Allcock Laight & Westwood Ltd. v. Patten*, [1967] 1 O.R. 18 (C.A.); *Dom. Chain Co. v. Eastern Const. Co.* (1976), 68 D.L.R. (3d) 385 (Ont. C.A.), affirmed (*sub nom. Giffels Assoc. Ltd. v. Eastern Const. Co.*) (1978), 4 C.C.L.T. 143 (S.C.C.); *Dabous v. Zuliani* (1976), 68 D.L.R. (3d) 414 (Ont. C.A.).

223 See, e.g., *Groves-Raffin Const. Ltd. v. Bank of N.S.* (1975), 51 D.L.R. (3d) 380 (B.C. S.C.), reversed in part on another point (1976), 64 D.L.R. (3d) 78 (B.C. C.A.).

224 That is, Alberta, Manitoba, New Brunswick, Nova Scotia.

225 Ontario, British Columbia, Saskatchewan, Prince Edward Island, and Newfoundland.

226 (1987), 47 D.L.R. (4th) 97 (B.C. S.C.).

227 See also *Anderson v. Stevens*, [1981] 5 W.W.R. 550 (B.C. S.C.), and the cases cited above dealing with contributory negligence. See also *Bains v. Hofs*, above, note 196, and *Brown v. Cole* (1995), [1996] 2 W.W.R. 567 (B.C. C.A.), where the court held that the word "fault" encompasses both intentional and negligent torts. An Ontario decision coming to the same conclusion is *Rabideau v. Maddocks* (1992), 12 O.R. (3d) 83 (Gen. Div.).

228 There is in the legislation of Ontario, Saskatchewan, and Nova Scotia. For example, s. 2 of the Ontario Negligence Act, R.S.O. 1990, c. N.1, provides that a tortfeasor may recover contribution by settling with the victim and thereafter commencing an action for contribution. Note the question as to whether the settlement must have been entered into before the claim for contribution can be made. See *Gevaert v. Arbuckle* (1998), 163 D.L.R. (4th) 762 (Ont.

Notwithstanding these omissions in the statutes, case law has permitted contribution in situations of settlement. In *A.R. (Al) Smith Ltd. v. Turner*,[229] for example, the court permitted a settling party to seek contribution despite the fact that the British Columbia statute did not provide for this. This has also been the case in Alberta.[230]

Is it necessary that the settling party be a party who would have been found liable to the victim had there been no settlement? In Ontario, where there is a specific provision entitling settling parties to seek contribution, case law has upheld the right of those who settled, even though they could not have been found liable to the victim, to claim contribution.[231] Despite the fact that the Ontario provision gives the right to seek contribution, in the case of settlement, only to tortfeasors, it has been held that the word tortfeasor must refer "not to a person who is held or admits liability at trial, but to a person who impliedly assumes or admits liability when he enters into a settlement."[232] The English jurisprudence, on the other hand, although conceding that settling parties could claim contribution, required that the settling party be able to prove, in their claim for contribution, that they were tortfeasors who would have been found liable to the victim had they not settled.[233] This would theoretically mean that unless settling parties could prove that they would have been held responsible in law for at least 1 per cent of the victim's damages, they could not require defendants who were fully responsible for the damages to pay for them. In an Alberta case, *Hannigan v. Edmonton*,[234] the plaintiff, believing that he was partly at fault, settled with the victim and claimed contribution from the defendant. The defendant, rather than denying its own liability to the victim, accepted 100 per cent liability for the accident. The defendant's contention that this assumption of full responsibility defeated the plaintiff's claim for contribution was properly rejected by the court. The court held that this interpretation of the legislative provision which allows tortfeasors to claim contribution would be contrary to the spirit of the legislation, would be a disincentive to early settlements, and would be inequitable. Persons who are involved in an accident and who reasonably believe that they would be found

---

Gen. Div.), which held that it must be. There are contrary authorities that are discussed in this judgment. Also see *Renaissance Leisure Group Inc. v. Frazer* (2001), 197 D.L.R. (4th) 336 (Ont. S.C.J.), reversed (2004), [2004] O.J. No. 3486, 2004 CarswellOnt 3468 (C.A.), where this issue is discussed.

229 [1985] 2 W.W.R. 424 (B.C. Co. Ct.).

230 An illustration is *Hannigan v. Edmonton* (1983), 1 D.L.R. (4th) 397 (Alta. Q.B.). See also *Tarnava v. Larson* (1956), 20 W.W.R. 538 (Alta. Dist. Ct.). An important English authority to the same effect is *Stott v. West Yorkshire Road Car Ltd.*, [1971] 2 Q.B. 561 (C.A.). The same ruling has been made in New Brunswick; see *LeBlanc v. LeBlanc* (1991), 115 N.B.R. (2d) 255, 291 A.P.R. 255 (Q.B.).

231 See *Marschler v. G. Masser's Garage* (1956), 2 D.L.R. (2d) 484 (Ont. H.C.). See Cheifetz, *Apportionment of Fault in Tort* (1981), at 147.

232 *Marschler v. G. Masser's Garage*, *ibid.*, at 490. Cheifetz argues, however, that at the least the person who settled must have been "a 'scientific' cause, a cause-in-fact, of the damages to be considered responsible for the damages." *Ibid.*, at 147-48.

233 See *Stott v. West Yorkshire Road Car Ltd.*, [1971] 2 Q.B. 651 (C.A.); *Littlewood v. George Wimpey & Co.* [1953] 2 Q.B. 501 (C.A.), affirmed (*sub nom. George Wimpey & Co. v. Br. Overseas Airways Corp.*) [1955] A.C. 169 (H.L.); and a New Zealand case, *Baylis v. Waugh*, [1962] N.Z.L.R. 44.

234 (1983), 1 D.L.R. (4th) 397 (Alta. Q.B.).

liable if sued should have a right to settle with the victim and subsequently to obtain contribution from other wrongdoers.[235] Whether contribution legislation should be extended to give this right of contribution to those who voluntarily settle the victim's claim without any reasonable grounds for considering that they were obliged to do so is more questionable.[236]

(iv) Obligation to Pay Contribution

In those provinces which use the wording of the tortfeasor legislation, contribution may be recovered "from any other tortfeasor who is, or would, if sued, have been liable in respect of the same damage. . . ." The negligence legislation imposes the contribution obligation on persons "who are found at fault or negligent."

As with the defence of contributory negligence, contribution between tortfeasors is only a concern when the *same injury* has been caused by the various parties. Where each party caused different injuries, each is responsible in full for that injury, and contribution cannot be claimed.

The Ontario case of *Katzman v. Yaeck*[237] illustrates this point. The plaintiff was injured in a motor vehicle accident, and as a result of these injuries he required dental treatment. The plaintiff instituted an action against the motorist, who in turn attempted to third-party the dentist for contribution, alleging the latter's negligence in exacerbating the original injuries. Whether or not a claim for contribution could be made against the dentist depended upon whether both the motorist and the dentist could be held liable for the injury allegedly caused by the dentist. If this injury was within the risk created by the motorist, i.e., was not too remote,[238] then both could be held liable for it, and a claim for contribution would be in order. The Ontario Court of Appeal allowed the third party claim to proceed on the basis that negligent medical treatment was not in law a *novus actus interveniens*. Thus, since both wrongdoers were potentially liable for the same injury, a claim for contribution could be made.[239]

---

235 A British Columbia decision, *Welk v. Mantelli,* [1995] 6 W.W.R. 485 (B.C. S.C.), came to the opposite conclusion. Errico J., after considering the *Hannigan* case, as well as other judgments, decided that under the B.C. legislation a party who settles cannot claim contribution, unless that party's fault contributed to the loss. The court noted that this decision was a matter of statutory interpretation, and that equitable relief or unjust enrichment were not pleaded in this case.

236 There may be a subrogation right, or some other equitable remedy available. However, legislation which permits contribution between tortfeasors seems to be an inappropriate vehicle to accomplish this. The Report of the Alberta Institute Of Law Research And Reform, No. 31, 1979, recommends that even those who settle without reasonable grounds for believing that they were liable ought to have a right to indemnity or contribution. Query whether this constitutes an assignment of a cause of action.

237 (1982), 136 D.L.R. (3d) 536 (Ont. C.A.), reversing (1981), 125 D.LR. (3d) 270 (Ont. H.C.).

238 See Chapter 12.

239 In *Sorenson v. Abrametz*, [1988] 1 W.W.R. 609 (Sask. C.A.), on the other hand, the injuries caused by two wrongdoers were different, and a claim for contribution was disallowed. The victim had been injured in a motor vehicle accident, but due to the alleged negligence of his lawyer, the limitation period for bringing a claim had expired. In an action brought by the victim against his lawyer, the court struck out the latter's third party notice claiming contribution from the motorist. The injuries caused by the motorist, that is, personal injuries and property damage, differed from that caused by the lawyer, namely the loss of a cause of action. Thus, the two alleged wrongdoers were neither joint nor several tortfeasors, and a claim for

It is clear in all the provisions that a person who has been sued by the victim and has been found liable is required to contribute to the victim's damages. Difficulties arise, however, with respect to those individuals against whom claims for contribution are made, either by means of third party notice or separate action, who have never been sued by the victim, or who, if they have been sued, have not been found liable to them.[240]

The problem arises in two situations. The first is one in which the victim's injuries have been caused by the fault of a person who was sued and found not liable by reason of a special defence. The defence can relate to a procedural defect in the victim's action, such as failure to give a timely notice, the expiration of a limitation period, dismissal for want of prosecution, or for substantive reasons, such as a statutory immunity, the defence of consent, or the existence of an exemption clause. The issue that these cases present is as follows. Should the special defence be respected, even in so far as claims for contribution are concerned, with the result that the remaining defendants are forced to absorb the extra burden, or should the defence be ignored, robbing the defendant of this special protection?[241]

In the two leading Canadian cases on this question, one decided under Ontario's Negligence Act,[242] and the other under Alberta's Tort-Feasors Act,[243] it was decided that a dismissal of the action against the defendant, even if based on a

---

contribution could not be made. See also *Wallace v. Litwiniuk*, 200 D.L.R. (4th) 534, [2001] 8 W.W.R. 84 (Alta. C.A.), which was a similar case. In *Leoppky v. McWilliams*, 202 D.L.R. (4th) 260, [2001] 9 W.W.R. 281 (Alta. C.A.), the court correctly disallowed a third-party claim to be made by a motorist who injured the plaintiff in a second car accident from a motorist who had injured the plaintiff in an earlier accident. Unless the injury caused in the second accident was factually and legally caused by the first motorist, the injuries were not the same. Also see *O'Neill v. Van Horne* (2002), 212 D.L.R. (4th) 558 (Ont. C.A.). The court disallowed a claim for contribution that was brought by a person who had allegedly sexually assaulted the plaintiff against others whom he claimed also had abused the plaintiff. The court stated that despite the difficulty inherent in determining which of the plaintiff's damages flowed from which of the acts committed against her, the torts were separate and the damages divisible.

240 Tortfeasors legislation requires that the person against whom a claim is made be a person who is "liable", or who "if sued", would "have been liable." Negligence legislation requires that the person is one who is "found at fault or negligent." No legislation elaborates on these rather vague requirements.

241 The fact that one of the defendants, despite being at fault, has a special defence which results in the dismissal of the action against it, does not mean that the remaining defendant can argue that it should only be liable for its share of the damages. It remains 100 per cent liable to the plaintiff. See, for example, *Horvath v. Thring* (2005), 30 C.C.L.T. (3d) 19 (B.C. C.A). One of the defendants, the Crown, though 50 per cent at fault, was relieved of its liability to the plaintiff due to a statutory provision. Nevertheless, the remaining defendant still was liable for the full claim. The court followed the Supreme Court's decision in *Stetar v. Poirier*, (*sub nom. Parkland No. 31 (County) v. Stetar*) [1975] 2 S.C.R. 884. For a full discussion of this and other issues raised by these provisions, see Kutner, "Contribution Among Tortfeasors" (1985), 63 Can. Bar Rev. 1; Cheifetz, *Apportionment of Fault in Tort* (1981), at 42-55, and Cheifetz's more recent articles referenced above, note 74. See also Klar, "Contribution Between Tort-Feasors" (1975), 13 Alta. L. Rev. 359. For a good discussion of the case law and issues see Elizabeth Pedersen Lewis, "Third Party Liability for Contribution and Indemnity — The Slings And Arrows Of Outrageous Circumstances" (1992), 10 Can. J. Ins. L. 33.

242 *Dom. Chain Co. v. Eastern Const. Co.* (1974), 46 D.L.R. (3d) 28 (Ont. H.C.), reversed (1976), 68 D.L.R. (3d) 385 (Ont. C.A.), which was affirmed (1978), 84 D.L.R. (3d) 344 (S.C.C.).

243 *Parkland v. Stetar*, [1975] 2 S.C.R. 884.

special defence, would relieve that defendant from its obligation to contribute to the victim's damages. In *Dom. Chain Co. v. Eastern Const. Co.*,[244] the defendant's special defence was a contractual clause limiting its liability to the plaintiff to defects in the construction of a project which appeared within one year from the time of the project's completion. Since the defects in issue in the case appeared after this time, the defendant was not liable. In *Parkland v. Stetar*,[245] on the other hand, the special defence involved the victim's failure to give timely notice of the accident to the defendant municipality. In both cases, the dismissal of the claim in the principal action was fatal to the claim for contribution. It has been suggested that the judgment in *Dominion Chain* would not prevent a claim for contribution against a defendant who, although relieved of liability in the principal action, was at one time potentially liable to the victim.[246] In other words, only if the special defence is one that has prevented any liability at any time, can there be no claim for contribution. If there could have been liability, the special defence, according to this view, would not be relevant to the contribution claim.[247] In *Re Urquhart and Hatt*,[248] the injured victim sued several persons allegedly responsible for the injuries he suffered in a motor vehicle accident. He settled with one of these parties and signed a release releasing all defendants. Two of these defendants moved to have the action which the injured party had brought against them dismissed for want of prosecution. After a notice of discontinuance was filed, an order was made dismissing the principal action. The court held that despite the release and eventual dismissal of the action, the defendants were still obliged to contribute to the victim's damages, which had been paid by the settling party. The court accepted the view that it is only a trial on the merits which finds that the defendant is not liable that affects the obligation to contribute.[249]

Cases have held that a settlement and release of one party by the plaintiff does not prevent another party from seeking contribution from the party who had been

244 Above, note 242.

245 Above, note 243.

246 See Cheifetz, above, note 1.

247 See also Kutner, above, note 241, who favours this approach. It must be stated, however, that there is nothing in the judgments of the two cases which endorses this distinction. In *Bill Thompson Transport Inc. v. Scarborough (City)* (1993), 14 M.P.L.R. (2d) 278 (Gen. Div.), the court allowed a contribution claim to be made against a party, even though the principal action was dismissed due to the expiration of the limitation period. The court distinguished *Dominion Chain*, stating that in the case before it there was potential liability of the third party to the principal claimant at one time. This interpretation of *Dominion Chain* was also supported by the Ontario Court of Appeal in *HSBC Securities (Canada) Inc. v. Davies, Ward & Beck* (2005), 249 D.L.R. (4th) 571 (Ont. C.A.), leave to appeal refused (2005), 2005 CarswellOnt 2737 (S.C.C.). That is, in *Dominion Chain*, the reason that the third party claim failed was not because the principal claim against the third party was dismissed, due to the expiration of a limitation period, but because the third party *could never have been liable* to the principal plaintiff. This differs from *Stetar*, where there was potential liability at some time, but a procedural defect gave the third party a special defence, which shielded it from this potential liability.

248 (1982), 132 D.L.R. (3d) 685 (Ont. Co. Ct.).

249 Cases from other jurisdictions on this point are inconsistent. See *Hart v. Hall and Pickles*, [1969] 1 Q.B. 405 (C.A.); *Harvey v. R.G. O'Dell Ltd.*, [1958] 2 Q.B. 78 (Q.B.); *George Wimpey & Co. v. Br. Overseas Airways Corp.*, [1955] A.C. 169 (H.L.); and *Castellan v. Elec. Power Transmission Pty. Ltd.* (1967), 69 S.R. (N.S.W.) 159 (C.A).

released. In *Tucker v. Asleson,*[250] for example, the plaintiff was injured in a motor vehicle accident caused by the fault of the driver of her car, who was her mother, the driver of a second vehicle, and the provincial Crown, which had the duty to maintain the road. The plaintiff settled with her mother's insurer, and proceeded to trial against the other two defendants. The trial judge found each of the three parties one-third at fault. The issue arose as to whether the settlement between the plaintiff and her mother severed the joint and several liability of the remaining two defendants. If it did not and they remained responsible for 100 per cent of the plaintiff's claim, less the settlement amount already received by the plaintiff, could they claim contribution from the settling party if the amount for which it settled was less than its one-third share of the judgment? The court held that the settlement did not sever the joint and several liability of the remaining defendants, nor did it prevent them from exercising their right to seek contribution from the party which had settled. On the facts of this case, however, these defendants had agreed to limit their rights to seek contribution and this agreement was enforced by the court. In a Manitoba case, *Fraternal Order of Eagles Winnipeg Aerie No. 23 v. Blumes,*[251] the court also held that a settlement and release of one party does not prevent another party from third-partying the former seeking contribution.[252]

Another problematic situation arises when a claim for contribution is brought against a person who was never actually sued by the victim. This claim can be brought by way of third party proceedings, or in a separate action. Since this party was never sued by the victim there is no judgment dismissing the principal action, as there is in the first situation discussed earlier.

Whether this party is required to contribute depends upon the court's interpretation of the tortfeasors legislation, and more particularly, on the meaning of the words, "would, if sued, have been liable." The question is: would, if sued, when?

---

250 (1991), 86 D.L.R. (4th) 73 (B.C. S.C.), reversed on another point [1993] 6 W.W.R. 45 (B.C. C.A.).

251 (1994), 95 Man. R. (2d) 92 (C.A.).

252 In *B.C. Ferry Corp. v. T & N plc*, [1994] 3 W.W.R. 245 (B.C. S.C.), affirmed as to this point (1995), 27 C.C.L.T. (2d) 287, [1996] 4 W.W.R. 161 (B.C. C.A.), the plaintiff released one party from its obligations and proceeded against other defendants only for their share of the responsibility. That being the case, these defendants, not being responsible for more than their shares, had no right of contribution against the third party. *Misko v. John Doe*, 2007 ONCA 660 (C.A.) is a similar case from Ontario, although as the discussion of Rosenberg J.A. indicates, "the cases in this area are not entirely consistent". The third-party claim was disallowed in this case because it was agreed that the plaintiff would only sue the defendant for its share of the damages. The court had to consider and distinguish another recent Ontario case, *Medeiros v. Dilworth* (2002), 59 O.R. (3d) 136 (S.C.J.), where a third-party claim was allowed in similar circumstances. An excellent review of this issue is found in *Viridian Inc. v. Dresser Canada Inc.* (1999), [2000] 2 W.W.R. 389 (Alta. Q.B.). The plaintiff sued two defendants and then settled with defendant 1. Defendant 2 brought a third-party application for contribution against defendant 1. The plaintiff and defendant 1 argued that under no circumstances could defendant 2 successfully claim contribution from defendant 1, and sought to strike out the third-party claim. The parties argued that the settlement agreement and the operation of law prevented a successful claim. The court held that these were arguable issues and that the third-party claim could proceed. Also see *Amoco Canada Petroleum Co. v. Propak Systems Ltd.* (2001), 200 D.L.R. (4th) 667 (Alta. C.A.), leave to appeal refused (2002), 292 N.R. 396 (note) (S.C.C.), where the effect of settlements on the rights of non-settling parties is explored further.

There are three possible answers. The first is that the tortfeasor ought to be required to contribute if there might have been liability to the victim *at any time.* In other words, even if the tortfeasor's potential liability had been extinguished before the victim either settled with, or brought action against the party claiming contribution, the tortfeasor can be brought back into the case by way of a claim for contribution. The second answer is to permit a contribution claim only if, at the time of the victim's settlement or action with the claimant, the tortfeasor against whom the claim for contribution is brought was still potentially liable to the victim. The third solution is to go even further and require a potential liability at the time that the claim for contribution itself is made. The issue is clear: should a person who can no longer be sued by the victim at the time a claim for contribution is made be forced to contribute to the victim's damages?

Logically, the courts should not approach the contribution issue differently depending upon whether there had been, or had not been, an actual unsuccessful suit against the tortfeasor. If, for example, the suit did fail, or would have failed, due to the expiration of a limitation period, the issue regarding the obligation to contribute is the same. Nevertheless, it appears that courts may be prepared to extend the obligation to contribute to tortfeasors who have never actually been sued and who would have had a successful defence had they been sued. In *MacKenzie v. Vance*,[253] for example, a defendant who was sued within the limitation period applicable to his case was allowed to third-party other tortfeasors for contribution, despite the fact that these tortfeasors could no longer have been sued by the victim, due to the expiration of the limitation period applicable to them. The court held that the claim for contribution arose independently from the tortfeasors legislation and could not be barred before it even accrued by a limitation period applicable to the potential action between the victim and the tortfeasors. In other words, as long as the tortfeasors would have been liable if they had been sued in the proper time by the victim, they are liable to contribute to that victim's damage via the contribution claim.[254]

---

253 (1977), 2 C.C.L.T. 63 (N.S. C.A.).

254 See Klar, "Annotation" (1977), 2 C.C.L.T. 63. For a similar Alberta decision, see *J.R. Paine & Assoc. Ltd. v. Strong, Lamb & Nelson*, [1979] 6 W.W.R. 353 (Alta. C.A.), and my criticism of that judgment in (1980), 18 Alta. L. Rev. 515. In *Canada Deposit Insurance Corp. v. Prisco*, [1996] 7 W.W.R. 30 (Alta. C.A.), leave to appeal refused [1996] 9 W.W.R. xlvi (S.C.C.), the argument that there can be no claim for contribution outside of the limitation period applicable to the plaintiff's claim was accepted. The court distinguished the *Paine v. Strong* case on the basis that in the latter case, the Limitation of Action Act specifically allowed the third-party claim for contribution outside of the limitation period in actions for personal injury or property damage. The *Canada Deposit Insurance Corp. v. Prisco* action was for pure economic loss. See also *Paquette v. Batchelor* (1980), 13 C.C.L.T. 237 (Ont. H.C.), and Cheifetz, "Annotation", 13 C.C.L.T. at 239; *Campbell v. Bartlett* (1979), 107 D.L.R. (3d) 591 (Sask. C.A.); and *Marelj v. Gosselin* (2001), 8 C.C.L.T. (3d) 260 (B.C. S.C.). These decisions have held that provisions, either in the apportionment legislation or limitations acts, which provide a limitation period for instituting contribution claims, permit claims for contribution to be made against tortfeasors who can at the time of the contribution claim no longer be sued by the principal victim. They, in effect, negate the defendant's limitation defence which would have been available at that time if the victim would have sued. The only requirements of the contribution claim are that there was a potential liability of the defendant and that the contribution claim itself is brought within the specified time. In *HSBC Securities*

As discussed elsewhere,[255] a possible solution to the above dilemma is to identify the victim with the tortfeasor who has a special defence by reducing the damages which may be recovered from the other defendants by the first tortfeasor's degree of fault.[256]

(v) *Basis of Apportionment*

Under negligence statutes, the basis of apportionment between concurrent tortfeasors is the same as in contributory negligence. The courts are directed to determine "the degree in which each of such persons is at fault or negligent." Tortfeasor statutes have adopted wording which is seemingly broader. Section 3(2) of the Alberta statute, for example, states that the amount of contribution recoverable is that amount which the court finds to be "just and equitable having regard to the extent of that person's responsibility for the damage."

As argued above, assessing degrees of fault or the extent of a person's responsibility must relate to the relative culpability or blameworthiness of the parties. The apportionment decision depends upon which of the defendants failed most markedly to live up to the standards of conduct expected.[257] In *T. (L.) v. T. (R.W.)*,[258] for example, the plaintiff sued her father for sexual assaults that he had

---

(Canada) Inc. v. Davies, Ward & Beck (2005), 249 D.L.R. (4th) 571 (Ont. C.A.), leave to appeal refused (2005), 2005 CarswellOnt 2737 (S.C.C.), the right to bring a claim for contribution outside of the limitation period which governed the victim's action against the contribution defendant was further qualified. The court held that both s. 5 (adding third parties for contribution) and s. 8 (suing for contribution) of the Ontario Act require that the principal victim must have settled with or sued the person who is claiming contribution in the prescribed limitation period for that claim. In this case, due to an agreement "to toll" the limitation period applicable to the claim between the victim and the defendant (the claimant for contribution), this was not done. This agreement precluded the operation of s. 8 and the court disallowed the claim for contribution. If, of course, the person who had not been sued could never have been found liable, due to a special defence, the claim for contribution will fail, as discussed above. See, for example, *Laing Property Corp. v. All Seasons Display Inc.* (2000), 190 D.L.R. (4th) 1 (B.C. C.A.). Section 8 of the Negligence Act, R.S.O. 1990, c. 91, was repealed on January 1, 2004. Cheifetz considers the implications of this repeal in "For Whom the Bell Tolled" (2007), 48 Advocates Q. 46-151.

255 See Klar, "Contribution Between Tort-Feasors" (1975), 13 Alta. L. Rev. 359.

256 See Law Reform Commission of B.C., *Report on Shared Liability*, 1986, where such a solution is proposed. Also see the Uniform Contributory Fault Act, 1985.

257 See *Clyke v. Blenkhorn* (1958), 13 D.L.R. (2d) 293 (N.S. C.A.); *Meyer v. Gordon* (1981), 17 C.C.L.T. 1 (B.C. S.C.); *Anderson v. Stevens* (1981), 125 D.L.R. (3d) 736 (B.C. S.C.). It has been argued, however, that, under tortfeasor acts, the courts can consider the defendants' "responsibility" for the injuries in the sense of its causal potency. See, e.g., Kutner, above, note 241, at 41 ff. Kutner argues that the courts can "make a judgment about the relative importance or directness of each party's conduct in causing the loss. Today, the prevailing view is that contribution under the tortfeasors acts is assessed on the basis of both culpability and causation, and it is unlikely that in practice either element will be ignored." It has also been suggested that tortfeasors legislation which permits the courts to apportion based on "just and equitable" considerations, allows other factors, such as the ability to pay, or the parties' motives, to be considered. See *Hawkins v. Ian Ross (Castings) Ltd.*, [1970] 1 All E.R. 180 (Q.B.); and *Stocker v. Norprint Ltd.* (1970), 10 K.I.R. 10 (C.A.). See, however, *Boothman v. Br. Northrop Ltd.* (1972), 13 K.I.R. 112 (C.A.), where this approach was disapproved. This suggestion, however, has not been taken up by the Canadian courts.

258 (1997), 36 C.C.L.T. (2d) 207 (B.C. S.C.).

committed against her when she was a child. The defendant father sought to third party the plaintiff's mother for contribution claiming that she had failed in her duty to her daughter by not protecting her against the abuse. The court held that the mother had not breached her duty, but raised the interesting question as to whether even if she had, a claim for contribution brought against her by the person who committed the assaults was appropriate. The court held that such a claim would be "ludicrous" although the trial judge stated that articulating in terms of law why such a claim should fail was difficult. It is suggested that although in principle a claim could be brought since the fault of both the father and mother contributed to the plaintiff's injuries, the fault of the mother in failing to prevent the abuse was trivial in comparison to the intentional misconduct of the abuser. That being the case no contribution by the father against the mother would be warranted.[259]

(vi) Other Matters

There are a host of other procedural and substantive questions which arise out of the contribution process. These detailed issues have been the subject of extensive analysis by other writers,[260] and law reform bodies.[261] Although a detailed discussion of these matters is beyond the scope of this text, it is useful to identify two of these other issues.

The common law rule which prevented a victim from suing a second joint tortfeasor after having sued to judgment a first, even if that judgment could not be satisfied, has been abolished by the tortfeasors legislation. Legislation provides that a judgment recovered against any tortfeasor liable in respect of the same damage is not a bar to an action against other potential tortfeasors. In order to discourage plaintiffs from instituting actions in order to search for the highest award, the legislation limits the award in subsequent actions so that it cannot exceed the award granted in the first judgment. It also disentitles the plaintiff from receiving the costs of the subsequent actions unless the court is of the opinion that there was a reasonable ground for bringing them.[262]

---

259 In jurisdictions that determine apportionment based on what would be "just and equitable", the argument that no contribution would be just is an appropriate response to this dilemma. If anything, the mother, if held liable to the daughter, should be ably to seek full indemnity from the abuser. Also see *Bouchard v. Carruthers* (2004), [2005] 2 W.W.R. 227 (Sask. C.A.). The court held that since a person who sexually abused the plaintiff could not seek contribution from her parents, claiming that they had breached their duty to her, neither could a party who was vicariously liable for the acts of the abuser.

260 See especially Cheifetz, *Apportionment of Fault in Tort* (1981), and Kutner, "Contribution Among Tortfeasors" (1985), 63 Can. Bar Rev. 1.

261 See, e.g., Alberta Institute of Law Research and Reform, *Contributory Negligence and Concurrent Wrongdoers*, Report No. 31, 1979; Law Reform Commission of B.C., *Report on Shared Liability*, 1986; Uniform Contributory Fault Act; Ontario Law Reform Commission, *Report on Contribution Among Wrongdoers and Contributory Negligence*, 1988.

262 There is no similar provision in the provinces which have negligence legislation. However, the common law rule forbidding a second action may be dealt with elsewhere. See, e.g., *Scarmar Const. Ltd. v. Geddes Contr. Co.* (1989), 61 D.L.R. (4th) 328 (B.C. C.A.), reversing (1987), 42 D.L.R. (4th) 565 (B.C. S.C.), where the B.C. Law and Equity Act, R.S.B.C. 1979, c. 224, s. 48, was applied to this situation.

Another procedural issue involves the question of the multiplicity of proceedings. Although the preferable method of claiming contribution is to do so in the principal action brought against the tortfeasor(s) by the victim, either by way of third party notice, or by the court adding parties, the question whether a court can permit a claim for contribution to be brought after the victim's principal action has been determined has been raised. In *Cohen v. S. McCord & Co.*,[263] decided under the Ontario Negligence Act,[264] the court held that a defendant who did not make a claim for contribution in the victim's principal action brought against him and a co-defendant could not do so in a subsequent separate action. This approach, although upheld in *Rickwood v. Aylmer (Town)*,[265] has been doubted by the Supreme Court of Canada in *R. v. Thomas Fuller Const. (1958) Ltd.*[266] and not followed in more recent cases.[267] The rule has also not been followed in other jurisdictions, where separate actions for contribution, following the victim's principal action, are permitted.[268]

---

263 [1944] 4 D.L.R. 753 (Ont. C.A.).

264 R.S.O. 1937, c. 115.

265 (1957), 8 D.L.R. (2d) 702 (Ont. C.A.).

266 (1979), 106 D.L.R. (3d) 193 (S.C.C.).

267 See *Cristovao v. Doran's Beverages Inc.* (1983), 143 D.L.R. (3d) 641 (Ont. H.C.). See also *McIntee v. Manzer*, [1993] O.J. No. 981 (Gen. Div.). The right to bring a claim for contribution in separate proceedings was reaffirmed in *Renaissance Leisure Group v. Frazer* (2004), [2004] O.J. No. 3486, 2004 CarswellOnt 3468 (Ont. C.A.). The Court of Appeal held, however, that a claimant for contribution cannot obtain a better result in the separate claim, than he could have obtained had he made the claim for contribution in the main action.

268 See, e.g., *Inglis Ltd. v. South Shore Sales & Service Ltd.* (1979), 104 D.L.R. (3d) 507 (N.S. C.A.). See discussion by Cheifetz, above, note 260, at 79-86. *Renaissance Leisure Group Inc. v. Frazer, ibid.*, illustrates difficult apportionment issues, which arise when a defendant in the principal action claims contribution in a separate action. The Court of Appeal held that the allocation of fault in the action for contribution should reflect the fault of all of the parties, whether they were sued or not in the main action. The Court of Appeal also qualified its earlier holding in *Martin* that the fault of "absent parties" ought not to be reflected in the principal action. See Cheifetz's comment on *Renaissance* in "Postcript # 2: The Retreat Continues" (2007), 29 Advocates Q. 276.

14

Proof

1. INTRODUCTION

Issues relating to problems of proof in civil litigation can be quite complex, and are generally outside the scope of a text on the substantive law of torts. There are, however, certain special problems relating particularly to tort law cases which arise frequently. These merit some attention in this text.

Certain difficult problems of proof have already been discussed in the context of previous topics. As we have seen, proving causation has been particularly difficult in some types of personal injury cases requiring the courts to develop new approaches.[1] Another issue of proof which was previously raised relates to the burden of proving intentional or negligent conduct in the context of actions based on trespass. Where a plaintiff can prove that a trespass has occurred, the burden of proving that the trespass was accidental shifts to the defendant.[2]

In this chapter, the matter of the burden of proof in tort cases will be briefly discussed. We will then turn to an issue that has been frequently raised in tort cases, the maxim *res ipsa loquitur*.

2. BURDEN OF PROOF IN GENERAL

The rule in tort is that the party who alleges a fact has the burden of proving it. Thus, in the context of the negligence action, the plaintiff has to prove all of the factual requirements necessary to support the cause of action, namely, that the plaintiff was a reasonably foreseeable victim, the defendant's conduct was negligent, the plaintiff suffered compensable injury, and this injury was caused by the defendant's negligence. Correspondingly, the defendant must prove those facts required to establish one of the available defences, namely that the plaintiff assumed the risk of injury, or was contributorily negligent.[3] The obligation on the parties to prove their facts, and on the trier of fact, be it judge or jury, to adjudicate on them, relates not only to the actual events of a dispute, but to the inferences

---

1 See Chapter 11.

2 See Chapter 2.

3 Neither party has to "prove" issues of law which run through the negligence action, although they will of course attempt to persuade the court as to their view of the applicable law.

which ought to be drawn from these events. In other words in determining the factual issues, parties must prove and triers must decide not only what did or did not occur, but as well what ought to have occurred.[4]

The rule that the person who alleges must prove is consistent with our sense of justice that one ought not to be required to defend oneself against unsubstantiated allegations of wrongdoing. In tort, as in criminal law, one is generally presumed to be innocent unless shown otherwise. It is also consistent with the general philosophy, which is still somewhat true of fault-based compensation, that losses should lie where they fall unless good reasons are shown for shifting them. One is not presumed to have an entitlement to tort-based compensation. One must prove one's entitlement by establishing the required elements of the cause of action. Of course, as tort law is seen more as a loss distribution system based on the need of the victim and the defendant's ability to distribute the loss, the requirements of proof are relaxed. This factor has been a feature of contemporary negligence law.

In order to discharge the civil law burden of proof, the party alleging facts must prove them on the balance of probabilities, or on the preponderance of the evidence. This burden cannot be translated with precision into mathematical terms.[5] It does, however, express a well understood principle. In a civil trial, although the trier of fact need not be absolutely convinced of the correctness of the facts as presented by the party who has the burden, and can harbour some reasonable doubts, the trier must, on balance, be more persuaded by the alleging party's evidence than by that of the adversary.

In theory, the fact that the burden of proof rests on the party who alleges has relevance in only one situation. In assessing conflicting evidence, triers of fact may find themselves in one of three positions. The trier may be more persuaded by the evidence of the plaintiff, by the evidence of the defendant, or by the evidence of neither. Only where the trier of fact cannot decide between the conflicting versions and is unable to determine which is probably correct will the burden of proof question become important. Where there is uncertainty, the party who had the burden of proof will lose.[6] Various terms have been used to describe

---

4 It is erroneous to assume that the factual issues include only the actual events, and beyond this, inferences and normative judgments involve issues of law. Thus, for example, in determining whether the defendant was negligent, the trier of fact is required not only to decide what the defendant did, but as well, what ought to have been done. See Klar, "Developments in Tort Law: The 1978-79 Term" (1980), 1 Sup. Ct. L. Rev. 311 at 332. See discussion in Chapter 9 with particular reference to the Supreme Court of Canada's decision in *Housen v. Nikolaisen* (2002), 211 D.L.R. (4th) 577 (S.C.C.).

5 Fleming, *The Law of Torts*, 9th ed. (1998), at 352, states that "a merely mathematical or statistical probability of barely 51 per cent is not sufficient because it carries no conviction that the case falls within the 51 rather than the 49." Fleming goes on to state that "empirical studies in the U.S. tend to confirm that judges and juries place the preponderance standard between 55-75%, compared with 'beyond all reasonable doubt' between 80-100%."

6 For example, in *Saillant v. Smith* (1973), 33 D.L.R. (3d) 61 (Ont. C.A.), the trial judge found that there were two equally convincing versions of why a saddle slipped and the plaintiff fell from his horse. That being the case, "the evidence is at best evenly balanced, and, accordingly, the plaintiff has not proved his case." It might be that as a practical matter, triers of fact will judge the evidence of the parties differently, being more critical and skeptical of the person who is alleging than they are of the person who is defending. This, however, would not be correct. Also note the statement by Lord Griffiths in *Ng Chun Pui v. Lee Chuen Tat*, [1988] R.T.R. 298

the matter of burden of proof. It is said that the primary burden or onus, or the legal burden, rests only on one party, generally the plaintiff, throughout the trial. This means that when all is said and done, and the evidence is weighed, the trier must be convinced of that person's case on the balance of probabilities, or that party will lose. The primary burden is fixed, and never shifts. It is conceded, however, that during the course of the trial, evidence introduced by either party might practically, if not necessarily, call for a reply by the other. This has been described as a secondary, or an evidential burden.[7] Part of the difficulty which arises in discussing matters of proof is that these, and other terms,[8] are not used in the same way by everyone.

3. THE MAXIM *RES IPSA LOQUITUR*

(a) Introduction

In *Fontaine v. British Columbia (Official Administrator),*[9] Major J. wrote the following:

> Whatever value *res ipsa loquitur* may have once provided is gone. Various attempts to apply the so-called doctrine have been more confusing than helpful. Its use has been restricted to cases where the facts permitted an inference of negligence and there was no other reasonable explanation for the accident. Given its limited use it is somewhat meaningless to refer to that use as a doctrine of law. It would appear that the law would be better served if the maxim was treated as expired and no longer used as a separate component in negligence actions. After all, it was nothing more than an attempt to deal with circumstantial evidence.[10]

---

at 301:

> Resort to the burden of proof is a poor way to decide a case; it is the duty of the judge to examine all the evidence at the end of the case and decide whether on the facts he finds to have been proved and on the inferences he is prepared to draw he is satisfied that negligence has been established.

Also see Sopinka J.'s statement in *Hollis v. Birch* (1995), [1996] 2 W.W.R. 77, 1995 CarswellBC 967, 1995 CarswellBC 1152 at 123 [W.W.R.]:

> Only if the evidence were so evenly balanced that a determinative conclusion could not be reached would resort to the legal burden of proof have been necessary.

7 For a clear discussion, see Addy J.'s judgment in *MacDonald v. York County Hosp.*, [1972] 3 O.R. 469 (H.C.), reversed in part (1973), 1 O.R. (2d) 653 (C.A.). Also see Lord Pearson's explanation in *Henderson v. Henry E. Jenkins & Sons*, [1970] A.C. 282 at 301 (H.L.), quoted with approval by Clement J.A. in *MacLachlan & Mitchell Homes v. Frank's Rentals & Sales Ltd.* (1979), 10 C.C.L.T. 306 at 317-18 (Alta. C.A.). Note, however, Sopinka J.'s criticism of these terms, in *Snell v. Farrell* (1990), 72 D.L.R. (4th) 289 at 301 (S.C.C.). Sopinka J. notes that "this is not a true burden of proof, and use of an additional label to describe what is an ordinary step in the fact-finding process is unwarranted."

8 Such as "presumption of law", "presumption of fact", "inference." See Cameron, "*Res Ipsa Loquitur* in Perspective" (1974), 6 Man. L.J. 39, for an excellent discussion of these evidentiary terms.

9 (1997), 156 D.L.R. (4th) 577, [1998] 7 W.W.R. 25, 41 C.C.L.T. (2d) 36 (S.C.C.).

10 (1997), 156 D.L.R. (4th) 577 (S.C.C.) at 585.

It is thus now clear, if it were not before, that despite a long and chequered history in tort law,[11] the maxim *res ipsa loquitur*[12] was neither a boon nor a great mystery to the solution of tort law disputes. The words essentially informed us that the plaintiff's burden of proving those facts necessary to support a cause of action in negligence can be discharged either by introducing positive, direct evidence, and/or circumstantial, indirect evidence as to how the injury was caused. In other words, although a trier of fact must be persuaded by the plaintiff's evidence that the injury complained of was caused by the defendant's negligence, it matters not whether this decision is arrived at as a result of direct proof of what occurred, or circumstantial proof, based on experience and common sense.[13] The maxim *res ipsa loquitur* performs the function of letting triers of fact know that as long as they are persuaded by the evidence that the defendant was probably negligent and caused the injury, the plaintiff has discharged the burden.

Difficulties concerning the effect of circumstantial evidence on a plaintiff's burden seem to have arisen either when judges have had to explain it to juries, or when motions for nonsuits or directed verdicts were brought.[14] As well, the issue of *res ipsa* takes on added dimensions when courts attempt to use the maxim to facilitate a plaintiff's burden of proof when multiple defendants are involved. It is for these reasons that Major J. considered that it was now advisable to stop using the maxim in a formulistic way and treating it as a separate doctrine.

Despite these sentiments, however, the role that circumstantial or indirect evidence should play in negligence lawsuits remains an important issue. It was this question that the maxim and the jurisprudence that surrounded it were meant to resolve. Thus although the maxim *res ipsa loquitur* may have expired, the use of circumstantial evidence to assist plaintiffs in proving their cases remains as important an issue today as it did before. This warrants taking a closer look at the maxim and the jurisprudence that applied it.[15]

---

11 Although the words had been spoken before, the emergence of *res ipsa loquitur* as a significant tort law doctrine is traced to the famous case of *Byrne v. Boadle* (1863), 2 H. & C. 722. There have been numerous commentaries on the maxim which trace its history and explain its meaning. See especially, Cameron, "*Res Ipsa Loquitur* in Perspective" (1974), 6 Man. L.J. 39; Wright, "*Res Ipsa Loquitur*", in Linden (ed.), *Studies in Canadian Tort Law* (1968), Chapter 3; Schiff, "A *Res Ipsa Loquitur* Nutshell" (1976), 26 U.T.L.J. 450. Commentaries on *Fontaine v. British Columbia (Official Administrator)* include Rafferty & Rowbotham, "Developments in Contract and Tort Law: The 1997-98 Term" (1999), 10 S.C.L.R. (2d) 169; S. Forbes, "Developments in the Law of Evidence: The 1997-98 Term" (1999), 10 S.C.L.R. 385; and M. McInnes, "The Death of RIL in Canada" (1998), 114 L.Q.R. 547. On recent English and Australian jurisprudence see M. McInnes, "RIL in the High Court of Australia – A Missed Opportunity" (2000), 8 Tort L. Rev. 162; C. and Witting, "RIL: Some Last Words?" (2001), 117 L.Q.R. 392.

12 Which translates into "the thing speaks for itself."

13 As stated by Lerner J. in *M. v. Sinclair* (1980), 15 C.C.L.T. 57 at 61 (Ont. H.C.): "The maxim is nothing more than a concise expression of common sense applied to circumstantial evidence."

14 See an Australian case, *Jones v. Dunkel* (1959), 101 C.L.R. 298 (Aust. H.C.), for a discussion of these applications.

15 This is stated by Major J. himself:

> The application of *res ipsa loquitur* in previous decisions may provide some guidance as to when an inference of negligence may be drawn but it does not serve to establish definitive categories of when *res ipsa loquitur* will apply; [At (1997), 156 D.L.R. (4th) 577 (S.C.C.) at 582.]

(b) When Does "A Thing Speak For Itself"?

(i) Introduction

The use of the expression *res ipsa loquitur* reminded the trier of fact that in certain cases proof of circumstantial or indirect evidence of the defendant's negligence will be enough to allow a plaintiff to discharge the burden of proof. Although one cannot define with precise rules when the happening of an event will speak for itself, one can identify common factual elements in the case law which have supported this inference.

These elements are traceable to the original fact pattern itself — the case of *Byrne v. Boadle*.[16] A barrel of flour fell out of a first-storey window of the defendant's warehouse and struck the plaintiff as he walked along the public highway below. The warehouse and the shop underneath it were occupied by the defendant. The defendant's employees would lower barrels of flour from the window of the warehouse into carts waiting on the street below. The plaintiff entered no positive evidence as to whose fault it was that this specific barrel fell.[17] Despite this, the Court of Exchequer entered a verdict for the plaintiff.[18] It was during the course of argument for the plaintiff's motion to obtain a rule *nisi* that the famous words were spoken. Pollock C.B., in response to defendant counsel's argument that, in so far as the cause of the accident was concerned, there was not "a scintilla of evidence, unless the occurrence is of itself evidence of negligence," stated:

> There are certain cases of which it may be said *res ipsa loquitur* and this seems to be one of them.[19]

Shortly thereafter, in *Scott v. London & St. Katherine's Docks Co.*[20] the elements of the maxim's application were described by Chief Justice Erle in the following terms:

> There must be reasonable evidence of negligence; but where the thing is shown to be under the management of the defendant or his servants, and the accident is such as in the ordinary course of things does not happen if those who have the management use proper care, it affords reasonable evidence, in the absence of explanation by the defendants, that the accident arose from want of care.[21]

---

16 (1863), 2 H. & C. 722. As discussed by Cameron, above, note 11, there were cases prior to *Byrne v. Boadle* where courts used circumstantial evidence of a defendant's negligence, where direct evidence was not available, to hold the defendant liable. However, for various reasons explained by Cameron, it is *Byrne v. Boadle* which is considered to be the origin of the maxim in so far as tort actions are concerned.

17 In other words, he did not know the cause of the accident. This is a problematic point for *res ipsa* cases, as we shall see. When is the cause of an accident unknown?

18 The Assessor had nonsuited the plaintiff, but gave leave to the plaintiff to move the Court of Exchequer to enter a verdict for him.

19 (1863), 2 H. & C. 722 at 725, cited by Cameron, above, note 11, at 52.

20 (1865), 3 H. & C. 596. The facts of this case were similar to *Byrne v. Boadle*. Instead of flour, bags of sugar fell from the defendant's warehouse injuring the plaintiff, who was walking below on the defendant's dock.

21 (1865), 3 H. & C. 596 at 600. This statement has been quoted with approval in several Supreme Court of Canada judgments. See, e.g., *United Motors Service Inc. v. Hutson*, [1937] 1 D.L.R. 737 at 738; *Walker v. Coates*, [1968] S.C.R. 599 at 602; *Hellenius v. Lees*, [1972] S.C.R. 165 at 172; *Finlay v. Auld* (1975), 43 D.L.R. (3d) 216 at 219; *Wilcox v. Cavan* (1974), 50 D.L.R. (3d) 687 at 695.

These factual elements have been recast in the following frequently quoted statement:

> The doctrine applies:
>
> (1) when the thing that inflicted the damage was under the sole management and control of the defendant, or of someone for whom he is responsible or whom he has a right to control; (2) the occurrence is such that it would not have happened without negligence. If these two conditions are satisfied it follows, on a balance of probability, that the defendant, or the person for whom he is responsible, must have been negligent. There is, however, a further negative condition; (3) there must be no evidence as to why or how the occurrence took place. If there is, then appeal to *res ipsa loquitur* is inappropriate, for the question of the defendant's negligence must be determined on that evidence.[22]

Prior to *Fontaine*, this statement had been consistently used by Canadian courts in setting down the requirements for the maxim's application. Let us examine its three elements.[23]

(ii) The Requirement of Control

As stated above, the maxim *res ipsa loquitur* informed the trier of fact that in certain cases the circumstances of an event might be such as to raise an inference that the plaintiff's injury was caused by the defendant's negligence. This explains the control requirement. Where the injury-producing event or thing was not under the defendant's control, or the control of someone for whom the defendant could be held legally liable, it will be more difficult for a reasonable trier of fact to link the injury to the defendant in the absence of positive evidence. This, however, is dependent on the particular facts of each case.[24] In the leading Canadian case on this issue, *Kirk v. McLaughlin Coal & Supplies Ltd.*,[25] the fact that a furnace which had been serviced and repaired by the defendant was not in the defendant's actual physical custody or possession did not mean that an inference of negligence could not be raised against the defendant when the furnace exploded. Since the evidence indicated that no one other than the defendant had tampered with the furnace, the court was satisfied that the explosion was probably linked to negli-

---

22 Clerk and Lindsell, *Torts*, 16th ed. (1989), at 569. This particular formulation has been quoted in numerous Canadian cases. See, e.g., *Jackson v. Millar*, [1976] 1 S.C.R. 225; *Hellenius v. Lees*, [1972] S.C.R. 165 at 172; *Chabot v. Ford Motor Co. of Can.* (1982), 22 C.C.L.T. 185 at 224 (Ont. H.C.); *Goldsworthy v. Catalina Agencies Ltd.* (1982), 142 D.L.R. (3d) 281 at 289 (Nfld. T.D.); *Sisters of Charity of the Immaculate Conception v. Robert J. Fudge Ltd.* (1988), 87 N.B.R. (2d) 119 (C.A.); *South v. Fuxa* (1986), 44 Sask. R. 130 (Sask. Q.B.); *Penn West Petroleum Ltd. v. Koch Oil Co.*, [1994] 4 W.W.R. 630 (Alta. Q.B.) and *Fischer v. Waller*, [1994] 1 W.W.R. 83 (Alta. Q.B.), among others.

23 In *Fontaine v. British Columbia (Official Administrator)*, Major J. approved of breaking down *res ipsa* into these elements although he cautioned against seeing this in too formulistic a way. It was for this reason that he thought that referring to *res ipsa* as a "doctrine of law", which is a "separate component in negligence actions", was more confusing than helpful.

24 As stated in *Westlake v. Smith Tpt. Ltd.* (1973), 42 D.L.R. (3d) 502 at 513 (Ont. H.C.), by Lieff J.:

> . . . it is not necessary . . . to establish that the article in question was within the sole control of the person against whom it is desired to apply the doctrine, in the sense of physical possession and control. The only necessity is that the article be linked to the defendant in such a way as to bespeak negligence on the part of the defendant . . .

25 (1967), 66 D.L.R. (2d) 321 (Ont. C.A.).

gence on the defendant's part.[26] This is a sensible view of the control requirement. If an inference of negligence cannot be raised once a defective product has left the manufacturer's hands, it would be impossible to establish the negligence liability of a producer, other than by the use of positive evidence.[27]

The control requirement illustrates the point that it is not enough to prove by circumstantial evidence that the plaintiff's injury was caused by someone's negligence. The circumstances of the case must point to the defendant. This conclusion can only be arrived at if other possible actors are reasonably excluded by the evidence.

Cases involving two or more defendants as potential wrongdoers vividly illustrate this aspect of the maxim's application. Despite some initial uncertainty, it became clear that where multiple defendants were involved, and the causes of action against them were independent, the maxim could only be applied to individual defendants against whom an inference of negligence was raised. The mere fact that one or other of two or more parties must have been negligent did not require an explanation from them all.[28] The following case illustrates this point.

---

26 Also see *South v. Fuxa* (1986), 44 Sask. R. 130 (Q.B.), where this view of control was applied to a car which unexpectedly accelerated; *Bishop v. Gander (Town)* (1986), 60 Nfld. & P.E.I.R. 310 (Nfld. T.D.), where a municipality was held to be in control of underground water pipes; *Lenz v. J.B.'s Automotive Service Centre Ltd.* (1987), 51 Alta. L.R. (2d) 16 (Q.B.), where an automobile repairer was held to be in control of the automobile, 3½ weeks after the car had been repaired and delivered to the plaintiff; *Pearson v. Fairview Corp.* (1974), 55 D.L.R. (3d) 522 (Man. Q.B.), where the owners of a shopping mall were held to be in control of the doors to the mall, even though they were being used by the public; and *Paravano v. El Mirador Apartments*, [1990] O.J. No. 532 (Dist. Ct.), where persons who did roofing work two years prior to materials being blown from the roof were held to be still in control of the roof for the purposes of the maxim. In *Clayton v. J.N.Z. Invt. Ltd.* (1968), 1 D.L.R. (3d) 440 (Ont. C.A.), on the other hand, the mere fact that a pipe which had been installed by the defendant contractor burst several months later did not infer negligence on the contractor's part. There was no evidence as to who supplied the pipe, and those responsible for its maintenance had not been sued.

27 One wonders, for example, how Mrs. Donoghue would have been able to establish negligence on the part of the manufacturer of her bottle of ginger beer if direct proof had been required. As stated by MacKeigan C.J.N.S. in *Smith v. Inglis Ltd.* (1978), 6 C.C.L.T. 41 at 48 (N.S. C.A.):

> Rarely could a plaintiff prove by direct evidence that a defect existed when the product containing it left the factory. Often that fact may be readily inferred and indeed be overwhelmingly obvious, e.g., where a sealed bottle contains a snail. . . .

See *Chabot v. Ford Motor Co. of Can.* (1982), 22 C.C.L.T. 185 (Ont. H.C.), for a discussion of the control requirement in product liability cases. See also *Goldsworthy v. Catalina Agencies Ltd.* (1982), 142 D.L.R. (3d) 281 (Nfld. T.D.); *MacLachlan & Mitchell Homes Ltd. v. Frank's Rentals & Sales Ltd.* (1979), 10 C.C.L.T. 306 (Alta. C.A.); *Farro v. Nutone Electrical Ltd.* (1990), 72 O.R. (2d) 637 (C.A.); *Pacific Lumber & Shipping Co. v. Western Stevedoring Co.*, [1995] B.C.J. No. 866, 1995 CarswellBC 1960 (S.C. [In Chambers]).

28 This was made clear by the Supreme Court of Canada in *Wotta v. Haliburton Oil Well Cementing Co*, [1955] S.C.R. 377. The court clarified the law as stated in the earlier case of *Leaman v. Rea*, [1954] 4 D.L.R. 423 at 426 (N.B. C.A.). That case had involved a two car collision, where the trial judge could not determine how the accident happened and who was at fault, and dismissed the actions. In reversing the trial judgment, Bridges J. stated:

> It is my opinion that where there has been a collision between two motor vehicles under such circumstances that there must have been negligence on the part of one or both drivers

In *Valleyview Hotel Ltd. v. Montreal Trust Co.*[29] a fire was started in a hotel room which had been occupied by two guests. The evidence indicated that the fire had started as a result of a cigarette; it did not indicate, however, which of the two guests had been smoking. Even conceding that the conduct of the guest who had been smoking was negligent, the court refused to apply *res ipsa loquitur*. Tallis J.A. stated that "the doctrine of res ipsa loquitur cannot be applied where any one of several defendants *wholly independent* of each other may be responsible for the plaintiff's injury and loss."[30] If, of course, the evidence did raise an inference of negligence against each of two or more independent wrongdoers, the maxim could be applied to each.[31]

The view that the control requirement should be relaxed in some cases of multiple defendants in order to allow *res ipsa* to be applied to them all has occasionally won favour in other jurisdictions. In *Ybarra v. Spangard*,[32] it was decided that a patient who was injured during an appendicitis operation ought to be permitted to use *res ipsa loquitur* to require the doctors and nurses who participated in the operation to exculpate themselves by disclosing the identity of the negligent individuals responsible for his injury. The court held that in the circumstances of this case, the control requirement should be modified, and that "all those defendants who had any control over [the patient's] body or the instrumentalities which might have caused the injuries may properly be called upon to meet the inference of negligence by giving an explanation of their conduct."[33] A similar issue came before the New South Wales Court of Appeal. In *Kilgannon v. Sharpe Bros. Pty. Ltd.*,[34] a plaintiff injured by an exploding bottle of carbonated beverage brought action against the manufacturer, the bottle/distributor and the retailer. Hope J.A.[35] held that *res ipsa loquitur* could only be applied against the defendants against whom a rational inference of fault could be raised. As explained by Hope J.A., it is not enough that one of the defendants must have been

---

and the Court is unable to distinguish between such drivers as to liability, both drivers should be found equally at fault.

The Supreme Court in *Wotta v. Haliburton* rejected this. The doctrine cannot apply where the evidence only infers negligence against one or the other party, but not both.

29 (1985), 33 C.C.L.T. 282 (Sask. C.A.).

30 *Ibid.*, at 286. The fact that both guests had died and were therefore not able to clarify the event might have influenced the court. Other cases which support this principle include *Haverkate v. Toronto Harbour Comm.* (1986), 30 D.L.R. (4th) 125 (Ont. H.C.), affirmed (1988), 46 D.L.R. (4th) 767 (Ont. C.A.); and *Prior v. Hanna* (1987), 43 D.L.R. (4th) 612 (Alta. Q.B.).

31 See discussion in *MacLachlan & Mitchell Homes v. Frank's Rentals & Sales Ltd.* (1979), 10 C.C.L.T. 306 at 324 (Alta. C.A.). The same problem arises when one of the parties responsible for the event may have been the plaintiff. In *Hollis v. Birch*, [1993] 6 W.W.R. 609 (B.C. C.A.), for example, the doctrine did not apply since the cause of the rupture of the plaintiff's breast implant may have been the plaintiff's own actions. The court held that the plaintiff failed to lead evidence eliminating this possibility, and thus could not rely on the maxim. The Court of Appeal's judgment was affirmed, on other issues, by the Supreme Court of Canada: (1995), [1996] 2 W.W.R. 77, 1995 CarswellBC 967, 1995 CarswellBC 1152.

32 154 P. 2d 687 (Cal. S.C., 1944).

33 *Ibid.*, at 691. This was followed in *Anderson v. Somberg*, 338 A. 2d 1 (N.J., 1975).

34 (1986), 4 N.S.W.L.R. 600.

35 With whom Priestly J.A. agreed.

and all of them may have been negligent; the plaintiff must be able to point to that particular defendant or defendants who was or were negligent.[36]

(iii) The Occurrence Would Not Ordinarily Happen Without Negligence

The second element of the above quoted *res ipsa loquitur* formulation merely described the nature of the maxim itself.[37] "A thing speaks for itself", in the sense that its mere occurrence raises an inference of negligence, when common experience or evidence indicates that the incident would not ordinarily have occurred in the absence of negligent conduct. As explained by one judge:

> The purpose of the rule is to enable an inference to be drawn from the mere occurrence of the event causing damage, even in the absence of evidence of the way in which it occurred, where in the ordinary affairs of mankind it can be said that such an event does not happen unless there is negligence or, if that cannot be said, where there is evidence that such an event does not occur in the absence of negligence. The very act must bespeak negligence.[38]

It is impossible to catalogue the types of accidents which by their very occurrence raise an inference of negligence. This is, in each case, a matter of common sense and evidence adduced by the plaintiff. It has been held in the cases, for example, that reasonably constructed chimneys do not get blown over, even in heavy winds,[39] that stirrups do not ordinarily fall off horses,[40] that fertilizer bags do not fall out of trucks,[41] that there would not be a hole in the ground,[42] that a light shield would not fall off a light,[43] and that a radio tower would not fall over,[44] in

---

36 Kirby P. disagreed, however, stating that for various policy reasons, as long as the plaintiff has brought before the court all those who on the evidence could be responsible for the negligence, he has done enough to call for an explanation from them. According to His Lordship, to require the plaintiff to "prove a positive case against each tortfeasor and identify which of a series of alleged tortfeasors is actually to blame" would be to impose "an unreasonable burden." See above, note 34, at 618.

37 As stated by Prosser, *The Law of Torts*, 4th ed. (1971), at 214:

> The requirement that the occurrence be one which ordinarily does not happen without negligence is of course only another way of stating an obvious principle of circumstantial evidence: that the event must be such that in the light of ordinary experience it gives rise to an inference that some one must have been negligent.

This was quoted in *Paquette v. Labelle* (1981), 17 C.C.L.T. 194 at 208-09 (Ont. C.A.).

38 Krever J. in *North York v. Kert Chem. Indust. Inc.* (1985), 33 C.C.L.T. 184 at 199 (Ont. H.C.). One of the problems raised by stating the issue in this way is that this factor overlaps with the defendant's need to produce a satisfactory explanation of why the injury occurred, once it is held that the maxim applies. In other words, the argument tends to become: the maxim only applies where the injury would not have occurred without negligence, but, if the maxim applies, a defendant can clear himself by showing that the injury could have occurred without negligence. See below.

39 *Gough v. Zwicker* (1979), 34 N.S.R. (2d) 624 (T.D.). Walls also do not collapse: *MacLaren v. Doyle*, (1990) 84 Nfld. & P.E.I.R. 91 (P.E.I. T.D.).

40 *M. v. Sinclair* (1980), 15 C.C.LT. 57 (Ont. H.C.).

41 *Fisher v. L.E. Matchett Trucking Co.* (1981), 14 Sask. R. 445 (Dist. Ct.).

42 *Taylor v. Husky Oil Operations Ltd.*, [1988] A.W.L.D. 423 (C.A.).

43 *Dauphinee v. Can. Life Assur. Co.* (1987), 78 N.S.R. (2d) 326 (C.A.).

44 *Cie D'Assurance du Qué. v. Can.* (1988), 23 F.T.R. 265 (T.D.).

the absence of negligence. Saddles, however, can slip,[45] and water-mains can break,[46] without there being negligence.[47]

There were four general areas where the maxim was raised frequently. These were cases dealing with fires, medical malpractice, product liability, and automobile accidents. The requirement that the maxim applied only where "the occurrence would not ordinarily happen without there being negligence" can best be understood by looking at the maxim's application in the context of these problem areas.

A. Fires

Claimants' attempts to use the maxim *res ipsa loquitur* to assist them in proving that those who occupy or control premises, or objects, should be held liable for fires which originated there, highlight this issue. Can it be claimed that fires ordinarily do not start unless there is negligence on the part of someone?

The numerous cases on this issue[48] established that since fires can originate without there having been any negligence on the part of those who occupy or control premises or things where the fires started, the mere fact of a fire having occurred does not raise an inference of negligence.[49] It is only where there was evidence in addition to the fact of the fire itself, from which it can be inferred that

---

45 *Sim v. Wardock* (1981), 29 A.R. 260 (Q.B.).

46 *Temple v. Melville* (1978), 7 C.C.L.T. 1 (Sask. Dist. Ct.), affirmed (1979), 11 C.C.L.T. 104 (Sask. C.A.).

47 Can a "parked" car roll down a hill without there having been any negligence on the driver's part? In *Noble (Guardian ad litem of) v. Bhumber* (1993), [1993] B.C.J. No. 1264, 1993 CarswellBC 2373 (S.C.), reversed (1996), [1996] B.C.J. No. 315, 1996 CarswellBC 314 (C.A.), the Court of Appeal reversed a trial judgment that had decided it could. The Court of Appeal held that even if the defendant's explanation that an intruder must have entered the car and shifted the gear into neutral was correct, this would indicate negligence on the defendant's part in not locking the car and leaving the wheels turned into the curb of the slope as required by legislation.

48 Fire damage litigation seems to be the area where *res ipsa* was most frequently raised. Some of the cases include *Paquette v. Labelle* (1981), 17 C.C.L.T. 194 (Ont. C.A.); *Ross v. Moore* (1982), 36 O.R. (2d) 464 (Co. Ct.); *Valleyview Hotel Ltd. v. Montreal Trust Co.* (1985), 33 C.C.L.T. 282 (Sask. C.A.); *Maron v. Baert & Siguaw Dev. Ltd.* (1981), 126 D.L.R. (3d) 9 (Alta. Q.B.); *Stern G.M.C. Trucks (1969) Ltd. v. L.P.Y. Caterers Ltd.* (1984), 27 Man. R. (2d) 298 (Co. Ct.); *Lenz v. J.B.'s Automotive Service Centre Ltd.* (1987), 51 Alta. L.R. (2d) 16 (Q.B.); *Can. Eductor Sales & Services Co. v. Horyn Hldg. Ltd.* (1986), 75 A.R. 23 (Q.B.); *Kish v. Prairie Harvestore Systems Ltd.* (1986), 48 Sask. R. 30 (Q.B.); *Sisters of Charity of the Immaculate Conception v. Robert J. Fudge Ltd.* (1988), 87 N.B.R. (2d) 119 (C.A.); *Chabot v. Ford Motor Co. of Can.* (1982), 39 O.R. (2d) 162; *Prior v. Hanna* (1987), 43 D.L.R. (4th) 612 (Alta. Q.B.); *Franks v. Sanderson* (1988), 44 C.C.L.T. 208 (B.C. C.A.); *Gale v. Box* (1987), 50 Man. R. (2d) 3 (Q.B.); *Walsh v. Import Doctor Ltd.* (1989), 78 Sask. R. 213 (Q.B.); *Satellite Const. Ltd. v. Glasgow Mercury Sales (1984) Ltd.* (1988), 84 N.S.R. (2d) 34 (T.D.); *Hunt v. Burgess*, [1993] 4 W.W.R. 1 (Man. C.A.); *Hunt v. Burgess*, [1993] 4 W.W.R. 1 (Man.C.A.); *Phoenix Sportswear of Canada Ltd. v. Intergold Jewellery Manufacturing Ltd.* (1995), [1996] 1 W.W.R. 740 (Alta. Q.B.); and *Hildebrandt v. Pavier*, [1997] 8 W.W.R. 470, 38 C.C.L.T. (2d) 159 (Sask. Q.B.).

49 As stated by Goddard C.J. in *Sochacki v. Sas*, [1947] 1 All E.R. 344 at 345 (K.B.): "Everyone knows fires occur through accidents which happen without negligence on anybody's part."

a specific defendant's negligence was the cause of the fire, that the maxim could be used.[50]

This has been found in a number of fire damage cases, including the leading one *United Motors Service Inc. v. Hutson.*[51] In this case, a fire started in a building in which the defendant had been using large quantities of gasoline to clean grease accumulations on a cement floor. The gasoline vapours ignited and an explosion occurred. The court was able to infer from these facts that the defendant had failed to take proper precautions in view of the danger of this operation, even though there was no direct evidence as to the precise cause of the initial fire. This was not merely an inexplicably caused fire; there was sufficient evidence of the defendant's negligence to require an explanation from it.

Following this principle, it was found, for example, that a fire which originated in a field where the defendant had previously been burning bushes indicated negligence on the defendant's part in having failed to ensure that the fire had been properly extinguished.[52] When a fire occurred in a kitchen near a deep fat fryer, the evidence that the fryer had been left on and unattended over a holiday period was sufficient to raise the maxim *res ipsa loquitur.*[53] Similarly, when a fire was discovered one day after the defendant's employees had been using carbon arc air torches to burn away the base of a silo, the court considered that the maxim applied and an explanation was required from the defendants.[54]

There were also been numerous fire cases where the maxim was not applied. In *Paquette v. Labelle*,[55] the mere fact that a fire originated in the defendant's shop where automobiles were repaired and painted did not raise an inference of negligence against the owners or employees of the body shop.[56] Similarly, in

---

50 For a good review of the authorities which establish this principle see Goodman J.A.'s judgment in *Paquette v. Labelle*, above, note 48.

51 [1937] 1 D.L.R. 737 (S.C.C.).

52 *Ross v. Moore*, above, note 48.

53 *Stern G.M.C. Trucks (1969) Ltd. v. L.P.Y. Caterers Ltd.*, above, note 48.

54 *Kish v. Prairie Harvestore Systems Ltd.* above, note 48. For other cases where the evidence required an explanation from the defendants, see *Sisters of Charity of the Immaculate Conception v. Robert J. Fudge Ltd.* (1988), 87 N.B.R. (2d) 119 (C.A.) — a fire started on a roof where workers were using hot tarred mops near combustible materials; *Interprovincial Pipe Line Co. v. Seller's Oil Field Service* (1975), 58 D.L.R. (3d) 719 (Man. Q.B.), affirmed (1976), 66 D.L.R. (3d) 360 (Man. C.A.) — oil tank caught on fire while being cleaned out by defendant; *Gale v. Box*, above, note 48 — fire started at precise spot where shortly before an acetylene torch with an open flame was being used in close proximity to floor joists; *Lenz v. J.B.'s Automotive Service Centre Ltd.*, above, note 48 — fire started in car in an area which had recently been worked on by defendant mechanics. In *Phoenix Sportswear of Canada Ltd. v. Intergold Jewellery Manufacturing Ltd.* (1995), [1996] 1 W.W.R. 740 (Alta. Q.B.), the court applied the maxim and required an explanation from the defendant. The defendant had no explanation. Despite this, the court held that the defendant's evidence convinced it that it was not negligent and the fire had some undetermined cause. A post-*Fontaine v. I.C.B.C.* case where the cause of a fire was determined on circumstantial evidence is *Furlong Estate v. Newfoundland Light & Power Co.* (2005), [2005] N.J. No. 146, 2005 CarswellNfld 120 (C.A.) affirming (2003), 230 Nfld. & P.E.I.R. 27 (Nfld. C.A.).There was an electrical fire which the trial judge determined was caused by the defendant's malfunctioning electrical equipment.

55 Above, note 48.

56 A similar autobody shop fire case is *Canadian Eductor Sales & Services Co. v. Horyn Hldg. Ltd.* (1986), 75 A.R. 23 (Q.B.). Also see *Satellite Const. Ltd. v. Glasgow Mercury*, above, note 48.

Pleasant Valley Motel (1972) Ltd. v. LePage,[57] the mere fact that a fire started in a truck which was carrying fuel for a camping stove, lantern and heater did not justify the application of *res ipsa loquitur*.

An interesting issue relating to liability for accidental fires is raised by an old English statute, the Fires Prevention (Metropolis) Act, 1774.[58] This statute, which is in effect in several Commonwealth and Canadian jurisdictions,[59] immunizes those who own certain types of premises[60] from liability for fires "accidentally" begun there. Critical to the operation of this provision, however, is the requirement that the fire be an accidental one.[61] The English cases have held that any fire deliberately started, even if innocently and non-negligently, is not accidental for the purposes of the statutory immunity. Thus, only spontaneous fires or fires begun by strangers will qualify for the immunity.[62] An "accidental fire" has also been described as "one that cannot, on a balance of probabilities, be traced to a particular cause".[63]

Although not effective in providing an immunity to defendants, the statutory provision has been interpreted as placing an onus on plaintiffs to prove that the fire in issue was not accidental.[64] Thus, in this way, the common law's strict liability for damage caused by fires has been transformed into a liability based on negligence.[65]

---

57 (1978), 94 D.L.R. (3d) 73 (B.C. S.C.).

58 14 Geo. 3, c. 78. See further discussion of this matter in Chapter 16.

59 See Irvine, "Annotation to *Franks v. Sanderson*" (1986), 35 C.C.L.T. 307. Irvine notes cases from Australia, New Zealand, British Columbia, Alberta, Saskatchewan, and Manitoba. Two Alberta cases referring to the statute are *Warkentin v. C. (M.)* (1998), [1998] A.J. No. 433, 1998 CarswellAlta 357 (Q.B.) and *Alberta v. Hay*, [2002] 5 W.W.R. 653 (Alta. Q.B.).

60 Namely, a "house, chamber, stable, barn or other building."

61 As stated by Professor Irvine, above, note 59, at 308, "these words have been accorded their most literal and inflexible meaning."

62 As noted by Irvine, above, note 59, this reduces the statute to a "superfluous and idle encumbrance", since defences were available at any event for these types of fires. Irvine also notes that to make matters worse, even if a fire began spontaneously, the failure to put it out could take it out of the category of an accidentally begun fire. Irvine cites *Musgrove v. Pandelis*, [1919] 2 K.B. 43 (C.A.); and *Goldman v. Hargrave*, [1967] 1 A.C. 645 (P.C.).

63 *Neff v. St. Catharines Marina Ltd.* (1998), 155 D.L.R. (4th) 647 (Ont. C.A.) at 650. One can infer the cause by the use of *res ipsa loquitur* if circumstantial evidence, other than the fact of the fire itself, exists. There was none in this case. Complicating the issue, however, was the fact that the plaintiffs were suing for the loss of their boats, which were destroyed in the fire. The law of bailment requires the bailee to disprove fault, if the goods are damaged or destroyed. The Court of Appeal held that if the bailee can prove that the fire was accidental, i.e., had no known source, it has satisfied this onus. In addition, the bailee can benefit from the immunity afforded by the Accidental Fires Act, R.S.O. 1990, c. A.4, repealed 1997, c. 4, s. 85. In *AXA Insurance (Canada) v. Brunetti* (1998), 62 O.T.C. 241 (Gen. Div.), the judgment in *Neff* was applied. Since the fire in this case had a known cause, the negligence of a tenant, the Act did not apply. The issue related to the landlord's liability. In this case the landlord was held not liable. See further discussion on liability for fires in Chapter 16.

64 See Irvine's discussion, above, note 59. As Irvine notes, there is contrary authority which places the onus on defendants to prove that the fire was accidental. However, according to Irvine, this authority has often been disregarded, and is against the tide of authority.

65 See Chapter 16.

B. Medical Malpractice

As with fire damage cases, courts generally resisted the application of *res ipsa loquitur* to the ordinary case of medical misadventure. Although the argument that the doctrine, as a matter of law, could not be applied to medical negligence cases was rejected,[66] the case law indicated that plaintiffs only rarely convinced courts that their medical mishaps would ordinarily not have occurred had their doctors not been negligent. Unless, therefore, common experience or the plaintiff's evidence took the case out of the ordinary, the maxim would not be applied for that plaintiff's benefit.

Based on this principle, it was found, for example, that the following medical mishaps did not raise an inference of negligence against the doctors involved: a patient's ureter was damaged in the course of the surgical removal of an ovary;[67] a patient became paralyzed after an angiogram;[68] a tubal ligation failed to render the patient sterile;[69] an artery was severed during spinal disc surgery;[70] and a baby was born with serious problems after a forceps delivery.[71] On the other side, *res ipsa loquitur* was applied when a patient developed tissue emphysema after a novel anaesthetic procedure was performed on her,[72] when a patient suffered a paralyzed vocal chord after an operation on her neck,[73] and when a needle was injected into the plaintiff's artery rather than his muscle.[74]

C. Products

An area where courts seemed to be more confident in their decisions to apply the maxim *res ipsa loquitur* was product liability.[75] The product liability area does

---

66 In *Nesbitt v. Holt*, [1953] 1 D.L.R. 671 (S.C.C.), Kerwin J. categorically rejected an earlier holding in *Clark v. Wansbrough*, [1940] O.W.N. 67 (H.C.), that *res ipsa loquitur* "has no application in malpractice cases." As stated by Kerwin J., at 673, "it may apply in malpractice cases depending upon the circumstances . . ." See also *Crits v. Sylvester*, [1956] S.C.R. 991.

67 *Hobson v. Munkley* (1976), 1 C.C.L.T. 163 (Ont. H.C.). See Picard, "Annotation", 1 C.C.L.T. 163.

68 *Ferguson v. Hamilton Civic Hosps.* (1983), 23 C.C.L.T. 254 (Ont. H.C.), affirmed (1985), 33 C.C.L.T. 56 (Ont. C.A.).

69 *Grey v. Webster* (1984), 14 D.L.R. (4th) 706 (N.B. Q.B.).

70 *Kapur v. Marshall* (1978), 4 C.C.L.T. 204 (Ont. H.C.).

71 *Goguen v. Crowe* (1987), 40 C.C.L.T. 212 (N.S. T.D.). See also *Schanilec Estate v. Harris* (1987), 39 C.C.LT. 279 (B.C. C.A.) — maxim not applied when plaintiff became paralyzed after cervical laminectomy; *Videto v. Kennedy* (1980), 107 D.L.R. (3d) 612 (Ont. H.C.), reversed on other grounds (1981), 17 C.C.L.T. 307 (Ont C.A.) — maxim not applied when bowel perforated during sterilization procedure; *Fischer v. Waller*, [1994] 1 W.W.R. 83 (Alta. Q.B.) — maxim not applied when needle used to administer anaesthetic perforated the patient's eye.

72 *Holmes v. London (City) Hosp. Bd.* (1977), 5 C.C.L.T. 1 (Ont. H.C.).

73 *Finlay v. Auld* (1973), 43 D.L.R. (3d) 216 (S.C.C.).

74 *Wilcox v. Cavan* (1974), 50 D.L.R. (3d) 687 (S.C.C.). Also see *Miles v. Judges* (1997), 37 C.C.L.T. (2d) 160 (Ont. Gen. Div.), where the circumstantial evidence supported an inference of negligence, and *Hassen v. Anvari* (2001), [2001] O.J. No. 6085, 2001 CarswellOnt 5325 (S.C.J.), additional reasons at (2002), 2002 CarswellOnt 3522 (S.C.J.), additional reasons at (2002), 2002 CarswellOnt 3523 (S.C.J.), affirmed (2003), 2003 CarswellOnt 3436 (C.A.), leave to appeal to S.C.C. refused (2004), 2004 CarswellOnt 1768 (S.C.C.) to the same effect. It is interesting to note that although *Hassen* post-dates *Fontaine v. I.C.B.C.*, we still see circumstantial evidence being used to discharge the plaintiff's burden of proof, without the court formally using the words *res ipsa loquitur*.

75 One might surmise why this is so. Perhaps it is because we expect more from the products we

highlight, however, some of the conceptual and practical difficulties courts had with *res ipsa loquitur.*

In order to establish a negligence action against the manufacturer of a product, a plaintiff has to prove that (1) the product was defective, (2) the defect was the result of the manufacturer's negligence, and (3) the defect caused the plaintiff's injury.[76] Depending on the circumstances of the case and the difficulties of proof faced by the plaintiff, the maxim could have been employed in relation to any of these elements.

Frequently it was clear that the product was defective and that this defect resulted in the plaintiff's injury. For example, a bottle that exploded was defective,[77] as was an improperly coiled capillary tube,[78] a bicycle manufactured without lock washers to hold the axle of the front wheel to the fork,[79] and a glass door that shattered when being opened in the normal way.[80] In these cases only two issues remained to be decided. Were the defects present when the products left their manufacturers, and did the defects arise as a result of the manufacturers' negligence? Since these questions were incapable of being answered by the introduction of direct evidence, the courts allowed inferences of negligence to arise from the facts. In *Smith v. Inglis Ltd.*,[81] for example, the court, conceding that "rarely could a plaintiff prove by direct evidence that a defect existed when the product containing it left the factory,"[82] considered the circumstantial evidence and concluded that the defect existed before the object left the factory. Once the court was satisfied as to this, the inference that the defect arose as a result of the manufacturer's negligence becomes, as one writer has put it, "practically irresistible."[83]

A more difficult case arose where the plaintiff was injured in a product-related accident but could not positively prove that the product was defective. In *McHugh v. Reynolds Extrusion Co.*,[84] for example, the plaintiff fell from a ladder manufactured by the defendant company. It could not be proven with direct evidence whether the fall was caused by a defect in the ladder, or by the way the plaintiff was climbing it. The court applied the maxim *res ipsa loquitur* and concluded that the evidence raised an inference that the problem lay with the ladder, and not with the plaintiff's use of it.[85] Similarly, in *South v. Fuxa*,[86] the unexpected and

---

buy than we are accustomed to receive, or because courts place a higher standard of care on manufacturers than on other defendants. Courts might also be more cognizant of the difficulties of proof that plaintiffs have in this area.

76 See Chapter 9. Negligence in the design of the product or in failing to market the product reasonably did not generally involve the maxim's use.

77 *Brunski v. Dom. Stores* (1981), 20 C.C.L.T. 14 (Ont. H.C.).

78 *Smith v. Inglis Ltd.* (1978), 6 C.C.L.T. 41 (N.S. C.A.).

79 *Goldsworthy v. Catalina Agencies Ltd.* (1982), 142 D.L.R. (3d) 281 (Nfld. T.D.).

80 *Pearson v. Fairview Corp.* (1974), 55 D.L.R. (3d) 522 (Man. Q.B.). Other examples of clearly defective products cited by Linden, *Canadian Tort Law*, 5th ed. (1993), at 226, include bread with glass found in it, a beer bottle which contains chlorine, and a bun which contains a stone.

81 Above, note 78.

82 *Ibid.*, at 48.

83 See Waddams, *Products Liability* 3rd ed. (1993), at 58.

84 (1974), 7 O.R. (2d) 336 (H.C.), affirmed (1976), 15 O.R. (2d) 325 (C.A.).

85 Although the defendant successfully negated this inference by its evidence.

86 (1986), 44 Sask. R. 130 (Q.B.).

unexplained acceleration of a vehicle raised an inference that the vehicle was defective. In *Stewart v. Chrysler Can. Ltd.*[87] on the other hand, the fact that the rear window of a car shattered did not, in view of the evidence, raise an inference that there was a manufacturer's defect in the product.

In another development, it was held that bottlers of drinks have the onus of disproving negligence once it had been shown that their products are defective.[88] Although, as noted above, a defect in any product which is causative of harm raised an inference of negligence against the manufacturer, the effect of this principle was to place an even greater onus of disproof on these defendants.

D. Automobile Accidents

A fourth area where the maxim *res ipsa loquitur* was frequently invoked was liability for unexplained automobile accidents.[89] Due to the inability of parties involved in some automobile accidents to explain their cause,[90] there may be no direct evidence for the courts to consider. In these cases, courts allowed the maxim *res ipsa loquitur* to apply. This has been done not only with respect to proof of negligence, but with respect to proof of gross negligence as well. As with all cases of *res ipsa loquitur*, evidence that the accidents would not ordinarily have occurred in the absence of the defendants' negligence has been a prerequisite to a finding of liability based on circumstantial evidence.

Many of the cases involved drivers who inexplicably have allowed their cars to swerve either off the road or across the middle line into the lane of oncoming traffic. Did these facts, without more, raise an inference of negligence? Was this conduct which would ordinarily not occur in the absence of negligence or gross negligence?

The courts were not fully consistent on this question. In most cases where negligence, or even gross negligence, was inferred, the courts have required additional circumstances to support this inference. In other words, merely losing control of one's car and driving it into danger did not by itself indicate gross negligence, or even negligence.[91] Thus, in *Kerr v. Cummings*,[92] the mere fact that

---

87 (1975), 13 N.B.R. (2d) 53 (Q.B.).

88 *Brunski v. Dom. Stores* (1981), 20 C.C.L.T. 14 (Ont. H.C.); *Zeppa v. Coca-Cola Ltd.*, [1955] 5 D.L.R. 187 (Ont. C.A.); *Varga v. John Labatt Ltd.* (1956), 6 D.L.R. (2d) 336 (Ont. H.C.).

89 In addition to *res ipsa loquitur*, there are specific highway traffic provisions which reverse the onus of proof in certain types of cases. For example, if a pedestrian is involved, there is an onus on the driver or owner of the car to prove that the damage did not arise through their improper conduct. See, e.g., Highway Traffic Act, R.S.O. 1990, c. H.8, s. 193(1).

90 Cases involve parties who have died, suffered amnesia, or simply slept through the accident.

91 This is in fact the *Fontaine v. British Columbia (Official Administrator)* scenario. Fontaine and Loewen went for a weekend hunting trip in Loewen's truck. They did not return from the trip on the expected date. More than two months later, their deceased bodies were found in Loewen's damaged truck, which lay in a creek bed adjacent to a highway. Loewen had been driving; his truck had gone off the road, down an embankment, and into a swollen creek. It was swept downstream until it came to rest. There was no clear evidence as to why the truck had left the road. There were no witnesses. The court knew that the weather at the time had been stormy and wet, the roads were very bad and the driving conditions terrible. Two of the truck's tires were excessively worn and one of the tires was cut and its rim damaged. The widow of the passenger Fontaine sued the estate of the driver Loewen for negligence. The trial dismissed the action based on lack of proof of negligence: (March 29, 1994), Doc. New Westminster S 0-

the driver's car inexplicably collided with the abutment of a bridge was not sufficient to raise an inference of gross negligence.[93] Where there has been additional evidence suggesting improper conduct on the driver's part, the maxim was employed. In *Walker v. Coates*,[94] for example, the evidence indicated that the driver probably fell asleep after he should have known that he was likely to be overcome by sleep. This raised an inference of gross negligence.[95] Other judges held, however, that merely losing control of one's car was sufficient in itself to raise an inference of negligence, or even gross negligence. In a leading case, *Goulais v. Restoule*,[96] the Supreme Court of Canada found a driver grossly negligent for inexplicably allowing her car to "slowly swerve" into the middle of the oncoming line of traffic.[97] As well, in *Lardner v. Canada Permanent Trust Co.*,[98] where there were no circumstances to suggest negligence other than the fact that the driver inexplicably drove his car into the lane of oncoming traffic, the court used the maxim to find the driver grossly negligent. In *Genik v. Ewanylo*,[99] where there was no evidence at all to explain why the driver might have suddenly veered off the road, the courts used the maxim *res ipsa loquitur* to raise an inference of gross negligence against the defendant.

One must also relate this discussion to the breach of statutory duty issue, discussed previously.[100] One might surmise that in most cases where an automobile accident has been caused by a driver's failure to remain in the appropriate driving lane, a breach of the relevant highway traffic provisions has occurred. If the breach itself is adopted by the courts as *prima facie* evidence of the driver's negligence, then resort to *res ipsa loquitur* to raise an inference of negligence becomes unnecessary. The mere fact of the breach of statutory duty will have the same effect. This approach was followed in some cases.[101] Although the decision

---

0386, [1994] B.C.J. No. 716 (S.C.). The Court of Appeal agreed: 18 M.V.R. (3d) 1, [1996] 9 W.W.R. 305 (B.C. C.A.). The Supreme Court affirmed, refusing to overturn the trial judge's findings and the inferences that were drawn from them.

92 [1953] 2 D.L.R. 1 (S.C.C.).

93 Also see *Primeau v. Morris* (1982), 54 N.S.R. (2d) 634 (T.D.).

94 (1968), 68 D.L.R. (2d) 436 (S.C.C.). See also *Van Der Zouwen v. Koziak* (1971), 25 D.L.R. (3d) 354 (Alta. C.A.); *Mabey v. Robertson* (1969), 8 D.L.R. (3d) 84 (Alta. C.A.); and *Jackson v. Millar*, [1976] 1 S.C.R. 225.

95 It has been held that merely falling asleep at the wheel is not gross negligence. There must be evidence or an inference that the driver had actual or constructive warning that he might fall asleep. See *Gunvaldsen v. Seward* (1969), 69 W.W.R. 366 (Sask. Q.B.), affirmed (1970), 74 W.W.R. 398 (Sask. C.A.), which was affirmed [1971] 4 W.W.R. 636 (S.C.C.); and *Jasper v. Deleau* (1967), 59 W.W.R. 24 (Man. Q.B.). It has also been held that one may lose control of one's car due to a "hypnoidal" state, and if one does not have knowledge or awareness of this, it cannot be deemed to be gross negligence. See *McDonald v. Little* (1970), 14 D.L.R. (3d) 114 (Alta. T.D.).

96 (1974), 48 D.L.R. (3d) 285 (S.C.C.).

97 Both lower courts had found for the driver. Note that Dickson J. in dissent referred both to *Kerr v. Cummings*, above, note 92, and *Walker v. Coates*, above, note 94, to support his opinion that the mere happening of the event did not raise an inference of gross negligence in this case.

98 (1969), 10 D.L.R. (3d) 753 (Man. Q.B.).

99 (1980), 12 C.C.L.T. 121 (Man. C.A.).

100 See Chapter 9.

101 Earlier authorities are *Baldwin v. Bell*, [1933] 1 D.L.R. 232 (S.C.C.); and *Gauthier & Co. v. R.*, [1945] 2 D.L.R. 48 (S.C.C.). A more recent case is *Rydzik v. Edwards* (1982), 138 D.L.R. (3d) 87 (Ont. H.C.).

in *Sask. Wheat Pool v. Canada*[102] has now lessened the effect of statutory breach in negligence actions, breaches of highway traffic legislation will undoubtedly continue to be treated with special respect by the courts.[103]

(iv) *The Cause of the Occurrence Must Not Be Known*

A sometimes confusing element of the *res ipsa loquitur* application was the condition that the maxim could only be applied where the cause of the occurrence was not known. As stated in the above formulation from Clerk and Lindsell,[104] "there must be no evidence as to why or how the occurrence took place."

In most cases, certainly the immediate cause of the plaintiff's injury is known. For example, in the case of *Byrne v. Boadle* itself, the cause of the plaintiff's injury was known — the defendant's barrel of flour fell from its warehouse window onto the plaintiff.[105] For *res ipsa*, however, the following question must be asked. Was what brought about the occurrence which resulted in the plaintiff's injury provable by direct evidence? If it was not, then the maxim was applicable. For example, using *Byrne v. Boadle* as an illustration, the fact that what caused the barrel to fall out of the window was not provable by direct evidence necessitated the adoption of the maxim.

The case of *Hellenius v. Lees*[106] illustrates the confusion. The plaintiff passenger was injured in a car accident. As the car was being driven by the defendant, a rear tire burst, the car swerved and rolled over on the highway. Was the cause of this accident known? Was *res ipsa loquitur* applicable? In the Ontario Court of Appeal, only Mr. Justice Laskin, in dissent, held that the facts of the case[107] provided sufficient circumstantial evidence to raise an inference of negligence against the defendant. Laskin J.A. held that the jury ought to have been so instructed; in other words, the maxim *res ipsa loquitur* applied. Mr. Justice Ritchie, however, in a judgment for the Supreme Court of Canada, stated that the rule did not apply. According to His Lordship, "the cause of the accident was known and was indeed apparent."[108] This, it is suggested, was the wrong question, and if asked in all cases, would have ruled out the maxim's use in almost every one.[109] A cause of an accident is not known when what precipitated the occurrence which led to the plaintiff's injury is not provable by direct evidence.

---

102 (1983), 143 D.L.R. (3d) 9 (S.C.C.). See Chapter 9.

103 See, e.g., *Hearn v. Rowland*, [1989] 3 W.W.R. 78 (B.C. C.A.), where a driver whose car skidded on ice and collided with an oncoming car was required to rebut an inference of negligence. The court accepted that he acted with reasonable care and dismissed the action.

104 Above, note 22.

105 One can see that this is true in almost every case. Usually the plaintiff knows what caused the injury. Only in the rare case, such as in *McGhee v. Nat. Coal Bd.*, or some of the medical misadventure cases, will the plaintiff not know at all what was the immediate cause of the injury, and in these cases *res ipsa* will likely not apply because it will be difficult to say that the accident ordinarily would not have occurred in the absence of negligence.

106 [1972] S.C.R. 165, affirming [1971] 1 O.R. 273 (C.A.).

107 Which included things like the age of the tire, its condition, the car's speed at the time, and so on.

108 As stated by Ritchie J., [1972] S.C.R. 165 at 172, "it was caused by the blow-out in the left rear tire of the car. . . ."

109 For example, the cause of the plaintiff's injury was also clear in *Byrne v. Boadle*, in this narrow sense.

Where there was direct evidence as to the cause of the occurrence, *res ipsa* was not necessary and could not be used. Thus, in *North York v. Kert Chem. Indust. Inc.*,[110] the evidence indicated that the plaintiff municipality's sewer was damaged as a result of the acidic wastes which had been discharged into it by the defendant company. The issues of the case concerned the plaintiff's appropriate causes of action and the determination as to whether the defendant was negligent. Krever J. correctly rejected the defendant's invocation of *res ipsa loquitur*, since there was, in this case, "ample evidence explaining the occurrence."[111]

One can also find numerous cases, however, where the maxim was used despite the fact that the cause of the accident was clearly known. In one of the more obvious examples, *res ipsa* was applied despite the evidence which indicated that the defendant driver was intoxicated and speeding.[112] In another case, *Van Der Zouwen v. Koziak*,[113] the defendant drove his vehicle in an erratic manner, weaving across the road for a period of 10 to 15 minutes, until finally striking an oncoming car. In this instance, was *res ipsa* applicable? Was the cause of the occurrence known? The majority of the court applied *res ipsa*; the dissenting judge held that the cause of the accident was known. In *Gough v. Zwicker*,[114] heavy winds blew over the top of a recently constructed brick chimney. The court found that there must have been a defect in the chimney, since otherwise it would have been able to withstand the winds. The court applied *res ipsa loquitur*, even though, it is suggested, the court already knew what the cause of the occurrence was. As well, in *Gale v. Box*,[115] despite the fact that the court found that a fire was caused by the careless use of an acetylene torch near to wooden joists, the court and counsel for both parties agreed that the maxim *res ipsa loquitur* applied.[116]

The mere fact that a plaintiff tendered evidence regarding the cause of the occurrence does not mean that the maxim could not be applied. It was held that

---

110 (1985), 33 C.C.L.T. 184 (Ont. H.C.).

111 *Ibid.*, at 199. There are many similar cases where the maxim has been held to be inapplicable since the cause of the accident was known. See, e.g., *Fairway Chev-Olds Ltd. v. Wilson Equip. Ltd.* (1980), 39 N.S.R. (2d) 421 (C.A.); *Perry v. Acker* (1983), 58 N.S.R. (2d) 206 (T.D.); and *Jones v. Green* (1993), 147 A.R. 199 (Q.B.), reversed on other grounds (1995), 162 A.R. 217 (C.A.). In *Penn West Petroleum Ltd. v. Koch Oil Co.*, [1994] 4 W.W.R. 630 (Alta. Q.B.), the court was able to determine from the evidence that the probable cause of an explosion was the defendant's negligence. It nevertheless used the maxim *res ipsa* as an additional ground to find in the plaintiff's favour. Also see *Sawler v. Franklyn Enterprises* (1992), 117 N.S.R. (2d) 316 (T.D.), for a similar approach.

112 *Stevens v. Hoeberg* (1972), 29 D.L.R. (3d) 673 (Ont. H.C.).

113 (1971), 25 D.L.R. (3d) 354 (Alta. C.A.).

114 (1979), 34 N.S.R. (2d) 624 (T.D.).

115 (1987), 50 Man. R. (2d) 3 (Q.B.).

116 In *Hann v. Blomidon Golf Club* (1994), 120 Nfld. & P.E.I.R. 278 (Nfld. Prov. Ct.), the plaintiff discovered her vehicle with a shattered windshield. The vehicle was parked in a lot across the road from a golf course. A golf ball was found lying near her car. The damage to the windshield was consistent with that caused by a golf ball. There were no "eyewitnesses.'qc Golf balls were regularly hit over the fence onto the parking lot and the golf course had failed to take reasonable measures to prevent this. Was *res ipsa* necessary in this case? Despite the fact that it was applied, I would argue that it was not needed. The plaintiff was able to prove, on a balance of probabilities, how the damage was caused. There was direct proof that the defendant was negligent. This was merely a case of drawing inferences from the facts.

the maxim, being "but a description of an instance of circumstantial evidence,"[117] could be utilized in conjunction with a plaintiff's attempts to prove, by the introduction of direct evidence, how and why the accident occurred.

(c) The Procedural Effect of the Maxim

Despite some seemingly contradictory statements in a few judgments,[118] it was generally agreed that the effect of the maxim *res ipsa loquitur* was to raise only an inference of negligence, while not displacing the primary burden of proof which rested on the plaintiff.[119] Circumstantial or indirect evidence can have no greater procedural effect than positive or direct evidence. The weight to be given to it in deciding whether the claimant has discharged the primary onus is a matter for the judgment of the trier of fact.

An understanding of what the maxim was intended to accomplish can be gained by considering how circumstantial evidence should be used during the course of a civil trial. This understanding is important because, despite the "expiration" of the use of the term *res ipsa loquitur*, circumstantial or indirect evidence will continue to have an important role in tort cases.

If the plaintiff has no direct or positive evidence which can explain the occurrence and prove that the defendant was negligent, appropriate circumstantial evidence, as previously defined by the maxim *res ipsa loquitur*,[120] may be introduced. Should the defendant, at this stage of the proceeding, move for a nonsuit, on the basis that the plaintiff's evidence has not even made out a *prima facie* case for it to answer, the practical effect of circumstantial evidence will come into play. The court will be required to judge whether a reasonable trier of fact could,

---

117 *Temple v. Melville* (1978), 7 C.C.L.T. 1 at 4 (Sask. Dist. Ct.), affirmed (1979), 11 C.C.L.T. 104 (Sask. C.A.), quoting Wright, "*Res Ipsa Loquitur*", above, note 11.

118 In *Bartlett v. Children's Hosp. Corp.* (1983), 40 Nfld. & P.E.I.R. 88 (Nfld. T.D.), reversed (1985), 55 Nfld. & P.E.I.R. 350 (Nfld. C.A.), for example, Hickman C.J.T.D. stated that the maxim shifts the burden of proof. According to the Chief Justice, at 105, it creates "a prima facie case . . . which thereupon burdens the defendant with the task of proving that he was not negligent." This onus, to rebut the probability of negligence, accords the maxim a more significant procedural effect than is usually admitted.

119 This was made clear in many leading cases. For example, in *Phillips v. Ford Motor Co.* (1971), 18 D.L.R. (3d) 641 (Ont. C.A.), quoted with approval in *Chabot v. Ford Motor Co. of Can.* (1982), 22 C.C.L.T. 185 at 223 (Ont. H.C.), Schroeder J.A. stated:

> . . . it is made clear that *res ipsa loquitur* has no effect on the burden of proof, and the plaintiff has to establish negligence on a balance of probabilities. It does not cast upon the defendant the burden of disproof of negligence . . .

In *Ng Chun Pui v. Lee Chuen Tat*, [1988] R.T.R. 298 at 300 (P.C.), this approach was affirmed. Lord Griffiths stated that "although it has been said in a number of cases, it is misleading to talk of the burden of proof shifting to the defendant in a *res ipsa loquitur* situation. The burden of proving negligence rests throughout the case on the plaintiff." See also Sopinka J. in *Snell v. Farrell* (1990), 72 D.L.R. (4th) 289 at 295 (S.C.C.): "In Canada, the rule has been generally regarded as a piece of circumstantial evidence which does not shift the burden of proof. . . ."

120 While Major J. thought that the law would be better served if we stopped elevating *res ipsa loquitur* to a doctrine, he did not quarrel with how circumstantial evidence, as defined by the maxim, should actually be used. He merely thought that using the words was confusing and unnecessary.

from the evidence introduced, find an inference of the defendant's negligence. If it could so find, the motion for a nonsuit must be dismissed. If such an inference could not reasonably be made, the motion must be granted. In other words, circumstantial evidence, at the least, may get the plaintiff past a nonsuit.[121]

This, however, does not end the matter. What, if anything, must the defendant do at this point? In theory, where the case is being tried by a judge and jury, the defendant still need not do anything. Although the judge has decided that as a matter of law it would not be an error for the trier of fact to find for the plaintiff on the basis of the circumstantial evidence which has been introduced, it is still up to the jury to decide whether it has been sufficiently persuaded by such evidence. In other words, the judge has decided that as a matter of law, there is sufficient evidence for a jury to find in the plaintiff's favour. Whether as a question of fact it does, is up to the jury.[122] The jury may decide, therefore, that even despite the defendant's failure to call evidence, the circumstantial evidence ought not to be given sufficient weight to discharge the plaintiff's onus. Thus, even if a defendant has decided not to introduce evidence, a trial judge should not, in an action tried by judge and jury, either take the case from the jury and enter judgment for the plaintiff, or direct the jury to return a verdict in favour of the plaintiff. It is up to the trial judge to determine whether the circumstantial evidence can be sufficient, but up to the jury to decide whether it is.[123] Where, on the other hand, the case is being tried by a judge alone, the situation would, of course, be different. The judge's finding that the circumstantial evidence raises an inference of negligence will place an evidential or secondary burden on the defendant, which he must discharge.

This approach was laid out in *Interlake Tissue Mills Co. v. Salmon*.[124] Roach J.A. held that where a trial judge decided that the maxim *res ipsa loquitur* was applicable,[125] the defendant's refusal to give evidence did not warrant that the trial judge either enter judgment for the plaintiff or direct the jury to return a verdict in favour of the plaintiff. As stated by Roach J.A.:

> Where the maxim is applicable, instead of that fact being a reason for taking the case from the jury it is a reason for leaving it with them. Furthermore where the maxim applies the question whether the *res* justifies an inference of negligence is a question of fact for the jury alone to determine.[126]

---

121 See, e.g., *McHugh v. Reynolds Extrusion Co.* (1974), 7 O.R. (2d) 336 (H.C.), affirmed (1976), 15 O.R. (2d) 325 (C.A.), where the maxim had precisely this effect.

122 This point is illustrated in *Cogar Estate v. Central Mountain Air Services Ltd.*, [1992] 3 W.W.R. 729 (B.C. C.A.). A plane carrying seven persons disappeared and was never found. In an action brought against the airline, the trial judge left the issue of *res ipsa* to the jury. The Court of Appeal held that the judge's instructions to the jury to the effect that the maxim might apply, but that it was up to the jury to decide whether it did, was correct. The jury found negligence.

123 This explanation of the effect of *res ipsa loquitur* was quoted with approval by Major J. in *Fontaine* at (1997), 156 D.L.R. (4th) 577 (S.C.C.) at 584-585. This reinforces my argument that the effect of circumstantial or indirect evidence on a trial still remains the same, even if we no longer call this *res ipsa loquitur*.

124 [1949] 1 D.L.R. 207 (Ont. C.A.).

125 In the sense that, as a matter of law, there was evidence to permit its application.

126 Above, note 124, at 210.

A further issue then arises. Should the trier of fact decide that there is sufficient circumstantial evidence to support the conclusion that an inference of the defendant's negligence emerges from the evidence, what must the defendant do to avoid an adverse judgment?[127] The cases have generally held that the defendant must, in the face of the inference of its negligence, adduce evidence which, as to the cause of the occurrence, reveals an "explanation equally consistent with the absence of negligence as with negligence."[128] In other words, the defendant's evidence must neutralize that of the plaintiff, by showing how the accident might have occurred despite the exercise of reasonable care. It has also been made clear that the defendant's case must be based on the evidence, and not on "mere speculation or conjecture"[129] or "scientific hypotheses."[130] It is not sufficient to merely advance "a theoretical explanation of how the accident might have happened." The defendant must prove facts in support of this theory.[131] As stated by one judge, "the explanation must be based on evidence, not imagination."[132] It has also been recognized that the burden on the defendant to neutralize the inference of its negligence will correlate with the strength of the inference itself. A very strong inference of the defendant's negligence will call for an equally strong explanation.[133]

Analyzed in this way, the apparent overlap between what plaintiffs must do to raise the maxim and what defendants must do to answer it becomes clear. As discussed above, the maxim did not apply unless the occurrence is one which ordinarily would not happen in the absence of the defendants' negligence. Once the maxim applied, however, defendants could clear themselves by evidence indicating how the accident might have occurred without their negligence. Although these statements seem to be inconsistent, they become logical in the context in which they are used. The plaintiffs' evidence and the use of the maxim

---

127 Of course, the defendant will not be able to know, until the jury renders its decision, whether it decided to apply the maxim or not. Therefore, to gamble that it will not find the inference, and not to call evidence upon this assumption, will be very risky.

128 To use Krever J.'s words in *Ferguson v. Hamilton Civic Hosps.* (1983), 23 C.C.L.T. 254 at 304 (Ont. H.C.), affirmed (1985), 33 C.C.L.T. 56 (Ont. C.A.). Or, as stated in another well-known case, *Cudney v. Clements Motor Sales Ltd.* (1969), 5 D.L.R. (3d) 3 at 11 (Ont. C.A.), the defendant must offer "a theory, consistent with the facts, of a way in which the accident may have happened without negligence on his part."

129 See *Tataryn v. Co-op. Trust* (1975), 65 D.L.R. (3d) 99 at 104 (Sask. C.A.).

130 See *Interprovincial Pipe Line v. Seller's Oil Field Service Inc.* (1975), 58 D.L.R. (3d) 719 at 723 (Man. Q.B.), affirmed (1976), 66 D.L.R. (3d) 360 (Man. C.A.).

131 See Lieff J. in *Westlake v. Smith Tpt. Ltd.* (1973), 42 D.L.R. (3d) 502 at 513 (Ont. H.C.). Also see Ayles J.A.'s judgment in *Sisters of Charity of the Immaculate Conception v. Robert J. Fudge Ltd.* (1988), 87 N.B.R. (2d) 119 at 153 (C.A.): ". . . the defendant must offer an explanation which is consistent with the facts — not a mere theoretical possibility. The explanation must be a probable cause of the incident not a mere possible cause."

132 Hutcheon J.A. in *Lee v. I.C.B.C.* (1986), 17 C.C.L.I. 124 at 129 (B.C. C.A.). In *Hanna v. M.D. Realty Canada Inc.*, [1996] 10 W.W.R. 37 (B.C. S.C.), an elevator door closed on the plaintiff's arm. The defendant's theory was that the plaintiff had tried to enter the elevator too late as the doors were closing. The trial judge held that this explanation was inconsistent with the evidence and the defendant was held negligent on the basis of *res ipsa*.

133 See Robins J. in *Holmes v. London (City) Hosp. Bd.* (1977), 5 C.C.L.T. 1 at 18 (Ont. H.C.); and *Kapur v. Marshall* (1978), 4 C.C.L.T. 204 at 213 (Ont. H.C.).

assisted them in surviving a nonsuit and taking the case to the trier of fact. It was then up to the defendants to adduce their own evidence to neutralize the inference, should the trier of fact have found one.[134]

(d) Conclusion

Aside from the instruction that the *res ipsa loquitur* is not a separate doctrine or rule that justifies having its own name, Major J.'s judgment in *Fontaine v. British Columbia (Official Administrator)* did not change the law with respect to *res ipsa loquitur* or prevent the continued use of circumstantial or indirect evidence in tort cases. Circumstantial or indirect evidence can, in the appropriate case, create an inference that the plaintiff's injury was caused by the defendant's negligence. The factors as discussed above such as 1) control; 2) the occurrence would not ordinarily happen without negligence; and 3) the absence of direct evidence, continue to be the relevant ones for courts to consider in deciding what weight is to be given to circumstantial evidence. The procedural effect of circumstantial evidence still remains the same. The advice given by Major J. was simply

---

134 The nature of the maxim *res ipsa loquitur* can be effectively summarized by quoting. Megaw L.J. in *Lloyde v. West Midlands Gas Bd.*, [1971] 1 W.L.R. 749 at 755 (C.A.):

> I doubt whether it is right to describe *res ipsa loquitur* as a "doctrine". I think it is no more than an exotic, although convenient, phrase to describe what is in essence no more than a common sense approach, not limited by technical rules, to the assessment of the effect of evidence in certain circumstances. It means that a plaintiff *prima facie* establishes negligence where: (i) it is not possible for him to prove precisely what was the relevant act or omission which set in train the events leading to the accident; but (ii) on the evidence as it stands at the relevant time it is more likely than not that the effective cause of the accident was some act or omission of the defendant or of someone for whom the defendant is responsible, which act or omission constitutes a failure to take proper care for the plaintiff's safety.

This was quoted with approval by Lord Bridge in *Ng Chun Pui v. Lee Chuen Tat*, [1988] R.T.R. 298. Megaw L.J. went on to explain that the words "at the relevant time" can refer either to the close of the plaintiff's case if the defendant moves for a nonsuit, at which time the court must decide whether *res ipsa loquitur* applies, or the close of the defendant's case, at which time the court must decide whether the defendant's evidence has significantly weakened or even silenced the *res* which previously spoke for itself.

to remind courts that this is not to be applied in a formulistic way but simply as a matter of a common sense approach to evidence.[135]

135 For example, in a post-*Fontaine v. British Columbia (Official Administrator)* case, *Bachalo v. Robson*, [1998] 10 W.W.R. 180 (Man. C.A.), Philp J.A. stated that since the maxim was expired, arguments relating to its application to the facts of the case need not be considered. Yet the court did consider the circumstantial evidence as a whole in deciding that a malfunctioning medical tool did not raise an inference of negligence. The court, in other words, applied the reasoning behind the maxim while stating that the maxim no longer was relevant. Also see *Jordan v. Power* (2002), [2002] A.J. No. 1080, 2002 CarswellAlta 1084 (Q.B.), additional reasons at (2002), 2002 CarswellAlta 1214 (Q.B.), which involved a fire that started in the defendant's car and spread to the plaintiff's condominium. Veit J. approved of the argument that although the maxim *res ipsa* was dead, it merely expressed the approach to circumstantial evidence that courts ought to take. This approach still prevails. She held that the fact of a fire alone, without any other evidence as to the defendant's negligence, did not create an inference of negligence. Veit J. referred to Klar, "The Death of *Res Ipsa Loquitur:* Long Live *Res Ipsa Loquitur*" (published in the Mid-Winter Proceedings of the Law Society of Alberta, 1999), a portion of which she appended to her judgment. In another fire case, *Marchuk v. Swede Creek Contracting Ltd.* (1998), 116 B.C.A.C. 318 (C.A.), Mackenzie J.A. stated that "while the Supreme Court of Canada was critical of the Latin maxim, the underlying principles governing use of circumstantial evidence in determining liability for negligence were not modified". In this case the court used the circumstantial evidence to find liability for an unexplained fire. Circumstantial evidence was also used to explain why a wheel flew off a truck — *Lemaire v. Ashabi* (2003), [2003] B.C.J. No. 2438, 2003 CarswellBC 2628 (C.A.), affirming (2002), [2002] B.C.J. No. 1396, 2002 CarswellBC 1478 (S.C.). Also see Fridman, *The Law of Torts*, 2nd ed. (Toronto: Carswell: 2002) at 416: "The use of the Latin expression may now be incorrect or outmoded: nonetheless the pragmatic idea which led to its emergence in the nineteenth century still operates".

15
Occupiers' Liability

1. INTRODUCTION

The law relating to the tort liabilities of occupiers to those injured while upon their property continues to be sufficiently idiosyncratic as to require separate attention by courts and commentators.[1] As well, given the large number of injuries and deaths caused by accidents occurring on private premises,[2] tort laws governing the compensation of these victims have particular relevance.

The tensions underlying occupiers' liability laws are easy to discern. It is undeniable that the freedom of those who occupy premises to act as they wish within the boundaries of their own domains is a cherished one in our system.[3] This factor, combined with the common law's traditional reluctance to require individuals, whether at home or not, to take affirmative steps to protect others, has resulted in what has generally been agreed to be an over-indulgence of the rights of land owners. On the other side, however, modern realities have moved the law in the opposite direction. The existence of liability insurance, and the desire to use it to compensate the disabled, has affected this area of the law, as it has in the road accident arena. As well, the increased public access to private property has long belied the belief that individuals should be the masters of their own domains. We are now all occupiers at some times and guests at others, just

---

1 See Di Castri, *Occupiers' Liability* (1980). There have been numerous articles on the subject, especially with regard to the legislative reforms. See, e.g., Osborne, "The Occupiers' Liability Act of Manitoba" (1986), 2 Man. L.J. 177. A useful article describing the common law position is Harris, "Occupiers' Liability in Canada," in Linden (ed.), *Studies in Canadian Tort Law* (1968), Chapter 11.

2 The Pearson Royal Commission Report on Compensation for Personal Injury, 1977 noted that 5 per cent of all tort claims in England involved occupiers' liability. Weiler, *Protecting the Worker from Disability* (1983), reports that 20 per cent of fatalities in Ontario occur from accidents in the home. Weiler also notes that U.S. studies indicate that about 40 per cent of temporary disabilities and 25 per cent of permanent disabilities result from accidents in the home.

3 As stated by Lord Uthwatt in *Read v. J. Lyons & Co.*, [1946] 2 All E.R. 471 at 483 (H.L.):

> The background is the original freedom of the landowner keeping within his own bounds to do what he liked with and on his own, the King's law save in felonies and trespass actions stopping at his boundary.

as likely to be defendants as we are victims. Thus, although still distinctive, this area of tort has gradually been melting into the general principles of negligence law.

From the perspective of the common law's ability to develop tort law, occupiers' liability law has been one of the common law's most significant failures. For some reason, contemporary courts, having been saddled with a hopelessly confusing set of nineteenth century rules spelling out the liabilities of occupiers to entrants, were unable to free themselves from this morass. Even worse, they became even more mired in it, adding new rules and distinctions. The courts, which had been able to break down barriers set up by earlier authorities with milestone decisions such as *Donoghue v. Stevenson* and *Hedley Byrne & Co. v. Heller & Partners*, were unable to do the same thing in the occupiers' liability area.[4] As a consequence, legislation has been gradually introduced into this area, and, in most cases, has completely taken over from the common law. At present, six of the common law provinces have comprehensive occupiers' liability legislation.[5] One province, New Brunswick, has gone so far as to abolish the law of occupier's liability as a special topic of liability.[6] It is therefore necessary, when dealing with the current law relating to occupiers' liability, to focus on the specific jurisdiction under consideration. In this chapter, an examination first will be made of the common law principles, followed by a review of the various legislative reforms.

2. THE COMMON LAW

(a) Definition of Occupier

For the purposes of liability at common law, an occupier has been defined as any person who had control over the premises on which the injury occurred.[7] It has frequently been held that for the purposes of liability, control need neither be exclusive nor complete. Thus, there can be more than one occupier of the same premises. This was expressed by Lord Denning in the leading case of *Wheat v. E. Lacon & Co.* as follows:

---

4 Except for Australia and Newfoundland, where in a series of cases, the courts have eliminated the complex categorization of the common law and replaced it with the general duty of care. The Newfoundland Court of Appeal proposed a reasonable care test for occupiers to all lawful visitors in *Stacey v. Anglican Churches of Canada (Diocesan Synod of Eastern Newfoundland & Labrador)* (1999), 47 C.C.L.T. (2d) 153 (Nfld. C.A.) at 164 and *Gallant v. Roman Catholic Episcopal Corp. for Labrador* (2001), 200 D.L.R. (4th) 643 (Nfld. C.A.). See discussion below.

5 Alberta: Occupiers' Liability Act, R.S.A. 2000 c. O-4; British Columbia: Occupiers Liability Act, R.S.B.C. 1996, c. 337; Manitoba: Occupiers' Liability Act, R.S.M. 1987, c. O8 (also C.C.S.M., c. O8) as amended S.M 1988-89, c. 13, s. 32; Nova Scotia: Occupiers' Liability Act, S.N.S. 1996, c. 27; Ontario: Occupiers' Liability Act, R.S.O. 1990, c. O.2; and Prince Edward Island: Occupiers' Liability Act, R.S.P.E.I. 1988, c. O-2. There is also comprehensive legislation in several other Commonwealth jurisdictions, including England, Scotland, and New Zealand.

6 Law Reform Act, S.N.B. 1993, c. L-1.2, s. 2. The section states that matters that "would have been determined in accordance with the law of occupier's liability shall be determined in accordance with other rules of liability".

7 See generally Di Castri, above, note 1, at 6-9; Rainaldi (ed.), *Remedies In Tort*, Vol. 3 (1988), at 18-24.

> Wherever a person has a sufficient degree of control over premises that he ought to realise that any failure on his part to use care may result in injury to a person coming lawfully there, then he is an "occupier" . . . In order to be an "occupier" it is not necessary for a person to have entire control over the premises. He need not have exclusive occupation. Suffice it to say that he has some degree of control. He may share the control with others. Two or more may be "occupiers".[8]

The requirement of control is consistent with the rationale of occupiers' liability law. Liability attaches not to the ownership of land. Rather it is based on the principle that the person who has the right to control the premises, in terms of determining the access of others to it, and regulating its condition and the activities conducted on it, ought to be liable to those injured when upon the property.[9] Although one might argue that the right to ownership of property, and the ability to acquire profits from it, even without control, ought to give rise to an obligation to ensure that the property is reasonably safe, this is not an aspect of occupiers' liability law.

Cases on the definition of occupier illustrate that the control requirement can be a problematic issue. What degree of control is required in order to constitute oneself as an occupier? In *Lavoie v. Lavoie*,[10] for example, it was determined that the defendant who owned property on which it conducted an agricultural fair was not the occupier of the area upon which, for a fee, a concessionaire operated mechanical rides. Rather the concessionaire, who as the tenant or licensee of the fair owner had the "exclusive control and supervision over it and the right to admit or refuse admittance to any prospective patron",[11] was the occupier.[12] In another case, *Couch v. McCann*,[13] auctioneers were held to have sufficient control

---

8 [1966] A.C. 552 at 578 (H.L.). Although the case came under the English Occupiers' Liability Act, 1957 (5 & 6 Eliz. 2, c. 31), the Act in s. 1(2) specifically provides that an "occupier" under the legislation includes only those who would be treated as occupiers at common law. This definition also has been used in Canadian cases decided under provincial occupiers' liability statutes. See, for example, *Peters v. A.B.C. Boat Charters Ltd.*, [1993] 2 W.W.R. 390 (B.C. S.C.). For a common law case affirming that there may be more than one occupier see *Cisecki v. Nipawin (Town)*, [2000] 7 W.W.R. 376 (Sask. Q.B.), where both a hockey team that used an arena, and the town that owned it, were held to be occupiers.

9 A frequently quoted explanation of the control requirement is that of Wrottesley J. in *Duncan v. Cammell Laird*, [1943] 2 All E.R. 621 at 627 (K.B.):

> The importance of control is that it affords the opportunity to know that the plaintiff is coming on to the premises, to know the premises, and to become aware of dangers whether concealed or not, and to remedy them, or at least to warn those that are invited on to the premises.

10 (1983), 145 D.L.R. (3d) 158 (N.B. C.A.).

11 *Ibid.*, at 163.

12 Contrast this with *Kohler v. Calgary* (1980), 28 A.R. 190 (Q.B.), a decision under the Alberta Occupiers' Liability Act, R.S.A. 1980, c. O-3. There the exhibition owners were occupiers and responsible for the condition of the grounds, and the types of activities which could be carried on on the grounds. *Kinsella v. Saint John Commercial Developers Ltd.* (1994), 155 N.B.R. (2d) 20 (Q.B.), both the landlord and tenant were "occupiers" and jointly liable. The landlord had control of an access ramp, on which the plaintiff fell. The tenant, under the contract, had the responsibility to remove snow from the ramp. The plaintiff's fall resulted from a combination of a depression in the ramp, and ice; thus, both landlord and tenant were liable. In *Richter v. Capri Holdings Inc.* (2001), 214 Sask. R. 109 (Q.B.), the landlord was held not to have been in control of the sidewalk of a tenant's house for the purpose of occupier's liability.

13 (1977), 77 D.L.R. (3d) 387 (Ont. C.A.).

of the barn in which the auction was being conducted so as to satisfy the requirement. This was so, and they were held liable, even though the decrepit state of the barn, which led to the injuries of the plaintiffs, was clearly not within their control. In *Sawler v. Franklyn Enterprises Ltd.*,[14] the company which was responsible for servicing and maintaining an elevator was held to be in control of the elevator and hence an occupier for the purposes of liability. This did not remove the responsibility from the owner of the building who was also defined as an occupier.[15]

The control requirement has been relaxed in cases where the defendant invites others to come onto its premises by means of other premises which are not themselves under its control. In *Snitzer v. Becker Milk Co.*,[16] the owner of a store was held under a duty to its invitee to ensure that a sidewalk, which was in no sense under its control but which accessed its store, was safe. The principle adopted by the court was that the "legal right to invite" persons onto property over which the invitor has no authority, right or possession or control, gives rise to a duty to ensure that the premises are safe for the invitee.[17] What must be highlighted, however, is that the standard of care required of such an occupier will reflect the degree of control which that individual was able to exercise over the property in question. The steps required to be taken to ensure the safety of vistors required of occupiers will vary according to the degree of control which they were able to exercise over the premises.

(b) Categories of Entrants

The principal difficulty with common law occupiers' liablity is the need to rigidly categorize the type of entrant who was injured while on the property. The common law distinguishes among three principal types of entrants with respect to the duty of care which is owed by the occupier to them: trespassers, licensees, and invitees. In addition, individuals who are allowed onto premises pursuant to

---

14 (1992), 117 N.S.R. (2d) 316 (T.D.).

15 The action against the owner failed since the court held that it did not and it ought not to have known of the problem with the elevator. The action against the elevator maintenance company succeeded. I would suggest, however, that the action against it also would have succeeded if based on normal negligence law.

16 (1976), 75 D.L.R. (3d) 649 (Ont. H.C.).

17 The court cited several previous authorities, principally *Drinkwalter v. Morand*, [1929] 4 D.L.R. 421 (Ont. C.A.). See, however, a Manitoba trial court decision, *Shwemer v. Odeon Morton Theatres Ltd.* (1985), 33 Man. R. (2d) 109 (Q.B.), affirmed (1985), 37 Man. R. (2d) 176 (C.A.). The trial court stated that the defendant theatre owner could not be held liable for the condition of the city sidewalk which accessed the theatre. The Court of Appeal, while agreeing with the dismissal of the action, clearly left open the possibility that the principle in *Snitzer v. Becker* might have applied, had negligence been proven. Also see *Trenholm v. Langham & West Ins. Co.* (1990), 106 N.B.R. (2d) 181, 265 A.P.R. 181 (Q.B.), where a tenant was held not to be the occupier of an entranceway leading to his leased premises. In *Reidy v. Kamloops Hotel Ltd.* (1997), 41 B.C.L.R. (3d) 338 (S.C.), *Snitzer v. Becker Milk* was applied to a fall on a public sidewalk accessing the defendant's hotel. Although there is occupiers' liability legislation in British Columbia, the court stated that the Act did not cover this incident, since the fall did not occur on the defendant's premises. The court applied the common law. One might argue that the effect of *Snitzer* is to extend the defendant's control to the sidewalk, in which case the Act should apply.

a contract are exempted from the restrictive tort rules. Their safety is assured by a more indulgent contractual obligation.

The difficulty of the classification requirement arises from the fact that the categories are not watertight. They are matters of degree, forming part of a continuum, thus shading into each other. Thus, although the *theory* of the common law assumes concrete categories which give rise to particular obligations, the reality is that the categories are not sufficiently distinctive.[18] Statutory reform permitted the flexibility which seemed to be precluded by the common law.

(i) Trespassers

At one end of the continuum is the trespasser, a person who has been defined as one "who goes on the land without invitation of any sort and whose presence is either unknown to the proprietor or, if known, is practically objected to."[19] At its most extreme, the trespasser's presence is not only unauthorized and unconsented to, but clearly unwanted and objectionable; the burglar, for example. Not only is a very low duty of care owed to this person, but, as previously discussed,[20] steps can be taken to remove the trespasser from the premises. Difficulties of classification and duty formulation arise, however, where the presence of the entrant, although neither authorized nor expressly agreed to, was also neither expressly objected to nor manifestly undesired. One may see why a court will want to distinguish between the "burglar or wandering child or irreproachable wayfarer"[21] and thus why the category of trespasser will be too crude to accommodate these differences. The duty owed to the trespasser has reflected the variable nature of the act of trespass itself, and this has been done by either reclassifying the trespasser into a higher category, or reformulating the duty owed to the trespasser.

(ii) Licensees

The second category of entrant is that of licensee. In general terms, the licensee is a person whose presence, while not of benefit to the occupier, is not objected to or undesired. Difficulties of classification arise in attempting to demarcate the

---

18 The problem was explained by Dean Wright, in *Cases on the Law of Torts*, 4th ed. (1967), at 667-68:

> . . . one can at least say, despite heroic judicial efforts to the contrary, that categories have a habit of shading one into the other. This is inevitable since categories attempt to confine facts and facts have an annoying habit of resisting confinement. It would seem reasonably obvious to anyone not familiar with this part of the law that what we need are either more categories to fit the facts — which makes categorizing futile since there may not be enough different rules of law to fit each category — or a principle of law as elastic as the facts to which it must apply. Strange as it may seem, we frequently need to remind ourselves that the function of law is not primarily to categorize but to categorize only if necessary to decide issues of fact on consistent legal principles. The question is, which shall be master, categories or facts?

19 Viscount Dunedin in *Robert Addie & Sons v. Dumbreck*, [1929] A.C. 358 at 371 (H.L.).

20 See Chapter 3.

21 To quote the words of Dickson J. in *Veinot v. Kerr-Addison Mines Ltd.* (1974), 51 D.L.R. (3d) 533 at 549 (S.C.C.).

boundaries between licensees and trespassers at one end of the line, and between licensees and invitees at the other end.

Where the entrant has received permission to be upon the premises, the distinction between trespasser and licensee is clear. Thus, a swimmer at a recreational pool,[22] and a daughter visiting her mother at home,[23] were clearly licensees as opposed to trespassers.[24] The problem arises where there has not been express permission, and where the fact-finder is called upon to decide whether the occupier had implicitly permitted the entrant to be there as opposed to having merely tolerated the entrant's presence. Since it is frequently impossible to keep determined visitors off private property, especially where these determined visitors are children, the courts must decide what steps must be taken by the occupier to signal objection to the entrant's presence.

McErlean v. Sarel[25] well illustrates this issue. The plaintiff, a 14-year-old trail bike rider, was injured while riding his bike on vacant land owned by the defendant municipality. The land, an abandoned gravel pit, was scheduled for park development, but was not at the time a public park. The Ontario Court of Appeal agreed with the trial judge that the plaintiff was a licensee, and not a trespasser. Since the defendant had "made no effort to exclude pedestrians, bikers or others from its property by means of signs . . . warning not to trespass, by the erection of adequate fencing, by supervision or by any other means,"[26] and since the presence of entrants was "readily ascertainable if not actually known,"[27] the court construed this "failure to object" as "tacit permission" to enter.[28]

The difficulty in deciding whether there was an implied licence as opposed to mere tolerance of a visitor's presence by the occupier was also a principal issue in the leading case of *Veinot v. Kerr-Addison Mines Ltd.*,[29] a factual situation which is typical of this problem. The plaintiff was injured when his snowmobile struck a pole that formed a gate across a private road. Was the plaintiff a trespasser or a licensee? The jury answered that the plaintiff was on the defendant's land with implied permission and was a licensee. This was reversed by the Ontario Court of Appeal,[30] but at the Supreme Court of Canada level, five of the justices restored the trial judgment, while four agreed with the Court of Appeal. In rejecting the plaintiff's claim of implied licence based upon the fact that there had been earlier intrusions onto the land, Martland J. argued that two things needed

---

22 *Wessell v. Kinsmen Club* (1982), 21 C.C.L.T. 10 (Ont. H.C.).

23 *Beaton v. MacMaster* (1986), 72 N.S.R. (2d) 336 (T.D.).

24 See also *Rau v. Rau*, [1993] 1 W.W.R. 701 (Sask. Q.B.) — plaintiff visiting her nephew and niece at their home is a licensee.

25 (1987), 42 C.C.L.T. 78 (Ont. C.A.), leave to appeal to S.C.C. refused (1988), 63 O.R. (2d) x (note) (S.C.C.).

26 *Ibid.*, at 92.

27 *Ibid.*

28 The court conceded that had the occupier attempted to prevent people from trespassing, even if these attempts were unsuccessful, or had the precautions against intrusion been "unduly burdensome or expensive or, based on past experience, likely to be futile," the entrant might not have been classified as a licensee.

29 (1974), 51 D.L.R. (3d) 533 (S.C.C.).

30 (1972), 31 D.L.R. (3d) 275 (Ont. C.A.).

to be shown: there must be knowledge of these instrusions, and evidence that they were permitted and not merely tolerated.[31]

The difficulties of categorization arise from the fact that rather than there being rigid categories, the distinctions between trespasser, licensee and invitee fall along the continuum. In the cases noted, the courts were dealing with entrants who fell into the gray areas. Were they at the top of the trespasser category, being those who were on property without permission but who were non-threatening to the occupier, or at the bottom of the category of licensee, i.e., those upon the property with implied permission?[32]

It is also interesting to note that, at common law, an entrant's status can change during the course of a visit. Thus, for example, in *Landry v. Cormier*,[33] a landscaper's status as licensee or invitee changed to that of trespasser when he entered his client's home without permission.[34]

(iii) Invitees

The invitee is a person whose presence on the property is not only permitted but, according to one view, of material benefit to the occupier, or, using a different test, of joint or mutual interest to the parties.[35] Whether the interest must be a business interest or a joint interest is not altogether clear from the case law.

In one of the leading Canadian cases on this matter, *Hillman v. MacIntosh*,[36] an employee of a parcel delivery service was injured while picking up a parcel from a tenant in the defendant's commercial building. Was this employee there to satisfy a business or material interest of the defendant? Certainly it was in the material interest of the plaintiff, and more precisely his employer, to be permitted to enter the defendant's building to service customers. As well, it was in the defendant's interest to facilitate the businesses carried out by its tenants. These benefits seemed sufficient to the Supreme Court of Canada to deem the parties

---

31 For a decision applying this, see *Rinas v. Regina* (1983), 26 Sask. R. 132 (Q.B.).

32 As we will discuss, the problem, even in those jurisdictions which have not adopted statutory reform, has been ameliorated by the courts' recognition that the duty owed by the occupier must also be placed along the continuum, and correspond to the entrant's place on it.

33 (1983), 45 N.B.R. (2d) 311 (Q.B.).

34 Lord Denning expressed this point nicely in *Dunster v. Abbott*, [1953] 2 All E.R. 1572 at 1574 (C.A.):

> A canvasser who comes onto your premises without your consent is a trespasser. Once he has your consent, he is a licensee. Not until you do business with him is he an invitee. Even when you have done business with him, it seems rather strange that your duty towards him should be different when he comes up to your door from what it is when he goes away. Does he change his colour in the middle of the conversation?

See Hertz, Study Paper, Nova Scotia Law Reform Advisory Commission, *Occupiers' Liability Law*, 1976, at 3.

35 See Hertz, *ibid.*, at 8. According to Hertz, some courts have required only the material interest of the occupier. Others have required a common interest, a common material interest, or a joint interest. In the Saskatchewan Law Reform Commission *Tentative Proposals for an Occupiers' Liability Act*, 1980 at 17, the test is said to be a common economic interest. Di Castri, above, note 1, at 33, talks about "some purpose connected, either directly or indirectly, with the business carried on by the occupier."

36 [1959] S.C.R. 384.

invitor/invitee based on a common interest test, although one can readily see the difficulties which this type of analysis causes.

As has been noted by others,[37] the lack of certainty as to the nature of the interest required by the parties has produced uncertainty in the case law. Some courts have required economic interest, whereas others have not.[38] For example, a person who fell in the parkade at the Calgary International Airport,[39] a person who fell at the entrance to the terminal building of the same airport,[40] a student who fell on the sidewalk leading to the entrance of a school,[41] and a shopper who drove her car into a concrete block on a mall's parking lot,[42] have all been considered to be invitees.[43] Fortunately, as will be discussed, the trend in those jurisdictions which have retained the common law is towards eliminating any distinction in the duty owed to licensees and invitees, making the task of categorization less important.

(iv) Contractual Entrants

A fourth category recognized in the case law is that of the contractual entrant. The contractual entrant has been described as a "person who had contracted for, and paid, to use the premises for a purpose mutually contemplated by him and the occupier."[44] When one looks more closely at this category, however, certain questions arise.

In its strictest sense, a contractual entrant is a person who has given consideration exclusively in return for the use of the premises. It thus becomes an implied term of the contract that the premises are safe, and when they are not, the plaintiff's action is based on breach of contract. Thus, for example, those who have paid to visit zoos,[45] or to stay at hotels,[46] or to view entertainments,[47] are contractual

---

37 See, e.g., Hertz, above, note 34, and Saskatchewan Law Reform Commission's *Tentative Proposals*, above, note 35.

38 Hertz notes cases where people going to public parks and washrooms were considered as licensees, whereas other non-business visitors, such as visitors at public libraries, hospitals and public schools, were considered invitees. See Hertz, above, note 34, at 8.

39 *Stuart v. Can.* (1988), 45 C.C.L.T. 290 (Fed. T.D.).

40 *Suche v. R.* (1987), 37 D.L.R. (4th) 474 (Fed. T.D.), affirmed (1988), 54 D.L.R. (4th) 384 (Fed. C.A.).

41 *Phillips v. Regina Bd. of Educ.* (1976), 1 C.C.L.T. 197 (Sask. Q.B.).

42 *Butler v. Caboway Development Ltd.* (1994), 117 Nfld. & P.E.I.R. 99 (Nfld. T.D.).

43 In *Richter v. Capri Holdings Inc.* (2001), 214 Sask. R. 109 (Q.B.), a person delivering a bundle of newspapers to the defendant's house so that the tenant's son could then deliver them to individual subscribers was held to be an invitee.

44 Boisvert J. in *Arseneau v. Fredericton Motor Inn* (1984), 59 N.B.R. (2d) 60 at 64 (Q.B.).

45 See *Maltais-Comeau v. Laliberté* (1986), 36 C.C.L.T. 26 (N.B. Q.B.).

46 See, e.g., *Arseneau v. Fredericton Motor Inn*, above, note 44; *Carriss v. Buxton*, [1958] S.C.R. 441.

47 See *Brown v. B. & F. Theatres Ltd.*, [1947] S.C.R. 486. Sporting events should fall into this category; see for example *Hawman v. Regina Exhibition Assn. Ltd.* (1999), [2000] 2 W.W.R. 669 (Sask. Q.B.).

entrants.[48] The principal purpose of these contracts is to permit individuals to enter, and use the facilities for their contemplated purpose, in safety. Frequently, however, the use of specified premises is merely ancillary to the contractual agreement. In other words, the individuals have not paid to enter and use the premises, but for the right to avail themselves of the services offered at these premises. In these cases, the entrants are better classified as invitees, and not contractual entrants.[49] Examples of these include people who go to a barn for an auction,[50] who go to a shopping mall,[51] or to restaurants.[52] In these cases, it is the service offered, and not the use of the premises, which is the purpose of the contract. Courts have not always kept this distinction in mind. In one case, for example, a fuel deliveryman was deemed to be a contractual entrant, even though it is clear that the purpose of the contractual relationship was the purchase and sale of fuel, and not the right of the plaintiff to enter the premises in order to deliver it.[53] As well, frequently the distinction is a difficult one to draw and the classification is arguable. Where individuals use recreational facilities, for example, bowling alleys, or health clubs,[54] the condition of the premises is integrally related to the service provided on these premises.[55] In addition, difficulties can arise when contractual entrants are injured while doing something which is incidental to the main purpose of the contract. In *Sinclair v. Hudson Coal & Fuel Oil*

---

48 An example is *Young v. A.G. Nfld.* (1990), 87 Nfld. & P.E.I.R. 163 (Nfld. T.D.) reversed (1993), 112 Nfld. & P.E.I.R. 245 (Nfld. C.A.), leave to appeal to S.C.C. refused (1994), 121 Nfld. & P.E.I.R. 136 (note) (S.C.C.). A visitor who paid a fee to enter a provincial park was classified as a contractual entrant. Also see *Can. Airlines Int. Ltd. v. Hudson General Aviation Services Inc.* (1994), 129 N.S.R. (2d) 223 (S.C.), additional reasons at (1994), 131 N.S.R. (2d) 210 (S.C.). An airline which paid fees for airport services was a contractual entrant.

49 This point was articulated by Klebuc J. in *Cisecki v. Nipawin (Town)*, [2000] 7 W.W.R. 376 (Sask. Q.B.) at 386: "If the contract is ancillary to a plaintiff's presence on the subject premises, that plaintiff is at best an invitee". The plaintiff in this case was asked to judge a hockey game. His seat collapsed. He was held to be a contractual entrant.

50 *Couch v. McCann* (1977), 77 D.L.R. (3d) 387 (Ont. C.A.).

51 *Jones v. Brunswick Square* (1985), 65 N.B.R. (2d) 27 (C.A.).

52 See, e.g., *MacKay v. McDonald's Restaurants of Can. Ltd.* (1984), 47 Nfld. & P.E.I.R. 150 (P.E.I. C.A.).

53 See *Chegwin v. Schwanke* (1985), 38 Sask. R. 277 (Q.B.). In *Minke v. Westfair Properties Ltd.* (1998), [1999] 5 W.W.R. 371 (Sask. Q.B.), affirmed (1999), [2000] 3 W.W.R. 292 (Sask. C.A.), the plaintiff was injured when she fell on rice on the floor of a store. The trial judge resisted the conclusion that the plaintiff was an invitee who was owed a lower duty of care than a contractual entrant. The plaintiff was therefore classified as a contractual entrant although in my opinion she clearly was not, at least according to the traditional definition. The Court of Appeal affirmed the judgment but did not comment specifically on this point. In a subsequent case, *Zoltan v. Saskatchewan (Liquor & Gaming Authority)* (2000), 198 Sask. R. 307 (Q.B.), the plaintiff injured himself when he was exiting from a liquor store. The court referred to *Minke* and other authorities and concluded that the plaintiff "at a minimum" was owed the invitee's duty.

54 See *Drodge v. St. John's Y.M.C.A.* (1987), 67 Nfld. & P.E.I.R. 57 (Nfld. T.D.); or *Trampe v. 21st Century Health Spas Ltd.* (1982), 16 Man. R. (2d) 34 (Q.B.), affirmed (1983), 22 Man. R. (2d) 308 (C.A.).

55 Similarly perhaps with students attending educational institutions; see, for example, *Dixon v. Cabot College of Applied Arts, Technology & Continuing Education* (1997), 177 Nfld. & P.E.I.R. 162 (Nfld. T.D.).

Ltd.,[56] the court held that a tenant's use of the sidewalk in front of the apartment building was incidental to the main purpose of the contract of letting. This being so, the court imposed a lower duty of care upon the occupier than would have applied had the use being made of the premises at the time of the injury been the main purpose of the contract.[57]

(c) Duties of Occupiers

Classification of entrant is important under the common law due to the fact that the nature of the occupiers' duty to the entrant is based entirely on the category in which the entrant falls.

(i) Duties Owed to Trespassers

The traditional duty owned to the trespasser was expressed by Lord Hailsham in *Robert Addie & Sons v. Dumbreck*:

> Towards the trespasser the occupier has no duty to take reasonable care for his protection or even to protect him from concealed danger. The trespasser comes on to the premises at his own risk. An occupier is in such a case liable only where the injury is due to some wilful act involving something more than the absence of reasonable care. There must be some act done with the deliberate intention of doing harm to the trespasser, or at least some act done with reckless disregard of the presence of the trespasser.[58]

This indifferent attitude towards trespassers is not consistent with the twentieth century loss distribution goals of tort law, and courts have developed various techniques to avoid it. Three approaches have been followed.

First, since the categories themselves are flexible, the courts will frequently reclassify a trespasser as a licensee. This is done especially with regard to children, where it can be more credibly argued that a young child has implicit permission to be on the premises, or that the child has been allured to the site by some attraction on it.[59]

A second approach followed by some courts is to restrict the application of occupiers' liability principles to injuries caused by the condition of premises, as contrasted with injuries caused by activities conducted thereon. In other words, while a trespasser receives the minimal protection afforded by the duty formulated in the *Addie* case with respect to the condition of the premises, the ordinary negligence law duty of care is owed to the trespasser with respect to injuries suffered as a result of the occupier's activities.

It has also been argued, particularly in the Australian cases, that a plaintiff at the same time can be both a trespasser and a neighbour; i.e., that the relationship of occupier/trespasser can stand alongside a neighbour relationship in certain

---

56 (1966), 56 D.L.R. (2d) 484 (Ont. C.A.).

57 Assume, for example, that a bowler is injured not while bowling but while getting a snack at the snack bar between games. Is the higher duty owed? This is precisely the type of hair splitting which legislative reform has sought to avoid.

58 [1929] A.C. 358 at 365 (H.L.).

59 See, e.g., *Mitchell v. C.N.R.*, [1975] 1 S.C.R. 592.

circumstances.[60] In short, it has been stated that the occupiers' liability duty "may be replaced by the general duty if the relationship between the parties is not simply that of occupier and trespasser and there are circumstances which give rise to a duty of care."[61]

The distinction between activity duties and occupancy duties can best be illustrated by looking at the cases dealing with injuries caused to trespassers by railway trains.[62] Although many of the railway accident cases involving trespassers have applied only the restricted duty of the occupier, not to recklessly or intentionally cause injury,[63] and did not distinguish between activity duties and occupancy duties, some courts have used this distinction in order to avoid applying the limited occupiers' liability duty owed to trespassers. In the leading case *Videan v. Br. Tpt. Comm.*,[64] Lord Denning held that an occupier owes a duty to foreseeable trespassers to conduct activities with reasonable care. While conceding that it may be difficult to distinguish the activities carried out on land from the static condition of premises, Lord Denning nevertheless stated:

> . . . whenever an occupier does things on land, whether he runs a moving staircase, or puts a bull into a field, or drives a railway engine, or uses land as a cinder tip, or even digs a hole, he is conducting activities on the land and he is under a duty of care, even to trespassers, if he ought to foresee their presence: and he is nonetheless under the duty because he is an occupier.[65]

It is obvious that, worded so broadly, this approach would classify almost every condition as activity-related and would virtually eliminate the restrictive occupiers' duty traditionally owed to trespassers.[66]

In *Wade v. C.N.R.*,[67] a trespassing youth was injured when he attempted to mount a moving freight train. The treatment of this youth by the three levels of

---

60 This approach has been followed in several Australian cases. For an excellent account, see *Hackshaw v. Shaw* (1985), 59 A.L.J.R. 156, and the cases cited therein: *Thompson v. Bankstown Mun. Council* (1953), 87 C.L.R. 619 (Aust. H.C.); *Rich v. Commrs. for Rys.* (1959), 101 C.L.R. 135 (Aust. H.C.); *Commrs. of Rys. v. Cardy* (1960), 104 C.L.R. 274 (Aust. H.C.); and *Pub. Tpt. Comm. of N.S.W. v. Perry* (1977), 137 C.L.R. 107 (Aust. H.C.).

61 *Hackshaw v. Shaw, ibid.*, at 161. The case concerned an occupier who deliberately fired at a car which was trespassing on his property, unintentionally hitting the plaintiff, who unbeknownst to the defendant, was hiding in the car. The majority of the High Court of Australia held that in these circumstances, a special duty to take care, outside the ordinary occupiers' liability duty owed to trespassers, applied.

62 See Klar, "A Comment on *Wade v. C.N.R.*" (1977-78), 3 C.C.L.T. 194.

63 See, e.g., *C.P.R. Co. v. Anderson*, [1936] S.C.R. 200; *Brisson v. C.P.R.* (1969), 69 W.W.R. 176 (Man. Q.B.), affirmed (1969), 70 W.W.R. 479 (Man. C.A.); *Pinkas v. C.P.R.*, [1928] 1 W.W.R. 321 (Man. K.B.); *Newell v. C.P.R.* (1906), 12 O.L.R. 21 (C.A.).

64 [1963] 2 Q.B. 650 (C.A.).

65 [1963] 2 Q.B. 650 at 667-68.

66 Lord Denning's approach was rejected in *Commr. for Rys. v. Quinlan*, [1964] A.C. 1054 at 1075 (P.C.). Viscount Radcliffe held that the limited duty owed to the trespasser, to avoid wilful or reckless injury, is the exclusive duty owed. There was, according to His Lordship, no distinction to be made between the duty owed by an occupier to a trespasser in one capacity or another. The duty is not "confined to the situation where injury arises from what is sometimes called the 'static condition' of the land . . . a trespasser must take the land as he finds it, but also he must take the occupier's activities as he finds them, subject to the restriction that the occupier must not wilfully or recklessly conduct them to his harm." See also *Commr. for Rys. v. McDermott*, [1967] 1 A.C. 169 (P.C.), where Viscount Radcliffe's views were adopted.

67 (1977), 3 C.C.L.T. 173 (S.C.C.).

court who tried the case is interesting, well illustrating the issues under discussion. The jury considered that the plaintiff was not a trespasser but a licensee, having been enticed onto the railway's property by the presence of sand and gravel piles and by the train itself. On appeal,[68] MacKeigan C.J.N.S. found that the plaintiff was a trespasser, but applied to him a more lenient duty than the traditional formula demanded.[69] At the Supreme Court of Canada level, the majority virtually ignored the occupiers' liability issue, and applied ordinary principles of negligence law. Chief Justice Laskin, in dissent, adopted the distinction between occupancy duties and activity duties, and held that since the plaintiff's injury did not arise from the condition of the railway's property, but from an activity carried on by the occupier, ordinary negligence law principles applied. In view of these varying approaches, one can well understand the need for legislative reform.[70]

The third approach to trespassers which greatly ameliorated their common law position was introduced in *Br. Ry. Bd. v. Herrington*.[71] As have so many of the important occupiers' liability cases, the *Herrington* case involved a child plaintiff who was injured while trespassing on railway property. Rather than applying the narrow duty owned by occupiers to trespassers formulated by *Robert Addie & Sons v. Dumbreck*,[72] the Lords developed a new duty, that of ordinary or common humanity. In arriving at its decision, the Lords agreed on certain points. They rejected as a fiction the approach which reclassified child trespassers as licensees with implicit permission to be on the property. They adopted, as the duty owed to trespassers, the duty of common humanity, which, although undefined, is taken to fall somewhere between the low duty of *Addie* and the general duty of *Donoghue v. Stevenson*.[73] Unlike the ordinary duty of care, which is tested objectively, the duty of common humanity is a subjective one, examined from the specific occupier's perspective. It depends on that occupier's knowledge, ability and resources. It essentially balances the court's desire to treat the trespasser with compassion, especially when that trespasser is a child, with its realization that occupiers ought not to be unfairly burdened by unwanted visitors. The duty is also premised on the fact that the occupier knew, or ought to have known, of the

---

68 14 N.S.R. (2d) 541.

69 The duty of common humanity. See discussion below.

70 Also see *Laviolette v. C.N.R. Co.* (1986), 36 C.C.L.T. 203 (N.B. Q.B.), affirmed (1987), 40 C.C.L.T. 138 (N.B. C.A.). Daigle J. reviewed the jurisprudence on this question and concluded that the plaintiff child, who was injured by a moving train, was subject to occupiers' liability principles, and not ordinary negligence law.

71 [1972] A.C. 877 (H.L.).

72 Above, note 58.

73 There are several statements which place the duty in this position of compromise. For example, Lord Morris of Borth-y-Gest stated, [1972] A.C. 877 at 899:

> In my view, while it cannot be said that the railways board owed a common duty of care to the young boy in the present case they did owe him at least the duty of acting with common humanity towards him.

Lord Wilberforce stated, [1972] A.C. 877 at 920:

> It must be remembered that we are concerned with trespassers, and a compromise must be reached between the demands of humanity and the necessity to avoid placing undue burdens on occupiers.

trespasser's presence.[74] In *Pannett v. McGuiness & Co.*,[75] Lord Denning enumerated those factors relevant to the determination. These included the gravity and probability of the injury, the character of the intrusion, the nature of the place and the foreseeability of the trespasser.

The duty of common humanity was accepted by Dickson J. in Canada's leading case, *Veinot v. Kerr-Addison*,[76] and it has generally been accepted, if not always enthusiastically,[77] by subsequent Canadian courts.[78] In view of this development, a credible argument can be made that the common law's current treatment of trespassers is no harsher than that provided by most of the statutory reforms.[79]

(ii) Duties Owed to Licensees

As with the duty owed to trespassers, the duty owed to licensees has been modified by the case law over time, so much so that it has now become indistinguishable from the duty owed to invitees. In its traditional and harshest form, the occupier was liable to licensees only for injuries caused to the latter by concealed dangers or traps of which the occupier had actual knowledge.[80] The actual knowledge requirement was gradually relaxed by numerous cases which held that

---

74 See *Southern Portland Cement Ltd. v. Cooper*, [1974] A.C. 623 (P.C.).

75 [1972] 3 W.L.R. 387 (C.A.).

76 [1975] 2 S.C.R. 311. The acceptance of the principle by the Supreme Court in the case was by no means convincing. The case concerned an adult snowmobiler. The majority of the court treated the plaintiff as a licensee and not a trespasser, and applied to him the traditional duty owed to licensees. Dickson J. held that even if the defendant was a trespasser, he ought to have been treated with common humanity.

77 See, e.g., *Eastwick v. N.B.* (1987), 45 C.C.L.T. 191 at 196 (N.B. Q.B.), where the trial judge stated that "the standards applied by Lord Wilberforce in the *Herrington* case can only lead to confusion if not chaos."

78 See, e.g., *Laviolette v. C.N.R. Co.* (1986), 36 C.C.L.T. 203 (N.B. Q.B.), affirmed (1987), 40 C.C.L.T. 138 (N.B. C.A.); *Smith v. Hudzik Estate* (1986), 38 Man. R. (2d) 115 (C.A.); *Parisian v. C.P. Ltd.* (1983), 25 C.C.L.T. 105 (Sask. Q.B.); *Rinas v. Regina (City)* (1983), 26 Sask. R. 132 (Sask. Q.B.); and *Walker v. Sheffield Bronze Powder Co.* (1977), 2 C.C.L.T. 97 (Ont. H.C.). In *Anderson v. Whitepass Transportation Ltd.*, [1994] Y.J. No. 9 (C.A.), the court made it clear that the duty of common or ordinary humanity applies only when the presence of trespassers on the property is foreseeable. As well, the duty is discharged if the trespasser is warned of the danger. Where the trespasser already knows of the danger, a warning is not necessary and the duty has not been breached. In this case, the trespasser ought to have known of the icy and dangerous conditions on the plaintiff's land, and the action was accordingly dismissed by the Court of Appeal. The duty of common humanity was discussed in *North King Lodge Ltd. v. Gowlland Towing Ltd.* (2005), 36 C.C.L.T. (3d) 47 (B.C. C.A.), reversing in part (2003), 24 C.C.L.T. (3d) 78 (B.C. S.C.). The case involved the right of the defendant to remove a boat which was moored without permission to the defendant's chattel, its anchored boomsticks. The Court of Appeal rejected the notion that the defendant owed the trespasser a duty of common humanity. The duty was not to recklessly or wilfully damage the plaintiff's boat. Although reasoned as a case of occupier's liability, this case can also be approached from the perspective of the right of an occupier to eject or remove a trespassing object. See Sigurdson J.'s judgment at trial where this matter is raised at 110-112. The trial judge based his decision, however, on his finding that the defendant did not "intentionally harm the plaintiff, act recklessly or without common humanity."

79 In fact, in some jurisdictions, such as Alberta, it is arguable that the trespasser is now worse off under the legislation than if the common law had been left in place.

80 See *Booth v. St. Catharines*, [1948] S.C.R. 564.

constructive knowledge could, in certain instances, suffice.[81] Finally, the requirement that the danger be hidden or concealed was abandoned, so that even warnings of it given to the licensee by the occupier would not be enough to discharge the latter's duty.

The traditional common law position regarding the duty owed to licensees was modified by the Supreme Court of Canada in *Mitchell v. C.N.R.*[82] Laskin J. held that a licensee's knowledge of the danger did not relieve the occupier of its duty of care, although it could constitute contributory negligence on the licensee's part. This decision in effect negated the requirement that the danger to a licensee be concealed or hidden and effectively approximated the duties owed to invitees and licensees.[83] As stated by Lord Denning, the distinction between the two categories "has now been reduced to vanishing point."[84] The only possible remaining distinction between the two categories relates to the issue of the occupier's knowledge. It has been suggested that occupiers are only liable to licensees for unusual dangers actually known to them, whereas with respect to invitees constructive knowledge will suffice.[85] Even on this point, however, there is disagreement, with some judgments holding that constructive knowledge will be sufficient even in so far as the duty to licensees is concerned.[86] A subtle distinction has been made between the duty of the invitor to inspect the premises to discover unusual dangers, i.e., dangers that the invitor ought to know, and the lesser duty of the licensor to be aware of dangers, not because of a duty to inspect, but because "he was aware of the circumstances."[87] This further refinement merely adds to the complexity of the common law.

---

81 See Rainaldi (ed.), *Remedies In Tort*, Vol. 3 (1988), Chapter 18 at 18-70.

82 (1974), 46 D.L.R. (3d) 363 (S.C.C.).

83 *Mitchell* was quickly followed in numerous Ontario judgments, although it has not been as well received in other provinces. See, e.g., *Bartlett v. Weiche Apts. Ltd.* (1974), 55 D.L.R. (3d) 44 at 48 (Ont. C.A.), where Jessup J.A. states that the occupier's duty to a licensee is "to take reasonable care to avoid foreseeable risk of harm from any unusual danger on the occupier's premises of which the occupier actually has knowledge or of which he ought to have knowledge because he was aware of the circumstances." See also *Alaica v. Toronto* (1976), 1 C.C.L.T. 212 (Ont. C.A.), and accompanying annotation at 213; and *Davies v. Day* (1977), 2 C.C.L.T. 91 (Ont. C.A.). In *Rau v. Rau*, [1993] 1 W.W.R. 701 (Sask. Q.B.), the court also adopted the judgment in *Bartlett*. Also see *Ackerman v. Wascana Centre Authority* (1997), [1998] 2 W.W.R. 678 (Sask. Q.B.), affirmed [1999] 6 W.W.R. 167 (Sask. C.A.) to the same effect.

84 *Slater v. Clay Cross Co.*, [1956] 2 Q.B. 264 at 269 (C.A.). Some courts, however, have clung to the distinction. See, e.g., *Beaton v. MacMaster* (1986), 72 N.S.R. (2d) 336 (T.D.); *Langille v. Walton* (1983), 55 N.S.R. (2d) 713 (T.D.); *Kucheran v. Yorkton Union Hosp.* (1983), 30 Sask. R. 68 (Q.B.); *Szabo v. Arne*, [1971] 5 W.W.R. 238 (Sask. Q.B.); and *Landry v. Cormier* (1983), 45 N.B.R. (2d) 311 (Q.B.).

85 See *Yelic v. Gimli (Town)*, [1987] 1 W.W.R. 537 (Man. C.A.); and *Moar v. Pesclovitch*, [1986] 5 W.W.R. 685 (Man. Q.B.).

86 For example, see Jessup J.A.'s judgment in *Bartlett v. Weiche Apts. Ltd.* (1974), 55 D.L.R. (3d) 44 (Ont. C.A.), approved by the Ontario Court of Appeal in *McErlean v. Sarel*, above, note 25. See also *Urzi v. North York Bd. of Educ.* (1980), 116 D.L.R. (3d) 687 (Ont. H.C.), affirmed (1981), 127 D.L.R. (3d) 768 (Ont. C.A.); *Wessell v. Kinsmen Club of Sault Ste. Marie* (1982), 21 C.C.L.T. 10 (Ont. H.C.), and the several other Ontario cases cited therein.

87 To use Jessup J.A.'s words in *Bartlett v. Weiche Apts.*, above, note 86. See discussion in Saskatchewan Law Reform Commission's *Tentative Proposals* at 20-21.

(iii) Duties Owed to Invitees

The occupier owes a duty to invitees to "use reasonable care to prevent damage from unusual danger, which he knows or ought to know."[88] Critical to this formulation is the requirement that the danger be an unusual one. This has been the principal issue in most of the cases.

It has been held that an unusual danger is a danger which the class of invitees, of which the claimant is one, does not usually encounter when visiting the premises.[89] The test of unusualness is thus objective. Other factors used by the courts are the ease with which the occupier might have resolved the danger, it being contemplated that invitees should be entitled to expect that dangers which could have been eliminated easily would have been,[90] and the nature and purpose of the premises.[91]

In *McErlean v. Sarel*,[92] the Ontario Court of Appeal, in considering whether a danger was unusual, placed particular emphasis on whether ordinary, reasonable persons would know or appreciate the danger. According to this approach, dangers which are common, and which are appreciated, are not unusual and no duty is owed with respect to them. This approach approximates the issues of unusual danger, contributory negligence, and voluntary assumption of risk. It may be suggested that the mere fact that a danger is known by an entrant ought not to eliminate the duty of care owed with respect to it.[93] Questions of the entrant's own conduct ought to be treated as issues of contributory negligence, or voluntary assumption of risk.[94]

The classic formulation of the duty owed to invitees found in *Indermaur v. Dames*,[95] implies that the duty is owed only to a person who is exercising reasonable care for his or her own safety. This raises the issue of the role of contributory negligence. Can a duty be owed to an invitee who fails to exercise reasonable

---

88 *Indermaur v. Dames* (1866), L.R. 1 C.P. 274 at 288, affirmed (1867), L.R. 2 C.P. 311 (Ex. Ch.), cited in Rainaldi (ed.), *Remedies In Tort*, Vol. 3 (1988), Chapter 18 at 18-42.

89 See *Campbell v. Royal Bank*, [1964] S.C.R. 85, and *Brandon (City) v. Farley* (1968), 66 D.L.R. (2d) 289 (S.C.C.), which adopted the definition from *London Graving Dock Co. v. Horton*, [1951] A.C. 737 (H.L.). For a recent case which adopts this, see *Butler v. Caboway Development Ltd.*, above, note 42. In *Francis v. ICPF Properties* (1993), 136 N.B.R. (2d) 215 (Q.B.), affirmed (1994), 146 N.B.R. (2d) 317 (C.A.), it was on the basis that icy parking lots are a normal feature of Canadian winters which convinced the court that this condition is not an "unusual" danger. In *Lakeman v. Pre-Con Ltd.* (2004), [2005] 4 W.W.R. 695 (Sask. Q.B.), the trial judge stated that it is not correct to make a sweeping statement that snow and ice on streets in a Saskatchewan winter can never constitute an unusual danger. It depends on the circumstances, including the expectation of the invitee. The action, nevertheless, was dismissed in this case as well.

90 See *Campbell v. Royal Bank*, *ibid.*, quoted in *Urzi v. North York Bd. of Educ.* (1980), 116 D.L.R. (3d) 687 at 693 (Ont. H.C.), affirmed (1981), 127 D.L.R. (3d) 768 (Ont. C.A.). See, however, *Stuart v. Can.* (1988), 45 C.C.L.T. 290 (Fed. T.D.), where this factor is discounted.

91 See Klar, "Annotation" (1976), 1 C.C.L.T. 213.

92 Above, note 25.

93 This position was supported in *Hale v. Westfair Foods Ltd.*, [1995] 3 W.W.R. 293 (Sask. Q.B.). The court held that the invitee's knowledge of the unusual danger does not dissolve the duty of care.

94 See *Gunn v. Halifax County Condo. Corp. No. 6* (1985), 67 N.S.R. (2d) 262 (T.D.); and *Vyas v. Colchester-East Hants Dist. Sch. Bd.* (1989), 65 D.L.R. (4th) 48 (N.S. C.A.).

95 (1866), L.R. 1 C.P. 274.

care, subject to the defence of contributory negligence, or is no duty owed if the invitee is not using reasonable care? Contributory negligence should be a defence here, as it currently is in all negligence actions and statutory occupiers' liability.[96]

Having determined that the danger is "unusual", the next issue is whether the occupier knew or ought to have known of it. In *St. Peter v. Atlantic Shopping Centres Ltd.*,[97] for example, the plaintiff injured herself as a result of a loose toilet seat in the mall's washroom. The court held that the plaintiff was an invitee, the loose toilet seat was unusual, and the defendant was not aware of it. It also held that the defendant had employed a good system of cleaning and inspecting its washroom facilities and therefore could not be faulted for not having been aware of this problem. In another bathroom case, *Saiville v. Dimar Foods Ltd.*,[98] the plaintiff hit her head on the plastic cover of a soap dispenser which had become unlatched. In deciding that this was not an unusual danger, the court considered the fact that the unhinged plastic cover, although perhaps unusual, was not dangerous.[99]

(iv) Duties Owed to Contractual Entrants

It has been stated that in the case of the contractual entrant, "there exists an implied warranty that the premises are as safe . . . as reasonable care and skill on the part of anyone can make them."[100] This has been seen as an exceptionally high duty of care, making the occupier liable not only for its own negligence, but for the negligence of independent contractors, and even applying to negligent acts which occurred before the defendant occupied the premises.[101] It has been held, however, that this does not mean that the occupier is an "insurer of the safety

---

96 See *Fehr v. O.T. Karz Kafe Ltd.* (1993), 110 Sask. R. 207 (Q.B.), where this position is supported. See also *Hale v. Westfair Foods Ltd.*, [1995] 3 W.W.R. 293 (Sask. Q.B.), where the court stated that, depending on the facts, an invitee can be held contributorily negligent, or, alternatively, it might be that the invitee's negligence was the sole and effective cause of the injuries. In this case, the latter finding was made.

97 (1999), 180 N.S.R. (2d) 121 (S.C.).

98 [2005] 8 W.W.R. 760 (Sask. Q.B.).

99 The plaintiff's injuries were caused by her own particular pre-existing medical problems. The court also found that even if it was an unusual danger, it was not one which the occupier ought to have known about. A recent Saskatchewan case which found that the danger presented to shoppers by a cardboard box was unusual and was known to the defendant is *Dehmke v. Westfair Foods Ltd.*, 2005 SKQB 309 (Q.B.).

100 See *Arseneau v. Fredericton Motor Inn* (1985), 59 N.B.R. (2d) 60 at 64 (Q.B.), and *McGinty v. Cook* (1989), 59 D.L.R. (4th) 94 (Ont. H.C.), [affirmed (1991), 79 D.L.R. (4th) 95 (Ont. C.A.], applying the leading case *Brown v. B. & F. Theatres Ltd.*, [1947] S.C.R. 486. Also see *Young v. A.G. Nfld.* (1990), 87 Nfld. & P.E.I.R. 163 (Nfld. T.D.), reversed (1993), 112 Nfld. & P.E.I.R. 245 (Nfld. C.A.); *Can. Airlines Int. Ltd. v. Hudson General Aviation Services Inc.* (1994), 129 N.S.R. (2d) 223 (S.C.). In *Young v. A.G. Nfld.*, the Court of Appeal took into account the fact that the defendant was a public authority in determining the standard of care required. See, generally, Rainaldi (ed.), *Remedies In Tort*, Vol. 3 (1988), Chapter 18 at 18-32.5.

101 See *Remedies In Tort, ibid.*, at 18-33.

of its guests".[102] Thus, where the occupier did not create a danger, was not aware of it, and had no reason to anticipate it, it was not held liable.[103]

3. OCCUPIERS' LIABILITY LEGISLATION

Six common law provinces, as well as several other common law jurisdictions, have replaced the common law of occupiers' liability with comprehensive statutory reform.[104] Although there are wide areas of similarity between the various statutes, differences do exist. Rather than examining each statute in detail, this section will highlight the major features of these statutory reforms.

(a) Definition of Occupier

The six provincial statutes define the occupier in virtually the same way. The occupier is a person who is in "physical possession" of the premises, or "who has

102 *McTaggart v. Commowealth Hospitality Ltd.* (1997), 38 C.C.L.T. (2d) 95 (Sask. Q.B.).

103 *Ibid.* The hotel was not liable when vandals removed a wall mirror and pushed it between the inner and outer elevator doors. The mirror crashed down onto the elevator resulting in an injury to a hotel guest who was in the elevator at the time.

104 See above, note 5. Note as well the statutory abolition of the law of occupiers' liability in New Brunswick; Law Reform Act, S.N.B. 1993, c. L-1.2, s. 2. See *Jones v. Richard* (2000), 226 N.B.R. (2d) 207 (C.A.), and *Reid v. Hatty* (2005), [2005] N.B.J. No. 20, 2005 CarswellNB 40 (C.A.), leave to appeal refused (2005), 2005 CarswellNB 509 (S.C.C.), recent decisions under this Act. The Court of Appeal noted that because of the New Brunswick approach, common law occupiers' liability cases are of limited assistance in New Brunswick. To the extent that the other provincial statutes impose a duty of reasonable care on occupiers, judgments from these provinces are useful. It is of note that in other common law jurisdictions that have not statutorily reformed occupiers' liability law, the courts have abandoned the common law special duties and have replaced them with ordinary principles of negligence law. In Australia, as a result of a series of decisions, the common law of occupiers' liability is now governed by the general duty established in *Donoghue v. Stevenson*. See *Hackshaw v. Shaw* (1984), 155 C.L.R. 614 (H.C.); *Papatonakis v. Australian Telecommunications Comm.* (1985), 156 C.L.R. 7 (H.C.), and *Australian Safeway Stores Pty. Ltd. v. Zaluzna* (1986), 69 A.L.R. 615 (H.C.). In *Austin v. Gendis Inc.* (1985), 68 N.B.R. (2d) 57 (Q.B.), Creaghan J. suggested that the standard negligence test ought to be used in occupiers' liability cases. This view was supported by Reed J. in *Stuart v. Can.* (1988), 45 C.C.L.T. 290 (Fed. T.D.). In Newfoundland, the Court of Appeal replaced the traditional common law formulae with a simplified one, similar to the one found in the statutes. See *Stacey v. Anglican Churches of Canada (Diocesan Synod of Eastern Newfoundland & Labrador)* (1999), 47 C.C.L.T. (2d) 153 (Nfld. C.A.) at 164. In *Gallant v. Roman Catholic Episcopal Corp. for Labrador* (2001), 200 D.L.R. (4th) 643 (Nfld. C.A.), the Court of Appeal held that this new duty formula applied even to causes of action arising prior to this restatement. In *Sheppard v. Empire Co.* (2001), 198 Nfld. & P.E.I.R. 53 (Nfld. C.A.), the trial occurred before *Stacey* and the appeal afterwards. The Court of Appeal was faced with the issue as to whether the old or new law should be applied in determining the appeal. The court decided that in the circumstances of this case it did not matter to the reasoning or result. The court reversed the trial judgment, which had found the defendant liable for injuries caused to the plaintiff while riding on an escalator. More recent Newfoundland judgments applying the new approach include *Hickey v. Fairview Investments Ltd.*, 2007 NLTD 85 (T.D.) and *Murphy v. Interprovincial Shopping Centres*, 2004 NLSCTD 210 (T.D.).

responsibility for, and control over, the condition of the premises, the activities conducted on those premises and the persons allowed to enter those premises."[105]

It is interesting to note that the Manitoba, Ontario, Nova Scotia and Prince Edward Island statutes use the word "or," whereas Alberta and British Columbia use the word "and" in describing the three responsibilities which define an occupier.[106] It may be questioned whether this was intended to be a significant difference. Even those provinces which use the word "and" admit that there may be more than one occupier of premises. Further, one can refer to cases such as *Meier v. Qualico Devs. Ltd.*,[107] where several persons were occupiers, even though they each did not possess all of the three responsibilities.[108] As well, case law dealing with the statutes accept the proposition that the common law precedents relating to the definition of occupier apply to the statutes,[109] and, at common law, "control" was the defining characteristic. As we have discussed above, "control" need not be exclusive nor complete in order to qualify a person as an occupier.[110]

---

105 This is the wording used in Alberta (R.S.A. 2000, c. O-4, s. 1(c)) and B.C. (R.S.B.C. 1996, c. 337, s. 1(a), (b)). Note that the Nova Scotia Act states that the "occupier" "means an occupier at common law. . ."; s. 2(a).

106 Thus in Ontario an "occupier" is defined as "a person who has responsibility for and control over the condition of premises *or* the activities there carried on, *or* control over persons allowed to enter the premises." [Emphasis added.] See *Moody v. Toronto (City)* (1996), 31 O.R. (3d) 53 (Gen. Div.); and *Lemieux v. Porcupine Snowmobile Club of Timmins Inc.* (1999), 120 O.A.C. 292 (C.A.), where the disjunctive approach was accepted. A recent case on the definition of "occupier" under the Ontario Act is *Davies v. Clarington (Municipality)* (2006), 266 D.L.R. (4th) 375 (Ont. S.C.J.), additional reasons at (2007), 2007 CarswellOnt 7413 (S.C.J.). The owner of land had a deeded right-of-way to use a farm crossing on a railway corridor owned by CN. A collision occurred between a passenger train and a truck which had become stuck on the corridor, after it had been hit by another train. The court decided that the land owner was not an occupier of the corridor. It was not in possession of it, had no responsibilities with respect to it, and could not control who used it.

107 40 A.R. 493 (Q.B.), reversed on other grounds [1985] 1 W.W.R. 673 (Alta. C.A.).

108 The defendants in the case were the owner of property on which a development was being constructed, the company hired to rough grade and strip the land, and an engineering consulting firm. All three were held to be occupiers by the trial judge. The Court of Appeal did not specifically deal with this aspect of the decision, although it was prepared to "assume" "without deciding" that they were all occupiers.

109 In interpreting who is an occupier under the legislative provisions, the common law cases are relevant. This is made explicit in the Manitoba legislation, in s. 1. See *Silva v. Winnipeg (City)*, [1993] 1 W.W.R. 691 (Man. Q.B.), where a corporation responsible for maintaining the sidewalk in front of its arena was deemed to be an "occupier" for the purpose of the statutory duty. In *Manitoba (Workers' Compensation Board) v. Podolsky* (2006), 41 C.C.L.T. (3d) 165 (Man. C.A.), a person who did not have actual physical possession of a house, but had the legal right to occupy it and a high degree of control over it was deemed to be an occupier at common law and hence also under the Manitoba Act. Also see *Bennett v. Kailua Estates Ltd.*, [1995] 2 W.W.R. 22 (B.C. S.C.), affirmed (1997), 32 C.C.L.T. (2d) 217 (B.C. C.A.), where the trial court resorts to the common law to define who is an occupier under the B.C. legislation. The court held that a person acting solely as an employee of the occupier is not himself an occupier for the purposes of the Act. The Court of Appeal affirmed the decision but on a different ground. Gibbs J.A. held that since the employee, who was a manager of a nightclub, was not on duty on the night of the incident, he could not be in "control" of the premises, the activities, or the persons allowed to enter at that time.

110 One should also recall that in addition to the "responsibility and control" provision, those in "physical possession" of premises are also occupiers. Depending upon how widely this is interpreted, it renders less important the "responsibility and control" provision.

Nevertheless, cases both from British Columbia[111] and Alberta[112] have held that the three responsibilities in the statutory definition must be read conjunctively and not disjunctively. In the British Columbia cases, landlords were held not to be occupiers under s. 1(b) since they did not possess all of the characteristics. One must keep in mind, however, that the law with regard to the liability of landlords is complex, since, in determining the liability of landlords, one must also consider the terms of the lease,[113] separate provisions of the occupiers' liability legislation dealing with landlords,[114] as well as provisions of other statutes, such as the Residential Tenancy Act.[115]

It is noteworthy that the statutes clearly eliminate the common law distinction between the condition of premises, to which occupiers' liability principles were said to apply, and the activities conducted thereon, to which ordinary negligence law applied. It seems irrefutable that the legislation was intended to be exclusive and comprehensive, in so far as the liability of occupiers is concerned.[116]

---

111 See *Goldmanis v. Mador* (1991), [1991] B.C.J. No. 3049, 1991 CarswellBC 1887 (S.C.); *Hodgson v. Christensen* (December 19, 1989), Doc. Vancouver C896385, [1989] B.C.J. No. 2322 (S.C.); and *Wiley v. Tymar Management Inc.* (1994), [1995] 3 W.W.R. 684 (B.C. S.C.), affirmed (1997), 1997 CarswellBC 854 (C.A.).

112 See, for example, *Kiceluk v. Oliverio* (2001), [2002] 1 W.W.R. 359 (Alta. Q.B.), *Koch v. Slave Lake Jewellers* (2001), [2001] A.J. No. 685, 2001 CarswellAlta 699 (Q.B.), *Pauk v. Catholic Parish of Saint Nykolaja of Greek Ruthenian Rite To Rome* (2006), [2006] A.J. No. 804, 2006 CarswellAlta 833 (Q.B.), affirmed (2007), 83 Alta. L.R. (4th) 1 (C.A.) and *Block v. Canadian Pacific Hotels Corp.* (2007), [2007] A.J. No. 295, 2007 CarswellAlta 340 (Q.B.).

113 In *Kiceluk v. Oliverio* (2001), [2002] 1 W.W.R. 359 (Alta. Q.B.), a tenant injured herself on the sidewalk leading to her duplex. Although the court held that the landlord was not responsible as an occupier under the Act, it was liable pursuant to an implied term of the lease respecting reasonable means of access to the leased property.

114 See, for example, s. 6 of the B.C. legislation. This section provides that "if premises are occupied or used under a tenancy under which a landlord is responsible for the maintenance or repair of the premises, it is the duty of the landlord to show toward any person who, or whose property, may be on the premises the same care in respect of risks arising from failure on the landlord's part in carrying out the landlord's responsibility, as is required by the Act to be shown by an occupier of premises toward persons entering on or using the premises." This section was applied in *Robertson v. Stang* (1997), 38 C.C.L.T. (2d) 62 (B.C. S.C.), and more recently in *Gagne v. Fourneau* (2005), 45 C.C.L.T. (3d) 248 (S.C.). In *Beheyt v. Chrupalo* (2004), [2006] 4 W.W.R. 654 (Man. C.A.), the relationship between the Occupiers' Liability Act, R.S.M. 1987, c. 08 and the Residential Tenancies' Act, S.M. 1990-91, c. 11, was considered. The Court of Appeal held that landlords who have not assumed responsibility for the maintenance of the let property and thus who do not have liability under the Occupiers' Liability Act cannot have their duties extended by considering them as landlords under the Residential Tenancies Act.

115 R.S.B.C. 1996, c. 406. See, for example, *Segstro v. McLean*, [1990] B.C.J. No. 2477; *Zavaglia v. MAQ Holdings Ltd.* (1983), 50 B.C.L.R. 204 (Co. Ct.), affirmed (1986), 6 B.C.L.R. (2d) 286 (C.A.). See Di Castri, *Occupiers' Liability* (1980), Chapter 6. In *Bueckert v. Mattison* (1996), [1997] 1 W.W.R. 430 (Sask. Q.B.), the court, while agreeing that a landlord normally does not have occupancy, it may have "control" for certain limited purposes. In this case, the landlord was responsible to ensure that the apartment had a smoke detector. The landlord had the necessary occupancy for this limited purpose.

116 That is, the debate raised, especially in the Australian jurisprudence, concerning co-existing duties, seems to be a non-issue under these statutes. It should be kept in mind that even though the defendant might not have been an occupier of the property in question, the defendant still owes a common law duty of care with respect to unreasonable risks created with regard to that property. See, for example, *Lytle v. Toronto (City)* (2004), [2004] O.J. No. 1570, 2004

(b) Common Duty of Care

The principal reform of the legislative provisions is the abandonment of the common law's classification of entrants, with the various duties owed to each, and the introduction of a common duty of care owed to all entrants, with a few exceptions. In Alberta, separate categories for trespassers and child trespassers are retained, and in other provinces trespassing snowmobilers or those in off-road vehicles are treated as a special category and receive less protection.[117] As well, the duty of care owed to entrants who are deemed to have accepted risks is very low.[118]

The common duty of care owed to entrants under the Ontario, Manitoba, British Columbia, Nova Scotia and Prince Edward Island statutes, and to visitors under Alberta's statute, is similarly worded. It is:

> to take such care as, in all the circumstances of the case, is reasonable to see that the person or property, as the case may be, will be reasonably safe while on the premises.[119]

It is made clear that the duty applies to persons and property,[120] to the condition of the premises,[121] to activities on the premises,[122] and to the conduct of third

---

CarswellOnt 1510 (S.C.J.), affirmed (2006), 2006 CarswellOnt 5886 (C.A.), and *Voulgaris v. Heartwood Construction Ltd.*, 2006 MBQB 52 (Man. Q.B.). In *Voulgaris*, a general contractor was liable in negligence for leaving debris on a parking lot during the course of doing renovations. In *Lytle*, a homeowner was liable in negligence for injuries suffered by a pedestrian when she fell over pipes which had been left by the homeowner on the public sidewalk in front of her house.

117 For example, in Manitoba, s. 3(4) of the Occupiers' Liability Act provides that the only duty owed to those trespassing in off-road vehicles is a duty not to deliberately harm them, or to act with reckless disregard of their presence. In Ontario, the Motorized Snow Vehicles Act, R.S.O. 1990, c. M.44, s. 22 provides that snowmobilers shall be taken to have assumed the risks of injury pursuant to s. 4 of the Occupiers' Liability Act. See *Cormack v. Mara (Twp.)* (1987), 50 M.V.R. 45 (Ont. Dist. Ct.), reversed (1989), 59 D.L.R. (4th) 300 (Ont. C.A.). See also the New Brunswick Motorized Snow Vehicles Act, R.S.N.B. 1973, c. M-18, s. 11.1 [en. 1975, c. 37, s. 3; repealed by All-Terrain Vehicle Act, S.N.B. 1985, c. A-7.11], applied in *Eastwick v. N.B.* (1987), 45 C.C.L.T. 191 (N.B. Q.B.).

118 See discussion below.

119 This is the Manitoba wording (R.S.M. 1987, c. O8 (also C.C.S.M., c. O8), s. 3(1)). The other statutes use very similar, but not identical, words. This is also the formulation adopted by the Newfoundland Court of Appeal in *Stacey v. Anglican Churches of Canada (Diocesan Synod of Eastern Newfoundland & Labrador)* (1999), 47 C.C.L.T. (2d) 153 (Nfld. C.A.) and subsequently reaffirmed in *Gallant v. Roman Catholic Episcopal Corp. for Labrador* (2001), 200 D.L.R. (4th) 643 (Nfld. C.A.).

120 Even if the individuals owning the property are not actually on the premises, their property is still protected. For a damage to property case under s. 14 of the Alberta Act, see *Vogel v. Can. Roxy Petroleum Ltd.*, [1995] 3 W.W.R. 49 (Alta. Q.B.).

121 It has been doubted in B.C. cases whether the duty applies to activities such as sitting in chairs, or climbing ladders. See *Howells v. Southland Can. Inc.*, [1995] B.C.J. No. 397 (S.C.); and *Wiley v. Tymar Management Inc.*, above, note 111. There is nothing in the legislation which suggests that the duty does not apply to such activities.

122 In *Downey v. St. Paul's Hospital* (2007), 47 C.C.L.T. (3d) 93 (B.C. S.C.), additional reasons at (2007), 2007 CarswellBC 1080 (S.C.), the plaintiff contracted TB after visiting his infected friend at the hospital. He sued the hospital. The court decided that treating patients was an activity which the hospital conducted on its premises and thus the British Columbia Act applied. The action was dismissed, however, on the basis that the duty of care imposed by the Act had not been breached. The hospital did not know that the patient had TB and had not been negligent in the way in which it dealt with the situation.

parties on the premises.[123] The Nova Scotia provision specifically outlines the factors that a court may consider in determining whether the duty of care has been discharged. These include the knowledge by the occupier of the likelihood of the visitor's presence, the circumstances of the entry, the age of the visitor, the ability of the visitor to appreciate the danger, the warning given, and the nature of the risk.[124]

Despite the inelegant wording,[125] the statutory duty of care is akin to the ordinary common law duty of care, as developed in the negligence action. The duty is based on an objective test of reasonable care, which includes factors such as reasonable foreseeability, reasonable risk, and so on.[126] Courts have had few difficulties in applying the new statutory duty. It has generally been agreed that the previous common law standards relating to unusual dangers, or concealed traps, are no longer relevant in determining liability under the statutory provisions.[127] As stated by the Ontario Court of Appeal in *McErlean v. Sarel*:

---

123 See British Columbia statute, s. 3(2); Ontario statute, s. 3(2); Manitoba statute, s. 3(2); Alberta statute, s. 6; Prince Edward Island statute, s. 3(2). Neither Ontario nor Prince Edward Island specifically refer to the conduct of third parties; however, the definitions of occupier do include those who control persons allowed to enter. Presumably, even in Ontario and P.E.I., therefore, there is a duty with respect to what these third parties do while upon the premises. See, e.g., *Allison v. Rank City Hall Can. Ltd.* (1984), 6 D.L.R. (4th) 144 (Ont. H.C.). In an unusual case, *H. (M.) v. Bederman* (1995), 27 C.C.L.T. (2d) 152 (Ont. Gen. Div.), additional reasons at (1995), 1995 CarswellOnt 642 (Gen. Div.), a doctor who owned and operated a private clinic was held liable in negligence for a sexual assault committed by one patient on another. Although the case was not pleaded as one of occupiers' liability, this could have been argued as such. The doctor's negligence did not relate in any way to his professional duties. The occupier's duty relating to the conduct of third parties does not extend so far as to require the occupier to take reasonable steps to ensure that the plaintiff can sue the third party. See *Hughson v. John Doe* (2005), 28 C.C.L.T. (3d) 123 (Ont. S.C.J.), affirmed (2006), 278 D.L.R. (4th) 575 (Ont. C.A.).

124 Section 4(3).

125 One wonders, for example, why it is necessary to use the word "reasonable" twice in framing the duty. As well, the notion of "reasonable care" inherently accounts for the "circumstances of the case."

126 See Chapter 9. That the standard of care under the B.C. Act, for example, is the standard applied to ordinary negligence actions was confirmed in *Rendall v. Ewert*, [1989] 6 W.W.R. 97 (B.C. C.A.), leave to appeal to S.C.C. refused [1990] 1 W.W.R. lxxii (note) (S.C.C.). In *Slaferek v. TCG International Inc.* (1997), [1998] 3 W.W.R. 600 (Alta. Q.B.), the court used the "foreseeability" test to determine the scope of the occupier's duty. In this case, liability was denied because the plaintiff's accident and injuries were not reasonably foreseeable. The plaintiff used a ski hill for tubing, a use that had not been foreseen by the defendant. Also see *Alchimowicz v. Schram* (1999), 49 M.P.L.R. (2d) 299 (Ont. C.A.), leave to appeal refused (1999), 133 O.A.C. 198 (note) (S.C.C.). The plaintiff dove from the top of a railing into a shallow lake. The Court of Appeal affirmed a trial judgment dismissing the action: (1997), [1997] O.J. No. 135, 1997 CarswellOnt 94 (Gen. Div.). The actions of the plaintiff were "beyond the scope of reasonable foreseeability". A contrary decision is *Woods v. Ontario (Ministry of Natural Resources)* (2001), 5 C.C.L.T. (3d) 142 (Ont. S.C.J.), affirmed (2003), 2003 CarswellOnt 1240 (C.A.), where the defendant was liable for failing to warn persons not to dive from a groyne, a low wall, into shallow waters.

127 Despite some earlier judgments which imported the common law concept into the application of the statutory duty, for example, *Story v. Prince George (City)* (1979), 99 D.L.R. (3d) 464 (B.C. S.C.), courts have made it clear that the common law categories, with their respective duties, are no longer relevant. See, e.g., *Johnson v. Creative Hobby Craft Stores* (1983), 53 B.C.L.R. 265 (C.A.); *Weiss v. Greater Vancouver Y.M.C.A.* (1979), 11 B.C.L.R. 112 (C.A.);

> . . . the measure of responsibility of those who occupy land to those who enter upon the land no longer depends on the rigid and formalistic common law classifications of trespassers, licensees and invitees . . . Rather than continue to predicate an occupier's duty on an entrant's status, the Act establishes a common duty of care.[128]

As well, it must be noted that the Ontario, Prince Edward Island, Nova Scotia and Manitoba statutes specifically provide that the common law rules have been replaced by the statutory duty of care,[129] thus ending all doubt on this question.

The statutes also provide that more onerous duties which may be imposed upon occupiers by other enactments or rules of law are not precluded by the common duty of care.[130] In Ontario and Alberta, specific examples of these higher duties of care are provided; they are the duties imposed on innkeepers, common carriers and bailees.[131] The section has been used to impose a high duty of care on an electric utility company which ran power lines over a public park area.[132] The contention that the section could operate to maintain the higher standard of care owed to contractual entrants at common law, however, has been rejected.[133]

It has been suggested in some cases that, because the statutes impose a duty on occupiers to ensure that their premises are reasonably safe for visitors, *positive* steps must always be taken by occupiers to fulfil their duties. The implication is that failing to do anything positive to remedy a potential danger automatically amounts to a breach of the statutory duty.[134] If this is what has been intended by

---

Preston v. Can. Legion of Br. Empire Service League, Kingsway Branch No. 175 (1981), 123 D.L.R. (3d) 645 (Alta. C.A.); *Waldick v. Malcolm* (1987), 43 D.L.R. (4th) 693 (Ont. H.C.), affirmed (1989), 63 D.L.R. (4th) 583 (Ont. C.A.), which was affirmed (1991), 8 C.C.L.T. (2d) 1 (S.C.C.); and *Smith v. Atlantic Shopping Centres Ltd.*, 2006 NSSC 133 (S.C.).

128 (1987), 42 C.C.L.T. 78 at 91 (Ont. C.A.).

129 See s. 2 of the Ontario Act, s. 3 of the Nova Scotia Act, s. 2 of the P.E.I. Act, and s. 2 of the Manitoba Act. Section 2 of the B.C. Act is somewhat less clear, and there is no similar provision in Alberta's Act.

130 See in Ontario, s. 9; P.E.I., s. 8; Manitoba, s. 3(5); B.C., s. 3(4); Nova Scotia, s. 4(4); and Alberta, in a more limited form, s. 14(4).

131 In *Mallais v. D.A. Campbell Amusements Ltd.* (2007), 45 C.C.L.T. (3d) 222 (Ont. C.A.), the plaintiff was injured on an amusement ride at a carnival. The action was dismissed at trial based on the application of negligence law and the ordinary duty of care imposed by the Occupiers' Liability Act. On appeal, the appellant submitted that the higher duty imposed on "common carriers" should have been applied. The Court of Appeal dismissed the appeal finding that the amusement ride did not qualify as a common carrier. It does not appear from the judgment, however, that s. 9 of the Act was specifically considered.

132 *Leischner v. West Kootenay Power & Light Co.* (1986), 24 D.L.R. (4th) 641 (B.C. C.A.). It has also been suggested that the section would apply to the higher standard of care imposed upon keepers of animals by the *scienter* principle: see Lambert J.A. in *Kirk v. Trerise* (1981), 17 C.C.L.T. 121 (B.C. C.A.). In an Alberta case, *Houle v. Calgary* (1985), 38 Alta. L.R. (2d) 331 (C.A.), the common duty of care provided in the Act was imposed. Note, however, that the legislation differs, particularly with respect to Alberta's narrow provision concerning the retention of higher duties of care. The standard of care with respect to operators of escalators is stated to be of the "highest order" and requires "the highest practical degree of care"; see *Naicken v. Edmonton (City)*, 32 C.C.L.T. (2d) 137, [1997] 4 W.W.R. 170 (Alta. Q.B.).

133 See *Wolf v. Airliner Motor Hotel (1972) Ltd.* (1988), 54 Man. R. (2d) 169 (Q.B.).

134 This appears to have been the view of the Ontario trial court in *Waldick v. Malcolm* (1987), 61 O.R. (2d) 624 (H.C.), which was affirmed by the Ontario Court of Appeal, at (1989), 2 C.C.L.T. (2d) 22, and approved by the Supreme Court of Canada (1991), 8 C.C.L.T. (2d) 1. See also the B.C. Court of Appeal decision in *Tutinka v. Mainland Sand & Gravel Ltd.*, [1994] 4 W.W.R. 580. In *Roasting v. Blood Band* (1999), 241 A.R. 171 (Q.B.), it is also stated that

these judgments, it is an approach which I would consider incorrect. The duty imposed by the legislation is to ensure that premises are reasonably safe for persons and their property. Depending on all of the circumstances of a case, it very well may be that premises are already reasonably safe, without any further positive action being required by an occupier.[135] Positive steps should only be required to remedy an unreasonably dangerous situation, where reasonable measures could have been taken.[136] As stated by Iacobucci J. in *Waldick v. Malcolm*, "the goals of the Act are to promote, and indeed require, *where circumstances warrant*, positive action on the part of the occupiers to make their premises reasonably safe."[137] As well, one must recall that the burden of proving that the premises were unreasonably safe and that the occupier thus has failed in its duty rests on the plaintiff.[138] A judge is, of course, entitled to infer from the plaintiff's evidence concerning the facts of the accident, that the occupier failed in its duty to ensure that the premises were reasonably safe. In this case, there would be an evidentiary burden on the defendant to prove that it had taken reasonable steps to avert the danger which faced the plaintiff.[139] Ultimately, however, it is the plaintiff's burden to prove the defendant's negligence.[140]

"it appears established that doing nothing falls short of the duty set out under the Occupiers' Liability Act".

135 See, for example, *Leweke v. Saanich School Board No. 63* (2005), 31 C.C.L.T. (3d) 1 (B.C. C.A.), affirming 2004 BCSC 1251 (S.C.). The mere fact that the plaintiff fell on the bleachers at the defendant's gym did not mean that they were unsafe. The accident was held to have been her own fault.

136 In *Mortimer v. Cameron* (1994), 111 D.L.R. (4th) 428 at 437 (Ont. C.A.), Robins J.A. correctly notes that an occupier "may be required in certain circumstances to take positive action to make the premises reasonably safe." An owner of a building was held liable for a defective condition of its building, even though the structural deficiency existed in the building prior to the defendant's purchase. It is clear, however, that the previous owner who created the defect cannot be liable as an occupier once the property has been sold. See, for example, *Ekkebus v. Lauinger* (1994), 22 C.C.L.T. (2d) 148 (Ont. Gen. Div.). In *Pope v. Route 66 Clothing Inc.* (1997), 41 C.C.L.T. (2d) 72 (Ont. Gen. Div.), a thief who was being detained in a store punched the plaintiff in the face as he fled the store. The plaintiff's claim that the defendant had breached the statutory duty by not preventing this from happening was rejected. The court held that the defendant acted reasonably in the circumstances and did not omit to do anything that it was required to do in order to prevent this from happening.

137 [1991] 2 S.C.R. 456 at 457 (emphasis added).

138 In *Tutinka v. Mainland Sand & Gravel*, above, note 134, at 598, the B.C. Court of Appeal stated that "it was not the responsibility of the trial judge or the plaintiff to dictate the steps Mainland could have or should have taken to make its property reasonably safe. The onus is on Mainland to take reasonable steps to make its property reasonably safe for persons on it." With respect, if this implies that the plaintiff need not prove that the defendant's conduct was unreasonable, but that the defendant must prove that it acted reasonably, it incorrectly reverses the burden of proof.

139 See, for example, *Howden v. Westfair Foods Ltd.* (2001), 154 Man. R. (2d) 118 (Q.B.), cited in *Ball v. Canada Safeway Ltd.* (2004), 28 C.C.L.T. (3d) 110 (Man. Q.B.). Spilled rice can raise a *prima facie* breach of the statute. The occupier must then show that it acted reasonably in the face of the danger which the rice presented to customers. It is the plaintiff, however, who ultimately has to prove that the defendant was negligent. See, for example, *Corbin v. Halifax (Regional Municipality)*, 2003 NSSC 121 (S.C.), at para. 56. In *Anderson v. Canada Safeway Ltd.*, 2004 ABCA 239 (C.A.), additional reasons at (2005), 2005 CarswellAlta 2 (C.A.), at para. 4, Paperny J.A. stated that "In Alberta, the Act does not make an occupier an insurer, but shifts the evidentiary burden to the occupier to show it exercised the degree of reasonable care called for by the foreseeable risk, sufficient to keep a visitor reasonably safe."

The issue as to whether the policy/operational dichotomy, which is used to resolve public tort liability cases framed in negligence, applies to occupiers' liability cases, has been raised in a few cases. In *Kennedy v. Waterloo (County) Board of Education*,[141] the Court of Appeal decided that the policy/operational dichotomy which applies to public tort liability cases to determine the standard of care issue does not apply to public authorities, who have a statutory occupier's liability duty. That is, the fact that the authority is making a policy decision does not relieve it of its statutory duty to make its premises reasonably safe. The authority cannot make a policy decision to exempt itself from this statutory duty, although the fact that the defendant is a public authority operating with scarce resources may be relevant in determining whether the duty was breached. In *Kennedy*, a school board was held liable for its failure to remove "bollards" from its property. In *Fox v. Vancouver (City)*,[142] on the other hand, the court suggested that *bona fide* policy decisions made by a municipality in order to discharge its statutory duty of care are not reviewable; only the operational aspects are. As discussed above in Chapter 8, attempting to resolve public tort liability issues by drawing a hard line between policy and operations is a frustrating exercise. The

---

The reverse burden of proof approach was also taken by Moreau J. in *Pauk v. Catholic Parish* (2006), [2006] A.J. No. 804, 2006 CarswellAlta 833 (Q.B.), affirmed on another issue (2007), 83 Alta. L.R. (4th) 1 (C.A.), at para. 29. The trial judge stated that "the Court must take into account the legislature's intention and the purpose of the *Act*, which is to shift the onus of proof of negligence from the Plaintiff to the occupier, who must disprove negligence." While I would agree that in certain cases the facts of a case might give rise to an inference of negligence on the part of an occupier, I would not agree that the Occupiers' Liability Act itself alters or shifts either the primary or secondary burden of proof. It imposes a duty of reasonable care on the occupier and, as in other types of negligence cases, it is the plaintiff who must prove, either by direct or indirect evidence, that the duty was breached.

140 See, for example, *Whitlow v. 572008 Ontario Ltd.* (1995), [1995] O.J. No. 77, 1995 CarswellOnt 2438 (Gen. Div.), where the court correctly notes that there is no presumption of negligence created whenever a person is injured on premises. The court, citing *Bauman v. Stein* (1991), 78 D.L.R. (4th) 118 (B.C. C.A.), at 127, states: "A plaintiff must still be able to point to some act or failure to act, on the part of the occupier which caused the injury complained of, before liability can be established." This was reaffirmed in *St. Louis-Lalonde v. Carleton Condominium Corp. No. 12* (2005), 2005 CarswellOnt 2731 (S.C.J.), additional reasons at (2005), 2005 CarswellOnt 4709 (S.C.J.), affirmed 2007 ONCA 108 (C.A.). Also see *Redman v. Saanich (District)*, [2006] 11 W.W.R. 424 (B.C. C.A.), leave to appeal refused (2007), 2007 CarswellBC 325 (S.C.C.) — the fact that an exercise ball burst causing injury to the plaintiff does not establish that the occupier was negligent. The burden of proving negligence and cause rests on the plaintiff, and was not discharged in this case. In *Atkins v. Jim Pattison Industries Ltd.* (1997), 39 B.C.L.R. (3d) 365 (S.C.), reversed (1998), 61 B.C.L.R. (3d) 183 (C.A.), the plaintiff slipped on a piece of lettuce which was on the floor of the defendant's store. The trial judge dismissed the action because the defendant had in place a reasonable inspection system. There was no evidence, however, whether the system had been followed in this case. The Court of Appeal held that, assuming that the existence of the lettuce on the floor raised a *prima facie* case of the defendant's negligence, the onus was on the defendant to prove that it not only had a system of inspection, but also that it was in fact used on this occasion. The judgment was reversed and the case sent back for a new trial.

141 (1999), 45 C.C.L.T. (2d) 169, 175 D.L.R. (4th) 106 (Ont. C.A.), leave to appeal refused (2000), 134 O.A.C. 397 (note) (S.C.C.).

142 (2003), 20 C.C.L.T. (3d) 123 (B.C. S.C.). Also see *Knodell v. New Westminster (City)* (2005), [2005] B.C.J. No. 2026, 2005 CarswellBC 2212 (S.C.). Joyce J. followed *Fox*, although reluctantly.

same point can be made with respect to occupiers' liability cases. Where public authorities have statutory duties under occupiers' liability legislation to ensure that their premises are reasonably safe, courts ought to examine all aspects of what they did in order to discharge their duties. The fact that the defendants are public authorities who must make "policy" decisions is certainly an important element in determining whether the statutory duties were properly discharged. It should not be used, however, as a reason to avoid the analysis.[143]

The issue as to whether an occupier has breached its statutory duty is similar to the issue of negligence in an action for negligence. It is a question of fact to be determined by the trier of fact. As long as the fact finder's decision is not perverse or manifestly unreasonable, and assuming there are no errors of law, an appeal court should not reverse a lower court's finding.[144]

(c) Acceptance of Risks

The statutes provide that in certain circumstances an entrant who has willingly assumed the risks presented by premises will be owed either no duty of care, or a very low duty of care, by the occupier. In Alberta,[145] Manitoba,[146] and British Columbia,[147] it is provided that "an occupier has no duty of care to a person in respect of risks willingly accepted by that person as his own risks."[148] Ontario,[149] Nova Scotia,[150] and Prince Edward Island[151] provide that, with respect to those who willingly assume risks, there is only a duty "not to create a danger with the deliberate intent of doing harm or damage to the person or his property and to not act with reckless disregard of the presence of the person or his property."[152]

Questions have been raised in the case law concerning these provisions. Is the provision dealing with the acceptance of risks a codification of the common law defence of *volenti*, or is it a new, and less demanding, provision? As we have

---

143 An expressed statutory duty under occupiers' liability statutes is in this sense no different than any other express liability provision imposed on public authorities. See discussion above in Chapter 8.

144 See *Anderson v. Anderson*, [1994] 4 W.W.R. 272 at 280 (Man. C.A.), where Huband J.A. states that although inferences and conclusions drawn from primary facts are more reviewable than primary findings of fact, "there should be no interference unless the trial judge has misunderstood or misconceived the evidence and thus has drawn erroneous inferences or conclusions." Also see *Kerr v. Loblaws Inc.*, 2007 ONCA 371 (C.A.) for a more recent affirmation of this point.

145 See s. 7.

146 See s. 3(3).

147 See s. 3(3).

148 To use the B.C. wording.

149 See s. 4.

150 See s. 5.

151 See s. 4.

152 These three statutes go even further, moreover, by deeming that certain types of entrants, for example, those who enter intending to commit crimes, those who trespass on certain types of lands, and those who enter for certain types of recreational purposes, have willingly assumed all risks, and are hence subject to the lower duty of care. It is apparent, in other words, that even though only Alberta formally retains a trespasser category and a low duty of care, other provinces have, through different provisions, separately dealt with the duty owed to unwanted entrants. See discussion below. For an application of this provision in Ontario, see *Cormack v. Mara (Twp.)* (1989), 59 D.L.R. (4th) 300 (Ont. C.A.).

seen,[153] mere knowledge of a risk is not sufficient to establish the *volenti* defence at common law. Until recently, the case law on the statutory provisions had been inconsistent. Most courts had decided that the rigorous requirements of *volenti* should apply to the statutes, otherwise the occupier's duty of care would be, in many instances, too easily negated.[154] A few judgments, on the other hand, decided that the statutory provision is a new provision which "cuts free from the previous common law and does not embrace or accept the defence of *volenti non fit injuria*."[155] The issue now has been resolved, at least in so far as the Ontario legislation is concerned, by the Supreme Court of Canada in *Waldick v. Malcolm.*[156] Iacobucci J. held that s. 4 of the Ontario Act "was intended to embody and preserve the *volenti* doctrine."[157] This would require consent to the physical and legal risks of injury. It would seem that, on this point, consistency with the general principle of negligence law is appropriate, and that, keeping within the spirit of the legislation, entrants should not be barred from recovery, unless the stringent requirements of the common law defence of *volenti* are met.[158]

As in the negligence action, a plaintiff's knowledge of the risks, although not amounting to *volenti*, can be a relevant factor in determining the standard of care owed under occupiers' liability legislation. In *Epp v. Ridgetop Builders Ltd.*,[159] Laycraft J. held that one of the circumstances which courts could take into consideration in determining the standard of care owed pursuant to s. 5 of the Alberta legislation was the entrant's familiarity with the premises and his appre-

---

153 Chapter 13.

154 See, e.g., *Epp v. Ridgetop Bldrs.* (1978), 7 C.C.L.T. 291 (Alta. T.D.); *Preston v. Can. Legion of Br. Empire Service League, Kingsway Branch No. 175* (1981), 123 D.L.R. (3d) 645 (Alta. C.A.); *Sandberg v. Steer Hldg. Ltd.*, [1987] 3 W.W.R. 732 (Man. Q.B.); *Beatty v. Brad-Lea Meadows Ltd.* (1986), 39 A.C.W.S. (2d) 334 (Ont. H.C.); *Waldick v. Malcolm* (1987), 43 D.L.R. (4th) 693 (Ont. H.C.), affirmed (1989), 63 D.L.R. (4th) 583 (Ont. C.A.), affirmed (1991), 8 C.C.L.T. (2d) 1 (S.C.C.).

155 Clements Co. Ct. J. in *Christie v. Toronto* (1983), 20 M.P.L.R. 145 at 157 (Ont. Co. Ct.). See also *Fraser v. McGee* (1985), 29 A.C.W.S. (2d) 480 (Ont. Dist. Ct.); *Abbott v. Silver Star Sports Ltd.* (1986), 6 B.C.L.R. (2d) 83 (S.C.); and *Samis v. Vancouver*, [1989] B.C.W.L.D. 1010, additional reasons [1989] B.C.W.L.D. 2064, leave to appeal to S.C.C. refused 102 N.R. 400n.

156 Above, note 1454.

157 *Ibid.*, 8 C.C.L.T. (2d) at 17.

158 Thus it is probable that the legislation in all provinces will be interpreted in this way. See, for example, *Bains v. Hill*, [1992] 5 W.W.R. 172 (B.C. C.A.), where the Court of Appeal followed *Waldick* in interpreting the B.C. legislation, and *Murray v. Bitango,* [1996] 7 W.W.R. 163, 135 D.L.R. (4th) 443 (Alta. C.A.), additional reasons at [1996] 8 W.W.R. 138 (Alta. C.A.), leave to appeal refused (1996), 139 D.L.R. (4th) vii (note) (S.C.C.), interpreting Alberta's provision in the same way. A British Columbia case that also applied the more restrictive defence is *Matharu v. Nam* (2006), [2006] B.C.J. No. 1383, 2006 CarswellBC 1534 (S.C.), affirmed (2007), [2007] B.C.J. No. 1223, 2007 CarswellBC 1301 (C.A.). See, however, *Laws v. Wright*, [2000] 5 W.W.R. 325 (Alta. Q.B.). The plaintiff was warned about the temperamental nature of a horse. Despite this warning, she fed the horse and was bitten. The court relieved the defendant of liability based upon s. 7 (willing acceptance of risks) and s. 9 (warnings). Also see *Block v. Canadian Pacific Hotels Corp.* (2007), [2007] A.J. No. 295, 2007 CarswellAlta 340 (Q.B.) where s. 7 was applied.

159 Above, note 154.

ciation of the dangers presented by them.[160] As well, all the provincial statutues provide that the contributory negligence legislation in force in the province applies to the action under the Occupiers' Liability Act.[161] Thus, an entrant who acts unreasonably in the face of obvious risks can properly be held to have been contributorily negligent.[162]

The case of *Roasting v. Blood Band*,[163] based on the Alberta Act, raises interesting questions relating to the interaction between various sections of the legislation. The facts of the case are as follows.

The plaintiff went to an area of a construction site—bleachers in a grandstand—that, because of the absence of guard railings, was off limits to workers. The plaintiff had been specifically warned not to go there. Despite these warnings, the plaintiff went to the bleachers, fell from them, and was seriously injured.

The court stated that in determining whether the occupier satisfied its statutory duty under section 5, it should consider whether the premises presented reasonably foreseeable risks to persons exercising ordinary diligence. In this respect unprotected bleachers did pose a foreseeable risk, which required the occupier to take reasonable steps. The steps taken here were to warn the plaintiff not to go to the bleachers because they were dangerous and off limits. The plaintiff's decision to disregard these warnings was held to have been not foreseeable. Hence the defendant had discharged its duty, under s. 5.

The court also relied on s. 9 of the Act dealing with warnings and held that the warnings given in this case were sufficient to enable the visitor to be reasonably safe. Dealing with s. 7 relating to acceptance of risks, the court adopted the position that, as with *volenti*, this requires an acceptance of not only physical risks, but legal risks as well. The court concluded that this did not happen in this case, and hence the court would not give effect to this section. In view of the fact that there was no breach of duty, the issue of contributory negligence was not addressed.

Where a plaintiff has been warned about risks, is told not to go to a specific area, but disregards these warnings, different sections of the Act seem to come into play. First there is the occupier's duty to take reasonable care (s. 5). Second, there is the section dealing with the modification or exclusion of liability by express agreement or notice (s. 8). Third, there is the section dealing with warnings (s. 9). Fourth, there is the section dealing with willing acceptance of risks (s. 7). Fifth, there is the section dealing with contributory negligence (s. 15). It is my

---

160 It is important to note that the Alberta Act, in s. 9, specifically provides that "a warning, without more, shall not be treated as absolving an occupier from discharging the common duty of care to the occupier's visitor unless in all the circumstances the warning is enough to enable the visitor to be reasonably safe."

161 See, in Ontario, s. 9(3); in Alberta, s. 15(1), (2); in British Columbia, s. 7; in Prince Edward Island, s. 8(3); in Manitoba, s. 7; and in Nova Scotia, s. 10.

162 See, e.g., *Tronrud v. French* (1989), 64 D.L.R. (4th) 498 (Man. C.A.); and *Lorenz v. Ed-Mon Developments Ltd.* (1991), 118 A.R. 201 (C.A.). A more recent example under the Ontario Act is *Litwinenko v. Beaver Lumber Co.* (2006), [2006] O.J. No. 3383, 2006 CarswellOnt 5061 (S.C.J.), additional reasons at (2007), 2007 CarswellOnt 2994 (S.C.J.), varied (2008), 2008 CarswellOnt 3155 (Div. Ct.).

163 (1999), [1999] A.J. No. 156, 1999 CarswellAlta 121 (Q.B.).

suggestion that since the Act deals with five separate issues, a logical approach in a case such as *Roasting* would be for the court, when dealing with such matters as warnings and off-limits areas, to keep these sections distinct.[164]

The first question should be whether the premises were reasonably safe as required by s. 5 of the Act, *without regard to the issue of warnings or the plaintiff's knowledge of risks.* In *Roasting,* for example, the premises were not reasonably safe. The second question should be whether there was a modification or exclusion of liability by an express agreement or notice. In *Roasting*, this was not an issue; there was no express agreement. The third question should be whether, despite a breach under s. 5, there was a warning sufficient to absolve the defendant from his obligation to discharge his s. 5 duty of care, pursuant to the terms of s. 9. In *Roasting*, for example, the court concluded that the warnings were sufficient.[165] The fourth question should ask whether there was an acceptance of the physical and legal risks. As *Roasting* concedes, this is difficult to establish and certainly cannot be determined merely by existing warnings or establishing an off-limit area. The fifth question should consider the contributory negligence of the plaintiff, assuming that based on the above, the defendant was liable. Certainly disregarding warnings or being on off-limit areas would be strong evidence of contributory negligence. This approach, it is suggested, would more clearly separate the application of each of the various sections of the legislation.

(d) Restrictive Duties

Although only the Alberta statute has specific provisions restricting the duty of care owed to trespassers,[166] provisions in other provincial statutes also introduce restrictive duties in certain cases.

In Alberta, the common duty of care is owed only to visitors, and it is clear from the definition of visitor that trespassers are excluded.[167] Trespassers are provided for in separate sections of the Alberta statute. To most trespassers, the occupier has no affirmative duty of care. The occupier must, however, not cause death or injury to trespassers by "wilful or reckless conduct."[168] This is equivalent to the traditional common law duty owed to trespassers, a factor which raises some intriguing questions. To what extent will the courts adopt the common law cases on the duty owed to trespassers in defining the statutory duty? As we have seen, the duty owed to trespassers at common law has been significantly modified

---

164 In extreme cases, the court might even consider the plaintiff a "trespasser" bringing yet another section of the Act into play.

165 Other cases have also held that putting the property "off-limits" and taking reasonable steps to ensure that visitors do not go there is one way of discharging the duty of care. See, for example, *Koperdak v. Wiesblatt* (2006), [2006] B.C.J. No. 888, 2006 CarswellBC 968 (S.C.). The court cited Iacobucci J's statement in *Waldick v. Malcolm* (1991), 83 D.L.R. (4th) 114 (S.C.C.), at 128, that "the occupier may, however, wish to put part of his property "off limits" rather than to make it safe, and in certain circumstances that might be considered reasonable."

166 New Brunswick has abolished the law of occupier's liability as a special area of law. However, it maintained a provision relating to trespassers, which states that the damages recoverable by a person injured on land may be reduced on account of the trespass. See Law Reform Act, S.N.B. 1993, c. L-1.2, s. 2(3).

167 S. 1(*e*).

168 S. 12(1), (2).

from its earlier formulation, and is now a duty to act with ordinary humanity. If the courts decide to strictly construe the statutory duty, trespassers may conceivably be worse off under the Alberta statute than they would have been had the common law been retained.[169]

As well, the interaction between the duty of an occupier under the statute not to cause injury or death by wilful or reckless conduct and the occupier's right to use reasonable force to eject a trespasser, as a defence to a battery action, is somewhat unclear. In *Cullen v. Rice,*[170] for example, the Alberta Court of Appeal relied upon both principles to exculpate an occupier who injured a trespasser while attempting to eject him from the premises. Presumably, the occupier's liability legislation was not intended to affect the right of an entrant to sue for the commission of an intentional tort, nor with the defences available to the occupier in such a case.

A separate provision is provided for child trespassers. The statute provides that when an occupier knows or has reason to know (a) that a child trespasser is on his premises, and (b) that the condition of, or activities on, the premises create a danger of death or serious bodily harm to that child, the occupier owes a duty to that child to take such care as in all the circumstances of the case is reasonable to see that the child will be reasonably safe from that danger.[171] The statute also provides that the child's age, the child's ability to appreciate the danger, and the burden on the occupier of eliminating the danger or protecting the child as compared to the risk of the danger to the child shall be considered by the courts in determining whether the duty of care has been discharged.[172] As well, the statute explains that constructive knowledge of a child trespasser's presence will be found where the occupier has knowledge of facts which would lead the reasonable man to infer the child's presence or the probability of a child's presence.[173]

Despite the absence of a specific trespasser provision, such as the one in Alberta, the other provinces have restricted duties and treat some entrants as trespassers. For example, Ontario, Prince Edward Island and British Columbia have sections providing that persons who (1) enter premises intending to commit criminal acts, (2) who trespass onto rural premises used for agricultural purposes, vacant premises, forested or wilderness premises, closed golf courses, utility rights-of-way, unopened road allowances, private roads, and recreational trails, (3) or who enter these mentioned premises for free recreational purposes, shall be deemed to have willingly assumed all risks.[174] These persons are owed no affirmative duty of care,

---

169 In one case under the statute, *Cullen v. Rice* (1981), 15 C.C.L.T. 180 (Alta. C.A.), the Court of Appeal did refer to the common law authorities regarding the duty owed to trespassers, with reference to *Herrington v. Br. Ry. Bd.*, [1972] A.C. 877 (H.L.). It is unclear, however, whether the duty of common humanity was being adopted.

170 *Ibid.*

171 S. 13(1).

172 S. 13(2).

173 The section was interpreted and applied in *Houle v. Calgary* (1985), 20 D.L.R. (4th) 15 (Alta. C.A.).

174 In Ontario, s. 4; in Prince Edward Island, s. 4, in British Columbia s. 3.1, 3.2. For a discussion of the Ontario section and its application to the criminal entrant, see D.S. Ferguson, "The Battered Burglar: An Analysis of Section 4 and the Position of the Criminal Entrant Under the Ontario Occupiers' Liability Act" (1991), 12 Advocates' Q. 257. For a case dealing with the definition of a "recreational trail" see *Moloney v. Parry Sound (Town)* (2000), 184 D.L.R.

but only the occupier's duty not to create a danger with the deliberate intent of doing harm or damage and not to act with reckless disregard of the person's presence.[175] The Nova Scotia provision also provides for a restrictive duty in a number of cases.[176] In Manitoba, the general duty of care applies to all persons, except for trespassing snowmobilers, who are owed the traditionally low common law duty owed to trespassers.[177]

In England, the Occupiers' Liability Act, 1957[178] maintained the common law with respect to the duty owed to trespassers, as the legislation dealt only with lawful visitors. This has been changed by the Occupiers' Liability Act, 1984, which introduced a duty of reasonable care owed to trespassers, in certain circumstances. The duty exists where the occupier has actual or constructive knowledge of dangers, of the existence of trespassers, and where he can reasonably offer protection against the risk.[179]

(e) Miscellaneous Provisions

There are a number of other provisions in the statutes which ought to be noted.

The statutes retain existing legal rights of occupiers to restrict the duties imposed by the statutes subject to certain conditions. Contractual restrictions shall not apply to those persons who are not party to the contract. As well, reasonable

---

(4th) 121 (Ont. C.A.). A recent case dealing with s. 4(3) of the Ontario Act respecting the use of rural premises for recreational purposes is *Denis v. Ontario (Ministry of Natural Resources)* (2005), [2005] O.J. No. 5261, 2005 CarswellOnt 7068 (S.C.J.). Alberta has enacted a similar provision treating persons who use certain types of properties for recreational purposes as trespassers except in certain cases; see Occupiers' Liability (Recreational Users) Amendment Act, 2003, S.A. 2003, c. 45. A recent case dealing with s. 3.3 of the B.C. Act is *Skopnik v. BC Rail Ltd.*, 2008 BCCA 331. The Court of Appeal reviewed the history of these restricted duty provisions and found that a railway right of way comes within them and is subject therefore to a lower duty of care.

175 A case which applied these provisions is *340812 Ontario Ltd. v. Canadian National Railway* (1997), 148 D.L.R. (4th) 351 (Ont. C.A.), additional reasons at (1997), 149 D.L.R. (4th) 575 (Ont. C.A.). The defendant's train hit the plaintiff's vehicle. The collision occurred on a privately owned siding located on a privately owned road. The occupier of the road and siding was not sued; the railway was (presumably as occupier of the right of way). The railway's defence was that the restrictive duty provisions in the Ontario Act dealing with persons who willingly accept risks when travelling on reasonably marked private roads applied. The Court of Appeal rejected this argument because the occupier permitted entry to this private road and siding, i.e., the owner of the private road. The limited duty only applies where "the occupier has posted no notice in respect of entry and has not otherwise expressly permitted entry". Another case dealing with an accident at a private crossing is *Coulter v. Canadian National Railway* (2000), [2000] O.J. No. 4277, 2000 CarswellOnt 4100 (C.A.), in which case the owner of the right of way, CN, was held partly responsible. *Dally v. London (City)* (2004), [2004] O.J. No. 3231, 2004 CarswellOnt 3179 (S.C.J.) applied the restrictive duty to a person injured while roller blading on a recreational trail. The plaintiff's action was dismissed, even though the occupier of the trail was found to have been in breach of the normal duty of care under the Act.

176 See s. 6.

177 Section 3(4) [re-en. 1988-89, c. 13, s. 32(2)].

178 5 & 6 Eliz. 2, c. 31.

179 See 1984 (Eng.), c. 3, s. 1(3), (4). See Samuels, "Occupiers' Liability Act 1984" (1984), 128 Sol. J. 308; and Jones, "The Occupiers' Liability Act 1984" (1984), 47 Mod. L. Rev. 713, for a detailed analysis of this legislation.

steps to notify the relevant parties of such restrictions shall be taken.[180] The Manitoba and Nova Scotia legislation go considerably further than the others, by specifically requiring that the restrictions of rights be reasonable. This will be determined by a variety of factors, including the relationship between the parties, the type of damage and risk, the scope of the restriction, and the steps taken to notify the affected persons.[181] As well, the Alberta, British Columbia, Nova Scotia and Manitoba statutes provide that the duty to those who are allowed to enter the property as of right cannot be restricted.

The statutes provide that an occupier is not liable for damage caused by the negligence of independent contractors engaged by the occupier, where there was reasonable care exercised in selecting and supervising the independent contractor, and where the work that the independent contractor was engaged to do reasonably should have been done.[182] This provision, however, does not override other statutes which provide liability by an occupier for the negligence of an independent contractor. It also does not apply where the occupier is liable for its own fault with reference to the work of the independent contractor.[183] As well, Ontario and Prince Edward Island provide that this does not affect the non-delegable duties imposed upon occupiers by the common law.[184]

The statutes also alter the common law position of landlords. The duty of landlords, contained in tenancy agreements, to maintain or repair premises, is

---

180 See: in Ontario, s. 5; in P.E.I., s. 5; in Alberta, ss. 8, 10; in Manitoba, s. 4; in British Columbia, s. 4. For a case upholding such a provision, see *McQuary v. Big White Ski Resort Ltd.*, [1993] B.C.J. No. 1956 (S.C.). An Alberta case held that a warning to a person not to use a cattle chute at a horse training arena and to use the arena at her own risk was not an effective restriction under s. 8 of the Act to reduce the defendant's liability. The chute fell onto the plaintiff after she had tied her horse to it. The court held that the restriction not to use the chute was not intended to cover this type of conduct. See *Murray v. Bitango*, [1996] 7 W.W.R. 163, 135 D.L.R. (4th) 443 (Alta. C.A.), additional reasons at [1996] 8 W.W.R. 138 (Alta. C.A.), leave to appeal refused (1996), 139 D.L.R. (4th) vii (note) (S.C.C.). As discussed above, this case illustrates how sections of the Act overlap in these types of cases.

181 See s. 7 of the Nova Scotia Act for example.

182 See: in Manitoba, s. 5; in B.C., s. 5; in Ontario, s. 6; in Alberta, s. 11; in Prince Edward Island, s. 6; in Nova Scotia, s. 8. A case under the B.C. Act is *Grochowich v. Okanagan University College*, 2004 BCCA 325 (C.A.). Rowles J.A. held that supervision of an independent contractor must include supervision with regard to safety. The occupier was held not liable on the facts of this case.

183 See for example *Carriere v. Schlachter* (1999), [2000] 1 W.W.R. 397 (Alta. Q.B.). The occupier hired roofing contractors. One of the employees of the contractor was electrocuted. The employee sued the occupiers. Although it is not totally clear from the judgment or the jury's findings, liability might have been based on the occupier's failure to properly advise the contractor concerning the dangers posed by nearby power lines. Section 11 of the Alberta legislation would clearly have no application to the facts of this type of case.

184 See *Crowe v. Dartmouth (City)* (1985), 69 N.S.R. (2d) 258 (T.D.), regarding liability of an occupier for negligence of independent contractor at common law. The question as to whether the common law regarding non-delegable duties overrides s. 5 of the B.C. Act so as to make an occupier responsible for the negligence of an independent contractor was discussed in *Dixon v. Eldorado Development Corp.* (1999), [2000] 1 W.W.R. 671 (B.C. S.C.). The court, relying on British Columbia jurisprudence, held that an occupier's liability for the acts of independent contractors is governed by the Act, which prevails over the common law. The matter was *obiter* since the court held that there was no non-delegable duty in this case at any event. In addition, liability was found based on the statutory provision.

extended for the protection of entrants. A landlord who has contractual duties to maintain or repair the premises is treated as an occupier, with the occupier's duty of care owed to entrants and their property. This duty, however, is derivative; the landlord must be in default to its tenants under the agreement in order for it to be held liable to entrants under the occupiers' liability legislation.[185]

The statutes also bind the Crown, with some exceptions. The principal exceptions relate to the Crown's occupation of public highways and roads.[186] As well, there are exceptions relating to the occupation of public highways, roads, and so on, by municipalities.[187]

---

185 See, in Prince Edward Island, s. 7; in Ontario, s. 8; in B.C., s. 6; in Nova Scotia, s. 9; and in Manitoba, s. 6. There is no provision in the Alberta Act. See *Zavaglia v. Maq Hldg. Ltd.* (1986), 6 B.C.L.R. (2d) 286 (C.A.).

186 See, however, *Lewis (Guardian and litem of) v. British Columbia* (1997), 153 D.L.R. (4th) 594, 40 C.C.L.T. 153 (S.C.C.), which holds that although the Occupiers' Liability Act, R.S.B.C. 1996, c. 337, s. 8 states that the Act does not apply to the Crown as an occupier of a public highway, it does not exempt the Crown from its duty with respect to repairing and maintaining highways, or reduce its common law duty. In other words, the issue of the Crown's liability for failing to repair or maintain highways must be considered without regard to the provision of the Occupier's Liability Act.

187 See, in Manitoba, ss. 8, 9; in British Columbia, s. 8; in Ontario, s. 10; in Prince Edward Island, s. 9; in Nova Scotia, ss. 11, 12; and in Alberta, ss. 4, 16. In *Larson v. Thunder Bay (City)* (2000), 132 O.A.C. 376 (C.A.), leave to appeal refused (2001), 147 O.A.C. 199 (note) (S.C.C.), the Act applied to the municipality's control over a walkway leading to a sports complex. The court decided that the walkway was not a sidewalk under the Municipal Act, which would have required "gross negligence" as opposed to the lower standard under the Occupiers' Liability Act. There is debate as to whether the federal Crown is bound by the legislation. See *Suche v. R.* (1987), 37 D.L.R. (4th) 474 (Fed. T.D.), affirmed (1988), 54 D.L.R. (4th) 384 (Fed. C.A.), where it was held that the Crown is not bound, and *Stuart v. Can.* (1988), 45 C.C.L.T. 290 (Fed. T.D.), where it was held that the Crown is bound. One must also keep in mind that when dealing with the liability of public authorities, the issue as to the applicable standard of care might arise. See, for example, *Vannan (Guardian ad litem of) v. Kamloops (City)*, [1992] 2 W.W.R. 759 (B.C. S.C.) and *Young v. A.G. Nfld.* (1993), 112 Nfld. & P.E.I.R. 245 (Nfld. C.A.), and discussion in Chapter 8.

16
Strict Liability

1. INTRODUCTION

Liability for injuries caused by non-negligent conduct can be termed strict liability. An individual will be said to be strictly liable when held liable for an injury caused, despite the fact that reasonable care was exercised in attempting to prevent it.

Strict liability, as a basis of liability, is relatively insignificant in contemporary tort law. It is clearly somewhat at odds with the values and objectives of fault-based compensation to hold a person liable for faultless behaviour. Different goals and values, other than the traditional ones associated with tort law, such as deterrence, education, and the punishment of wrongdoers, the creation of acceptable standards of conduct, and the assertion of the moral principle of the accountability of wrongdoers, must be advanced in support of strict liability. There are strong advocates of strict liability as a basis of tort liability.[1] Nevertheless, liability without fault[2] is the exception, and not the rule, in contemporary tort law.

The relative insignificance of strict liability can be explained by the growth and fluidity of the negligence law principle itself. Not content to merely allow negligence law to occupy a reasonably sized middle ground between strict liability torts at one end and intentional torts at the other, courts have nurtured negligence law, so much so that it now occupies most of the available space. There has been little room, and less need, for the development of strict liability torts. Most

---

1 See, for example, the work of Epstein, especially *A Theory of Strict Liability: Toward a Reformulation of Tort Law* (1980), whose principal thrust is that tort liability should, for ideological reasons, be based upon causation. Alternatively, others argue for strict liability based upon economic theory: see, for example, Calabresi and Hirschoff, "Toward a Test for Strict Liability in Torts" (1972), 81 Yale L.J. 1055. There are, of course, strong critiques of these works. See Weinrib, "Toward a Moral Theory of Negligence Law" (1983), 2 Law and Philosophy 37; and Perry, "The Impossibility of General Strict Liability" (1988), Can. J. of Law And Jurisprudence 147. In Honore, "Responsibility and Luck" (1988), 104 L.Q.R. 530, strict liability is defended upon the grounds that persons should be responsible for the outcomes of their choices.

2 Which is, of course, fault as defined by negligence law, whether or not this corresponds to everyone's satisfaction with moral fault. See, e.g., Glasbeek and Hasson, "Fault — The Great Hoax" in Klar (ed.), *Studies in Canadian Tort Law* (1977), Chapter 14.

accidentally caused injuries which merit compensation have been comfortably encompassed by the welcoming arms of negligence law.[3]

This chapter will examine the principal areas of strict liability in tort; namely, the rule in *Rylands v. Fletcher*,[4] liability for fires, and liability regarding animals. It will also discuss the concept of vicarious liability.

2. THE PRINCIPLE OF *RYLANDS v. FLETCHER*

(a) Introduction

Strict liability in contemporary tort law principally stems from the judgments of Blackburn J. and Lord Cairns in the classic case of *Rylands v. Fletcher*.[5] The facts of this case are as follows.[6] The defendants, Rylands and Horrocks, respectively the owner and manager of a textile mill, received permission from the Earl of Wilton to construct a reservoir, which was necessary to provide water for their mill, on land owned by the Earl. They hired an engineer and contractors for this project, and the reservoir was completed. In close proximity to the reservoir and mill, and also on lands owned by Lord Wilton, were the coal mining operations of the plaintiff, Fletcher. The problem occurred when water in the reservoir, which had been constructed in ground where unused blocked vertical mining shafts were located, burst into one of these shafts. These unused shafts were connected to the underground workings of Fletcher's active operations, and as a result, Fletcher's mine was flooded. Fletcher sued both Rylands and Horrocks, framing his action in negligence.

It is generally agreed that an innovative judgment was required from the judges if the plaintiff was to succeed on these facts.[7] Neither negligence,[8] nuisance,[9] nor

---

3 See Picard J. in *Acheson v. Dory* (1993), 138 A.R. 241 (Q.B.), affirmed (1994), 157 A.R. 187 (C.A.). In this case, rather than resorting to strict liability in an animal injury case, the court utilized the "more modern and flexible parameters" of negligence law.

4 (1868), L.R. 3 H.L. 330, affirming (1866) L.R. 1 Ex. 265.

5 There is extensive literature on this case. Legal historians have found it to be an especially fascinating study. See, e.g., Heuston, "Judges and Judgments in Torts" (1986), 20 U.B.C. L. Rev. 33; Simpson, "Legal Liability for Bursting Reservoirs: The Historical Context of *Rylands v. Fletcher*" (1984), 13 J. Leg. Stud. 209; and Spencer, "Motor-Cars and the Rule in *Rylands v. Fletcher*" (1983), 42 Cambridge L.J. 65.

6 The history of the event and the litigation are described by Simpson, *ibid*.

7 Although it must be noted that it has been argued that "the legal principle which underlies the decision in *Rylands v. Fletcher* was well known in English law from a very early period, but it was explained and formulated in a strikingly clear and authoritative manner in that case and therefore is usually referred to by that name." See Lord Moulton in *Rickards v. Lothian*, [1913] A.C. 263 (P.C.).

8 The defendants themselves had not been negligent, the contractors were not sued, and there would have been no vicarious liability for the acts of independent contractors. It has been suggested, for example, by Sellers J. in *Dunne v. North Western Gas Bd.*, [1964] 2 Q.B. 806 (C.A.), that, in contemporary tort law, the defendants would have been liable in negligence for their failure to take reasonable care to protect adjacent mines which were known to be there or which ought to have been discovered with reasonable care, and that it would be no answer to them to say that this was the independent contractor's failure.

9 The interference with the use of the plaintiff's mines was not a continuous interference, but a one-time affair, which, at that time, seemed to rule out nuisance. See the judgments of Pollock C.B. and Martin B. in the Court of Exchequer. Also see Windeyer J.'s judgment in *Benning v. Wong* (1969), 122 C.L.R. 249 at 296 (Aust. H.C.). Nuisance would now be an available remedy. See Chapter 18. Note as well the view that *Rylands v. Fletcher* was really only "a simple case

trespass[10] seemed to fit.[11]

The judgments in the case which formulated the principle of *Rylands v. Fletcher* are those of Blackburn J., in the Court of Exchequer Chamber, and Lord Cairns, on appeal to the House of Lords. It is the difference in the wording used by these two justices, in defining the conditions necessary to invoke the principle of *Rylands v. Fletcher*, which has been responsible for creating much of the subsequent debate concerning the principle's proper application.[12]

Blackburn J. articulated the principle of *Rylands v. Fletcher* in the following terms:

> . . . the person who for his own purposes brings on his lands and collects and keeps there anything likely to do mischief if it escapes, must keep it in at his peril, and if he does not do so, is *prima facie* answerable for all the damage which is the natural consequence of its escape. He can excuse himself by shewing that the escape was owing to the plaintiff's default; or perhaps that the escape was the consequence of *vis major*, or the act of God.[13]

It is evident from this passage, as well as from other parts of Blackburn J.'s judgment, that it was principally the hazardous nature of the defendant's activity, in terms of its potential damage to neighbouring land occupiers, that led Blackburn J. to formulate a standard of strict liability for these types of activities.[14] The principle was not only clear but commendable. Those who engage for their own benefit in highly dangerous, although lawful, activities ought to bear the accident costs of these activities. It is an early theory of enterprise liability, which certainly has its modern day adherents.

In the House of Lords, the focus changed slightly and a new element was added. Although upholding Blackburn J., Lord Cairns drew a different distinction, not between dangerous and ordinarily safe activities, but between the natural and non-natural uses of land. In this respect, Lord Cairns was clear. The non-natural use of land involved the introduction onto the land of something that in the land's natural condition was not there. For example, the distinction was drawn between water which was on land as a result of natural gravitation, and water which had been brought there by the land owner.[15] Although the dangers from both would be the same, strict liability would apply only to the non-natural use. New questions thus arose. Would the principle be restricted to activities which not only bring

---

of nuisance" all along. See Newark, "The Boundaries of Nuisance" (1949), 65 L.Q.R. 480 at 488. Also see *Danku v. Fort Frances (Mun.)* (1976), 73 D.L.R. (3d) 377 at 381 (Ont. Dist. Ct.), where it stated that "it seems generally accepted that the rule in *Rylands v. Fletcher* is probably no more than a specialized form of nuisance restricted to cases involving the user of land and the escape of some substance accumulated thereon".

10 The interference was indirect. Moreover, there was no wrongdoing.

11 Simpson's account of the various judgments indicates that the judges considered these other causes of action, and disagreed between themselves concerning their applicability. See Simp son, above, note 5, at 243.

12 Although it is interesting to note that in a New Zealand case, *A.G. v. Geothermal Produce N.Z. Ltd.*, [1987] 2 N.Z.L.R. 348 (C.A.), Mr. Justice Cook states that Blackburn J.'s judgment "has hardly been taken seriously by modern English Courts", all the attention having been focussed on Lord Cairns' non-natural use requirement.

13 (1866), L.R. 1 Ex. 265 at 279.

14 For example, Blackburn J. talked about things which were dangerous, mischievous if they escape, and drew analogies to filth, fumes and noisome vapours, the vicious propensity of certain beasts, the damage done by trespassing cattle, and so on. These activities are unusual, not in terms of their unique character *per se*, but in terms of their potential for damage.

15 By reference to the case of *Baird v. Williamson* (1863), 15 C.B. (N.S.) 376.

increased risks to others, but are as well unusual or special in respect of their frequency, or novelty? Would ordinary, albeit risky activities, be subject to the principle of *Rylands v. Fletcher*, or the ordinary principles of negligence law?

The treatment by subsequent courts of the judgments in *Rylands v. Fletcher* has reflected ambiguity concerning the purpose of the principle of *Rylands v. Fletcher*. Unlike negligence law and other specific tort actions whose objectives have been relatively clear, enabling courts to reach decisions in individual disputes by reference to them, the same cannot be said with respect to the principle of *Rylands v. Fletcher*. Too frequently, the principle, with its various requirements, has been applied almost mechanically, cases being resolved by focussing on the specific elements articulated in the initial judgments, without adequate consideration being given to the purpose of the principle. *Rylands v. Fletcher* has been applied at some times as the basis for a common law theory of liability for ultrahazardous or dangerous activities,[16] and at other times as a narrow and quite inconsequential principle of liability to regulate the activities of neighbouring land occupiers in rather unique situations. As well, it must be recognized from the outset that, in the large majority of the cases, discussion of the principle of *Rylands v. Fletcher* has been unnecessary, the courts being able to adequately resolve disputes by the application of the ordinary principles of negligence or nuisance law.[17]

(b) Non-Natural Use

The non-natural use requirement introduced by Lord Cairns into Blackburn J.'s formula of strict liability has been the most troublesome aspect of the *Rylands v. Fletcher* principle. The meaning given to this concept has determined how important a role *Rylands v. Fletcher* has played in the resolution of tort disputes.[18]

The non-natural use requirement has been defined in a broad and in a more narrow manner. More broadly, a non-natural use has been seen as any use which introduces special dangers to the neighbourhood, the accident costs of which ought to be borne by the person who is conducting, and in most cases, profiting from the use. More narrowly, a non-natural use has been defined as a use which is not only hazardous, but also unusual or special, in the sense that it is not one ordinarily conducted on land.

The case of *Rickards v. Lothian*[19] indicated that, for the English courts at least, the principle of *Rylands v. Fletcher* would be given a narrow, more restricted interpretation. The case involved a plugged basin in the lavatory of a commercial building. Water overflowed from the basin, and caused damage to the stock-in-trade belonging to the plaintiff, who occupied a lower space in the building. One

---

16 See Linden, "Whatever Happened to *Rylands v. Fletcher*"? in Klar (ed.), *Studies in Canadian Tort Law* (1977), at 325.

17 A very thorough review of the evolving meaning of the elements of the "rule" is found in *Burnie Port Authority v. General Jones Pty. Ltd.* (1994), 120 A.L.R. 42 (H.C.). The Court ultimately decided that "ordinary negligence has encompassed and overlain the territory in which the rule in *Ryland v. Fletcher* operates".

18 See the list of cases in Rainaldi (ed.), *Remedies in Tort*, Vol. 3 (1988), at 21-20. Also see Linden and Feldthusen, *Canadian Tort Law*, 8th ed. (2006), at 532-537. See Newark, "Non-Natural User and *Rylands v. Fletcher*" (1961), 24 Mod. L. Rev. 557.

19 [1913] A.C. 263 (P.C.).

of the reasons used by the court to reject the application of *Rylands v. Fletcher* to the facts of this case was expressed by Lord Moulton in the following terms:

> The provision of a proper supply of water to the various parts of a house is not only reasonable, but has become, in accordance with modern sanitary views, an almost necessary feature of town life. It is recognized as being so desirable in the interests of the community that in some form or other it is usually made obligatory in civilized countries. . . . In having on his premises such means of supply he is only using those premises in an ordinary and proper manner, and, although he is bound to exercise all reasonable care, he is not responsible for damage not due to his own default, whether that damage be caused by inevitable accident or the wrongful acts of third persons.[20]

This was a clear rejection of an enterprise theory of liability. The potential of the principle of *Rylands v. Fletcher* becoming a vehicle to spread the costs of socially useful and desirable, but dangerous, activities was severely restricted by this approach. The removal of the strict liability principle from activities which are ordinary or socially useful has had a limiting effect on the growth of *Rylands v. Fletcher*.[21]

The Canadian case of *Tock v. St. John's Metro. Area Bd.*[22] supports the narrow approach. The case involved the flooding of the plaintiffs' home as a result of an obstructed storm sewer system, during an exceptionally heavy rain storm. Both the Newfoundland Court of Appeal[23] and the Supreme Court of Canada held that the operation of public sewerage and drainage systems did not constitute a non-natural use of land, and was not subject to the principle of *Rylands v. Fletcher*. Mr. Justice La Forest's rejection of the principle of strict liability was based upon the fact that these systems "are an indispensable part of the infrastructures necessary to support urban life," and are "ordinary and proper for the general benefit of the community."[24] Consideration was not paid to the dangers presented by this use.[25]

There have been many other cases in which the principle of *Rylands v. Fletcher* has not been applied because the defendant's use of the land, although dangerous, was normal. In *St. Anne's Well Brewery Co. v. Roberts*,[26] Scrutton L.J. refused to

---

20 *Ibid.*, at 281-82.

21 For a similar Canadian case involving a leaky toilet tank, see *Guerard Furniture Co. v. Horton* (1978), 90 D.L.R. (3d) 379 (B.C. Co. Ct.). The issue of what constitutes a "non-natural" use of land was revisited by the House of Lords in *Cambridge Water Co. v. Eastern Counties Leather plc.*, [1994] 1 All E.R. 53. Although the case was decided upon another ground, Lord Goff implied that the "general benefit of the community" exception should not be interpreted too broadly. He held, in an *obiter dictum*, that the storage of chemicals in substantial quantities and their use in an industrial process was not a natural use of land, even though the factory employed many persons in the community.

22 (1989), 64 D.L.R. (4th) 620 (S.C.C.).

23 (1986), 40 C.C.L.T. 55 (Nfld. C.A.).

24 (1989), 64 D.L.R. (4th) 620 at 638.

25 A case applying *Tock* is *Ratko v. Woodstock (City) Public Utility Commission* (1994), 111 D.L.R. (4th) 375 (Ont. Div. Ct.). See also *Gambo (Town) v. Dwyer* (1990), 82 Nfld. & P.E.I.R. 232 (Nfld. T.D.), where the same reasoning was used to find that drainage ditches were not non-natural uses of land. A more recent case supporting this approach is *John Campbell Law Corp. v. Strata Plan 1350* (2001), 8 C.C.L.T. (3d) 226 (B.C. S.C.). There was reference to other similar judgments, including *Stachniak v. Thorhild No. 7 (County)* (2001), [2001] A.J. No. 423, 2001 CarswellAlta 411 (Prov. Ct.); and *McKellar v. Saint John (City)* (1997), 189 N.B.R. (2d) 49 (Q.B.), reversed (1998), 196 N.B.R. (2d) 393 (C.A.).

26 (1928), 140 L.T. 1 (C.A.).

apply the principle to a case where a brick wall fell and completely demolished the plaintiff's inn, since the principle was said not to apply "to the normal use of land."[27] And, in this respect, "one of the most normal uses of land . . . is to put buildings on it."[28] A clear articulation of this approach to the *Rylands v. Fletcher* principle can be found in *Gertsen v. Metro. Toronto*.[29] The case involved the explosion of methane gas, which had been created by the decomposition of organic material deposited on a land-fill site. Despite the admittedly dangerous nature of the substance, Lerner J. explained:

> When the use of the element or thing which the law regards as the potential source of mischief is an accepted incident of some ordinary purpose to which land is reasonably applied by the occupier, the *prima facie* rule of absolute responsibility for the consequences of its escape must give way. In applying this qualification, the Courts have looked not only to the thing or activity in isolation, but also to the place and manner in which it is maintained and its relation to its surroundings. Time, place and circumstance, not excluding purpose, are most material. The distinction between natural and non-natural user is both relative and capable of adjustment to the changing patterns of social existence. . . .[30]

The argument that a *Rylands v. Fletcher* activity must be not only dangerous, but unusual as well, has been the basis of its rejection in numerous cases; for example, those dealing with domestic and industrial fires,[31] domestic gas appliances,[32] and even explosives.[33] One can hardly contend that these activities are not unusually hazardous. They are, however, in other respects, not unusual activities. The issue was addressed squarely in *Smith v. Widdicombe*.[34] Was a scrub fire, deliberately set on a farmer's land to burn off debris, a non-natural use of land? Having conceded "that fire is a dangerous thing and there is a high risk involved with its use,"[35] the trial judge rejected the application of the *Rylands* principle. The court found that "the action of the defendant was a recognized natural user and act of proper husbandry and so prevalent in the community" that the principle in *Rylands* would not apply.[36]

On the other hand, there have been cases which have supported the broader view and where the non-natural use requirement has focussed primarily on the dangerous nature of the use in question without regard to whether it is usual or not. This can be illustrated by *Metson v. R.W. DeWolfe Ltd.*[37] The plaintiff's domestic water supply became contaminated when animal manure which the

---

27 *Ibid.*, at 6.

28 *Ibid.*

29 (1973), 2 O.R. (2d) 1 (H.C.).

30 *Ibid.*, at 19-20, also referring to Fleming, *The Law of Torts*, 4th ed. (1971), at 283. The trial judge considered this to be a non-natural use.

31 E.g., *Dudek v. Brown* (1980), 124 D.L.R. (3d) 629 (Ont. H.C.); *Maron v. Baert & Siguaw Dev. Ltd.* (1981), 126 D.LR. (3d) 9 (Alta. Q.B.).

32 E.g., *O'Neill v. Esquire Hotels Ltd.* (1972), 30 D.L.R. (3d) 589 (N.B. C.A.).

33 *Peitrzak v. Rocheleau*, [1928] 2 D.L.R. 46 (Alta. C.A.). See Rainaldi (ed.), *Remedies in Tort*, Vol. 3 (1988), at 21-26.

34 (1987), 39 C.C.L.T. 98 (Man. Q.B.), affirmed [1987] 6 W.W.R. 687 (Man. C.A.).

35 39 C.C.L.T. 98 at 105.

36 *Ibid.*, at 116. The court cited other supporting cases, including a B.C. case, *Dahler v. Bruvold*, [1981] 5 W.W.R. 706 (B.C. S.C.). See also *Modern Livestock Ltd. v. Elgersma* (1989), 50 C.C.L.T. 5 (Alta. Q.B.), for support of the narrow approach.

37 (1980), 14 C.C.L.T. 216 (N.S. T.D.). See Irvine, "Case Comment", at 14 C.C.L.T. 225.

defendant had spread on his agricultural fields was washed by heavy rains into the plaintiff's well. Despite the fact that the court conceded that the defendant's activity was "normal agricultural husbandry," it applied the principle of *Rylands v. Fletcher* to it. In another agricultural case, *Cruise v. Niessen*,[38] the principle was applied to the aerial spraying of herbicides. In arriving at this decision, the trial judge conceded that the aerial spraying of herbicides was not an unusual operation. It was, in fact, "standard good farming management on cereal growing farms."[39] However, as stated by Solomon J.:

> It is not the aerial application that makes the user of herbicide liable for damages, it is the action of allowing the herbicide, a dangerous substance, to escape beyond the boundaries of his own property that makes the user liable for damage to neighbours' crops. . . . The aerial type of spraying is much more likely to result in an escape of herbicide beyond the boundaries of the land being sprayed and that is why it is considered more dangerous.[40]

Perhaps the most unusual case, however, is that of *Chu v. Dawson*.[41] In this case, earth which had been dug from the defendant's land and deposited on the boundaries of his lot overlooking a ravine became saturated with water and slid down the banks of the ravine onto houses lying below. Despite the fact that this was conceded to have been an ordinary use of land, something which many people situated as were the defendants had done, the trial judge adopted the test of increased danger, and declared the use to be non-natural.[42] These cases illustrate that the strict liability principle can be used to shift the costs of dangerous activities to those who profit from them.[43]

There have been several other cases where *Rylands v. Fletcher* has been applied to dangerous, although entirely usual and beneficial, activities. Perhaps the natural gas explosion cases provide the best examples of these. It surely must be conceded that the use of natural gas for heating is a beneficial and ordinary activity. Nevertheless, some courts have not hesitated in applying the principle of *Rylands v. Fletcher* in this area.[44]

---

38 (1977), 2 C.C.L.T. 53 (Man. Q.B.), reversed on other grounds (1978), 4 C.C.L.T. 58 (Man. C.A.). For a more recent case applying *Rylands v. Fletcher* to damage caused by herbicide drift, see *Fondrick v. Gross* (2003), [2004] 6 W.W.R. 367 (Sask. Q.B.).

39 2 C.C.L.T. 53 at 57.

40 *Ibid.*, at 57-58. See Klar, "Annotation", 2 C.C.L.T. 53.

41 (1984), 31 C.C.L.T. 146 (B.C. C.A.), affirming (1982), 21 C.C.L.T. 228 (*sub nom. Chu v. North Vancouver*) (B.C. S.C.).

42 More interesting, perhaps, was the fact that the "object" which slipped was of course not brought to the land by the defendants; it was not something "not naturally there." The trial judge noted that its placement on the land was non-natural. The Court of Appeal affirmed the trial judgment.

43 Although it has been argued that this approach ignores the non-natural use requirement, by treating all objects which are dangerous as non-natural. The non-natural use requirement simply reiterates the requirement that the object be one which is likely to do mischief if it escapes. See Irvine, "Case Comment" (1980), 14 C.C.L.T. 225."Another unusual case is *Calgary (City) v. Yellow Submarine Deli Inc.* (1994), 158 A.R. 239 (Prov. Ct.), which held that an advertising balloon which escaped and damaged transmission wires fell under *Rylands v. Fletcher*.

44 See *Northwestern Utilities Ltd. v. London Guar. & Accident Co.*, [1936] A.C. 108 (P.C.), and *Fenn v. Peterborough (City)* (1979), 9 C.C.L.T. 1 (Ont. C.A.), affirmed (*sub nom. Consumers' Gas Co. v. Fenn*) (1981), 18 C.C.L.T. 258 (S.C.C.). The same can be said about the water leaking cases. See, e.g., *Wei's Western Wear v. Yui Hldg. Ltd.* (1983), 27 C.C.L.T. 292 (Alta.

What conclusions can be drawn from the case law? What is a non-natural use? It must be conceded that, at this point in time, there is no clear answer. For some courts, the *Rylands v. Fletcher* principle has opened the way to a common law rule of strict liability for dangerous activities. Others have been more resistent to this and have used the non-natural use requirement to restrict *Rylands v. Fletcher* to marginal, and unusual, activities. There are difficulties of interpretation within each approach. If strict liability is applicable to dangerous activities, how does one draw the line between dangerous and safe activities? If strict liability is restricted to unusual activities, how are these to be defined? It must be conceded that, even after almost a century and a quarter, the non-natural use requirement remains as vague as ever.

(c) Escape

The second requirement of *Rylands v. Fletcher* is that the object escape from the defendant's land.

If the principle of *Rylands v. Fletcher* is seen as a narrow doctrine governing disputes between neighbouring land owners, the escape requirement is meaningful. Individuals must not allow the non-natural and dangerous use of their land to damage neighbouring properties. Most of the cases to which the principle of *Rylands v. Fletcher* has been applied have satisfactorily met this escape requirement.

The question of a wider use of *Rylands v. Fletcher* as a principle of strict liability for dangerous activities is raised, however, where there has been no escape. For example, can strict liability apply when a dangerous activity conducted on the defendant's land injures another person while present on the defendant's land? Is this a case for strict liability or does the reasonable care standard of occupiers' liability apply?[45]

In the well-known English case of *Read v. J. Lyons & Co.*,[46] the House of Lords gave a restricted role to *Rylands v. Fletcher*. The plaintiff, an inspector at a munitions factory,[47] was injured on the work site by an exploding shell. Although the trial judge had applied the principle of strict liability,[48] this judgment was reversed by the Court of Appeal.[49] The thorough judgment of Scott L.J. clearly accepted the narrow view of the principle of *Rylands v. Fletcher*. It is, according to His Lordship, a principle limited

> to the case where the escaping water gets out of the defendant's land, and on to the plaintiff's land and there does damage . . . The vital feature in *Rylands v. Fletcher* which gave the plaintiff his cause of action was the defendant's interference with the plaintiff's right to enjoy his land without interference by the defendant.[50]

Q.B.). A case which held that gasoline escaping from a gasoline bar came under *Rylands v. Fletcher* is *Bisson v. Brunette Holdings Ltd.* (1993), 15 C.E.L.R. (N.S.) 201 (Ont. Gen. Div.), additional reasons at (1994), 15 C.E.L.R. (N.S.) 201 at 219 (Ont. Gen. Div.).

45 As we have seen, occupiers' liability legislation permits higher or more onerous duties being placed upon occupiers by other rules of law. See Chapter 15.

46 [1946] 2 All E.R. 471 (H.L.).

47 The plaintiff was not employed by the factory but by the Crown.

48 [1944] 2 All E.R. 98.

49 [1945] 1 All E.R. 106.

50 *Ibid.*, at 115.

Escape is thus essential to this concept, one which is narrow and not capable of extension to a wider principle of strict liability for ultrahazardous activities.[51] In the House of Lords, this position was strongly reaffirmed. According to Viscount Simon, this case fell to be decided by the duty imposed by occupiers' liability principles. Escape was seen as being essential to the invocation of the principle of *Rylands v. Fletcher* and was defined as "escape from a place which the defendant has occupation of, or control over, to a place which is outside his occupation or control."[52] Lord MacMillan explained that the *Rylands* principle derived "from a conception of the mutual duties of adjoining or neighbouring landowners and its congeners are trespass and nuisance."[53] Lord Simonds expressly rejected a doctrine of strict liability for ultrahazardous activities, where there was no escape.[54] Lord Uthwatt reiterated the narrow view of *Rylands v. Fletcher*, as a case not "laying down any principle other than a principle applicable between occupiers in respect of their lands" and not "reflecting an aspect of some wider principle applicable to dangerous businesses or dangerous things."[55] This view was reaffirmed by Lord Goff for the House of Lords in *Cambridge Water Co. v. Eastern Counties Leather plc.*[56] Rather than the common law developing a general theory of strict liability for ultrahazardous activities, Lord Goff's view was that this was a matter best left to Parliament.

Although never as clearly in issue, Canadian courts generally have required an escape for purposes of a *Rylands* application.[57] However, the escape requirement has been relaxed, especially when compared to the stringent interpretation given to it in *Read v. Lyons*.[58] An escape of gas or water, running through pipes under

---

51 MacKinnon L.J. notes in his judgment that "escape" and "escaping" are repeated 10 times in Blackburn J.'s judgment, and repeated in other terms throughout the judgment. *Ibid.*, at 117.

52 [1946] 2 All E.R. 471 at 474.

53 *Ibid.*, at 477. His Lordship also stated that the doctrine "is truly a case on the mutual obligations of owners or occupiers of neighbouring closes . . .", at 478.

54 *Ibid.*, at 481.

55 *Ibid.*, at 484. In another English case, *Rigby v. Chief Constable of Northamptonshire*, [1985] 2 All E.R. 985 (Q.B.D.), the fact that a gas cannister was thrown by police from the highway into a store was not, on account of this, seen as denying the application of the *Rylands* principle. For, as stated by Taylor J. at 996:

> I can see no difference in principle between allowing a man-eating tiger to escape from your land onto that of another and allowing it to escape from the back of your wagon parked on the highway.

56 [1994] 1 All E.R. 53.

57 See, e.g., *Maron v. Baert & Siguaw Dev. Ltd.* (1981), 126 D.L.R. (3d) 9 at 17 (Alta. Q.B.); *Seneka v. Leduc* (1985), 59 A.R. 284 at 289 (Q.B.); and *Blyth (Village) v. G.L Hubbard Ltd.* (1997) 29 O.T.C. 283 (Gen. Div.). In *Hoffman v. Monsanto Canada Inc.*, [2005] 7 W.W.R. 665 (Q.B.), leave to appeal allowed (2005), 2005 CarswellSask 572 (C.A. [In Chambers]), affirmed (2007), 283 D.L.R. (4th) 190 (Sask. C.A.), leave to appeal refused (2007), 2007 CarswellSask 725 (S.C.C.), a *Rylands v. Fletcher* claim brought against manufacturers of genetically modified seeds by organic farmers who claimed that the seeds had escaped from the fields of conventional farmers onto their fields was struck out. The trial judge held that there was no escape from lands owned or controlled by the defendant manufacturers. Also see *Brooks v. Canadian Pacific Railway*, [2007] 11 W.W.R. 436 (Sask. Q.B.) to the same effect. There was a train derailment resulting in train cars carrying anhydrous ammonia tipping over. The gaseous substance did not escape from either the cars or the railroad's property. Because of this the court held that the principle of *Rylands v. Fletcher* did not apply.

58 Above, note 46.

public streets, or stored in underground tanks, for example, has frequently been satisfactory for the application of the *Rylands* principle.[59]

Another interesting question has been raised in the cases in relation to the escape requirement. Does the principle of *Rylands v. Fletcher* apply to the situation of intentional discharges of dangerous substances, or must the escape be inadvertent or careless for the application of its principle? One would have thought that an individual who is strictly liable for the inadvertent escape of a dangerous substance should be held strictly liable when that same substance is intentionally released. Curiously, however, in two cases, the opposite opinion was offered. In *North York v. Kert Chem. Indust.*,[60] which involved the deliberate discharge of acidic wastes into a sewer system, Mr. Justice Krever suggested that the principle of *Rylands v. Fletcher* "may not be entirely appropriate for a case in which the discharges of the offending substances were intentional."[61] Similarly, in *Rigby v. Chief Constable of Northamptonshire*,[62] the court was inclined to agree with the defendant's argument that the doctrine did not apply to the intentional, and direct, as opposed to the accidental, and indirect, release of a gas cannister into a building. Although the question as to whether the *Rylands* principle applied to these two incidences was academic, since in both cases the intentional discharges were actionable in negligence,[63] the point raised is an interesting one, going to the foundation of the principle of *Rylands v. Fletcher*. As a narrow principle of strict liability for innocent but damaging uses of land by neighbours, the requirement of an accidental release is explicable. As a wider principle of strict liability for dangerous activities, it is not.[64]

(d) Anything Likely to Do Mischief

The principle of *Rylands v. Fletcher* applies only to things likely to do mischief if they escape. The importance of this requirement depends upon the court's interpretation of the non-natural use requirement. If a non-natural use is one which must be dangerous or hazardous, the requirement that the thing be likely to do mischief if it escapes is mere surplusage. Dangerous or hazardous uses are, by definition, likely to do mischief. If the more narrow interpretation is ascribed to the non-natural use requirement, that is, any use conducted on land which is not ordinary or common, the mischief requirement becomes meaningful. The principle will apply only to uses which are both unusual and dangerous.[65] In *Schenck*

---

59 Cases include *Doherty v. Allen* (1987), 86 N.B.R. (2d) 361 (Q.B.), affirmed (1988), 55 D.L.R. (4th) 746 (N.B. C.A.); *B.C. Tel. v. Shell Can. Ltd.* (1987), 13 B.C.L.R. (2d) 210 (S.C.); *Adilman's Ltd. v. Bill Boyd's Radio (T.V.) Clinic* (1982), 19 Sask. R. 215 (Q.B.); and *Newell v. R.E. Newell Fisheries Ltd.* (1982), 54 N.S.R. (2d) 652 (T.D.).

60 (1985), 33 C.C.L.T. 184 (Ont. H.C.).

61 *Ibid.*, at 200.

62 Above, note 55.

63 Trespass and nuisance might also have been available.

64 Also interesting was the English court's preoccupation with the correct form of action, *Rylands v. Fletcher* being confined to indirect releases, trespass to direct releases. Will the gains which were made by *Fowler v. Lanning*, [1959] 1 Q.B. 426, and *Letang v. Cooper*, [1965] 1 Q.B. 232 (C.A.), in terms of eliminating the direct and indirect distinction in terms of trespass and negligence, now be lost by resurrecting this distinction for trespass and strict liability?

65 Or, at least, "likely to do mischief if it escapes," even if not inherently dangerous in its natural state.

v. Ont.,[66] for example, salt used to de-ice highways was considered to be a common and normal use in Ontario, and hence, not non-natural. The salt was also considered not to be inherently dangerous nor extrahazardous if it escaped. Thus both requirements were considered separately.

In most cases, the mischief requirement has been ignored. Almost everything is capable of being mischievous in certain circumstances, and where damage has already been caused, it is difficult to deny an activity's damaging propensities.

(e) Type of Compensable Damage

Despite unequivocal *dicta* in *Read v. J. Lyons & Co.*[67] that the principle of *Rylands v. Fletcher* protects only the *proprietary* interests of adjoining land owners and is not applicable to cases of personal injuries, the subsequent jurisprudence has not restricted the principle to property damage claims. There are numerous cases in which the principle has been applied to claims for personal injuries.[68] It would be an undesirable aspect of the common law if one could be held strictly liable for property damage, but not for personal injuries, caused by dangerous activities conducted on land.[69]

(f) Remoteness

In *Cambridge Water Co. v. Eastern Counties Leather plc.*,[70] the House of Lords faced the question of remoteness of damages within the context of a *Rylands v. Fletcher* claim. Over a period of years, the defendant leather manufacturer had allowed a solvent, which it used in its tanning process, to spill onto the concrete floor of its tannery. Several years after the spillage ended, it was discovered that the the water supply used by the plaintiff had been contaminated by the solvent. It appeared that the solvent had been seeping through the tannery floor deep into the soil and had found its way through the ground until it reached the strata from which the plaintiff extracted its water.

Conceding that this was a classic case of non-natural use for the purposes of *Rylands v. Fletcher,* Lord Goff, for the House of Lords, faced the issue of remoteness of damage. The evidence indicated that at the time that the solvent was being spilled, it was not reasonably foreseeable that the solvent would enter the aquifer or, having done so, would contaminate water down-catchment. The only damage foreseeable was that a person might be overcome by fumes if a sufficient quantity of solvent were spilled. This being the case, could this defendant, in a *Rylands v. Fletcher* claim, be liable for the unforeseeable damage of the escaping substance?

---

66 (1981), 20 C.C.L.T. 128 (Ont. H.C.), additional reasons at (1982), 23 C.C.L.T. 147 (Ont. H.C.), affirmed (1985), 49 O.R. (2d) 556 (C.A.), which was affirmed [1987] 2 S.C.R. 289.

67 Above, note 46.

68 See Rainaldi (ed.), *Remedies in Tort*, Vol. 3 (1988), at 21-48.

69 *Rylands v. Fletcher* was applied in a damage to chattels case. In *Richard v. New Brunswick Power Corp.* (1993), 131 N.B.R. (2d) 153 (Q.B.), damage to the finish of the plaintiff's fibreglass sailboat caused by chemical emissions, was dealt with as a case of strict liability. In *Brooks v. CPR*, above, note 57, the fact that the train derailment did not cause any personal injury or property damage, but pure economic losses, was another reason for the court's rejection of *Rylands v. Fletcher*.

70 [1994] 1 All E.R. 53 (H.L.).

The House of Lords answered that it could not. Lord Goff, upon a consideration of the decision in *Rylands v. Fletcher* itself,[71] the law of remoteness as it applies to nuisance,[72] and other authorities which have restricted the application of the principle of *Rylands v. Fletcher*,[73] concluded that "foreseeability of damage of the relevant type should be regarded as a prerequisite of liability in damages under the rule."[74] The main logic behind the introduction of this restriction was the desire to establish a coherent body of law which viewed *Rylands v. Fletcher* "essentially as an extension of the law of nuisance to cases of isolated escapes from land."[75] Hence, foreseeability, already an element of nuisance, should be an element of *Rylands v. Fletcher*.[76]

The decision to require foreseeability of the type of damage further restricts the utility of the *Rylands v. Fletcher* principle. It also introduces into the area the same uncertainties and policy issues which afflict negligence law in relation to the remoteness issue.[77]

3. DEFENCES

Although liability under *Rylands v. Fletcher* is strict, it is not absolute. Defences are admitted. If successful, the defence will relieve the defendant of strict liability. The defendant may still be held liable on some other grounds, however, most frequently for negligence.

(a) Consent

Although not frequently employed, a defendant may be relieved of strict liability if it can be shown that the plaintiff consented to the presence of the non-natural use and agreed to assume the risks presented by it. There is no reason to assume that the courts would be more willing to uphold the defence of consent in the context of strict liability torts than as a defence to negligence. Thus, for the defence of consent to succeed, there ought to be consent to both the physical and legal risks created by the defendant's activity.[78] It must be conceded, however, that as with *volenti* as a defence to negligence, it will be only rarely decided that

---

71 For example, Lord Goff noted that the principle was said to apply to things *likely* to do mischief if they escaped, or things *known* to be mischievous.

72 The judgment contained significant discussion on how nuisance and *Rylands v. Fletcher* interact. On nuisance, see the discussion in Chapter 18.

73 For example, Lord Goff considered the requirement that there be an "escape". According to Lord Goff, this effectively had precluded the development of a general principle in English law of strict liability for ultrahazardous activities.

74 [1994] 1 All E.R. at 76.

75 *Ibid.*

76 It is interesting to note that no reference was made to strict liability for wild animals. As we will discuss, a keeper of a wild animal is strictly liable for damages caused by the animal, even if those damages were not the ordinary ones which could have been anticipated.

77 A Canadian case which approves of the principles of *Cambridge Water Co.* is *Smith Bros. Excavating Windsor Ltd. v. Camion Equipment & Leasing Inc. (Trustee of)* (1994), 21 C.C.L.T. (2d) 113 (Ont. Gen. Div.). The case concerned the escape of methanol from tanks, which contaminated the soil of neighbouring properties. Although foreseeability of damage was not in issue, the court approved of the statements of Lord Goff. The court held that the principle of *Rylands v. Fletcher* applied although the action was dismissed due to lack of damages.

78 See, e.g., *Pattison v. Prince Edward Region Conservation Authority* (1988), 45 C.C.L.T. 162 (Ont. C.A.), affirming (1984), 30 C.C.L.T. 305 (Ont. H.C.), where there was a written consent.

a plaintiff has implicitly consented not only to the existence of the physical risks, but to waive the legal right to compensation should these risks eventuate. One must also add, moreover, that consent to the risks of an accidental escape will not relieve a defendant guilty of negligence.[79]

(b) Act of God, of the Plaintiff or of Strangers

From the outset, it was stated by Blackburn J. that if an escape was due to (1) the plaintiff's own fault, or (2) an act of God, the defendant, otherwise liable on the principle of *Rylands v. Fletcher*, would be excused.[80] As well, the Privy Council, in *Rickards v. Lothian*,[81] added yet a third defence — that of an escape caused by the malicious act of a third person. In view of the modern trend towards apportioning liability and reducing, rather than eliminating, compensation, when the plaintiff or others have contributed to the injuries, one must examine the effect of these three defences on the principle of *Rylands v. Fletcher*.

An act of God has been defined as a natural and extraordinary event which could not have been foreseen by the defendant, even as a possibility, and thus could not have been guarded against.[82] In an Alberta case,[83] the court noted that, with regard to natural events, persons are expected to anticipate not only normal occurrences, but extremes as well, and "when the extremes are ascertained, it must still be contemplated that the extremes may be exceeded."[84] A more liberal view of what constitutes an act of God has been suggested. In *Nichols v. Marsland*,[85] the fact that the defendant could not reasonably have anticipated the extraordinary event was sufficient to establish the defence. Since this, however, imported a concept of fault into liability which is theoretically strict, the more stringent test is preferable.

Whether an act of God should be a defence to a strict liability tort raises a question of policy. Where a defendant has introduced a dangerous substance onto land which escapes due to an unforeseeable natural event should the defendant or an innocent victim bear the loss? As with issues of remoteness of damage within the context of the negligence action,[86] causation language has been used to resolve these policy issues in the strict liability context. It has been argued that where an escape of an offensive substance was brought about as a result of an act of God, the real cause of the escape was that act, and not the defendant's activity.[87] One might usefully apply the principles of intervening cause or *novus actus interveniens* to this issue,[88] and ask whether the possibility of an act of God was

79 See, e.g., *Holinaty v. Hawkins* (1965), 52 D.L.R. (2d) 289 (Ont. C.A.).

80 Blackburn J., in *Rylands v. Fletcher* (1866), L.R. 1 Ex. 265 at 279.

81 [1913] A.C. 263 (P.C.).

82 See *Tennent v. Earl of Glasgow* (1864), 2 Macph. 22; *Greenock v. Glasgow & Southwestern Ry.*, [1917] A.C. 556 (H.L.).

83 *Seneka v. Leduc* (1985), 59 A.R. 284 (Q.B.).

84 *Ibid.*, at 287.

85 (1876), 2 Ex. D. 1 (C.A.).

86 See Chapter 12.

87 See, e.g., *Nichols v. Marsland*, above, note 85, and *Rickards v. Lothian*, above, note 81.

88 This suggestion was made by Windeyer J. in *Benning v. Wong* (1969), 122 C.L.R. 249 at 298 (Aust. H.C.). His Lordship submitted that the defences of act of God, the act of the plaintiff himself, and the act of a third party, displace the liability of the defendant because they are a *novus actus interveniens*.

within the risk created by the defendant's activity. If it ought to have been anticipated by the defendant that an act of God could intervene and cause the escape of the object, the risk of that occurring ought to be borne by the defendant. If, on the other hand, the act of God was so extraordinary as to not have been foreseeable, it was outside the risk, and not the responsibility of the defendant. Although this test is useful, one must emphasize that this area is one governed not by negligence law, but by principles of strict liability. Accordingly, the act of God must have been an extremely remote possibility, before the defence should be accepted. This being the case, the defence is unlikely to succeed in most cases.[89]

The same approach and reasoning can be applied to the defences of fault of the plaintiff and act of strangers. Where the escape of the object was the result of the plaintiff's negligent or even deliberate act, one must ask whether this could be viewed as having been within the risks created by the defendant's activity. If the defendant ought to have anticipated and provided against the occurrence, liability ought to be imposed. In this instance, however, the plaintiff's own fault ought to be considered as contributory, and a reduction of damages would be appropriate. Similarly, where the negligent or malicious act of a stranger resulted in the object's escape, the question whether this was within the risk of the activity must be determined. In *Hale v. Jennings Bros.*,[90] the defendants were held liable when a mechanically operated chair came free from an amusement park ride and struck the plaintiff. The chair had been tampered with by an exuberant rider. Scott L.J. recognized that the inherent dangers of the defendant's activity included the possibility that third parties would not behave properly and disallowed the defence of act of a stranger. In *Perry v. Kendricks Tpt. Ltd.*,[91] on the other hand, the court held that the explosion of petrol in a car's tank was caused not by the defendant's activity in parking the disused coach on its lot, but by the young boy who threw a match into the gas tank. Using the language of remoteness, one can argue that the possibility of the stranger's intervention was not within the risks created by the defendant's activity. Thus it was the stranger's act, and not the defendant's, which was the effective cause of the explosion. Although it has been stated that only the deliberate acts of strangers can qualify for the defence,[92] a court ought not to exonerate the defendant where deliberate acts of strangers were anticipated and within the risks created by the defendant's activity.[93]

If a defendant ought to have reasonably foreseen and guarded against the intervening act, the failure to do so can be considered within the context of the

89 Note, however, that in view of the fact that the House of Lords now has adopted the foreseeability test as a test of remoteness for strict liability, in *Cambridge Water Co. v. Eastern Counties Leather plc.*, above, note 70, it would be consistent with that position to argue that an act of God which is not reasonably foreseeable is a successful defence.

90 [1938] 1 All E.R. 579 (C.A.).

91 [1956] 1 All E.R. 154 (C.A.).

92 See Linden and Feldthusen, *Canadian Tort Law*, 8th ed. (2006), at 548.

93 See *Smith Bros. Excavating Windsor Ltd. v. Camion Equipment & Leasing Inc. (Trustee of)* (1994), 21 C.C.L.T. (2d) 113 (Ont. Gen. Div.). Methane gas escaped from tanks due to the wilful and malicious acts of vandals. The court stated that the "highest standard of care" was required. The defendants failed to prove that they used every effort to avoid the escape, and that they secured their premises by imposing "all known and available security." The action failed, however, due to lack of provable damages.

negligence action as well. It is submitted, however, that in the context of a dangerous activity, the degree of anticipation required of the defendant ought to be significantly higher than in the case of ordinary activities.

(c) Statutory Authority

Since several of the activities encompassed by the principle of *Rylands v. Fletcher* are normally statutorily authorized,[94] the question of the defence of statutory authority has frequently arisen. Should statutorily authorized activities be subject to the rules of strict liability?

As a matter of fairness and economics, there are no reasons to exclude statutorily authorized activities from the principle of *Rylands v. Fletcher*, unless the statute which authorizes the activity so provides.[95] The idea of the principle of *Rylands v. Fletcher* is to require dangerous activities to absorb their own accident costs, while recognizing their utility and lawfulness. Activities authorized by statute for the public's benefit ought not to be treated differently than private profit activities in this respect. There is, in fact, much to be said for the proposition that the costs of statutorily authorized activities ought to be distributed equitably amongst all who benefit from them.

Despite this, the case law has held that activities conducted pursuant to statutory authority are not subject to strict liability.[96] As pointed out by Linden, however, this immunity has been narrowed by several techniques.[97] Courts have strictly construed statutes so as to avoid the immunity, and have distinguished between statutes which merely permit activities as opposed to those which authorize or mandate them.[98] With respect to statutorily authorized activities, the liability issue

---

94 For example, the provision of natural gas, water and electricity, or the running of trains.

95 In *Form-Rite Contracting Ltd. v. Prince George (City)* (1999), 69 B.C.L.R. (3d) 372 (S.C. [In Chambers]), the plaintiff's property was damaged as a result of flooding, due to an alleged malfunctioning of the city's water drainage system. The city relied on s. 288 of the Local Government Act, R.S.B.C. 1996, c. 322, which provides that the city is not liable in an action based on nuisance or *Rylands v. Fletcher* for damage caused directly or indirectly by the breakdown or malfunction of a water drainage system. The court strictly construed this provi sion and held that it only applied if the defendant exercised reasonable care and the malfunction was an inevitable consequence. The court accordingly rejected the defendant's motion for a summary dismissal of the action. As noted below in Chapter 17, Nuisance, there are a number of statutory immunity provisions which protect municipalities from liability from flooding and other types of damage claims.

96 See Linden, "Strict Liability, Nuisance and Legislative Authority" (1966), 4 Osgoode Hall L.J. 196, for an excellent discussion and review of the leading cases. See especially *North western Utilities Ltd. v. London Guar. & Accident Co.*, [1936] A.C. 108 (P.C.); *Green v. Chelsea Waterworks Co.* (1895), 65 L.J.Q.B. 126 (C.A.); *Dunn v. Birmingham Canal Co.* (1872), 27 L.T. 683 (Ex. Ch.); *Benning v. Wong* (1969), 122 C.L.R. 249 (Aust. H.C.); *Allen v. Gulf Oil Refining Ltd.*, [1981] 1 All E.R. 353 (H.L.); and *Tock v. St. John's Metro. Area Bd.* (1989), 64 D.L.R. (4th) 620 (S.C.C.). In the latter case, La Forest J. stated, at 638-39, that "the rule cannot be invoked where a municipality or regional authority, acting under the warrant of statute and pursuant to a planning decision taken in good faith, constructs and operates a sewer and storm drain system in a given locality."

97 See Linden, *ibid.*

98 See, for example, the classic case of *Metro. Asylum v. Hill* (1881), 6 App. Cas. 193 at 213; or *C.P.R. Co. v. Parke*, [1899] A.C. 535 at 544-45 (P.C.). The issue was fully explored by the Supreme Court of Canada in relation to a nuisance action in *Tock v. St. John's Area Metro. Area Bd.*, above, note 96. See discussion in Chapter 18.

has been formally resolved by resorting to strict rules of statutory construction. In this respect, three cardinal rules are said to apply.[99] First, it will not be assumed that a statute has abrogated common law rights of action, without unambiguous and compelling language. Second, the statutory activities in issue must have been expressly authorized or necessarily incidental to the execution of those which were so authorized. Third, a statute only authorizes the careful execution of its activities. These propositions have accordingly led to the conclusion that although a statutory authority cannot be held strictly liable for damage caused by authorized acts, it can be held liable for the negligent performance of these acts. In essence, negligence law,[100] and not strict liability, applies to statutorily authorized activities.

A variant of the defence of statutory authority is the defence of "general benefit of the community." It has been suggested that, apart from the question of the statutory exemption, a local authority is exempt from the principle of *Rylands v. Fletcher* where the use of land "is proper for the general benefit of the community."[101] The argument suggested is that where a public authority conducts an activity for the community's benefit, it has not made a use of the land for its own purposes.[102] This argument has not been generally accepted.[103] The general benefit of the community argument has rather been subsumed into the non-natural use element of the *Rylands v. Fletcher* formulation.[104]

An interesting question concerns the burden of proof, about which two views have been expressed. The first is that a defendant who pleads statutory authority must not only establish all the elements of the defence,[105] but, as well, must prove that the statutory activity was carried out in a careful manner.[106] It has been reasoned that since a statute authorizes only the careful execution of its activities, the defence of statutory authority cannot apply unless it is established by the defendant that the activities were conducted reasonably. A contrary view, how-

99 See Barwick C.J. in *Benning v. Wong* (1969), 122 C.L.R. 249 at 256 (Aust. H.C.). See also Robins J. in *Schenck v. Ont.* (1981), 20 C.C.L.T. 128 (Ont. H.C.), additional reasons at (1982), 23 C.C.L.T. 147 (Ont. H.C.), affirmed (1985), 15 D.L.R. (4th) 320 (Ont. C.A.), which was affirmed (1987), 50 D.L.R. (4th) 384 (S.C.C.).

100 Or perhaps nuisance; see *Tock v. St. John's Metro. Area Bd.*, above, note 96.

101 See Denning L.J. in *Pride of Derby v. Br. Celanese*, [1953] 1 Ch. 149 at 189 (C.A.). See also *Danku v. Fort Frances (Mun.)* (1977), 73 D.L.R. (3d) 377 (Ont. Dist. Ct.).

102 Note that the original formulation of the rule in *Rylands v. Fletcher* referred to a person who "for his own purposes brings on his land."

103 See, e.g., Upjohn J.'s discussion in *Smeaton v. Ilford Corp.*, [1954] 1 All E.R. 923 at 931 (Ch. D.).

104 As was done by La Forest J. in the *Tock* case, above, note 96.

105 For example, that the statute authorized the activity in question.

106 See, e.g., Barwick C.J. and Windeyer J. in *Benning v. Wong*, above, note 99, and the judgment of Lord Wright in *Northwestern Utilities Ltd. v. London Guar. & Accident Co.*, [1936] A.C. 108 (P.C.). In *Benning v. Wong*, Windeyer J. cited several Canadian cases in suppport of this position: *Crossman v. Moncton Elec. & Gas Co.*, [1940] 4 D.L.R. 127 (N.B. C.A.), reversed on other grounds [1941] 4 D.L.R. 433 (S.C.C.); *J.P. Porter v. Bell*, [1955] 1 D.L.R. 62 (N.S. C.A.); *Turpin v. Halifax-Dartmouth Bridge Comm.* (1959), 21 D.L.R. (2d) 623 (N.S. C.A.); and *B.C. Pea Growers Ltd. v. Portage La Prairie* (1963), 43 D.L.R. (2d) 713 (Man. Q.B.), affirmed (1964), 49 D.L.R. (2d) 91 (Man. C.A.), which was affirmed (1966), 54 D.L.R. (2d) 503 (S.C.C.).

ever, also has considerable support.[107] It is submitted that once the defendant's statutory authority has been established, the principle of *Rylands v. Fletcher* does not apply to the case. The plaintiff's action can then only be based on a duty of care in negligence, and in line with ordinary negligence law, the burden of proving the negligence will lie upon the plaintiff. It is submitted that one cannot argue that strict liability applies to statutory activities subject to the defence of reasonable care.

The weight of the authorities, including the Canadian cases, support the view that a defendant who pleads statutory authority must prove that the activity was conducted with care.[108] It has also been suggested[109] that the degree of care required by the defendant is very high. This is consistent with the ordinary measurement of the standard of care, which requires that the care taken be commensurate with the possible risks. In the area of dangerous activities, one can expect that the highest standard of care will be required.

4. LIABILITY FOR FIRES

(a) Introduction

Although sometimes considered simply as an aspect of the strict liability principle of *Rylands v. Fletcher*, the law concerning the liability for damage caused by fires is a distinct and somewhat complicated area of tort law.[110] Not only does the topic have a long and interesting judicial and legislative history, but even today different remedies seem to be available to a person damaged by a fire which emanated from a neighbouring property.

As with most other personal injury and property damage claims, negligence law dominates the question of liability for fires. The ordinary principles of negligence law will apply to all fire cases, and the highly dangerous nature of fire will always ensure that a high standard of care will be imposed on defendants. It will usually be unnecessary, therefore, for plaintiffs to seek more stringent tort liability rules to succeed in fire damage claims.

In addition to negligence law, nuisance law will also be available to plaintiffs in some fire or smoke damage cases. As will be discussed,[111] negligent conduct is not a necessary element of the nuisance action. This will assist plaintiffs in some situations.

This section will briefly examine the strict liability aspect of the fire liability issue. The principle of *Rylands v. Fletcher* will be available in some cases of fire

107 See, e.g., the judgments of Menzies J. and Owen J., in *Benning v. Wong, ibid.*, and the numerous cases cited by them to suppport their positions.

108 See Rainaldi (ed.), *Remedies in Tort*, Vol. 3 (1988), Chapter 21, for several case references.

109 See Linden and Feldthusen, *Canadian Tort Law*, 8th ed. (2006), at 551; Fleming, *The Law of Torts*, 9th ed. (1998), at 390.

110 See Ogus, "Vagaries in Liability for the Escape of Fire", [1969] Cambridge L.J. 104. Ogus refers to Winfield's description of liability for the escape of fire as "confusing medleys of remedies for the same wrong." See also Fleming, *ibid.*, Chapter 17; Irvine, "Annotation" (1986), 35 C.C.L.T. 307. An excellent historical review is provided by the Australian High Court judgment in *Burnie Port Authority v. General Jones Pty. Ltd.* (1994), 120 A.L.R. 42 (H.C.) at 45 and following.

111 See Chapter 18.

damage. As well, more stringent principles of common law liability for fire damage may assist plaintiffs in other cases.

(b) Special Action on the Case

The early common law liability for damage caused by fire was based on an action on the case *pur negligent garder son few*.[112] Liability, although nominally predicated upon the defendant's negligence, was strict.[113] The action depended upon proof that the fire was in the defendant's control, and that it caused the plaintiff's damage. If the fire was caused by an act of God or an act of a stranger, it was not within the defendant's control, and the defendant was accordingly not liable.[114]

With the growth of negligence law principles in the nineteenth century, this general strict liability position for damage done by fire was abandoned in favour of a fault-based approach.[115] Although the common law liability of occupiers for fire started on their property is no longer strict,[116] tort law still imposes upon occupiers a high degree of responsibility for fires started on their property. In *H & N Emanuel Ltd. v. GLC*,[117] Lord Denning held that occupiers are liable for the escape of fires which are due not only to the negligence of servants, for which there would ordinarily be vicarious liability, but which arise also as a result of the negligent acts of independent contractors and guests of the occupier. Only the negligence of persons who are considered strangers[118] will relieve the occupier of liability. Lord Denning made it clear, however, that the occupier is not liable for the escape of fire which is not due to anyone's negligence.[119]

This common law liability of occupiers for the negligent acts of all but strangers has been accepted in Canadian cases.[120] It is a liability which is distinct both from

---

112 See Ogus, Winfield, and Fleming, above, note 110.

113 See the authors cited above, note 110. See also Irvine, "Annotation" (1986), 35 C.C.L.T. 307. Note, however, contrary views. For example, in *McAuliffe v. Hubbell*, [1931] 1 D.L.R. 835 at 838 (Ont. C.A.), Middleton J.A. states that "the statements sometimes rather recklessly made are found to have very slender foundations" and that the liability of land owners arose in situations where "the owner himself or by his servants has intentionally ignited a fire for his own purposes and negligently failed to guard it safely." This was cited in *Hallick v. Doroschuk* (1985), 41 Sask. R. 151 at 156 (Q.B.). See also Lord Goddard C.J. in *Balfour v. Barty-King*, [1957] 1 Q.B. 496 at 504-05.

114 See Duff J. in *Port Coquitlam v. Wilson*, [1923] S.C.R. 235. Thus this was known as the "*ignis suus*" rule; it must have been the occupier's fire. See *Burnie Port Authority v. General Jones*, above, note 110 at 45.

115 See, e.g., *Vaughan v. Menlove* (1837), 132 E.R. 490.

116 With the exception of those cases to which *Rylands v. Fletcher* applies. See discussion below.

117 [1971] 2 All E.R. 835 (C.A.).

118 Lord Denning, [1971] 2 All E.R. 835 at 839, defined a stranger as "anyone who in lighting a fire or allowing it to escape acts contrary to anything which the occupier could anticipate that he would do."

119 Lord Denning cited the well-known cases of *Tuberville v. Stamp* (1697), 91 E.R. 1072, and *Vaughan v. Menlove*, above, note 115, among others.

120 See, e.g., *Wager v. Molyneaux* (1988), 47 C.C.L.T. 73 (Alta. Q.B.); *Gallo v. St. Cyr*, [1983] 2 W.W.R. 395 (Alta. Q.B.); *Franks v. Sanderson* (1988), 44 C.C.L.T. 208 (B.C. C.A); *Iversen v. Purser* (1990), 73 D.L.R. (4th) 33 (B.C. S.C.); and *Alberta v. Hay*, [2002] 5 W.W.R. 653 (Alta. Q.B.). In *Millan v. Hulsman* (1990), 104 A.R. 228 (Q.B.), although the principle was

the principle of *Rylands v. Fletcher*, and occupiers' liability laws, either at common law or imposed by statute.

(c) *Rylands v. Fletcher*

The judgment in *Rylands v. Fletcher* gave new life to strict liability for damages caused by fire. Shortly after the decision in *Rylands v. Fletcher*, Blackburn J.[121] applied his new principle of strict liability to a fire caused by sparks which escaped from a locomotive's engine.[122] Later, in *Musgrove v. Pandelis*,[123] this strict liability position was reaffirmed by Bankes L.J., who stated:

> A man was liable at common law for damage done by fire originating on his own property (1) for the mere escape of the fire; (2) if the fire was caused by the negligence of himself or his servants, or by his own wilful act; (3) upon the principle of *Rylands v. Fletcher*. This principle was not then known by that name, because *Rylands v. Fletcher* was not then decided; but it was an existing principle of the common law. . . .[124]

Since these decisions, there have been numerous fire damage cases which have been decided upon the application of the *Rylands v. Fletcher* strict liability principle.[125]

In so far as fires which are deliberately set for a specific purpose, for example, for heating, lighting, or cooking, are concerned, whether *Rylands v. Fletcher* applies depends upon the requirement that they be a non-natural use. The cases have distinguished between fires which are natural as opposed to non-natural uses of land, *Rylands v. Fletcher* applying only in the latter case. In *Sochacki v. Sas*,[126] for example, Lord Goddard refused to apply the *Rylands* principle to a fire which emanated from a fireplace in a lodger's room. The lodger was using his room "in the ordinary, natural way in which the room could be used," and this was "an ordinary, natural, proper, everyday use of a fireplace in a room."[127] In *Dudek v. Brown*,[128] the court, on this basis, declined to apply the *Rylands* principle to a

---

accepted, the occupier was relieved of liability since he could not anticipate the activities of his subtenant which led to the fire. In *Alberta v. Hay* the issue was whether three defendants were "occupiers". The person who started the fire was a co-tenant with the other two defen dants. He was clearing land. All three were signatories on a grazing lease, but the other two defendants played no role in the clearing. They were simply co-tenants, with no control over the acts of the other party. The court concluded that they were therefore not vicariously liable for his acts.

121 In *Jones v. Festiniog Ry. Co.* (1868), L.R. 3 Q.B. 733.

122 For a similar Canadian case, see *Can. Southern Ry. Co. v. Phelps* (1884), 14 S.C.R. 132.

123 [1919] 2 K.B. 43 (C.A.).

124 *Ibid.*, at 46.

125 Many of these have actually involved not fires, *per se*, but dangerous *objects*, such as trains, cars, blow torches, matches, gases, and other flammable materials which have exploded or otherwise caused fires. In these instances, it is in fact the dangerous substance or activity, and not the fire, which is considered from the perspective of the principle in *Rylands v. Fletcher*. *Musgrove v. Pandelis, ibid.*, itself is in fact a good illustration of this point. Bankes L.J. asked not whether the fire, but whether the "motor car, with its petrol tank full or partially filled with petrol, was a dangerous thing to bring into the garage within the principle of *Rylands v. Fletcher*?"

126 [1947] 1 All E.R. 344 (K.B.D.).

127 *Ibid.*, at 345.

128 (1980), 124 D.L.R. (3d) 629 (Ont. H.C.).

case of a fire emanating from a wood-burning stove,[129] and in *Smith v. Widdicombe,*[130] a fire started for purposes of husbandry was not subject to this principle of strict liability.[131] In one other case, however, *Hudson v. Riverdale Colony of Hutterian Brethren*,[132] a "slough grass" fire which was deliberately set to prevent the expansion of an initial fire was considered to be a non-natural user of land, to which the principle of strict liability applied.

(d) The Fires Prevention (Metropolis) Act, 1774

A complicating factor in the area of liability for fires is the effect of the Fires Prevention (Metropolis) Act, 1774.[133] This statute, which was a re-enactment of the Statute of Anne, 1707,[134] provides that:

> No action, suit or process whatever shall be had, maintained or prosecuted against any person in whose house, chamber, stable, barn or other building any fire . . . accidentally begin, nor shall any recompense be made by such person for any damage suffered thereby; any law, usage or custom to the contrary notwithstanding.[135]

This provision, which is still in effect in several Canadian provinces,[136] and has been in issue in some of the cases,[137] was originally enacted in order to mitigate the strict liability position of the common law, by ensuring that defendants would not be held liable for fires which were outside their control. Commentators have noted that the statute was not utilized by the courts for several decades,[138] by which time the strict liability position of the earlier common law had been over-

---

129 See also *Millan v. Hulsman* (1990), 104 A.R. 228 (Q.B.), where the same reasoning was applied to a furnace, or to *AXA Insurance (Canada) v. Brunetti* (1998), 62 O.T.C. 241 (Gen. Div.), where it was applied to a cooking fire.

130 (1987), 39 C.C.L.T. 98 (Man. Q.B.), affirmed [1987] 6 W.W.R. 687 (Man. C.A.).

131 Numerous other cases are cited in support, for example, *Dahler v. Bruvold*, [1981] 5 W.W.R. 706 (B.C. S.C.); *Lickoch v. Madu*, [1973] 2 W.W.R. 127 (Alta. C.A.); *Dean v. McCarty* (1846), 2 U.C.Q.B. 448 (C.A.); *Curtis v. Lutes*, [1953] 4 D.L.R. 188 (Ont. C.A.). For a recent case, see *Alberta v. Hay*, above, note 120. In *Denys v. Gabel* (2003), [2003] S.J. No. 428, 2003 CarswellSask 450 (Prov. Ct.), the defendant, although not a farmer, started a fire on his land to clear brush. This was held to be an ordinary use of land.

132 (1980), 114 D.L.R. (3d) 352 (Man. C.A.).

133 14 Geo. 3, c. 78. For a useful commentary, see Irvine, "Annotation", above, note 110. See also Ogus, "Vagaries in Liability for the Escape of Fire", above, note 110.

134 Act of 1707 (6 Anne, c. 31).

135 S. 86.

136 Professor Irvine notes that there are reported cases affirming the statute's validity in British Columbia, Alberta, Saskatchewan, and Manitoba, and that it has been re-enacted in Ontario as the Accidental Fires Act, R.S.O. 1990, c. A.4, since repealed and replaced by the Fire Protection and Prevention Act, S.O, 1997, c.4, s. 76, 85. There are also cases in Australia and New Zealand. See Irvine, above, note 113, at 312, note 1. Alberta cases discussing the Act include *Warkentin v. C. (M.)* (1998), [1998] A.J. No. 433, 1998 CarswellAlta 357 (Q.B.); *Alberta v. Hay,* [2002] 5 W.W.R. 653 (Alta. Q.B.); and *Jordan v. Power* (2002), 325 A.R. 60 (Q.B.), additional reasons at (2002), 2002 CarswellAlta 1214 (Q.B.). In Ontario see *AXA Insurance (Canada) v. Brunetti* (1998), 62 O.T.C. 241 (Gen. Div.) and *Neff v. St. Catharines Marina Ltd.* (1998), 155 D.L.R. (4th) 647 (Ont. C.A.).

137 See *Franks v. Sanderson* (1986), 35 C.C.L.T. 307 (B.C. S.C.), affirmed (1988), 44 C.C.L.T. 208 (B.C. C.A.); *Hallick v. Doroschuk* (1985), 41 Sask. R. 151 (Q.B.); *Dudek v. Brown* (1980), 124 D.L.R. (3d) 629 (Ont. H.C.); and *Prior v. Hanna* (1988), 55 Alta. L.R. (2d) 276 (Q.B.).

138 Ogus, above, note 110, states that it was not used in any reported case until 1842.

taken by negligence law, and, shortly thereafter, by *Rylands v. Fletcher*. Since it has consistently been held that the statute was inapplicable to actions based on negligence,[139] and to liability under the principle of *Rylands v. Fletcher*,[140] the role of the provision was extremely limited. The only fires which are neither intentionally nor negligently started by the property owner, or, by those for whom the property owner is responsible, are fires started spontaneously by acts of nature, or by strangers, and, as we have seen, defendants were already protected from liability in these cases. The role of the statute became even more limited when it was held, in *Musgrove v. Pandelis*,[141] that an accidental fire which spreads due to the negligence of the defendant in failing to control it is also outside the statute's protection.[142]

The statutory provision has, however, played an important role in one respect. Although it has not provided the defendant with defences not otherwise available at common law, it has, according to most authorities,[143] placed the onus of proving that the fire was not caused accidentally upon the plaintiff. This will be of significance where a fire is of unknown origin. A plaintiff who has been damaged by a fire emanating from the defendant's property will only be able to succeed by proving that (1) *Rylands v. Fletcher* applies, or (2) the fire was started or was not controlled as a result of the defendant's negligence, or the negligence of a person, including a guest, for whom the defendant was responsible.

5. LIABILITY FOR ANIMALS

(a) Introduction

As with the law relating to the liability of occupiers for fires, the law relating to the liability of those who own or keep animals which injure others or damage

---

139 See, e.g., *Walt v. Newton Motors*, [1950] 1 W.W.R. 721 (Sask. C.A.); *Filliter v. Phippard* (1847), 116 E.R. 506; and *Port Coquitlam v. Wilson*, [1923] S.C.R. 235. More recently see *AXA Insurance (Canada) v. Brunetti* (1998), 62 O.T.C. 241 (Gen. Div.). In *Neff v. St. Cath arines Marina Ltd.* (1998), 155 D.L.R. (4th) 647 (Ont. C.A.), an unexplained fire destroyed three boats in a marina. The bailors sued, alleging a breach of the bailee's obligations. The trial judge allowed the action but this was reversed on appeal. The Court of Appeal held that the Accidental Fires Act, R.S.O. 1990, c. A.4, s. 1 (repealed and replaced by the Fire Protection and Prevention Act, S.O., 1997, c.4, s. 76, 85) applied as the fire in this case was of unexplained origin; it was incapable of being traced to any cause. Thus the occupier was not liable. The Court of Appeal also held that the law of bailment, which requires the bailee to prove that the required care was taken when the bailed goods are damaged, must be interpreted consistently with the Act. That is, the law of bailment cannot render a bailee liable for damage caused by an accidental fire.

140 Since the courts agreed that the Act could not apply to intentionally lit fires.

141 [1919] 2 K.B. 43 (C.A.).

142 See also *Goldman v. Hargrave*, [1966] 2 All E.R. 989 (P.C.); *Burnie Port Authority v. General Jones Pty. Ltd.* (1994), 120 A.L.R. 42 (H.C.), and discussion by Irvine, above, note 110, at 309. For a Canadian case, see *Dibartolo Estate v. Avanti Tavern*, [1994] O.J. No. 191 (Gen. Div.).

143 See Canadian and English cases discussed by Irvine, *ibid.* Notably, in Canada: *McAuliffe v. Hubbell*, [1931] 1 D.L.R. 835 (Ont. C.A.); *Paquette v. Labelle* (1981), 17 C.C.L.T. 194 (Ont. C.A.); *Hallick v. Doroschuk* (1986), 41 Sask. R. 151 (Q.B.); and a concession by Duff J. in *Port Coquitlam v. Craig*, [1923] S.C.R. 235, that although he was inclined to disagree, the "weight of dicta" places the onus on the plaintiff.

their property has a long and interesting judicial history.[144] Various actions seem to be available to claimants, depending upon the particular circumstances of the case. There is, of course, the action in negligence, which will resolve most claims.[145] As well, the action in nuisance may apply, or the laws relating to occupiers' liability.[146] In addition to these, however, there are peculiar common law rules of liability. There is the *scienter* action, the action for cattle trespass, and the rule in *Searle v. Wallbank*.[147] Overriding all of this are numerous legislative enactments which bear upon this area.

In this chapter, we will briefly examine the strict liability aspects of the animal liability issue.

(b) The *Scienter* Action[148]

At common law, a keeper of a dangerous animal is held strictly liable for injuries caused by it. In respect of this principle, the common law recognizes two classes of dangerous animals.[149] The first are animals *ferae naturae*, or wild animals.[150] These animals, such as lions, bears, tigers, zebras, and monkeys, are irrebuttably presumed to be vicious or dangerous, and their keepers are accordingly strictly liable for all injuries or damage which they cause, whether it be

---

144 There are several textbooks dealing with the general subject. See, e.g., North, *The Modern Law of Animals* (1972), and Williams, *Liability for Animals* (1939). See also Fleming, *The Law of Torts*, 9th ed. (1998), Chapter 18.

145 Note, however, the suggestion raised in some cases that for a defendant to be liable in negligence for injuries caused by an animal, there must exist "special circumstances." See especially Picard J.'s discussion of this issue in *Acheson v. Dory* (1993), 8 Alta. L.R. (3d) 128 (Q.B.), affirmed (1994), 24 Alta. L.R. (3d) 187 (C.A.). The point seems to be that an owner of an animal cannot be held negligent if the animal acts in an unexpected way and injures someone. I would interpret this as illustrating the point that for a person to be held negligent there must be foreseeability of harm and unreasonable conduct in relation to the risk. See Conrad J.'s judgment in *Bates (Guardian of) v. Horkoff* (1991), 119 A.R. 270 at 276 (Q.B.), where this is expressed as follows: "could the owner of the particular animal, with its particular characteristics, in the particular circumstances, have reasonably foreseen the danger that could result in damage." A similar approach is found in *Hare v. Onofrychuk* (1999), 252 A.R. 279 (Prov. Ct.). Also see *Taller v. Goldenshtein*, [1994] 3 W.W.R. 557 (B.C.C.A.) and *Janota-Bzowska v. Lewis* (1997), 43 B.C.L.R. (3d) 352 (C.A.), where actions in negligence were dismissed because the dogs' owners could not have foreseen the injury. In *D"Aoust v. Lindsay*, [2000] 4 W.W.R. 255 (Alta. Q.B.), the action was also dismissed due to the absence of foreseeability of harm to the plaintiff.

146 See, e.g., *Maltais-Comeau v. Laliberté* (1986), 36 C.C.L.T. 26 (N.B. Q.B.). In *Bates v. Horkoff* (1991), 119 A.R. 270 (Q.B.), it was unclear whether the plaintiff child put her hand through the defendant's fence and was bitten by the dog, or whether the dog put its head through the fence and grabbed the plaintiff's arm. The court stated that in the first scenario the case would be decided by the law relating to occupiers' liability, since the injury occurred on the defen dant's premises, whereas in the second scenario, ordinary negligence law would apply.

147 [1947] A.C. 341 (H.L.).

148 See Williams, above, note 144, Chapter XV.

149 See Lord Esher's judgment in *Filburn v. People's Palace & Aquarium Co.* (1890), 25 Q.B.D. 258 (C.A.).

150 It has been argued that the use of the term wild is misleading, since all of the animals in this category are not necessarily wild. They may in fact be quite tame, and very unable to survive in the wilds. See Fleming and Williams, above, note 144.

personal injury or property damage.[151] It does not matter if the harm caused by an animal *ferae naturae* is the ordinary type of harm one can anticipate from that type of animal.[152] An animal falls into the category of *ferae naturae* as a matter of law and not fact. Therefore, the court cannot consider a specific animal's disposition in order to transfer it out of this category.[153] Since it is unusual[154] for animals *ferae naturae* to be kept as pets by ordinary urban dwellers, actions brought with respect to injuries caused by these types of animals are rare. Those that are brought usually involve animals being kept for display in circuses, zoos, animal parks, and other amusement centres.[155]

The second category of dangerous animals are animals *mansuetae naturae* which have known vicious or mischievous propensities. Animals *mansuetae naturae*, although not necessarily harmless by nature, have become harmless through domestication.[156] Unlike the case of animals which are, as a species, naturally dangerous, the principle of strict liability only applies to animals *mansuetae naturae*, when the animal has vicious or mischievous propensities, which are known to its owner or keeper.[157] The burden of proving this knowledge falls on the plaintiff.[158] As well, strict liability applies only with respect to those injuries caused by the vicious propensities.[159] The strict liability rule applied to keepers

---

151 See Devlin J. in *Behrens v. Bertram Mills Circus Ltd.*, [1957] 2 Q.B. 1. See also Fleming, *The Law of Torts*, 9th ed. (1998), at 401. Fleming notes that the modern formulation of this ancient rule stems from *May v. Burdett* (1846), 115 E.R. 1213. See also *Knott v. London County Council*, [1934] 1 K.B. 126; *McNeill v. Frankenfield* (1963), 44 D.L.R. (2d) 132 (B.C. C.A.).

152 Devlin J. in *Behrens v. Bertram Mills Circus Ltd., ibid.*, suggests that a keeper of a tiger, for example, would be strictly liable even if the injury it caused was to give a shocked individual a heart attack.

153 See Devlin J. in *Behrens v. Bertram Mills Circus, ibid.*, Devlin J. was not even prepared to treat Burmese elephants as harmless in England, since all elephants, no matter where in the world they are found, are considered by English law to be dangerous.

154 In some jurisdictions, it may even be unlawful.

155 For example, of the classic cases, *Filburn v. People's Palace & Aquarium Co.* (1890), 25 Q.B.D. 258 (C.A.), involved a trained elephant in a public exhibition; *Behrens v. Bertram Mills Circus Ltd.*, [1957] 2 Q.B. 1, a circus elephant; and *Marlor v. Ball* (1900), 16 T.L.R. 239 (C.A.), a zebra in an exhibition ground. The recent case of *Cowles v. Balac* (2005), 29 C.C.L.T. (3d) 284 (Ont. S.C.J.), additional reasons at (2005), 2005 CarswellOnt 4545 (S.C.J.), affirmed (2006), 42 C.C.L.T. (3d) 161 (Ont. C.A.), additional reasons at (2006), 2006 CarswellOnt 7936 (C.A.), leave to appeal refused (2007), 2007 CarswellOnt 1359 (S.C.C.) involved a tiger in a wildlife park. There are cases involving animals *ferae naturae* in other settings: see, e.g., *Rands v. McNeil*, [1955] 1 Q.B. 253 (C.A.), which involved a bull on a farm.

156 In this respect, harmless is used with reference to personal injuries, not property damage. See Fleming, *The Law of Torts*, 9th ed. (1998), at 401, and Bankes L.J. in *Buckle v. Holmes*, [1926] 2 K.B. 125 at 129 (C.A.). But see Williams' definition of dangerous animals, above, note 144, at 298.

157 In *Bacon (Litigation Guardian of) v. Ryan* (1995), 27 C.C.L.T. (2d) 308, [1996] 3 W.W.R. 215 (Sask. Q.B.), the court stressed that possession or control of the dog is the key to responsibility, not ownership.

158 See *Laws v. Wright*, [2000] 5 W.W.R. 325 (Alta. Q.B.).

159 See *Sgro v. Verbeek* (1980), 111 D.L.R. (3d) 479 (Ont. H.C.); *Konkin v. Bartel*, [1988] B.C.W.L.D. 3169. In *Laws v. Wright, ibid.*, the defendant's horse was known to have "nipped" people but never to have bitten anyone. The plaintiff was bitten. The court held that a nip is a bite, albeit a "gentle" one, and therefore the defendant had knowledge of this dangerous or mischievous propensity. In *Janota-Bzowska v. Lewis* (1997), 43 B.C.L.R. (3d) 352 (C.A.),

of dangerous animals, although undoubtedly based on the same policy which underlies the principle of *Rylands v. Fletcher*, is not an instance of it.[160] There is no concern over the concept of non-natural use,[161] and more importantly, the dangerous animal need not escape from its keeper's land to the land of the plaintiff for liability to ensue. Many of the cases which have been brought with respect to injuries caused by these animals have involved injuries suffered by plaintiffs while on the defendants' lands.

Although an escape *per se* is not required, it has been stated in several of the earlier cases,[162] and stressed in the more recent ones,[163] that an escape from control, even if not from custody, is required before strict liability can be applied to the keeper of a dangerous animal.[164] Although a somewhat ambiguous notion, the escape from control requirement suggests that an animal who is reasonably secured on its keeper's property will not attract strict liability if, despite the control, a person is injured. As pointed out by one commentator,[165] this requirement, a "recent and contentious one", which has been rejected by at least one common law court,[166] significantly diminishes the relevance of strict liability, approximating it quite closely to the ordinary standard of negligence law. It is likely that a defendant who has permitted a dangerous animal to be out of control would be found liable either under negligence law or occupiers' liability principles. A more satisfactory approach would be to reject the requirement of escape from control as an element of the principle of strict liability, but to recognize the defence of fault of the plaintiff once the strict liability principle has been admitted.[167]

There appear to be few defences to the strict liability action brought against keepers of dangerous animals.[168] Fault of the plaintiff is no defence, although, as noted above, it could be considered as a factor in determining whether or not the animal has escaped from its keeper's control. The issue was recently considered in *Cowles v. Balac*.[169] The plaintiffs were injured when a tiger got into their car

---

the court held that it is not necessary for the defendant to know the specific type of harm that its dog had a propensity to do; knowledge of the "kind of harm" suffices. On the facts of the case, the owner's knowledge that his dog liked to chase deer was insufficient to establish *scienter* for an injury caused by the dog jumping up on the claimant.

160 It has been called "a branch of the rule in *Rylands v. Fletcher*." See Devlin J. in *Behrens v. Bertram Mills Circus*, above, note 155.

161 Unless one wishes to suggest that keeping a dangerous animal is by definition non-natural.

162 See, e.g., *Rands v. McNeil*, above, note 155; *Knott v. London County Council*, [1934] 1 K.B. 126.

163 See *Maynes v. Galicz* (1975), 62 D.L.R. (3d) 385 (B.C. S.C.); and *Lewis v. Oeming* (1983), 24 C.C.L.T. 81 (Alta. Q.B.).

164 See discussion by Irvine at 24 C.C.L.T. 82 at 85.

165 See Irvine, *ibid.*

166 *Higgins v. William Inglis & Son Pty. Ltd.*, [1978] 1 N.S.W.L.R. 649 (C.A.).

167 In other words, if a person keeps a dangerous animal, there will in all cases be strict liability. However, if the defendant can prove that the plaintiff's injury was brought about by the plaintiff's own fault, and not due to the fact that the animal was out of control, the strict liability claim would be rejected. See *McNeill v. Frankenfield* (1963), 44 D.L.R. (2d) 132 at 147 (B.C. C.A.), where Lord J.A. stated that absolute liability "may be rebutted by showing that the plaintiff was the author of her own misfortune, in that she *meddled with or provoked the dog*." This was cited with approval by Taylor J. in *Hall v. Sorley* (1980), 23 B.C.L.R. 281 at 283 (S.C.). (Emphasis added by Taylor J.)

168 See Fleming, *The Law of Torts*, 9th ed. (1998), at 405.

169 Above, note 155.

in a wildlife park. The trial judge found the owner of the park strictly liable and rejected the defence of contributory negligence. Not only did the trial judge find it "contradictory" to apply the defence to an action for strict liability, but she concluded that there was no negligence on the plaintiffs' part in any event. The majority of the Court of Appeal did not consider the issue, in view of the trial judge's findings. The dissent, however, after a review of both case law and texts, stated that "functional and fairness considerations strongly suggest that comparative negligence principles are appropriate where a plaintiff's misconduct or want of care is a contributing factor to his or her damages".[170] Although I am sympathetic to this approach, it is difficult to reconcile it with Canadian apportionment legislation, which specifically apportions liability based on the degrees of "fault" of the parties. Where only one of the parties is at fault, the other party being only strictly liable, there is no apportionment possible.[171] It may be that the defendant in a strict liability claim can also be considered negligent for not having taken reasonable steps to foresee and prevent a negligent plaintiff from exposing himself to the dangers posed by a wild animal. In this case, there could be apportionment, since the cause of action would be one of negligence, and not strict liability. Otherwise, the court's decision should be to either accept the plaintiff's strict liability claim in full, or to dismiss it where the injury suffered by the plaintiff was caused not by the defendant's failure to control the wild animal, but by the plaintiff's own unreasonable behaviour. Voluntary assumption of risk, although theoretically available, will be at least as strictly interpreted here as it is in negligence law.[172] Act of a stranger or act of God seem not to be defences, but here again, the recent emphasis on the escape from control requirement may permit these defences under this guise.[173]

The common law *scienter* action has drawn considerable criticism. It has been the subject of several studies,[174] and legislative reforms have been enacted with respect to it.[175] Difficulties of classification of animals, the knowledge requirement with respect to animals *mansuetae naturae*, the ambiguous escape requirement, and the uncertain defences have all been cited as defects of this action.[176] The general complaint has been that the action has become too complex and rigid,[177] and ought to be simplified, if not replaced, by ordinary negligence law.

---

170 At 42 C.C.L.T. (3d) 218.

171 Note, however, that in *Blackwater v. Plint* (2005), 258 D.L.R. (4th) 275, 35 C.C.L.T. (3d) 161, [2006] 3 W.W.R. 401 (S.C.C.), fault was apportioned between two defendants who were only vicariously liable. See discussion below on vicarious liability.

172 See, however, *Laws v. Wright*, [2000] 5 W.W.R. 325 (Alta. Q.B.), where the court used the defence of voluntary assumption of risk to exculpate the defendant. The court stressed accep tance of the physical risk and did not refer to acceptance of the legal risk.

173 Fleming, *The Law of Torts*, 9th ed. (1998), at 406, states that it is doubtful whether act of God is a defence, but that act of a stranger might be a possible defence, although the authorities are conflicting.

174 Note, for example, in England, the Goddard Committee, 1953, and the Law Commission Report, No. 14; in New South Wales, the N.S.W. Law Reform Commission, 1970; in Scotland, 12th Law of the Law Reform Committee for Scotland.

175 See, e.g., the Animals Act, 1971 (Eng.), c. 22, or Animal Liability Act, S.M. 1998, c. 8, s. 2(2), among others.

176 See North, *The Modern Law of Animals* (1972), at 4.

177 See Devlin J. in *Behrens v. Bertram Mills Circus Ltd.*, [1957] 2 Q.B. 1 at 14.

In Canada, legislation concerning the liability for animals exists in all provinces. The liability of dog owners in particular has been regulated. There is considerable variance in what the different statutes seek to accomplish, and the statutes themselves have created additional problems and confusion. Some of the statutes maintained the strict liability position of the common law, while reversing the burden of proof and requiring that owners of dogs establish that they did not know of their animals' vicious or mischievous propensities. Other legislation abolished the *scienter* requirement entirely.[178]

(c) Cattle Trespass

At common law, an owner of cattle[179] is strictly liable for trespasses committed by them in leaving their owner's fields and wandering onto the land of others.[180] Unlike other actions based on trespass, liability is based neither on fault nor intentional wrongdoing. As well, unlike strict liability actions based on *Rylands v. Fletcher*, non-natural use is not an element of this tort. Adding to the responsibility of the cattle owner is the fact that there is no common law duty for neighbours to fence and thus to protect their property from wandering cattle.[181]

(d) The Rule in *Searle v. Wallbank*

In the well-known case of *Searle v. Wallbank*,[182] the House of Lords held that owners of land abutting highways are under no duty to users of highways to exercise reasonable care to prevent their animals from straying onto them. Accordingly, an action brought by a cyclist injured in a collision with the defendant's horse which had wandered onto the highway was dismissed. A duty of care to users of highways, however, is imposed upon those who deliberately bring cattle onto highways in order to move them about.[183]

The Supreme Court of Canada rejected the rule of *Searle v. Wallbank* in the case of *Fleming v. Atkinson*.[184] The court held that ordinary negligence law applied to the case of animals which stray onto highways and cause accidents.[185]

---

178 In view of the differences in the provincial legislation, and the fact that they are frequently modified, those faced with animal liability issues are well advised to consult the relevant legislative changes which have been made.

179 This did not include cats and dogs, who were entitled to roam at will, according to *Buckle v. Holmes*, [1926] 2 K.B. 125 (C.A.).

180 The owner is not liable, however, for trespassing cattle who were lawfully on the highway before their intrusion. See Williams, *Liability for Animals* (1939), at 197-99; Fleming, *The Law of Torts*, 9th ed. (1998), at 396.

181 The cattle trespass rule, and other matters relating to the keeping of cattle, have been significantly affected by legislation, and should be consulted by those dealing with these issues.

182 [1947] A.C. 341 (H.L.).

183 See *Desmond v. Scott*, [1951] 3 D.L.R. 418 (N.B. K.B.). Note that there is legislation in this area as well.

184 [1959] S.C.R. 513. Also note that legislation has altered *Searle v. Wallbank* in England and other Commonwealth countries.

185 This judgment related to Ontario and has not been universally accepted. See, e.g., *Lane v. Biel* (1970), 17 D.L.R. (3d) 632 (Sask. Dist. Ct.), where it was rationalized that Rand J. in *Fleming v. Atkinson* dealt only with cattle whose presence on the highway was tolerated by their owner, and not with cattle who stray onto highways. It was held that *Searle v. Wallbank* was still applicable in Saskatchewan. Case law from Newfoundland indicates an acceptance of *Fleming*

Since *Fleming v. Atkinson*, negligence law has been applied to numerous cases involving collisions between cars, or other vehicles, and animals.[186] It has been explained that the duty of care to prevent cattle from wandering onto highways will be based on several factors, including the type of highway involved, and the amount and nature of the traffic one would expect to be on it.[187]

6. VICARIOUS LIABILITY

(a) Introduction

The liability of a person is termed vicarious when it is based not on any personal wrongdoing by that individual, but on the tortious conduct of someone else.[188] Unlike the other examples of strict liability discussed in this chapter, vicarious liability does not relate to a specific cause of action in tort against a particular defendant arising from an injury caused by that defendant. Rather, it is based upon a relationship the defendant has with another individual involved in tortious conduct.[189] It is, nonetheless, an illustration of strict liability, because the defendant will be vicariously liable in the absence of any personal wrongdoing.[190] It is

---

v. Atkinson: see *Rowe v. Canning* (1994), 117 Nfld. & P.E.I.R. 353 (Nfld. T.D.). Also see a recent Manitoba case, *Manitoba Public Insurance Corp. v. Lamb* (2004), [2006] 2 W.W.R. 136 (Q.B.). An owner was held liable in an action for negligence for failing to adequately fence in his cattle. The court rejected the owner's statutory defence under the Animal Liability Act, C.C.S.M, c. 495, s. 2(3), since the defendant failed to control his livestock "in accordance with generally accepted agricultural practices." The court held that the action in negligence is not precluded by the Act, at any event. Thus presumably even if there were no liability under the Act, there could be a successful negligence claim. This implies that even if the animal was controlled in accordance with generally accepted agricultural practices, the owner can still be found negligent.

186 For example, a pig in *Rozon v. Patenaude* (1982), 35 O.R. (2d) 619 (Co. Ct.); a horse in *Reynoldson v. Simmons* (1982), 14 Sask. R. 257 (Q.B.); a cow in *Pellizzari v. Miller* (1981), 35 O.R. (2d) 700 (H.C.); and in *Haley v. Reade* (2000), 228 N.B.R. (2d) 359 (Q.B.); a bull in *Young v. Glenburn Ranches Ltd.* (1984), 49 A.R. 154 (Q.B.); and a dog in *Ruckheim v. Robinson*, [1995] 4 W.W.R. 284 (B.C. C.A.).

187 See *Baty v. Parkdale Farms* (1986), 37 C.C.L.T. 9 (Man. Q.B.); *Gash v. Wood* (1960), 67 Man. R. 193 (Co. Ct.); and *Penner v. Allan* (1963), 43 W.W.R. 244 (Man. Co. Ct.). Here as well one must be alert to the plethora of legislative enactments which directly or indirectly bear upon this issue.

188 See Atiyah, *Vicarious Liability in the Law of Torts* (1967). There are several useful articles on this topic. See, for example, Flannigan, "Enterprise Control: The Servant-Inde pendent Contractor Distinction" (1987), 37 U.T.L.J. 25; Neyers, "A Theory of Vicarious Liability" (2005), 43 Alta. L. Rev. 287; Wingfield, "Perish Vicarious Liability?" in Neyers, Pitel, Chamberlain, eds., *Emerging Issues in Tort Law* (2007), Chapter 15; Giliker, "Comparative Perspectives on Vicarious Liability: Defining the Scope of Employment", in *Emerging Issues in Tort Law, ibid.*, Chapter 16.

189 As stated by Major J. in *671122 Ontario Ltd. v. Sagaz Industries Canada Inc.* (2001), 204 D.L.R. (4th) 542 (S.C.C.), reconsideration refused (2001), 10 C.C.L.T. (3d) 292 (S.C.C.) at 551 [D.L.R.]:

> Vicarious liability is not a distinct tort. It is a theory that holds one person responsible for the misconduct of another because of the relationship between them.

190 A question which has been raised in cases and the literature is whether vicarious liability is based upon one person's liability for the *tort* of another person or one person's responsibility for the *act* of another person. The question may be important when considering whether a person can be vicariously liable even though the person who committed the act cannot be held liable. The prevailing view seems to be that an immunity from suit in favour of one party does

useful, therefore, to include in this chapter a discussion of this very important and somewhat contentious issue.[191]

In the context of tort law, vicarious liability is primarily applied in the employer/employee relationship.[192] Stated generally, an employer is vicariously liable to third parties for torts committed by employees in the course of their employment.[193] The determination of when an employer/employee relationship exists,

---

not protect another party, where a tort has in fact been committed. See, for example, *Wadsworth v. Hayes*, [1996] 3 W.W.R. 561 (Alta. C.A.), leave to appeal refused [1996] 9 W.W.R. xlvii (S.C.C.); *Rayani v. Yule & Co. (Hong Kong) Ltd.*, [1996] 3 W.W.R. 574 (Alta. C.A.) — immunity from suit due to Workers' Compensation scheme does not preclude owner's vicar ious liability; and *Wowk v. Edmonton Board of Health*, [1994] 7 W.W.R. 78 (Alta. Master) — immunity from suit for acts done in good faith does not preclude vicarious liability. See Fleming, *The Law of Torts*, 9th ed. (1998), at 412, who argues that despite these exceptional situations, vicarious liability is based upon one person's liability for the *tort* of another. The Saskatchewan Court of Appeal, in *Bouchard v. Carruthers* (2004), [2005] 2 W.W.R. 227 (Sask. C.A.), stated that vicarious liability is based upon one person's liability for another person's "liability for the wrong". In the context of this case, this meant that if the wrongdoer could not reduce her liability for a sexual assault by third partying the victim's parents for contribution, neither could her employer. The Court relied on *dicta* in *Bluebird Cabs Ltd. v. Guardian Insurance Co. of Canada* (1999), 173 D.L.R. (4th) 318 (B.C. C.A). It should, however, be noted that *Bluebird* was a duty to defend insurance law case. *Query:* does this imply that if the wrongdoer was immune from liability that it would preclude vicarious liability? In *McVea (Guardian ad litem of) v. B. (T.)*, [2005] 8 W.W.R. 149 (B.C. C.A), reconsideration refused (2006), 2006 CarswellBC 956 (C.A.), additional reasons at (2006), 2006 CarswellBC 2951 (C.A.), leave to appeal refused (2007), 2007 CarswellBC 270 (S.C.C.), affirmed (2008), 2008 CarswellBC 212 (S.C.C.), the A.G. of British Columbia was held vicariously liable for the negligence of a police officer even though the officer had a statutory immunity from suit. Note, however, that the Police Act, R.S.B.C. 1996, c. 367, s. 21(4)(c), specifically provided that the statutory immunity of the police officer did not affect the applicability of vicarious liability, which was provided for in s. 11(1) of the Act.

191 The distinction between vicarious liability and personal liability can be blurred in some types of cases. For example, where the negligence of an employee becomes the negligence of a corporate employer, the liability of the employer is personal, and not vicarious. See, for example, the discussion of this matter in *ACA Cooperative Assn. v. Associated Freezers of Can. Inc.* (1992), 93 D.L.R. (4th) 559 (N.S. C.A.).

192 There is no vicarious liability between parents and children. See, for example, *Segstro v. McLean*, [1990] B.C.J. No. 2477 (S.C.). Vicarious liability also arises in tort with respect to automobile accidents. This area however is now regulated by legislation. See discussion below. In *Fullowka v. Royal Oak Ventures Inc.* (2005), [2005] 5 W.W.R. 420 (N.W.T. S.C.), additional reasons at (2005), 2005 CarswellNWT 55 (S.C.), reversed (2008), 2008 CarswellNWT 32 (C.A.), a labour union was held vicariously liable at trial for the acts of union members, who were not employees or agents of the union. Cases referred to by Lutz J. in support of this finding were ones in which unions were held liable for the acts of their representatives, agents or employees. The Court of Appeal reversed the judgment. The Court stated, at para. 148, that "the relationship between a member and his or her union is not characterized by the level of control, unity of purpose and proximity needed to generate vicarious liability. Unions are not vicariously liable for the acts of their members per se." If, on the other hand, a union member was given a specific task to do on behalf of the union, the union could be held vicariously liable for a tort committed by that union member during the course of the assignment, depending upon the "strong connection" test. This was not true of this case. Those union members who had set the bomb or incited violence during a strike were not acting within the tasks assigned to them by the union.

193 It has been held that vicarious liability has no relevance when an employer sues an employee for injuries suffered by the employer as a result of the employee's tortious conduct. It only applies when the employee injures a third party. See *Savoie v. Bouchard* (1982), 23 C.C.L.T. 83 at 109 (N.B. Q.B.), affirmed (1983), 26 C.C.L.T. 173 (N.B. C.A.).

and to which of the employee's acts the doctrine of vicarious liability will apply, are highly contentious issues. There have been several concrete factors and tests that courts have adopted to resolve these issues which have been useful. Ultimately, however, decision-making in this area boils down to an assessment of the facts in each case.

What are the policy objectives of the common law in imposing liability on an employer for the torts of employees? Identifying the policies underlying the doctrine of vicarious liability will assist courts in formulating those factors which ought to be relevant to decision-making in this area.[194]

Several policies have been suggested. It has been argued that vicarious liability is fair since it places the losses which are created by an activity on the person who benefits from it. This rationale assumes a "for profit" or commercial defendant and would not thereby apply to a charitable or not-for-profit foundation.[195] A variant of this theme that would apply to non-profit foundations, however, is "the idea that the person who introduces a risk incurs a duty to those who may be injured [by it]".[196] The doctrine may also ensure that there will be a "deep pocket" from which an injured victim will more easily obtain compensation.[197] Economic efficiency is achieved by permitting the shifting of losses to those who can more easily distribute them through insurance or the pricing of goods and services. The doctrine also encourages accident prevention by deterring employers from engaging in unsafe enterprises or from using inexperienced employees.[198]

These rationales are only partly convincing.[199] Although the doctrine of vicarious liability allows victims to recover their losses from employers, employees

---

194 See Flannigan, above, note 188, whose article elaborates on this theme. In the recent vicarious liability judgements from the Supreme Court of Canada, *B. (P.A.) v. Curry* (1999), 46 C.C.L.T. (2d) 1, 174 D.L.R. (4th) 45 (S.C.C.) at 13 [C.C.L.T.], and *T. (G.) v. Griffiths* (1999), 46 C.C.L.T. (2d) 49, 174 D.L.R. (4th) 71 (S.C.C.), McLachlin C.J. noted that "[v]icarious liability has always been concerned with policy. . ." Also note Major J.'s comment in *671122 Ontario Ltd. v. Sagaz Industries Canada Inc.* (2001), 204 D.L.R. (4th) 542 (S.C.C.), reconsideration refused (2001), 10 C.C.L.T. (3d) 292 (S.C.C.) at 552 [D.L.R.] that the "[i]dentification of the policy considerations underlying the imposition of vicarious liability assists in determining whether the doctrine should be applied in a particular case. . ."

195 This was of course a serious concern of the Supreme Court of Canada in the *Curry* and *Griffiths* cases, which involved non-profit defendants.

196 McLachlin C.J. in the *Curry* case at (1999), 46 C.C.L.T. (2d) 1 (S.C.C.), at 15. McLachlin C.J. noted that this idea "lies at the heart of tort law". It must be stated, however, that it is the fault principle that lies at the heart of tort law. It is only when the risk introduced is an "unreasonable" one that liability will flow.

197 This was also mentioned by the Supreme Court of Canada in the *Curry* and *Griffiths* cases. Again it must be noted, however, that with non-insured defendants or charitable foundations the pocket might in fact not be so deep.

198 An extensive analysis of the theory and policies of vicarious liability is contained in La Forest J.'s dissenting judgment in *London Drugs Ltd. v. Kuehne & Nagel International Ltd.*, [1993] 1 W.W.R. 1 (S.C.C.). La Forest J. identifies the policy concerns as being compensation, deterrence, and loss internalization. In the *Curry* and *Griffiths* cases, the Supreme Court of Canada saw the twin policies of "just and fair compensation" and "deterrence" as supporting the imposition of vicarious liability.

199 In Neyers' article, above, note 188, the author critiques all of the policies or goals that are said to underlie vicarious liability. He persuasively argues that none of the existing theories adequately explain why vicarious liability is applied in some situations, but not in others. Neyers ultimately concludes that vicarious liability is explained by the theory that in certain types of employment situations there is an implied contractual obligation on the part of an

may still be required to indemnify employers for what was paid out on their account.[200] Thus, the goal of requiring persons who profit from activities to pay their costs, or the goal of deterrence, may not in fact always be achieved. As well, any unreasonable conduct on the part of an employer which ought to be deterred would most likely lead to personal liability on the part of the employer at any event. Finally, policies which relate to the deep pocket or loss distribution theories fail to explain why our existing rules of vicarious liability apply in the case of some, but not all employers.[201] Despite its inadequacies, the doctrine of vicarious liability is firmly entrenched in Canadian tort law.[202]

---

employer to indemnify its employee for its liability to third parties. The third party is subrogated to this right and can therefore sue the employer directly.

200 The leading authority is *Lister v. Romford Ice & Cold Storage Ltd.*, [1957] A.C. 555. In Canadian case law see, for example, *McFee v. Joss*, [1925] 2 D.L.R. 1059 (Ont. C.A.), cited by Ritchie J. in *Co-operators Ins. Assn. v. Kearney* (1964), 48 D.L.R. (2d) 1 at 8 (S.C.C.). It has been held that this right is forfeited if the employer was also partly at fault. See *McCrindle v. Westin Ltd.* (1985), 35 C.C.L.T. 183 (Ont. H.C.). See also Lambert J.A. in *London Drugs Ltd. v. Kuehne & Nagel Int. Ltd.* (1990), 2 C.C.L.T. (2d) 161 (B.C. C.A.), who stated that the employer and negligent employee must bear the burden equally. The existing law, which requires that an employee be vulnerable to suit either at the instance of the injured party, or the employer, was objected to by La Forest J. in his dissenting judgment in *London Drugs*, *ibid.* This type of loss shifting was stated to upset the very policy foundations of vicarious liability. La Forest J. would go even further, however, and require an employer to indemnify its employee whenever the employee is held liable in tort to a third party. In other words, not only would the employer be vicariously liable for the torts of its employee, but the employee in turn would be immune from all personal liability. This would operate only where the employee's tort is not an "independent" tort and falls within the range of the employer's liability under the vicarious liability regime. This is similar to Neyers' theory, above, note 188. Neyers argues that contrary to *Lister*, an employer should not be able to sue its employee for indemnification. The Ontario Court of Appeal in *Douglas v. Kinger (Litigation Guardian of)*, 2008 ONCA 452 (Ont. C.A.) was critical of *Lister*, noting that it provoked a strong negative reaction and led to "gentleman's agreements" whereby insurers agree not to enforce their rights of subrogation against employees. *Douglas v. Kinger* involved not an action for indemnity, but a subrogated action brought by an employer's insurer against the employee whose negligence damaged the employer's property. The claim failed, the Court of Appeal holding that the employee owed no duty to his employer, due to lack of proximity and for policy reasons.

201 See Flannigan, above, note 188, at 28. The goals of vicarious liability, and accordingly the limits of its application, have been usefully discussed by Professor Flannigan in his recent article. According to Flannigan, the doctrine of vicarious liability exists as an effective means to regulate the risk-taking activities of employers. When employers are in a position to control the activities of employees, they can, by positive and negative steps, reduce risks, and, hence, reduce accident costs. Vicarious liability will encourage them to take these steps. This explanation finds judicial support and was one of the policy rationales adopted by the Supreme Court of Canada in *Bazely*. In *Lapensée v. Ottawa Day Nursery Inc.* (1986), 35 C.C.L.T. 129 at 155 (Ont. H.C.), varied as to damages (1986), 38 C.C.L.T. 113 (Ont. H.C.), Sutherland J. held the defendant vicariously liable because it was "in a far better position . . . to make provision for the fact that some accidents are virtually inevitable in that line of work, to devise and implement practices calculated to reduce the risk of accidents and to distribute the risk."

202 As I noted in Klar, "Recent Developments in Canadian Law: Tort Law" (1991), 23 Ottawa L. Rev. 177 at 251, the rationales explaining vicarious liability are different, and depending on which the court emphasizes, the applications will differ. See Rowles J.A.'s judgment in *British Columbia Ferry Corp. v. Invicta Security Service Corp.* (1998), [1999] 4 W.W.R. 536, 167 D.L.R. (4th) 193, 43 C.C.L.T. (2d) 194 (B.C. C.A.), for an excellent review of the history of vicarious liability, the various rationales used to justify it, and the academic literature. The

(b) Who is an Employee?

One of the most problematic issues in the area of vicarious liability has been to distinguish between employees, for whose torts employers are vicariously liable, and independent contractors, for whose actions there is no vicarious liability.[203] Various factors and tests have been suggested by the leading judgments in this area to define the essentials of the employer/employee relationship.[204]

The traditional test that has been applied to determine whether a party hired by another is an employee or an independent contractor is the control test. The adoption and formulation of this test can be found in numerous Canadian cases. The control test has evolved and been modified to reflect contemporary realities in the market place, and "remains the starting place" for any inquiry into vicarious liability, being "sufficient to dispose of many cases."[205] As stated by Major J. in the Supreme Court of Canada's most recent pronouncement on this matter, the question as to the nature of the relationship "lies with the element of control that the employer has over the direct tortfeasor (the worker). If the employer does not control the activities of the worker, the policy justifications underlying vicarious liability will not be satisfied".[206]

In its most orthodox form, the control test posits that an individual will be considered to have been hired as an employee, for the purposes of the doctrine of vicarious liability, when the employer not only tells that person *what* to do, but *how* to do it as well. An independent contractor, on the other hand, is hired to do a certain job and to produce a certain result, without being required to accomplish the task in a specified manner.[207]

Court of Appeal decided 2-1 that a defendant security company was vicariously liable for a fire deliberately set by one of its employees. This was prior to the Supreme Court of Canada's most recent judgments, discussed below.

203 Another way of stating the same thing is to contrast a contract of service, upon which an employee is hired, and a contract for services in relation to the independent contractor.

204 The distinction between employees and independent contractors usually arises in the context of vicarious liability; i.e., should the person who engaged the wrongdoer be responsible for its acts? It can also arise however for other reasons. In *M.A.N. - B & W Diesel v. Kingsway Transports Ltd.* (1997), 35 C.C.L.T. (2d) 30 (Ont. C.A.), the plaintiffs were arguing that the defendant truck driver, whose negligent driving resulted in damage to the plaintiffs' goods, was not an employee of the carrier but an independent contractor. The issue was whether the defendant truck driver, if an employee, could be protected by a limitation of liability clause in the contract between the plaintiffs and the carrier. The court held that the driver was an employee and therefore was protected.

205 Sutherland J. in *Lapensée v. Ottawa Day Nursery*, above, note 201, at 153.

206 *671122 Ontario Ltd. v. Sagaz Industries Canada Inc.* (2001), 204 D.L.R. (4th) 542 (S.C.C.) at 553-54. The policies were those highlighted by the Supreme Court in its *Curry* and *Bazely* cases, namely "just and practical" compensation and "deterrence of future harm".

207 The following explanation from *Salmond on Torts*, which has been approved of by Canadian courts, articulates this approach:

> A servant may be defined as any person employed by another to do work for him on the terms that he, the servant, is to be subject to the control and directions of his employer in respect of the manner in which his work is to be done.

This was quoted in *Armstrong v. Mac's Milk Ltd.* (1975), 55 D.L.R. (3d) 510 at 513 (Ont. H.C.). Flannigan traces the origin of the control test to Bramwell B. in *Yewens v. Noakes* (1880), 6 Q.B.D. 530 at 532-33: "A servant is a person subject to the command of his master as to the manner in which he shall do his work."

One of the leading cases propounding the control test is *Performing Right Soc. Ltd. v. Mitchell & Booker (Palais de Danse) Ltd.*[208] The case involved the vicarious liability of the occupiers of a dance hall for a breach of copyright by a band hired by them. McCardie J., while conceding that factors such as the nature of the task assigned to the workers, the freedom of action given to them, the size of the contract amount, and the circumstances under which payment could be withheld, related to the distinction between employees and independent contractors, these factors alone could not be decisive. Employers might, by contract, reserve the right to control similar aspects of their relationship with independent contractors. For McCardie J., the final test was "the nature and degree of detailed control over the person alleged to be a servant."[209] The occupiers of the dance hall were accordingly held vicariously liable, since their agreement with the band gave them "the right of continuous, dominant, and detailed control on every point. . . ."[210]

Control over the manner and modes by which workers will perform their tasks, although appropriate in some circumstances, will obviously not aptly describe many employer/employee relationships. This is true, for example, with reference to the professional employee. It cannot be suggested that hospitals control the manner in which interns, residents, anaesthetists, nurses, or other professional full-time staff, should perform their tasks. Yet vicarious liability has been held to exist in these cases.[211] In one Canadian case, *Robitaille v. Vancouver Hockey Club*,[212] a hockey team was held vicariously liable for the staff doctor's negligence, in view of the team's right to select the doctor, to control certain aspects of his employment relating to non-professional matters, and to dismiss him.[213] In recognition of this, courts, eager to pursue the objectives of vicarious liability,[214] have been willing to broaden the range of factors relevant to establishing an employer/employee relationship. In a leading case, *Montreal v. Montreal Locomotive Works Ltd.*,[215] Lord Wright, in recognition of what he termed "the more complex conditions of modern industry,"[216] suggested factors other than control to define the employer/employee relationship. Ownership of the tools, chance of profit, and risk of loss were said to be of importance.[217] For Lord Wright the

---

208 [1924] 1 K.B. 762.

209 *Ibid.*, at 767.

210 *Ibid.*, at 771.

211 See, e.g., *Savoie v. Bouchard* (1982), 23 C.C.L.T. 83, affirmed 26 C.C.L.T. 173 (N.B.C.A.); *Aynsley v. Toronto Gen. Hosp.* (1969), 7 D.L.R. (3d) 193, affirmed 25 D.L.R. (3d) 241 (S.C.C.).

212 (1979), 19 B.C.L.R. 158, affirmed 16 C.C.L.T. 225 (C.A.).

213 For an unsuccessful suit brought against the same defendant in relation to another doctor, see *Wilson v. Vancouver Hockey Club* (1983), 5 D.L.R. (4th) 282, affirmed 22 D.L.R. (4th) 516 (B.C.C.A.). The cases were distinguished on the facts.

214 In *P.C. Kooragang Ltd. v. Richardson*, [1981] 3 All E.R. 65 (P.C.), Lord Wilberforce admits that the law has moved toward "more liberal protection" of third parties.

215 [1946] 3 W.W.R. 748 (P.C.).

216 *Ibid.*, at 756.

217 These factors were used by Picard J. in *Food Giant Markets Ltd. v. Watson Leaseholds Ltd.* (1987), 43 C.C.L.T. 152 at 157 (Alta. Q.B.).

question was not necessarily one of control but of profit and loss. "Whose business is it?" was the more apt question.[218]

The inadequacy of a simple control test to distinguish between an employee and an independent contractor was highlighted in the Supreme Court of Canada judgment, *671122 Ontario Ltd. v. Sagaz Industries Canada Inc.*[219] The tortfeasor in this case was a marketing company hired by a supplier to market its product to a major retail chain of stores. The marketing company engaged in illegal activities to win the contract for the supplier. The plaintiff company accordingly lost its earlier contract to supply the product and it sued the successful company alleging that it was vicariously liable for the torts of its marketing company. While acknowledging that control was an important factor in distinguishing between employees and independent contractors, Major J. recognized that other factors leading to other tests were also important. These included the "entrepreneur test",[220] the "organization or integration test",[221] and "the enterprise test".[222] While conceding that "there is no one conclusive test which can be universally applied to determine whether a person is an employee or an independent contractor",[223] Major J. adopted the following position:

> The central question is whether the person who has been engaged to perform the services is performing them as a person in business on his own account. In making this determination, the level of control the employer has over the worker's activities will always be a factor. However, other factors to consider include whether the worker provides his or her own equipment, whether the worker hires his or her own helpers, the degree of financial risk taken by the worker, the degree of responsibility for investment and management held by the worker, and the worker's opportunity for profit in the performance of his or her tasks.[224]

Based on this analysis, the Court concluded that the marketing company was an independent contractor.

---

218 A Canadian case which reviews the various tests is *Lake v. Callison Outfitters Ltd.* (1991), 7 C.C.L.T. (2d) 274 (B.C. S.C.). A guide-outfitter sold his company to the corporate defendant. He also had entered into a contract with the corporate defendant to remain person ally involved in the operations. An accident occurred during a fishing excursion. The court held that the corporate defendant was vicariously liable for the negligence of the guide. In coming to this conclusion, the court relied on the terms of the employment contract and the manner in which the guide's services were integrated into the defendant's business. Another interesting case is *Parker v. Blencoe* (2000), 193 D.L.R. (4th) 752 (B.C. S.C.): Crown not vicariously liable for sexual assaults committed by the defendant when he was an M.L.A. and Cabinet Minister due to absence of employer/employee relationship.

219 (2001), 204 D.L.R. (4th) 542, 8 C.C.L.T. (3d) 60 (S.C.C.), reconsideration refused (2001), 10 C.C.L.T. (3d) 292 (S.C.C.).

220 Major J. cited *Montreal v. Montreal Locomotive Works Ltd.*, above, note 215.

221 Major J. cited *Stephenson, Jordan & Harrison Ltd. v. MacDonald & Evans*, [1952] 1 T.L.R. 101 (Eng. C.A.).

222 Major J. cited Flannigan, "Enterprise Control: The Servant-Independent Contractor Distinc tion" (1987), 37 U.T. L.J. 25.

223 (2001), 204 D.L.R. (4th) 542 (S.C.C.) at 557-58.

224 *Ibid.* Major J. referred approvingly to the judgment of Cooke J. in *Market Investigations Ltd. v. Minister of Social Security*, [1968] 3 All E.R. 732 (Q.B.). This approach was applied in *Jans v. Ducks Unlimited Canada* (2006), [2007] 2 W.W.R. 154 (Sask. Q.B.), where it was decided that a person hired to remove a fence was an independent contractor and not an employee.

In *B. (K.L.) v. British Columbia*,[225] the nature of the relationship that must exist between the parties to justify the imposition of vicarious liability was further explored by the Supreme Court. The plaintiffs had been foster children who experienced physical abuse and, in the case of one plaintiff, sexual abuse in foster homes. Although the judgment dealt with several issues,[226] on the matter of the vicarious liability of the government for the acts of foster parents, the Supreme Court, with one dissent, rejected the claim. This was based on the court's conclusion that there was not a sufficiently close connection between the government and the foster parents who committed the torts. Utilizing the policy rationales which it articulated in the *Bazely* and *Curry* judgments,[227] namely that of "fair and effective compensation and deterrence of future harm",[228] the court concluded that since foster parents operated outside of day-to-day government control, in a "highly independent manner", in their own homes, and in their own way, that it would not be fair to hold government vicariously liable for the wrongs committed by foster parents and would not effectively deter foster parents from committing their wrongdoing.[229]

The case of the "borrowed servant" raises issues which shed light on the definition of the employer/employee relationship. When an employee, ordinarily under the control of one employer, is transferred, frequently in order to operate equipment for example, to another employer, the question as to whose employee that individual is, arises. In the leading case on this issue, *Mersey Docks v. Coggins*,[230] Lord Porter noted the various factors relevant to this question. Factors such as who the paymaster is, who has the right to dismiss, the length of time of the transfer, who owns the machinery used, and who can tell the employee how to do the work, are critical.[231] In *McKee v. Dumas*,[232] Dubin J.A. noted that the burden of proving that the control over an employee has been transferred from a general employer to a temporary employer is a heavy one, which must be discharged by the general employer. Control in respect of the manner in which work is to be done is only one factor. The authority to fire, hire, suspend or reprimand, the manner of payment and the right of selection are also to be considered.[233] In

225 230 D.L.R. (4th) 513, [2003] 2 S.C.R. 403, 19 C.C.L.T. (3d) 66.

226 Including the direct liability of the government under the Protection of Children Act, R.S.B.C. 1960, c. 303, breach of fiduciary duty, breach of non-delegable duty, and the applicable limitation period. Ultimately the actions, other than one for sexual assault, were dismissed due to the expiration of the limitation period.

227 See discussion below.

228 230 D.L.R. (4th) 523.

229 There was a vigorous dissent by Arbour J. *B. (M.) v. British Columbia* (2003), 230 D.L.R. (4th) 567 (S.C.C.) was released at the same time. It also dealt with the vicarious liability of government for the torts of foster parents and for the reasons given in *B. (K.L.)*, the claim was rejected.

230 [1974] A.C. 1 (H.L.).

231 *Ibid.*, at 17.

232 (1976), 70 D.L.R. (3d) 70 (Ont. C.A.).

233 See also *James Street Hardware & Furniture Co. v. Spizziri* (1985), 33 C.C.L.T. 209 (Ont. H.C.), affirmed on this point (1987) 43 C.C.L.T. 9 (Ont. C.A.); *Short v. J. & W. Henderson Ltd.* (1946), 174 L.T. 417 (H.L.); and *Baldwin v. Lyons and Erin Dist. High School Bd.* (1961), 29 D.L.R. (2d) 290 (Ont. C.A.), affirmed (*sub nom. Baldwin v. Erin Dist. High Sch. Bd.*) (1962), 36 D.L.R. (2d) 244 (S.C.C.).

Hardisty v. 851791 N.W.T. Ltd.,[234] Vertes J. in applying the above factors and finding the general, and not the temporary, employer liable for the negligence of the borrowed employee noted that this was consistent with the enterprise theory of vicarious liability. The general employer was being paid for the transfer of its employee to the temporary employer. Part of these costs, namely liability insurance premiums, had therefore theoretically already been passed on to and paid for by the temporary employer.[235]

In sum, it is clear that while control will remain an important factor in distinguishing between employees and independent contractors, the courts will consider a broad range of other factors in order to determine whether the party who engaged the tortfeasor ought to be held financially responsible for its wrongdoing. These factors must ultimately relate to the essential policy goals of vicarious liability; namely to provide just and fair compensation to the victims of the wrongdoing and to deter future harms. It must be conceded, however, that since the policy goals themselves are not crystal clear, there remains ambiguity. For example, the argument that it is fair to impose vicarious liability on the person who introduces the risk or who benefits from the activity seems to support imposing liability on those who engage independent contractors to further their business goals. In the *Sagaz* case, for example, it was the supplier who directly benefited from the illegal activities of its marketing company. It was also in the best position to spread the losses through the pricing of its goods. If the primary goal is deterrence, however, the control requirement is more defensible. What one ultimately concludes is that there are a variety of goals and factors, they do not all point in the same direction, and judgments are based on the relative importance of these factors to the decision makers.

(c) Course of Employment

An employer is vicariously liable only for the torts of employees which were committed during the course of their employment. Which torts are these?

This is a difficult question to answer with clarity, despite the best efforts of courts and commentators in suggesting tests. The issue is a question of fact, which depends on the particular circumstances of each case. Like many other issues in tort law, this is a matter of drawing lines, and where the court will draw the line in marginal cases is difficult to predict.

Tortious conduct of employees can range from activities which are expressly condoned or authorized by employers to those that are expressly prohibited and clearly outside the range of the employers' reasonable anticipation. The doctrine of vicarious liability is inapplicable to extreme conduct at both ends of the line.

---

234 (2004), 26 C.C.L.T. (3d) 305 (N.W.T. S.C.), additional reasons at (2005), 2005 CarswellNWT 118 (S.C.), affirmed (2005), 35 C.C.L.T. (3d) 100, [2006] 4 W.W.R. 199 (N.W.T. C.A.).

235 Cases cited by Vertes J. in support of his judgment included *Trans Canada Forest Products Ltd. v. Heaps, Waterous Ltd.*, [1954] S.C.R. 240, and *Earthworm Red River Ltd. v. Underwood, McLellan and Associates* (1971), [1972] 1 W.W.R. 362 (Man. Q.B.), affirmed [1972] 3 W.W.R. 400 (Man. C.A.), affirmed [1973] 2 W.W.R. 576 (S.C.C.). The same type of question of "whose employee is it?" was raised in *Nielsen Estate v. Epton* (2006), 45 C.C.L.T. (3d) 31 (Alta. C.A.). Costigan J.A. held that the negligent employee worked for the company, and hence a director of the company could not be held vicariously liable for that person.

When an employer authorizes, instructs, or in some other way participates with an employee in tortious activity, the doctrine of vicarious liability is unnecessary. The employer's liability will be personal and direct.[236] In a similar vein, tortious acts done by agents for the benefit of their principals will directly implicate the principal in the wrongdoing.[237]

Vicarious liability will apply to the torts of employees which were not authorized by their employers and for which they cannot be held personally responsible, if these torts were committed within the course of the employee's employment. Where will the courts draw the line between conduct committed within or outside the scope of the employee's employment?

The traditional approach has been to distinguish between conduct the courts will regard as the "unauthorized mode of committing an authorized act," and conduct which is so unconnected to the employee's job as to be separate from it.[238] Various factors can be suggested as being relevant to the determination of this issue. Certainly, the degree of the employee's wrongdoing will be important. Mere carelessness in the performance of tasks which were authorized, albeit authorized to be performed carefully, will result in vicarious liability. The more serious the wrongdoing the less likely it will be that the courts will consider the conduct to be merely an unauthorized mode of performing an authorized act. Deliberate wrongdoing, unlawful conduct, wilful or malicious conduct, or acts done incontravention of express instructions, will incline to the rejection of vicarious liability.[239] As well, the context of the employee's tort will be relevant. Consideration must be given to the time of its commission, its place, and its

---

236 This was explained by Anglin C.J.C. in the frequently quoted case of *Saint John (City) v. Donald*, [1926] S.C.R. 371 at 383-84, as follows:

> Injuries due to improper acts authorized by the employer, to his negligence in the selection of the contractor, to his failure to impart proper instructions, to his neglect to prevent the creation on his own property by the contractor of a nuisance, or its continuance, or to his giving employment to do acts which, though lawful, can be done only at the peril of him who does them, are really not within the purview of the doctrine imputing vicarious re sponsibility. In these cases the responsibility is rather direct and rests on personal acts or omissions.

For an application of this, see *Travois Hldg. Ltd. v. Adanac Tile & Marble Co.* (1987), 52 Alta. L.R. (2d) 108 (Q.B.).

237 See, e.g., *Brown & Huston Ltd. v. York (Borough)* (1985), 17 C.L.R. 193 (Ont. C.A.).

238 In *Triplett v. Steadman*, [1982] 1 W.W.R. 266 at 269 (Alta. Q.B.), the principle was stated as follows:

> . . . an employer is liable for acts he has not authorized provided they are so connected with acts he has authorized that they might rightly be regarded as modes, although improper modes, of doing them. However, the employer is not responsible if the wrongful act of a servant is not so connected with that authorized by or within the scope of the employment as to be a mode of carrying out the employment. If the act can be viewed as an independent act of the employee, the master will not be responsible, as the servant has gone outside the scope of his employment.

Although this clearly states the issue, it fails to provide guidance as to how to determine these questions.

239 The term frequently used to define conduct which falls outside of the course of employment is an employee's "frolic of his own." See, for example, *Krokosz Estate v. Soucy Estate* (1992), 82 Man. R. (2d) 124 (Q.B.), where the employee's decision to give passengers a ride in his employer's helicopter was considered to constitute such conduct.

purpose. This will give an indication as to whether the tort was committed as part of the employee's job, or whether it was unconnected to and independent from it.[240]

The case law reveals that although these factors are helpful, the results of cases are inconsistent and can be surprising.[241] For example, although vicarious liability was rejected where an employee had disregarded express instructions,[242] disregarding express instructions will not necessarily place an employee's tort outside the scope of the employment.[243]

Although vicarious liability has generally been rejected in cases of intentional and deliberate wrongdoing by employees,[244] there are cases where deliberate wrongdoing has resulted in the vicarious liability of employers.[245] This issue of wilful wrongdoing has been particularly problematic.[246] It is clear that merely because the wrongdoing of an employee is deliberate does not, *per se*, preclude the application of vicarious liability. It certainly, however, makes it much less likely that vicarious liability will be applied.[247] The connection of the employee's

---

240 Although the issue generally concerns whether the employee's conduct was part of the employment, a separate issue which can arise is whether the employee was even at work at the time of the tort. For example, is driving to and from work part of the employment? In *Lockhart v. Christie* (1994), 148 N.B.R. (2d) 81 (Q.B.), affirmed (1994), 155 N.B.R. (2d) 26 (C.A.), the defendant left the job site driving his own car. He went to the bank, and then either was planning to go home or to another job for the same employer. He was paid for the whole day. The court held, "not without some reservation," that his work only commenced when he arrived at the job site, and that there accordingly was no vicarious liability for a car accident which happened en route.

241 This was commented on by Comyn J. in *Harrison v. Michelin Tyre Co.*, [1985] 1 All E.R. 918 at 920: "One is constantly surprised in the law at reading the facts of a reported case and jumping ahead, as one will, to guessing the answer that the court gave; in no field has it proved more surprising than in this."

242 See, e.g., *R. v. Crown Diamond Paint Co.*, [1983] 1 F.C. 837 (C.A.); and *Bickman v. Smith Motors Ltd.*, [1955] 5 D.L.R. 256 (Alta. C.A.).

243 See, e.g., *Lockhart v. C.P.R.*, [1942] 3 W.W.R. 149 (P.C.).

244 See, e.g., *Q v. Minto Mgmt. Ltd.* (1984), 15 D.L.R. (4th) 581 (Ont. H.C.), affirmed (1986), 34 D.L.R. (4th) 767 (Ont. C.A.); *Heasmans v. Clarity Cleaning Co.*, [1987] I.R.L.R. 286 (C.A.); *Irving v. Post Office*, [1987] I.R.L.R. 289 (C.A.); *P.C. Kooragang v. Richardson*, [1981] 3 All E.R. 65 (P.C.); *Plains Engr. Ltd. v. Barnes Security Services Ltd.* (1987), 43 C.C.L.T. 129 (Alta. Q.B.); and *Barrett v. "Arcadia" (The)* (1977), 2 C.C.L.T. 142 (B.C. S.C.). Where the employee's job involves deliberate force, the case for vicarious liability is stronger. See, for example, the "bouncer" cases, discussed in *Ecuimates v. Rix*, [1993] O.J. No. 2905 (Gen. Div.).

245 See, e.g., *Lloyd v. Grace, Smith*, [1912] A.C. 716 (H.L.), and Lord Denning's judgment in *Photo Production v. Securicor*, [1978] 3 All E.R. 146 at 150, reversed on other grounds [1980] 1 All E.R. 556 (H.L.). These, and other cases, are discussed in *Plains Engr. Ltd. v. Barnes Security Services Ltd.* (1987), 43 C.C.L.T. 129 (Alta. Q.B.). A recent case involving thefts by an employee of a security provider where vicarious liability was not found is *Royal Bank v. Intercon Security Ltd.* (2005), [2005] O.J. No. 4700, 2005 CarswellOnt 5922 (S.C.J.).

246 See discussion below on cases involving sexual and physical abuse.

247 As well, as discussed by Hutchinson J. in *Plains Engr., ibid.*, cases which have found employers vicariously liable for the intentional wrongdoing of employees may be explained on other bases: holding out by the employers, agency, or non-delegable duties, for example. Cases such as *Lloyd v. Grace, Smith, ibid.*, *Morris v. C.W. Martin & Sons*, [1965] 2 All E.R. 725 (C.A.), and *Photo Production v. Securicor*, [1980] 1 All E.R. 556 (H.L.), which involved employers' liability for the deliberate wrongdoing of employees were explained on these grounds by Hutchinson J. who, at 43 C.C.L.T. at 150, proposed the following rule regarding

tort to the authorized job has clearly been one of the most important factors. Nevertheless, even where tortious acts have been integrally related to the employee's job, decisions as to vicarious liability have been inconsistent. For example, the conduct of a fire brigade in purposely driving slowly to a fire, in furtherance of an industrial dispute, was held to be outside the scope of the employment.[248] Horseplay at work has been considered to be outside the scope of employment in some cases,[249] but within the course of employment in others.[250]

(d) Vicarious Liability for Sexual and Physical Abuse: The Supreme Court of Canada's "Strong Connection" Test

The vicarious liability of employers for sexual assaults committed against children by employees highlights the difficulties with the traditional "in the course of employment" test. For it is clearly so that if anything lies outside the course of employment of those hired to care for children, it is their egregious abuse of these children.

The Supreme Court of Canada has been called upon to deal with the issue of vicarious liability in these extreme situations in a number of cases.[251] In the first two, *Bazley v. Curry*[252] and *T. (G.) v. Griffiths*,[253] the policies justifying vicarious liability and its applicability to these types of cases were thoroughly reviewed. Both cases concerned sexual assaults committed by employees of non-profit defendants on children in their care.[254] Although these cases represent the most serious types of intentional wrongs committed by employees, the general policies

---

vicarious liability for wrongful acts which are wilful or deliberate:

> . . . the employer will only be liable if the *tortious* act by the employee is of the same general kind as the employee was authorized to carry out on behalf of the employer, and where the resultant loss can be connected to the employer. Foreseeability also plays a part as to whether the wrongful unauthorized act was a normal or expected incident of the act which the employee was engaged to perform. This may be answered by asking whether the employer could have reasonably foreseen the wrongful act as a risk which might be expected in the typical performance by the employee in the course of performing his appointed tasks.

248 *General Engr. Services Ltd. v. Kingston & Saint Andrew Corp.*, [1988] 3 All E.R. 867 (P.C.).

249 *Smith v. Crossley Bros.* (1951), 95 S.J. 655 (C.A.); and *Aldred v. Nacanco*, [1987] I.R.L.R. 292 (C.A.).

250 See, e.g., *Harrison v. Michelin Tyre Co.*, above, note 241.

251 They are *Bazley v. Curry* (1999), 46 C.C.L.T. (2d) 1, 174 D.L.R. (4th) 45 (S.C.C.); *T. (G). v. Griffiths* (1999), 46 C.C.L.T. (2d) 49, 174 D.L.R. (4th) 71, [1999] 9 W.W.R. 1 (S.C.C.); *B. (K.L.) v. British Columbia*, 230 D.L.R. (4th) 513, [2003] 2 S.C.R. 403, 19 C.C.L.T. (3d) 66, [2003] 11 W.W.R. 203; *G. (E.D.) v. Hammer*, 230 D.L.R. (4th) 554, [2003] 2 S.C.R. 459, 19 C.C.L.T. (3d) 38, [2003] 11 W.W.R. 244; *B. (M.) v. British Columbia* (2003), 230 D.L.R. (4th) 567; *John Doe v. Bennett* (2004), 236 D.L.R. (4th) 577; *B. (E.) v. Order of the Oblates of Mary Immaculate (British Columbia)* (2005), 258 D.L.R. (4th) 385, 35 C.C.L.T. (3d) 1, [2006] 3 W.W.R. 1 (S.C.C.); and *Blackwater v. Plint* (2005), 258 D.L.R. (4th) 275, [2006] 3 W.W.R. 401 (S.C.C.). *B. (K.L.) v. B.C.* and *B. (M.) v. British Columbia* were discussed above in relation to whether the government and foster parents were in a sufficiently close relationship to warrant the imposition of vicarious liability.

252 (1999), 46 C.C.L.T. (2d) 1, 174 D.L.R. (4th) 45 (S.C.C.).

253 (1999), 46 C.C.L.T. (2d) 49, 174 D.L.R. (4th) 71, [1999] 9 W.W.R. 1 (S.C.C.).

254 The *Curry* case concerned a residential facility for emotionally troubled children. The *Griffiths* case involved a daily recreational program operated by a boys and girls club.

underlying the imposition of vicarious liability for any type of case were reviewed by the Court.[255]

The Court outlined the approach that ought to be taken to determine whether vicarious liability should be imposed on employers. First is the matter of precedent—"a court should determine whether there are precedents which unambiguously determine on which side of the line between vicarious liability and no liability the case falls".[256] Second, and assuming there are no precedents, the court must consider the policy reasons for imposing vicarious liability. As noted above, these are "the concern to provide a just and practical remedy to people who suffer as a consequence of wrongs perpetrated by an employee"[257] and "the deterrence of future harm".[258] These policies supported the principle that employers should be held vicariously liable where the wrongdoing fell "within the ambit of the risk" created or exacerbated by the employer's enterprise.[259] This can be said to exist "where the wrong is so connected with the employment that it can be said that the employer has introduced the risk of wrong".[260]

The "strong connection" test is based on a factual determination that the enterprise "materially enhanced the risk" rather than providing the "mere opportunity" for the employee to commit the wrong. The factors which the court identified as being relevant to this determination included (a) the opportunity that the enterprise afforded the employee to commit the tort; (b) the extent to which the wrongful act furthered the employer's aims; (c) the extent to which the wrongful act was related to friction, confrontation or intimacy inherent in the enterprise; (d) the extent of the power conferred upon the employee by the job; and (e) the vulnerability of the victims to the wrongful exercise of that power.[261] Based on these indicia a unanimous Court found that there was vicarious liability in the residential school case. A strongly divided Court, however, found that there was no vicarious liability in the recreational day program setting.[262]

---

255 The importance of these judgments is reflected in the extensive commentary that has resulted from them. See V. Black & S. Wilderman, "Parsing the Supreme Court's New Pronouncements on Vicarious Liability for Sexual Battery" (1999), 46 C.C.L.T. (2d) 126; P. Cane, "Vicarious Liability for Sexual Abuse" (2000), 116 L.Q.R. 21; K.E. Davis, "Vicarious Liability, Judgment Proofing and Non-Profits" (2000), 50 U.T. L.J. 407; N. Des Rosiers, "From Precedent to Prevention—Vicarious Liability for Sexual Abuse" (2000), 8 Tort L. Rev. 27; G.M. Dickinson, "Precedent or Public Policy? Supreme Court Divided on Rules for Vicarious Liability" (2000), 10 Educ. & L.J. 137; B. Feldthusen, "Vicarious Liability for Sexual Abuse" (2001), 9 Tort L. Rev. 173; among others. Also see B. Feldthusen, "Vicarious Liability For Sexual Torts" in Mullany & Linden, eds., *Tort Tomorrow: A Tribute to John Fleming* (1998), Chap.12, written after the Court of Appeal judgments in the two cases. The Canadian judgments were also relied upon by the House of Lords in its own recent judgment *Lister v. Hesley Hall Ltd.*, [2001] UKHL 22 (H.L.); and by the Australian High Court in *New South Wales v. Lepore*, [2003] H.C.A. 4. See discussion below.

256 (1999), 46 C.C.L.T. (2d) 1 (S.C.C.) at 10.

257 *Ibid.*, at 15.

258 *Ibid.*, at 16.

259 *Ibid.*, at 17.

260 *Ibid.*

261 *Ibid.*, at 20.

262 The court was divided 4-3.

The next three Supreme Court of Canada judgments were *B. (K.L.) v. British Columbia*,[263] *G. (E.D.) v. Hammer*,[264] and *B. (M.) v. British Columbia*.[265] As discussed above, *B. (K.L.) v. B.C.* and *B. (M.) v. B.C.* dealt not with whether the torts committed by foster parents were committed in the course of their employment, but whether the foster parents and the government were in a sufficiently close relationship to warrant the imposition of vicarious liability. The court concluded that there was not a sufficiently close connection between the government and the foster parents who committed the torts. *G. (E.D.) v. Hammer* dealt with sexual assaults committed by a school janitor on a grade three student. The assaults took place at school during school hours. The trial judge had dismissed all actions against the school board, including the vicarious liability claim.[266] In the Supreme Court of Canada's judgment in *Jacobi v. Griffiths*,[267] Justice Binnie referred approvingly to the trial judgment in *Hammer* as an illustration of the principle that "creation of opportunity without job-created power over the victim or other link between the employment and the tort will seldom constitute the 'strong connection' required to attract vicarious liability." As a result of that statement, the plaintiff in *Hammer* did not appeal the trial judge's vicarious liability decision. Despite the fact, therefore, that vicarious liability was not in issue in *G. (E.D.) v. Hammer* when the case reached the Supreme Court, both McLachlin C.J.C. and Arbour J. referred to Binnie J.'s earlier statement rejecting vicarious liability on the facts of this case.[268]

John Doe v. Bennett[269] dealt with sexual assaults committed by a priest on young boys. The Supreme Court, applied the guidelines articulated in *Bazely*, and held that the bishop's relationship with the wrongdoing priest and the connection between the priest's torts and his employment as a priest were sufficiently close to warrant the imposition of vicarious liability on the bishop.[270] *Blackwater v. Plint*[271] and *B. (E.) v. Order of the Oblates of Mary Immaculate (British Columbia)*[272] dealt with allegations of sexual abuse brought by former residents of residential schools. In *Blackwater*, the claims for vicarious liability were brought against both the government, which was statutorily responsible for establishing

---

263 230 D.L.R. (4th) 513, [2003] 2 S.C.R. 403, 19 C.C.L.T. (3d) 66, [2003] 11 W.W.R. 203.

264 230 D.L.R. (4th) 554, [2003] 2 S.C.R. 459, 19 C.C.L.T. (3d) 38, [2003] 11 W.W.R. 244.

265 (2003), 230 D.L.R. (4th) 567 (S.C.C.).

266 (1998), [1998] B.C.J. No. 992, 1998 CarswellBC 902 (S.C.), affirmed (2001), 2001 CarswellBC 721 (C.A.), leave to appeal allowed (2001), 2001 CarswellBC 2756 (S.C.C.), affirmed (2003), 2003 CarswellBC 2407 (S.C.C.).

267 Above, note 253.

268 One cannot go so far as to say that McLachlin C.J.C. and Arbour J. thought that Binnie J. was correct in his view. However, they did feel that in light of Binnie J.'s comments in *Jacobi v. Griffiths*, with reference to the trial judge's decision in *G. (E.D.) v. Hammer*, it was correct for the plaintiff in *Hammer* not to have pursued the vicarious liability issue on appeal. The claims against the school board for breach of non-delegable duty and breach of fiduciary duty were also rejected by all three courts.

269 (2004), 236 D.L.R. (4th) 577 (S.C.C.).

270 The Roman Catholic Episcopal corporation that had oversight over the priest, and the bishop of the corporation were viewed as synonymous entities for the purpose of the suit.

271 (2005), 258 D.L.R. (4th) 275 (S.C.C.).

272 (2005), 258 D.L.R. (4th) 385 (S.C.C.).

and regulating boarding schools for Aboriginal children, and the Church, which ran the school under an agreement with the government. The sexual assaults were committed by a dormitory supervisor hired by a Principal employed by the Church. The interesting aspect of the case was whether the court could find both the government and the Church vicariously liable for the tort committed by the wrongdoer. In this case, not only were both parties found vicariously liable, based on the idea that they were "partners" in running the school, but the trial judge's decision to apportion liability for the tort 75 per cent to the government and 25 per cent to the Church was affirmed by the Supreme Court. While conceding that using legislation which apportions liability based upon "fault" to parties whose liabilities are not based on fault, but on strict liability, may be seen as problematic, the Supreme Court affirmed the trial judge's unequal distribution based on the notion of varying degrees of control. This is consistent with the Supreme Court's policy rationales for the imposition of vicarious liability. The party with the greater control over the wrongdoing employee and his activities was in the better position to take steps to prevent this wrongdoing, and thus a greater portion of "fault" was attributed to it.

B. (E.) v. Order of the Oblates of Mary[273] dealt with the vicarious liability of a Church for sexual assaults committed against a resident of a residential school by a lay employee, who worked in the school bakery and operated the school's motorboat. In rejecting vicarious liability, Binnie J. emphasized that in determining whether there was a strong connection between the wrongdoing and the employer's enterprise, attention must not only be paid to the nature of the enterprise but also to the "job-created power and duties" assigned to the wrongdoing employee. After considering a number of vicarious liability cases, Binnie J., for the majority of the court, held that there was insufficient connection between what the wrongdoing employee was asked to do by his employer and his acts of wrongdoing to justify the imposition of vicarious liability.[274]

(e) The "Strong Connection" Test in Practice

Despite the considerable effort by the Supreme Court to provide a useful guide to the resolution of vicarious liability cases, especially in cases of intentional wrongdoing, difficulties remain. The new "strong connection" test, with the Court's suggested indicators, does more clearly point the way than did the traditional "unauthorized mode of committing an authorized act" test. Courts must now look for factors which suggest that the employment not only provided the opportunity for an employee to commit an intentional wrong, but as well significantly enhanced the employee's opportunity to do so. The employer's responsibility to pay damages in these cases emanates from the principle that since it was the enterprise which created the risk, the enterprise should pay its costs. This is based not on a "deep pocket" rationale, since even if the enterprise cannot afford to pay these costs or is no position to distribute them, it will still be held

273 *Ibid.*

274 There was a vigorous dissent by Abella J. who would not have reversed the trial judge's conclusion that based on the factors enumerated by the Supreme Court in *Bazely*, vicarious liability existed.

vicariously liable.[275] It is based on the view that where there is a strong connection between the employee's tasks and the employee's wrongdoing, both fairness and the ability to deter point to the liability of the employer.

It must be stated that despite the new clarity, the strong connection test has not been easy for courts to apply. This is evident from the fact that the Supreme Court itself was almost evenly divided on the question whether there was a sufficiently strong connection between the employee's duties and the sexual abuse in the *Griffiths* case to justify the imposition of vicarious liability.[276]

Finally there is the matter of precedent. Despite the fact that the unanimous Court in *Curry* conceded that the first things courts must do is look for precedents, the Court found no precedents. This can be contrasted with the Court's judgment in the *Griffiths* case, where the majority acknowledged that "Canadian courts have in fact examined a variety of circumstances in which it has been sought to make employers liable for sexual assaults committed by employees".[277] This difference in view again demonstrates a division in the Court regarding the applicability of previous judgments in emerging areas.[278]

One can illustrate the application of the strong connection test in practice by looking at the results of some of the decisions which have applied it since it was introduced by the Supreme Court. Vicarious liability has been found for sexual assaults committed by a residential school administrator,[279] a priest,[280] a dormitory supervisor,[281] a country camp volunteer,[282] a boxing instructor,[283] a technologist at a private health care clinic,[284] a high school teacher,[285] and a probation officer.[286]

---

275 It must be recognized that there is some division in the Court on this matter. In *Curry*, the Court specifically rejected the argument that special consideration should be paid to the fact that the defendant was a non-profit foundation. In *Griffiths,* the majority of the Court, while not specifically using the defendant's non-profit status as a reason to deny vicarious liability, expressed doubt whether the policies furthered by vicarious liability of just compensation, loss spreading, and deterrence are met when non-profit defendants are held vicariously liable.

276 One surmises that the Court realized that a divided Court on this question would not send out a clear message and must have desperately sought to reach a consensus in both cases. They could not, and now there are two judgments which lower courts and counsel can rely upon, depending on which result they prefer. And, as we have seen above, the Supreme Court has been divided in a number of its own judgments on vicarious liability decided since *Bazely v. Curry* guidelines were articulated.

277 46 C.C.L.T. (2d) 71.

278 The issue of precedents is a troubling one. Rarely do courts find exact factual situations to the one before them. Nevertheless, the facts frequently are significantly similar. In my opinion, the search for the "exact" case will destroy a system based on precedent.

279 *P. (V.) v. Canada (Attorney General)*, [2000] 1 W.W.R. 541, 47 C.C.L.T. (2d) 249 (Sask. Q.B.).

280 *John Doe v. Bennett*, above, note 269; and *Swales v. Glendinning* (2004), 237 D.L.R. (4th) 304 (Ont. S.C.J.).

281 *Blackwater v. Plint*, above, note 271.

282 *S. (C.) (Next Friend of) v. Miller*, [2002] 6 W.W.R. 148 (Alta. Q.B.), additional reasons at (2003), 2003 CarswellAlta 1901 (Q.B.).

283 *H.L. v. Canada* (2001), 5 C.C.L.T. (3d) 186, [2001] 7 W.WE.R. 722, varied as to damages [2002] S.J. No. 702 (Sask.C.A.), varied as to damages (2005), 251 D.L.R. (4th) 604 (S.C.C.).

284 *Weingerl v. Seo* (2005), 256 D.L.R. (4th) 1 (Ont. C.A.), additional reasons at (2005), 2005 CarswellOnt 3323 (C.A.).

285 *Bouchard v. Carruthers* (2004), [2005] 2 W.W.R. 227 (Sask. C.A.); and *John Doe v. Avalon East School Board* (2004), 28 C.C.L.T. (3d) 88 (N.L. T.D.).

286 *G. (B.M.) v. Nova Scotia (Attorney General)* (2007), 260 N.S.R. (2d) 257 (C.A.).

It has not been imposed in cases involving assaults committed by foster parents,[287] a school janitor,[288] a lay employee,[289] a lay minister,[290] a physical education teacher,[291] a manager of a recreation centre,[292] a manager of an apartment complex,[293] and an army corporal.[294] Although each case is, of course, fact specific, it is interesting to note the divergence of judicial opinions on its application to fairly similar situations.[295]

Subsequent to the Supreme Court of Canada's judgments, the English House of Lords decided *Lister v. Hesley Hall Ltd.*[296] The case involved sexual assaults committed by an employee, a warden of a school boarding house, on children under his care. The lower courts had dismissed a vicarious liability claim brought against the warden's employer for these sexual assaults. These dismissals were based on an earlier Court of Appeal decision, *T. (S.) v. North Yorkshire County Council.*[297]

In a unanimous decision, the House of Lords decided that the lower courts had properly applied *T. (S.)*, but that *T. (S.)* had been incorrectly decided. Taking its lead from the Supreme Court of Canada judgments, the "strong connection" test appealed to the Lords. The Lords examined the nature of the employer's enterprise, which in *Lister* was to take care of students, the duties of the employee in relation to the achievement of this objective, and the type of wrongdoing that occurred. The fact that there was a sufficiently close connection between these elements justified imposing vicarious liability.[298]

---

287 *B. (K.L.) v. B.C.* and *B.(M.) v. B.C.* above, note 251 .

288 *G. (E.D.) v. Hammer*, above, note 266.

289 *B. (E.) v. Order of the Oblates*, above, note 273.

290 *Wilson v. United Church of Canada* (2005), 30 C.C.L.T. (3d) 314 (B.C. S.C.).

291 *H. (S.G.) v. Gorsline*, 5 C.C.L.T. (3d) 65, [2001] 6 W.W.R. 132 (Alta. Q.B.), additional reasons at (2001), 2001 CarswellAlta 1009 (Q.B.), affirmed (2004), [2005] 2 W.W.R. 716 (Alta. C.A.), leave to appeal refused (2005), 2005 CarswellAlta 62 (S.C.C.).

292 *H. (T.E.G.) v. K. (P).*, [2001] 6 W.W.R. 546 (Alta. Q.B.)

293 *Armstutz v. McGregor* (2003), [2006] 3 W.W.R. 98 (Alta. Q.B.).

294 *S. (K.) v. McLean* (1999), [1999] O.J. No. 4085, 1999 CarswellOnt 3511 (Gen. Div.).

295 For example, it was applied to a priest but not to a lay minister; to a boxing coach but not to a physical education teacher, and so on.

296 [2001] UKHL 22 (H.L.).

297 (1998), [1999] L.G.R. 584 (Eng. C.A.). The case involved sexual assaults committed on a mentally handicapped child by the deputy headmaster of a school that the plaintiff child had attended. The county council that operated the school was sued and its vicariously liability was rejected.

298 Lord Steyn stated it this way: ". . .the employers entrusted the care of the children in Axeholme House to the warden. The question is whether the warden's torts were so closely connected with his employment that it would be fair and just to hold the employers vicariously liable. On the facts of the case the answer is yes. After all, the sexual abuse was inextricably interwoven with the carrying out by the warden of his duties in Axeholme House". Lord Clyde also noted "the sufficient connection between the acts of abuse which he [the warden] com mitted and the work which he had been employed to do". Lord Hobhouse approached the case from the perspective of a specific duty that had been entrusted to the employer, which the employer had then delegated to the employee; i.e., the language of non-delegable duties was used. See discussion below. Lord Millett emphasized the connection between the enterprise, the employee's duties and the nature of the wrongdoing.

(f) Vicarious Liability for "Independent Contractors"

It has been suggested that notwithstanding the designation of the wrongdoer as an "independent contractor" and not an "employee", the person who engages the wrongdoer can still be held vicariously liable. In two British Columbia cases, *A. (C.) v. C. (J.W.)*[299] and *B. (M.) v. British Columbia*,[300] judges held that the Crown was vicariously liable for the wrongs committed by foster parents over children in their care despite the fact that the foster parents were designated as independent contractors. In another British Columbia case, *Thiessen v. Mutual Life Assurance Co. of Canada*,[301] a financial investment company was held vicariously liable for the fraud of a sales representative who was clearly an independent contractor. It is my assessment that this approach complicates an already difficult jurisprudence and should be resisted. If the wrongdoer is a true independent contractor, as determined by the factors suggested by the Supreme Court of Canada in *Sagaz*, vicarious liability ought not to be applicable. Rather, the court can find liability based on other theories; for example, negligence, breach of fiduciary duty, agency or breach of non-delegable duty.[302] In the absence of the control or other factors set out by the Supreme Court of Canada in the *Sagaz* case to establish the wrongdoer as an employee, it is difficult to justify imposing vicarious liability on those who are truly independent contractors.[303]

(g) Non-delegable Duties

The vicarious liability issues discussed above will be avoided in those cases where the court finds that the employee's breach involved a non-delegable or personal duty imposed on the employer. In this situation, liability will be imposed on the employer without regard to the status of the employee or the nature of the employee's tort. The breach of the duty will result in the personal liability of the employer, and therefore the restrictions of the doctrine of vicarious liability do not apply.[304]

---

299 (1998), 166 D.L.R. (4th) 475, 43 C.C.L.T. (2d) 223 (B.C. C.A.). This case was decided before the Supreme Court of Canada judgments in *Curry*, *Griffiths* and *Sagaz Industries*. Leave to appeal was sought but abandoned in *A. (C.) v. C. (J.W.)*.

300 [2001] 5 W.W.R. 6 (B.C. C.A.). This case was decided after *Curry* and *Griffiths*, but before *Sagaz*. As discussed above, *B. (M.) v. British Columbia* was reversed by the Supreme Court of Canada.

301 (2001), 8 C.C.L.T. (3d) 134 (B.C. S.C.), varied (2002), 13 C.C.L.T. (3d) 30 (B.C. C.A.). The Court of Appeal affirmed the judgment based not on vicarious liability, however, but on the liability of a principle for the acts of its agent.

302 Where the liability of the defendant is based on its own fault, or a breach of a statutory or other duty, it is incorrect to categorize this as vicarious liability. Sometimes courts do this; see for example *Carriere v. Schlachter* (1999), [2000] 1 W.W.R. 397 (Alta. Q.B.), where the occupier was liable for the wrong of an independent contractor not based on vicarious liability but because it breached its own occupiers' duty to the plaintiff. See also *Dixon v. Eldorado Development Corp.* (1999), [2000] 1 W.W.R. 671 (B.C. S.C.).

303 The view that independent contractors can be held vicariously liability was not shared by all of the justices who heard these cases. Mackenzie J.A. stated explicitly that he "would limit vicarious liability to cases where there is an employer-employee relationship", at [2001] 5 W.W.R. 6 (B.C. C.A.) at 33.

304 See Williams, "Liability for Independent Contractors", [1956] Cambridge L.J. 180; Stevens, "Non-Delegable Duties and Vicarious Liability" in Neyers, Pitel, Chamberlain, eds., *Emerging Issues in Tort Law* (2007), Chapter 13; and Murphy, "Juridical Foundations of Common Law Non-Delegable Duties", *ibid.*, Chapter 14.

The essential feature of a non-delegable duty is that responsibility for its execution always rests on the person upon whom the duty is imposed. Although it may be delegated to another, the breach, no matter how committed, by the delegatee, will be treated as a breach by the delegator.[305] In the leading case on this issue, *Wilsons & Clyde Coal Co. v. English*,[306] Lord Wright held that the fundamental obligations of employment owed by an employer to its employee — the duty to provide competent staff, adequate material, and a proper system of effective supervision — were personal to the employer. They could not be delegated to others so as to absolve the employer of the legal responsibility for them.[307] Another instance has arisen with respect to the duty imposed upon the Crown, and presumably other public authorities, to maintain roads under their jurisdiction. The fact that the Crown has hired an independent contractor to perform functions with respect to road maintenance does not relieve the Crown of its personal liability should the functions be performed carelessly.

The Supreme Court of Canada expounded on this matter in *Lewis (Guardian ad litem of) v. British Columbia*.[308] Cory J. noted, "a party upon whom the law has imposed a strict statutory duty to do a positive act cannot escape liability

---

305 As explained by Prowse J.A. in *B. (M.) v. British Columbia*, [2001] 5 W.W.R. 6 (B.C. C.A.), leave to appeal allowed (2001), 2001 CarswellBC 2754 (S.C.C.), reversed (2003), 230 D.L.R. (4th) 567 (S.C.C.), at 29 [W.W.R.]:

> it is important to bear in mind that the words "non-delegable duty" are somewhat misleading. To call a duty non-delegable does not mean that the duty cannot be delegated, but, rather, that ultimate responsibility for the performance of the duty cannot be delegated. Respon sibility for the performance of the duty remains with the delegator who will be held liable in the event that the duty is not performed, or is performed negligently or tortiously.

306 [1938] A.C. 57 (H.L.).

307 This approach was important to defeat the doctrine of common employment, which precluded an employee from suing an employer for the torts of a fellow employee. If the employee could establish that the breach involved a personal duty of the employer, the suit was not precluded. As noted by Mason J. in the Australian High Court case *Kondis v. State Tpt. Authority* (1984), 55 A.L.R. 225, this judgment has been followed in subsequent employment cases, well as being applied in other contexts. It was reaffirmed by the House of Lords in *McDermid v. Nash Dredging Ltd.*, [1987] 2 All E.R. 878 at 887, where Lord Brandon explained the position as follows:

> First, an employer owes to his employees a duty to exercise reasonable care to ensure that the system of work provided for him is a safe one. Second, the provision of a safe system of work has two aspects: (a) the devising of such a system and (b) the operation of it. Third, the duty concerned has been described alternatively as either personal or non-delegable. The meaning of these expressions is not self-evident and needs explaining. The essential characteristic of the duty is that, if it is not performed, it is no defence for the employer to show that he delegated its performance to a person, whether his servant or not his servant, whom he reasonably believed to be competent to perform it. Despite such delegation the employer is liable for the non-performance of the duty.

In two Canadian cases, *Boothman v. Canada*, [1993] 3 F.C. 381 (T.D.), and *Clark v. Canada* (1994), 20 C.C.L.T. (2d) 241 (Fed. T.D.), the Crown was held vicariously liable for torts committed by supervisors against employees. Although the vicarious liability was sup ported by the ordinary application of the doctrine, it might have been more appropriately justified in terms of the employer's nondelegable duties vis-à-vis its employees. The issue of a non-delegable duty was thoroughly reviewed by the Australian High Court in *New South Wales v. Lepore*, [2003] H.C.A. 4. The case concerned the liability of a school authority for a sexual assault committed on a pupil by a teacher.

308 (1997), 40 C.C.L.T. (2d) 153 (S.C.C.).

simply by delegating the work to an independent contractor".[309] Where, on the other hand, the defendant's duty is merely one of reasonable care, as a general rule exercising reasonable care in the selection and in some cases the supervision of an independent contractor will discharge this duty. Nevertheless, there may be situations where due to the nature of the statute that has authorized the activity, or because of policy considerations, even a party, whose duty is merely one of reasonable care, will be held liable for the negligence of an independent contractor. The Court held that the Crown's duty to exercise reasonable care in discharging its statutory discretion to repair and maintain highways is one such circumstance. According to Cory J., not only do the relevant statutory provisions[310] properly interpreted place liability for the negligence of independent contractors on the Ministry, but also for reasons of fairness liability should be so placed. These related to the reasonable expectations of highway users and their reliance upon the Ministry with respect to the safety of highways.[311]

The nature of a non-delegable duty was further explored by the Supreme Court of Canada in three of the recent sexual abuse cases discussed above. In *B. (K.L.) v. British Columbia*[312] and *B. (M.) v. British Columbia,*[313] involving abuse by foster parents, and *G. (E.D.) v. Hammer*,[314] involving sexual abuse by a school's

309 (1997), 40 C.C.L.T. (2d) 153 (S.C.C.) at 164.

310 Primarily s. 48 of the Ministry of Transportation Highways Act, R.S.B.C. 1979, c. 280:

> The minister shall direct the construction, maintenance and repair of all government build ings, highways and public works in progress, or constructed or maintained at the expense of the Province, and which are under his control.

311 Other policy considerations were that it would be difficult for the public to know which contractor to sue, and the Ministry can protect itself by providing for insurance and indemnity in its contract with contractors. McLachlin J. concurred with Cory J. but affirmed that she preferred to leave the issue of when common law duties arising from the exercise of statutory powers as non-delegable open. A companion case to *Lewis (Guardian ad litem of) v. British Columbia* is *Mochinski v. Trendline Industries Ltd.* (1997), 154 D.L.R. (4th) 212, [1998] 5 W.W.R. 756 (S.C.C.). The case also involved the liability of the Ministry for a contractor's negligence relating to highway safety, in this instance removing overhanging ice from rock faces. Cory J. found the Ministry liable for the reasons set out in the *Lewis* case. Note the "Annotation" by Professor Irvine at (1996), 29 C.C.L.T. (2d) 2, to the Court of Appeal's judgment finding that the duty was non-delegable. Professor Irvine opined "that in the near future, academic lawyers and the judiciary will take up the challenge and assign to the device of the 'non-delegable duty" a reasoned, politic and predictably-located place in our law of torts". This the Supreme Court of Canada has now attempted in these judgments. In an earlier case, *Piercey (Guardian ad litem of) v. Lunenburg (County) District School Board* (1997), 41 C.C.L.T. (2d) 163 (N.S. S.C.), affirmed (1998), 41 C.C.L.T. (2d) 60 (N.S. C.A.) it was held that a school board's duties under the Education Act, R.S.N.S. 1989, c. 136, with relation to the education of students were non-delegable. *Lewis (Guardian ad litem of) v. British Colum bia* was applied in another road maintenance case, *Truong v. Saskatoon (City)* (2001), [2002] 2 W.W.R. 290 (Sask. Q.B.). Although the court held that the city's responsibilities under The Urban Municipality Act 1984, S.S. 1983-84, c. U-11, were non-delegable, the city was ultimately protected by a statutory indemnity provision.

312 Above, note 251.

313 Above, note 251.

314 Above, note 251.

janitor, the Supreme Court rejected liability via the route of non-delegable duty.[315] Basing her conclusion on an interpretation of the statutes which defined the duties and responsibilities of the Superintendent of Child Welfare, namely the Protection of Children Act,[316] and on the school board, namely the School Act,[317] McLachlin C.J.C. held that, unlike the statute in *Lewis*, these statutes could not be interpreted as imposing non-delegable duties on the defendants for the type of harms which befell the plaintiffs. For example, while the Superintendent of Child Welfare had non-delegable duties with respect to the apprehension of a child and its care while in custody, to the placement of the child, and to certain aspects of the child's care after placement, it did not have such a duty with respect to the day-to-day care of the child. Similarly, while the School Act imposed a number of specific duties on school boards, some even relating to student health and safety, it could not be interpreted as imposing a non-delegable duty to ensure that children are not abused at the hands of a school employee.

This approach fails, in my view, to articulate a principle which can explain, in general terms, the nature of a non-delegable duty. For even if the above statutes could have been interpreted as imposing specific duties on the defendants to have prevented the harms in question, why these duties would automatically have been considered as "non-delegable", is not clear, unless it is to be concluded that all statutory duties which can give rise to civil liability are non-delegable.[318] Thus, the principle which declares that some duties are non-delegable remains unclear.

Another approach to the liability of employers for the torts of either employees or independent contractors, which avoids the problems of vicarious liability, relates to the problem of intrinsically dangerous or ultrahazardous activities. It has been held in several judgments that where a person hires someone to engage in intrinsically dangerous work, the employer will be held liable if injury results from the negligent performance of that work.[319] This principle has been applied in several Canadian cases,[320] but has been rejected in Australia.[321]

---

315 As noted by McLachlin C.J.C. in *B. (K.L.)*, the issue of non-delegable duty was not before the court in that case. It had, however, been in issue before the Court of Appeal, two of the three justices there finding that a non-delegable duty was breached. The Crown did not appeal this finding. The Supreme Court, however, decided to deal with the matter despite this, since it was an issue in the other two cases with which they were dealing.

316 R.S.B.C. 1960, c. 303.

317 R.S.B.C. 1996, c. 412.

318 It is also open to the objection that it does not explain why the statutory duty, whether non-delegable or not, even gives rise to a private law remedy in the first place. See Chapter 8.

319 The leading case is *Bower v. Peate* (1876), 1 Q.B.D. 321 at 326, where Cockburn C.J. stated:

> . . . a man who orders a work to be executed, from which, in the natural course of things, injurious consequences to his neighbour must be expected to arise, unless means are adopted by which such consequences may be prevented, is bound to see to the doing of that which is necessary to prevent the mischief, and cannot relieve himself of his responsibility by employing someone else — whether it be the contractor employed to do the work from which the danger arises or some independent person — to do what is necessary to prevent the act he has ordered to be done from becoming wrongful.

Another frequently cited case which articulates this principle is *Honeywill & Stein v. Larkin Bros. Ltd.*, [1934] 1 K.B. 191 at 199 (C.A.).

320 See, e.g., *Peters v. North Star Oil Ltd.* (1965), 54 D.L.R. (2d) 364 (Man. Q.B.), a case which involved the delivery of oil; *Bristow v. Urban Contr. (J.J. Walsh) Ltd.* (1984), 49 Nfld. &

(h) Statutory Vicarious Liability

In addition to the common law doctrine of vicarious liability, liability for the torts of others may be imposed by statute.

The liability of owners of automobiles for the torts committed by those driving their vehicles with their consent is regulated by statute in Canadian provinces.[322] As well, vicarious liability has been imposed by statute in other relationships.[323] These cases will be decided upon the application of principles of statutory interpretation, although the common law principles of vicarious liability may be of assistance in interpreting statutory language which raises the issues discussed above.

P.E.I.R. 155 (Nfld. Dist. Ct.), a case which involved the demolition of a house; *Ostapowich v. Benoit* (1982), 14 Sask. R. 233 (Q.B.), a case involving the taking down and removal of telephone poles and wires; *Doyle v. Chester Dawe Ltd.* (1980), 29 Nfld. & P.E.I.R. 113 (Nfld. Dist. Ct.), in relation to blasting operations; *A.G. Can. v. Biggar* (1981), 10 Sask. R. 401 (Sask. Dist. Ct.), in relation to highway excavations; and *Dendewicz v. B.C. Tel. Co.*, [1994] B.C.J. No. 221 (S.C.) in relation to the removal of utility cables. In *C.N.R. Co. v. di Domen icantonio* (1988), 49 D.L.R. (4th) 342 (N.B. C.A.), it was held that the principle did not apply to the running of trains, since this was considered not to be an intrinsically dangerous activity. The principle also did not apply in *Sun-Can. Pipeline Co. v. Lockwood*, [1993] O.J. No. 3089 (Gen. Div.) with regard to work on a pipe line right-of-way; or in *Gilbert Plains (Rural Municipality) v. Rohl Construction Ltd.* (1999), 45 M.V.R. (3d) 169 (Man. Q.B.), affirmed (2000), [2000] M.J. No. 607, 2000 CarswellMan 673 (C.A.) with regard to the laying of cables. It was applied in *Scarmer Const. Ltd. v. Geddes Contr. Ltd.* (1989), 61 D.L.R. (4th) 328 (B.C. C.A.), a case involving the use of explosives. This latter case also held that the employer and independent contractor, in the case of work involving special dangers, are joint tortfeasors, and not several, concurrent wrongdoers.

321 See *Stevens v. Brodribb Sawmilling Co. Pty.* (1986), 63 A.L.R. 513 (Aust. H.C.).

322 The "deemed agency" provisions of highway traffic legislation have been interpreted in numerous motor vehicle accident cases. The legislation is not uniform and has been given different interpretations. See Segal, *Manual of Motor Vehicle Law*, 3rd ed. (1982); Phelan, *Highway Traffic Law*, 3rd ed. (1969). See the Law Reform Commission of B.C., *Report on Vicarious Liability under the Motor Vehicle Act*, 1989.

323 For example, in relation to torts committed by policemen. See *Aziz v. Adamson* (1979), 11 C.C.L.T. 134 (Ont. H.C.); *Williams v. Saint John* (1983), 27 C.C.L.T. 247 (N.B. Q.B.), affirmed (*sub nom. Williams v. N.B.*) (1985), 34 C.C.L.T. 299 (N.B. C.A.). The common law status of the police was discussed in *Jane Doe v. Metro. Toronto Commrs. of Police* (1989), 48 C.C.L.T. 105 (Ont. H.C.), affirmed (1990), 72 D.L.R. (4th) 580 (Ont. Div. Ct.) and *Tasse v. Hoveland* (1992), 3 Alta. L.R. (3d) 323 (Master). Apart from statute, there is no vicarious liability for the torts of the police. The independence of the office of Commis sioner of Police was reviewed by Lord Denning in *R. v. Metro. Police Commr.; Ex parte Blackburn*, [1968] 1 All E.R. 763 (C.A.). As far as police constables are concerned, see *Re St. Catharines Police Assn. and St. Catharines Bd. of Police Commrs.*, [1971] 1 O.R. 430 (H.C.); and *Re Metro. Toronto Police Commrs. and Metro. Toronto Police Assn.* (1974), 5 O.R. (2d) 285 (Div. Ct.), affirmed (1975), 8 O.R. (2d) 65 (C.A.). The duties of a police officer are said to be public, and not owed to the municipality or board which employs or appoints them. The Ontario Police Services Act, R.S.O. 1990, c. P.15, s. 50(1), imposes vicarious liability on the "board or the Crown in right of Ontario" for "torts committed by members of the police force in the course of their employment." Also see the Police Act, R.S.A. 2000, c. P-17, s. 39(2), as well as other provincial legislation.

17
Business Torts

1. INTRODUCTION

Somewhat ignored within contemporary tort law, the business or economic torts are available to furnish occasional relief to business people who feel that the conduct of their competitors or associates has gone beyond the limits acceptable even to a capitalist, free enterprise economy. Despite the fact that these torts have a relatively long history, and exist in a society where questionable business conduct is undoubtedly not exceptional, the low profile of the business torts is not surprising. Much of the field in which the business torts would ordinarily operate has been usurped by other forms of legal control. Disputes between employers and employees are highly regulated by labour laws. Even in the context of tort, other causes of action, and particularly negligence law, provide complainants with more familiar avenues for redress. Patent, trademark, copyright, and industrial design laws also are relevant here. Other legislation, dealing with combines, illegal trade practices, criminal law and international trade, also exists. Contract law and the law relating to fiduciaries also have an important impact in ordering business relationships. The business torts thus compete in a crowded field, and play only a peripheral role.

Broadly defined, the business torts include those individual torts which are concerned not with damage which has been caused to a person's body or property but with damage which has been inflicted on a person's economic interests, usually in the context of business relationships. Although this definition covers a wide range of remedies, the discussion in this chapter will be confined to the following torts: (1) deceit; (2) interference with contractual relations; (3) intimidation; (4) conspiracy; and (5) interference with economic interests by unlawful means.[1]

---

1 English texts on the economic torts include H. Carty, *An Analysis of the Economic Torts* (Oxford

2. DECEIT

(a) Introduction

Deceit,[2] as an independent tort, must be distinguished from deceitful or fraudulent conduct, as a type of dishonest behaviour. Its existence as an independent tort, not linked to a contractual relationship between two parties, was confirmed in the case of *Pasley v. Freeman.*[3] This case decided that an individual could be held liable for a fraudulent misrepresentation made by that person to another, even though the representor had no direct interest in the matter at hand, nor was in collusion with the party who had an interest.[4] The tort is based on a false representation made by one person to another, knowingly, whereby damage is caused to the other.

Apart from the tort itself, deceitful or fraudulent behaviour has relevance in many areas of the law. It is, most importantly, relevant in the law of contracts leading to rescission of contracts,[5] and affecting the validity of contractual clauses dealing with warranties and representations.[6] It is a relevant consideration in other tort actions, for example, in respect of the validity of consent as a defence in the tort of battery. It can also affect consent as a requirement for the validity of marriage,[7] is of vital importance to insurance law principles, and so on. Although the issue of deceitful or fraudulent behaviour in these areas has a close connection to the notion of fraud in the tort of deceit, and cases in these other areas can be useful in defining the term, they are strictly outside the scope of the tort itself.[8]

University Press, 2001); T. Weir, *Economic Torts* (Clarendon Press, 1997), and Heydon, *Economic Torts*, 2nd ed. (1978). There are as of yet no Canadian texts dedicated to this topic.

2 Sometimes called fraud, or fraudulent misrepresentation. In *Bozzo, Re* (2005), [2005] O.J. No. 2037, 2005 CarswellOnt 1996 (S.C.J.), Stinson J. traces the origins of the torts of deceit and fraudulent misrepresentation. He concludes that the tort of fraudulent misrepresentation "grew from the older cause of action referred to as the tort of deceit" and that "courts have tended to treat the two causes of action similarly, if not the same", at para. 23. The court decided that the tort of fraudulent misrepresentation, as is the tort of deceit, is an action upon the case for the purpose of the applicable limitation period.

3 (1789), 100 E.R. 450.

4 There was one dissent, Grose J., who held that the previous authorities supported an action for deceit only when linked to a contractual relationship between the parties, whereby one party falsely represented a fact of the contract.

5 For example, see *Mooney v. Orr*, [1995] B.C.J. No. 1094 (S.C.). In fact, the topic is frequently seen as a matter of contract law; see, e.g., *Metropolitan Stores of Canada Ltd. v. Nova Construction Co.* (1988), 49 R.P.R. 81 (N.S. C.A.).

6 For example, fraud will negate contractual terms denying the existence of warranties or representations. It can also create liability for inaccuracies in pre-tender construction contracts in circumstances where, absent fraud, liability would not exist. See, e.g., *K.R.M. Const. Ltd. v. B.C. Ry. Co.* (1982), 40 B.C.L.R. 1 (C.A.). It has been held that one cannot have judgment for breach of warranty and fraud in the same action. See *Link v. Schaible* (1961), 27 D.L.R. (2d) 461 (B.C. C.A.).

7 See *Said v. Said* (1986), 38 C.C.L.T. 260 (B.C. C.A.).

8 The distinction between the tort of deceit *per se*, and fraudulent conduct which ought to lead to a remedy for the defrauded party, whether by way of an equitable claim for unjust enrichment, or simply as a tort in itself, was discussed by D.S. Ferguson J. in *Harland v. Fancsali* (1993), 102 D.L.R. (4th) 577 (Ont. Gen. Div.). The defendant purchasers "tricked" the vendor into selling the property to them at $10,000 less than a previously agreed to price, by making an offer to him under the maiden name of one of the parties. This appeared to the vendor to be a new offer from a different person, which he accepted. The trial judge thought that this was fraudulent, but that it did not fit within the requirements of the tort of deceit, especially with regard to the

(b) Elements of the Tort

To succeed in deceit, a plaintiff must prove that (1) a false representation or statement was made by the defendant, (2) which was knowingly false, (3) was made with the intention to deceive the plaintiff, and (4) which materially induced the plaintiff to act, resulting in damage.

(i) False Representation or Statement

In its most orthodox form, the tort of deceit involves a false statement of fact made by the defendant directly to the plaintiff. This positive misrepresentation can be in either verbal or written form. In the leading case on the tort of deceit, *Derry v. Peek*,[9] the deceit was contained in a company's written prospectus. In its judgments defining the tort, the Lords repeatedly referred to false "statements", or "representations", as constituting the basic element of the tort.[10]

The majority of the reported cases on deceit involve misstatements of fact made by the defendant directly to the plaintiff. For example, in *Sugar v. Peat Marwick Ltd.*,[11] the defendants were liable on account of falsified books which overstated accounts receivable. In *Underwood v. Ocean City Realty Ltd.*,[12] liability resulted from false statements concerning the state of a septic system, in *Francis v. Dingman*[13] from false statements concerning the terms of a stock sale, and in *Wishloff v. Boyko*[14] from false statements concerning the adequacy of wells.[15]

The direct lie, however, is not the only form of actionable misrepresentation. A successful action for deceit can be based on an incomplete disclosure — the so-called half-truth. Thus, in *C.R.F. Hldg. Ltd. v. Fundy Chem. Int. Ltd.*,[16] a

---

requirement of a false "representation." The action was upheld, therefore, on the notion of fraud, as a broader cause of action dealing with dishonesty. The Divisional Court upheld the decision, based on the tort of deceit. See (1994), 21 O.R. (3d) 798. Also see *Kelemen v. El-Homeira* (1999), 49 C.C.L.T. (2d) 188 (Alta. C.A.), leave to appeal refused (2000), 271 A.R. 398 (note) (S.C.C.). The court noted that the deceit action is founded in law, the contract action in equity. Either can lead to damages, but recission is available only in the contract action. There is a duty to mitigate in both. The case concerned the tort action. In *Perry, Farley & Onyschuk v. Outerbridge Management Ltd.* (2001), 54 O.R. (3d) 131 (C.A.), Sharpe J.A. notes that the action for deceit developed as an action on the case. This is further elaborated upon by Stinson J. in *Bozzo, Re* (2005), [2005] O.J. No. 2037, 2005 CarswellOnt 1996 (S.C.J.). The tort of deceit has also been employed outside of the business context. For example, see *Raju v. Kumar* (2006), 265 D.L.R. (4th) 632 (B.C. S.C.), where a wife sued her husband for deceit and *Auch v. Wolfe*, [2003] 9 W.W.R. 140 (Man. Q.B.), where a person with cancer sued defendants who falsely represented that they could arrange for alternative treatment which could cure it.

9 (1889), 14 App. Cas. 337 (H.L.).

10 *Pasley v. Freeman*, above, note 3, also based the tort on a direct lie, a fraudulent affirmation of fact.

11 (1988), 55 D.L.R. (4th) 230 (Ont. H.C.).

12 (1985), 34 C.C.L.T. 128 (B.C. S.C.), affirmed (1987), 12 B.C.L.R. (2d) 199 (C.A.).

13 (1983), 2 D.L.R. (4th) 244 (Ont. C.A.).

14 (1984), 52 A.R. 260 (Q.B.).

15 Other cases of the same type involve a false statement concerning the previous sales of a food kiosk — *TWT Enterprises Ltd. v. Westgreen Developments (North) Ltd.* (1992), 3 Alta. L.R. (3d) 124 (C.A.); a false financial statement given by a vendor to a purchaser of a business — *System Contractors Ltd. v. 2349893 Manitoba Ltd.*, [1994] 4 W.W.R. 488 (Man. Q.B.); and a false description of a printing press given by the vendor to its purchaser — *473759 Alberta Ltd. v. Heidelberg Canada Graphic Equipment Ltd.*, [1995] 5 W.W.R. 214 (Alta. Q.B.).

16 (1981), 19 C.C.L.T. 263 (B.C. C.A.).

representation made to the plaintiff that slag would make "excellent fill" was fraudulent, since, although partly true, the fact that the slag was radioactive was not disclosed to the questioning purchaser.[17]

Active concealment by conduct may also constitute a fraudulent misrepresentation. In *Brown & Assoc. Advertising Inc. v. Farmco Steel Bldgs. Ltd.*,[18] for example, liability flowed from conduct which implicitly misrepresented facts. The manager of a company was held liable when he placed advertisements with the plaintiff even though he was aware at the time of the company's inability to pay for these services.[19]

In some situations, the courts have been prepared to depart from the narrow requirement of a positive misstatement, whether in the form of a direct lie or a half-truth, or active concealment of the truth by conduct, in order to constitute the tort. It is now conceded that positive assertions or misrepresentations are not essential to the tort, since the truth can be misrepresented in other ways. Although the principle that mere silence or concealment is not sufficient to give rise to a cause of action in deceit is of long-standing authority,[20] and is still supported in current law,[21] it is a principle which has been increasingly more narrowly confined. In *Sidhu Estate v. Bains*,[22] for example, a defendant who remained silent when a misrepresentation that he had initiated was passed on by an innocent party to the

---

17 The trial judgment at (1980), 14 C.C.L.T. 87 (B.C. S.C.), traces the law with respect to deceit by half-truths to the *dicta* of Chambre J. in *Tapp v. Lee* (1803), 127 E.R. 200 at 203:

> Fraud may consist as well in the suppression of what is true, as in the representation of what is false. If a man, professing to answer a question, selects those facts only which are likely to give a credit to the person of whom he speaks, and keep back the rest, he is a more artful knave than he who tells a direct falsehood.

For a more recent discussion of what constitutes a "half-truth", see *Freeman v. Perlman* (1999), 169 D.L.R. (4th) 133 (B.C. C.A.); and *Alevizos v. Nirula* (2003), 234 D.L.R. (4th) 352 (Man. C.A.).

18 (1983), 26 Sask. R. 305 (Q.B.).

19 See, however, the cautionary note by Lambert J.A. in *Burns v. Kelly Peters & Assoc.* (1987), 41 C.C.L.T. 257 at 319 (B.C. C.A.):

> It is possible to found an action in deceit without an express representation, but only where the course of conduct of the defendant is so unequivocal in its meaning that a failure to explain it leaves an impression, taking the conduct and the lack of explanation together, that is equivalent in effect to an express false and fraudulent representation.

20 See the judgment of Lord Chelmsford in *Peek v. Gurney* (1873), L.R. 6 H.L. 377 at 391 (H.L.).

21 See, e.g., Macdonnell J. in *Canson Ent. Ltd. v. Boughton & Co.* (1988), 45 C.C.L.T. 209 at 219 (B.C. S.C.), affirmed (1989), 39 B.C.L.R. (2d) 177 (C.A.), affirmed [1991] 3 S.C.R. 534: "Simple reticence or silence does not amount to fraud. There must be a positive assertion which amounted to a misrepresentation. . . ." See also Lambert J.A. in *Sorensen v. Kaye Hldg.*, [1979] 6 W.W.R. 193 at 225 (B.C. C.A.):

> The first question is whether silence constituted a misrepresentation. This is not a contract of utmost good faith, nor was there a fiduciary relationship between the parties. In the absence of such a special contract or relationship, it is not deceit for a vendor to fail to decry his own wares unless he makes some positive assertion that becomes distorted by the failure.

See also *Alevizos v. Nirula* (2003), 234 D.L.R. (4th) 352 (Man. C.A.) at 358.

22 [1996] 10 W.W.R. 590 (B.C. C.A.), leave to appeal refused (1997), 89 B.C.A.C. 240 (note) (S.C.C.).

plaintiff was held liable for an actionable misrepresentation.[23] It must be realized, however, that the less direct the misrepresentation, and the less active the concealment, the more difficult will it be to establish that the defendant acted dishonestly with the intention to deceive the plaintiff, which is crucial to the success of the action. Mere forgetfulness, or even negligence, will not support the tort.

The issue arises in its most contentious form when the courts are called upon to balance the obligation of vendors to refrain from dishonestly representing their wares with the obligation of purchasers to assess for themselves the qualities of the products they purchase. While it is true that the maxim *caveat emptor* does not apply in cases of fraud,[24] what constitutes fraud for this purpose remains the important question.

Several Canadian cases have dealt with this concern. In *Abel v. McDonald*,[25] the defendants were liable for fraud based upon "active non-disclosure." The defendants, vendors of property, aware of the fact that the property had been damaged after an agreement of sale for it had been entered into, but before the closing date, prevented the purchaser from gaining access to the property so that the damage could not be discovered.[26]

An actionable deceit also occurs when a defendant remains silent after a change in circumstances renders a previously true representation false.[27] In *K.R.M. Const. Ltd. v. B.C. Ry. Co.*,[28] for example, the defendants were liable when the representations they made during the beginning of negotiations and upon which the plaintiffs relied became untrue due to a change of plans prior to the time the agreement was concluded. The court held that the defendants' failure to inform the plaintiffs of the change was fraudulent.[29]

---

23 The defendant had misrepresented to an investor that he himself had invested money in a company. On the basis of this, the investor not only invested his own money but also convinced his sister to do so in a telephone conversation. The defendant was present at the time of the call but said nothing to correct the misrepresentation.

24 See *Redican v. Nesbitt*, [1924] 1 D.L.R. 536 (S.C.C.).

25 (1964), 45 D.L.R. (2d) 198 (Ont. C.A.).

26 A similar case is *Reid v. Prowse* (1983), 45 Nfld. & P.E.I.R. 216 (Nfld. Dist. Ct.), where the vendors of a car stated that it was in perfect shape, and actively concealed its rust by painting it over.

27 The principle stems from Lord Blackburn's judgment in *Brownlie v. Campbell* (1880), 5 App. Cas. 925 at 950:

> . . . when a statement or representation has been made in the *bona fide* belief that it is true, and the party who has made it afterwards comes to find out that it is untrue, and discovers what he should have said, he can no longer honestly keep up the silence on the subject after that has come to his knowledge, thereby allowing the other party to go on. . . .

This was quoted with approval in *K.R.M. Const. Ltd. v. B.C. Ry. Co.* (1982), 40 B.C.L.R. 1 at 18 (C.A.), and *Rainbow Indust. Caterers v. C.N.R.* (1988), 46 C.C.L.T. 112 at 119 (B.C. C.A.).

28 *Ibid.*

29 See also *Jones v. Dumbrell*, [1981] V.R. 199 (Vict. S.C.), a similar Australian case. The same principle applies when a representor remains silent knowing that a representation previously made is no longer true or was never true: see *Toronto-Dominion Bank v. Leigh Instruments Ltd. (Trustee of)* (1991), 4 B.L.R. (2d) 220 (Ont. Gen. Div.); *Toronto-Dominion Bank v. Leigh Instruments Ltd. (Trustee of)* (1998), 40 B.L.R. (2d) 1 (Ont. Gen. Div. [Commercial List]), additional reasons at (1998), 78 O.T.C. 134 (Gen. Div. [Commercial List]), affirmed (1999), 45 O.R. (3d) 417 (C.A.), leave to appeal refused (2000), 139 O.A.C. 399 (note) (S.C.C.); and

A further extension of deceit by non-disclosure has arisen with respect to cases involving latent defects in realty sold by vendors to unsuspecting purchasers. In one of the leading cases on this issue, *McGrath v. MacLean*,[30] Dubin J.A., in *obiter*, conceded that "a vendor may be liable to a purchaser with respect to premises which are not new if he knows of a latent defect which renders the premises unfit for habitation."[31] This liability extends to non-disclosed latent defects which are known to the vendor, and which render the premises either actually or potentially dangerous.[32] In *C.R.F. Hldg. Ltd. v. Fundy Chem. Int. Ltd.*,[33] Anderson J.A. held that the following rule was applicable to cases of this kind:

> The vendor of land on which is situate an inherently dangerous substance is guilty of fraud if he sells such land to a purchaser, without warning the purchaser that if the dangerous substance is not used or disposed of in a specified manner, or in the manner prescribed by statute, the purchaser and/or strangers to the contract may suffer a serious risk of injury.[34]

In *Sevidal v. Chopra*,[35] this duty to disclose was extended. The vendor was held to be under a duty to disclose not only those matters which rendered the property dangerous but "unfit for habitation" as well.[36] This rule was applied in *Jung v. Ip*,[37] where silence concerning a termite infestation was considered to be

---

862590 Ontario Ltd. v. Petro Canada Inc. (2000), 33 C.E.L.R. (N.S.) 107 (Ont. S.C.J.), additional reasons at (2000), 2000 CarswellOnt 1783 (S.C.J.) for a discussion of these principles. See, however, *Crozman v. Ruesch*, [1994] 4 W.W.R. 116 (B.C. C.A.), where the court did not fault the vendors for failing to reveal discoveries of additional cracks in their house to the purchasers. There was, at the time, an already executed contract of purchase and sale. In addition, there was no fraudulent intent.

30 (1979), 95 D.L.R. (3d) 144 (Ont. C.A.).

31 *Ibid.*, at 151. Dubin J.A. referred to Laskin, "Defects of Title and Quality: *Caveat Emptor* and the Vendor's Duty of Disclosure", [1960] Spec. Lect. L.S.U.C. 389. The judgment in *McGrath* and Laskin's article frequently are referred to in the numerous judgments concerning fraudulent representations in connection with the sale of realty. Many of these cases deal with real estate contracts in general and "disclosure statements" in particular and are outside the scope of this text. See Perell & England, *Remedies and the Sale of Land*, 2nd ed. (Markham: Butterworths, 1998); Oosterhoff & Rayner, *Anger & Honsberger Law of Real Property* (Aurora: Canada Law Book, 1985); and other specialized texts on this topic. For a good discussion of the vendor's obligations with respect to information given in a "Property Condition Statement" see *Alevizos v. Nirula* (2003), 234 D.L.R. (4th) 352 (Man. C.A.). Both Scott C.J.M. and Kroft J.A. expressed serious concerns relating to the use of these types of disclosure statements.

32 Note that liability in tort for falsely representing the safety of dangerous chattels was the basis of *Langridge v. Levy* (1837), 150 E.R. 863, affirmed (1838), 150 E.R. 1458. This was significant in that it permitted liability in tort, despite the lack of contractual privity. Weatherston J.A., in *McGrath v. MacLean*, in dissent, reviewed the law applicable to non-disclosure of latent defects with respect to realty. The courts have held that *caveat emptor* was the rule, subject only to a few exceptions, one of which related to fraudulent misrepresentation. Other exceptions related to defects in title, and defects which rendered the premises uninhabitable. With respect to fraud, however, mere silence not accompanied by active concealment or suggestions of the non-existence of the defect did not amount to fraud; see Williams, "Non-disclosure, Upon the Sale of Land, of a Latent Defect Known to Vendor" (1906), 50 Sol. J. 611. Weatherston J.A. would have maintained the action, not on fraud principles, however, but on negligence.

33 (1981), 19 C.C.L.T. 263 (B.C. C.A.).

34 *Ibid.*, at 309-10.

35 (1987), 41 C.C.L.T. 179 (Ont. H.C.).

36 See Irvine's cautions about this extension, *ibid.*, at 181.

37 (1988), 47 R.P.R. 113 (Ont. Dist. Ct.).

a fraudulent misrepresentation.[38] In *Jakubke v. Sussex Group — SRC Realty Corp.*,[39] the rule may have been extended further. The vendor was liable in fraud for failing to disclose to the purchasers that renovations had been completed to the house without the required building permits, and in direct contravention of stop work orders. This was said to constitute a latent defect, the conscious non-disclosure of which constituted a fraudulent misrepresentation. What is interesting to note, however, is that although these defects resulted in financial losses to the purchasers, there was no discussion in the case as to whether this rendered the property dangerous or unfit for habitation.[40]

A principal can be held liable in deceit for remaining silent and permitting an innocent agent to represent facts which the principal knows are false. In *Sugar v. Peat Marwick Ltd.*,[41] the defendant bank was held liable for allowing a receiver/manager who was acting as the bank's agent to furnish the plaintiff with a financial statement which overstated the accounts receivable of a bankrupt company. This was a personal liability of the principal for fraud, which depended upon proof that the principal remained silent, knowing that his agent was misrepresenting the truth, in order to deceive the representee.[42]

---

38 Note, however, these additional findings: the vendors had concealed the termite damage by replacing flooring and installing drywall, the damage was considered to be so bad as to render the property uninhabitable and "dangerous to life and limb", and the purchasers had specifically asked the unaware agent about termites. It is not surprising that in view of these findings, fraud was found. A judgment of an Alberta court, in *Modern Livestock Ltd. v. Elgersma* (1989), 50 C.C.L.T. 5 (Alta. Q.B.), has held that this "new species of deceit" by failing to disclose ought not to be extended to a vendor of hogs which were infected with a disease. There was liability in negligence, however, based on a duty to warn.

39 (1993), 15 C.C.L.T. (2d) 298 (B.C. S.C.).

40 The judgment indicates that the affected rooms — a bedroom and bathroom — were not built to Code, *vis-à-vis* height requirements, and could not lawfully be used for these purposes, although they could be used for other purposes, storage, for example. Would this qualify them as being "unfit for habitation"? Also see *Brown v. Fritz*, [1993] B.C.J. No. 2182 (S.C.), where the failure to inform purchasers that their property substantially encroached on Crown land led to a successful tort claim for fraudulent misrepresentation. In *Alevizos v. Nirula* (2003), 234 D.L.R. (4th) 352 (Man. C.A.), at 360, Scott C.J.M. stated that active concealment of a patent defect so as to render it latent is fraudulent. The difference between a patent defect and one which is latent was discussed by Ballance J. in *Cardwell v. Perthen* (2006), 38 C.C.L.T. (3d) 210 (B.C. S.C.), additional reasons at (2007), 2007 CarswellBC 566 (S.C.), affirmed (2007), 48 C.C.L.T. (3d) 137 (B.C. C.A.). If the defect, although not observable "on a casual inspection. . .would have been discoverable upon a reasonable inspection by a qualified person", it is not a latent defect. The court found the defendant liable for failing to disclose the existence of certain latent defects that rendered the property unfit for human habitation and in one case posed a significant health risk. The cost for remedying these defects was awarded. The action for negligent or fraudulent misrepresentations inducing the plaintiff to purchase the house was dismissed due to lack of reliance. The Court of Appeal affirmed, although it noted that the trial judge was not implying that there is always an absolute obligation on a purchaser to obtain an inspection. This depends on the circumstances including the knowledge and qualifications of the purchaser to recognize obvious, visible and readily observable defects.

41 (1988), 55 D.L.R. (4th) 230 (Ont. H.C.).

42 It is to be distinguished from the vicarious liability of the principal for the deceitful conduct of its agent committed during the course of its employment. See Fleming, *The Law of Torts*, 9th ed. (1998), at 700. The principal will also be held personally liable for authorizing an agent to make false statements, or for purposely employing an innocent agent to make false statements, in order to deceive the representee. As well, a company can be liable for a fraud committed by

(ii) Knowledge

The tort of deceit depends upon strict proof that the defendant's representations were made fraudulently.[43] In *Derry v. Peek*,[44] the Lords made it clear this required that the defendant must have made the statement knowing that it was false, or with reckless disregard of the truth or falsity of the representations. Mere negligence with respect to the truth of the representation was not sufficient.[45] Canadian courts have affirmed this aspect of the tort. It has been held that negligence, carelessness and wishful thinking do not amount to fraud. There must be "moral recklessness and a callous disregard as to whether the statement is true or false."[46] Although the defendant's assertions of an honest belief in the truth of the statements will be tested by reference to a standard of reasonableness, the issue ultimately is not whether the defendant was unreasonable, but whether knowingly, or with careless disregard for the truth, the defendant made the false statements.[47] Once fraud is established, the defendant's motive for making the statement is irrelevant. A dishonest defendant will be liable, whether or not the statements were intended to harm the representee.[48]

(iii) Intention to Deceive

The representation must be made in order to deceive the plaintiff. In other words, the defendant must have intended that the plaintiff act upon the representation.[49]

---

its officers, when the operating, or directing, mind of the company commits a fraud which "by design or result" benefits the company, and was not in fraud of the company. See *Dixon v. Deacon Morgan McEwen Easson* (1993), 102 D.L.R. (4th) 1 (B.C. C.A.). See also *Standard Investments Ltd. v. C.I.B.C.* (1985), 22 D.L.R. (4th) 410 (Ont.C.A.); and *R. v. Canadian Dredge & Dock Co.* (1985), 19 D.L.R. (4th) 314 (S.C.C.).

43 It has been held that fraud must be "strictly pleaded and strictly proven." See *Rainbow Indust. Caterers v. C.N.R.* (1988), 46 C.C.L.T. 112 at 143 (B.C. C.A.).

44 (1889), 14 App. Cas. 337 (H.L.).

45 This judgment blocked the development of liability for negligent statements, until *Hedley Byrne & Co. v. Heller & Partners*, [1964] A.C. 465 (H.L.). See Reed, "*Derry v. Peek* and Negligence" (1987), 8 J. of Leg. History 64.

46 *McLaughlin v. Colvin*, [1941] 4 D.L.R. 568 at 583 (Ont. C.A.), affirmed [1942] 3 D.L.R. 292 (S.C.C.).

47 See Lord Herschell's judgment, 14 App. Cas. 337 at 374. The Lords struggled with distinguishing between defendants who were simply unreasonable in their beliefs, for which liability would not lie, and defendants whose assertions of an honest belief in the truth of their statements could not, based on an objective test, be upheld. For a good discussion on this point, see Feehan J.'s judgment in *Opron Construction Co. v. Alberta* (1994), 151 A.R. 241 (Q.B.). More recently see A.F. Wilson J.'s judgment in *Pacific Playground Holdings Ltd. v. Endeavour Developments Ltd.* (2002), [2002] B.C.J. No. 1109, 2002 CarswellBC 1159 (S.C.), additional reasons at (2003), 2003 CarswellBC 281 (S.C.), who discusses both the issue of silence amounting to fraud and reckless disregard for the truth. It is stressed that the "will to mislead" must be established in order for the representor to be guilty of fraud. See L. Hoyano, "Lies, Recklessness and Deception: Disentangling Dishonesty in Civil Fraud" (1996), 75 Can. Bar Rev. 474.

48 See Lord Herschell, *ibid.*, at 374. See *Opron Construction v. Alberta*, *ibid.*, and *Thomas J. Lipton Inc. v. Spada*, [1992] O.J. No. 572 (Gen. Div.). There need not be an intention to cheat or injure. There must, however, be an intention to deceive. One must concede that, ordinarily, where one makes a knowingly false statement which damages another, a good motive is unlikely to be present.

49 See discussion of this point by Southin and Hinkson JJ.A. in *BG Checo International Ltd. v.*

In the ordinary case, where a knowingly false representation is made directly to the plaintiff, this requirement is easily satisfied. A defendant may still be held liable, however, for a false representation not made directly to the plaintiff, as long as the statement was made in order to deceive that person.[50] For example, a statement not made directly to the plaintiff, but to a banker in the plaintiff's presence, was held to have been made in order to induce the plaintiff to act.[51]

(iv) Material Inducement Causing Damage

In order to be actionable, the deceit must have materially induced the plaintiff to act detrimentally. The question as to whether the test of materiality is an objective one, i.e., would the deceit have been relied on by the "reasonable" person, or a subjective one, did this representee rely on the deceit, was in issue in *Keleman v. El-Homeira.*[52] In an earlier Alberta Court of Appeal judgment, *TWT Enterprises Ltd. v. Westgreen Developments (North) Ltd.*,[53] an objective test of materiality was applied.[54] In *Kelemen*, however, the Alberta Court of Appeal held that although the objective test of materiality is correct in the contract action for fraudulent misrepresentation, the test for the tort action for deceit is the subjective one; i.e., was the representation a true inducement as between the parties themselves?[55] This creates an anomalous situation. It requires the parties and the court to carefully distinguish between the two actions,[56] and it creates the result that on the same facts damages for fraudulent misrepresentation in a contract action might

---

B.C. Hydro & Power Authority (1990), 4 C.C.L.T. (2d) 161 (B.C. C.A.), and Feehan J. in *Opron Construction Co. v. Alberta, ibid.* The Supreme Court of Canada agreed with the B.C. Court of Appeal in *BG Checo* that there was no intention to deceive and thus that fraud could not be made out in that case, but without extensive discussion of this point. In *40 Sunpark Plaza Inc. v. 850453 Alberta Inc.*, [2007] 7 W.W.R. 339 (Alta. Q.B.), the trial judge noted that the tort requires an intention to deceive, and not an intention to cheat. That is, the defendant's motive is irrelevant.

50 See *Peek v. Gurney* (1873), L.R. 6 H.L. 377, and *Barry v. Croskey* (1861), 70 E.R. 945, cited in *Cherewick v. Moore*, [1955] 2 D.L.R. 492 at 494 (B.C. S.C.).

51 See *Smith v. Porter* (1979), 27 N.B.R. (2d) 439 (C.A.).

52 (1999), 49 C.C.L.T. (2d) 188 (Alta. C.A.), leave to appeal refused (2000), 271 A.R. 398 (note) (S.C.C.).

53 (1992), 127 A.R. 353, 3 Alta. L.R. (3d) 124 (C.A.).

54 In this case the plaintiffs leased a food kiosk in a mall. They alleged that false representations were made to them inducing them to enter into the lease and they sued for damages. The court described the actions as actions for fraud and negligent misrepresentation. The trial judge applied a subjective test of materiality. The Court of Appeal described this as a "dubious manner" in which to deal with this issue, but nevertheless agreed with the result because the objective test of materiality was met.

55 The court cites several leading texts in support of this approach. The court viewed the *TWT Enterprises Ltd.* case as a contracts case, not a tort case.

56 For example, on the surface both the *TWT Enterprises Ltd.* and *Kelemen* actions are for damages caused by fraudulent misrepresentations leading to contracts. The Court of Appeal explained however that in *TWT* the allegation was that the fraud was used directly by the defendant as an inducement to the plaintiff to enter into the contract, whereas in *Kelemen* the representation was made in order to convince the plaintiff to consult an advisor who was not independent. With respect, this appears to be an overly subtle distinction. The gravamen of both actions was that the defendants used fraudulent representations to induce parties to enter into unfavourable contracts.

be denied, which would be recovered if the complaint was framed as a tort action for deceit.

The court must determine whether the plaintiff did actually rely on the statement to its detriment. There are several aspects to this requirement. Ordinarily, the action for deceit will be based on misrepresentations of fact, rather than on mere opinions, promises, or "puffery."[57] This can be explained on the basis that statements of fact will more likely be a material inducement upon which others act than will be unenforceable promises, opinions, or self-serving descriptions.[58] The "puffing" which is commonly expected of parties to transactions will generally not be considered as a material inducement for serious transactions. In *Semkuley v. Clay*,[59] for example, a realtor's statement of opinion concerning the possibility of obtaining rezoning approval was held not to have been a fraudulent misrepresentation. The trial judge stated that "in order for a misrepresentation to be operative, it must be shown that it was a statement of fact, rather than a statement of law, or of intention, or a promise or a mere commendatory puff."[60]

It has been held that statements of opinion may constitute fraud where the representor does not actually hold the opinion professed, or where there is the implication that the individual offering the opinion is possessed of facts which the representee does not have, and which substantiate the validity of the opinion.[61] It has also been stated that "a statement of law cannot be treated as an operative misrepresentation."[62] However, where a person fraudulently represents to another knowledge of the law in order to induce that individual to enter into a transaction, there is no reason to reject the tort's application.

The misrepresentation must have been made with the intention of inducing the representee to act in the transaction which constitutes the object of the complaint. Thus, in *Peek v. Gurney*,[63] a plaintiff was shown a false prospectus prepared in order to induce the public to take shares in a new company. The plaintiff did not acquire shares. However, at a later date, the plaintiff acquired the shares of the company on the stock exchange. It was held that the plaintiff could no longer base an action on deceit on the false prospectus, as the prospectus had not been acted upon in the manner intended. The plaintiff's decision to buy the shares and

---

57 See *Daeyoo Ent. Co. v. Long* (1986), 75 A.R. 47 (Q.B.).

58 See *Kerr on Fraud and Mistake*, 5th ed. at 45, cited in *Barmettler v. Endicott* (1983), 29 Sask. R. 192 at 193 (Q.B.), where it is stated that:

> A misrepresentation goes for nothing unless it is a proximate and immediate cause of the transaction. It is not enough that it may have remotely or indirectly contributed to the transaction and may have supplied a motive to the other party to enter into it. The representation must be the very ground on which the transaction has taken place.

59 (1982), 140 D.L.R. (3d) 489 (Alta. Q.B.).

60 *Ibid.*, at 493.

61 *Semkuley v. Clay, ibid.* Authorities cited by the court included *Smith v. Land & House Property Corp.* (1884), 28 Ch. 7 (C.A.); *Bisset v. Wilkinson*, [1927] A.C. 177 (P.C.); and *Brown v. Raphael*, [1958] 2 All E.R. 79 (C.A.). See also *Ballard v. Gaskill*, [1954] 4 D.L.R. 427 at 431 (B.C. S.C.): "An expression of opinion concerning a present or future event may be a representation of fact if it implies that it is an opinion presently held."

62 *Semkuley v. Clay, ibid.*, at 495.

63 (1873), L.R. 6 H.L. 377.

his resultant losses were not the immediate, but the remote consequences of the false prospectus.[64]

It has been held that a fraudulent defendant cannot defend the action on the grounds that the plaintiff was unwise in acting upon the representation, or had the opportunity, which was not taken up, of verifying the information.[65] Consistent with the approach the courts have adopted with reference to the intentional torts, contributory negligence has been held to be inapplicable to actions for deceit.[66]

Once it is proven that material false statements were made in order to induce the plaintiff to act, the onus of proving that the plaintiff did not actually rely on those representations in deciding to act falls upon the defendant.[67]

(c) Assessment of Damage

Damages for deceit are assessed on a tort rather than on a contract basis. Plaintiffs are entitled to be put back into the position in which they would have been had the false representation not been made, not into the position they would have been in had the representation been true.[68]

The case law illustrates this approach. Where, for example, the plaintiff would not have entered into the transaction had the representation not been made, he

---

64 See also *Currie v. MacFarlane* (1989), 6 R.P.R. (2d) 243 (N.S. T.D.). There was no liability where the representation was made after the plaintiff entered into the agreement.

65 See *Siametis v. Trojan Horse (Burlington) Inc.* (1979), 104 D.L.R. (3d) 556 (Ont. H.C.), affirmed (1981), 123 D.L.R. (3d) 767 (Ont. C.A.); *United Services Funds (Trustees of) v. Richardson Greenshields of Can. Ltd.* (1988), 48 D.L.R. (4th) 98 (B.C. S.C.); and *Midland Doherty Ltd. v. Fasken*, [1993] O.J. No. 2510 (Gen. Div.); reversed on other grounds and new trial ordered (1997), [1997] O.J. No. 4097, 1997 CarswellOnt 3759 (C.A.). The Supreme Court of Canada affirmed this approach in *Sylvan Lake Golf & Tennis Club Ltd. v. Performance Industries Ltd.* (2002), 209 D.L.R. (4th) 318 (S.C.C.), a case that dealt with the rectification of a contract. For a contrary decision, see *Laird Group Inc. v. Astral Bellevue Pathe Inc.*, [1990] O.J. No. 47 (Dist. Ct.).

66 *Ibid.*

67 See *Baker v. Guar. Savings & Loan Assn.*, [1931] 1 D.L.R. 968 (S.C.C.); *Siametis v. Trojan Horse (Burlington) Inc.*, above, note 65; *Barron v. Kelly* (1918), 41 D.L.R. 590 (S.C.C.); *System Contractors Ltd. v. 2349893 Manitoba Ltd.*, [1994] 4 W.W.R. 488 (Man. Q.B.); *Sidhu Estate v. Bains*, [1996] 10 W.W.R. 590 (B.C. C.A.), leave to appeal refused (1997), 89 B.C.A.C. 240 (note) (S.C.C.); *Weibe v. Gunderson* (2003), 13 R.P.R. (4th) 78 (S.C.), additional reasons at (2003), 2003 CarswellBC 3158 (S.C. [In Chambers]), varied (2004), 27 C.C.L.T. (3d) 159 (B.C. C.A.), additional reasons at (2004), 2004 CarswellBC 2816 (C.A.), additional reasons at (2004), 2004 CarswellBC 3094 (S.C. [In Chambers]); and *3Com Corp. v. Zorin International Corp.* (2004), 2004 CarswellOnt 1685 (S.C.J.), affirmed (2006), 2006 CarswellOnt 3333 (C.A.). There are, however, authorities to the contrary; see, for example, *L.K. Oil & Gas Ltd. v. Canalands Energy Corp.* (1989), 68 Alta. L.R. (2d) 269 (C.A.), leave to appeal refused [1990] 1 W.W.R. lxxi (S.C.C.), cited in *Sidhu Estate*.

68 They are, in other words, not entitled to the "lost bargain." See *Metropolitan Stores of Can. Ltd. v. Nova Const. Co.* (1987), 39 C.C.L.T. 185 (N.S. T.D.), reversed on other grounds (1988), 49 R.P.R. 81 (N.S. C.A.); *V.K. Mason Const. Ltd. v. Bank of Nova Scotia*, [1985] 1 S.C.R. 271; *Rainbow Industrial Caterers v. C.N.R.*, [1991] 3 S.C.R. 3; *Toronto Dominion Bank v. Mapleleaf Furniture Manufacturing Ltd.* (2003), [2003] O.J. No. 4719, 2003 CarswellOnt 4601 (S.C.J.); and *Weibe v. Gunderson* (2004), 27 C.C.L.T. (3d) 159 (B.C. C.A.), additional reasons at (2004), 2004 CarswellBC 2816 (C.A.). In a proper case, however, the court may rectify a contract and thereby put a plaintiff into the position it would have been in had the representation been true. See, e.g., the Court of Appeal decision in *Metropolitan Stores of Can. Ltd., ibid.*

was entitled to receive back the investment which he had lost.[69] Where the misrepresentation concerns the value of property purchased by the plaintiff, the damages represent the difference between what the plaintiff paid for the property and what it was actually worth.[70] If, therefore, the property is worth the price paid for it, despite the fraud, the plaintiff can recover nothing, even though it would have been worth more had the representation been true.[71] It has also been held, however, that one method of assessing the actual value of the property is by calculating how much it would cost to make the representation true and deducting this amount from the purchase price.[72]

Although the authorities are not uniform, it has been held in several cases that, in addition to the above assessment, a plaintiff is entitled to the consequential damages suffered as a result of the fraudulent misrepresentation. The leading authority is *Doyle v. Olby (Ironmongers) Ltd.*,[73] where Lord Denning held that "the defendant is bound to make reparation for all the actual damages directly flowing from the fraudulent inducement",[74] whether reasonably foreseeable or not. Although several Canadian cases have accepted the principle of awarding consequential damages,[75] some judges have suggested that they should be limited, as in negligence actions, by the reasonable foreseeability test.[76] Consequential damages have included such things as the expenses incurred in order to attempt to make a business successful,[77] and the moving expenses, legal fees and the real estate commission pertaining to a house purchase.[78] In the appropriate case of

---

69 See *Sugar v. Peat Marwick* (1988), 55 D.L.R. (4th) 230 (Ont. H.C.).

70 See, e.g., *Underwood v. Ocean City Realty Ltd.* (1985), 34 C.C.L.T. 128 (B.C. S.C.), affirmed (1987), 12 B.C.L.R. (2d) 199 (C.A.); *Hepting v. Schaaf*, [1964] S.C.R. 100; *McConnel v. Wright*, [1903] 1 Ch. 546 (C.A.). This has been described by Newbury J.A. as the "traditional approach" to assessing damages in these types of cases; see *Weibe v. Gunderson*, above, note 68, at 167. As stated by Newbury J.A., the question to be asked is "what a hypothetical, willing but not anxious buyer, informed of the true picture, would have paid a willing but not anxious seller for the 'package' of assets in a competitive market at the time", at 176.

71 See *Sorensen v. Kaye Hldg.*, [1979] 6 W.W.R. 193 (B.C. C.A.).

72 See *Chua v. Van Pelt* (1977), 74 D.L.R. (3d) 244 (B.C. S.C.).

73 [1969] 2 Q.B. 158 (C.A.).

74 *Ibid.*, at 167, quoted with approval in *C.R.F. Hldg. Ltd. v. Fundy Chem. Int. Ltd.* (1981), 19 C.C.L.T. 263 at 274-75 (B.C. C.A.).

75 See, e.g., *Siametis v. Trojan Horse (Burlington) Inc.*, above, note 66, *K.R.M. Const. Ltd. v. B.C. Ry. Co.* (1982), 40 B.C.L.R. 1 (C.A.), and *Weibe v. Gunderson*, above, note 66.

76 See *Sevidal v. Chopra* (1987), 41 C.C.L.T. 179 (Ont. H.C.); Craig J.A. in *C.R.F. Hldg Ltd.*, above, note 74. Irvine notes in his Annotation at 41 C.C.L.T. 179 at 184 that other judges seem to have accepted Lord Denning's views in their entirety. Irvine cites Anderson J.A. in the *C.R.F. Hldg.* case and in *Jacks v. Davis* (1980), 12 C.C.L.T. 298 (B.C. S.C.), affirmed (1983), 22 C.C.L.T. 266 (B.C. C.A.), as well as Prowse J. in *Morin Technical Services (1978) Ltd. v. Morin* (1982), 40 A.R. 15 at 34 (Q.B.). Not all courts, however, seem to have accepted the principle that consequential damages themselves can be awarded. See *Underwood v. Ocean City Realty Ltd.* (1985), 34 C.C.L.T. 128 (B.C. S.C.), affirmed (1987), 12 B.C.L.R. (2d) 199 (C.A.).

77 *Siametis v. Trojan Horse*, above, note 65.

78 See *Sevidal v. Chopra*, above, note 76. The question of whether "loss of profits" should be awarded in addition to diminution in the value of the land was a difficult and controversial issue in *Weibe v. Gunderson*, above, note 68. The trial judge awarded a substantial amount under this head. As pointed out by Newbury J.A., however, this gave the plaintiff a contract measure for damage assessment. The plaintiffs did not seek to rescind the purchase, were already awarded damages for the diminution in the value of the land, and now were given a

sufficiently outrageous behaviour, punitive damages may also be awarded.[79]

3. INTERFERENCE WITH CONTRACTUAL RELATIONS

(a) Introduction

The case law recognizes as tortious various types of conduct which involve the interference by one party, the defendant, with a contractual relationship existing between the plaintiff and a third party. Traditionally this tort has been called inducing breach of contract, but due to its expanding, although still uncertain ambit, this name no longer accurately represents its true scope.[80] The action, broadly described, involves interferences with contractual relations. The following issues, however, must be resolved: Is this tort confined to conduct which is intentional, or will negligent conduct suffice? Does it apply to only existing and binding contracts, or to commercial relationships in general? Does a remedy exist only where a contract has been breached, or as well where contractual performance has been affected, short of an actual breach? This section will examine these issues.

(b) Inducing Breach of Contract by Direct Interference[81]

(i) Introduction

The source of any contemporary trend towards the development of a general principle of tortious liability for interfering with contractual relations is the well-known case of *Lumley v. Gye*.[82] The defendant persuaded an opera singer who was under contract to sing exclusively at the theatre managed by the plaintiff to break her contract so that she could sing instead at the theatre managed by the defendant. The plaintiff sued the defendant for damages and succeeded, the majority of the court holding that the principle which allowed a master to sue

---

sum representing what they would have earned had the representations been true. The trial judge had awarded the plaintiff over $1,000,000 in damages, which was far more than what they had paid for the land. Thus they had their full purchase money back, the land with all of its assets, and a substantial sum extra. The Court of Appeal reduced the award.

79 See, e.g., *Denison v. Fawcett*, [1957] O.W.N. 393 (H.C.), affirmed [1958] O.R. 312 (C.A.).

80 See Burns, "Tort Injury to Economic Interests: Some Facets of Legal Response" (1980), 58 Can. Bar Rev. 103, where the author notes that this action has been called "interference with contract", "inducement of breach of contract", "interference with contractual relations", and "procuring a breach of contract."

81 In addition to the textbooks, there are several useful articles which discuss the elements of this tort. See Burns, "Tort Injury to Economic Interests: Some Facets of Legal Response" (1980), 58 Can. Bar Rev. 103; Richardson, "Interference With Contractual Relations: Is Torquay Hotel the Law in Canada?" (1983), 41 U. of T. Fac. L. Rev. 1; and Stevens, "Interference With Economic Relations — Some Aspects of the Turmoil in the Intentional Torts" (1974), 12 Osgoode H.L.J. 595.

82 (1853), 118 E.R. 749. As noted by the authors, prior to this case liability was confined to actions brought by masters for the enticement by others of their servants. *Lumley v. Gye* recognized a general principle of liability applicable to contracts of personal service. *Bowen v. Hall* (1881), 6 Q.B.D. 333 (C.A.), and *Temperton v. Russell*, [1893] 1 Q.B. 715 (C.A.), extended it to other classes of contract. See *Clerk and Lindsell on Torts*, 11th ed. at 319-20, cited in *Dirassar v. Kelly, Douglas & Co.* (1966), 59 D.L.R. (2d) 452 at 485-86 (B.C. C.A.), affirmed (1967), 64 D.L.R. (2d) 456 (S.C.C.).

when his servants were enticed away ought to be applied whenever someone maliciously procured a party under contract with the plaintiff to break that contract, thereby causing damage to the plaintiff.[83]

Lumley v. Gye illustrates the tort of inducing or procuring a breach of contract by *direct* means. This action has persisted with only some modification and can be broken down into the following elements.

(ii) The Existence of a Contract

In order for a defendant to be liable for inducing breach of contract or unlawfully interfering with contractual relations, there must be an existing contract between the plaintiff and a co-contractant. Although this point seems obvious and easily satisfied in most cases, it can give rise to difficulties.

In *Royal Bank v. Wilton*,[84] for example, the plaintiff received and accepted an offer to purchase its land from potential purchasers. The purchase was conditional upon a visual inspection of the property and satisfactory financing, within a definite period. Prior to the expiration of that period, an employee of the defendant bank telephoned the potential purchaser and informed him that the bank was about to foreclose on the property and that the purchaser had only seven days to close the deal. Due to its inability to obtain the financing within the seven days, the purchaser abandoned his offer to purchase. In actual fact, the bank did not foreclose until well over a year later.

The disappointed vendor brought an action against the bank for inducing breach of contract. One of the issues raised was whether there was an enforceable contract whose breach was induced. While recognizing the difficult contract law issue inherent in this matter, the Court of Appeal upheld the trial court's finding that there had been an executory contract in this case which was breached as a result of the defendant bank's intervention.[85]

A more unusual case is *Potter v. Rowe*.[86] The plaintiff was engaged as a volunteer manager of the defendant hospital's gift shop. Due to problems with her performance, the hospital asked the auxiliary, which ran the gift shop, to dismiss her. The plaintiff sued the hospital for inducing breach of contract. The case focussed on whether the hospital was justified in its actions, and the court

---

83 Crompton J. and Erle J. wrote judgments in the plaintiff's favour. Coleridge J. wrote a strong dissent, holding that the law regarding enticement ought not to be extended. Note as well that in the companion case, *Lumley v. Wagner* (1852), 42 E.R. 687, an injunction was obtained to prevent Miss Wagner from singing for the defendant Gye's theatre.

84 (1995), 165 A.R. 261 (C.A.), leave to appeal refused [1995] 9 W.W.R. lxxix (note) (S.C.C.).

85 Authorities cited in support include *United Enterprises Ltd. v. Bronze Motor Inn Ltd.* (1987), 63 Sask. R. 244 (Q.B.) [affirmed (1988), 71 Sask. R. 79 (C.A.)], and contract texts. Another case is *Duke v. Puts* (2004), 21 C.C.L.T. (3d) 181 (Sask. C.A.). The parties had entered into a contractual relationship which provided for the sale of a pharmacy. The terms involved a period of payments over a number of years based on the profits, the lease of the building, and the eventual purchase of it. The sale of the vendor's home was also a term of the arrangement. After several months of running the pharmacy, the purchaser ultimately decided that due to harassment by the defendant, he could not carry on with the arrangement and complete the purchase. The court, without stating that the purchaser had breached the contract, held that the defendant had sufficiently interfered with the purchaser's contractual relations with the vendor, the plaintiff in this action, to constitute the tort.

86 [1990] B.C.J. No. 2912 (S.C.).

decided that it was.[87] The court accepted that there was a valid contract between the plaintiff and the auxiliary and that it was breached. But was there? Were there any contractual relations in this case? The plaintiff's services were unpaid, and purely voluntary. Without a breach of contract, there were no damages and a successful action could not have been maintained, defences aside.

Where there are no contractual relations between the plaintiff and another person, the tort of inducing breach of contract cannot be maintained.[88] It may, however, be possible in such a case to sue for some other tort, such as unlawful interfence with economic interests.[89]

(iii) Intention

Although the judgments in *Lumley v. Gye* stated that the action was available for the malicious procurement of a contractual breach, it soon became clear that the principle of the action does not require malice, in the sense of an action initiated principally to cause damage to the plaintiff. This was established by the House of Lords in *Allen v. Flood*[90] and *Quinn v. Leathem*.[91] Lord McNaghten, in the latter case, stated that the decision in *Lumley v. Gye* was rightly decided:

> not on the ground of malicious intention — that was not, I think, the gist of the action — but on the ground that a violation of legal right committed knowingly is a cause of action, and that it is a violation of a legal right to interfere with contractual relations recognized by law if there be no sufficient justification for the interference.[92]

In order to succeed, a plaintiff must prove that the defendant intended to procure a breach of contract. In this respect, intention is proven by showing that the defendant acted with the desire to cause a breach of contract, or with the substantial certainty that a breach of contract would result from the defendant's conduct.[93]

---

87 See discussion on defence of "justification" below.

88 See, for example, *Pepsi-Cola Canada Beverages (West) Ltd. v. R.W.D.S.U., Local 558* (2002), 208 D.L.R. (4th) 385 (S.C.C), affirming (1998), 167 D.L.R. (4th) 220, [1999] 8 W.W.R. 429 (Sask. C.A.). As will be discussed below, this case involved secondary picketing. In the absence of evidence establishing that there were existing contracts between the parties that were interfered with as a result of the secondary picketing, the tort could not be made out.

89 See discussion below.

90 [1898] A.C. 1.

91 [1901] A.C. 495.

92 *Ibid.*, at 510.

93 See, for example, *Fasson Canada Inc. v. Mediacoat Inc.*, [1993] O.J. No. 2228 (Gen. Div.), *Walsh v. Nicholls* (2004), 25 C.C.L.T. (3d) 33 (N.B. C.A.) at 57, and *Drouillard v. Cogeco Cable Inc.* (2007), 86 O.R. (3d) 431 (C.A.), additional reasons at (2007), 2007 CarswellOnt 4106 (C.A.) at para. 29, where this definition of intention is used. Note, however, Fleming, *The Law of Torts*, 8th ed. (1992), at 694. While Fleming agrees that the tort is an intentional tort, and that the defendant must have acted with the necessary knowledge and intent to procure a breach, Fleming states that for a direct inducement cause of action, all that is required is that the breach was a *foreseeable*, and not a *necessary* consequence. See Picard J.'s judgment in *Atcheson v. College of Physicians & Surgeons (Alta.)*, [1994] 6 W.W.R. 239 (Alta. Q.B.). Also see *369413 Alberta Ltd. v. Pocklington* (2000), 194 D.L.R. (4th) 109, [2001] 4 W.W.R. 423 (Alta. C.A.), where "intention" is defined rather broadly to include "reasonably foreseeable" results, as well as recklessness or wilful blindness to the results. This is also the definition used by Milanetti J. in *Homelife Realty Services Inc. v. Homelife Performance Realty Inc.* (2007), [2007] O.J. No. 4846, 2007 CarswellOnt 8011 (S.C.J.). I would resist this interpretation as it converts what is an intentional tort into a negligent one. In *OBG Ltd. v. Allan*, [2007] UKHL

Even if the defendant's motive was not to harm the plaintiff but to further personal interests, the defendant will be held liable when the contractual breach was intended. Despite *dicta* in some of the case law that an intention to damage or harm the plaintiff is an element of the tort,[94] numerous Canadian and Commonwealth cases have made it clear that a malicious motive is not an element of the tort.[95] In one of the leading Canadian cases, *Posluns v. Toronto Stock Exchange*,[96] Gale J. stated:

> While a contract cannot impose the burden of an obligation on one who is not a party to it, a duty is undoubtedly cast upon any person, although extraneous to the obligation, to refrain from interfering with its due performance unless he has a duty or a right in law to so act. Thus, if a person without lawful justification knowingly and intentionally procures the breach by a party to a contract which is valid and enforceable and thereby causes damage to another party to the contract, the person who has induced the breach commits an actionable wrong. *That wrong does not rest upon the fact that the intervenor has acted in order to harm his victim, for a bad motive does not per se convert an otherwise lawful act into an unlawful one, but rather because there has been an unlawful invasion of legal relations existing between others.*[97]

Where the evidence indicates that the defendant did not know that the conduct would result in a contractual breach, or that there was a contract in force, the

---

21 (H.L.) at para. 43, Lord Hoffman states that the breach of contract must have been what the defendant intended. Being merely "a foreseeable consequence" would not be sufficient.

94 For example, in *D.C. Thomson & Co. v. Deakin*, [1952] 2 All E.R. 361 at 367 (C.A.), Sir Evershed M.R. states that "the actor must have acted with the intention of doing damage to the person damaged."

95 See *Parks West Mall Ltd. v. Jennett* (1995), 28 C.C.L.T. (2d) 1 (Alta. C.A.), additional reasons at (1996), 38 Alta. L.R. (3d) 423 (C.A.), leave to appeal refused [1996] 10 W.W.R. lix (note) (S.C.C.), where this is quoted with approval; and *Ed Miller Sales & Rentals Ltd. v. Caterpillar Tractor Co.*, 30 C.C.L.T. (2d) 1, [1996] 9 W.W.R. 449 (Alta. C.A.), leave to appeal refused (1997), 209 A.R. 400 (note) (S.C.C.), additional reasons at [1998] 10 W.W.R. 736 (Alta. C.A.). This was also cited with approval in a rather strange case. The plaintiff was a season ticket holder to Ottawa Senator hockey games. The defendant was a star player who was refusing to honour his contract. The defendant and his agent were sued for interfering with the contractual relations between the ticket holders and the hockey team. It was alleged that an implied term of the season ticket was that Yashin, the marquis player, would play for the team. A motion to strike out the claim as being frivolous was dismissed. See: *Potechin v. Yashin* (January 4, 2000), Doc. 99-CV-11500-CP, [2000] O.J. No. 2 (S.C.J.).

96 (1964), 46 D.L.R. (2d) 210 (Ont. H.C.), affirmed (1966), 53 D.L.R. (2d) 193 (Ont. C.A.), which was affirmed (1968), 67 D.L.R. (2d) 165 (S.C.C.).

97 46 D.L.R. (2d) 210 at 261 (emphasis added). Also see *Dirassar v. Kelly, Douglas & Co.* (1966), 59 D.L.R. (2d) 452 (B.C. C.A.), affirmed (1967), 64 D.L.R. (2d) 456 (S.C.C.); *Thermo King Corp. v. Prov. Bank of Can.* (1981), 130 D.L.R. (3d) 256 (Ont. C.A.); *Engr. & Plumbing Supplies (Vancouver) Ltd. v. Intercan Accept. Corp.* (1981), 30 B.C.L.R. 170 (C.A.); and *Bank of N.S. v. Gaudreau* (1985), 48 O.R. (2d) 478 (H.C.). For a reaffirmation of this point in English authority, see *Edwin Hill & Partners v. FNFC*, [1988] 3 All E.R. 801 at 808 (C.A.). See, however, *Canadian Direct Insurance Inc. v. Insurance Corp. of British Columbia* (1998), 60 B.C.L.R. (3d) 1 (S.C.). The defendant entered into contracts with repair shops on condition that they would stop giving an advantage to the defendant's competitors. The plaintiff was one of these competitors. The defendant knew that contracts existed that in fact did just that. Repair shops entered into contracts with the defendant and then breached existing contracts with the defendant's competitors. The plaintiff sued for inducing breach of contract. The court dismissed the action on the ground that it was not the defendant's intention to procure breaches of contract. The court relied on considerations such as the fact that the defendant was pursuing its own interests, and that repair shops were not required to contract with the defendant, in dismissing the claim. This, with respect, seems to be a questionable result in this case. Self-interest is not a justification to commit this tort. See discussion below.

intention to cause harm to the contractual relationship will be absent, and the action will fail.[98]

The cause of action is predicated upon intentional conduct — a deliberate interference with the plaintiff's interests — and despite some case law to the contrary,[99] its extension to negligent conduct ought to be resisted. As discussed previously,[100] purely economic losses suffered as a result of negligent conduct have been a matter of great concern to the courts. The issue of recovery for losses emanating from negligent interference with contractual relations can best be dealt with within the context of negligence law, rather than the business torts.[101]

An apparent exception to the general principle that motive is not an element of the tort of inducing breach of contract has arisen with respect to the conduct of directors or officers of companies.[102] Since the decisions of companies to sever contractual relations with others is made upon the advice and initiative of the companies' officers and employees, it would be harsh if these agents could be sued for inducing breach of contract in every case where the decision to terminate the contract resulted in contractual breach. The cases have held that a servant will only be liable for inducing breach of contract where the conduct was not *bona fide* within the scope of employment.[103] It has also been held that in addition to a lack of *bona fides*, a director cannot be held liable for inducing the breach of a contract between the company and a third party, unless it can be

---

98 See, e.g., *Matsushita Elec. of Can. Ltd. v. Central Trust Co.* (1986), 73 N.S.R. (2d) 250 (T.D.); *Allister Harlow Const. Ltd. v. Shelburne Shopping Centre Ltd.* (1981), 45 N.S.R. (2d) 271 (C.A.); and *Yellow Submarine Deli Inc. v. AGF Hospitality Associates Inc.* (1997), [1998] 2 W.W.R. 701, 40 C.C.L.T. (2d) 111 (Man. C.A.).

99 *Nicholls v. Richmond (Twp.)* (1983), 24 C.C.L.T. 253 (B.C. C.A.). Note, however, *Pearl v. Pac. Enercon Inc.* (1985), 19 D.L.R. (4th) 464 (B.C. C.A.), where Hinkson J.A., without elaboration, reversed a trial judgment holding the president of a company personally liable for negligently inducing the breach of an employment contract with an employee. In *ACL Holdings Ltd. v. St. Joseph's Hospital of Estevan*, [1996] 6 W.W.R. 207, 29 C.C.L.T. (2d) 150 (Sask. Q.B.), the court refused to strike out a statement of claim for negligently inducing breach of contract.

100 See Chapter 7.

101 See Berger J.'s judgment in *Ed Miller Sales & Rentals Ltd. v. Caterpillar Tractor Co.*, [1994] 5 W.W.R. 473 at 541 (Alta. Q.B.), where the restriction of this tort to intentional conduct is accepted as being the prevailing view. The trial judgment was reversed on other grounds at 30 C.C.L.T. (2d) 1, [1996] 9 W.W.R. 449 (Alta. C.A.), leave to appeal refused (1997), 209 A.R. 400 (note) (S.C.C.), additional reasons at [1998] 10 W.W.R. 736 (Alta. C.A.). Also see Blair J.'s judgment in *131843 Canada Inc. v. Double "R" Toronto Ltd.*, [1991] O.J. No. 2015 (Gen. Div.), B. Wright J.'s judgment in *Conquest Tours (Toronto) v. Intair Inc.*, [1994] O.J. No. 1141 (Gen. Div.), and Twaddle J.A. in *Yellow Submarine Deli Inc. v. AGF Hospitality Associates Inc.* (1997), 40 C.C.L.T. (2d) 111 (Man. C.A.) where there is agreement with this position.

102 See Richardson, "Making an End Run Around the Corporate Veil: The Tort of Inducing Breach of Contract" (1984-85), 5 Advocates' Q. 103.

103 See *Said v. Butt*, [1920] 3 K.B. 497; *McFadden v. 481782 Ont. Ltd.* (1984), 27 B.L.R. 173 (Ont. H.C.); *Kepic v. Tecumseh Road Bldrs.* (1985), 29 B.L.R. 85 (Ont. H.C.), varied (1987), 18 C.C.E.L. 218 (Ont. C.A.); *Mentmore Mfg. Co. v. Nat. Merchandising Mfg. Co.* (1978), 89 D.L.R. (3d) 195 (Fed. C.A.); *Lehndorff Can. Pension Properties Ltd. v. Davis & Co.* (1987), 39 C.C.L.T. 196 (B.C. S.C.); *Truckers Garage Inc. v. Krell* (1993), 3 C.C.E.L. (2d) 157 (Ont. C.A.); *Ashdown v. Jumbo Video Inc.*, [1993] O.J. No. 1169 (Gen. Div.); and *Polimeni v. Danzinger* (1995), [1996] 1 W.W.R. 305 (Man. Q.B.), affirmed [1997] 10 W.W.R. 357, 32 C.C.L.T. (2d) 113 (Man. C.A.), leave to appeal refused (1997), 123 Man. R. (2d) 80 (note) (S.C.C.).

shown that the director's "dominating concern was focussed upon depriving the complainant of its contractual benefits."[104] In *369413 Alberta Ltd. v. Pocklington*,[105] it was held that in order for a director to be held liable, the burden is on the plaintiff to prove that the director was not acting in the best interests of the company. The plaintiff, according to this interpretation, need not go so far as proving that the director acted in order to harm the plaintiff. The defendant director, however, can restore the defence of justification by showing that a legitimate interest of the company's was served by its conduct. In this case the plaintiff must go further and prove that the director's dominating motive was to deprive the plaintiff of its contractual rights.[106]

(iv) Knowledge

Since the tort of inducing breach of contract is predicated upon the defendant's intention to induce a party to breach its contract with the plaintiff, it follows that the defendant's knowledge of the existence of a contract, and its terms, is an

---

104 See *Imp. Oil Ltd. v. C & G Hldg. Ltd.* (1989), 62 D.L.R. (4th) 261 at 266 (Nfld. C.A.). The court was concerned that if *bona fides* were the only test, this would permit the complainant to scrutinize the internal affairs of a company and require directors to justify their corporate actions in order to protect themselves against tort suit. See *Levi v. Chartersoft Canada Inc.*, [1995] 2 W.W.R. 279 (Man. Q.B.), where the principle was applied and a president of a company relieved of liability since he was acting *bona fide* and in the best interests of his company. A case where a director of a company was personally liable for inducing breach of contract is *Jackson v. Trimac Industries Ltd.*, [1993] 2 W.W.R. 209 (Alta. Q.B.), varied [1994] 8 W.W.R. 237 (Alta. C.A.). The trial court held that the defendant director's "compelling motivation", his "dominating concern or dominant purposes", were to deny the plaintiff his contractual benefits. The Court of Appeal upheld this action, noting that the defendant was taking "advantage of his employment to commit a tort for his own ends", and accordingly was not protected from personal liability. Also see *United Cooler (Niagara 1980) Ltd. v. Zafir*, [1992] O.J. No. 1258 (Gen. Div.) where the defendant who was the president, sole shareholder and directing mind of a company was held liable personally for inducing a breach of contract between his company and the plaintiff. The court held that the purpose of the breach was to protect the personal assets and liability of the defendant. Also see *Heslop v. Cooper's Crane Rental Ltd.* (1994), 6 C.C.E.L. (2d) 252 (Ont. Gen. Div.), reversed (1997), 30 C.C.E.L. (2d) 279 (Ont. C.A.), where the president and controlling shareholder was held liable personally for inducing breach of contract, since his involvement had become "personal" and his acts were not in the best interests of his company. See also *ADGA Systems International Ltd. v. Valcom Ltd.* (1999), 44 C.C.L.T. (2d) 174 (Ont. C.A.), leave to appeal refused (2000), 134 O.A.C. 400 (note) (S.C.C.) where the court refused to extend this immunity where the tortious act committed was intentional and was directed at a competitor corporation that had no relationship with the corporation for which the defendant director and employees worked. The court stated that the protection should be a limited one applicable only to parties "who have voluntarily chosen to accept the ambit of risk of a limited liability company". See E.M. Iacobucci, "Unfinished Business: An Analysis of Stones Unturned in *ADGA Systems v. Valcom*" (2001), 35 Can. Bus. L.J. 39.

105 (2000), 194 D.L.R. (4th) 109, [2001] 4 W.W.R. 423 (Alta. C.A.).

106 The Court of Appeal was attempting to strike a balance between the director's defence of justification and the plaintiff's right not to have its contractual benefits tortiously interfered with. It was concerned that requiring the plaintiff to prove in all cases that the director's dominating motive was to harm it would be to create too difficult a burden. Requiring a defendant director, however, to prove on a balance of probabilities why it advised the company not to fulfil its contractual obligations would be to unduly expose the company's affairs to outsider's scrutiny.

essential element of the cause of action. It has been held that knowledge of the precise terms of a contract is not required, as long as the defendant had "the means of knowledge" yet deliberately disregarded them.[107] A party who induces another to terminate its contract with the plaintiff, without regard to whether this can lawfully be done, runs the risk that the contract will be breached as a result of this inducement.[108] Reckless indifference as to whether conduct will result in an interference with the plaintiff's contractual relations will result in liability, although a reasonable belief that there is either no contract to be interfered with, or that the act induced is not inconsistent with it, will not.[109]

(v) Conduct Inducing Breach

The tort of inducing breach of contract by direct intervention occurs when a defendant directly persuades or induces a third party to break a contract with the plaintiff.

It has been suggested that there is a distinction between statements which persuade and thereby induce someone to break a contract and statements which merely advise a contractual breach or inform a party of reasons why a contractual

---

107 Lord Denning M.R. in *Emerald Const. Co. v. Lowthian*, [1966] 1 W.L.R. 691 at 700 (C.A.). See also Gale J. in *Posluns v. Toronto Stock Exchange* (1964), 46 D.L.R. (2d) 210 at 268 (Ont. H.C.), affirmed (1966), 53 D.L.R. (2d) 193 (Ont. C.A.), which was affirmed (1968), 67 D.L.R. (2d) 165 (S.C.C.). See also Lord Pearce's judgment in *J.T. Stratford & Son v. Lindley*, [1964] 3 All E.R. 102 at 112 (H.L.): "It is no answer to a claim based on wrongfully inducing a breach of contract, to assert that the defendants did not know with exactitude all the terms of the contract. The relevant question is whether they had sufficient knowledge of the terms to know they were inducing a breach of contract." In *Ed Miller Sales & Rentals Ltd. v. Caterpillar Tractor Co.*, [1994] 5 W.W.R. 473 at 541 (Alta. Q.B.), reversed 30 C.C.L.T. (2d) 1, [1996] 9 W.W.R. 449 (Alta. C.A.), leave to appeal refused (1997), 209 A.R. 400 (note) (S.C.C.), additional reasons at [1998] 10 W.W.R. 736 (Alta. C.A.), Berger J. at trial stated that the plaintiff "need not prove that the defendants had knowledge of the details of the contract or its terms". I would suggest, however, that there must be sufficient knowledge of the terms to support the inference that the defendant knew that, by its conduct, the contract would be breached. The Court of Appeal agreed with this view holding that without knowledge that one's conduct would lead to a breach of a contract there can be no tort.

108 Diplock L.J. in *Emerald Const. Co. v. Lowthian*, *ibid.*, at 704. Note, however, the caution by Jenkins L.J. in *D.C. Thomson & Co. v. Deakin*, [1952] 2 All E.R. 361 at 380 (C.A.), that if a person advocates lawful means, and the person persuaded takes unlawful means, there is no cause of action against the former. In *Drouillard v. Cogeco* (2007), 86 O.R. (3d) 431 (C.A.), additional reasons at (2007), 2007 CarswellOnt 4106 (C.A.), it was held that the intention to cause a breach existed even though there was no direct evidence that the defendant wanted the plaintiff's contract to be terminated without reasonable notice.

109 See Norris J.'s dissenting judgment in *Dirassar v. Kelly, Douglas & Co.* (1966), 59 D.L.R. (2d) 452 (B.C. C.A.), affirmed (1967), 64 D.L.R. (2d) 456 (S.C.C.); *Short v. City Bank of Sydney* (1912), 15 C.L.R. 148 (Aust. H.C.); *Br. Indust. Plastics Ltd. v. Ferguson*, [1940] 1 All E.R. 479 (H.L.). This principle was applied in *Super-Save Enterprises Ltd. v. 249513 B.C. Ltd.* (2004), 23 C.C.L.T. (3d) 202 (B.C. C.A.), affirming (2003), 36 B.L.R. (3d) 52 (S.C.). The plaintiff, a supplier of propane, sued another supplier, alleging that it induced one of its former customers to switch suppliers. The court found that the defendant did not know that there had been a supply contract in place, nor did it act with wilful blindness concerning the existence of a contract. In *Homelife Realty Services Inc. v. Homelife Performance Realty Inc.* (2007), [2007] O.J. No. 4846, 2007 CarswellOnt 8011 (S.C.J.) at para. 219, on the other hand, the court held that the corporate defendant "should have known that a contract existed and/or had the means to ascertain its terms".

breach may be a desirable option.[110] Statements which induce a contractual breach are said to be distinguished by the fact that they provide the party induced with an incentive to break the contract with the plaintiff.[111] Statements which merely point out existing reasons for not abiding by the terms of the contract are said to constitute merely information, and not an inducement. In *Brown v. Spamberger*,[112] for example, a vendor orally agreed to pay a commission to a realtor should he find a purchaser for his property. The defendant, a potential purchaser, advised the vendor that this oral agreement was not enforceable, as it was not in writing, and that, accordingly, the realtor's commission need not be paid if the two dealt directly with each other. The parties contracted for the sale of the property, and the realtor's commission was not paid. The realtor sued for breach of contract, and for inducing breach of contract. Were the defendant's representations an inducement to the vendor not to fulfil a valid, albeit unenforceable, contractual obligation, or merely advice to him pointing out his options? Roach J.A. held that it was not actionable to point out the vendor's legal options, even if this resulted in a disadvantage to the plaintiff and a benefit for the advisor. LeBel J.A., in dissent, held that it was tortious for the purchaser to have induced a breach of the oral contract. The facts that there was no malice, that the contract was unenforceable, and that the vendor willingly agreed to the arrangement, were of no legal consequence with respect to the tort claim.

The distinction between inducement and advice is a subtle one, which ought to be avoided.[113] It is arguably preferable to accept the proposition that any statement made by the defendant with the intention of encouraging another party not to fulfil its contract with the plaintiff, whether it provides new incentives or merely states existing reasons, is *prima facie* actionable conduct. If it can be shown, however, that the statements made by the defendant did not cause the party's actions, were not made with the intention of advocating a contractual breach, or were justified, the action will then fail on these grounds.[114] Thus where

---

110 See *Salmond on Torts*, 17th ed. (1977), at 371-72, quoted with approval by Cameron J.A. in *Garry v. Sherritt Gordon Mines* (1987), 42 C.C.L.T. 241 at 274 (Sask. C.A.). The distinction between procuring a breach, and advising a breach, has been raised in several cases. See, e.g., Romer L.J.'s judgment in *Glamorgan Coal Co. v. South Wales Miners' Fed.*, [1903] 2 K.B. 545 at 575 (C.A.), affirmed [1905] A.C. 239 (H.L.).

111 See *Parks West Mall Ltd. v. Jennett*, above, note 96, where this statement is quoted with approval.

112 (1959), 21 D.L.R. (2d) 630 (Ont. C.A.).

113 As conceded by Evershed M.R. in *D.C. Thomson & Co. v. Deakin*, [1952] 2 All E.R. 361 at 373 (C.A.), the point at which advice becomes persuasion is a difficult question. See *Royal Bank v. Wilton*, above, note 84, at 293. The bank informed the potential purchaser that it was about to foreclose on property which the vendor was selling. Was this merely "advice" or an "inducement" which led to a breach? The court accepted the argument made in this text, and concluded that this conversation was not merely "advice."

114 For example, Cameron J.A. in *Garry v. Sherritt Gordon Mines Ltd.* (1987), 42 C.C.L.T. 241 (Sask. C.A.), cites *Becker Const. Co. v. U.A., Loc. 170* (1958), 15 D.L.R. (2d) 354 (B.C. C.A.), where the tradesmen refused to cross the picket line, not because they were encouraged to do so by the picketers, but based on their own individual judgment. Contrast this, however, with Bayda C.J.S.'s judgment at 42 C.C.L.T. 241 at 284 and following. Union sympathy and respect for picket lines does not mean that the picketer has not caused the breach of contract. There are numerous cases on point. See, e.g., *Alltrans Express v. Gen. Truck Drivers' & Helpers' Union, Loc. 213* (1982), 20 C.C.L.T. 164 (B.C. S.C.), where secondary picketing set up to encourage the plaintiff's employees not to cross the picket line was held to be

a party to a contract has already decided not to honour it, a person subsequently dealing with the contract breaker cannot be said to have induced or advised a breach.[115]

Direct intervention to procure a contractual breach will also arise where a defendant deals with a third party in a way known to be inconsistent with the contractual terms between that party and the plaintiff. The defendant need not initiate or encourage the inconsistent dealings, as long as, with knowledge of the contract, the defendant deals with the contract breaker in a manner which constitutes a breach of the contract.[116] It has also been held that the defendant's acts need not be done with the knowledge or complicity of the contract breaker in order to be actionable.[117]

(vi) Damage

The action for inducing breach of contract requires that the plaintiff suffer damage. Since, however, the plaintiff's action frequently coincides with a successful action for breach of contract against the contract breaker, the issue of overlap between the two actions arises.[118]

A plaintiff cannot receive the same damages twice; overlap must be avoided.[119] However, as in *Vale v. I.L.W.U., Loc. 508*,[120] a court may find that some damages which are not recoverable in the contract action ought to be recoverable in tort. Thus, damages for a wrongful dismissal did not include an assessment for the lost opportunity to earn an income in a chosen job, which damages were awarded on the tort claim. As well, punitive damages may be awarded for the tort claim.

It has been stated that damages for inducing breach of contract are "at large"; their assessment is "a matter of impression and not addition."[121] Matters such as

---

interference with the plaintiff's contractual relations with its employees. Also *West. Stevedoring Co. v. Pulp, Paper & Woodwkrs. of Can.* (1975), 61 D.L.R. (3d) 701 (B.C. C.A.); *Mark Fishing Co. v. U.F.A.W.*, [1972] 3 W.W.R. 641 (B.C. C.A.), affirmed [1973] 3 W.W.R. 13 (S.C.C.); among others. On the legality of "secondary picketing" at common law, see the Supreme Court of Canada's judgment in *Pepsi-Cola Canada Beverages (West) Ltd. v. R.W.D.S.U., Local 558* (2002), 208 D.L.R. (4th) 385 (S.C.C.). See discussion below.

115 See *Harry Winton Investments Ltd. v. CIBC Development Corp.* (2001), 199 D.L.R. (4th) 709 (Ont. C.A.); and *Homelife Realty Services Inc. v. Homelife Performance Realty Inc.* (2007), [2007] O.J. No. 4846, 2007 CarswellOnt 8011 (S.C.J.).

116 See Jenkins L.J. in *D.C. Thomson & Co. v. Deakin*, above, note 114, at 378. Even if the defendant did not initially realize that the dealings were inconsistent, once notice of the contract is acquired, continuing the dealings constitutes the tort. See *Ernst & Young v. Stuart*, [1994] 8 W.W.R. 431 (B.C. C.A.), varied as to damages [1997] 5 W.W.R. 253 (B.C. C.A), where a defendant firm hired the defendant accountant even though the firm knew that the accountant was in breach of a notice clause with its former employer. The defendant firm was held liable for inducing breach of contract.

117 See *G.W.K. Ltd. v. Dunlop Rubber Co.* (1926), 42 T.L.R. 376.

118 It can be that although the contract was breached, it was unenforceable and the action for breach of contract fails. See, e.g., *Unident Ltd. v. DeLong* (1981), 131 D.L.R. (3d) 225 (N.S. T.D.); and *Brown v. Spamberger*, above, note 112.

119 See Ford J.A. in *Garbutt Bus. College Ltd. v. Henderson*, [1939] 4 D.L.R. 151 at 179 (Alta. C.A.).

120 (1979), 9 C.C.L.T. 262 (B.C. C.A.).

121 Seaton J.A. in *Vale v. I.L.W.U., ibid.*, at 271, and Rouleau J.A. in *Drouillard v. Cogeco Cable Inc.* (2007), 86 O.R. (3d) 431 (C.A.), additional reasons at (2007), 2007 CarswellOnt 4106 (C.A.), at para. 42, citing *Cassell & Co. v. Broome*, [1972] A.C. 1027 at 1072 (H.L.). It has

the plaintiff's loss of reputation, injured feelings, the nature of the conduct, or punishment are said to be legitimate considerations.[122] While it has been conceded that proof of special damages need not support the action, substantial damages will not be awarded in the absence of actual damages.[123]

(vii) Justification

One of the most uncertain issues in relation to the tort of inducing breach of contract relates to the defence of justification. When is a defendant entitled to deliberately interfere in the contractual relationship existing between the plaintiff and a third party?

That a defendant may be justified in deliberately interfering with the plaintiff's contractual relations was conceded in several of the early, leading cases.[124] What constitutes justification, however, was, and remains, unclear. In *Glamorgan Coal Co. v. South Wales Miners' Fed.*,[125] Romer L.J. admitted that, although justification was clearly a defence, "it would be extremely difficult, even if it were possible, to give a complete and satisfactory definition of what is 'sufficient justification' and most attempts to do so would probably be mischievous."[126] The following factors, however, were suggested as relevant: the nature of the contract broken, the position of the parties to the contract, the grounds for the breach, the means employed to procure the breach, the relationship of the person procuring the breach to the person who breaks the contract, and the object of the person procuring the breach.[127] Romer L.J. held that, at least in so far as employment contracts are concerned, the absence of malice, or the fact that the breach of the contract was in the contract breaker's interest, does not justify the tort. Romer L.J. dismissed the defendant union's argument that it had a duty to persuade its members to break their contracts with the plaintiff, and hence, were justified in so doing.[128] In *Edwin Hill Partners v. FNFC*,[129] the English authorities on the defence of justification were reviewed. It was noted that the following arguments for the defence have not been successful: (1) absence of malice, (2) interests of the contract breaker, or (3) retaliatory conduct.[130] On the other hand, a moral duty

---

also been stated at 9 C.C.L.T. 271 that "the plaintiff is to be compensated for the invasion of a right, and need not be put to strict proof of specific damage."

122 Lord Hailsham in *Cassell & Co. v. Broome, ibid.*, at 1073, cited in *Vale v. I.L.W.U., ibid.*

123 Ford J.A. in *Garbutt Business College v. Henderson*, above, note 119.

124 See, e.g., *Quinn v. Leathem*, [1901] A.C. 495 at 510: "A violation of legal right committed knowingly is a cause of action, and . . . it is a violation of legal right to interfere with contractual relations recognised by law if there be no sufficient justification for the interference."

125 [1903] 2 K.B. 545 (C.A.), affirmed [1905] A.C. 239 (H.L.).

126 *Ibid.*, at 573.

127 *Ibid.*, at 574.

128 The object of the action was to reduce the output of coal, thus keeping the price of coal up and protecting the workers' jobs.

129 [1988] 3 All E.R. 801 (C.A.).

130 In *Walker v. Stern*, [1993] Y.J. No. 169 (S.C.), defendant 1 owned a dental practice and shared space with defendant 2. An employee of defendant 2 informed defendant 1's wife that defendant 1 was having an extra-marital affair. Due to this, defendant 1 asked defendant 2 to dismiss the employee. The court held that his personal concerns with the employee's conduct did not justify defendant 1 inducing defendant 2 to breach his contract with the employee. Also see *Payjack v. Springhill Farms*, [2002] 7 W.W.R. 354 (Man. Q.B.). The fact that the plaintiff and the defendant were having a dispute in relation to another matter did not justify the defendant's act in inducing the plaintiff's employer to fire him.

to intervene,[131] and action taken to protect interference with the defendant's own rights, when they are equal or superior to the rights of the plaintiff, have been recognized as constituting sufficient justification. In *Edwin Hill & Partners*,[132] for example, the defendants had the legal right to call in a loan and preclude the third party from continuing with a property development. The third party had a contract with the plaintiff architect, which contract would necessarily come to an end if the defendants foreclosed. Rather than exercising their power of sale, the defendants decided to finance the development themselves, but insisted that the plaintiff architect be discharged. The court held that the defendants had a superior legal right to the plaintiff, and could not be held liable for inducing breach of contract by exercising this right.[133] In another interesting case, *Soroka v. Skjoth*,[134] a Master in Chambers held that a purchaser who buys land knowing that there is an unregistered lease that will be terminated by the sale is not liable for inducing breach of contract. The legislation protecting the purchaser from the lease[135] was stated to serve as a defence to the tort.[136]

Another instance of a justification for inducing a breach of contract has arisen with respect to "professional advice-givers", such as lawyers, doctors, bankers and others. In *Spectra Architectural Group Ltd. v. Eldred Sollows Consulting Ltd.*,[137] the defendants were architectural consultants who had been retained by a party which was involved in a dispute with its architect. The consultants' advice was that the architect had breached its contract with their client and that their client should accordingly terminate the contract which it had with the architect, and engage another architect. The client followed this advice and the consultants were sued for inducing breach. The Master in Chambers, noting the absence of Canadian authorities on this point, was persuaded by American authorities that a

131 The well-known case of *Brimelow v. Casson*, [1924] 1 Ch. 302, is frequently cited. Here the defendant was justified in inducing a breach of contract between the plaintiff, an owner of a burlesque troupe, and owners of theatres, in order to protect the interests of the plaintiff's chorus girls, who were being underpaid for their services. See, however, *Babcock v. Carr* (1981), 127 D.L.R. (3d) 77 (Ont. H.C.), where it was held that a daughter did not act out of a sense of familial duty when she induced her mother to breach a contract of sale which her mother had with the plaintiff. See also *Crofter Hand Woven Harris Tweed Co. v. Veitch*, [1942] A.C. 435 (H.L.), where in an *obiter dictum*, Viscount Simon suggested that a father would be justified in persuading his daughter to break her engagement to marry a scoundrel.

132 Above, note 129.

133 Also see *Atcheson v. College of Physicians & Surgeons (Alta.)*, [1994] 6 W.W.R. 239 (Alta. Q.B.). The defendant College required a doctors' clinic to terminate an arrangement which it had with the plaintiff, a registered nurse working for the clinic. This led to the discharge of the plaintiff by the clinic. She sued the College for inducing breach of contract. The court held that the College's actions were protected by the defence of justification. It was exercising its statutory responsibility to prevent the unauthorized practice of medicine.

134 37 C.C.L.T. (2d) 197, [1997] 9 W.W.R. 341 (Alta. Master).

135 Land Titles Act, R.S.A. 2000, c. L-4.

136 In *Even v. El Al Israel Airlines Ltd.* (2006), [2006] O.J. No. 711, 2006 CarswellOnt 1046 (S.C.J.), the defence of justification was carefully considered. Klowack J. suggested that the following factors are relevant to the defence of justification: the grounds for the interference, whether legal or social; the purpose of the interference; the means used; and the nature of the contract being interfered with, including the consequences. In this case, the defendant airlines refused to do business with any travel agency that employed the plaintiff. This was as a result of difficulties which the airline had with the plaintiff in previous transactions. On the facts of the case, the defence of justification succeeded.

137 (1991), 7 C.C.L.T. (2d) 169 (Alta. Master).

"privilege" should be conferred on professionals who give advice, which is within the scope of their retainer, and which is honestly given.[138] This is similar to the privilege which protects officers or directors of companies from being sued for this tort,[139] and is sensible.[140]

(c) Procuring Breach of Contract by Indirect Means

The possibility that a breach of contract can be procured by a defendant not by means of direct persuasion or intervention, but indirectly, by preventing a party from fulfilling the terms of a contract, was established in *D.C. Thomson & Co. v. Deakin*.[141] Unfortunately, here as elsewhere in the law of torts, the distinction between a direct and indirect interference is ambiguous, and the reasons for making the distinction somewhat questionable.[142]

An indirect interference with a contractual relationship between the plaintiff and a third party can be said to arise where the defendant, rather than applying

---

138 In *ACL Holdings Ltd. v. St. Joseph's Hospital of Estevan*, 29 C.C.L.T. (2d) 150, [1996] 6 W.W.R. 207 (Sask. Q.B.), the court refused to strike out a statement of claim for inducing breach of contract brought against an architect by an unsuccessful bidder. The court allowed the possibility that the action could succeed if the architect did not exercise reasonable care in advising his client.

139 See discussion above.

140 In *Walsh v. Nicholls* (2004), 25 C.C.L.T. (3d) 33 (N.B. C.A), reversing 2003 NBQB 259 (Q.B.), an insurance adjuster was sued when the insurance company for which he worked discontinued the plaintiff's income and medical benefits. Although the motions judge dismissed the action, the Court of Appeal allowed it to proceed as an action for intentional procurement of breach of contract. Drapeau C.J.N.B. noted that in order to succeed the plaintiff would be required to prove bad faith on the part of the adjuster. In this respect, bad faith is not limited to acting out of personal gain or in order to cause injury to the insured. The denial of benefits on spurious grounds, frivolous objections and so on could constitute bad faith.

141 [1952] 2 All E.R. 361 (C.A.).

142 In *OBG and Others v. Allan and Others*, [2007] UKHL 21, the Lords rejected the extension of the *Lumley v. Gye* tort of inducing breach of contract tort into a tort of indirect interference with contractual relations by the use of unlawful means. Rather they see two distinct and separate torts, each with its own elements. The first is the *Lumley v. Gye* direct inducement tort; the second the tort of intentionally causing loss by unlawful means. *Lumley v. Gye* was described as a tort of "accessory liability"; that is, the defendant is liable as an accessory to the breach of contract committed by the contract breaker. The "unlawful means" tort is based on "primary liability"; that is, the defendant's liability does not require a wrongful act by anyone else, but is based on its own independent unlawful act. The Lords reviewed the development of the economic torts, concluding that there is one tort of inducing breach of contract by direct persuasion, and a separate tort of causing loss by unlawful means, each with their own rationale and requirements. Canadian law has not yet engaged in this rationalization of these closely related torts. It still maintains a tort of inducing breach of contract by direct persuasion (*Lumley v. Gye)*, an action for indirectly interfering with contractual relations by using unlawful means (the extension of *Lumley v. Gye)*, and perhaps even an action for interference with contractual relations short of breach (the *Torquay Hotel* tort). There is also a residual tort of unlawful interference with economic interests, which may be broader than the *OBG* tort of intentionally causing loss by unlawful means, at least in so far as the definition of unlawful means is concerned. See Carty, "*OBG Ltd v. Allan*: The House of Lords Shapes the Economic Torts and Explores Commercial Confidences and Image Rights" (2007), 15 Torts L.J. 283, where the English developments are discussed. Also see Neyers, "Rights-based justification for the tort of unlawful interference with economic interests" (2008) Legal Studies 1, for a discussion of the theoretical justification of the unlawful means tort.

direct pressure on the contract breaker, or working with the latter to effect a breach of the contract, deliberately creates an intervening event which renders the contract breaker's performance of the contract impossible or necessarily impractical. Various scenarios of the indirect action have been suggested. The defendant intervenor may make the performance of the contract impossible by physically detaining the contracting party,[143] by removing or damaging tools,[144] or even by kidnapping a necessary and irreplaceable servant.[145] Indirect interference can also occur where the defendant makes the performance of the contract impossible by inducing employees of a contracting party to deprive the latter of their services, thereby preventing the employer from performing its contract with the plaintiff. It is this last illustration of the tort which has been the most significant, certainly in so far as the labour relations context is concerned.[146]

It has generally been held that whereas to directly persuade a party to breach a contract with the plaintiff is an act which is wrongful in itself, the tort of procuring breach of contract by indirect means requires that the indirect means which are employed be unlawful in themselves.[147] It is, however, somewhat unclear as to the meaning of "unlawfulness" for this purpose. The commission of a tort which

---

143 See Sir Evershed M.R.'s judgment, at [1952] 2 All E.R. 361 at 368.

144 See Jenkins L.J.'s judgment, *ibid.*, at 379.

145 *Ibid.*, at 385. Note the disagreement concerning characterization which arises here. Some characterize these as indirect interferences, others as direct. Fleming, *The Law of Torts*, 9th ed. (1998), at 760, for example, describes these as examples of indirect interference with contractual relations. Jenkins L.J. in *D.C. Thomson & Co. v. Deakin*, on the other hand, cites these as illustrations of a direct invasion of the plaintiff's rights, as does Norris J.A. in *Dirassar v. Kelly, Douglas & Co.* (1966), 59 D.L.R. (2d) 452 at 471 (B.C. C.A.), affirmed (1967), 64 D.L.R. (2d) 456 (S.C.C.). The difficulty in distinguishing between direct and indirect interferences is one of the reasons given by Lord Hoffman in *OBG v. Allan* for separating the *Lumley v. Gye* tort from the unlawful means tort. In *Lumley v. Gye*, the inducement of the breach constitutes the unlawful act. In the unlawful means tort, the prevention of performance by using independent, unlawful means is the gist of the action, without regard to whether this was accomplished through a direct or indirect act.

146 In *Ed Miller Sales & Rentals Ltd. v. Caterpillar Tractor Co.*, [1994] 5 W.W.R. 473, reversed 30 C.C.L.T. (2d) 1, [1996] 9 W.W.R. 449 (Alta. C.A.), leave to appeal refused (1997), 209 A.R. 400 (note) (S.C.C.), additional reasons at [1998] 10 W.W.R. 736 (Alta. C.A.), the defendant manufacturer of equipment parts adopted a new parts policy which effectively prevented one of its dealers from continuing to supply parts to the plaintiff. This was analyzed as a "direct" interference with the contractual relations between the plaintiff and its dealer, although an argument could be made that this was an "indirect" interference. The Court of Appeal held, however, that the defendant had done nothing unlawful and therefore there was no unlawful interference with economic relations or presumably procuring breach of contract by unlawful means. In *Duke v. Puts* (2004), 21 C.C.L.T. (3d) 181 (Sask. C.A.), the defendant's actions in harassing a purchaser of a pharmacy and an employee of that pharmacy, led to the purchaser's decision not to complete the sale. The court treated this as a "direct" interference with the contractual relations between the vendor plaintiff and his lost purchaser, although indirect interference might have been a more appropriate characterization.

147 See Lord Denning's judgment in *Torquay Hotel v. Cousins*, [1969] 1 All E.R. 522 at 530 (C.A.), where it is stated that "indirect interference is only unlawful if unlawful means are used." It has been suggested, however, that there has been a relaxation of the requirement that unlawful means must be proved in order to support the indirect form of the action. See *Fraser v. Central United Church* (1982), 38 O.R. (2d) 97 at 104 (H.C.). Unfortunately, however, the issue is somewhat obscured by the lack of agreement concerning the distinction between direct and indirect interferences.

renders it impossible for a third party to perform a contract with the plaintiff clearly qualifies.[148] In the labour relations context, inducing one group of employees to break their contracts with their employer, making it impossible for a contract which their employer has with the plaintiff from being performed, will also qualify. In *D.C. Thomson & Co. v. Deakin*,[149] for example, the defendants wished to disrupt the contractual relationship which the plaintiff, a firm of printers, had with the B company, a company which supplied the plaintiff with paper. The defendants accomplished this, not by directly persuading B not to fulfil its contract with the plaintiff, but by inducing the employees of the B company not to deliver or load paper destined for the plaintiff. Because its employees refused to work, B was unable to continue supplying paper to the plaintiff. Was the defendants' conduct actionable? The judges, while conceding that the tort of inducing breach of contract may be committed by a defendant who indirectly procures its breach, imposed the requirement that the indirect means used be tortious. Since in this case the evidence did not support the proposition that the defendants had induced B's employees to breach their contract with B, the defendants had not acted wrongfully and could not be held liable.[150]

In *Merkur Island Corp. v. Laughton*,[151] the cause of action was extended. Not only was it held to be actionable to prevent a contracting party from performing

---

148 For example, a trespass, as in *G.W.K. Ltd. v. Dunlop Rubber Co.* (1926), 42 T.L.R. 376; or fraud, as in *Nat. Phonograph Co. v. Edison-Bell Consol.*, [1908] 1 Ch. 335 (C.A.). Note that now, as a result of *OBG v. Allan*, these would be examples of the unlawful means tort, a tort of primary liability, and not *Lumley v. Gye*. As stated by Lord Nicholls in *OBG v. Allan* at para. 178:

> the application of the *Lumley v Gye* tort to a "prevention" case was unfortunate. There is a crucial difference between cases where the defendant induces a contracting party not to perform his contractual obligations and cases where the defendant prevents a contracting party from carrying out his contractual obligations. In inducement cases the very act of joining with the contracting party and inducing him to break his contract is sufficient to found liability as an accessory. In prevention cases the defendant does not join with the contracting party in a wrong (breach of contract) committed by the latter. There is no question of accessory liability.

149 Above, note 141.

150 The cause of action was described by Jenkins L.J., [1952] 2 All E.R. 361 at 379 as follows:

> . . . an actionable interference with contractual relations may be committed by a third party who, with knowledge of a contract between two other persons and with the intention of causing its breach, or preventing its performance, persuades, induces or procures the servants of one of those parties, on whose service he relies for the performance of his contract, to break their contracts of employment with him, either by leaving him without notice or by refusing to do what is necessary for the performance of his contract, provided that the breach of the contract between the two other persons intended to be brought about by the third party does in fact ensue as a necessary consequence of the third party's wrongful interference with the contracts of employment.

Jenkins L.J. was insistent that to persuade someone to commit a lawful act in order to prevent a third party from performing a contract with the plaintiff is not, and ought not to be, tortious. See also *J.T. Stratford & Son v. Lindley*, [1964] 3 All E.R. 102 (H.L.). It is Jenkins L.J.'s "unified theory" approach, lumping together the *Lumley v. Gye* inducing breach of contract tort with other unlawful acts of interference into a general tort of actionable interference with contractual rights, which the Lords in *OBG v. Allan* rejected.

151 [1983] 2 A.C. 570 (H.L.).

a contract with the plaintiff, by inducing the former party's employees to breach their contracts, but it is actionable as well to induce a breach of contract at a more remote stage.[152]

Canadian courts have recognized the action for inducing breach of contract by indirect unlawful means. Thus, in *Dirassar v. Kelly, Douglas & Co.*,[153] the defendant's action in asserting its legal right to acquire title to a property being developed, which resulted in the breach of a contract between the developer and its architect, not being unlawful, was not actionable.[154] In *Garry v. Sherritt Gordon Mines Ltd.*,[155] Cameron J.A. confirmed that the two causes of action existed; the first, the "direct persuasion", and the second, "the doing of an unlawful act."[156]

Aside from the unlawful means requirement, the cause of action for procuring a breach of contract by indirect means has the same elements as inducing breach of contract by direct persuasion. The defendant must be shown to have acted with the intention of disrupting the plaintiff's contractual relations. The defendant must have known of the existence of the contract. The breach of contract must have occurred, causing damage to the plaintiff. With the indirect form of the tort, causation may be more difficult to prove. It has been held that the breach of the contract must have ensued as a "necessary consequence" of the defendant's conduct, a necessary consequence being defined as the contract breaker's inability to perform "as a matter of practical possibility."[157]

---

152 On the facts of the case, the contracting party, A, required the services of another party, B, in order to enable A to perform its contract with the plaintiff. The defendant induced B's employees to breach their contract with B. The court held that since the defendant's acts were unlawful, the tort of inducing breach of the more remote contract was actionable. See Dillon J.'s judgment in the Court of Appeal, [1983] 2 A.C. 570 at 587. It was, however, conceded by Sir John Donaldson M.R. that the more indirect the action of the defendant, the more difficult will it be to prove the defendant's knowledge and intention to interfere with the performance of the principle contract. As a result of *OBG v. Allan*, the Lords would now regard this as an example of the "unlawful means" tort.

153 (1966), 59 D.L.R. (2d) 452 (B.C. C.A.), affirmed (1967), 64 D.L.R. (2d) 456 (S.C.C.).

154 Note that Norris J.A. dissented, treating this as an example of a direct interference with contractual relations.

155 (1987), 42 C.C.L.T. 241 (Sask. C.A.).

156 *Ibid.*, at 262. Since picketing by the defendants was not unlawful, Cameron J.A. dismissed the action. Bayda J.A. upheld it, since in his opinion the picketing was unlawful, being an intentional inducement of breach of contract. The case of *Thermo King Corp. v. Prov. Bank of Can.* (1981), 130 D.L.R. (3d) 256 (Ont. C.A.), illustrates the difficulty of characterization. The defendant bank refused to issue a draft on its customer's instructions, which, to the bank's knowledge, resulted in a breach of contract between the customer and the plaintiff. The action was characterized as inducing breach of contract, without reference to whether this was in the direct or indirect form. The court upheld the action based upon the wrongfulness of the bank's decision not to issue the draft. It was conceded that had this been a lawful act, the action could not succeed, on the basis that it would have constituted a "reasonable justification." Also see *Great West Marketing Inc. v. Connell* (2002), [2003] 6 W.W.R. 101 (Alta. Q.B.), where the court dismissed the action because the indirect interference was not unlawful.

157 See *D.C. Thomson & Co. v. Deakin*, [1952] 2 All E.R. 361 at 380. Under the *OBG v. Allan* reformulation, the "unlawful means" tort does not require that the unlawful act resulted in a

(d) Interferences with Contractual Relations not Involving Breach

In *Torquay Hotel Co. v. Cousins*,[158] Lord Denning M.R. extended the tort of inducing breach of contract to the case "where a third person *prevents* or *hinders* one party from performing his contract, even though it be not a breach."[159] As with inducing breach of contract, the tort of interfering with the performance of a contract, short of actual breach, can be committed directly or indirectly, although in the latter case, the indirect means used must be unlawful. On the facts of *Torquay Hotel*, the defendants were liable for directly persuading a contracting party not to perform a contract with the plaintiff, even though the failure to perform due to a *force majeure* clause in the contract, was not, according to Lord Denning, a breach of the contract.[160] In *Merkur Island Corp. v. Laughton*,[161] Lord Diplock accepted the principle of *Torquay Hotel*, holding that it is actionable to procure the breach of a primary obligation under a contract, even though the contract breaker could not be held responsible for the "secondary obligation" of making monetary compensation by way of damages to the affected party, because this obligation was excluded by a *force majeure* clause.[162] *OBG v. Allan*[163] has, however, at least in so far as English law is concerned, reversed this position. Lord Nicholls, characterizing the *Torquay* principle has having taken the law "a step too far", stated that an action based on *Lumley v. Gye* cannot be successful in the absence of the defendant having induced an actual breach of contract. Acting unlawfully with the intention to inflict harm on the plaintiff is actionable, not, however, as an extension of *Lumley v. Gye*, but under the unlawful means tort.[164]

---

breach of the contract; only that it was intended to and did in fact harm the plaintiff's economic interests.

158 [1969] 1 All E.R. 522 (C.A.).

159 *Ibid.*, at 530. For commentary on this case see Richardson, "Interference With Contractual Relations: Is Torquay Hotel the Law in Canada?" (1983), 41 U. of T. Fac. L. Rev. 1; and Burns, "Tort Injury to Economic Interests: Some Facets of Legal Response" (1980), 58 Can. Bar Rev. 103.

160 Note that the other judges in the case, Russell L.J. and Winn L.J., did not consider that the *force majeure* clause meant that there was no breach, only that there could be no liability for the breach. Thus, they did not see a need to extend the tort. For criticism of Lord Denning's approach, see Richardson, *ibid.* Richardson argues that the judgment was *obiter*, since there was a breach, that the judgment was not supported by previous authorities, and most significantly, that where there has in fact been no breach, or a failure to perform which amounts to a breach, the contracting party has no damages on which to base a tort claim.

161 [1983] 2 All E.R. 189 (H.L.).

162 It is important to note, however, that, on the facts of the case, it was the party who was unable to perform its primary obligation because of the acts of the defendants who was the plaintiff here, and not, as in *Torquay*, the intended beneficiary of the contractual obligation.

163 Above.

164 Lord Nicholls went so far as to characterize Lord Denning's extension of the law as "irrational" and declared that there is no "hybrid tort of 'interfering with contractual relations'", short of breach. "In so far as authorities suggest or decide otherwise they should not now be followed." The refusal to extend the *Lumley v. Gye* tort to conduct which did not amount to breach of contract was a view shared by Lord Hoffman and Lord Walker. The Lords did not agree, however, on what constitutes unlawful means for the "unlawful means tort". Lord Hoffman's view, which was agreed to by the majority, was that only those acts which are actionable by the third party against whom they were directed, or would be if the third party had suffered loss, constitute unlawful means for the purpose of the plaintiff's unlawful means tort. Lord

The principle of *Torquay Hotel* has been approved of in a few Canadian cases.[165] It was reviewed by the Saskatchewan Court of Appeal in *College of Dental Surgeons (Saskatchewan) v. Thorvaldson.*[166] In this case, an action was brought by plaintiffs, who were dental therapists and a dental assistant, against the College of Dental Surgeons of Saskatchewan. The College had proposed to the Government of Saskatchewan that its members provide dental services which were then being provided by the plaintiffs. The government accepted the proposal and terminated the plaintiffs' employment. This termination was made pursuant to the agreement between the government and the plaintiffs. The Court of Appeal, although accepting the principle of *Torquay Hotel*, rejected its application to this case. The College had not hindered or prevented the government from performing its contract with the plaintiffs. It merely had proposed an alternative scheme to the government, which the government decided to adopt, without there having been any breach of its existing contract with the plaintiffs.

The ambit of the *Torquay* principle remains somewhat unclear. It has been applied, for example, to assist a plaintiff whose complaint was not that there was an interference with the performance of a contract by its co-contractant, but with its own obligation to perform.[167] It would have been more appropriate in this latter

---

Nicholl's broader view was that unlawful means "embraces all acts a defendant is not permitted to do whether by the civil law or the criminal law."

165 For a discussion of five of these cases, see Burns, and Richardson, above, note 158. The five cases are *Einhorn v. Westmount Invt. Ltd.* (1969), 6 D.L.R. (3d) 71 (Sask. Q.B.), affirmed (1970), 11 D.L.R. (3d) 509 (Sask. C.A.); *Mark Fishing Co. v. U.F.A.W.*, [1972] 3 W.W.R. 641 (B.C. C.A.), affirmed [1973] 3 W.W.R. 13 (S.C.C.); *Celona v. Kamloops Centennial (Pac. No. 269) Branch of Royal Can. Legion*, [1974] 2 W.W.R. 144 (B.C. S.C.); *McKenzie v. Peel County Bd. of Educ.* (1974), 51 D.L.R. (3d) 33 (Ont. C.A.); and *West. Stevedoring Co. v. Pulp, Paper & Woodwkrs. of Can.* (1975), 61 D.L.R. (3d) 701 (B.C. C.A.). Richardson analyzes each case, arguing that the *Torquay* principle was, despite the *dicta* in the judgments, not actually applied in reaching the decisions. *Torquay* was approved of by Bayda C.J.S. in *Garry v. Sherritt Gordon Mines Ltd.* (1987), 42 C.C.L.T. 241 at 294ff (Sask. C.A.); by Wakeling J.A. for the Saskatchewan Court of Appeal in *College of Dental Surgeons (Sask.) v. Thorvaldson*, [1991] 5 W.W.R. 436; and by Berger J. in *Ed Miller Sales & Rentals v. Caterpillar Tractor Co.*, above, note 146, at 542 [5 W.W.R.]. The issue was raised but left unresolved by the Manitoba Court of Appeal in *Merchants Consolidated Ltd. (Receiver of) v. Canstar Sports Group Inc.*, [1994] 5 W.W.R. 210. It was also raised in Ontario in *A.G. Ont. v. Dieleman* (1994), 117 D.L.R. (4th) 449 (Gen. Div.). The question was whether anti-abortion protesters could be liable for inducing breach of contract, or interfering with contracts, between would-be patients and an abortion clinic. Since there was no evidence establishing what were the contractual relationships between patients and the clinics or patients and their doctors, the matter was not pursued by the court. In *Daishowa Inc. v. Friends of the Lubicon* (1996), 29 C.C.L.T. (2d) 76 (Ont. Div. Ct.), leave to appeal refused (1996), 1996 CarswellOnt 1553 (C.A.), leave to appeal refused (1997), 107 O.A.C. 160 (note) (S.C.C.), Corbett J. held that "interference with a contract or an existing contractual relationship which falls short of causing an actual breach but results in the untimely conclusion of relations is nonetheless actionable".

166 *Ibid.*

167 See *Alltrans Express Ltd. v. Gen. Truck Drivers' & Helpers' Union, Loc. 213* (1982), 20 C.C.L.T. 164 (B.C. S.C.); *Verchere v. Greenpeace Canada* (2003), 16 C.C.L.T. (3d) 236 (B.C. S.C.), additional reasons at (2003), 2003 CarswellBC 2539 (S.C.), affirmed (2004), 241 D.L.R. (4th) 327, 233 C.C.L.T. (3dd) 208 (B.C. C.A.), additional reasons at (2004), 2004 CarswellBC 2007 (C.A.), leave to appeal refused (2004), 2004 CarswellBC 2715 (S.C.C.); and *Peter Kiewit Sons Co. v. U.A., Local 740* (2004), [2004] N.J. No. 359, 2005 CarswellNfld 35 (T.D.)), leave to appeal refused (2005), 244 Nfld. & P.E.I.R. 342 (C.A.). In *Verchere v. Greenpeace Canada*, for example, the action for interference with contractual relations was

case for the court to have applied the action for unlawful interference with economic interests,[168] rather than the cause of action for inducing breach of contract.[169] One can also argue that unlawful conduct directed against a party to prevent others from contracting with that party is better dealt with by a general principle of liability for unlawful interference with economic interests than by a tort whose object is the recognition and protection of the sanctity of contract. The issue of damages also presents problems. Where a party is persuaded by the defendant not to perform non-contractual obligations for, or enter into a contract with, the plaintiff, has the plaintiff lost something worthy of tort law's protection? If unlawful means have been used, an argument for compensation can be made under a more general principle of liability.

4. INTIMIDATION

(a) Introduction

The tort of intimidation, which has been called "a rare and peculiar cause of action",[170] was only solidly established in the relatively recent case of *Rookes v. Barnard*.[171] Its essence lies in threats of unlawful acts directed by A against B in order to coerce B into doing something which is damaging either to B's own interests, or those of a third party. A two party intimidation occurs where the threats are directed against the plaintiff, who suffers damages as a result of the threats. A three party intimidation occurs where the threats are directed against a third party and where, as a result of these threats, the plaintiff's interests are damaged. In either case, the elements of the cause of action are the same.

(b) Threat

The essence of the tort of intimidation is that an individual acts in a way which is either self-damaging or damaging to the interests of another, due to coercion by the defendant's express or implied threats.[172] A threat has been defined as "a pre-intimation of proposed action of some sort",[173] or "an intimation by one to

---

applied to plaintiffs who were suing because they were forced to breach their own contracts with their employer, due to the conduct of the defendants. The plaintiffs were loggers who were unable to work because of a protest staged by the defendants. The protest involved preventing the loggers from using the equipment necessary to do their work. In my view, the more appropriate action would have been unlawful interference with economic interests. Strictly speaking, the more narrow tort of interference with contractual relations applies where the plaintiff is claiming that a third party was unable to perform its contract with it due to the actions of the defendant; not where the plaintiffs themselves were unable to perform their contractual obligations.

168 See below.

169 The inappropriateness of using this tort when it is the complainant who was unable to perform was commented upon by O'Sullivan J.A. in *Mintuck v. Valley River Band No. 63A* (1977), 2 C.C.L.T. 1 at 26 (Man. C.A.).

170 Pearson L.J. in *Rookes v. Barnard*, [1963] 1 Q.B. 623 at 688 (C.A.).

171 [1964] A.C. 1129 (H.L.). The judicial history is reviewed by Pearson L.J.'s judgment in the Court of Appeal, *ibid.*, at 689 ff.

172 One can see a close connection between intimidation and inducing breach of contract. In intimidation, the act which is damaging to a third party is forced onto the immediate actor. In inducing breach of contract, the damaging act is encouraged or otherwise procured.

173 Lord Dunedin in *Sorrell v. Smith*, [1925] A.C. 700 at 730 (H.L.).

another that unless the latter does or does not do something the former will do something which the latter will not like."[174] The threat may be made expressly in a demand, or implicitly in conduct, as long as the threatened party has reason to believe that the conduct will continue until the demanded course of action is followed.[175]

(c) Unlawful Act

In order to be liable, the defendant must have intimidated the party concerned with threats of unlawful acts. Threats of tortious and criminal acts clearly qualify in this regard. In *Mintuck v. Valley River Band No. 63A*,[176] for example, the defendant committed the tort of two party intimidation by harassing the plaintiff with threats of damage to his property and physical harm to him and his family. These were clearly threats of unlawful acts which supported the tort claim for intimidation.[177] Where the acts threatened are not unlawful, the cause of action will fail.[178]

In *Rookes v. Barnard*,[179] the House of Lords extended the tort by including in the range of unlawful acts threats of breach of contract. The case illustrates the tort of a three party intimidation. The trade union defendant coerced an employer into discharging the plaintiff employee by threatening the employer with an illegal strike, a breach of contract, unless the employee was discharged. The plaintiff was discharged with due notice, and sued the union for intimidation. The Lords held that the threat of an unlawful act included the threat of a breach of contract and upheld the claim. Although the decision has been criticized,[180] it has been applied to subsequent cases.[181]

---

174 Peterson J. in *Hodges v. Webb*, [1920] 2 Ch. 70 at 89, cited by Matas J.A. in *Mintuck v. Valley River Band No. 63A*, [1977] 2 W.W.R. 309 at 323 (Man. C.A.), and Legg J. in *Circuit Graphics Ltd. v. C.A.I.M.A.W., Loc. 1* (1981), 31 B.C.L.R. 5 at 9 (S.C.).

175 See, e.g., *Circuit Graphics v. C.A.I.M.A.W., Loc. 1, ibid.*

176 [1977] 2 W.W.R. 309 (Man. C.A.).

177 Also see *Boychuk v. N.W.T. Housing Corp.* (1985), 33 C.C.L.T. 28 (N.W.T. S.C.), where threats of violence were directed at the plaintiff, compelling him to discontinue working on a construction project.

178 See, e.g., *Vancouver Museums & Planetarium Assn. v. Vancouver Mun. & Regional Employees' Union* (1981), 27 B.C.L.R. 73 (C.A.) and *Sandy Ridge Sawing Ltd. v. Norrish*, [1996] 4 W.W.R. 528 (Sask. Q.B.). In *Skybridge Investments Ltd. v. Metro Motors Ltd.*, 2006 BCCA 500 (C.A.), the plaintiff entered into an agreement with a car dealership in Canada to buy 31 vehicles for resale to a car dealership in the United States. This was disallowed by the terms of the Dealers Sales and Service Agreement (DSSA), which the Canadian dealer had with Ford Motor Company. The cars were never delivered to the plaintiff. The plaintiff sued the manufacturer and dealer for intimidation and conspiracy. Both claims were struck out. The court held that the DSSA was not a breach of the Competition Act, R.S.C. 1985, c. 34, and thus there was no unlawful act. In addition, the plaintiff did not plead that the predominant purpose of the agreement was to cause injury to the plaintiff and thus the tort of conspiracy to injure could not succeed. See discussion below.

179 Above, note 171.

180 See, e.g., Wedderburn, "Intimidation and the Right to Strike" (1964), 27 Mod. L. Rev. 257.

181 See *Morgan v. Fry*, [1968] 3 All E.R. 452 (C.A.). See, however, the case of *Roehl v. Houlahan*

In *Central Can. Potash Co. v. Sask.*,[182] the applicability of *Rookes v. Barnard*, with its extension to threats of breach of contract, was considered by the Supreme Court of Canada, in relation to a two party intimidation. The defendant, the Government of Saskatchewan, threatened to cancel the plaintiff's licence and mineral leases unless it complied with a statutorily enacted scheme restricting potash production. Although the plaintiff complied with the request, it challenged the validity of the scheme and claimed damages for intimidation. Despite the fact that the Supreme Court ruled that the production scheme was invalid, and hence that the government could not lawfully terminate the leases of those who refused to comply with it, the claim for intimidation failed. Martland J. held that, since at the time of the demand, the scheme had not yet been ruled invalid, the government had not acted wrongfully. The minister was properly discharging his duty in enforcing the statutory provisions.[183] More significantly, however, Martland J. expressed serious reservations about the application of the *Rookes v. Barnard* extension to cases of two party intimidation. While conceding that a remedy ought to be provided to a plaintiff whose interests are injured because of unlawful threats made against a third party, even if these threats are merely threats of breach of contract, Martland J. did not agree that this ought to be the case in the two party tort.[184] Martland J. agreed with a passage in *Winfield and Jolowicz on Tort*[185] that in cases of two party intimidation, where the threat is one of breach of contract, the intimidated party ought to resist the threat, and pursue the available contractual remedies should the threat be carried out.[186] Martland J. did recognize, however, that the tort of two party intimidation should be available where the party is threatened "with violence or perhaps with any other tort."[187]

In *Central Can. Potash*,[188] Martland J. also held that the tort of intimidation is not made out where "a party to a contract asserts what he reasonably considers to be his contractual right."[189] This was applied in *J.C. Kerkhoff & Sons Contr. Ltd. v. XL Ironworks Co.*,[190] in relation to a three party intimidation. The defendant

---

(1990), 74 D.L.R. (4th) 562 (Ont. C.A.), where it was held that a threat to resign was not the threat of an unlawful act which could support the tort of intimidation.

182 (1978), 6 C.C.L.T. 265 (S.C.C.).

183 See also *White Hatter Limousine Service Ltd. v. Calgary (City)* (1993), 17 C.C.L.T. (2d) 309 at 314 (Alta. Q.B.): "public officials charged with enforcing legislation cannot be held liable in damages for purporting to lawfully enforce legislation which is later determined to be invalid. It is not intimidation to make threats of certain acts if the intent is not to injure, but merely to ensure compliance of legislation."

184 In the three party situation, where the party threatened acts lawfully in relation to the plaintiff, the plaintiff's only recourse will be against the intimidator for intimidation. In the two party situation, however, the intimidated party will have a remedy against the defendant, should the threatened unlawful act be carried out, and thus there is no need for the additional intimidation remedy.

185 10th ed. at 458.

186 For comment see Klar, "Annotation" (1978), 6 C.C.L.T. 266.

187 (1978), 6 C.C.L.T. 265 at 307. For a discussion of what constitutes an "unlawful act" for the purposes of the tort of intimation and other economic torts, see Lambert J.A.'s dissenting judgment in *No. 1 Collision Repair & Painting (1982) Ltd. v. Insurance Corp. of British Columbia* (2000), 1 C.C.L.T. (3d) 1 (B.C. C.A.), leave to appeal refused (2001), 155 B.C.A.C. 320 (note) (S.C.C.). The majority of the Court of Appeal upheld the trial judgement that there were no threats of unlawful acts made.

188 (1978), 6 C.C.L.T. 265 (S.C.C.).

190 (1983), 26 C.C.L.T. 1 (B.C. S.C.), reversed on other grounds (1984), 11 C.L.R. 230 (B.C. C.A.).

union was relieved of liability for threatening to withdraw its labour, on the basis of a "reasonable belief" in its right to do so, even though, as it later was shown, the collective agreement did not support the union's position.

(d) Submission to Threat

Unless the party threatened complies with the threat, there can be no tort of intimidation. In *Fouillard Implement Exchange Ltd. v. Kello-Bilt Indust. Ltd.*,[191] for example, the defendant threatened to terminate its contractual relationship with the plaintiff unless the plaintiff agreed to comply with what was alleged to be a price-fixing scheme. The plaintiff refused to comply, and the threat was executed. The action for intimidation was accordingly dismissed.[192]

It has also been held that the intimidated party's damaging conduct must occur as a result of the threat. As stated by Martland J., "if the course of conduct which the person making the threat seeks to induce is that which the person threatened is obligated to follow, the tort of intimidation does not arise."[193] Thus in *Henuset Bros. Ltd. v. I.U.O.E., Loc. 955*,[194] the court dismissed the action for intimidation because it found that the decision of the party upon whom pressure was exerted not to contract with the plaintiff "was a straightforward business decision made by him in the absence of threatening circumstances and on the basis of the best interests of his companies. . . ."[195]

(e) Intention

Although the cause of action for intimidation is based upon an act of the defendant which is directed at causing injury to the plaintiff's interests, there is, as with the tort of inducing breach of contract, no need to establish malice on the defendant's part. The defendant will be liable even if the predominant purpose was the promotion of self-interests, and not the causing of injury to the plaintiff. The wrong lies not in the defendant's motive, but in the deliberate act of interfering with the plaintiff's interests through threats of unlawful acts.[196]

As with the tort of inducing breach of contract, the circumstances in which a person may be justified in issuing threats of unlawful acts are unclear. In *Morgan v. Fry*,[197] Lord Denning, while conceding that the courts have not yet been called on to indicate the role of justification in the tort of intimidation, intimated that there might be legitimate reasons to threaten to withdraw one's labour, for example.[198] Undoubtedly factors such as the nature of the threatened reprisals, the motives for the threats, and their goals, will be considered by the courts in developing the defence of justification in respect of this tort.[199]

---

191 [1985] 6 W.W.R. 548 (Man. Q.B.), affirmed [1986] 2 W.W.R. 93 (Man. C.A.).

192 See also *Roth v. Roth* (1991), 9 C.C.L.T. (2d) 141 (Ont. Gen. Div.).

193 Above, note 188, at 307.

194 (1986), 73 A.R. 194 (Q.B.).

195 *Ibid.*, at 222.

196 *Ibid.*, at 205.

197 [1968] 3 All E.R. 452 at 458 (C.A.).

198 If, for example, the workers were being required to work with "troublemakers."

199 Note, however, *Bartrop v. Sweetgrass Band No. 113* (1987), 54 Sask. R. 213 (Q.B.), where it was held that if illegal means are used, there is no defence of justification.

5. CONSPIRACY

(a) Introduction

Of all the business torts, the cause of action for conspiracy has provoked the most controversy. A conspiracy has been defined as an "agreement of two or more to do an unlawful act, or to do a lawful act by unlawful means."[200] As with the other business torts, the gravamen of the wrong in conspiracy is that the defendant engaged in unlawful conduct, the task of the courts therefore being to determine the nature of this unlawfulness requirement.

Canadian law recognizes two types of conspiracy actions.[201] The first is a conspiracy to injure, whereby two or more persons combine in order to effect the unlawful purpose of causing injury to the plaintiff. The second is a conspiracy to use unlawful means which are directed at the plaintiff, and thus cause the plaintiff injury.[202]

Where a defendant's actions are tortious in themselves, without regard to the fact that they were committed in combination with others, the claim of conspiracy is unnecessary.[203] The unique nature of the conspiracy action resides in the notion that it is the combination of persons which has converted an otherwise non-tortious activity into a tort. Whether the factor of numbers ought to convert a lawful activity into an unlawful one has been the subject of much debate. The principal argument in favour of the tort has been that an act may become more oppressive or dangerous when done by a combination of persons than it would

---

200 Willes J. in *Mulcahy v. R.* (1868), L.R. 3 H.L. 306 at 317.

201 For an excellent analysis, see Burns, "Civil Conspiracy: An Unwieldy Vessel Rides a Judicial Tempest" (1982), 16 U.B.C. L. Rev. 229.

202 Another useful way of characterizing these two types of conspiracy claims is to say that the first involves "a wrongful objective" — namely to injure the plaintiff, and the second involves a "wrongful act" — namely the use of unlawful means. See Vancise J.A. in *O.K. Economy Stores v. R.W.D.S.U. Local 454* (1994), 23 C.C.L.T. (2d) 233 at 259 (Sask. C.A.).

203 See, for example, *G. (R.) v. Christison* (1996), [1997] 1 W.W.R. 641 (Sask. Q.B.), additional reasons at [1997] 3 W.W.R. 604 (Sask. Q.B.), where the court dismissed a claim for conspiracy to commit defamation since it added nothing to the plaintiff's actions for defamation; and *Guccione v. Bell* (1998), 229 A.R. 365 (Master), varied (1999), 239 A.R. 277 (Q.B. [In Chambers]), affirmed (2001), 2001 CarswellAlta 1402 (C.A.). In *Accord Planners Insurance Agencies Ltd. v. Wise / Riddell Insurance Agency Inc.* (1997), [1997] O.J. No. 2423, 1997 CarswellOnt 2403 (Gen. Div.), pleadings of conspiracy to breach a contract were struck. Note however that in *Berry v. Pulley* (2000), 48 O.R. (3d) 169 (C.A.), leave to appeal allowed (2001), 146 O.A.C. 198 (note) (S.C.C.), affirmed (2002), 211 D.L.R. (4th) 651 (S.C.C.), the Ontario Court of Appeal held that a tortious conspiracy to deprive a party of contractual rights is different than a claim for breach of contract. Also see *Andersen Consulting Ltd. v. Canada (Attorney General)* (2001), 13 C.P.C. (5th) 251 (Ont. C.A.) to the same effect. In *Dionisio v. Lucas* (2006), [2006] O.J. No. 1212, 2006 CarswellOnt 1906 (S.C.J.), Ground J. allowed a plaintiff to plead conspiracy to commit other nominate torts, on the basis that it could not be said at this stage whether the plaintiff would succeed in proving that these other torts were committed, although a conspiracy might be proved. The claim was struck, however, since the plaintiff failed to allege damage resulting from the conspiracy. In *Toronto Dominion Bank v. Mapleleaf Furniture Manufacturing Ltd.* (2003), [2003] O.J. No. 4719, 2003 CarswellOnt 4601 (S.C.J.), Sutherland J., although supporting the view that where other torts have been proven, finding that a conspiracy to commit these torts was unnecessary, did so nevertheless. Sutherland J. wanted to make it clear that the facts of the case did support the existence of a conspiracy tort.

have been had the act been committed by a single individual.[204] One can certainly agree with the view that in many instances a group acting together against the plaintiff will be more damaging than would be the act of a single individual. In general we regard it as unfair when a group of individuals combine together and gang up against the single individual. Nonetheless, as has been recognized by eminent judges,[205] there clearly is no necessary magic in numbers. Considerable harm can be wrought upon the plaintiff by a single individual or company, depending upon its personality, influence and size. It is illogical, for example, that the action of a few small merchants acting together could be considered to be tortious when the same act carried out by one large, national supermarket would not be. On balance, it may be preferable for the law to abandon conspiracy as a separate tort, and to disregard the fact of a combination in determining the lawfulness of conduct. If an act is tortious when done by many, it should be tortious if done by one.[206]

The nature of the conspiracy action has made it particularly relevant in the labour relations context. Since the interests of employees are most effectively furthered by their combining together and exerting their collective strength, the conspiracy tort offers their adversaries a powerful countervailing option. Several successful common law conspiracy actions demonstrate the importance of this weapon.[207] Legislation has accordingly been enacted to limit this possibility.[208] Despite judicial[209] and academic[210] criticism, the conspiracy action is still part of contemporary tort law, and has been frequently utilized in recent years.[211]

---

204 See Bowen L.J. in *Mogul S.S. Co. v. McGregor, Gow & Co.*, (1889), 23 Q.B.D. 598 at 616 (C.A.). See also Lord Bramwell's judgment in the House of Lords at [1892] A.C. 25 at 45, and Lord Macnaghten's judgment in *Quinn v. Leathem*, [1901] A.C. 495 at 511.

205 See, e.g., Viscount Simon's judgment in *Crofter Hand Woven Harris Tweed Co. v. Veitch*, [1942] A.C. 435 at 443 (H.L.), and Lord Diplock's judgment in *Lonrho Ltd. v. Shell Petroleum Co.*, [1981] 2 All E.R. 456 (H.L.).

206 The matter can best be resolved as a matter of damages. If the single actor did not detrimentally affect the plaintiff's interests, because of a lack of size and influence, the action could be dismissed on this account.

207 See, e.g., *Gagnon v. Foundation Maritime Ltd.* (1961), 28 D.L.R. (2d) 174 (S.C.C.); *Mark Fishing Co. v. U.F.A.W.* (1972), 24 D.L.R. (3d) 585 (B.C. C.A.), affirmed (1973), 38 D.L.R. (3d) 316 (S.C.C.); *West. Stevedoring Co. v. Pulp, Paper & Woodwkrs. of Can.* (1975), 61 D.L.R. (3d) 701 (B.C. C.A.); and *Central Native Fishermen's Co-op. v. B.C. Prov. Council* (1975), 61 D.L.R. (3d) 677 (B.C. S.C.).

208 See discussion by Burns, above, note 201. See generally Christie, *The Liability of Strikers in the Law of Tort* (1967). A recent case dealing with such legislation in the context of a claim for conspiracy is *Pepsi-Cola Canada Beverages (West) Ltd. v. R.W.D.S.U., Local 558* (1998), [1999] 8 W.W.R. 429 (Sask. C.A.), affirmed (2002), 208 D.L.R. (4th) 385 (S.C.C.).

209 The Supreme Court of Canada has on at least two recent occasions called the tort anomalous and anachronistic. See *Frame v. Smith* (1987), 42 C.C.L.T. 1 (S.C.C.), and *Can. Cement LaFarge Ltd. v. B.C. Lightweight Aggregate Ltd.* (1983), 24 C.C.L.T. 111 (S.C.C.).

210 See Burns, above, note 201; and Heffey, "The Survival of Civil Conspiracy: A Question of Magic or Logic" (1975), 1 Monash U. L. Rev. 136.

211 For a good review of the authorities and the elements of the action for conspiracy, see Berger J.'s judgment in *Ed Miller Sales & Rentals v. Caterpillar Tractor Co.*, above, note 146; and the Nova Scotia Court of Appeal's judgment in *Coughlan v. Westminer Canada Holdings Ltd.* (1994), 127 N.S.R. (2d) 241. Also see Mesbur J.'s judgment in *Duca Community Credit*

(b) Agreement and Execution

The tort of conspiracy involves an agreement between two or more persons to act, followed by an execution of that agreement. As pointed out in the leading action on conspiracy, *Crofter Hand Woven Harris Tweed Co. v. Veitch*,[212] the agreed combination must be carried into effect in a greater or lesser degree in order for conspiracy to be actionable as a civil cause of action.

Parties who act independently, each with the intention of injuring the plaintiff but not having agreed together in advance to do so, cannot be sued for conspiracy. As explained by McLachlin J. in *Nicholls v. Richmond (Twp.)*,[213] the agreement need not be in any specific form or constitute a binding contract.[214] It is a matter of a "joint plan or common design." It can be established by either direct evidence or inferred from the facts of the case.[215] For example, the fact that a joint decision was taken by municipal officials,[216] or by directors of an organization,[217] did not indicate a conspiracy, since the element of an agreement in advance to act together was absent. It has also been stated that to be a party to a conspiracy, one must know the facts of the alleged agreement or combination *and* have intended to be a party to the combination.[218] "Mere knowledge, acquiescence, or approval of the act, without co-operation or agreement to co-operate" has been stated to be insufficient for a conspiracy.[219] Thus, where one of the parties goes beyond the acts which were known and agreed to, the other parties cannot be held liable as conspirators in those acts.[220]

(c) Conspiracy to Injure

The first type of conspiracy is a conspiracy "to effect an unlawful purpose", namely, to cause injury to the plaintiff.[221] Despite the *dicta* in *Allen v. Flood*[222]

Union Ltd. v. Giovannoli (2000), [2000] O.J. No. 1199, 2000 CarswellOnt 1170 (S.C.J.), additional reasons at (2000), 2000 CarswellOnt 4814 (S.C.J.) for a good discussion of the tort.

212 [1942] A.C. 435 (H.L.).

213 [1984] 3 W.W.R. 719 at 730-31 (B.C. S.C.).

214 See Lowry J.A. in *Golden Capital Securities Ltd. v. Holmes* (2004), 28 C.C.L.T. (3d) 31 at 42 (B.C. C.A.). The agreement need not be contractual. The parties must have "combined or conspired. . .to carry out a common design or a means of achieving a common objective, which is then implemented with resulting injury to the plaintiff."

215 McLachlin J., *ibid.*, citing *Sweeney v. Coote*, [1907] A.C. 221 (H.L.).

216 See *Nicholls v. Richmond (Twp.)*, above, note 213.

217 *Posluns v. Toronto Stock Exchange* (1964), 46 D.L.R. (2d) 210 (Ont. H.C.), affirmed (1965), 53 D.L.R. (2d) 193 (Ont. C.A.), which was affirmed (1968), 67 D.L.R. (2d) 165 (S.C.C.).

218 *Maguire v. Calgary*, [1983] 4 W.W.R. 342 (Alta. C.A.).

219 See *Culzean Inventions Ltd. v. Midwestern Broom Co.*, [1984] 3 W.W.R. 11 at 40 (Sask. Q.B.), and *Star Cabs v. Casawn Ent. Inc.* (1982), 21 Sask. R. 182 (Q.B.).

220 See, for example, *Golden Capital Securities Ltd. v. Holmes* (2004), 28 C.C.L.T. (3d) 31 (B.C. C.A.), additional reasons at (2005), 2005 CarswellBC 1276 (C.A.) — parties participated in an unlawful trading scheme. Although held liable at trial, the Court of Appeal dismissed the action for conspiracy brought by a brokerage house who had lost money. The parties did not know that it was likely that the scheme would result in losses suffered by the broker, nor did it know and agree to acts perpetrated by one of the parties.

221 The leading authorities are *Crofter Hand Woven Harris Tweed Co. v. Veitch*, [1942] A.C. 435

that motive cannot turn an otherwise lawful act into a unlawful one, the leading conspiracy cases have long held that where persons combine together for the predominant purpose of causing injury to the plaintiff, the combination is unlawful, and actionable in tort.

The difficulty in establishing the tort of conspiracy to injure resides in the requirement of proving that the predominant purpose of the defendants was to cause injury to the plaintiff, as opposed to promoting their own interests. Acting in order to improve one's own interests, even if this is accomplished by damaging the plaintiff's, has always been regarded as legitimate.[223] The test is a subjective one. What matters is not what the defendants ought to have realized would occur, nor what would naturally occur, as a result of their actions, but what their purpose or object was in acting. It is clear that in the rare case where defendants act in order to injure the plaintiff, not to advance their own interests, but out of spite or ill-will, an unlawful purpose has been established.[224] Conversely, where the defendants' principal goal is to further or advance their own interests, even if this was at the expense of the plaintiff's, the unlawfulness requirement has not been made out.[225] In this latter respect, it has been stated that it is not necessary that all of the conspirators have precisely the same interest or object, it being sufficient that "the various combining parties have their own legitimate trade or business interests to gain."[226] It has also been conceded that the court is concerned with the defendants' predominant purpose, recognizing that often the combiners may have had more than one purpose.[227]

A complicating question is introduced if one, by narrowly defining the concept of self-interest, finds that the conspirators' predominant purpose was neither to injure the plaintiff, nor to further their own interests, but to accomplish some other object. The conspirators, for example, may have wished to promote the interests of a third person, to demonstrate their power, or to express a political or ideological view, not directly in furtherance of their own interests, at least in a

---

(H.L.), *Mogul S.S. Co. v. McGregor*, [1892] A.C. 25 (H.L.), *Quinn v. Leathem*, [1901] A.C. 495 (H.L.), and *Sorrell v. Smith*, [1925] A.C. 700 (H.L.).

222 [1898] A.C. 1 (H.L.).

223 Unless, of course, unlawful means are used. See, e.g., *Dusessoy's Supermarkets St. James Ltd. v. Retail Clerks' Union, Loc. 832* (1961), 30 D.L.R. (2d) 51 (Man. Q.B.), where a secondary boycott which involved threats of violence, untrue statements, and conduct amounting to a nuisance was held to be an actionable conspiracy to injure. See also *Moffat Communications Ltd. v. Hughes* (1975), 55 D.L.R. (3d) 701 (B.C. S.C.).

224 Most conspiracy cases flounder on this issue, unless unlawful acts can be shown. One recent case which did succeed in establishing a predominant purpose to injure is *Coughlan v. Westminer Canada Holdings Ltd.*, above, note 211.

225 This has been the typical finding in the cases. See, e.g., *Crofter Hand Woven Harris Tweed Co. v. Veitch*, above, note 221; *Mogul S.S. Co. v. McGregor*, above, note 221; *Lonrho v. Shell Petroleum Co.*, [1982] A.C. 173 (H.L.); and *Can. Cement LaFarge Ltd. v. B.C. Lightweight Aggregate Ltd.* (1983), 24 C.C.L.T. 111 (S.C.C.), as leading examples of this. A notable exception is *Quinn v. Leathem*, above, note 221, where the court viewed the union's conspiracy as an act of "vengeance", as opposed to promoting its own interests. The *ratio* of the case is somewhat unclear, since the facts also supported the torts of interference with contractual relations, and intimidation.

226 Viscount Maugham in *Crofter Hand Woven Harris Tweed Co. v. Veitch*, above, note 221, at 453.

227 See Viscount Simon L.C. in *Crofter, ibid.*, at 445. Even if one of the purposes was to damage the plaintiff for spite, as long as this was not the predominant purpose, the combination is lawful.

commercial sense.[228] Since their predominant goal was neither to injure the plaintiff, nor to advance their self-interest, is this conspiracy actionable?[229] It would be consistent with the concern of recent authorities that the tort of conspiracy is anomalous, to take the more restricted view, and to hold that unless the predominant purpose of the combiners was to cause injury to the plaintiff, the action should fail. Thus, any predominant purpose other than causing injury should legitimate a combination, unless unlawful means are used. The task of the courts in this area is essentially to determine how far the notion of the legitimate self-interests of the conspirators can be stretched, until the point is reached when the causing of injury to the plaintiff, and not some alleged self-interest, is deemed to be the conspirators' main objective.

There is the matter of the burden of proof. Must the plaintiff establish both the conspiracy and its unlawful purpose, or having proved the conspiracy, must the defendants justify it by proving a lawful purpose? Again there seem to be divergent views.[230] Some have held that the plaintiff must prove all of the elements of the case, including the unlawful object;[231] others have seen the lawful purpose as a defence or justification to be proved by the defendant, once the combination to cause damage has been established.[232] It is consistent with tort principles that the plaintiff ought to be required to establish all of the elements of the case, including the unlawful purpose of the conspiracy, in order to succeed.[233] This is also consistent with the desire of contemporary law to confine the action narrowly.

---

228 A good example of this might be the actions of the defendants in *A.G. Ont. v. Dieleman* (1994), 117 D.L.R. (4th) 449 (Ont. Gen. Div.). The defendants were anti-abortion protesters. They picketed clinics, homes and offices of physicians, and hospitals. One might argue that their predominant purpose was not to injure the doctors or patients, or to advance their own self-interests, but to promote their ideological, political or religious positions on abortion. Conspiracy as a cause of action failed, because their predominant purpose was not to injure.

229 See Burns, above, note 201, at 239, for a discussion of this point. Burns notes that several of the Justices in the *Crofter* case admitted that this third possibility exists, but were not in agreement as to how the law should deal with it.

230 See discussion by Burns, *ibid.*, at 237.

231 Burns cites Lords Wright and Porter in *Crofter*, Lord Watson in *Mogul* and Dunedin L.J. in *Sorrell v. Smith*, above, note 221; and Salmon L.J. in *J.T. Stratford & Son v. Lindley*, [1965] A.C. 269 (C.A.), reversed on other grounds [1965] A.C. 269 at 307 (H.L.). See also *Tree Savers International Ltd. v. Savoy* (1991), 81 Alta. L.R. (2d) 325 (Q.B.), varied in part (1992), 84 Alta. L.R. (2d) 384 (C.A.), where the court held that the onus of proving all elements of the action, including the predominant purpose to injure, rests on the plaintiff.

232 Burns submits that this is the view of Heydon, "The Defence of Justification in Cases of Intentionally Caused Economic Loss" (1970), 20 U.T.L.J. 139; and Fleming, *The Law of Torts*, 8th ed. (1992).

233 The question arises as to the nature of the burden. When unlawful conduct is alleged in the context of a civil case, does the burden of proof remain the civil burden, or does it approximate the burden in a criminal case? The issue is discussed in *Ed Miller Sales & Rentals Ltd. v. Caterpillar Tractor Co.*, above, note 146. Berger J. concludes that the burden remains the

Although the usual case of conspiracy involves competition between traders or labour disputes, the tort is not to be confined to these matters.[234] For example, passengers on an airline affected by an illegal strike of air traffic controllers were able to sue for a conspiracy.[235] The Supreme Court of Canada has decided, however, that the action ought not to be extended into the family law context as a means of resolving disputes concerning the custody of, and access to, children.[236]

(d) Conspiracy to Use Unlawful Means

A second type of tortious conspiracy arises where parties combine in the use of unlawful means and the plaintiff suffers damage as a result. If the unlawful means used are in themselves tortious and would give rise to a cause of action, even if done by a single party acting alone, the claim of a conspiracy adds nothing to the cause of action itself, although the damages caused because of the conspiracy may be more serious.[237] It is where the unlawful act would not normally give rise to a tort claim, if done by a single party, that the issue becomes important.[238] Should the combining together to commit an unlawful act give rise to a civil cause of action for conspiracy?

This issue has been dealt with both in England and in Canada. The first important English case to deal with the issue was *Lonrho v. Shell Petroleum Co.*[239] In this judgment, the House of Lords seemed to decide that the tort of conspiracy to use unlawful means, where the predominant purpose of the conspiracy was not

---

balance of probabilities, with a higher degree of proof required, commensurate with the severity of the wrongdoing alleged.

234 This was made clear by Viscount Simon in *Crofter*, [1942] A.C. 435 at 446-47. See also *McKinnon v. F.W. Woolworth Co.* (1968), 66 W.W.R. 205 (Alta. C.A.). See, however, *Surrey (Dist.) v. Marall Homes Ltd.* (1988), 48 C.C.L.T. 70 at 78 (B.C. S.C.), where it is stated that the tort should be confined to labour and commercial disputes.

235 See *Can. Training & Dev. Group v. Air Can.* (1986), 39 C.C.L.T. 72 (Ont. Div. Ct.). The action was dismissed due to a statutory defence.

236 See *Frame v. Smith* (1987), 42 C.C.L.T. 1 (S.C.C.). On the question of the scope of the conspiracy action, see also *Hunt v. Carey Can. Inc.*, [1990] 6 W.W.R. 385 (S.C.C.). An action for conspiracy was brought by a cancer victim against the defendants, who allegedly had conspired to withhold information concerning the dangers of exposure to asbestos. The Supreme Court refused to strike out the statement of claim, since it was not "plain and obvious" that an action for personal injury could not be brought in conspiracy. Another interesting conspiracy case is *Helmy v. Helmy* (2000), 36 E.T.R. (2d) 100 (Ont. S.C.J.). Family members conspired with a husband to conceal from his wife the fact that he had won $2.5 million in a lottery. The court upheld the claim. It is unclear whether the decision was based on a conspiracy to injure or a conspiracy to use unlawful means. Arguably the second form of conspiracy would be more appropriate on the facts of the case, as the parties conspired together by using various schemes to prevent the wife from gaining her fair share of the family property as provided for by the Family Law Act, R.S.O. 1990, c. F.3.

237 The tortious means may involve the other economic torts, such as conspiracy to induce breach of contract, to unlawfully interfere with contractual relations, or to intimidate. Thus here the conspiracy may be pleaded in addition to the other tort. Other torts may also be involved, such as conspiracy to commit a nuisance. It has been held that when the unlawful means used by the conspirators are themselves tortious, the conspiracy "merges" into the torts committed, and thus the allegation of the prior conspiracy to commit the tort adds nothing. See, for example, *Franklin Supply Co. v. Midco Supply Co.* (1995), 33 Alta. L.R. (3d) 362 (Q.B.).

238 Especially for the labour relations context. Unlawful means may involve breaches of labour relations legislation, the Criminal Code, licensing regulations, or trade laws.

239 [1981] 2 All E.R. 456 (H.L.).

to injure the plaintiff, ought not to exist. While conceding that the tort of conspiracy to injure the plaintiff's commercial interests is "too well-established to be discarded, however anomalous it may seem today",[240] Lord Diplock held that it ought not to be extended beyond these narrow limits. The tort of conspiracy to use unlawful means was accordingly rejected.[241]

The question was revisited, however, by the House of Lords in *Lonrho plc. v. Fayed.*[242] Lord Bridge challenged and rejected the interpretation given to Lord Diplock's *Lonrho* judgment. According to Lord Bridge, the earlier House of Lords' decision did not rule out conspiracy as a viable cause of action if it could be shown that (a) unlawful means were used by conspirators and (b) there was an intention to injure the plaintiff. This would be actionable, even if the predominant purpose was not to injure the plaintiff.[243]

The same issue arose in Canada in *Can. Cement LaFarge Ltd. v. B.C. Lightweight Aggregate Ltd.*[244] The defendants were sued for a civil conspiracy to breach the Combines Investigation Act.[245] Since it could not be established that the defendants conspired to injure the plaintiff's interests, rather than to further their own, the plaintiff relied on this second type of conspiracy action. The lower courts affirmed this action, Callaghan J. stating that "if two or more persons combine to do an unlawful act or to do a lawful act by unlawful means and in the carrying out of the act or acts damage results to another person then that other person will have an action in conspiracy for damages."[246] Callaghan J. made it clear that in this conspiracy action, "when unlawfulness is found, the object of the conspirators

---

240 *Ibid.*, at 464.

241 Lord Diplock stated, *ibid.*:

> I am against extending the scope of the civil tort of conspiracy beyond acts done in execution of an agreement entered into by two or more persons for the purpose not of protecting their own interests but of injuring the interests of the plaintiff.

Lord Diplock accordingly decided that even though the defendants' acts were unlawful, since they were not done with the intent to harm the plaintiff and were not in themselves actionable, merely being a breach of penal legislation, no tort of conspiracy lay. The subsequent case of *Metall and Rohstoff AG v. Donaldson, Lufin & Jenrette Inc.*, [1990] 1 Q.B. 391 (C.A.), interpreted *Lonrho* in this way and dismissed a claim for conspiracy, since the defendants' conduct, although unlawful, did not have as its sole or predominant purpose the injuring of the plaintiff.

242 [1991] 3 W.L.R. 188 (H.L.).

243 The merits of the particular case were not dealt with, since the question arose on an interlocutory motion to strike. The merits of the particular case were not dealt with, since the question arose on an interlocutory motion to strike. The House of Lords revisited the tort of conspiracy in *Total Network SL v. Her Majesty's Revenue and Customs*, [2008] UKHL 19. One of the issues dealt with was the nature of the 'unlawful means' requirement. Were unlawful means restricted to conduct which gave rise to a separate action in tort against at least one of the conspirators or did it include criminal conduct? The Lords were unanimous in holding that criminal conduct, although not actionable in tort against any of the conspirators, could form the basis of the "unlawful means" form of conspiracy. In so deciding, the Lords were cognizant of the fact that unlawful means in conspiracy had a broader meaning than that agreed to in *OBG v. Allan* for the unlawful means tort.

244 (1983), 24 C.C.L.T. 111 (S.C.C.), reversing (1981), 123 D.L.R. (3d) 66 (B.C. C.A.), which affirmed (1979), 103 D.L.R. (3d) 587 (B.C. S.C.).

245 R.S.C. 1970, c. C-23, ss. 31.1, 32.

246 (1979), 103 D.L.R. (3d) 587 at 620.

becomes irrelevant."[247] The lower courts[248] found that the plaintiff was one of the targets of the conspiracy and had suffered damages.

The Supreme Court of Canada reversed the lower courts' judgments, and in so doing narrowed, without altogether eliminating, the tort of conspiracy to use unlawful means. Estey J. held that the action requires that the defendants combine together to commit an unlawful act, which "is directed towards the plaintiff (alone or together with others), and the defendants should know in the circumstances that injury to the plaintiff is likely to and does result."[249] Although their predominant purpose need not have been the plaintiff's injury, they must have intended to cause the plaintiff injury, by knowing that injury to the plaintiff would likely ensue.[250] On this test, the Supreme Court found that the facts did not support the case, and rejected the action.[251]

The tort of conspiracy to use unlawful means has been applied in cases subsequent to the Supreme Court judgment. Its most liberal application occurred in *Can. Training & Dev. Group v. Air Can.*,[252] where an illegal strike by air traffic controllers, which was entered into in order to put pressure on their employer, was deemed to constitute the unlawful means for the purposes of the tort. More surprisingly, it was held to have been directed at the plaintiffs who were passengers, even though the defendants did not know of, or single out, the plaintiff passengers specifically. Since the defendants should have known that injuries were likely to result to passengers from the strike, and damages were suffered, the action for conspiracy was complete.[253]

---

247 *Ibid.*, at 623.

248 See the B.C. Court of Appeal judgment at (1981), 123 D.L.R. (3d) 66.

249 24 C.C.L.T. 111 at 126.

250 This has been characterized by subsequent case law as constituting a "constructive" intent to injure. See, for example, *Lokos v. Manfor Ltd.*, [1995] 2 W.W.R. 709 at 719 (Man. C.A.). In view of the second *Lonrho* decision and the decision in *Canada Cement* it now appears that the English and Canadian positions on this second type of conspiracy tort are consistent. In *Golden Capital Securities v. Holmes* (2004), 28 C.C.L.T. (3d) 31 (B.C. C.A.), at 44, additional reasons at (2005), 2005 CarswellBC 1276 (C.A.), Lowry J.A. defined constructive intent as requiring that the conspirators had a "clear expectation" that the plaintiff would be injured. In other words, merely thinking that there was a better than 50 per cent chance that injury would occur would not be enough. The defendants must have been more certain than that.

251 The court held that the conspiracy was not directed at the plaintiff, and that there was no causal connection between the defendants' unlawful activities and the plaintiff's damages. The Supreme Court did not deal with the scope of the unlawful means requirement. One is left to conclude, therefore, that in line with existing Canadian authorities, a conspiracy to commit any unlawful act, or to commit a lawful act by unlawful means, is actionable. It is noteworthy that the case dealt with a breach of the Combines Investigation Act, and there was no suggestion that this was not within the scope of the civil conspiracy claim. See also *Westfair Foods Ltd. v. Lippens Inc.* (1989), 64 D.L.R. (4th) 335 (Man. C.A.), where it was held that the Competition Act, R.S.C. 1985, c. C-34, could support an action. See *Apotex Inc. v. Hoffman-La-Roche Ltd.* (2000), 195 D.L.R. (4th) 244 (Ont. C.A.).

252 (1986), 39 C.C.L.T. 72 (Ont. Div. Ct.).

253 Although the suit was dismissed on the basis of a defence provided for by the Rights of Labour Act, R.S.O. 1980, c. 456. Also see *Culzean Inventions Ltd. v. Midwestern Broom Co.*, [1984] 3 W.W.R. 11 (Sask. Q.B.), where a breach of a licensing agreement constituted unlawful means for the purpose of the tort of conspiracy. In *671122 Ontario Ltd. v. Sagaz Industries Canada Inc.* (1998), 42 C.C.L.T. (2d) 50 (Ont. Gen. Div.), additional reasons at (1998), 1998 CarswellOnt 5010 (Gen. Div.), reversed (2000), 48 C.C.L.T. (2d) 79 (Ont. C.A.), leave to

As with conspiracy to injure, the tort of conspiracy to use unlawful means is anomalous. An unlawful act which is not tortious *vis-à-vis* the plaintiff when done by one person ought not to become tortious merely because it is done by several people in concert with each other.[254]

(e) Damage

The plaintiff must suffer damage in order to have an action for conspiracy.[255] Whether actual pecuniary losses must be established by the plaintiff is not altogether clear. In *Valley Salvage Ltd. v. Molson Brewery*,[256] the court reviewed the authorities, finding that they supported the view that "where a plaintiff claims damages for injury to his business, actual pecuniary loss must be shown."[257] It has been held that where the conspiracy relates to the violation of a plaintiff's "legal right", and not to interference with trade or commercial interests, pecuniary damages need not be proved, since the violation of the right itself is sufficient injury.[258] In addition to compensatory damages, exemplary damages can be awarded in cases of conspiracy.[259]

---

appeal allowed [2000] 2 S.C.R. 983, reversed (2001), 8 C.C.L.T. (3d) 60 (S.C.C.), reconsideration refused (2001), 10 C.C.L.T. (3d) 292 (S.C.C.), the payment of bribes constituted the unlawful means to support the conspiracy claim. But see *Rogers v. Bank of Montreal*, [1985] 5 W.W.R. 193 (B.C. S.C.), affirmed [1987] 2 W.W.R. 364 (B.C. C.A.), where the court held that shareholders could not sue for conspiracy directed at their company, since *vis-à-vis* them, the defendants' actions were not unlawful. An interesting recent case is *Fraser v. Westminer Canada Ltd.* (2001), 199 N.S.R. (2d) 1 (S.C.), additional reasons at (2002), 2002 CarswellNS 547 (S.C.). This action stemmed from an earlier successful action brought by the CEO and directors of a company (Seabright) in conspiracy against a group of companies (Westminer) that had executed an unfriendly takeover of Seabright. See above, note 210. This action for conspiracy was brought by plaintiffs who lost money in another venture in which the CEO of Seabright had been involved. Their claim was that the conspiratorial actions of Westminer in relation to Seabright was the cause of the failed venture. The court dismissed the claim based on the fact that none of Westminer's actions, whether lawful or unlawful, were directed against the plaintiffs.

254 One should also note that the decision that a breach of a statute, when committed by several persons rather than merely one, can become a tort, is not in the spirit of the Supreme Court's decision in *R. v. Sask. Wheat Pool* (1983), 143 D.L.R. (3d) 9, regarding the effect of statutory breach on civil causes of action. See Chapter 9. See, however, *Westfair Foods Ltd. v. Lippens Inc.* (1989), 64 D.L.R. (4th) 335 (Man. C.A.), where this argument was rejected.

255 See, e.g., Lord Diplock's statement in *Lonrho v. Shell Petroleum*, [1981] 2 All E.R. 456 at 463: "The gist of the cause of action is damage to the plaintiff. . . ." See also Estey J.'s statement in *Can. Cement LaFarge*, 24 C.C.L.T. 111 at 123.

256 (1975), 64 D.L.R. (3d) 734 (B.C. S.C.).

257 *Ibid.*, at 751. See also *Peterborough (City) v. Mann* (1991), 4 C.P.C. (3d) 81 (Ont. Gen. Div.), and cases cited therein on question of whether "special damages" must be shown to support a successful action for conspiracy to injure. Also see *Positive Seal Dampers Inc. v. M & I Heat Transfer Products Ltd.* (1991), 2 O.R. (3d) 225 (Gen. Div.): damages for conspiracy must be "real", and not "nominal."

258 See *Shaw v. Lewis*, [1948] 2 D.L.R. 189 (B.C. C.A.). See also *Hunt v. T. & N. plc.*, [1989] B.C.W.L.D. 1516, affirmed (*sub nom. Carey Can. Inc. v. Hunt*) [1990] 6 W.W.R. 385 (S.C.C.).

259 See, e.g., *Claiborne Indust. v. Nat. Bank of Can.* (1989), 59 D.L.R. (4th) 533 (Ont. C.A.). The court applied the tort of conspiracy to use unlawful means and awarded significant exemplary damages against the defendant, which were designed to ensure that the defendant did not profit from its wrong. In *Colborne Capital Corp. v. 542775 Alberta Ltd.*, [1995] 7 W.W.R. 671 (Q.B.), additional reasons at (June 27, 1995), Doc. Calgary 9301-12382, 9301-13674

6. INTERFERENCE WITH ECONOMIC INTERESTS BY UNLAWFUL MEANS

The above discussion illustrates that when defendants engage in unlawful acts, with the intention of damaging another party's economic interests, and damage does result, this will, in some circumstances, constitute a tort. As we have seen, to threaten a person with unlawful acts constitutes the tort of intimidation. To conspire with others in the use of unlawful means constitutes the tort of conspiracy, and to use unlawful means to interfere with contractual relations is also tortious. The question has been raised whether there exists a general principle of tort liability which subsumes these nominate torts, whereby any use of unlawful means by an individual with the intention of causing injury to another, without justification, can be considered to be tortious. Is there a tort of interference with economic interests by unlawful means?[260]

Dicta in a few Canadian and Commonwealth cases suggest that such a tort is emerging. In *I.B.T., Loc. 213 v. Therien*,[261] Locke J. stated that a person is "not entitled to interfere with another man's method of gaining his living by illegal means."[262] More recently, the existence of such a cause of action was accepted by O'Sullivan J.A. in *Gershman v. Man. Vegetable Producers' Marketing Bd.*,[263] Matas J.A. in *Mintuck v. Valley River Band No. 63A*,[264] and Cooper J.A. in *Volkswagen Can. Ltd. v. Spicer*.[265] In a recent important "secondary picketing"

(Alta. Q.B.), varied [1999] 8 W.W.R. 222 (Alta. C.A.), leave to appeal allowed (1999), 266 A.R. 335 (note) (S.C.C.), additional reasons at (1999), [2000] 2 W.W.R. 715 (Alta. C.A.), a trial judgment awarding $1,000,000 in punitive damages for conspiracy and other tortious conduct was reversed by the appellate court. The court expressed concern over excessively large punitive damage awards and their appropriateness in tort cases where compensatory damages and costs will adequately deter wrongful behaviour.

260 A good discussion of this tort is provided by Cumming J. in *671122 Ontario Ltd. v. Sagaz Industries Canada Inc.* (1998), 42 C.C.L.T. (2d) 50 (Ont. Gen. Div.), additional reasons at (1998), 1998 CarswellOnt 5010 (Gen. Div.), reversed (2000), 48 C.C.L.T. (2d) 79 (Ont. C.A.), leave to appeal allowed [2000] 2 S.C.R. 983, reversed (2001), 8 C.C.L.T. (3d) 60 (S.C.C.), reconsideration refused (2001), 10 C.C.L.T. (3d) 292 (S.C.C.). Especially useful is reference to a number of American cases that recognize it. As discussed above, in England, *OBG and Others v. Allen and Others* rejected a broad tort action for causing economic loss by unlawful means. Unlawful means were restricted to actions directed against a third party, which were intended to harm the plaintiff's economic interests, which are actionable by that third party, or would have been had there been loss.

261 (1960), 22 D.L.R. (2d) 1 (S.C.C.).

262 *Ibid.*, at 13. Note, however, that the facts of the case seemed to fit within the torts of intimidation and conspiracy. See also Locke J.'s judgment in *Gagnon v. Foundation Maritime Ltd.* (1961), 28 D.L.R. (2d) 174 at 180-81 (S.C.C.), where the same principle is expressed. See also *Mark Fishing Co. v. U.F.A.W.* (1972), 24 D.L.R. (3d) 585 at 599 (B.C. C.A.), affirmed (1973), 38 D.L.R. (3d) 316 (S.C.C.), where the principle was applied by Davey C.J.B.C.

263 [1976] 4 W.W.R. 406 (Man. C.A.).

264 (1977), 2 C.C.L.T. 1 (Man. C.A.). Note, however, that other nominate torts existed on the facts of these cases.

265 (1978), 91 D.L.R. (3d) 42 (N.S. C.A.). More recently, see *White Hatter Limousine Service Ltd. v. Calgary (City)* (1993), 17 C.C.L.T. (2d) 309 (Alta. Q.B.). The plaintiff claimed that overly zealous city taxi inspectors "hindered or interfered" with his livelihood. Several unlawful acts were complained of, some of which may have constituted other torts, some not. The action was upheld. The plaintiff's proposition was that "a person who suffers harm or loss from the unlawful acts of another is entitled to recover damages." Also see *Cheticamp*

case, *Daishowa Inc. v. Friends of the Lubicon*,[266] the Court, while accepting the principle, rejected an application to restrain picketing in the absence of proof that the defendants had employed unlawful means.[267] In England, the principle was expressed in *J.T. Stratford & Son v. Lindley*.[268]

In *Ed Miller Sales & Rentals Ltd. v. Caterpillar Tractor Co.*,[269] the elements of this emerging tort were discussed by Berger J.[270] Referring to both Commonwealth and Canadian authorities,[271] Berger J. described the tort as "unlawful

---

Fisheries Co-operative Ltd. v. Canada (1994), 21 C.C.L.T. (2d) 151 (N.S. S.C.), reversed (1995), 26 C.C.L.T. (2d) 40 (N.S. C.A.), leave to appeal refused (1995), 26 C.C.L.T. (2d) 40 (note) (S.C.C.). The plaintiffs complained that the Federal Department of Fisheries levied unlawful fees against them. The trial court upheld the action as an "interference with economic relations" consisting of three elements: (i) unlawful conduct, (ii) deliberately done with the intention to damage the plaintiff's business, and (iii) damage. The most difficult element was (ii), but the court concluded that the officials knew that the fees were unlawful or were reckless as to whether they were or not. The decision was subsequently reversed on appeal. Although agreeing that the tort comprises these three elements, Chipman J.A. held that element (ii) had not been proved. According to the Court of Appeal, the defendant did not intend to inflict injury upon the plaintiff, "constructive" intent not being sufficient for this tort. Also see *Rowe v. De Salaberry (Rural Municipality)* (1995), 104 Man. R. (2d) 235 (Master), affirmed [1997] 9 W.W.R. 42 (Man. C.A.), reversed (1997), [1998] 4 W.W.R. 416 (Man. C.A.). A frequently referred to case for the elements of this tort is *Barretts & Baird (Wholesale) Ltd. v. Institution of Professional Civil Servants*, [1987] 1 I.R.L.R. 3. The elements described therein are:

(i) interference with plaintiff's trade or business;
(ii) unlawful means;
(iii) intent to injure;
(iv) actual injury.

266 Interlocutory injunction to restrain picketing granted at (1996), 29 C.C.L.T. (2d) 76 (Ont. Div. Ct.), leave to appeal refused (1996), 1996 CarswellOnt 1553 (C.A.), leave to appeal refused (1997), 107 O.A.C. 160 (note) (S.C.C.). Permanent injunction refused: (1998), 158 D.L.R. (4th) 699, 41 C.C.L.T. (2d) 193 (Ont. Gen. Div.).

267 See discussion on secondary picketing below.

268 [1965] A.C. 307 (H.L.). See also *Associated British Ports v. TGWU*, [1989] 3 All E.R. 796 (C.A.), reversed [1989] 3 All E.R. 822 (H.L.), and discussion by Professor Fridman (1993), 1 Tort Law Review 99, at 104. This is referred to with approval by Berger J. in *Ed Miller Sales & Rentals Ltd. v. Caterpillar Tractor Co.*, above, note 146, at 564-65 [5 W.W.R.].

269 *Ibid.*, at 564-67. Also see *A. & B. Sound Ltd. v. Future Shop Ltd.* (1995), 25 C.C.L.T. (2d) 1 (B.C. S.C.). This case dealt with whether certain activities done in connection with "comparison shopping" could constitute this tort. The court held that there was a fair action to be tried.

270 Also see Cumming J.'s judgment in *671122 Ontario Ltd. v. Sagaz Industries Canada Inc.* (1998), 42 C.C.L.T. (2d) 50 (Ont. Gen. Div.), additional reasons at (1998), 1998 CarswellOnt 5010 (Gen. Div.), reversed (2000), 48 C.C.L.T. (2d) 79 (Ont. C.A.), leave to appeal allowed [2000] 2 S.C.R. 983, reversed (2001), 8 C.C.L.T. (3d) 60 (S.C.C.), reconsideration refused (2001), 10 C.C.L.T. (3d) 292 (S.C.C.). Six elements of the tort were noted:

(1) the existence of a valid business relationship or expectancy;
(2) knowledge of this by the defendant;
(3) intentional interference that induces or causes a termination on the relationship or expectancy;
(4) unlawful means;
(5) proximate cause; and
(6) loss.

271 *Merkur Island Shipping Corp. v. Laughton*, [1983] A.C. 570 (H.L.); and *Dufferin Real Estate Ltd. v. Giralico*, [1989] O.J. No. 1525 (H.C.), affirmed [1992] O.J. No. 947 (C.A.).

interference with trade, business or economic interests."[272] The value of such a broadly defined tort to plaintiffs is apparent. Freed from the restrictive elements of the other economic torts, it can provide a successful avenue for relief where otherwise none might be available.[273] Conversely, the danger of recognizing and applying a tort of such undefined limits is to risk making superfluous the other economic torts and permitting their prudently considered limits to be too easily ignored.

On balance, this development is positive. Certainly one can agree with the view that unlawful acts directed at individuals with the intention of causing injury to their interests ought to be tortious.[274] This would be clearly consistent with the expansion of negligence law into the economic loss area. If negligent conduct which causes economic losses is now actionable, *a fortiori* intentional conduct ought to be as well.[275]

Two features of this new tort would have to be clarified. The type of unlawful means necessary to constitute it must be delineated. Is, for example, every breach of statute *prima facie* going to qualify in terms of establishing a cause of action? Will conduct, which is not strictly unlawful,[276] but at most unethical, or contrary

---

272 The Court of Appeal reversed the trial judgment, holding that since the conduct of the defendant was not unlawful, the tort could not be made out in any event.

273 For example, conspiracy to injure requires that the predominant purpose of the conspirators was to cause injury to the plaintiff. Apparently, this tort does not. Inducing breach of contract, or unlawfully interfering with contractual relations, requires that the plaintiff be in a valid contractual relationship. Again, this tort seems broader, and does not require proof of breach of contract. The issue as to what interests qualify as being "economic interests" for the purpose of this tort was raised by Virtue J. in *Colborne Capital Corp. v. 542775 Alberta Ltd.*, [1995] 7 W.W.R. 671 (Q.B.), additional reasons at (June 27, 1995), Doc. Calgary 9301-12382, 9301-13674 (Alta. Q.B.), varied [1999] 8 W.W.R. 222 (Alta. C.A.), leave to appeal allowed (1999), 266 A.R. 335 (note) (S.C.C.), additional reasons at (1999), [2000] 2 W.W.R. 715 (Alta. C.A.) at 749 [7 W.W.R.], Virtue J.'s suggested definition was that an economic interest "is an inherent right to carry out some type of economic activity which is so entrenched in the Canadian economic community that it will be recognized and protected by the courts."

274 One must be careful, however, not to confuse "intention" with "motive". The tort requires that the intention was to cause injury; i.e., that it was desired or substantially certain by the defendant that injury would be caused to the plaintiff by the defendant's unlawful act. It does not require a "bad" motive, i.e., malice. The question of motive or purposes of the defendant's act ought to be treated as an element of the justification defence. See, for example, *Daishowa Inc. v. Friends of the Lubicon* (1996), 29 C.C.L.T. (2d) 76 (Ont. Div. Ct.), leave to appeal refused (1996), 1996 CarswellOnt 1553 (C.A.), leave to appeal refused (1997), 107 O.A.C. 160 (note) (S.C.C.), where Corbett J. correctly distinguishes between the defendant's intention; i.e., to interfere with the plaintiff's contractual relations, with the defendant's motive, to assist the Lubicon. The motive goes only to a possible defence of justification.

275 It has been held that even if the predominant purpose of the defendant's act was to advance its own interests and not to cause injury to the plaintiff, if the act was "in some measure" directed against the plaintiff, the requirement of intention to injure has been met. See *Reach M.D. Inc. v. Pharmaceutical Manufacturers Assn. of Canada* (2003), 17 C.C.L.T. (3d) 149 (Ont. C.A.). This approach was followed in *Even v. El Al Israel Airlines Ltd.* [2006] O.J. No. 711. The Manitoba Court of Appeal left this issue open in *Conversions by Vantasy Ltd. v. GM of Canada Ltd.* (2006), 40 C.C.L.T. (3d) 28, although the trial judge in that case had opted for the more rigorous definition. See [2002] M.J. No. 343, para. 43. The Court of Appeal decided the case based on the absence of an unlawful act and concluded that even if the broader test of intention were applied it would fail on the facts of the case.

276 That is not a breach of statute, a tort, a breach of contract, or any other legal or equitable duty.

to a voluntary code of conduct or internal policy, satisfy the unlawfulness requirement?[277] As well, the defences must be established. Justification as a defence to the existing torts is, as we have seen, poorly defined. With the expansion of an unlawful means tort, the defences would have to be more carefully articulated, so that every unlawful act which is not otherwise actionable by the alleged victim of this developing tort, would not automatically give rise to a claim for damages in tort.[278]

---

277 As discussed in Chapter 9, as a result of *Sask. Wheat Pool v. Canada*, [1983] 1 S.C.R. 205, there is no tort of breach of statutory duty in Canada. However, if the courts hold that a breach of a statute can provide the unlawful means for a tort of unlawfully interfering with economic interests, there is the danger that the decision of *Sask. Wheat Pool* will become undermined. See *Whistler Cable Television v. Ipec Canada Inc.*, [1993] 3 W.W.R. 247 (B.C. S.C.). In this case the court agreed that there is no tort of breach of statutory duty, but that there is a tort of breach of statutory provision. Somewhat confusing, however, was the court's assertion that this latter tort is separate from the tort of unlawful interference with economic interests. In another recent case, *Tran v. Financial Debt Recovery Ltd.* (2000), 193 D.L.R. (4th) 168 (Ont. S.C.J.), reversed (October 24, 2001), Doc. 751/00, [2001] O.J. No. 4103 (Div. Ct.), a breach of the Collection Agencies Act, R.S.O. 1990, c. C.14, constituted the unlawful means. It should be noted however that the defendant was also liable for defamation and other torts. The trial judgment was overturned based on a reasonable apprehension of bias on the part of the trial judge and a new trial was ordered. A very useful discussion of what constitutes an unlawful act for the purposes of the economic torts is found in Lambert J.A.'s dissenting judgment in *No. 1 Collision Repair & Painting (1982) Ltd. v. Insurance Corp. of British Columbia* (2000), 1 C.C.L.T. (3d) 1 (B.C. C.A.), leave to appeal refused (2001), 2001 CarswellBC 670 (S.C.C.). Lambert J.A. adopted Lord Denning's approach articulated in *Torquay Hotel v. Cousins* that any "act which a person is not at liberty in law or equity to commit without being at risk of being found liable at the suit of the person wronged" is an unlawful act. This view was adopted by the Ontario Court of Appeal in *Reach M.D. Inc. v. Pharmaceutical Manufacturers Assn. of Canada* (2003), 17 C.C.L.T. (3d) 149 (Ont. C.A.). A ruling by a committee of a voluntary trade association which it was not authorized to make was held to constitute an unlawful act for the purposes of making out a successful claim. In a subsequent case, however, *Drouillard v. Cogeco Cable Inc.* (2007), 86 O.R. (3d) 431 (C.A.), additional reasons at (2007), 2007 CarswellOnt 4106 (C.A.), the Ontario Court of Appeal held that a breach of an unwritten internal policy by the defendant company was not a sufficiently unlawful act to constitute this tort. The Court distinguished this breach from the nature of the breach committed in *Reach*. In *Kotch v. Casino St. Albert Inc.* (2005), [2005] A.J. No. 1122, 2005 CarswellAlta 1900 (Q.B.), the unlawful means which supported the tort included acts which breached an injunction order, imposing terms on the use of the plaintiffs' services which were not authorized by statute or regulation, and inducing parties to breach their contracts with the plaintiffs.

278 The broader the definition of "unlawful", the more extensive must be the defence of justification. It will be more difficult for a defendant to justify its commission of serious breach of the law, even if it is not independently actionable at the suit of the plaintiff, then it will be to justify a breach of a lesser moral or ethical obligation. Thus, the two issues of what is "unlawful" and what is "justified" or inextricably connected. In addition, as with the tort of conspiracy, where another established action exists, it is questionable whether this developing tort should be used. For example, the tort was applied in *Flintoft v. Quai* (2004), 27 C.C.L.T. (3d) 308 (Ont. S.C.J.) to a case of defamation. A winery was defamed by a competitor in letters sent to several third parties. The two principals of the winery succeeded in a defamation claim; the company in the tort of unlawful interference with economic relations. The unlawful act was the defamatory material. Arguably all of the plaintiffs, including the winery, could have succeeded under defamation. Also see *Duke v. Puts* (2004), 21 C.C.L.T. (3d) 181 (Sask. C.A) where defamation and interference with contractual relations constituted the unlawful means for this tort. If the plaintiff had been defamed by the defendant, and the defendant had

7. SECONDARY PICKETING

In *Pepsi-Cola Canada Beverages (West) Ltd. v. R.W.D.S.U., Local 558*,[279] the Supreme Court of Canada dealt with the legality of secondary picketing at common law. Although principally an issue of labour law, its interaction with several of the torts discussed in this chapter warrants a brief examination of this issue.

The case involved a lawful strike by the employees of Pepsi-Cola against their employer. In the course of this strike, workers picketed some of the retail outlets that sold the product, a hotel where substitute workers were staying, and the homes of the employer's managers. This type of picketing is commonly known as "secondary" picketing, as it occurs not at the employer's place of business, but at the location of others who are not involved in the labour dispute. Its purpose is to put pressure on those who deal with the employer, i.e., the principle target of the strike, not to continue to deal with it. This is done by encouraging or persuading the customers of these other parties not to deal with them. In essence it targets businesses and others who are not involved in the labour dispute. Is it legal?

The Supreme Court of Canada held that it is, as long as the secondary picketing does not involve activities that in and of themselves are criminal or tortious.[280] In arriving at this decision the Court was highly influenced by the value of freedom of expression as enshrined in the Canadian Charter of Rights and Freedoms. The practical effect of this decision on the law of torts will be to enhance the importance of the economic torts and other torts within the labour law field.[281] This will

---

also directly interfered with the plaintiff's contractual relations with a third party, did the claim for unlawful interference with economic interests add anything to the plaintiff's action?

279 (2002), 208 D.L.R. (4th) 385 (S.C.C.).

280 The Supreme Court considered and rejected two other approaches adopted with reference to secondary picketing in the jurisprudence. The first was that secondary picketing is illegal *per se*, attributed to *Hersees of Woodstock Ltd. v. Goldstein* (1963), 38 D.L.R. (2d) 449 (Ont. C.A.). The second was to allow secondary picketing at other businesses allied with the principle targeted employer, as long as it did not involve illegal acts.

281 The Supreme Court, per McLachlin C.J.C. and LeBel J., calmed fears that this approach would not offer adequate protection to those affected by secondary picketing by relying on tort law; at (2002), 208 D.L.R. (4th) 385 (S.C.C.) at 421:

> Picketing which breaches the criminal law or one of the specific torts like trespass, nuisance, intimidation, defamation or misrepresentation, will be impermissible, regardless of where it occurs. Specific torts known to the law will catch most of the situations which are liable to take place in a labour dispute. In particular, the breadth of the torts of nuisance and defamation should permit control of most coercive picketing. Known torts will also protect property interests. They will not allow for intimidation, they will protect free access to private premises and thereby protect the right to use one's property. Finally, rights arising out of contracts or business relationships also receive basic protection through the tort of

require that close attention be paid to defining the limits and requirements of these torts.[282]

---

inducing breach of contract.

It also noted that provinces are at liberty to legislate in this area, while respecting, of course, Charter concerns.

282 Based on this analysis, the Supreme Court affirmed the Court of Appeal judgment, reported at 167 D.L.R. (4th) 220, [1999] 8 W.W.R. 429 (Sask. C.A.). The Court of Appeal refused the injunction relating to secondary picketing at the retail outlets, but did enjoin the picketing which occurred at the homes of the managers. In *Telus Communications Inc. v. T.W.U.* (2005), [2005] A.J. No. 1314, 2005 CarswellAlta 1436 (Q.B.), affirmed (2007), 2006 CarswellAlta 1687 (C.A.), the court denied an application to extend an injunction to enjoin all picketing at the homes of employees of the targeted employer. The court did not find that any torts had been committed against the company in the course of this picketing, although tortious conduct with respect to the residents had occurred; e.g., trespass and nuisance. Although these residents were not parties to this application, the court nevertheless amended the terms of the injunction to prevent these activities from occurring in the future.

18
Nuisance

1. INTRODUCTION

The law of nuisance is comprised of two distinct causes of action which, aside from sharing a common name, otherwise bear little resemblance to each other.

The first, and by far the less important of the two, is the private law cause of action for public nuisance. Public nuisances, broadly viewed, constitute a host of troublesome and frequently criminal activities which detrimentally affect the public's interests. They can, in the occasional case, constitute the basis for a private right of action for damages or injunction. Due, however, to this tort's peculiar nature, its special requirements, and the law of negligence's overwhelming influence, the tort of public nuisance plays a peripheral role in contemporary law.

The common law cause of action for private nuisance, on the other hand, is significantly more important and interesting. Principally concerned with regulating the conflicting uses of land which invariably arise in an increasingly urbanized and crowded society, the law of private nuisance plays an important role, alongside negligence law, in modern tort. In addition, the principles of nuisance law have been used by contemporary courts to shift the accident costs of socially beneficial although occasionally harmful activities from individual victims to the general public which benefits from these services. As with negligence law, the law of nuisance is open-ended. Having adopted principles which balance conflicting uses of land, the common law has been able to apply these principles to land use conflicts in new and changing circumstances.

2. PUBLIC NUISANCE

(a) Introduction

A public nuisance has been defined as any activity which unreasonably interferes with the public's interest in questions of health, safety, morality, comfort or convenience.[1] Public nuisances were originally crimes, implicating the offenders

1 See Reynolds, "Public Nuisance: A Crime in Tort Law" (1978), 31 Okla. L. Rev. 318. Quoted with approval by Major J. in *Ryan v. Victoria (City)* (1999), 4 C.C.L.T. (2d) 1 (S.C.C.) at 25,

in criminal and not in civil liability.[2] In 1535, however, it was decided that if by an obstruction of the highway "one man has suffered greater hurt or inconvenience than the generality have . . . he who has suffered such greater displeasure or hurt can have an action to recover the damage which he has by reason of this special hurt";[3] and thus started the hybrid or "schizophrenic" tort of public nuisance.[4] Still a crime[5] and a tort, public nuisance occupies a peripheral and increasingly insignificant role in contemporary law.

(b) Types of Activities

As one might expect, the types of activities which can be said to detrimentally affect the public's "morality, comfort, convenience, health or safety" cannot be neatly categorized. Originally designed to deal with obstructions of public highways or rights of way, the scope of activities which have been dealt with as public nuisances significantly grew over time.[6] As a result, public nuisance has been rather meaninglessly defined as "an offence against the publick, either by doing a thing which tends to the annoyance of all the King's subjects, or by neglecting to do a thing which the common good requires."[7] As the history of the offence demonstrates, the types of annoyances which have fallen into this net have been remarkably wide and varied.[8]

In determining whether an activity constitutes a public nuisance, both elements of the offence must be examined: that is, (1) does the activity affect the public?; and (2) is the activity a nuisance?

---

and by Binnie J. in *British Columbia v. Canadian Forest Products Ltd.*, [2004] 9 W.W.R. 1 (S.C.C.), at 28. There are several articles which discuss this cause of action. In addition to Reynolds, see Spencer, "Public Nuisance — A Critical Examination", [1989] Cambridge L.J. 55; Cassels, "Prostitution and Public Nuisance: Desperate Measures and the Limits of Civil Adjudication" (1985), 63 Can. Bar Rev. 764; McLaren, "The Modern Law of Nuisance" (1980), 3 *Alberta Law For The 80's*, Chapter 1; Jones, "Public Rights, Private Rights, and Particular Damage" (1983), 34 N.I. Leg. Q. 341; and Bilson, The Canadian Law of Nuisance (1990), Chapter 3.

2 For an excellent historical account, see Spencer, *ibid.* As noted by Spencer, they were originally called "common nuisances."

3 Y.B. Mich., 27 Hen. 8, f. 27, pl. 10. See Simpson, *ibid.*, at 73.

4 In Newark, "The Boundaries of Nuisance" (1949), 65 L.Q.R. 480 at 483, this case is described as having "set the law of nuisance on the wrong track." Fitzherbert J., in *obiter*, extended nuisance actions, which were hitherto confined to interferences with interests in land, to cases of personal injury caused by, for example, obstructions on the road. According to Newark, this illustration "sent subsequent generations wrong in their law."

5 For example, the Criminal Code, R.S.C. 1985, c. C-46, has a provision regarding common nuisance, s. 180, and a host of other provisions dealing with various types of public nuisances, such as causing a disturbance (s. 175), vagrancy (s. 179), and indecency (s. 173).

6 See especially Spencer, above, note 1, where this process of expansion is explained.

7 William Hawkins, *Pleas of the Crown*, 2nd ed. (1724), at 197, cited by Spencer, above, note 1, at 65.

8 Spencer, above, note 1, colourfully illustrates this point by noting all of the following activities which have at some time been said to be a common or public nuisance: making obscene phone calls, laying manure in the street, importing cattle, building a thatched house, digging up the wall of a church, helping a murderer escape, and depositing a mutilated corpse on a doorstep.

(i) What is Public?

Whether enough members of the public were detrimentally affected by a nuisance in order to constitute the activity as a public nuisance is a question of fact. It has been held that it is clearly not necessary that the nuisance affect all of Her Majesty's subjects, "for otherwise no public nuisance could ever be established at all."[9] The number of persons required, however, is somewhat unclear. In one case, where a nuisance only affected three houses, this was insufficient,[10] whereas in another, involving seven, the nuisance was sufficiently public.[11] It has also been stated that as long as the activity interfered "with the comfort and convenience of life of the persons residing in or coming within the sphere of the influence of that which has been done by the defendants as their works",[12] the nuisance is sufficiently public.[13] Lord Denning, conceding that the question of numbers is a difficult one, provided his own test: "a public nuisance is a nuisance which is so widespread in its range or so indiscriminate in its effect that it would not be reasonable to expect one person to take proceedings on his own responsibility to put a stop to it."[14]

The problem with the numbers issue in relation to the tort of public nuisance is that unlike the criminal offence, where action is taken by the prosecutor to protect the interests of the public,[15] the private action for public nuisance is initiated in order to protect not the public's interest, but the personal interests of the complainant. The requirement, therefore, that a civil action for public nuisance proceed only on the basis that the nuisance was, in the first instance, a public one is illogical. It is an illustration of the schizophrenic nature of the tort. The odd result is that a public nuisance becomes actionable at the instigation of a private complainant only if the nuisance interfered with the public interest while at the same time damaging the claimant's own interests in a unique way.[16]

(ii) What is a Nuisance?

More significant is the requirement that the activity constitutes a nuisance, that is, an unreasonable interference with the public interest. As with the tort of private nuisance, this involves the need to balance several factors. The defendant's right to conduct an activity without impediment must be weighed against the public's

---

9 Romer L.J. in *A.G. v. P.Y.A. Quarries Ltd.*, [1957] 1 All E.R. 894 at 900 (C.A.).

10 *R. v. Lloyd* (1802), 4 Esp. 200.

11 *A.G. B.C. v. Haney Speedways Ltd.* (1963), 39 D.L.R. (2d) 48 (B.C. S.C.).

12 *A.G. v. Keymer Brick & Tile Co.* (1903), 67 J.P. 434 at 435.

13 Romer L.J., in *A.G. v. P.Y.A. Quarries Ltd.*, above, note 9, at 902, stated that the neighbourhood must have been affected, not everyone but "a representative cross-section of the class."

14 *Ibid.*, at 908. These factors were considered in the recent case of *Newmarket (Town) v. Halton Recycling Ltd.* (2006), [2006] O.J. No. 3918, 2006 CarswellOnt 5920 (S.C.J.) with reference to an organic waste processing facility which emitted odours. The facility was declared to be a public nuisance for the purposes of enforcement provisions granted to municipalities under the Municipal Act, 2001, S.O. 2001, c. 25.

15 Hence it is logical to require that the public be affected.

16 One must keep in mind, however, that if the nuisance was not sufficiently public to constitute a public nuisance, but the plaintiff suffered damages from the activity, other causes of action may be available, such as private nuisance, or negligence.

right to have its interests protected. In general, several factors may be relevant, such things as the trouble and inconvenience caused by the activity, the ease or difficulty involved in taking steps to lessen or avoid the risk, the general practice of others, the utility of the activity, and the character of the neighbourhood.[17] The more harmful and less useful the activity, the more likely it is that it will be termed a nuisance. Where the activity results not in material damage to public property, but to questions of the public's comfort and sensibilities, the balancing is more difficult.

As with private nuisance, public nuisance seems to rest on the fact that a proprietary interest has been interfered with. In the case of public nuisance, "the injury is to the property of mankind."[18] This fact may be seen as limiting the types of offensive activities which can be considered as public nuisances. The effectiveness of this limiting device is somewhat minimal, however, as most activities which interfere with the public interest probably have some connection with public property or resources.[19]

A somewhat unclear aspect of the tort of public nuisance is whether the activity complained of must constitute an actual criminal offence.[20] Although public nuisance is generally seen first as a crime, and then, if certain requirements are met, a tort,[21] it is interesting to note that tort judgments dealing with public nuisance frequently ignore the requirement of criminality. Recent Canadian cases validate the observation that "no case has been found in which an action for public nuisance has failed because the defendant's conduct has not been proven criminal."[22] In *A.G. Man. v. Campbell*,[23] an injunction was obtained by the provincial Attorney General which compelled the owner of a tower which interfered with the use of an airport at night to dismantle the tower. The trial judge who granted the order specifically noted that the tower in this case did not breach any legal

---

17 See *Chessie v. J.D. Irving Ltd.* (1982), 140 D.L.R. (3d) 501 (N.B. C.A.) and *Ryan v. Victoria (City)*, 168 D.L.R. (4th) 513, 44 C.C.L.T. (2d) 1, [1999] 6 W.W.R. 61 (S.C.C.).

18 See *A.G. v. Sheffield Gas Consumers Co.* (1853), 3 De G.M. & G. 304 at 320, cited by Cassels, above, note 1, at 783.

19 For example, it was found that the defendant's railway tracks, which caused a personal injury to a motorcyclist, constituted a public nuisance since it interfered with the public's right to use the street. See *Ryan v. Victoria (City)*, above, note 17. This is a very broad interpretation of the concept of "nuisance." A similar case is *Danco v. Thunder Bay (City)* (2000), 13 M.P.L.R. (3d) 130 (Ont. S.C.J.), affirmed (2001), 21 M.P.L.R. (3d) 18 (Ont. C.A.). In *Zsoldos v. Canadian Pacific Railway* (2007), [2007] O.J. No. 942, 2007 CarswellOnt 1511 (S.C.J.), on the other hand, a railway crossing was held not to constitute a public nuisance.

20 See especially Cassels' discussion, above, note 1, at 777 ff. Cassels notes that in the 1953-54 revision of the Criminal Code, S.C. 1953-54, c. 51, s. 8, common law offences were abolished. Thus, if a public nuisance must first be a crime in order to be a tort, it would now have to be a statutory offence.

21 Cassels, *ibid.*, at 779, notes that "all writers on the subject continue to assert that public nuisance provides a civil remedy in respect of criminal conduct only." See as well judicial comments, such as McLachlin J.'s statement in *Stein v. Gonzales* (1984), 14 D.L.R. (4th) 263 at 265 (B.C. S.C.): "Private nuisance is a civil wrong. Public nuisance is a criminal offence."

22 Cassels, *ibid.*, at 782, speaking of the English and Canadian case law. Note, however, the opposite statement coming from the American experience: "no case has been found of tort liability for a public nuisance which was not a crime": Stone, "Touchstones of Tort Liability" (1950), 2 Stan. L. Rev. 259, cited in Reynolds, above, note 1.

23 (1983), 26 C.C.L.T. 168 (Man. Q.B.).

enactment whatever. Nevertheless, the existence of the tower was said to constitute a public nuisance. In another case, *A.G. Man. v. Adventure Flight Centres Ltd.*,[24] the nuisance complained of concerned the operation of an airfield for ultra-light aircraft. Again the activity was considered to constitute a public nuisance, as a result of the noise generated by it, without any concern being paid to issues regarding the legality or illegality of the activities. In *Chessie v. J.D. Irving Ltd.*,[25] whether a wharf was a public nuisance was at issue, and although the court held that it did not in this case constitute one, this decision was made without any regard to the criminality requirement.[26] It thus appears that although one generally thinks of public nuisance as being "a crime in tort law",[27] when a civil action for an injunction or damages is taken with respect to an activity on the basis that it is a public nuisance, the criminality element of the offence is frequently ignored.[28]

What is an unreasonable interference with public rights is clearly a matter of judgment, and as indicated before, the cases have dealt with a wide range of problems. The classic public nuisance cases have involved the obstruction of highways and navigable rivers.[29] The pollution of beaches and shoreline properties has also been held to be a public nuisance.[30] Activities which create excessive noise have also been enjoined as a public nuisance.[31] Interesting developments in the area concerned the efforts by Attorneys General and private complainants to control street prostitution by the use of this action.[32] While an injunction was granted in only one of these cases,[33] the courts generally agreed that these activities fell within the boundaries of public nuisance.[34]

---

24 (1983), 25 C.C.L.T. 295 (Man. Q.B.).

25 Above, note 17.

26 See also *Ryan v. Victoria (City)*, above, note 17. Railway tracks which crossed a street were stated to constitute a public nuisance. There was no suggestion in this case that the tracks were illegal or that the defendant's acts were in any other way criminal.

27 To use the title from Reynolds' article, above, note 1.

28 Cassels cites *A.G. Ont. v. Canadian Wholesale Grocers Assn.* (1922), 52 O.L.R. 536 at 547 (H.C.), affirmed [1923] 2 D.L.R. 617 (Ont. C.A.), where there are specific *dicta* to the effect that a public nuisance need not be an illegal act.

29 See Jones, "Public Rights, Private Rights and Particular Damage", above, note 1, where the point is made that these activities are *prima facie* public nuisances. See, e.g., *Tate & Lyle Indust. Ltd. v. Greater London Council*, [1983] 1 All E.R. 1159 (H.L.).

30 See *R. v. Sun Diamond (The)* (1983), 25 C.C.L.T. 19 (Fed. T.D.); and *Blanchard v. Cormier* (1979), 25 N.B.R. (2d) 496 (Q.B.), affirmed (1980), 112 D.L.R. (3d) 667 (N.B. C.A.).

31 *A.G. Man. v. Adventure Flight Centres Ltd.* (1983), 25 C.C.L.T. 295 (Man. Q.B.).

32 See *A.G. N.S. v. Beaver* (1984), 31 C.C.L.T. 54 (N.S. T.D.), affirmed (1985), 32 C.C.L.T. 170 (N.S. C.A.); *A.G. B.C. v. Couillard* (1984), 31 C.C.L.T. 26 (B.C. S.C.); and *Stein v. Gonzales* (1984), 31 C.C.L.T. 19 (B.C. S.C.). See Cassels, above, note 1; and MacLauchlan, "Criminal Law Meets Civil Law" (1985), 42 C.R. (3d) 284.

33 *A.G. B.C. v. Couillard, ibid.*

34 The actions failed on other grounds, namely no special damage in the case of private litigants, and the impropriety of the Attorney General using the civil injunction to combat prostitution. Also see *A.G. Ont. v. Dieleman* (1994), 117 D.L.R. (4th) 449 (Ont. Gen. Div.). The court held that anti-abortion protests and pickets outside of clinics and the homes and offices of physicians constituted both public and private nuisances. Since the action was brought by the Attorney-General, the issue of "special damages" did not arise. Injunctions were granted to prevent picketing at numerous locations, such as clinics, doctors' offices and homes. Picketing at hospitals was not enjoined, due to their size, and the numbers of entrances which could be used by patients.

(c) The Negligence Requirement

The role which negligence plays in the private action for public nuisance is unclear. Where, as is the most common case, the defendant's activity was itself the public nuisance, the issue does not arise. Thus, if street prostitution, the deliberate discharge of pollutants into the air or water, the erection of a steel tower, or the construction of a wharf which obstructs water navigation, constitute public nuisances, negligence is not in issue. The defendants in these cases have in fact intentionally created the public nuisances, and only the extent of their liability for damages remains to be determined.[35] However, where what is complained of as a public nuisance is not the activity itself but the inadvertent results of an activity, the situation is different. If, for example, pollutants are inadvertently discharged into a stream, or a highway is accidentally obstructed, can there be liability for a public nuisance in the absence of fault?

In general, it appears that the courts are not prepared to impose liability in public nuisance for the inadvertent results of an activity, unless the defendant's conduct was negligent. The leading contemporary case on the role of negligence within the action for nuisance is *Wagon Mound (No. 2)*,[36] where it was held that "although negligence may not be necessary, fault of some kind is almost always necessary"[37] for a private party to recover damages for a nuisance.[38]

The issue has arisen most frequently with respect to activities conducted on, adjacent to, or over public highways or streets, which although not public nuisances in themselves, result in a public nuisance.[39] In *Ross v. Wall*,[40] for example, a canvas awning on a tubular metal frame, which was erected over a public sidewalk, collapsed and injured the plaintiff. The facts, as found by the jury, established that the collapse was not the result of the defendant's negligence, the defendant neither having created the dangerous condition nor having failed to take reasonable steps to abate it. Under these circumstances, it was held at trial, and affirmed on appeal, that there could be no liability for public nuisance. The courts rejected a more stringent standard of care for such activities which had been adopted in earlier English cases,[41] to ensure that the activities were as safe as reasonable care could make them,[42] opting instead for a negligence law stan-

35 Subject to any defences that may be raised, such as the defence of necessity, or lawful authority. See, e.g., Denning L.J.'s judgment in *Southport Corp. v. Esso Petroleum Co.*, [1954] 2 Q.B. 182 (C.A.), reversed on other grounds [1955] 3 All E.R. 864 (H.L.).

36 [1966] 2 All E.R. 709 (P.C.). See Glasbeek, "Wagon Mound II — Re Polemis Revived; Nuisance Revised" (1967), 6 U.W.O. L. Rev. 192.

37 *Ibid.*, at 716.

38 See also *Maitland v. Raisbeck*, [1944] 2 All E.R. 272 (C.A.), cited by Spencer, above, note 1, at 66.

39 Note, however, the argument that personal injury cases are not the proper prerogative of nuisance law to begin with, and therefore, that these cases are essentially cases of negligence or trespass law. See Newark, above, note 4.

40 (1980), 14 C.C.L.T. 243 (B.C. C.A.).

41 See *Mint v. Good*, [1950] 2 All E.R. 1159 (C.A.); *Wringe v. Cohen*, [1939] 4 All E.R. 241 (C.A.); *Heap v. Ind. Coope & Allsopp Ltd.*, [1940] 3 All E.R. 634 (C.A.); and *Tarry v. Ashton* (1876), 1 Q.B.D. 314. See Annotation by Irvine at 14 C.C.L.T. 243.

42 Thus, the defendant would be liable even for the negligence of an independent contractor, for example.

dard. In another decision, *Assie v. Sask. Telecommunications*,[43] guy wires which had been strung over the highway sagged six feet and became entangled with the plaintiff's cultivator. Although the trial judge found the defendant liable in public nuisance, even though there had been no negligence,[44] the decision was reversed on appeal, and the strict liability aproach was rejected. It thus appears that, unless a defendant has deliberately created a public nuisance, there will be no liability for the accidental results of a lawful activity, even if those results otherwise qualify as a public nuisance.[45]

(d) The Special Damages Requirement

What has made public nuisance a particularly ineffective private law remedy is the special damages requirement.[46]

As we have seen, public nuisance is an activity which offends the interests of the public, and, accordingly, actions taken in order to enjoin public nuisances are generally taken by the representative of the public, i.e., the Attorney General. Actions may be taken by the Attorney General *ex officio* or by way of a relator action.[47]

The principle that private individuals may sue in their own right for an injunction or damages arising out of a public nuisance, when they are able to establish special or particular damage, was established in the sixteenth century.[48] The

---

43 (1978), 7 C.C.L.T. 39 (Sask. C.A.), reversing (1977), 2 C.C.L.T. 256 (Sask. Q.B.).

44 At trial, only negligence was pleaded and the judge held that the defendant had not been negligent. An amendment to the pleading was allowed, so that public nuisance could be claimed. See Annotation by McLaren at 2 C.C.L.T. 256.

45 In *McNee v. Northrop* (2004), [2004] B.C.J. No. 295, 2004 CarswellBC 313 (S.C.), a diseased tree fell from the defendant's land onto the plaintiff's wharf causing it damage. The court held that there was no duty on the landowner to routinely hire inspectors to examine its trees for decay. There was no visible sign of decay and the tree was located in a dense, forested area. There was no discussion in the judgment as to the precise cause of action in this case, although in my view negligence is the most appropriate cause of action in a case such as this.

46 This is noted by Binnie J. in *B.C. v. Canadian Forest Products*, above, note 1, at 29.

47 See Cassels, above, note 1, at 785, and Spencer, above, note 1, at 80. The role of the Attorney General in suing for the abatement of a public nuisance and for compensatory damages is discussed by Binnie J. for the majority and LeBel J. in dissent in *British Columbia v. Canadian Forest Products Ltd.*, above, note 1, at 28 and 49 respectively. Binnie J. referred to McLachlin J.'s judgment in *Stein v. Gonzales* (1984), 31 C.C.L.T. 19 (B.C. S.C.). It has been held that the Attorney General's discretion to decide in what cases it is proper to institute proceedings is absolute: see *Grant v. St. Lawrence Seaway Authority*, [1960] O.R. 298 (C.A.). See, however, *Hollick v. Metropolitan Toronto (Municipality)* (1999), 181 D.L.R. (4th) 426 (Ont. C.A.), affirmed (2001), 205 D.L.R. (4th) 19 (S.C.C.) where it is pointed out that the Environmental Protection Act, R.S.O. 1990, c. E.19, s. 99(2) and the Environmental Bill of Rights 1993, S.O. 1993, c. 28, as. 103(1) eliminated the need to proceed by way of relator proceedings in a claim for public nuisance. Certification of a class action on behalf of 30,000 residents complaining of noxious odours emanating from a waste disposal site was denied due to the inevitable differences in the situations of the various parties.

48 Y.B. Mich., 27 Hen. 8, f. 27, pl. 10. The rationale generally put forth for not giving everyone who suffered damage from a public nuisance a right of action is that this would result in a multiplicity of proceedings. See Estey, "Public Nuisance and Standing to Sue" (1972), 10 Osgoode Hall L.J. 563. There are several statements in the case law which support this, e.g., *Walsh v. Ervin*, [1952] V.L.R. 361, and *Fillion v. N.B. Int. Paper Co.*, [1934] 3 D.L.R. 22 (N.B. C.A.).

difficulty since then has been to determine the meaning of the special damage requirement.

If a public nuisance results in a personal injury to the plaintiff, then the special damage requirement is clearly met.[49] Damage to, or interference with, the plaintiff's property, whether real or personal, also qualifies as special damage, as does interfering with the plaintiff's right of ingress or egress to private property.[50] The special damage requirement becomes more difficult, however, when the plaintiff's complaint relates to less tangible injuries, namely, purely economic losses, or personal discomfort and inconvenience. In this case, several questions arise. Can the plaintiff even claim in public nuisance for purely economic losses, such as loss of business profits? Must the plaintiff's damages be special or particular in kind, when compared to the damage suffered by others, or is a greater degree of damage of the same kind sufficient? When comparing the plaintiff's damages with that suffered by others, is the plaintiff compared only with the class of persons who suffered damage, or with the general public?

In several pollution cases,[51] the courts have narrowly defined the special damages requirement. It has been held that in order to sue for a public nuisance, a plaintiff must establish that the injury which was suffered was "particular, direct and substantial, over and above the injury" suffered by the public in general.[52] Moreover, even where the plaintiffs, as a class of the public, suffered damage which was different from that suffered by the public in general, individuals in that class could not be said to have suffered particular damage.[53] The judgments also cast doubt upon the ability of plaintiffs to even claim damages for purely economic losses, as these could not be considered to be direct damage.

This restrictive view of the special damage requirement has been carried over into some of the more recent cases. In *Stein v. Gonzales*,[54] McLachlin J. denied the action brought by the proprietors of businesses affected by street prostitution on the basis that the damage suffered by the plaintiffs was not "special and unique." Their damages were no different from those suffered by other businesses

---

49 One must assume this to be so even if many people suffer similar personal injuries. See *Palmer v. Stora Kopparbergs Bergslags Aktiebolag* (1983), 26 C.C.L.T. 22 (N.S. T.D.), where it was stated that "an allegation of serious health risks is always a matter of special damage", even where there are numerous plaintiffs. See *Ryan v. Victoria (City)*, above, note 17, where a plaintiff injured while driving across the defendant's railway tracks on his motorcycle was said to have suffered "special" damage, giving him standing to sue for a public nuisance.

50 See, e.g., *Hagel v. Yellowknife* (1962), 35 D.L.R. (2d) 110 (N.W.T. C.A.), and the numerous cases cited therein. It has been stated that it is the depreciation of the value of the land caused by interfering with the access which constitutes the special damage: see Kodilnye, "Public Nuisance and Particular Damage in the Modern Law" (1986), 6 Leg. Stud. 182 at 183. See, however, the statements in *Hagel* which lend support to the view that it is the interference with the plaintiff's private right of ingress and egress *per se* which entitles the plaintiff to sue to have the obstruction removed.

51 *Hickey v. Elec. Reduction Co.* (1970), 21 D.L.R. (3d) 368 (Nfld. T.D.); *McRae v. Br. Norwegian Whaling Co.*, [1927-31] Nfld. L.R. 274; and *Fillion v. N.B. Int. Paper Co.*, [1934] 3 D.L.R. 22 (N.B. C.A.).

52 *McRae v. Br. Norwegian Whaling Co.*, [1927-31] Nfld. L.R. 274 at 283. See also *Chiswell v. Charleswood*, [1935] 3 W.W.R. 217 (Man. K.B.), where a similar test is suggested.

53 See *Hickey v. Elec. Reduction Co.*, above, note 51. But see *Hill v. Vernon (City)* (1989), 43 M.P.L.R. 177 (B.C. S.C.).

54 (1984), 31 C.C.L.T. 19 (B.C. S.C.).

and, applying the test of the *Hickey* case,[55] were common to all persons of the same class. Even though the damages suffered by businesses were, as in the case of commercial fishermen, greater in degree than those suffered by the general public who did not operate businesses, the right to operate a business was a public right available to all. Thus, all who would have undertaken this activity would have suffered the same damage.[56] While it has been suggested that Canadian courts are prepared to take a more liberal view of the special damage requirement, and allow recovery for damages not only different in kind, but in degree as well,[57] these recent cases do not encourage this view.

Where the plaintiff has suffered damage which is either different in kind from that suffered by others, or, if the more liberal view is accepted, substantially different in degree, the fact that the damage takes the form of a purely economic loss does not appear to disentitle the plaintiff from recovery, at least in so far as the English cases are concerned. Thus, in *Tate & Lyle Indust. Ltd. v. Greater London Council*,[58] the House of Lords, upon finding that the defendant's activity, which resulted in a partial obstruction of the Thames River by causing siltation, was a public nuisance which uniquely affected the plaintiff's business, allowed the plaintiff to recover its purely economic losses, i.e., expenses incurred to dredge the river.[59] Economic loss recovery, which poses such a conundrum for the law of negligence, is evidently not of concern here. This may be explained by the fact that since the scope of recovery for public nuisance is already severely limited by the special damage requirement, the fear of indeterminate liability, which is present in the negligence law area, does not concern the courts in this area.

3. PRIVATE NUISANCE

(a) Introduction

The tort of private nuisance is the fourth and last of the torts this text will consider which protect those with proprietary or possessory interests in land.

---

55 Above, note 51.

56 See also *A.G. Man. v. Adventure Flight Centres Ltd.* (1983), 25 C.C.L.T. 295 (Man. Q.B.), where neighbours of a noisy airfield were held not to have suffered particular, direct and substantial damages above those sustained by the public at large. If, however, there has been an interference with the use and enjoyment of their property, there is no reason why these claimants should not have a claim for private nuisance, subject to any available defences. See, for example, *Sutherland v. Canada (Attorney General)*, 12 C.C.L.T. (3d) 106, 215 D.L.R. (4th) 1, [2002] 10 W.W.R. 1 (B.C. C.A.), additional reasons at (2003), 2003 CarswellBC 288 (C.A.), leave to appeal refused (2003), 2003 CarswellBC 1102, 2003 CarswellBC 1103 (S.C.C.).

57 See McLaren, "The Modern Law of Nuisance", above, note 1, at 10. McLaren cites *Newell v. Smith* (1971), 20 D.L.R. (3d) 598 (N.S. T.D.), where Dubinsky J. is sympathetic to the wider approach. Note, however, that the case concerned interference with the plaintiff's access to property caused by an obstruction on the road.

58 [1983] 1 All E.R. 1159 (H.L.).

59 Numerous cases have held that a person's loss of business or custom caused as a result of a public nuisance, such as an obstruction on a public road, can constitute special damage. See cases cited by Kodilnye, above, note 50, at 184. Three conditions are said to be required: (1) that the loss cannot be suffered by the public in general; (2) that the loss is direct and not consequential; and (3) that it is not "fleeting or evanescent." Note, however, *Hickey*, above, note 51, and the other Canadian cases which stated that only direct losses are recoverable, not consequential losses. If by direct losses, the courts were, as it appeared, referring to tangible damages, the Canadian jurisprudence is at odds with these English cases.

Since the boundaries of the other three — trespass, the principle of *Rylands v. Fletcher*, and negligence — are not themselves clearly defined, it is not then surprising to find that the modern tort of nuisance suffers from a similar lack of focus.[60]

The historical origins of the tort of nuisance have been explored by several authors.[61] Originally, individuals who were totally dispossessed of land had available to them the assize of novel disseisin. Persons whose rights were interfered with, but not totally taken away, had either an action of trespass to land, if the interference actually occurred on their lands, or the remedy for assize of nuisance, if the interference was the result of something that took place off their lands, on the neighbouring lands.[62] Nuisance involved interferences with persons' enjoyment of rights over land, and this extended not only to interferences with the plaintiffs' lands *per se*, but with rights the plaintiffs had over other lands, by way of easement or profit.[63] The assize for nuisance was later superseded by the action on the case for nuisance.[64]

In contemporary law, the nuisance action operates in two different contexts. In its more traditional role, nuisance law protects interests in land from indirect and continuing interferences emanating from neighbouring lands.[65] In this vein, it has

---

60 See Newark, "The Boundaries of Nuisance" (1949), 65 L.Q.R. 480; Gearty, "Private Nuisance in a Modern Law of Torts", [1989] Cambridge L.J. 214; and Lee, "What Is Private Nuisance?" (2003), 119 L.Q.R. 298, which deal particularly with the problem of the boundaries of these torts. The House of Lords judgment in *Hunter v. Canary Wharf Ltd.* [1997] A.C. 655 (U.K. H.L.) is especially important in this regard. Commentaries on *Canary Wharf Ltd.* include S. Blay, "The House of Lords and the Lord of the House: Making Sense of Nuisance" (1999), 73 Aust. L.J. 275; K. Oliphant, "Unblurring the Boundaries of Nuisance" (1998), 6 Tort L. Rev. 21; J. Wightman, "Nuisance—The Environmental Tort" (1998), 61 Mod. L. Rev. 870; and M. Lee, "What is Private Nuisance" (2003), 119 L.Q.R. 298.

61 See, e.g., Newark, *ibid.*; Gearty, *ibid.*; Winfield, "Nuisance as a Tort" (1931), 4 Cambridge L.J. 189; or any of the major texts.

62 Newark, above, note 60, illustrates this point with these examples. To go onto a plaintiff's land and demolish a weir was a trespass; to stay on one's own land and demolish a weir to the detriment of the plaintiff was a nuisance.

63 Newark, above, note 60, at 482. As stated by Lord Wright in *Sedleigh-Denfield v. O'Callaghan*, [1940] A.C. 880 at 903 (H.L.), "'Property' means land and should be amplified to include rights over or in connection with it."

64 Fleming, *The Law of Torts*, 9th ed. (1998), at 459. See also Lord Wright's judgment in *Sedleigh-Denfield v. O'Callaghan*, [1940] A.C. 880 at 902 ff., for a brief historical review. The judgments in *Hunter v. Canary Wharf Ltd.*, [1997] 1 A.C. 655 (H.L.) provide an excellent account of the development of nuisance.

65 The interference need not be indirect to constitute a nuisance. Direct interferences can also constitute a nuisance. See, for example, Lord Goff's judgment in *Hunter v. Canary Wharf Ltd.*, *ibid.*, at 695: "Private nuisances are of three kinds. They are (1) nuisance by encroachment on a neighbour's land; (2) nuisance by direct physical injury to a neighbour's land; and (3) nuisance by interference with a neighbour's quiet enjoyment of his land." Thus, there can be an overlap between trespass and nuisance. For example, golf balls being hit onto one's property can constitute a nuisance: see, for example, *Schneider v. Royal Wayne Motel Ltd.* (1995), 164 A.R. 68 (Prov. Ct.); *Transcona Country Club v. Transcona Golf Club (1982) Inc.*, [2000] 8 W.W.R. 259 (Man. Q.B.); and *Carley v. Willow Park Golf Course Ltd.* (2002), [2003] 2 W.W.R. 659, 2002 CarswellAlta 1209 (Alta. Q.B.). As we have discussed in Chapter 2, however, an indirect interference cannot be a trespass. As well, the nuisance need not emanate from private land in occupation of the defendant. The defendant can commit a nuisance from a public place. See *A.G. Ont. v. Dieleman* (1994), 117 D.L.R. (4th) 449 at 688 (Ont. Gen. Div.). In *Doug Boehner Trucking & Excavating Ltd. v. United Gulf Developments Ltd.* (2007), [2007] N.S.J. No. 360,

been stated that "the paramount problem in the law of nuisance is . . . to strike a tolerable balance between conflicting claims of landowners, each invoking the privilege to exploit the resources and enjoy the amenities of his property without undue subordination to the reciprocal interests of the other."[66] Nuisance law requires those who wish to exploit their lands without interference to respect this same desire by their neighbours. The philosophy of live and let live and give and take is illustrated by the vocabulary of traditional nuisance law cases. The classic problems of competing neighbours — those of excessive noises, odours, fumes, vibrations or other causes of annoyance, inconvenience, or discomfort, caused by ongoing activities — form the stuff of mainstream nuisance law.

Two factors, however, have contributed to the creation of another role for nuisance law. Rather than dealing simply with problems of land use conflict and resource allocation, nuisance law increasingly has been used as a vehicle to provide compensation for property damage and personal injury caused by accidental occurrences.[67] Foremost in this development has been contemporary tort law's overriding concern with compensation and the shifting of accident costs. Tort law's earlier focus on fault and the protection of proprietary interests has been replaced with a concern for adjusting and allocating accident costs. Thus all torts, and especially those whose strict liability principles seem to facilitate these objectives, have been called into play. The second factor in nuisance law's growth has been the absence in the common law of an alternative strict liability principle designed to deal with the allocation of accident costs arising from socially beneficial, although inevitably harmful, activities. In response to the common law's unduly restrictive interpretation of the principle of *Rylands v. Fletcher*, the much less constrained principles of nuisance law have been put to use.

2007 CarswellNS 379 (C.A.), additional reasons at (2007), 2007 CarswellNS 542 (C.A.), contaminated soil was used as residential fill for the plaintiff's development. The plaintiff sued the parties who were responsible for providing the fill. One of the claims was in nuisance against the party who provided the fill. Cromwell J.A. rejected the nuisance claim on the basis that it was a "direct" and not "indirect" interference — the contaminated soil was dumped on the plaintiff's land. In explaining the requirement of directness, Cromwell J.A. stated the following, at para. 128:

> there is virtually no doubt that nuisance is concerned with indirect, not direct interference with the plaintiff's enjoyment of his or her land *in the sense that the interference must originate elsewhere than on the affected land itself.* [Emphasis added.]

Understood in this way, I would agree with the proposition. However, direct interferences emanating from a neighbour's land can constitute a nuisance; e.g., the golf ball or flooding cases.

66 *Pugliese v. Nat. Capital Comm.* (1977), 3 C.C.L.T. 18 at 51-52 (Ont. C.A.), varied (1979), 8 C.C.L.T. 69 (S.C.C.), cited by the Supreme Court of Canada in *St. Pierre v. Ont. (Min. of Tpt. & Communications)* (1987), 40 C.C.L.T. 200 at 206.

67 Whether nuisance law should be used for personal injury claims at all has been subject to recent judicial and academic debate. Although most nuisance cases have dealt with damage to property or diminution of the enjoyment of property, personal injury claimants, for example asthmatics, have sued for nuisance. In addition, the plaintiff in *Ryan v. Victoria (City)*, above, note 17, successfully sued for his personal injuries based, in part, on an action for public nuisance. The majority of the House of Lords in *Hunter v. Canary Wharf Ltd.*, above, note 60, was quite clear that personal injuries cannot in and of themselves be the subject of a private nuisance claim, although one might claim for the diminution in one's use and enjoyment of land as manifested by the personal injury. See Martin Davies, "Private Nuisance, Fault and Personal Injuries" (1990), 20 U.W.A. L. Rev. 129 for a good discussion of this issue.

The result is that nuisance law today is made up of two broad categories, which should be kept separate. The first comprises the more traditional cases where defendants have been accused of having deliberately engaged in activities which constitute continuing nuisances in so far as the defendants' neighbours are concerned. Courts in these cases face the classical task of weighing the conflicts and deciding which uses to sanction. The second comprises those cases where nuisance law has been applied to compensate victims of property damage or personal injury which are the inadvertent results of activities which could not in themselves be described as nuisances. These are the cases which deal not with the resolution of land use conflicts, but with problems of accident compensation and loss distribution.

(b) Deliberate and Continuing Nuisances

In its most general formulation, nuisance can be defined as an activity which results in an unreasonable and substantial interference with the use and enjoyment of land.[68] Which interferences, however, qualify in this respect cannot be restricted within fixed boundaries. As stated by Lord Evershed M.R., "the forms which activities constituting actionable nuisance may take are exceedingly varied, and there is the highest authority for saying that they are not capable of precise or close definition."[69] Or, as put by Lord Wright, "the forms which nuisance may take are protean."[70] Where the gist of a plaintiff's complaint is that the defendant has intentionally made a use of land in a way which by its very nature constitutes a nuisance, what concerns the court is "the impact of the defendant's activity on the plaintiff's interest . . . and not the nature of the defendant's conduct."[71] Although, as has been pointed out, in nuisance it is important to focus on the effect of the defendant's conduct on the plaintiff, and not on the conduct itself,[72] the nuisance must be caused by some thing or some conduct traceable to the defendant.[73]

---

68 This is a fairly standard definition. See, e.g., Stratton J. in *Gray's Velvet Ice-Cream Ltd. v. Campbellton* (1981), 36 N.B.R. (2d) 288 at 302 (C.A.).

69 In *Thompson-Schwab v. Costaki*, [1956] 1 All E.R. 652 at 653-54 (C.A.).

70 In *Sedleigh-Denfield v. O'Callaghan*, [1940] 3 All E.R. 349 at 364 (H.L.).

71 *Gray's Velvet Ice-Cream v. Campbellton*, above, note 68.

72 Fleming, *The Law of Torts*, 9th ed. (1998) at 457 puts it this way:

> . . .the crucial point is easily missed that nuisance is a field of tort liability rather than any particular type of tortious conduct. Its unifying element resides in the general kind of harm caused, not in any particular kind of conduct causing it.

73 This becomes an important issue when the nuisance emanates from a thing on the defendant's land. In *Hunter v. Canary Wharf Ltd.*, [1997] A.C. 655 (U.K. H.L.), for example, the House of Lords decided that the mere presence of a building on the defendant's land, which allegedly interfered with the plaintiffs' use and enjoyment of its lands, could not constitute a nuisance. The presence of the building interfered with television reception. Compare this, however, to *White v. LeBlanc* (2004), [2004] N.B.J. No. 384, 2004 CarswellNB 483 (Q.B.), where the presence of a large commercial highway trailer parked on the land owned by the defendants' father was held to be a nuisance. The effect of the trailer was to block the plaintiffs' scenic view of Shediac Bay. *Query* whether this is consistent with *Hunter v. Canary Wharf* or other cases which have dismissed claims for loss of a view? See *Strachan v. Sterling*, 2004 BCPC 203 (Prov. Ct.) for a discussion of some these right of view cases.

In considering whether a use of land is sufficiently unreasonable to constitute a nuisance, the courts have broken down the nature of interferences into two broad categories. The first involves interferences which result in material injury to property, and in light of recent extensions of the tort, to persons themselves. The second types of interferences affect less visible and tangible interests. They produce sensible, personal discomforts, annoyances, and inconveniences. In short, while not damaging their neighbours' actual property, or physically injuring them, they affect their neighbours' enjoyment of life, and invariably, therefore, the value of their properties.[74]

Firmly entrenched in the jurisprudence is the principle that no use of land is reasonable if it produces substantial discomfort to others, or materially damages their property.[75] No matter the character of the neighbourhood, who was there first, the standard of conduct of the defendant, the utility of the activity, or the suitability of the neighbourhood for that type of activity, "no use of property is reasonable which causes substantial discomfort to others or is a source of damage to their property."[76] Thus, foundries which emitted particles of iron, manganese sulphide and other materials which damaged the finish on motor-cars[77] or impeded the growth of flowers,[78] and insecticide spray which reduced the number of pollinating bees,[79] poplar tree roots which damaged a lawn[80] or the foundation of a house,[81] and salt sprayed on roads which damaged the growth of fruit trees,[82] have all been found to constitute nuisances.[83]

---

74 Note, however, the admonition of Lord Hoffman in *Canary Wharf*, *ibid.*, at 705-706. Whether dealing with a nuisance that causes material damage to property or one that merely results in "sensible personal discomfort" to those on the land, there is still only one tort of nuisance. It is a wrong against the land, by either diminishing its capital or its amenity value. This led to the House of Lords' decision that only those with an interest in the land can sue. The difference between the two "types" of nuisances is only relevant to determining whether the activity was unreasonable and was indeed therefore a nuisance.

75 The judgment of Lord Westbury L.C. in *St. Helen's Smelting Co. v. Tipping* (1865), 11 H.L. Cas. 642 at 650, is frequently cited in support of this proposition. See *Walker v. McKinnon Indust. Ltd.*, [1949] 4 D.L.R. 739 at 763 (Ont. H.C.); *Russell Tpt. Ltd. v. Ont. Malleable Iron Co.*, [1952] 4 D.L.R. 719 at 730 (Ont. H.C.); *Royal Anne Hotel Co. v. Ashcroft* (1979), 8 C.C.L.T. 179 at 182-83 (B.C. C.A.); and Mr. Justice La Forest's judgment in *Tock v. St. John's Metro. Area Bd.* (1989), 64 D.L.R. (4th) 620 at 640 (S.C.C.). See, however, *Miller v. Jackson*, [1977] 3 All E.R. 338 (C.A.), where Lord Denning sought to dislodge this principle by arguing that a person who comes to a nuisance cannot complain of it, and secondly that the interests of the public can be a factor in denying that the activity was a nuisance, even in this type of case.

76 *Russell Tpt. Ltd. v. Ont. Malleable Iron Co., ibid.*, at 728, quoting from *Salmond on Torts*, 10th ed. at 228-31.

77 *Russell Tpt. Ltd. v. Ont. Malleable Iron Co., ibid.*

78 *Walker v. McKinnon Indust. Ltd.*, above, note 75.

79 *Bridges Bros. Ltd. v. Forest Protection Ltd.* (1977), 72 D.L.R. (3d) 335 (N.B. Q.B.).

80 *Mendez v. Palazzi* (1976), 68 D.L.R. (3d) 582 (Ont. Co. Ct.).

81 *Black v. Zager* (1982), 22 C.C.L.T. 231 (Man. Q.B.).

82 *Schenck v. Ont.* (1981), 20 C.C.L.T. 128 (Ont. H.C.), additional reasons at (1982), 23 C.C.L.T. 147 (Ont. H.C.), affirmed (1984), 15 D.L.R. (4th) 320 (Ont. C.A.), which was affirmed (1987), 50 D.L.R. (4th) 384 (S.C.C.).

83 Note the view of Gearty, "Private Nuisance in a Modern Law of Torts", [1989] Cambridge L.J. 214, that nuisance law ought to be reserved for cases of non-physical damage alone, the law of negligence or the principle of *Rylands v. Fletcher* being more than adequate to deal with these property damage cases. Note, as well, that the requirement that the nuisance must emanate from private as opposed to public lands seems to have been ignored in contemporary law. See

Activities which produce less visible and tangible effects on the plaintiff's use and enjoyment of land have been treated with more circumspection by the courts. Since "it is certainly not every smell, whiff of smoke, sound of machinery or music which will entitle the indignant plaintiff to recover" in nuisance,[84] the courts must now decide where to draw the line between the tolerable and intolerable neighbour. It is here that the real balancing and weighing take place. It must also be recalled that, unlike trespass, nuisance is not actionable without proof of damage. It has been said that, in this respect, the damage must be material or substantial: "it must not be merely sentimental, speculative or trifling, or damage that is merely temporary, fleeting or evanescent."[85]

Whether an activity constitutes an unreasonable interference with personal sensibilities is tested objectively. It is the "ordinary usages of mankind living . . . in a particular society"[86] which is relevant, and not the "elegant or dainty modes and habits of living"[87] of the overly fastidious person which count.[88] Unfortunately, as in other areas of tort,[89] attempting to determine the reactions of "normal" individuals is somewhat of a dubious exercise.[90]

The character of the neighbourhood also has been an important factor when individuals are complaining of mere personal discomforts. The well-known quote of Thesiger L.J. in *Sturges v. Bridgman* that "what would be a nuisance in *Belgrave Square* would not necessarily be so in *Bermondsey*"[91] has been accepted into Canadian law.[92] Thus, persons who live near gravel quarries or mixed use com-

---

Motherwell v. Motherwell, [1976] 6 W.W.R. 550 (Alta. C.A.); and *A.G. Ont. v. Dieleman* (1994), 117 D.L.R. (4th) 449 (Ont. Gen. Div.).

84 McIntyre J.A. in *Royal Anne Hotel Co. v. Ashcroft* (1979), 8 C.C.L.T. 179 at 186 (B.C. C.A.).

85 *Halsbury's Laws of England*, 4th ed., vol. 34, at 105, quoted in *Palmer v. N.S. Forest Indust.* (1983), 60 N.S.R. (2d) 271 at 345 (T.D.).

86 Lord Wright in *Sedleigh-Denfield v. O'Callaghan*, [1940] 3 All E.R. 349 at 364 (H.L.).

87 *Royal Anne Hotel Co. v. Ashcroft* (1979), 8 C.C.L.T. 179 at 186 (B.C. C.A.), quoting from *Walter v. Selfe* (1851), 64 E.R. 849 at 852.

88 Surprisingly, asthmatics have been put into the category of the overly sensitive and have been barred from relief. See, e.g., *O'Regan v. Bresson* (1977), 3 C.C.L.T. 214 (N.S. Co. Ct.), and *MacNeill v. Devon Lumber Co.* (1987), 42 C.C.L.T. 192 (N.B. C.A.). Also, a plaintiff who developed a profound and pathological fear of airplanes: see *Lewis v. St. Stephen* (1981), 34 N.B.R. (2d) 508 (C.A.). The plaintiff's "airplanephobia" was somewhat understandable, considering that one of the low flying aircraft actually hit the antennae on the roof of her house.

89 For example, the nervous shock cases.

90 In *Mandrake Management Consultants Ltd. v. T.T.C.* (1993), 102 D.L.R. (4th) 12 (Ont. C.A.), Galligan J.A. was prepared to consider the abnormal sensitivity to noise, not of the occupants of a building, but of the building itself, as a factor in deciding whether there was a nuisance. That is, an older building, with inadequate insulation and support, is more vulnerable to noise and vibrations than a more modern building. Although not determinative, this was held to be a legitimate factor in determining whether there was a nuisance. In *Pinewood Recording Studios Ltd. v. City Tower Development Corp.* (1996), 31 C.L.R. (2d) 1 (B.C. S.C.), additional reasons at (1997), 1997 CarswellBC 1290 (S.C.), varied (1998), 61 B.C.L.R. (3d) 110 (C.A.), additional reasons at (1998), 115 B.C.A.C. 33 (C.A.), the court held that a recording studio was unusually sensitive to construction noise. The court also added however that where the noise was transmitted as a result of negligence, both nuisance and negligence are available causes of action.

91 (1879), 11 Ch. D. 852 at 865.

92 See, e.g., Morden J.'s judgment in *Walker v. Pioneer Const. Co.* (1975), 56 D.L.R. (3d) 677 at 680 (Ont. H.C.). As stated in another case, *Colls v. Home & Colonial Stores*, [1904] A.C. 179 at 185 (H.L.), quoted in *Appleby v. Erie Tobacco Co.* (1910), 22 O.L.R. 533 at 536, "a dweller in towns cannot expect to have as pure air, as free from smoke, smell and noise as if he lived in the country, and distant from other dwellings. . . ."

munities must put up with some irritations.[93] As well, people who operate businesses in commercial areas "are required to put up with a considerably greater intrusion on their sensibilities than do people living in a locality which is residentially oriented or substantially residential."[94] In the same vein, an acreage owner who builds his residence across the road from a hog farm, in an area which has been designated as agricultural, cannot complain about the odours and flies which result from that kind of operation.[95] On the other hand, a person can complain when a kitchen cabinet factory is established in a predominantly residential area.[96] In considering the character of the neighbourhood, who was there first will be a relevant, although not a determinative, factor. Merely because one knew of the existence of the defendant's operations before moving in, does not mean that one appreciated the full extent of their effects, or agreed to tolerate them.[97]

Excessive noise and odours frequently are the objects of complaints in nuisance actions. In determining what are reasonable levels of noise, courts have considered not only the intensity, duration and frequency, but the time of day or night when the noise occurs.[98] Although technical reports and scientific studies regarding acceptable levels of noise, according to community standards, have been accepted into evidence, ultimately it is the court and not the expert which must decide when a noise becomes a nuisance.[99] In terms of smells, those who live near such places

93 See, e.g., *Muirhead v. Timbers* (1977), 3 C.C.L.T. 1 (Ont. H.C.).

94 *Mandrake Management Consultants Ltd. v. T.T.C.* (1993), 102 D.L.R. (4th) 12 at 21 (Ont. C.A.). The case concerned complaints from a business operated near a subway. The complainants were bothered by noise and vibrations.

95 See *MacGregor v. Penner*, [1993] 1 W.W.R. 245 (Man. Q.B.), affirmed [1994] 2 W.W.R. 251 (Man. C.A.).

97 See *Compton v. Superior Manufacturing Ltd.* (1993), 107 Nfld. & P.E.I.R. 70 (Nfld. T.D.).

97 See, for example, *Ward v. Magna International Inc.* (1994), 21 C.C.L.T. (2d) 178 (Ont. Gen. Div.). The plaintiffs knew that there was a private park next to their house, but did not know its function. As well, activities can change after one moves in, which make the situation worse. Also see *Schneider v. Royal Wayne Motel Ltd.*, [1995] 4 W.W.R. 760 at 767 (Alta. Prov. Ct.), citing McRuer C.J. in *Russell Transport Ltd. v. Ontario Malleable Iron*, [1952] 4 D.L.R. 719 at 729 (Ont. H.C.).

98 See, e.g., *Cloutier v. Carrefour Assomption Ltée* (1984), 55 N.B.R. (2d) 114 (Q.B.); *La-Ko Ent. v. Van Wart* (1981), 124 D.L.R. (3d) 553 (N.B. C.A.); *Walker v. Pioneer Const. Co.*, above, note 92; *Ward v. Magna International Inc.* (1994), 21 C.C.L.T. (2d) 178 (Ont. Gen. Div.); *340909 Ont. Ltd. v. Huron Steel Products (Windsor) Ltd.* (1990), 73 O.R. (2d) 641 (H.C.), affirmed (1992), 10 O.R. (3d) 95 (C.A.); and *Laing v. St. Thomas Dragway* (2005), 30 C.C.L.T. (3d) 127 (Ont. S.C.J.). A good discussion of noise as a nuisance, relating to living under an airport's flight path, is found in *Sutherland v. Canada (Attorney General)*, [2001] 10 W.W.R. 328 (B.C. S.C.), additional reasons at (2002), 212 D.L.R. (4th) 378 (B.C. S.C.), reversed [2002] 10 W.W.R. 1, 215 D.L.R. (4th) 1, 12 C.C.L.T. (3d) 106 (B.C. C.A.), additional reasons at (2003), 2003 CarswellBC 288 (C.A.). The court reviewed the various factors discussed above and concluded that the airplane noise was a nuisance. The judgment was reversed, however, based on the defence of statutory authority.

99 See *Acciaroli v. R.* (1988), 49 R.P.R. 277 (Fed. T.D.); and *Banfai v. Formula Fun Centre Inc.* (1984), 34 C.C.L.T. 171 (Ont. H.C.). An interesting discussion about those factors which people find most annoying about noise is found in *Popoff v. Krafczyk*, [1990] B.C.J. No. 1935 (S.C.). The plaintiffs complained about the noises made by the defendants' macaws. The defendants countered by claiming that the plaintiffs were unduly sensitive and lived in an area with a lot of other types of noises. After considering an expert's report about noises the court concluded that the plaintiffs were not overly sensitive and that the squawking birds were a nuisance.

as piggeries or garbage dumps must put up with some irritation, but even here there are limits beyond which the courts will not require individuals to go.[100]

In balancing conflicting uses, courts will consider the utility of the parties' conduct, and the *bona fides* of the parties themselves. Therefore, except in the rare case where the common law has given the defendant an absolute right to do something, irrespective of the purpose in so doing,[101] the defendant's purposes will be taken into account.[102] Maliciously making noises merely to irritate one's neighbour,[103] or worse yet, to damage a neighbour's business,[104] have been considered to be nuisances. As well, putting up an otherwise useless high tower in order to interfere with a neighbouring airport was enjoined.[105] Whereas the absence of negligent conduct on the defendant's part is not a factor when substantial damage or injury has been caused, it is a legitimate consideration in cases involving less serious interferences with the plaintiff's use and enjoyment of its land. As well, as has been previously discussed, reasonable foreseeability of the type of injury caused by the activity is a requirement of a successful nuisance claim.[106]

Since "the category of interests covered by the tort of nuisance ought not be and need not be closed . . . to new or changing developments associated from time to time with normal usage and enjoyment of land",[107] the courts have been able to use the nuisance action to deal with new concerns. In *Nor-Video Services Ltd. v. Ont. Hydro*,[108] for example, the right to receive and broadcast television signals was considered worthy enough to be protected from interference. As well, harassment by the use of the telephone has also constituted a nuisance.[109] The

---

100 See *Sullivan v. Desrosiers* (1986), 40 C.C.L.T. 66 (B.C. C.A.), and *Soucy v. Breau* (1983), 27 C.C.L.T. 168 (N.B. C.A.) — smell from piggery unacceptable. See *Wiebe v. De Salaberry (Rural Mun.)* (1979), 11 C.C.L.T. 82 (Man. Q.B.) — smell from garbage dump unacceptable, and *Nippa v. C.H. Lewis (Lucan) Ltd.* (1991), 82 D.L.R. (4th) 417 (Ont. Gen. Div.) — odours, litter, noise, and dust from landfill site unacceptable.

101 *Bradford Corp. v. Pickles*, [1895] A.C. 587 (H.L.), is the classic case. The defendant was said to have an absolute right to abstract the subterranean water percolating through his soil, and it mattered not what his object and purpose were in so doing. The "right to prospect" cases also can be analyzed in this way. Since the common law does not recognize the right to have a nice view from one's property — see *Walker v. Pioneer Const. Co.* (1975), 56 D.L.R. (3d) 677 at 768 (Ont. H.C.), or *St. Pierre v. Ont. (Min. of Tpt. & Communications)* (1987), 40 C.C.L.T. 200 (S.C.C.) — it presumably does not matter why your neighbours decided to erect particularly ugly things on their property. Also see *Olah v. Cadillac Fairview Corp.*, [1990] S.J. No. 344 (Q.B.) — "compensation cannot be awarded merely because a defendant allows his property to become an eyesore." Also see *Becze v. Edmonton (City)* (1993), 144 A.R. 321 (Q.B.). See, however, *Chan v. Familton*, [1994] B.C.J. No. 2804 (Prov. Ct.), where a court did declare an ugly fence put up very close to the plaintiff's house in order to annoy him to be a nuisance.

102 See, for example, *Mandrake Management Consultants Ltd. v. T.T.C.*, above, note 94, where the fact that the alleged nuisance was emanating from a subway system was considered to be an important factor.

103 See *Christie v. Davey*, [1893] 1 Ch. 316.

104 See *Hollywood Silver Fox Farm v. Emmett*, [1936] 1 All E.R. 825 (K.B.D.), which involved fox breeding, and *MacGibbon v. Robinson*, [1953] 2 D.L.R. 689 (B.C. C.A.), which involved mink breeding.

105 *A.G. Man. v. Campbell* (1983), 26 C.C.L.T. 168 (Man. Q.B.).

106 See *Cambridge Water Co. v. Eastern Counties Leather plc.*, [1994] 1 All E.R. 53 (H.L.), discussed in Chapter 16.

107 Robins J. in *Nor-Video Services Ltd. v. Ont. Hydro* (1978), 4 C.C.L.T. 244 at 256 (Ont. H.C.).

108 *Ibid.*

109 See *Motherwell v. Motherwell*, [1976] 6 W.W.R. 550 (Alta. C.A.).

nuisance action has also been used to protect those without proprietary or possessory interests in land, as long as the complainants have established a "right of occupation."[110] This approach, however, has been rejected by the English House of Lords in *Hunter v. Canary Wharf Ltd.*[111] The House of Lords, with the exception of a vigorous dissent by Lord Cooke, made it clear that since the action for nuisance is a tort "directed against the plaintiff's enjoyment of land",[112] only those with an interest in the land can sue. This will include those in actual possession, as freeholder or tenant, or even licensees with exclusive possession, but not those simply in occupation.[113]

The judgments in *Canary Wharf Ltd.* usefully highlight and explore the role of nuisance law in the context of modern tort law. If it is confined to a tort committed against those with interests in property, then it is logical that only those with the interest in the property, which has been damaged by the nuisance, should be able to sue. This will not only restrict the nuisance action to those with proprietary or possessory interests, but it would also exclude nuisance actions for personal injuries in all cases. Those who are personally injured or affected in some way by the activities of others, despite the fact that these losses occur on private land, would have to resort to other tort claims, principally negligence law, to recover compensation, leaving nuisance law with its advantage of strict liability to its traditional setting. As will be commented upon shortly, this is a rationalization of the law that I find attractive.[114]

The persons who are liable for the nuisance are those who are conducting the offensive activities in question or those who are responsible for them.[115] Thus in

---

110 Notably, spouses and children of the proprietor. See, e.g., *MacNeill v. Devon Lumber Co.* (1987), 42 C.C.L.T. 192 (N.B. C.A.); *Motherwell v. Motherwell, ibid.*; *O'Regan v. Bresson* (1977), 3 C.C.L.T. 214 (N.S. Co. Ct.); and *Lewis v. St. Stephen* (1981), 34 N.B.R. (2d) 508 (C.A.). Note that mere licensees with a right to fish and trap were not able to sue in nuisance: see *Bolton v. Forest Pest Mgmt. Inst.* (1985), 21 D.L.R. (4th) 242 (B.C. C.A.).

111 [1997] A.C. 655 (U.K. H.L.).

112 Lord Goff at [1997] A.C. 655 (U.K. H.L.) at 687, quoting from Newark, "The Boundaries of Nuisance" (1949), 65 L.Q.R. 480.

113 There was an extensive discussion of this issue by the Lords in five separate judgments. The jurisprudence and textual authorities are carefully reviewed. The Alberta Court of Appeal decision in *Motherwell v. Motherwell,* above, is specifically discussed and rejected, with the one dissent.

114 The impact of *Canary Wharf Ltd.* on Canadian jurisprudence is already being seen. In *Sutherland v. Canada (Attorney General)*, [2001] 10 W.W.R. 328 (B.C. S.C.), additional reasons at (2002), 212 D.L.R. (4th) 378 (B.C. S.C.), reversed 12 C.C.L.T. (3d) 106, 215 D.L.R. (4th) 1, [2002] 10 W.W.R. 1 (B.C. C.A.), additional reasons at (2003), 2003 CarswellBC 288 (C.A.), although property owners were able to sue for nuisance caused by the noise of aircraft, the children of the owners were not.

115 Thus in cases concerning persons who live next to golf courses, the defendant is the entity responsible for operating the course, even though the acts of individual golfers interfere with the plaintiffs' ability to use and enjoy their homes. See, for example, *Carley v. Willow Park Golf Course Ltd.* (2002), [2003] 2 W.W.R. 659 (Alta. Q.B.), where golf balls coming from the defendant's driving range constituted a nuisance. The golf club had created the nuisance by allowing its users to drive their golf balls onto the plaintiff's property. Other cases of nuisances created by golf balls include *Segal v. Derrick Golf & Winter Club* (1977), 76 D.L.R. (3d) 746 (Alta. Q.B.); *Lakeview Gardens Ltd. v. Regina (City)* (2003), [2003] S.J. No. 364, 2003 CarswellSask 366 (Q.B.), additional reasons at (2003), 2003 CarswellSask 436 (Q.B.), reversed (2004), 2004 CarswellSask 563 (C.A.), and *Sammut v. Islington Golf Club Ltd.* (2005), [2005] O.J. No. 2674, 2005 CarswellOnt 3199 (S.C.J.).

a landlord/tenant situation, for example, it is ordinarily the occupier of the land and not its owner who is liable for the nuisance. In cases, however, where an owner of land or landlord has authorized the nuisance or knew of it before letting the property, the landlord may also be held liable.[116]

(c) Continuing or Adopting a Nuisance

Unlike the situation of the individual who deliberately engages in an activity which constitutes a nuisance, the law's treatment of an occupier who in some way inherits a nuisance is considerably more sympathetic. The liability of a person who occupies property on which a nuisance, or a potential nuisance, which was created by a previous owner, a trespasser, an act of nature, or a latent defect in the property, is discovered, is essentially a matter not of strict liability, but of negligence law.[117] In a series of English decisions,[118] it was determined that an occupier of land has a duty only to take reasonable steps to abate a nuisance, or a potential nuisance, discovered on the occupied land, where the occupier did not create the nuisance or continue it by use. Liability is predicated on actual or constructive knowledge of the hazardous condition, and the occupier's lack of reasonable care in responding to it. In view of the fact that the hazardous condition was thrust upon the innocent occupier, a more lenient duty of care than that ordinarily imposed by negligence law has been laid down. The defendant's particular circumstances, including the financial and physical capacity to abate the nuisance, will be considered.[119]

Courts must be careful, however, to avoid extending this approach too far. The *Sedleigh-Denfield* approach should be used only where the occupier did not, by

---

116 See *Kenny v. Shuster*, [1990] B.C.J. No. 1420 (S.C.), citing *Banfai v. Formula Fun Centre Inc.* (1984), 34 C.C.L.T. 171 (Ont. H.C.), and *Winfield On Tort*, 9th ed. (1971) at 347. A mortgagee not in possession or control of property is not liable in nuisance for activities which emanate from it; see *A.G. Ont. v. Tyre King Tyre Recycling Ltd.* (1992), 9 O.R. (3d) 318 (Gen. Div.).

117 See Chapter 6.

118 See *Sedleigh-Denfield v. O'Callaghan*, [1940] A.C. 880 (H.L.); *Goldman v. Hargrave*, [1967] 1 A.C. 645 (P.C.); and *Leakey v. Nat. Trust*, [1980] Q.B. 485 (C.A.).

119 See *Leakey v. Nat. Trust*, [1980] Q.B. 485 at 526. The *Leakey* principle was applied in *PPG Can. Inc. v. R.B. Colwell Ltd.* (1991), 7 C.C.L.T. (2d) 31 (N.S. T.D.). The defendant, an owner of land, was responsible for remedial work necessary to provide lateral support for the plaintiff's higher land. The "reasonableness" standard was applied. Also see *Turner v. Delta Shelf Co.* (1995), [1995] B.C.J. No. 75, 1995 CarswellBC 135 (S.C.); *Doucette v. Parent* (1996), 31 C.C.L.T. (2d) 190 (Ont. Gen. Div.); *Lee v. Shalom Branch No. 178 Building Society* (2001), 8 C.C.L.T. (3d) 276 (B.C. S.C.); and *Kraps v. Paradise Canyon Holdings Ltd.* (1998), [1998] B.C.J. No. 709, 1998 CarswellBC 703 (S.C.). In *Bowes v. Edmonton (City)* (2005), [2006] 4 W.W.R. 112 (Alta. Q.B.), additional reasons at (2005), 2005 CarswellAlta 1557 (Q.B.), affirmed (2007), [2007] A.J. No. 1500, 2007 CarswellAlta 1851 (C.A.), the defendant city was sued for permitting the construction of homes on unstable land. The action was brought both in negligence and nuisance. The trial judge considered whether the defendant's failure to secure its own lands and thereby prevent the plaintiffs' land from sliding raised a *Leakey* claim, and if so, whether *Leakey* was a negligence or nuisance action. He decided that lack of reasonable care was required in a successful *Leakey* action, and that lack of reasonable care had not been established. The actions were dismissed due to the expiration of the Alberta ten-year ultimate limitation period and as to this point, the decision was affirmed by the Court of Appeal.

its own conduct, create the nuisance or the potential nuisance. In the latter case, strict liability must be applied. Difficulties can arise if one fails to distinguish the occupier who innocently inherits a nuisance and fails to deal with it, from the occupier who actually creates the nuisance by positive conduct. The failure of courts to make this distinction is becoming a problem in Canadian law. In *McKenzie Barge & Marine Ways Ltd. v. North Vancouver*,[120] for example, the British Columbia Court of Appeal applied the principle established in *Sedleigh-Denfield v. O'Callaghan*[121] to a nuisance seemingly caused by natural forces occurring on the defendant's lands. The defendant had dug a drainage ditch in order to drain a highway. The ditch resulted in erosion of soil, which was carried down the ditch and accumulated on the plaintiff's water lot. The court held that, on the basis of *Sedleigh-Denfield*, the defendant could not be held liable for the damage caused until it was notified of the situation and failed to abate the nuisance. It is questionable whether the principle of *Sedleigh-Denfield* ought to have been applied to this situation at all. The nuisance was caused initially by the defendant's positive act, and not by its omission.[122] A similar observation can be made regarding *Guerard Furniture Co. v. Horton*.[123] The court relieved the defendant of liability in nuisance for damages caused to the plaintiff's premises by water which leaked from the defendant's defective toilet tank. The court held that the defendant was not liable, since it had no knowledge of the defect and thus could not have prevented the nuisance. It is suggested that this is an undue extension of the principle of *Sedleigh-Denfield*. The nuisance in this case was created by a positive act of the defendant in building and maintaining the potential threat.[124] One can make the same argument about the recent decision in *Pitt v. Koch*.[125] The defendant had an underground pipe installed. The pipe fitting became defective and water gradually leaked out, causing damage to the plaintiff's property. The court held that since the defendant did not create the nuisance, nor allow it to continue once it became aware of it, nor fail to exercise reasonable care in not becoming aware of it earlier, it could not be held liable for nuisance. The defendant did, however, by its own conduct, install the pipe, thereby creating a potential nuisance, and in my opinion the strict liability approach ought to have prevailed.[126]

---

120 (1964), 44 D.L.R. (2d) 382 (B.C. C.A.), reversed (1965), 49 D.L.R. (2d) 710 (S.C.C.).

121 Above, note 118.

122 The Supreme Court of Canada dismissed the action, however, on the basis of the defence of statutory authority.

123 (1978), 90 D.L.R. (3d) 379 (B.C. Co. Ct.).

124 See also *Wayen Diners Ltd. v. Hong Yick Tong Ltd.* (1987), 39 C.C.L.T. 176 (B.C. S.C.), for a similar decision. One must always keep in mind that it is not every positive activity of the defendant which constitutes a nuisance, even if it does damage one's neighbour. The notion of "unreasonable" interference is still critical. Thus, it is not a nuisance to cut down one's trees, even if this does cause damage to one's neighbour. See *Zbarsky v. Lukashuk* (1991), 61 B.C.L.R. (2d) 349 (B.C. C.A.).

125 [1992] A.J. No. 268 (Prov. Ct.).

126 As it did in *Philip v. Smith* (May 4, 1994), Doc. Nanaimo 01593, [1994] B.C.J. No. 1086 (S.C.), varied (1996), [1996] B.C.J. No. 1863, 1996 CarswellBC 1913 (C.A.), additional reasons at (1997), 1997 CarswellBC 92 (C.A.). The defendant removed soil from the bank leading to the plaintiff's property, and built a retaining wall. This resulted in damage to the plaintiff's property when a heavy rain caused the plaintiff's land to slide. The court, rather than applying the principle of *Sedleigh-Denfield*, held that the defendant created the nuisance

Consider, however, the case of *A.G. Canada v. Ottawa-Carleton (Regional Municipality).*[127] The defendant regional municipality was found liable on the strict liability principle of nuisance for a water main break. The pipe which burst was defective. It had been installed 58 years before the defendant regional authority was assigned the responsibility for the water distribution in the region.[128] The Court of Appeal rejected the defendant's contention that it could not be liable unless it knew or ought to have known of the defect in time to take remedial action. In other words, the fact that the defendant inherited the potential nuisance did not relieve it of responsibility in this type of case. The court was rightly concerned not to lessen the responsibility on a public authority merely by a legislative scheme which transferred responsibility for waterworks from one authority to another.[129]

(d) Accident Compensation and Loss Distribution

Contemporary nuisance law increasingly has been used, alongside negligence, as a means of shifting the accident costs of activities from individual victims to those actors who are best equipped to distribute them among the activities' beneficiaries. Due to the common law's narrow interpretation of the principle of *Rylands v. Fletcher* and, in particular, its non-natural use requirement, the common law has found itself devoid of a principle of strict liability applicable to cases of property damage caused by hazardous but, at the same time, ordinary and beneficial uses of land. Not satisfied with resort to the law of negligence, with its requirement of fault for the resolution of these disputes, and interested in promoting the goal of loss distribution for the damaging effects of socially beneficial activities, the common law is adopting nuisance law to deal with these cases.

This use of nuisance law is best illustrated in the numerous property damage cases involving the bursting of water mains,[130] and the backup of sewage or drainage systems.[131] In view of the socially beneficial nature of water, sewage

---

and should be held strictly liable for it. On appeal, the contractor who built the wall was also held liable for trespass.

127 (1991), 8 C.C.L.T. (2d) 256 (Ont. C.A.).

128 The Regional Municipality of Ottawa-Carleton Act, R.S.O. 1980, c. 439 transferred responsibility for waterworks to the regional authority.

129 A similar case is *Jones v. Mobil Oil Canada Ltd.* (1999), [2000] 1 W.W.R. 479 (Alta. Q.B.). The defendant was strictly liable for a nuisance caused by a "flare pit" buried in the ground by its predecessor company with which it merged. It was held to have created the condition that led to the nuisance as opposed to having merely adopted or inherited a nuisance.

130 See, e.g., *Bishop v. Gander (Town)* (1986), 60 Nfld. & P.E.I.R. 310 (Nfld. T.D.); *Dressew Supply Ltd. v. Vancouver (City)*, [1989] 6 W.W.R. 73 (B.C. C.A.); *A.G. Can. v. Ottawa-Carleton (Reg. Mun.)* (1988), 44 C.C.L.T. 242 (Ont. H.C.); *Wayen Diners Ltd. v. Hong Yick Tong Ltd.*, above note 124; *Campbellton (City) v. Gray's Velvet Ice Cream Ltd.* (1981), 127 D.L.R. (3d) 436 (N.B. C.A.); *Temple v. Melville* (1979), 11 C.C.L.T. 104 (Sask. C.A.); and *Ratko v. Woodstock (City) Public Utility Commission* (1994), 111 D.L.R. (4th) 365 (Ont. Gen. Div.).

131 See, e.g., *Tock v. St. John's Metro. Area Bd.* (1989), 64 D.L.R. (4th) 620 (S.C.C.); *Danku v. Fort Frances (Mun.)* (1976), 73 D.L.R. (3d) 377 (Ont. Dist. Ct.); *Royal Anne Hotel Co. v. Ashcroft* (1979), 8 C.C.L.T. 179 (B.C. C.A.); *Dartmouth (City) v. Fairview Suede & Leather Specialists Ltd.* (1980), 115 D.L.R. (3d) 364 (N.S. C.A.); *Buysse v. Shelburne (Town)* (1984), 28 C.C.L.T. 1 (Ont. Div. Ct.); *Malenfant v. Edmundston (City)* (1983), 51 N.B.R. (2d) 1 (Q.B.); and *Wait v. Prince Albert (City)*, [2003] 7 W.W.R. 187 (Sask. Q.B.).

and drainage systems, and thus considering themselves unable to apply the strict liability principle of *Rylands v. Fletcher* to them,[132] the courts have resorted to nuisance law to distribute the accident costs resulting from these activities among the public.[133]

The principles and reasoning which have supported liability in these cases are straightforward. Despite the fact that the activities themselves, i.e., the maintenance and operation of water, sewage, and drainage systems, are not nuisances and do not unreasonably interfere in an ongoing manner with the use and enjoyment of land,[134] the courts have consistently held that should these activities inadvertently misfire in some way and cause damage, their failure to operate properly will be considered to constitute a nuisance. The courts have specifically rejected the contention that an activity must result in continuous damage which is occasioned for a substantial period of time in order to constitute a nuisance.[135] It has been stated that "one incident of physical damage to property may constitute nuisance."[136] This being the case, courts have been quick to conclude that an activity conducted on land which materially damages the property of one's neighbour, whether continuously, intermittently, or even on a single occasion, constitutes a nuisance. Consistent with the nuisance principles discussed previously, the effect of this reasoning has been to eliminate from consideration factors such as the defendant's reasonable care, or the utility and public benefits derived from the activity, when determining the defendant's liability.

Why has this development occurred? It certainly must be viewed as somewhat curious that activities which create risks of harm but which are not conducted on land are judged according to the fault requirements of negligence law, while single, calamitous accidents emanating from land-based activities are judged on the stricter liability principles of nuisance law. This approach generally has been

---

132 The courts have frequently held that *Rylands v. Fletcher* does not apply to "ordinary and proper uses of land for the general benefit of the community." See, e.g., La Forest J.'s judgment in *Tock v. St. John's Metro. Area Bd.* (1989), 64 D.L.R. (4th) 620 at 638 (S.C.C.); or Barry J.'s judgment in *Bishop v. Gander (Town)* (1986), 36 C.C.L.T. 208 at 234 (Nfld. T.D.).

133 Note, however, statutory immunities from suit which have been enacted in order to counter this trend. See discussion below and in Chapter 8.

134 In fact, the opposite is true. These activities are highly useful and ordinarily result in no harm at all.

135 See, e.g., *Buysse v. Shelburne (Town)* (1984), 28 C.C.L.T. 1 at 7 (Ont. Div. Ct.).

136 *Ibid.* Thus, even damage caused by a stock-car which crashed through the fence of a race track and injured the plaintiff was considered to have been actionable as a nuisance. See *Aldridge v. Van Patter*, [1952] 4 D.L.R. 93 (Ont. H.C.). One ought to note that the argument that a single isolated act causing direct damage from adjacent property can constitute a nuisance was specifically rejected by Jenkins L.J. in the famous case of *Bolton v. Stone*, [1949] 2 All E.R. 851 at 855, reversed on other grounds [1951] 1 All E.R. 1078 (H.L.). According to Jenkins L.J., the gist of nuisance is "causing or permitting a state of affairs from which damage is likely to result." Also see the recent case of *Copithorne v. Transalta Utilities Corp.* (2005), [2005] A.J. No. 252, 2005 CarswellAlta 303 (Q.B.), additional reasons at (2007), 2007 CarswellAlta 184 (Q.B.), where Bensler J. rejected the action for nuisance in a case involving the defendant's failure to maintain its power line equipment resulting in a fire to the plaintiff's property. The court held that nuisance required a pattern of misconduct that resulted in the loss, and there was none established in this case. Reference was made to an earlier case, *Dingwall v. Transalta Utilities Corp.* (1996), [1996] A.J. No. 821, 1996 CarswellAlta 759 (Q.B.), to the same effect. In my view, this is an approach which is more consistent with the classical view of the purpose of nuisance law.

justified on the basis of the goal of loss distribution in relation to those activities which are viewed as necessary activities undertaken for the general public's benefit. Judicial expressions of this philosophy are found in several of the cases. In one of the leading cases, *Royal Anne Hotel Co. v. Ashcroft*,[137] for example, McIntyre J.A. stated:

> There is no reason why a disproportionate share of the cost of such a beneficial service should be visited upon one member of the community by leaving him uncompensated for damage caused by the existence of that which benefits the community at large.[138]

Or, more recently, in *Tock v. St. John's Metro. Area Bd.*, La Forest J. stated:

> The costs of damage that is an inevitable consequence of the provision of services that benefit the public at large should be borne equally by all those who profit from the service.[139]

While one might agree with the sentiments expressed and the approach of the courts in these instances, there are difficulties to consider. There is no reason why the strict liability approach should be confined to claimants with proprietary or possessory interests in land. If the rationale for applying strict liability is the distribution of accident costs resulting from socially beneficial activities, this principle ought not to be restricted to problems associated only with the use and enjoyment of property. As well, it must be recognized that this justification would be absent in those cases of accidental damage caused by activities on land which do not involve a public benefit, and hence do not have a public authority defendant who can distribute its costs.[140] It is difficult to justify the imposition of strict liability for accidents which cause damage to those with proprietary or possessory interests in land, while requiring proof of negligence for damages caused in other contexts by equally, if not more risky, conduct.[141] While the efforts of the courts to utilize strict liability principles to better distribute the costs of accidents are laudable, their linkage with nuisance law creates problems. What is needed is a rationalization of the principles of both negligence law and strict liability, which must take place outside the domain of the law of nuisance.

(e) The Defence of Statutory Authority

The principal defence in the law of nuisance is the defence of statutory authority. Applicable to cases of activities conducted by public authorities pursuant to statute, the defence has been significantly narrowed by modern case law. This is consistent with contemporary nuisance law's concern that the costs of activities undertaken for the benefit of the general public ought to be absorbed by the public, and not remain the burden of individual victims.

---

137 (1979), 8 C.C.L.T. 179 (B.C. C.A.).

138 *Ibid.*, at 187.

139 (1989), 64 D.L.R. (4th) 620 at 647 (S.C.C.).

140 For example, in *Barbour v. G.H. Heating & Air Conditioning Ltd.* (1981), 15 C.C.L.T. 168 (Ont. H.C.), the defendant inadvertently poured heating oil into the plaintiff's basement. Is this a case of negligence or nuisance? See Annotation by Irvine at 15 C.C.L.T. 169.

141 For example if a farmer's tractor accidentally rolls down his hill onto his neighbour's land, killing the neighbour's cow and damaging crops, will nuisance law be applied? Consider the fact that negligence will be required if the farmer, while driving a tractor on the highway, runs over the neighbour. See Martin Davies, "Private Nuisance, Fault and Personal Injuries" (1990), U.W.A.L. Rev. 129, where this issue is discussed.

The Supreme Court of Canada has reviewed the defence in the following two cases. In the first, *Tock v. St. John's Metro. Area Bd.*,[142] the defence of statutory authority was carefully analysed. The case involved a claim brought by home owners against a public board which was given the statutory authority to operate public water and sewerage systems. As a result of an obstruction in the system and an exceptionally heavy rainfall, the system overflowed and the basement of the plaintiffs' home was flooded. The plaintiffs sued in negligence, on the principle of *Rylands v. Fletcher*, and in nuisance. The trial court dismissed the negligence claim,[143] but allowed the claim on the basis of *Rylands v. Fletcher*. The Court of Appeal reversed the trial judgment, holding that *Rylands v. Fletcher* did not apply, and that although the nuisance was established, the defence of statutory authority relieved the defendant of its liability.[144] The case was appealed to the Supreme Court.

The Supreme Court agreed with the Court of Appeal that the rule in *Rylands v. Fletcher* did not apply. It also agreed that the flooding constituted a nuisance. However, it very narrowly interpreted the scope of the defence of statutory authority and held that it was inapplicable on the facts of this case.

As discussed by La Forest J., the defence of statutory authority was originally developed in order to protect important public and semi-public industries, such as railways, road and water works, and hospitals from legal liability for damages flowing from their non-negligent operation.[145] Where a statute authorized public works to be undertaken, but did not provide an express immunity from suit if these activities resulted in what ordinarily would have been considered to be an unreasonable interference with the use and enjoyment of private lands, the courts were prepared to imply such an immunity in certain circumstances.

According to Wilson J.,[146] the conditions required for the implication of such an immunity were originally quite narrow, and despite the fact that these conditions have not consistently been required by the courts, they ought to be reaffirmed in Canadian law.[147] Pursuant to this approach, the defence of statutory authority is applied to relieve a defendant who was operating under statutory direction of liability only where two conditions are met. First, the statutory provisions must be mandatory in their direction and not merely permissive. This means that they must either expressly impose a duty on the authority to conduct the specific activity in question, or failing that, at least empower the authority to do something with specific direction as to how or where it is to be done. Merely permitting a public authority to do something without either ordering it to do it, or directing

---

142 (1989), 64 D.L.R. (4th) 620 (S.C.C.). See Klar, "The Supreme Court of Canada: Extending the Tort Liability of Public Authorities" (1990), 28 Alta. L. Rev. 648 at 658.

143 (1983), 45 Nfld. & P.E.I.R. 197 (Nfld. T.D.).

144 (1986), 62 Nfld. & P.E.I.R. 133 (Nfld. C.A.).

145 La Forest J. referred to Linden, "Strict Liability, Nuisance and Legislative Authorization" (1986), 4 Osgoode Hall L.J. 196.

146 Concurred in by Lamer and L'Heureux-Dubé JJ.

147 Wilson J. referred to the early English cases dealing with railways: *R. v. Pease* (1832), 110 E.R. 366; *Vaughan v. Taff Vale Ry. Co.* (1860), 29 L.J. Ex. 247; *Hammersmith & City Ry. Co. v. Brand* (1869), 38 L.J.Q.B. 265; the reservoir case of *Geddis v. Bann Reservoir* (1878), 3 App. Cas. 430 (H.L.); and the hospital case of *Metro. Asylum Dist. v. Hill* (1861), 6 App. Cas. 193. She also referred to the later case of *Manchester Corp. v. Farnworth*, [1930] A.C. 171 (H.L.).

that it be done in a certain way or place, is, according to Wilson J., not sufficient to allow the defendant to raise the defence. If the first condition is satisfied, the defendant must then also satisfy the court that the nuisance was the inevitable consequence of the mandated activity. This doctrine, whose formulation stems from Viscount Dunedin's judgment in *Manchester Corp. v. Farnworth*,[148] holds that there will be no liability for a nuisance which was the inevitable consequence of a statutorily mandated activity. Inevitable consequence, in this context, means that considering the existing state of scientific knowledge, the feasible alternatives, the costs, and also common sense, the nuisance could not have possibly been avoided.[149] Since Wilson J. decided that the statutory directives in the *Tock* case were framed in permissive and not in mandatory terms, it was not necessary for her to consider the application of the inevitable consequences doctrine to the facts of this case.

As noted by Sopinka J., Wilson J.'s approach to the defence of statutory authority marks a departure from existing Canadian case law.[150] The tendency in Canadian cases has been to apply the doctrine of inevitable consequences to all statutorily authorized activities, whether the statutes have been framed in mandatory or permissive terms.[151] According to Sopinka J., Wilson J.'s approach will have the effect of virtually abrogating the defence of statutory authority in Canada, since "modern legislation authorizing the provision of the type of works which frequently give rise to nuisance is almost invariably permissive."[152] Sopinka J.'s approach is to apply the doctrine of inevitable consequences to all statutorily authorized activities. Having said that, however, his interpretation of the doctrine is so restrictive as to make it almost impossible to establish. The defendant has to establish that there were virtually no alternative ways to conduct the activity in question. The damage must have been practically impossible to avoid. As the Canadian case law indicates,[153] defendants invariably fail to execute this duty, which is substantially more burdensome than one of ordinary reasonable care.[154]

La Forest J. proposed a more radical approach.[155] The application of the defence of statutory authority ought to be limited to cases where legislation has expressly authorized the construction of a public work at a particular place. Otherwise it is abrogated. The liability of public bodies for nuisances caused by socially beneficial activities should be resolved on the basis of the principle of loss distribution. The court must ask whether, given all of the circumstances, it would be reasonable

---

148 *Ibid.*

149 Note, however, that in *Allen v. Gulf Oil Refining Ltd.*, [1981] 1 All E.R. 353 (H.L.), Lord Edmund-Davies stated that the question of the unavoidability of the consequences must be considered without regard to the expense that might necessarily be involved in its avoidance.

150 This was even conceded by Wilson J.

151 See, e.g., *Portage La Prairie v. B.C. Pea Growers Ltd.*, [1966] S.C.R. 150, or *Royal Anne Hotel Co. v. Ashcroft* (1979), 8 C.C.L.T. 179 (B.C. C.A.).

152 (1989), 64 D.L.R. (4th) 620 at 649.

153 See, e.g., *Portage La Prairie v. B.C. Pea Growers Ltd.*, [1966] S.C.R. 150; *Royal Anne Hotel Co. v. Ashcroft* (1979), 8 C.C.L.T. 179 (B.C. C.A.); *Wiebe v. De Salaberry (Rural Mun.)* (1979), 11 C.C.L.T. 82 (Man. Q.B.); among many others.

154 See, however, *Allen v. Gulf Oil Refining Ltd.*, [1981] 1 All E.R. 353 (H.L.), where the defence did succeed. Also see *Mandrake Management Consultants Ltd. v. T.T.C.* (1993), 102 D.L.R. (4th) 12 (Ont. C.A.), where the Court of Appeal held that noise and vibrations are an inevitable consequence of running a subway system.

155 Concurred in by Dickson C.J.C.

to refuse to compensate a victim for damage suffered as the result of an activity carried out by a public body. Factors such as the nature of the conduct, the alternatives available, the costs of avoiding the damage, the severity of the plaintiff's damage, and the social utility of the activity will be relevant. While private individuals might be required to tolerate the ordinary disturbances or loss of amenities incidental to the conducting of socially beneficial programs, heavy material damages suffered in a single, calamitous event should be shifted to the defendant and redistributed to the public.[156]

The uncertainty created by having three separate approaches to the defence led the Supreme Court to revisit the matter in *Ryan v. Victoria (City)*.[157] The defence was raised by a railway company that had been sued for public nuisance by a motorcyclist who was injured when the wheel of his cycle got stuck in the flangeway gap in the rail tracks. The building of the tracks had been statutorily authorized.[158] Major J. writing for a unanimous Court noted that neither Wilson J.'s or La Forest J.'s judgments in *Tock* had carried a majority of the Court. That being the case, it was Major J.'s opinion that the judgment of Sopinka J. expressed the traditional view of the defence, and should be retained. For the defence to succeed the defendant must prove not only that its activity was statutorily authorized,[159] but also that there were no alternative methods to carry out the activity and it was practically impossible to avoid the nuisance. This the defendant could not establish in *Ryan* and the defence of statutory authority was accordingly rejected.[160]

---

156 For a useful discussion of the judgments, see Kurisko J. in *Oosthoek v. Thunder Bay (City)* (1994), [1994] O.J. No. 2619, 1994 CarswellOnt 632 (Gen. Div.). The defendant city was held liable in nuisance for damage caused by sewer back-up. The court held that the city failed to satisfy the onus of proving that the flooding occurred as an inevitable consequence of its activity. The trial judgment was affirmed at (1996), 139 D.L.R. (4th) 611 (Ont. C.A.), leave to appeal refused (1997), 104 O.A.C. 240 (note) (S.C.C.).

157 168 D.L.R. (4th) 513, 44 C.C.L.T. (2d) 1, [1999] 6 W.W.R. 61 (S.C.C.).

158 The relevant legislation was the Railway Act, 1919, S.C. 1919, c. 68 pursuant to which the "Board of Railway Commissioners of Canada" had authorized the construction of the tracks.

159 The issue of when an activity is "statutorily authorized" was discussed in *Sutherland v. Canada (Attorney General)*, [2001] 10 W.W.R. 328 (B.C. S.C.), additional reasons at (2002), 212 D.L.R. (4th) 378 (B.C. S.C.), reversed [2002] 10 W.W.R. 1, 12 C.C.L.T. (3d) 106, 215 D.L.R. (4th) 1 (B.C. C.A.), additional reasons at (2003), 2003 CarswellBC 288 (C.A.). Neighbours complained of airplane noise caused by the construction of a new runway. The issue was complicated because the Minister of Transport, who had statutory authority to construct the offensive runway, had transferred the responsibility for construction, management and operation to an Airport Authority. The trial court concluded that the Authority was not operating under statutory authority and if it were, the nuisance was not an "inevitable consequence" of the exercising that authority. I would suggest, however, that the construction of the runway in this case was statutorily authorized in the sense that the Authority's right or permission to construct it derived from a statutory base. There are two distinct questions here: (i) was the activity (not the nuisance) statutorily authorized? and (ii) was the nuisance the inevitable consequence of carrying out the activity? The Court of Appeal reversed the trial judge and held that the activity was statutorily authorized, even though it was carried out by the Authority and not by the government.

160 The "practical impossibility" test will make it very difficult for defendants to be successful. Even if the plaintiff fails to prove negligence on the defendant's part, the defendant may still be unable to prove that the nuisance was unavoidable. See, for example, *Rideau Falls Generating Partnership v. Ottawa (City)* (1999), 174 D.L.R. (4th) 160 (Ont. C.A.); and *Wait v. Prince Albert (City)*, [2003] 7 W.W.R. 187 (Sask. Q.B.). A case where the defence did succeed was *St. John's (City) v. Lake* (2000), 191 D.L.R. (4th) 616 (Nfld. C.A.). The court held that

(f) Other Defences

Due to the fact that most of the justifications which can be raised by a defendant to defeat liability for a nuisance are subsumed in the balancing of factors which determines the lawfulness of the defendant's activity in the first instance, there are few available defences to a nuisance claim. The following, however, have occasionally been raised.

(i) Prescription

In those jurisdictions where property rights still can be acquired by prescription,[161] the defence of prescription can be used in respect of a private nuisance after an activity has been carried on continuously for 20 years.[162] The defence depends upon the fact that the activity was open, and actionable for the full 20-year period.[163] As well, the nuisance claimed must be one which can legitimately be converted into an easement.[164] In *Schenck v. R.*,[165] the defendant government's claim that it had acquired the right to use salt as a de-icing agent on the highway by prescription was categorically rejected by the court. Robins J. noted that even assuming that this type of nuisance could be converted into an easement, the government had not enjoyed 20 years of uninterrupted use. There had been continuing negotiations, settlement proposals, and a general course of dealings in this dispute which undermined the defendant's argument.

(ii) Acquiescence

There is also the defence of acquiescence or consent. In *Pattison v. Prince Edward Region Conservation Authority*,[166] the plaintiffs, both by conduct and in

---

although it was theoretically possible for the city to have prevented melting snow from flooding the plaintiff's basement, it was not "practically feasible in view of situation and expense". Also see *Sutherland v. Canada (Attorney General), ibid.* The runway construction, at the location in which it was constructed, was authorized by statute. Noise by aircraft using that runway was the inevitable result. The defence of statutory authority succeeded.

161 For example, see in Ontario the Limitations Act, R.S.O. 1990, c. L.15, s. 31, discussed by Linden and Feldthusen, *Canadian Tort Law*, 8th ed. (2006), at 590. The authors note that in Ontario, s. 51 of the Land Titles Act, R.S.O. 1990, c. L.5, prevents title from being acquired by prescription or possession on land registered under the Land Titles Act. Note that in certain provinces which have adopted a Torrens system of land registration, e.g., British Columbia, Alberta, and Saskatchewan, the right to claim prescriptive rights has been abolished. See, for example, Land Title Act, R.S.B.C. 1996, c. 250, s. 24.

162 See Rainaldi (ed.), *Remedies in Tort*, Vol. 3 (1988), Chapter 17 at 17-54.6; Fleming, *The Law of Torts*, 9th ed. (1998), at 490.

163 For a good discussion, see McRuer C.J.H.C.'s judgment in *Russell Tpt. Ltd. v. Ont. Malleable Iron Co.*, [1952] 4 D.L.R. 719 at 733 ff (Ont. H.C.).

164 See McLaren, "Nuisance in Canada", in *Studies in Canadian Tort Law*, Linden ed. (1967), at 373. McLaren states that this is a problematic issue. Canadian courts have recognized prescriptive rights for the discharge of rain and snow onto land by overhanging eaves: *Wood v. Gibson* (1897), 30 N.S.R. 15 (C.A.); *Hall v. Alexander* (1902), 3 O.L.R. 482 (C.A.); *De Vault v. Robinson* (1920), 54 D.L.R. 591 (Ont. C.A.).

165 (1981), 20 C.C.L.T. 128 (Ont. H.C.), additional reasons at (1982), 23 C.C.L.T. 147 (Ont. H.C.), affirmed (1985), 15 D.L.R. (4th) 320 (Ont. C.A.), which was affirmed (1987), 50 D.L.R. (4th) 384 (S.C.C.).

166 (1984), 23 D.L.R. (4th) 201 (Ont. H.C.), affirmed (1988), 45 C.C.L.T. 162 (Ont. C.A.).

writing, consented to the building of a dam which resulted in the flooding of their lands. The trial judge applied the principle that consent which takes the form of active encouragement, as opposed to mere passive acquiescence, will constitute a defence to a claim in nuisance.[167] The judgment was affirmed by the Court of Appeal on the basis of the plaintiffs' encouragement given for the dam's construction and acquiescence in its design.

(iii) Contributory Negligence

As discussed earlier,[168] the contributory negligence legislation is not restricted to actions in negligence, but applies to all causes of action in tort where fault is in issue. Thus, the fact that the plaintiff's cause of action is brought in nuisance ought not to prevent the plaintiff's own negligence from being taken into account if the essence of the plaintiff's complaint is that the injury was caused by the negligent act of the defendant.[169] As long as the action is essentially fault-based, contributory negligence ought to be a relevant defence.[170]

(iv) Acts of Normal Husbandry

It has been suggested in a few Canadian cases that acts of normal husbandry which result in what otherwise would be considered an unreasonable interference with the use and enjoyment of land ought not to be actionable in nuisance. In *Lickoch v. Madu*,[171] and *Zaruk v. Schroderus*,[172] it was held that the practice of farmers burning off dry grass and weeds was an act of normal husbandry and not subject to a claim for a nuisance created by drifting smoke. The actors could only be liable in such cases if negligence could be proved. In *Metson v. R.W. DeWolfe Ltd.*,[173] the defence of normal husbandry was rejected, at least in so far as the strict liability principle of *Rylands v. Fletcher* was concerned. The defendant was accordingly held liable for allowing contaminated water to run off his property, damaging the plaintiff's domestic water supply.[174]

It has also been stated that conduct which can be characterized as "a natural use of land" is exempt from liability for nuisance. Thus, a defendant nursery was not liable for nuisance caused by water run-off from its land onto the plaintiff's golf course.[175] This was so even though the run-off may have been worsened by

---

167 The trial judge cited *Heenan v. Dewar* (1870), 17 Gr. 638 (Ch. Div.), affirmed (1871), 18 Gr. 438 (C.A.); *Radenhurst v. Coate* (1857), 6 Gr. 139 at 142 (C.A.); and *Breathour v. Bolster* (1864), 23 U.C.Q.B. 317 at 320 (C.A.).

168 See Chapter 13.

169 For example, failing to take reasonable care to abate a nuisance.

170 See, e.g., *Koch Indust. v. Vancouver*, [1982] 4 W.W.R. 92 (B.C. S.C.), where the defence was used in a nuisance action, which was essentially based on the defendant's negligence.

171 [1973] 2 W.W.R. 127 (Alta. C.A.).

172 (1976), 71 D.L.R. (3d) 216 (Alta. T.D.).

173 (1980), 14 C.C.L.T. 216 (N.S. T.D.).

174 It has been suggested that the immunity in nuisance for normal acts of husbandry is a uniquely Canadian development which ought to be confined to the incendiary side of agricultural practice and not extended to other normal farming practices. See Irvine, "Case Comment", 14 C.C.L.T. 225.

175 *270233 Ont. Ltd. v. Weall & Cullen Nurseries Ltd.* (1993), 17 C.C.L.T. (2d) 176, affirmed on other grounds (1997), 41 C.C.L.T. (2d) 239 (Ont. C.A.).

the defendant's clearing of vegetation on its property, which caused increased volumes of mud and silt to flow onto the golf course. As we have seen, the difficult concept of "natural use" is critical to the issue of liability under *Rylands v. Fletcher.* It is not generally relevant to the law of nuisance, and its introduction into nuisance law ought to be rejected. One will concede, however, that the fact that the defendant's conduct is consistent with ordinary uses of land is a factor in determining whether it is a reasonable or unreasonable interference for the purpose of balancing conflicting uses.[176]

(v) Statutory Immunity

In addition to the defence of statutory authority, a statute may provide an express immunity from suit for nuisance. In *Pyke v. Tri Gro Enterprises Ltd.*[177] for example, a section of the Farm Practices Protection Act[178] was raised as a defence by mushroom farmers against a claim for nuisance. The legislation immunizes persons who carry on agricultural operations from nuisance claims for odours, noise or dust as a result of "normal farm practices". The Court of Appeal held that the defendants' operations failed to meet the standards set by the Act and the defence was accordingly rejected.[179]

(g) Remedies

The two remedies which are available for a successful action in nuisance are damages and injunctive relief.

Where a plaintiff has suffered property damage or personal injury as a result of the defendant's activity, compensatory damages will be awarded. It has long

---

176 This was the position adopted by the Court of Appeal in the *270233 Ontario Ltd.* case. It held that the trial judge's approach of dismissing the nuisance claim based on a "natural user" ground was not appropriate. Rather the nuisance action was dismissed because the defendant's use of its property was "reasonable". In another flooding case, *Eagle Forest Products Inc. v. Whitehorn Investments Ltd.* (1992), 12 M.P.L.R. (2d) 18 (Ont. Gen. Div.), a developer which added fill to its property, thereby increasing its elevation, and which created an artificial ditch, was liable in nuisance for the flooding of its neighbour's land. This was said to constitute an unreasonable interference with the plaintiff's enjoyment and use. Also see *Flaro v. Roffey*, [1993] O.J. No. 562 (Gen. Div.), and the cases cited therein, which deal with liability arising from the diversion of natural surface water caused by the defendant's activities. In *Doucette v. Parent* (1996), 31 C.C.L.T. (2d) 190 (Ont. Gen. Div.), the "natural use of land" defence was one of the approaches used to exculpate the defendant for damage done to the plaintiff's property by a falling tree. The court also held that the "reasonable use" test also applied.

177 (2001), 204 D.L.R. (4th) 400 (Ont. C.A.), leave to appeal refused (2002), 294 N.R. 394 (note) (S.C.C.).

178 R.S.O. 1990, c. F.6, repealed and replaced by the Farming and Food Production Protection Act, 1998, S.O. 1998, c. 1.

179 There are a number of statutory immunity cases. See, for example, *Port Alberni (City) v. Moyer* (1999), 65 B.C.L.R. (3d) 352 (S.C. [In Chambers]); *Hewson v. Whistler (Resort Municipality)* (2006), [2006] B.C.J. No. 1789, 2006 CarswellBC 1949 (Prov. Ct.), with reference to s. 288 of Local Government Act, R.S.B.C. 1996, c. 323; *Bavelas v. Copley* (2001), 87 B.C.L.R. (3d) 374 (C.A.), with reference to s. 596(6) of the Municipal Act, R.S.B.C. 1979, c. 290, and *Moakler v. Conception Bay South (Town)*, 2006 NLCA 72 (C.A.), with reference to Municipalities Act, 1999, S.N.L. c. M-24, s. 411(2), among others. The issue of statutory immunities is jurisdictional specific; readers are advised to consult with the appropriate provincial legislation on this matter.

been recognized, however, that in cases of continuing interferences with the plaintiff's use and enjoyment of land, damages may not be an adequate remedy.[180] The authorities have held that unless the injury to the plaintiff's legal rights is small, is capable of being estimated in money, can be adequately compensated by a small money payment, and unless it would be oppressive to the defendant to grant an injunction, an injunction should be awarded. It has also been stated that unless there is something special in the case, a plaintiff is entitled "as of course to an injunction to prevent the recurrence" of the violation of his rights.[181] As a result, the injunction is generally granted in cases of continuing nuisances. This approach is reflected in current Canadian case law.[182] The court may grant an injunction which either completely prevents the continuation of the activity, or allows it to continue as long as certain conditions are met. As well, the time for enforcement of the injunction may be suspended to allow the defendant time to alter its activities.[183]

Whether an injunction should be granted, almost as of right, in cases of continuing interferences which materially affect the interests of individual complainants, even in those cases where the activity is of important public benefit, is a controversial matter.[184] Innovation and flexibility have been suggested as being necessary in this area.[185] Courts have proposed different solutions.[186] Canadian courts

---

180 The leading case is *Shelfer v. London Elec. Lighting Co.*, [1895] 1 Ch. 287 (C.A.). Canadian cases have affirmed this approach; see, e.g., *McKie v. K.V.P. Co.*, [1948] 3 D.L.R. 201 (Ont. H.C.); *Walker v. McKinnon Indust. Ltd.*, [1949] 4 D.L.R. 739 (Ont. H.C.); *Walker v. Pioneer Const. Co.* (1975), 56 D.L.R. (3d) 677 (Ont. H.C.); and *Russell Tpt. v. Ont. Malleable Iron Co.*, [1952] 4 D.L.R. 719 (Ont. H.C.).

181 Lord Kingsdown in *Imp. Gas, Light & Coke Co. v. Broadbent* (1859), 7 H.L. Cas. 600, quoted in *McKie v. K.V.P. Co., ibid.*

182 See, e.g., *Cloutier v. Carrefour Assomption Ltée* (1982), 55 N.B.R. (2d) 114 (Q.B.); *Soucy v. Breau* (1983), 27 C.C.L.T. 168 (N.B. C.A.); and *Carley v. Willow Park Golf Course Ltd.*, [2003] 2 W.W.R. 659, 2002 CarswellAlta 1209 (Alta. Q.B.); among others.

183 The circumstances that will allow a plaintiff to obtain an interim injunction were discussed in *Palmer v. Burnaby (City)*, 2006 BCSC 165 (S.C.). The court held that the ordinary tests which determine this matter, as developed in the case law, apply to this issue. The interim injunction was denied.

184 See Tromans, "Nuisance — Prevention or Payment?", [1982] Cambridge L.J. 87.

185 The law and economics theorists have thoroughly explored the possibilities. See, e.g., Prichard, "An Economic Analysis of *Miller v. Jackson*", [1985] Cambridge Lectures 71.

186 Especially in the United States. In *Boomer v. Atl. Cement Co.*, 309 N.Y.S. 2d 312 (1970), the court ordered that in lieu of an injunction which would close down a large cement plant, permanent damages should be awarded to the plaintiffs. In another case, *Spur Indust. Inc. v. Del E. Webb Dev. Co.*, 494 P. 2d 700 (Ariz., 1972), the court granted the plaintiff an injunction only on the condition that the plaintiff compensate the defendant for the costs in preventing the nuisance. In a Canadian case, *Kerlenmar Holdings Ltd. v. Matsqui (Dist.)* (1991), 81 D.L.R. (4th) 334 (B.C. C.A.), a municipality was held liable in nuisance for flooding caused to the plaintiff's lower lying farm lands. The trial judge ordered the municipality to build dykes to prevent further flooding. The Court of Appeal held that this relief was improper, but it ordered the municipality to purchase the plaintiff's land at a price fixed on the basis of lands not affected by flooding. It should be noted that the defendant consented to this order being made. A similar case of flooding is *Medomist Farms Ltd. v. Surrey (Dist.)*, [1992] 2 W.W.R. 303 (B.C. C.A.). In this case, the court ordered the construction of a permanent pumping station. It should also be noted that s. 755.3 of the Municipal Act, en. 1987, c. 14, s.7, which seems to immunize a municipality from actions based on the breakdown or malfunction of sewer systems, drainage facilities and the like, was held not to apply to the simple overflowing

have been prepared to consider the hardship which would be caused to a defendant or to the public if an injunction were granted. In *Black v. Can. Copper Co.*,[187] for example, it was stated that "there are circumstances in which it is impossible for the individual so to assert his individual rights as to inflict a substantial injury upon the whole community." As well, in *Bottom v. Ont. Leaf Tobacco Co.*,[188] the court considered the disastrous consequences of closing down the defendant's factory to the community, in deciding to deny the injunction. In *Soucy v. Breau*,[189] the court considered the public interest issues of the location of a municipal garbage dump in determining its order. Even in England, where the law generally has not been flexible, the Court of Appeal, in *Miller v. Jackson*,[190] considered the public interest in maintaining the defendant's cricket field, in deciding to reject the complainant's request for injunctive relief.[191]

In addition to judicial remedies, the extra-judicial remedy of self-help to abate a nuisance may be available to the complainant. Thus, it is clearly legitimate for persons to cut branches or roots of neighbours' trees which extend over or under their own land.[192] Whether this can be done without regard to the survival of the offending tree, where there are proper techniques which can be used which will save the tree, was left unanswered in the British Columbia case of *Anderson v. Skender*.[193] On balance, one would think that where proper techniques can be used, they should be. More serious is the issue of the victim's right to commit a trespass in order to remove the offending tree at its source, i.e. on its owner's land. Although the right to do so exists, it is a restricted one. Reasonable force must be used, there must not be any unnecessary damage caused, and notice may be required.[194]

---

of these systems. This was stated not to be a "malfunction" or "breakdown." Another case to this effect is *Port Alberni (City) v. Moyer* (1999), 65 B.C.L.R. (3d) 352 (S.C. [In Chambers]). In *British Columbia v. Vancouver (City)* (2005), [2005] B.C.J. No. 1140, 2005 CarswellBC 1196 (S.C.), the court held that flooding from a sewer was the result of a malfunction and applied the immunity provision contained in s. 294(9) of the Vancouver Charter, S.B.C. 1953, c. 55.

187 (1917), 12 O.W.N. 243 at 244 (H.C.), affirmed (*sub nom. Taillifer v. Can. Nickel Co.*) (1920), 17 O.W.N. 399 (C.A.).

188 [1935] 2 D.L.R. 699 (Ont. C.A.).

189 Above, note 182.

190 [1977] 3 All E.R. 338 (C.A.).

191 See, however, *Kennaway v. Thompson*, [1980] 3 All E.R. 329 (C.A.), where the more traditional approach of granting injunctions was adopted. See Tromans, above, note 184, and Markesinis and Tettenborn, "Cricket, Power Boat Racing and Nuisance" (1981), 131 N.L.J. 108, for commentary.

192 See *Anderson v. Skender* (1993), 17 C.C.L.T. (2d) 160 (B.C. C.A.), varied on reconsideration (1993), 36 B.C.A.C. 79 (C.A.). Cases cited in support of this proposition are *Lemmon v. Webb*, [1894] 3 Ch. 1 (C.A.); *Butler v. Standard Telephones & Cables Ltd.*, [1940] 1 K.B. 399; *McCombe v. Read*, [1955] 2 Q.B. 429; *Davey v. Harrow Corp.*, [1958] 1 Q.B. 60 (C.A.); and *Morgan v. Khyatt*, [1964] 1 W.L.R. 475 (P.C.).

193 *Ibid.*

194 See Fleming, *The Law of Torts*, 9th ed. (1998), at 496-498. In *Anderson v. Skender*, *ibid.*, Taylor J.A. stated that there is "generally" no right to enter another's property to remove a tree. The defendant who did so in this case was liable for trespass.

19
Defamation

1. INTRODUCTION

The law of defamation plays a distinctive and fascinating role within the tort law family. Unlike most of tort, defamation law has little to do with protecting the security of persons or their property and, in most respects, has no interest in notions of fault or wrongdoing. Based almost entirely on rules of strict liability, defamation law seeks to protect the reputation of individuals against unfounded and unjustified attacks. What troubles the law of defamation, however, is that the protection of reputation comes only at a very high cost — the need to restrict freedom of speech.[1]

In view of the numerous outstanding texts devoted to the topic of defamation law,[2] this chapter will present but a brief overview of the principles of defamation law.[3]

---

1 The balance between freedom of speech and the protection of the reputation of the individual is at the core of the defamation issue. It is explored by Cory J. in *Hill v. Church of Scientology of Toronto* (1995), 25 C.C.L.T. (2d) 89 (S.C.C.). Mr. Justice Cory reviews the history of laws and attitudes towards defamation in his judgment, particularly with respect to the importance of reputation and the need to protect it. It is interesting to note the following recent comment by Sharpe J.A. in *Cusson v. Quan*, 2007 ONCA 771 (C.A.), leave to appeal allowed (2008), 2008 CarswellOnt 1862 (S.C.C.), at para. 37: "In its traditional formulation, the common law of defamation clearly favours the protection of reputation over freedom of expression." This is a view which I believe is borne out by the jurisprudence in this area.

2 The Canadian text, Brown, *The Law of Defamation in Canada*, 2nd. ed. (1999), four-volume loose-leaf set, provides an exhaustive treatment of the topic. This text was extremely helpful in the preparation of this chapter. In addition, there are numerous other texts, the most authoritative of which is *Gatley on Libel and Slander*, 9th ed. (1998). See also Duncan and Neill, *Defamation*, 2nd ed. (1983); Carter-Ruck, *Libel and Slander*, 4th ed. (1991); and Williams, *The Law of Libel and Slander in Canada*, 2nd ed. (1988), among others. Recent Canadian texts include Peter Downward, *Libel* (2003); and McConchie & Potts, *Canadian Libel and Slander Actions* (2004).

3 It is evident from the cases that aside from the substantive principles of law which apply to defamation actions, the correctness of the pleadings is a critical matter for the litigants. As stated recently by Rosenberg J.A. in *Lysko v. Braley* (2006), 70 O.R. (3d) 721 (Ont. C.A.), at para. 91: "Both courts and leading authors on the law of defamation repeatedly state that pleadings in defamation cases are more important than in any other class of actions. The statement of claim must contain a concise statement of the material facts." Also see *Astley v. Verdun* (2007), 49

2. SOURCES OF DEFAMATION LAW

Defamation law is still principally a common law subject, despite the intrusion into the law of some statutory reforms.[4] The statutes modify the common law principles in several respects. First, the distinction between libel and slander has been abolished by statute in several provinces.[5] Second, the liability of broadcasters and the print media has been modified by providing these defendants with a qualified privilege with respect to certain kinds of publications,[6] and an absolute privilege with respect to others.[7] The defence of fair comment has also been altered in certain respects. As well, the damages which can be recovered against media defendants will be affected by the publication of apologies and retractions if certain conditions are met. Finally, legislative provisions deal with various procedural aspects and pleadings in defamation litigation.[8]

It is important to emphasize that, notwithstanding the statutory modifications, the fundamentals of defamation law have not been altered, and are still to be found in the case law. This is significant for at least two reasons. Control of the defamation action and the critical decision as to how to satisfactorily provide for the appropriate balance between the values of reputation and speech still remain firmly in the hands of the judges, and have not been taken away from them by legislators. As well, the impact that the Charter of Rights and Freedoms can have on defamation law is limited by the fact that defamation law is principally judge-made and not statutory law.[9]

It is also interesting to note the heavy reliance by Canadian judges on principles of law developed in English decisions, many of them several decades old. One

---

C.C.L.T. (3d) 96 (Ont. S.C.J.) where this view is re-iterated. Readers are advised to consult the specialized works on defamation law for the pleading requirements relating to this action. Brown, above, note 2; Volume 3 is particularly useful.

4 Every common law province, and the territories, have enacted defamation statutes which modify the common law. They are: Defamation Act, R.S.A. 2000, c. D-7; Libel and Slander Act, R.S.B.C. 1996, c. 263; Defamation Act, R.S.M. 1987, c. D20 (also C.C.S.M. c. D20); Defamation Act, R.S.N.B. 1973, c. D-5; Defamation Act, R.S.N. 1990, c. D-3; Defamation Act, R.S.N.S. 1989, c. 122; Libel and Slander Act, R.S.O. 1990, c. L.12; Defamation Act, R.S.P.E.I. 1988, c. D-5; Libel and Slander Act, R.S.S. 1978, c. L-14; Defamation Act, R.S.N.W.T. 1988, c. D-1; Defamation Act, R.S.Y. 1986, c. 41. In Quebec, there is no specific defamation law. Rather the general principles of the Civil Code of Quebec, S.Q. 1991, c. 64, and other relevant laws, such as the Quebec Charter of Human Rights and Freedoms, are applied to defamation actions. See *Prud'homme c. Prud'homme* (2002), [2002] S.C.J. No. 86, 2002 CarswellQue 2710, 2002 CarswellQue 2711 for the application of these laws to a defamation action brought against a municipal councillor. The approach to defamation actions is very different in the two systems of law on a theoretical level, although as a practical matter the same values and considerations are employed in resolving defamation actions. Also see *Gilles E. Néron Communication Marketing inc. c. Chambre des notaires du Québec* (2004), 26 C.C.L.T. (3d) 161 (S.C.C.), another recent Supreme Court of Canada case dealing with defamation under the civil law of Quebec. According to LeBel J., the test for liability under Quebec law is "fault" and the question to be asked when suing a journalist for defamation is whether "the journalist has fallen below the standard of the reasonable journalist."

5 Namely, Alberta, Manitoba, New Brunswick, Newfoundland, Prince Edward Island and the Northwest and Yukon Territories. It has been abolished in Nova Scotia for purposes of its statute.

6 For example, fair and accurate reports of legislative proceedings, public meetings.

7 For example, fair and accurate reports of judicial proceedings.

8 Discussion of these specific provisions will be left for the specialized texts.

9 See especially *Hill v. Church of Scientology*, above, note 2, and the discussion of tort law and the Charter in Chapter 1.

can argue that in this area of law, even more so than in others, Canadian law ought to be developed independently of foreign influences. The balance between protecting reputation and protecting speech ought to be reflective of contemporary Canadian values. Technological advances in modes of communication, the increased public interest in current affairs,[10] and the introduction of the Charter with its emphasis on individual freedoms, all point to the greater importance of free speech in Canadian society. These changes must be reflected in Canadian defamation laws.

3. THE DISTINCTION BETWEEN LIBEL AND SLANDER

Although of diminishing importance, in view of statutory interventions which have eliminated it in some jurisdictions, the common law makes a distinction between actions for libel and for slander.[11] Libel is treated by the common law as being more serious than slander, which, except for certain cases, is only actionable upon proof of special damage. The distinction relates to the permanence and tangible nature of the defamatory material. A libel involves material exhibited in written or some other concrete form, such as in film, pictures, or statues.[12] Slanders are defamations which have been spoken or are "embodied in some transitory form."[13] Although the distinction, with its practical consequences, can be explained by reference to historical factors and the separate lineage of the two forms of defamation,[14] most would agree that the continuation of the distinction cannot be justified in view of modern realities. While it has been argued in support of the distinction that slander will not by its nature damage a person's reputation as much as libel,[15] the argument is unpersuasive. Both oral and written defamations damage reputation; the one which is more serious depends on the facts of the case.[16] Rather than rigidly distinguishing between defamatory material only on

---

10 Witness the advent of all-news channels on television.

11 See *Meldrum v. Australian Broadcasting Co.*, [1932] V.L.R. 425, for a good discussion of the distinction.

12 See Linden and Feldthusen, *Canadian Tort Law*, 8th ed. (2006), at 774. The essence seems to be that the material is visible and concrete, not that it is permanent, since very few things last forever, and most can disappear or be destroyed very quickly. For example, it has been held in an old case that burning a person in effigy is a libel, despite the fact that it is clearly a transitory event: see *Eyre v. Garlick* (1878), 42 J.P. 68.

13 Brown, above, note 2, at 8-2. Slanders are not necessarily invisible, since slander can consist of "looks, signs or gestures", which of course must be seen to be communicated. See *Piasta v. Stewart* (1986), 48 Sask. R. 56 at 60 (Q.B.).

14 See Brown, above, note 2, at 8-2, and the authorities cited therein.

15 On the theory, as stated in Latin, "*scripta manent, verba volant*": "spoken words fly away, the written ones abide": see Brown, above, note 2, at 8-20. Or, as stated by Cardozo J. in *Ostrowe v. Lee*, 175 N.E. 505 (N.Y., 1931): "The spoken word dissolves, but the written one abides and 'perpetuates the scandal' . . ." There are two aspects to this: the permanence of the written word and ease of its transmission.

16 A letter written by one person to another defaming the plaintiff will probably be much more insignificant, for example, than a public lecture repeating the same information. The same can be said for the argument that libel is more serious than slander because "a libel written and published shows more deliberate malignity than a mere oral slander, and requires some degree of premeditation and design": see Macdonald J.A. in *CBC v. MacIntyre* (1985), 34 C.C.L.T. 243 at 250 (N.S. C.A.), who cites this as the principal historical reason for considering libel to be more serious than slander.

the basis of form, several jurisdictions wisely have decided to abandon the distinction.[17]

The practical consequences of the distinction are as follows. Libel is actionable *per se*, whereas slander only on proof of special damages,[18] except in certain cases. In this respect, four types of slander are actionable *per se*. They are statements which impute to the plaintiff the commission of a crime,[19] a loathsome disease, unchastity (in relation to a female),[20] or unfitness to practise a trade or profession.[21] In all other cases of slander, a suit will be successful only if special

---

17 Two provinces which have not eliminated the distinction between libel and slander have provided that broadcasting defamatory words by means of radio and television shall be considered to constitute libel. See Libel and Slander Act, R.S.O. 1990, c. L.12, s. 2; Libel and Slander Act, R.S.B.C. 1996, c. 263, s. 2. Whether speaking into a microphone at a public meeting constituted a "broadcast" for the purpose of the Ontario provision was raised in *Romano v. D'Onofrio* (2005), 262 D.L.R. (4th) 181 (Ont. C.A.), reversing (2004), 246 D.L.R. (4th) 720 (Ont. S.C.J.). The motions judge had decided that it was not a broadcast, therefore it was slander and required special damages. The Court of Appeal decided that this issue should not have been resolved in a Rule 20 summary motion proceeding. The Court of Appeal also held that whether the plaintiff, who was a law student at the time of the alleged defamation, could take advantage of s. 16 of the Ontario Act, which eliminated the need for professionals and certain others to prove special damages, should not have been determined by the motions judge. The motions judge had decided that the plaintiff did not qualify under this provision.

18 Note that the statutes which define defamation as meaning libel or slander specify that an action lies for defamation and may be brought without alleging or proving special damages.

19 See, for example, *Skomar v. Rachinski* (1990), 88 Sask. R. 177 (Q.B.). The parties were disputing neighbours. The plaintiff was called a "thief" by the defendant. The court held that since this slander imputed a criminal offence, it was actionable without proof of special damages. An opposite case is *Maher v. K Mart Canada Ltd.* (1990), 84 Nfld. & P.E.I.R. 271 (Nfld. T.D.). The plaintiff's allegation was that the store security officer slandered him by imputing that he had committed a crime, namely an offence under the Liquor Control Act, S.N. 1973, No. 103. The plaintiff argued that therefore special damages need not be proved. The court rejected the plaintiff's contention. It held that the defendant merely had raised a suspicion that the plaintiff had committed a crime, which was insufficient. The court also held that the imputation must relate to a crime punishable directly or alternatively by imprisonment.

20 See, e.g., *Maietta v. Bennett* (1988), 72 Nfld. & P.E.I.R. 185 (Nfld. T.D.). Brown, above, note 2, notes that this exception stems not from the common law, which required proof of special damage in this type of case, but from the English Slander of Women Act, 1891 (54 & 55 Vict., c. 51). Various Canadian provinces passed legislation starting with Ontario in 1889. The situation now is that those provinces which have eliminated the libel/slander distinction do not need such a provision. Ontario, which maintains the libel/slander distinction, has a provision which states that special damage is not required in relation to slanders of women imputing unchastity or adultery. See Brown, above, note 2, at 8.5, fn. 123.

21 See, e.g., *Colliar v. Robinson Diesel Injection Ltd.* (1988), 72 Sask. R. 81 (Q.B.). As Brown, above, note 2, notes, this category is not limited to certain jobs or professions, but applies to every type of office, profession, calling, trade or business. One of the controversial issues has been to decide how close a connection is required between the defamatory words and the plaintiff *qua* worker, as opposed to the plaintiff *qua* person. This is, of course, no longer an issue in provinces which have eliminated the distinction between libel and slander, and, even in Ontario, where the distinction has been maintained, the statute provides that the slander need not be "spoken of the plaintiff in the way of his office, profession, calling trade or business . . ." (s. 18). Note that for the common law exception to apply, the person must have been engaged in the profession at the time the slanderous words were spoken. See *Hicks v. Stephens* (1997), 40 C.C.L.T. (2d) 223 (Ont. Gen. Div.). The case decided that this is also true of the statutory provision.

damages, meaning a pecuniary loss,[22] have been suffered by the plaintiff as a result of the slander.[23]

4. ELEMENTS OF THE PLAINTIFF'S CASE

(a) What is Defamatory?

To say that the purpose of defamation law is to protect one's right to reputation masks several important concerns. While the question of whether material was defamatory ought to be one of the most important aspects of defamation litigation, the reality is that invariably it is not. The question is generally glossed over by the courts, and is usually a non-issue.

There are several traditional explanations of what constitutes defamatory material. Defamatory words are said to be those which tend "to lower the plaintiff in the estimation of right-thinking members of society generally",[24] which hold the person named up to contempt, hatred, scorn or ridicule, or which cause a person to be discredited, detested, shunned and avoided.[25] Clearly, all of these explanations of the defamatory statement are not the same,[26] and thus the extent of damage which must result to an individual's reputation before material will be considered to be defamatory depends upon which threshold is adopted. In this respect, it is suggested that the threshold which has been adopted by Canadian courts is *extremely minimal*. The cases indicate that virtually all critical comment, whether it be in the form of fact or opinion,[27] which portrays a person in an uncomplimentary light will be considered to be defamatory. The battle lines in defamation cases are not fought out at the threshold level of "what is defamatory?" but with reference to the defences. This is significant. It has the effect of quickly shifting the burden of proof to defendants in defamation cases, encourages litigation, and creates an atmosphere in which plaintiffs in defamation cases are more easily seen as victims, in need of legal protection.[28]

---

22 See *Piasta v. Stewart* (1986), 48 Sask. R. 56 (Q.B.).

23 This is so no matter "how grossly insulting, scurrilous or demeaning" the slander may have been. See Brown, above, note 2, at 8-114.

24 Lord Atkin in *Sim v. Stretch*, [1936] 2 All E.R. 1237 at 1240 (H.L.).

25 See Cory J. in *Botiuk v. Toronto Free Press Publications Ltd.* (1995), 126 D.L.R. (4th) 609 at 622-23:

> a publication which tends to lower a person in the estimation of right-thinking members of society, or to expose a person to hatred, contempt or ridicule, is defamatory and will attract liability.

26 For example, a statement may lower a person's reputation in the eyes of others, while not resulting in that person being despised, shunned, or avoided. An interesting article on this issue is J. Harkness, "A Linguistic Inspection of the Law of Defamation" (1998), 8 Auckland Univ. L. Rev. 653. The author notes the differences between the legal approach to words and linguistic analysis. Linguistic analysis can teach us how allegedly "defamatory" statements actually affect the reader or listener.

27 As stated by Belzil J.A. in *Christie v. Geiger* (1986), 38 C.C.L.T. 280 at 290 (Alta. C.A.): "In determining whether words are capable of being defamatory, the distinction [between fact and comment] is one without a difference. . . ."

28 That this is the approach which courts follow in defamation cases was conceded by Dickson J. in *Cherneskey v. Armadale Publishers Ltd.* (1978), 7 C.C.L.T. 69 at 94-95 (S.C.C.):

> The law of defamation must strike a fair balance between the protection of reputation and the protection of free speech, for it asserts that a statement is not actionable, in spite of

In addition to the low threshold requirement, other factors contribute to the ease of establishing that most critical material is defamatory. The test of whether or not material lessened a plaintiff's reputation is an objective one. The court is not concerned with whether material *actually did* lower the person's reputation amongst those who actually were aware of the material, but whether it *would have had* that effect on the reasonable person.[29] It is a question of law whether material is capable of being considered to be defamatory,[30] and a question of fact whether in the circumstances of the case, a reasonable person would so consider it. Even if a plaintiff's reputation was not affected by the material, since the persons to whom it was published did not believe it,[31] or in fact actually knew

---

> the fact that it is defamatory, if it constitutes the truth, or is privileged, or is fair comment on a matter of public interest, expressed without malice by the publisher. These defences are of crucial importance in the law of defamation because of the low level of the threshold which a statement must pass in order to be defamatory. The virtually universally accepted test is that expressed by Lord Atkin "after collating the opinions of many authorities" in *Sim v. Stretch*, [1936] 2 All E.R. 1237 at 1240 (H.L.). He stated that the test of whether a statement is defamatory is [at p. 1240]: "would the words tend to lower the plaintiff in the estimation of right-thinking members of society generally?" In the earlier case of *O'Brien v. Clement* (1846), 15 M. & W. 435 at p. 437, 153 E.R. 920, Baron Parke said that, subject to any available defences, "[e]verything printed or written, which reflects on the character of another" is a libel. It is apparent that the scope of defamatory statements is very wide indeed. In particular, a great deal of what is printed in the letters to the editor columns of newspapers unquestionably has the effect of lowering the subject's reputation in the estimation of right-thinking people generally. In all cases, nevertheless, the statement is not actionable if it is the truth, or fair comment, or protected by privilege. This is the reason why most defamation actions centre on the defences of justification, fair comment, or privilege. It is these defences which give substance to the principle of freedom of speech.

Also see Adams J. in *A.G. Ont. v. Dieleman* (1994), 117 D.L.R. (4th) 449 at 673 (Ont. Gen. Div.). Adams J., while conceding the low threshold argument, states that "the defences of justification and fair comment are quite robust, particularly in light of the Charter . . .".

29 See *O'Malley v. O'Callaghan*, [1992] 4 W.W.R. 81 at 85 (Alta. Q.B.):

> The essential question to be asked is how a reasonable person would construe the words used . . .

30 See, for example, *Colour Your World Corp. v. Canadian Broadcasting Corp.* (1998), 156 D.L.R. (4th) 27, 41 C.C.L.T. (2d) 11 (Ont. C.A.), leave to appeal refused (1998), 119 O.A.C. 397 (note) (S.C.C.) where the Ontario Court of Appeal reversed a trial judge's finding that the material complained of was capable of conveying a defamatory meaning. Also see *Laufer v. Bucklaschuk* (1999), [2000] 2 W.W.R. 462 (Man. C.A.), leave to appeal refused (2000), 160 Man. R. (2d) 115 (note) (S.C.C.) where the "two stage process" is described. The judge must decide as a matter of law "whether the words cited are capable of a defamatory meaning in relation to the plaintiff". Only if the answer to this is yes should the matter be put to the jury to determine whether the words were in fact defamatory of the plaintiff. The court noted how critical the pleadings are in a defamation action and how the judge must determine whether the words are capable of bearing the meanings relied upon by the plaintiff in its pleadings. See also *Young v. Toronto Star Newspapers Ltd.* (2005), 259 D.L.R. (4th) 127 (Ont. C.A.), at 149.

31 See *Sydney Post Publishing Co. v. Kendall* (1910), 43 S.C.R. 461 at 475. In *Pochwalowski v. Tsai* (2003), 41 C.C.L.T. (3d) 124 (Ont. S.C.J.), additional reasons at (2003), additional reasons at (2003), 2003 CarswellOnt 8562 (S.C.J.), affirmed (2003), 2003 CarswellOnt 4713 (Div. Ct.), leave to appeal refused (2004), 2004 CarswellOnt 1313 (C.A.), leave to appeal refused (2004), 2004 CarswellOnt 3464 (S.C.C.), the defendant, who was mentally ill, distributed a defamatory letter to his neighbours concerning the plaintiff. Despite the fact that the court doubted that the plaintiff's reputation was "in any way tarnished as a result of the letter", because his neighbours "as reasonable people recognized immediately the falsehoods contained in the letter", the

that it was false, it would still be considered to be defamatory, as long as the objective test was met.[32] The same is true of material which did not lower a person's reputation in the eyes of the recipient, because the latter already knew of the material, and consequently already had a very low opinion of the plaintiff. Where words are considered to be defamatory in their ordinary and natural meaning, not only is the meaning in which they were understood by their recipients irrelevant, but evidence as to how they were understood by their recipients is inadmissible.[33] Conversely, where the material, although highly critical of the plaintiff, could not, because of the circumstances under which it was published or due to the character of its publisher, have the effect on the reasonable person of damaging the plaintiff's reputation, it will not be considered to be defamatory.[34] Thus, very unflattering words spoken in the course of a heated argument, for their effect, or in political debate, will not be considered to be defamatory if those who heard them, as reasonable persons, would not, due to the special circumstances, think less of the plaintiff.[35] Where, however, the allegation is that the words, although not defamatory in their ordinary meaning, were defamatory due to a special meaning known to the recipients, evidence must be entered to establish this.[36] The test, however, is still objective, except now the court is concerned with the reasonable person who is aware of the special circumstances.[37]

Since the test of whether material was defamatory is not based on actual damage to reputation, the courts have had to develop rules of construction to answer the question: "if a right-minded person were to be made aware of this material, would this person think less of the plaintiff?" Considerable attention has been paid to

---

defendant was found liable. In addition, the defendant's mental illness did not prevent him from being held liable.

32 See *Kerr v. Conlogue*, [1992] 4 W.W.R. 258 at 268 (B.C. S.C.):

> Moreover, to prove that the article is capable of being defamatory or in fact is defamatory, there is no onus on the plaintiff to prove that reasonable people actually understood the words in a defamatory sense. Rather, the plaintiff is only required to prove that the ordinary reasonable person might have understood it in a defamatory sense. The plaintiff does not have to prove that persons to whom it was published in fact did think less of him; indeed a person may be defamed even though those to whom the statement is published know it to be untrue.

Another somewhat interesting recent case is *Ralston v. Fomich*, [1992] 4 W.W.R. 284 (B.C. S.C.). In addition to confirming that the test of what is defamatory is an objective one, the court had to consider whether the words "son of a bitch" were defamatory. It concluded that this could depend upon the tone of voice of the speaker or the adjective which accompanied the words. The adjective "sick" son of a bitch was considered to be defamatory in this case.

33 See, e.g., *John Fairfax & Sons Ltd. v. Hook* (1983), 47 A.L.R. 477 at 480 (Fed. Ct.), cited by Brown, above, note 2, at 5-101, n. 401.

34 But see the case of *Pochwalski v. Tsai*, above, note 31, where the action succeeded despite the fact that the court doubted that reasonable people would have been influenced by the material.

35 There are numerous cases which affirm that the context and circumstances are important. See, e.g., Britton J. in *Ward v. McBride* (1911), 24 O.L.R. 555 at 569 (C.A.): "The time when, the place where, and all the undisputed facts and circumstances attending the speaking, must be taken into consideration . . ."

36 For example, when the issue relates to the legal innuendo, the recipients of the defamatory must be aware of the extrinsic facts which make the words defamatory: see *Cassidy v. Daily Mirror Newspapers Ltd.*, [1929] 2 K.B. 331 (C.A.).

37 See Brown, above, note 2-114 *et seq.*

the definition of the right-minded or reasonable person. For example, the courts have emphasized that they are concerned with ordinary, average, right-thinking, and reasonable persons, and not those who are unusually suspicious or unusually naive.[38] The various rules of construction have been summarized as follows:

> . . . a court will take into consideration the plain, fair, natural and ordinary meaning, or popular construction, of the words which persons "of common and reasonable understanding would ascribe to them", read or heard in the context in which they were spoken or written, and applying "their general knowledge and common sense", after taking into consideration the reasonable implications of the words and all the surrounding circumstances of the case, including the subject matter, the audience to whom they were published and the mode and manner in which they were presented.[39]

A second factor, which renders establishing that the material was defamatory much easier, is that truth or falsity is not relevant to the issue. As stated by Lacourcière J.A. in *Elliott v. Freisen*,[40] "if the words complained of are defamatory, the law presumes that they are false." Thus the law assumes that an individual is entitled to a good reputation.

A defendant's intention to defame or knowledge that the material which is published is defamatory have no bearing on the action. As stated by Jessup J.A., "the test is not of intent but rather what reasonable persons would understand from the allegedly defamatory words."[41] The defendant's honesty, careful research, or motives do not impinge upon the issue of "what is defamatory?". This is significant, especially where words are not obviously defamatory, but only can be proved to be so because of an innuendo. An innuendo exists where words are not defamatory in their ordinary and natural meaning but "because of special facts and circumstances known by those to whom the words are published."[42] For example, where a newspaper reported the marriage of two persons, extraneous

---

38 See *Rubber Improvement v. Daily Telegraph*, [1964] A.C. 234 (H.L.); and *Thomas v. CBC*, [1981] 4 W.W.R. 289 (N.W.T. S.C.), and cases cited therein.

39 Brown, above, note 2, at 5-62 to 5-63. (citations omitted). A leading case, frequently cited, is *Rubber Improvement v. Daily Telegraph, ibid.* In *Colour Your World Corp. v. Canadian Broadcasting Corp.*, above, note 30, the court noted that the material "should be assessed from the perspective of someone reasonable, that is, a person who is reasonably thoughtful and informed, rather than someone with an overly fragile sensibility. A degree of common sense must be attributed to viewers"; at (1998), 156 D.L.R. (4th) 27 (Ont. C.A.) at 36-37.

40 (1984), 6 D.L.R. (4th) 338 at 340 (Ont. C.A.).

41 *Stopforth v. Goyer* (1979), 8 C.C.L.T. 172 at 179 (Ont. C.A.).

42 Salmon L.J. in *Slim v. Daily Telegraph Ltd.*, [1968] 2 Q.B. 157 at 183 (C.A.). This is called the true or legal innuendo. The other type of innuendo, known as the false or popular innuendo, is really nothing more than an allegation that the words, on their face, can be interpreted by reasonable persons in a defamatory sense. No extraneous facts, outside the statement itself, need be established to construe this type of statement in a defamatory way. In *Lions Gate Marketing Co. v. Used Car Dealers Assn. of Ontario*, 2005 BCCA 274 (C.A.), the material alleged to be defamatory was the statement that the plaintiff's car warranties were uninsured. The Court of Appeal held that on its face this statement was not defamatory. If the plaintiff pled and could prove that this meant that the plaintiff was uninsurable, or was acting unlawfully in not having insurance, then the statement could be defamatory. However, these extrinsic facts or circumstances were not pled and the Court of Appeal reversed a judgment in the plaintiff's favour and dismissed the action.

evidence indicating that the parties were already married created the innuendo that the crime of bigamy had been committed.[43]

The case law illustrates how low the threshold requirement for establishing that material is defamatory is in Canadian law. Plaintiffs have been able to easily establish that almost all uncomplimentary comment is defamatory. Cases have turned not on the plaintiff's *prima facie* case but on the defences. In *Russell v. Pawley*,[44] for example, words stated within the context of a vigorous public debate, expressing surprise that the plaintiff, who was on sick leave from his job, could find so much time for his cause rather than going back to work, were held to be defamatory.[45] In *Moores v. Salter*,[46] a letter of reprimand by a superior stating that an argument between employees involved "violent displays of temper and the use of language not conducive to civilized human beings" was held to have been defamatory because it "would lead the general public to think less of" the plaintiff.[47] In *Bennett v. Stupich*,[48] a political newsletter from an opposition member suggesting that the Premier had Scotch with his dinner, and thus was at times in no position to attend evening sittings of the legislature, was held to be defamatory. This was so even though the plaintiff himself had commenced the debate by earlier stating that drinking at dinner time by various members of the legislature was interfering with the evening sittings. In *Upton v. Better Bus. Bureau of B.C. Mainland*,[49] a statement written in a bulletin of the Better Business Bureau to the effect that the bureau had received unanswered complaints concerning the plaintiff and that other estimates ought to be obtained by customers contemplating work, was held to be defamatory, despite the acknowledgment by the court that the criticism was mild.[50] In *Whitaker v. Huntington*,[51] statements by a Member of Parliament, spoken in the context of a controversial debate, expressing the view that a radical group was running a union's affairs, and that, because of this, the

43 *Duval v. O'Beirne* (1912), 20 O.W.R. 884 (H.C.). Another case of defamatory innuendo is *Bordeleau v. Bonnyville Nouvelle Ltd.*, [1993] 1 W.W.R. 634 (Alta. Q.B.). The defendant newspaper, at the behest of an unknown party, published a notice congratulating the plaintiff on the surprising event of her "newcoming BABY." The plaintiff was 18, single, and living in a small town. The court held that this notice was defamatory. The defences of qualified privilege and fair comment failed. The action was dismissed, however, because the newspaper published a full and fair retraction and apology and there were no special damages shown.

44 [1986] 4 W.W.R. 172 (Man. Q.B.), reversed (1987), 36 D.L.R. (4th) 625 (Man. C.A.).

45 There was a dissent in the Court of Appeal. Monnin C.J.M. stated that in view of all of the "very unparliamentary, intemperate, derogatory and vituperative language" which was being used by all parties to the debate over French language rights in Manitoba, it was amazing to note that the plaintiff felt himself defamed by what was said in this instance. According to Monnin C.J.M., at 36 D.L.R. (4th) at 626, "democratic debate in a free and open civilized society, such as ours, has the necessary tolerance to accept such statements and it does not offend my sense of justice, fair play or democratic principles to say so."

46 (1982), 37 Nfld. & P.E.I.R. 128 (Nfld. Dist. Ct.).

47 *Ibid.*, at 134-35. Note that the letter of reprimand was not made public, but was published only to the employees involved, and their superiors.

48 (1981), 125 D.L.R. (3d) 743 (B.C. S.C.).

49 (1980), 114 D.L.R. (3d) 750 (B.C. S.C.).

50 The court itself interpreted the words as meaning that the plaintiffs were "untrustworthy and are prone to overcharge", and then found *these* implications to be defamatory.

51 (1980), 15 C.C.L.T. 19 (B.C. S.C.).

union was undemocratic and unresponsive to the wishes of its membership, were held to be defamatory. In *Hanly v. Pisces Prod. Inc.*,[52] a frank letter written in response to a union's request for reasons explaining why the plaintiff was not hired by the defendant was held to be defamatory.[53] In *Vander Zalm v. Times Publishers*,[54] a political cartoon depicting the Minister of Human Resources gleefully plucking the wings off a fly was considered by the trial judge to have been defamatory.[55] In *Holt v. Sun Publishing Co.*,[56] an editorial which was critical of the manner in which two politicians were exercising their responsibilities was held to be defamatory. In *Murray Alter's Talent Associates Ltd. v. Toronto Star Newspapers*,[57]one sentence in an article in the fashion section of a newspaper stating that when the plaintiff band started playing rock music at a ball, it "cleared the floor, sending many home before the 1 a.m. finish", was considered to be defamatory. In *Teamsters, Local 987 v. U.F.C.W., Local 401*,[58] statements to the effect that a union had agreed to a "quick and easy" deal with management to settle a strike and that the deal was "substandard" were held to be defamatory. In *Robbins v. Pacific Newspaper Group Inc.*,[59] calling someone a "hypocite" was held to be defamatory although stating that he "stole" someone else's wife was not.[60] Even a plaintiff's own words can be presented in a way that is defamatory

---

52 [1981] 1 W.W.R. 369 (B.C. S.C.).

53 The defendant explained that the plaintiff was not hired because of her lack of self-confidence, her failure to provide positive work references, and her previous unsatisfactory work experiences.

54 [1980] 4 W.W.R. 259 (B.C. C.A.), reversing [1979] 2 W.W.R. 673 (B.C. S.C.).

55 Although members of the Court of Appeal expressed doubts regarding this finding, this aspect of the decision was upheld. Only Aitkins J.A. was prepared to find that the trial judge erred and should be reversed on this question. The remaining members, although expressing reservations, did not feel able to say that the trial judge was wrong. The judgment was reversed on other grounds. Another case in which a cartoon was found to be defamatory is *Mitchell v. Nanaimo District Teachers' Association* (1994), 94 B.C.L.R. (2d) 81 (C.A.). The parties were involved in a labour strike. The plaintiff, a school principal, was depicted in a cartoon, submitted to a newspaper by the teachers' union, as a greedy person. The trial judge found the cartoon to be defamatory. The Court of Appeal upheld the trial judgment, although Southin J.A. did say that it was unfortunate that the case was not tried by a jury. *Ross v. N.B.T.A.* (2001), 6 C.C.L.T. (3d) 171 (N.B. C.A.) also dealt with the issue of cartoons as defamations. The cartoon depicted the plaintiff and Josef Goebbels, drawing a comparison between them. The trial judge held that the cartoon was defamatory, implying that the plaintiff was a Nazi who supported the policy of the extermination of Jews. The Court of Appeal interpreted the cartoon differently as representing that both the plaintiff and Goebbels had a conspiracy theory relating to Jews. The Court of Appeal held, however, that the cartoon and the accompanying commentary at the workshop where the cartoon was presented were defamatory.

56 (1978), 83 D.L.R. (3d) 761 (B.C. S.C.), varied as to damages (1979), 100 D.L.R. (3d) 447 (B.C. C.A.).

57 (1995), 124 D.L.R. (4th) 105 (Ont. Div. Ct.).

58 (2003), [2004] 10 W.W.R. 574 (Alta. Q.B.), reversed (2005), 258 D.L.R. (4th) 33 (Alta. C.A.). The judgment was reversed with regard to the defence of qualified privilege.

59 2005 BCSC 1634 (S.C.), additional reasons at (2006), 2006 CarswellBC 873 (S.C.), additional reasons at (2006), 2006 CarswellBC 1393 (S.C.).

60 The judgment discussed the concept of "bane and antidote". That is, a publication must be read as a whole and the harm caused by a negative part may be cancelled out by something stated elsewhere in the publication. This did not occur in this case.

of the speaker or writer. In *Carter v. Gair*,[61] the defamation occurred when the defendant newspaper edited the plaintiff's humorous open letter in a way that allegedly made the plaintiff writer appear irrational and perhaps even violent. In *Myers v. Canadian Broadcasting Corp.*,[62] statements by a physician were presented in a television documentary in such a way as to defame him. It is in fact difficult to find many reported cases where actions were dismissed because material was found not to be defamatory.[63]

The existing threshold of what constitutes defamatory material is too low. This has significant consequences for freedom of speech in Canada. It encourages litigation and stifles expression because it places the burden on defendants to justify critical comment. If the courts were to indicate that critical comment is *prima facie* justifiable in a free society, rather than the reverse being true, the balance between protecting reputation and protecting speech would be altered.

An alternative solution is to reject the objective test of what is defamatory, and require complainants to prove not only that impugned material was capable of being defamatory, but that it actually did affect their reputation in the minds of those who were made aware of it. It might be objected, with some justification, that this would create a serious evidentiary problem in defamation litigation. How would the credibility of witnesses who testified that they did, or did not, think less of the plaintiff, due to the allegedly defamatory material, be tested? One can suggest, however, that courts, in other contexts, are able to establish issues of credibility, and could do so in these cases.[64] As well, the issue of whether material is capable of being defamatory would remain a question of law. Only if the threshold objective standard were met would the subjective issue be determined as a question of fact.

---

61 (1999), 170 D.L.R. (4th) 204 (B.C. C.A.).

62 (1999), 47 C.C.L.T. (2d) 272 (Ont. S.C.J.), additional reasons at (2000), 2000 CarswellOnt 13 (S.C.J. [In Chambers]), varied as to damages (2001), 6 C.C.L.T. (3d) 112 (Ont. C.A.), leave to appeal refused (2002), 163 O.A.C. 400 (note) (S.C.C.).

63 Although it is true that in some of these cases the actions were dismissed based on a successful defence, the actions, as indicated above, were fought out at that level. A case where the comments were found not to be capable of being considered defamatory is *Crandall v. Atlantic School of Theology* (1993), 120 N.S.R. (2d) 219, 332 A.P.R. 219. The defendant made suggestions of sexual misconduct on the plaintiff's part. The judge ruled that the words used were not capable of being viewed as defamatory and refused to put the issue to the jury. Also see *Pollock v. Winnipeg Free Press* (1996), 34 C.C.L.T. (2d) 203 (Man. Q.B.); *Colour Your World Corp. v. Canadian Broadcasting Corp.*, above, note 30, and *Roth v. Aubichon* (1998), 171 Sask. R. 271 (Q.B.), where the material was held not to be defamatory. In view of the jurisprudence, the *Roth* case is particularly surprising since the words spoken of a lawyer impugned his knowledge and competence. In *P.G. Restaurant Ltd. v. Northern Interior Regional Health Board* (2005), 30 C.C.L.T. (3d) 55 (B.C. C.A.), reconsideration refused (2005), 2005 CarswellBC 1219 (C.A.), leave to appeal refused (2005), 2005 CarswellBC 2711 (S.C.C.), additional reasons at (2006), 2006 CarswellBC 1388 (C.A.), reversing 22 C.C.L.T. (3d) 153, [2004] 4 W.W.R. 287 (B.C. C.A.), the Court of Appeal reversed a trial judge's decision that a newspaper article contained defamatory material. The Court of Appeal held that the article was not capable of "bearing the sting attached to it by the trial judge" when read as a whole. The part of the article that was held to be defamatory was found to be true.

64 For example, if witnesses claim that they thought less of the plaintiff, this might be tested by examining their conduct. For example, did they stop associating with the plaintiff?

(b) Reference to the Plaintiff

An essential aspect of the *prima facie* case is proof that the defamatory material adversely affected the plaintiff's reputation because it referred, either expressly or by implication, to the plaintiff. In other words, the defamation must have been "published of and concerning the plaintiff."[65]

Where the plaintiff was expressly named or identified by the defamatory material, as is frequently the case, this aspect of the plaintiff's *prima facie* case poses no difficulty. The plaintiff's burden will be discharged without the necessity of further proof. This will be so even if the persons to whom the material was published had no knowledge of the plaintiff.[66] This is consistent with the approach that whether a person's reputation has been damaged by material is tested not by the subjective belief of those who were aware of the material, but by a hypothetical reasonable person.

Where the plaintiff was not expressly identified, however, the situation differs. The courts, in this circumstance, have imposed a two stage test.[67] The court first asks whether, as a question of law, the material can be regarded as being capable of referring to the complainant. If the answer to this is in the affirmative, the trier must determine, as a matter of fact, whether the material would lead reasonable people who know the plaintiff to the conclusion that it does refer to the plaintiff. In *Dale's Trad'n Post v. Rhodes*,[68] for example, the defamatory material impugned the quality and manner of installation of a fireplace insert purchased and installed by an unnamed "local vendor." Since there was only one local vendor who sold and installed the material in question, the court held that the material was capable of referring to that individual.[69] In deciding the question of fact, i.e., whether reasonable persons who were aware of the material would consider that it referred to the plaintiff, the court emphasized the objective nature of this issue. As with the question of whether material is in fact defamatory, the question of reference to the plaintiff depends upon the understanding of the reasonable person, and not necessarily the actual witnesses to the material.[70] Again the question is a hypo-

---

65 See Brown, above, note 2, at 6-2. This issue is known as the "colloquium." In the ordinary case, it is the person who is defamed who must bring the action. In *A.G. Ont. v. Dieleman* (1994), 117 D.L.R. (4th) 449 (Ont. Gen. Div.), the court held that the Attorney General could bring an action to restrain the further publications of defamations concerning other persons in her capacity as *parens patriae* in pursuit of regulating a nuisance.

66 See *Consol. Trust Co. v. Browne* (1948), 49 S.R. (N.S.W.) 86 (C.A.).

67 The leading authority is *Knupffer v. London Express Newspaper Ltd.*, [1944] 1 All E.R. 495 (H.L.), which has been cited with approval in numerous Canadian cases, including *Butler v. Southam Inc.* (2001), 197 N.S.R. (2d) 97 (C.A.); *Lennon v. Harris* (1999), 45 O.R. (3d) 84 (S.C.J.); *Dale's Trad'n Post v. Rhodes* (1987), 43 C.C.L.T. 37 (B.C. S.C.); *Booth v. B.C.T.V. Broadcasting Systems* (1982), 139 D.L.R. (3d) 88 (B.C. C.A.); *Halprin v. Sun Publishing Co.*, [1978] 4 W.W.R. 685 (B.C. S.C.); and *Arnott v. College of Physicians & Surgeons (Sask.)*, [1954] S.C.R. 538. See also Ritchie J. in *Fraser v. Sykes*, [1974] S.C.R. 526.

68 *Ibid.*

69 The court, on the other hand, held that the words were not capable of referring to a foreign manufacturer.

70 The court cited *Halprin v. Sun Publishing Co.*, [1978] 4 W.W.R. 685 (B.C. S.C.), where the trial judge refused to rely upon the plaintiff's nine witnesses, with regard to their understanding of the impugned material, since they were close friends, associates and former associates of the plaintiff who would not read the material in the same way as would the average reader.

thetical one: *if* a reasonable person, with knowledge of the special facts of the case, was made aware of the material, would this person think it referred to the plaintiff?[71] The trial judge concluded that there was no evidence establishing how the "average sensible reader" would have interpreted the material, and that therefore the plaintiff had failed to discharge the burden of proving that the material had been published of the plaintiff.[72]

Where there is nothing in the material itself which either expressly or implicitly identifies the person to whom the material refers, the plaintiff must introduce evidence of special facts which, although extraneous to the material, would lead reasonable persons aware of such facts to realize that the material refers to the plaintiff.[73]

As with the defamatory imputation, the intention or knowledge of the defendant is not relevant with respect to the issue of whether the defamatory material referred to the plaintiff. Nor is it relevant that the defendant acted totally reasonably and without fault, if it transpires that the material is understood by reasonable people to be referable to the plaintiff. Defamation law is not concerned with what a speaker subjectively meant to say, but with the meaning reasonable persons would take from what was said.[74] In determining this, it has been stated that the court will consider all of the circumstances of the communication, including the kind

71 See *Morgan v. Odhams Press Ltd.*, [1971] 2 All E.R. 1156 (H.L.), cited in *Dale's Trad'n Post* (1987), 43 C.C.L.T. 37 at 49 (B.C. S.C.), where Lord Morris stated that the issue must be judged from the point of view of a "hypothetical sensible reader who knew the special facts to be proved."

72 Compare this case to *P.G. Restaurant Ltd. v. Northern Interior Regional Health Board* (2004), 22 C.C.L.T. (3d) 153, [2004] 4 W.W.R. 287, reversed on another issue (2005), 30 C.C.L.T. (3d) 55 (B.C. C.A.), reconsideration refused (2005), 2005 CarswellBC 1219 (C.A.), leave to appeal refused (2005), 2005 CarswellBC 2711 (S.C.C.), additional reasons at (2006), 2006 CarswellBC 1388 (C.A.). The defendant, an employee of a Board of Health, told a reporter that there was a health-related incident "at a restaurant in Prince George that offers a buffet and that had had a good record with the Board prior to the incident", at 22 C.C.L.T. 176. He did not identify the restaurant. The trial judge noted that there were "countless restaurants in Prince George" and found that as a matter of fact the statement would not lead reasonable people to conclude that it was the defendant restaurant.

73 As Brown, above, note 2, at 6-34 *et seq.*, notes, however, if the special facts were not generally known, the plaintiff must prove that the facts were known by those to whom the material was published. Brown cites *Consol. Trust Co. v. Browne* (1948), 49 S.R. (N.S.W.) 86 (C.A.); and *Arnott v. College of Physicians & Surgeons (Sask.)*, above, note 67. See discussion at 6.4. It has also been held that where there are a series of publications, some of which name the plaintiff and others of which do not, it is possible by reading the publications together to find references to the plaintiff even in the ones in which the plaintiff was not named. See *Misir v. Toronto Star Newspapers Ltd.* (1997), 105 O.A.C. 270 (C.A.) and *Butler v. Southam Inc.*, above, note 67. In *Dinyer-Fraser v. Laurentian Bank of Canada* (2005), 28 C.C.L.T. (3d) 205 (B.C. S.C.), additional reasons at (2005), 2005 CarswellBC 2365 (S.C.), the reverse argument was used. A letter was sent to the plaintiff's clients incorrectly informing them that "your agent/financial advisor" was named in a Temporary Order restricting her right to deal in certain securities. Had her clients actually read the Temporary Order, they would have seen that she was not one of the persons named. Despite this, the court did not think that this eliminated the defamatory reference to the plaintiff contained in the letter.

74 *Booth v. B.C.T.V. Broadcasting Systems* (1982), 139 D.L.R. (3d) 88 at 94 (B.C. C.A.). Or, as stated in an Alberta judgment, "the intention of the author is of no consequence on the issue of identification if the words used by him include individuals he did not intend to include": see *A.U.P.E. v. Edmonton Sun* (1986), 39 C.C.L.T. 143 at 155 (Alta. Q.B.).

of person the speaker was and the kind of knowledge that people would anticipate that the speaker would have.[75] In the leading case, *E. Hulton & Co. v. Jones*,[76] an article written about a person whom the author considered to have been fictitious was alleged to have been defamatory of a real person of the same name. Lord Loreburn L.C. noted that, as with the defamatory imputation, the intention of the defendant is not relevant to whether the material was defamatory of and concerning the plaintiff.[77]

When a group of individuals has been defamed, individuals in that group cannot sue for defamation unless they can prove that the statements identified or referred to them in the minds of the reasonable person.[78] The test remains the same: would the reasonable person think less of the particular complainant due to the material? In *A.U.P.E. v. Edmonton Sun*,[79] the fact that the size of the group was 200 persons was not considered to have been an obstacle to defamation actions brought by 25 individual members of that group.[80] It is fair to state, however, that generally defamatory comments aimed at groups of persons containing numerous members will not be actionable by individual group members,[81] even though they personally

---

75 *Booth v. B.C.T.V.*, *ibid.*, at 94.

76 [1910] A.C. 20 (H.L.).

77 See also *Newstead v. London Express Newspapers Ltd.*, [1940] 1 K.B. 377 (C.A.), another case involving an innocent but nevertheless actionable confusion as to names. Nova Scotia has a provision in its legislation which protects innocent publication of defamatory words if certain conditions are met. Basically, where the publisher did not intend to publish the words of and concerning the other person, and did not know of the circumstances by virtue of which they might be understood to refer to that person, or, where the words were not *ex facie* defamatory, and the publisher did not know of the circumstance by virtue of which they might be understood to be defamatory, and, there was in either case reasonable care, an offer of amends, by way of an apology or other corrective steps, can serve as a defence. See Defamation Act, R.S.N.S. 1989, c. 122, s. 16.

78 See *Masters v. Fox* (1978), 85 D.L.R. (3d) 64 (B.C. S.C.); *S.I.U. v. Lawrence* (1979), 97 D.L.R. (3d) 324 (Ont. C.A.); or the other authorities cited by Brown, above, note 2, at 6-53 *et seq.* For reaffirmation of this point see *A.G. Ont. v. Dieleman* (1994), 117 D.L.R. (4th) 449 at 673 (Ont. Gen. Div.); *Elliott v. C.B.C.* (1993), 16 O.R. (3d) 677 (Gen. Div.), affirmed on other grounds (1995), 125 D.L.R. (4th) 534 (Ont. C.A.), leave to appeal refused (1996), 131 D.L.R. (4th) vii (note) (S.C.C.); and *Aiken v. Ontario (Premier)* (1999), 177 D.L.R. (4th) 489 (Ont. S.C.J.). *Butler v. Southam Inc.*, above, note 67, contains an excellent discussion of the matter of "group" defamation with reference to numerous cases and academic commentary. Cromwell J.A. discusses the "intensity of suspicion" approach and the various factors that go into determining whether the plaintiff is identifiable as a result of a defamatory statement being made in reference to a group of which the plaintiff is a member. Factors identified are, among others: (i) nature of group; i.e., size, identity, organizational structure; and (ii) nature of statement; i.e., seriousness of statement, importance to free speech. The parties in this case were current and former employees of a school for boys. They were suing in reference to articles concerning physical and sexual abuse at five provincially run institutions involving hundreds of children over many years. The motion was to strike out the statement of claim and dismiss the action based on the lack of reference to the plaintiffs. Some of the pleadings were struck while the action was permitted to continue for others. In *Gauthier et al v. Toronto Newspapers Ltd.* (2004), 245 D.L.R. (4th) 169 (Ont. C.A.), leave to appeal refused (2005), 2005 CarswellOnt 274 (S.C.C.), affirming (2003), 228 D.L.R. (4th) 748 (Ont. C.A.), a class action brought by police officers and civilian personnel, numbering at least 7,000, was struck for defamatory material aimed at the "Toronto police".

79 (1986), 39 C.C.L.T. 143 (Alta. Q.B.).

80 The group consisted of the guards at a local prison.

81 Unless certain individuals can prove that they were actually singled out from the larger group and thus identifiable.

felt very offended and hurt by the remarks.[82] This has led some jurisdictions to statutorily provide that individuals belonging to a racial or religious group libelled by racist comments may sue for an injunction to prevent the continuation of the libel, under certain conditions.[83]

(c) Publication

Defamatory material is not actionable unless the plaintiff can prove that it has been published, i.e., communicated to at least one person who is not the person defamed.[84] In order to be communicated, the person to whom the material was published must have been aware of it and understood it. It has been stated that this person must have understood the material in a defamatory sense and that it referred to the plaintiff,[85] but as argued by Brown,[86] this must be regarded as questionable. As noted previously, whether material is defamatory and refers to the plaintiff does not depend upon the subjective understanding of individual witnesses, but on the understanding of the ordinary, reasonable person.[87]

---

82 For example, in *Elliott v. C.B.C.*, above, note 78, the action was brought by one man on behalf of the 25,000 surviving airmen of Bomber Command. The defamatory material was contained in a made-for-T.V. film and book concerning these World War II fighting men. The statement of claim was struck out at first instance, on the basis that no single person could be considered to have been singled out. The Court of Appeal affirmed the decision on the ground that, the issue of the number of persons aside, the material was not defamatory. A significantly more trivial defamation of a group occurred in *McCann v. The Ottawa Sun* (1993), 16 O.R. (3d) 672 (Gen. Div.). The mayor of Pembroke took offence at a sports column containing derogatory comments about the behaviour of hockey fans, "coming from places like Embrum, Arnprior, Renfrew and Pembroke." The court struck out the statement of claim on the basis that no particular resident of Pembroke, including the mayor, was singled out by the defamation. In *Aiken v. Ontario (Premier)* (1999), 177 D.L.R. (4th) 489 (Ont. S.C.J.), the group defamed were striking teachers. One hundred and five sued although it is not stated in the case how large the group itself was. In *Bai v. Sing Tao Daily Ltd.* (2003), 226 D.L.R. (4th) 477 (Ont. C.A.), leave to appeal refused (2004), 2004 CarswellOnt 234 (S.C.C.), an action brought by Canadian practitioners of Falun Gong was struck out, due to the large size of that group.

83 See Manitoba's Defamation Act, C.C.S.M., c. D20, s. 19(1).

84 See, e.g., Locke J. in *Arnott v. College of Physicians & Surgeons (Sask.)*, [1954] S.C.R. 538 at 565: "There can be no cause of action in libel unless the writing complained of is published." Publication was defined by Duff J. in *McNichol v. Grandy*, [1931] S.C.R. 696 at 704: ". . . the defamatory matter is brought by the defendant or his agent to the knowledge or understanding of some person other than the plaintiff." See, however, *O'Malley v. O'Callaghan*, [1992] 4 W.W.R. 81 (Alta. Q.B.), which seems to widen the concept of publication. The defendant wrote a series of letters to the plaintiff, the coordinator of Calgary Coalition for Life. The letters were addressed to the plaintiff in his capacity as coordinator. They contained defamatory material concerning the plaintiff. The court held that since it was "reasonably foreseeable" that the letters "could" be opened by a third party, or that their contents "would" or "could" be communicated to other members of the organization, these letters were published. I would argue that actual publication to a third party is necessary and must be shown. Publication by the plaintiff to a third party may suffice. See discussion below.

85 See Wetmore J. in *Wood v. Mackey* (1881), 21 N.B.R. 109 (C.A.); Eldredge, *The Law of Defamation* (1978), at 206; and *Gatley on Libel and Slander*, 8th ed. (1981), at 101, para. 221, and at 102, para. 223, cited by Brown, above, note 2, at 7-48, fn. 225 and 226.

86 *Ibid.*

87 See discussion by Brown, *ibid.* Brown cites Locke J. in *Arnott v. College of Physicians & Surgeons (Sask.)*, [1954] S.C.R. 538 at 566, which supports Gatley that there must be evidence that someone understood the language complained of in a defamatory sense. Brown notes, however, that this is inconsistent with other statements by Gatley that the test is that of the

The issue of publication also arises when the author's defamatory material is transcribed or printed by another party for the benefit of the author. While early cases have held that dictation to a stenographer constitutes publication, it has recently been held that communications between lawyers and their secretaries does not.[88] In addition, a defendant printer who had been hired to print and bind into books defamatory material was held not to be a publisher of the material when it delivered these books to their author.[89]

Each time defamatory material is communicated to a new person, a fresh and actionable publication takes place.[90] However, in order to avoid a multiplicity of proceedings against all those who participated in the publication and distribution of defamatory material, it has been held that "all those who participated in or were responsible for the original publication and its distribution must be joined as joint tortfeasors in the original cause of action."[91] As well, secondary disseminators of defamatory material, i.e., those who sell, loan, or distribute books, are given special consideration in terms of liability for their role in the publication process. As held in *Vizetelly v. Mudie's Select Library Ltd.*,[92] if parties who played a subordinate role in disseminating material can show that they did not and could not reasonably have known of the libellous material when they disseminated the

---

hypothetical reasonable person. See also *Faryna v. Chorny* (1951), 4 W.W.R. (N.S.) 171 (B.C. C.A.), which supports the view that the test is an objective one.

88 See *Simons v. Carr & Co.*, [1996] 10 W.W.R. 64 (Alta. Q.B.). The court held that the letter dictated by a lawyer to his secretary and read by the secretary of the lawyer to whom it was addressed was also protected by an absolute privilege. One should note that even in the case of clerks or stenographers, if the material is written in the ordinary course of business, it would be protected. See the cases relied on regarding stenographers or clerks: *Puterbaugh v. Gold Medal Furniture Manufacturing Co.* (1904), 7 O.L.R. 582 (C.A.); and *Moran v. O'Regan* (1907), 38 N.B.R. 189 (S.C.). The case of *Best v. Spasic* (2004), [2004] O.J. No. 5765, 2004 CarswellOnt 6107 (S.C.J.), additional reasons at (2005), 2005 CarswellOnt 994 (S.C.J.) dealt with the principle of "intra corporate communication". The argument is that communications between employees of a corporation concerning the business of the corporation are not publications. The court rejected this principle as not being part of Canadian law. It does not apply to the case of one employee suing another employee, which was the issue in the case. Harris J. also doubted whether it even applied to suits against the corporation itself for intra corporate communications. The court felt that the defence of qualified privilege was adequate to deal with these types of defamatory communications. The court also rejected the argument that the fact of incorporation protected the defendant, who was the president, from personal liability for defamations published by her.

89 *Menear v. Miguna* (1996), 32 C.C.L.T. (2d) 35 (Ont. Gen. Div.), reversed (1997), 33 O.R. (3d) 223 (C.A.). The Court of Appeal reversed the judgment holding that the trial judge erred in dealing with this issue in summary judgment proceedings.

90 As stated in *Basse v. Toronto Star Newspapers Ltd.* (1983), 44 O.R. (2d) 164 at 165 (H.C.): "Every republication of a libel is a new libel and each publisher is answerable for his act." The question as to whether the "single publication" rule, which has been adopted in some American states, and treats all continuing publications of defamatory material by the same defendant as one, for the purposes of determining when the limitation of action period begins to run, should be adopted in British Columbia, was considered in *Carter v. B.C. Federation of Foster Parents Assn.*, 257 D.L.R. (4th) 133, [2005] 10 W.W.R. 427 (B.C. C.A.), reversing as to another issue [2004] 7 W.W.R. 319, 21 C.C.L.T. (3d) 307 (B.C. S.C.). The Court of Appeal rejected it. Both English and Australian authorities were relied on in the Court's decision.

91 Brown, *The Law of Defamation in Canada*, 2nd ed. (1994), at 17-110. The leading case is *Thomson v. Lambert*, [1938] S.C.R. 253.

92 [1900] 2 Q.B. 170 at 180 (C.A.).

material, they will not be considered to have published it.[93] In a somewhat similar vein, a defendant who published a newsletter which contained a reference to a website was held not to have republished the defamatory material which was contained on that website.[94]

An individual who originally published defamatory material generally is not held liable for the republication of that material. There are, however, exceptions to this rule.[95] If the defendant intended or authorized the republication, if the defendant published the material to someone who was under a moral, legal, or social duty to repeat or publish the words to someone else, or if the republication was the natural and probable result of the original publication, then the defendant will be liable for the republication.[96] A case illustrating this problem is *Smith v. Matsqui (Dist.)*.[97] The court held that a mayor who had written an allegedly defamatory memorandum to a municipal employee concerning the plaintiff was not responsible for this memorandum's republication in the local newspaper. There was no evidence of negligence on the part of the mayor, nor any explanation concerning the newspaper's sources. In another case, *Basse v. Toronto Star Newspapers*,[98] it was held that the defendant newspaper was not liable for the republication of material, which it originally published, by other media. The court held that "there is no liability upon the original publisher of the libel when the repetition is the voluntary act of a free agent, over whom the original publisher had no control and for whose acts he is not responsible."[99]

The Supreme Court of Canada dealt with the issues of joint publication and republication in *Botiuk v. Toronto Free Press Publications Ltd.*[100] Three separate

---

93 This rule has been applied to printers of defamatory material who have no knowledge of the defamatory material. This is reflective of the fact that modern day printing takes place without the printer having any editorial or other role that would require it to read the material. See *Menear v. Miguna* (1996), 32 C.C.L.T. (2d) 35 (Ont. Gen. Div.), reversed (1997), 33 O.R. (3d) 223 (C.A.) and the accompanying annotation by Roger Harris and Petrillo Bujold at 35.

94 *Carter v. B.C. Federation of Foster Parents Assn.*, above, note 90. The trial judge had held that there was no republication, stating, among other factors, that the defendant had no knowledge that the website contained defamatory material. The Court of Appeal did not raise the knowledge issue, but noted that the defendant had no control over the website. The Court of Appeal specifically refrained from deciding whether the same result would follow in the case of one website referring to another website.

95 The leading case is *Speight v. Gosnay* (1891), 60 L.J.Q.B. 231 (C.A.).

96 See, for example, *O'Malley v. O'Callaghan*, [1992] 4 W.W.R. 81 (Alta. Q.B.). *McNabb v. Equifax Canada Inc.* (1999), [2000] 6 W.W.R. 562 (Man. Q.B.) distinguishes between publication by the plaintiff to a third party and republication by a third party to another party. Beard J. suggests a stricter test when the plaintiff itself publishes to a third party; namely was this publication "necessary"? When it is a case of republication, the test suggested is whether the republication was the "natural and probable consequences" of the initial publication. Beard J. notes that this matter is not clearly resolved by either the texts or the case law. Beard J. favoured the approach that the test for publication by the plaintiff himself should be stricter, i.e., a test of necessity or compulsion, but since this matter was not argued by counsel it was left open.

97 (1986), 4 B.C.L.R. (2d) 342 (S.C.).

98 Above, note 90.

99 *Ibid.*, at 166. On the other hand, see *St. Michael's Extended Care Centre Society v. Frost*, [1994] 6 W.W.R. 718 (Alta. Q.B.), where the defendant was liable for the publication of his defamatory statements which appeared in a newspaper. He had given an interview to a reporter and he should have known that anything he said would be published.

100 (1995), 126 D.L.R. (4th) 609 (S.C.C.).

documents were published which contained material defamatory of the plaintiff. The first was a report, produced by defendant M, accusing the plaintiff lawyer of reneging on a promise to return money he had received as legal fees to a nonprofit committee he had represented. The second was a declaration, produced by other defendants, who were lawyers, which confirmed the allegation contained in the first report. The third was another document, produced by defendant M, which incorporated the lawyers' declaration. Rather than limiting the defendant lawyers' liability for damages to those which flowed from the publication of their declaration, Cory J., for the Supreme Court of Canada, considered the parties to be "joint concurrent" tortfeasors. They were accordingly all held liable for the damages which flowed fromthe three defamatory publications. The defendant lawyers were held liable for the defamatory material contained in the first document, since they had adopted its contents in their declaration.[101]

Unlike the strict liability approach applied to the issues of the defamatory meaning, and reference to the plaintiff, the fault of the defendant is a requirement with respect to the issue of publication. The defendant must have intended to publish the material, or failing that, must have been unreasonable with respect to the risk of its publication, in order to be responsible for its publication. The leading case in Canada is *McNichol v. Grandy*,[102] where the Supreme Court of Canada held that the accidental publication of defamatory material will not lead to liability. It appears, however, that the burden of disproving fault rests with the defendant.[103]

The principle of liability for republication is also illustrated in the *Botiuk* case.[104] The defendant lawyers were responsible for the republication of their defamatory declaration by the other defendant, since its republication was "a natural and logical consequence of the lawyers signing it without placing any restrictions on its use."[105]

With the advent of radio or television "call-in" shows, the question as to who is responsible for defamatory remarks made by a caller to the show's host or guest

---

101 It was held in *Brown v. Cole* (1995), [1996] 2 W.W.R. 567 (B.C. C.A.) that the provisions of the Negligence Act, R.S.B.C. 1979, c. 298 allowing for defendants to claim contribution from each other applied to defamation actions. Thus original publishers were allowed to claim contribution by means of a third party procedure for damages payable to the plaintiff from others who republished the defamation.

102 [1931] S.C.R. 696.

103 Also see *Skomar v. Rachinski* (1990), 88 Sask. R. 177 (Q.B.). The defendant called the plaintiff a thief, in a loud and angry exchange. This was overheard by parties, relatives of the disputants, who were present at the scene. The court held that the words were not overheard accidentally, and thus that they were published by the defendant. Also see *Carter v. B.C. Federation of Foster Parents*, above note 90, where the B.C. Court of Appeal reversed the trial judge's finding that the publication was innocent, noting the heavy burden that rests on a defendant to establish this.

104 Above, note 100.

105 *Ibid.*, at 626. Another case is *Peters-Brown v. Regina District Health Board* (1995), [1996] 1 W.W.R. 337 (Sask. Q.B.), affirmed (1996), [1997] 1 W.W.R. 638 (Sask. C.A.). A list containing names or persons with infectious diseases, which was originally published in a hospital, ended up being posted in the staff room of a remand centre, where the plaintiff worked. The court held that the republication was not "the natural and probable result" of the original publication and not therefore the hospital's responsibility.

arises. In *Smith v. Matsqui (Dist.)*,[106] for example, the silence of the radio guest host following an allegedly defamatory statement by a caller was held not to have constituted his tacit agreement with the remark. As well, neither the radio station not its host were held liable for the unsolicited and unconfirmed remarks of the caller.[107] In *Syms v. Warren*,[108] on the other hand, the court held that permitting defamatory remarks to be made by a caller, especially where the host had the ability to censor calls and stop them from being broadcast, was actionable. The internet and the ability of persons to post material anonymously also has resulted in new legal issues. In *Vaquero Energy Ltd. v. Weir*,[109] defamatory material was published on an internet stock "chat room" under anonymous names. The plaintiff sued the defendant, alleging that he was responsible for the postings. Despite the defendant's denials, the plaintiff was able to adduce convincing evidence tracing the postings to the defendant's computer and he was accordingly held liable.

5. DEFENCES

(a) Justification

Justification or truth is a complete defence to an action for defamation.

This position has been defended in different ways. First, it has been stated that something which is true cannot be defamatory.[110] This explanation, however, seems flawed. Certainly, even true information about an individual can lower that person's reputation in the eyes of others, especially where this information was not generally known. It seems to be an unnecessary complexity to add the element of falsity to the definition of what constitutes defamatory material.[111] It has also been argued that, as a matter of principle, reputations which are not deserved ought not to be protected.[112] However, this explanation is also unsatisfactory. A person may deserve a good reputation based on existing characteristics, even though there is true information based on past events which, if known, would lower the esteem in which that individual is held by others. It probably is best to simply concede that, as a matter of policy, the law has decided to protect free

---

106 Above, note 97.

107 This is questionable. The radio station clearly published the remarks. The fact that the defendants did not know that the remarks were defamatory ought not to have been relevant. As stated by Brown, above, note 2, at 7-12, "a defendant may be liable for the publication of a defamatory statement by another where he has some control over the machinery that produces it, or the place where it originated, or some responsibility for the persons publishing it." In *Stanley v. Shaw*, 2006 BCCA 467 (C.A.), the Court of Appeal held that the defendants who said and did nothing when they became aware of defamatory material published of the plaintiff, who was an employee of their company, could not be held liable for defamation. Their silence could not be construed as a publication of the material.

108 (1976), 71 D.L.R. (3d) 558 (Man. Q.B.).

109 [2006] 5 W.W.R. 176 (Alta. Q.B.), additional reasons at (2004), 2004 CarswellAlta 389 (Q.B.).

110 See Tritschler C.J.Q.B. in *Courchene v. Marlborough Hotel Co.* (1971), 20 D.L.R. (3d) 109 (Man. Q.B.), affirmed (1971), 22 D.L.R. (3d) 157 (Man. C.A.).

111 It is clear that something can be defamatory without it being false: see, e.g., *Elliott v. Freisen* (1982), 136 D.L.R. (3d) 281 (Ont. H.C.), affirmed (1984), 6 D.L.R. (4th) 338 (Ont. C.A.).

112 See Littledale J. in *M'Pherson v. Daniels* (1829), 109 E.R. 448.

speech over the right to reputation, where material which damages reputation is true, no matter why it is published, and no matter how unfair this may be to the person defamed.[113] While one can certainly sympathize with those who are critical of this, the defence ought to be maintained. Free speech suffers sufficiently from the existing defamation laws, without exacerbating the problem by requiring those who speak truly about others to justify their speech by proving good motives. Good reputations which are based upon solid achievements ought to be able to withstand malevolent gossiping concerning past wrongs. Tolerance for the failings of all persons will be better promoted by standing firm against those who seek to promote ill will, rather than by attempting to silence these individuals.

In considering the defence, it is the substance of the defamatory material which must be examined, and not the manner in which it is presented. Thus a defendant will be liable for repeating defamatory material, even though truthfully reporting what was actually heard.[114] A person who wishes to publish material originating from others must be prepared to prove the truth of that material.[115]

The defence of justification does not inquire into questions of good intentions or reasonable care. Material is either substantially true or false. It is no excuse to allege that the defendant had every reason to believe that what was published was true, that all reasonable care was exercised, or that the publisher had excellent motives, when material has not been shown to have in fact been true.[116]

Whether defamatory material is true is a matter of context and degree. In determining what message is conveyed by material, the law looks to the ordinary

---

113 This approach is not universally supported. There are some who feel that gratuitous defamations about persons should not be permitted simply because they are true, where no benefit is served by such communication. See, e.g., Ray, "Truth: A Defence to Libel" (1931), 16 Minn. L. Rev. 43. It should be noted that under Quebec civil law "truth and public interest are merely factors to consider in the overall contextual analysis of fault in an action in defamation" and "are not necessarily the determinative factors"; see Lebel J. in *Gilles E. Neron inc. v. Chambre des notaires* (2004), 26 C.C.L.T. (3d) 161 (S.C.C.). The Supreme Court held a broadcaster liable in defamation despite the fact that the information broadcast may have been true in part and in the public interest, because of the faulty manner in which the show was prepared and broadcast. Binnie J. dissented.

114 See, e.g., Greer L.J. in *Cookson v. Harewood*, [1932] 2 K.B. 478 at 485n (C.A.): "If you repeat a rumour you cannot say it is true by proving that in fact the rumour existed; you have to prove that the subject-matter of the rumour was true."

115 See, e.g., *Farrell v. St. John's Publishing Co.* (1986), 58 Nfld. & P.E.I.R. 66 (Nfld. C.A.). As we shall discuss below, the media has defences relating to fair and accurate reports, which allow them to publish defamatory material under certain conditions. In addition, depending upon context, the repetition of what appears to be defamatory might be done in such a way as to not cause the reader to think less of the subject. In this case, there is no defamation. This might be the reason for the judgment in *Silva v. Toronto Star Newspapers Ltd.* (1998), 167 D.L.R. (4th) 554 (Ont. Gen. Div.), affirmed (2002), 215 D.L.R. (4th) 77 (Ont. C.A.), which exonerated a newspaper from defamation when it published allegations about the plaintiff that were, at least in so far as their original publisher was concerned, defamatory. The Court of Appeal, in a brief judgment affirming the decision, noted that s. 3(2) of the Libel and Slander Act, R.S.O. 1990, c. L.12, might have been applicable. The Court of Appeal referred to the House of Lords decision in *McCarton Turkington Breen v. Times Newspapers Ltd.* (2000), [2001] 2 A.C. 277 (U.K. H.L.). See discussion below.

116 See, e.g., *Caldwell v. McBride* (1988), 45 C.C.L.T. 150 (B.C. S.C.) — honest belief is irrelevant; and *Peterkin v. Union of Northern Workers* (2006), 40 C.C.L.T. (3d) 319 (N.W.T. S.C.), additional reasons at (2006), 2006 CarswellNWT 78 (S.C.).

and natural meaning of the material, as understood by reasonable persons.[117] It is this which is tested by the defences. It has been stated that "it is not necessary for the defendant to prove the truth of every detail of the words used, but only the sting of the charge."[118] In this respect, "regard must be had not only to the words complained of but also to the context in which the words were used and to all of the relevant circumstances."[119] As well, not every detail of the material need be true, as long as "the whole of the defamatory material is substantially true."[120]

A plea of justification will aggravate damages if the defence is unsuccessful.[121] It is considered as a republication of the original defamation. This approach is inconsistent with the absolute privilege given to defamatory statements in judical proceedings, and is undesirable. Defendants should not be discouraged from attempting to establish the truth of their assertions by being required to assume the risk of higher damage awards should the defence be rejected.[122]

(b) Absolute Privilege

Certain types of communications are protected by an absolute privilege. This means that no defamation action can be successfully brought in these cases, notwithstanding that the material communicated met all the requirements of the plaintiff's *prima facie* case, was false, and may even have been published maliciously. In these cases, freedom of speech prevails entirely over the protection of reputation. Although the contexts to which absolute privilege applies are different, the policy underlying its application is consistent. The common law has taken the

---

117 See, e.g., *DeMoor v. Harvey* (1989), 24 C.C.E.L. 293 (B.C. S.C.).

118 *Baxter v. CBC* (1979), 28 N.B.R. (2d) 114 at 151 (Q.B.), affirmed (1980), 30 N.B.R. (2d) 102 (C.A.).

119 *Ibid.*

120 See Brown above, note 2, at 10-29, and the numerous authorities cited therein. Also note statutory provisions which provide that where there are two or more distinct charges against the plaintiff, "a defence of justification shall not fail by reason only that the truth of every charge is not proved if the words not proved to be true do not materially injure the plaintiff's reputation having regard to the truth of the remaining charges": Libel and Slander Act, R.S.O. 1990, c. L.12, s. 22. See also the Defamation Act, R.S.N.S. 1989, c. 122, s. 9. For a recent case affirming this see *Sidorsky v. CFCN Communications Ltd.* (1994), 158 A.R. 161 at 207 (Q.B.): "It is not necessary to prove the truth of each word. It is sufficient if the substance of the allegations is justified"; varied (1997), [1998] 2 W.W.R. 89 (Alta. C.A.), reconsideration refused (1998), 216 A.R. 151 (C.A.), additional reasons at (1999), 232 A.R. 189 (C.A.).

121 See, e.g., *Knott v. Telegram Printing Co.*, [1917] 1 W.W.R. 974 (Man. C.A.), affirmed [1917] 3 W.W.R. 335 (S.C.C.). Also see *Hill v. Church of Scientology of Toronto* (1995), 126 D.L.R. (4th) 129 (S.C.C.).

122 Another important issue raised in recent case law deals with the matter of pleadings and the meaning to be given to the alleged defamatory material. In *Pizza Pizza Ltd. v. Toronto Star Newspapers Ltd.* (1998), 42 O.R. (3d) 36 (Div. Ct.), affirmed (2000), 49 O.R. (3d) 254 (C.A.), the court held that the defendant's pleadings were not restricted to justifying the truth of the material as determined by the plaintiff, but that the defendant could plead an alternate meaning and seek to justify that meaning. On this matter also see *Asper v. Lantos* (February 28, 2000), Doc. 99-CV-162816 (Ont. S.C.J.) 2000 CarswellOnt 505, reversed (2000), 2000 CarswellOnt 3509, [2000] O.J. No. 3712, 51 O.R. (3d) 215, 138 O.A.C. 378, 3 C.P.C. (5th) 330 (Ont. Div. Ct.) 2000 CarswellOnt 3509, [2000] O.J. No. 3712; and *Clement v. McGuinty* (2000), [2000] O.J. No. 2466, 2000 CarswellOnt 2252 (S.C.J.), additional reasons at (2000), 2000 CarswellOnt 2617 (S.C.J.), reversed (2001), [2001] O.J. No. 1400, 2001 CarswellOnt 1275 (C.A.). As noted above, pleadings are extremely important in defamation actions.

view that certain types of communications are so vital that they must not be fettered by even the threat of a legal action for defamation. Speakers must be free to say what they wish, and for whatever reason they wish, without fear of legal action.

An absolute privilege applies to defamatory material published in the following contexts. It extends "to the acts of high executive officers in the performance of their official duties."[123] This defence was considered in Canada in *Dowson v. R.*[124] The case concerned allegedly defamatory material concerning the plaintiff published to the Assistant Deputy Attorney General of Ontario by a chief superintendent of the R.C.M.P. The publication concerned an investigation by the R.C.M.P. into allegedly subversive political activities. Le Dain J., in applying *Chatterton v. Secretary of State for India*,[125] noted that three conditions were necessary for this category of absolute privilege: (1) the statement must have been made by one officer of state to another officer of state, (2) it must have related to state matters, and (3) it must have been made by an officer of state in the course of his official duty. After reviewing the authorities, and while conceding that it was arguable whether a chief superintendent of the R.C.M.P. was a sufficiently high official to qualify for an absolute privilege, Le Dain J. held that the chief superintendent made the statement as an agent of the Federal Solicitor General, and could therefore benefit from the absolute privilege which would undoubtedly apply to the latter. Similarly, the Acting Assistant Deputy Attorney General of Ontario was considered to have been the agent of the Attorney General, who was clearly an officer of the state.[126] Whether the statements were made for some illegitimate purpose was held not to have been relevant. The statement was absolutely privileged, being made in the course of official duties.

An absolute privilege also applies to statements made during parliamentary proceedings. In *Stopforth v. Goyer*,[127] Lieff J. stated that "the proceedings of a legislative body are absolutely privileged and words spoken in the course of a proceeding in Parliament can neither form the basis of nor support either a civil action or a criminal prosecution."[128] As Lieff J. noted, this privilege has been extended to apply to proceedings which are an extension of the Parliamentary proceedings, carried on outside the House, although the scope of this extension is unsettled.[129] Lieff J. refused, however, to extend the absolute privilege to statements made by a parliamentarian outside the House in response to journalists' questions, even though the statements made were substantially the same as those which had previously been read to the House.[130] The privilege applies not only to statements made in the House, but to a committee of the House.[131]

---

123 Brown, above, note 2, at 12-3.

124 (1981), 124 D.L.R. (3d) 260 (Fed. C.A.).

125 [1895] 2 Q.B. 189 (C.A.).

126 Le Dain J. also held that the other two conditions were satisfied.

127 (1978), 4 C.C.L.T. 265 (Ont. H.C.), reversed (1979), 8 C.C.L.T. 172 (Ont. C.A.).

128 4 C.C.L.T. 265 at 274.

129 Lieff J. cites *Roman Corp. v. Hudson's Bay Oil & Gas Co.*, [1973] S.C.R. 820, although, as noted by Lieff J., this was not a defamation case.

130 The trial judgment was reversed on the issue of qualified privilege, which the Court of Appeal held was applicable to this case.

131 See Brown, above, note 2, at 12-22.

An absolute privilege applies to all statements made within the context of judicial proceedings.[132] It has been held that the privilege applies to three categories of proceedings: (1) to all matters done *coram judiciam*, (2) to everything said during the actual proceeding including documents put in as evidence, and (3) to the precognition or proof of evidence, which was given in court, taken by a solicitor.[133] The absolute privilege applies to statements made by all participants to the proceedings, including the judge, jury, witnesses, parties, and counsel.[134] Judicial proceedings include not only the trial itself, but pre-trial proceedings, preliminary motions, and so forth.[135] It has also been stated that the privilege probably applies to all communications between lawyers and their clients, whether made with respect to impending or contemplated litigation.[136]

The degree to which communications, whether made by a lawyer or other interested party, must be connected to impending or contemplated litigation, in order to attract an absolute privilege, was considered by Cullity J. in *Moseley-Williams v. Hansler Industries Ltd.*[137] After an extensive review of the authorities, Cullity J. decided that merely because the maker of the statement is contemplating "the possibility of litigation and threatens that proceedings may be commenced" does not mean that an absolute privilege applies. The occasion must be one which is "'incidental' or 'preparatory' to judicial proceedings"; it must not be "too remote".[138] On the facts of this case, Cullity J. decided that a letter sent by the defendant's solicitor, on the instructions of his client, to the plaintiff and several other parties alleging improper conduct by the plaintiff, was not protected by an absolute privilege. Although the letter was sent to assert the rights of the defendant,

---

132 It has been held that this absolute privilege applies to all causes of action based upon statements in a pleading, statements made in court, evidence of witnesses, and submissions. That is, it not only applies to defamation actions, but to actions such as intentional infliction of mental suffering, intentional interference with economic interest, or abuse of process. See *Dooley v. C.N. Weber Ltd.* (1994), 19 O.R. (3d) 779 (Gen. Div.). Whether the privilege applies to "all" statements, even irrelevant ones, is an interesting question. See discussion below.

133 See *Lincoln v. Daniels*, [1962] 1 Q.B. 237 (C.A.), cited in *Dingwall v. Lax* (1988), 47 D.L.R. (4th) 604 (Ont. H.C.).

134 See Brown, above, note 2, at 12-71. See Lopes L.J. in *Royal Aquarium v. Parkinson*, [1892] 1 Q.B. 431 at 451 (C.A.). The absolute privilege protects both duty counsel and the counsel of record. See *Barber v. Baird* (1993), 144 A.R. 7 (Master). The absolute privilege applies to information provided to a lawyer in connection with the proceedings by a potential witness; see *Web Offset Publications Ltd. v. Vickery* (1999), 43 O.R. (3d) 802 (C.A.), leave to appeal refused (2000), 43 O.R. (3d) 802 (note) (S.C.C.). The witness immunity rule was recently applied in *Howatt v. Klassen* (2005), 31 C.C.L.T. (3d) 54 (Ont. S.C.J.).

135 This does not extend, however, so far as to include cries of "rape" and accusations made on the scene of the alleged crime before the police arrived: see *Can. v. Lukasik* (1985), 18 D.L.R. (4th) 245 (Alta. Q.B.).

136 See Brown, above, note 2, at 12-95, n. 446, citing *More v. Weaver*, [1928] 2 K.B. 520 (C.A.). Fleming notes the uncertainty but expresses preference for the view that a qualified privilege is sufficient to protect the solicitor/client relationship, where the matter does not relate to actual or intended litigation. See Fleming, *The Law of Torts*, 9th ed. (1998), at 619.

137 (2004), 32 C.C.L.T. (3d) 266 (Ont. S.C.J.), affirmed (2005), 2005 CarswellOnt 991 (Ont. C.A.). The matter came before Cullity J. on the defendant's motion for summary judgment, which Cullity J. denied. The Court of Appeal made it clear that Cullity J.'s judgment was restricted to the motion and was interlocutory. This therefore did not resolve the issue for trial.

138 32 C.C.L.T. (3d) 282.

it "was not necessary or properly incidental to the institution of a judicial proceeding."[139]

An absolute privilege has been applied to a written report prepared by a doctor with respect to litigation in which he was to act as a witness,[140] to a draft statement of claim and accompanying letter sent by a lawyer representing one party to the lawyers acting for the adverse party,[141] as well as to statements made in a statement of claim and examination for discovery.[142] The privilege has also been held to extend to documents used in the course of proceedings before a legally recognized tribunal carrying out judicial or quasi-judicial functions, for example, a written complaint sent to the Complaints Committee of the Royal College of Dental Surgeons.[143] In a similar vein, a written complaint to the Chief of Police, who was given statutory functions with respect to such matters by the Police Act,[144] was

---

139 *Ibid.* Cullity J. also held that where the absolute privilege exists, it is not limited to solicitors, but applies to the clients on whose behalf the letter was sent, as well as unrepresented parties.

140 See *Fabian v. Margulies* (1985), 53 O.R. (2d) 380 (C.A.).

141 See *Dingwall v. Lax* (1988), 47 D.L.R. (4th) 604 (Ont. H.C.).

142 See *Razzell v. Edmonton Mint Ltd.*, [1981] 4 W.W.R. 5 (Alta. Q.B.). See also *Foran v. Richman* (1975), 64 D.L.R. (3d) 230 (Ont. C.A.), where an absolute privilege applied to a letter written by a doctor to the plaintiff's solicitor regarding the plaintiff's condition, in the context of impending litigation. Note, however, that in *Davies & Davies Ltd. v. Kott* (1979), 9 C.C.L.T. 249 (S.C.C.), the court applied a qualified and not an absolute privilege to a letter written by one party to a dispute concerning a mortgage, to the lawyer for the adverse party.

143 See *Sussman v. Eales* (1985), 33 C.C.L.T. 156 (Ont. H.C.), reversed in part (1986), 25 C.P.C. (2d) 7 (Ont. C.A.). *Dechant v. Stevens*, [2001] 5 W.W.R. 405 (Alta. C.A.), additional reasons at [2001] 5 W.W.R. 448 (Alta. C.A.), leave to appeal refused (2001), 283 N.R. 394 (note) (S.C.C.) dealt with complaints to the Law Society of Alberta and s. 112 of the Legal Professions Act, S.A. 1990, c. L-9.1. This provision protects the Society and others for acts done "in good faith". The issue arose as to whether this over-rides the absolute privilege available at common law. The majority of the Court of Appeal held that it did and that therefore the Chambers Judge was correct in allowing the action to proceed to trial. The majority held as well that, even apart from the statute, there were legitimate questions to resolve concerning the extent and applicability of the common law absolute privilege. In *Schut v. Magee*, 2003 CarswellBC 79, 14 C.C.L.T. (3d) 301 (B.C. S.C. [In Chambers]) affirmed (2003), 19 C.C.L.T. (3d) 233 (B.C. C.A.), it was held that a similar provision in the Medical Practitioners Act, R.S.B.C. 1996, c. 285, s. 70(2) dealing with complaints to the College of Physicians and Surgeons did not over-ride the common law absolute privilege. In *Hung v. Gardiner*, 2003 CarswellBC 1060, 2003 BCCA 257 (C.A.), the British Columbia Court of Appeal held that a report prepared by an investigator for the Professional Conduct Inquiry Committee of the Institute of Chartered Accountants of British Columbia, which was sent to the Law Society and to the Certified General Accountants Association for their information, was protected by an absolute privilege. This was so even though the professional bodies did not investigate or take any disciplinary action against the subject of the report. In *Richardson v. Vancouver (City)* (2006), 264 D.L.R. (4th) 669 (B.C. C.A.), leave to appeal refused (2006), 2006 CarswellBC 1602 (S.C.C.), a complaint sent to the Law Society was protected by an absolute privilege even though copies of the complaint were sent to other interested parties. Although the Court of Appeal considered the argument that this deprived the complaint of its confidential nature and hence the absolute privilege, it rejected it since the publication to others "was kept within such a narrow compass." In *Hamouth v. Smart Video Technologies Inc.* (2005), 253 D.L.R. (4th) 372 (B.C. C.A.), an absolute privilege was held to apply to correspondence sent by the defendant law firm in the course of representing their client in a regulatory, quasi-judicial proceeding; in this case an investigation by the securities exchange commission.

144 R.S.A. 1980, c. P-12 [see now R.S.A. 2000, c. P-17].

held to have been protected by an absolute privilege.[145] In *Stark v. Auerbach*,[146] an absolute privilege was held to extend to a decision of a board of review established pursuant to the Workers' Compensation Act.[147] The privilege applies to judicial or quasi-judicial bodies acting in a judicial as opposed to an administrative capacity. In determining this, one must have regard to the authority under which the tribunal acts, the nature of its inquiry, the nature of its procedures, and the legal consequences which attach to its conclusions.[148]

Whether the absolute privilege applies to all statements made in judicial or quasi-judicial proceedings, even those that are irrelevant to the proceedings, was considered by the Saskatchewan Court of Appeal in *Duke v. Puts*.[149] The defamatory material in issue was directed at the plaintiff, who was a pharmacist. It was contained in a letter of complaint which the defendant had sent to the College of Physicians and Surgeons accusing a doctor of unethical conduct. Vancise J.A. held that although statements made in judicial or quasi-judicial proceedings need not be relevant, in the sense that they contribute to the resolution of the matter, in order to be protected by an absolute privilege, "they must have some nexus or be connected to the proceedings."[150] Gratuitous or irrelevant statements which have no reference to the inquiry are not protected. The Court of Appeal found that portions of the complainant's statement fell into that category and hence were not privileged.[151]

---

145 See *Boyachyk v. Dukes* (1982), 136 D.L.R. (3d) 28 (Alta. Q.B.). See, however, cases cited in *Boyachyk*, which held that the procedures were not protected: *O'Connor v. Waldron*, [1935] 1 D.L.R. 260 (P.C.), and *Lincoln v. Daniels*, [1961] 3 All E.R. 740 (C.A.). In another case, *Kazas v. Peterson*, [1992] O.J. No. 1666 (Gen. Div.), an absolute privilege was held to apply to oral and written statements given to the police by a person complaining that the plaintiff had assaulted her.

146 (1979), 98 D.L.R. (3d) 583 (B.C. S.C.).

147 S.B.C. 1968, c. 59. The court applied *Perry v. Heatherington* (1971), 24 D.L.R. (3d) 127 (B.C. S.C.), which dealt with a Court of Revision.

148 See Lord Diplock in *Trapp v. Mackie*, [1979] 1 W.L.R. 377 at 379 (H.L.). Lord Diplock noted 10 factors which he considered relevant in deciding whether the tribunal was judicial in nature. For a case discussing this distinction and applying an absolute privilege to material relating to a complaint to the Canadian Human Rights Commission, see *Ayangma v. NAV Canada* (2001), 203 D.L.R. (4th) 717 (P.E.I. C.A.), leave to appeal refused (2001), 205 Nfld. & P.E.I.R. 180 (note) (S.C.C.), reconsideration refused (2002), 2002 CarswellPEI 96, 2002 CarswellPEI 97 (S.C.C.). The court considered an important recent House of Lords judgment on absolute privilege, *Taylor v. Director of the Serious Fraud Office*, [1998] 4 All E.R. 801 (C.A.).

149 [2004] 6 W.W.R. 208 (Sask. C.A.), affirming (2001), 204 Sask. R. 130 (Q.B.).

150 [2004] 6 W.W.R. 233.

151 In an odd case, *Big Pond Communications 2000 Inc. v. Kennedy* (2004), 22 C.C.L.T. (3d) 315 (Ont. S.C.J.), the alleged defamatory material was found in the "pathname" at the bottom of a statement of claim. A pathname is a series of words which tells a reader where to find a file which had been produced and stored electronically. Although the pathname was not part of the statement of claim, in the sense that it was relevant to its contents, the court held that it was still protected by absolute privilege. The judgment contained an interesting discussion of the history of the privilege. In another recent case, *Liboiron v. Majola* (2007), 46 C.C.L.T. (3d) 34 (Alta. C.A.), the defendant pled guilty to a speeding ticket by sending in the offence notice and the fine to the clerk of the Provincial Court. Accompanying this was a letter which was highly critical and defamatory of the officer who issued the ticket. This letter was held

The cases have distinguished between judicial proceedings in superior as opposed to inferior courts. It has been held that an absolute privilege extends to *all* statements made by a judge sitting in a superior court, even if that judge "abuses his judicial office, by using slanderous words maliciously and without reasonable and probable cause."[152] However, with respect to courts of inferior jurisdiction, it has been stated that the doctrine of *ultra vires* applies.[153] This means that if a judge in such a court or tribunal acts with respect to a matter which is not within the court's jurisdiction at all, as a matter of law, the protection of the absolute privilege is lost.[154]

Communications between spouses are absolutely privileged. This has been explained in different ways. It has been stated that the immunity applies on the basis that a statement made by one spouse to the other has not been published.[155] It has also been argued, however, that the absence of publication approach is a "threadbare fiction."[156] The immunity has been categorized as an instance of absolute privilege based on the policy of protecting the confidential relationship between spouses.

(c) Qualified Privilege

The defence of qualified privilege applies to protect defamatory material published on certain occasions. As explained by Cory J. in *Hill v. Church of Scientology of Toronto,*[157] and *Botiuk v. Toronto Free Press Publications,*[158] "qualified privilege attaches to the occasion upon which the communication is made, and not to the communication itself." As with absolute privilege, the defence applies notwithstanding that the plaintiff's *prima facie* case has been made out, and the material cannot be shown to have been true. Unlike an absolute privilege, however, the privilege on these occasions is qualified by the requirement that there has been no malice on the part of the publisher of the material. Once an occasion

---

not to be part of the judicial proceedings related to the speeding offence and hence not protected by an absolute privilege.

152 See *Anderson v. Gorrie*, [1895] 1 Q.B. 668 at 671, cited in *MacKenzie v. McArthur*, [1981] 4 W.W.R. 692 at 694 (B.C. S.C.). See, however, Brown, above, note 2, at 12-87, who states that the comments made by the judge must "have at least some connection with the case."

153 See *MacKenzie v. McArthur, ibid.*

154 See *MacKenzie v. Martin*, [1952] O.R. 849 (C.A.), affirmed [1954] S.C.R. 361. See, however, *Sirros v. Moore*, [1975] Q.B. 118 (C.A.), and discussion in Chapter 8, where this issue is more fully explored. In a similar vein, the issue as to whether a statement made in a quasi-judicial proceeding that had nothing to do with the proceeding should be protected by absolute privilege was raised in *M. (M.J.). v. M. (D.J.)* (2000), 187 D.L.R. (4th) 473 (Sask. C.A.). In a complaint made to the law society about her lawyer, the complainant alleged that her husband had sexually assaulted their son. This had nothing to do with the complaint. The chambers judge struck out the husband's defamation action against his wife, but the Court of Appeal reversed this decision. The court held that it was not plain and obvious that absolute privilege applied to this irrelevant statement.

155 See Brown, above, note 2, at 7-57, citing *Wennhak v. Morgan* (1888), 20 Q.B.D. 635; *Huth v. Huth*, [1915] 3 K.B. 32 (C.A.).

156 See Fleming, *The Law of Torts*, 9th ed. (1998), at 621.

157 (1995), 126 D.L.R. (4th) 129 at 170 (S.C.C.).

158 (1995), 126 D.L.R. (4th) 609 at 626 (S.C.C.).

of qualified privilege has been shown to have existed, the plaintiff has the onus to defeat the defence by proving malice.

The defence of qualified privilege is based on the policy of allowing freedom of speech to prevail over the protection of reputation due to the perceived importance of communication in certain circumstances. In general terms, the protection of a qualified privilege extends to publications "fairly made by a person in the discharge of some public or private duty, whether legal or moral, or in the conduct of his own affairs, in matters where his interest is concerned."[159] Unlike the case with absolute privilege, however, there are no fixed and well-defined occasions to which the defence of qualified privilege applies.[160] Whether or not the relationship between the parties and the conditions of the publication give rise to an occasion of qualified privilege is a question of law.

The fundamental basis of all occasions of qualified privilege is the notion that the publisher had an interest or duty to convey the material to a person who had a reciprocal interest or duty to receive it. One of the classic formulations was stated by Lord Atkinson in the leading case of *Adam v. Ward*:

> . . . a privileged occasion is, in reference to a qualified privilege, an occasion where the person who makes the communication has an interest or duty, legal, social, or moral, to make it to the person to whom it is made, and the person to whom it is so made has a corresponding interest or duty to receive it. This reciprocity is essential.[161]

It is generally agreed that the existence of a duty is based on an objective test. What is important is whether "people of ordinary intelligence and moral principles" would have considered there to have been a duty, not whether the defendant honestly believed that one existed.[162]

Occasions of qualified privilege can be classified into four general categories for purposes of analysis. It must be underscored, however, that these are merely rough groupings of the types of occasions in which there exist a legal, moral, or social duty to communicate information to those with an interest or duty in receiving it.[163]

---

159 Baron Parke in *Toogood v. Spyring* (1834), 149 E.R. 1044 at 1049-50.

160 See, e.g., the statement by Lindley L.J. in *Stuart v. Bell*, [1891] 2 Q.B. 341 at 346 (C.A.): ". . . it is obvious that no definite line can be drawn as to mark off with precision those occasions which are privileged, and separate them from those which are not."

161 [1917] A.C. 309 at 334 (H.L.).

162 See *Halls v. Mitchell*, [1928] S.C.R. 125. Brown, above, note 2, at 13-44 *et seq.*, notes that there were contrary judgments in earlier cases. The recent judgments, however, support the view that the defendant's belief does not create the duty, although it may go to the issue of malice. See, e.g., *Whitaker v. Huntington* (1980), 15 C.C.L.T. 19 at 25 (B.C. S.C.). In *Dinyer-Fraser v. Laurentian Bank of Canada* (2005), 28 C.C.L.T. (3d) 205 (B.C. S.C.), additional reasons at (2005), 2005 CarswellBC 2365 (S.C.), the court seems to favour the objective test. The problem in the case, however, was that the defamatory letter was sent to the wrong persons. That being the case, the court concluded that whatever the test was, the defendant had no belief that it had any interest in communicating with the recipients of the letter and did not hold an honest belief in the truth of the communication. Thus, it had no defence of qualified privilege.

163 In fact, frequently the decision as to where to categorize a case is somewhat arbitrary. Occasions of qualified privilege can frequently be rationalized on more than one basis. For example, in *McKinnon v. Dauphin (Rural Municipality)*, [1996] 3 W.W.R. 127 (Man. Q.B.),

(i) Protection of One's Own Interests

It has been held that "statements which are fairly made by a person in the conduct of his own affairs in matters where his own interest is concerned are *prima facie* privileged."[164] In *Pleau v. Simpsons-Sears Ltd.*,[165] for example, a department store was entitled to protect its economic interests in preventing forged cheques from being accepted, by posting a notice to its employees to detain any person attempting to pass off a cheque with the forged name.[166] In protecting its interests, an individual must only act with that purpose in mind. Thus, the communication must be made in such a way, and to such persons, which promote the protection of that interest.

Where the statements made in reply to an attack are either excessive, or not relevant to the criticism, the defence will not be applied. Thus, in *Bennett v. Stupich*,[167] the court rejected the defendant's arguments that attacks made against the Premier were made in order to defend the former's reputation. The court held that the reply did not seek to deny or refute the original attacks, but merely took the form of launching similar criticisms against the Premier and others. As well, in *Whitaker v. Huntington*,[168] the defendant was held to have stepped beyond "the legitimate bounds of refutation", and "entered upon the area of gratuitous insult and defamation" by his choice of words used to defend himself from a prior attack.[169] It has also been stated, however, that where a party is acting in order to defend his interests, the words "must not be weighed too delicately in considering the intent and motives of the writer."[170]

---

affirmed (1997), [1998] 1 W.W.R. 309 (Man. C.A.), a city councillor defamed a contractor while discussing the awarding of a contract in a meeting of council. This was stated to be protected by qualified privilege, although it was not pigeon-holed into a specific category. One could argue that it was a matter of protection of the public interest, one's own interest, or a common interest.

164 Spence J. in *Sun Life Assur. Co. v. Dalrymple* (1965), 50 D.L.R. (2d) 217 at 220 (S.C.C.), citing *Toogood v. Spyring* (1834), 1 C.M. & R. 181 at 193; *Halls v. Mitchell*, [1928] 2 D.L.R. 97 at 101-02. See also Buckmaster L.C. in *London Assn. for Protection of Trade v. Greenlands Ltd.*, [1916] 2 A.C. 15 at 22 (H.L.).

165 (1976), 2 C.C.L.T. 28 (Ont. C.A.).

166 See also *Netupsky v. Craig*, [1973] S.C.R. 55, affirming [1971] 1 O.R. 51 (C.A.), where supervising architects to a project were entitled to reply to attacks made upon their professional integrity and competence by the engineer to that project; *Wooding v. Little* (1982), 24 C.C.L.T. 37 (B.C. S.C.), where it was held that the chairman of the Workers' Compensation Board was entitled to defend his board and his position as chairman from attacks made upon it; *Davies & Davies Ltd. v. Kott* (1979), 9 C.C.L.T. 249 (S.C.C.), where a letter sent by one party in a dispute concerning a mortgage, to the lawyer for the adversarial party, was held to be protected by a qualified privilege; and *Hanly v. Pisces Productions Inc.*, [1981] 1 W.W.R. 369 (B.C. S.C.), where a motion picture producer and director's response to complaints concerning his decision not to hire the plaintiff was also protected.

167 (1981), 125 D.L.R. (3d) 743 (B.C. S.C.).

168 (1980), 15 C.C.L.T. 19 (B.C. S.C.).

169 *Ibid.*, at 30. See also *Douglas v. Tucker*, [1952] 1 D.L.R. 657 at 665 (S.C.C.), where Cartwright J. rejected the defence of qualified privilege on the basis that the defendant's reply "went beyond matters which were reasonably germane to the charge which had been brought against him."

170 McIntyre J. in *Davies & Davies Ltd. v. Kott* (1979), 9 C.C.L.T. 249 at 260 (S.C.C.).

(ii) Protection of Another's Interest

It has been stated that where a person "has, by his situation, to protect the interests of another, that which he writes under such circumstances is a privileged communication."[171] Any situation which imposes upon a person a legal or moral duty to protect the interests of another will qualify in this respect. Where there is a legal duty to protect another's interests by communicating information to a person who has a reciprocal duty in receiving the information, the case is not difficult. It is in defining social or moral duties that courts have had difficulties.

In one of the leading cases, *Watt v. Longsdon*,[172] the English Court of Appeal held that a friend of the plaintiff's wife did not have a moral or social duty to inform the wife of the plaintiff's alleged infidelity. Applying the test of the "reasonably right-minded person", Greer L.J. held that such a person would not have felt obliged to pass on these stories, especially without having first attempted to research their accuracy more carefully.[173] In another leading case, *Adam v. Ward*,[174] the House of Lords gave a qualified privilege to an Army Council which had the moral and legal duty[175] to inquire into allegations made concerning a general of the army, and to report accordingly. Because the charges made against the general had been made in the House of Commons, and hence published "to the world", it was held to have been appropriate that the refutation of these charges, which contained the defamatory material, could also be published as widely as possible. It must be stressed, however, that consistent with the basis of qualified privilege in general, there must be a reciprocity of interests. Thus those to whom the communication is made, if not the persons whose interests are actually being protected, must have some interest or duty in receiving that information.

Information given to a person with respect to the character, competence or credit-worthiness of the plaintiff can qualify for a privilege on the basis that there is a duty on the part of the publisher to protect the interests of the recipient of the information. Thus, in *Gillett v. Nissen Volkswagen Ltd.*,[176] the plaintiff's previous employer was said to have been "exercising a social or moral duty in providing information to a person who was seeking that information for a prospective employer. . . ."[177] The transmission of character and credit references was stated to be "for the common convenience and welfare of society."[178] It has also been held, on the other hand, that mercantile agencies which are in the business of

171 Baron Parke in *Cockayne v. Hodgkisson* (1833), 5 C. & P. 543 at 548, cited by Scrutton L.J. in *Watt v. Longsdon*, [1930] 1 K.B. 130 at 143 (C.A.).

172 *Ibid.*

173 This might have been more appropriately an issue of malice, if the qualified privilege was first deemed to have existed.

174 [1917] A.C. 309 (H.L.).

175 According to Lord Dunedin, there was a legal duty under military law.

176 [1975] 3 W.W.R. 520 (Alta. T.D.).

177 *Ibid.*, at 528. Also see *Phutela v. University of Alberta* (1996), [1996] A.J. No. 1052, 1996 CarswellAlta 933 (C.A.).

178 Another type of case which might be said to fit into this category are statements made to parents about the activities or conduct of their children. See, for example, *Chrispen v. Novak*, [1995] 5 W.W.R. 752 (Sask. Q.B.), where statements made by a police officer to a mother concerning allegations of criminal activities by her son were protected by a qualified privilege.

collecting credit information and supplying this information to their customers do not do so under the protection of a qualified privilege.[179] Thus, although the information given to the commercial agency by a previous employer was protected by a qualified privilege, the transmission of this information by the agency to its customer, a prospective employer, was not.

(iii) Protection of Common Interests

It has been stated that "a communication is protected by a qualified privilege if it is made in furtherance of a common or mutual interest shared by the publisher and recipient of the communication."[180] As with all occasions of qualified privilege, there must be a reciprocity of interests between the parties. As well, the interest or duty to communicate can be a legal, moral, or social one. The following cases illustrate this type of occasion. In *Leverman v. Campbell Sharp Ltd.*,[181] the publication of a bankruptcy notice by a trustee in bankruptcy to creditors of the alleged bankrupt, made pursuant to a statutory duty, was an occasion of qualified privilege. In *Camporese v. Parton*,[182] the publishers of a consumer column and the readers of this column were said to have "a legitimate common interest" in the adequacy of a product which had previously been recommended by the publishers.[183] In *Moores v. Salter*,[184] a letter of reprimand concerning the behaviour of the employees being supervised by the defendant which was circulated internally to the employees and to their supervisors was held to have been published on an occasion of qualified privilege. In *Hanly v. Pisces Productions Inc.*,[185] a letter sent by a movie producer to the plaintiff's union outlining his reasons for not having hired the plaintiff was given the protection of a qualified privilege. In *McLoughlin v. Kutasy*,[186] a report by the project physician, in the course of his duties, to a government department concerning the plaintiff's suitability for prospective employment was held to have the protection of a qualified privilege.[187]

---

179 *Macintosh v. Dun*, [1908] A.C. 390 (P.C.), applied in *Gillett v. Nissen Volkswagen*, above, note 176. See also, however, *London Assn. for Protection of Trade v. Greenlands Ltd.*, [1916] 2 A.C. 15 (H.L.), which allowed a qualified privilege for credit reports produced within the context of a mutual trade protective society.

180 Brown, above, note 2, at 13-187. Brown cites *Booth v. Passmore* (1924), 27 O.W.N. 113 (H.C.).

181 (1987), 40 C.C.L.T. 73 (B.C. C.A.).

182 (1983), 150 D.L.R. (3d) 208 (B.C. S.C.).

183 *Ibid.*, at 225.

184 (1982), 37 Nfld. & P.E.I.R. 128 (Nfld. Dist. Ct.).

185 [1981] 1 W.W.R. 369 (B.C. S.C.).

186 (1980), 97 D.L.R. (3d) 620 (S.C.C.).

187 A similar type of case is *Muller v. Canada* (1991), 48 F.T.R. 215 (T.D.). The R.C.M.P. were held to be protected by a qualified privilege with respect to security information which they passed on to the army, or to government departments, concerning the plaintiff. The court stated that the R.C.M.P. had a legal duty to convey the information to parties who had a legal duty to receive it. It is an occasion of qualified privilege whether one sees it as protection of a common interest, or protection of the public interest. Another "common interest" case is *N. (R.) v. S. (S.L.)*, [1993] N.S.J. No. 99 (T.D.). Statements by a woman to her best friend stating that she had been sexually abused by her father, who was a clergyman, were protected by a qualified privilege. Also see *Cronk v. Cundall* (1993), 87 Man. R. (2d) 141 (Q.B.), where a

In *C. (L.G.) v. C. (V.M.)*,[188] statements made by children to their mother and therapist alleging that their father had sexually abused them were held to have the protection of a qualified privilege.

In *Teamsters, Local 987 v. U.F.C.W., Local 401*,[189] statements made by a union to its members were held to be protected by a qualified privilege. In *Hill v. Johnston*,[190] a notice sent out by one pharmacist to many other pharmacists alerting them to a person who the notice alleged was bringing in a forged prescription was held to be protected by a qualified privilege.[191] In *Porter v. Robinson Sheppard Shapiro*,[192] a summary of an important Supreme Court of Canada judgment[193] which the defendant law firm posted on its website for the advantage of its clients was held to be protected by a qualified privilege.[194]

(iv) Protection of the Public Interest

The broadest category of qualified privilege is that of "protection of the public interest."[195] This occasion of qualified privilege arises when the law considers that there was a duty or interest on a publisher to convey information to the public, which had a reciprocal duty or interest in receiving it.

Politicians have frequently claimed the benefit of this privilege, with varying degrees of success. In *Douglas v. Tucker*,[196] Cartwright J. rejected the defence of qualified privilege for statements made by the defendant, the Premier of the Province of Saskatchewan, with regard to the plaintiff, the leader of the opposition, during an election campaign. Without defining the extent of the qualified privilege which protected publications made by one elector to other electors concerning a candidate for office, the court found that the privilege was lost once the material

---

report commissioned by a city council to review the management and operation of city departments was held to be protected by a qualified privilege.

188 (1996), 33 C.C.L.T. (2d) 286 (B.C. S.C. [In Chambers]).

189 (2005), 258 D.L.R. (4th) 33 (C.A.), reversing (2003), [2004] 10 W.W.R. 574 (Alta. C.A.).

190 2006 ABQB 212 (Q.B.).

191 The prescription was in fact not a forgery. The judgment by Slatter J. contains a good discussion regarding the respective roles of judge and jury when the defence of qualified privilege and the existence of malice are in issue. The existence of a qualified privilege was upheld on these facts, presumably based on the protection of a common interest, although it was arguably also a matter of public interest. An interesting issue in the case was the fact that the notices were faxed to pharmacy fax machines, where persons other than pharmacists could read them. Did this defeat the privilege? The court held no; the fact that organizations have "clerks, secretaries, messengers, and other employees" who can see the information as part of their employment does not defeat the privilege.

192 (2004), [2004] O.J. No. 2809, 2004 CarswellOnt 2734 (S.C.J.), additional reasons at (2004), 2004 CarswellOnt 3570 (S.C.J.), reversed (2005), 2005 CarswellOnt 45 (C.A.).

193 Namely *Whiten v. Pilot Insurance Co.*, [2002] 1 S.C.R. 595.

194 The plaintiff in the defamation suit was one of the persons who worked for the defendant insurance company in the *Whiten* case. He alleged that the summary of the facts of *Whiten* published on the firm's website defamed him. The court held that the words were not defamatory and were protected by a qualified privilege in any event.

195 In a sense, protection of the public interest is the underlying premise of all qualified privilege occasions. It is the fact that it is considered to be in the public interest that persons be allowed to speak freely when the law considers that there is a duty to do so, which supports all occasions of qualified privilege.

196 [1952] 1 S.C.R. 275.

was published to the world at large, via a newspaper.[197] In a later decision, *Jones v. Bennett*,[198] Cartwright C.J.C. reaffirmed this position, this time in relation to statements made by the Premier of British Columbia. Cartwright C.J.C. rejected the defendant's argument that a qualified privilege applies "whenever the holder of high elective political office sees fit to give an account of his stewardship and of the actions of the government of which he is a member to supporters of the political party to which he belongs. . . ."[199]

Recently, courts have been more receptive to the defence of qualified privilege as it pertains to statements made by politicians. In *Stopforth v. Goyer*,[200] a qualified privilege was applied to statements made to the media by the Federal Minister of Supply and Services, Jessup J.A. stated:

> . . . the electorate, as represented by the media, has a real and bona fide interest in the demotion of a senior civil servant for an alleged dereliction of duty. It would want to know if the reasons given in the House were the real and only reasons for the demotion. The appellant had a corresponding public duty and interest in satisfying that interest of the electorate.[201]

This reasoning was applied in *Parlett v. Robinson*,[202] *Loos v. Robbins*,[203] *Milgaard v. Saskatchewan (Minister of Justice)*,[204] and *B.S.O.I.W., Local 97 v. Campbell*,[205] which also involved statements by a members of legislatures and Cabinet Ministers published to the public at large through the media.[206] The public interest rationale has been extended to non-politicians as well. In *Campbell v. Jones*,[207] a qualified privilege was extended to a press conference called by lawyers to condemn the treatment of their clients by the police. Young female students had been strip-searched at school in order to determine whether they were responsible for a theft of a small amount of money. The lawyers alleged that the motivation

---

197 The defendant knew that a reporter was present during the election meeting, and knew that a report of the meeting would be published.

198 [1969] S.C.R. 277.

199 *Ibid.*, at 284. The fact that the defendant knew that his statements would be reported to the public at large through the media would, at any event, have been fatal to any privilege which might otherwise have existed.

200 (1979), 8 C.C.L.T. 172 (Ont. C.A.).

201 *Ibid.*, at 178.

202 [1986] 5 W.W.R. 586 (B.C. C.A.).

203 [1987] 4 W.W.R. 469 (Sask. C.A.).

204 [1997] 3 W.W.R. 82 (Sask. Q.B.).

205 (1997), 152 D.L.R. (4th) 547 (B.C. S.C.).

206 See, however, *Russell v. Pawley*, [1987] 3 W.W.R. 442 (Man. C.A.), where the Premier of Manitoba was successfully sued for defamation based on his public remarks. The defence of qualified privilege, however, was not argued, the defendant relying on the defence of fair comment. As well, in *Bennett v. Stupich* (1981), 125 D.L.R. (3d) 743 (B.C. S.C.), and *Whitaker v. Huntington* (1980), 15 C.C.L.T. 19 (B.C. S.C.), the defence of qualified privilege failed, on the reasoning of *Jones v. Bennett*, above, note 198. A B.C. case that followed *Parlett v. Robinson* is *Baumann v. Turner* (1993), 105 D.L.R. (4th) 37 (B.C. C.A.). The case concerned correspondence between the district mayor and a government Minister that was published in the newspaper. The Court of Appeal, with one dissent, upheld the defence of qualified privilege. One must also keep in mind that in these cases the privilege was the politician's, not the media's. In *Puddister v. Wells*, 2007 NLCA 25 (C.A.), the Court of Appeal recognized the existence of a qualified privilege with respect to statements made by politicians to the public at large through the media, without deciding whether it applied on the facts of the case. The court concluded that even if it did apply, it was defeated by malice.

207 (2001), [2001] N.S.J. No. 595, 2001 CarswellNS 534 (S.C.).

of the police underlying this strip search was racist. The majority of the Court of Appeal held that the fact that the allegations were made to the public at large was not fatal to a claim of qualified privilege. The Court recognized the specific responsibilities of lawyers to improve the administration of justice and their "special relationship with and responsibility to the public to speak out when those involved in enforcing our laws violate the fundamental rights of citizens". Finally the Court was highly influenced by the Charter values and rights that were implicated by the facts of this case.[208]

A major area of contention with respect to the defence of qualified privilege in Canadian defamation law has involved the role of the media, and particularly newspapers, in communicating information to the public.[209] The Supreme Court of Canada, in *Globe & Mail Ltd. v. Boland*,[210] held that a newspaper has the same *right* as any other person to report truthfully and comment fairly upon matters of public interest, but has no special *duty* to do so. Cartwright J. held that it would not be in the best interests of society to grant a qualified privilege to the press,[211] and rejected this defence. In a second Supreme Court of Canada judgment several months later, *Banks v. Globe & Mail Ltd.*,[212] Cartwright J. restated this position, which has since then consistently been maintained.[213]

An apparently contrary decision is *Silva v. Toronto Star Newspapers*.[214] A newspaper that wrote a story about tenants' complaints was relieved of liability because of a qualified privilege. It was held to have had a "social and moral

---

208 There was one dissent. The dissent agreed with the trial judgment that publishing to the world at large in the circumstances of this case was not protected. The timing of the press conference was premature, as the complaint process respecting the police's conduct had only just commenced. The dissenting judgment is lengthy and deals with several other issues.

209 It is on this issue that one often compares the U.S. law on defamation of public figures and the Canadian approach. The case of *New York Times Co. v. Sullivan*, 376 U.S. 254 (U.S. Ala., 1964) disallowed public officials from suing for defamation unless they could establish malice. This has been resisted by Canadian courts. For commentary on the two positions see C. Tingley, "Reputation, Freedom of Expression and the Tort of Defamation in the US and Canada: A Deceptive Polarity" (1999), 37 Alta. L. Rev. 620.

210 [1960] S.C.R. 203.

211 The issue involved a defamatory editorial written by the defendant newspaper concerning the plaintiff, who was a candidate for federal office.

212 [1961] S.C.R. 474.

213 In *Moises v. Canadian Newspaper Co.* (1993), 1993 CarswellBC 1768 (S.C.), varied (1996), 30 C.C.L.T. (2d) 145 (B.C. C.A.), leave to appeal refused (1997), 86 B.C.A.C. 240 (note) (S.C.C.), the trial court granted the defence of qualified privilege to a newspaper. The issue was on a matter of public interest, and had been discussed by the media on previous occasions. It concerned an alleged terrorist who had immigrated to Canada. The court held that there was "a common interest between the defendant and its readers in respect of the administration of the Immigration Department. . ." which gave rise to the qualified privilege. The court also held that the defendant newspaper had a "duty and an interest in the subject matter and a corresponding public interest in matters involving immigration". The Court of Appeal reversed the decision, at (1996), 30 C.C.L.T. (2d) 145 (B.C. C.A.). Williams J.A. reaffirmed the traditional position that newspapers do not have a qualified privilege based on a "duty" to report to the public. The balance between freedom of expression and the right to reputation struck by Canadian defamation law was stated to be the correct one. See discussion below, however, on the "Reynolds privilege".

214 (1998), 167 D.L.R. (4th) 554 (Ont. Gen. Div.), affirmed on other grounds (2002), 215 D.L.R. (4th) 77 (Ont. C.A.).

purpose" in writing the article. Although it is difficult to reconcile this decision with the traditional view of the newspaper's role expressed above, one might argue that in certain cases, where there is an interest of pressing public concern, and where the defendant newspaper is in a unique position to protect the public, it has a social or moral duty to do so. One would say that in this type of case, the newspaper is not being given any special privilege, because everyone has a qualified privilege to protect the interests of others in certain situations.[215]

This approach, of not creating a special privilege for the media, but recognizing that depending upon the circumstances there might to be a privilege based on a social or moral duty to convey information to the public, was adopted by the House of Lords in *Reynolds v. Times Newspapers Ltd.*[216] The case involved a defamation action brought by the Taoiseach (Prime Minister) of Ireland against a newspaper. The suit claimed that the newspaper had defamed the plaintiff by reporting that he had deliberately and dishonestly misled political colleagues and the Dail (House of Representatives). The question for the House of Lords was whether this type of political discussion should be protected by a qualified privilege.

All of the Lords agreed that there should not be a new category of qualified privilege for political discussion. Rather the Lords held that the ordinary test for qualified privilege, that is, whether the publisher of the statement had a duty to publish the material to recipients who had an interest in receiving it, adequately dealt with the matter of political discussion. Although it was agreed that the specific "circumstantial test" as articulated by the Court of Appeal should not be added to the analysis as a third requirement of qualified privilege, the Lords did acknowledge that the circumstances of each case are critical to determining whether a qualified privilege should be recognized or not.[217] Lord Nicholls, for example, stated that the courts could consider the following circumstances on a case-by-case basis to determine whether a qualified privilege should be recognized: (1) the seriousness of the allegation; (2) the nature of the information; (3) the source of the information; (4) steps taken to verify the information; (5) status of the information; (6) urgency; (7) whether comment was sought from plaintiff; (8) content—was plaintiff's side adequately presented?; (9) tone of article; and (10) circumstances, including timing. The Lords agreed that the circumstances were important to the duty-interest analysis but thought that calling this

---

215 Note that while the Court of Appeal affirmed the trial judgment it did not do so based upon the recognition of a qualified privilege. In fact, the Court of Appeal made a point of stating that it was not necessary to deal with qualified privilege and added that "we should not, however, be taken as agreeing with [the trial judge's findings]."

216 [1999] 3 W.L.R. 1010 (U.K. H.L.).

217 The Court of Appeal had decided that there was no generic qualified privilege but that depending upon the circumstances of the publication there could be one. The circumstances included not only the normal duty and interest requirements, but also the "nature, status and source of the material, and the circumstances of the publication". See [1998] 3 W.L.R. 862 (Eng. C.A.) at 899-900, quoted by Lord Steyn in the House of Lords' judgment at [1999] 3 W.L.R. 1010 (U.K. H.L.) at 1033.

a new test was confusing and unnecessary. A qualified privilege was not granted in this case.[218]

In a subsequent judgment, *Jameel v. Wall Street Journal Europe SPRL (No.3)*,[219] the House of Lords further elaborated on the so-called "*Reynolds* privilege". While there was some disagreement as to whether the *Reynolds* defence should be characterized as an instance of qualified privilege, in the traditional duty/interest sense, or as a "different jurisprudential creature", there was agreement as to the nature and requirements of this defence.[220] The publication must be of something which is in the public interest.[221] The impugned material must be looked at as a whole; not every statement must be put under scrutiny. It is not limited to newspapers, but is "available to anyone who publishes materials of

---

218 This approach was applied by Lysyk J. in *Grassi v. WIC Radio Ltd.*, [2000] 5 W.W.R. 119 (B.C. S.C.), reversed on the matter of costs (2001), 6 C.C.L.T. (3d) 118 (B.C. C.A.). It was also discussed with approval in *Myers v. Canadian Broadcasting Corp.* (1999), 47 C.C.L.T. (2d) 272 (Ont. S.C.J.), and *Leenen v. Canadian Broadcasting Corp.* (2000), 50 C.C.L.T. (2d) 213 (Ont. S.C.J.), additional reasons at (2000), 2000 CarswellOnt 3327 (S.C.J.), affirmed (2001), 6 C.C.L.T. (3d) 97 (Ont. C.A.), leave to appeal refused (2002), 164 O.A.C. 200 (note) (S.C.C.), although not applied to the facts of those cases. The House of Lords' rejection of a special qualified privilege for political discussion was followed in *Goddard v. Day* (2000), [2001] 5 W.W.R. 651 (Alta. Q.B.). In contrast, the Australian High Court in *Lange v. Australian Broadcasting Corp.* (1997), 189 C.C.L.R. 520 (Australia H.C.) has accepted a qualified privilege for discussion on political matters, subject to the publisher proving reasonableness of conduct. The New Zealand Court of Appeal also has looked at this question; see *Lange v. Atkinson*, [2000] 3 N.Z.L.R. 385 (New Zealand C.A.), and has adopted its own approach to the defence of qualified privilege for political discussion. There has been extensive commentary on these decisions. See "A Symposium on Defamation and Political Expression" [2000] N.Z.L. Rev. 385, which contains five commentaries on the New Zealand decision; Atkins, Evans, McLay and Petersson, *Torts in New Zealand: Cases and Materials*, 3rd ed. (2002) at 636-653; J.F. Burrows, "Defamation and Politicians" (1999), 7 Tort L. Rev. 8; M. Chesterman, "The Common Law Rules in Defamation—OK?" (1998), 6 Tort L. Rev. 9; D. Crerar, "Recent Developments in the Defamation Defence of Qualified Privilege" (2001), 59 The Advocate 683; M. Tilbury, "Uniformity, the Constitution and Australian Defamation Law at the Turn of the Century" in Mullany and Linden, eds., *Torts Tomorrow: A Tribute to John Fleming* (1998), Chapter 13; among others.

219 [2006] UKHL 44 (H.L.).

220 Lord Bingham stated that the *Reynolds* decision "built on the traditional foundations of qualified privilege but carried the law forward in a way which gave much greater weight than earlier law had done to the value of informed public debate of significant issues", at para. 28. Lord Hoffman preferred to characterize it as not a "privilege" in the "old sense". This is because it is "the material which is privileged, not the occasion on which it is published", at para. 46. Malice does not defeat it, "because the propriety of the conduct of the defendant is built into the conditions under which the material is privileged", at para. 46. Lord Hoffman preferred to call it "the *Reynolds* public interest defence". Lord Hope characterized the defence as "a new category of privileged subject matter — a generic qualified privilege of political speech". Lord Scott saw the defence as a broadening of the traditional qualified privilege as it recognized that journalists may have a "professional duty" to publish material, not to specific individuals who have a reciprocal interest in receiving it, but to the world at large. Baroness Hale viewed the defence as "a different jurisprudential creature" from the law of privilege — a defence which can be termed as a "defence of publication in the particular interest", at para. 146.

221 As contrasted with something which may merely interest the public; such as titillating gossip.

public interest in any medium".[222] Most importantly, the test of liability is that of "responsible journalism". As explained by Lord Hoffman "the question in each case is whether the defendant behaved fairly and responsibly in gathering and publishing the information."[223] Thus, while unlike the traditional defence of qualified privilege, where once the qualified privilege is established it can be defeated upon the plaintiff proving malice, "the propriety of the conduct of the defendant is built into the conditions upon which the material is privileged. The burden is upon the defendant to prove that these conditions are satisfied."[224]

The Ontario Court of Appeal adopted the "public interest defence of responsible journalism" as part of Ontario law in *Cusson v. Quan*.[225] After a review of the English, Australian, New Zealand, South African and American case law, Sharpe J.A. held that although the defence of qualified privilege "in its traditional form" should not be extended "to all media reports on matters of public interest" the public interest defence of responsible journalism along the lines of *Reynolds* and *Jameel* should be adopted.[226] The court was concerned that a wide defence of qualified privilege to all media reports on matters of public interest would place too difficult a burden on plaintiffs who would have to prove malice to defeat the privilege. The lack of a defence, however, for the publishing of matters of public interest,[227] was seen to be inconsistent with Charter values and contemporary trends towards greater protection of freedom of expression. The new defence was seen, therefore, as occupying a sound middle ground between these two extreme positions. In general terms, the defence requires proof by the defendant both that the material be a matter of public interest and that the publisher acted in accordance with the standards of responsible journalism. It is not limited to political speech. It applies despite the falsity of the statements published as long as the "media defendant. . .took reasonable steps to ensure that the story was fair and its contents were true and accurate."[228] Important issues will have to be faced in the development of this defence. To which "media" defendants does it apply? What factors determine whether matters are of sufficient "public interest"? How are the standards of "responsible journalism" to be determined? If confirmed by the Supreme Court of Canada, the defence will represent a significant change in the common law tort of defamation, converting what has traditionally been seen as a no fault

---

222 Lord Hoffman, at para. 54.

223 *Ibid.*

224 *Ibid.*, at para 46. The defence was recognized by the Lords on the facts and the plaintiff's action was dismissed.

225 2007 ONCA 771 (C.A.), leave to appeal allowed (2008), 2008 CarswellOnt 1862 (S.C.C.). The case concerned a story in the *Ottawa Citizen* concerning the plaintiff police constable. The story was about the plaintiff's trip to New York, in order to participate in the "9/11" rescue efforts. Although the defence was adopted by the court, it was not applied in this case. According to Sharpe J.A., the defendants relied on qualified privilege. The trial judge rejected the defence. The Court of Appeal held that it would not be fair to allow the defence of responsible journalism to be raised on appeal, or to allow the defendants the opportunity to re-litigate the matter. The Supreme Court of Canada has granted leave to appeal; see (2008), [2008] S.C.C.A No. 11, 2008 CarswellOnt 1862 (S.C.C.).

226 *Ibid.*, at para. 137.

227 Other than the traditional ones of truth, fair comment, or other common law or statutory defences.

228 *Ibid.*, at para. 144.

tort into a tort requiring fault, at least in so far as the limited area covered by this new defence. It will also depart from long-standing Canadian authority that the media has no special duty to report on matters of public interest to the public at large.

There have been some protections given to the media, principally through statutory reform, but also by case law. Statutory protection is given in all Canadian common law jurisdictions to newspapers and broadcasters with respect to the fair and accurate reporting of judicial and legislative proceedings. Although the statutory privilege governing the reporting of judicial proceedings is, in most jurisdictions, absolute, the statutes clearly limit the conditions under which this privilege shall apply. The statutes generally require that the report of judicial proceedings be (1) fair and accurate,[229] (2) without comment,[230] and (3) published contemporaneously with the proceedings.[231] If requested, the defendant must publish or broadcast a reasonable statement of explanation or contradiction by or on behalf of the plaintiff. The privilege does not protect blasphemous, seditious or indecent matter.[232]

The statutes provide a qualified privilege for fair and accurate reports of legislative proceedings. As with the statutory protection for judicial proceedings, the statutes define the conditions under which this protection will operate. According to the Ontario statute,[233] for example, the report must (1) be fair and accurate, (2) be published without malice, (3) concern the proceedings of any legislative body or committee, (4) not contain blasphemous, seditious or indecent matter,

---

229 A case on this point is *Wenman v. Pacific Press Ltd.*, [1991] B.C.J. No. 186 (S.C.). The plaintiff, an M.P., testified as a witness in proceedings to set aside an injunction regarding anti-abortion protesters. The newspaper article reporting on his testimony stated that the plaintiff, in his testimony, condoned breaking the law. The court held that this was not a "fair and accurate" report of what he actually stated, and therefore that the article was not protected by the Libel and Slander Act, R.S.B.C. 1979, c. 234, s. 3. As well, an editorial concerning the matter was held to be defamatory and not protected by fair comment since it relied upon untrue facts. More recently, see *M.D. Mineralsearch Inc. v. East Kootenay Newspapers Ltd.* (2002), 209 D.L.R. (4th) 375 (B.C. C.A), additional reasons at (2002), 2002 CarswellBC 2085 (C.A.). The plaintiff had been convicted of a "deceptive act" although the provincial court judge had found that it's act was unintentional; the result of a clerical error. The judicial proceedings were reported but the report did not make it clear that the judge had found that despite it's guilt the plaintiff did not have a deceitful intention. The trial court found that the report was not fair, but this was reversed on appeal.

230 In *Ager v. Canjex Publishing Ltd.* (2005), 259 D.L.R. (4th) 727 (B.C. C.A.), varying as to damages (2003), 16 C.C.L.T. (3d) 188 (B.C. S.C.), the court held that a defamatory report of legal proceedings can be defended on the basis of both fair reporting and fair comment. That is, the defence of fair reporting would apply to the parts of the article that report the proceedings, and the defence of fair comment to the part that comments on them. Both defences failed in this case. The Court of Appeal held that the report of the proceedings was not fair and accurate and that the commentary was so intertwined with the reporting that the reader would not distinguish between the two. Also see *Young v. Toronto Star Newspapers Ltd.* (2005), 259 D.L.R. (4th) 127 (Ont. C.A.), where the defence failed under the Ontario Act since the report was not fair and accurate.

231 The provision only applies to hearings in open court; see *Taylor-Wright v. CHBC-TV* (1999), 1999 CarswellBC 344 (S.C.), affirmed 194 D.L.R. (4th) 621, [2000] 11 W.W.R. 250 (B.C. C.A.), additional reasons at (2001), 199 D.L.R. (4th) 292 (B.C. C.A.).

232 See, e.g., Libel and Slander Act, R.S.O. 1990, c. L.12, s. 3(5).

233 *Ibid.*, s. 3.

and (5) concern matters of public interest for the public benefit. The plaintiff must be permitted to provide a reasonable statement of explanation or contradiction. Statutory protections are also given to newspapers and broadcasters with respect to the fair and accurate reporting of public meetings, and other reports.[234]

At common law, publication without malice of a fair and accurate report of judicial proceedings before a properly constituted judicial tribunal exercising its jurisdiction in open court is protected.[235] This common law privilege applies as well to fair and accurate reports of parliamentary proceedings.[236] There is also a common law defence for fair and accurate reporting of public documents.[237] The common law defence of qualified privilege as it relates to a *report* of judicial proceedings was in issue in *Hill v. Church of Scientology of Toronto*.[238] One of the defendants in this defamation case was a lawyer, Manning, who had represented the other defendant, the Church of Scientology, in contempt proceedings which the Church had brought against a second lawyer, Hill, the plaintiff in this defamation suit. Prior to the actual filing of the notice of motion for the contempt application, the defendant lawyer Manning had held a press conference. During this conference, the defendant read aloud a passage from the notice of motion. Copies of the notice of motion also were distributed to the media. The material contained in the notice of motion was defamatory. The defendant lawyer Manning was sued for publishing this material by reading it out at the press conference.

The Supreme Court of Canada applied the defence of qualified privilege to the lawyer's decision to read the notice of motion out at the press conference. This was seen as a report of judicial proceedings.[239] In his judgment, Cory J. noted that

---

234 For a case involving a report of a city council meeting see *Cardwell v. Hutchinson* (1997), 36 C.C.L.T. (2d) 183 (B.C. C.A.). In *Silva v. Toronto Star Newspapers Ltd.*, above, note 214, the trial court held that a press conference organized by tenants to publicize their concerns about public housing did not qualify as a "meeting lawfully held for a lawful purpose and for the furtherance of discussion of any matter of public concern" under s. 3(2) of the Libel and Slander Act, R.S.O. 1990, c. L.12. It was thought that the composition of the meeting and the views represented there were not sufficiently broad. The Court of Appeal, referring to *McCarton Turkington Breen v. Times Newspapers Ltd.* (2000), [2001] A.C. 277 (U.K. H.L.) suggested that s. 3(2) might indeed have applied to this meeting, although it did not specifically decide this point.

235 See Lord Esher M.R. in *Kimber v. Press Assn. Ltd.*, [1893] 1 Q.B. 65 at 68 (C.A.), cited in *Wesolowski v. Armadale Publishers Ltd.* (1980), 112 D.L.R. (3d) 378 (Sask. Q.B.), and approved in *Gazette Printing Co. v. Shallow* (1909), 41 S.C.R. 339 at 347.

236 See *Cook v. Alexander*, [1974] Q.B. 279 (C.A.), and discussion by Brown, above, note 2, at 14-79 ff. Brown notes that the immunity was established in *Wason v. Walter* (1868), L.R. 4 Q.B. 73.

237 See, for example, *Fletcher-Gordon v. Southam Inc.*, [1997] 6 W.W.R. 155 (B.C. S.C.). The case concerned publication by the media of public documents obtained under the Freedom of Information and Privacy Act, S.B.C. 1992, c. 61. The judgment referred to the leading case of *Fleming v. Newton* (1848), 9 E.R. 797, 1 H.L.C. 363 (H.L.). As the judgment notes, this is not a defence restricted to the media but available to the general public, including the media. Also see Freedom of Information and Protection of Privacy Act, R.S.B.C. 1996, c. 165, s. 46, which grants a privilege to information or records produced during investigations or inquiries.

238 (1995), 126 D.L.R. (4th) 129 (S.C.C.).

239 The trial judge had refused to put the defence of qualified privilege to the jury. This was upheld by the Court of Appeal at (1994), 20 C.C.L.T. (2d) 129. The Court of Appeal noted that the law distinguished between publication of proceedings in open court and publication of statements in pleadings, the privilege attaching to the first occasion but not to the latter. The court was also concerned that the contempt proceedings had not actually been instituted

the purpose of the qualified privilege which protects reports of judicial proceedings is to safeguard the public's right to be informed about judicial proceedings to which the public has access, even if these proceedings deal with private litigation. This encompasses pleadings and court documents filed before trial. The privilege accordingly does not extend to reports on material which are not part of the proceedings. The fact that the notice of motion in the *Hill* case had not yet been filed in court before it was read out publicly did not, in the majority of the Supreme Court of Canada' opinion, prevent the operation of the qualified privilege. The documents were filed and served the next morning, and it was clear that it was the intention of the defendant to initiate the proceedings when he read from the document.[240] What did defeat the qualified privilege, however, was that the defendant had exceeded the privilege.[241]

What is important to highlight about the *Hill* case is that the notice of motion itself, from which the defendant lawyer read, was protected by an absolute privilege. However, the defendant's reporting, republishing, or even *verbatim* repeating of the contents of the notice were not. This was protected only by a qualified privilege. The rationale behind this is that the law's policy to allow those involved in judicial proceedings to publish whatever they wish absolutely, without fear of repercussion, in the course of the proceedings themselves, differs from the law's policy in relation to the reporting of such proceedings. In the latter case, the publisher can report,[242] but its right to do so is qualified by the defence of malice or excess of privilege.

The public interest rationale has been used to support the existence of a qualified privilege in other settings. For example, in *Upton v. Better Bus. Bureau of B.C. Mainland*,[243] the court held that it was in the public interest that a consumer's protection organization provide information to the public.[244] As well, lesser legislative bodies, such as municipal councils, which are not protected by an absolute privilege, can claim the benefit of qualified privilege.[245] In a similar vein, lower political officials, who cannot claim the benefit of an absolute privilege for internal communications, will benefit from a qualified privilege.[246] In attempting to catalogue instances of qualified privilege based on public interest grounds, it is always important to recall that there is no fixed list of occasions of qualified

---

in accordance with the Rules of Practice. As well, the notice of motion had not been filed. For all of these reasons, the Court of Appeal held that there was no qualified privilege.

240 L'Heureux-Dubé J. dissented on this matter. She agreed with the Court of Appeal that the qualified privilege does not apply to reports of pleadings in purely private litigation upon which no judicial action has yet been taken. In *Taylor-Wright v. CHBC-TV* (2000), 194 D.L.R. (4th) 621 (B.C. C.A.), additional reasons at (2001), 199 D.L.R. (4th) 292 (B.C. C.A.), the majority decision in *Hill* to extend the privilege to documents filed or intended to be filed but not yet referred to in open court was critically analysed by Esson J.A. Despite the criticism, the court held that since these documents were privileged, the fair and accurate reporting of them by the media was also privileged. The privilege was denied in this case, however, since the Court of Appeal held that the report was not fair.

241 See discussion below.

242 As long as the report is fair and accurate.

243 (1980), 114 D.L.R. (3d) 750 (B.C. S.C.).

244 The court went so far as to suggest that the defendant had a duty to provide this information because its objects mandated it to do so.

245 See *Ward v. McBride* (1911), 24 O.L.R. 555 (C.A.); and *Horrocks v. Lowe*, [1975] A.C. 135 (H.L.).

246 See, e.g., *Smith v. Matsqui (Dist.)* (1986), 4 B.C.L.R. (2d) 342 (S.C.).

privilege, the courts being free to apply the defence to any occasion which they consider appropriate.

(d) Exceeding the Privilege and Malice

The defence of qualified privilege will fail if (1) the defendant exceeded the purpose for which the qualified privilege was created, or (2) the defendant was malicious.[247]

The defendant will exceed the purpose of the qualified privilege and lose its protection either by using words which were not relevant to the occasion, or communicating the material to those who were not entitled to receive it. In *Pleau v. Simpsons-Sears*,[248] for example, the defendant department store was allowed to protect its economic interests by notifying its employees that cheques bearing the plaintiff's name were forged documents. The question in dispute, however, was whether the manner by which this information was passed on to the staff — the posting of notices at each cash register whereby they were visible to all customers — was excessive. Did the publication go "beyond the exigencies of the privileged occasion so as to constitute 'publicity incommensurate to the occasion'"?[249] The majority of the Ontario Court of Appeal, per Lacourcière J.A., held that whether the defendant exceeded the privilege was a matter of law for the judge alone.[250] On the facts of this case, the majority held that the issue of excess of privilege is a matter of degree and that in this case it had not been exceeded.[251]

---

247 The issue arises as to whether exceeding the privilege is separate from malice, or is evidence of malice. There appear to be several different approaches. The first approach distinguishes between two situations. Material may be relevant to the privileged occasion, but excessive, i.e., stronger than that which was required. This is evidence of malice. Or, information may not be relevant to the occasion, or be published to someone who was not entitled to receive it. This is excess of privilege. See Brown, above, note 2, at 13-354 to 13-355, n. 2199; Lord Esher in *Nevill v. Fine Arts & Gen. Ins. Co.*, [1895] 2 Q.B. 156, affirmed [1897] A.C. 68 (H.L.). Another view is to treat only "wholly irrelevant and improper" communication as exceeding the privilege and malicious, while "marginally" irrelevant material is to be used within the context only of malice. See Duncan and Neill, *Defamation* (1979), discussed by Brown, *ibid.* Yet a third approach is to treat the whole issue of irrelevant material as going to the question of malice. See *Horrocks v. Lowe*, [1957] A.C. 135 (H.L.), per Lord Diplock. Brown's view is that irrelevant material goes to excess of privilege, and that malice is a separate issue. In *Botiuk v. Toronto Free Press Publications Ltd.* (1995), 126 D.L.R. (4th) 609 at 627 (S.C.C.), Cory J. treated malice as being a situation of ill will, indirect motive, purposeful dishonesty, or reckless dishonesty, and excess of privilege as being material not "reasonably appropriate to the legitimate purposes of the occasion." Cory J. reiterated the points which he had made in *Hill v. Church of Scientology of Toronto* (1995), 126 D.L.R. (4th) 129. However, as shall be discussed below, the *Hill* judgment illustrates the confusion between "malice" and "exceeding the privilege."

248 (1976), 2 C.C.L.T. 28 (Ont. C.A.).

249 Lacourcière J.A., *ibid.*, at 35, quoting from Earl Loreburn in *Adam v. Ward*, [1917] A.C. 309 at 321 (H.L.).

250 Thus distinguishing the issue of excess privilege from the issue of malice.

251 Lacourcière J.A. cited *Tench v. Great Western Ry. Co.* (1873), 33 U.C.Q.B. 8 (C.A.). Brooke J.A. dissented, holding that the manner of posting the notice communicated the information to the public, which had no interest in this information. A recent excess of privilege case is *Ward v. Clark* (2000), 50 C.C.L.T. (2d) 288 (B.C. S.C.), reversed (2001), [2001] B.C.J. No. 2687, 2001 CarswellBC 2846 (C.A), leave to appeal refused (2002), 295 N.R. 199 (note)

A qualified privilege may be exceeded where defamatory material is published to the "world at large" through the press.[252] In these cases, both the original publisher and the newspaper will be held liable. However, where the publisher of defamatory material has a qualified privilege to publish the material to the public, publication in a newspaper will protect not only the person who is privileged, but the newspaper as well.[253]

The Supreme Court of Canada case, *Hill v. Church of Scientology of Toronto*,[254] dealt with excess of privilege. As noted above, the defendant lawyer's conduct in reading out the contents of a notice of motion for a contempt application to the press was declared to be an occasion protected by a qualified privilege. However, Cory J. held that the defendant had been unreasonable in publishing these contents without first having taken steps to confirm them, or to await the outcome of an investigation concerning them. The defendant's conduct was considered to have been "highhanded and careless", although not malicious. It was concluded that the defendant had exceeded the privilege. The characterization of the defendant's conduct, however, seemed to more aptly fit the notion of malice, rather than excess of privilege.

A qualified privilege will also be defeated by proof of the defendant's malice. Since material published on the occasion of a qualified privilege is presumed to have been published without malice, the onus of proving malice rests upon the plaintiff.[255] It is a question of law whether there is sufficient evidence of malice to go to the jury, and a question of fact whether the defendant was actuated by malice.[256]

(S.C.C.). The defendant Cabinet Minister made comments to the press about the plaintiff. The issue concerned the construction of ferries. The plaintiff had been a critic of the government's policies. The defendant called the plaintiff "a disgruntled bidder on this project who is constantly feeding misinformation on this issue". The trial court held that the words were defamatory, were protected by qualified privilege, there was no malice, but that the words were disproportionate and thus exceeded the privilege. The Court of Appeal reversed, holding that the statements were germane and reasonably appropriate to the occasion. That being the case, and there being no malice, the qualified privilege applied.

252 See *Douglas v. Tucker*, [1952] 1 S.C.R. 275; and *Jones v. Bennett*, [1969] S.C.R. 277.

253 See, e.g., *Loveday v. Sun Newspapers Ltd.* (1938), 59 C.L.R. 503 at 519 (Aust. H.C.), where Dixon J. stated: "A privilege would be of no value if the means of exercising it were also not protected."

254 (1995), 126 D.L.R. (4th) 129.

255 See *Moores v. Salter* (1982), 37 Nfld. & P.E.I.R. 128 (Nfld. Dist. Ct.); *Foran v. Richman* (1975), 64 D.L.R. (3d) 230 (Ont. C.A.); *Hanly v. Pisces Productions Inc.*, [1981] 1 W.W.R. 369 (B.C. S.C.); and numerous other supporting authorities cited by Brown, above, note 2, at 16-102, n. 596. In *Davies & Davies Ltd. v. Kott* (1979), 9 C.C.L.T. 249 at 256-57 (S.C.C.), McIntyre J. stated:

> . . . the privilege of which the defendant has the benefit creates a presumption against malice. In this context, the word "malice" is used to connote malice in fact, actual malice, or express malice which goes beyond the malice ordinarily presumed upon the mere publication of libellous words.

256 See *Sun Life Assur. Co. v. Dalrymple*, [1965] S.C.R. 302, cited with approval in *Davies & Davies Ltd. v. Kott*, *ibid.*, at 258. *Hill v. Johnston*, 2006 ABQB 212 (Q.B.), affirmed that the issue of malice should only be put to the jury if there was a "probable case" of malice. This does not mean, however, that the judge must be convinced that there is probably malice; only that the evidence is "finely balanced". That is, there must be more than "a mere scintilla of evidence". In *Teskey v. Toronto Transit Commission* (2003), [2003] O.J. No. 5315, 2003

There have been numerous explanations of what constitutes malice. For example, not having an honest belief in the material published will constitute conclusive proof of malice.[257] Abusing an occasion "by using it for an improper purpose, personal spite or ill will, or by excessive or irrelevant publication, or by a lack of belief in the truth of what was written"[258] is evidence of malice. Publishing material "recklessly, without considering or caring whether it be true or not"[259] is evidence of malice. Mere "carelessness, impulsiveness, or irrationality in arriving at a positive belief that it is true"[260] is, however, not sufficent.[261] In short, malice goes to the "state of mind of the defendant at the time the words were published"[262] and includes any improper or indirect motive for publishing the material.[263]

CarswellOnt 5273 (S.C.J.), at para. 21, it was stated that "probability requires that the evidence should be more consistent with the existence of malice than its non-existence."

257 See *Horrocks v. Lowe*, [1975] A.C. 135 (H.L.), cited with approval in *Davies & Davies Ltd. v. Kott, ibid.*; and in *Leverman v. Campbell Sharp Ltd.* (1987), 40 C.C.L.T. 73 (B.C. C.A.). In *Hill v. Church of Scientology of Toronto* (1995), 126 D.L.R. (4th) 129 at 171, Cory J. stated that malice may be established "by showing that the defendant spoke dishonestly, or in knowing or reckless disregard for the truth."

258 *Camporese v. Parton* (1983), 150 D.L.R. (3d) 208 at 226 (B.C. S.C.). See also *Bennett v. Stupich* (1981), 125 D.L.R. (3d) 743 at 750 (B.C. S.C.): "The use of an occasion of qualified privilege for an indirect purpose in law means malice." Note that these judgments treat this as a question of malice, and not as a matter of exceeding a privilege.

259 *Horrocks v. Lowe*, [1975] A.C. 135 at 150 (H.L.), per Lord Diplock, cited with approval in *Camporese v. Parton, ibid.* See also *Fraser v. Sykes*, [1971] 1 W.W.R. 246 at 271 (Alta. S.C.), affirmed [1971] 3 W.W.R. 161 (Alta. C.A.), which was affirmed [1973] 5 W.W.R. 484 (S.C.C.): ". . . the recklessness and carelessness of the defendant in making the untruthful statements may well be construed as malice sufficient to defeat this defence."

260 *Horrocks v. Lowe, ibid.* See, for example, *McKinnon v. Dauphin (Rural Municipality)*, [1996] 3 W.W.R. 127 (Man. Q.B.), affirmed (1997), [1998] 1 W.W.R. 309 (Man. C.A.).

261 Note, however, that "carelessness in the publication of the statement so that it does not express the honest belief, or shows that the honest belief was never formed, takes away the defence of qualified privilege": Lambert J.A. in *Leverman v. Campbell Sharp Ltd.* (1987), 40 C.C.L.T. 73 at 77 (B.C. C.A.). Also note that there is disagreement concerning the issue of negligence in forming the honest belief. Some cases have held that it is not enough for the defendant to have an honest belief; it must have been formed reasonably. See, e.g., *Gillett v. Nissen Volkswagen Ltd.*, [1975] 3 W.W.R. 520 (Alta. T.D.); *Netupsky v. Craig*, [1973] S.C.R. 55; and other cases cited by Brown, above, note 2, at 16-43, n. 227. This issue was dealt with recently in *Korach v. Moore* (1991), 1 O.R. (3d) 275 (C.A.). The Court of Appeal held that reasonableness is not in issue in malice; only honesty. Thus if the defendant had an honest belief in his statements, there is no malice, notwithstanding the reasonableness of this belief. Thus negligence or carelessness cannot constitute malice. Also see *Peterkin v. Union of Northern Workers* (2006), 40 C.C.L.T. (3d) 319 (N.W.T. S.C.), additional reasons at (2006), 2006 CarswellNWT 78 (S.C.), where Vertes J. states that "an error of judgment, carelessness, negligence or even gross negligence, is not sufficient to establish malice if the defendant otherwise had an honest belief", although "reckless indifference to the truth" would be. A union official processing a grievance on behalf of a union member is not a neutral party and was not obligated to investigate the complaint before presenting it to the employer. Although the defamation action failed against him, it succeeded against a shop steward based on proof of malice relating to other defamatory material.

262 Brown, above, note 2, at 16-11.

263 In *Teamsters, Local 987 v. U.F.C.W., Local 401* (2005), 258 D.L.R. (4th) 33 (Alta. C.A.), Berger J.A. stated that malice is established if the predominant motive of the defendant was to injure (express malice), or if the defendant had an indirect motive or ulterior purpose which conflicted with the sense of duty or mutual interest that the occasion created. The Court of

(e) Fair Comment

The defence of fair comment allows persons to comment on matters of public interest, even if their comments are defamatory of other persons,[264] if certain conditions are met.

There have been numerous statements explaining the lofty purposes of the defence of fair comment. It has been stated that the purpose of the defence is to permit "a free and general discussion of public matters", as a "fundamental" feature of a democratic society.[265] It is to allow "untrammelled discussion of public affairs and of those participating in them" in order to "safeguard against irresponsible political power."[266] It is to afford "everyone an equal opportunity of participating in the process of self-government."[267] There is no question that, at least on a theoretical level, the defence of fair comment gives wide scope for criticism of public officials and for political dissent.[268] The extent to which the defence has *in fact* achieved these goals can only be judged by analyzing the conditions of the defence, and the way in which these conditions have been interpreted by the courts. It is suggested that as with the other aspects of the defamation action, the approach in Canadian case law has been a conservative one.[269]

Appeal reversed the trial judge's decision that found malice, finding that the trial judge had failed to fully consider "the context of the occasion, the dominant motive, the protection of legitimate interests, and the sense of duty and mutual interest which the occasion created" at 258 D.L.R. (4th) 340. Also see *Wells v. Sears*, [2007] NLCA 21, where the Court of Appeal stressed that malice must be the "dominant motive" in order for the defence of qualified privilege to be defeated. For this reason, the trial judge's finding of malice was rejected.

264 The fact that there is a defence which protects critical comment indicates that the law considers not only statements of fact, but also expressions of opinion, as being capable of being defamatory, and satisfying the plaintiff's *prima facie* case.

265 Dickson J. in *Cherneskey v. Armadale Publishers Ltd.*, [1979] 1 S.C.R. 1067 at 1096.

266 Fleming, *The Law of Torts*, 9th ed. (1998), at 648.

267 Weiler, "Defamation, Enterprise Liability, and Freedom of Speech" (1967), 17 U.T.L.J. 278 at 327. The defence applies, of course, to more mundane concerns, for example to reviews of theater, films, and restaurants. See, for example, *Sara's Pyrohy Hut v. Brooker* (1991), 83 Alta. L.R. (2d) 131 (Q.B.), affirmed [1993] 3 W.W.R. 662 (Alta. C.A.). The plaintiff complained of the defendant's restaurant review which, among other things, characterized the plaintiff's pyroghies as "bland." See also *Kerr v. Conlogue*, [1992] 4 W.W.R. 258 (B.C. S.C.), a case which involved a critical theater review.

268 One can find many statements which stress this. For example, see *Martin v. Man. Free Press Co.* (1892), 8 Man. R. 50 at 71-72, per Bain J.:

> It is not now open to question that publishers, editors and proprietors of newspapers, and indeed all other citizens, have the fullest and freest liberty to discuss and comment upon the public acts and conduct of a public man, and, if they see fit, not only to criticise his acts and conduct in the most hostile spirit and in the severest terms, but also to assail and denounce the man himself as unfit for his position for the want of such qualities as wisdom, judgment, discretion or skill and the like, as evidenced by his acts and conduct. One who undertakes to fill a public office offers himself to public attack and criticism; and it is now admitted and recognized that the public interest requires that a man's conduct shall be open to the most searching criticism.

269 Lord Denning M.R. in *Slim v. Daily Telegraph Ltd.*, [1968] 1 All E.R. 497 at 503 (C.A.), warned that the defence of fair comment, being "one of the essential elements which go to make up our freedom of speech . . . must not be whittled down by legal refinements." It is this writer's opinion that this warning too frequently has been ignored.

The conditions for the successful application of the defence of fair comment have been laid out as follows:

(a) the comment must be on a matter of public interest;
(b) the comment must be based on fact;
(c) the comment, though it can include inferences of fact, must be recognizable as comment;
(d) the comment must satisfy the following *objective* test: could any man honestly express that opinion on the proved facts?
(e) even though the comment satisfies the objective test the defence can be defeated *if the plaintiff proves that the defendant was actuated by express malice.*[270]

(i) Comment and Fact

It has generally been recognized that it is very difficult to distinguish between statements which allege fact from those which merely express opinion.[271] It has been suggested that statements of fact and statements of opinion "exist on a spectrum with little hard indication of where an opinion stops and an assertion of fact starts."[272] There are factors, however, which can be used to locate the statement on the spectrum. For example, an unqualified statement of a past event and an implied allegation of a past event have been stated to be clearly statements of fact, whereas general and evaluative statements, without reference to actual events, fall more on the side of comment.[273] A statement which asserts something which can be objectively tested with reference to its truth is a statement of fact. An opinion, however, is not capable of being tested by reference to truth or falsity, although it can be evaluated in terms of its reasonableness. The same words can be considered either statements of fact or opinion, depending upon the context in which they appear. For example, to state that a specific event has occurred and then to draw certain conclusions from that event will allow the conclusions to be treated as comment.[274] However, merely to state the conclusion without asserting the existence of any objective event from which it is drawn will lead to the

---

270 Dickson J. in *Cherneskey v. Armadale Publishers Ltd.*, [1979] 1 S.C.R. 1067 at 1099-1100, adopting Duncan and Neill, *Defamation* (1978), at 62, para. 12.02. This has been quoted in several other Canadian decisions. It was reaffirmed by the Supreme Court of Canada in *WIC Radio Ltd. v. Simpson*, 2008 SCC 40, reversing [2006], 10 W.W.R. 460, reversing 31 B.C.L.R. (4th) 285.

271 See, e.g., Lord Porter in *Kemsley v. Foot*, [1952] A.C. 345 at 356-57 (H.L.): "Sometimes, however, it is difficult to distinguish an allegation of fact from an expression of opinion." In *Christie v. Geiger* (1986), 38 C.C.L.T. 280 at 290 (Alta. C.A.), Belzil J.A. stated that "the distinction between comment on facts and statement of facts is not always apparent, but is one which must absolutely be made in defamation actions." The issue is a question of fact: see Nemetz C.J.B.C. in *Vander Zalm v. Times Publishers* (1980), 12 C.C.L.T. 81 at 86 (B.C. C.A.). A useful discussion of this aspect of the defence is found in *Ross v. N.B.T.A.* (2001), 6 C.C.L.T. (3d) 171 (N.B. C.A.). The case involved a cartoon that was held to be defamatory, although the defence of fair comment succeeded.

272 Trelawney, "Rethinking the Standard of Liability in Defamation", LL.M. Thesis, University of Alberta, 1989. Trelawney refers to Weiler's suggestion that fact and opinion exist along a spectrum ranging from "brute data" to inferences of fact to clear evaluations or opinions; see Weiler, "Defamation, Enterprise Liability and Freedom of Speech", above, note 267.

273 See Trelawney, *ibid.*

274 For example, to say that Mr. X refused to sell his house to an immigrant, and therefore is a racist, will allow the latter conclusion to be treated as comment.

conclusion being treated as a statement of fact.[275] In the first case, the material is presented as a comment or opinion upon facts. In the second case, the material is presented as a matter of fact.[276]

The defence requires that the material be "recognizable to the ordinary reasonable man as a comment upon true facts, and not as a bare statement of fact."[277] If the facts upon which the comment is based are not true, the defence will fail.[278] As with other elements of the defamation action, it is not the defendant's intention which is important, but the meaning derived from the statement by the reasonable person.[279] Thus where the trial judge finds that the comments contain a defamatory meaning, one which was not intended to be conveyed by the defendant, it is the fairness of that meaning which must satisfy the elements of the defence of fair comment.[280] Where the facts are not stated with the comment, or were not otherwise known by the recipients of the material, the comment will be treated as a statement of fact.[281]

---

275 For example, to simply state that Mr. X is a racist.

276 The practical difference to the defendant will be important. In the first case, the defendant will merely have to prove the truth of the assertion that the plaintiff refused to sell his house to an immigrant. He will not have to prove that the defendant was a racist. In the second case, the defendant will have to prove that the plaintiff was in fact a racist. A useful discussion of the difference between comment and fact is found in Bellamy J.'s judgment in *Myers v. Canadian Broadcasting Corp.* (1999), 47 C.C.L.T. (2d) 272 (Ont. S.C.J.). The key is whether the statement appears to the reader or viewer as an opinion based on true facts that are accessible to the viewer or an assertion without facts provided.

277 Nemetz C.J.B.C. in *Vander Zalm v. Times Publishers* (1980), 12 C.C.L.T. 81 (B.C. C.A.), at 86.

278 See, for example, *Makow v. The Winnipeg Sun,* [2004] 6 W.W.R. 45 (Man. C.A.), affirming [2003] 11 W.W.R. 166 (Q.B.). The Court of Appeal held that for the defence of fair comment to succeed "the material and essential facts upon which the comment is based must be proved to be substantially true", at [2004] 6 W.W.R. 53. It rejected a more rigid standard which would require that the defendant prove "that each and every statement of fact upon which the comment is based is true."

279 Thus, where the statements of comment are intertwined with the statements of fact, the defendant bears the risk that statements intended as opinion will be treated as fact. See, e.g., *Paletta v. Lethbridge Herald Co. (No. 2)* (1976), 4 Alta. L.R. (2d) 97 (T.D.).

280 See *WIC Radio Ltd. v. Simpson*, 2008 SCC 40, reversing [2006], 10 W.W.R. 460, reversing 31 B.C.L.R. (4th) 285. The meaning intended to be conveyed by the defendant was that the plaintiff was an "intolerant bigot". The meaning which the trial judge held that it did convey, however, was that the plaintiff condoned violence. The trial judge applied the defence of fair comment and dismissed the action. The Court of Appeal reversed, holding that since there was no evidentiary basis for the meaning ascribed to the defendant's comments, and the defendant did not honestly believe it, the defence of fair comment failed. The Supreme Court of Canada restored the trial judgment on the basis of the fair comment defence. See discussion below.

281 In *Vander Zalm v. Times Publishers* (1980), 12 C.C.L.T. 81 (B.C. C.A.), reversing (1979), 8 C.C.L.T. 144 (B.C. S.C.), for example, the trial judge was receptive to the plaintiff's assertion that the defence of fair comment could not apply to a political cartoon depicting the plaintiff in a derogatory manner, since "there were no facts before the reader" and therefore the cartoon stood in the same position as facts. On appeal, the decision was reversed, partly because the facts about the plaintiff had been publicized, allowing the cartoon to become a commentary upon those facts. See also *Christie v. Geiger*, above, note 271, where Belzil J.A. cited *Kemsley v. Foot*, [1952] A.C. 345 at 354 (H.L.), to support the view that the facts necessary to justify a comment may in certain cases be implied from the terms of the comment. If the facts are

(ii) Public Interest

The defence of fair comment does not apply to all opinions. They must concern a matter of public interest. In *McLoughlin v. Kutasy*,[282] Ritchie J. stated that an "essential ingredient of [the] defence is that the comment was made on a matter of public interest."[283] Cases in which the defence of fair comment is raised generally relate to comments by, or concerning, politicians, those involved in political disputes, those with celebrity status, and other public figures. As well, a private individual who becomes involved in a publicissue may "cease to be a private person and enter the public domain."[284] It is not sufficient, however, that the matter commented upon involves a public figure. The matter must also be one of relevant public interest.[285] In *Russell v. Pawley*,[286] for example, it was held that merely because the defendant injected himself into a matter of public controversy, his personal ethics did not become a matter of public interest.[287]

(iii) Fairness

Even if a defamatory statement can be categorized as a comment on a matter of public interest, a third requirement must be met. The comment must be fair.[288]

What this requirement implies is subject to different interpretations. One is that unless a comment is in fact the "honest expression of the real view of the person making the comment",[289] it cannot be a fair comment. Accordingly, the beliefs and *bona fides* of the publisher of a comment, i.e., the publisher's honesty, is an element of the defence, and must be established by each publisher who wishes to

---

well known, or can be readily ascertained by those who were reading the comment, it is not necessary that the facts be restated with the comment.

282 (1979), 97 D.L.R. (3d) 620 at 623 (S.C.C.).

283 The case concerned a report prepared by a doctor for a company regarding the suitability of an applicant for a job. This was held not to have been a matter of public interest, and therefore the defence of fair comment did not apply.

284 See *Russell v. Pawley*, [1986] 4 W.W.R. 172 at 180 (Man. Q.B.), reversed [1987] 3 W.W.R. 442 (Man. C.A.).

285 Thus the private lives of public figures may not be matters of legitimate public interest. Although the public undoubtedly is interested in gossip, this does not convert gossip into a matter of public interest, at least in so far as the defence of fair comment is concerned. In *Vander Zalm v. Times Publishers* (1980), 12 C.C.L.T. 81 at 86 (B.C. C.A.), Nemetz C.J.C.B. stated:

> . . . the matter commented upon must be one of public interest. There must, in short, be a public nexus between the matter and the person caricatured. In a case such as this, the cartoonist may not intrude upon the private life of a public man, no matter how interesting such an intrusion may be to the public, nor may he expose a private person to unsought publicity.

286 [1987] 3 W.W.R. 442 (Man. C.A.).

287 The debate concerned French language rights. The defendant made a remark suggesting that the plaintiff was acting improperly in accepting sick-leave pay, even though he was evidently not so sick that he could not work for his cause. This was not related to the controversy, and the Court of Appeal reversed the trial judge's decision to protect the statement by fair comment.

288 This has been stated to be a question of fact. See, e.g., Nemetz C.J.B.C. in *Vander Zalm v. Times Publishers* (1980), 12 C.C.L.T. 81 at 86 (B.C. C.A.).

289 See *Russell v. Pawley*, [1986] 4 W.W.R. 172 at 179 (Man. Q.B.).

utilize the defence.[290] Under this approach, the honesty of the commentator is an issue separate and distinct from the issue of malice, which only arises once the honest belief of the defendant has been established.[291] This was the principal issue in *Cherneskey v. Armadale Publishers Ltd.*[292] A newspaper published a letter to the editor which contained opinions held to have been defamatory of the plaintiff. The newspaper was sued and claimed the defence of fair comment. The majority of the Supreme Court of Canada held that since the opinions did not express the honest beliefs of the publisher of the letter, i.e., the newspaper, it could not avail itself of the defence.[293] The majority of the court held that since the fairness of the comment, based upon the honesty of the defendant, had not been established, the issue of malice, which is only relevant once the basic elements of the defence have been made out, ought not to have been put to the jury.

The dissenting justices in *Cherneskey* suggested quite a different view of the fairness requirement. Dickson J. stated that "the test of whether a comment is 'fair comment' in law is an 'objective test', i.e., is the comment one that an honest, albeit prejudiced, person might make in the circumstances?"[294] According to this approach, the objective fairness of a comment raises an issue which is different from that of the subjective fairness of the commentator. The former issue alone must be proved by the defendant who raises the defence of fair comment. The latter issue, relating to the honesty and *bona fides* of the publisher, goes to the question of malice, which must be proved by the plaintiff once the defence of fair comment has been established.[295] With respect to the objective fairness of the comment, different tests have been suggested. One formula has been to ask whether "a fair-minded man, holding a strong view, holding perhaps an obstinate view, holding perhaps a prejudiced view — could a fair-minded man have been capable of writing this?"[296]

The Supreme Court of Canada re-visited this issue in *WIC Radio Ltd. v. Simpson*.[297] The defendant's comment concerning the plaintiff was given a meaning

290 See Ritchie J. in *Cherneskey v. Armadale Publishers Ltd.* (1978), 7 C.C.L.T. 69 at 77 (S.C.C.). This view seems to be the predominant one, especially where the defendant is the originator of the statement.

291 As stated by Ritchie J.: "As honesty of belief is an essential component of the defence of fair comment, that defence involves at least some evidence that the material complained of was published in a spirit of fairness.": *ibid.*, at 87.

292 Above, note 290.

293 The judgment was somewhat ambiguous on this issue. The judgment could also be interpreted as holding that the opinions had to represent either the honest belief of the newspaper, or the honest belief of those who wrote the letter. Since there was evidence that the opinions expressed in the letter were not those of the newspaper, and no evidence was introduced showing that they were the genuine opinions of the letter writers, the defence failed to satisfy either test.

294 7 C.C.L.T. 69 at 97.

295 This was the view of the three dissenting judges in *Cherneskey*, as well as that of Hall J.A. in the Court of Appeal decision, [1977] 5 W.W.R. 155 (Sask. C.A.). As well, Dickson J. cited *Merivale v. Carson* (1887), 20 Q.B.D. 275 (C.A.); *Lyon v. Daily Telegraph*, [1943] 1 K.B. 746 (C.A.), and *Slim v. Daily Telegraph*, [1968] 1 All E.R. 497 (C.A.), in support of this approach.

296 Diplock J. in *Silkin v. Beaverbrook Newspapers Ltd.*, [1958] 2 All E.R. 516 at 520 (Q.B.D.), cited by Dickson J. in *Cherneskey*, 7 C.C.L.T. 69 at 105.

297 2008 SCC 40, reversing [2006], 10 W.W.R. 460, reversing 31 B.C.L.R. (4th) 285.

by the trial judge which was not the meaning intended by the defendant. The defendant did not subjectively hold an honest belief in that meaning.[298] In view of this, could the defence of fair comment succeed? The Supreme Court of Canada held that it could. Binnie J., writing for the majority of the court, adopted Dickson J.'s dissenting view in *Cherneskey* that as long as the comment was one which, on an objective test, could honestly be held by anyone, the defence of fair comment was available. The test succeeded on the facts of this case and the trial judgment was restored.[299]

This change in Canadian defamation law is welcomed. As I have have argued previously, the defence of fair comment should only require proof that a comment was objectively fair, with the issue of a publisher's *bona fides* going to the question of malice, proof of which should rest upon the plaintiff.[300] The defence of fair comment is meant to encourage the participation of everyone in discussions on matters of public importance, and, accordingly, the rules for its successful application ought to promote this goal. When defamatory material constitutes statements of opinion on true facts, and the comments are objectively fair, they should be protected, subject to the occasion being abused by the publisher. In this respect, evidence that the publisher was dishonest may be evidence of malice, the burden of proving which ought, as is normally the case, to be on the person so alleging. Where a publisher publishes the opinions of another person, and portrays them as such, the same rules ought to govern. The defence of fair comment ought to prevail once its required elements have been established, and the dishonesty of the publisher ought to be considered only within the context of malice.[301]

A comment will be deemed to be unfair if the facts upon which it has been based are untrue.[302] It has been stated that "a comment based on facts untruly

---

298 The defendant had intended to convey the meaning that the plaintiff was an intolerant bigot. The meaning ascribed to the comment was that the plaintiff condoned violence against gays.

299 Lebel J. and Rothstein J., writing separate judgments, would have eliminated the requirement of honest belief altogether. In their view, as long as the statement was a comment, had a basis in true facts, and concerned a matter of public interest, the defence should be available. It then can be defeated by malice. Lack of honest subject belief can be evidence of malice. Lebel J. argued as well that the impugned statement failed to meet the threshold test of what is defamatory.

300 See Klar, "Developments in Tort Law: The 1978-79 Term" (1980), 1 Sup. Ct. L. Rev. 310, and Klar, "The Defence of 'Fair Comment' " (1979), 8 C.C.L.T. 149. This approach was applied in *Pilot Insurance Co. v. Jessome*, [1993] O.J. No. 172 (Gen. Div.). Also see *Myers v. C.B.C.*, above, note 276.

301 As a result of the *Cherneskey* decision, numerous provinces amended their legislation to ensure that the opinions of others could be published in newspapers, without the requirement that the newspapers shared the opinions expressed. The Ontario Libel and Slander Act, R.S.O. 1990, c. L.12, s. 24, for example, states that the publisher's defence of fair comment is not defeated by reason only that neither the publisher nor the third party held the opinion if a person could honestly hold the opinion. See *AssessMed Inc. v. Canadian Broadcasting Corp.* (2004), 22 C.C.L.T. (3d) 89 (Ont. S.C.J.), additional reasons at (2004), 2004 CarswellOnt 2307 (Ont. S.C.J.), affirmed (2006), [2006] O.J. No.2226, 2006 CarswellOnt 3392 (Ont. C.A.), leave to appeal refused (2006), 2006 CarswellOnt 7954 (S.C.C.).

302 See *Holt v. Sun Publishing Co.* (1980), 100 D.L.R. (3d) 447 (B.C. C.A.). Also see *Wenman v. Pacific Press Ltd.*, [1991] B.C.J. No. 186 (S.C.), where an editorial on the controversial issue of abortion was deemed defamatory of the plaintiff. The defence of fair comment failed because the court held that the editorial relied upon untrue facts concerning the plaintiff's role in court proceedings.

stated cannot be fair."[303] In *Pearlman v. CBC*,[304] Morse J. stated that "in order to establish the defence of fair comment, the defendants must prove that each and every statement of fact in the words complained of was true. . . ."[305] As with the defence of justification, what is important is whether the facts were true, and not whether the publisher believed them to be true.[306] The facts must also be stated, unless they are known, so that the recipient can determine the fairness of the comment.[307] Where a comment contains an imputation of corrupt or dishonest motives, the comment must be shown to be justifiable in order for it to be considered fair.[308]

(iv) Malice

As with the defence of qualified privilege, the defence of fair comment can be defeated by proof that the defendant was malicious. In *Cherneskey v. Armadale Publishers Ltd.*,[309] Dickson J. noted that malice includes spite, ill will, and any indirect motive or ulterior purpose. In *Parlett v. Robinson*,[310] the trial judge rejected the plaintiff's contention that the defendant was malicious, and that his real purpose in making his statements was to attract publicity to himself, rather than fulfilling a duty to inform the public. The trial judge stated that to prove improper motive, the defendant's "predominant purpose" must be identified. In *Vogel v. CBC*,[311] on the other hand, the court held that although the purported purpose of the defendant broadcaster was to serve the public interest by exposing corruption in high places, its real motive was to enhance its reputation by producing a sensational programme. This attitude amounted to malice.

---

303 Lord Oaksley in *Kemsley v. Foot*, [1952] A.C. 345 at 361 (H.L.), quoted with approval by Aikins J.A. in *Holt v. Sun Publishing Co., ibid.*, at 450. It has been stated that a defendant must "get his facts right": see *Whitaker v. Huntington* (1980), 15 C.C.L.T. 19 at 33 (B.C. S.C.), citing Lieberman J. in *Fraser v. Sykes*, [1971] 1 W.W.R. 246 at 248 (Alta. S.C.); and that "it is trite law that no comment can be fair if it is based upon facts which are invented or mis-stated": Tallis J. in *England v. CBC* (1979), 97 D.L.R. (3d) 472 at 489 (N.W.T. S.C.).

304 (1981), 13 Man. R. (2d) 1 at 10 (Q.B.).

305 Note that there are statutory provisions in some jurisdictions which state that where the action consists partly of allegations of fact and partly of expressions of opinion, fair comment shall not fail merely because the truth of every allegation of fact is not proved, if the expression of opinion is fair comment having regard to such of the facts alleged or referred to in the words complained of as are proved. See, e.g., s. 24 of the Ontario Libel and Slander Act, R.S.O. 1990, c. L.12. See *Myers v. C.B.C.*, above, note 276.

306 In fact, if the facts were true, it does not matter if the publisher did not know they were true. See *Russell v. Pawley*, [1986] 4 W.W.R. 172 at 178 (Man. Q.B.).

307 If the facts are expressly stated, implicit from the comment itself, have been previously publicized, or are readily ascertainable, the test is met.

308 See *Parlett v. Robinson* (1985), 33 C.C.L.T. 161 at 177 (B.C. S.C.), citing *Gatley on Libel and Slander*, 8th ed. (1981), at 300-01, para. 709. See also Esson J., citing Gatley, in *Vogel v. CBC* (1982), 21 C.C.L.T. 105 at 192 (B.C. S.C.):

> To be fair, comment must be based on facts truly stated and must not contain imputations of corrupt or dishonourable motives on the person whose conduct is criticized, save insofar as such imputations are warranted by the facts.

309 [1979] 1 S.C.R. 1067.

310 (1985), 33 C.C.L.T. 161 (B.C. S.C.), reversed on other grounds (1986), 37 C.C.L.T. 281 (B.C. C.A.).

311 (1982), 21 C.C.L.T. 105 (B.C. S.C.).

Proof that the opinion expressed was not the honest opinion of the commentator will be evidence of malice.

(f) Consent

Consent can constitute an absolute defence to an action for defamation. Although there have been very few Canadian cases on point,[312] it has been accepted that the defence can be raised in limited circumstances. In *Hanly v. Pisces Productions Inc.*,[313] for example, the fact that the plaintiff asked a third party to obtain, from the defendant, an explanation as to why the plaintiff had not been hired by the defendant was considered to be express consent to the publication of the defamatory material. The plaintiff ought to have reasonably anticipated that the defendant's response to the request might be defamatory. In *Syms v. Warren*,[314] the fact that the plaintiff willingly participated in a radio show to discuss rumours which had been circulating concerning him was held to have constituted consent to a discussion of these rumours. However, when the discussion continued beyond the point which could have reasonably been anticipated, the defence of consent no longer applied. The court held that the "consent must be given or be able to be inferred with respect to each publication of defamatory material",[315] otherwise "consent to the merest publication would open the door to wide dissemination that might be very damaging and never intended to be authorized by the person giving the initial consent."[316] In *Jones v. Brooks*,[317] the plaintiff's act in hiring private detectives in order to engage the defendants in conversation and to tape their slanderous remarks about the plaintiff, so that he could discover what they had been saying about him, was held to have constituted consent to these defamations.

6. REMEDIES

Compensatory and punitive damages may be awarded in defamation cases.

A plaintiff is entitled to be compensated for the actual monetary losses suffered as a result of the defamation. As well, since the real damage suffered as a result of defamatory material cannot be ascertained, it has been held that damages in defamation cases are "at large."[318] This generally is taken to mean that the damages are assessed without regard to the need to prove actual monetary losses.[319] In

312 There have been some; see, for example, *Hanly v. Pisces Productions Inc.*, [1981] 1 W.W.R. 369 (B.C. S.C.); *Syms v. Warren* (1976), 71 D.L.R. (3d) 558 (Man. Q.B.); and *Jones v. Brooks* (1974), 45 D.L.R. (3d) 413 (Sask. Q.B.).

313 *Ibid.*

314 Above, note 312.

315 (1976), 71 D.L.R. (3d) 558 at 563.

316 *Ibid.*

317 Above, note 312.

318 See *Vogel v. CBC* (1982), 21 C.C.L.T. 105 at 198 (B.C. S.C.), citing Lord Atkin in *Ley v. Hamilton* (1935), 153 L.T. 384 at 386 (H.L.). See Cory J. in *Hill v. Church of Scientology of Toronto* (1995), 126 D.L.R. (4th) 129 (S.C.C.).

319 In *Farrell v. CBC* (1987), 43 D.L.R. (4th) 667 at 669 (Nfld. C.A.), Goodridge C.J.N. stated that this term generally means "general damages consisting of non-economic loss and exemplary damages in appropriate cases." See also Lord Hailsham's judgment in *Cassell & Co. v. Broome*, [1972] A.C. 1027 at 1073 (H.L.). In *Murphy v. Alexander* (2004), 21 C.C.L.T. (3d) 226 (Ont. C.A.) at 234, Cronk J.A. points out that although general damages are presumed

considering the size of the award, the court will consider the seriousness of the defamatory material, the breadth of its publication, the extent of the demonstrable damage, and the malice of the defendant.[320] The court can consider "the entire conduct of the defendant, both before and after an action is commenced as well as in court during the trial" in assessing damages, particularly aggravated damages, although no damages can be awarded for defamatory remarks which are not the subject-matter of the cause of action.[321] The court will also consider the deterrent effect provided by a sizeable award.[322] The plaintiff is entitled to be compensated for damage to reputation, and the resultant injury to feelings and health.[323] It has been held that there is "little justification for extravagant awards" in Canadian law, and that when assessing damages in one case, reference should be had to other comparable cases, so as to ensure some predictability and consistency.[324]

The issue of quantum of damages was one of the major issues in *Hill v. Church of Scientology of Toronto.*[325] The damages awarded in the case: $300,000 against one of the defendants and $1.6 million against the other, represent the largest

---

from the fact of the slander or publication of the false statement, the presumption of damages may be rebutted.

320 See *Vogel v. Canadian Broadcasting Corp.* (1982), 21 C.C.L.T. 105 (B.C. S.C.), at 202. In *Munro v. Toronto Sun Publishing Corp.* (1982), 21 C.C.L.T. 261 (Ont. H.C.), Holland J. quoted from Odgers, *The Law of Libel and Slander*, 5th ed. (1912), at 373, where the author indicated that the jury can consider things such as the rank and position of the parties, the mode of publication, the extent of the circulation, the tardiness, inadequacy or absence of an apology, and the negligence of the defendant, in determining the award. Also see Cunningham J.'s judgment in *Leenen v. Canadian Broadcasting Corp.* (2000), 50 C.C.L.T. (2d) 213 (Ont. S.C.J.), additional reasons at (2000), 2000 CarswellOnt 3327 (S.C.J.), affirmed (2001), 6 C.C.L.T. (3d) 97 (Ont. C.A.), leave to appeal refused (2002), 164 O.A.C. 200 (note) (S.C.C.) for a good discussion of the factors to be considered in assessing the appropriate level of compensation.

321 See Cronk J.A. in *Murphy v. Alexander* (2004), 21 C.C.L.T. (3d) 226 (Ont. C.A.). Cronk J.A. referred to Brown, as well as judicial decisions in support of her propositions. The court held that the trial judge erred in awarding damages resulting from a defamatory publication regarding which the plaintiff's claim was statute barred. In *Rogacki v. Belz* (2004), 243 D.L.R. (4th) 585 (Ont. C.A.), leave to appeal refused (2005), 2005 CarswellOnt 1110 (S.C.C.), the Ontario Court of Appeal held that although a jury did not find malice with respect to the defence of fair comment, it could find malice with respect to an award of aggravated damages. The court's reasoning was that for malice to defeat the defence of fair comment, the malice must exist at the time of publication. However, malice as a factor going to aggravated damages is based on the defendant's conduct in a broader time frame. In other words, post-publication malice could lead to an award of aggravated damages, even if malice did not exist at the time of publication.

322 This will be considered within the context of punitive damages.

323 See Irvine, "Annotation" (1982), 21 C.C.L.T. 264 at 265, quoting from Samuels, "Problems of Assessing Damages in Defamation" (1963), 79 L.Q.R. 63.

324 See Goodridge C.J.N.'s judgment in *Farrell v. CBC*, above, note 319, at 668. Another plea for moderate awards came from Wood J.A. in *Westbank Band of Indians v. Tomat* (1992), 10 C.C.L.T. (2d) 1 at 28 (B.C. C.A.). Wood J.A. stated that the appropriate balance between the protection of speech and reputation "lies in a realistic appreciation of the rehabilitative effect which may reasonably be expected to result from a finding against the defendant and the award of significant monetary damages." Particularly with regard to political debate, "the courts must be careful not to award damages which may tend more to stifle the free expression of opinion than to rehabilitate the reputation of the defamed", *ibid.*, at 29.

325 (1995), 126 D.L.R. (4th) 129 (S.C.C.).

award of damages ever made in a Canadian defamation case.[326] More important, however, the Supreme Court has by its judgment signalled an increase of damages in this area. Cory J. rejected the notion of any cap on general damages for defamation, as there is on non-pecuniary damages for personal injury actions.[327] The rejection of a cap was a reflection of the seriousness with which Cory J. views defamation,[328] the different policy issues which are present in the two types of claims,[329] and of Cory J.'s view that defamation results from more serious misconduct than that which occurs in ordinary negligence actions.[330]

Where the conduct of the defendant was particularly reprehensible, aggravated or punitive damages can be awarded.[331] Factors which can be considered as aggravating the plaintiff's injury, such as the defendant's high-handedness, malice, insulting or oppressive behaviour, refusal to apologize, or even pleading justification, may increase the award.[332] The fact that the defamatory material was

---

326 The award was made up of $300,000 in general damages, for which both defendants were responsible, plus $500,000 in aggravated and $800,000 in punitive damages, for which only the defendant church was liable.

327 The cap was established in the Supreme Court's 1977 "trilogy": *Andrews v. Grand & Toy Alberta Ltd.* (1978), 3 C.C.L.T. 225; *Thornton v. Prince George Board of Education*, [1978] 2 S.C.R. 267; and *Arnold v. Teno*, [1978] 2 S.C.R. 287. The cap was $100,000. It is now in the range of $300,000 due to the effects of inflation.

328 For example, Cory J. stated at 126 D.L.R. (4th) at 176 that "A defamatory statement can seep into the crevasses of the subconscious and lurk there ever ready to spring forth and spread its cancerous evil."

329 For example, Cory J. noted that personal injury cases are more frequent, require more consistent treatment by courts, and have more significant liability insurance implications. He also noted how the awards have been traditionally very small in defamation cases, averaging $30,000 or less. Whether this changes due to the *Hill* decision itself remains to be seen.

330 This is a surprising statement on several accounts. First, defamation is essentially a strict liability tort — fault is not even required. Cory J. states that negligent conduct "does not usually arise from any desire to injure the plaintiff", implying that in defamation cases there is an intention to injure. Secondly, general damages for tort actions are not awarded based on the nature of the misconduct, but on the nature of the plaintiff's injury. If Cory J. is concerned with punishing outrageous behaviour, this is the function of aggravated or punitive damages, and not general damages. Cory J. also stated that a cap on defamation damages might be seen as a licence to defame which would "amount to a radical change in policy and direction for the courts."

331 See Southin J.A.'s judgment in *Brown v. Cole* (1998), [1999] 7 W.W.R. 703 (B.C. C.A.), leave to appeal refused (1999), 133 B.C.A.C. 143 (note) (S.C.C.) for a useful discussion concerning aggravated and general damages in defamation actions.

332 See *Farrell v. CBC* (1987), 43 D.L.R. (4th) 667 at 679 (Nfld. C.A.). See also Robins J.A. in *Walker v. CFTO Ltd.* (1987), 39 C.C.L.T. 121 at 130 (Ont. C.A.):

> The damages may be aggravated by the manner in which, or the motives with which, the statement was made or persisted in. Where the defendant is guilty of insulting, high-handed, spiteful, malicious or oppressive conduct which increases the mental distress — the humiliation, indignation, anxiety, grief, fear and the like — suffered by the plaintiff as a result of being defamed, the plaintiff may be entitled to what has come to be known as "aggravated damages." Aggravated damages are damages which take into account the additional harm caused to the plaintiff's feelings by such reprehensible or outrageous conduct on the part of the defendant. Their purpose is compensatory and, being compensatory, they properly form part of a general damage award.

Also see Cory J.'s judgment in *Hill v. Church of Scientology*, above, note 325. In *Myers v. Canadian Broadcasting Corp.* (2001), 6 C.C.L.T. (3d) 112 (Ont. C.A.), leave to appeal refused (2002), 163 O.A.C. 400 (note) (S.C.C.), the Ontario Court of Appeal added $150,000 in

published on the Internet may increase the size of the award. In *Barrick Gold Corp. v. Lopehandia*,[333] Blair J.A. stated that "communication via the Internet is instantaneous, seamless, interactive, blunt, borderless and far-reaching. It is also impersonal, and the anonymous nature of such communications may itself create a greater risk that the defamatory remarks are believed."[334]

Various legislative provisions enacted in every common law province allow for the mitigation of the damages to be assessed against defendants in certain circumstances. An offer of an apology given to the plaintiff may mitigate damages.[335] In the case of defamatory material published in newspapers, or broadcast, evidence that the material was published without actual malice and without gross negligence, and that a full and fair retraction and apology were offered, may also mitigate damages.[336] In the case of defamatory material published in good faith, where there was reasonable ground to believe that the publication was for the public benefit, where the publication did not impute the commission of a crime, where the defendant mistook or misapprehended the facts, and where there was a full and fair apology and retraction, a plaintiff may be limited to special damage.[337] The fact that the plaintiff has already recovered damages or has received

---

aggravated damages to the trial judge's award of $200,000 for general damages. In a companion action brought by another doctor defamed by the same broadcast, *Leenen v. Canadian Broadcasting Corp.* (2000), 50 C.C.L.T. (2d) 213 (Ont. S.C.J.), additional reasons at (2000), 2000 CarswellOnt 3327 (S.C.J.), affirmed (2001), 6 C.C.L.T. (3d) 97 (Ont. C.A.), leave to appeal refused (2002), 164 O.A.C. 200 (note) (S.C.C.), $950,000 including $400,000 general, $350,000 aggravated and $200,000 punitive were awarded.

333 (2004), 239 D.L.R. (4th) 577, 23 C.C.L.T. (3d) 273 (Ont. C.A.).

334 *Ibid.*, at 590. Blair J.A. referred to *Vaquero Energy v. Weir*, [2004] A.J. No. 84 (Alta. Q.B.). The majority of the Court of Appeal found fault with several aspects of the trial judge's decision, increased the trial judge's award, and awarded punitive damages. Doherty J.A. dissented in part, finding that the trial judge was aware of the factors enumerated by the Court of Appeal, and thus he refused to, in the absence of misapprehension of the evidence or errors in principle, vary her award for general damages.

335 See, e.g., Manitoba's Defamation Act, R.S.M. 1987, c. D20 (also C.C.S.M., c. D20), s. 4. The comparable Ontario provision, the Libel and Slander Act, R.S.O. 1980, c. 237, s. 9(1), (now R.S.O. 1990, c. L.12) was considered in *Munro v. Toronto Sun Publishing Corp.*, above, note 320. It was also held that even if the statutory requirements are not satisfied, the common law allows for an apology to be taken into consideration in the mitigation of damages. See also *Tait v. New Westminster Radio Ltd.*, [1985] 1 W.W.R. 451 (B.C. C.A.), to the same effect. In *Carter v. Gair* (1999), 170 D.L.R. (4th) 204 (B.C. C.A.), although an apology was offered, it was not actually published because counsel had not accepted it. Damages were only slightly reduced.

336 See, e.g., Manitoba's Defamation Act, *ibid.*, s. 16.

337 See, e.g., Manitoba's Defamation Act, *ibid.*, s. 17. See *Teskey v. Can. Newspapers Co.* (1989), 59 D.L.R. (4th) 709 (Ont. C.A.), *Wiley v. Toronto Star Newspapers Ltd.* (1988), 51 D.L.R. (4th) 439 (Ont. H.C.), varied as to costs (1990), 69 D.L.R. (4th) 448 (Ont. C.A.), *Murray Alter's Talent Associates v. Toronto Star Newspapers Ltd.* (1995), 124 D.L.R. (4th) 105 (Ont. Gen. Div.) and *Ungaro v. Toronto Star Newspapers Ltd.* (1997), 144 D.L.R. (4th) 84 (Ont. Gen. Div.) for a discussion of the comparable Ontario provision: Libel and Slander Act, R.S.O. 1990, c. L.12, s. 5; and *Snider v. Calgary Herald* (1985), 34 C.C.L.T. 27 (Alta. Q.B.), re Alberta's Defamation Act, R.S.A. 2000, c. D-7, s. 16. In *Fulton v. West End Times Ltd.* (1998), 45 B.C.L.R. (3d) 288 (S.C.), it is noted that the newspaper cannot take advantage of these defences unless its name and address are stated "either at the head of the editorials or on the front page of the newspaper": s. 12(1) Libel and Slander Act, R.S.B.C. 1996, c. 263. In this case the required information was at the foot of the editorial page. See also *Weiss v. Sawyer* (2002), [2002] O.J. No. 3570, 2002 CarswellOnt 3003 (C.A.) dealing with a similar provision

compensation in respect of the defamation which forms the basis of the action brought can mitigate the damages.[338]

While damages are the normal remedy for a defamation action, the courts may in the exceptional case grant an injunction to restrain the publication of defamatory material in advance of trial. It has been held, however, that an injunction should only issue "where the words complained of are so manifestly defamatory that any jury verdict to the contrary would be considered perverse by the Court of Appeal."[339]

7. SLANDER OF GOODS

Where false statements have been made disparaging not a person, but that person's business or trade, an action similar to defamation may be instituted.[340]

---

in Ontario's act (s. 8(1)) and accepting as sufficient "substantial compliance" with the requirements. The case also dealt with the notice requirement of the Act (s. 5(1)) and held that it applied even to non-media defendants where the alleged libel was published in a newspaper or broadcast. It applied as well to a newspaper published on an on-line website. The notice provision did not apply however to faxes or e-mails sent to the newspaper. The Court of Appeal reaffirmed these positions in *Janssen-Ortho Inc. v. Amgen Canada Inc.* (2005), 256 D.L.R. (4th) 407 (Ont. C.A.). In *Bahlieda v. Santa* (2003), 64 O.R. (3d) 599, 16 C.C.L.T. (3d) 108 (Ont. S.C.J.), reversed (2003), 20 C.C.L.T. (3d) 297 (Ont. C.A.), the notice and limitation provisions of Ontario's Act were applied to material placed on a website. The court held that placing material on the Internet constitutes a "broadcast" under the Act. The Ontario Court of Appeal reversed, holding that this matter ought not to have been resolved in a summary judgment application. The court noted that there were several unresolved and important policy issues which should be decided at trial. See *MCF Capital Inc. v. Canadian Broadcasting Corp.* (2003), [2004] 3 W.W.R. 508 (Man. Q.B.) for a discussion of the notice requirement under the Manitoba Act.

338 See, e.g., Defamation Act, R.S.A. 2000, c. D-7, s. 15, raised in *A.U.P.E. v. Edmonton Sun* (1986), 39 C.C.L.T. 143 (Alta. Q.B.), and *Snider v. Calgary Herald* (1985), 34 C.C.L.T. 27 (Alta. Q.B.).

339 *Rapp v. McClelland & Stewart Ltd.* (1981), 19 C.C.L.T. 68 at 74 (Ont. H.C.). Also see *A.G. Ont. v. Dieleman* (1994), 117 D.L.R. (4th) 449 at 669 (Ont. Gen. Div.) where the court stated that "the granting of an injunction to restrain the publication of an alleged libel is an exceptional remedy granted only in the rarest and clearest of cases." See, to the same effect, *John Doe v. C.B.C.*, [1994] 2 W.W.R. 666 (B.C. S.C.). In *Pilot Insurance Co. v. Jessome*, [1993] O.J. No. 172 (Gen. Div.), the court held that if the material was manifestly defamatory, an injunction will be granted even if the plaintiff cannot show that there is "no reasonable possibility" of a defence. The court held that this is too high a burden. The matter was also addressed by the Supreme Court of Canada in *Canada (Human Rights Commission) v. Canadian Liberty Net* (1997), 157 D.L.R. (4th) 385 (S.C.C.). Although not a defamation action, Bastarache J. likened the enjoining of discriminatory speech with defamatory speech. In respect of the latter, Bastarache J. approved of the high threshold that must be met before defamatory speech will be enjoined, as expressed in *Rapp* and other cases. Also see *Coltsfoot Publishing Ltd. v. Harris* (1999), 180 N.S.R. (2d) 238 (S.C.).

340 A corporation can sue for defamation if the business reputation of the corporation as a legal entity has been defamed. See for example *Walker v. CFTO Ltd.* (1987), 59 O.R. (2d) 104 (C.A.). In *Halton Hills (Town) v. Kerouac* (2006), 270 D.L.R. (4th) 479 (Ont. S.C.J.) it was decided that governments, including municipal corporations, cannot sue in defamation. The decision was based on the Charter value of freedom of speech. Corbett J. held that "an absolute privilege attaches to statements made about government". Also see Pedlar J.'s decision in *Montague (Township) v. Page* (2006), 2006 CarswellOnt 451 (S.C.J.) to the same effect. This

This action, known as slander of goods or malicious falsehood,[341] can be brought if the following elements can be shown: (1) there must have been a statement made of and concerning the goods of the plaintiff, (2) the statement must have been false, (3) the statement must have been published maliciously, that is to say, dishonestly or with improper motive, and (4) the plaintiff must have suffered special damage.[342]

Comparisons which point out truthful differences between the plaintiff's goods and those of the defendant are legitimate. Statements which falsely disparage the plaintiff's goods are not. It has been stated that "the line between what constitutes permissible comparison, on the one hand, and impermissible disparagement, on the other, however difficult to identify in individual cases, is generally drawn upon the basis of whether a reasonable person with knowledge of the facts would take the claim being made to be a serious one."[343]

Although the disparaging statement must be made about and concerning the plaintiff's goods, it has been held that this does not necessarily mean that the plaintiff must be identified by name.[344] Where the plaintiff controls the market place for the product, and the implication will be drawn by the public that the disparaging comments must therefore be referring to the plaintiff's product, the requirement of identification has been satisfied. As well, the disparagement of a plaintiff's product might be construed in some contexts as the disparagement of the plaintiff manufacturer, so as to give the latter a cause of action for defamation.[345]

Two aspects of the action seem to have posed difficulty. It may be difficult for a plaintiff to establish a loss of specific business, i.e., customers or contracts, as a result of the defendant's statements, although a decline in sales can be shown.

---

does not preclude actions by public officials as opposed to the government itself. The judgments contain an excellent discussion of the issues and policies at stake in this debate.

341 See Irvine, "Annotation" (1982), 20 C.C.L.T. 246. Irvine notes that this tort has several names: slander of goods, slander of title, injurious falsehood, or malicious falsehood have been used. "Slander of title" deals with defamatory material which disparage a person's property. See *Western Surety Co. v. Hancon Holdings Ltd.*, [2007] 6 W.W.R. 630 (B.C. S.C.) which discusses the requirements for this cause of action.

342 See *Rust Check Can. Inc. v. Young* (1988), 47 C.C.L.T. 279 at 299 (Ont. H.C.); *Frank Flaman Wholesale Ltd. v. Firman* (1982), 20 C.C.L.T. 246 (Sask. Q.B.). Note the requirement that the exact words alleged to be defamatory must be stated in the Statement of Claim: see *Paragon Properties (Finance) Ltd. v. Del Swan Trucking Inc.* (1998), [1999] 7 W.W.R. 224 (Alta. Q.B.). Note as well legislation: see, for example, Libel and Slander Act, R.S.O. 1990, c. L.12, s. 17, which states that it is not necessary to prove special damages if the words are published in writing or other permanent form and are calculated to cause pecuniary damage to the plaintiff.

343 Watt J. in *Rust Check Can. Inc. v. Young, ibid.*, at 299-300.

344 See *Church & Dwight Ltd. v. Sifto Canada Inc.* (1994), 22 C.C.L.T. (2d) 304 (Ont. Gen. Div.).

345 In *Color Your World Corp. v. Canadian Broadcasting Corp.* (1998), 156 D.L.R. (4th) 27, 41 C.C.L.T. (2d) 11 (Ont. C.A.), leave to appeal refused (1998), 119 O.A.C. 397 (note) (S.C.C.), reversing (1994), 17 O.R. (3d) 308 (Gen. Div.), for example, a television broadcast claiming that there was an unacceptably high level of mercury in the plaintiff company's paint was seen by the trial court as defamatory of the plaintiff company itself. The trial court held that the broadcast implied that the plaintiff company had acted improperly and was unconcerned with public safety. The Ontario Court of Appeal reversed the decision based on its conclusion that the words complained of were not defamatory.

Is this sufficient? In *Frank Flaman Wholesale Ltd. v. Firman*,[346] the court, relying on an earlier English authority,[347] held that in the circumstances of the case, "a general loss of custom or business, as distinct from loss of specific customers", was admissible in evidence, and was "sufficient special damage to maintain an action of this kind."[348] In *Church & Dwight v. Sifto Canada*,[349] it was held that an injunction can be granted where the court is satisfied that actual loss will occur, if the disparagement is not prohibited. As well, the malice element has been described as "a matter not entirely free from controversy."[350] Malice is, however, a requirement for a successful action. In the leading Canadian case, *Man. Free Press Co. v. Nagy*,[351] the court held that there must be an absence of *bona fides* which imports malice in order to successfully bring this action. In this respect, publishing the material knowing that it was false, or with a reckless disregard as to its truth or falsity, will be evidence of malice. There is no need, however, to prove that the material was published with the predetermined intention to injure the plaintiff.[352]

8. CONCURRENT ACTIONS IN DEFAMATION AND NEGLIGENCE

Recent case law has dealt with the question as to whether a plaintiff can bring actions in both defamation and negligence relating to the same defamatory material. At the heart of this issue is whether a plaintiff can avoid the defences to defamation, by arguing that the defendant was negligent in publishing the impugned material.

The leading judgment is *Spring v. Guardian Assurance plc*.[353] The case involved a defamatory employment reference made by the defendants concerning the plaintiff, resulting in the plaintiff's inability to obtain employment. The defendants were under a duty to give the reference and the trial judge had found that they were not malicious in doing so. Thus the defence of qualified privilege applied and the defamation action could not succeed. Could the claim proceed in negligence? The Court of Appeal had held that it could not and the plaintiff appealed its decision to the House of Lords.[354]

---

346 Above, note 342.

347 *Ratcliffe v. Evans*, [1892] 2 Q.B. 524 at 533-34.

348 20 C.C.L.T. 246 at 258. Irvine notes in his annotation that the circumstances of the case are relevant. He cites these other cases on point: *Perestrello & Comphania Limitada v. United Paint Co.*, [1969] 3 All E.R. 479 (C.A.); and *Glo-Klen Distributors v. B.C. Chem. Ltd.* (1959), 19 D.L.R. (2d) 635 (B.C. C.A.). He also refers to Heydon, *Economic Torts*, 2nd. ed. (1978), at 85.

349 (1994), 22 C.C.L.T. (2d) 304 (Ont. Gen. Div.).

350 *Rust Check Can. Inc. v. Young*, above, note 342, at 300.

351 (1907), 39 S.C.R. 340.

352 See *Procor Ltd. v. U.S.W.A.* (1989), 65 D.L.R. (4th) 287 (Ont. H.C.), additional reasons at (1990), 65 D.L.R. (4th) at 310 (Ont. H.C.), for a recent successful action for injurious falsehood. The defendants, a union and employees of the plaintiff company, had alleged that the plaintiff company was guilty of customs fraud. The court found that the statements were made with wilful blindness to the truth and for indirect and improper motives. In addition to compensatory damages of $100,000, punitive damages of $100,000 were also awarded.

353 (1994), [1995] A.C. 296 (H.L.).

354 See [1993] I.C.R. 412.

The majority in the House of Lords allowed the action to proceed in negligence. The essence of their opinions[355] was that there was, on the facts of this case, a *Hedley-Byrne* duty of care owed by the defendants to the plaintiff with respect to the employment reference made by them.[356] This was seen as something different than, and independent from, their potential liability under defamation law. The plaintiff, in other words, was not merely alleging that he had been defamed by the defendants resulting in a loss to his reputation, but that a tort law duty of care which was owed to him at common law had been beached.[357] The Lords did not see any inconsistency in recognizing a duty of care owed in the circumstances of this case despite the fact that defamation law protected the occasion in which these statements were made. Lord Keith dissented. According to him, the same policy reasons which, under defamation law, protect defamatory references if malice is not proved, should apply to negligence claims. Lord Keith pointed to authorities in other Commonwealth jurisdictions which supported the view that the negligence action should not "introduce a distorting element" into defamation law.[358]

The matter of possible concurrent claims in both defamation and negligence has been considered in a several Canadian cases. Two recent judgments in particular have given careful thought to this issue, and have come down on different sides of this contentious issue. In the first, *P.G. Restaurant Ltd. v. Northern Interior Regional Health Board*,[359] Goepel J., at trial, rejected a plaintiff's claim for negligence against a defendant who allegedly published defamatory and inaccurate statements.[360] The defamation action against the defendant failed on the basis that the impugned statements did not sufficiently refer to the plaintiff.[361] Could, however, a negligence claim be brought? Goepel J. held that it could not. After an extensive review of the authorities,[362] Goepel J. expressed his preference for Lord Keith's dissent in *Spring*, stating that "as a matter of policy, it is preferable

355 There were five opinions. Lord Goff, Lord Lowry, Lord Slynn, and Lord Woolf wrote in favour of the appeal; Lord Keith dissented.

356 The possibility of a contractual duty of care was also raised in the judgments.

357 The Lords applied *Hedley-Byrne v. Heller* and the more contemporary notion of proximity; i.e., was there a sufficiently proximate relationship between the parties to make it just and fair to impose a duty of care on the defendants for the protection of the plaintiff.

358 Quoting Sir Robin Cooke in *Bell-Booth Group Ltd. v. Attorney General*, [1989] 3 N.Z.L.R. 148 (C.A.). Other cases cited included *South Pacific Manufacturing Co. Ltd. v. New Zealand Security Consultants & Investigations Ltd.* (1991), [1992] 2 N.Z.L.R. 282 (C.A.) and *Balfour v. Attorney-General*, [1991] 1 N.Z.L.R. 519 (C.A.).

359 (2004), 22 C.C.L.T. (3d) 153, [2004] 4 W.W.R. 287 (B.C. S.C.), reversed on the issue of defamation (2005), 30 C.C.L.T. (3d) 55 (B.C. C.A.), reconsideration refused (2005), 2005 CarswellBC 1219 (C.A.), leave to appeal refused (2005), 2005 CarswellBC 2711 (S.C.C.), additional reasons at (2006), 2006 CarswellBC 1388 (C.A.).

360 The plaintiff restaurant brought a defamation and negligence action against a Board of Health and a separate defamation action against a newspaper and several of its employees. The action against the Board for defamation and negligence failed. The action against the newspaper for defamation succeeded at trial, but was reversed on appeal. This discussion relates only to the dismissal of the negligence claim, concerning which there was no appeal.

361 See discussion above.

362 Goepel J. considered the *Spring* judgment and several of the Commonwealth authorities discussed therein. He also referred to a number of Canadian cases, several of which were also referred to in *Dinyer-Fraser*, below, note 365.

to resolve the tensions between freedom of speech and protection of one's reputation using the law of defamation."[363] Goepel J. was reluctant to allow the "long standing" defences of qualified privilege and fair comment to be overridden by the law of negligence.[364]

In *Dinyer-Fraser v. Laurentian Bank of Canada*,[365] Ballance J. was supportive of the majority's view in *Spring*, even outside of the context of defamatory employment references. He, as did Goepel J. in *P.G. Restaurant Ltd.*, carefully considered this issue, including a comprehensive review of many of the authorities, both Commonwealth and Canadian.[366] In Ballance J.'s view, Canadian law has not rejected *Spring* "or the possibility that the claims of negligence and defamation, which arise out of the same facts, may stand together in certain circumstances."[367] Where there is a duty in tort, based on proximity, and not "merely on the duty not to defame", an action in negligence can succeed, even if there might not have been liability in defamation.[368]

---

363 (2004), 22 C.C.L.T. (3d) 153 (B.C. S.C.), reversed (2005), 2005 CarswellBC 799 (C.A.), reconsideration refused (2005), 2005 CarswellBC 1219 (C.A.), leave to appeal refused (2005), 2005 CarswellBC 2711 (S.C.C.), additional reasons at (2006), 2006 CarswellBC 1388 (C.A.).

364 Goepel J. limited his objections by noting that he refrained from deciding whether the majority in *Spring* was correct in regard to employer references. He also would have dismissed the negligence claim on its merits.

365 (2005), 28 C.C.L.T. (3d) 205 (B.C. S.C.), additional reasons at (2005), 2005 CarswellBC 2365 (S.C.).

366 As is evident from the review, Canadian courts have for the most part, not been favourably inclined to recognize plaintiffs' concurrent claims in negligence and defamation. Ballance J. discussed the following cases, among others. In *Fulton v. Globe & Mail (The)* (1997), 207 A.R. 374 (Q.B.), affirming (1996), 194 A.R. 254 (Alta. Master), Master Funduk rejected the plaintiff's claim that the defendant had engaged in negligent research and investigation leading to a defamatory article. Master Funduk termed this as a defamation action "dressed up" as a negligence claim. In a subsequent case, *Guccione v. Bell* (1998), 229 A.R. 365 (Master), varied (1999), 1999 CarswellAlta 238 (Q.B. [In Chambers]), affirmed (2001), 2001 CarswellAlta 1402 (C.A.), Master Funduk makes the same point when he says that "a claim for damages for loss of reputation cannot be slid in under the guise of a different tort", at para. 18. In *Butler v. Southam Inc.* (2000), 191 N.S.R. (2d) 158 (S.C. [In Chambers]), reversed (2001), 2001 CarswellNS 297 (C.A.), the plaintiff's claim for negligence failed due to lack of proximity and duty. Similarly in *Jurcevic v. Thidrickson* (2001), 159 Man. R. (2d) 176 (Master), where the plaintiffs failed to plead duty and the negligence action was struck. In *Haskett v. Trans Union of Canada Inc.* (2003), 63 O.R. (3d) 577 (Ont. C.A), additional reasons at (2003), 2003 CarswellOnt 1295 (C.A.), leave to appeal refused (2003), 2003 CarswellOnt 4754 (S.C.C.), the issue was raised in the context of a motion to strike out an action for negligence in credit reporting. The Court of Appeal allowed the action to proceed, holding that at this stage in the proceedings, it could not be said that the claim was bound to fail, even if "truth" would have prevented a successful defamation action. A negligent credit rating action succeeded in *Clark v. Scotiabank* (2004), 25 C.C.L.T. (3d) 109 (Ont. S.C.J.), additional reasons at (2005), 2005 CarswellOnt 1529 (S.C.J.), although there was no discussion concerning its overlap with defamation law.

367 (2005), 28 C.C.L.T. (3d) 205 (S.C.), additional reasons at (2005), 2005 CarswellBC 2365 (S.C.). Ballance J. considered Goepel J.'s judgment in *P.G. Restaurants* noting that it did not hold that *Spring* was wrongly decided on its facts, and was in any event plainly *obiter dicta*, as the case would have failed on its merits.

368 In this case, however, there was liability in defamation, unlike the *Spring* situation. Thus, the only issue with respect to concurrent liability in both defamation and negligence related to the assessment of damages. In my view, this therefore avoided the basic policy problem at the heart of this issue; i.e., should free speech which is protected by the law of defamation

The Supreme Court of Canada had the opportunity to consider the matter in *Bella v. Young*.[369] The case concerned a negligence action brought by a student against a university and its employees. The defendant had reported the student to the Child Protection Services as a potential child abuser. The report was found by a jury to have been produced as a result of the defendants' negligent and unfounded suspicions, created by a professor's misunderstanding of a footnote reference in one of the student's submitted papers. This mistaken report led to significant damages suffered by the plaintiff. Although defamation was pled along with negligence, the trial judge withdrew the defamation issue from the jury on the basis that the letter which had been sent was not capable of giving rise to a defamatory meaning. The jury found for the plaintiff on the basis of negligence. The Court of Appeal reversed the trial judgment, basing its judgment on an immunity provision contained in the Child Welfare Act.[370]

Although the appeal to the Supreme Court revolved around the action for negligence and the applicability of the immunity provision, the matter of the interaction between defamation and negligence was raised. McLachlin C.J.C. and Binnie J. rejected the defendants' contention that the plaintiff's claim was "really an action for defamation, dressed up as a negligence action."[371] Supporting the approach of the majority in *Spring v. Guardian Assurance*, the court held that where there is a negligence action based on proximity and foreseeability, and the damages cover more than just harm to the plaintiff's reputation, there is no reason in principle why negligence actions should not be allowed to proceed.[372] On the facts of this case, the court found that there was a duty of care relationship between the plaintiff and the defendants, not restricted to the accusatory report itself, but based on their broader relationship of professor and student, including its implied contractual terms. In other words, the essence of the plaintiff's complaint was not that the defendants had defamed her, but that they had duties of care with respect to her education and career, based on a professor-teacher relationship, which they breached.[373]

Seen in this way, the Supreme Court of Canada's support of *Spring* is understandable. The courts will have to be careful, however, not to too easily find a duty of care relationship between the parties merely on the basis that the defendant failed to take reasonable care not to defame the plaintiff. The duty must be based on proximity between the parties which exists independently of the relationship between defamer and defamed. Otherwise, the important protections given under defamation law in order to promote free speech will be seriously eroded.

---

become secondary if the plaintiff's complaint relates not to a loss of reputation, but to economic losses caused by negligent conduct?

369 (2006), 261 D.L.R. (4th) 516 (S.C.C.), reversing (2004), 241 Nfld. & P.E.I.R. 35 (C.A.).

370 R.S.N.L. 1990, c. C-12. The court held that this provision applied to all legal proceedings including defamation. It required proof of malice or lack of reasonable cause.

371 (2006), 261 D.L.R. (4th) 516 (S.C.C.), at 535.

372 (2006), 261 D.L.R. (4th) 516 (S.C.C.), at 536.

373 The court did concede, however, that issues of freedom of speech and the policies underlying qualified privilege can be taken into account in determining the appropriate standard of care, at 261 D.L.R. (4th) 516 (S.C.C.), at 536.

INDEX